# 26th EDITION

# GUNS
## ILLUSTRATED®

# 1994

**Edited by Harold A. Murtz**
and the Editors of Gun Digest

MEMBER OF THE

NATIONAL
SHOOTING
SPORTS
FOUNDATION
INC.

# DBI BOOKS, INC.

# STAFF

## GUNS ILLUSTRATED

**EDITOR**
Harold A. Murtz

**ASSOCIATE EDITOR**
Robert S.L. Anderson

**PRODUCTION MANAGER**
John L. Duoba

**EDITORIAL/PRODUCTION ASSOCIATE**
Jamie L. Puffpaff

**ASSISTANT TO THE EDITOR**
Lilo Anderson

**ELECTRONIC PUBLISHING MANAGER**
Nancy J. Mellem

**GRAPHIC DESIGN**
Jim Billy

**MANAGING EDITOR**
Pamela J. Johnson

**PUBLISHER**
Sheldon L. Factor

## DBI BOOKS, INC.

**PRESIDENT**
Charles T. Hartigan

**VICE PRESIDENT & PUBLISHER**
Sheldon L. Factor

**VICE PRESIDENT—SALES**
John G. Strauss

**TREASURER**
Frank R. Serpone

## ABOUT OUR COVERS

European American Armory Corp. is still a relatively young name in the gun business, but they are far from unknown. This Florida-based firm brings firearms enthusiasts some of the best shooting equipment money can buy, like the Witness and Astra series of pistols.

At right on our covers is the E.A.A. Witness in stainless steel. This gun is available not only in 9mm Parabellum, but also 38 Super, 40 S&W, 41 AE and 45 ACP; soon to be released is a 10mm version. The Witness is truly a high-capacity proposition. Standard magazines hold sixteen rounds of 9mm, nineteen of 38 Super, twelve 40 S&W, eleven 41 AE, ten for 45 ACP.

Barrel length of the basic Witness is 4.50 inches, overall length 8.10 inches, and the gun weighs 33 ounces.

This is one of the few high-capacity pistols that can be converted with off-the-shelf factory parts into a full-house competition gun. It features excellent three-dot standard sights, cocked and locked carry system, finely tuned double- or single-action trigger, fore and aft slide and grip serrations, internal firing pin block and frame-mounted sear-block safeties, and one of the most comfortable grip configurations for a high-capacity pistol on the market today. Finishes available are blue, chrome, blue and chrome combination and stainless steel.

It's easy to understand why so many shooters have taken to the Witness pistols in such a big way—they're loaded with features and they *work*.

Also shown is the latest offering from the great Spanish gun maker, Astra—the A-75 autoloader.

Currently offered in 9mm Parabellum and 40 S&W, this new gun will soon be available in 45 ACP. Magazine capacity in 9mm is eight rounds; for 40 S&W it's seven shots. Barrel length is 3.5 inches, overall length is 6.5 inches, and the gun weighs 31 ounces.

The A-75 has a lot of good features: all-steel construction; automatic firing pin safety; selective double/single action mechanism; decocking lever; an easily accessible button-style magazine release; checkered frontstrap, back strap and trigger guard; and low-profile, three-dot sights adjustable for windage. Either caliber is available in blue or nickel finish.

However you slice it, European American Armory offers today's market some of the best values in handgunnery.

Photo by John Hanusin.

**ISBN 0-87349-142-4**          **Library of Congress Catalog #69-11342**

# CONTENTS

## FEATURES

## DEPARTMENTS

Frank Conway on his way to winning both pistol ammo events at the Picacho Gun Club's fourth annual machinegun match, Las Cruces, New Mexico. He's firing a 1928 A-1 Thompson with altered buttstock of his design.

# THE MACHINEGUN
## AS A
# PRECISION WEAPON

"THEY'RE IMPROVING," is how Bill Madden described the performance of the shooters at the Picacho Gun Club's fourth annual machinegun match. It was the 16th of May, 1992, and the place was the Butterfield Trail Shooting Range, 11 miles west of Las Cruces, New Mexico. The sixteen contestants were from several cities in the Southwest, and among them were a couple of engineers, a secretary, a dentist, a rancher, a retired Army officer, a college student, and a fellow who owns an oil well supply company. Yes, they were something of a cross-section of American society, and they were all firing for accuracy against the clock with their favorite automatic weapons.

Bill Madden continued: "That first year we held the machinegun match, 1989, some folks would even shoot from the hip and spray the general target area, waste a lot of ammo. Now they're learning what it's all

**Though interesting and fun, spray and pray is far from the order of the day for these serious shooters who are trying to legitimize the full-auto gun.**

about, and what firing an automatic weapon is all about is short, aimed, controlled bursts."

Madden was standing just behind the firing line with his 1916 Lewis gun, and he was dressed in a campaign hat, 1918 officers' britches, and leather puttees. He looked like he might have been in training for either the Punitive Expedition or what used to be called the Great War, and he surely *looked* like he knew what he was talking about. Just a little later, with the classic Lewis pop-popping along at what might be described as a "resolute" rate of fire, Madden took second place in the rifle ammo event although he was using just the original iron sights. At 200 meters, he knocked over five 7x11-inch metal targets with five consecutive two-shot bursts. Madden's Lewis gun is chambered for the 30-06, and he was shooting 1953 GI Ball ammo he had stripped from M-1 clips just before

## by ALBERT MANCHESTER

A wide array of full-auto guns showed up at the match, including, from left: HK MP-5, AK-47, HK 94, M-16, Ruger AC556 and an Uzi. Others included Thompsons, U.S. M-60, FN FAL, Lewis gun, M-3 Grease Guns, and British Stens.

loading the Lewis' pans.

John Mathis, who won the rifle ammo event, didn't mind admitting that Bill Madden's shooting was probably the best in that event. Mathis: "Bill shot high at the paper target at 200 meters, otherwise he might have taken first place." (Score: Mathis, 4.392; Madden, 4.209.) Mathis likes the older machineguns: "They're heavier, easier to hold on target, and they have a slower rate of fire than modern 'spray-and-pray' weapons." In spite of his affinity for older machineguns, Mathis shot the event with a heavy-barreled M-16 with a bipod and Colt 3x scope. His ammo was 55-grain full-metal-jacket reloads in front of 26 grains of H-335. Mathis is a Distinguished Rifleman, and when he was on active duty in the Army, he engaged in pistol competition.

The match started at 1:00 p.m. and the pistol ammo and rifle ammo events were run at the same time. Madden allowed as how the weather was a trifle warm for his period outfit. Indeed, it was a typically hot day for southern New Mexico, and although thunderheads were building all afternoon in the northwest and over the Organ Mountains to the east, shooting conditions at the range were just about perfect. That is, as long as you like your weather hot and dry. Wind was not a factor.

As in any shooting match, the main factors were the skill, talent, experience and training of the participants, as well as their emotional and mental condition on the day of the shoot. First prizes did not go to people who had picked up their first automatic just the week before. Frank Conway took first prize in both of the pistol ammo events with a Model 1928 A-1 Thompson; he had fired his first Thompson over 50 years ago.

Frank Conway: "About 95 percent of good marksmanship is between your ears. Mental control. Learn to control your emotions. When you're firing in competition, isolate yourself. Ignore everything else except the person who is in charge of the firing line. And learn to take advice. Don't try to invent anything; it's all been tried before. Read books on marksmanship, read all you can—and find out what works best for *you.*"

Although Conway retired from the Army as a lieutenant colonel, he started his military career during World War II as an armorer with an armored division. Back in those days, at the very beginning of the war, he was responsible for the functioning of no less than 2300 Thompsons. He still regrets the day the division had to turn in their Thompsons and accept the M-3 Grease Gun in its place. Conway holds expert badges for the submachine gun, heavy machinegun, carbine, pistol and rifle; he is a Distinguished Rifleman; he took first place at Wimbledon two years in a row, the only person to have done so.

One might say that on that hot day in May there was a world of firearms savvy on the firing line at the Butterfield Shooting Range.

Yes, a lifetime of shooting experience, but that didn't stop Frank Conway from practicing for the event. Not by a long chalk, as the British say. During the ten days

In stage two of the first submachine gun event, contestants had to fire at pepper poppers from behind a wall. A paper target for another stage can be seen at far left.

Coralie Carrier posts scores at the match. She was the only woman to compete in the match and used an Uzi. This is serious business!

prior to the match, Frank burned up 1400 rounds as he worked to get himself in shape. One might conjecture, too, that Conway is a pro right down to his bone marrow.

Conway's ammunition for the match was 230-grain, out-of-the-box, 1966 Match ammo by Remington, 45-caliber, of course, and his Thompson is a weapon he resurrected from a welded-together hulk from about 1941 that he purchased some years ago. The barrel is one he made, and the buttstock is just like the one he designed fifty years ago as an improvement over the issued 1928 A-1 stock. (A military board would not accept the change.) The Conway buttstock is straighter than the original design, creating a more direct line of thrust. During long bursts, a Conway-altered Thompson will not climb as rapidly as one with the old-style butt. And, speaking of the British, Conway prefers the British-style front hand grip for his Thompson. Whatever the reason, Frank's score in Event I (Sub Gun)

was 15.393; the score of his nearest competitor, Dave D., 12.559. Event II (Sub Gun) was closer, with Conway scoring 11.327, and the second place man, Mark J., scoring 11.143.

The idea for the annual machinegun match was born in the late 1980s when members of the Picacho Gun Club (Picacho Peak is a conical hill of volcanic origin which intrudes on the horizon just northwest of Las Cruces) got to discussing machinegun matches in other parts of the country they had read about. "Those matches seemed like just a bunch of people getting together to shoot up an old car," Coralie Carrier explained. Carrier is spokesperson for the gun club, and she competes in the machinegun match with an Uzi—tenth place, Event I (Sub Gun); sixth place, Event II (Sub Gun). "We decided we could do better than just shooting an old car to pieces. We would promote proficiency with automatic weapons. We wanted to create events in which the contestants

would have to be fast *and* accurate. Actually, we have quite a few shooting events during the year at the club. The only difference here is that the guns shoot a lot faster." Besides being spokesperson for the gun club, Carrier teaches firearms skill and safety at the local community college.

Well, there is one big difference between the gun club's machinegun match and their other matches. The machinegun match was designed to have the contestants under control at all times. Coming as they do from distant parts of the Southwest, many of the participants are relative

Bill Madden fired his 1916 Lewis and took second place in the rifle ammo event in spite of using only the issue iron sights. The campaign hat adds to the fun.

strangers to the gun club members. Their ability and training with automatic weapons is unknown. In the machinegun match, then, two gun club members are assigned to each shooter on the line to ensure that he or she does not make a dangerous mistake. As far as safety is concerned, absolutely nothing is left to chance. However, it is readily apparent that the machinegun match is a gathering of capable and conservative firearms enthusiasts.

Although the events will change a bit from year to year so that the contestants can't practice for the upcoming match, the courses for 1992 are fairly typical of what the gun club has devised. There were two pistol ammo events and one rifle ammo event, each featuring two stages.

Event I (Sub Gun): In the first stage of the first event, the shooter fired at pieces of 11x14$\frac{1}{2}$-inch computer paper at 15, 25 and 35 meters. The paper was stapled to targets about 5 feet off the ground. One clip of twenty rounds was fired at each target, and the contestant changed clips while the clock ran.

In stage two of the first event, the contestant fired on seven pepper poppers (falling targets) set randomly between 15 and 35 meters. At least one participant in the match was able to put down all of the pepper poppers with less than twenty rounds. In this part of the first event, the shooter had to fire from behind a wall and keep at least one foot behind that wall at all times.

All firing in all of the events was measured with electronic timers. Because this was a match for automatic weapons, each burst (except the last in a clip) had to be of at least two rounds. Clips, belts, drums and pans were limited to twenty rounds.

Although the rules were sent out with the invitations, the Match Director gathered the contestants together before the match and went over all the rules very carefully. Eye and ear protection was a must. Any decisions by the Match Director or Safety Officer were final. But there were no arguments, no discussion whatsoever about the outcome of the match.

The match organizers decided to use "generic" targets—no silhouettes of humans or animals. Observers were kept away from the shooting by yellow plastic tape strung out behind the firing line.

Event II (Sub Gun): Steel plates of 8-inch diameter were set on rebar

Just for safety's sake, each shooter had two gun club members behind them at all times while shooting. Eye and ear protection were required. Gun is a scoped M-60.

stands about 1$\frac{1}{2}$ feet above ground at 15 to 35 meters and staggered randomly. Shooting against the clock, the contestant used as many rounds as necessary to knock down the plates.

In stage two of the second event, six steel plates hinged to a rebar base about 5 feet off the ground at 30 meters were the targets. Ed Carrier was seen smoking his pipe as he shot the pistol ammo events, the very picture of a contented, relaxed shooter (sixth place, Event I; fourth place, Event II).

Event III (Machine Gun): The rifle ammo contestant would set up his

weapon before taking his (no women competed in this event in 1992) turn at the targets. He settled his weapon on its bipod, loaded the gun, adjusted the sights, and then stood up. He would go into action from a standing position.

Out in front, to the north, were two groups of targets, the first set at 100 meters, the second at 200 meters. He would fire on a piece of computer paper at 100 meters, then shift to steel plates cut to 11x7 inches and set about 2 feet apart on individual rebar bases. The steel plate in the middle was set somewhat lower than the others so the shooter would be forced to adjust his sights a couple of times. At the sound of the elec-

Todd Bensley holds a typical target from the 100-meter position of the rifle ammo event. Bensley was an Olympic shooter at the 1984 and 1988 Games

tronic timer, the shooter fell to his weapon and went to work. As in the other events, any jams had to be cleared while the clock continued to run. He emptied twenty rounds at the paper target, loaded, and then fired on the steel plates. Paper target dealt with as best he could, all of the plates knocked down, the shooter reloaded for the targets at 200 meters and stood again behind his weapon. The targets at 200 meters were the same as those at 100. At the sound of the timer, he dropped to his weapon and did the best he could at the longer range.

Because setting up the targets again at 200 meters was so time consuming, two groups of targets were organized for the rifle ammo contestants. That is, two contestants were able to shoot the course before the targets would have to be set up again.

During one of the set-up periods, a rifle ammo contestant said that he would like to take a look at the metal targets. He was shooting 223-caliber SS109 armor-piercing ammo, he announced, and wanted to see how much damage he had done to the plates. To his chagrin, he discovered that his vaunted SS109 ammo had just barely nicked the metal. The plates had been cut from an old road grader blade, steel so hard that it was difficult to see where his rounds had hit.

After the plaques and a little prize money were handed out, the contestants demonstrated their firearms for the onlookers, and some were able to shoot the weapons. One young man who said that he had never expected to see a Lewis gun outside of the movies got a chance to fire off a few rounds with Madden's gun. If you could judge by the look of utter bliss on his face as he cuddled the warm wood of the stock against his cheek, you might have thought the fellow had just fallen in love.

The machinegun match was designed to a certain extent for viewer interest. After the match, a couple of 50-caliber M2HBs were demonstrated, and, although it wasn't a machinegun, a 20mm 1934 Lahti anti-tank gun was cut loose a few times. For noise and recoil, there wasn't anything else quite like it at the match. Viewers and contestants felt that it had been a very good day indeed. A few folks who had come out to the range apparently expecting to see something quite different—maybe like an old car being shot up?—exclaimed at how well

Match Director John Mathis demonstrates his 50-caliber M2HB after the official events of the match. Note the rifle scope and ejected case falling from the gun.

organized the match was.

Over to the right of the pistol ammo course, and way down at the end of the range, an old, white Rambler station wagon had been waiting for the official events of the match to end. To be absolutely minced by machinegun fire was the glorious fate of that plebian automobile. The 50s ripped apart its innards. The car was so badly torn up that it had to be chained together to be towed away. Well, when you come right down to it, it *is* a lot of fun to shoot up an old car...

Another difference between a machinegun match and any other kind of firearms event is the advanced planning; contestants must file for permission to take automatics across a state line, a process which can take weeks or months. If you plan to use a *public* shooting range, find out well in advance whether you will be able to use that public property for a machinegun shoot.

Two of the purposes behind the gun club's machinegun match are to help take automatic weapons out of the disrespectable category, and establish the use of them on the firing range as a legitimate sport. The very first year, news media types from several places showed up to report on the event and film it for the evening news. This year, no newspaper or TV people came. This annual match in southern New Mexico is now rather old hat, an established event of little interest to very few except the participants, and that's exactly the attitude the Picacho Gun Club is trying to establish.

Now let's see, I spotted another old car in a field . . .  •

Yes, it's fun to shoot up an old car. Bill Madden empties a pan of 30-06 from his Lewis gun just for fun.

DEVELOPED IN 1978 by long-time gun guru Ken Waters as a better round for lever guns like the Model 94 Winchester, the 7-30 Waters offers higher velocity, greater energy, flatter trajectory and less recoil than its 30-30 parent. On top of that, it does all those things using bullets with better ballistic properties than the 30-30. In addition, it is one of the premier chamberings for the Thompson/Center Contender.

Never heard of it, you say? That's exactly the problem.

I, for one, cannot understand why the shooting world hasn't taken this beautifully balanced cartridge to its heart, but Western hunters, at least, seem largely unaware of its existence. Long-range Contender shooters, however, are another story. Fred Smith of Bullberry Arms (2430 W. Bullberry Ln., #67-5, Hurricane, UT 84737, phone 801/635-9866), a maker of custom Contender barrels, tells me it's one of their hottest sellers here in the West. And when you consider its record, that's not hard to understand. According to Smith, a shooter named Robert Campbell won the Colorado Long Range Competition three times with a Bullberry 7-30 Waters barrel, most recently with a three-shot group of $^{31}/_{32}$-inch—fired from 500 meters!

Despite these impressive credentials, there's been hardly any hoopla in the gun media about the 7-30 Waters. Perhaps that's because, at the moment, it is chambered only in the Winchester Model 94 Angle Eject and in the T/C Contender. Lever guns are an action type that usually draws yawns from most of the shooting press. Then, too, the cartridge wears a rim instead of a belt; the word "magnum" is nowhere to be heard in its neighborhood.

I view the 7-30 as a superb deer round for both lever rifles and the Contender. It is ideal for youths, women and men

# WATERS
## The Unknown Wonder

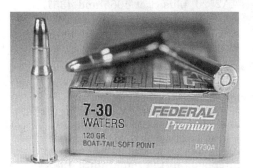

A relative newcomer, this beautifully balanced cartridge flat outperforms its 30-30 parent in every way, but few shooters have discovered its virtues.

## by ROCKY RAAB

Chambered in the Winchester Model 94 Angle Eject and the Thompson/Center Contender, Raab feels the 7-30 Waters may be the finest deer caliber available in either gun.

Federal is the only ammunition maker producing the 7-30 Waters, but its Premium offering carries a reliable Nosler bullet. This load gave the second best accuracy in the author's Contender—.88-inch at 100 yards.

who don't like recoil. It is eminently useful for antelope, black bear, wild boar, caribou and possibly even smallish elk. Although available in only a single factory loading, the Federal ammo (catalog number P730A) carries the excellent 120-grain Nosler flat-tip boattail.

For Model 94 owners who hand-load, either that Nosler bullet (#41722) or the 139-grain flat point from Hornady will have to do. Those are the only flat-tip bullets in 7mm listed by bullet makers that I could locate. Such a lack of bullets compatible with tubular magazines makes the 7-30's anonymity a Catch-22 scenario. If there were more Model 94/7-30 Waters shooters, there'd be a broader selection of bullets, but shooters won't be attracted unless there are more bullets. Contender shooters (and Model 94 owners who load their guns as two-shooters only), however, aren't limited to flatpoint bullet designs. Such shooters are free to use any of the great bullets available in 7mm diameter. Virtually every bullet manufacturer makes several choices from 100 to 140 grains, the 7-30's useful range. A quick scan of catalogs on my shelf shows four each from Sierra, Speer and Nosler, plus seven from Hornady and two from

Barnes. Of special note is the Hornady 120-grain spitzer (#2811), which is designed for big game use in single shot pistols.

Created by necking down the 30-30 case and moving the shoulder forward, 7-30 Waters brass has an average water capacity of 40 grains. Now that Federal has stopped supplying virgin brass, reloaders can get cases by shooting factory ammo or reforming 30-30 brass. To do the latter, just run unfired or once-fired 30-30 cases through your regular 7-30 sizing die. This will reduce the case neck to 7mm. Now select nearly any *starting* load from a current loading manual, preferably using one of the faster powders. Starting loads will give good loading density in the reduced capacity case, yet will give sufficient pressure to fire-form the brass. After firing, the case that comes out of the chamber will be a fully formed 7-30 Waters. From here on, work up your load as usual. But be sure to keep reformed cases separate from those with original 7-30 Waters headstamps. Reformed cases

can vary in capacity, which can sometimes change pressures drastically.

Powder choices for the 7-30 Waters include medium-fast to medium-slow burners, a very large range indeed. Proven choices for the 7-30 Waters include Reloder 7 and 12, IMR-4320 and IMR-4064, H-335 and H-414, both of the 4895s, W-748 and W-760, AA2015BR and AA2520, plus Scot 4065 and 4351. Some slightly slower powders also give good results, but at the expense of added muzzle flash and blast, especially in short barrels. Standard primers are sufficient. I used CCI Bench Rest or Federal 210 primers for all loads tested here.

Although Ken Waters began developing his 7mm wildcat in 1977 using a rebarreled Marlin Model 336A, no gun manufacturer seemed interested in the round until 1982. At that time, the folks at U.S. Repeating Arms announced that they would manufacture rifles for a slightly altered version of the round. In 1984, U.S.R.A. fulfilled their

Making cases is easy and begins with the fired 30-30 (left). A 7-30 Waters sizing die reduces the neck diameter to 7mm in preparation for loading a reduced powder charge and 7mm bullet (center). After fire-forming, the case is ready for regular load development (right).

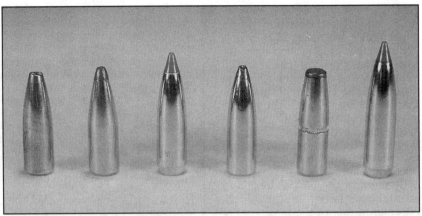

Bullets used in the author's handloads, from left: Speer 115 HP, Hornady 120 Single Shot Pistol, Nosler 120 BT, Speer 130 SP, Hornady 139 FP, and Nosler 140 BT.

promise and listed the 7-30 Waters as an option for the Winchester Model 94. The offering was initially available only with a 24-inch barrel, but now the 7-30 Waters Model 94 wears only the handier 20-inch tube. To date, Marlin hasn't offered their strong and popular Model 336 in 7-30, but I'd be willing to bet it would be a good seller if they did.

But if Marlin hasn't yet seen the light at the end of the 7mm tunnel, Thompson/Center has. T/C offers 7-30 barrels for their extremely popular Contender in both 10- and 14-inch lengths. In addition, they also offer 20-inch barrels for the Contender carbine in the caliber. Other lengths, plus a variety of barrel contours, finishes and options, are available from Fox Ridge Outfitters, T/C's official custom house.

Several independent custom houses also produce drop-in barrels for the Contender pistol and carbine. The better of these outfits, like SSK Industries (721 Woodvue Ln., Wintersville, OH 43952, phone 614/264-7217) and Bullberry, offer match-grade barrel blanks, custom chambering, muzzle brakes, replacement stocks and more. The 7-30 Waters is one of the more popular calibers requested from these custom shops, and if you're serious about the Contender you should have their catalogs.

To review the 7-30 Waters, I obtained a Winchester Model 94 Angle Eject as well as a Contender barrel from Thompson/Center. The

Model 94 hardly needs a lengthy description for most readers, as it is one of the most popular firearms ever produced. Mine has the current-production 20-inch barrel. Angle Eject models are drilled and tapped for scope bases on the receiver. Taking advantage of this, I mounted a venerable 4x Weaver K4 scope on the rifle using Millett bases and rings. The rifle comes with a hammer extension that simply screws onto the hammer. The extension makes both manual cocking and uncocking easier and safer, and Winchester deserves credit for supplying it at no charge.

For the Contender, I got a regular Super 14 model barrel from T/C, of bull contour. Such a short, fat barrel is conducive to accuracy, and its weight aids in recoil reduction. Because the 7-30 Contender is ideal for heavy varminting as well as deer hunting, I fitted it with a Burris 2-7x variable scope using Burris base and rings.

To test factory ammo in both guns, and to obtain brass for reloading, I bought five boxes of Federal Premium 7-30 ammo. The first shots with both guns verified what I'd read and heard about the 7-30—it's a very pleasant round to shoot. Mild of both shout and shove, it just begs to be shot again and again. This project was already fun. After initial sight-in, I tacked up targets at the 100-yard line and got serious.

I started with my favorite firearm, the Contender. From the 14-inch barrel, the 120-grain Noslers delivered an average of 2415 fps with a standard deviation of only 18—very consistent performance. Cases expanded to .4208-inch after firing, measured just ahead of the base web. This measurement established the "standard" pressure in this bar-

rel, for later reloading work.

This load proved to be highly accurate in the Contender, producing the second best average groups of all loads tested. Five-shot groups averaged 0.88-inch, well under the magic MOA. The cartridge is obviously capable of fine accuracy, certainly good enough for deer hunting out to 200 yards. The drop and energy numbers bear this out, too.

With a ballistic coefficient of .217 and sighted 2 inches high at 100 yards, the Nosler flatpoint will strike at 2078/1151, the numbers referring to velocity/energy. Dead-on target will be at 168 yards and our maximum point blank range is 194 yards. At 175 yards, it's still doing 1820/883 and is .46-inch low. At 200 yards, we're still getting 1740/807 and the bullet is only 2.55 inches below line of sight. Way out at 225, we still get 1663/737 with only 5.37 inches of drop. This is more velocity and nearly the same energy as the 41 Magnum gives at the muzzle. And the 41 Magnum is certainly an effective deer cartridge.

Next, I fired the factory loads from the Model 94. As expected, the gun functioned perfectly and ammo fed smoothly from the magazine. I experienced no malfunctions of any kind. Also as expected, the longer barrel produced higher velocity, with my Oehler 35P chronograph reporting an average of 2611 fps with a standard deviation of only 16. This translates to a muzzle energy of 1802 foot pounds. If we again sight in 2 inches high at 100, we'll get 2215/1307 at that range. At 150, the numbers are 2035/1103 and 1.24 inches high. The zeroed range is 177 yards. At 200, we'll get 1862/924 at 1.56 inches low; max point blank is 205. At 225, it's 1781/845 at -3.91 inches. Even at 250 yards, we're still getting 1702/772 with a drop of -6.97. Again, it's 41 Magnum muzzle performance, but out at 250 yards.

But, as with many cartridges, it's with reloads that the true potential comes out. I did test some 139-grain loads with the Hornady flatpoint for the Model 94, which I'll describe later. But because the Contender's single shot action offers the most leeway in bullet type and overall cartridge length, I concentrated my reloading efforts there.

By the way, the 7-30 Waters has a normal case length of 2.030-inch. Cases grow *fast* to the maximum of 2.040. Some of the factory loads I fired reached this length on their first firing! Trim to 2.020 and you should get three or four firings before they hit 2.040 again. Case stretching is definitely slowed if you lubricate the insides of case necks during resizing. Using a dry lube like mica or graphite makes things easy. The elliptical expander in my Hornady New Dimension dies also helped reduce drag considerably.

Lightest and first to be tested was the Speer 115-grain hollowpoint. Loaded over 32.0 grains of Reloder 7, this load averaged an even 2500 fps with a standard deviation of 36 from the Contender. Groups ran 1.43 inches and were very consistent. Recoil with this load was light, and expansion of the fired cases was well under that of factory loads at .4205-inch. I was limited by time from doing any additional work up with this bullet and powder, but I believe some improvement is possible.

With the Hornady 120-grain Single Shot Pistol bullet and 36.5 grains of AA2520, velocity ran 2503 with an s.d. of 15. Muzzle blast and fireball were significantly greater with this slow powder, and case expansion was .4210-inch, some .002-inch greater than factory ammo. This indicates a warmish load in this gun, because factory ammo is already loaded to near-maximum pressures. Indeed, some cases were slightly sticky to extract with this load. Groups ran 1.77-inch on average, with some evidence of vertical stringing, another indication that this concoction was crowding maximum.

The Nosler Ballistic Tip in 120 grains was the next bullet to be tested. I loaded it over 34.5 grains of H-335, a load Ken Waters himself developed. From the Contender, this load churns up 2445 fps with an s.d. of 16. Groups ran around 1.8 inches. Both muzzle blast and fireball are

The author likes to glass for deer from a location where a firm rest can be taken. Bullets of high ballistic coefficient make shots of 250 yards possible if the game is not alerted. A wrist bandolier keeps extra ammo handy for fast reloading.

Factory ammo is accurate as well as fast and consistent. This 100-yard group shot with the Contender shows the combination can perform!

large, almost the norm with H-335. Case expansion ran .4206-inch, making it a moderate-pressure loading. This would be a good load for deer if you wear electronic ear protection to cope with the heavy blast.

Venturing above factory bullet weight, the Speer 130-grain spitzer was next. The Hercules data book suggested 34.0 grains of Reloder 12, and this turned out to be a conservative load. Velocity ran only 2192 fps with a 37 s.d., and cases expanded to only .4195-inch. Groups ran almost exactly 2.00 inches, but usually had four in about an inch plus a flyer. I intend to work this load up a bit in my Contender to see if that flyer will join the crowd. I think the velocity could possibly be upped by another 100 fps, as well.

The final combination tested in the Contender was the Nosler 140-grain Ballistic Tip. With it I tried 33.0 grains of a powder I'd never used before—Scot 4065. Said to burn one to two grains faster than the venerable IMR 4064, Scot claims this coarse, extruded powder is a very consistent and clean burner. Boy, is it. The *largest* group I fired with this recipe was 0.74-inch; the smallest went into 0.68, the tiniest cluster of the series. Velocity ran 2125 fps with a 22 s.d. and cases

dropped out of the chamber with moderate expansion of .4206-inch. Would I mess with this load? I'd sooner send donations to Sarah Brady and Cleveland Amory.

For the Contender, then, I'd not hesitate to use the Federal factory ammo for deer out to 200 yards if I didn't reload. But to take advantage of a bullet with much better ballistics, I'd load the Nosler 140 Ballistic Tip over Scot 4065. If I wanted to use but a single load for varmints as well as deer, I'd work with either the Hornady 120 Single Shot Pistol bullet or the Nosler 120 Ballistic Tip. And I'd try both of them over 4065 and Reloder 12 until I found a recipe my barrel would like. Judging from my first efforts, I think that would be a short search.

Based on the excellent results I'd obtained with Scot 4065 under the 140-grain Nosler, I began my Model 94 loads with exactly the same 33.0-grain charge under the Hornady 139-grain flat-tip. I also wanted to see if AA2520 might boom a little less in the Winchester's longer barrel, so I also decanted 33.0 grains of that. Along with those medium and slow burners, respectively, I tried one fast powder that I've had good luck with in a variety of calibers—AA2015BR. According to Accurate

## 7-30 Waters Load Data

| Bullet/Type | Weight | Powder | Weight (grs.) | Velocity (fps) | Standard Deviation | Case Expansion | 100-yd. Group | Remarks |
|---|---|---|---|---|---|---|---|---|
| **T/C Contender** | | | | | | | | |
| Nosler FP | 120 | — | — | 2411 | 18 | .4208 | 0.88 | Factory load |
| Speer HP | 115 | RL-7 | 32.0 | 2500 | 36 | .4205 | 1.43 | |
| Hornady SSP | 120 | AA2520 | 36.5 | 2503 | 15 | .4210 | 1.77 | Heavy blast, fireball |
| Nosler BT | 120 | H-335 | 34.5 | 2445 | 16 | .4206 | 1.81 | Heavy blast, fireball |
| Speer SP | 130 | RL-12 | 34.0 | 2192 | 37 | .4195 | 2.02 | |
| Nosler BT | 140 | 4065 | 33.0 | 2125 | 22 | .4206 | 0.78 | Best accuracy |
| **Winchester Model 94** | | | | | | | | |
| Nosler FP | 120 | — | — | 2611 | 16 | .4208 | 2.05 | Factory load |
| Hornady FP | 139 | AA2015 | 30.0 | 2416 | 14 | .4212 | 1.11 | Best accuracy |
| Hornady FP | 139 | AA2520 | 33.0 | 2470 | 16 | .4212 | 1.75 | |
| Hornady FP | 139 | 4065 | 33.0 | 2290 | 26 | .4208 | 1.70 | |

All loads in Contender used CCI BR-2 primers; Model 94 loads used Federal 210.
Velocity and s.d. measured with an Oehler 35P chronograph.

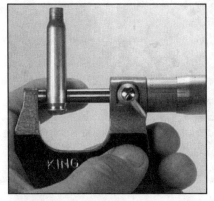

Case expansion is measured at the bright expansion ring just forward of the web area. Measurement of factory ammo gives a "standard" pressure level for that barrel.

Arms' data, 31.0 grains of this fine-grained tubular powder is maximum in the 7-30 Waters, so I tried 30.0 even.

The only change in loading procedure from short gun to long gun was to crimp the case lightly into the cannelure. Such a crimp is necessary in lever-action rifles to keep the magazine spring tension and recoil from driving the bullet deeper into the case. Don't try for a hard crimp. The shoulder will distort, making it impossible to chamber that cartridge. I know; the first case I ran into the die did just that because I'd turned the seating die down an eighth-turn too far. Once corrected, loading was normal.

The Scot 4065 load clocked only 2290 fps with an s.d. of 26. That's only 165 fps faster from a barrel a full 6 inches longer than the Contender's. The difference is proba-bly due to the significantly longer bearing surface on the Hornady bullet. This 33.0-grain load expanded cases to .4208-inch, the same reading I got with factory ammo in the Model 94. So this load delivers factory-equivalent pressures even though velocities are lower than expected. Accuracy was fine, though, with groups that ran about 1.70-inch.

With 30.0 grains of AA2015BR, the Model 94 achieved 2416 fps with an s.d. of just 14. Accuracy also improved, with groups averaging 1.10-inch. On one target, three shots went into an incredible 0.31-inch cloverleaf. The remaining two shots took the group out to 0.94-inch. That would be outstanding for a bolt action. From an out-of-the-box lever action with only a 4x scope, it's phenomenal. This load was maximum in this rifle, though. Cases miked an average of .4212-inch and extraction was a little bit sticky. This is yet another instance where a published load exceeds what is prudent in a given firearm, and illustrates why reloaders should *always* begin with the starting load.

Incidentally, I have found Accurate Arms' published maximum loads to be very "hot" in several calibers and with numerous powder and bullet combinations. In a few cases, even the starting loads turned out to be warm, especially if bullets were seated out to touch the lands. With normal bullet seating, pressures are distinctly lower. In all cases, the published starting loads have been safe. But it certainly wouldn't pay to ignore those loads and jump right in at the maximum listed charge.

That left 33.0 grains of AA2520. As I suspected, muzzle blast was distinctly less with the longer barrel. This powder produced the highest velocity with the 139-grain bullet, a respectable 2470 fps with an s.d. of 16. That's only 140 fps less than the factory load delivers with a 120-grain bullet. It also just about duplicates what Ken Waters achieved with a 139-grain bullet during his initial load development work. Groups averaged 1.75-inch with a few called flyers marked and discounted, still less than 2 MOA. Once again, cases were expanded to .4212-inch, making this another maximum load. I range tested at about 80 degrees Fahrenheit, so for hunting in really cold conditions, I'd use this load just as is. But if I thought I'd be out on a warm weather hunt, I'd back the charge down at least a half-grain just to be sure of easy extraction.

Unfortunately, the seasons didn't cooperate with me for this review as my deadline fell about a month before the opening of deer season here in Utah. But when the third Saturday in October rolls around, you can bet the barrel on my Contender will carry the 7-30 Waters roll mark. And you can also bet that if the occasion arises, this wonderfully balanced cartridge will get the job done efficiently and humanely. Fast and accurate, yet mild of recoil, ballistically superior and with a wide range of truly excellent bullets, Ken Water's creation just might be the very best choice yet for the Model 94 or the Contender. ●

# Today's Mausers

**Mauser-Werke has always been known for its high quality and military firearms, but today the focus is on sporting guns, both long and short.**

## by ROBERT T. SHIMEK

FOR WELL OVER a century, the name Mauser has been synonymous with success in arms manufacture. The firm is probably best known for the series of turnbolt service rifles that, many decades ago, it sold both at home and to foreign governments. At one time, a Mauser rifle was military issue in Germany, in a half-dozen other European nations, in almost all of South America, much of Latin America and the Far East, and in parts of Africa. Few companies have ever so dominated the world's service rifle market. Mauser pistols were big sellers too: The famed

Broomhandle sold very well to WWI Germany and to China and other countries; the 32-caliber blowbacks gleaned significant contracts from the German armed forces. Mauser was an important producer of sporting rifles as well: they offered high-quality centerfires in a variety of European and American calibers suitable for everything from varmints to African game. The massive company also produced fine rimfire sporters.

Nowadays, Mauser no longer courts the world's military procurers, but she remains a prolific source of sporting arms. Her present-day products are not as well known in this country as they should be because, in keeping with Mauser tradition, they are usually costly premi-

The Mauser Model 80 SA fed full-jacket ammo flawlessly and grouped well. This 25-yard magazineful (thirteen shots) was fired with Federal 124-grain FMJs, and measures 3 inches.

The Mauser Model 80 SA is a military-style Hi-Power copy built by FEG of Hungary. It seems a bit strange to see the Mauser banner on this design.

The Mauser Model 90 DA pistol is also from FEG of Hungary. It has a fourteen-shot magazine, blued finish, and lines reminiscent of the Hi-Power. It's a moderately priced Wonder-Nine.

um-quality instruments. But they are superb performers, as I recently discovered when I sampled several of them, sent on loan by Mauser's exclusive U.S. importer, Precision Imports Inc. (5040 Space Center Drive, San Antonio, Texas 78218).

### Handguns

Mauser-Werke today builds but a single handgun only on a limited, custom-shop basis. The gun is the Mauser Parabellum 08/73—in essence, the German service version of Herr Georg Luger's classic toggle-actioned auto pistol. "Shooting" versions of this arm were sold in this country in very limited numbers not too many years ago by Interarms, but now Precision Imports is the only distributor, and special gussied-

up commemorative versions are the only Parabellums available. These commemoratives are superbly crafted and handsomely decorated, but also very expensive. The suggested retail price for the "cheapest" model is just under $6000! Among the pistols offered are an 8-inch-barreled Artillery Model commemorative, a 4-inch-barreled gun honoring the International Weapons Exposition, etc. I have examined the cased Artillery Model and found it to be breathtakingly beautiful.

More affordable and shootable handguns bearing the Mauser trade-name are available, but they are not made by Mauser. The guns are made by FEG of Hungary and rollstamped and marketed by Mauser; they carry moderate suggested retail price tags

in the high-$300/low-$400 range and thus represent a departure from Mauser's traditional appeal to the high-priced end of the market. Models include the 80 SA, a Hungarian-built copy of the classic military Hi-Power, and the 90 DA, Hungary's now-well-recognized Wonder-Nine. There is also a Compact version of the 90 DA.

My shooting sample was a FEG 80 SA. The gun showed classic old-model/military features: the small and low profile left-side-only safety-lever, the service sights with hemispherical front post and tiny fixed U-notch rear, and a rounded hammer spur. Examination revealed high standards of fit and external finish. The gun was only a little inferior in this regard to a new Browning I

The Mauser Model 201 Luxus represents their costliest rimfire sporter. The gun's lines suggest a miniaturized centerfire hunting rifle. It's a handsome rifle.

Four different 22 Long Rifle loads were tried in the Model 201, and all printed five shots under 1 inch from the 50-yard bench with open sights.

recently tried. As to internal polish, the FEG's moving part articulations were noticeably grittier than on the super-slick Browning, but I certainly would not deem the Hungarian pistol rough.

Shooting tests of the FEG showed perfect functionality with W-W 115-grain FMJ and Federal 124-grain FMJ ammunition. Accuracy with either round was "good" by military pistol standards. Five-shot groups with either load averaged somewhere over 2.5 inches center to center from the 25-yard bench, and an entire thirteen-shot magazine with either load would go into 3.0 to 3.5 inches. With W-W 115 Silvertip HPs and Federal 115 JHPs, similar good groups were recorded, with thirteen shots going into 3.2 and 3.3 inches respectively; however, with these hollowpoint rounds, one frequently had trouble cycling the first round from a fully loaded magazine into the chamber. This problem seemed related to a certain amount of "play" when the magazine was locked in place and presumably is not universal. I note that another reviewer described no feeding problems with JHPs in his 80 SA. The military pistol personality carried over to other shooting qualities—the hammer bit me and the sight picture was "close." However, the only truly egregious quality I noted was that the trigger was heavy and exceedingly rough. All in all, I thought the 80 SA represented good value in a low-priced 9mm.

### Rimfire Rifles

Mauser builds a pair of bolt-action rimfire hunting rifles. Both are quality items, but they differ conceptually. The Model 107 is a traditional rimfire, weighing just over 5 pounds. The action locks closed via the base of the bolt handle entering a receiver groove; feeding is via detachable five-shot box magazine; the trigger is adjustable and is of the two-stage variety. Open sights are de rigeur, and the rear sight is adjustable for elevation to 200 meters. The receiver is grooved to accept rail-type scope mounts. Suggested retail is in the $330 range. Sole caliber available in this country is 22 Long Rifle, though a 22 WMR version does exist. The only variation to be had from Precision Imports is the basic model with beechwood stock, machine-cut checkering, and satin blue finish, though a premium "Luxus" version is described in the M107 owner's manual.

The second Mauser rimfire is, in essence, a miniaturized rimfire version of a centerfire hunting rifle; such guns have long been prized by serious rimfire riflemen, which is why a few 22 versions of centerfire favorites have occasionally been available on costly special order. This Mauser is called the Model 201; it weighs 6.2 pounds and—suggestive of many of history's Mauser centerfires—it sports a bolt with dual front-mounted locking lugs. Feeding, as with the M107, is via detachable five-shot box magazine. The trigger is an adjustable single stage unit, though a "French hair" trigger or double-set type are available. Open sights are provided, but it is obvious the owner will want to mount a premium-grade scope. The rear sight is adjustable only for windage and the receiver is grooved for a rail mount, and drilled and tapped for a base and rings mount as well. A version with no sights is available, if desired. Suggested retail varies from $490 to $670, depending upon which of two calibers—22 Long Rifle or 22 WMR—and which of two versions— Standard or Luxus—is selected. The Standard model features hand-checkered beechwood furniture and satin-blued steel; the Luxus shows hand-checkered walnut stocking, a rosewood forend tip, and high-polish blued steel.

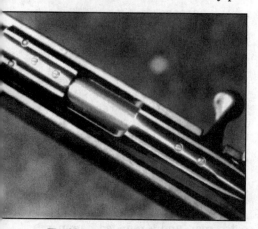

The Mauser Model 201 receiver is grooved for a rail-type scope mount, as well as being drilled and tapped for a base and rings mount. Nice touch!

The Mauser Model 66-S shows unusual receiver lines; note that the bolt handle is forward of the trigger.

My sample Model 201 was a Luxus version in Long Rifle chambering. Everything about this rifle suggested "class," from the superb metal finishing to the skillful checkering. The stock showed some nice figuring and a well-done satiny oil finish.

Accuracy was sampled from the 50-yard bench and was predictably exemplary: Each of four different loads tried—Federal Hi-Power HVHP, W-W Silhouette, Federal Target and CCI Mini-Mag HP— would print a five-shot magazineful under an inch when the author did his part. The tightest cluster printed was .8-inch center to center, fired with the Federal hollowpoint; worst group recorded in all of shooting was 1.4 inches center to center. The fine creep-free, superbly adjusted trigger bears much of the credit for the fine groups. Functioning throughout the range session was flawless. The only Model 201 quality I didn't like was the rear sight. While I recognize that a 201 Luxus is intended for use with a premium-quality glass (Heaven knows what sort of groups I would have printed with glass sights!), I couldn't help but feel that a best-grade fully adjustable rear sight should appear on open-sighted Model 201 rifles.

All in all, I found the Model 201 Luxus an impressive item. A squirrel hunter would be well pleased.

### Centerfire Rifles

Mauser builds a pair of fine big game hunting rifles—one being an older (and quite unusual) design, the other newer and more conventional looking. The older gun is the Model 66-S. It is available in a wide variety of calibers ranging from 243 Winchester to 458 Winchester, and in a variety of metric rounds from 5.6x57mm to 9.3x64mm. Pricewise, the 66-S is Mauser's more costly sporting centerfire offering, with a suggested retail from $1783 to $2079, depending upon caliber and styling. The Model 66-S's unique fea-

tures include a very unusual telescoping-bolt action, involving a "telescopic slide" which cycles part way with the bolt when the action is opened or closed. The advantage is that the receiver is about 2 inches shorter than normal, making the Model 66-S significantly handier than competitive rifles. The overall length goes 42 inches with a 24-inch barrel, versus about 44 inches for other makes with similar barrel length. The only disadvantages I could think of for the telescoping action are that the bolt handle is placed rather far forward and that the rifle's appearance is unusual (some love its looks, others don't).

Other interesting Model 66-S features include a manual safety that uses a secondary lock to resist inad-

This view of the Model 66-S with the bolt opened shows the unique telescoping action; this allows a receiver 2 inches shorter than on most competitive rifles and, therefore, less overall length.

The Mauser Model 99 in 308 Winchester doted on match ammo to perform its best. The average for these three consecutive 100-yard groups, fired with Federal Match fodder, was .65-inch!

vertant release, a bolt with dual-opposed front-mounted locking lugs, a three-shot magazine, full-length Stutzen stock option, and the availability of a highly engraved presentation edition.

The newer Mauser centerfire sporter—and the less costly, with suggested retail varying from $1130 to $1322—is the Model 99. This gun is very similar to the Voere-made Kleingunther rifles offered in this country some years back. A call to Precision Imports confirmed that Mauser bought the rights to the Voere design in 1986 and now produces it—with some alteration—as the Model 99. This is hardly disappointing since the Voere/Kleingunther was one of the most accurate bolt-guns ever. American calibers available in the Model 99 range from 243 Winchester to 375 H&H; metric offerings go from 5.6x57mm to 9.3x64mm.

In contrast to the Model 66-S, the gun represents one of the best looking hunting rifles extant in my opinion. Dimensions and weights are robust: A 24-inch-barreled Model 99 measures about 44 inches long and weighs around 8 pounds, which is somewhat longer and heavier than

The author tries the Mauser Model 86-SR from the bench. The gun proved a gentle kicker, thanks to its 14-pound weight.

the Model 66-S. Notable Voere/Kleingunther design features include a bolt with three symetrically placed front-mounted locking lugs that engage a special Stellite insert. The Stellite adds both wear resistance and slickness of bolt operation to the design. A two-stage floating firing pin is incorporated which, in combination with a dual-cocking cam, allows for a very fast lock time; this is part of the reason the Mauser 99 is advertised as producing "benchcrest accuracy right out of the box." There are no open sights, this

gun being meant exclusively for scoping. The M99's magazine, while it does not protrude below the stock, is detachable; capacity is three or four rounds, depending upon caliber. A manual safety of standard pattern is fitted.

My sample Mauser Model 99 was in 308 Winchester. This gun was cosmetically equal to other modern commercial Mausers I've seen; I especially admired the fine figuring of the oil-finished walnut stock. Sighting equipment sent along by Precision Imports was a Swarovski 6x scope, a premium Austrian-made glass of outstanding light-gathering qualities and reputation.

The Model 99/Swarovski combo proved magnificently groupable, provided one fed the rifle the match-grade ammunition it demanded. The accuracy load was Federal's 168-grain Boattail Hollowpoint Match round, which averaged a stunning .65-inch for three consecutive three-shot groups from 100 yards. Also delightfully accurate was the Remington 168-grain Boattail Hollowpoint Match round, which averaged .85-inch for three consecutive groups. Standard hunting ammo didn't do quite as well: The best performer in this genre was the Winchester 150-grain Power-Point Softpoint round, which averaged

1.73 inches from 100 yards; however, one group miked over 3 inches. Remington 180-grain Core-Lokt softpoints shot some fine groups, but some poor ones, too, marred by uncalled flyers that spread groups as large as 4 inches. There were no functioning problems at all during my tests. Noteworthy shooting characteristics of the Mauser 99 included a rather long reach for the trigger and a very smooth action.

All things considered, I liked the 99, in spite of its gourmet ammo tastes. An accuracy average of .65-inch at 100 yards, coming from a standard-barrel-profile hunting rifle of reasonable weight, is worth taking the trouble to cater to.

### Specialty Rifle

Mauser's speciality rifle is (for me) probably the most appealing item in an appealing line, though this model is at once Mauser's most expensive item and the one most limited in its application. The gun is called the "Prazisiongewehr 86" ("Precision Rifle 86") or "Model 86-SR," and it is a serious long-range bolt-gun intended both for the police sharpshooter and the serious civilian rifleman.

The list of its specifications suffices to impress. The barrel is a match-grade cold-forged affair that measures almost 29 inches from breech to the tip of the integral muzzle brake/flash suppressor. Overall length of the rifle is a long 48 inches; all-up weight, sans accessories, is over 13 pounds. The receiver is an enormous, weighty forging. The stock—the buyer chooses between a laminated wood thumbhole design and McMillan fiberglass unit—features an adjustable cheekpiece and buttplate, as well as provision for a bipod. The trigger, of staight international match pattern, is adjustable for weight, and for double or single stage. Caliber is 308 Winchester, a good choice for distance work and a police/military favorite. Capacity of the detachable box magazine is a surprising nine rounds, which also enhances police/military appeal. The scope mount system is readily detachable and promises a return to zero when replaced. Night vision and laser range-finding equipment are available, but are sold only to government agencies. Accuracy on the order of .8-inch at 100 meters, using match ammo, is expected and is even listed on the specification sheet.

My sample Prazisiongewehr came with the camo-painted McMillan fiberglass stock, not as attractive as

Phenomenal groups were the rule for the Prazisiongewehr: With match ammo from either Federal or Remington, 100-yard benchrest accuracy averaged just over 1/2-inch.

the wood-laminate, but it is far more functional, and the McMillan name is synonymous with fine accuracy. All metal parts were done up in a gray phosphate to kill reflections, but quality of fit and polish was obvious despite the G.I. dress. The mounting of accessories was carried out easily: The bipod locked into its stock slot; the receiver accepted the specially-crafted base of roughly Weaver pattern, and the base in turn accepted the slide-on upper component which holds the scope rings, and that locked solidly into place courtesy of its thumb lever. The scope supplied was a trusty Swarovski straight 6x; yes, a glass of higher magnification is indicated on a shooting machine like the 86-SR, but the hunting-oriented Swarovski was all that was available.

Zeroing went without incident. Impressions gained during early firing were that this was the gentlest 308 this writer had ever fired (not much kick in a 14-pound gun!) and that this was possibly the most ergonomic 308 extant, at least after the cheekpiece and buttplate were adjusted. Accuracy was what you expect from a super-rifle bearing a suggested retail price of (take a deep

breath now...) $4145, sans accessories. Even standard commercial hunting rounds would shoot right around 1 inch from 100 yards. An example here was the Winchester 180-grain Silvertip, which averaged .9-inch for three consecutive three-shot groups, and on one occasion I shot a group miking .65-inch. Very nearly as accurate was Remington's 150-grain PSP Core-Lokt ammo, which averaged 1.1 inches c-c for its three consecutive 100-yard groups. This represents near half-minute of angle performance! Also quite accurate was Remington 168-grain Boattail HP Match ammo, which averaged .55-inch for its three groups. Ten-shot benchrest exercises with either match round yielded groups measuring under .8-inch.

All things considered, my experience with the 86-SR was positive and showed me why someone might be willing to part with big bucks for a shooting machine like this. One-half-MOA with factory ammo! Impressive!

Many things have changed for Mauser-Werke over the past 100-plus years. The company's appeal now is almost exclusively to sporting interests, rather than to the interna-

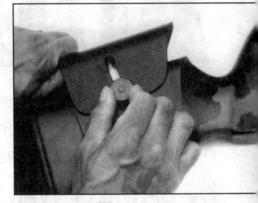

A handy feature on the Model 86-SR is the adjustable cheekpiece, especially with the high-mounted scope. The palm-swell pistol grip has a textured finish.

tional military market. Additionally, some moderately priced items have been introduced to attract buyers who otherwise might have no interest in Mauser's traditionally high-priced line. And some promising designs that didn't originate in the Mauser stable are now seen wearing the Mauser tradename. But one thing remains unchanged: Mauser-Werke of Oberndorf-am-Neckar is still a producer of fine-quality arms, and its name still works magic wherever firearms are sold. May the company prosper yet another century-plus.

●

# AIRGUN ACCURACY

Many factors contribute to the overall accuracy of an airgun whether it's a rifle or pistol. Here are the basics.

## by JAMES WALKER

THE AIRGUN is a hunting instrument, a paper-punching machine, a pastime tool of the marksman. Rifle or pistol puts small game in the pot, discourages varmints from the garden, wins shooting tournaments and affords inexpensive, quiet and safe practice on indoor as well as outdoor shooting ranges. It's a pleasure to watch the bullseye change into a ragged hole at the 10-meter basement gallery. But without accuracy, the airgun represents no more than an exercise in pulling the trigger.

Most air-powered arms do not have the power of the most anemic rimfire cartridge. A shooter wants to enjoy the potential of hitting a matchstick at 10 feet or cleanly harvesting a cottontail with a head shot at 20 yards. Failing these demands, the airgun has no more shooting interest than chucking a spear and probably less fascination. Today, there are numerous air pistols and air rifles that have the inherent accuracy to deliver their tiny bullets to the same locus point on the target every shot.

The engineering mechanics of the airgun are fascinating, especially the double-piston, spring-powered target models. The ability of the system to put a lead pellet in the bullseye every time is worthy of attention. There is a touch of magic—spelled "precision"—in airgun accuracy, and it all starts with the pellet. A scale tells the story about pellet unformity by weight. When that scale is an

A contributing factor to airgun accuracy is good sights. This fully adjustable micrometer peep rear on the RWS Model 75 rifle is a precision instrument that works in concert with a front sight that accepts different inserts for varying sight pictures.

These RWS Meisterkugeln match pellets are intended for competition, but they're a lot of fun to shoot informally, too. Author found them extremely consistent in weight.

which lacks ideal aerodynamic design, does not fare well in the wind. But indoor testing is no problem, and indoors the pellet proves itself an excellent missile in terms of accuracy potential.

After long study, Dr. Franklin Mann concluded that good bullets from good barrels were primarily responsible for accuracy. Of course, he didn't exclude the many other factors that pertain to accuracy, but his pronouncement was broth from the boiling pot of ideas. Coupled with a near-perfect projectile, the accurate airgun possesses a precision barrel, correctly rifled with sufficient rate of twist to stabilize the pellet.

Another link in the airgun accuracy chain is the manner in which power is transmitted to the pellet. The spring-piston design is one of three good ones. The double-piston offshoot of this type is even more intriguing than the single-piston model. If my information is correct, the Giss contra piston system of the early 1960s is the basis for the current double-piston design.

The basic idea is simple. It's predicated on Newton's Third Law of Motion, which states that every action has an opposite and equal reaction. That's why a rocket works in space. After all, there's no atmosphere to push on, but a jet of gas expelled from the back end sends the rocket forward. A good example to explain how this works is the fellow standing in a boat near shore. He tosses his coat to a friend on shore. As he does so, the boat moves out and away from shore in the opposite direction of his tossed coat. Action—reaction. Same for recoil. The bullet goes thataway and the buttplate heads in the opposite direction (not as fast because the rifle is far heavier than the bullet).

The double-piston target air rifle takes advantage of Newton's Third. The uncoiling of a powerful spring produces recoil, but recoil in a fine target rifle shooting a lightweight pellet is undesirable. So why not have an opposing piston of the same mass taking off at the same time as the power piston, but in the opposite direction? Should work. And it does. Two pistons and three springs complete the mechanical plan. The pistons are timed to reach the end of their respective travel simultaneously. Timing is the key. The recoil-piston is not independently driven or timing would be nearly impossible. Rather, toothed quadrants and rods are used for syncopation, to steal a

RCBS Electronic Balance, the impact is even greater because this first-class device offers not only high accuracy, but instant results that appear on a readout screen. The only pellets I had on hand were from RWS, but I'm certain other brands follow the same tradition of manufacturing perfection.

Here is how the electronic scale read for ten RWS Superpoints of .177-inch diameter: 8.0, 8.0, 7.9, 8.0, 7.8, 8.0, 7.9, 7.9, 7.9, 8.0. The spread between the lightest and heaviest pellet from the ten-sample test ran .2-grain—two-tenths of one grain weight (7000 grains per pound). Ten 17-caliber RWS Superdomes ran thusly: 8.4, 8.3, 8.4, 8.4, 8.3, 8.3, 8.4, 8.3, 8.4 and 8.4, a .1-grain variation. Meisterkugeln RWS match pellet samples went: 8.4, 8.4, 8.4, 8.4, 84. 8.5, 8.4, 8.4, 8.4, and 8.4. That is the same .1-grain spread; however, the mode is superior. In other words, without that one 8.5 grain pellet out of the ten weighed, these pellets would have read perfectly. Just for curiosity, a ten-sample run of RWS Meisterkugeln 17-caliber Extra 530 pellets were weighed. The results: 8.2, 8.2, 8.2, 8.2, 8.2, 8.2, 8.2, 8.2, 8.2, and 8.2—it doesn't get any better than that. I repeated the last sample with ten new pellets taken randomly from the tin container. Results: the same.

The accuracy of any gun is no better than its bullet, with, of course, the minor exception of imperfections balanced on a common axis through rotation. Since the airguns of interest here are precision rifled, there is a gyroscopic effect on the pellet in flight, so lack of homogeneity, as minute as it must be, is somewhat overcome through stabilization on a common axis via projectile spinning. As a joke more than test, I extracted five paper clips from a box and weighed them on the RCBS Electronic scale. Results: 7.5, 6.5, 6.6, 7.6, and 7.5 grains for a variation of 1.1 grains weight for a mass-produced item not requiring perfection, but still a far cry from modern pellet weight consistency.

A projectile weight test does not, of course, speak of bullet concentricity, and a bullet spinner is impractical for testing pellet uniformity of configuration. However, results at the target prove pellet concentricity. Naturally, the lightweight pellet,

Pellets are inserted one at a time into the breech of the air rifle. The pellet skirt is slightly compressed, which effects an air seal and engraves the rifling, which can be easily seen.

Anschutz Model 2002.

term from music. The front piston provides the compressed air, the rear piston serves as the opposite and equal force. Bingo. The match double-piston air rifle is recoilless due to counter-inertia.

There are a few more players on the double-piston stage, but the show's leading actors are the two opposing pistons. The power piston goes faster than a perigrine falcon in a hurricane, moving 2 to 3 inches, depending upon the exact rifle, in about 6 milliseconds. The point of peak pressure is reached about a millisecond after the power piston achieves maximum acceleration. The pellet's inertia is not overcome until peak pressure is reached. In effect, the pellet remains motionless for a fraction of a second.

Also aiding accuracy is the fact that there is virtually no air leakage in the system, which promotes accuracy for the reason already stated: A constant pressure applied to the pellet achieves a velocity with a low standard deviation. In other words, there is uniformity of thrust on the pellet from one shot to the next. The

regular spring-piston system in our high-class pellet guns also offers uniformity of thrust, albeit without the benefit of the double-piston recoilless advantage.

The spring-piston is not the only pellet gun system that provides accuracy. Pneumatic or pump-action guns can also be highly accurate. One advantage of the pneumatic design is the absence of the powerful spring, hence there is light recoil without going to double-piston designs.

Not to make too much of this recoil business, but remember that a standard spring-piston pellet rifle can eventually scramble the innards of an inexpensive scope sight meant for low-recoil arms, namely 22 rimfires. That's why special air rifle scopes are available. These are built for the single-piston spring-type air rifle (and pistol) and are engineered to withstand the effects of the rapidly uncoiling spring.

The smooth-shooting $CO_2$ airgun system also enjoys a potential for phenomenal accuracy. Obviously, there is no uncoiling spring. A varied amount of gas can be introduced behind the pellet to achieve what may be ideal pellet velocity for accuracy. The Crosman Model 84 $CO_2$ match grade air rifle was noted for one-hole accuracy, as was the same

Author found that match grade pellets were near perfection in terms of consistent weight. They are individually packed to prevent deformation.

company's Skanaker air pistol, also $CO_2$-powered. Another fantastic $CO_2$ match rifle is the Beeman/FWB C60. And don't forget the Beeman Crow Magnum with the "gas-spring." It would be difficult to choose any system over the other in terms of inherent accuracy. All types have proven they can produce one-hole results at 10 meters.

And they do their amazing work with little lead pellets—a sub-topic difficult to stay away from when looking into airgun accuracy. Incidentally, the skirt on a pellet is remindful of the skirt on the old-style Minie ball, a conical projectile made of lead with a hollow base. The idea of the hollow base on the Minie is to force the skirt area, which flares out due to pressure from the powder charge, to make full contact with the rifling (called projectile obturation). The soft lead pellet has this capability, but I do not believe that very much skirt expansion is achieved with such low pressure pushing on its hollow base. Rather, I see the skirt effecting an air seal when the pellet is seated in the chamber of the airgun due to a swaging effect. That seems a more practical explanation of the pellet skirt.

There are accurate pellets without skirts. The SABO Pellet from Sussex Armoury, Ltd., of England is an example. It's a solid bullet that is

Beeman/FWB 65 Mk. II.

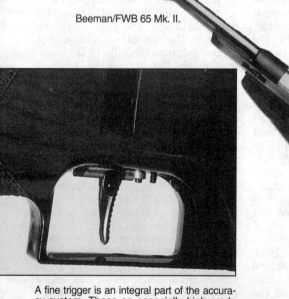

A fine trigger is an integral part of the accuracy system. Those on especially high-grade airguns are adjustable in many ways, including for position.

Beeman Crow Magnum.

fired from an airgun, but with a plastic sabot in which a 4mm (.157-inch diameter) bullet is seated. This 13.8-grain solid conical is cold swaged from a lead alloy (not pure lead) and has a boattail design. The SABO Pellet shows good accuracy in some rifles, but I have no data to support accuracy in match air rifles.

Overall firearm precision of manufacture is certainly evident in pneumatic and $CO_2$ airguns as well as the spring-piston models. This factor can never be left out of the overall accuracy picture.

Lubrication of the pellet gun is also important to accuracy. There may be auto-igntion or diesel explosions when the wrong lubricant is used, for example. That situation cannot promote accuracy. Internal pressure produces a temperature that is above the flashpoint of the lube, high enough to ignite the lubricant vapor in the compression chamber. The piston seal may be damaged from such an explosion and consequent residue in the combustion chamber may also affect accuracy due to varied thrust on the pellet.

There may also be a velocity parameter that promotes pellet accuracy—pure speculation on my part. The latest tests I've run with a Model 75 RWS match air rifle gave a consistent pellet speed of 650 fps. If pellets are like other projectiles, this means that the slipstream behind the missile is definitely well below the speed of sound. A bullet leaving the muzzle at around 900 fps may still suffer from base disturbance because the slipstream behind that missile may be over the speed of sound. This whole speed-of-sound issue is slightly suspect in light of the fact that our most accurate cartridge—currently—is the 6mm PPC USA with the 22 PPC USA close behind, and both shoot fast bullets.

The 6mm PPC is most often in the winner's circle at high-competition benchrest matches and, of course, the bullet leaves the muzzle at close to three times the speed of sound. At the same time, there is ample evidence that a region of disturbance exists within a specific velocity range that appears to be slightly higher than the speed of sound but well below the 2000 fps realm. It's seen at work with the 22 Long Rifle. Shooters imagined that the high-velocity Long Rifle bullet would drift less than the standard-velocity bullet, but this was not the case. The region of disturbance was singled out as the cause for the high-speed bullet to drift off course more than the standard-velocity missile.

But with pellets, perhaps the lower velocity factor is important due to the extreme lightness of the projectile as well as its form. I only know that at 10 meters my RWS match rifle cuts a 20-caliber hole in the bullseye with the rifle rested, shooting indoors, of course, without atmospheric disturbance.

Another factor that must play a role in airgun accuracy is the absence of bore fouling, but this is not to suggest that there is no fouling. I make certain the bores of all test rifles are clean before attempting to shoot groups with them. Certainly there is no copper fouling in the bore because there is no copper jacket as on a centerfire bullet. As for lead fouling, the low-velocity pellet doesn't do much of that either. Lubricating oil can burn in the bore, however, and its residue should be removed. In short, the airgun bore doesn't suffer from rifling that is coated with copper, lead or powder residue. Nor does the rifling or throat of the pellet gun suffer rapid wear, as is the case with gas cutting from an exploding powder charge.

Other pellet gun accuracy attributes include good sights, irons or scopes, and fine triggers. Heavy stocks and overall rifle weight also affect accuracy favorably. The RWS Micro Peep sight on one of my test rifles offered an excellent sight picture, for example, and, of course, the addition of a glass sight improved

Beeman Feinwerkbau 100.

grouping even further. Triggers on all test arms, including the pistol, were of match quality. Everyone knows that a poor trigger pull only serves to disrupt aim, so the fine trigger system is definitely another aspect of high accuracy in the airgun. The heavy stock of the target rifle helped bring total weight to a stable 10-plus pounds.

I found the entire airgun accuracy profile interesting, especially considering that one of my test rifles, the Model 75 RWS, had over 100 working parts, all synchronized to do their respective jobs in concert with each other.

With fewer near-city shooting ranges these days, the air rifle and air pistol are increasingly important to marksmen who want to shoot often without long drives. But the airgun would offer little if it didn't have a remarkable ability to group its tiny bullets on the target. Even in playing games, such as airgun silhouette shooting, it is that high level of accuracy that keeps the entire sub-sport of airgunning interesting and worthwhile. Practice is meaningful because a hit denotes good aim, not random chance, and a miss means you did it, not the shooting instrument. That's the beauty of fine accuracy in any gun.

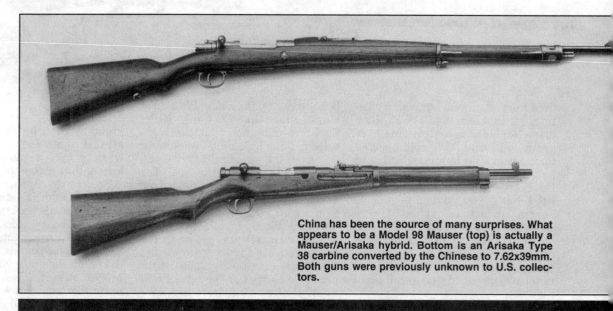

China has been the source of many surprises. What appears to be a Model 98 Mauser (top) is actually a Mauser/Arisaka hybrid. Bottom is an Arisaka Type 38 carbine converted by the Chinese to 7.62x39mm. Both guns were previously unknown to U.S. collectors.

# SURPLUS Surprises

## Previously unknown military surplus guns are showing up in the U.S., making the collectors drool and ponder.

## by CHARLES W. KARWAN

WHEN THE IMPORTATION of military surplus arms was opened up again in 1984 after a hiatus of sixteen years, it turned the collector's market for such guns topsyturvy. Formerly rare or totally unavailable models suddenly became common. There are myriad examples like the Finnish variations of the Mosin-Nagant rifles, Australian-made Lee-Enfields, Czech Vz 52 carbines and pistols, Russian SKS carbines, Swedish Ljungman rifles,

Spanish Destroyer carbines and many more.

At the same time, much to the dismay of many collectors, some formerly expensive models became inexpensive almost overnight. A prominent example is the Czech Vz 52 7.62x25mm pistol that had a market value of $750 and could suddenly be purchased in beautiful condition for well under $200, complete with a holster, cleaning rod, lanyard and spare magazine. Similarly, an East

German Makarov pistol once worth nearly $1000 could be bought for under $200 with a spare magazine and holster in beautiful condition.

All of this has been grand, except for the poor guys who bought their specimens at pre-'84 prices, but the real treat during the current run of military surplus importation has been the surplus surprises. These are the guns and model variations that previously were virtually unknown to exist in the U.S. Invariably, the reason they were unknown is that they do not appear in the standard references, or if they do it is the barest mention.

The Spanish FR8, shown with bayonet and sling, looks more like an assault rifle than a bolt-action carbine. The sights, flash hider, sling, bayonet, grenade launching ability and 7.62mm NATO chambering allowed easy transition to the CETME auto rifle.

The least significant of these surplus surprises are the previously unknown minor variations of well-known models that have shown up. In many cases, they were just as much a surprise to the importer as everyone else. A good example are the many Swedish Mausers that showed up with threaded muzzles. No English-language reference mentions these guns, and speculation over the purpose of the threads ran rampant. Collectors thought it was for the fitting of noise suppressors, muzzle brakes, grenade launchers, etc. Actually, the threads were put on the Swedish Model 96, 96/38 and 38 rifles, primarily to allow the fitting of a blank adapter for the safe firing of blanks during training. It was necessary to prevent accidents from the wooden bullets used in the Swedish training ammunition. The blank adapter stopped the wooden bullet from going downrange.

Similarly, a number of previously unknown variations showed up among the many surplus Chinese Type 56 (SKS) rifles that have been recently imported. Some have shown up with pressed-in and pinned barrels instead of being threaded; some have brown plastic stocks and ribbed plastic handguards; a few have gas cut-off levers, and a significant number of other variations have been encountered. Indeed, a substantial collection could be made up just of Chinese SKS variations.

Another interesting and previously unknown variation of an existing rifle model that has appeared is the French MAS 36/51. This is a post-World War II modification of the familiar French MAS 36. It differs from the standard model only in that it has an integral grenade launcher mounted on the barrel. Prior to their recent importation, just about no one knew of this model's existence.

A good many of the surplus surprises have been well-known military models converted into interesting previously unknown variations or even new models. One of the more intriguing is a variation of the familiar British No. 5 "Jungle Carbine."

On the surface, these rifles look pretty much like a conventional No. 5. However, close inspection reveals that they are actually No. 4 rifles converted into the No. 5 carbine configuration. On the left side of the receiver they are pantograph-engraved NO 5 CONV-CYP/NIC.

The barrel was shortened to carbine length and fitted with a No. 5 flash-hider assembly. The forend and rear handguard were shortened to approximate No. 5 specifications, and the buttstock was fitted with a No. 5 buttpad/sling loop assembly. In the process, the cut for the No. 4 sling swivel base has been plugged with a piece of wood. The net result is a Jungle Carbine with a heavier barrel and without the lightening cuts in the action.

No one seems to know the exact story behind these carbines. Some research has turned up pictures of Cyprus police carrying No. 5 carbines. It was a logical choice due to the paramilitary-type operations they have had to conduct, and the fact that there has been strong British Commonwealth influence there for decades, including the U.N.

peace-keeping force located there since 1964.

Considering this and the markings on these guns, I am relatively certain that these No. 5-type carbines were made by or for the Nicosia police on Cyprus. They probably tried to acquire additional No. 5 carbines some time after gaining independence and found that none were available. Since parts to do conversions of readily available No. 4 rifles were available, that route was taken. Regardless of the reason behind these conversions, they are an interesting and previously unknown field variation.

Due to their stiff and short barrel and unlightened action, they should shoot great, too. These rifles should not be confused with similar commercial conversions of Mk. III and possibly No. 4 Lee-Enfields to No. 5 configuration by Golden State Arms, Santa Fe Arms, and maybe others.

Many of the surplus surprises are guns converted to different chamberings. Two such conversions have shown up among the imports from China. The first were a number of M1911A1 pistols that had been converted by the Chinese to take the 7.62x25mm (7.62mnm Tokarev pistol) cartridge. The major modifications made were that the breech face was welded and recut for the smaller diameter cartridge case, the extractor claw was extended, the barrel replaced or relined, and the magazine well opened up front-to-rear to take the standard Chinese Type 54 (Russian TT-33) pistol magazine. These are neat pistols and a natural for 1911 collectors. In addition, they

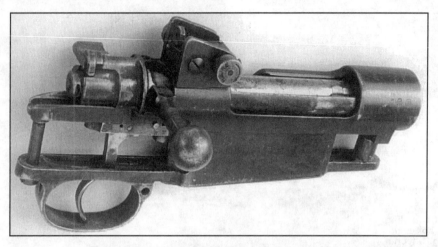

Though few complete Danish Model 52 rifles were imported, a fair number of actions made it to the U.S. market. The peep sight is very similar to the U.S. Garand and give a like picture. Action is standard German Gew. 98.

make a great basis for a multi-caliber pistol. The addition of a 38 Super barrel and magazine allows conversion to that chambering. Likewise for the 9mm Parabellum round. To go back to a 45 ACP requires a barrel, slide assembly, and magazine for that round. With a little imagination, other chamberings can be added

The other previously unknown Chinese chambering conversion of a known model was quite a surprise when they arrived. These were Japanese Type 38 6.5mm rifles and carbines modified into 7.62x39mm carbines. These were obviously made from some of the many thousands of Japanese Arisaka rifles captured and inherited by China at the close of World War II. The huge Mukden arsenal in Manchuria even manufactured Arisakas during the Japanese occupation of that area prior to and during World War II, and quite likely afterward.

The Chinese had so many Type 38 Arisakas that they equipped entire military units with these rifles and made ammunition for them until at least the late 1950s. They were frequently encountered by our troops fighting against the Chinese in Korea. Evidently, when they began switching to the 7.62x39mm cartridge in their Type 56 SKS rifles and AK-47 assault rifles, they decided to get even more mileage out of the Arisakas on hand. They rebored them, modified the magazine for the shorter round, and, if the Arisaka was a rifle, reconfigured them into carbine status, even to include shortening the rear sight. Unfortunately, the workmanship on these was marginal at best.

At least two other unique Arisaka variations came out of China as surplus surprises. The first is a small number of Type 38 6.5mm rifles that were cut down into carbines like the previously mentioned guns, but left in their original chambering and with an SKS folding bayonet added. The other was a group of Type 99 7.7mm Arisaka short rifles in their original chambering that also had SKS folding bayonets added. All of these variations were new ones for the Arisaka collectors.

Getting extra mileage out of older rifles seems to have been a common theme with many of the surplus surprises. A good example are the 7.62mm NATO (308) Spanish Mausers that appeared on the market. There were a number of different models that showed up. First, there were Model 1916 Mauser carbines converted from 7x57 to 7.62mm NATO. Another variation is the same rifle bearing the Spanish Guardia Civil (Civil Guard) crest on the receiver. These rifles are pretty straight-forward conversions that look externally like a standard Model 1916 except for their sights. Obviously, they were made to use standard ammunition once the 7.62mm CETME rifle was adopted.

More interesting is what the Spanish called the FR7. These, too, are Model 1916 carbines that have been converted to 7.62mm NATO, but in this case they have also been totally reconfigured so they look more like assault rifles than bolt-action rifles.

The stocks were shortened to a half-stock. They were rebarreled with 7.62mm NATO barrels that are configured like that of the standard Spanish CETME Model C assault

rifle with rings on the barrel to support the use of rifle grenades. They have a front sight, sling mounts and flash suppressor like a CETME. In addition, a tube is mounted under the barrel that looks all the world like the gas cylinder on an M-14. Instead, it serves as a mounting base for the standard CETME bayonet (one of the neater bayonets around) as well as a reservoir for a cleaning kit. To top it off, there is a rotating multi-aperture peep sight welded to the action's rear receiver ring. All the metal is refinished with a dull phosphate-type finish. The obvious intention was to make the old Spanish Mauser rifles as much like the CETME assault rifle as possible, most likely for training purposes or for use by reserve or paramilitary forces. This is an exotic and racy looking rifle!

All the above mentioned Spanish rifles were converted from Model 1916s which have the old model 1893 Mauser-type action. As a pre-98 Mauser type, it is not considered as strong or safe as the Model 98. This was not a problem for the Spanish because their standard military 7.62mm loading is quite mild and not nearly as hot as NATO standard or even commercial 308 Winchester ammunition.

As a consequence, I highly recommend staying with mild loadings when shooting these rifles. According to several independent tests, they *appear* to be safe enough with NATO-spec 7.62mm and commercial 308 SAAMI-spec ammunition, but there is 7.62mm machinegun ammunition out there that is not recommended for use in these guns. Also, it is prudent to keep all handloads on the mild side. It is quite unlikely that any of these rifles would actually blow up if heavy loads were used in them. However, the bolt locking lug seats might set back, resulting in excessive headspace and making the bolt extremely difficult to open after shooting.

When the FR7 rifles appeared, I found them to be fascinating, but I also found myself wishing that the Spanish had built them on Model 98-type actions. No sooner than I made my wish, I found out that the Spanish made an almost identical rifle called the FR8, using their Model 98-type M43 Mauser rifle as a base. About the only difference between the FR7 and FR8, beside the action, is that the former has a turned-down bolt handle and the latter has a bolt handle straight out to the side, just like the rifle from which it was converted. Similarly, the FR7 has the straight-grip stock of its parent while the FR8 has a pistol grip.

Since the Spanish M43 is a 98 Mauser-type action, it is significantly stronger and safer than the 93. As a consequence, they are far more desirable for shooting purposes than any of the previously mentioned Spanish conversions. The FR8s were eventually imported in quantity, and I was one of the first in line to get one. To this day, I have not found one word of mention of these interesting rifles in any English-language reference.

A surplus surprise called the M52 turned up among a lot of Mausers that were recently imported from Denmark. Post-World War II Denmark had an organization similar to our National Rifle Association (NRA) and Director of Civilian Marksmanship (DCM) combined. They had just re-equipped their military forces with M-1 Garand rifles and, in light of their recent World War II experience, they wanted to get their population as proficient with arms as possible.

Denmark had inherited large numbers of 98 Mauser rifles from the withdrawn German occupation forces, and these rifles were used as a basis to build the M52 rifle. The gun consists of a G.98 Mauser action with a straight bolt handle and is fitted with a 21.6-inch medium-weight, target-grade barrel made by the famous Danish firm of Schultz & Larsen. Chamberings were either 6.5x55mm or 30-06, at the choice of the shooter. The original rifle stock

was shortened to half-stock configuration. An interesting set of sights were fitted that give the same sight picture as that of an M-1 Garand. The rear sight is a peep that has click adjustment knobs for elevation and windage, just like the M-1, while the front sight has a post with ears, again like the M-1 sight. The idea was to make transition to the use of the then-standard Garand as easy as possible. These rifles were supplied at nominal cost to members of the Danish equivalent of the NRA, in much the same way our DCM has supplied surplus rifles like Model 1903A3s, M-1 Garands and M-1 Carbines to members of DCM-affiliated clubs to this day.

Just a few of these M52 rifles made it into the U.S., but one U.S. importer offered the actions from these rifles, complete with the unique adjustable rear peep sight, at quite reasonable prices.

When a large number of Mauser rifles were imported from Chile, there were a number of surprises. While most of us were familiar with the Chilean Model 95 7x57mm rifles and carbines, we were completely surprised to find there was also a Chilean Model 1912 7x57mm rifle (29.1-inch barrel), short rifle (23.6-inch barrel), and carbine (21.3-inch barrel). All are marked WAFFENFABRIK STEYR AUSTRIA on the left side of the receiver. Unlike the Model 95s, these have Model 98-type Mauser actions. Export Mausers made by Steyr are pretty uncommon and desirable, particularly carbines. However, the surprises from Chile didn't end there.

Chile, like most other Western

countries, adopted the 7.62mm NATO cartridge in the late 1950s or early 1960s. As a result, they also converted many of their bolt-action rifles to that caliber. Prior to their recent importation, these conversions were totally unknown in this country.

It would appear that the model designations for these rifles are the same as their original designation with the addition of a "-61." Thus, a Model 95 became a Model 95-61 and the Model 1912 became the Model 1912-61. The Model 1912 rifles converted to 7.62mm NATO appear to either have been shortened to short rifle configuration, or, possibly, only short rifles were converted, while the Model 95 rifles were left in full length configuration.

In both cases, the barrels were rebored and rechambered to 7.62mm NATO. On the Model 95-61 rifles, the rear receiver bridge is stamped "7.62" over an "N." In addition, material is added to the top of the front sight by welding to help compensate for the much flatter trajectory of the NATO round over the old 175-grain round-nosed 7x57 round for which the rifle's sights were originally regulated. The same recommendations for ammunition hold for the Model 95-61 as the previously mentioned Spanish conversions of pre-Model 98 Mauser rifles.

The Model 1912 rifles have a "-61" added to the already present MODELO 1912 on the rifle's receiver, and NATO is stamped under that. Also, a spacer is added to the front of the magazine well to improve feeding of the shorter cartridge.

In the case of the Model 1912-61,

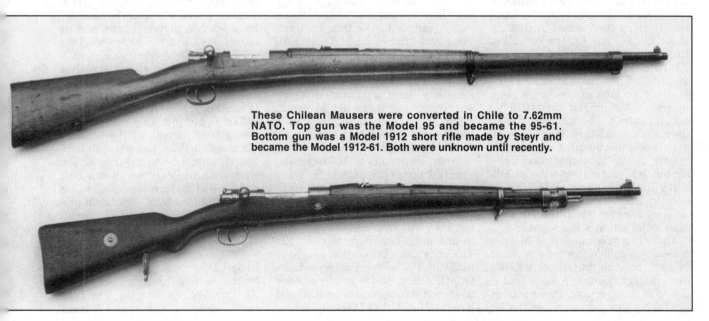

These Chilean Mausers were converted in Chile to 7.62mm NATO. Top gun was the Model 95 and became the 95-61. Bottom gun was a Model 1912 short rifle made by Steyr and became the Model 1912-61. Both were unknown until recently.

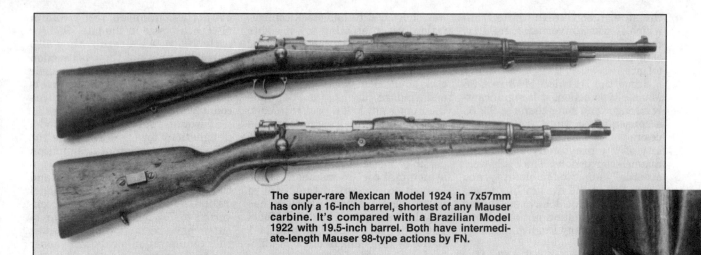

The super-rare Mexican Model 1924 in 7x57mm has only a 16-inch barrel, shortest of any Mauser carbine. It's compared with a Brazilian Model 1922 with 19.5-inch barrel. Both have intermediate-length Mauser 98-type actions by FN.

we have the interesting situation of a previously unknown conversion of a previously almost unknown model. In effect, a double whammy.

Latin America has been particularly fertile ground for the discovery of previously unknown Mauser rifle variations. From Mexico came a substantial number of Mexican Mausers. Most such guns were fairly well known in the U.S., even though they were not common. However, among the Mexican Mausers was a real surprise.

Only particularly knowledgeable Mauser collectors know that the Mexicans bought a substantial number of Model 1924 Mauser rifles from FN of Belgium. But, until they hit the U.S. surplus market, even these collectors didn't know there was also a small lot of interesting Model 1924 carbines purchased as well.

Both the Mexican Model 24 rifle and carbine have the beautiful Mexican eagle crest on the front receiver ring surrounded by REBPUBLICA MEXICANA 1924. On the left side of the receiver, in two lines, is FAB.NAT.D'ARMSS DE GUERRE HERSTAL-BELGIQUE. They have Model 98-type Mauser actions of the large ring, intermediate-length variety. This action is about .25-inch shorter than the standard military 98 action, with a bolt about .20-inch shorter in length. It was developed specifically for the 7x57mm spitzer-bulleted military load which is significantly shorter than the German 8x57mm military load for which the standard Mauser 98 action was designed.

These intermediate-length Mauser actions are sometimes referred to as "short" actions, but there was an even smaller sporting Mauser that is the true short action. These actions are highly favored by gunsmiths for

building rifles chambered for cartridges shorter than 30-06, such as 6mm Remington, 257 Roberts, 7x57mm, 308, 243 and others.

The Mexican Model 1924 carbine is a real collector's treat for a number of reasons. First, *true* military carbines (less than 23-inch barrel) built on a Mauser 98-type action are quite uncommon in any model variation. Second, the total production of the Mexican Model 1924 carbine appears to be not more than 1200 guns total. In the world of military long arms, that is minuscule and genuinely rare by any standard. Finally, the Mexican carbine has an original barrel length of only 16 inches. To the best of my knowledge, that is the shortest barrel of any standard-production Mauser carbine ever made. The next shortest I can identify are a number of different carbines with a 17.3-inch barrel length. Naturally, shooting a military load in that short barrel lends new meaning to the terms muzzle blast and muzzle flash! These neat carbines have a pistol grip stock and no provision to mount a bayonet.

Unfortunately, these carbines must have been popular because the surviving specimens are in pretty rough shape. Regardless, they are a pleasant surprise and a rare and desirable collectible.

When shipments of Mauser rifles started entering the U.S. from Brazil, there were a couple more surplus surprises, and both of them were highly desirable Model 98-type carbines. The first was the previously unknown Brazilian Model 1922 7x57 carbine. This little gem was made by FN with an intermediate-length action and a mildly turned down bolt handle, and is marked just like the Model 1924 Mexican carbine

The Mexican Model 1924 rifle and carbine both have receiver markings as shown, the handsome Mexican crest of an eagle holding a snake in its mouth. All specimens seen so far are in pretty rough condition.

on the left side of its receiver. It wears the Brazilian star crest on its front receiver ring top and MOD. 1922 on the right side of the receiver. Its stock has no pistol grip, and its barrel is 19.5 inches in length. Like the Mexican Mauser carbine, most of these are in rough shape, but they are still a rare collectible.

The other previously unknown Brazilian gun is the Model 1935 7x57mm carbine. This rare Mauser was actually made by the original Mauser factory. It has the standard-length Model 98 large ring action with a sharply turned down bolt handle and 22-inch barrel. It has a very distinctive front sight with protective ears that is extremely uncommon on Mausers.

The front top of the receiver ring wears the attractive United States of Brazil star crest. On the right is MOD.1935. On the left is MAUSER-WERKE A.G.OBERNDORF A/N. The rear receiver ring has the famous Mauser banner insignia on top. Its stock has a pistol grip and provision for a sling on both the bottom and left side.

This is one of the best fitted and finished military rifles ever made, easily on par with the German-made Argentine Mausers which are equally well made and smooth in operation. It is basically a carbine version of the Mauser "Standard Modell" or later Kar. 98k. This is my favorite of all the military Mausers because of its handiness, quality, chambering and unique features.

Total production appears to be quite small since no specimen observed to date by the author has had more than a four digit serial number, and the highest seen has been under 2000.

Out of Colombia came several more previously unknown Mauser models. Two are 7x57mm short rifles with 23.6-inch barrels. Both wear the Colombian crest on their receiver ring. One, designated the Modelo 1940, was made by FN of Belgium and is so marked on the left side of the receiver, like the Mexican Model 24. The other, designated Modelo 1934, was made by Steyr of Austria and is marked STEYR-SOLOTHURN WAFFEN, quite an uncommon marking. Total production of the Modelo 1940 had to be small, considering Belgium fell to the German invaders in the spring of that year.

While both of the above are interesting, the one that was a real surprise was the Colombian Model 53 Mauser carbine in 30-06 with only a 17.3-inch barrel. This is a post-World War II model made by FN of Belgium for the Colombians in quite small numbers, supposedly for issue to non-commissioned officers. I suspect they may have been carried, but I doubt that they were fired much! Recoil, muzzle blast and muzzle flash would be high enough to make a brass monkey flinch!

Latin America hasn't been the only source for previously unknown Mauser models. Recently, a large group of Mausers were imported from Turkey. Included were some Gew. 98 rifles of the type used by the Germans in World War I, except these were made by BRNO of Czechoslovakia in the 1920s. This variation is yet another one unknown in the U.S. until now. Best of all, they are in great shape.

Among the many Mauser and Arisaka rifles recently imported from China, there were a few guns that had features of both that were virtually unknown in the U.S. These are

Mauser-type rifles made in Manchuria after the Japanese occupation of the area in the 1930s, and probably after the creation of the Japanese puppet state of Manchukuo.

Externally, the gun appears to be a Model 98-type long rifle and is chambered for the 8x57mm cartridge. However, close inspection reveals many differences from a standard Mauser. The top of the receiver has two gas escape holes similar to those of a Type 38 Arisaka, and it is fitted with a sheet steel bolt cover, also like that rifle. The bolt shows even more Arisaka influence in that the firing pin is of the hollow Arisaka type with the mainspring inside. The bolt retains the Mauser wing safety, but the bolt sleeve is not threaded to the bolt body as in the Mauser; it's attached by lugs similar to the way the Arisaka safety is held to its bolt body.

The uniqueness of this rifle makes it a desirable collectible to both Mauser and Arisaka collectors, as well as military rifle collectors in general. I recently encountered one of these that had been rebarreled to the Japanese 6.5x50mm cartridge and fitted with a late Arisaka Type 38 front sight assembly and front band to take the Arisaka bayonet. This was undoubtedly done by the Japanese to make better use of these rifles when they got short of arms toward the end of World War II.

Until they were offered on the U.S. surplus market, the Indian 2A and 2A1 rifles were also almost completely unknown here. These extremely interesting rifles were made from about 1962 until at least into 1968. They are little more than a Short Magazine Lee-Enfield No. 1 Mark III made at the Indian Ishapore Arsenal in 7.62mm NATO, instead of 303 British. Except for the parts changed to handle the shorter, higher-pressure and rimless NATO cartridge, the two rifles are nearly identical. The changes are the magazine, the extractor, the location of the ejector screw, the stripper clip guide, sights, and the metallurgy and heat-treatment of the bolt and receiver.

The original No. 1 Mark III action is not strong enough to handle the 7.62mm NATO cartridge with a sufficient margin of safety. To gain the necessary strength, the Indians took the simple expedient of making the receiver and bolt out of a stronger alloy and gave it a more sophisticated heat-treatment.

It is a significant rifle in a variety of ways: It was the only rifle in the Lee-Enfield family that was made originally in 7.62mm NATO, rather than being a conversion; its 12-round magazine had the highest capacity ever fielded on a standard military bolt-action rifle; it was the last non-sniper military bolt-action rifle ever produced; and, finally, it was the last of the noble Lee-Enfield line of mili-

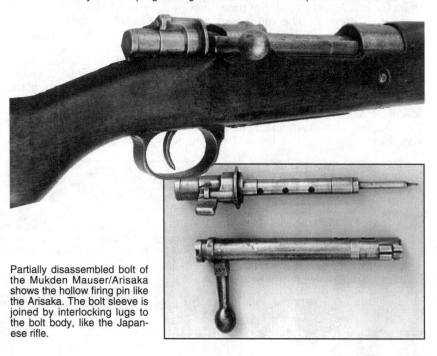

Made at the Mukden arsenal in China, small quantities of the Mauser/Arisaka showed up in shipments from China. What looks like a cocking piece on the rear of the bolt is actually the mainspring housing. Even the bolt knob is shaped like the Arisaka's.

Partially disassembled bolt of the Mukden Mauser/Arisaka shows the hollow firing pin like the Arisaka. The bolt sleeve is joined by interlocking lugs to the bolt body, like the Japanese rifle.

Though it looks like a World War II Ishapore No. 1 Mark III Lee-Enfield, the squared magazine gives it away as an Indian 2A1 in 7.62mm NATO. Made from about 1962 until at least 1968, these are the last of the military Lee-Enfield rifle variations to be produced.

Typical markings on the Indian 2A1. R.F.I. stands for Rifle Factory Ishapore. Other than the magazine, the other giveaway as to its identity is the squared nose cap. All specimens seen to date are in pretty rough shape.

tary rifles to be produced. For more information on this fascinating rifle, see my piece on it in the 1993 GUNS ILLUSTRATED.

I am convinced that the main importer of these Indian 2A and 2A1 rifles mistakenly believed they were just conversions of No. 1 Mark III rifles. They were such an unknown that even the importer didn't know what they had!

This is not the first time that has happened. When the Finnish variations of the Mosin-Nagant rifle began to be imported in quantity by a couple of different firms, they offered the Finnish Model 91, Model 27, Model 28, Model 28/30 and the Model 39. This included all the standard Mosin-Nagant infantry rifles of the Finnish Army and Civil Guard except one, the obscure Model 24, which is not even mentioned in some references.

I wanted one of each of the Finnish Mosin-Nagant models to study, shoot and write about. I called the importers and asked if they had seen any Model 24s go through. In both cases, I was told they had not seen any at all. Then I ran into one at a gun show mislabeled as a Model 91 Mosin-Nagant made in Switzerland. You guessed it, the importer had Model 24s all the time and didn't know it! The confusion came from the fact that most Finnish Model 24s have barrels that were made in Switzerland by SIG, and the barrels are so marked under the wood.

Though it looks externally like a Model 91 Mosin-Nagant, the Model 24 is the first significant and distinctive Finnish variation from the

Russian model. The Finnish 91s are just mildly reworked or rebuilt Russian guns with minor changes in sights, sight markings or sling mountings. In contrast, the Finnish Civil Guard Model 24 has a completely different barrel configuration and specifications.

The barrel of the Model 24 is of the medium-heavy target type from the receiver all the way out to just behind the front sight. From there forward, it drops down in size to the specifications of the standard Model 91 so it can mount the regular-issue Model 91 bayonet. This distinctive 31.5-inch-long heavy barrel causes the rifle to weigh 10.3 to 10.5 pounds. To the best of my knowledge, that makes it the heaviest smokeless powder bolt-action infantry rifle ever fielded. Evidently, the Finns were willing to put up with the heavier weight to achieve a higher level of accuracy.

The ironic thing about the Finnish Model 24 is that even though a substantial number of them have been imported, they are still relatively unknown because their owners mistakenly believe they are Swiss-made Model 91s.

Not all of the surplus surprises in the rifle department have been bolt actions. Several have been semi-automatics. Most students of recent military weaponry know that the French adopted a semi-automatic rifle in the post-World War II era called the MAS Model 1949, chambered for 7.5mm. However, out of the clear blue, an MAS Model 1944 appeared on the market and caught most of us by surprise. The virtually unknown 1944 gun was the little-

known predecessor to the Model 1949. It is virtually identical and most parts will interchange between the two rifles. The main differences are that the Model 1944 mounts the MAS Model 1936 bayonet, while the 1949 gun does not, and the 1949 has provision and sights to launch rifle grenades.

Evidently, the French ordnance people had the design for the MAS Model 1944 ready to go even while the Germans occupied their country. Once France was liberated, they lost little time in getting the rifle into production. Certainly, in spite of its 1944 designation, the gun was produced after the war was over, but you have to give the French credit for moving quickly. The fact that the Model 1944 rifles appearing on the surplus market seemed to all be in great shape was an added treat.

Another unknown from France that surfaced out of the blue was the

The Finnish Model 24 (top) looks like a Russian or Finnish Model 91 Mosin-Nagant, but it weighs a few pounds more due to it's heavier barrel. Below it is the Finnish Model 39, last of the Finnish Mosin-Nagant military models.

The 22-caliber MAS 45 looks more like a modern sporter than a military trainer. The iron sights are excellent, but B-Square makes a no drill/tap scope mount that replaces the rear sight should a scope be desired.

If the Egyptian Hakim (top) in 8x57mm wasn't a surprise for the military rifle buff, its little brother, the 7.62x39mm Rashid (bottom), almost certainly was. Only about 6500 Rashids were made, making it an uncommon to rare rifle.

extremely interesting MAS Model 45 22-caliber rimfire military training rifle. During World War II, it was Free French forces that captured the Mauser plant in Oberndorf. The French used the plant to produce P-38 pistols and Kar. 98k Mauser rifles for their own use from parts on hand. They then packed up parts and manufacturing equipment and sent it back to France. Among this booty was the needed parts to produce bolt-action 22 Long Rifle training rifles like the Mauser KKW.

The French ordnance people at Manufacture d'Armes Saint-Étienne (MAS) very cleverly modified the Mauser tangent sight, usually mounted in front of the receiver into a receiver-mounted peep, and approximating that of the MAS Model 1936 rifle, and mounted it on the KKW action. They also modified the action to a repeater using a detachable magazine much like some of the Mauser 22 sporters. This action was mated to a medium-heavy barrel just short of 24 inches long and a well-proportioned, plain, half-stock with a pistol grip. The net result is a man-sized 22 rifle suitable for marksmanship training and practice. It also makes a dandy hunting rifle as is.

Most examples are marked MAS in an oval with MOD.45 just under it on the front receiver ring. Occasionally, specimens are found with receivers that had already been marked with the Mauser banner insignia before they were captured. In these cases, the MAS marking was deleted. The rear sight is calibrated from 30 to 150 meters and has windage adjustment through the use of opposing screws. The specimen I have worked with is superbly accurate.

It appears that the French used these rifles for training and marksmanship practice for many years, though many specimens are in like-new condition.

A couple of other semi-automatic unknowns that surfaced as surplus surprises came out of Egypt. They are the Hakim and Rashid rifles. Since they are mentioned in one of the major military arms references, avid students of military arms knew they existed, but the guns were totally unknown to the general gun-buying public before they appeared on the market.

The Hakim is a line-for-line copy of the Swedish Ljungman Model 42 rifle with only minor differences, except for the chambering being 8x57mm instead of 6.5x55mm. Like its Swedish brother, the Hakim is an accurate, rugged and reliable rifle. This should not be a surprise since it was built on Swedish equipment with Swedish technical help. It has the same bolt system as the Russian Tokarev, Belgian FAL and several other successful semi-autos, as well as the same gas system as the M-16 and MAS Model 1949.

If the Hakim was relatively unknown, the Rashid was even more so. Basically, the Rashid is a Hakim re-engineered to shoot the shorter and less powerful 7.62x39mm cartridge. It would seem that the Russians supplied the Egyptians

with some SKS rifles and they were well liked. Rather than completely retool to make the SKS, the Egyptians chose to make an equivalent using their Hakim tooling. I'm sure some feeling of national pride in their own design enters into the equation, too.

The Rashid is a short carbine similar in size to the SKS. It even has a folding bayonet like the SKS. It uses a conventional cocking handle to cycle the bolt rather than the unconventional moving bolt cover of the Ljungman and Hakim. However, it is also a whole pound heavier than an SKS, so it is not as handy. On the other side of the coin, the Rashid has truly minuscule recoil and an excellent detachable ten-round magazine, as opposed to the non-detachable variety of the SKS.

It is important to be aware that much of the 7.62x39mm ammunition on the market has corrosive priming, and the Rashid does not have the chrome-lined bore of the SKS. Consequently, it must be cleaned properly as soon after shooting as possible or the bore will be ruined. Also, remember that cleaning must include places where the gas meets the bolt carrier as well. My recommendation is to only shoot non-corrosive ammunition in the Rashid and save yourself some potential grief.

Total production of the Rashid is estimated to be only 6500 pieces, a

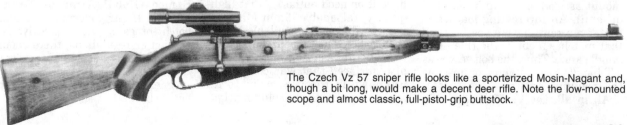

The Czech Vz 57 sniper rifle looks like a sporterized Mosin-Nagant and, though a bit long, would make a decent deer rifle. Note the low-mounted scope and almost classic, full-pistol-grip buttstock.

drop in the bucket in military terms. Both the Hakim and Rashid are desirable collectibles and fun shooters.

The opening up of trade with many of the former Eastern Bloc countries has turned up some more surplus surprises. From Czechoslovakia, a small quantity of heretofore unknown Vz 57 sniper rifles has surfaced. This is an extremely interesting rifle in a number of ways.

It uses the basic Model 91/30 Mosin-Nagant action which has proven to be incredibly durable and long lived in service. Naturally, it is chambered for the 7.62x52R Russian cartridge, the original Mosin-Nagant chambering back in 1891. The bolt handle is extended in length and turned down sharply, allowing the scope to be mounted lower than has ever been done on any other sniper rifle based on the Mosin-Nagant action.

The rifle's stock has a high, straight comb and full pistol grip, making it much like a modern sporting rifle stock. The forend is of the half-stock variety, further promoting the sporting rifle appearance of the gun. The barrel is of medium weight and about 28 inches long with a tangent open rear sight and hooded post front sight mounted on it. The sling loops are on the left side of the rifle, indicating the designer did not intend for the sling to be used as a shooting aid.

The telescopic sight of this rifle has only 2.5x magnification, adequate for most police sniping purposes, but inadequate for military sniping. It has excellent clarity, good resolution, but poor mechanical design. Like most World War II-era scopes, when adjustments are made to the rifle's zero, the reticle appears to move within the scope's field of view. That is, if you adjust the scope to cause the rifle to shoot higher and to the right, the reticle will appear to be to be in the upper right-hand quadrant of the field. This is crude by modern optical standards with our constantly centered reticles.

The scope is mounted quite low over the bore using a dovetail-type side mount. The mount is held to the dovetail via two screws that both mechanically position and secure the mount as well as clamp it onto the dovetail. An interesting feature is that the screws have a special head that matches a cut in the rifle's bolt handle knob. Thus, the bolt serves as a T-handle tool to tighten or unscrew the mounting screws.

All in all, the Vz 57 sniper rifle

The Hungarian PA-63 is nearly identical to the Walther PP except for longer slide and barrel, and the aluminum frame.

The Model 74 in 32 ACP is from Hungary, but might have been designed/made in Romania. It's another Walther PP derivative with an aluminum frame.

impresses me as being one of the most modernized and sophisticated of all the Mosin-Nagant family, a fascinating collectible that would be fun to shoot and a decent hunting rifle to boot.

From Hungary, we have seen several surplus surprises appear on the market. The first was the Hungarian PA-63 pistol chambered for the 9mm Makarov round. This cartridge has about the same overall length as the 380 ACP, but has a case length 1 millimeter longer and a larger head size. In addition, the bore size is larger, .363-inch versus .355-inch for the 380 ACP, and it has a 150 to 200 fps velocity advantage over the 380 as well.

The PA-63 is a direct copy of the Walther PP with a slightly longer barrel and slide, as well as an aluminum frame. It is well made and finished. Some of the examples that have been imported have been rebarreled to 380 ACP for ease of ammunition procurement. Personally, I prefer the original 9mm Makarov chambering for its added power. I have it on good authority that high-quality, reloadable, 9mm Makarov ammo will soon be available loaded with jacketed hollowpoint bullets.

A smaller version of the PA-63 also surfaced that was completely unknown in the U.S. prior to its appearance on the surplus market.

Called the R61, this little pistol is just a tad larger than a Walther PPK and is chambered for the same 9mm Makarov round, though many were also rebarreled to 380 ACP to make them more saleable. Everything said about the PA-63 as to quality also applies to this handy little piece.

The third surplus surprise pistol that came out of Hungary, but may have had Romanian origins, is the Model 74 in 32 ACP. In most ways, it is a close relative to the previously mentioned pistols in that it is a Walther PP derivative with an aluminum frame. Beside the chambering, it is basically the same as the other two except it is slightly larger than the R61 in both length and height, and it uses a butt-type magazine catch. Because of the way its grip frame is contoured, and the larger spur on the backstrap to protect the shooter's hand from the slide, I like this one the best of the three, except for its wimpy chambering.

All three of these neat guns are desirable collectibles and shooters, and they are extremely inexpensive for their quality.

Though I have covered a pile of guns that have appeared on the U.S. surplus market that were virtually unknown here before they arrived, there have been more and there undoubtedly will be others. In many cases, the above guns were only available in small quantities and the importer has already sold out. Others are still available as this is written. Mostly, though, they have come and gone with little or no fanfare or, in the case of the Finnish Model 24, without even a mention. It pays to watch the advertisements in the trade journals, and collectors should not delay should something appear at a good price.

By far, it appears the largest importer of surplus surprises has been Century International Arms of St. Albans, Vermont, and I want to give them particular thanks for their help in preparing this article. Some other importers that have brought in surplus surprises are the Gibbs Rifle Co. (Navy Arms) of Martinsburg, West Virginia; Springfield Sporters of Penn Run, Pennsylvania; and Samco Global Arms of Miami, Florida. If our government doesn't botch things up with restrictive legislation or regulations, there should be many more surplus surprises in the future.

American collectors can only hope for the best. ●

# House Gun, Plinker Gun:
## *An Economy Shooter*

### by J.B. WOOD

**Not everyone can afford a new Colt or Smith & Wesson, so here's a low-cost alternative that shoots straight and reliably.**

Not everyone can start their shooting "career" with a Smith & Wesson, a Colt or a Ruger. This is true of those who want a handgun for recreational shooting and those who buy one for home defense. If the choice is a revolver, even a used gun with any of the above names will have a substantial price. For some, even that brand-name used revolver will take too big a bite out of the family's grocery money.

Fortunately, there is an easy answer: the surplus gun market.

The term "surplus" can take a couple of different meanings. Some of the offerings can be revolvers sold by a domestic police department be-cause they've chosen to update their sidearms and rearm with automatic pistols. In this case, the revolvers will more than likely be well-used brand-name guns, but still priced out of range for many folks. The alternative surplus guns are those from foreign lands whose police and/or military have re-equipped with more modern artillery. Often, the names on these guns won't be as familiar as our home-grown types, but they can still be good buys.

There is a pretty good supply of various models and "off-brand" names available from a number of sources, and though some of these

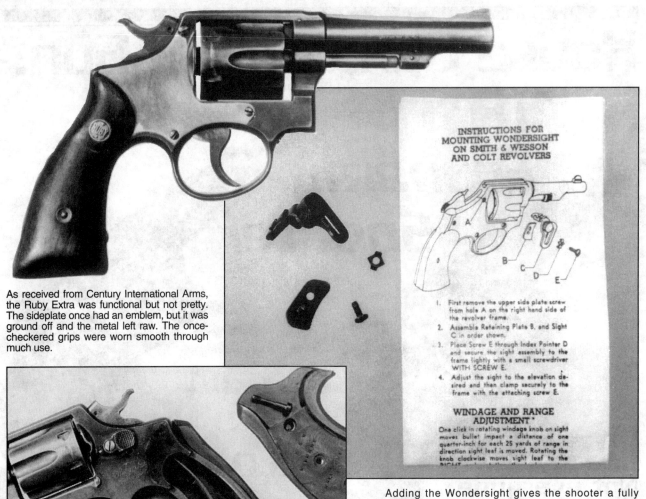

As received from Century International Arms, the Ruby Extra was functional but not pretty. The sideplate once had an emblem, but it was ground off and the metal left raw. The once-checkered grips were worn smooth through much use.

INSTRUCTIONS FOR
MOUNTING WONDERSIGHT
ON SMITH & WESSON
AND COLT REVOLVERS

1. First remove the upper side plate screw from hole A on the right hand side of the revolver frame.
2. Assemble Retaining Plate B, and Sight C in order shown.
3. Place Screw E through Index Pointer D and secure the sight assembly to the frame lightly with a small screwdriver WITH SCREW E.
4. Adjust the sight to the elevation desired and then clamp securely to the frame with the attaching screw E.

WINDAGE AND RANGE ADJUSTMENT

One click in rotating windage knob on sight moves bullet impact a distance of one quarter-inch for each 25 yards of range in direction sight leaf is moved. Rotating the knob clockwise moves sight leaf to the

Adding the Wondersight gives the shooter a fully adjustable rear sight. It was a simple matter to fit the unit to the right side of the gun, as can be seen in the diagram.

The Ruby's frame is almost identical to the S&W K-frame, so Pachmayr's rubber grips fit nicely. The hammer spring screw area needed to be relieved slightly. Groups improved with this addition alone.

guns are a little rough in appearance, most are mechanically sound. Recently, I decided to find out if one of them would make a decent shooter. The subject revolver, from Century International Arms, was a "Ruby Extra" made by Gabilondo y Compania in Spain, in 38 Special chambering. It was definitely not a hand-picked "writer's gun."

Well-used by some South American police agency, its grips had most of the checkering worn off. On the right side, some national or police emblem had been somewhat crudely removed from the sideplate, and this part had been left in the white. Although it probably had been done

fairly recently, some surface rust was beginning to appear. The rest of the original blue was faded and beginning to go brown. There was holster and general handling wear at the edges, and some other small areas of light rust. This poor thing had obviously been carried quite a bit.

Internally, though, it seemed all right. The cylinder was timed correctly, and the bore and chambers were all nice and bright. The trigger pull on both single and double action was smooth and pretty even. Test-fired with ordinary 38 Special loads from Black Hills, the Ruby functioned perfectly, and it even grouped

acceptably well, considering the sights.

The as-issued sighting equipment consisted of a low ramped front with a square blade, and a square notch groove in the topstrap at the rear. On the credit side, the heavy barrel had a low rib, and both rib and topstrap had lengthwise grooving to prevent glare. The problem, of course, was that they were non-adjustable. On 25-yard targets, the gun shot low and to the right.

As many readers will know, the older Llama revolvers were fairly close copies of the earlier Smith & Wessons. This includes the early-style "four screw" sideplate, and this feature gave me an idea. I recalled an accessory adjustable rear sight that was once offered called the "Wondersight." It attached by replacing the upper sideplate screw with a longer one, supplied with the sight. Was this thing still available?

The answer to that is maybe. The Wondersight was made in earlier times by another company, but by

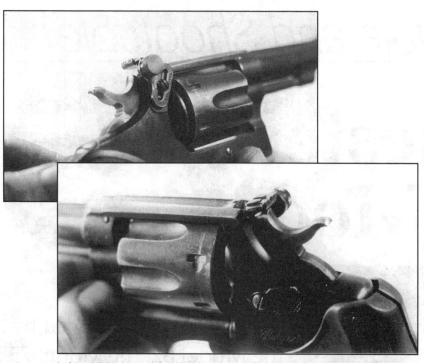

Left and right views of the Wondersight installed on the Ruby Extra show that it mounts fairly low on the frame. It adds versatility for the shooter who wants to try different loads which give differing points of impact.

1990 it was being turned out by Andy Evans in Magalia, California. At that time, it sold for around $25. A recent attempt at contacting Mr. Evans was unsuccessful, and he has apparently moved. If any reader knows the present address for the Wondersight company, please write to me at DBI Books. It's too neat an item to just fade away.

Fortunately, I had one of the sights on hand. The sideplate mounting screw is a #3-48, and I assumed that the screws on the Ruby Extra were all metric. That being the case, the hole would have to be re-tapped. Not so. The screw for the Wondersight went in easily, and snugged up tightly. With full vertical and horizontal adjustment now possible, it was easy to center the groups. The gun aver-aged 2 inches at 25 yards, and I thought this was quite acceptable.

Next, a cosmetic touch. The bare steel sideplate was removed and brightened with some 400-grade emery cloth stapled to a block of wood to keep the surface as flat as possible. It was then given a dose of Birchwood Casey cold blue. The problem now is that the sideplate looks somewhat better than the rest of the gun. Maybe I'll refinish the whole thing sometime.

Then I found, as I had suspected, that the grip frame was almost exactly the same as a S&W K-series gun. A set of Pachmayr Presentation grips was tried and the fit was nearly perfect. The hammer spring screw "pooches" the rubber out a bit, and that area inside the grip will have to be recessed. A little judicious work with a sharp knife will take care of that quite easily. Otherwise, no problem.

After the grips were installed, I went back to the range and found that now all groups were staying inside 2 inches, with most near 1½ inches. Give this old Llama an adjustable rear sight and some decent grips, and it will *shoot*. It already has what could be termed a "heavy" barrel, and I'm sure this aids the accuracy.

I'm planning to do some other things to the little Ruby. The trigger return spring is a bit stiff, and I will probably reduce it by a couple of coils. The trigger face has those terrible vertical grooves on it, and it is going to be polished smooth. The action is not bad at all, but a little stoning will make it even smoother. And, the whole thing would look nice in electroless nickel, I think...

At this point, though, the total investment, including the gun, has been less than $150. I have several revolvers that cost more than twice this amount, and they will shoot as well, but no better. They are, of course, a lot prettier. Still, for a beginning shooter with limited funds, this Ruby Extra from Century International Arms is a real bargain, and it's been a fun project. ●

With the addition of the new rear sight and Pachmayr grips, and by refinishing the side-plate, the Ruby Extra takes on a more pleasing and business-like appearance. It's an accurate plinker or low-cost defense gun at an affordable price.

# Collectible and Shootable

# Winchester's Model 75

Author's shooting partner, John Gentry, tries the Model 75 Target from the sitting position. This would be an excellent entry-level target rifle for the neophyte wanting to try his hand at the sport.

Always overshadowed by the Model 52, the Model 75 is often overlooked by both collectors and shooters.

## by GERRY BANDY

**D**O YOU HAVE an older brother or sister who has cast a long shadow on your self-esteem? Did they make As in school while you were solidly committed to Bs and Cs? Could they run faster? If so, read on, Bunkie, because now you know how Winchester's Model 75 rimfire rifles might feel if they had emotions. With an older sibling like the Model 52, could the Model 75 ever excel in anything? For years, the answer has been no, but that may be changing with some shooters—at least this one.

Winchester's Model 75 Target and Model 75 Sporter might be termed "shootable collectibles." Although a bit scarce with only about 89,000 made, these rifles remain relatively affordable and extremely usable.

The Model 75, introduced in 1938 and discontinued in 1958, was a less expensive alternative to the Model 52. My 1958 *Sports Afield Gun Annual* shows a suggested retail price of $197.25 for a Model 52

Sporter with sights, versus $79.95 for a Model 75 Sporter equally equipped. The price differential for the Model 52 Target ($157.50) and Model 75 Target ($80.85) was similar. (Those interested in more historical information should consult sources such as George Madis' *The Winchester Book* and R. L. Wilson's *Winchester: An American Legend.*)

Both models have increased substantially in value. S.P. Fjestad's *Blue Book of Gun Values* (Thirteenth Edition) shows a Model 52C Sporter in 100 percent condition at $2950! A Model 75 Sporter has also appreciated ($625 for a 100 percent specimen), but nice examples are available for prices I consider very reasonable for shooters.

Both versions of the Model 75 are bolt-action 22 Long Rifle repeaters with five-shot detachable magazines. Single-shot converters and ten-shot magazines were also available. The trigger is adjustable for weight of pull. The thumb safety is on the

right rear at the top of the receiver. The magazine release is recessed in the left side of the stock, above and behind the magazine.

The Model 75 Target variant weighs 8 pounds, 10 ounces; overall length is 44³/₄ inches. Length of pull is 13¹/₂. The heavy barrel is 28 inches long with a diameter of ¹¹/₁₆-inch at the muzzle. The uncheckered walnut stock is a straight, target style with a beavertail forend. Swivels are provided for a 1¹/₄-inch leather sling. The front swivel is adjustable for position along a metal rail.

Several sights were offered, including Winchester's own as well as Lyman, Redfield, Marble Wittek and Vaver. My Model 75 Target has a Lyman Model 58E with globe front sight. A variety of front sight inserts was available. The barrel is drilled and tapped for scope mounting (7¹/₄ inches center-to-center), but will require target-type mounting blocks and a long, Unertl-style target scope. With the forward mounting of the

The Model 75 Sporter (top) has a slim, walnut stock with checkered pistol grip and forend. The Target model is uncheckered and shows its function.

Ammunition brands and types come and go, but good rifles like the Model 75 Sporter are timeless. This is a gun made to be shot, not relegated to the gun rack as simply a showpiece.

scope blocks, eye relief on contemporary shorter scopes likely won't suffice. Some later models have receivers grooved for scope mounting.

Internally, the Model 75 is somewhat unsophisticated by current standards. Like other rimfire bolt actions, it is a rear-locking design; however, it has a single locking lug, part of the bolt handle base. Removal of the bolt is accomplished by pulling it back while depressing the trigger.

In spite of this unpretentious bolt design, the Model 75 has other redeeming features. These include sturdy twin extractors and an ejector of machined steel—no stampings for these rifles.

The Model 75 Sporter is function-ally identical to the Target version. Dimensionally, it's clearly sporting in intent. Weight is 5½ pounds; over-all length is 40½ inches; length of pull is just short of 13½ inches; and the barrel length is 24 inches. The barrel tapers to $^{17}/_{32}$-inch at the crowned muzzle. The walnut stock has a checkered forend and pistol grip. The style is classic with swivels for a 1-inch sling.

The front sight on the Sporter is a hooded, post-mounted bead. The standard rear sight is a semi-buck-horn type, step-adjustable for elevation. Aperture rear sights were commonly ordered, and my Model 75 Sporter has a Lyman 57ES. Madis' book notes that Sporter models rarely had grooved receivers until

after serial number 40,000; however, mine is numbered in the 60,000+ range and still lacks this feature.

The Model 75 Target was intended for just that—target shooting—but on a budget. Its heavy barrel enhances stability, and its straight stock, beavertail forend, and adjustable-position front sling swivel facilitate prone shooting. It's still a good choice for the neophyte who wants to try target competition without taking out a home equity loan to buy equipment. Its heft and weight distribution invite consideration by those desiring to try rimfire silhou-ette or benchrest shooting.

The Model 75 Sporter is also pur-pose-built. It is an easy-handling field piece. With the right aperture, its sights are quick enough to make it a viable rabbit rifle. It's a natural for small varmints at rimfire ranges. If you prefer scope use, find a grooved receiver variant or expect to have the receiver drilled and tapped.

Triggers of Model 75s show their "poor relations" position versus late Model 52s. We've all read about, and some have experienced, the latter's Micro-Motion trigger which "broke like glass." My Model 75 triggers break cleanly with no take-up, but have some over-travel. Trigger pull on the Sporter runs a bit over 3 pounds. On the Target, it's a bit lighter at 2 pounds, 12 ounces.

The trigger pull adjustment screw is vertically mounted and loosens downward to reduce pull weight. Its travel is limited by the depth of stock inletting. Running it out too far pro-duces failures to function, i.e. the round chambers but the rifle fails to cock. A little trial and error is in order here to achieve minimum pull weight with maximum reliability.

I tested the Model 75s on the out-door range at my local shooting club, the Fairfield (Ohio) Sportsman's As-sociation. Thirteen ammo types were used as a representative sample.

Chronograph results using PACT equipment show that the longer bar-rel of the Target reduced velocities, but the amounts weren't significant in many instances, and averaged less than three percent for each ammo class used. Standard-velocity ammo averaged 1117 fps from the 24-inch barrel Sporter and 1086 fps from the 28-inch Target barrel. Results from the Sporter and Target for high-velocity hollowpoints were 1259 and 1230 fps, respectively, and for hyper velocity, 1533 and 1503 fps.

In deference to the lack of scopes

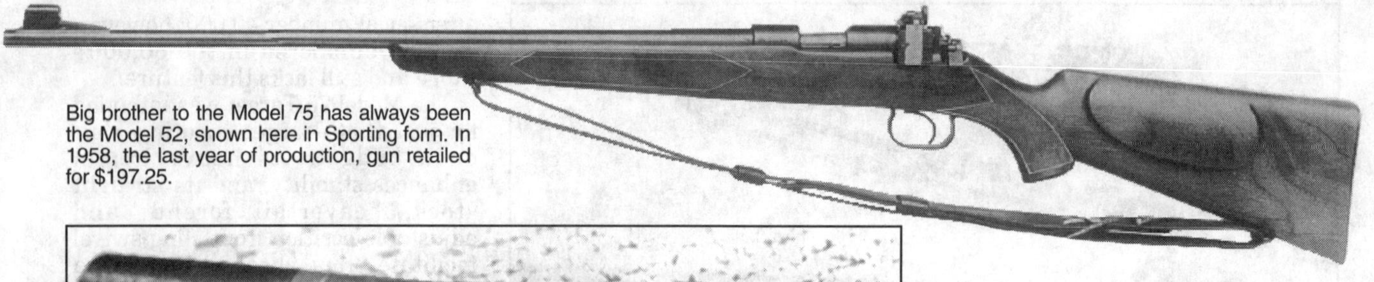

Big brother to the Model 75 has always been the Model 52, shown here in Sporting form. In 1958, the last year of production, gun retailed for $197.25.

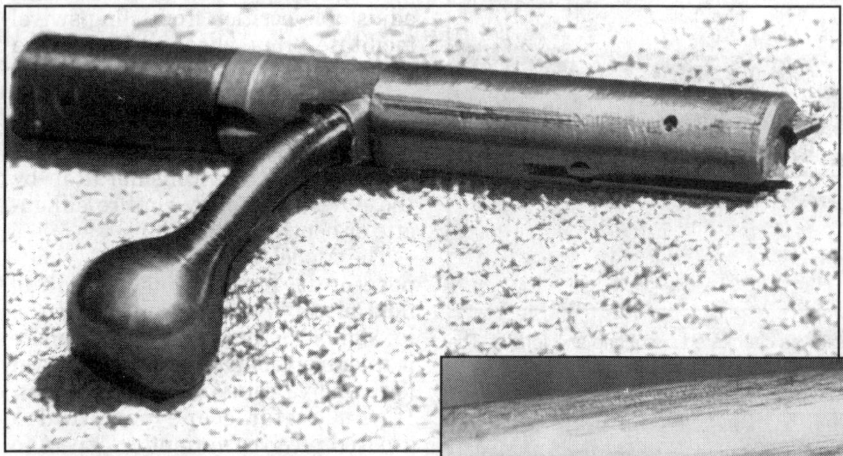

Model 75 bolt design is simple but reliable. The twin extractors assure positive operation.

The Model 75 Target has an adjustable sling rail to allow the most comfortable shooting position. Inletting of the rail is excellent.

on either rifle, and my nearly fifty-year-old myopic eyes, I tested accuracy at 25 yards. Five-shot strings were fired from a Hoppe's Expert Rifle Rest. Results are shown in the table nearby.

### WINCHESTER MODEL 75 SPORTER & TARGET ACCURACY RESULTS

| Ammunition | Sporter | Target |
|---|---|---|
| **22 LR Standard Velocity** | | |
| CCI Green Tag | .87 | 1.15 |
| Fed. Champion | .94 | 1.11 |
| Rem. Target | 1.06 | .75 |
| RWS Target | .68 | .73 |
| Win. T-22 | .73 | .57 |
| Average | .86 | .86 |
| **22 LR High Velocity** | | |
| CCI Mini-Mag HP | 1.02 | .85 |
| Fed. Hi-Power HP | 1.45 | .47 |
| Rem. Hi-Vel. HP | 1.22 | .63 |
| Win. Super Sil. | .86 | .68 |
| Win. Super-X HP | 1.03 | .47 |
| Average | 1.12 | .62 |
| **22 LR Hyper Velocity** | | |
| CCI Stinger | 1.04 | .91 |
| Fed. Spitfire HP | .99 | .65 |
| Rem. Yellow Jacket | 1.07 | .96 |
| Average | 1.03 | .84 |

Five-shot groups fired at 25 yards. Measurements shown in inches.

The Model 75 Sporter was more difficult to shoot at paper. Its post-mounted bead subtended more than the bullseye on my targets and allowed shooter-induced fliers to spoil some pretty good groups. Best five-shot group was .68-inch with RWS Target ammo. Averages for ammo types tested were .86-inch (standard velocity), 1.12 inches (high velocity), and 1.03 inches (hyper velocity).

By comparison, I recently tested a Ruger 77/22RSP with a Burris 4x scope. I obtained the following averages for five-shot groups at 25 yards: .76-inch for standard velocity, .78-inch for high velocity, and 1.03 inches for hyper velocity. All in all, I think the iron-sighted Winchester acquitted itself well versus the scoped, modern bolt gun.

With a front sight designed for paper-punching, results for the Model 75 Target were very good, considering yours truly at the trigger. Standard velocity averaged .86-inch with a best of .57-inch (Winchester T-22). High velocity was its preferred ammo, averaging .62-inch with bests of .47-inch from Federal

Hi-Power hollowpoints and Winchester Super-X hollowpoints. Hyper-velocity types averaged .84-inch with Federal Spitfire hollowpoints showing best at .65-inch.

Returning to my original thesis, Winchester's Model 75 Target and Sporter rimfire rifles may ultimately come out of the Model 52's shadow, at least with shooters. Too often, the Model 52 Sporter is relegated to investment status. Many are only cleaned and admired.

While not cheap, Model 75s can be found for what I consider reasonable prices. My Model 75 Target and Sporter, for example, are both in very good condition. The former was obtained for less than $250 at a gun show. The Sporter was pricier at around $400, but that's competitive with retail prices for a Browning A-Bolt, a Remington 541T or a Ruger 77/22. That's not bad for a collectible, shootable rimfire rifle with a nicely checkered walnut stock, sling swivels, aperture sights and an adjustable trigger. Both my Model 75s are over forty years old and going strong. I think they truly can last a lifetime.     ●

This single barrel shotgun has been color case-hardened using the method described in the text. The colors here are actually vivid and long lasting.

by BILL HOLMES

# Case-Coloring

Here's an easy way to case-harden and color gun parts to give them that classy, old-time look.

CASE-HARDENING is a process whereby the exposed surfaces of low carbon steel parts are given a very hard, thin surface that is resistant to wear. However, the interior steel of the part retains its original "soft" properties. The steel parts are brought to a high heat and treated with carbon, which is absorbed into the surface of the metal. As practiced many years ago, cyanide was the coloring agent applied to the heated metal, but non-toxic materials are used these days.

The case-hardening process often produces pleasing red, blue, yellow and gray colors in swirling patterns. The "case" can be quite thin for purely decorative purposes or it may be quite deep for functional hardness. Depending on the procedure used, the patterns and colors can be tailored to suit individual needs and desires.

Years ago, this was usually accomplished by placing the parts to be treated in metal boxes or "pots" with a carbonaceous compound packed around them. Such compounds consisted variously of such materials as animal charcoal, wood charcoal, bone, leather, coal, beans and nuts, coke, sodium cyanide, as well as various combinations of these things. The box containing the parts and carburizing materials was sealed and placed in an oven or furnace maintained at a temperature of about 1650 to 1700 degrees Fahrenheit. The heating duration depended on the extent of the carburizing action desired.

Modern versions of the process, including variations such as nitriding, liquid carburizing and gas carburizing, utilizing suitable alloy steels, result in highly sophisticated applications. As originally used before the turn of the century, its primary purpose was to permit the use of cheaper and easier-to-machine low carbon steel to be used in such items as concern us here: gun frames and other parts.

Somewhere along in the process it was discovered that through the use of assorted mixes of packing compounds and quenching methods, various mottled colors could be imparted on the surface of the steel. These colors ranged from yellow to brown, and red to blue, with other tints showing up at times. To many people, this was, and is, the most attractive finish ever put on a gun frame, and is still highly sought after by collectors and shooters.

The sad part, as regards the small shop, is that this process is not foolproof. Even major gun manufacturing firms including Winchester, Marlin, Savage and others lose a sizable percentage of parts so treated due to warping, cracking, and changing dimensions. Equally important, at least some of the packing materials formerly used are now considered hazardous to the environment.

The process described here, while it has little or no effect on the heat-treatment of the steel, has certain

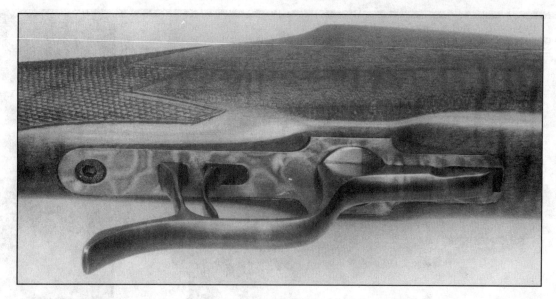

The trigger guard and trigger plate of this single shot rifle were case-colored in a soft pattern that gives a very pleasing effect. It contrasts nicely with the blued trigger and screw.

advantages over the original method. Properly done, there is no danger of warping, cracking or dimensional changes. Colors are more vivid than the original procedure gave, color patterns are controllable, and they are as durable, or more so, than the originals.

To refer to this process as "imitation" would be misleading since the term suggests inferiority. In truth, this method is in many ways superior, both for the reasons given above, and the fact that the only equipment required is a bucket of water and a gas welding outfit. The only material required is a small amount of tincture of benzoin compound which is available at most drugstores.

I say gas welding outfit because propane and oxygen works as well, or better than, an oxygen/acetylene combination. Small propane torches are not suitable since they spread

the heat too much. A combination two-bottle set up is required.

As with other types of finish such as bluing or plating, the quality of the end-result depends mostly on how well the metal is prepared. It should be polished or finished just as if it were to be plated or blued.

When polished to your satisfaction, the work is given a coating of the tincture of benzoin using a small brush or cotton swab and allowed to dry. All exposed surfaces should be coated.

The welding torch and bucket of water should be placed in close proximity and the torch lit and adjusted to give a slightly oxidizing flame. This means a slight excess of oxygen, as compared to a neutral flame.

The part to be colored can be held in the hand if it is of fairly good size. Small parts can be held in pliers or clamped to a handle of some sort.

The torch flame is brought into contact with the part and a small area heated until it just changes color. It is then plunged into the water to cool it and keep the heat from spreading. This process is repeated until the entire surface is colored. Properly done, the temperature of the part being colored will not exceed 400 degrees Fahrenheit. If it is allowed to get too hot, the coloring compound will char and flake off. The metal must be heated quickly and only to a point where the color appears, then quenched. It's easy to see how the color pattern can be "worked" to nearly any form you want.

As with most other phases of gunsmith work, proficiency will improve with practice. As one gains experience, complete control of color patterns is possible, with vivid red, yellow, green, brown and blue colors imparted.

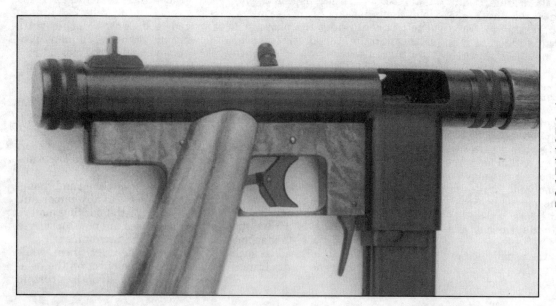

The lower receiver of this semi-auto pistol was case-colored in muted tones for a decorative touch. The colors break up what would otherwise be quite a lot of blued metal.

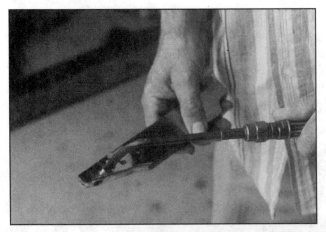

After proper polishing and coating with tincture of benzoin, the torch is applied to a small area, heating quickly until it just changes color.

The part is then quenched in water to cool and prevent the spread of heat. Large parts can be held by hand; small pieces need to be clamped or held with non-marring pliers.

The process is repeated on an adjacent area, usually using a slightly different stroke to vary the pattern and colors. Black and white photos don't show the effects very well.

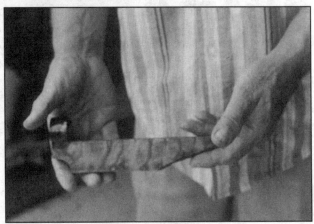

The heating and quenching procedure is repeated until the entire part is treated. After drying, the metal is coated with a preservative to protect the finish.

When the coloring process is finished, any remaining moisture from the quench should be allowed to dry. The part is then rubbed down with a soft cloth and given a thin coating of some sort of sealer such as Tru-Oil to seal and protect the finish. This is in keeping with the older methods. In fact, the instruction booklets that came with many of the higher grade British and other double guns suggested that the action be returned to the factory periodically for revarnishing to protect the colored finish and keep it from fading.

This case-hardening process is especially useful on the cast frames of the cheaper small-caliber rifles and shotguns produced mainly before World War II. It is also invaluable for use on modern gun frames which resist conventional bluing methods. Post-1964 Model 94 Winchesters are a good example of this. The frame, or receiver, of these guns, which usually turns all sorts of color rather than the desired blue, can be polished bright and case-colored. In many cases, this actually enhances the value of the refinished gun.

As a case in point, several years ago I took in trade a post-'64 Winchester 94 which had been allowed to rust, damaging the original finish. I polished and blued this gun in the usual manner, only to find the receiver had turned a deep pink color. I simply polished the receiver again and gave it a case-color treatment. I later sold or traded the gun for a good profit.

Sometime later, I attended a firearms auction where I spotted this same gun among the firearms to be sold. Two of the bargain-hunting, speculating, semi-gun experts who are the primary patrons of auctions of this type were examining this gun and discussing it between them.

"That's a real old gun," I heard one tell the other. "Look at that case-hardening, they don't do that any more".

I tried to tell them it wasn't real, but they simply looked at me like I was an idiot.

They paid more than three times what a new gun would have cost!

The process described here is not original with me. An old-time blacksmith who I only remember as "Pete" showed me how to do it in Sunland, California, back during World War II, and I've used the procedure many times to dress up what were otherwise plain-Jane guns with great success. ●

# The FBI's

# Latest Wondernine

In a move little noticed by most everyone, the nation's top law enforcement agency has begun issuing a semi-auto-only version of the MP5 submachine gun.

# by FRANK JAMES

With the exception of the trigger group, the H&K MP5 SF is the same gun as seen here in the hands of Chief Deputy John Roberts of the White County (Indiana) Sheriff's Department. The SF version is semi-auto only.

IT WAS AN EVENT that passed with the minimum of notice, but the nation's leading law enforcement agency recently adopted an additional high capacity "Wondernine." No, it's not some new polymer and steel handgun featuring the latest in ergonomics, but rather a semi-auto-only version of the finest submachine gun ever made—the Heckler & Koch MP5 SF.

The Federal Bureau of Investigation has taken a giant leap forward by equipping a large number of their agents and their corresponding vehicles with this semi-auto rendition of the most successful 9mm submachine gun in modern history.

The H&K MP5 SF is the same submachine gun seen so often in the hands of expert SWAT team members or counter-terrorist strike teams,

law enforcement agencies moved toward SMGs. Detailed examination of this trend shows it has been a slow movement that has only recently gained wide acceptance. The prejudice against submachine guns created during the 1930s has been hard to overcome.

The standard long gun for police use in this country has always been the 12-gauge shotgun, most frequently a pump-action Cylinder-bore gun with the most rudimentary sighting systems.

The police shotgun has always been a weapon valued for its intimidation effect. We've all heard the locker-room saying that the mere sound of a 12-gauge pump being actioned on a dark night is enough to make the bad guy wet his pants.

While this philosophy has little

wise. Sport shooting, whether on the target range or in a field of corn stalks hunting pheasants, is not practiced to the extent it once was.

It wasn't that long ago when young people were taught firearms safety and marksmanship in the public school system, even in urban/suburban areas. Many high schools still have disused small-bore ranges in their basements, but the demographic changes over the last few decades reveal there are fewer farms, fewer youngsters growing up on farms, and there are also fewer youngsters with the opportunity to use a firearm in a safe and wholesome manner. Shopping malls and urban development are partly to blame here because they eliminate not only the animals and their habitat, but the gulleys and pastures

Heckler & Koch has developed two new MP5s, one in 10mm Auto, and this one chambered for the extremely popular 40 S&W round. Despite the more powerful chambering, balance and weight are the same as the original 9mm gun.

but there are specific differences between the FBI model and those used elsewhere.

But first, why would this country's top law enforcement agency choose a type of weapon that has been surrounded by so much controversy? There are a number of important reasons, so bear with me and you'll see why this is such a significant step toward bringing the Bureau's front-line troops up to snuff with current technology.

Submachine guns, in this country at least, have seldom been accepted as legitimate tools for law enforcement. SMGs are often associated with military operations or seen by the public and general media as a tool of terrorists or criminals, even if they admit they can't properly define what a submachine gun is.

Only with the advent and development of SWAT teams have American

validity when up against a hardened foe, it is true the visual image of the 12-gauge bore diameter at close range can be one of the most daunting situations ever experienced. Up close, the riot shotgun muzzle resembles the snout of a 16-inch gun on the battleship Missouri, but the most intimidating thing about the police shotgun to today's police recruits is *shooting* it!

Demographics is the study and science of vital and social statistics, like births, deaths, diseases, marriages and social trends of various populations, and any demographic study of today's beginning police recruit classes would quickly reveal major differences between the current freshmen class and those seen, say, just two or three decades ago.

Few people going into law enforcement today have prior experience with firearms—sporting or other-

that years before were safe places to shoot for most town kids.

This can be seen in the number of police recruits that lack even the most rudimentary of firearms experience that only a short time before would have been part of every child's background.

This lack of experience deprives these people of the necessary reference knowledge and, combined with other aspects of the modern world, makes it difficult for some to transition from their non-gun civilian world to this firearms-oriented line of work.

There is no way to say it without sounding politically incorrect, but many women who are new to shooting shotguns, especially those loaded with buckshot, can't qualify with them.

I've talked to a number of police firearms instructors (who speak

A number of trigger groups are available for the MP5 series of guns. This trigger group permits either semi-auto fire or two-round bursts (note markings). The FBI opted for the semi-auto-only assembly.

about this subject only with the condition of anonymity), and each one can relate a litany of problem shooters who would otherwise be excellent police officers. The kicker in each case is they are women who have no firearms experience and can't master a gun with significant recoil.

One instructor told me, "You've always heard that you can't miss with a shotgun. Well, I can show you a number of people who not only can miss, but can miss every time with a 12-gauge and buckshot at *any* range."

Though the length of pull from trigger to butt is fairly close between these two guns, the MP5 is lighter, shorter and better balanced than the pump-action Mossberg police shotgun.

He related the number of different teaching techniques he tried in an attempt to get his pupils accustomed to the shotgun. He would do everything he could to make them hold the gun tight against the shoulder, but the basic problem was the student failed to relax and work with the gun. They were scared of it and nothing he could say or do would erase that fear from their subconscious. In the most extreme cases, he had women who had been through the qualification process three times and still failed to make the grade.

Up to this point, it would be easy to dismiss this instructor as a prejudicial sexist, but then he mentioned an experience where he handed one of these female recruits an H&K Model 94 (the 9mm semi-auto, civilian-legal car-

bine) his department had in inventory. She qualified with it quickly and with a good score.

The FBI's move to the MP5 SF could be a reflection of this situation. By adopting this short-barreled carbine, they have avoided the firestorm of politically correct theory and the difficulties experienced while training people with the hard-kicking shotgun.

But, there are other factors at work here also. The argument for shotguns has always been that since most of them hold six rounds, and each 2³/₄-inch 00 buck shell holds either nine or twelve pellets depending upon the load, the officer has the equivalent of fifty-four

projectiles (seventy-two with the 2³/₄-inch magnum) at his disposal.

The problem here is the question of marksmanship and the ability to aim and hit the target exactly where the projectile is needed to neutralize the felon.

Launching nine 33-caliber pellets from a short-barreled riot gun at a subject in a lethal force situation is seldom precise.

This load of heavy pellets is designed primarily to overwhelm the subject's central nervous system, or to create sufficient damage that all further resistance or threat ceases.

Generally, the 12-gauge shotgun loaded with 00 buckshot is very successful in attaining these goals at short range, but as the distance increases it becomes more difficult to maintain point of aim confidence, even for an experienced shooter. Simply, the shotgun is not a precision instrument.

To try to overcome this lack of accuracy, many departments are now loading their shotguns with slugs, but even their use doesn't guarantee target neutralization. Bad shooting and poorly hit targets will still produce unsatisfactory results.

Additionally, when using slugs, the shooter has only six rounds available, or nine if the gun has an extended magazine.

Now, compare that to the 30-round magazine found in the MP5 SF, and you can begin to understand the reasoning behind this move by the FBI.

Describing the H&K MP5 SF as a submachine gun is not entirely correct because the "SF" in its title stands for Single Fire, or semi-auto. The MP5 SF is *not* capable of full-auto fire, and that is a prime criteria for a *true* submachine gun.

But, the MP5 SF is a submachine gun by legal BATF definition in that it has a machine gun receiver, the full-auto bolt carrier, and the short 8.9-inch barrel.

The MP5 SF would be capable of full-auto fire if the SF 0-1 trigger group were replaced with the S-E-F trigger group, or the three-position pictogram "Navy" trigger group, or the four-position pictogram trigger assembly.

One of the advantages of the MP5 submachine gun is the fact that six different trigger groups are available. The MP5 Deputy Roberts is holding in a nearby photo is capable of semi-auto, three-round burst, as well as full-auto fire, depending upon the selector position. Other possible combinations include the 0-1-2 combination, as well as the original S-E-F trigger group which stands for *Sicher* (or Safe), *Einselfeuer* (or Single Fire), and *Feuerstoss* which literally means Fire Burst.

The FBI selected the 0-1 trigger group for a number of reasons, but the primary one has to be the fact it is an expensive proposition to train personnel in full-auto fire, both in terms of ammunition expenditure and training time requirements.

With the MP5 SF, they gain the best of both worlds and in the process acquire a short, handy carbine with a large ammunition capacity.

But the biggest advantage is that the MP5 SF is an easy gun for all shooters to master, regardless of their proficiency or experience level.

The FBI's MP5 SF differs from the standard MP5 in two more minor details: one is the removable flash hider, and the second is the A-2 fixed stock.

The MP5 SF has the same three-lug barrel like all the other MP5s, and one purpose of these three lug-like features behind the muzzle is to serve as anchor points for different muzzle-mounted devices. The flash hider is the most commonly encountered accessory, but there are other attachments such as a blank firing device and a grenade launcher for delivery of chemical agents in a crowd control situation.

The biggest advantage to the flash hider, however, is not in terms of reducing the muzzle flash, but in the fact it adds a bit of length to the barrel. This makes it a little more difficult for the operator to put his hand in front of the muzzle, increasing operator safety.

The weight of the MP5 with the fixed A-2 buttstock is actually lighter than the same gun with the A-3 retractable stock. The MP5 SF(A2) weighs 5.59 pounds, while the retractable buttstock increases the weight to 6.34 pounds.

The overall length of the MP5 in A-2 configuration is only 26.77 inches. The fixed stock is more often appreciated by Americans because of its longer length of pull.

When compared with the typical police shotgun, the HK's length of pull is very close to the scattergun, but the overall length is significantly shorter. This shorter length, combined with the lighter weight and higher ammunition capacity, makes the MP5 SF better suited for deployment from vehicles or in building searches.

In terms of recoil management, there is literally nothing to control. The recoil impulse is light, the straight stock is more in line with the center of the bore, and all this combines to make a firearm that even a neophyte can control with ease and excellence.

Because the MP5 SF is a carbine, the shooter now has the benefit of a weapon with greater range, and a greater degree of accuracy than that found with the common police shotgun.

While most experts limit the effective range of the 9x19mm caliber MP-5 SMG to 100 meters, it can be extended to 150 meters, or even 200 meters in extreme cases when used by an expert. In contrast, the shotgun with slugs is seldom accurate past 100 yards.

The A-2 fixed stock of the MP5 has a slightly longer length of pull than the heavier A-3 retractable stock. The FBI chose the A-2 version for its SF guns, and most U.S. shooters find it more comfortable to shoot.

Which gun has more firepower? This police-issue shotgun holds four slug and two 00 buck loads, while the MP5 holds 30 rounds of 9mm ammunition in a magazine that can be reloaded in less than 2 seconds.

The FBI learned from the Dade County disaster in 1986 that for any carbine, shotgun or rifle to be utilized in a developing situation, they must accessible to the driver of the vehicle—while the car is moving. That precludes storage in the conventional gun case in the cruiser's trunk.

What the FBI is doing is mounting these new Wondernine carbines to the car's headliner, above the driver and his front seat passenger's head. The mount is fastened to the door posts behind the driver and it allows removal of the gun even while the officer is driving at 60 mph.

This is an important benefit. It means the weapon can be utilized almost instantly, if needed. It also means the carbine is out of view of the general public and doesn't by its mere presence alert the neighborhood to the presence of an unmarked police car.

The MP5 SF also has its own intimidation effect. One department in a Southern state has purchased a limited number of these carbines for the express purpose of arming their uniformed female officers. It is a firearm that inspires confidence due to its excellent handling characteristics, light weight, low recoil and good accuracy—when an officer is confidant about her equipment, that can be intimidating!

The FBI has always been instrumental in initiating new trends in American law enforcement, both in terms of techniques and science, and it looks like they're on the leading edge again.

Who knows, maybe these light and handy carbines will replace pump-action shotguns in the same way semi-auto pistols have supplanted the conventional double-action police revolver?　●

Deputy Roberts has the cocking handle back and the magazine out to render the gun safe, but this gives a felon's view of the MP5 in action. It's just as intimidating as the shotgun!

# THE CLASSIC LEWIS GUN

## The World's First Light Machinegun

Sworn by and sworn at, the Lewis gun proved itself through two world wars and beyond.

ARABIA, 1917. They set off the explosive charge just as the second engine of the Turk train rumbled onto the bridge. As the dust cleared, T.E. Lawrence's men opened fire on the now stationary carriages and wagons. His two Lewis guns, set up about 300 yards from the train, went into action, and "long rows of Turks on the carriage roofs rolled over and were swept off the top like bales of cotton before the furious shower of bullets which stormed along the roofs and splashed clouds of yellow chips from the planking."

An Australian was at one of the Lewis guns, an Arab tribesman on the other. A stalwart British

sergeant was there to handle the Stokes gun (a mortar), and when his well-placed shells chased some of the Turks from behind the far side of the railroad line, the Lewis gunners "grimly traversed with drum after drum, till the open sand was littered with bodies." This description of Lewis guns in action is in Lawrence's *Seven Pillars of Wisdom,* a book which manages to be at the same time a swashbuckling yarn and a classic of the English language.

The Lewis gun had gone into action in the first days of World War I, and by 1917 it was fighting on every front on land, in the air, and

at sea. The U.S. Cavalry carried Lewis guns with them when they chased Pancho Villa's boys through Chihuahua. Why, even the boys at the Harvard Travellers Club were familiar with the Lewis. In the Club's *Handbook of Travel* for 1917, they advise: "On caravan journeys across open dangerous country, a light machine-gun, such as the Lewis, might be extremely desirable." For example, a chap could surprise a band of marauding Tuaregs with a few bursts from a handy Lewis, which could be put into action in seconds. The life of a brigand, even in truly remote country, would never be quite the same. The Lewis gun was one of Lawrence of Arabia's favorite weapons; on those hit-and-run raids across the desert, an overburdened camel could mean the difference between life or death. During the battle described here, when Turk soldiers from another railroad station started to close in on Lawrence's men, the two Lewis guns were simply tied together at their shoulder stocks and thrown scissor-like over the back of a camel for the getaway.

Although the Lewis gun is often

## by ALBERT MANCHESTER

(Left) Bill Madden with his 1916 Lewis gun. This example was made by Savage Arms for the U.S. Navy and is chambered for 30-06.

(Below) A lot of folks wonder what is down the Lewis stovepipe barrel. The actual barrel is in the center and is inside an aluminum "radiator," which is encased by the barrel jacket.

thought of as a European (British) weapon, it was, as the men at the Harvard Club probably knew, as American as the Model T Ford. Indeed, the Lewis gun was born just a few years after the Model T started rolling in 1908, and, like the ubiquitous flivver, it came from the heartland of America. The Lewis gun would be one of America's greatest contributions to the Allied war effort in World War I.

Isaac N. Lewis was born in Pennsylvania in 1858, moved to Kansas in 1879, and graduated from West Point in 1884. Lewis was a benign-looking fellow with a fashionably large mustache, big ears and hair parted in the middle. He spent most of his military career in ordnance; he is credited with several military inventions and innovations before he became involved with what would become known as the Lewis gun. He was certainly aware of the burgeoning interest in automatic weapons, especially in Europe where the great powers were starting the monotonous drum beats of their countdown to the Great War. Lewis had toured Europe in an official capacity; he developed ideas of his own as to what a machinegun should be. When the call came from a Cleveland, Ohio, arms manufacturer to help them perfect a machinegun, Lewis was ready.

The call came from a group of investors who had been backing Samuel N. McLean, an Iowan who had been trying to make a machinegun that would impress somebody. Hundreds of thousands of dollars went into his inventions; McLean had a few examples and some patents, but by 1906 he was broke. His investors, who would become the Automatic Arms Company, of Cleveland, took over the patents and started searching the horizon for somebody with ordnance expertise. They focused on Isaac N. Lewis.

Although Lewis had his own ideas about automatic weapons, he did take what he needed from McLean's patents. However, it is generally conceded that the Lewis gun is at least as much Lewis as it is McLean. Lewis went to work for the Automatic Arms Company in 1910, and in the spring of 1911, he was ready to start marketing the new light machinegun.

The Lewis is air-cooled, gas-operated, and fed from a drum (or pan) magazine. The two distinguishing characteristics which make it imme-diately recognizable are the magazine and the large barrel jacket. The barrel looks the way it does because there is an aluminum "radiator" inside the steel jacket. The barrel itself is inside the radiator which has seventeen cooling fins extending the length of the barrel. The idea behind the design is that, theoretically, the muzzle exhaust sucks cool air into the rear of the radiator cover and, as the air passes along the fins, it helps dissipate heat from the barrel. It should be noted that there is some discussion about how necessary this expensive setup is. We will not take part in that controversy here. Suffice it to say that no true aficionado of the Lewis gun would ever be caught in public without his radiator and radiator jacket.

In any case, the Lewis gun will operate perfectly well without its radiator. Thousands of Lewis guns that were stripped of radiators and radiator jackets were used on airplanes in World War I. It was thought that a 100 mph wind should be enough cooling for almost any machine gun. They were right.

The Lewis magazine comes in 47- and 96-round versions, the larger drum intended mainly for aircraft use. On the ground, an experienced gunner could change magazines in four seconds. In the air, in a swooping, plunging aircraft, wrestling a heavy magazine onto a gun could take a matter of seconds—or the rest of eternity. With a loaded magazine in place, the charging handle, generally on the right side of the gun but not always, is pulled to the rear as far as it will go and released. The gun can then be fired, and it fires from an open bolt. When the trigger is pulled, the bolt moves forward and its top edge engages the lower edge of a cartridge that will be in the feedway. The cartridge is driven forward and downward into the firing chamber. When the cartridge fires, and the bullet reaches the end of the barrel, some of the gas will be pushed down into what is called the gas regulator cup. The gas is then driven into the gas chamber, just below the barrel, and the piston is forced to the rear. The machinegun's action is thrown in reverse, the cartridge is ejected, and as the bolt once again comes forward it engages a fresh cartridge. And so forth. (This is, of course, an extremely simplified explanation of the operation.)

The gas regulator cup is interesting: There are four ports of different sizes in it, and the gunner aligns the port he wants to give him a slower or faster rate of fire. The larger the port, the faster the rate of fire.

The basic Lewis gun has sixty-two parts, weighs 26 pounds, and is almost 51 inches long with the shoulder stock. The gun can be shortened by removing the shoulder stock and substituting a spade grip, an acces-

The Lewis went into the air in the early days of World War I. This is probably 1914 or early 1915. Later, the aluminum radiator and barrel jacket were stripped for aviation use.

sory recommended for a gun that was to be mounted on an aeroplane. Another early accessory was a light folding bipod. So, even at the beginning of World War I, the Allies had a light automatic weapon which could go forward with assault troops or, which was too often the situation, could be used with deadly effect in rear guard actions.

The Europeans had the Lewis gun because Lewis was unable to sell it at home. This in spite of the fact that one of his weapons was taken into the air on a Signal Corps airplane on the 7th of June, 1912, and the daring young men cut loose with it at a ground target. The first machinegun ever in the air. The aviators were thrilled. The Board of Ordnance was not. The Lewis had not done well during some ground tests, and in 1912 almost nobody in the military had any reason to believe that a machinegun would be of any use on airplanes, for which no useful role had yet been developed. A light machinegun was a revolutionary idea. The Lewis invention was unac-

ceptable to the Board of Ordnance. Frustrated, Lewis resigned his commission in 1913 and headed for Europe to see if he could do business over there.

Autumn, 1913. The drum beats were becoming louder and more insistent in Europe. Vast armies were wound up tight and ready to start spinning. Enter Yankee inventor Isaac N. Lewis with a brand new machinegun concept. (This has to be *the* classic example of a man and his invention being in the right place at the right time.) The Brits and the Belgians must have tugged at their mustaches and said things like "whizzer" and *epatant*. The Lewis went into production in Belgium and then at the Birmingham Small Arms plant in England. Lewis guns were coming off the line when in August of 1914 millions of men started marching.

This could be a short war, the soldiers thought, so they rushed to it as if they were going to a picnic, fired by thoughts of revenge (the French) or dreams of glory (the Germans). The Germans pounded through Belgium on their way to the channel. That was the idea, sweep the beaches of the channel with their right wing and pounce on Paris from the northwest. But it was a hot August, and the Belgians—and then the British—were aggravatingly tenacious. Weary, behind schedule, the Germans swung to the south. Too soon. And the French, sensing an opening with Napoleonic insight, rebounded from slogging retreat with incredible elan and fell on the Germans, stopping them at the Marne. No, nobody would have to be left out as far as this war was concerned. (It has been argued that the Battle of the Marne was the most

Loading the Lewis magazine. The latch that secures the magazine to the gun is held back by the tool at right. The pan can then be turned by hand as cartridges are fed into place.

# Field-Stripping:

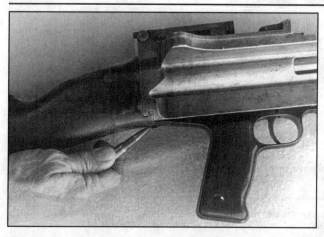

**1.** Insert the point of a bullet into the slot leading to the butt latch and push forward against the force of the latch spring. At the same time, twist the buttstock up and to the left, then remove it to the rear.

**2.** Hold back the trigger and pull the guard/grip to the rear until clear of the receiver. Pull down on the gear casing (right) until it drops clear of the rack.

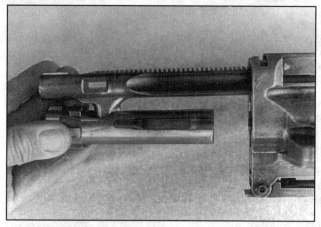

**3.** Pull back the charging handle (not shown) until it reaches the end of its slot, then withdraw by pulling it out away from the receiver. Withdraw the operating rod and bolt (shown) by pulling them both together to the rear until clear of the receiver.

**4.** With the point of a bullet, push back on the receiver lock pin, then twist the receiver up and to the left and unscrew it from the barrel. Gun is now field-stripped.

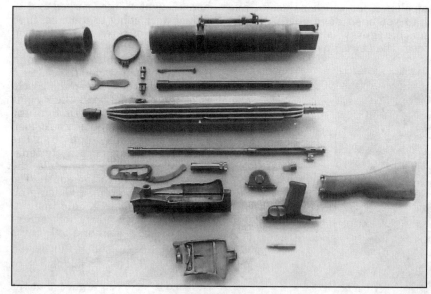

The Lewis gun nearly completely dismantled.

fateful battle of the 20th century.) In any case, there would be plenty of time to manufacture Lewis guns.

Tens of thousands of Lewis guns were made in England, the French produced it, and the Savage Arms Company of Utica, New York, was licensed to make the gun for the British and Canadians. Several Lewis guns could be manufactured in the time it took to make one heavy Vickers machinegun, and, of course, the cost per gun was much less. As the trench war ground tediously on, the troops learned how to use the light machinegun. The Lewis guns went forward with attacking troops; thousands of Lewis guns were involved in the Battle of Cambrai, for example (which, by the way, was also the first time tanks were used en masse). One man could put a Lewis gun into action. He took up no more room than a rifleman and, at a quick glance, appeared to be a rifle-man, but the sudden shock of unexpected automatic fire could be terminal. When it was discovered that No Man's Land was more user friendly if just small groups rushed forward, one group covering the other, the Lewis gun served for covering fire. The Lewis, the world's first light machinegun, was well field-tested during 1914-1918.

The Lewis gun was mounted on every kind of motor vehicle from motorcycles to tanks, and it went into the air in 1914 and flew until 1918. Before machineguns were synchronized to fire through propellers, the Lewis was mounted on the top wing of fighters, and they were mounted singly or as a pair for the use of the observer in two-place machines. But during World War I, Lewis guns were bolted to airplanes in almost every conceivable location.

Was the Lewis gun a success? Certainly. It was a Model T kind of machinegun, but World War I was a Model T kind of war. (Was the flivver a success? But would you buy one today for commuting to work?) Legend has it that the Lewis was prone to an "astonishing variety" of stoppages. Now that sounds like a Model T. Or a Sopwith Camel, for that matter.

New Mexico resident William Madden, who owns and operates a Lewis gun, has noticed that when he's firing his on windy days—and in New Mexico windy means dusty—the gun seems to slow down, as if some of the flying grit is seeping into the mechanism and setting up resistance. Madden says, too, that a dented magazine—and those pan magazines are certainly exposed—will stop the gun. But Madden claims that he has had little trouble with his Lewis, which was made by Savage Arms in 1916 for the U.S. Navy, and is chambered for the 30-06.

The Western Front was the ultimate test for many weapons. The Canadian Ross, a bolt-action rifle, wouldn't work out there, and one would think that a bolt action could be kept operating under the most abominable conditions. But the Lewis chugged along through battle after dreary battle—until one day the war just stopped. The alleged crankiness of the old gun may have some basis in fact, but one must always keep in mind the wretched living and fighting conditions on the Western Front.

Probably the main thing the Lewis

U.S. troops apparently on maneuvers with a Lewis gun. The photo could have been staged by the Savage Arms Co. because the U.S. Ordnance Dept. didn't like the gun.

had going for it was that it was the world's first light machinegun. At the time, there were no real competitors. The Lewis gun was officially adopted by the armed forces of Belgium, Great Britain, France, Russia, Portugal, Holland, Nicaragua, Italy and Japan. The U.S. Navy, Marines, Coast Guard and Army Air Corps used the Lewis. Unofficially, however, the Lewis has fought all over the world. You can bet your last round that the muzzle blast of Lewis guns echoed through the mountains of Afghanistan just a few years ago. But even by the 1930s, the Lewis was obsolescent. Lighter, simpler light machineguns were developed between the big wars.

Dunkirk. The Brits who miraculously escaped came home with little of their equipment. Thousands of Lewis guns were unpacked for their second big war, and, once again, saw action all over the world. British seamen in the Channel fought the low-flying Luftwaffe intruders with their Lewis guns. Lewis guns fought across North Africa. The British made do with what they had; thousands of Lewis guns helped hold the line until they could be replaced by handier weapons.

Several other countries put their own Lewis guns into the field in World War II. And, as with any weapon that had served for many years and with several countries, there are many models with slight variations. The basic mechanism of

all of these weapons is thought, however, to be the same. Most of the countries chambered the Lewis for their own cartridges.

But it was World War I that was truly the Lewis gun's war. The timing was absolutely right for it. Historians have decried the fact American troops in France were denied the use of the Lewis gun, an American invention, and had to fight the *boches* with the disdained French Chauchat (pronounced show-shah) light machinegun. But it's true that the Lewis did not do well in some Ordnance Department tests, and there is evidence that Colonel Isaac Lewis himself, not just his machinegun, was not popular at the Ordnance Department.

Whatever the case, the doughboys went over the top with their Chauchats. But that wasn't the only foreign weapon the Americans had to use; the doughboys fought with French 75s, French tanks, French airplanes, other French machineguns, and in some cases they had to wear bits and pieces of French and British uniforms. World War I is simply another war we weren't ready for.

Yes, World War I was the Lewis gun's war, and it's really interesting to note how much this American invention contributed to the Allied victory. The Great War wouldn't have been the same without the Lewis gun. On the other hand, without that war there might not have been a Lewis gun. •

# Scoping The SKS Carbine

**Here's a do-it-yourself gunsmithing project that'll add versatility to the popular and handy SKS carbine.**

## by NORMAN E. JOHNSON

**A**T FIRST GLANCE, attaching a suitable scope mount on the SKS 7.62x39mm carbine didn't seem practical. Top mounts weren't applicable and the narrow band of exposed side receiver metal didn't appear to provide adequate surface for a scope base. But a second look at a Remington 1100 shotgun side mount was the answer.

With the removal of a small strip of stock wood to expose additional receiver surface, and the addition of a spacer between mount and receiv-er, a very attractive and sturdy mounting job was possible, and the total cost was well under $50 for the mount, scope rings and miscellaneous materials.

No special talent is required to accomplish the scope mounting job, just common shop tools and close attention to detail will get the job done. I used a side mount I had on hand marked "05-1100" which had a one-piece integral Weaver base attached. This mount base was removed from a Model 1100

The side mount intended for the Remington Model 1100 shotgun. Holes at far left and top right were drilled to adapt the unit to the SKS.

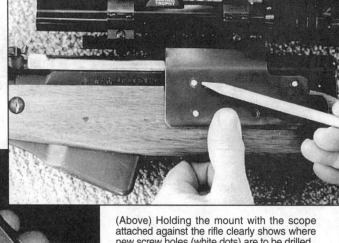

(Above) Holding the mount with the scope attached against the rifle clearly shows where new screw holes (white dots) are to be drilled.

(Left) The spacer used to interface the mount to the SKS receiver can be made from $3/16$-inch scrap aluminum or soft steel. The small lip is not absolutely necessary, but looks better.

Remington shotgun. Standard Weaver quick-detachable rings fit this base.

The basic tools needed will include a drill press or electric drill, #18 and #29 drill bits, an 8-32 tap, small rasp, fine-tooth hacksaw, flat file, machinist's rule, a screwdriver and Allen wrench. The only materials required are two 8-32x$1/2$-inch socket-head screws, two $1/2$-inch number 8 round-head sheet metal screws and a length of flat metal stock $9/16$x-$3/16$x4$3/8$ inches in length. This piece of metal is used as an interface spacer between the side mount and the flat surface at the side of the receiver, to hold the base out flush with the gun stock, and is cut to exact size later.

Before removing the action from the stock, attach the scope and rings to the base and carefully lay the mount exactly in position where it will later be permanently mounted. At this time, be sure the scope has sufficient clearance for clear viewing and the objective lens clears the lowered rear sight. Also, be sure the scope is aligned with the axis of the bore. Use of a straightedge is helpful here. It is also important at this time to check that the bottom of the extended scope base is positioned approximately 1$1/4$ inches above the lower portion of the cartridge loading port. This clearance will permit ample room for loading and cartridge ejection without scope or mount interference. This will also help assure that the underside of the scope base clears the receiver.

With the mount thus placed and the scope height where you want it, the mount should also be carefully positioned front to rear. If the center of the mount flange is positioned about 3 inches from the rear of the receiver, screw application will be

very workable, and optimal scope eye relief will be attained. With the mount placed and held where you want it, carefully mark the outer borders of the mount on the side of the stock. A light pencil marking here will permit easy replacing for screw hole location and later drilling.

As the photos show, approximately $3/16$-inch of wood will later be cut out at the top left side of the stock to square things up and expose a bit more receiver metal for a very rigid

Spacer in place after a bit of wood was removed from the top of the stock. Holes in the spacer match those drilled in the receiver; holes in the stock are for screws to add rigidity.

mounting. But first, with the scope base aligned and held temporarily in position, carefully mark the screw hole positions so the through-holes will be located as required on the side of the receiver. Ideally, the tapped holes should be located $1/4$-inch below the square surface of the top of the receiver. If the rear screw hole is centered 1$3/8$-inch from the back of the receiver and the forward hole centered 3$1/16$-inch forward of this hole, this will be ideal. There is

some margin for variation in screw hole location, but not much, as you will later see as you look inside the receiver. The gun can now be disassembled.

Field-stripping the action and removing the action from the stock on the SKS carbine is simple. Just lower the trigger assembly by depressing the lock—located at the rear of the trigger guard—and pull downward on the trigger guard. With the trigger assembly removed, pull down on the magazine assembly and remove it as it pivots out of the front cam-lock position. The barreled action is now floating in the stock and can be removed by gently working the screw-slotted cam (located on the left side of the stock under the rear sight) as the barreled action is lowered out of the stock from the rear.

Removing the bolt assembly is accomplished by lifting and pulling outward on the receiver cap lock pin located at the very rear right side of the receiver. The receiver cap, which covers the bolt thrust spring and plunger, is then slid off for removal of the bolt and spring assembly. The inner receiver is now exposed and free of parts and can be worked on. Assembly is just the reverse of takedown and takes but a minute once you've done it.

At this time, the spacer which is used as an interface between the scope mount flange and the receiver should be made. Just cut a piece of $3/8$-inch-thick aluminum or steel to a width of $7/16$-inch and to a length of $4 3/8$ inches. As the illustration shows,

a slightly raised lip extending $9/16$-inch at the front top side of the spacer sort of fills in where the receiver is raised, but is not absolutely required. After the spacer is rough cut, mill or file the piece to uniform dimensions.

The spacer can now be mortised into the stock so the upper surface of the spacer is exactly flush with the top of the gun's receiver. This is best accomplished by laying the spacer at the side of the stock, with the barreled action in place, and sighting along the top of the receiver rail. When the spacer and receiver rail are perfectly parallel, mark the spacer position on the stock with a pencil. Then, carefully remove enough stock wood to fit the spacer so it lays correctly in place with its upper surface at the same height as the receiver rail. With the

spacer in position, I used a small C-clamp to hold it in place and drilled the holes through the spacer to a depth sufficient to just mark the receiver metal to indicate screw hole position. Here I used a #29 drill and later enlarged the spacer holes to size 18 body drill to fit the 8-32 screws for mounting.

Drilling and tapping the receiver should be done with care. While the receiver does not appear to be case-hardened, it is made of fairly hard metal and care should be exercised to drill and tap slowly to avoid breaking a drill or tap. Use a good quality, sharp drill and tap, along with proper drill or tap lubricant. A two-flute tap is stronger and will help prevent breakage.

The receiver wall is fully .110-inch thick where it is tapped, providing sufficient screw thread depth

(Right) There's plenty of room for eye relief adjustments with this scope/mount arrangement. The low recoil, power and decent accuracy make the rig ideal for serious plinking and small game.

(Below) These 75-yard groups show impressive accuracy for the SKS. Author used Speer 125-grain, .311-inch bullets, Federal 210 primers, 25 grains of Hodgdon 4198 powder.

for hardened socket-head screws. I started with screws a bit over length and, as the mount and spacer were tightened in position, I later cut the screws to exact length. As you do this, be sure the threaded holes are clean and lubricated to avoid wear on the threads. As the screws are fitted, leave as much clean thread length as possible for optimal strength, and then cut to exact flush fit with the inside of the receiver wall.

Having drilled and tapped the mount and receiver holes, clean the inside of the receiver and replace the barreled action in the stock. Do not replace the bolt and receiver cap at this time—you just want to see how the scope base and spacer fit as a unit. Tighten the screws with enough torque to see they don't protrude further than flush with the inside of the receiver wall. Screws should be fitted to exact length at this time.

With the scope base attached, a look inside the open receiver shows a perfect place where two additional sheet metal screws can be effectively used to hold the scope base flange to the stock. A close look at the side mount shows the two holes used to attach this base to a Remington Model 1100 shotgun. The smaller (front) of these two holes is ideally located to place a $1/2$-inch number 8 metal screw into the stock wood. Then, exactly $1^{13}/_{16}$ inches forward of this existing hole, drill another hole through the base flange using the #18 drill for the second metal screw. As a lead hole into the wood, use a #29 or #30 drill for a perfect screw fit.

Though the recoil on this little rifle is light, the addition of two extra screws into the stock wood really provide a solid mount—and it looks good too. I would advise the use of a thread-bonding material on the two socket-head screws on final application of the mount. The scope mounts perfectly over the bore line to enhance the aesthetic appearance of the gun.

This rifle is very well made with few shortcuts in workmanship. At the time of this writing, unissued SKS carbines can be purchased for around $100. Scoped, this little rifle can provide a lot of sporting and recreational shooting pleasure at low cost. Though these handy little guns aren't known for pin-point accuracy, you'll be able to gain some useful yardage in your plinking and small game hunting. And, by mounting the scope yourself, there is additional self-satisfaction to be gained. ●

Thompson/Center offers 45 Colt barrels in 10-, 14-, and 16-inch lengths for use on the basic Contender frame. The combination makes an extremely accurate handgun and a good one for short-range hunting.

THERE'VE BEEN at least a few hundred articles written about the 45 Colt cartridge and the various firearms (mostly handguns) chambered for it. Is there room for one more manuscript on the subject? Perhaps there is, if we don't simply do another rubber-stamp treatise as so many gunwriters have unenthusiastically accomplished over the years.

As with many other topics, we gun scribes often get in a rut. Consequently, the important aspects and/or attributes of the 45

# The 45 Colt Again

Now going into its second century, this still-popular revolver round has a lot to offer the handgunner who likes big-bore plinking and hunting.

## by MIKE THOMAS

Colt cartridge and the firearms either go unmentioned or do not receive what can be deemed as adequate treatment.

The 45 Colt or 45 "Long" Colt? Does it make a difference? No, of course not. We are talking about the same cartridge, but it's officially known as, simply, 45 Colt. Where I type "45 Colt," please feel free to read "45 Long Colt" if so inclined. It won't bother me a bit.

A long, long time before anyone ever used smokeless powder or jacketed bullets in the 45 Colt cartridge, its enviable reputation as an effective round was firmly entrenched in both the real American West and the embellished American West of legend.

The "mystique" of the 45 Colt is shared by few other handgun or rifle cartridges. Comparatively, that may not make it any more powerful or accurate, but anything so rich in history and lore that's still popular after 120 years must have something going for it.

Okay, what's so great about the 45 Colt anyway? In commercial loadings, this cartridge develops very mild chamber pressure.

recommended for use only in strong Ruger single-action revolvers or Thompson/Center Contender single shots. I briefly experimented with higher-pressure loads some years ago and found no real advantage to their use. Now, hopefully somewhat wiser, it becomes difficult to imagine why anyone would want to hotrod a 45 Colt. It makes far more sense to use a 44 Magnum! In this case, both the cartridge and the gun were *designed* for high-pressure loads.

against other cartridges? It certainly holds its own, that's for sure. I mentioned in the beginning of this article that I would not rehash material already done to death for generations. That is exactly what a comparison ballistic table would do here. For those so inclined, tables galore can be found in the myriad reloading manuals and other gun books. Let it suffice to say that a 250- to 260-grain bullet at 850-900 feet per second muzzle velocity does excellent service as a defense round or

Typical of today's 45 Colt revolvers are these in the author's battery (from top): Smith & Wesson Model 25-5 with 6-inch barrel, a nickeled Model 25-5 with 4-inch barrel and stag grips, and a Ruger Blackhawk with 7½-inch barrel.

That's an important point, more important, in fact, than many of us realize. It's no secret that mild pressures are far easier on gun metal than high chamber pressures. And, while on the subject of pressure, I know that many overzealous handloaders have been running some rather hot (and potentially dangerous) loads through their 45 Colt handguns. This is not entirely their own fault, as some of the recipes published in handloading manuals actually advocate the practice. Fortunately, such loads are usually listed in a separate section and

An advantage of the 45 Colt cartridge is one that's sometimes overlooked and difficult to pin down. "Shootability" is perhaps as accurate a description as any. Unlike a magnum, recoil is not severe, nor is muzzle blast. Recovery from recoil for accurate repeat shots is very quick. Flinching normally is not a problem with any firearm chambered for such a mild cartridge. This all means better shooting for most of us. Even most magnum enthusiasts will readily admit they become better shooters when using a non-magnum cartridge like the 45 Colt.

How does the old Colt stack up

as a short-range hunting load. Cartridges in this same general category include the 44 Special and the 44-40 Winchester (44 WCF). Actually, the 45 ACP probably should be included as well. These are all very fine, useful cartridges despite the fact that they, like the 45 Colt, are rather elderly.

Heavy, large-diameter bullets at moderate velocities need not depend on jacketed softpoint or hollow-point construction for performance, as is often necessary with bullets of smaller diameter and much lighter weight. Modern jacketed bullets will certainly

The Winchester 94 Angle Eject Trapper is chambered for 45 Colt and has a 16-inch barrel.

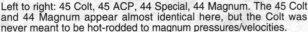

Left to right: 45 Colt, 45 ACP, 44 Special, 44 Magnum. The 45 Colt and 44 Magnum appear almost identical here, but the Colt was never meant to be hot-rodded to magnum pressures/velocities.

The author's favorite bullet for use in the 45 Colt is cast from wheelweights using Lyman's #454424 mould. Depending on the alloy, bullets weigh 250-260 grains.

work in the 45 Colt, but their use is superfluous. In fact, a moderately hard cast bullet (or a moderately soft one) will perform at least as well, if not better, than a jacketed bullet in the aging Colt cartridge, in many instances. I'm talking about overall performance here, accuracy included.

The 45 Colt loaded with heavy lead bullets is still available commercially. And, for those handloaders who don't cast their own bullets, such slugs can be had from a number of commercial casters.

I have been working with the 45 Colt since 1977, when I bought my first handgun in this chambering, a Ruger Blackhawk single action with the 7½-inch barrel. Cast bullet loads have been used exclusively. There has been some question as to the proper cast bullet diameter for use in various 45 Colt firearms. Many say to use .454-inch bullets in pre-World War II guns as their bores were larger than guns of more recent manufacture. I'll take a different approach as to my recommendations, based solely on my own experience with "recent" guns. Thus far, I have

found the difference between the two diameters to be a subtle one at best. I hope one day to do more extensive testing in this area than what I have done already, but I can report now that .454-inch cast bullets rank the best in overall performance. The .452-inch bullets are either close or identical in accuracy in many instances. For the caster who wants to invest in only one bullet sizing die, there should be no regrets with the purchase of one in .454-inch. By the way, the 45 Colt is a very forgiving cast bullet cartridge. Wheelweight alloy and practically any bullet lubricant will work effectively at 45 Colt velocities.

Unique powder has been a favorite propellant in the 45 Colt for years. A load of 9 grains of Unique with the 255- to 260-grain plainbase semi-wadcutter cast from a Lyman mould (#454424) is a very fine combination, and my favorite. Depending on barrel length, muzzle velocity usually runs from 830 fps to 925 fps.

The "power" terms like killing, stopping, shocking and knockdown are floating around in myriad

handgun/cartridge articles these days. Various formulas for figuring these things are out there, too. Though it might hurt the feelings of textbook theorists, these terms mean little in the real world, and they are hardly worth cluttering a practical mind with. Even "foot pounds of energy" does not tell us a great deal, though this one may not be as worthless as the rest. The point here is that these idioms only merit argument among the ranks of the misinformed. To my way of thinking, for defense or close-range hunting, a heavy bullet that's almost ½-inch in diameter *before* it leaves the muzzle need not lower itself to the level of the various "power and formula" theories.

For hunting game to the size of whitetail deer at ranges not exceeding 50 yards, a 45 Colt handgun with proper loads would be quite adequate in the hands of an experienced shooter. With the Trapper carbine offered by Winchester in its Model 94 lever-action series, the range could be extended to perhaps 75 yards or so. I will qualify these statements

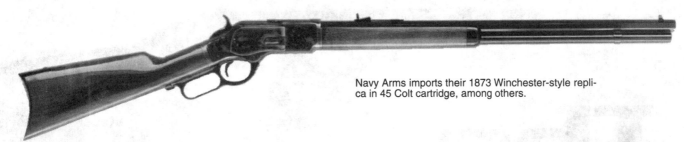

Navy Arms imports their 1873 Winchester-style replica in 45 Colt cartridge, among others.

by saying that I hunt deer in Texas. Most of our deer are comparatively small and are often taken at close range using cartridges considered to be on the very light side for deer in other states. In the interest of humane kills, it would be untrue to say that the 45 Colt is an ideal deer cartridge. It is not, of course, but keeping in mind the range limitation, I've found it is more than adequate for small deer-size game.

The little carbine's 16-inch barrel accounts for a muzzle velocity increase of about 25 percent over that of most handguns. The 850 fps from a 4-inch barrel increases to around 1125 fps in the carbine. Recoil in the Winchester is slight and muzzle blast is certainly not of the magnum variety.

Let's look at what's presently available in the way of guns chambered for the 45 Colt. This is only one of many chamberings that can be had in the Thompson/Center Contender single shot pistol. The Ruger Blackhawk comes with either a 4⅝-inch or 7½-inch barrel. The Dan Wesson 45V, a big double-action revolver, can be had with interchangeable barrels starting at 4 inches. There are several foreign-made copies of the Colt single action, all of which are available in 45 Colt. These are marketed by such companies as E.A.A., EMF, Cimarron Arms, American Arms, Mitchell Arms, Navy Arms, etc. Colt reintroduced their Single-Action Army revolver in 1992. Of course, it's still made in this country, as is the beautiful Freedom Arms single action. Both guns approach or perhaps exceed $1000, but quality is excellent as one would certainly expect. Surprisingly, Smith & Wesson's

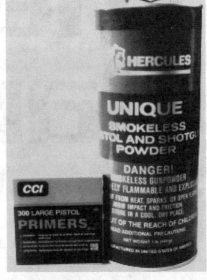

There are a number of acceptable powders and primers that can be effectively used in the 45 Colt, but Thomas favors Unique and CCI-300s for the bulk of his handloads.

Model 25-5 revolver is no more. Used ones, however, are not difficult to locate.

Some of the same folks who manufacture the European single actions also produce some reproduction rifles in 45 Colt. These are based on the 1873 Winchester lever-action pattern. And then there's the Winchester Trapper made by U.S. Repeating Arms. I might mention that the Winchester is the least expensive of the longarms available for 45 Colt.

Well, there you have it. Perhaps the 45 Colt is not the "all-round" handgun cartridge, but it's quite likely nothing else fills that bill either if we look at things objectively. Now, that's a rather esoteric, gunwriter-type statement that doesn't mean too much. Right? Right. The real point is that the 45 Colt is a very useful cartridge in the *practical* realm of the shooting sports. Its usefulness overshadows magnum handgun rounds by a considerable margin, though some of us have failed to notice this. Not too bad for a 120 year-old cartridge...  ●

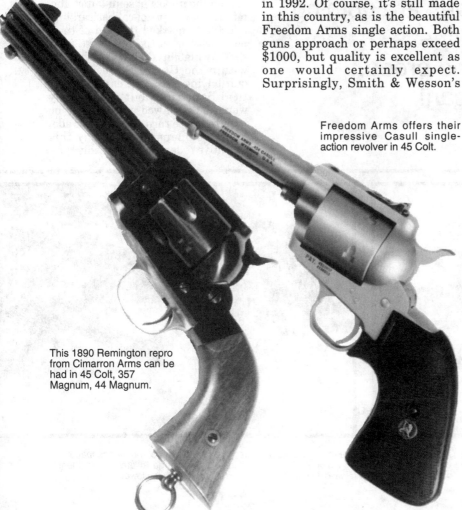

Freedom Arms offers their impressive Casull single-action revolver in 45 Colt.

This 1890 Remington repro from Cimarron Arms can be had in 45 Colt, 357 Magnum, 44 Magnum.

# The Claridge Carbine

Pistol-caliber carbines are nothing new, but this Nifty Nine is one of the best of the breed. Get one while you can!

## by JACK STEIN

PRESIDENT GEORGE Bush's ban on the import of semi-automatic, military-style, pistol-caliber carbines effectively marked the end of their popularity or, at the very least, their wide availability to civilian shooters within the United States. People quit buying these popular and practical light rifles out of fear they would be outlawed and possibly be required to be turned in without adequate compensation. To say this executive order by a supposedly "pro-

Claridge's safety-lever is at the top of the left grip. Operation is effortless and the shooter's thumb finds it easily. The lever protruding from the receiver above the safety is the manual bolt hold-open.

The magazine release button is on the left grip and mimics that of the Colt Model 1911. It is protected by a ridge to prevent accidental release. Comfortable grip is cast integral with the lower receiver.

gun" president was an inane, knee-jerk reaction to the irrational hysteria promoted by the anti-gun media and politicians would simply be a statement of the obvious.

Pistol-caliber carbines have always been popular with Americans. One need only look to the lever-action series of carbines in 44-40, 38-40, and other common revolver calibers found during the late 1800s to prove the point. One hundred years later, importers provided the semi-auto Uzi carbine, the H&K Model 94 carbine, and a few semi-auto, civilian-legal versions of the British Sterling SMG to meet the need for a pistol-caliber carbine.

With the banning of these late model light rifles, Americans were left to search the used gun market and pay premium prices for these new collector items. A number of American manufacturers started producing new products to fill the void, but none of them ever caught the eye, nor the imagination, as the formerly imported models did.

Colt introduced their 9mm carbine based on the AR-15 and it probably comes the closest to achieving the former glory of these firearms, but one of the better examples of the breed is the Claridge Hi-Tec.

This semi-auto carbine in 9mm Parabellum has captured much of the essence of the old, previously available Uzi semi-auto and the HK 94 carbine. The Claridge is a light and handy gun with a double-stack magazine, and it can easily be operated with reasonable accuracy while held with only one hand.

Are these small rifles really worth-while? Their value depends upon your point of view, but their purpose is no different than that of any firearm.

Pistol-caliber semi-auto carbines are still as viable and useful today as they have been in the past. They are easy to shoot because of their low recoil and quiet muzzle report in comparison to more powerful rifles or the ever-faithful short-barreled shotgun. They have a shorter overall length than full-blown rifles, and they are lighter, too.

Additionally, in some jurisdictions, they are easier to own than handguns, but that has changed drastically in the last few years because of legislation prohibiting possession of "assault weapons." The reader should check local and state laws in his area to determine if a firearm like the Claridge fits the legal definition of a prohibited "assault weapon."

The Claridge is a striker-fired gun and, like the semi-auto-only Uzi, it lacks a hammer to strike the firing pin. In fact, this aspect of the Claridge is very similar in mechanical theory to that gun.

The civilian-legal Uzi was a striker-fired carbine operating from a closed bolt. The original full-auto Uzi fired from an open bolt, which could best be described as a wrap-around bolt that actually surrounded the rear portion of the barrel. It extended past the bolt face and enclosed the chamber portion of the barrel.

When the Uzi was first imported into the United States, the BATF stipulated the semi-auto version be designed so as not to be readily convertible into a full-auto version, so a number of significant changes were mandated in its design. What they actually were is not germane to the discussion here, but the closed-bolt, striker-fired system used for the semi-auto Uzi is.

The Uzi carbine employed an L-shaped strut that had its longer portion of the L running down one side on the bottom of the semi-auto bolt. When released by the trigger sear, the spring-powered firing pin would move forward to strike the primer of the chambered cartridge.

The Claridge employs a firing system that is identical in practice. Here, the bolt is round, instead of the Uzi's rectangular shape, but the Claridge's striker system uses two springs like the Uzi. One is used to power the firing pin assembly, the other is the recoil spring.

The firing pin assembly is something of a U-shaped piece with the firing pin itself forming one leg of the U, while the other leg extends both below the U and forward to make contact with the sear. Unlike the Uzi, on the Claridge this is a one-piece unit with the firing pin welded to the sear release leg.

The Claridge recoil spring is of small diameter, tightly wound, that surrounds a guide rod $7\frac{1}{8}$ inches in length. The guide rod is permanently fastened to a circular metal disc. This disc has a thin, blue rubber buffer between it and the bolt, and it also has the firing pin spring and extension rod welded to it. The extension rod and spring power the firing pin forward for firing.

Everything is held in place by a small spring clip that secures the end of the recoil spring guide rod through the front of the bolt assembly. A very clean and neat design, provided you don't lose the clip pin; if you do, a small piece of wire will serve the same purpose.

Once this spring clip is secured to the end of the recoil spring guide rod, the whole bolt assembly (and striker firing assembly) is self-contained.

The Claridge Hi-Tec field-strips easily. To get to the bolt assembly, make sure the chamber is empty and the gun clear of any cartridges, then move the safety off and pull the trigger. There is a cross-pin located at the front of the lower receiver. Pull it out and separate the upper receiver from the lower receiver. Retract the cocking knob to the rear of its travel slot in the upper receiver and pull out to remove it from the bolt. The bolt assembly will now lift out of the

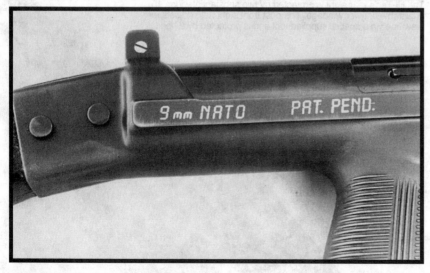

The Claridge is built for high-pressure 9x19mm ammunition. The 9mm NATO is among the highest-pressure of its type available. Owner's manual warns against the use of aluminum-cased ammo, however.

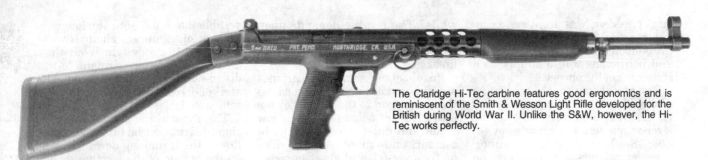

The Claridge Hi-Tec carbine features good ergonomics and is reminiscent of the Smith & Wesson Light Rifle developed for the British during World War II. Unlike the S&W, however, the Hi-Tec works perfectly.

upper receiver.

The Claridge, like the Uzi, has the magazine located within the pistol grip, and the advantage here is the operator can easily reload in low light or dark conditions with the "hand finds hand" principle.

The Claridge is oriented for the right-handed shooter because the magazine release button is on the upper left side of the grip and operates in the same fashion as that used on the Colt Model 1911 automatic pistol. It is not reversible on the Claridge. The grip is cast as an integral part of the lower receiver.

The upper receiver is formed from thin-wall steel tube. In this respect, it shares a similarity with many submachine guns seen during World War II, like the Sten, the German MP-40, and the post-war Swedish K. The barrel is held in position by a circular block fastened within this tube. Forward of this block are 28 ventilation holes to help cool the barrel ahead of the chamber.

The cocking handle is nothing more than a knob that sticks out of the left side of the upper receiver at a 45-degree angle. It is connected directly to the bolt assembly, so it reciprocates when the carbine fires.

The rear sight is protected by two vertical wings that are part of the lower receiver. It is adjustable for windage, but not elevation. The front sight is adjustable for elevation and consists of a round post that operates like the one used on the Chinese SKS rifle, but it still requires a special tool to change settings.

The safety-lever is on the left side of the lower receiver and above the grip. It is easily reached by the right thumb when the shooter holds the gun.

The Claridge owner's manual said the magazine was one of Claridge's own design, but it looks strangely like the one used on the Beretta Model 92F pistol. It holds 15 rounds and falls freely from the magazine well when the latch is released.

A nylon sling was provided that fastens to the carbine by quick-detachable swivels at the front and rear. The rear attachment point is on the left side of the receiver, at the very back. The front swivel is a clamp mounted to the barrel just forward of the polymer handguard.

During testing of the Claridge Hi-Tec, we immediately noted the gun's superb accuracy. The test target shown nearby was shot with ten rounds of Eldorado's 124-grain Starfire ammunition from a standing position at 25 yards, and only one round out of ten strayed out of the nine ring.

We soon learned this was rather typical performance for the Claridge, and it is the major reason why we recommend this handy little carbine.

The synthetic stock of the Claridge is comfortable and has a natural feel to it during shooting. It has a dog-leg appearance to it. In fact, the whole rifle looks a lot like the old Smith & Wesson Light Rifle that was built for

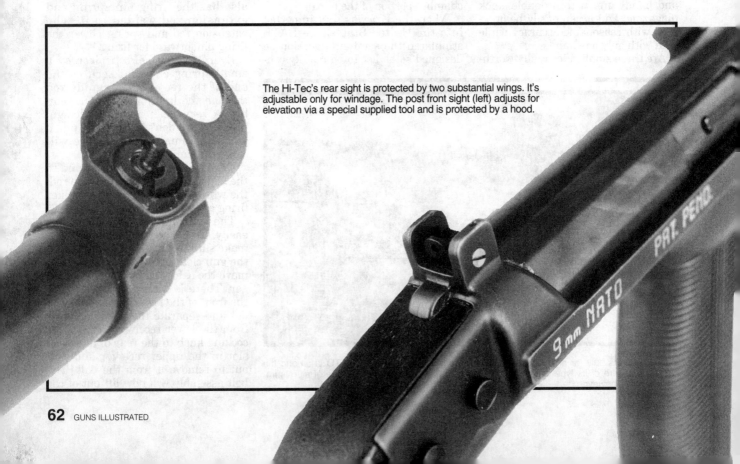

The Hi-Tec's rear sight is protected by two substantial wings. It's adjustable only for windage. The post front sight (left) adjusts for elevation via a special supplied tool and is protected by a hood.

At 25 yards from a standing position, the Claridge produced this impressive ten-shot group with Eldorado Starfire ammunition. The gun is also highly reliable.

the British at the beginning of World War II, and that's not all bad. Different, but not bad.

The Claridge handled a variety of ammunition types with equal aplomb and always performed with good accuracy. The owner's manual warns against the use of aluminum-cased ammunition, so CCI Blazer was not tested, but we did use Action Arms Uzi and Samson brands to good effect.

The only comment we could voice that would even come close to sounding like a complaint concerns the pull weight on the trigger.

Shooting the Claridge in cold weather with gloved hands made it difficult to know when the trigger was going to break. The trigger has a long travel and there is no pre-travel in the conventional sense. The trigger just has to move a bit more than on most rifles. The trigger pull measured 12 pounds on our trigger pull gauge. It felt heavy, but not *that* heavy.

Is there a need for these light-weight, handy carbines? You bet there is. They are easier to learn than a 12-bore shotgun and shorter to move through a doorway than a rifle. They make great home defense firearms and good casual, plinking, family recreational guns.

For home defense, all one has to do is add an auxiliary light, available

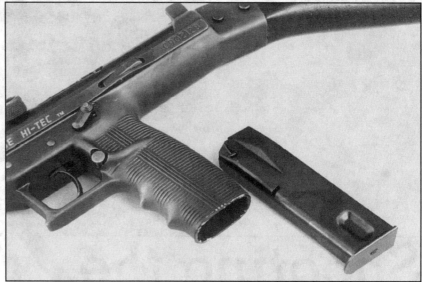

Like the Uzi before it, the Claridge houses the magazine in the grip. The system works well for recharging the gun in the dark as one hand can always find the other.

from either Laser Products or Tac Star, and you have a firearm that is superior to any handgun because you can identify your target. This is an important point for a home defense firearm, both to avoid accidental shootings and for later court testimony.

The status of the Claridge company and carbine is unclear. Reports of

the firm's demise have been widely circulated, but others say production has only been placed on hold pending better financing.

Whatever the outcome, the Claridge has many good attributes, and like the semi-auto Uzi before it, it makes a good pistol-caliber carbine for the American shooter. My advice is to pick one up when you see it.  ●

# Offbeat Handgun Fun

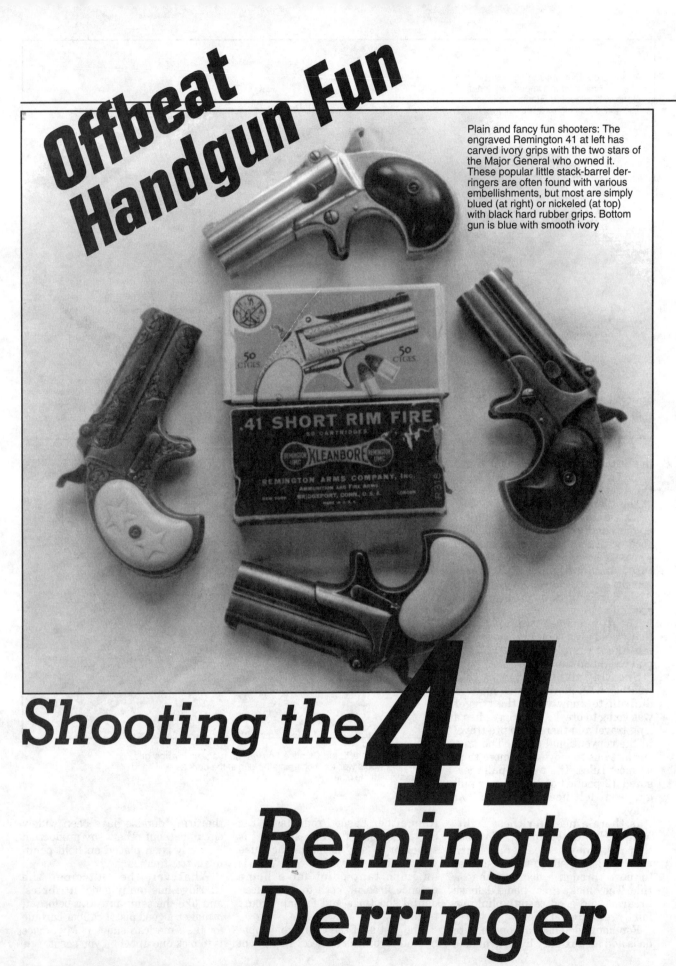

Plain and fancy fun shooters: The engraved Remington 41 at left has carved ivory grips with the two stars of the Major General who owned it. These popular little stack-barrel derringers are often found with various embellishments, but most are simply blued (at right) or nickeled (at top) with black hard rubber grips. Bottom gun is blue with smooth ivory

# Shooting the 41 Remington Derringer

# by JIM McCOSKEY

It's a rimfire, but reloadable cases make these over/unders bark and blast again.

FAVORITE GUNS, like horses, cars, golf clubs and bird dogs acquire their preeminent status through a complex synthesis of objective and subjective factors, mostly the latter. This may be the case with one of my favorite guns—the venerable 41-caliber rimfire Remington over/under derringer. Certainly, the 41 has little to recommend it as a practical handgun nowadays, but I find it lots of fun to play with.

Introduced in 1866, Remington 41s were instantly popular and justly so. The little pistol is sleek, compact, and mechanically reliable. Over 150,000 of them were produced before the gun was dropped from production in 1935. Its heyday spanned the most colorful era of American history. It, along with the Winchester '73, Colt Single Action Army, and Model 1911 Colt 45 auto must be considered an American firearms classic.

Despite the impressive size of the holes in those twin bores, the little 41 is anything but a powerhouse. Originally, the load was a pointed 130-grain lead bullet ahead of 10 grains of blackpowder. Sometime after the turn of the century, the load was modernized with smokeless powder, but no increase in power resulted. Loads of all original varieties I have tested, including some vintage blackpowder cartridges, will not quite bury the bullet out of sight in a pine 2x4 at a range of 2 to 3 feet. It is, however, a matter of historical fact that the round has been sufficient to do a lethal job when fired into the human torso at card table range. This so-called "pipsqueak" accounted for enough casualties to earn a popularity among hideout gun toters that was uneclipsed until 25-caliber automatic pistols came along at the turn of the century.

Although popularized in Old West literature as the "gambler's gun," gaslight-era pistol packers from all walks of life probably

The classic 41 Remington and an example of the early Colt 25 ACP auto which hastened the 41's demise. The Remington design lives on to this day, however, and is chambered for a wild variety of calibers.

owned at least one Remington 41. Actually, the 41 remained fairly popular up through the World War II period. General Douglas MacArthur regularly carried a Remington 41 in his pocket during the War. Apparently the General had good cause for confidence in his 41. During the 1914 crisis with Mexico at Vera Cruz, then Captain MacArthur made a daring scout into hostile territory during which he reportedly dropped two bandits with his derringer. Author William Manchester related this story in his book *American Caesar*, and does not specifically say so, but that "derringer" was in all probability a Remington 41. Lesser military lights, including yours truly, have also carried 41s as wartime backups. During the Vietnam War, I often carried a nice old nickel-plated Remington 41 or a Browning 25 auto in addition to my 45.

However obsolete as a serious weapon, the little stack-barrel 41 is still a lot of fun to own and shoot—sort of like driving around in a

restored Model T Ford; nostalgia along with some practical utility. Because so many were made for so long, Remington 41s are still commonly available at reasonable prices. Most, owing to simple design and quality manufacture, are still in shooting condition. Although 41 rimfire ammo has not been made by domestic concerns for many years, new imported cartridges are readily available through numerous sources, including the famous Dixie Gun Works of Union City, Tennessee. I now also see plenty of it at gun shows and even in some local gun shops. However, this new factory fodder is by no means cheap. At $25 or so dollars per box of 50, the cost is steep enough to take the gun out of this impecunious shooter's plinking category.

Happily for the state of the family finances and peace on the home front, I have discovered an alternative which enables me to enjoy shooting my 41s with less damage to the budget. Rimfires like the 41 are normally considered nonreloadable. However, where there is a will there is a way, as the old saw goes. Some years ago, I spotted an advertisement for "reloadable rimfire" cases. Promptly, I ordered a few samples in 41-caliber.

The idea with these cases is ingeniously simple. A brass case is turned out with a 22-caliber chamber bored into the case head so that a 22 rimfire case (minus powder and bullet) can serve as the primer for the 41.

Now that I had reloadable cases, the next step was to develop a load. Of course, there is no published loading data for the 41 rimfire—the ammo was never meant to be reloaded. Dixie Gunworks, who later marketed the reloadable rimfire cases, recommends a system of filling cases with blackpowder for round ball loads, but offers no detailed instructions as to the loading process. By dint of trial

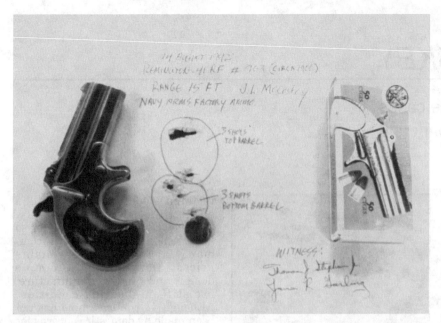

Shooting the current Navy Arms ammunition, the author produced this target with one of his Remingtons that dates to about 1900. Three shots from each barrel printed surprisingly close to each other.

and error, I developed a workable loading method.

The first point I must make is that *extreme caution* must be exercised. There is a definite possibility that in the process of trying to seat a ball in a primed case, the 22 rimfire priming case could be fired from pressure or shock.

I offer an easy fix for this safety problem: Merely reverse the normal cartridge loading sequence. First, seat the projectile in the *empty* case. I do this simply by squeezing a ball into the case up to the ogive in a small vise. No special loading tools are required. After seating all the balls, pour in the powder through the 22-size hole in the base of the cases. Finally, gently insert an *empty* 22 Short case (from which the bullet and powder have been removed) with the fingers. At first, I found these 22 cases had a tendency to fall out in the box or pocket. This was easy to cure by brushing a little clear fingernail polish around the 22 case rim just prior to inserting it—works like a charm and helps seal the finished 41 case against moisture. Another wrinkle I found helpful was to substitute an RWS BB Cap case for the 22 Short case. It is an aggravation to pull bullets out of 22 Shorts. With the BB Cap, the little round ball is easily rolled out of the case mouth with a nut-pick or screwdriver.

To my knowledge, bullets in any standard commercial form are not available for the 41 rimfire. Nor do I know of any mould to cast the rather weird 130-grain pointed bullet with which the factory 41 is loaded. It is, however, easy and practical to use .395-inch round balls.

In summary, simply seat one of these round balls up to the ogive in the vise, fill the case through the priming hole with FFFg, then, using finger pressure, seat the empty 22 Short or BB Cap case with fingernail polish. Load the completed cartridge into the derringer with the primer aligned so that the firing pin will hit it squarely. You are in business and will be rewarded with a highly impressive flash, bang, and

## Step 1

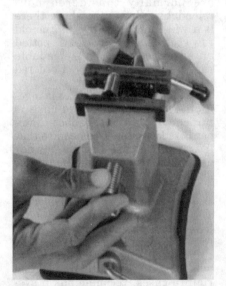

Seat a round ball up to the ogive in the empty case. Seating too deep can cause chambering problems. These reloadable cases may need to be shortened and polished a bit to fit some guns.

## Step 2

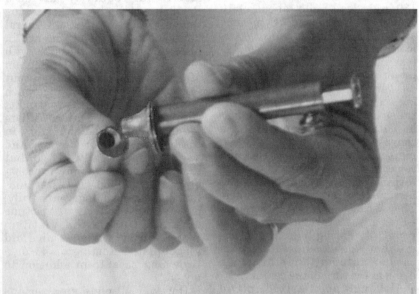

Pour in the powder charge of about 10 grains of FFFg blackpowder through the rear of the case, where the empty 22 BB Cap will be seated. You'll have to devise a suitable cartridge block to hold the rounds until completion.

smoke—decent plinkin' accuracy too!

Now that we have a "shootin' recipe," some thoughts on carrying, managing, and shooting these interesting little pistols are in order. Remington 41s are simple and reliable in operation. All that notwithstanding, they can easily be abused and even broken if not handled with reasonable care.

The structural Achilles heel on the Remington is the hinge upon which the barrels pivot to open and close. Lots of these nice little guns have been broken over the years by careless people who tried to "throw" them open. That hinge will take any amount of shooting, but it was never designed to withstand the impact of that heavy set of barrels being snapped back against it. I have never seen or heard of an original Remington breaking at the hinge in normal use.

One often encounters a derringer that shows a crack in the left-side hinge ring adjacent to the screw head. I believe this is due to over tightening the screw when there is excessive play between barrels and frame. Logically, such guns command lower prices than their pristine brethren in otherwise equivalent condition. In my experience, these guns work just fine. I have owned and extensively shot many of them with minor hinge ring

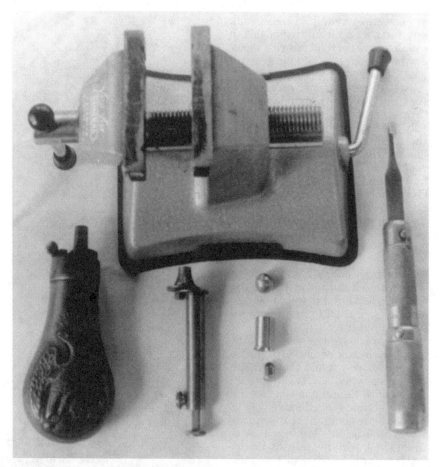

Here's all you need to assemble round ball loads: FFFg blackpowder, powder measure, small vise, .395-inch balls, reloadable cases (see text), BB Caps, and a screwdriver for removing balls. Minimum equipment, maximum fun!

## Step 3

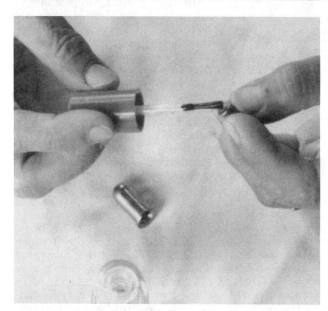

Swab a bit of nail polish around the head of the BB Cap from which the lead ball has been removed. The polish acts to hold the Cap in place and seal the load from moisture.

## Step 4

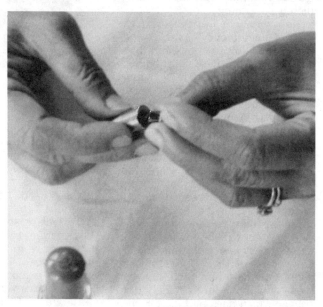

Immediately insert the BB Cap into the loaded 41 case and set aside for the nail polish to dry. That's all there is to reloading 41 rimfire ammunition.

cracks and never had one break any further. As a matter of fact, a couple of my current favorite shooters have such cracks and are still going strong.

Just to confirm my impression that the top hinge undergoes very little stress from shooting, I repeatedly fired a Remington 41 on which the top hinge was completely broken off the frame. This specimen was in good shape otherwise, and I had picked it up for spare parts. Over the course of 10 shots, this broken pistol stayed together just fine, firing both barrels just like it was supposed to, even though it was held together only by the locking lug.

Safety in carrying is a point where the Remington is usually faulted. Certainly, it would be possible for the pistol to fire if dropped hard enough on the hammer to break or dislodge the sear from the simple half-cock notch. Such probably has happened and the possibility has spawned safety catches on the modern Remington-type copies. A very simple but effective way to prevent an accidental discharge with the original Remington is to insert a 1/4-inch strip of heavy leather down in front of the hammer. With the hammer let down on the leather, there is no possibility of the firing pin reaching the case. Yet, when the pistol is cocked, the little strip will fall out or it can be easily pulled free with virtually no loss of time. I have pocket-carried my Remingtons for years with this leather hammer block and feel completely safe doing so.

Now, what can be expected in the way of accuracy? Naturally, we can't hope for full-size handgun accuracy out of these short barrels. However, I can tell you that most Remingtons will shoot far better than you might think.

I find that most 41s shoot well enough to ventilate tin cans at 10 feet and beyond. Accuracy such as this is, in my opinion, sufficient for this type of handgun. Now, inherent accuracy is one thing, but "shootability," which includes such practical factors as trigger pull and sights, is the paramount consideration. Some Remingtons will be found with an excellent trigger pull, and they're easy to hit with if the sights are right. On the other hand, many of these guns have an extremely hard trigger which does nothing for good shooting. A good gunsmith can easily correct a hard pull if need be.

In his tests, the author found his round ball handloads superior to the Navy Arms factory ammo. At 3 feet, factory loads went flush with the surface of the wood, whereas reloads penetrated 1/4-inch below surface.

Sights on the Remington are simply a blade front integral to the barrels, with the rear only a notch atop the hinge. Some of these little guns shoot right on with one barrel or the other. The second barrel is generally 2 to 3 inches high or low at 10 feet or so. If you get one of these inherently good shooters, you have a prize indeed. Of the others, most seem to shoot high—some as much as a foot at 10 or 12 feet. Oddly, I have yet to encounter one that was off significantly in windage. Of course, the high shooters are caused by front sights

which are too low or, less likely, the rear notch too shallow. Low shooters can be corrected by carefully filing down the front sight. High shooters are a bit more complicated but there is a way to do this without permanently altering the gun.

I have had great success in bringing down the point of impact by making a little brass bead which is affixed atop the front sight with Acraweld, a high quality epoxy product available from Brownells (222 W. Liberty, Montezuma, Iowa 50171; 515/623-5401). Basically, the system is this: Turn down a piece of brass welding rod with an electric drill and a file to about 1/16-inch diameter. Then, with a slotting file, carefully cut a slit in the bottom to fit over the top of the sight blade. This takes a bit of careful work. After a good fit is achieved, cut off the leftover rod. You will have a little piece about 3/16-inch or so long. Epoxy this on top of the sight. When dry, the bead can be shaped to follow the general contours of the original sight. This accomplishes two things: point of impact is lowered and you now have a nice "gold" bead which is easy to see. Restoration to original can be readily accomplished by laying a hot soldering iron on top of the brass bead to break the epoxy bond. I have so modified several Remingtons and have yet to have one of these beads come off when shooting. Although there is no permanent alteration to the pistol, I would not do this to a gun in pristine collector condition—just as I would not shoot such a fine piece either. There are plenty of "shooter" grade Remingtons available to play with.

With sights regulated and trigger adjusted (if necessary), the old Remington 41 will certainly shoot accurately enough for plenty of fun shooting. Even Ed McGivern thought so. Noted author of *Fast and Fancy Revolver Shooting*, and most scholarly of our old-time handgun experts, McGivern had nice things to say about the 41 Remington derringer. In his book, he featured a pair of 41s of which he stated: "We find that very good shooting at average defense ranges (15 to 25 feet) can be done with these two guns. This may be contrary to general belief, but is no less a fact."

Ed, I believe you! •

THERE ARE MANY different categories in the world of firearms. One of the most interesting is pistol-caliber carbines and rifles. They have been made in a wide variety of action types, including single shots like the Thompson/Center Contender Carbine chambered for 45 Colt and the Uberti Rolling Block Baby Carbine in 357 Magnum, lever-actions like the Winchester Model 94 in 45 Colt and the Marlin Model 1894CS 357 Magnum, pump-actions such as the Action Arms Timber Wolf 357 Magnum and 44 Magnum, and the Remington Model 14 1/2 38-40; then there are semi-automatics like the Marlin Camp Carbine in 9mm and 45 ACP and the Uzi carbine in 9mm Parabellum. The one action type that is not well represented in pistol-caliber carbines or rifles is the bolt action.

There were a few Savage Model 23C bolt actions made in 32-20, but the 32-20 was originally designed as a rifle cartridge, and it was far more useful as such, even though many handguns have been so chambered. There was also the Remington 788, a small number of which were chambered for the 44 Magnum round. However, the 44 Magnum is powerful enough to double as a big game cartridge in the 30-30 class in a rifle, and it certainly is not a typical handgun round with regard to performance. The British De Lisle 45 ACP silenced carbine, based on the Lee-Enfield action, is another example, but it was made only in small numbers and has never been available to civilians.

The only bolt-action, pistol-caliber carbine ever made in significant numbers is the subject of this article, the Spanish Destroyer carbine. It was most commonly chambered for the 9mm Bergmann-Bayard cartridge, but occasionally also for 9mm Parabellum and 38 ACP/Super, probably for export. Indeed, unlike the limited production of the other bolt actions chambered for handgun cartridges, the Destroyer carbine was in production from the early 1920s until at least well into the 1960s, and quite possibly much later. Also, unlike the other bolt-action pistol-caliber rifles mentioned, it was made in fairly substantial numbers.

There seems to be at least two major variations of the Destroyer. The earliest, which is sometimes called the Model 1921, has a rudimentary design reminiscent of a bolt-action 410-bore shotgun in that

## by CHARLES W. KARWAN

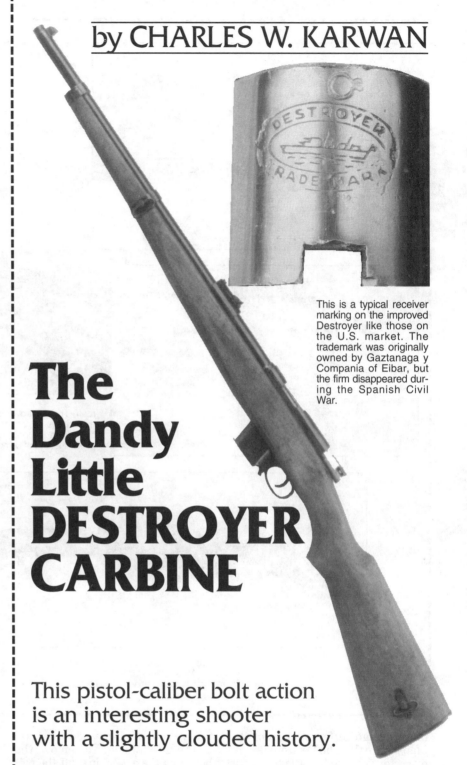

This is a typical receiver marking on the improved Destroyer like those on the U.S. market. The trademark was originally owned by Gaztanaga y Compania of Eibar, but the firm disappeared during the Spanish Civil War.

# The Dandy Little DESTROYER CARBINE

This pistol-caliber bolt action is an interesting shooter with a slightly clouded history.

the root of the bolt handle also serves as the only locking lug. It is rather crude in construction as well as design. The vast majority feed from a single-column box magazine, but I have seen a picture of one made with a tubular magazine much like that found on a typical Winchester lever-action rifle.

The early Destroyer was superseded by a much improved model some time before World War II. It was upgraded in both design and quality of construction. This is by far the most commonly encountered of the Destroyers, and this is the one that is currently on the U.S. market as imported by Century Arms International. It is also our subject gun.

The improved Destroyer has an interesting action quite similar to a miniaturized Model 93 Mauser. The

(Left) In many ways, the Destroyer is a miniaturized Model 1893 Mauser action. It has an extremely short bolt throw, which makes aimed rapid-fire quite easy. Magazine fits into the well in front of the trigger guard.

(Below) As seen here, the Destroyer's bolt throw is quite short. With practice, it can be fired as fast as a pump- or lever-action carbine with good accuracy.

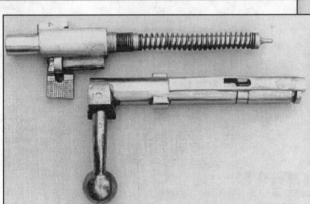

(Left) The Destroyer bolt is similar to the 1893 Mauser except the extractor is on top, and the locking lugs are two-thirds of the way back from the bolt face. Also, the firing pin is screwed into the striker instead of being held by lugs.

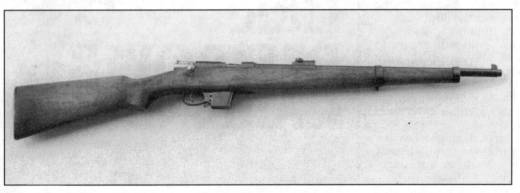

The Destroyer carbine is a lightweight, handy little gun that is a cousin to the Model 1893 Spanish Mauser. In spite of its military configuration, it was primarily a police gun.

main design differences from the Mauser are that the Destroyer's claw extractor is located on the top of the bolt instead of on the side, and the Destroyer's dual opposing locking lugs are not located at the front of the bolt. Instead, they are about two-thirds of the way toward the rear of the bolt body so as to lock into recesses in the rear receiver ring. Interestingly, this is similar in function and location to the locking lugs on the ultra-modern Ruger 77/22.

This bolt configuration allows a unique and simple bolt removal and retention system that adds no parts to the mechanism. To remove the bolt from the action, just lift the bolt handle and pull the bolt back. Just before you reach full rearward travel, the locking lugs will line up with a notch cut into the left side of the bolt track. When this happens, just rotate the bolt 90 degrees clockwise and pull it out. It couldn't be simpler. Naturally, reverse the procedure to reinsert the bolt.

Bolt disassembly is virtually identical to that of the Model 93 Mauser with one minor exception. First, cycle the bolt so the striker is cocked, then put the safety in the vertical position. Next, remove the bolt from the rifle as previously described. The bolt sleeve/striker assembly can then be unscrewed from the bolt body. Move the safety to the fire position. This will allow the firing pin to go forward and take most of the tension off the firing pin spring. The firing pin can then be unscrewed from the striker. This is the aforementioned difference from the 93 Mauser which has the firing pin held to the striker via lugs that only require a 90-degree rotation of the striker to separate it from the firing pin.

When reassembling the firing pin to the striker, be sure to screw the firing pin in so that the rear of the pin is flush with the rear of the striker. This accomplished, push the firing pin against a wooden surface while holding the bolt sleeve. Once the striker is pushed back far enough, move the safety to the vertical position. The firing pin assembly can then be screwed into the bolt body. Screw it in all the way and then back it off so the vertical safety lines up with the extractor. The bolt can then be reinserted into the rifle, turning the locking lugs in at the dismounting notch. Once the bolt is in all the way, disengage the safety.

Like the Model 93 Mauser, the Destroyer cocks on the closing of the bolt. The combination of locking lug position and short cartridge allow for an extremely short bolt throw. This, in turn, allows an excellent high rate of aimed fire by a trained operator. I found that I could empty the magazine of the Destroyer with aimed rapid-fire in an average of well under two seconds per shot. For all practical purposes, it is just as fast as a lever-action or pump-action rifle for *aimed* fire.

The six-shot magazine of the improved Destroyer is little more than a shortened Colt Government Model 38 Super magazine. In fact, such a Colt magazine can be easily modified to be used in a Destroyer carbine by simply drilling and filing a rectangular notch in the appropriate place in the back of the magazine to accept the Destroyer's magazine catch. However, Century has many of these magazines in stock at a very moderate price, so such efforts are not necessary unless you want a magazine of larger capacity.

Not surprisingly, the sights on the Destroyer are miniaturized copies of that of the Mauser 93. There is a fixed "battle sight" apparently zeroed for 25 to 50 meters and a folding sight ladder with markings in 100-meter increments out to 700 meters. Using the rather crude V-notch and barleycorn front sight, one can't expect much in the way of grouping beyond 150 meters or so, let alone 700 meters. That is not to say the basic rifle doesn't have good mechanical accuracy. Even with the crude sights, I was easily able to get sub-2-inch groups at 50 yards with my specimen, using military ball ammunition. I strongly suspect that use of a good aperture or telescopic sight with selected ammunition would get the same size groups at double that distance.

All the recently imported Destroyer carbines, and the vast majority of those produced, have a military-styled stock that runs out to within 3.5 inches of the muzzle. However, there is no bayonet lug or cleaning rod as found on most Mauser military rifles. Examples are known that have factory "sporter"-type stocks. These were probably made for sale as sporting rifles, whereas the vast majority of Destroyer carbines were purchased and issued by police agencies in Spain and, to some extent, Latin American.

In the U.S., the dominant police long arm since the late 1800s has been the shotgun. In most of Europe and much of the rest of the world prior to World War II, police used either no long gun at all or some version of the standard or obsolescent military rifle of that country. Since the war, there has been a move to submachine guns and assault rifles as the preferred police long arm in much of the world,

including Spain and, to some degree, in the U.S.

Spain's choice of a bolt-action pistol-caliber carbine for police use started in the 1920s and lasted through the first several decades following World War II. It is unique, but actually well thought out.

Prior to the adoption of the Destroyer carbine by Spanish police, a major police long arm in Spain was the 44-40 El Tigre lever-action carbine. These were good quality piece-for-piece copies of the Winchester Model 92 carbine that were made in Spain and often exported to Latin American countries. While the 44-40 cartridge was originally brought out as a rifle round, it has handgun-type ballistics and was widely chambered in a variety of revolvers.

Evidently, the Spanish police found from their experience with the El Tigre that they did not need the power, penetration and range of the 7x57mm Spanish service rifle cartridge they had been using. Indeed, such power and penetration is actually a detriment for police use because of its likelihood of over-penetration and endangerment of innocent bystanders. At the same time, the standard Spanish service pistol cartridge was the 9mm Bergmann-Bayard. What could be more natural for police use than a miniaturized Model 93 Mauser chambered for 9mm Bergmann-Bayard? This is particularly so since at the time there was no semi-automatic rifle design available in Spain. Thus was the Destroyer carbine concept brought about and implemented.

The manufacturers of the Destroyer carbines are a bit obscure. It is known that Gaztanaga y Compania of Eibar at one time owned the Destroyer name and trademark. They made and market-

Like the rest of the gun, the Destroyer's sights are miniaturized versions of the Model 1893 Mauser. The "battle sight" is zeroed for 25 to 50 meters, while the ladder goes up to a wishful 700 meters.

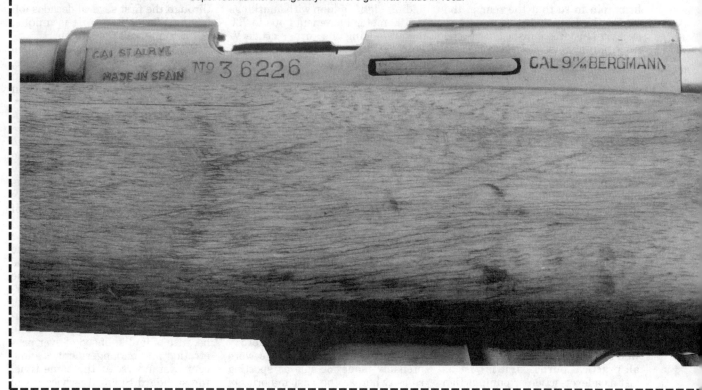

Most Destroyers are chambered for 9mm Bergmann, but they are also found in 9mm Parabellum and 38 Super. The latter are usually marked "9mm/.38" and will handle both Bergmann and Super rounds interchangeably. Author's gun was made in 1962.

ed a line of small Browning-pattern blowback pistols marked "Destroyer" from 1913 until the firm disappeared in the morass of the Spanish Civil War in the mid-1930s. One source claims Gaztanaga was the original manufacturer of the Destroyer and the company Ayra Duria of Eibar took over later manufacture.

Part of the confusion comes from the fact that much of the firearms manufacture in Eibar was by the cottage industry method. One family specialized in the manufacture of barrels, another in stocks, another in magazines, and several different such businesses may make the various other parts. All these were delivered to one central "manufacturer" where they were assembled and marketed. Consequently, virtually the same model of gun may have been marketed by more than one "manufacturer."

Typical markings found on the improved Destroyer carbine consist of an oval containing a stylized naval Destroyer surrounded by the words DESTROYER TRADE MARK on the receiver ring. On the left side of the receiver, there is the serial number and the caliber designation, usually CAL 9M/M. There are various proof-

marks on the barrel, one of which can tell you the date of manufacture if you know the code used. My specimen was made in 1962 and has a serial number of over 36000.

The 9mm Bergmann-Bayard cartridge, which is also commonly called just 9mm Bergmann, 9mm Bayard, 9mm Largo, 9x23mm and 9mm Astra M1921, was developed by Theodor Bergmann circa 1903. However, it was not actually fielded in quantity until it was adopted by Spain in 1908 in the Belgian-made Bergmann-Bayard pistol. It was also adopted by Denmark in 1910. It remained the standard Spanish service pistol cartridge until it was replaced by the 9mm NATO (Parabellum) in the 1980s.

The 9mm Bergmann cartridge is quite an excellent round that is ballistically similar to the 9mm Parabellum. Physically, it is extremely close in dimensions to the 38 ACP and the 9mm Steyr rounds. Many guns chambered for the 9mm Bergmann will fire and function properly with the latter two rounds as well. However, in the case of the Destroyer carbine chambered for the 9mm Bergmann, the 38 ACP's semirim is too large to fit into the bolt

face. The Steyr will fit and function fine, but the cases may swell slightly just in front of the cartridge's head.

When the 9mm Bergmann cartridge is fired in the Destroyer, the report from its 21.5-inch barrel is extremely mild and the recoil is minuscule. There is a good deal of military surplus Bergmann ammunition on the market as this is written, but it all has corrosive priming and care must be taken to clean the gun thoroughly and properly after shooting it. Remember that most modern bore cleaners *do not* remove corrosive priming residue. If in doubt with your bore cleaner, clean the bore thoroughly with hot water-soaked patches after you have cleaned it with your normal bore cleaner, and then dry and oil the bore. The corrosive salts are dissolved by water, even though many oils and solvents won't touch it.

Since all of the military 9mm Bergmann ammunition is loaded with fully jacketed bullets and is not particularly accurate, the best way to get the most out of the round is to handload it. This is particularly so since the Destroyer's action is capable of safely handling ammunition loaded up to 357 Magnum levels of

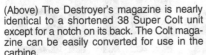

(Above) The Destroyer's magazine is nearly identical to a shortened 38 Super Colt unit except for a notch on its back. The Colt magazine can be easily converted for use in the carbine.

The standard Destroyer magazine holds only six rounds and fits flush with the bottom of the magazine well. A converted Colt pistol magazine increases capacity to nine shots.

(Left) The 9mm Largo (Bergmann-Bayard, etc.) is the most common chambering for the Destroyer. It served the Spanish military from about 1908 until the 1980s. Box says ammo is for use in automatic pistols, carbines and "sub-rifles"—pistol-caliber carbines.

performance. To efficiently handload the round requires the acquisition of Boxer-primed cases, and this can be done in several ways.

A number of years back, Midway Arms offered a large quantity of newly made, Boxer-primed Bergmann brass and loaded ammunition. Much of this is still around, and it is excellent for reloading if you can find some. Another approach is to make 9mm Bergmann cases from an existing round, and there are several possibilities. The 9mm Winchester Magnum case can be shortened into perfect Bergmann cases, though you may have to do a little reaming to thin the case mouth. Another way is to turn off the semi-rim on 38 Super or 38 ACP brass. Yet another avenue is to use 223 brass by shortening and reaming it. You can also take Boxer-primed 30 Mauser brass, neck it up and trim to 9mm Bergmann specs. Finally, you can purchase some Fiocchi 9mm Steyr ammunition and use it for your brass. Though it is slightly undersize at the head, it shouldn't cause a problem in most instances.

As you can see, obtaining 9mm Bergmann ammunition to shoot in a Destroyer carbine is no great task,

particularly if you are a handloader. One point of caution, however: If you load your ammunition to above normal levels for use in the Destroyer, make sure that it is identifiable and never fired in a handgun. The most common handgun chambered for the Bergmann round is the Astra 400, and it is a straight blowback. It is doubtful that it would react favorably to ammunition loaded much above normal levels.

Until recently, the Destroyer carbine was fairly rare and high priced in the U.S. With the recent imports by Century, they have extremely attractive prices. What are they good for besides their obvious collector value? They are an extremely fun plinker that gets far more reaction out of tin cans and such than any 22-caliber rimfire rifle. They are also dandy for close-range small game and varmint hunting. One example is for hunting turkeys where the use of rifles is legal. Likewise for shooting called predatory varmints like coyotes and fox, as well as the larger rodents like nutria and marmots at close range. Because of its light weight of only just over 6 pounds, and its short length, it is also a handy gun around the farm. It is easy to put a loaded

magazine into it on the way out to dispatch a fox in the hen house or a nutria in the orchard.

There are also jurisdictions in the U.S. where possession of a handgun is difficult to impossible, and ownership of a semi-automatic long gun is also restricted. In such a case, the Destroyer would make an excellent home-defense weapon. Likewise for someone traveling through such restrictive jurisdictions. Were I to use the Destroyer in that way, I would probably have a gunsmith open up the bolt face slightly so that it would chamber 38 Super ammunition and then modify a nine-shot Colt 38 Super Government Model magazine to work in the gun. Loaded with one of the better 38 Super hollowpoint loads like that offered by Cor-Bon, this would be a mighty effective rig. Naturally, you would have to practice bolt manipulation to be fast and sure in its operation.

No matter how you look at it, the Destroyer is a light, handy little carbine with a lot of charm, and that's good enough for me. If you want to acquire one, have your dealer contact Century Arms. As this is written, they have a fair number still available.

•

# Volquartsen's Custom 10/22 Rifle

Volquartsen's glass fiber reinforced thumb-hole stock, precision stainless steel barrel, and a fine scope change the entire character of the Ruger 10/22.

## Superb accuracy, dashing good looks and Tom Volquartsen's magic touch, all add up to one fine rifle for hunting or small bore competition.

## by RALPH C. GLAZE

**H**AVE YOU EVER been out hunting varmints with a 22 rimfire single shot or repeater and missed a second shot while working the bolt, slide or lever, or lost even more time stuffing another round into a single-loader? If your answer, like mine, is yes, then that is reason enough for wishing you had a tight-grouping autoloader. Since recoil in a 22 auto is practically nil, you need never lose sight of the target because it loads as fast as you can pull the trigger. But most autoloaders do not produce target accuracy as they come from the factory. The Volquartsen Custom rifle seen here is a super-accurate modification of the Ruger 10/22, which is a fine little rifle in its own right, but is hardly a target-quality tackdriver. Tom Volquartsen, of Carroll, Iowa, who built our test rifle, has made every effort to create a super shooting firearm that has many characteristics of a single-shot target rifle combined with the obvious advantages of an autoloader.

The Ruger 10/22 action has a well-deserved reputation for reliable functioning in fair weather or foul, and that is the reason it was selected for accurizing. The results would seem to be well worth the time and labor required to produce this little jewel. Volquartsen guarantees $1/2$-inch groups at 100 yards, from machine rest using the proper ammunition. That is *accuracy!*

Accuracy in a rifle is, perhaps, like beauty, in the eye of the beholder. What one shooter might consider quite accurate, another could just as

easily find totally inadequate. Many hunters may be satisfied with a medium or large game rifle that groups inside an 8-inch circle at 200 yards, and rightly so, because with a proper hold, accuracy of this order is plenty good enough to down a deer or other large game. On the other hand, however, a benchrest or Olympic-class marksman would be rather displeased by a group that doesn't show up as a single hole in a target 50 yards (or meters) downrange. Most of us would think of a $1/2$-inch group at 50 yards from a 22 rimfire as being remarkably accurate. The rifle described here is capable of $1/2$-inch groups or better when

supplied with proper ammunition and a steady hand on the trigger. We make no claim that it will outshoot a highly tuned Olympic-type rimfire rifle—it won't! But it does bring a most refined standard of accuracy to the hunting fields, combined with an ease of handling that makes it a delight to shoot.

What makes one rifle more accurate than another? There are many factors, the most important of which is the person behind the gun. We all know that no one can hold a rifle as firmly as a massive machine rest anchored in a ton of concrete. So, leaving the shooter out of the picture, what determines accuracy?

First, a barrel that is straight, consistent in bore diameter, smoothly finished from muzzle to breech and heavy enough to resist flexing and vibration. A superior barrel must have a chamber that is correctly shaped and finished to allow the bullet to be driven forward without deformation resulting from tipping or yawing. The throat (the region directly ahead of the chamber) must be designed in a manner that allows the bullet to engage the rifling with a minimum of commotion. After traveling through the bore, the bullet must leave the muzzle cleanly, without tilting. Therefore, the muzzle must be square to the bore and evenly finished all around. Obviously, a barrel has to be tightly attached to the receiver, and both need to be solidly mated to the stock. Any movement here can negate the gains attained by a super barrel.

Next, the face of the breechblock or bolt has to be held snugly against the barrel breech so that no movement can occur during ignition. Strong firing pin action is needed to ensure efficient initiation of combustion. Lock time should be minimal, so that movement is limited in the interval between release of the sear and ignition of the powder charge.

A good trigger is an absolute necessity. A great many otherwise

Test firing was done from a sandbag rest on an outdoor range at 50 yards. The thumbhole stock adds to the stability of this shooting position.

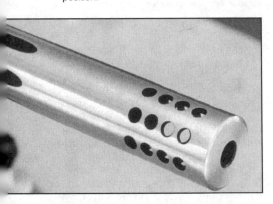

Barrel flutes and an integral muzzle brake/expansion chamber both contribute to the accuracy and appearance of the Douglas Premium barrel on Volquartsen's Custom 22 rifle.

fine and accurate firearms are spoiled by a lousy trigger. Huge numbers of guns leave the factories with triggers that grate, rasp, snag and chatter, making one wonder if those who make them know how to shoot them. A good trigger should have a smooth, short take-up, an unhesitating release and virtually no over-travel. All this with a pull that is as light as possible within the limits of safety and convenience.

The contribution of correct ammunition to firearm accuracy cannot be too strongly emphasized. Some ammunition is simply made better than others. In the ammo line we have our Rolls-Royces and we have our Yugos. In general, you get what you pay for—but not always! Even the very finest ammo will sometimes perform poorly in a particular rifle, and vice versa. I once bought 10,000 rounds of outdated British Army surplus Eley Mark 2 rimfire cartridges for a ridiculously low price. It worked beautifully in one of my target pistols, but less than not so hot in most of the others. Conversely, I have one pistol that prefers Federal Champions to Eley Pistol Match. So price is not necessarily the criterion. It is necessary to try many different brands to determine what variety makes a given firearm happy.

There are other more esoteric factors involved in determining accuracy in firearms, but those noted above will be sufficient for our purposes.

In building his custom 22, Tom Volquartsen starts with a factory-fresh Ruger 10/22, removes the stock and barrel, then strips the action. Careful attention is paid to the fit of the breechblock, with emphasis on the front face. As part of the trigger tune-up, he installs a custom hammer made from 440C stainless steel coated with titanium nitride, heat-treated to a hardness of about 80 on the Rockwell scale. This assures a slick surface that will not wear with age and use. When the trigger group is reassembled, a near-miraculous change has occurred. What was once a typical so-so production trigger now has a smooth take-up with a crisp let-off at a pull of about 32 ounces. This modification in itself could make a vast improvement in an otherwise standard Ruger 10/22.

The barrel on our test rifle is turned from a Douglas stainless steel blank having a twist of one turn in 16 inches. Diameter of the barrel is .920-inch with six lightening flutes running for most of its $19^{1}/_{4}$-inch length. The front $1^{1}/_{2}$ inches is taken up by an expansion chamber muzzlebrake, leaving the effective barrel length at $17^{3}/_{4}$ inches. To create the muzzlebrake, the barrel is bored out, leaving a wall of about $^{1}/_{16}$-inch thickness. The front wall of the expansion chamber is left at about $^{1}/_{8}$-inch thickness. There are 32 holes of .180-inch diameter encircling the chamber in eight rows of four openings each. The exit opening of the chamber is a tad over 30-caliber. The muzzlebrake provides an expansion chamber that holds undisturbed air, allowing the bullet to exit under similar conditions at each shot. It perhaps gives some recoil reduction, but not so you could notice it. Besides, who needs it on a 22 rimfire? In my opinion, the jury is still out on the effectiveness of this little

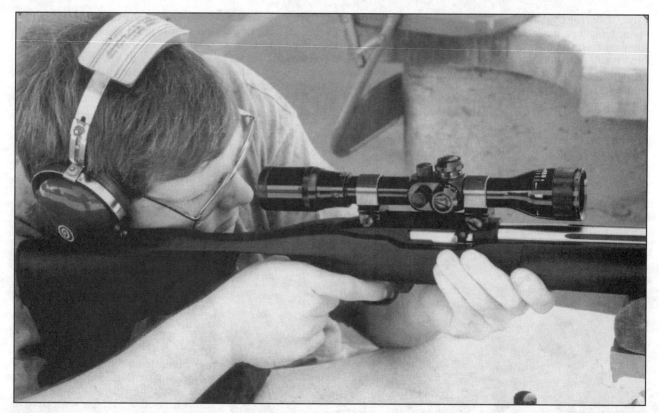

The Volquartsen Custom 10/22 was topped by a Shepherd Model 27-4 2.5-7.5x variable scope using Weaver rings and base. This would make an excellent small game and varmint rig.

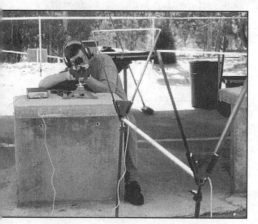

Velocities of 20 brands of ammunition were recorded with an Oehler Model 33 chronograph set 5 feet from the muzzle.

A 100-round string of CCI Green Tag ammo placed all but three shots inside a 1⁵/₁₆-inch circle at 100 yards, despite gusty winds.

item. Besides which, it is a real beast to clean! It must be admitted, however, that it sure looks neat.

Volquartsen's barrels are air-gauged to less than .0002-inch tolerance. Barrel groove diameter is a tight .221-inch, one to three thousandths less than most production 22s. Chambers are tight, too, which adds to accuracy, but requires more frequent and thorough cleaning to facilitate feeding and ejection. During our firing tests, we switched to Federal's new Gold Medal UltraMatch cartridges after firing some 100 rounds of other ammo.

Three of the first ten cases did not completely eject, remaining cross-wise in the ejection port. However, a careful cleaning of barrel and chamber cured the problem. Then, too, this is a brand new gun needing a bit of break-in.

The thumbhole stock on our test rifle is a product of Volquartsen's Custom Shop. It is glass fiber reinforced, painted black with a nice pebbly grain, making it easy to grip and hold. Not being addicted to thumbhole stocks, I was at first a bit dubious about it, but a few days' use was quite convincing. It is comfortable to shoulder, partly because of its cast-off or slight bending to the right of the butt, which keeps the shooter's head more erect and makes it easier to line up the scope sight. The thumbhole provides a good carrying handle and aids in getting into action quickly. The stock design adds considerably to the appearance of this little rifle, as well as contributes to its accuracy. The 10/22 action is not firmly bedded into the stock, but is allowed to "free-float." The barrel is supported only at the forend and under the stock mounting bolt. Sling swivel studs are installed, making

for easier carrying in the field.

Overall length of the rifle is 38 inches, and it weighs a mite over 6³/₄ pounds with a Shepherd Shooting Star Model 27-4 scope attached.

Since our test was primarily concerned with accuracy and functioning, we selected twenty different types of ammo to fire from the 50-yard bench. Our selection included low-velocity target ammunition, high-speed and hyper-velocity rounds. At least fifty rounds were fired with each brand, a total of over 2000 rounds in all. Our test was not intended to extol or condemn any

The butt of the Volquartsen stock is cast off to the right, allowing the shooter's eye to line up behind the scope with a minimum of head tilt. It's built for right-handers, obviously.

the wind had an adverse effect on many of the groups fired.

There were not a few surprises when all results were tabulated. The smallest group we were able to achieve was not with special rifle ammo, but with Eley Pistol Match, which printed one group measuring .380-inch. In all, fifty rounds of this fine Eley ammo were fired, but we could never get another group that small. Another interesting finding was that Federal American Eagle gave us the same size group as Remington Rifle Match—.582-inch.

The most outstandingly consistent ammunition was Federal's new (relatively) Gold Medal UltraMatch. We shot our second smallest group with this brand which was developed especially for our Olympic and International marksmen (and women). We fired fifty rounds with the Federal UltraMatch, ten groups of five shots each. The smallest was

The best group fired measured .380-inch at 50 yards using Eley Pistol Match ammunition. Other groups with this ammo were not quite as tight—but close. Impressive performance!

| TEST FIRE DATA | | |
|---|---|---|
| Ammunition Type | Group Size (in.) | MV (fps) |
| Eley Pistol Match | .380 | 1060 |
| Fed. Gold Medal UltraMatch | .438 | 1114 |
| Fed. Champion | .495 | 1108 |
| Rem. Yellow Jacket | .516 | 1398 |
| CCI Green Tag | .575 | 1089 |
| Win. HP | .580 | 1241 |
| Rem. Rifle Match | .582 | 1094 |
| Fed. American Eagle | .582 | 1228 |
| Rem. 22 Target | .595 | 1189 |
| CCI Stinger | .600 | 1621 |
| Win. Super Silhouette | .604 | 1118 |
| Fed. Silhouette | .618 | 1127 |
| Fed. Spitfire | .686 | 1368 |
| Win. T-22 | .689 | 1096 |
| Rem. High Velocity HP | .750 | 1252 |
| CCI Standard Velocity | .861 | 1145 |
| CCI Mini-Mag SP | .880 | 1272 |
| Fed. American Eagle HP | .916 | 1266 |
| Eley Mark 2 | 1.032 | 1083 |
| Win. 22 High Velocity | 1.050 | 1239 |

Results show the size of the best five-shot group with each type of ammunition. At least fifty rounds were fired using each brand of ammo. Chronograph figures are averages of three shots over an Oehler Model 33 at five feet from the muzzle. All groups were fired at 50 yards.

than most 22s. Case heads have a dimple pressed into them, making them similar in appearance to the Russian Olympic round. The dimple serves to concentrate the flash of the primer more directly into the propellant powder mass.

Based on our brief experience with Federal Gold Medal UltraMatch ammunition, we would have to rank these superbly made little target cartridges along with the world's best. Federal is to be congratulated for developing this highly accurate round that frees our championship shooters from dependence upon

The most consistent ammunition was Federal's Gold Medal UltraMatch. Groups measured between .438 and .542-inch.

brand. The results given are taken from our own experience, and it is admitted that other shooters might not agree with our findings. The figures shown in the accompanying table should be a fair indication of the relative accuracy of the brands tested, however.

All shooting was done at the Angeles Shooting Range a few miles north of Los Angeles. Weather was clear and cool, temperature between 55 and 65 degrees, with winds from 5 to 15 miles per hour. Shots were taken when the wind was as calm as possible, but there is no doubt that

.438-inch, and the largest measured .542-inch, which we think is remarkably consistent for 22 rimfire ammunition fired from a sandbag rest. If there is one special secret ingredient that assures the remarkable precision of Federal's UltraMatch ammunition, it is the meticulous care that goes into its manufacturing process. Bullet weight is a consistent 38.5 grains, and propellant and priming charges are measured to a level of accuracy rarely achieved in run-of-the-mill rimfire cartridges. Cases are carefully crafted to exacting tolerances and are perhaps a bit heavier

## The Shepherd Scope

Anyone who hasn't seen a Shepherd rifle scope should take a good long look at one before plunking down the considerable amount of cash it takes these days to buy a fine shooting glass. Shepherd scopes are not only bright and clear, but they are waterproof, virtually shockproof, and are nitrogen-filled to prevent fogging. Other scope makers may say the same about their wares, but Shepherds have some added features that set them apart.

Instead of just one crosshair reticle, Shepherd scopes have two reticles. One is a conventional crosshair with three limbs, fine in the center and broader in the peripheral field. The second reticle has a small circle at the center from which radiate short, fine crosshairs. Below this small circle is a series of circles, growing smaller as they go down toward the bottom of the field. Each circle is marked for a particular range and, on the Model 27-4 scope, represents the apparent size of a 9-inch object at the designated distance. Nine inch-

The Shepherd scope has two reticles controlled by two sets of external knobs. Windage and elevation adjustments can be made with one reticle, while the other holds the zero setting

es is about the height of a prairie dog, so all that is required is to estimate the range, place the proper circle over the little varmint and fire away. Holdover for a given cartridge is automatically correct for that range. Other Shepherd scopes have larger circles for larger game.

In addition, the two-reticle system with its two sets of adjustment screws allows for one-shot zeroing of the scope as follows: Place the large crosshair squarely on the target and fire one shot. While holding the crosshair on the target, move the small central circle to cover the bullet hole, using the large adjustment knobs. Now, turn the small adjustment knobs until the crosshair centers on the small circle. The rifle is now zeroed in. In practice, a few more clicks may be necessary to find a perfect zero, but the system produces surprisingly accurate results.

A scale runs across the top and right-hand side of the visible field within the scope. Each mark on these scales is equivalent to 1 minute of angle, or about 1 inch at 100 yards. Thus, it is possible to adjust for windage or ammunition variations with one reticle, while retaining the scope's zero with the other.

Shepherd's Model 27-4 is a 2.5-7.5x variable with a parallax adjustable objective and a focusing eyepiece. The eyepiece is rimmed with rubber to prevent injury, which should not be a problem since eye relief is a good 3 inches.

We can't say that a miss is impossible with a Shepherd scope, but one can certainly increase the chances of a sure hit.

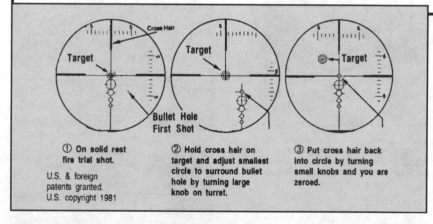

① On solid rest fire trial shot.

U.S. & foreign patents granted. U.S. copyright 1981

② Hold cross hair on target and adjust smallest circle to surround bullet hole by turning large knob on turret.

③ Put cross hair back into circle by turning small knobs and you are zeroed.

Zeroing a Shepherd scope is easy as 1-2-3 with the two-reticle system. Fire one shot, keep the crosshairs on target, adjust the small circle over the bullet hole, move the crosshairs over the small circle, and it's zeroed!

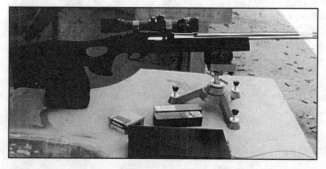

The Volquartsen Custom 10/22 all set up on the bench presents a handsome sight for any shooter. This gun would be loads of fun for prairie dog or ground squirrel control.

European sources for their match ammunition.

All brands of ammunition tested produced satisfactory results, and all of them functioned perfectly, with the exception previously noted. The Volquartsen Custom 22, like the Ruger from which it sprang, is a reliable and consistent performer as well as being a delight to shoot. It's also a very handsome rifle.

For a hunting rifle with near match quality accuracy, the Volquartsen Custom 22 is very hard to beat. A firearm of this nature must of necessity be relatively expensive, although when the amount of work involved is considered, the gun does not seem to be over-priced at about $900. When performance is compared with other rifles in this category, Tom V's big little rifle may be a bargain at that. More information can be had from Volquartsen Custom, Ltd., P.O. Box 271, Carroll, Iowa 51401. A catalog is available. ●

Sorry, Linnea, this 250 is already spoken for. The author argued that it would make a good starter gun for his daughter, but some things just don't work as planned.

# "Sorry Linnea, I'm Keeping This One!"

***Really good guns come along only every so often, and despite all good intentions, this one will not be passed along to the budding hunter.***

## by LEE ARTEN

I WALKED INTO the gunshop, looked in the used rack, and didn't want to ask. Maybe you know the feeling: You've bought a new barrel for the Contender, picked up a lot of reloading supplies, or a spotting scope, and now it's time to back off and let the domestic climate cool. I had passed up several interesting guns in an effort to slow spousal warming and conserve cash. I thought I was resigned to looking, and not touching the checkbook for a time. Still, I looked into the used-gun rack and had to ask. Maybe you know that feeling too.

"What caliber is that Ruger lightweight?" I asked, pretty sure I already knew the answer.

"250 Savage," was the reply.

When I heard that I went into the "Plotting and Scheming" mode, even before I got my hands on the gun.

That might seem strange, considering that the 250-3000 Savage has been heading for relic status since the 243 Winchester and 6mm Remington were introduced in 1955. At the time I went into the P&S mode at the gunshop, I don't think Savage was even chambering the 25-caliber that bears its name. It might seem even stranger if you knew that one of the rifles I'd passed up was an early Remington 700 in 6mm. The 700 was nice, but I'd wanted a Ruger 77 since shortly after they came out. Recently, I'd been after a Ruger Ultra Light in 250-3000. I'd never fired one, never seen one in the deer

The author sights in the Ruger before Michigan's deer season. The little rifle has a history of one-shot kills on deer over five seasons.

woods, and they weren't easy to find on the used gun market. I was having a fine time looking for one, until I walked into the shop that day.

You might say I'd been looking for a Ruger 250-3000 since before Ruger made one. My craving began after I read a Larry Koller story of killing a bull moose with two shots from a Savage 99 in 250. He used the 250 because his 30-06 was still buried under gear in his canoe. Koller's story, in which the 250 Savage did fine work, appeared in *The Treasury Of Hunting*, published by The Ridge Press in 1965. In May, 1987, John Wooters had an article on the 250-3000 in *Guns & Ammo*. That story rekindled the flame. A few months after I read it, my Ruger turned up at Firearms & Supplies, the local gun shop just down the road.

"How does it shoot?" I asked Frank.

"Oh, it'll shoot," he said. I looked it over some more. It was in much nicer shape than an M77 in 243 that I'd passed up during my economy period.

"If it'll shoot," I asked, "why did the other guy get rid of it?" I handed it back.

Frank wiped *my* Ruger down with a rag.

"Well," he said, "the way I heard it, he was reducing his collection

from 20 rifles to a dozen or so. This was one he decided had to go."

I had to go then. Home, I talked to my wife, stressing that I was going to get a Ruger M77 sometime, and that a new one would be more expensive than the used one available now. Shortly after that conversation, I was back at the gun shop picking at small imperfections, then writing out a fairly large check.

I've had my 250 for five seasons and killed five deer with it. Despite the mumblings of some 30-caliber fans I know, the farthest a deer shot with it has ever run is 100 yards. (That was with a shot that turned out to have hit too far back.) The first deer I took with my M77RL just fell on its side. The next ran 40 yards after a heart shot. The third managed a half step. The fourth walked in a half circle, fell, got up while I was moving to retrieve it, ran 100 yards across a field and died just inside a cedar swamp. The fifth, which my family is eating now, crumpled at the shot, then rolled half onto its back and was still. Besides the 250, I've taken deer with a Browning 30-06 and a Winchester Model 12 in 16-gauge. Of the three guns, the 250 has made the quickest kills. I think the overburdened rifle collector should have kept my Ruger and dumped another 30-06.

My 250-3000 sports a black forend tip and a slim 20-inch barrel. It goes 6 pounds even on my bathroom scale, unloaded, but with scope and

All-up weight of the M77 Ultra Light is 6 pounds, less ammo, but with scope and sling. Author believes gun feels much like his 20-gauge O/U in the field.

sling. It also shoots like a house afire. I have only used Remington 100-grain factory ammunition in it so far. It shoots so well that pre-season sighting-in targets often have two shots of a three-shot group touching. The third shot is usually high and an inch, or a bit more, right. I attribute the fliers to the Ruger's light barrel heating as I hurry to zero it, pack, and hit the road to deer camp.

One of my summer projects next year will be to bench the 250 and sing the national anthem, or maybe "100 Bottles Of Beer On The Wall," between each shot. That should tell me if my Ruger will really shoot. However, even when I have to fire in a hurry, it does well enough to spook some other hunters sighting-in along with me.

Before the 1989 deer season, I was at a makeshift 100-yard range shooting over the top of my car. A man and his son were next to me, popping away at a sheet of typing paper with a lever-action carbine. We shot, then walked down to the sandbank together. I picked up my target, showed it to them and complained about it. Two of the shots were touching, the other was a bit over an inch away. The father looked as taken aback as I am at a high-power match when one of the hotshots moans about his lone low nine.

"A deer's vital area is about as big as this," the man said, pointing at the sheet of paper, "so I guess we're okay."

There's something about having a rifle that is accurate enough to let me complain about groups larger than an inch. I have my lines down pat. After flashing the target, I say, "If the guy behind it could, I think this gun would really shoot." It's immodest, but I love it, and I can't resist.

In the field, my Ruger carries easily. It comes to my shoulder more smoothly than any of my other rifles, and feels more like my 20-gauge over/under than anything else in the rack. Like my best grouse gun, it has a tang safety, something I find comfortable and a help when switching guns with the changing seasons.

I was cluttering up the aisle of another local firearms emporium recently. Leafing through a Ruger catalog, I noticed something that made my palms sweat, my heart palpitate, and my face pale. The symptoms would be familiar to my wife, but, for once, it wasn't a new model that I had to plot and scheme over.

(Above) With a steady rest, the author can take advantage of the 250's accuracy. Leaning on a hay bale in August, waiting for a shootable deer, is a lot more comfortable than some of the places he's waited during the traditional November season.

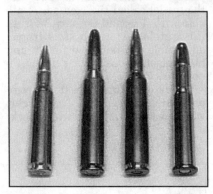

(Left) This line-up of cartridges in the 250-3000 class reveals some of the usual deer and deer/varmint suspects. From left: 250-3000 Savage, 257 Roberts, 6mm Remington, 30-30 Winchester.

Instead, it was the lack of the 250-3000 chambering in the latest models of the Ruger 77RL. I thought I detected something of a 250 renaissance lately, but maybe I was wrong. I was glad I found my 250 when Ruger was still making them. Now that they seem to have stopped, I'm even happier.

The 250 found after 22 years of looking is a good one, too good, in fact, for one of the plans I had for it. An argument I used when I was talking about buying it was that it would be the perfect rifle for my daughter, Linnea, to use when she started hunting deer. She was almost 2 then, and whether she'd take up deer hunting was uncertain. She's nearly 7 now, and still making up her mind. The possibility that she'll start with my 250-3000 is getting increasingly remote. My Ruger is going to stay mine. I have 7 years, so maybe I can find another 250 for her.

Sorry, Linnea! ●

Two groups shot with the Ruger during pre-season sight-in. Group just above the scope went into about an inch at 50 yards; the other group, with two touching shots and one flier, was done at 200 yards.

# Browning's

## MICRO BUCK MARK PISTOL

This pleasant-shooting little 22 fills the bill for semi-serious plinking, target shooting or small game hunting.

MOST OF US need little introduction to the Browning name. It has meant quality firearms and sporting goods for many generations. Forty years ago, during my pre-teen years, I can vividly remember my dad occasionally allowing me to hold, caress and admire his Browning A-5 Sweet Sixteen. Since then, I have owned many Brownings and am still impressed with their quality and good looks.

Browning's entry into the rimfire handgun market came in 1962 with the model called the Nomad. Available with 4½- and 6¾-inch barrels, this autoloader had a steel frame, adjustable sights, blued finish, and black plastic grips. It was discontinued in 1975.

During the same period, the company also offered the Challenger, which was an upgrade with checkered wrap-around walnut grips and gold-plated trigger.

Up through 1975, FN of Belgium was producing virtually all of the Browning firearms line. In 1975, the Challenger II was introduced with a 6¾-inch barrel only, and with an alloy frame. Unlike its predecessors, this gun was manufactured by ATI, Inc., in Salt Lake City, Utah. This model was discontinued in 1982, at which time the Challenger III came upon the scene. This version had a 5½-inch bull barrel and was made through 1985.

This historical summary brings us to the introduction of the Browning Buck Mark 22. Originally made with a 5½-inch bull barrel, the first Buck Mark also sported composite grips with skip-line checkering and matte blue finish.

Several versions have been offered

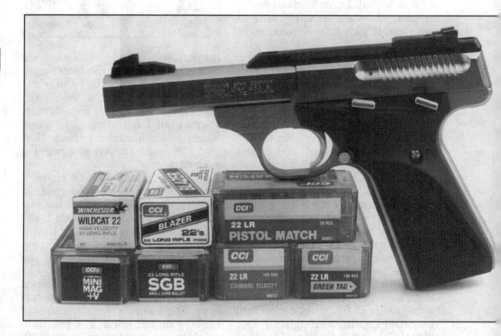

## by JERRY HORGESHEIMER

over the past few years. The company's 1993 catalog lists a total of twelve different models. Choices in the standard series include two barrel lengths of either 4 or 5½ inches, matte blue or nickel finish, and black moulded composite or laminated wood grips.

The Buck Mark 5.5 is more of a target version than the standard model and has a .900-inch diameter 5½-inch barrel. This model is available in matte blue or a combination of blue and gold with either contoured walnut slabs or walnut wraparound grips.

Last but not least is the Hi-Performance series which includes the Unlimited Match, the Silhouette, and the Varmint models. The first comes with a 14-inch barrel, while the others have tubes that measure 9⅞ inches. Actually, 5½- and 10-inch versions are also available. A special clip-on shell deflec-

tor can also be purchased as an option for any of the Buck Mark models.

One of the later additions to the Buck Mark series of 22 autoloaders is called the Micro Buck Mark. It follows the lines of the standard model, but with blue or nickel finish, 4-inch barrel and black moulded composite grips. The Pro Target sight, which is standard on all Buck Marks, is adjustable for both windage and elevation with very precise controls. The total weight of the Micro version is a comfortable 32 ounces.

The safety and slide latch are in the proper place for an autoloader (above the thumb) and so is the magazine release. I am not overly fond of magazine releases located on the underside of the grip. The Buck Mark allows an easy, one-handed magazine drop for fast and easy reloading.

The trigger pull on my sample weighed just under 4 pounds and had an almost imperceptible amount

of creep. For a 22-caliber plinker that has a suggested retail price of $274.95, I consider this completely acceptable. The blued Buck Mark standard sells for just $234.95.

Other than its looks, the most attractive feature of the Micro Buck Mark is its feel. For my average-sized hands, this autoloader fits and feels good. The composite grips with skip-line checkering feel just like a good set of Pachmayr grips.

How does it shoot? I tested my sample with Winchester Wildcats and six types of CCI ammo. All shooting was conducted at 25 yards using an Outers Pistol Perch on the shooting bench. Though not as precise as using a machine rest, this is a fairly sturdy setup. I did not expect pinpoint accuracy from this short-barreled plinker with its 6½-inch sight radius, but was pleasantly surprised at its ability to shoot small groups.

The biggest surprise came when the CCI Blazer 22s actually generated the best group with ten shots measuring 1.2 inches. The Blazer line is CCI's most economically priced ammo, so you would ordinarily not expect it to be the most accurate. The largest group came from the CCI SGB (Small Game Bullet)

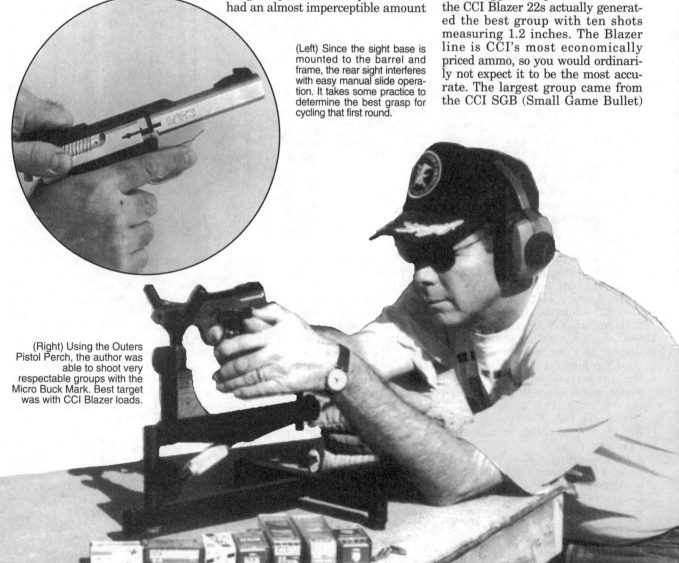

(Left) Since the sight base is mounted to the barrel and frame, the rear sight interferes with easy manual slide operation. It takes some practice to determine the best grasp for cycling that first round.

(Right) Using the Outers Pistol Perch, the author was able to shoot very respectable groups with the Micro Buck Mark. Best target was with CCI Blazer loads.

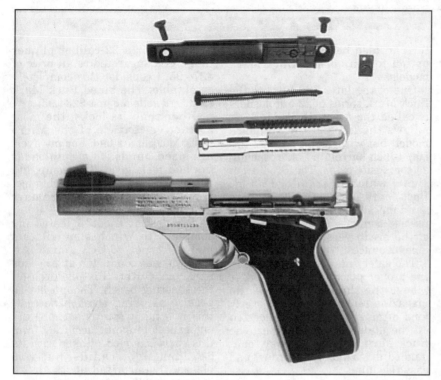

| PERFORMANCE RESULTS | |
|---|---|
| Cartridge | Group Size (in.) |
| Winchester Wildcat | 1.7 |
| CCI Standard | 1.8 |
| CCI Mini-Mag+V | 2.1 |
| CCI SGB (Small Game Bullet) | 2.5 |
| CCI Green Tag | 1.8 |
| CCI Blazer | 1.2 |
| CCI Pistol Match | 1.5 |
| Mean (70 rounds) | 1.8 |

### BROWNING
### Micro Buck Mark
### 22 LR Semiauto Pistol

| | |
|---|---|
| Manufacturer: | Browning |
| | Route One |
| | Morgan, Utah 84050 |
| Model: | Micro Buck Mark |
| Type: | Straight blowback |
| Operation: | Single action |
| Caliber: | 22 Long Rifle |
| Barrel Length: | 4 inches |
| Overall Length: | 8 inches |
| Weight Empty: | 32 ounces |
| Safety: | Manual sear blocking |
| Rear Sight: | Pro Target, fully adjustable |
| Front Sight: | Post on serrated ramp |
| Sight Radius: | $6^1/_2$ inches |
| Stocks: | Black moulded composite |
| Magazine Capacity: | 10 rounds |
| Finish: | Blue or nickel |
| Price: | $274.95 |

Disassembly for cleaning the Micro Buck Mark is easy. The two Allen-head sight base screws must be removed with the provided wrench to get at the slide. The square buffer (top right) may or may not come off with the slide, so keep track of it.

Rapid-fire shooting is easy with the Micro Buck Mark. The balance and grip angle allow for good control for quick follow-up shots whether you're hunting small game or tin cans.

and measured 2.5 inches. The Winchester Wildcat ammo also performed impressively with a 1.7-inch ten-shot group.

After firing 500 rounds through the Micro Buck Mark and experiencing only one failure to feed, I am impressed with this handgun's reliability, accuracy, performance, handling and looks. The only criticism I have relates to the manual operation of the slide when chambering the first round from the magazine. The front of the sight mounting base is attached to the breech end of the barrel, while the rear is attached to the frame using Allen-head screws. This sight base actually bridges the slide, so the slide can operate smoothly while the sight base is stationary. However, I find it difficult to cycle the slide without getting hung up on the sight. It takes a pretty good forefinger and thumb grip on the slide serrations to cock the recoil spring and feed the first round from the magazine. With the sight and its base in the way of easy slide operation, loading that first round can be a bit frustrating.

Disassembly for cleaning is relatively easy, although the two screws holding the sight base in place must be removed. An Allen wrench is supplied for this purpose. After removing the magazine and making sure the pistol is empty, the sight base is detached. Then pull the slide back about an inch and lift the recoil spring guide and spring upward from the slide. Take care during this step to watch the buffer at the rear end of the spring guide, just in front of the guide post. It may stay in position or it may come off with the rod. The slide can now be lifted from the frame, exposing most parts that need periodic cleaning. Browning suggests that any further disassembly be completed by a gunsmith.

Although the Micro Buck Mark was not designed for competition, it certainly has the potential for highly refined plinking. One of my favorite informal targets is called the Qualifier, made by World of Targets (9200 Floral Ave., Cincinnati, Ohio 45242). It is made up of three different-sized steel plates hanging from a steel frame with the smallest plate being $1^5/_8$ inches in diameter, the largest measuring $3^5/_8$ inches. Offhand shooting at 75 feet is challenging, especially on the smaller plates, and hits are immediately apparent.

The nickel plating and contrasting black grips make an attractive combination for the Micro Buck Mark. This autoloader is nicely finished, functional and very accurate—in addition to being reasonably priced. It makes a nice addition to my battery of handguns and would probably add to yours also. ●

# THE COMPLETE COMPACT CATALOG

## A listing of all the guns in the catalog, by name and model, alphabetically and numerically.

Includes models suitable for several forms of competition and other sporting purposes.

### ACCU-TEK MODEL AT-9 AUTO PISTOL
**Caliber:** 9mm Para., 7-shot magazine.
**Barrel:** 3.2".
**Weight:** 28 oz. **Length:** 6.25" overall.
**Stocks:** Black checkered nylon.
**Sights:** Blade front, rear adjustable for windage; three-dot system.
**Features:** Stainless steel construction. Double action only. Firing pin block with no external safeties. Lifetime warranty. Introduced 1992. Made in U.S. by Accu-Tek.
**Price:** Satin stainless . . . . . . . . . . . . . . . . . . . . . . . . . . **$270.00**
**Price:** Black finish over stainless . . . . . . . . . . . . . . . . . . . **$275.00**

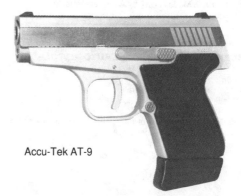

Accu-Tek AT-9

### Accu-Tek AT-40 Auto Pistol
Same as the Model AT-9 except chambered for 40 S&W. Introduced 1992.
**Price:** Stainless . . . . . . . . . . . . . . . . . . . . . . . . . . . . **$270.00**
**Price:** Black finish over stainless (AT-40B) . . . . . . . . . . . . . **$275.00**

### ACCU-TEK MODEL HC-380SS AUTO PISTOL
**Caliber:** 380 ACP, 13-shot magazine.
**Barrel:** 2.75".
**Weight:** 28 oz. **Length:** 6" overall.
**Stocks:** Checkered black composition.
**Sights:** Blade front, rear adjustable for windage.
**Features:** External hammer; manual thumb safety with firing pin and trigger disconnect; bottom magazine release. Stainless finish. Introduced 1993. Made in U.S. by Accu-Tek.
**Price:** . . . . . . . . . . . . . . . . . . . . . . . . . . . . . . . . **$230.00**

Accu-Tek HC-380SS

### ACCU-TEK MODEL AT-380SS AUTO PISTOL
**Caliber:** 380 ACP, 5-shot magazine.
**Barrel:** 2.75".
**Weight:** 20 oz. **Length:** 5.6" overall.
**Stocks:** Grooved black composition.
**Sights:** Blade front, rear adjustable for windage.
**Features:** Stainless steel frame and slide. External hammer; manual thumb safety; firing pin block, trigger disconnect. Lifetime warranty. Introduced 1992. Made in U.S. by Accu-Tek.
**Price:** Satin stainless . . . . . . . . . . . . . . . . . . . . . . . . . **$182.00**
**Price:** Black finish over stainless (AT-380SSB) . . . . . . . . . . . **$187.00**

### Accu-Tek Model AT-32SS Auto Pistol
Same as the AT-380SS except chambered for 32 ACP. Introduced 1990.
**Price:** Satin stainless . . . . . . . . . . . . . . . . . . . . . . . . . **$176.00**
**Price:** Black finish over stainless (AT-32SSB) . . . . . . . . . . . . **$181.00**

Accu-Tek AT-380SS

### Accu-Tek Model AT-25SS Auto Pistol
Similar to the AT-380SS except chambered for 25 ACP with 7-shot magazine. Also available with aluminum frame and slide with 11-oz. weight. Introduced 1991.
**Price:** Satin stainless . . . . . . . . . . . . . . . . . . . . . . . . . **$158.00**
**Price:** Black finish over stainless (AT-25SSB) . . . . . . . . . . . . **$163.00**

### AMERICAN ARMS MODEL CX-22 DA AUTO PISTOL
**Caliber:** 22 LR, 8-shot magazine.
**Barrel:** 3⅓".
**Weight:** 22 oz. **Length:** 6⅓" overall.
**Stocks:** Checkered black polymer.
**Sights:** Blade front, rear adjustable for windage.
**Features:** Double action with manual hammer-block safety, firing pin safety. Alloy frame. Has external appearance of Walther PPK. Blue/black finish. Introduced 1990. Made in U.S. by American Arms, Inc.
**Price:** . . . . . . . . . . . . . . . . . . . . . . . . . . . . . . . . **$198.00**

American Arms PK22

### AMERICAN ARMS MODEL PK22 DA AUTO PISTOL
**Caliber:** 22 LR, 8-shot magazine.
**Barrel:** 3.3".
**Weight:** 22 oz. **Length:** 6.3" overall.
**Stocks:** Checkered plastic.
**Sights:** Fixed.
**Features:** Double action. Polished blue finish. Slide-mounted safety. Made in the U.S. by American Arms, Inc.
**Price:** . . . . . . . . . . . . . . . . . . . . . . . . . . . . . . . . **$198.00**

**CAUTION:** PRICES CHANGE, CHECK AT GUNSHOP.

## AMERICAN ARMS MODEL P-98 AUTO PISTOL
**Caliber:** 22 LR, 8-shot magazine.
**Barrel:** 5".
**Weight:** 25 oz. **Length:** 8⅛" overall.
**Stocks:** Grooved black polymer.
**Sights:** Blade front, rear adjustable for windage.
**Features:** Double action with hammer-block safety, magazine disconnect safety. Alloy frame. Has external appearance of the Walther P-38 pistol. Introduced 1989. Made in U.S. by American Arms, Inc.
**Price:** . . . . . . . . . . . . . . . . . . . . . . . . . . . . . . . . . . . **$213.00**

## AMERICAN ARMS MODEL PX-22 AUTO PISTOL
**Caliber:** 22 LR, 7-shot magazine.
**Barrel:** 2.85".
**Weight:** 15 oz. **Length:** 5.39" overall.
**Stocks:** Black checkered plastic.
**Sights:** Fixed.
**Features:** Double action; 7-shot magazine. Polished blue finish. Introduced 1989. Made in U.S. From American Arms, Inc.
**Price:** . . . . . . . . . . . . . . . . . . . . . . . . . . . . . . . . . . . **$193.00**

American Arms P-98

American Arms PX-22

American Arms Spectre

## AMERICAN ARMS SPECTRE DA PISTOL
**Caliber:** 9mm Para., 30-shot; 45 ACP, 30-shot magazine.
**Barrel:** 6".
**Weight:** 4 lbs., 8 oz. **Length:** 13.75".
**Stocks:** Black nylon.
**Sights:** Post front adjustable for windage and elevation, fixed U-notch rear.
**Features:** Triple action blowback fires from closed bolt; ambidextrous safety and decocking levers; matte black finish; magazine loading tool. For standard velocity ammunition only. From American Arms, Inc.
**Price:** 9mm . . . . . . . . . . . . . . . . . . . . . . . . . . . . . **$429.00**
**Price:** 45 ACP . . . . . . . . . . . . . . . . . . . . . . . . . . . **$457.00**

## AMT AUTOMAG II AUTO PISTOL
**Caliber:** 22 WMR, 9-shot magazine (7-shot with 3⅜" barrel).
**Barrel:** 3⅜", 4½", 6".
**Weight:** About 23 oz. **Length:** 9⅜" overall.
**Stocks:** Grooved carbon fiber.
**Sights:** Blade front, adjustable rear.
**Features:** Made of stainless steel. Gas-assisted action. Exposed hammer. Slide flats have brushed finish, rest is sandblast. Squared trigger guard. Introduced 1986. From AMT.
**Price:** . . . . . . . . . . . . . . . . . . . . . . . . . . . . . . . . . . **$375.95**

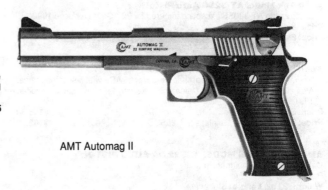

AMT Automag II

## AMT AUTOMAG III PISTOL
**Caliber:** 30 Carbine, 9mm Win. Mag., 8-shot magazine.
**Barrel:** 6⅜".
**Weight:** 43 oz. **Length:** 10½" overall.
**Stocks:** Carbon fiber.
**Sights:** Blade front, adjustable rear.
**Features:** Stainless steel construction. Hammer-drop safety. Slide flats have brushed finish, rest is sandblasted. Introduced 1989. From AMT.
**Price:** . . . . . . . . . . . . . . . . . . . . . . . . . . . . . . . . . . **$465.95**

## AMT AUTOMAG IV PISTOL
**Caliber:** 10mm Magnum, 45 Winchester Magnum, 6-shot magazine.
**Barrel:** 6.5" (45), 8⅝" (10mm only).
**Weight:** 46 oz. **Length:** 10.5" overall with 6.5" barrel.
**Stocks:** Carbon fiber.
**Sights:** Blade front, adjustable rear.
**Features:** Made of stainless steel with brushed finish. Introduced 1990. Made in U.S. by AMT.
**Price:** . . . . . . . . . . . . . . . . . . . . . . . . . . . . . . . . . . **$679.99**

AMT Automag III

## AMT BACKUP AUTO PISTOL
**Caliber:** 380 ACP, 5-shot magazine.
**Barrel:** 2½".
**Weight:** 18 oz. **Length:** 5" overall.
**Stocks:** Carbon fiber.
**Sights:** Fixed, open, recessed.
**Features:** Concealed hammer, blowback operation; manual and grip safeties. All stainless steel construction. Smallest domestically-produced pistol in 380. From AMT.
**Price:** . . . . . . . . . . . . . . . . . . . . . . . . . . . . . . . . . . $295.99

AMT Backup DAO

## AMT Backup Double Action Only Pistol
Similar to the standard Backup except has double-action-only mechanism, enlarged trigger guard, slide is rounded ar rear. Has 6-shot magazine. Introduced 1992. From AMT.
**Price:** . . . . . . . . . . . . . . . . . . . . . . . . . . . . . . . . . . $295.99

## AMT ON DUTY DA PISTOL
**Caliber:** 9mm Para., 15-shot; 40 S&W, 11-shot; 45 ACP, 9-shot magazine.
**Barrel:** 4½".
**Weight:** 32 oz. **Length:** 7¾" overall.
**Stocks:** Smooth carbon fiber.
**Sights:** Blade front, rear adjustable for windage; three-dot system.
**Features:** Choice of DA with decocker or double action only. Inertia firing pin, trigger disconnector safety. Aluminum frame with steel recoil shoulder, stainless steel slide and barrel. Introduced 1991. Made in the U.S. by AMT.
**Price:** 9mm, 40 S&W . . . . . . . . . . . . . . . . . . . . . $469.99
**Price:** 45 ACP . . . . . . . . . . . . . . . . . . . . . . . . . . $529.99

AMT On Duty

## AMT 45 ACP HARDBALLER
**Caliber:** 45 ACP.
**Barrel:** 5".
**Weight:** 39 oz. **Length:** 8½" overall.
**Stocks:** Wrap-around rubber.
**Sights:** Adjustable.
**Features:** Extended combat safety, serrated matte slide rib, loaded chamber indicator, long grip safety, beveled magazine well, adjustable target trigger. All stainless steel. From AMT.
**Price:** . . . . . . . . . . . . . . . . . . . . . . . . . . . . . . . $529.99
**Price:** Government model (as above except no rib, fixed sights) . . $475.95

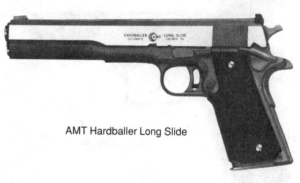

AMT Hardballer Long Slide

## AMT 45 ACP HARDBALLER LONG SLIDE
**Caliber:** 45 ACP.
**Barrel:** 7". **Length:** 10½" overall.
**Stocks:** Wrap-around rubber.
**Sights:** Fully adjustable rear sight.
**Features:** Slide and barrel are 2" longer than the standard 45, giving less recoil, added velocity, longer sight radius. Has extended combat safety, serrated matte rib, loaded chamber indicator, wide adjustable trigger. From AMT.
**Price:** . . . . . . . . . . . . . . . . . . . . . . . . . . . . . . . $575.95

Consult our Directory pages for the location of firms mentioned.

## ASTRA A-70 AUTO PISTOL
**Caliber:** 9mm Para., 8-shot; 40 S&W, 7-shot magazine.
**Barrel:** 3.5".
**Weight:** 29.3 oz. **Length:** 6.5" overall.
**Stocks:** Checkered black plastic.
**Sights:** Blade front, rear adjustable for windage.
**Features:** All steel frame and slide. Checkered grip straps and trigger guard. Nickel or blue finish. Introduced 1992. Imported from Spain by European American Armory.
**Price:** Blue, 9mm Para. . . . . . . . . . . . . . . . . . . . $495.00
**Price:** Blue, 40 S&W . . . . . . . . . . . . . . . . . . . . . $495.00
**Price:** Nickel, 9mm Para. . . . . . . . . . . . . . . . . . . $540.00
**Price:** Nickel, 40 S&W . . . . . . . . . . . . . . . . . . . . $540.00

## Astra A-75 Decocker Auto Pistol
Same as the A-70 except has decocker system, different trigger, contoured pebble-grain grips. Introduced 1993. Imported from Spain by European American Armory.
**Price:** Blue, 9mm or 40 S&W . . . . . . . . . . . . . . . $575.00
**Price:** Nickel, 9mm or 40 S&W . . . . . . . . . . . . . . $620.00
**Price:** Blue, 45 ACP . . . . . . . . . . . . . . . . . . . . . . $595.00
**Price:** Nickel, 45 ACP . . . . . . . . . . . . . . . . . . . . . $640.00

Astra A-75

**CAUTION:** PRICES CHANGE, CHECK AT GUNSHOP.

## ASTRA A-100 AUTO PISTOL
**Caliber:** 9mm Para., 17-shot; 40 S&W, 13-shot; 45 ACP, 9-shot magazine.
**Barrel:** 3.9".
**Weight:** 29 oz. **Length:** 7.1" overall.
**Stocks:** Checkered black plastic.
**Sights:** Blade front, interchangeable rear blades for elevation, screw adjustable for windage.
**Features:** Selective double action. Decocking lever permits lowering hammer onto locked firing pin. Automatic firing pin block. Side button magazine release. Introduced 1993. Imported from Spain by European American Armory.
**Price:** Blue, 9mm, 40 S&W, 45 ACP . . . . . . . . . . . **$625.00**
**Price:** As above, nickel . . . . . . . . . . . . . . . . . . . **$660.00**
**Price:** Blue with night sights . . . . . . . . . . . . . . . . **$750.00**
**Price:** Nickel with night sights . . . . . . . . . . . . . . . **$785.00**

## AUTO-ORDNANCE 1911A1 AUTOMATIC PISTOL
**Caliber:** 9mm Para., 38 Super, 9-shot; 10mm, 45 ACP, 7-shot magazine.
**Barrel:** 5".
**Weight:** 39 oz. **Length:** 8½" overall.
**Stocks:** Checkered plastic with medallion.
**Sights:** Blade front, rear adjustable for windage.
**Features:** Same specs as 1911A1 military guns—parts interchangeable. Frame and slide blued; each radius has non-glare finish. Made in U.S. by Auto-Ordnance Corp.
**Price:** 45 cal. . . . . . . . . . . . . . . . . . . . . . . . . . **$388.95**
**Price:** 9mm, 38 Super . . . . . . . . . . . . . . . . . . . . **$415.00**
**Price:** 10mm (has three-dot combat sights, rubber wrap-around grips) **$420.95**
**Price:** 45 ACP General Model (Commander style) . . . . **$427.95**
**Price:** Duo Tone (nickel frame, blue slide, three-dot sight system, textured black wrap-around grips) . . . . . . . . . . . . . . . **$575.00**

Baby Eagle Auto

## BERETTA MODEL 80 SERIES DA PISTOLS
**Caliber:** 380 ACP, 13-shot magazine (8-shot for M85F); 22 LR, 7-shot (M87), 22 LR, 8-shot (M89).
**Barrel:** 3.82".
**Weight:** About 23 oz. (M84/85); 20.8 oz. (M87). **Length:** 6.8" overall.
**Stocks:** Glossy black plastic (wood optional at extra cost).
**Sights:** Fixed front, drift-adjustable rear.
**Features:** Double action, quick takedown, convenient magazine release. Introduced 1977. Imported from Italy by Beretta U.S.A.
**Price:** Model 84F (380 ACP) . . . . . . . . . . . . . . . . **$525.00**
**Price:** Model 84F wood grips . . . . . . . . . . . . . . . . **$555.00**
**Price:** Model 84F nickel finish . . . . . . . . . . . . . . . **$600.00**
**Price:** Model 85F nickel finish, 8-shot . . . . . . . . . . **$550.00**
**Price:** Model 85F plastic grips, 8-shot . . . . . . . . . . **$485.00**
**Price:** Model 85F wood grips, 8-shot . . . . . . . . . . . **$510.00**
**Price:** Model 87, 22 LR, 7-shot magazine, wood grips . . . . **$490.00**
**Price:** Model 87 Long Barrel, 22 LR, single action . . . **$510.00**
**Price:** Model 89 Sport Wood, single action, 22 LR . . . . **$735.00**

## BERETTA MODEL 92FS PISTOL
**Caliber:** 9mm Para., 15-shot magazine.
**Barrel:** 4.9".
**Weight:** 34 oz. **Length:** 8.5" overall.
**Stocks:** Checkered black plastic; wood optional at extra cost.
**Sights:** Blade front, rear adjustable for windage.
**Features:** Double action. Extractor acts as chamber loaded indicator, squared trigger guard, grooved front- and backstraps, inertia firing pin. Matte finish. Introduced 1977. Made in U.S. and imported from Italy by Beretta U.S.A.
**Price:** With plastic grips . . . . . . . . . . . . . . . . . . . **$625.00**
**Price:** With wood grips . . . . . . . . . . . . . . . . . . . . **$645.00**

Auto-Ordnance 1911A1

## Auto-Ordnance ZG-51 Pit Bull Auto
Same as the 1911A1 except has 3½" barrel, weighs 36 oz. and has an over-all length of 7¼". Available in 45 ACP only; 7-shot magazine. Introduced 1989.
**Price:** . . . . . . . . . . . . . . . . . . . . . . . . . . . . . . **$420.95**

## Auto-Ordnance 40 S&W 1911A1
Similar to the standard 1911A1 except has 4½" barrel giving overall length of 7¾", and weighs 37 oz. Has three-dot combat sight system, black rubber wrap-around grips, 8-shot magazine. Introduced 1991.
**Price:** . . . . . . . . . . . . . . . . . . . . . . . . . . . . . . **$427.95**

## BABY EAGLE AUTO PISTOL
**Caliber:** 9mm Para., 40 S&W, 41 A.E.
**Barrel:** 4.37".
**Weight:** 35 oz. **Length:** 8.14" overall.
**Stocks:** High-impact black polymer.
**Sights:** Combat.
**Features:** Double-action mechanism; polygonal rifling; ambidextrous safety. Introduced 1992. Imported by Magnum Research.
**Price:** 9mm Para., 40 S&W, 41 A.E. . . . . . . . . . . . **$569.00**
**Price:** Conversion kit, 9mm Para. to 41 A.E. . . . . . . . **$239.00**

Beretta Model 84F

## Beretta Model 86
Similar to the 380-caliber Model 85 except has tip-up barrel for first-round loading. Barrel length is 4.33", overall length of 7.33". Has 8-shot magazine, walnut or plastic grips. Introduced 1989.
**Price:** . . . . . . . . . . . . . . . . . . . . . . . . . . . . . . **$510.00**

Beretta Model 92FS

## Beretta Model 92FC Pistol
Similar to the Beretta Model 92FS except has cut down frame, 4.3" barrel, 7.8" overall length, 13-shot magazine, weighs 31.5 oz. Introduced 1989.
**Price:** With plastic grips . . . . . . . . . . . . . . . . . . . $625.00
**Price:** With wood grips . . . . . . . . . . . . . . . . . . . $645.00
**Price:** For Trijicon sights, add . . . . . . . . . . . . . . . $65.00

## Beretta Models 92FS/96 Centurion Pistols
Same as the Model 92FS and 96 except uses slide and barrel (4.3") of the Compact version. Trijicon or three-dot sight systems. Plastic or wood grips. Available in 9mm or 40 S&W. Introduced 1992.
**Price:** Model 92FS Centurion, three-dot sights, plastic grips . . . . . $625.00
**Price:** Model 92FS Centurion, wood grips . . . . . . . . $645.00
**Price:** Model 96 Centurion, three-dot sights, plastic grips . . . . . . $640.00
**Price:** For Trijicon sights, add . . . . . . . . . . . . . . . $65.00

## Beretta Model 92F Stainless Pistol
Same as the Model 92FS except has stainless steel barrel and slide, and frame of aluminum-zirconium alloy. Has three-dot sight system. Introduced 1992.
**Price:** . . . . . . . . . . . . . . . . . . . . . . . . . . $755.00
**Price:** Model 92F-EL Stainless (gold trim, engraved barrel, slide, frame, gold-finished safety-levers, trigger, magazine release, grip screws) . $1,240.00
**Price:** For Trijicon sights, add . . . . . . . . . . . . . . . $65.00

## Beretta Model 92D Pistol
Same as the Model 92FS except double action only and has bobbed hammer, no external safety. Introduced 1992.
**Price:** With plastic grips, three-dot sights . . . . . . . . . $585.00
**Price:** As above with Trijicon sights . . . . . . . . . . . . $650.00

## BERETTA MODEL 950 BS AUTO PISTOL
**Caliber:** 25 ACP, 8-shot.
**Barrel:** 2.5".
**Weight:** 9.9 oz. **Length:** 4.5" overall.
**Stocks:** Checkered black plastic or walnut.
**Sights:** Fixed.
**Features:** Single action, thumb safety; tip-up barrel for direct loading/unloading, cleaning. From Beretta U.S.A.
**Price:** Blue, 25 . . . . . . . . . . . . . . . . . . . . . $180.00
**Price:** Nickel, 25 . . . . . . . . . . . . . . . . . . . . . $210.00
**Price:** Engraved . . . . . . . . . . . . . . . . . . . . . $260.00
**Price:** Matte blue . . . . . . . . . . . . . . . . . . . . . $150.00

## Beretta Model 21 Pistol
Similar to the Model 950 BS. Chambered for 22 LR and 25 ACP. Both double action. 2.5" barrel, 4.9" overall length. 7-round magazine on 22 cal.; 8-round magazine; available in nickel or blue finish. Both have walnut grips. Introduced in 1985.
**Price:** 22-cal. . . . . . . . . . . . . . . . . . . . . . . . $235.00
**Price:** 22-cal., nickel finish . . . . . . . . . . . . . . . . $260.00
**Price:** 25-cal. . . . . . . . . . . . . . . . . . . . . . . . $235.00
**Price:** 25-cal., nickel finish . . . . . . . . . . . . . . . . $260.00
**Price:** EL model, 22 or 25 . . . . . . . . . . . . . . . . $285.00
**Price:** Matte blue, plastic grips, 22 or 25 . . . . . . . . . . $185.00

## BERSA MODEL 23 AUTO PISTOL
**Caliber:** 22 LR, 10-shot magazine.
**Barrel:** 3.5".
**Weight:** 24.5 oz. **Length:** 6.6" overall.
**Stocks:** Walnut with stippled panels.
**Sights:** Blade front, notch rear adjustable for windage; three-dot system.
**Features:** Double action; firing pin and magazine safeties. Available in blue or nickel. Introduced 1989. Distributed by Eagle Imports, Inc.
**Price:** Blue . . . . . . . . . . . . . . . . . . . . . . . . $281.95
**Price:** Nickel . . . . . . . . . . . . . . . . . . . . . . . . $314.95

## BERSA MODEL 83, 85 AUTO PISTOLS
**Caliber:** 380 ACP, 7-shot (M83), 13-shot magazine (M85).
**Barrel:** 3.5".
**Weight:** 25.75 oz. **Length:** 6.6" overall.
**Stocks:** Walnut with stippled panels.
**Sights:** Blade front, notch rear adjustable for windage; three-dot system.
**Features:** Double action; firing pin and magazine safeties. Available in blue or nickel. Introduced 1989. Distributed by Eagle Imports, Inc.
**Price:** Model 85, blue . . . . . . . . . . . . . . . . . . . $331.95
**Price:** Model 85, nickel . . . . . . . . . . . . . . . . . . $391.95
**Price:** Model 83 (as above, except 7-shot magazine), blue — . . . . $281.95
**Price:** Model 83, nickel . . . . . . . . . . . . . . . . . . $314.95

Beretta Centurion

## Beretta Model 96 Auto Pistol
Same as the Model 92F except chambered for 40 S&W. Ambidextrous triple safety mechanism with passive firing pin catch, slide safety/decocking lever, trigger bar disconnect. Has 10-shot magazine. Available with Trijicon or three-dot sights. Introduced 1992.
**Price:** Model 96F, plastic grips . . . . . . . . . . . . . . . $640.00
**Price:** Model 96D, double action only, three-dot sights . . . . . . . . $605.00
**Price:** For Trijicon sights, add . . . . . . . . . . . . . . . $65.00

Beretta 950BS

Consult our Directory pages for the location of firms mentioned.

Bersa Model 85

## BERSA MODEL 86 AUTO PISTOL
**Caliber:** 380 ACP, 13-shot magazine.
**Barrel:** 3.5".
**Weight:** 22 oz. **Length:** 6.6" overall.
**Stocks:** Wraparound textured rubber.
**Sights:** Blade front, rear adjustable for windage; three-dot system.
**Features:** Double action; firing pin and magazine safeties; combat-style trigger guard. Matte blue or satin nickel. Introduced 1992. Distributed by Eagle Imports, Inc.
**Price:** Matte blue . . . . . . . . . . . . . . . . . . . . . $366.95
**Price:** Satin nickel . . . . . . . . . . . . . . . . . . . . . $399.95

### BERSA THUNDER 9 AUTO PISTOL
**Caliber:** 9mm Para., 15-shot magazine.
**Barrel:** 4".
**Weight:** 30 oz. **Length:** 7⅜" overall.
**Stocks:** Checkered black polymer.
**Sights:** Blade front, rear adjustable for windage and elevation; three-dot system.
**Features:** Double action. Ambidextrous safety, decocking levers and slide release; internal automatic firing pin safety; reversible extended magazine release; adjustable trigger stop; alloy frame. Link-free locked breech design. Matte blue finish. Introduced 1993. Imported from Argentina by Eagle Imports, Inc.
**Price:** Blue only . . . . . . . . . . . . . . . . . . . . . . . . . . . $414.95

Bersa Thunder 9

Browning BDA-380

### BROWNING BDM DA AUTO PISTOL
**Caliber:** 9mm Para., 15-shot magazine.
**Barrel:** 4.73"
**Weight:** 31 oz. **Length:** 7.85" overall.
**Stocks:** Moulded black composition; checkered, with thumbrest on both sides.
**Sights:** Low profile removable blade front, rear screw adjustable for windage.
**Features:** Mode selector allows switching from DA pistol to "revolver" mode via a switch on the slide. Decocking lever/safety on the frame. Two redundant, passive, internal safety systems. All steel frame; matte black finish. Introduced 1991. Made in the U.S. From Browning.
**Price:** . . . . . . . . . . . . . . . . . . . . . . . . . . . . . . $559.95

### BROWNING HI-POWER 9mm AUTOMATIC PISTOL
**Caliber:** 9mm Para., 13-shot magazine.
**Barrel:** 4²¹⁄₃₂".
**Weight:** 32 oz. **Length:** 7¾" overall.
**Stocks:** Walnut, hand checkered, or black Polyamide.
**Sights:** ⅛" blade front; rear screw-adjustable for windage and elevation. Also available with fixed rear (drift-adjustable for windage).
**Features:** External hammer with half-cock and thumb safeties. A blow on the hammer cannot discharge a cartridge; cannot be fired with magazine removed. Fixed rear sight model available. Ambidextrous safety available only with matte finish, moulded grips. Imported from Belgium by Browning.
**Price:** Fixed sight model, walnut grips . . . . . . . . . . . **$524.95**
**Price:** 9mm with rear sight adj. for w. and e., walnut grips . . . . . **$571.95**
**Price:** Mark III, standard matte black finish, fixed sight, moulded grips, ambidextrous safety . . . . . . . . . . . . . . . . . . . . **$493.95**
**Price:** Silver chrome, adjustable sight, Pachmayr grips . . . . . . **$581.95**

Browning Hi-Power HP

### BROWNING BDA-380 DA AUTO PISTOL
**Caliber:** 380 ACP, 13-shot magazine.
**Barrel:** 3¹³⁄₁₆".
**Weight:** 23 oz. **Length:** 6¾" overall.
**Stocks:** Smooth walnut with inset Browning medallion.
**Sights:** Blade front, rear drift-adjustable for windage.
**Features:** Combination safety and de-cocking lever will automatically lower a cocked hammer to half-cock and can be operated by right- or left-hand shooters. Inertia firing pin. Introduced 1978. Imported from Italy by Browning.
**Price:** Blue . . . . . . . . . . . . . . . . . . . . . . . . . . . . $592.95
**Price:** Nickel . . . . . . . . . . . . . . . . . . . . . . . . . . . $624.95

Browning BDM

### Browning Capitan Hi-Power Pistol
Similar to the standard Hi-Power except has adjustable tangent rear sight authentic to the early-production model. Also has Commander-style hammer. Checkered walnut grips, polished blue finish. Reintroduced 1993. Imported from Belgium by Browning.
**Price:** . . . . . . . . . . . . . . . . . . . . . . . . . . . . . . $619.95

### Browning Hi-Power HP-Practical Pistol
Similar to the standard Hi-Power except has silver-chromed frame with blued slide, wrap-around Pachmayr rubber grips, round-style serrated hammer and removable front sight, fixed rear (drift-adjustable for windage). Introduced 1991.
**Price:** . . . . . . . . . . . . . . . . . . . . . . . . . . . . . . $565.95
**Price:** With fully adjustable rear sight . . . . . . . . . . . . . . . $612.95

### Browning 40 S&W Hi-Power Pistol
Similar to the standard Hi-Power except chambered for 40 S&W, 10-shot magazine, weighs 35 oz., and has 4¾" barrel. Comes with matte blue finish, low profile front sight blade, drift-adjustable rear sight, ambidextrous safety, moulded polyamide grips with thumb rest. Introduced 1993. Imported from Belgium by Browning.
**Price:** . . . . . . . . . . . . . . . . . . . . . . . . . . . . . . $612.95

Browning Micro Buck Mark

Browning Buck Mark Varmint

## BROWNING BUCK MARK 22 PISTOL

**Caliber:** 22 LR, 10-shot magazine.
**Barrel:** 5½".
**Weight:** 32 oz. **Length:** 9½" overall.
**Stocks:** Black moulded composite with skip-line checkering.
**Sights:** Ramp front, Browning Pro Target rear adjustable for windage and elevation.
**Features:** All steel, matte blue finish or nickel, gold-colored trigger. Buck Mark Plus has laminated wood grips. Made in U.S. Introduced 1985. From Browning.
**Price:** Buck Mark, blue . . . . . . . . . . . . . . . . . . . . . . . . **$234.95**
**Price:** Buck Mark, nickel finish with contoured rubber stocks . . . . **$274.95**
**Price:** Buck Mark Plus . . . . . . . . . . . . . . . . . . . . . . . **$284.95**

## Browning Micro Buck Mark

Same as the standard Buck Mark and Buck Mark Plus except has 4" barrel. Available in blue or nickel. Has 16-click Pro Target rear sight. Introduced 1992.
**Price:** Blue . . . . . . . . . . . . . . . . . . . . . . . . . . . . . **$234.95**
**Price:** Nickel . . . . . . . . . . . . . . . . . . . . . . . . . . . . **$274.95**
**Price:** Micro Buck Mark Plus . . . . . . . . . . . . . . . . . . . **$284.95**

## Browning Buck Mark Varmint

Same as the Buck Mark except has 9⅞" heavy barrel with .900" diameter and full-length scope base (no open sights); walnut grips with optional forend, or finger-groove walnut. Overall length is 14", weight is 48 oz. Introduced 1987.
**Price:** . . . . . . . . . . . . . . . . . . . . . . . . . . . . . . . . **$354.95**

## BRYCO MODEL 38 AUTO PISTOLS

**Caliber:** 22 LR, 32 ACP, 380 ACP, 6-shot magazine.
**Barrel:** 2.8".
**Weight:** 15 oz. **Length:** 5.3" overall.
**Stocks:** Polished resin-impregnated wood.
**Sights:** Fixed.
**Features:** Safety locks sear and slide. Choice of satin nickel, bright chrome or black Teflon finishes. Introduced 1988. From Jennings Firearms.
**Price:** 22 LR, 32 ACP, about . . . . . . . . . . . . . . . . . . . . **$109.95**
**Price:** 380 ACP, about . . . . . . . . . . . . . . . . . . . . . . . **$129.95**

Bryco Model 48

## BRYCO MODEL 48 AUTO PISTOLS

**Caliber:** 22 LR, 32 ACP, 380 ACP, 6-shot magazine.
**Barrel:** 4".
**Weight:** 19 oz. **Length:** 6.7" overall.
**Stocks:** Polished resin-impregnated wood.
**Sights:** Fixed.
**Features:** Safety locks sear and slide. Choice of satin nickel, bright chrome or black Teflon finishes. Announced 1988. From Jennings Firearms.
**Price:** 22 LR, 32 ACP, about . . . . . . . . . . . . . . . . . . . . **$139.00**
**Price:** 380 ACP, about . . . . . . . . . . . . . . . . . . . . . . . **$139.00**

Calico M-110

## CALICO MODEL 110 AUTO PISTOL

**Caliber:** 22 LR, 100-shot magazine.
**Barrel:** 6".
**Weight:** 3.7 lbs. (loaded). **Length:** 17.9" overall.
**Stocks:** Moulded composition.
**Sights:** Adjustable post front, notch rear.
**Features:** Aluminum alloy frame; flash suppressor; pistol grip compartment; ambidextrous safety. Uses same helical-feed magazine as M-100 Carbine. Introduced 1986. Made in U.S. From Calico.
**Price:** . . . . . . . . . . . . . . . . . . . . . . . . . . . . . . . . **$301.90**

Calico M-950

## CALICO MODEL M-950 AUTO PISTOL

**Caliber:** 9mm Para., 50- or 100-shot magazine.
**Barrel:** 7.5".
**Weight:** 2.25 lbs. (empty). **Length:** 14" overall (50-shot magazine).
**Stocks:** Glass-filled polymer.
**Sights:** Post front adjustable for windage and elevation, fixed notch rear.
**Features:** Helical feed 50- or 100-shot magazine. Ambidextrous safety, static cocking handle. Retarded blowback action. Glass-filled polymer grip. Introduced 1989. From Calico.
**Price:** . . . . . . . . . . . . . . . . . . . . . . . . . . . . . . . . **$572.90**

## CENTURY MODEL P9R PISTOL

**Caliber:** 9mm Para., 15-shot magazine.
**Barrel:** 4.6".
**Weight:** 35 oz. **Length:** 8" overall.
**Stocks:** Checkered walnut.
**Sights:** Blade front, rear drift adjustable for windage.
**Features:** Double action with hammer-drop safety. Polished blue finish. Comes with spare magazine. Imported from Hungary by Century International Arms.
**Price:** About . . . . . . . . . . . . . . . . . . . . . . . . . . . . . **$263.00**
**Price:** Chrome finish, about . . . . . . . . . . . . . . . . . . . . **$375.00**

## CLARIDGE HI-TEC MODEL S, L, T PISTOLS

**Caliber:** 9mm Para., 18-shot magazine.
**Barrel:** 5" (S model); 7.5" (L model); 9.5" (T model).
**Weight:** 3 lbs., 2 oz. (L model). **Length:** 15.1" overall (L model).
**Stocks:** Moulded composition.
**Sights:** Adjustable post front in ring, open rear adjustable for windage.
**Features:** Aluminum or stainless frame. Telescoping bolt; floating firing pin. Safety locks the firing pin. Also available in 40 S&W and 45 ACP. Made in U.S. by Claridge Hi-Tec, Inc.
**Price:** Model S (5") . . . . . . . . . . . . . . . . . . . . . . . . . $419.50
**Price:** Model L (7.5") . . . . . . . . . . . . . . . . . . . . . . . $466.50
**Price:** Model T (target, 9.5") . . . . . . . . . . . . . . . . . $466.50
**Price:** Model ZL-9 (7.5" with laser sight) . . . . . . . . . . . . $776.50
**Price:** Model ZT-9 (9.5" with laser sight) . . . . . . . . . . . . $776.50

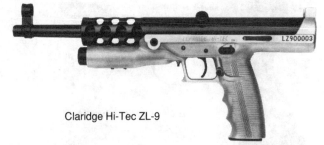

Claridge Hi-Tec ZL-9

## COLT ALL AMERICAN MODEL 2000 DA AUTO

**Caliber:** 9mm Para., 15-shot magazine.
**Barrel:** 4.5".
**Weight:** 29 oz. (polymer frame); 33 oz. (aluminum frame). **Length:** 7.5" overall.
**Stocks:** Checkered polymer.
**Sights:** Ramped blade front, rear drift-adjustable for windage. Three dot system.
**Features:** Double-action only. Moulded polymer or aluminum frame, blued steel slide. Internal striker block safety. Introduced 1991. Made in U.S. by Colt's Mfg. Co., Inc.
**Price:** Polymer frame . . . . . . . . . . . . . . . . . . . . . . . $575.00
**Price:** Aluminum frame . . . . . . . . . . . . . . . . . . . . . . . NA
**Price:** 3¾" barrel and bushing kit . . . . . . . . . . . . . . . NA

Colt All American 2000

## COLT COMBAT COMMANDER AUTO PISTOL

**Caliber:** 38 Super, 9-shot; 45 ACP, 8-shot.
**Barrel:** 4¼".
**Weight:** 36 oz. **Length:** 7¾" overall.
**Stocks:** Rubber combat.
**Sights:** Fixed, glare-proofed blade front, square notch rear; three-dot system.
**Features:** Long trigger; arched housing; grip and thumb safeties.
**Price:** 45, blue . . . . . . . . . . . . . . . . . . . . . . . . . . $694.95
**Price:** 45, stainless . . . . . . . . . . . . . . . . . . . . . . . $749.95
**Price:** 38 Super, stainless . . . . . . . . . . . . . . . . . . . $749.95

### Colt Lightweight Commander MK IV/Series 80

Same as Commander except high strength aluminum alloy frame, rubber combat grips, weight 27½ oz. 45 ACP only.
**Price:** Blue . . . . . . . . . . . . . . . . . . . . . . . . . . . . . $694.95

## COLT DOUBLE EAGLE MKII/SERIES 90 DA PISTOL

**Caliber:** 45 ACP, 8-shot magazine.
**Barrel:** 4½", 5".
**Weight:** 39 ozs. **Length:** 8½" overall.
**Stocks:** Black checkered Xenoy thermoplastic.
**Sights:** Blade front, rear adjustable for windage. High profile three-dot system. Colt Accro adjustable sight optional.
**Features:** Made of stainless steel with matte finish. Checkered and curved extended trigger guard, wide steel trigger; decocking lever on left side; traditional magazine release; grooved frontstrap; bevelled magazine well; extended grip guard; rounded, serrated combat-style hammer. Announced 1989.
**Price:** . . . . . . . . . . . . . . . . . . . . . . . . . . . . . . . $695.95
**Price:** Combat Comm., 45, 4½" bbl. . . . . . . . . . . . . . $695.95

Colt Double Eagle Mk II

### Colt Double Eagle Officer's ACP

Similar to the regular Double Eagle except 45 ACP only, 3½" barrel, 34 oz., 7¼" overall length. Has 5¼" sight radius. Also offered in Lightweight version weighing 25 oz. Introduced 1991.
**Price:** Standard or Lightweight . . . . . . . . . . . . . . . . $695.95

## COLT GOVERNMENT MODEL MK IV/SERIES 80

**Caliber:** 38 Super, 9-shot; 45 ACP, 8-shot magazine.
**Barrel:** 5".
**Weight:** 38 oz. **Length:** 8½" overall.
**Stocks:** Rubber combat.
**Sights:** Ramp front, fixed square notch rear; three-dot system.
**Features:** Grip and thumb safeties and internal firing pin safety, long trigger.
**Price:** 45 ACP, blue . . . . . . . . . . . . . . . . . . . . . . . $693.95
**Price:** 45 ACP, stainless . . . . . . . . . . . . . . . . . . . . $738.95
**Price:** 45 ACP, bright stainless . . . . . . . . . . . . . . . . $813.95
**Price:** 38 Super, blue . . . . . . . . . . . . . . . . . . . . . . $704.95
**Price:** 38 Super, stainless . . . . . . . . . . . . . . . . . . . $727.95
**Price:** 38 Super, bright stainless . . . . . . . . . . . . . . . $819.95

Colt Government Model

## Colt 10mm Delta Elite
Similar to the Government Model except chambered for 10mm auto cartridge. Has three-dot high profile front and rear combat sights, rubber combat stocks with Delta medallion, internal firing pin safety, and new recoil spring/buffer system. Introduced 1987.
**Price:** Blue . . . . . . . . . . . . . . . . . . . . . . . . . . . . . . . **$765.95**

## Colt Combat Elite MK IV/Series 80
Similar to the Government Model except has stainless frame with ordnance steel slide and internal parts. High profile front, rear sights with three-dot system, extended grip safety, beveled magazine well, rubber combat stocks. Introduced 1986.
**Price:** 45 ACP, STS/B . . . . . . . . . . . . . . . . . . . . . . . . **$841.95**
**Price:** 38 Super, STS/B . . . . . . . . . . . . . . . . . . . . . . . **$852.95**

## COLT GOVERNMENT MODEL 380
**Caliber:** 380 ACP, 7-shot magazine.
**Barrel:** 3¼".
**Weight:** 21¾ oz. **Length:** 6" overall.
**Stocks:** Checkered composition.
**Sights:** Ramp front, square notch rear, fixed.
**Features:** Scaled-down version of the 1911A1 Colt G.M. Has thumb and internal firing pin safeties. Introduced 1983.
**Price:** Blue . . . . . . . . . . . . . . . . . . . . . . . . . . . . . . **$432.95**
**Price:** Nickel . . . . . . . . . . . . . . . . . . . . . . . . . . . . . . **$483.95**
**Price:** Stainless . . . . . . . . . . . . . . . . . . . . . . . . . . . . **$463.95**
**Price:** Pocketlite 380, blue . . . . . . . . . . . . . . . . . . . . . **$432.95**

## Colt Mustang Plus II
Similar to the 380 Government Model except has the shorter barrel and slide of the Mustang. Introduced 1988.
**Price:** Blue . . . . . . . . . . . . . . . . . . . . . . . . . . . . . . . **$432.95**
**Price:** Stainless . . . . . . . . . . . . . . . . . . . . . . . . . . . . **$463.95**

## COLT MODEL 1991 A1 AUTO PISTOL
**Caliber:** 45 ACP, 7-shot magazine.
**Barrel:** 5".
**Weight:** 38 oz. **Length:** 8.5" overall.
**Stocks:** Checkered black composition.
**Sights:** Ramped blade front, fixed square notch rear, high profile.
**Features:** Parkerized finish. Continuation of serial number range used on original G.I. 1911-A1 guns. Comes with one magazine and moulded carrying case. Introduced 1991.
**Price:** . . . . . . . . . . . . . . . . . . . . . . . . . . . . . . . . . **$499.95**

## Colt Model 1991 A1 Commander Auto Pistol
Similar to the Model 1991 A1 except has 4¼" barrel. Parkerized finish. 7-shot magazine. Comes in moulded case. Introduced 1993.
**Price:** . . . . . . . . . . . . . . . . . . . . . . . . . . . . . . . . . **$499.95**

## COLT OFFICER'S ACP MK IV/SERIES 80
**Caliber:** 45 ACP, 6-shot magazine.
**Barrel:** 3½".
**Weight:** 34 oz. (steel frame); 24 oz. (alloy frame). **Length:** 7¼" overall.
**Stocks:** Rubber combat.
**Sights:** Ramp blade front with white dot, square notch rear with two white dots.
**Features:** Trigger safety lock (thumb safety), grip safety, firing pin safety; long trigger; flat mainspring housing. Also available with lightweight alloy frame and in stainless steel. Introduced 1985.
**Price:** Blue . . . . . . . . . . . . . . . . . . . . . . . . . . . . . . **$694.95**
**Price:** L.W., blue finish . . . . . . . . . . . . . . . . . . . . . . . **$694.95**
**Price:** Stainless . . . . . . . . . . . . . . . . . . . . . . . . . . . . **$739.95**
**Price:** Bright stainless . . . . . . . . . . . . . . . . . . . . . . . . **$814.95**

## COONAN 357 MAGNUM PISTOL
**Caliber:** 357 Mag., 7-shot magazine.
**Barrel:** 5".
**Weight:** 42 oz. **Length:** 8.3" overall.
**Stocks:** Smooth walnut.
**Sights:** Interchangeable ramp front, rear adjustable for windage.
**Features:** Stainless and alloy steel construction. Unique barrel hood improves accuracy and reliability. Linkless barrel. Many parts interchange with Colt autos. Has grip, hammer, half-cock safeties, extended slide latch. Made in U.S. by Coonan Arms, Inc.
**Price:** 5" barrel . . . . . . . . . . . . . . . . . . . . . . . . . . . . **$720.00**
**Price:** 6" barrel . . . . . . . . . . . . . . . . . . . . . . . . . . . . **$755.00**
**Price:** With 6" compensated barrel . . . . . . . . . . . . . . . . . **$999.00**

Colt Government Pocketlite

## Colt Mustang 380, Mustang Pocketlite
Similar to the standard 380 Government Model. Mustang has steel frame (18.5 oz.), Pocketlite has aluminum alloy (12.5 oz.). Both are ½" shorter than 380 G.M., have 2¾" barrel. Introduced 1987.
**Price:** Mustang 380, blue . . . . . . . . . . . . . . . . . . . . . . **$432.95**
**Price:** As above, nickel . . . . . . . . . . . . . . . . . . . . . . . . **$483.95**
**Price:** As above, stainless . . . . . . . . . . . . . . . . . . . . . . **$463.95**
**Price:** Mustang Pocketlite, blue . . . . . . . . . . . . . . . . . . . **$432.95**
**Price:** Mustang Pocketlite STS/N . . . . . . . . . . . . . . . . . . **$463.95**

Colt 1991A1 Compact

## Colt Model 1991 A1 Compact Auto Pistol
Similar to the Model 1991 A1 except has 3½" barrel. Overall length is 7", and gun is ⅜" shorter in height. Comes with one 6-shot magazine, moulded case. Introduced 1993.
**Price:** . . . . . . . . . . . . . . . . . . . . . . . . . . . . . . . . . **$499.95**

Coonan Compact 357

## Coonan Compact 357 Magnum Cadet Pistol
Similar to the 357 Magnum full-size gun except has 3.9" barrel, shorter frame, 6-shot magazine. Weight is 39 oz., overall length 7.8". Linkless bull barrel, full-length recoil spring guide rod, extended slide latch. Introduced 1993. Made in U.S. by Coonan Arms, Inc.
**Price:** . . . . . . . . . . . . . . . . . . . . . . . . . . . . . . . . . **$841.00**

**CAUTION:** PRICES CHANGE, CHECK AT GUNSHOP.

## CZ 75 AUTO PISTOL

**Caliber:** 9mm Para., 15-shot magazine.
**Barrel:** 4.7".
**Weight:** 34.3 oz. **Length:** 8.1" overall.
**Stocks:** High impact checkered plastic.
**Sights:** Square post front, rear adjustable for windage; three-dot system.
**Features:** Single action/double action design; choice of black polymer, matte or high-polish blue finishes. All-steel frame. Imported from the Czech Republic by Action Arms, Ltd.
**Price:** Black polymer finish . . . . . . . . . . . . . . . . . . . . . **$485.00**
**Price:** Matte blue . . . . . . . . . . . . . . . . . . . . . **$505.00**
**Price:** High-polish blue . . . . . . . . . . . . . . . . . . . . . **$519.00**

CZ 75 Compact

## CZ 75 Compact Auto Pistol

Similar to the CZ 75 except has 13-shot magazine, 3.9" barrel and weighs 32 oz. Has removable front sight, non-glare ribbed slide top. Trigger guard is squared and serrated; combat hammer. Introduced 1993. Imported from the Czech Republic by Action Arms, Ltd.
**Price:** Black polymer finish . . . . . . . . . . . . . . . . . . . . . **$519.00**
**Price:** Matte blue . . . . . . . . . . . . . . . . . . . . . **$545.00**
**Price:** High-polish blue . . . . . . . . . . . . . . . . . . . . . **$565.00**

## CZ 85 Auto Pistol

Same gun as the CZ 75 except has ambidextrous slide release and safety-levers; non-glare, ribbed slide top; squared, serrated trigger guard; trigger stop to prevent overtravel. Introduced 1986. Imported from the Czech Republic by Action Arms, Ltd.
**Price:** Black polymer finish . . . . . . . . . . . . . . . . . . . . . **$515.00**
**Price:** Matte blue . . . . . . . . . . . . . . . . . . . . . **$529.00**
**Price:** High-polish blue . . . . . . . . . . . . . . . . . . . . . **$559.00**

## CZ 85 Combat Auto Pistol

Same as the CZ 85 except has walnut grips, round combat hammer, fully adjustable rear sight, extended magazine release. Trigger parts coated with friction-free beryllium copper. Introduced 1992. Imported from the Czech Republic by Action Arms, Ltd.
**Price:** Black polymer finish . . . . . . . . . . . . . . . . . . . . . **$625.00**

## CZ 83 DOUBLE-ACTION PISTOL

**Caliber:** 380 ACP, 12-shot magazine.
**Barrel:** 3.8".
**Weight:** 26.2 oz. **Length:** 6.8" overall.
**Stocks:** High impact checkered plastic.
**Sights:** Removable square post front, rear adjustable for windage; three-dot system.
**Features:** Single action/double action; ambidextrous magazine release and safety. Blue finish; non-glare ribbed slide top. Imported from the Czech Republic by Action Arms Ltd.
**Price:** . . . . . . . . . . . . . . . . . . . . . **$389.00**

CZ 83 DA

## DAEWOO DP51 AUTO PISTOL

**Caliber:** 9mm Para., 13-shot magazine.
**Barrel:** 4.1".
**Weight:** 28.2 oz. **Length:** 7.48" overall.
**Stocks:** Checkered composition.
**Sights:** Blade front, square notch rear drift adjustable for windage.
**Features:** Patented tri-action mechanism. Ambidextrous manual safety and magazine catch, half-cock and firing pin block. Alloy frame, squared trigger guard. Matte black finish. Introduced 1991. Imported from Korea by Firstshot.
**Price:** . . . . . . . . . . . . . . . . . . . . . **$369.50**

Daewoo DP51

Davis P-32

## DAVIS P-32 AUTO PISTOL

**Caliber:** 32 ACP, 6-shot magazine.
**Barrel:** 2.8".
**Weight:** 22 oz. **Length:** 5.4" overall.
**Stocks:** Laminated wood.
**Sights:** Fixed.
**Features:** Choice of black Teflon or chrome finish. Announced 1986. Made in U.S. by Davis Industries.
**Price:** . . . . . . . . . . . . . . . . . . . . . **$87.50**

## DAVIS P-380 AUTO PISTOL

**Caliber:** 380 ACP, 5-shot magazine.
**Barrel:** 2.8".
**Weight:** 22 oz. **Length:** 5.4" overall.
**Stocks:** Black composition.
**Sights:** Fixed.
**Features:** Choice of chrome or black Teflon finish. Introduced 1991. Made in U.S. by Davis Industries.
**Price:** . . . . . . . . . . . . . . . . . . . . . **$98.00**

**CAUTION:** PRICES CHANGE, CHECK AT GUNSHOP.

Desert Eagle Magnum

Desert Industries Double Deuce

E.A.A. Witness

## DESERT EAGLE MAGNUM PISTOL
**Caliber:** 357 Mag., 9-shot; 41 Mag., 44 Mag., 8-shot; 50 Magnum, 7-shot.
**Barrel:** 6", 10", 14" interchangeable.
**Weight:** 357 Mag.—62 oz.; 41 Mag., 44 Mag.—69 oz.; 50 Mag.—72 oz.
**Length:** 10¼" overall (6" bbl.).
**Stocks:** Wraparound plastic.
**Sights:** Blade on ramp front, combat-style rear. Adjustable available.
**Features:** Rotating three-lug bolt; ambidextrous safety; combat-style trigger guard; adjustable trigger optional. Military epoxy finish. Satin, bright nickel, hard chrome, polished and blued finishes available. Imported from Israel by Magnum Research, Inc.
**Price:** 357, 6" bbl., standard pistol . . . . . . . . . . . . . . . . . . **$789.00**
**Price:** As above, stainless steel frame . . . . . . . . . . . . . . . . **$839.00**
**Price:** 41 Mag., 6", standard pistol . . . . . . . . . . . . . . . . . . **$799.00**
**Price:** 41 Mag., stainless steel frame . . . . . . . . . . . . . . . . . **$849.00**
**Price:** 44 Mag., 6", standard pistol . . . . . . . . . . . . . . . . . . **$899.00**
**Price:** As above, stainless steel frame . . . . . . . . . . . . . . . . **$949.00**
**Price:** 50 Magnum, 6" bbl., standard pistol . . . . . . . . . . . . **$1,249.00**

## DESERT INDUSTRIES WAR EAGLE PISTOL
**Caliber:** 9mm Para., 14-shot magazine; 10mm, 13-shot; 40 S&W, 14-shot; 45 ACP, 12-shot.
**Barrel:** 4".
**Weight:** 35.5 oz. **Length:** 7.5" overall.
**Stocks:** Rosewood.
**Sights:** Fixed.
**Features:** Double action; matte-finished stainless steel; slide mounted ambidextrous safety. Announced 1986. From Desert Industries, Inc.
**Price:** . . . . . . . . . . . . . . . . . . . . . . . . . . . . . . . . . . **$795.00**

## DESERT INDUSTRIES DOUBLE DEUCE, TWO BIT SPECIAL PISTOLS
**Caliber:** 22 LR, 6-shot; 25 ACP, 5-shot.
**Barrel:** 2½".
**Weight:** 15 oz. **Length:** 5½" overall.
**Stocks:** Rosewood.
**Sights:** Special order.
**Features:** Double action; stainless steel construction with matte finish; ambidextrous slide-mounted safety. From Desert Industries, Inc.
**Price:** 22 . . . . . . . . . . . . . . . . . . . . . . . . . . . . . . . . **$399.95**
**Price:** 25 (Two-Bit Special) . . . . . . . . . . . . . . . . . . . . . . **$399.95**

**Price:** 9mm, blue slide, chrome frame . . . . . . . . . . . . . . . **$595.00**
**Price:** 9mm Compact, blue, 13-shot . . . . . . . . . . . . . . . . . **$550.00**
**Price:** As above, blue slide, chrome frame, or all-chrome . . . . **$595.00**
**Price:** 40 S&W or 41 A.E., blue . . . . . . . . . . . . . . . . . . . . **$595.00**
**Price:** As above, blue slide, chrome frame, or all-chrome . . . . **$650.00**
**Price:** 40 S&W or 41 A.E. Compact, 8-shot, blue . . . . . . . . . **$595.00**
**Price:** As above, blue slide, chrome frame, or all-chrome . . . . **$650.00**
**Price:** 45 ACP, blue . . . . . . . . . . . . . . . . . . . . . . . . . . . **$695.00**
**Price:** As above, blue slide, chrome frame, or all-chrome . . . . **$750.00**
**Price:** 45 ACP Compact, 8-shot, blue . . . . . . . . . . . . . . . . **$695.00**
**Price:** As above, blue slide, chrome frame or all-chrome . . . . **$750.00**
**Price:** 9mm/40 S&W Combo, blue, compact or full size . . . . **$825.00**
**Price:** As above, blue/chrome, compact or full size . . . . . . . **$875.00**
**Price:** 9mm/40 S&W/41 A.E. Tri Caliber, blue, compact or full size . **$995.00**
**Price:** As above, blue/chrome . . . . . . . . . . . . . . . . . . . . **$1,050.00**
**Price:** 9mm or 40 S&W Carry Comp, blue . . . . . . . . . . . . . **$775.00**
**Price:** As above, blue/chrome . . . . . . . . . . . . . . . . . . . . . **$825.00**
**Price:** As above, 45 ACP . . . . . . . . . . . . . . . . . . . . . . **$1,010.00**

## E.A.A. WITNESS DA AUTO PISTOL
**Caliber:** 9mm Para., 16-shot magazine; 10mm Auto, 10-shot magazine; 38 Super, 40 S&W, 12-shot magazine; 45 ACP, 10-shot magazine.
**Barrel:** 4.72".
**Weight:** 35.33 oz. **Length:** 8.10" overall.
**Stocks:** Checkered rubber.
**Sights:** Undercut blade front, open rear adjustable for windage.
**Features:** Double-action trigger system; squared-off trigger guard; frame-mounted safety. Introduced 1991. Imported from Italy by European American Armory.
**Price:** 9mm, blue . . . . . . . . . . . . . . . . . . . . . . . . . . . . **$550.00**
**Price:** 9mm, satin chrome . . . . . . . . . . . . . . . . . . . . . . . **$595.00**

## E.A.A. EUROPEAN MODEL AUTO PISTOLS
**Caliber:** 32 ACP or 380 ACP, 7-shot magazine.
**Barrel:** 3.88".
**Weight:** 26 oz. **Length:** 7⅜" overall.
**Stocks:** European hardwood.
**Sights:** Fixed blade front, rear drift-adjustable for windage.
**Features:** Chrome or blue finish; magazine, thumb and firing pin safeties; external hammer; safety-lever takedown. Imported from Italy by European American Armory.
**Price:** Blue . . . . . . . . . . . . . . . . . . . . . . . . . . . . . . . . **$225.00**
**Price:** Blue/chrome . . . . . . . . . . . . . . . . . . . . . . . . . . . **$249.00**
**Price:** Chrome . . . . . . . . . . . . . . . . . . . . . . . . . . . . . . **$249.00**
**Price:** Blue/gold . . . . . . . . . . . . . . . . . . . . . . . . . . . . . **$260.00**
**Price:** Ladies Model . . . . . . . . . . . . . . . . . . . . . . . . . . . **$299.00**

Consult our Directory pages for the location of firms mentioned.

## E.A.A. European 380/DA Pistol
Similar to the standard European except in 380 ACP only, with double-action trigger mechanism. Available in blue, chrome or blue/chrome finish. Introduced 1992. From European American Armory.
**Price:** Blue . . . . . . . . . . . . . . . . . . . . . . . . . . . . . . . . **$275.00**
**Price:** Chrome . . . . . . . . . . . . . . . . . . . . . . . . . . . . . . **$299.00**
**Price:** Blue/chrome . . . . . . . . . . . . . . . . . . . . . . . . . . . **$299.00**
**Price:** Blue/gold . . . . . . . . . . . . . . . . . . . . . . . . . . . . . **$310.00**
**Price:** Ladies Model . . . . . . . . . . . . . . . . . . . . . . . . . . . **$365.00**

**CAUTION:** PRICES CHANGE, CHECK AT GUNSHOP.

## ERMA KGP68 AUTO PISTOL
**Caliber:** 32 ACP, 6-shot, 380 ACP, 5-shot.
**Barrel:** 4".
**Weight:** 22½ oz. **Length:** 7⅜" overall.
**Stocks:** Checkered plastic.
**Sights:** Fixed.
**Features:** Toggle action similar to original "Luger" pistol. Action stays open after last shot. Has magazine and sear disconnect safety systems. Imported from Germany by Mandall Shooting Supplies.
**Price:** . . . . . . . . . . . . . . . . . . . . . . . . . . $499.95

## ERMA SPORTING PISTOL MODEL ESP 85A
**Caliber:** 22 LR, 8-shot; 32 S&W Long, 5-shot.
**Barrel:** 6".
**Weight:** 39.9 oz. **Length:** 10" overall.
**Stocks:** Checkered walnut with thumbrest. Adjustable target stocks optional.
**Sights:** Interchangeable blade front, micro. rear adjustable for windage and elevation.
**Features:** Interchangeable caliber conversion kit available; adjustable trigger, trigger stop. Imported from Germany by Precision Sales Int'l. Introduced 1988.
**Price:** 22 LR . . . . . . . . . . . . . . . . . . . $1,228.00
**Price:** 32 S&W Long . . . . . . . . . . . . . . . $1,284.00
**Price:** 22 LR, chrome . . . . . . . . . . . . . . . $1,449.00
**Price:** 22 LR conversion unit . . . . . . . . . . . $689.00
**Price:** 32 S&W conversion unit . . . . . . . . . . $746.00

## FALCON AUTO PISTOL
**Caliber:** 10mm, 40 S&W, 10-shot magazine, 45 ACP, 8-shot magazine.
**Barrel:** 5".
**Weight:** 37.5 oz. **Length:** 8.5" overall.
**Stocks:** Black Du Pont Zytel with stipple finish.
**Sights:** Post front, rear adjustable for windage and elevation; Tri-Square system.
**Features:** Double-action with passive firing pin lock, decocking lever, ambidextrous thumb safety levers; reversible magazine release; beveled magazine well; stainless steel magazine. Black slide, stainless frame. Announced 1990. Made in U.S. by Falcon Industries.
**Price:** 10mm, 40 S&W, 45 ACP . . . . . . . . . . . $795.00

## FEG B9R AUTO PISTOL
**Caliber:** 380 ACP, 15-shot magazine.
**Barrel:** 4".
**Weight:** 25 oz. **Length:** 7" overall.
**Stocks:** Hand-checkered walnut.
**Sights:** Blade front, drift-adjustable rear.
**Features:** Hammer-drop safety; grooved backstrap; squared trigger guard. Comes with spare magazine. Introduced 1993. Imported from Hungary by Century International Arms.
**Price:** About . . . . . . . . . . . . . . . . . . . . $312.00

## FEG FP9 AUTO PISTOL
**Caliber:** 9mm Para., 14-shot magazine.
**Barrel:** 5".
**Weight:** 35 oz. **Length:** 7.8" overall.
**Stocks:** Checkered walnut.
**Sights:** Blade front, windage-adjustable rear.
**Features:** Full-length ventilated rib. Polished blue finish. Comes with extra magazine. Introduced 1993. Imported from Hungary by Century International Arms.
**Price:** About . . . . . . . . . . . . . . . . . . . . $269.00

Erma ESP 85A

FEG B9R

FEG PJK-9HP

## FEG PJK-9HP AUTO PISTOL
**Caliber:** 9mm Para., 13-shot magazine.
**Barrel:** 4.75".
**Weight:** 32 oz. **Length:** 8" overall.
**Stocks:** Hand-checkered walnut.
**Sights:** Blade front, rear adjustable for windage.
**Features:** Single action; polished blue or hard chrome finish; rounded combat-style serrated hammer. Comes with two magazines and cleaning rod. Imported from Hungary by K.B.I., Inc.
**Price:** Blue . . . . . . . . . . . . . . . . . . . . . $329.00
**Price:** Hard chrome . . . . . . . . . . . . . . . . . $435.00

## FEG PMK-380 AUTO PISTOL
**Caliber:** 380 ACP, 7-shot magazine.
**Barrel:** 4".
**Weight:** 21 oz. **Length:** 7" overall.
**Stocks:** Checkered black nylon with thumbrest.
**Sights:** Blade front, rear adjustable for windage.
**Features:** Double action; anodized aluminum frame, polished blue slide. Comes with two magazines, cleaning rod. Introduced 1992. Imported from Hungary by K.B.I., Inc.
**Price:** . . . . . . . . . . . . . . . . . . . . . . . . $249.00

## FEG SMC-380 AUTO PISTOL
**Caliber:** 380 ACP, 6-shot magazine.
**Barrel:** 3.5".
**Weight:** 18.5 oz. **Length:** 6.1" overall.
**Stocks:** Checkered composition with thumbrest.
**Sights:** Blade front, rear adjustable for windage.
**Features:** Patterned after the PPK pistol. Alloy frame, steel slide; double action. Blue finish. Comes with two magazines, cleaning rod. Imported from Hungary by K.B.I.
**Price:** . . . . . . . . . . . . . . . . . . . . . . . . $299.00

FEG PMK-380

**CAUTION:** PRICES CHANGE, CHECK AT GUNSHOP.

Glock 19

Glock 21

**Glock 21 Auto Pistol**
Similar to the Glock 17 except chambered for 45 ACP, 13-shot magazine. Overall length is 7.59", weight is 25.2 oz. (without magazine). Fixed or adjustable rear sight. Introduced 1991.
**Price:** . . . . . . . . . . . . . . . . . . . . . . . . . . . . . . **$638.49**

**Glock 23 Auto Pistol**
Similar to the Glock 19 except chambered for 40 S&W, 13-shot magazine. Overall length is 6.85", weight is 20.6 oz. (without magazine). Fixed or adjustable rear sight. Introduced 1990.
**Price:** . . . . . . . . . . . . . . . . . . . . . . . . . . . . . . **$579.95**

Grendel P-12

Grendel P-31

## FEG P9R AUTO PISTOL
**Caliber:** 9mm Para., 15-shot magazine.
**Barrel:** 4.6".
**Weight:** 35 oz. **Length:** 7.9" overall.
**Stocks:** Checkered walnut.
**Sights:** Blade front, rear adjustable for windage.
**Features:** Double-action mechanism; slide-mounted safety. All-Steel construction with polished blue finish. Comes with extra magazine. Introduced 1993. Imported from Hungary by Century International Arms.
**Price:** About . . . . . . . . . . . . . . . . . . . . . . . . . . **$262.00**

## GLOCK 17 AUTO PISTOL
**Caliber:** 9mm Para., 17-shot magazine.
**Barrel:** 4.49".
**Weight:** 21.9 oz. (without magazine). **Length:** 7.28" overall.
**Stocks:** Black polymer.
**Sights:** Dot on front blade, white outline rear adjustable for windage.
**Features:** Polymer frame, steel slide; double-action trigger with "Safe Action" system; mechanical firing pin safety, drop safety; simple takedown without tools; locked breech, recoil operated action. Adopted by Austrian armed forces 1983. NATO approved 1984. Imported from Austria by Glock, Inc.
**Price:** With extra magazine, magazine loader, cleaning kit . . . . . . **$579.95**
**Price:** Model 17L (6" barrel) . . . . . . . . . . . . . . . . . . **$768.25**

## Glock 19 Auto Pistol
Similar to the Glock 17 except has a 4" barrel, giving an overall length of 6.85" and weight of 20.99 oz. Magazine capacity is 15 rounds. Fixed or adjustable rear sight. Introduced 1988.
**Price:** . . . . . . . . . . . . . . . . . . . . . . . . . . . . . . **$579.95**

## Glock 20 10mm Auto Pistol
Similar to the Glock Model 17 except chambered for 10mm Automatic cartridge. Barrel length is 4.60", overall length is 7.59", and weight is 26.3 oz. (without magazine). Magazine capacity is 15 rounds. Fixed or adjustable rear sight. Comes with an extra magazine, magazine loader, cleaning rod and brush. Introduced 1990. Imported from Austria by Glock, Inc.
**Price:** . . . . . . . . . . . . . . . . . . . . . . . . . . . . . . **$638.49**

## Glock 22 Auto Pistol
Similar to the Glock 17 except chambered for 40 S&W, 15-shot magazine. Overall length is 7.28", weight is 22.3 oz. (without magazine). Fixed or adjustable rear sight. Introduced 1990.
**Price:** . . . . . . . . . . . . . . . . . . . . . . . . . . . . . . **$579.95**

## GRENDEL P-12 AUTO PISTOL
**Caliber:** 380 ACP, 11-shot magazine.
**Barrel:** 3".
**Weight:** 13 oz. **Length:** 5.3" overall.
**Stocks:** Checkered DuPont ST-800 polymer.
**Sights:** Fixed.
**Features:** Double action only with inertia safety hammer system. All steel frame; grip forms magazine well and trigger guard. Introduced 1992. Made in U.S. by Grendel, Inc.
**Price:** Blue . . . . . . . . . . . . . . . . . . . . . . . . . . . . **$175.00**
**Price:** Electroless nickel . . . . . . . . . . . . . . . . . . . . **$195.00**

## GRENDEL P-30 AUTO PISTOL
**Caliber:** 22 WMR, 30-shot magazine.
**Barrel:** 5", 8".
**Weight:** 21 oz. (5" barrel). **Length:** 8.5" overall (5" barrel).
**Stocks:** Checkered Zytel.
**Sights:** Blade front, fixed rear.
**Features:** Blowback action with fluted chamber; ambidextrous safety, reversible magazine catch. Scope mount available. Introduced 1990.
**Price:** With 5" barrel . . . . . . . . . . . . . . . . . . . . . . **$225.00**
**Price:** With removable muzzlebrake (Model P-30M) . . . . . . . . **$235.00**
**Price:** With 8" barrel (Model P-30L) . . . . . . . . . . . . . . . **$280.00**

## GRENDEL P-31 AUTO PISTOL
**Caliber:** 22 WMR, 30-shot magazine.
**Barrel:** 11".
**Weight:** 48 oz. **Length:** 17.5" overall.
**Stocks:** Checkered black Zytel grip and forend.
**Sights:** Blade front adjustable for windage and elevation, fixed rear.
**Features:** Blowback action with fluted chamber. Ambidextrous safety. Matte black finish. Muzzlebrake. Scope mount optional. Introduced 1991. Made in the U.S. by Grendel, Inc.
**Price:** . . . . . . . . . . . . . . . . . . . . . . . . . . . . . . **$345.00**

**HAMMERLI MODEL 212 AUTO PISTOL**
**Caliber:** 22 LR, 8-shot magazine.
**Barrel:** 4.9".
**Weight:** 31 oz.
**Stocks:** Checkered walnut.
**Sights:** Blade front, rear adjustable for windage only.
**Features:** Polished blue finish. Imported from Switzerland by Mandall Shooting Supplies and Hammerli Pistols USA.
**Price:** About . . . . . . . . . . . . . . . . . . . . . . . $1,395.00

**HASKELL JS-45 CALIBER PISTOL**
**Caliber:** 45 ACP, 7-shot magazine.
**Barrel:** 4.5".
**Weight:** 44 oz. **Length:** 7.95" overall.
**Stocks:** Checkered acetal resin.
**Sights:** Fixed; low profile.
**Features:** Internal drop-safe mechanism; all aluminum frame. Introduced 1991. From MKS Supply, Inc.
**Price:** Matte black . . . . . . . . . . . . . . . . . . . $149.95
**Price:** Brushed nickel . . . . . . . . . . . . . . . . . $159.95

Hammerli Model 212

Heckler & Koch P7M10

Heckler & Koch SP89

Heckler & Koch USP

**HECKLER & KOCH P7M8 AUTO PISTOL**
**Caliber:** 9mm Para., 8-shot magazine.
**Barrel:** 4.13".
**Weight:** 29 oz. **Length:** 6.73" overall.
**Stocks:** Stippled black plastic.
**Sights:** Blade front, adjustable rear; three dot system.
**Features:** Unique "squeeze cocker" in frontstrap cocks the action. Gas-retarded action. Squared combat-type trigger guard. Blue finish. Compact size. Imported from Germany by Heckler & Koch, Inc.
**Price:** P7M8, blued . . . . . . . . . . . . . . . . . $1,059.00
**Price:** P7M8, nickel . . . . . . . . . . . . . . . . . $1,059.00
**Price:** P7M13 (13-shot capacity, ambidextrous magazine release, forged steel frame), blued . . . . . . . . . . . . . . $1,284.00
**Price:** P7M13, nickel . . . . . . . . . . . . . . . . . $1,284.00

**Heckler & Koch P7M10 Auto Pistol**
Similar to the P7M8 except chambered for 40 S&W with 10-shot magazine. Weighs 43 oz., overall length is 6.9". Introduced 1992. Imported from Germany by Heckler & Koch, Inc.
**Price:** Blue . . . . . . . . . . . . . . . . . . . . . . . $1,314.00
**Price:** Nickel . . . . . . . . . . . . . . . . . . . . . . $1,314.00

**Heckler & Koch P7K3 Auto Pistol**
Similar to the P7M8 and P7M13 except chambered for 22 LR or 380 ACP, 8-shot magazine. Uses an oil-filled buffer to decrease recoil. Introduced 1988.
**Price:** . . . . . . . . . . . . . . . . . . . . . . . . . $1,059.00
**Price:** 22 LR conversion unit . . . . . . . . . . . . $524.00
**Price:** 32 ACP conversion unit . . . . . . . . . . . $228.00

**HECKLER & KOCH SP89 AUTO PISTOL**
**Caliber:** 9mm Para., 15- or 30-shot magazine.
**Barrel:** 4.5".
**Weight:** 4.4 lbs. **Length:** 12.8" overall.
**Stocks:** Black high-impact plastic.
**Sights:** Post front, diopter rear adjustable for windage and elevation.
**Features:** Semi-auto pistol inspired by the HK94. Has special flash-hider forend. Introduced 1989. Imported from Germany by Heckler & Koch, Inc.
**Price:** . . . . . . . . . . . . . . . . . . . . . . . . . $1,324.00

**HECKLER & KOCH USP AUTO PISTOL**
**Caliber:** 9mm Para., 16-shot magazine, 40 S&W, 13-shot magazine.
**Barrel:** 4.13".
**Weight:** 28 oz. (USP40). **Length:** 6.9" overall.
**Stocks:** Non-slip stippled black polymer.
**Sights:** Blade front, rear adjustable for windage.
**Features:** New HK design with polymer frame, modified Browning action with recoil reduction system, single control lever. Special "hostile environment" finish on all metal parts. Available in SA/DA, DAO, left- and right-hand versions. Introduced 1993. Imported from Germany by Heckler & Koch, Inc.
**Price:** Right-hand . . . . . . . . . . . . . . . . . . . $624.00
**Price:** Left-hand . . . . . . . . . . . . . . . . . . . . $644.00

**HELWAN "BRIGADIER" AUTO PISTOL**
**Caliber:** 9mm Para., 8-shot magazine.
**Barrel:** 4.5".
**Weight:** 32 oz. **Length:** 8" overall.
**Stocks:** Grooved plastic.
**Sights:** Blade front, rear adjustable for windage.
**Features:** Polished blue finish. Single-action design. Cross-bolt safety. Imported by Interarms.
**Price:** . . . . . . . . . . . . . . . . . . . . . . . . . . $262.00

## HERITAGE MODEL HA25 AUTO PISTOL
**Caliber:** 25 ACP, 6-shot magazine.
**Barrel:** 2½".
**Weight:** 12 oz. **Length:** 4⅝" overall.
**Stocks:** Smooth walnut.
**Sights:** Fixed.
**Features:** Exposed hammer, manual safety; open-top slide. Polished blue or chrome finish. Introduced 1993. Made in U.S. by Heritage Mfg., Inc.
**Price:** . . . . . . . . . . . . . . . . . . . . . . . . . **$69.95** to **$89.95**

Hi-Point C-9MM

## HI-POINT FIREARMS MODEL C-9MM PISTOL
**Caliber:** 9mm Para., 8-shot magazine.
**Barrel:** 3.5".
**Weight:** 35 oz. **Length:** 6.7" overall.
**Stocks:** Textured acetal plastic.
**Sights:** Combat-style fixed three-dot system; low profile.
**Features:** Single-action design; frame-mounted magazine release. Scratch-resistant matte finish. Introduced 1993. From MKS Supply, Inc.
**Price:** . . . . . . . . . . . . . . . . . . . . . . . . . . . **$129.95**

## HUNGARIAN T-58 AUTO PISTOL
**Caliber:** 7.62mm and 9mm Para., 8-shot magazine.
**Barrel:** 4.5".
**Weight:** 31 oz. **Length:** 7.68" overall.
**Stocks:** Grooved composition.
**Sights:** Blade front, rear adjustable for windage.
**Features:** Comes with both barrels and magazines. Thumb safety locks hammer. Blue finish. Imported by Century International Arms.
**Price:** About . . . . . . . . . . . . . . . . . . . . . . . . **$187.00**

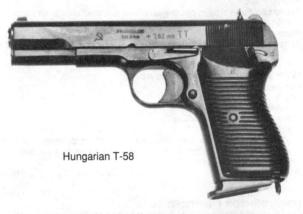

Hungarian T-58

## IBERIA FIREARMS JS-40 S&W AUTO
**Caliber:** 40 S&W, 8-shot magazine.
**Barrel:** 4.5".
**Weight:** 44 oz. **Length:** 7.95" overall.
**Stocks:** Checkered acetal resin.
**Sights:** Fixed; low profile.
**Features:** Internal drop-safe mechansim; all aluminum frame. Introduced 1991. From MKS Supply, Inc.
**Price:** Matte black . . . . . . . . . . . . . . . . . . . . . **$149.95**
**Price:** Brushed nickel . . . . . . . . . . . . . . . . . . . **$159.95**

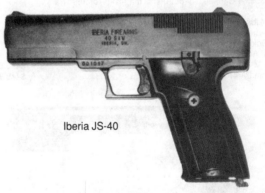

Iberia JS-40

## INTRATEC CATEGORY 9 AUTO PISTOL
**Caliber:** 9mm Para., 8-shot magazine.
**Barrel:** 3".
**Weight:** 21 oz. **Length:** 5.5" overall.
**Stocks:** Textured black polymer.
**Sights:** Fixed channel.
**Features:** Black polymer frame. Announced 1993. Made in U.S. by Intratec.
**Price:** About . . . . . . . . . . . . . . . . . . . . . . . . **$200.00**

## INTRATEC PROTEC-22, 25 AUTO PISTOLS
**Caliber:** 22 LR, 10-shot; 25 ACP, 8-shot magazine.
**Barrel:** 2½".
**Weight:** 14 oz. **Length:** 5" overall.
**Stocks:** Wraparound composition in gray, black or driftwood color.
**Sights:** Fixed.
**Features:** Double-action only trigger mechanism. Choice of black, satin or TEC-KOTE finish. Announced 1991. Made in U.S. by Intratec.
**Price:** 22 or 25, black finish . . . . . . . . . . . . . . . . **$99.95**
**Price:** 22 or 25, satin or TEC-KOTE finish . . . . . . . . . . **$104.95**

Intratec TEC-DC9

## INTRATEC TEC-DC9 AUTO PISTOL
**Caliber:** 9mm Para., 32-shot magazine.
**Barrel:** 5".
**Weight:** 50 oz. **Length:** 12½" overall.
**Stock:** Moulded composition.
**Sights:** Fixed.
**Features:** Semi-auto, fires from closed bolt; firing pin block safety; matte blue finish. Made in U.S. by Intratec.
**Price:** . . . . . . . . . . . . . . . . . . . . . . . . . . . **$260.00**
**Price:** TEC-DC9S (as above, except stainless) . . . . . . . . . **$353.00**
**Price:** TEC-DC9K (finished with TEC-KOTE) . . . . . . . . . . **$290.00**

## Intratec TEC-DC9M Auto Pistol
Similar to the TEC-DC9 except smaller. Has 3" barrel, weighs 44 oz.; 20-shot magazine. Made in U.S. by Intratec.
**Price:** . . . . . . . . . . . . . . . . . . . . . . . . . . . **$239.00**
**Price:** TEC-DC9MS (as above, stainless) . . . . . . . . . . . **$330.00**
**Price:** TEC-DC9MK (finished with TEC-KOTE) . . . . . . . . . **$270.00**

# HANDGUNS—AUTOLOADERS, SERVICE & SPORT

Jennings J-25

## JENNINGS J-22, J-25 AUTO PISTOLS
**Caliber:** 22 LR, 25 ACP, 6-shot magazine.
**Barrel:** 2½".
**Weight:** 13 oz. (J-22). **Length:** 4¹⁵⁄₁₆" overall (J-22).
**Stocks:** Walnut on chrome or nickel models; grooved black Cycolac or resin-impregnated wood on Teflon model.
**Sights:** Fixed.
**Features:** Choice of bright chrome, satin nickel or black Teflon finish. Introduced 1981. From Jennings Firearms.
**Price:** J-22, about . . . . . . . . . . . . . . . . . . . **$75.00**
**Price:** J-25, about . . . . . . . . . . . . . . . . . . . **$89.95**

## IVER JOHNSON COMPACT 25 ACP
**Caliber:** 25 ACP.
**Barrel:** 2".
**Weight:** 9.3 oz.
**Stocks:** Checkered composition.
**Sights:** Fixed.
**Features:** Ordnance steel construction with bright blue slide, matte blue frame, color case-hardened trigger. Comes in jewelry-type presentation box. Introduced 1991. From Iver Johnson.
**Price:** . . . . . . . . . . . . . . . . . . . . . . **$199.95**

## IVER JOHNSON ENFORCER AUTO
**Caliber:** 30 M-1 Carbine, 15- or 30-shot magazine, or 9mm Para.
**Barrel:** 10½".
**Weight:** 4 lbs. **Length:** 18½" overall.
**Stocks:** American walnut with metal handguard.
**Sights:** Gold bead ramp front. Peep rear.
**Features:** Accepts 15- or 30-shot magazines. From Iver Johnson.
**Price:** 30 M-1 . . . . . . . . . . . . . . . . . . **$416.50**
**Price:** 9mm Para. . . . . . . . . . . . . . . . . **$448.95**

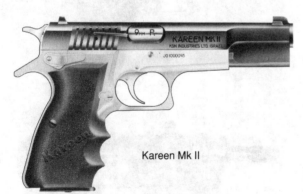

Kareen Mk II

## L.A.R. GRIZZLY WIN MAG MK I PISTOL
**Caliber:** 357 Mag., 357/45, 10mm, 44 Mag., 45 Win. Mag., 45 ACP, 7-shot magazine.
**Barrel:** 5.4", 6.5".
**Weight:** 51 oz. **Length:** 10½" overall.
**Stocks:** Checkered rubber, non-slip combat-type.
**Sights:** Ramped blade front, fully adjustable rear.
**Features:** Uses basic Browning/Colt 1911A1 design; interchangeable calibers; beveled magazine well; combat-type flat, checkered rubber mainspring housing; lowered and back-chamfered ejection port; polished feed ramp; throated barrel; solid barrel bushings. Available in satin hard chrome, matte blue, Parkerized finishes. Introduced 1983. From L.A.R. Mfg., Inc.
**Price:** 45 Win. Mag. . . . . . . . . . . . . . . **$920.00**
**Price:** 357 Mag. . . . . . . . . . . . . . . . . **$933.00**
**Price:** Conversion units (357 Mag.) . . . . . **$228.00**
**Price:** As above, 45 ACP, 10mm, 45 Win. Mag., 357/45 Win. Mag. . . **$214.00**

## INTRATEC TEC-22T AUTO PISTOL
**Caliber:** 22 LR, 30-shot magazine.
**Barrel:** 4".
**Weight:** 30 oz. **Length:** 11³⁄₁₆" overall.
**Stocks:** Moulded composition.
**Sights:** Protected post front, front and rear adjustable for windage and elevation.
**Features:** Ambidextrous cocking knobs and safety. Matte black finish. Accepts any 10/22-type magazine. Introduced 1988. Made in U.S. by Intratec.
**Price:** . . . . . . . . . . . . . . . . . . . . . . **$157.00**
**Price:** TEC-22TK (as above, TEC-KOTE finish) . . . . . . . . . . **$178.95**

Iver Johnson Compact

## KAREEN MK II AUTO PISTOL
**Caliber:** 9mm Para., 13-shot magazine.
**Barrel:** 4.75".
**Weight:** 32 oz. **Length:** 8" overall.
**Stocks:** Textured composition.
**Sights:** Blade front, rear adjustable for windage.
**Features:** Single-action mechanism; external hammer safety; magazine safety; combat trigger guard. Blue finish standard, optional two-tone or matte black. Optional Meprolight sights, improved rubberized grips. Comes with two magazines. Imported from Israel by J.O. Arms & Ammunition. Introduced 1969.
**Price:** . . . . . . . . . . . . . . . . $389.00 to **$525.00**

## KIMEL AP9 AUTO PISTOL
**Caliber:** 9mm Para., 20-shot magazine.
**Barrel:** 5".
**Weight:** 3.5 lbs. **Length:** 11.8" overall.
**Stocks:** Checkered plastic.
**Sights:** Adjustable post front in ring, fixed open rear.
**Features:** Matte blue/black or nickel finish. Lever safety blocks trigger and sear. Fires from closed bolt. Introduced 1988. Made in U.S. Available from Kimel Industries.
**Price:** Matte blue/black . . . . . . . . . . . . **$264.00**
**Price:** Nickel finish . . . . . . . . . . . . . . . **$274.00**
**Price:** Mini AP9 (3" barrel) . . . . . . . . . . . **$258.00**
**Price:** Nickel finish . . . . . . . . . . . . . . . **$268.00**
**Price:** Target AP9 (12" bbl., grooved forend), blue . . . . . . . . **$279.00**

L.A.R. Grizzly Win Mag

## L.A.R. Grizzly Win Mag 8" & 10"
Similar to the standard Grizzly Win Mag except has lengthened slide and either 8" or 10" barrel. Available in 45 Win. Mag., 45 ACP, 357/45 Grizzly Win. Mag., 10mm or 357 Magnum. Introduced 1987.
**Price:** 8", 45 ACP, 45 Win. Mag., 357/45 Grizzly Win. Mag. . . . . **$1,313.00**
**Price:** As above, 10" . . . . . . . . . . . . . . **$1,375.00**
**Price:** 8", 357 Magnum . . . . . . . . . . . . . **$1,337.50**
**Price:** As above, 10" . . . . . . . . . . . . . . **$1,400.00**

**110** GUNS ILLUSTRATED

**CAUTION:** PRICES CHANGE, CHECK AT GUNSHOP.

Laseraim Arms Series I

## Laseraim Arms Series II Auto Pistol

Similar to the Series I except without compensator, has matte stainless finish. Standard Series II has 5" barrel, weighs 46 oz., Compact has 3⅜" barrel, weighs 43 oz. Blade front sight, rear adjustable for windage. Introduced 1993. Made in U.S. by Emerging Technologies, Inc.

**Price:** Standard or Compact . . . . . . . . . . . . . . . . . . . . . **$529.00**

## LLAMA COMPACT FRAME AUTO PISTOL

**Caliber:** 9mm Para., 9-shot, 40 S&W, 8-shot, 45 ACP, 7-shot.
**Barrel:** 4¼" (40 S&W), 4⁵⁄₁₆" (9mm, 45).
**Weight:** 37 oz.
**Stocks:** Smooth walnut.
**Sights:** Blade front, rear adjustable for windage.
**Features:** Scaled-down version of the Large Frame gun. Locked breech mechanism; manual and grip safeties. Introduced 1985. Imported from Spain by SGS Importers Int'l., Inc.
**Price:** Model XI-B (9mm Para.), blue . . . . . . . . . . . . . **$314.95**
**Price:** As above, nickel . . . . . . . . . . . . . . . . . . . . . **$363.95**
**Price:** Model XII-B (40 S&W), blue . . . . . . . . . . . . . **$324.95**
**Price:** As above, nickel . . . . . . . . . . . . . . . . . . . . . **$363.95**
**Price:** Model IX-B (45 ACP), blue . . . . . . . . . . . . . . **$324.95**
**Price:** As above, nickel . . . . . . . . . . . . . . . . . . . . . **$363.95**

## LLAMA LARGE FRAME AUTO PISTOL

**Caliber:** 38 Super, 40 S&W, 45 ACP.
**Barrel:** 5" (38 Super, 45 ACP), 5⅛" (40 S&W).
**Weight:** 40 oz. **Length:** 8½" overall.
**Stocks:** Checkered walnut.
**Sights:** Fixed.
**Features:** Grip and manual safeties, ventilated rib. Imported from Spain by SGS Importers Int'l., Inc.
**Price:** Model VIII (38 Super), blue . . . . . . . . . . . . . **$324.95**
**Price:** As above, nickel . . . . . . . . . . . . . . . . . . . . . **$363.95**
**Price:** Model XII-A (40 S&W), blue . . . . . . . . . . . . . **$324.95**
**Price:** As above, nickel . . . . . . . . . . . . . . . . . . . . . **$363.95**
**Price:** Model IX-A (45 ACP), blue . . . . . . . . . . . . . . **$324.95**
**Price:** As above, nickel . . . . . . . . . . . . . . . . . . . . . **$363.95**

## LLAMA XV, III-A SMALL FRAME AUTO PISTOLS

**Caliber:** 22 LR, 380.
**Barrel:** 3¹¹⁄₁₆".
**Weight:** 23 oz. **Length:** 6½" overall.
**Stocks:** Checkered plastic, thumbrest.
**Sights:** Fixed front, adjustable notch rear.
**Features:** Ventilated rib, manual and grip safeties. Imported from Spain by SGS Importers Int'l., Inc.
**Price:** Blue . . . . . . . . . . . . . . . . . . . . . . . . . . . **$281.95**
**Price:** Satin Chrome . . . . . . . . . . . . . . . . . . . . . **$314.95**

## LLAMA M-82 DA AUTO PISTOL

**Caliber:** 9mm Para., 40 S&W, 15-shot magazine.
**Barrel:** 4¼".
**Weight:** 39 oz. **Length:** 8" overall.
**Stocks:** Matte black polymer.
**Sights:** Blade front, rear drift adjustable for windage. High visibility three-dot system.
**Features:** Double-action mechanism; ambidextrous safety. Introduced 1987. Imported from Spain by SGS Importers Int'l., Inc.
**Price:** . . . . . . . . . . . . . . . . . . . . . . . . . . . . . **$584.95**

## L.A.R. Grizzly 44 Mag MK IV

Similar to the Win. Mag. Mk I except chambered for 44 Magnum, has beavertail grip safety. Matte blue finish only. Has 5.4" or 6.5" barrel. Introduced 1991. From L.A.R. Mfg., Inc.
**Price:** . . . . . . . . . . . . . . . . . . . . . . . . . . . . . **$933.00**

## L.A.R. Grizzly 50 Mark V Pistol

Similar to the Grizzly Win Mag Mark I except chambered for 50 Action Express with 6-shot magazine. Weight, empty, is 56 oz., overall length 10⅝". Choice of 5.4" or 6.5" barrel. Has same features as Mark I, IV pistols. Introduced 1993. From L.A.R. Mfg., Inc.
**Price:** . . . . . . . . . . . . . . . . . . . . . . . . . . . . . **$1,060.00**

## LASERAIM ARMS SERIES I AUTO PISTOL

**Caliber:** 10mm Auto, 40 S&W, 8-shot, 45 ACP, 7-shot magazine.
**Barrel:** 5.5", with compensator.
**Weight:** 52 oz. **Length:** 10.5" overall.
**Stocks:** Pebble-grained black composite.
**Sights:** Blade front, fully adjustable rear.
**Features:** Single action; barrel compensator; stainless steel construction; ambidextrous safety-levers; extended slide release; matte black Teflon finish; integral mount for laser sight. Introduced 1993. Made in U.S. by Emerging Technologies, Inc.
**Price:** Standard . . . . . . . . . . . . . . . . . . . . . **$599.00**
**Price:** Compact (3⅞" barrel, 40 S&W, 45 ACP only) . . . . . . . . . **$599.00**

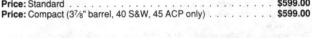

Llama Large Frame

Llama Small Frame

Llama M-82

## LORCIN L-22 AUTO PISTOL
**Caliber:** 22 LR, 9-shot magazine.
**Barrel:** 2.5".
**Weight:** 16 oz. **Length:** 5.25" overall.
**Stocks:** Black combat, or pink or pearl.
**Sights:** Fixed three-dot system.
**Features:** Available in chrome or black Teflon finish. Introduced 1989. From Lorcin Engineering.
**Price:** About . . . . . . . . . . . . . . . . . . . . . . . . . . . . **$79.95**

## LORCIN L-25, LT-25 AUTO PISTOLS
**Caliber:** 25 ACP, 7-shot magazine.
**Barrel:** 2.4".
**Weight:** 14.5 oz. **Length:** 4.8" overall.
**Stocks:** Smooth composition.
**Sights:** Fixed.
**Features:** Available in choice of finishes: chrome, black Teflon or camouflage. Introduced 1989. From Lorcin Engineering.
**Price:** . . . . . . . . . . . . . . . . . . . . . . . . . . . . . . **$79.95**

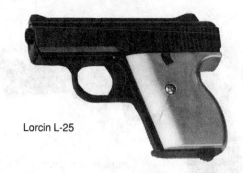
Lorcin L-25

## LORCIN L-32, L-380 AUTO PISTOLS
**Caliber:** 32 ACP, 380 ACP, 7-shot magazine.
**Barrel:** 3.5".
**Weight:** 27 oz. **Length:** 6.6" overall.
**Stocks:** Grooved composition.
**Sights:** Fixed.
**Features:** Black Teflon or chrome finish with black grips. Introduced 1992. From Lorcin Engineering.
**Price:** 32 ACP . . . . . . . . . . . . . . . . . . . . . . . . **$85.00**
**Price:** 380 ACP . . . . . . . . . . . . . . . . . . . . . . . **$95.00**

Lorcin L-32

## MAUSER MODEL 80 SA AUTO PISTOL
**Caliber:** 9mm Para., 13-shot magazine.
**Barrel:** 4.67".
**Weight:** 31.7 oz. **Length:** 8" overall.
**Stocks:** Checkered beechwood.
**Sights:** Blade front, rear adjustable for windage.
**Features:** Uses basic Hi-Power design. Polished blue finish. Introduced 1992. Imported from Germany by Precision Imports, Inc.
**Price:** . . . . . . . . . . . . . . . . . . . . . . . . . . . . . **$372.00**

### Mauser Model 90 DA Auto Pistols
Similar to the Mauser Model 80 except has double-action trigger system. Has 14-shot magazine, weighs 35.2 oz. Introduced 1992. Imported from Germany by Precision Imports, Inc.
**Price:** Model 90 DA . . . . . . . . . . . . . . . . . . . . . **$399.00**
**Price:** Model 90 DA Compact (4.13" bbl., 7.4" overall, 33.5 oz.) . . . **$425.00**

Mitchell American Eagle

## MITCHELL ARMS AMERICAN EAGLE AUTO
**Caliber:** 9mm Para., 7-shot magazine.
**Barrel:** 4".
**Weight:** 29.6 oz. **Length:** 9.6" overall.
**Stocks:** Checkered walnut.
**Sights:** Blade front, fixed rear.
**Features:** Recreation of the American Eagle Parabellum pistol in stainless steel. Chamber loaded indicator. Made in U.S. From Mitchell Arms, Inc.
**Price:** . . . . . . . . . . . . . . . . . . . . . . . . . . . . . **$695.00**

## MITCHELL ARMS SHARPSHOOTER AUTO PISTOL
**Caliber:** 22 LR, 10-shot magazine.
**Barrel:** 5.5" bull.
**Weight:** 42 oz. **Length:** 10.25" overall.
**Stocks:** Checkered walnut with thumbrest.
**Sights:** Ramp front, slide-mounted square notch rear adjustable for windage and elevation.
**Features:** Military grip. Slide lock; smooth gripstraps; push-button takedown. Announced 1992. From Mitchell Arms, Inc.
**Price:** Stainless steel . . . . . . . . . . . . . . . . . . . . **$364.00**

## MITCHELL ARMS TROPHY II AUTO PISTOL
**Caliber:** 22 LR, 10-shot magazine.
**Barrel:** 5.5" bull, 7.25" fluted.
**Weight:** 44.5 oz. (5.5" barrel). **Length:** 9.75" overall (5.5" barrel).
**Stocks:** Checkered walnut with thumbrest.
**Sights:** Undercut ramp front, click-adjustable frame-mounted rear.
**Features:** Grip duplicates feel of military 45; positive action magazine latch; front- and backstraps stippled. Trigger adjustable for pull, over-travel; gold-filled roll marks, gold-plated trigger, safety, magazine release; push-button barrel takedown. Available in stainless steel. Announced 1992. From Mitchell Arms, Inc.
**Price:** Stainless steel . . . . . . . . . . . . . . . . . . . . **$479.00**

Mitchell Trophy II

### Mitchell Arms Citation II Auto Pistol
Same as the Trophy II except has nickel-plated trigger, safety and magazine release, and has silver-filled roll marks. Available in stainless steel. Announced 1992. From Mitchell Arms, Inc.
**Price:** Stainless steel . . . . . . . . . . . . . . . . . . . . **$454.00**

Mountain Eagle

## NAVY ARMS TT-OLYMPIA PISTOL
**Caliber:** 22 LR.
**Barrel:** 4.6".
**Weight:** 28 oz. **Length:** 8" overall.
**Stocks:** Checkered hardwood.
**Sights:** Blade front, rear adjsutable for windage.
**Features:** Reproduction of the Walther Olympia pistol. Polished blue finish. Introduced 1992. Imported by Navy Arms.
**Price:** . . . . . . . . . . . . . . . . . . . . . . . . . . . . . . **$300.00**

## NORINCO NP-15 TOKAREV AUTO PISTOL
**Caliber:** 7.62x25mm, 8-shot magazine.
**Barrel:** 4.5".
**Weight:** 29 oz. **Length:** 7.7" overall.
**Stocks:** Grooved black plastic.
**Sights:** Fixed.
**Features:** Matte blue finish. Imported from China by China Sports, Inc.
**Price:** . . . . . . . . . . . . . . . . . . . . . . . . . . . . . . **NA**

## NORINCO MODEL 59 MAKAROV DA PISTOL
**Caliber:** 9x18mm, 380 ACP, 8-shot magazine.
**Barrel:** 3.5".
**Weight:** 21 oz. **Length:** 6.3" overall.
**Stocks:** Checkered plastic.
**Sights:** Blade front, adjustable rear.
**Features:** Blue finish. Double action. Introduced 1990. Imported from China by China Sports, Inc.
**Price:** . . . . . . . . . . . . . . . . . . . . . . . . . . . . . . **NA**

Norinco 77B

## OLYMPIC ARMS OA-93 AR PISTOL
**Caliber:** 223, 20- or 30-shot, 7.62x39mm, 5- or 30-shot magazine.
**Barrel:** 6", 9", 14"; 4140 steel or 416 stainless.
**Weight:** 4 lbs. 15 oz. **Length:** 15.75" overall (6" barrel).
**Stocks:** A2 stowaway pistol grip.
**Sights:** Cut-off carrying handle with scope rail attached.
**Features:** AR-15 receiver with special bolt carrier; short slotted aluminum handguard; button-cut 4140 chrome moly or broach-cut stainless barrel, Vortex flash suppressor. Introduced 1993. Made in U.S. by Olympic Arms, Inc.
**Price:** . . . . . . . . . . . . . . . . . . . . . . . . . . . . . . **$952.00**

## MITCHELL ARMS SPORT-KING AUTO PISTOL
**Caliber:** 22 LR, 10-shot magazine.
**Barrel:** 4.5", 6.75".
**Weight:** 39 oz. (4.5" barrel).**Length:** 9" overall (4.5" barrel).
**Stocks:** Checkered black plastic.
**Sights:** Blade front, rear adjustable for windage.
**Features:** Military grip; standard trigger; push-button barrel takedown. All stainless steel. Announced 1992. From Mitchell Arms, Inc.
**Price:** . . . . . . . . . . . . . . . . . . . . . . . . . . . . . . **$299.00**

## MOUNTAIN EAGLE AUTO PISTOL
**Caliber:** 22 LR, 15-shot magazine.
**Barrel:** 6.5".
**Weight:** 21 oz. **Length:** 10.6" overall.
**Stocks:** One-piece impact-resistant polymer in "conventional contour"; checkered panels.
**Sights:** Serrated ramp front with interchangeable blades, rear adjustable for windage and elevation; interchangeable blades.
**Features:** Injection moulded grip frame, alloy receiver; hybrid composite barrel replicates shape of the Desert Eagle pistol. Flat, smooth trigger. Introduced 1992. From Magnum Research.
**Price:** . . . . . . . . . . . . . . . . . . . . . . . . . . . . . . **$239.00**

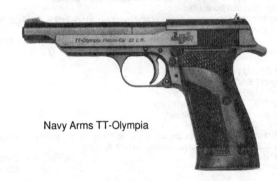

Navy Arms TT-Olympia

## NORINCO MODEL 77B AUTO PISTOL
**Caliber:** 9mm Para., 8-shot magazine.
**Barrel:** 5".
**Weight:** 34 oz. **Length:** 7.5" overall.
**Stocks:** Checkered wood.
**Sights:** Blade front, adjustable rear.
**Features:** Uses trigger guard cocking, gas-retarded recoil action. Front of trigger guard can be used to cock the action with the trigger finger. Introduced 1989. Imported from China by China Sports, Inc.
**Price:** . . . . . . . . . . . . . . . . . . . . . . . . . . . . . . **NA**

> Consult our Directory pages for the location of firms mentioned.

## NORINCO M93 SPORTSMAN AUTO PISTOL
**Caliber:** 22 LR, 10-shot magazine.
**Barrel:** 4.6".
**Weight:** 26 oz. **Length:** 8.6" overall.
**Stocks:** Checkered composition.
**Sights:** Blade front, rear adjustable for windage.
**Features:** All steel construction with blue finish, Introduced 1992. Imported from China by Interarms.
**Price:** . . . . . . . . . . . . . . . . . . . . . . . . . . . . . . **$238.00**

## NORINCO M1911A1 AUTO PISTOL
**Caliber:** 45 ACP, 7-shot magazine.
**Barrel:** 5".
**Weight:** 39 oz. **Length:** 8.5" overall.
**Stocks:** Checkered wood.
**Sights:** Blade front, rear adjustable for windage.
**Features:** Matte blue finish. Comes with two magazines. Imported from China by China Sports, Inc.
**Price:** . . . . . . . . . . . . . . . . . . . . . . . . . . . . . . **NA**

Para-Ordnance P12.45

## PARA-ORDNANCE P14.45 AUTO PISTOL
**Caliber:** 45 ACP, 13-shot magazine.
**Barrel:** 5".
**Weight:** 28 oz. (alloy frame). **Length:** 8.5" overall.
**Stocks:** Textured composition.
**Sights:** Blade front, rear adjustable for windage. High visibility three-dot system.
**Features:** Available with alloy, steel or stainless steel frame with black finish (silver or stainless gun). Steel and stainless steel frame guns weigh 38 oz. (P14.45), 35 oz. (P13.45), 33 oz. (P12.45). Grooved match trigger, rounded combat-style hammer. Double column, high-capacity magazine gives 14-shot total capacity (P14.45). Beveled magazine well. Manual thumb, grip and firing pin lock safeties. Solid barrel bushing. Introduced 1990. Made in Canada by Para-Ordnance.
**Price:** P14.45 . . . . . . . . . . . . . . . . . . . . . . . . . . . . . **$716.25**
**Price:** P12.45 (11-shot magazine, 3½" bbl., 24 oz., alloy) . . . . . **$650.00**
**Price:** P14.45E steel frame . . . . . . . . . . . . . . . . . . . . . **$716.25**
**Price:** P12.45E steel frame . . . . . . . . . . . . . . . . . . . . . **$708.75**

## PHOENIX ARMS MODEL RAVEN AUTO PISTOL
**Caliber:** 25 ACP, 6-shot magazine.
**Barrel:** 2⁷⁄₁₆".
**Weight:** 15 oz. **Length:** 4¾" overall.
**Stocks:** Smooth walnut, ivory-colored or black slotted plastic.
**Sights:** Ramped front, fixed rear.
**Features:** Available in blue, nickel or chrome finish. Made in U.S. Available from Phoenix Arms.
**Price:** . . . . . . . . . . . . . . . . . . . . . . . . . . . . . . . . . **$69.95**

## PSP-25 AUTO PISTOL
**Caliber:** 25 ACP, 6-shot magazine.
**Barrel:** 2⅛".
**Weight:** 9.5 oz. **Length:** 4⅛" overall.
**Stocks:** Checkered black plastic.
**Sights:** Fixed.
**Features:** All steel construction with polished finish. Introduced 1990. Made in the U.S. under F.N. license; distributed by K.B.I., Inc.
**Price:** Blue . . . . . . . . . . . . . . . . . . . . . . . . . . . . . . . **$249.00**
**Price:** Hard chrome . . . . . . . . . . . . . . . . . . . . . . . . . . **$329.99**

## ROCKY MOUNTAIN ARMS PATRIOT PISTOL
**Caliber:** 223, 5-, 20-, 30-shot magazine.
**Barrel:** 7", with Max Dynamic muzzle brake.
**Weight:** 6.5 lbs. **Length:** 21" overall.
**Stocks:** Black composition.
**Sights:** None furnished.
**Features:** Uses AR-type receiver with flat top for optical sight mount with Weaver-style bases. Finished in DuPont Teflon-S matte black or NATO green. Comes with black nylon case, one magazine. Introduced 1993. From Rocky Mountain Arms, Inc.
**Price:** . . . . . . . . . . . . . . . . . . . . . . . . . . . . . . . **$1,095.00**

## RUGER P89 AUTOMATIC PISTOL
**Caliber:** 9mm Para., 15-shot magazine.
**Barrel:** Weight: 32 oz. **Length:** 7.84" overall.
**Stocks:** Grooved black Xenoy composition.
**Sights:** Square post front, square notch rear adjustable for windage, both with white dot inserts.
**Features:** Double action with ambidextrous slide-mounted safety-levers. Slide is 4140 chrome moly steel or 400-series stainless steel, frame is a lightweight aluminum alloy. Ambidextrous magazine release. Blue or stainless steel. Introduced 1986; stainless introduced 1990.
**Price:** P89, blue, with extra magazine and magazine loading tool, plastic case . . . . . . . . . . . . . . . . . . . **$410.00**
**Price:** KP89, stainless, with extra magazine and magazine loading tool, plastic case . . . . . . . . . . . . . . . . . . . **$452.00**
**Price:** KP89X Convertible 30 Luger/9mm Para. . . . . . . . . . . . **$497.00**

### Ruger P89D Decocker Automatic Pistol
Similar to the standard P89 except has ambidextrous decocking levers in place of the regular slide-mounted safety. The decocking levers move the firing pin inside the slide where the hammer can not reach it, while simultaneously blocking the firing pin from forward movement—allows shooter to decock a cocked pistol without manipulating the trigger. Conventional thumb decocking procedures are therefore unnecessary. Blue or stainless steel. Introduced 1990.
**Price:** P89D, blue with extra magazine and loader, plastic case . . . **$410.00**
**Price:** KP89D, stainless, with extra magazine, plastic case . . . . . **$452.00**

Phoenix Arms Model Raven

## PHOENIX ARMS HP22, HP25 AUTO PISTOLS
**Caliber:** 22 LR, 11-shot (HP22), 25 ACP, 10-shot (HP25).
**Barrel:** 2⁷⁄₁₆".
**Weight:** 20 oz. **Length:** 5½" overall.
**Stocks:** Checkered composition.
**Sights:** Blade front, adjustable rear.
**Features:** Single action, exposed hammer; manual hold-open; button magazine release. Available in bright chrome, satin nickel, polished blue finish. Introduced 1993. Made in U.S. by Phoenix Arms.
**Price:** . . . . . . . . . . . . . . . . . . . . . . . . . . . . . . . . . **$99.95**

> Consult our Directory pages for the location of firms mentioned.

## ROCKY MOUNTAIN ARMS 1911A1-LH PISTOL
**Caliber:** 40 S&W, 45 ACP, 7-shot magazine.
**Barrel:** 5¼".
**Weight:** 37 0z. **Length:** 8¹³⁄₁₆" overall.
**Stocks:** Checkered walnut.
**Sights:** Red insert Patridge front, white outline rear click adjustable for windage and elevation.
**Features:** Fully left-handed pistol. Slide, frame, barrel made from stainless steel; working parts coated with Teflon-S. Single-stage trigger with 3½ lb. pull. Introduced 1993. Made in U.S. by Rocky Mountain Arms, Inc.
**Price:** . . . . . . . . . . . . . . . . . . . . . . . . . . . . . . . **$1,395.00**

Ruger KP89D

**CAUTION:** PRICES CHANGE, CHECK AT GUNSHOP.

## Ruger P89 Double-Action Only Automatic Pistol

Same as the KP89 except operates only in the double-action mode. Has a bobbed, spurless hammer, gripping grooves on each side of the rear of the slide; no external safety or decocking lever. An internal safety prevents forward movement of the firing pin unless the trigger is pulled. Available in 9mm Para., stainless steel only. Introduced 1991.

**Price:** With lockable case, extra magazine, magazine loading tool . **$452.00**

## Ruger P93 Compact Automatic Pistol

Similar to the P89 except has 3.9" barrel, 7.3" overall length, and weighs 31 oz. The forward third of the slide is tapered and polished to the muzzle. Front of the slide is crowned with a convex curve. Slide has seven finger grooves. Trigger guard bow is higher for better grip. Square post front sight, square notch rear drift adjustable for windage, both with white dot inserts. Slide is 400-series stainless steel, black-finished alloy frame. Available as decocker-only or double action-only. Introduced 1993.

**Price:** KP93DAO (double action only), KP93 (decocker) . . . . . . . **$452.00**

## RUGER P90 AUTOMATIC PISTOL

**Caliber:** 45 ACP, 7-shot magazine.
**Barrel:** 4.50".
**Weight:** 33.5 oz. **Length:** 7.87" overall.
**Stocks:** Grooved black Xenoy composition.
**Sights:** Square post front, square notch rear adjustable for windage, both with white dot inserts.
**Features:** Double action with ambidextrous slide-mounted safety-levers which move the firing pin inside the slide where the hammer can not reach it, while simultaneously blocking the firing pin from forward movement. Stainless steel only. Introduced 1991.

**Price:** KP90 with lockable case, extra magazine . . . . . . . . . . **$488.65**

## Ruger P90 Decocker Automatic Pistol

Similar to the P90 except has a manual decocking system. The ambidextrous decocking levers move the firing pin inside the slide where the hammer can not reach it, while simultaneously blocking the firing pin from forward move-ment—allows shooter to decock a cocked pistol without manipulating the trigger. Available only in stainless steel. Overall length 7.87", weight 34 oz. Introduced 1991.

**Price:** P90D with lockable case, extra magazine, and magazine loading tool . . . . . . . . . . . . . . . . . . . . . . . **$488.65**

## RUGER P91 DECOCKER AUTOMATIC PISTOL

**Caliber:** 40 S&W, 11-shot magazine.
**Barrel:** 4.50".
**Weight:** 33 oz. **Length:** 7.87" overall.
**Stocks:** Grooved black Xenoy composition.
**Sights:** Square post front, square notch rear adjustable for windage, both with white dot inserts.
**Features:** Ambidextrous slide-mounted decocking levers move the firing pin inside the slide where the hammer can not reach it while simultaneously blocking the firing pin from forward movement. Allows shooter to decock a cocked pistol without manipulating the trigger. Conventional thumb decocking procedures are therefore unnecessary. Stainless steel only. Introduced 1991.

**Price:** KP91D with lockable case, extra magazine, and magazine loading tool . . . . . . . . . . . . . . . . . . . . . . . . **$488.65**

Ruger 22/45 Mark II

## Ruger 22/45 Mark II Pistol

Similar to the other 22 Mark II autos except has grip frame of Zytel that matchs the angle and magazine latch of the Model 1911 45 ACP pistol. Available in 4¾" standard, 5¼" tapered and 5½" bull barrel. Introduced 1992.

**Price:** KP4 (4¾" barrel) . . . . . . . . . . . . . . . . **$280.00**
**Price:** KP514 (5¼" barrel) . . . . . . . . . . . . . . . . **$330.00**
**Price:** KP512 (5½" bull barrel) . . . . . . . . . . . . . . **$330.00**

Ruger KP90C

Ruger KP93DC

## Ruger P91 Double-Action-Only Automatic Pistol

Same as the KP91D except operates only in the double-action mode. Has a bobbed, spurless hammer, gripping grooves on each side at the rear of the slide, no external safety or decocking levers. An internal safety prevents forward movement of the firing pin unless the trigger is pulled. Available in 40 S&W, stainless steel only. Introduced 1992.

**Price:** KP91DAO with lockable case, extra magazine, and magazine loading tool . . . . . . . . . . . . . . . . . . . . . . . **$488.65**

## RUGER MARK II STANDARD AUTO PISTOL

**Caliber:** 22 LR, 10-shot magazine.
**Barrel:** 4¾" or 6".
**Weight:** 36 oz. (4¾" bbl.). **Length:** 8⁵⁄₁₆" (4¾" bbl.).
**Stocks:** Checkered plastic.
**Sights:** Fixed, wide blade front, square notch rear adjustable for windage.
**Features:** Updated design of the original Standard Auto. Has new bolt hold-open latch. 10-shot magazine, magazine catch, safety, trigger and new receiver contours. Introduced 1982.

**Price:** Blued (MK 4, MK 6) . . . . . . . . . . . . . . . . . . . **$252.00**
**Price:** In stainless steel (KMK 4, KMK 6) . . . . . . . . . . . . . **$330.25**

## SAFARI ARMS CREST SERIES PISTOLS

**Caliber:** 9mm Para., 38 Super, 45 ACP, 7-shot magazine (standard), 6-shot (4-Star).
**Barrel:** 5" (standard), 4.5" (4-Star); 416 stainless steel.
**Weight:** 39 oz. (standard), 35.7 oz. (4-Star). **Length:** 8.5" overall (standard).
**Stocks:** Checkered walnut.
**Sights:** Ramped blade front, fully adjustable rear.
**Features:** Right- or left-hand models available. Long aluminum trigger, long recoil spring guide, extended safety and slide stop. Stainless steel. Introduced 1993. Made in U.S. by Safari Arms, Inc.

**Price:** Right-hand, standard . . . . . . . . . . . . . . . . **$740.00**
**Price:** Left-hand, standard . . . . . . . . . . . . . . . . . **$880.00**
**Price:** Right-hand, 4-Star . . . . . . . . . . . . . . . . . . **$770.00**
**Price:** Left-hand, 4-Star . . . . . . . . . . . . . . . . . . . **$910.00**

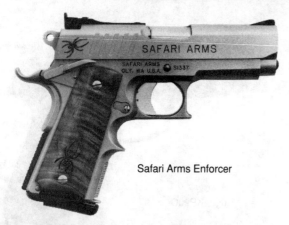

Safari Arms Enforcer

## SEECAMP LWS 32 STAINLESS DA AUTO
**Caliber:** 32 ACP Win. Silvertip, 6-shot magazine.
**Barrel:** 2", integral with frame.
**Weight:** 10.5 oz. **Length:** 4⅛" overall.
**Stocks:** Glass-filled nylon.
**Sights:** Smooth, no-snag, contoured slide and barrel top.
**Features:** Aircraft quality 17-4 PH stainless steel. Inertia-operated firing pin. Hammer fired double-action only. Hammer automatically follows slide down to safety rest position after each shot—no manual safety needed. Magazine safety disconnector. Polished stainless. Introduced 1985. From L.W. Seecamp.
**Price:** . . . . . . . . . . . . . . . . . . . . . . . . . . . $375.00

## SIG P-210-2 AUTO PISTOL
**Caliber:** 7.65mm or 9mm Para., 8-shot magazine.
**Barrel:** 4¾".
**Weight:** 31¾ oz. (9mm). **Length:** 8½" overall.
**Stocks:** Checkered black composition.
**Sights:** Blade front, rear adjustable for windage.
**Features:** Lanyard loop; matte finish. Conversion unit for 22 LR available. Imported from Switzerland by Mandall Shooting Supplies.
**Price:** P-210-2 Service Pistol . . . . . . . . . . . $3,000.00

## SIG SAUER P220 "AMERICAN" AUTO PISTOL
**Caliber:** 9mm, 38 Super, 45 ACP, (9-shot in 9mm and 38 Super, 7 in 45).
**Barrel:** 4⅜".
**Weight:** 28¼ oz. (9mm). **Length:** 7¾" overall.
**Stocks:** Checkered black plastic.
**Sights:** Blade front, drift adjustable rear for windage.
**Features:** Double action. De-cocking lever permits lowering hammer onto locked firing pin. Squared combat-type trigger guard. Slide stays open after last shot. Imported from Germany by SIGARMS, Inc.
**Price:** "American," blue (side-button magazine release, 45 ACP only) $780.00
**Price:** 45 ACP, blue, Siglite night sights . . . . . . . . . $880.00
**Price:** K-Kote finish . . . . . . . . . . . . . . . . . . $850.00
**Price:** K-Kote, Siglite night sights . . . . . . . . . . . $950.00

## SIG SAUER P225 DA AUTO PISTOL
**Caliber:** 9mm Para., 8-shot magazine.
**Barrel:** 3.8".
**Weight:** 26 oz. **Length:** 7³⁄₃₂" overall.
**Stocks:** Checkered black plastic.
**Sights:** Blade front, rear adjustable for windage. Optional Siglite night sights.
**Features:** Double action. De-cocking lever permits lowering hammer onto locked firing pin. Square combat-type trigger guard. Shortened, lightened version of P220. Imported from Germany by SIGARMS, Inc.
**Price:** . . . . . . . . . . . . . . . . . . . . . . . . . $775.00
**Price:** With Siglite night sights . . . . . . . . . . . . $875.00
**Price:** K-Kote finish . . . . . . . . . . . . . . . . . . $845.00
**Price:** K-Kote with Siglite night sights . . . . . . . . $945.00

## SIG SAUER P230 DA AUTO PISTOL
**Caliber:** 32 ACP, 8-shot; 380 ACP, 7-shot.
**Barrel:** 3¾".
**Weight:** 16 oz. **Length:** 6½" overall.
**Stocks:** Checkered black plastic.
**Sights:** Blade front, rear adjustable for windage.
**Features:** Double action. Same basic action design as P220. Blowback operation, stationary barrel. Introduced 1977. Imported from Germany by SIGARMS, Inc.
**Price:** Blue . . . . . . . . . . . . . . . . . . . . . . . $510.00
**Price:** In stainless steel (P230 SL) . . . . . . . . . . . $595.00

## SAFARI ARMS ENFORCER PISTOL
**Caliber:** 45 ACP, 6-shot magazine.
**Barrel:** 3.8".
**Weight:** 36 oz. **Length:** 7.5" overall.
**Stocks:** Smooth walnut with etched black widow spider logo.
**Sights:** Ramped blade front, rear adjustable for windage and elevation.
**Features:** Extended safety, extended slide release; Commander-style hammer; beavertail grip safety; throated, ported, tuned, with cone-shaped barrel, no bushing. Parkerized matte black or satin stainless steel. From Safari Arms, Inc.
**Price:** . . . . . . . . . . . . . . . . . . . . . . . . . $690.00

## Safari Arms Enforcer Carrycomp II Pistol
Similar to the Enforcer except has Wil Schueman-designed hybrid compensator system. Introduced 1993. Made in U.S. by Safari Arms, Inc.
**Price:** . . . . . . . . . . . . . . . . . . . . . . . . $1,010.00

## SAFARI ARMS G.I. SAFARI PISTOL
**Caliber:** 45 ACP, 7-shot magazine.
**Barrel:** 5".
**Weight:** 39.9 oz. **Length:** 8.5" overall.
**Stocks:** Checkered walnut.
**Sights:** Blade front, fixed rear.
**Features:** Beavertail grip safety, extended safety and slide release, Commander-style hammer. Barrel is chrome-lined 4140 steel; National Match 416 stainless optional. Parkerized matte black finish. Introduced 1991. Made in U.S. by Safari Arms, Inc.
**Price:** . . . . . . . . . . . . . . . . . . . . . . . . . $430.00

## SIG P-210-6 AUTO PISTOL
**Caliber:** 9mm Para., 8-shot magazine.
**Barrel:** 4¾".
**Weight:** 36.2 oz. **Length:** 8½" overall.
**Stocks:** Checkered black plastic; walnut optional.
**Sights:** Blade front, micro. adjustable rear for windage and elevation.
**Features:** Adjustable trigger stop; target trigger; ribbed frontstrap; sandblasted finish. Conversion unit for 22 LR consists of barrel, recoil spring, slide and magazine. Imported from Switzerland by Mandall Shooting Supplies.
**Price:** P-210-6 . . . . . . . . . . . . . . . . . . . . $3,200.00
**Price:** P-210-5 Target . . . . . . . . . . . . . . . . . $3,500.00

SIG Sauer P220 "American"

SIG Sauer P230

**CAUTION:** PRICES CHANGE, CHECK AT GUNSHOP.

SIG Sauer P228

## SIG Sauer P229 DA Auto Pistol

Similar to the P228 except chambered for 40 S&W with 12-shot magazine. Has 3.86" barrel, 7.08" overall length and 3.35" height. Weight is 30.5 oz. Introduced 1991. Imported from Germany by SIGARMS, Inc.

**Price:** Blue . . . . . . . . . . . . . . . . . . . . . . . . . . . . . . . . . **$875.00**
**Price:** Blue, double-action only . . . . . . . . . . . . . . . . . . . **$875.00**

## SMITH & WESSON MODEL .356 TSW LIMITED PISTOL

**Caliber:** 356 TSW, 15-shot magazine.
**Barrel:** 5".
**Weight:** 44 oz. **Length:** 8.5" overall.
**Stocks:** Checkered black composition.
**Sights:** Blade front drift adjustable for windage, fully adjustable Bo-Mar rear.
**Features:** Single action trigger. Stainless steel frame and slide, hand-fitted titanium-coated stainless steel bushing, match grade barrel. Extended magazine well and oversize release; magazine pads; extended safety. Checkered front strap. Introduced 1993. Available from Lew Horton Dist.

**Price:** About . . . . . . . . . . . . . . . . . . . . . . . . . . . . . . $1,300.00

## Smith & Wesson Model .356 TSW Compact Pistol

Similar to the .356 TSW Limited except has 3½" barrel, 12-shot magazine, Novak LoMount combat sights. Overall length 7", weight 37 oz. Introduced 1993. Available from Lew Horton Dist.

**Price:** . . . . . . . . . . . . . . . . . . . . . . . . . . . . . . . . . . . . **NA**

## SMITH & WESSON MODEL 915 DA AUTO PISTOL

**Caliber:** 9mm Para., 15-shot magazine.
**Barrel:** 4".
**Weight:** 28.5 oz. **Length:** 7.5" overall.
**Stocks:** One-piece Xenoy, wraparound with straight backstrap.
**Sights:** Post front with white dot, fixed rear.
**Features:** Alloy frame, blue carbon steel slide. Slide-mounted decocking lever. Introduced 1992.

**Price:** . . . . . . . . . . . . . . . . . . . . . . . . . . . . . . . . . . **$467.00**

## SMITH & WESSON MODEL 422, 622 AUTO

**Caliber:** 22 LR, 10-shot magazine.
**Barrel:** 4½", 6".
**Weight:** 22 oz. (4½" bbl.). **Length:** 7½" overall (4½" bbl.).
**Stocks:** Checkered plastic (Field), checkered walnut (Target).
**Sights:** Field—serrated ramp front, fixed rear; Target—Patridge front, adjustable rear.
**Features:** Aluminum frame, steel slide, brushed blue finish; internal hammer. Introduced 1987. Model 2206 introduced 1990.

**Price:** Blue, 4½", 6", fixed sight . . . . . . . . . . . . . . . . . **$225.00**
**Price:** As above, adjustable sight . . . . . . . . . . . . . . . . **$278.00**
**Price:** Stainless (Model 622), 4½", 6", fixed sight . . . . . . . . . . **$272.00**
**Price:** As above, adjustable sight . . . . . . . . . . . . . . . . **$324.00**

## Smith & Wesson Model 2214 Sportsman Auto

Similar to the Model 422 except has 3" barrel, 8-shot magazine; dovetail Patridge front sight with white dot, fixed rear with two white dots; matte blue finish, black composition grips with checkered panels. Overall length 6⅛", weight 18 oz. Introduced 1990.

**Price:** . . . . . . . . . . . . . . . . . . . . . . . . . . . . . . . . . . **$258.00**

## SIG Sauer P226 DA Auto Pistol

Similar to the P220 pistol except has 15-shot magazine, 4.4" barrel, and weighs 26½ oz. 9mm only. Imported from Germany by SIGARMS, Inc.

**Price:** Blue . . . . . . . . . . . . . . . . . . . . . . . . . . . . . . . . **$805.00**
**Price:** With Siglite night sights . . . . . . . . . . . . . . . . . **$905.00**
**Price:** Blue, double-action only . . . . . . . . . . . . . . . . . **$805.00**
**Price:** Blue, double-action only, Siglite night sights . . . . . **$905.00**
**Price:** K-Kote finish . . . . . . . . . . . . . . . . . . . . . . . . . **$875.00**
**Price:** K-Kote, Siglite night sights . . . . . . . . . . . . . . . . **$975.00**
**Price:** K-Kote, double-action only . . . . . . . . . . . . . . . . **$875.00**
**Price:** K-Kote, double-action only, Siglite night sights . . . . . . . **$975.00**

## SIG Sauer P228 DA Auto Pistol

Similar to the P226 except has 3.86" barrel, with 7.08" overall length and 3.35" height. Chambered for 9mm Para. only, 13-shot magazine. Weight is 29.1 oz. with empty magazine. Introduced 1989. Imported from Germany by SIGARMS, Inc.

**Price:** Blue . . . . . . . . . . . . . . . . . . . . . . . . . . . . . . . . **$805.00**
**Price:** Blue, with Siglite night sights . . . . . . . . . . . . . . . **$905.00**
**Price:** Blue, double-action only . . . . . . . . . . . . . . . . . . **$805.00**
**Price:** Blue, double-action only, Siglite night sights . . . . . **$905.00**
**Price:** K-Kote finish . . . . . . . . . . . . . . . . . . . . . . . . . **$875.00**
**Price:** K-Kote, Siglite night sights . . . . . . . . . . . . . . . . **$975.00**
**Price:** K-Kote, double-action only . . . . . . . . . . . . . . . . **$875.00**
**Price:** K-Kote, double-action only, Siglite night sights . . . . . . . **$975.00**

Smith & Wesson .356 TSW

Smith & Wesson Model 915

Smith & Wesson Model 2214

## Smith & Wesson Model 2206 Auto

Similar to the Model 422/622 except made entirely of stainless steel with non-reflective finish. Weight is 35 oz. with 4½" barrel, 39 oz. with 6" barrel. Other specs are the same. Introduced 1990.

**Price:** With fixed sight . . . . . . . . . . . . . . . . . . . . . $314.00
**Price:** With adjustable sight . . . . . . . . . . . . . . . . . $370.00

## SMITH & WESSON MODEL 3913/3914 DOUBLE ACTIONS

**Caliber:** 9mm Para., 8-shot magazine.
**Barrel:** 3½".
**Weight:** 26 oz. **Length:** 6¹³⁄₁₆" overall.
**Stocks:** One-piece Delrin wraparound, textured surface.
**Sights:** Post front with white dot, Novak LoMount Carry with two dots, adjustable for windage.
**Features:** Aluminum alloy frame, stainless slide (M3913) or blue steel slide (M3914). Bobbed hammer with no half-cock notch; smooth .304" trigger with rounded edges. Straight backstrap. Extra magazine included. Introduced 1989.

**Price:** Model 3913 . . . . . . . . . . . . . . . . . . . . . $597.00
**Price:** Model 3914 . . . . . . . . . . . . . . . . . . . . . $539.00

Smith & Wesson 3913 LadySmith

## Smith & Wesson Model 3953DA Pistol

Same as the Models 3913/3914 except double-action only. Model 3953 has stainless slide with alloy frame. Overall length 7"; weight 25.5 oz. Extra magazine included. Introduced 1990.

**Price:** . . . . . . . . . . . . . . . . . . . . . . . . . . . . $597.00

## Smith & Wesson Model 3913-NL Pistol

Same as the 3913/3914 LadySmith autos except without the LadySmith logo and it has a slightly modified frame design. Right-hand safety only. Has stainless slide on alloy frame; extra magazine included. Introduced 1990.

**Price:** . . . . . . . . . . . . . . . . . . . . . . . . . . . . $597.00

## Smith & Wesson Model 3913 LadySmith Auto

Similar to the standard Model 3913/3914 except has frame that is upswept at the front, rounded trigger guard. Comes in frosted stainless steel with matching gray grips. Grips are ergonomically correct for a woman's hand. Novak LoMount Carry rear sight adjustable for windage, smooth edges for snag resistance. Extra magazine included. Introduced 1990.

**Price:** . . . . . . . . . . . . . . . . . . . . . . . . . . . . $615.00

## SMITH & WESSON MODEL 4006 DA AUTO

**Caliber:** 40 S&W, 11-shot magazine.
**Barrel:** 4".
**Weight:** 36 oz. **Length:** 7½" overall.
**Stocks:** Xenoy wraparound with checkered panels.
**Sights:** Replaceable post front with white dot, Novak LoMount Carry fixed rear with two white dots, or micro. click adjustable rear with two white dots.
**Features:** Stainless steel construction with non-reflective finish. Straight backstrap. Extra magazine included. Introduced 1990.

**Price:** With adjustable sights . . . . . . . . . . . . . . . $743.00
**Price:** With fixed sight . . . . . . . . . . . . . . . . . . . $715.00
**Price:** With fixed night sights . . . . . . . . . . . . . . . $820.00

Smith & Wesson Model 4006

## Smith & Wesson Model 4046 DA Pistol

Similar to the Model 4006 except is double-action only. Has a semi-bobbed hammer, smooth trigger, 4" barrel; Novak LoMount Carry rear sight, post front with white dot. Overall length is 7½", weight 39 oz. Extra magazine included. Introduced 1991.

**Price:** . . . . . . . . . . . . . . . . . . . . . . . . . . . . $715.00
**Price:** With fixed night sights . . . . . . . . . . . . . . . $820.00

## SMITH & WESSON MODEL 4013/4014, 4053 AUTOS

**Caliber:** 40 S&W, 7-shot magazine.
**Barrel:** 3½".
**Weight:** 26 oz. **Length:** 7" overall.
**Stocks:** One-piece Xenoy wraparound with straight backstrap.
**Sights:** Post front with white dot, fixed Novak LoMount Carry rear with two white dots.
**Features:** Models 4013/4014 are traditional double action; Model 4053 is double-action only; Models 4013, 4053 have stainless slide on alloy frame; 4014 has blued steel slide. Introduced 1991.

**Price:** Models 4013, 4053 . . . . . . . . . . . . . . . . . $693.00
**Price:** Model 4014 . . . . . . . . . . . . . . . . . . . . . $635.00

Smith & Wesson Model 4506

## SMITH & WESSON MODEL 4026 DA AUTO

**Caliber:** 40 S&W, 11-shot magazine.
**Barrel:** 4".
**Weight:** 39 oz. **Length:** 7.5" overall.
**Stocks:** Xenoy one-piece wraparound.
**Sights:** Post front with white dot, Novak LoMount Carry rear with two white dots.
**Features:** Stainless steel. Has spring-loaded, frame-mounted decocking lever, magazine disconnector safety and firing pin safety. Matte finish. Bobbed hammer, smooth trigger. Introduced 1992.

**Price:** . . . . . . . . . . . . . . . . . . . . . . . . . . . . $731.00

## SMITH & WESSON MODEL 4500 SERIES AUTOS

**Caliber:** 45 ACP, 8-shot magazine (M4506, 4566/4586).
**Barrel:** 5" (M4506).
**Weight:** 41 oz. (4506). **Length:** 7⅛" overall (4516).
**Stocks:** Delrin one-piece wraparound, arched or straight backstrap on M4506, straight only on M4516.
**Sights:** Post front with white dot, adjustable or fixed Novak LoMount Carry on M4506.
**Features:** M4506 has serrated hammer spur. Extra magazine included. Contact Smith & Wesson for complete data. Introduced 1989.

**Price:** Model 4506, fixed sight . . . . . . . . . . . . . . $742.00
**Price:** Model 4506, adjustable sight . . . . . . . . . . . $773.00
**Price:** Model 4566 (stainless, 4¼", traditional DA, ambidextrous safety) . . . . . . . . . . . . . . . . . $742.00
**Price:** Model 4586 (stainless, 4¼", DA only) . . . . . . . . . . $742.00

**CAUTION:** PRICES CHANGE, CHECK AT GUNSHOP.

### Smith & Wesson Model 1006 Double-Action Auto

Similar to the Model 4506 except chambered for 10mm auto with 9-shot magazine. Available with either Novak LoMount Carry fixed rear sight with two white dots or adjustable micrometer-click rear with two white dots. All stainless steel construction; one-piece Delrin stocks with straight backstrap; curved backstrap available as option. Has 5" barrel, 8½" overall length, weighs 38 oz. with fixed sight. Rounded trigger guard with knurling. Extra magazine included. Introduced 1990.

**Price:** With fixed sight . . . . . . . . . . . . . . . . . . . . **$769.00**
**Price:** With adjustable sight . . . . . . . . . . . . . . . . . **$796.00**

### Smith & Wesson Model 1076 Auto

Same as the Model 1006 except has frame-mounted decocking lever, fixed sight only; traditional double-action mechanism. Extra magazine included. Introduced 1990.

**Price:** . . . . . . . . . . . . . . . . . . . . . . . . . . . . . **$778.00**

### SMITH & WESSON MODEL 5900 SERIES AUTO PISTOLS

**Caliber:** 9mm Para., 15-shot magazine.
**Barrel:** 4".
**Weight:** 28½ to 37½ oz. (fixed sight); 29 to 38 oz. (adj. sight). **Length:** 7½" overall.
**Stocks:** Xenoy wraparound with curved backstrap.
**Sights:** Post front with white dot, fixed or fully adjustable with two white dots.
**Features:** All stainless, stainless and alloy or carbon steel and alloy construction. Smooth .304" trigger, .260" serrated hammer. Extra magazine included. Introduced 1989.

**Price:** Model 5903 (stainless, alloy frame, traditional DA, adjustable sight, ambidextrous safety) . . . . . . . . . . . . . . . . . . . . . **$693.00**
**Price:** As above, fixed sight . . . . . . . . . . . . . . . . . **$662.00**
**Price:** Model 5904 (blue, alloy frame, traditional DA, adjustable sight, ambidextrous safety) . . . . . . . . . . . . . . . . . . . . . **$645.00**
**Price:** As above, fixed sight . . . . . . . . . . . . . . . . . **$616.00**
**Price:** Model 5906 (stainless, traditional DA, adjustable sight, ambidextrous safety) . . . . . . . . . . . . . . . . . . . . . . . . . **$711.00**
**Price:** As above, fixed sight . . . . . . . . . . . . . . . . . **$679.00**
**Price:** With fixed night sights . . . . . . . . . . . . . . . . **$784.00**
**Price:** Model 5946 (as above, stainless frame and slide) . . . . . **$679.00**

### Smith & Wesson Model 6904/6906 Double-Action Autos

Similar to the Models 5904/5906 except with 3½" barrel, 12-shot magazine (20-shot available), fixed rear sight, .260" bobbed hammer. Extra magazine included. Introduced 1989.

**Price:** Model 6904, blue . . . . . . . . . . . . . . . . . . . **$590.00**
**Price:** Model 6906, stainless . . . . . . . . . . . . . . . . . **$650.00**
**Price:** Model 6946 (stainless, DA only, fixed sights) . . . . . . . **$650.00**
**Price:** With fixed night sights . . . . . . . . . . . . . . . . **$756.00**

> Consult our Directory pages for the location of firms mentioned.

### SPHINX AT-380M AUTO PISTOL

**Caliber:** 380 ACP, 10-shot magazine.
**Barrel:** 3.27".
**Weight:** 25 oz. **Length:** 6.03" overall.
**Stocks:** Checkered plastic.
**Sights:** Fixed.
**Features:** Double-action-only mechanism, Chamber loaded indicator; ambidextrous magazine release and slide latch. Blued slide, bright Palladium frame, or bright Palladium overall. Introduced 1993. Imported from Switzerland by Sile Distributors, Inc.

**Price:** Two-tone . . . . . . . . . . . . . . . . . . . . . . . **$571.95**
**Price:** Palladium finish . . . . . . . . . . . . . . . . . . . . **$629.95**

### SPHINX AT-2000S DOUBLE-ACTION PISTOL

**Caliber:** 9mm Para., 9x21mm, 15-shot, 40 S&W, 11-shot magazine.
**Barrel:** 4.53".
**Weight:** 36.3 oz. **Length:** 8.03" overall.
**Stocks:** Checkered neoprene.
**Sights:** Fixed, three-dot system.
**Features:** Double-action mechanism changeable to double-action-only. Stainless frame, blued slide. Ambidextrous safety, magazine release, slide latch. Introduced 1993. Imported from Switzerland by Sile Distributors, Inc.

**Price:** 9mm, two-tone . . . . . . . . . . . . . . . . . . . . **$902.95**
**Price:** 9mm, Palladium finish . . . . . . . . . . . . . . . . **$989.95**
**Price:** 40 S&W, two-tone . . . . . . . . . . . . . . . . . . . **$911.95**
**Price:** 40 S&W, Palladium finish . . . . . . . . . . . . . . . **$998.95**

Smith & Wesson Model 1006

Smith & Wesson Model 6904

Sphinx AT-380M

Sphinx AT-2000S

**CAUTION:** PRICES CHANGE, CHECK AT GUNSHOP.

## Sphinx AT-2000H Auto Pistol

Similar to the AT-2000P except has shorter slide with 3.54" barrel, shorter frame, 10-shot magazine, with 7" overall length. Weight is 32.2 oz. Stainless frame with blued slide, or overall bright Palladium finish. Introduced 1993. Imported from Switzerland by Sile Distributors, Inc.

Price: 9mm, two-tone . . . . . . . . . . . . . . . . . . . $858.95
Price: 9mm, Palladium finish . . . . . . . . . . . . . . . . . $945.95
Price: 40 S&W, two-tone . . . . . . . . . . . . . . . . . $867.95
Price: 40 S&W, Palladium . . . . . . . . . . . . . . . . . $954.95

## Sphinx AT-2000P, AT-2000PS Auto Pistols

Same as the AT-2000S except AT-2000P has shortened frame (13-shot magazine), 3.74" barrel, 7.25" overall length, and weighs 34 oz. Model AT-2000PS has full-size frame. Both have stainless frame with blued slide or bright Palladium finish. Introduced 1993. Imported from Switzerland by Sile Distributors, Inc.

Price: 9mm, two-tone . . . . . . . . . . . . . . . . . . . $858.95
Price: 9mm, Palladium finish . . . . . . . . . . . . . . . . . $945.95
Price: 40 S&W, two-tone . . . . . . . . . . . . . . . . . $867.95
Price: 40 S&W, Palladium finish . . . . . . . . . . . . . $954.95

## SPORTARMS TOKAREV MODEL 213

Caliber: 9mm Para., 8-shot magazine.
Barrel: 4.5".
Weight: 31 oz. Length: 7.6" overall.
Stocks: Grooved plastic.
Sights: Fixed.
Features: Blue finish, hard chrome optional. 9mm version of the famous Russian Tokarev pistol. Made in China by Norinco. Imported by Sportarms of Florida. Introduced 1988.

Price: Blue, about . . . . . . . . . . . . . . . . . . . $150.00
Price: Hard chrome, about . . . . . . . . . . . . . . . $179.00

## SPRINGFIELD INC. 1911A1 AUTO PISTOL

Caliber: 9mm Para., 9-shot; 38 Super, 10-shot; 45 ACP, 8-shot.
Barrel: 5".
Weight: 35.06 oz. Length: 8.59" overall.
Stocks: Checkered walnut.
Sights: Fixed low-profile combat-style.
Features: Beveled magazine well. All forged parts, including frame, barrel, slide. All new production. Introduced 1990. From Springfield Inc.

Price: Basic, 45 ACP, Parkerized . . . . . . . . . . . . . $449.00
Price: Standard, 45 ACP, blued . . . . . . . . . . . . . . $489.00
Price: Basic, 45 ACP, stainless . . . . . . . . . . . . . . $532.00

## Springfield Inc. 1911A1 Custom Carry Gun

Similar to the standard 1911A1 except has fixed three-dot low profile sights, Videki speed trigger, match barrel and bushing; extended thumb safety, beavertail grip safety; beveled, polished magazine well, polished feed ramp and throated barrel; match Commander hammer and sear, tuned extractor; lowered and flared ejection port; Shok Buff, full-length spring guide rod; walnut grips. Comes with two magazines with slam pads, plastic carrying case. Available in 45 ACP only. Introduced 1992. From Springfield Inc.

Price: . . . . . . . . . . . . . . . . . . . . . . . . . P.O.R.

Springfield Inc. 1911A1 Factory Comp

## STALLARD JS-9MM AUTO PISTOL

Caliber: 9mm Para., 8-shot magazine.
Barrel: 4.5".
Weight: 41 oz. Length: 7.72" overall.
Stocks: Textured acetal plastic.
Sights: Fixed, low profile.
Features: Single-action design. Scratch-resistant, non-glare blue finish. Introduced 1990. From MKS Supply, Inc.

Price: Matte black . . . . . . . . . . . . . . . . . . . $139.95
Price: Brushed nickel . . . . . . . . . . . . . . . . . $149.95

Sphinx AT-2000H

Springfield Inc. 1911A1

## Springfield Inc. 1911A1 High Capacity Pistol

Similar to the Standard 1911A1 except available in 45 ACP and 9x21mm with 10-shot magazine (45 ACP), 16-shot magazine (9x21mm). Has Commander-style hammer, walnut grips, ambidextrous thumb safety, beveled magazine well, plastic carrying case. Blue finish only. Introduced 1993. From Springfield, Inc.

Price: 45 ACP . . . . . . . . . . . . . . . . . . . . . $799.00
Price: 9x21mm . . . . . . . . . . . . . . . . . . . . . $879.00
Price: 45 ACP Factory Comp$999.00

## Springfield Inc. 1911A1 Factory Comp

Similar to the standard 1911A1 except comes with bushing-type dual-port compensator, adjustable rear sight, extended thumb safety, Videki speed trigger, and beveled magazine well. Checkered walnut grips standard. Available in 38 Super or 45 ACP, blue only. Introduced 1992.

Price: 38 Super . . . . . . . . . . . . . . . . . . . . $899.00
Price: 45 ACP . . . . . . . . . . . . . . . . . . . . . $869.00

## Springfield Inc. 1911A1 Champion Pistol

Similar to the standard 1911A1 except slide and barrel are ½" shorter. Has low-profile three-dot sight system. Comes with Commander hammer and walnut stocks. Available in 45 ACP only; blue or stainless. Introduced 1989.

Price: Blue . . . . . . . . . . . . . . . . . . . . . . $513.00
Price: Stainless . . . . . . . . . . . . . . . . . . . . $558.00
Price: Blue, comp . . . . . . . . . . . . . . . . . . . $829.00

## Springfield Inc. Product Improved 1911A1 Defender Pistol

Similar to the 1911A1 Champion except has tapered cone dual-port compensator system, rubberized grips. Has reverse recoil plug, full-length recoil spring guide, serrated frontstrap, extended thumb safety, Commander-style hammer with modified grip safety to match and a Videki speed trigger. Bi-Tone finish. Introduced 1991.

Price: 45 ACP . . . . . . . . . . . . . . . . . . . . . $959.00

## Springfield Inc. 1911A1 Compact Pistol

Similar to the Champion model except has a shortened slide with 4.025" barrel, 7.75" overall length. Magazine capacity is 7 shots. Has Commander hammer, checkered walnut grips. Available in 45 ACP only. Introduced 1989.

Price: Blued . . . . . . . . . . . . . . . . . . . . . . $509.00
Price: Bi-Tone (blue slide, stainless frame) . . . . . . . . . . $829.00
Price: Stainless . . . . . . . . . . . . . . . . . . . . $558.00

**CAUTION:** PRICES CHANGE, CHECK AT GUNSHOP.

## STAR FIRESTAR AUTO PISTOL
**Caliber:** 9mm Para., 7-shot; 40 S&W, 6-shot.
**Barrel:** 3.39".
**Weight:** 30.35 oz. **Length:** 6.5" overall.
**Stocks:** Checkered rubber.
**Sights:** Blade front, fully adjustable rear; three-dot system.
**Features:** Low-profile, combat-style sights; ambidextrous safety. Available in blue or weather-resistant Starvel finish. Introduced 1990. Imported from Spain by Interarms.
**Price:** Blue, 9mm . . . . . . . . . . . . . . . . . . . . . . **$460.00**
**Price:** Starvel finish 9mm . . . . . . . . . . . . . . . . . **$492.00**
**Price:** Blue, 40 S&W . . . . . . . . . . . . . . . . . . . . **$488.00**
**Price:** Starvel finish, 40 S&W . . . . . . . . . . . . . . **$517.00**

### Star Firestar M45 Auto Pistol
Similar to the standard Firestar except chambered for 45 ACP with 6-shot magazine. Has 3.6" barrel, weighs 35 oz., 6.85" overall length. Reverse-taper Acculine barrel. Introduced 1992. Imported from Spain by Interarms.
**Price:** Blue . . . . . . . . . . . . . . . . . . . . . . . . . . **$525.00**
**Price:** Starvel finish . . . . . . . . . . . . . . . . . . . . . **$553.00**

## STAR MEGASTAR 45 ACP AUTO PISTOL
**Caliber:** 10mm, 45 ACP, 12-shot magazine.
**Barrel:** 4.6".
**Weight:** 47.6 oz. **Length:** 8.44" overall.
**Stocks:** Checkered composition.
**Sights:** Blade front, adjustable rear.
**Features:** Double-action mechanism; steel frame and slide; reverse-taper Acculine barrel. Introduced 1992. Imported from Spain by Interarms.
**Price:** Blue, 10mm . . . . . . . . . . . . . . . . . . . . . **$693.00**
**Price:** Starvel finish, 10mm . . . . . . . . . . . . . . . . **$725.00**
**Price:** Blue, 45 ACP . . . . . . . . . . . . . . . . . . . . . **$693.00**
**Price:** Starvel finish, 45 ACP . . . . . . . . . . . . . . . **$725.00**

## STAR MODEL 31P & 31PK DOUBLE-ACTION PISTOLS
**Caliber:** 9mm Para., 15-shot magazine.
**Barrel:** 3.86".
**Weight:** 30 oz. **Length:** 7.6" overall.
**Stocks:** Checkered black plastic.
**Sights:** Square blade front, square notch rear click-adjustable for windage and elevation.
**Features:** Double or single action; grooved front- and backstraps and trigger guard face; ambidextrous safety cams firing pin forward; removable backstrap houses the firing mechanism. Model 31P has steel frame; Model PK is alloy. Introduced 1984. Imported from Spain by Interarms.
**Price:** Model 31P, 40 S&W, blue, steel frame . . . . . . . . . **$643.00**
**Price:** Model 31P, 40 S&W, Starvel finish, steel frame . . . **$675.00**
**Price:** Model 31P, 9mm, blue, steel frame, . . . . . . . . . **$580.00**
**Price:** Model 31P, 9mm, Starvel finish, steel frame . . . . **$612.00**
**Price:** Model 31PK, 9mm only, blue, alloy frame . . . . . . . **$580.00**

## STEYR SSP SEMI-AUTOMATIC PISTOL
**Caliber:** 9mm Para., 15- or 30-shot magazine.
**Barrel:** 5.9".
**Weight:** 42 oz. **Length:** 12.75" overall.
**Stocks:** Grooved synthetic.
**Sights:** Post front adjustable for elevation, open rear adjustable for windage.
**Features:** Delayed blowback, rotating barrel operating system. Synthetic upper and lower receivers. Drop and cross-bolt safeties. Rail mount for optics. Introduced 1993. Imported from Austria by GSI, Inc.
**Price:** . . . . . . . . . . . . . . . . . . . . . . . . . . . . . **$895.00**

Star Firestar

Star Model 31P

Steyr SSP

Sundance BOA

## SUNDANCE BOA AUTO PISTOL
**Caliber:** 25 ACP, 7-shot magazine.
**Barrel:** 2½".
**Weight:** 16 oz. **Length:** 4⅞".
**Stocks:** Grooved ABS or smooth simulated pearl; optional pink.
**Sights:** Fixed.
**Features:** Patented grip safety, manual rotary safety; button magazine release; lifetime warranty. Bright chrome or black Teflon finish. Introduced 1991. Made in the U.S. by Sundance Industries, Inc.
**Price:** . . . . . . . . . . . . . . . . . . . . . . . . . . . . . **$95.00**

## SUNDANCE MODEL A-25 AUTO PISTOL
**Caliber:** 25 ACP, 7-shot magazine.
**Barrel:** 2.5".
**Weight:** 16 oz. **Length:** 4⅞" overall.
**Stocks:** Grooved black ABS or simulated smooth pearl; optional pink.
**Sights:** Fixed.
**Features:** Manual rotary safety; button magazine release. Bright chrome or black Teflon finish. Introduced 1989. Made in U.S. by Sundance Industries, Inc.
**Price:** . . . . . . . . . . . . . . . . . . . . . . . . . . . . . **$79.95**

## TAURUS MODEL PT 22/PT 25 AUTO PISTOLS
**Caliber:** 22 LR, 9-shot (PT 22); 25 ACP, 8-shot (PT 25).
**Barrel:** 2.75".
**Weight:** 12.3 oz. **Length:** 5.25" overall.
**Stocks:** Smooth Brazilian hardwood.
**Sights:** Blade front, fixed rear.
**Features:** Double action. Tip-up barrel for loading, cleaning. Blue only. Introduced 1992. Made in U.S. by Taurus International.
**Price:** 22 LR or 25 ACP . . . . . . . . . . . . . . . . . . . . . **$182.00**

---

Consult our Directory pages for the location of firms mentioned.

---

## TAURUS MODEL PT 92AF AUTO PISTOL
**Caliber:** 9mm Para., 15-shot magazine.
**Barrel:** 4.92".
**Weight:** 34 oz. **Length:** 8.54" overall.
**Stocks:** Brazilian hardwood.
**Sights:** Fixed notch rear. Three-dot sight system.
**Features:** Double action, exposed hammer, chamber loaded indicator. Inertia firing pin. Imported by Taurus International.
**Price:** Blue . . . . . . . . . . . . . . . . . . . . . . **$473.00**
**Price:** Blue, Deluxe Shooter's Pak (extra magazine, case) . . . . **$501.00**
**Price:** Nickel . . . . . . . . . . . . . . . . . . . . . **$511.00**
**Price:** Nickel, Deluxe Shooter's Pak (extra magazine, case) . . . **$539.00**
**Price:** Stainless steel . . . . . . . . . . . . . . . . . . **$538.00**
**Price:** Stainless, Deluxe Shooter's Pak (extra magazine, case) . . . **$564.00**

### Taurus PT 92AFC Compact Pistol
Similar to the PT-92 except has 4.25" barrel, 13-shot magazine, weighs 31 oz. and is 7.5" overall. Available in stainless steel, blue or satin nickel. Introduced 1991. Imported by Taurus International.
**Price:** Blue . . . . . . . . . . . . . . . . . . . . . . **$473.00**
**Price:** Blue, Deluxe Shooter's Pak (extra magazine, case) . . . . **$501.00**
**Price:** Nickel . . . . . . . . . . . . . . . . . . . . . **$511.00**
**Price:** Nickel, Deluxe Shooter's Pak (extra magazine, case) . . . **$539.00**
**Price:** Stainless steel . . . . . . . . . . . . . . . . . . **$538.00**
**Price:** Stainless, Deluxe Shooter's Pak (extra magazine and case) . **$564.00**

## TAURUS PT 100 AUTO PISTOL
**Caliber:** 40 S&W, 11-shot magazine.
**Barrel:** 5".
**Weight:** 34 oz.
**Stocks:** Smooth Brazilian hardwood.
**Sights:** Fixed front, drift-adjustable rear. Three-dot combat.
**Features:** Double action, exposed hammer. Ambidextrous hammer-drop safety; inertia firing pin; chamber loaded indicator. Introduced 1991. Imported by Taurus International.
**Price:** Blue . . . . . . . . . . . . . . . . . . . . . . **$482.00**
**Price:** Blue, Deluxe Shooter's Pak (extra magazine, case) . . . . **$510.00**
**Price:** Nickel . . . . . . . . . . . . . . . . . . . . . **$521.00**
**Price:** Nickel, Deluxe Shooter's Pak (extra magazine, case) . . . **$548.00**
**Price:** Stainless . . . . . . . . . . . . . . . . . . . . **$547.00**
**Price:** Stainless, Deluxe Shooter's Pak (extra magazine, case) . . . **$575.00**

### Taurus PT 101 Auto Pistol
Same as the PT 100 except has micro-click rear sight adjustable for windage and elevation, three-dot combat-style. Introduced 1991.
**Price:** Blue . . . . . . . . . . . . . . . . . . . . . . **$522.00**
**Price:** Blue, Deluxe Shooter's Pak (extra magazine, case) . . . . **$549.00**
**Price:** Nickel . . . . . . . . . . . . . . . . . . . . . **$564.00**
**Price:** Nickel, Deluxe Shooter's Pak (extra magazine, case) . . . **$592.00**
**Price:** Stainless . . . . . . . . . . . . . . . . . . . . **$592.00**
**Price:** Stainless, Deluxe Shooter's Pak (extra magazine, case) . . . **$623.00**

## TAURUS MODEL PT-908 AUTO PISTOL
**Caliber:** 9mm Para., 8-shot magazine.
**Barrel:** 3.8".
**Weight:** 30 oz. **Length:** 7.05" overall.
**Stocks:** Checkered black composition.
**Sights:** Drift-adjustable front and rear; three-dot combat.
**Features:** Double action, exposed hammer; manual ambidextrous hammer-drop; inertia firing pin; chamber loaded indicator. Introduced 1993. Imported by Taurus International.
**Price:** Blue . . . . . . . . . . . . . . . . . . . . . . **$473.00**
**Price:** Nickel . . . . . . . . . . . . . . . . . . . . . **$511.00**
**Price:** Stainless steel . . . . . . . . . . . . . . . . . . **$538.00**

## TAURUS MODEL PT58 AUTO PISTOL
**Caliber:** 380 ACP, 12-shot magazine.
**Barrel:** 4.01".
**Weight:** 30 oz. **Length:** 7.2" overall.
**Stocks:** Brazilian hardwood.
**Sights:** Integral blade on slide front, notch rear adjustable for windage. Three-dot system.
**Features:** Double action with exposed hammer; inertia firing pin. Introduced 1988. Imported by Taurus International.
**Price:** Blue . . . . . . . . . . . . . . . . . . . . . . **$423.00**
**Price:** Satin nickel . . . . . . . . . . . . . . . . . . . **$454.00**
**Price:** Stainless steel . . . . . . . . . . . . . . . . . . **$481.00**

### Taurus PT 99AF Auto Pistol
Similar to the PT-92 except has fully adjustable rear sight, smooth Brazilian walnut stocks and is available in stainless steel, polished blue or satin nickel. Introduced 1983.
**Price:** Blue . . . . . . . . . . . . . . . . . . . . . . **$512.00**
**Price:** Blue, Deluxe Shooter's Pak (extra magazine, case) . . . . . **$540.00**
**Price:** Nickel . . . . . . . . . . . . . . . . . . . . . **$554.00**
**Price:** Nickel, Deluxe Shooter's Pak (extra magazine, case) . . . . **$583.00**
**Price:** Stainless steel . . . . . . . . . . . . . . . . . . **$582.00**
**Price:** Stainless, Deluxe Shooter's Pak (extra magazine, case) . . . **$609.00**

Taurus PT92C

Taurus PT101

Taurus PT-908

**CAUTION:** PRICES CHANGE, CHECK AT GUNSHOP.

## WALTHER PP AUTO PISTOL
**Caliber:** 22 LR, 15-shot; 32 ACP, 380 ACP, 7-shot magazine.
**Barrel:** 3.86".
**Weight:** 23½ oz. **Length:** 6.7" overall.
**Stocks:** Checkered plastic.
**Sights:** Fixed, white markings.
**Features:** Double action; manual safety blocks firing pin and drops hammer; chamber loaded indicator on 32 and 380; extra finger rest magazine provided. Imported from Germany by Interarms.
**Price:** 22 LR . . . . . . . . . . . . . . . . . . . . . . . . . . . . . . . **$948.00**
**Price:** 32 . . . . . . . . . . . . . . . . . . . . . . . . . . . . . . . **$1,448.00**
**Price:** 380 . . . . . . . . . . . . . . . . . . . . . . . . . . . . . . **$1,492.00**
**Price:** Engraved models . . . . . . . . . . . . . . . . . **On Request**

### Walther PPK/S American Auto Pistol
Similar to Walther PP except made entirely in the United States. Has 3.27" barrel with 6.1" length overall. Introduced 1980.
**Price:** 380 ACP only . . . . . . . . . . . . . . . . . . . . . . . **$627.00**
**Price:** As above, stainless . . . . . . . . . . . . . . . . . . . **$627.00**

## WALTHER P-38 AUTO PISTOL
**Caliber:** 9mm Para., 8-shot.
**Barrel:** 4¹⁵⁄₁₆".
**Weight:** 28 oz. **Length:** 8½" overall.
**Stocks:** Checkered plastic.
**Sights:** Fixed.
**Features:** Double action; safety blocks firing pin and drops hammer. Matte finish standard, polished blue, engraving and/or plating available. Imported from Germany by Interarms.
**Price:** . . . . . . . . . . . . . . . . . . . . . . . . . . . . . . . **$1,000.00**
**Price:** Engraved models . . . . . . . . . . . . . . . . . **On Request**

### Walther P-5 Auto Pistol
Latest Walther design that uses the basic P-38 double-action mechanism. Caliber 9mm Para., barrel length 3½"; weight 28 oz., overall length 7".
**Price:** . . . . . . . . . . . . . . . . . . . . . . . . . . . . . . . **$1,257.00**
**Price:** P-5 Compact . . . . . . . . . . . . . . . . . . . . . . . **$1,257.00**

## WALTHER MODEL TPH AUTO PISTOL
**Caliber:** 22 LR, 25 ACP, 6-shot magazine.
**Barrel:** 2¼".
**Weight:** 14 oz. **Length:** 5⅜" overall.
**Stocks:** Checkered black composition.
**Sights:** Blade front, rear drift-adjustable for windage.
**Features:** Made of stainless steel. Scaled-down version of the Walther PP/PPK series. Made in U.S. Introduced 1987. From Interarms.
**Price:** Blue or stainless steel, 22 or 25 . . . . . . . . . . . . **$473.00**

Walther P88 Compact

Wildey Auto

Walther PPK/S American

### Walther PPK American Auto Pistol
Similar to Walther PPK/S except weighs 21 oz., has 6-shot capacity. Made in the U.S. Introduced 1986.
**Price:** Stainless, 380 ACP only . . . . . . . . . . . . . . . . $627.00
**Price:** Blue, 380 ACP only . . . . . . . . . . . . . . . . . . $627.00

Walther P-38

Walther TPH

## WALTHER P-88 AUTO PISTOL
**Caliber:** 9mm Para., 15-shot magazine.
**Barrel:** 4".
**Weight:** 31½ oz. **Length:** 7⅜" overall.
**Stocks:** Checkered black composition.
**Sights:** Blade front, rear adjustable for windage and elevation.
**Features:** Double action with ambidextrous decocking lever and magazine release; alloy frame; loaded chamber indicator; matte finish. Imported from Germany by Interarms.
**Price:** . . . . . . . . . . . . . . . . . . . . . . . . . . . . . . . **$1,200.00**
**Price:** P-88 Compact (14-shot) . . . . . . . . . . . . . . . **$1,200.00**

## WILDEY AUTOMATIC PISTOL
**Caliber:** 10mm Wildey Mag., 11mm Wildey Mag., 30 Wildey Mag., 357 Peter-built, 45 Win. Mag., 475 Wildey Mag., 7-shot magazine.
**Barrel:** 5", 6", 7", 8", 10", 12", 14" (45 Win. Mag.); 8", 10", 12", 14" (all other cals.). Interchangeable.
**Weight:** 64 oz. (5" barrel). **Length:** 11" overall (7" barrel).
**Stocks:** Hardwood.
**Sights:** Ramp front (interchangeable blades optional), fully adjustable rear. Scope base available.
**Features:** Gas-operated action. Made of stainless steel. Has three-lug rotary bolt. Double or single action. Polished and matte finish. Made in U.S. by Wildey, Inc.
**Price:** . . . . . . . . . . . . . . . . . . . . . . . **$1,175.00 to $1,495.00**

Wilkinson "Sherry"

### WILKINSON "SHERRY" AUTO PISTOL
**Caliber:** 22 LR, 8-shot magazine.
**Barrel:** 2⅛".
**Weight:** 9¼ oz. **Length:** 4⅜" overall.
**Stocks:** Checkered black plastic.
**Sights:** Fixed, groove.
**Features:** Cross-bolt safety locks the sear into the hammer. Available in all blue finish or blue slide and trigger with gold frame. Introduced 1985.
**Price:** . . . . . . . . . . . . . . . . . . . . . . . . . . . . . . . . $169.95

### WILKINSON "LINDA" AUTO PISTOL
**Caliber:** 9mm Para., 31-shot magazine.
**Barrel:** 8⁵⁄₁₆".
**Weight:** 4 lbs., 13 oz. **Length:** 12¼" overall.
**Stocks:** Checkered black plastic pistol grip, maple forend.
**Sights:** Protected blade front, aperture rear.
**Features:** Fires from closed bolt. Semi-auto only. Straight blowback action. Cross-bolt safety. Removable barrel. From Wilkinson Arms.
**Price:** . . . . . . . . . . . . . . . . . . . . . . . . . . . . . . . . $412.00

# HANDGUNS—COMPETITION HANDGUNS

Models specifically designed for classic competitive shooting sports.

Benelli MP90S

### BENELLI MP90S MATCH PISTOL
**Caliber:** 22 Short, 22 LR, 32 S&W wadcutter, 5-shot magazine.
**Barrel:** 4.33".
**Weight:** 38.8 oz. **Length:** 11.81" overall.
**Stocks:** Stippled walnut match type with fully adjustable palm shelf; anatomically shaped.
**Sights:** Match type. Blade front, click-adjustable rear for windage and elevation.
**Features:** Fully adjustable trigger for pull and position, and is removable. Special internal weight box on sub-frame below barrel. Comes with loading tool, cleaning rods. Introduced 1993. Imported from Italy by European American Armory.
**Price:** . . . . . . . . . . . . . . . . . . . . . . . . . . . . . . . . $1,895.00

### BF SINGLE SHOT PISTOL
**Caliber:** 22 LR, 357 Mag., 44 Mag., 7-30 Waters, 30-30 Win., 375 Win., 45-70; custom chamberings from 17 Rem. through 45-cal.
**Barrel:** 10", 10.75", 12", 15+".
**Weight:** 52 oz. **Length:** NA.
**Stocks:** Custom Herrett finger-groove grip and forend.
**Sights:** Undercut Patridge front, ½-MOA match-quality fully adjustable RPM Iron Sight rear; barrel or receiver mounting. Drilled and tapped for scope mounting.
**Features:** Rigid barrel/receiver; falling block action with short lock time; automatic ejection; air-gauged match barrels by Wilson or Douglas; matte black oxide finish standard, electroless nickel optional. Barrel has 11-degree recessed target crown. Introduced 1988. Made in U.S. by E.A. Brown Mfg.

BF Single Shot

**Price:** 10", no sights . . . . . . . . . . . . . . . . . . $499.95
**Price:** 10", RPM sights . . . . . . . . . . . . . . . . . $564.95
**Price:** 10.75", no sights . . . . . . . . . . . . . . . . $529.95
**Price:** 10.75", RPM sights . . . . . . . . . . . . . . . $594.95
**Price:** 12", no sights . . . . . . . . . . . . . . . . . . $562.95
**Price:** 12", RPM sights . . . . . . . . . . . . . . . . . $627.95
**Price:** 15", no sights . . . . . . . . . . . . . . . . . . $592.95
**Price:** 15", RPM sights . . . . . . . . . . . . . . . . . $658.95
**Price:** 10.75" Ultimate Silhouette (heavy barrel, special forend, RPM rear sight with hooded front, gold-plated trigger) . . . . . . . . . . $687.95

Consult our Directory pages for the location of firms mentioned.

### BERETTA MODEL 89 TARGET PISTOL
**Caliber:** 22 LR, 8-shot magazine.
**Barrel:** 6"
**Weight:** 41 oz. **Length:** 9.5" overall.
**Stocks:** Target-type walnut with thumbrest.
**Sights:** Interchangeable blade front, fully adjustable rear.
**Features:** Single-action target pistol. Matte blue finish. Imported from Italy by Beretta U.S.A.
**Price:** . . . . . . . . . . . . . . . . . . . . . . . . . . . . . . . . $735.00

Beretta Model 89

**CAUTION:** PRICES CHANGE, CHECK AT GUNSHOP.

## BROWNING BUCK MARK SILHOUETTE

**Caliber:** 22 LR, 10-shot magazine.
**Barrel:** 9⅞".
**Weight:** 53 oz. **Length:** 14" overall.
**Stocks:** Smooth walnut stocks and forend, or finger-groove walnut.
**Sights:** Post-type hooded front adjustable for blade width and height; Pro Target rear fully adjustable for windage and elevation.
**Features:** Heavy barrel with .900" diameter; 12½" sight radius. Special sighting plane forms scope base. Introduced 1987. Made in U.S. From Browning.
**Price:** . . . . . . . . . . . . . . . . . . . . . . . . . . . . **$394.95**

## Browning Buck Mark Target 5.5

Same as the Buck Mark Silhouette except has a 5½" barrel with .900" diameter. Has hooded sights mounted on a scope base that accepts an optical or reflex sight. Rear sight is a Browning fully adjustable Pro Target, front sight is an adjustable post that customizes to different widths, and can be adjusted for height. Contoured walnut grips with thumbrest, or finger-groove walnut. Matte blue finish. Overall length is 9⅝", weight is 35½ oz. Has 10-shot magazine. Introduced 1990. From Browning.
**Price:** . . . . . . . . . . . . . . . . . . . . . . . . . . . **$374.95**
**Price:** Target 5.5 Gold (as above with gold anodized
frame and top rib) . . . . . . . . . . . . . . . . . . . **$399.95**

## Browning Buck Mark Field 5.5

Same as the Target 5.5 except has hoodless ramp-style front sight and low profile rear sight. Matte blue finish, contoured or finger-groove walnut stocks. Introduced 1991.
**Price:** . . . . . . . . . . . . . . . . . . . . . . . . . . . **$374.95**

## COLT GOLD CUP NATIONAL MATCH MK IV/SERIES 80

**Caliber:** 45 ACP, 8-shot magazine.
**Barrel:** 5", with new design bushing.
**Weight:** 39 oz. **Length:** 8½".
**Stocks:** Rubber combat with silver-plated medallion.
**Sights:** Patridge-style front, Colt-Elliason rear adjustable for windage and elevation, sight radius 6¾".
**Features:** Arched or flat housing; wide, grooved trigger with adjustable stop; ribbed-top slide, hand fitted, with improved ejection port.
**Price:** Blue . . . . . . . . . . . . . . . . . . . . . . **$885.95**
**Price:** Stainless . . . . . . . . . . . . . . . . . . . . **$948.95**
**Price:** Bright stainless . . . . . . . . . . . . . . . . **$1,018.95**
**Price:** Delta Gold Cup (10mm, stainless) . . . . . . **$975.95**

## COMPETITOR SINGLE SHOT PISTOL

**Caliber:** 22 LR through 50 Action Express, including belted magnums.
**Barrel:** 14" standard; 10.5" silhouette; 16" optional.
**Weight:** About 59 oz. (14" bbl.). **Length:** 15.12" overall.
**Stocks:** Ambidextrous; synthetic (standard) or laminated or natural wood.
**Sights:** Ramp front, adjustable rear.
**Features:** Rotary canon-type action cocks on opening; cammed ejector; interchangeable barrels, ejectors. Adjustable single stage trigger, sliding thumb safety and trigger safety. Matte blue finish. Introduced 1988. From Competitor Corp., Inc.
**Price:** 14", standard calibers, synthetic grip . . . . . . . . . . . . **$364.90**
**Price:** Extra barrels, from . . . . . . . . . . . . . . . . . . . . . **$132.95**

## E.A.A. EUROPEAN EA22T TARGET AUTO

**Caliber:** 22 LR, 12-shot.
**Barrel:** 6".
**Weight:** 40 oz. **Length:** 9.10" overall.
**Stocks:** Checkered walnut, with thumbrest.
**Sights:** Blade on ramp front, rear adjustable for windage and elevation.
**Features:** Blue finish. Finger-rest magazine. Imported by European American Armory Corp.
**Price:** . . . . . . . . . . . . . . . . . . . . . . . . . . . **$399.00**

Browning Buck Mark Target 5.5

## Browning Buck Mark Unlimited Match

Same as the Buck Mark Silhouette except has 14" heavy barrel. Conforms to IHMSA 15" maximum sight radius rule. Introduced 1991.
**Price:** . . . . . . . . . . . . . . . . . . . . . . . . . . . **$469.95**

Colt Gold Cup National Match

E.A.A. European EA22T

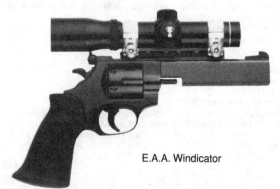

E.A.A. Windicator

## E.A.A. WINDICATOR TARGET GRADE REVOLVERS

**Caliber:** 22 LR, 8-shot, 38 Special, 357 Mag., 6-shot.
**Barrel:** 6".
**Weight:** 50.2 oz. **Length:** 11.8" overall.
**Stocks:** Walnut, competition style.
**Sights:** Blade front with three interchangeable blades, fully adjustable rear.
**Features:** Adjustable trigger with trigger stop and trigger shoe; frame drilled and tapped for scope mount; target hammer. Comes with barrel weights, plastic carrying box. Introduced 1991. Imported from Germany by European American Armory.
**Price:** . . . . . . . . . . . . . . . . . . . . . . . . . . . **$499.00**

## E.A.A. WITNESS GOLD TEAM AUTO

**Caliber:** 9mm Para., 9x21, 10mm Auto, 38 Super, 40 S&W, 45 ACP.
**Barrel:** 5.1".
**Weight:** 41.6 oz. **Length:** 9.6" overall.
**Stocks:** Checkered walnut, competition style.
**Sights:** Square post front, fully adjustable rear.
**Features:** Triple-chamber compensator; competition SA trigger; extended safety and magazine release; competition hammer; beveled magazine well; beavertail grip. Hand-fitted major components. Hard chrome finish. Match-grade barrel. From E.A.A. Custom Shop. Introduced 1992. From European American Armory.
**Price:** . . . . . . . . . . . . . . . . . . . . . . . . . . . . . . . . . **$2,195.00**

E.A.A. Witness Gold Team

## E.A.A. Witness Silver Team Auto

Similar to the Wittness Gold Team except has double-chamber compensator, paddle magazine release, checkered walnut grips, double-dip blue finish. Comes with Super Sight or drilled and tapped for scope mount. Built for the intermediate competition shooter. Introduced 1992. From European American Armory Custom Shop.
**Price:** 9mm Para., 9x21, 10mm Auto, 38 Super, 40 S&W, 45 ACP   **$1,195.00**

## ERMA ER MATCH REVOLVERS

**Caliber:** 22 LR, 32 S&W Long, 6-shot.
**Barrel:** 6".
**Weight:** 47.3 oz. **Length:** 11.2" overall.
**Stocks:** Stippled walnut, adjustable match-type.
**Sights:** Blade front, micrometer rear adjustable for windage and elevation.
**Features:** Polished blue finish. Introduced 1989. Imported from Germany by Precision Sales International.
**Price:** 22 LR or 32 S&W Long . . . . . . . . . . . . . . . . . . **$1,345.00**

Erma ER Match

## ERMA ESP 85A COMPETITION PISTOL

**Caliber:** 22 LR, 8-shot; 32 S&W, 5-shot magazine.
**Barrel:** 6".
**Weight:** 39 oz. **Length:** 10" overall.
**Stocks:** Match-type of stippled walnut; adjustable.
**Sights:** Interchangeable blade front, micrometer adjustable rear with interchangeable leaf.
**Features:** Five-way adjustable trigger; exposed hammer and separate firing pin block allow unlimited dry firing practice. Blue or matte chrome; right- or left-hand. Introduced 1988. Imported from Germany by Precision Sales International.
**Price:** 22 LR . . . . . . . . . . . . . . . . . . . . . . **$1,345.00**
**Price:** 22 LR, left-hand . . . . . . . . . . . . . . . . **$1,375.00**
**Price:** 22 LR, matte chrome . . . . . . . . . . . . . **$1,568.00**
**Price:** 32 S&W . . . . . . . . . . . . . . . . . . . . . . **$1,400.00**

> Consult our Directory pages for the location of firms mentioned.

## FAS 602 MATCH PISTOL

**Caliber:** 22 LR, 5-shot.
**Barrel:** 5.6".
**Weight:** 37 oz. **Length:** 11" overall.
**Stocks:** Walnut wraparound; sizes small, medium or large, or adjustable.
**Sights:** Match. Blade front, open notch rear fully adjustable for windage and elevation. Sight radius is 8.66".
**Features:** Line of sight is only $^{11}/_{32}$" above centerline of bore; magazine is inserted from top; adjustable and removable trigger mechanism; single lever takedown. Full 5-year warranty. Imported from Italy by Nygord Precision Products.
**Price:** . . . . . . . . . . . . . . . . . . . . . . . . . . . . . . . **$995.00**

## FAS 601 Match Pistol

Similar to Model 602 except has different match stocks with adjustable palm shelf, 22 Short only for rapid fire shooting; weighs 40 oz., 5.6" bbl.; has gas ports through top of barrel and slide to reduce recoil; slightly different trigger and sear mechanisms. Imported from Italy by Nygord Precision Products.
**Price:** . . . . . . . . . . . . . . . . . . . . . . . . . . . . . . **$1,095.00**

## FAS 603 Match Pistol

Similar to the FAS 602 except chambered for 32 S&W with 5-shot magazine; 5.3" barrel; 8.66" sight radius; overall length 11.0"; weighs 42.3 oz. Imported from Italy by Nygord Precision Products.
**Price:** . . . . . . . . . . . . . . . . . . . . . . . . . . . . . . **$1,050.00**

## FREEDOM ARMS CASULL MODEL 252 SILHOUETTE

**Caliber:** 22 LR, 5-shot cylinder.
**Barrel:** 9.95".
**Weight:** 63 oz. **Length:** NA
**Stocks:** Black micarta, western style.
**Sights:** $^{1}/_{8}$" Patridge front, Iron Sight Gun Works silhouette rear, click adjustable for windage and elevation.
**Features:** Stainless steel. Built on the 454 Casull frame. Two-point firing pin, lightened hammer for fast lock time. Trigger pull is 3 to 5 lbs. with pre-set overtravel screw. Introduced 1991. From Freedom Arms.
**Price:** Silhouette Class . . . . . . . . . . . . . . . . . . . **$1,295.00**
**Price:** Extra fitted 22 WMR cylinder . . . . . . . . . . . . . . **$213.00**

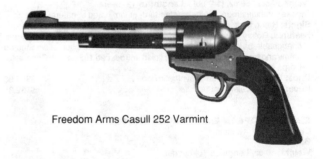

Freedom Arms Casull 252 Varmint

## Freedom Arms Casull Model 252 Varmint

Similar to the Silhouette Class revolver except has 7.5" barrel, weighs 59 oz., has black and green laminated hardwood grips, and comes with brass bead front sight, express shallow V rear sight with windage and elevation adjustments. Introduced 1991. From Freedom Arms.
**Price:** Varmint Class . . . . . . . . . . . . . . . . . . . **$1,248.00**
**Price:** Extra fitted 22 WMR cylinder . . . . . . . . . . . . . . **$213.00**

## HAMMERLI MODEL 160/162 FREE PISTOLS

**Caliber:** 22 LR, single shot.
**Barrel:** 11.30".
**Weight:** 46.94 oz. **Length:** 17.52" overall.
**Stocks:** Walnut; full match style with adjustable palm shelf. Stippled surfaces.
**Sights:** Changeable blade front, open, fully adjustable match rear.
**Features:** Model 160 has mechanical set trigger; Model 162 has electronic trigger; both fully adjustable with provisions for dry firing. Introduced 1993. Imported from Switzerland by Hammerli Pistols USA.
**Price:** Model 160, about . . . . . . . . . . . . . . . . . . **$1,910.00**
**Price:** Model 162, about . . . . . . . . . . . . . . . . . . **$2,095.00**

**CAUTION:** PRICES CHANGE, CHECK AT GUNSHOP.

## HAMMERLI MODEL 208s PISTOL

**Caliber:** 22 LR, 8-shot magazine.
**Barrel:** 5.9".
**Weight:** 37.5 oz. **Length:** 10" overall.
**Stocks:** Walnut, target-type with thumbrest.
**Sights:** Blade front, open fully adjustable rear.
**Features:** Adjustable trigger, including length; interchangeable rear sight elements. Imported from Switzerland by Hammerli Pistols USA, Mandall Shooting Supplies.
**Price:** About . . . . . . . . . . . . . . . . . . . . . . . . . . . **$1,695.00**

Hammerli 208s

Hammerli 280

## GAUCHER GP SILHOUETTE PISTOL

**Caliber:** 22 LR, single shot.
**Barrel:** 10".
**Weight:** 42.3 oz. **Length:** 15.5" overall.
**Stocks:** Stained hardwood.
**Sights:** Hooded post on ramp front, open rear adjustable for windage and elevation.
**Features:** Matte chrome barrel, blued bolt and sights. Other barrel lengths available on special order. Introduced 1991. Imported by Mandall Shooting Supplies.
**Price:** . . . . . . . . . . . . . . . . . . . . . . . . . . . . . . . . **$323.00**

Glock 17L

## MITCHELL ARMS OLYMPIC I.S.U. AUTO PISTOL

**Caliber:** 22 Short, 10-shot magazine.
**Barrel:** 6.75" round tapered, with stabilizer.
**Weight:** 40 oz. **Length:** 11.25" overall.
**Stocks:** Checkered walnut with thumbrest.
**Sights:** Undercut ramp front, frame-mounted click adjustable square notch rear.
**Features:** Integral stabilizer with two removable weights. Trigger adjustable for pull and over-travel; blue finish; stippled front and backstraps; push-button barrel takedown. Announced 1992. From Mitchell Arms.
**Price:** . . . . . . . . . . . . . . . . . . . . . . . . . . . . . . . . **$599.00**

Ram-Line Exactor

## HAMMERLI MODEL 280 TARGET PISTOL

**Caliber:** 22 LR, 6-shot; 32 S&W Long WC, 5-shot.
**Barrel:** 4.5".
**Weight:** 39.1 oz. (32). **Length:** 11.8" overall.
**Stocks:** Walnut match-type with stippling, adjustable palm shelf.
**Sights:** Match sights, micrometer adjustable; interchangeable elements.
**Features:** Has carbon-reinforced synthetic frame and bolt/barrel housing. Trigger is adjustable for pull weight, take-up weight, let-off, and length, and is interchangeable. Interchangeable metal or carbon fiber counterweights. Sight radius of 8.8". Comes with barrel weights, spare magazine, loading tool, cleaning rods. Introduced 1990. Imported from Switzerland by Hammerli Pistols USA and Mandall Shooting Supplies.
**Price:** 22-cal., about . . . . . . . . . . . . . . . . . . . . **$1,465.00**
**Price:** 32-cal., about . . . . . . . . . . . . . . . . . . . . **$1,650.00**

## GLOCK 17L COMPETITION AUTO

**Caliber:** 9mm Para., 17-shot magazine.
**Barrel:** 6.02".
**Weight:** 23.3 oz. **Length:** 8.85" overall.
**Stocks:** Black polymer.
**Sights:** Blade front with white dot, fixed or adjustable rear.
**Features:** Polymer frame, steel slide; double-action trigger with "Safe Action" system; mechanical firing pin safety, drop safety; simple takedown without tools; locked breech, recoil operated action. Introduced 1989. Imported from Austria by Glock, Inc.
**Price:** . . . . . . . . . . . . . . . . . . . . . . . . . . . . . . . . **$768.25**

## McMILLAN SIGNATURE JR. LONG RANGE PISTOL

**Caliber:** Any suitable caliber.
**Barrel:** To customer specs.
**Weight:** 5 lbs.
Stock: McMillan fiberglass.
**Sights:** None furnished; comes with scope rings.
**Features:** Right- or left-hand McMillan benchrest action of titanium or stainless steel; single shot or repeater. Comes with bipod. Introduced 1992. Made in U.S. by McMillan Gunworks, Inc.
**Price:** . . . . . . . . . . . . . . . . . . . . . . . . . . . . . . . . **$2,370.00**

## McMILLAN WOLVERINE AUTO PISTOL

**Caliber:** 9mm Para., 10mm Auto, 38 Wadcutter, 38 Super, 45 Italian, 45 ACP.
**Barrel:** 6".
**Weight:** 45 oz. **Length:** 9.5" overall.
**Stocks:** Pachmayr rubber.
**Sights:** Blade front, fully adjustable rear; low profile.
**Features:** Integral compensator; round burr-style hammer; extended grip safety; checkered backstrap; skeletonized aluminum match trigger. Many finish options. Announced 1992. Made in U.S. by McMillan Gunworks, Inc.
**Price:** Combat or Competition Match . . . . . . . . . . . . . . . **$1,500.00**

## RAM-LINE EXACTOR TARGET PISTOL

**Caliber:** 22 LR, 15-shot magazine.
**Barrel:** 8.0".
**Weight:** 23 oz. **Length:** 12.3" overall.
**Stocks:** One-piece injection moulded in conventional contour; checkered side panels, ridged front and backstraps.
**Sights:** Ramp front with interchangeable .125" blade, rear adjustable for windage and elevation.
**Features:** Injection moulded grip frame, alloy receiver; hybrid composite barrel. Constant force sear spring gives 2.5-lb. trigger pull. Adapt-A-Barrel allows mounting weights, flashlight. Drilled and tapped receiver for scope mounting. Jewelled bolt. Comes with carrying case, test target. Introduced 1990. Made in U.S. by Ram-Line, Inc.
**Price:** . . . . . . . . . . . . . . . . . . . . . . . . . . . . . . . . **$279.97**

Remington XP-100 Silhouette

## Ruger Mark II Bull Barrel

Same gun as the Target Model except has 5½" or 10" heavy barrel (10" meets all IHMSA regulations). Weight with 5½" barrel is 42 oz., with 10" barrel, 52 oz.
**Price:** Blued (MK-512) . . . . . . . . . . . . . . . . . . . . . . **$310.50**
**Price:** Blued (MK-10) . . . . . . . . . . . . . . . . . . . . . . . . **$294.50**
**Price:** Stainless (KMK-10) . . . . . . . . . . . . . . . . . . . . **$373.00**
**Price:** Stainless (KMK-512) . . . . . . . . . . . . . . . . . . **$389.00**

Ruger Government Target

Safari Arms Matchmaster

## SMITH & WESSON MODEL 41 TARGET

**Caliber:** 22 LR, 10-shot clip.
**Barrel:** 5½", 7".
**Weight:** 44 oz. **Length:** 9" overall.
**Stocks:** Checkered walnut with modified thumbrest, usable with either hand.
**Sights:** ⅛" Patridge on ramp base; S&W micro-click rear adjustable for windage and elevation.
**Features:** ⅜" wide, grooved trigger; adjustable trigger stop.
**Price:** S&W Bright Blue, satin matted top area . . . . . . . . . . . **$753.00**

## SMITH & WESSON MODEL 52 38 MASTER AUTO

**Caliber:** 38 Special (for mid-range W.C. with flush-seated bullet only), 5-shot magazine.
**Barrel:** 5".
**Weight:** 40 oz. with empty magazine. **Length:** 8⅝" overall.
**Stocks:** Checkered walnut.
**Sights:** ⅛" Patridge front, S&W micro-click rear adjustable for windage and elevation.
**Features:** Top sighting surfaces matte finished. Locked breech, moving barrel system; checked for 10-ring groups at 50 yards. Coin-adjustable sight screws. Dry-firing permissible if manual safety on.
**Price:** S&W Bright Blue . . . . . . . . . . . . . . . . . . . . . . **$908.00**

## REMINGTON XP-100 SILHOUETTE PISTOL

**Caliber:** 7mm BR Rem., single shot.
**Barrel:** 10½".
**Weight:** 3⅞ lbs. **Length:** 17¼" overall.
**Stock:** American walnut.
**Sights:** Blade front, fully adjustable square notch rear.
**Features:** Mid-handle grip with scalloped contours for left- or right-handed shooters; match=type trigger; two-postion thumb safety. Matte blue finish.
**Price:** . . . . . . . . . . . . . . . . . . . . . . . . . . . . . . . **$613.00**

## RUGER MARK II TARGET MODEL AUTO PISTOL

**Caliber:** 22 LR, 10-shot magazine.
**Barrel:** 5¼", 6⅞".
**Weight:** 42 oz. **Length:** 11⅛" overall.
**Stocks:** Checkered hard plastic.
**Sights:** .125" blade front, micro-click rear, adjustable for windage and elevation. Sight radius 9⅜".
**Features:** Introduced 1982.
**Price:** Blued (MK-514, MK-678) . . . . . . . . . . . . . . . . **$310.50**
**Price:** Stainless (KMK-514, KMK-678) . . . . . . . . . . . . . . **$389.00**

## Ruger Mark II Government Target Model

Same gun as the Mark II Target Model except has 6⅞" barrel, higher sights and is roll marked "Government Target Model" on the right side of the receiver below the rear sight. Identical in all aspects to the military model used for training U.S. armed forces except for markings. Comes with factory test target. Introduced 1987.
**Price:** Blued (MK-678G) . . . . . . . . . . . . . . . . . . . . . **$356.50**
**Price:** Stainless (KMK-678G) . . . . . . . . . . . . . . . . . . **$427.29**

## Ruger Stainless Government Competition Model 22 Pistol

Similar to the Mark II Government Target Model stainless pistol except has 6⅞" slab-sided barrel; the receiver top is drilled and tapped for a Ruger scope base adaptor of blued, chromemoly steel; comes with Ruger 1" stainless scope rings with integral bases for mounting a variety of optical sights; has checkered laminated grip panels with right-hand thumbrest. Has blued open sights with 9¼" radius. Overall length is 11⅛", weight 44 oz. Introduced 1991.
**Price:** KMK-678GC . . . . . . . . . . . . . . . . . . . . . . . . **$441.00**

## SAFARI ARMS MATCHMASTER PISTOL

**Caliber:** 45 ACP, 7-shot magazine.
**Barrel:** 5"; National Match, stainless steel.
**Weight:** 38 oz. **Length:** 8.5" overall.
**Stocks:** Smooth walnut with etched scorpion logo.
**Sights:** Ramped blade front, rear adjustable for windage and elevation.
**Features:** Beavertail grip safety, extended safety, extended slide release, Commander-style hammer; throated, ported, tuned. Finishes: Parkerized matte black, or satin stainless steel. Available from Safari Arms, Inc.
**Price:** . . . . . . . . . . . . . . . . . . . . . . . . . . . . . . . **$670.00**

## Safari Arms Matchmaster Carrycomp I Pistol

Similar to the Matchmaster except has Wil Schueman-designed hybrid compensator system. Introduced 1993. Made in U.S. by Safari Arms, Inc.
**Price:** . . . . . . . . . . . . . . . . . . . . . . . . . . . . . . **$1,010.00**

Smith & Wesson Model 52

**CAUTION:** PRICES CHANGE, CHECK AT GUNSHOP.

## SPHINX AT-2000C COMPETITOR PISTOL
**Caliber:** 9mm Para., 9x21mm, 15-shot, 40 S&W, 11-shot.
**Barrel:** 5.31".
**Weight:** 40.56 oz. **Length:** 9.84" overall.
**Stocks:** Checkered neoprene.
**Sights:** Fully adjustable Bo-Mar or Tasco Pro-Point dot sight in Sphinx mount.
**Features:** Extended magazine release. Competition slide with dual-port compensated barrel. Two-tone finish only. Introduced 1993. Imported from Switzerland by Sile Distributors, Inc.
**Price:** With Bo-Mar sights (AT-2000CS) . . . . . . . . . . . . . **$1,902.00**
**Price:** With Tasco Pro-Point and mount . . . . . . . . . . . . . **$2,189.00**

### Sphinx AT-2000GM Grand Master Pistol
Similar to the AT-2000C except has single-action-only trigger mechanism, squared trigger guard, extended beavertail grip, safety and magazine release; notched competition slide for easier cocking. Two-tone finish only. Has dual-port compensated barrel. Available with fully adjustable Bo-Mar sights or Tasco Pro-Point and Sphinx mount. Introduced 1993. Imported from Switzerland by Sile Distributors, Inc.
**Price:** With Bo-Mar sights (AT-2000GMS) . . . . . . . . . . . . **$2,893.00**
**Price:** With Tasco Pro-Point and mount (AT-2000GM) . . . . . **$2,971.00**

## SPRINGFIELD INC. 1911A1 BULLSEYE WADCUTTER PISTOL
**Caliber:** 45 ACP.
**Barrel:** 5".
**Weight:** 45 oz. **Length:** 8.59" overall (5" barrel).
**Stocks:** Checkered walnut.
**Sights:** Bo-Mar rib with undercut blade front, fully adjustable rear.
**Features:** Built for wadcutter loads only. Has full-length recoil spring guide rod, fitted Videki speed trigger with 3.5-lb. pull; match Commander hammer and sear; beavertail grip safety; lowered and flared ejection port; tuned extractor; fitted slide to frame; Shok Buff; beveled and polished magazine well; checkered front strap and steel mainspring housing (flat housing standard); polished and throated National Match barrel and bushing. Comes with two magazines with slam pads, plastic carrying case, test target. Introduced 1992. From Springfield Inc.
**Price:** . . . . . . . . . . . . . . . . . . . . . . . . . . . . . . . . **P.O.R.**

### Springfield Inc. Entry Level Wadcutter Pistol
Similar to the 1911A1 Bullseye Wadcutter Pistol except has low-mounted Bo-Mar adjustable rear sight, undercut blade front; match throated barrel and bushing; polished feed ramp; lowered and flared ejection port; fitted Videki speed trigger with tuned 3.5-lb. pull; fitted slide to frame; Shok Buff; Pachmayr mainspring housing; Pachmayr grips. Comes with two magazines with slam pads, plastic carrying case, test target. Introduced 1992. From Springfield Inc.
**Price:** 45 ACP, blue, 5" only . . . . . . . . . . . . . . . . . . . **P.O.R.**

### Springfield Inc. 1911A1 N.M. Hardball Pistol
Similar to the 1911A1 Entry Level Wadcutter Pistol except has Bo-Mar adjustable rear sight with undercut front blade; fitted match Videki trigger with 4-lb. pull; fitted slide to frame; throated National Match barrel and bushing; polished feed ramp; Shok Buff; tuned extractor; Herrett walnut grips. Comes with one magazine, plastic carrying case, test target. Introduced 1992. From Springfield Inc.
**Price:** 45 ACP, blue . . . . . . . . . . . . . . . . . . . . . . . . **P.O.R.**

### Springfield Inc. Trophy Master Expert Pistol
Similar to the 1911A1 Trophy Master Competition Pistol except has triple-chamber tapered cone compensator on match barrel with dovetailed front sight; lowered and flared ejection port; fully tuned for reliability. Comes with two magazines, plastic carrying case. Introduced 1992. From Springfield Inc.
**Price:** 45 ACP, Duotone finish . . . . . . . . . . . . . . . . . . **P.O.R.**

Sphinx AT-2000C Competitor

Sphinx AT-2000 GM Grand Master

### Springfield Inc. Trophy Master Competition Pistol
Similar to the 1911A1 Entry Level Wadcutter Pistol except has brazed, serrated improved ramp front sight; extended ambidextrous thumb safety; match Commander hammer and sear; serrated rear slide; Pachmay flat mainspring housing; extended magazine release; beavertail grip safety; full-length recoil spring guide; Pachmayr wrap-around grips. Comes with two magazines with slam pads, plastic carrying case. Introduced 1992. From Springfield Inc.
**Price:** 45 ACP, blue . . . . . . . . . . . . . . . . . . . . . . . . **P.O.R.**

### Springfield Inc. Trophy Master Distinguished Pistol
Has all the features of the 1911A1 Trophy Master Expert except is full-house pistol with Bo-Mar low-mounted adjustable rear sight; full-length recoil spring guide rod and recoil spring retainer; beveled and polished magazine well; Pachmayr grips. Duotone finish. Comes with five magazines with slam pads, plastic carrying case. From Springfield Inc.
**Price:** 45 ACP . . . . . . . . . . . . . . . . . . . . . . . . . . . . **P.O.R.**
**Price:** Trophy Master Distinguished Limited . . . . . . . . . . . **P.O.R.**

## THOMPSON/CENTER SUPER 14 CONTENDER
**Caliber:** 22 LR, 222 Rem., 223 Rem., 7mm TCU, 7-30 Waters, 30-30 Win., 35 Rem., 357 Rem. Maximum, 44 Mag., 10mm Auto, 445 Super Mag., single shot.
**Barrel:** 14".
**Weight:** 45 oz. **Length:** 17¼" overall.
**Stocks:** T/C "Competitor Grip" (walnut and rubber).
**Sights:** Fully adjustable target-type.
**Features:** Break-open action with auto safety. Interchangeable barrels for both rimfire and centerfire calibers. Introduced 1978.
**Price:** . . . . . . . . . . . . . . . . . . . . . . . . . . . . . . . . **$425.00**
**Price:** Extra barrels, blued . . . . . . . . . . . . . . . . . . . . . **$200.00**

### Thompson/Center Super 16 Contender
Same as the T/C Super 14 Contender except has 16¼" barrel. Rear sight can be mounted at mid-barrel position (10¾" radius) or moved to the rear (using scope mount position) for 14¾" radius. Overall length is 20¼". Comes with T/C Competitor Grip of walnut and rubber. Available in 22 LR, 22 WMR, 223 Rem., 7-30 Waters, 30-30 Win., 35 Rem., 44 Mag., 45-70 Gov't. Also available with 16" vent rib barrel with internal choke, caliber 45 Colt/410 shotshell.
**Price:** . . . . . . . . . . . . . . . . . . . . . . . . . . . . . . . . **$430.00**
**Price:** 45-70 Gov't . . . . . . . . . . . . . . . . . . . . . . . . . . **$435.00**
**Price:** Extra 16" barrels (blued) . . . . . . . . . . . . . . . . . . **$205.00**
**Price:** As above, 45-70 . . . . . . . . . . . . . . . . . . . . . . . **$210.00**
**Price:** Super 16 Vent Rib (45-410) . . . . . . . . . . . . . . . . **$460.00**
**Price:** Extra vent rib barrel . . . . . . . . . . . . . . . . . . . . . **$235.00**

Thompson/Center Super 14 Contender

Unique D.E.S. 69U

Unique Model 2000-U

## WALTHER GSP MATCH PISTOL
**Caliber:** 22 LR, 32 S&W wadcutter (GSP-C), 5-shot.
**Barrel:** 5¾".
**Weight:** 44.8 oz. (22 LR), 49.4 oz. (32). **Length:** 11.8" overall.
**Stocks:** Walnut, special hand-fitting design.
**Sights:** Fixed front, rear adjustable for windage and elevation.
**Features:** Available with either 2.2 lb. (1000 gm) or 3 lb. (1360 gm) trigger. Spare mag., bbl. weight, tools supplied in Match Pistol Kit. Imported from Germany by Interarms.
**Price:** GSP, with case . . . . . . . . . . . . . . . . . . **$1,843.00**
**Price:** GSP-C, with case . . . . . . . . . . . . . . . . **$2,545.00**
**Price:** 22 LR conversion unit for GSP-C (no trigger unit) . . . . **$1,053.00**
**Price:** 22 Short conversion unit for GSP-C (with trigger unit) . . . **$1,495.00**
**Price:** 32 S&W conversion unit for GSP-C (no trigger unit) . . . . **$1,400.00**

## Walther OSP Rapid-Fire Pistol
Similar to Model GSP except 22 Short only, stock has adjustable free-style hand rest.
**Price:** . . . . . . . . . . . . . . . . . . . . . . . . **$2,275.00**

## WESSON FIREARMS MODEL 22 SILHOUETTE REVOLVER
**Caliber:** 22 LR, 6-shot.
**Barrel:** 10", regular vent or vent heavy.
**Weight:** 53 oz.
**Stocks:** Combat style.
**Sights:** Patridge-style front, .080" narrow notch rear.
**Features:** Single action only. Available in blue or stainless. Introduced 1989. From Wesson Firearms Co., Inc.
**Price:** Blue, regular vent . . . . . . . . . . . . . . . . **$459.72**
**Price:** Blue, vent heavy . . . . . . . . . . . . . . . . . **$478.10**
**Price:** Stainless, regular vent . . . . . . . . . . . . . . **$488.84**
**Price:** Stainless, vent heavy . . . . . . . . . . . . . . . **$516.40**

## WESSON FIREARMS MODEL 40 SILHOUETTE
**Caliber:** 357 Maximum, 6-shot.
**Barrel:** 4", 6", 8", 10".
**Weight:** 64 oz. (8" bbl.). **Length:** 14.3" overall (8" bbl.).
**Stocks:** Smooth walnut, target-style.
**Sights:** ⅛" serrated front, fully adjustable rear.
**Features:** Meets criteria for IHMSA competition with 8" slotted barrel. Blue or stainless steel. Made in U.S. by Wesson Firearms Co., Inc.
**Price:** Blue, 4" . . . . . . . . . . . . . . . . . . . . **$488.00**
**Price:** Blue, 6" . . . . . . . . . . . . . . . . . . . . **$508.00**
**Price:** Blue, 8" . . . . . . . . . . . . . . . . . . . . **$550.94**
**Price:** Blue, 10" . . . . . . . . . . . . . . . . . . . **$579.20**
**Price:** Stainless, 4" . . . . . . . . . . . . . . . . . . **$550.00**
**Price:** Stainless, 6" . . . . . . . . . . . . . . . . . . **$569.00**
**Price:** Stainless, 8" slotted . . . . . . . . . . . . . . . **$571.57**
**Price:** Stainless, 10" . . . . . . . . . . . . . . . . . **$651.16**

## UNIQUE D.E.S. 32U RAPID FIRE MATCH
**Caliber:** 32 S&W Long wadcutter.
**Barrel:** 5.9".
**Weight:** 40.2 oz.
**Stocks:** Anatomically shaped, adjustable stippled French walnut.
**Sights:** Blade front, micrometer click rear.
**Features:** Trigger adjustable for weight and position; dry firing mechanism; slide stop catch. Optional sleeve weights. Introduced 1990. Imported from France by Nygord Precision Products.
**Price:** Right-hand, about . . . . . . . . . . . . . . . . **$1,295.00**
**Price:** Left-hand, about . . . . . . . . . . . . . . . . . **$1,345.00**

## UNIQUE D.E.S. 69U TARGET PISTOL
**Caliber:** 22 LR, 5-shot magazine.
**Barrel:** 5.91".
**Weight:** 35.3 oz. **Length:** 10.5" overall.
**Stocks:** French walnut target-style with thumbrest and adjustable shelf; hand-checkered panels.
**Sights:** Ramp front, micro. adj. rear mounted on frame; 8.66" sight radius.
**Features:** Meets U.I.T. standards. Comes with 260-gram barrel weight; 100, 150, 350-gram weights available. Fully adjustable match trigger; dry-firing safety device. Imported from France by Nygord Precision Products.
**Price:** Right-hand, about . . . . . . . . . . . . . . . . **$1,195.00**
**Price:** Left-hand, about . . . . . . . . . . . . . . . . . **$1,245.00**

## UNIQUE MODEL 2000-U MATCH PISTOL
**Caliber:** 22 Short, 5-shot magazine.
**Barrel:** 5.9".
**Weight:** 43 oz. **Length:** 11.3" overall.
**Stocks:** Anatomically shaped, adjustable, stippled French walnut.
**Sights:** Blade front, fully adjustable rear; 9.7" sight radius.
**Features:** Light alloy frame, steel slide and shock absorber; five barrel vents reduce recoil, three of which can be blocked; trigger adjustable for position and pull weight. Comes with 340-gram weight housing, 160-gram available. Introduced 1984. Imported from France by Nygord Precision Products.
**Price:** Right-hand, about . . . . . . . . . . . . . . . . **$1,350.00**
**Price:** Left-hand, about . . . . . . . . . . . . . . . . . **$1,400.00**

Walther GSP Match

Wesson Firearms Model 40

## Wesson Firearms Model 445 Supermag Revolver
Similar size and weight as the Model 40 revolvers. Chambered for the 445 Supermag cartridge, a longer version of the 44 Magnum. Barrel lengths of 4", 6", 8", 10". Contact maker for complete price list. Introduced 1989. From Wesson Firearms Co., Inc.
**Price:** 4", vent heavy, blue . . . . . . . . . . . . . . . **$539.00**
**Price:** As above, stainless . . . . . . . . . . . . . . . . **$615.00**
**Price:** 8", vent heavy, blue . . . . . . . . . . . . . . . **$594.00**
**Price:** As above, stainless . . . . . . . . . . . . . . . . **$662.00**
**Price:** 10", vent heavy, blue . . . . . . . . . . . . . . . **$615.00**
**Price:** As above, stainless . . . . . . . . . . . . . . . . **$683.00**
**Price:** 8", vent slotted, blue . . . . . . . . . . . . . . . **$575.00**
**Price:** As above, stainless . . . . . . . . . . . . . . . . **$632.00**
**Price:** 10", vent slotted, blue . . . . . . . . . . . . . . . **$597.00**
**Price:** As above, stainless . . . . . . . . . . . . . . . . **$657.00**

**CAUTION:** PRICES CHANGE, CHECK AT GUNSHOP.

**WESSON FIREARMS MODEL 322/7322 TARGET REVOLVER**
**Caliber:** 32-20, 6-shot.
**Barrel:** 2.5", 4", 6", 8", standard, vent, vent heavy.
**Weight:** 43 oz. (6" VH). **Length:** 11.25" overall.
**Stocks:** Checkered walnut.
**Sights:** Red ramp interchangeable front, fully adjustable rear.
**Features:** Brigh blue or stainless. Introduced 1991. From Wesson Firearms Co., Inc.
**Price:** 6", blue . . . . . . . . . . . . . . . . . . . . $355.00
**Price:** 6", stainless . . . . . . . . . . . . . . . . . $384.00
**Price:** 8", vent, blue . . . . . . . . . . . . . . . . . $404.55
**Price:** 8", stainless . . . . . . . . . . . . . . . . . $434.71
**Price:** 6", vent heavy, blue . . . . . . . . . . . . . $412.20
**Price:** 6", vent heavy, stainless . . . . . . . . . . $441.32
**Price:** 8", vent heavy, blue . . . . . . . . . . . . . $422.94
**Price:** 8", vent heavy, stainless . . . . . . . . . . $459.72

**WICHITA INTERNATIONAL PISTOL**
**Caliber:** 22 LR, 22 WMR, 32 H&R Mag., 357 Super Mag., 357 Mag., 7R, 7mm Super Mag., 7-30 Waters, 30-30 Win., single shot.
**Barrel:** 10", 10½", 14".
**Weight:** 3 lbs. 2 oz. (with 10", 10½" barrels).
**Stocks:** Walnut grip and forend.
**Sights:** Patridge front, adjustable rear. Wichita Multi-Range sight system optional.
**Features:** Made of stainless steel. Break-open action. Grip dimensions same as Colt 45 Auto. Drilled and tapped for furnished see-thru rings. Extra barrels are factory fitted. Introduced 1983. Available from Wichita Arms.
**Price:** International 10" . . . . . . . . . . . . . . . $550.00
**Price:** International 14" . . . . . . . . . . . . . . . $585.00
**Price:** Extra barrels, 10" . . . . . . . . . . . . . . $325.00
**Price:** Extra barrels, 14" . . . . . . . . . . . . . . $355.00

**WICHITA SILHOUETTE PISTOL**
**Caliber:** 308 Win. F.L., 7mm IHMSA, 7mm-308.
**Barrel:** 14¹⁵⁄₁₆".
**Weight:** 4½ lbs. **Length:** 21⅜" overall.
**Stock:** American walnut with oil finish. Glass bedded.
**Sights:** Wichita Multi-Range sight system.
**Features:** Comes with left-hand action with right-hand grip. Round receiver and barrel. Fluted bolt, flat bolt handle. Wichita adjustable trigger. Introduced 1979. From Wichita Arms.
**Price:** Center grip stock . . . . . . . . . . . . . . $1,150.00
**Price:** As above except with Rear Position Stock and target-type Lightpull trigger . . . . . . . . . . . . . . . . . . . . . . $1,150.00

**WICHITA CLASSIC SILHOUETTE PISTOL**
**Caliber:** All standard calibers with maximum overall length of 2.800".
**Barrel:** 11¼".
**Weight:** 3 lbs., 15 oz.
**Stocks:** AAA American walnut with oil finish, checkered grip.
**Sights:** Hooded post front, open adjustable rear.
**Features:** Three locking lug bolt, three gas ports; completely adjustable Wichita trigger. Introduced 1981. From Wichita Arms.
**Price:** . . . . . . . . . . . . . . . . . . . . . . . . $2,950.00

Wichita International

Wichita Silhouette

# HANDGUNS—DOUBLE ACTION REVOLVERS, SERVICE & SPORT

Includes models suitable for hunting and competitive courses for fire, both police and international.

**CHARTER BULLDOG PUG REVOLVER**
**Caliber:** 44 Spec., 5-shot.
**Barrel:** 2½".
**Weight:** 19½ oz. **Length:** 7" overall.
**Stocks:** Checkered walnut Bulldog.
**Sights:** Ramp-style front, fixed rear.
**Features:** Blue or stainless steel construction. Fully shrouded barrel. Reintroduced 1993. Made in U.S. by Charco, Inc.
**Price:** Blue . . . . . . . . . . . . . . . . . . . . . . $278.75
**Price:** Stainless steel . . . . . . . . . . . . . . . . $334.33

**CHARTER OFF DUTY REVOLVER**
**Caliber:** 22 LR, 6-shot, 38 Spec., 5-shot.
**Barrel:** 2".
**Weight:** 17 oz. (38 Spec.). **Length:** 6¼" overall.
**Stocks:** Checkered walnut.
**Sights:** Ramp-style front, fixed rear.
**Features:** Available in blue, stainless or electroless nickel. Fully shrouded barrel. Introduced 1993. Made in U.S. by Charco, Inc.
**Price:** Blue, 22 or 38 Spec. . . . . . . . . . . . . $208.83
**Price:** Stainless steel, 22 or 38 Spec. . . . . . . . $267.83
**Price:** Electroless nickel, 22 or 38 Spec. . . . . . . $243.00

Consult our Directory pages for the location of firms mentioned.

**CHARTER POLICE UNDERCOVER REVOLVER**
**Caliber:** 32 H&R Mag., 38 Spec., 6-shot.
**Barrel:** 2½".
**Weight:** 16 oz. (38 Spec.). **Length:** 6¼" overall.
**Stocks:** Checkered walnut.
**Sights:** Ramp-style front, fixed rear.
**Features:** Blue or stainless steel. Fully shrouded barrel. Reintroduced 1993. Made in U.S. by Charco, Inc.
**Price:** Blue . . . . . . . . . . . . . . . . . . . . . . $250.00
**Price:** Stainless . . . . . . . . . . . . . . . . . . . $275.88

## COLT ANACONDA REVOLVER
**Caliber:** 44 Rem. Magnum, 45 Colt, 6-shot.
**Barrel:** 4", 6", 9".
**Weight:** 53 oz. (6" barrel). **Length:** 11⅝" overall.
**Stocks:** Combat-style black neoprene with finger grooves.
**Sights:** Red insert front, adjustable white outline rear.
**Features:** Stainless steel; full-length ejector rod housing; ventilated barrel rib; offset bolt notches in cylinder; wide spur hammer. Introduced 1990.
**Price:** . . . . . . . . . . . . . . . . . . . . . . . . . . . . **$584.95**
**Price:** 45 Colt, 6" barrel only . . . . . . . . . . . . . . . . . . . **$584.95**

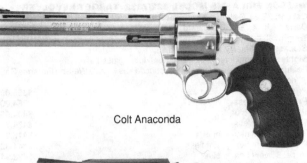

Colt Anaconda

## COLT DETECTIVE SPECIAL REVOLVER
**Caliber:** 38 Special, 6-shot.
**Barrel:** 2".
**Weight:** 22 oz. **Length:** 6⅝" overall.
**Stocks:** Black composition.
**Sights:** Fixed. Ramp front, square notch rear.
**Features:** Glare-proof sights, grooved trigger, shrouded ejector rod. Colt blue finish. Reintroduced 1993.
**Price:** . . . . . . . . . . . . . . . . . . . . . . . . . . . . **$383.95**

Colt Detective Special

## COLT KING COBRA REVOLVER
**Caliber:** 357 Magnum, 6-shot.
**Barrel:** 4", 6".
**Weight:** 42 oz. (4" bbl.). **Length:** 9" overall (4" bbl.).
**Stocks:** Checkered rubber.
**Sights:** Red insert ramp front, adjustable white outline rear.
**Features:** Full-length contoured ejector rod housing, barrel rib. Introduced 1986.
**Price:** Stainless . . . . . . . . . . . . . . . . . . . . . . . . . **$434.95**

## COLT PYTHON REVOLVER
**Caliber:** 357 Magnum (handles all 38 Spec.), 6-shot.
**Barrel:** 4", 6" or 8", with ventilated rib.
**Weight:** 38 oz. (4" bbl.). **Length:** 9¼" (4" bbl.).
**Stocks:** Rubber wraparound.
**Sights:** ⅛" ramp front, adjustable notch rear.
**Features:** Ventilated rib; grooved, crisp trigger; swing-out cylinder; target hammer.
**Price:** Royal blue, 4", 6", 8" . . . . . . . . . . . . . . . . **$791.95**
**Price:** Stainless, 4", 6", 8" . . . . . . . . . . . . . . . . . . **$882.95**
**Price:** Bright stainless, 4", 6", 8" . . . . . . . . . . . . . . **$912.95**

Colt Python

## E.A.A. STANDARD GRADE REVOLVERS
**Caliber:** 22 LR, 22 LR/22 WMR, 8-shot; 32 H&R Mag., 7-shot; 38 Special, 6-shot.
**Barrel:** 4", 6" (22 rimfire); 2" (32 H&R Mag.); 2", 4" (38 Special).
**Weight:** 38 oz. (22 rimfire, 4"). **Length:** 8.8" overall (4" bbl.).
**Stocks:** Hardwood with finger grooves.
**Sights:** Blade front, fixed or adjustable on rimfires; fixed only on 32, 38.
**Features:** Swing-out cylinder; hammer block safety; blue finish. Introduced 1991. Imported from Germany by European American Armory.
**Price:** 22 LR 4", 32 H&R 2", 38 Special 2" . . . . . . . . . **$250.00**
**Price:** 38 Special, 4" . . . . . . . . . . . . . . . . . . . . . **$275.00**
**Price:** 22 LR, 6" . . . . . . . . . . . . . . . . . . . . . . . . **$295.00**
**Price:** 22 LR/22 WMR combo, 4" . . . . . . . . . . . . . . . **$350.00**
**Price:** As above, 6" . . . . . . . . . . . . . . . . . . . . . . **$375.00**

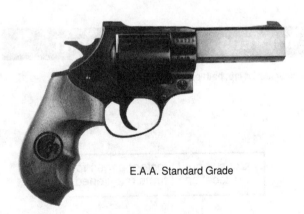

E.A.A. Standard Grade

## E.A.A. Tactical Grade Revolvers
Similar to the Standard Grade revolvers except in 38 Special only, 2" or 4" barrel, fixed sights. Compensator on 4", bobbed hammer (DA only) on 2" model. Introduced 1991. Imported from Germany by European American Armory.
**Price:** 2", bobbed hammer . . . . . . . . . . . . . . . . . . **$275.00**
**Price:** 4", compensator . . . . . . . . . . . . . . . . . . . . **$350.00**

## ERMA ER-777 SPORTING REVOLVER
**Caliber:** 22 LR, 32 S&W, 357 Mag., 6-shot.
**Barrel:** 4", 5½".
**Weight:** 43.3 oz. **Length:** 9½" overall (4" barrel).
**Stocks:** Stippled walnut service-type.
**Sights:** Interchangeable blade front, micro-adjustable rear for windage and elevation.
**Features:** Polished blue finish. Adjustable trigger. Imported from Germany by Precision Sales Int'l. Introduced 1988.
**Price:** . . . . . . . . . . . . . . . . . . . . . . . . . . **$1,200.00**
**Price:** ER-772 (22 LR), ER-773 (32 S&W) . . . . . . . . . . **$1,265.00**

Erma ER-777

## HARRINGTON & RICHARDSON SPORTSMAN 999 REVOLVER
**Caliber:** 22 Short, Long, Long Rifle, 9-shot.
**Barrel:** 4", 6".
**Weight:** 30 oz. (4" barrel). **Length:** 8.5" overall.
**Stocks:** Walnut-finished hardwood.
**Sights:** Blade front adjustable for elevation, rear adjustable for windage.
**Features:** Top-break loading; polished blue finish; automatic shell ejection. Reintroduced 1992. From H&R 1871, Inc.
**Price:** . . . . . . . . . . . . . . . . . . . . . . . . . . . . . **$279.95**

Harrington & Richardson Sportsman 999

## HERITAGE SENTRY DOUBLE-ACTION REVOLVERS
**Caliber:** 38 Spec., 6-shot.
**Barrel:** 2", 4".
**Weight:** 23 oz. (2" barrel). **Length:** 6¼" overall (2" barrel).
**Stocks:** Magnum-style round butt; checkered plastic.
**Sights:** Ramp front, fixed rear.
**Features:** Pill-pin-type ejection; serrated hammer and trigger. Polished blue or chrome finish. Introduced 1993. Made in U.S. by Heritage Mfg., Inc.
**Price:** . . . . . . . . . . . . . . . . . **$104.95 to $129.95**

Heritage Sentry

## KORTH REVOLVER
**Caliber:** 22 LR, 22 Mag., 32 H&R Mag., 32 S&W Long, 357 Mag., 9mm Parabellum.
**Barrel:** 3", 4", 6".
**Weight:** 33 to 38 oz. **Length:** 8" to 11" overall.
**Stocks:** Checkered walnut, sport or combat.
**Sights:** Blade front, rear adjustable for windage and elevation.
**Features:** Four interchangeable cylinders available. Major parts machined from hammer-forged steel; cylinder gap of .002". High polish blue finish. Presentation models have gold trim. Imported from Germany by Mandall Shooting Supplies.
**Price:** With two cylinders . . . . . . . . . . . . . . . . . . **$3,300.00**

## LLAMA COMANCHE REVOLVER
**Caliber:** 22 LR, 357 Mag.
**Barrel:** 4", 6".
**Weight:** 28 oz. **Length:** 9¼" (4" bbl.).
**Stocks:** Checkered walnut.
**Sights:** Fixed blade front, rear adjustable for windage and elevation.
**Features:** Ventilated rib, wide spur hammer. Satin chrome finish available. Imported from Spain by SGS Importers International., Inc.
**Price:** Blue finish . . . . . . . . . . . . . . . . . . . . . **$274.95**

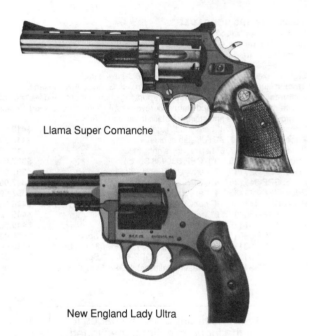

Llama Super Comanche

### Llama Super Comanche Revolver
Similar to the Comanche except: large frame, 44 Mag. with 6", 8½" barrel, 6-shot cylinder; smooth, extra wide trigger; wide spur hammer; over-size walnut, target-style grips. Weight is 3 lbs., 2 oz. Blue finish only.
**Price:** 44 Mag. . . . . . . . . . . . . . . . . . . . . . . **$366.95**

New England Lady Ultra

## NEW ENGLAND FIREARMS STANDARD REVOLVERS
**Caliber:** 22 LR, 9-shot; 32 H&R Mag., 5-shot.
**Barrel:** 2½", 4".
**Weight:** 26 oz. (22 LR, 2½"). **Length:** 8½" overall (4" bbl.).
**Stocks:** Walnut-finished American hardwood with NEF medallion.
**Sights:** Fixed.
**Features:** Choice of blue or nickel finish. Introduced 1988. From New England Firearms Co.
**Price:** 22 LR, 32 H&R Mag., blue . . . . . . . . . . . . . . **$119.95**
**Price:** 22 LR, 2½", 4", nickel, 32 H&R Mag. 2½" nickel . . . . . . . **$129.95**

## NEW ENGLAND FIREARMS LADY ULTRA REVOLVER
**Caliber:** 32 H&R Mag., 5-shot.
**Barrel:** 3".
**Weight:** 31 oz. **Length:** 7.25" overall.
**Stocks:** Walnut-finished hardwood with NEF medallion.
**Sights:** Blade front, fully adjustable rear.
**Features:** Swing-out cylinder; polished blue finish. Comes with lockable storage case. Introduced 1992. From New England Firearms Co.
**Price:** . . . . . . . . . . . . . . . . . . . . . . . . . . . . **$149.95**

## NEW ENGLAND FIREARMS ULTRA REVOLVER
**Caliber:** 22 LR, 9-shot; 22 WMR, 6-shot.
**Barrel:** 4", 6".
**Weight:** 36 oz. **Length:** 10⅝" overall (6" barrel).
**Stocks:** Walnut-finished hardwood with NEF medallion.
**Sights:** Blade front, fully adjustable rear.
**Features:** Blue finish. Bull-style barrel with recessed muzzle, high "Lustre" blue/black finish. Introduced 1989. From New England Firearms.
**Price:** . . . . . . . . . . . . . . . . . . . . . . . . . . . . **$149.95**
**Price:** Ultra Mag 22 WMR . . . . . . . . . . . . . . . . . . **$149.95**

## ROSSI MODEL 68 REVOLVER
**Caliber:** 38 Spec.
**Barrel:** 2", 3".
**Weight:** 22 oz.
**Stocks:** Checkered wood.
**Sights:** Ramp front, low profile adjustable rear.
**Features:** All-steel frame, thumb latch operated swing-out cylinder. Introduced 1978. Imported from Brazil by Interarms.
**Price:** 38, blue, 3" . . . . . . . . . . . . . . . . . . . **$227.00**
**Price:** M68/2 (2" barrel), wood or rubber grips . . . . . . . . . **$238.00**
**Price:** 3", nickel . . . . . . . . . . . . . . . . . . . . . **$232.00**

## ROSSI MODEL 88 STAINLESS REVOLVER
**Caliber:** 32 S&W, 38 Spec., 5-shot.
**Barrel:** 2", 3".
**Weight:** 22 oz. **Length:** 7.5" overall.
**Stocks:** Checkered wood, service-style.
**Sights:** Ramp front, square notch rear drift adjustable for windage.
**Features:** All metal parts except springs are of 440 stainless steel; matte finish; small frame for concealability. Introduced 1983. Imported from Brazil by Interarms.
**Price:** 3" barrel . . . . . . . . . . . . . . . . . . . . . . . **$262.00**
**Price:** M88/2 (2" barrel), wood or rubber grips . . . . . . . . . . . **$275.00**

## ROSSI MODEL 720 REVOLVER

**Caliber:** 44 Special, 5-shot.
**Barrel:** 3".
**Weight:** 27.5 oz. **Length:** 8" overall.
**Stocks:** Checkered rubber, combat style.
**Sights:** Red insert front on ramp, fully adjustable rear.
**Features:** All stainless steel construction; solid barrel rib; full ejector rod shroud. Introduced 1992. Imported from Brazil by Interarms.
**Price:** . . . . . . . . . . . . . . . . . . . . . . . . . . . . . . **$332.00**

Rossi 971 Comp

## RUGER GP-100 REVOLVERS

**Caliber:** 38 Special, 357 Magnum, 6-shot.
**Barrel:** 3", 3" heavy, 4", 4" heavy, 6", 6" heavy.
**Weight:** 3" barrel—35 oz., 3" heavy barrel—36 oz., 4" barrel—37 oz., 4" heavy barrel—38 oz.
**Sights:** Fixed; adjustable on 4" heavy, 6", 6" heavy barrels.
**Stocks:** Ruger Santoprene Cushioned Grip with Goncalo Alves inserts.
**Features:** Uses action and frame incorporating improvements and features of both the Security-Six and Redhawk revolvers. Full length and short ejector shroud. Satin blue and stainless steel. Introduced 1988.
**Price:** GP-141 (357, 4" heavy, adj. sights, blue) . . . . . . . . . . **$413.50**
**Price:** GP-160 (357, 6", adj. sights, blue) . . . . . . . . . . **$413.50**
**Price:** GP-161 (357, 6" heavy, adj. sights, blue) . . . . . . . . . . **$413.50**
**Price:** GPF-330 (357, 3"), GPF-830 (38 Spec.) . . . . . . . . . . **$397.00**
**Price:** GPF-331 (357, 3" heavy), GPF-831 (38 Spec.) . . . . . . . **$397.00**
**Price:** GPF-340 (357, 4"), GPF-840 (38 Spec.) . . . . . . . **$397.00**
**Price:** GPF-341 (357, 4" heavy), GPF-841 (38 Spec.) . . . . . . **$397.00**
**Price:** KGP-141 (357, 4" heavy, adj. sights, stainless) . . . . . **$446.50**
**Price:** KGP-160 (357, 6", adj. sights, stainless) . . . . . **$446.50**
**Price:** KGP-161 (357, 6" heavy, adj. sights, stainless) . . . . . **$446.50**
**Price:** KGPF-330 (357, 3", stainless), KGPF-830 (38 Spec.) . . . . **$430.00**
**Price:** KGPF-331 (357, 3" heavy, stainless), KGPF-831 (38 Spec.) . **$430.00**
**Price:** KGPF-340 (357, 4", stainless), KGPF-840 (38 Spec.) . . . . **$430.00**
**Price:** KGPF-341 (357, 4" heavy, stainless), KGPF-841 (38 Spec.) . **$430.00**

> Consult our Directory pages for the location of firms mentioned.

Ruger SP101 DAO

## ROSSI MODEL 851 REVOLVER

**Caliber:** 38 Special, 6-shot.
**Barrel:** 3" or 4".
**Weight:** 27.5 oz. (3" bbl.). **Length:** 8" overall (3" bbl.).
**Stocks:** Checkered Brazilian hardwood.
**Sights:** Blade front with red insert, rear adjustable for windage.
**Features:** Medium-size frame; stainless steel construction; ventilated barrel rib. Introduced 1991. Imported from Brazil by Interarms.
**Price:** . . . . . . . . . . . . . . . . . . . . . . . . . . . . . . **$280.00**

## ROSSI MODEL 971 REVOLVER

**Caliber:** 357 Mag., 6-shot.
**Barrel:** 2½", 4", 6", heavy.
**Weight:** 36 oz. **Length:** 9" overall.
**Stocks:** Checkered Brazilian hardwood. Stainless models have checkered, contoured rubber.
**Sights:** Blade front, fully adjustable rear.
**Features:** Full-length ejector rod shroud; matted sight rib; target-type trigger, wide checkered hammer spur. Introduced 1988. Imported from Brazil by Interarms.
**Price:** 4", stainless . . . . . . . . . . . . . . . . . . **$315.00**
**Price:** 6", stainless . . . . . . . . . . . . . . . . . . **$315.00**
**Price:** 4", blue . . . . . . . . . . . . . . . . . . . . . **$280.00**
**Price:** 2½", stainless . . . . . . . . . . . . . . . . . . **$320.00**

### Rossi Model 971 Comp Gun

Same as the Model 971 stainless except has 3¼" barrel with integral compensator. Overall length is 9", weight 32 oz. Has red insert front sight, fully adjustable rear. Checkered, contoured rubber grips. Introduced 1993. Imported from Brazil by Interarms.
**Price:** . . . . . . . . . . . . . . . . . . . . . . . . . . . . . . **$320.00**

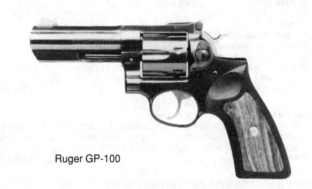

Ruger GP-100

## RUGER SP101 REVOLVERS

**Caliber:** 22 LR, 32 H&R Mag., 6-shot, 9mm Para., 38 Special +P, 357 Mag., 5-shot.
**Barrel:** 2¼", 3¹/₁₆", 4".
**Weight:** 2¼"—25 oz.; 3¹/₁₆"—27 oz.
**Sights:** Adjustable on 22, 32, fixed on others.
**Stocks:** Ruger Santoprene Cushioned Grip with Xenoy inserts.
**Features:** Incorporates improvements and features found in the GP-100 revolvers into a compact, small frame, double-action revolver. Full-length ejector shroud. Stainless steel only. Introduced 1988.
**Price:** KSP-821 (2½", 38 Spec.) . . . . . . . . . . . **$408.00**
**Price:** KSP-831 (3¹/₁₆", 38 Spec.) . . . . . . . . . . . **$408.00**
**Price:** KSP-221 (2¼", 22 LR) . . . . . . . . . . . . . **$408.00**
**Price:** KSP-240 (4", 22 LR) . . . . . . . . . . . . . . **$408.00**
**Price:** KSP-241 (4" heavy bbl., 22 LR) . . . . . . . . **$408.00**
**Price:** KSP-3231 (3¹/₁₆", 32 H&R) . . . . . . . . . . . **$408.00**
**Price:** KSP-921 (2¼", 9mm Para.) . . . . . . . . . . . **$408.00**
**Price:** KSP-931 (3¹/₁₆", 9mm Para.) . . . . . . . . . . **$408.00**
**Price:** KSP-321 (2¼", 357 Mag.) . . . . . . . . . . . **$408.00**
**Price:** KSP-331 (3¹/₁₆", 357 Mag.) . . . . . . . . . . . **$408.00**
**Price:** KSP-821L (2½", 38 Spec., double action only) . . . . . **$408.00**
**Price:** KSP-32LXL (2½", 357 Mag., double action only) . . . . . **$408.00**

### Ruger SP101 Double-Action-Only Revolver

Similar to the standard SP101 except is double action only with no single-action sear notch. Has spurless hammer for snag-free handling, floating firing pin and Ruger's patented transfer bar safety system. Available with 2½" barrel in 38 Special +P and 357 Magnum only. Weight is 25½ oz., overall length 7.06". Natural brushed satin stainless steel. Introduced 1993.
Price: KSP821L (38 Spec.), KSP321XL (357 Mag.) . . . . . . . . . **$408.00**

Ruger Redhawk

## SMITH & WESSON MODEL 10 M&P REVOLVER
**Caliber:** 38 Special, 6-shot.
**Barrel:** 2", 4".
**Weight:** 30½ oz. **Length:** 9¼" overall.
**Stocks:** Checkered walnut, Service. Round or square butt.
**Sights:** Fixed, ramp front, square notch rear.
**Price:** Blue . . . . . . . . . . . . . . . . . . . . . . . . . $361.00

## Smith & Wesson Model 10 38 M&P Heavy Barrel
Same as regular M&P except: 4" heavy ribbed bbl. with ramp front sight, square rear, square butt, wgt. 33½ oz.
**Price:** Blue . . . . . . . . . . . . . . . . . . . . . . . . . $361.00

## SMITH & WESSON MODEL 13 H.B. M&P
**Caliber:** 357 and 38 Special, 6-shot.
**Barrel:** 3" or 4".
**Weight:** 34 oz. **Length:** 9⁵⁄₁₆" overall (4" bbl.).
**Stocks:** Checkered walnut, Service.
**Sights:** ⅛" serrated ramp front, fixed square notch rear.
**Features:** Heavy barrel, K-frame, square butt (4"), round butt (3").
**Price:** Blue . . . . . . . . . . . . . . . . . . . $367.00
**Price:** Model 65, as above in stainless steel . . . . . . . . . . . $402.00

## SMITH & WESSON MODEL 14 FULL LUG REVOLVER
**Caliber:** 38 Special, 6-shot.
**Barrel:** 6", full lug.
**Weight:** 47 oz. **Length:** 11⅛" overall.
**Stocks:** Combat-style Morado with square butt.
**Sights:** Pinned Patridge front, adjustable micrometer click rear.
**Features:** Has .500" target hammer, .312" smooth combat trigger. Polished blue finish. Reintroduced 1991. Limited production.
**Price:** . . . . . . . . . . . . . . . . . . . . . . . . $442.00

## SMITH & WESSON MODEL 15 COMBAT MASTERPIECE
**Caliber:** 38 Special, 6-shot.
**Barrel:** 4".
**Weight:** 32 oz. **Length:** 9⁵⁄₁₆" (4" bbl.).
**Stocks:** Checkered walnut. Grooved tangs.
**Sights:** Front, Baughman Quick Draw on ramp, micro-click rear, adjustable for windage and elevation.
**Price:** Blued . . . . . . . . . . . . . . . . . . . . . . $391.00

## SMITH & WESSON MODEL 17 K-22 FULL LUG
**Caliber:** 22 LR, 6-shot.
**Barrel:** 4", 6".
**Weight:** 39 oz. (6" bbl.). **Length:** 11⅛" overall.
**Stocks:** Square butt Goncalo Alves, combat-style.
**Sights:** Patridge front with 6", serrated on 4", S&W micro-click rear adjustable for windage and elevation.
**Features:** Grooved tang, polished blue finish, full lug barrel. Introduced 1990.
**Price:** 4" . . . . . . . . . . . . . . . . . . . . $410.00
**Price:** 6" . . . . . . . . . . . . . . . . . . . . $449.00

## Smith & Wesson Model 617 Full Lug Revolver
Similar to the Model 17 Full Lug except made of stainless steel. Has semi-target .375" hammer, .312" smooth combat trigger on 4"; 6"; 8⅜" available with either .312" smooth combat trigger or .400" serrated trigger and .500" target hammer. Introduced 1990.
**Price:** 4" . . . . . . . . . . . . . . . . . . . . . . . . $432.00
**Price:** 6", semi-target hammer, combat trigger . . . . . . . . . . . $432.00
**Price:** 6", target hammer, target trigger . . . . . . . . $466.00
**Price:** 8⅜" . . . . . . . . . . . . . . . . . . . . . $476.00

## RUGER REDHAWK
**Caliber:** 44 Rem. Mag., 6-shot.
**Barrel:** 5½", 7½".
**Weight:** About 54 oz. (7½" bbl.). **Length:** 13" overall (7½" barrel).
**Stocks:** Square butt Goncalo Alves.
**Sights:** Interchangeable Patridge-type front, rear adjustable for windage and elevation.
**Features:** Stainless steel, brushed satin finish, or blued ordnance steel. Has a 9½" sight radius. Introduced 1979.
**Price:** Blued, 44 Mag., 5½", 7½" . . . . . . . . . . . . . . . . $458.50
**Price:** Blued, 44 Mag., 7½", with scope mount, rings . . . . . . . . $496.50
**Price:** Stainless, 44 Mag., 5½", 7½" . . . . . . . . . . . . $516.75
**Price:** Stainless, 44 Mag., 7½", with scope mount, rings . . . . . . . $557.25

## Ruger Super Redhawk Revolver
Similar to the standard Redhawk except has a heavy extended frame with the Ruger Integral Scope Mounting System on the wide topstrap. The wide hammer spur has been lowered for better scope clearance. Incorporates the mechanical design features and improvements of the GP-100. Choice of 7½" or 9½" barrel, both with ramp front sight base with Redhawk-style Interchangeable Insert sight blades, adjustable rear sight. Comes with Ruger "Cushioned Grip" panels of Santoprene with Goncalo Alves wood panels. Satin polished stainless steel, 44 Magnum only. Introduced 1987.
**Price:** KSRH-7 (7½"), KSRH-9 (9½") . . . . . . . . . . . . $589.00

Smith & Wesson Model 65

Smith & Wesson Model 15

## Smith & Wesson Model 648 K-22 Masterpiece MRF
Similar to the Model 17 except made of stainless steel and chambered for 22 WMR cartridge. Available with 6" full-lug barrel only, combat-style square butt grips, combat trigger and semi-target hammer. Introduced 1991.
**Price:** . . . . . . . . . . . . . . . . . . . . . . . . . $437.00

Smith & Wesson Model 19

## SMITH & WESSON MODEL 19 COMBAT MAGNUM
**Caliber:** 357 Magnum and 38 Special, 6-shot.
**Barrel:** 2½", 4", 6".
**Weight:** 36 oz. **Length:** 9⁹⁄₁₆" (4" bbl.).
**Stocks:** Checkered hardwood, target. Grooved tangs.
**Sights:** Serrated ramp front 2½" or 4" bbl., red ramp on 4", 6" bbl., micro-click rear adjustable for windage and elevation.
**Price:** S&W Bright Blue, adj. sights . . . . . . . . . $388.00 to $420.00

### SMITH & WESSON MODEL 27 357 MAGNUM REVOLVER
**Caliber:** 357 Magnum and 38 Special, 6-shot.
**Barrel:** 6".
**Weight:** 45½ oz. **Length:** 11⁵⁄₁₆" overall.
**Stocks:** Checkered walnut, Magna. Grooved tangs and trigger.
**Sights:** Serrated ramp front, micro-click rear, adjustable for windage and elevation.
**Price:** . . . . . . . . . . . . . . . . . . . . . $462.00

Smith & Wesson Model 27

### SMITH & WESSON MODEL 29 44 MAGNUM REVOLVER
**Caliber:** 44 Magnum, 6-shot.
**Barrel:** 6", 8⅜".
**Weight:** 47 oz. (6" bbl.). **Length:** 11⅜" overall (6" bbl.).
**Stocks:** Oversize target-type, checkered hardwood. Tangs and target trigger grooved, checkered target hammer.
**Sights:** ⅛" red ramp front, micro-click rear, adjustable for windage and elevation.
**Price:** S&W Bright Blue, 6", 8⅜" . . . . . . . . . . . $526.00
**Price:** Model 629 (stainless steel), 4", 6" . . . . . . $557.00
**Price:** Model 629, 8⅜" barrel . . . . . . . . . . . . . $575.00

Smith & Wesson Model 629

### Smith & Wesson Model 29, 629 Classic Revolvers
Similar to the standard Model 29 and 629 except has full-lug 5", 6½" or 8⅜" barrel; chamfered front of cylinder; interchangable red ramp front sight with adjustable white outline rear; Hogue square butt Santoprene grips with S&W monogram; the frame is drilled and tapped for scope mounting. Factory accurizing and endurance packages. Overall length with 5" barrel is 10½"; weight is 51 oz. Introduced 1990.
**Price:** Model 29 Classic, 5", 6½" . . . . . . . . . . $567.00
**Price:** As above, 8⅜" . . . . . . . . . . . . . . . . . $578.00
**Price:** Model 629 Classic (stainless), 5", 6½" . . . . . . $598.00
**Price:** As above, 8 ⅜" . . . . . . . . . . . . . . . . . $617.00

### Smith & Wesson Model 629 Classic DX Revolver
Similar to the Classic Hunters except offered only with 6½" or 8⅜" full-lug barrel; comes with five front sights: 50-yard red ramp; 50-yard black Patridge; 100-yard black Patridge with gold bead; 50-yard black ramp; and 50-yard black Patridge with white dot. Comes with combat-type grips with Carnuba wax finish and Hogue combat-style square butt conversion grip. Introduced 1991.
**Price:** Model 629 Classic DX, 6½" . . . . . . . . . . $786.00
**Price:** As above, 8⅜" . . . . . . . . . . . . . . . . . $811.00

Smith & Wesson Model 629 Classic DX

### SMITH & WESSON MODEL 36, 37 CHIEFS SPECIAL & AIR-WEIGHT
**Caliber:** 38 Special, 5-shot.
**Barrel:** 2", 3".
**Weight:** 19½ oz. (2" bbl.); 13½ oz. (Airweight). **Length:** 6½" (2" bbl. and round butt).
**Stocks:** Checkered walnut, round or square butt.
**Sights:** Fixed, serrated ramp front, square notch rear.
**Price:** Blue, standard Model 36, 2" . . . . . . . . . . $366.00
**Price:** As above, 3" . . . . . . . . . . . . . . . . . . $378.00
**Price:** Blue, Airweight Model 37, 2" only . . . . . . . $394.00
**Price:** As above, nickel, 2" only . . . . . . . . . . . $410.00

### Smith & Wesson Model 36LS, 60LS LadySmith
Similar to the standard Model 36. Available with 2" barrel. Comes with smooth, contoured rosewood grips with the S&W monogram. Has a speedloader cutout. Comes in a fitted carry/storage case. Introduced 1989.
**Price:** Model 36LS . . . . . . . . . . . . . . . . . . $398.00
**Price:** Model 60LS (as above except in stainless) . . . . $450.00

Smith & Wesson Model 36LS LadySmith

### Smith & Wesson Model 60 3" Full-Lug Revolver
Similar to the Model 60 Chief's Special except has 3" full-lug barrel, adjustable micrometer click black blade rear sight; rubber Uncle Mike's Custom Grade combat grips. Overall length 7½"; weight 24½ oz. Introduced 1991.
**Price:** . . . . . . . . . . . . . . . . . . . . . $443.00

### Smith & Wesson Model 60 Chiefs Special Stainless
Same as Model 36 except all stainless construction, 2" bbl. and round butt only.
**Price:** Stainless steel . . . . . . . . . . . . . . . . . . $417.00

### SMITH & WESSON MODEL 38 BODYGUARD
**Caliber:** 38 Special, 5-shot.
**Barrel:** 2".
**Weight:** 14½ oz. **Length:** 6⁵⁄₁₆" overall.
**Stocks:** Checkered walnut.
**Sights:** Fixed serrated ramp front, square notch rear.
**Features:** Alloy frame; internal hammer.
**Price:** Blue . . . . . . . . . . . . . . . . . . . . . $418.00
**Price:** Nickel . . . . . . . . . . . . . . . . . . . . . $433.00

Smith & Wesson Model 60 3"

**CAUTION:** PRICES CHANGE, CHECK AT GUNSHOP.

## Smith & Wesson Model 49, 649 Bodyguard Revolvers
Same as Model 38 except steel construction, weight 20½ oz.
**Price:** Blued, Model 49 . . . . . . . . . . . . . . . . **$389.00**
**Price:** Stainless, Model 649 . . . . . . . . . . . . . **$441.00**

## SMITH & WESSON MODEL 57, 657 41 MAGNUM REVOLVERS
**Caliber:** 41 Magnum, 6-shot.
**Barrel:** 6".
**Weight:** 48 oz. **Length:** 11⅜" overall.
**Stocks:** Oversize target-type checkered Goncalo Alves.
**Sights:** ⅛" red ramp front, micro-click rear adjustable for windage and elevation.
**Price:** S&W Bright Blue, 6" . . . . . . . . . . . . . . **$466.00**
**Price:** Stainless, Model 657, 6" . . . . . . . . . . . . **$497.00**

## SMITH & WESSON MODEL 63, 22/32 KIT GUN
**Caliber:** 22 LR, 6-shot.
**Barrel:** 2", 4".
**Weight:** 24 oz. (4" bbl.). **Length:** 8⅜" (4" bbl. and round butt).
**Stocks:** Checkered walnut, round or square butt.
**Sights:** Front, serrated ramp, micro-click rear, adjustable for windage and elevation.
**Features:** Stainless steel construction.
**Price:** 4" . . . . . . . . . . . . . . . . . . . . . . . . **$435.00**
**Price:** 2" round butt . . . . . . . . . . . . . . . . . . **$435.00**

## SMITH & WESSON MODEL 65LS LADYSMITH
**Caliber:** 357 Magnum, 6-shot.
**Barrel:** 3".
**Weight:** 31 oz. **Length:** 7.94" overall.
**Stocks:** Rosewood, round butt.
**Sights:** Serrated ramp front, fixed notch rear.
**Features:** Stainless steel with frosted finish. Smooth combat trigger, service hammer, shrouded ejector rod. Comes with soft case. Introduced 1992.
**Price:** . . . . . . . . . . . . . . . . . . . . . . . . . **$450.00**

## SMITH & WESSON MODEL 66 STAINLESS COMBAT MAGNUM
**Caliber:** 357 Magnum and 38 Special, 6-shot.
**Barrel:** 2½", 4", 6".
**Weight:** 36 oz. **Length:** 9⁹⁄₁₆" overall.
**Stocks:** Checkered Goncalo Alves target.
**Sights:** Ramp front, micro-click rear adjustable for windage and elevation.
**Features:** Satin finish stainless steel.
**Price:** . . . . . . . . . . . . . . **$437.00 to $447.00**

## SMITH & WESSON MODEL 586, 686 DISTINGUISHED COMBAT MAGNUMS
**Caliber:** 357 Magnum.
**Barrel:** 4", 6", full shroud.
**Weight:** 46 oz. (6"), 41 oz. (4").
**Stocks:** Goncalo Alves target-type with speed loader cutaway.
**Sights:** Baughman red ramp front, four-position click-adjustable front, S&W micrometer click rear (or fixed).
**Features:** Uses new L-frame, but takes all K-frame grips. Full-length ejector rod shroud. Smooth combat-type trigger, semi-target type hammer. Trigger stop on 6" models. Also available in stainless as Model 686. Introduced 1981.
**Price:** Model 586, blue, 4", from . . . . . . . . . . . **$439.00**
**Price:** Model 686, stainless, from . . . . . . . . . . **$467.00**
**Price:** Model 686, 6", adjustable front sight . . . . . **$499.00**
**Price:** Model 686, 8⅜" . . . . . . . . . . . . . . . . . **$489.00**
**Price:** Model 686, 2½" . . . . . . . . . . . . . . . . . **$457.00**

## SMITH & WESSON MODEL 625-2 REVOLVER
**Caliber:** 45 ACP, 6-shot.
**Barrel:** 5".
**Weight:** 46 oz. **Length:** 11.375" overall.
**Stocks:** Pachmayr SK/GR Gripper rubber.
**Sights:** Patridge front on ramp, S&W micrometer click rear adjustable for windage and elevation.
**Features:** Stainless steel construction with .400" semi-target hammer, .312" smooth combat trigger; full lug barrel. Introduced 1989.
**Price:** . . . . . . . . . . . . . . . . . . . . . . . . . **$562.00**

## Smith & Wesson Model 442 Centennial Airweight
Similar to the Model 640 Centennial except has alloy frame giving weight of 15.8 oz. Chambered for 38 Special, 2" carbon steel barrel; carbon steel cylinder; concealed hammer; Uncle Mike's Custom Grade Santoprene grips. Fixed square notch rear sight, serrated ramp front. Introduced 1993.
**Price:** Blue . . . . . . . . . . . . . . . . . . . . . . . **$418.00**
**Price:** Nickel . . . . . . . . . . . . . . . . . . . . . . . **$433.00**

Smith & Wesson Model 49

## SMITH & WESSON MODEL 64 STAINLESS M&P
**Caliber:** 38 Special, 6-shot.
**Barrel:** 2", 3", 4".
**Weight:** 34 oz. **Length:** 9⁵⁄₁₆" overall.
**Stocks:** Checkered walnut, Service style.
**Sights:** Fixed, ⅛" serrated ramp front, square notch rear.
**Features:** Satin finished stainless steel, square butt.
**Price:** . . . . . . . . . . . . . . . . . . . . . . . . . **$402.00**

Smith & Wesson Model 65LS

Smith & Wesson Model 625-2

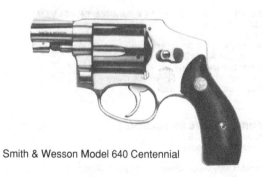

Smith & Wesson Model 640 Centennial

## SMITH & WESSON MODEL 640, 940 CENTENNIAL
**Caliber:** 38 Special, 9mm Para., 5-shot.
**Barrel:** 2", 3".
**Weight:** 20 oz. **Length:** 6⁵⁄₁₆" overall.
**Stocks:** Round butt hardwood (M640), Santoprene (M940).
**Sights:** Serrated ramp front, fixed notch rear.
**Features:** Stainless steel version of the original Model 40 but without the grip safety. Fully concealed hammer, snag-proof smooth edges. Model 640 introduced 1990; Model 940 introduced 1991.
**Price:** Model 640 (38 Special) . . . . . . . . . . . . **$441.00**
**Price:** Model 940 (9mm Para., rubber grips) . . . . . . **$446.00**

## SMITH & WESSON MODEL 651 REVOLVER
**Caliber:** 22 WMR, 6-shot cylinder.
**Barrel:** 4".
**Weight:** 24½ oz. **Length:** 8¹¹⁄₁₆" overall.
**Stocks:** Checkered service Morado; square butt.
**Sights:** Red ramp front, adjustable micrometer click rear.
**Features:** Stainless steel construction with semi-target hammer, smooth combat trigger. Reintroduced 1991. Limited production.
**Price:** . . . . . . . . . . . . . . . . . . . . . . . . . . . $428.00

Smith & Wesson Model 651

Consult our Directory pages for
the location of firms mentioned.

## SPORTARMS MODEL HS38S REVOLVER
**Caliber:** 38 Special, 6-shot.
**Barrel:** 3", 4".
**Weight:** 31.3 oz. **Length:** 8" overall (3" barrel).
**Stocks:** Checkered hardwood; round butt on 3" model, target-style on 4".
**Sights:** Blade front, adjustable rear.
**Features:** Polished blue finish; ventilated rib on 4" barrel. Made in Germany by Herbert Schmidt; Imported by Sportarms of Florida.
**Price:** About . . . . . . . . . . . . . . . . . . . . . $150.00

Taurus Model 66

## TAURUS MODEL 66 REVOLVER
**Caliber:** 357 Magnum, 6-shot.
**Barrel:** 2.5", 4", 6".
**Weight:** 35 oz.(4" barrel).
**Stocks:** Checkered Brazilian hardwood.
**Sights:** Serrated ramp front, micro-click rear adjustable for windage and elevation. Red ramp front with white outline rear on stainlees models only.
**Features:** Wide target-type hammer spur, floating firing pin, heavy barrel with shrouded ejector rod. Introduced 1978. Imported by Taurus International.
**Price:** Blue, 2.5" . . . . . . . . . . . . . . . . . . . $292.00
**Price:** Blue, 4", 6" . . . . . . . . . . . . . . . . . . $290.00
**Price:** Blue, 4", 6" compensated . . . . . . . . . . $299.00
**Price:** Stainless, 2.5" . . . . . . . . . . . . . . . . $371.00
**Price:** Stainless, 4", 6" . . . . . . . . . . . . . . . $368.00
**Price:** Stainless, 4", 6" compensated . . . . . . . $375.00

### Taurus Model 65 Revolver
Same as the Model 66 except has fixed rear sight and ramp front. Available with 2.5" or 4" barrel only, round butt grip. Imported by Taurus International.
**Price:** Blue, 2.5" . . . . . . . . . . . . . . . . . . . $266.00
**Price:** Blue, 4" . . . . . . . . . . . . . . . . . . . . $264.00
**Price:** Stainless, 2.5", 4" . . . . . . . . . . . . . . $338.00

Taurus Model 82

## TAURUS MODEL 80 STANDARD REVOLVER
**Caliber:** 38 Spec., 6-shot.
**Barrel:** 3" or 4".
**Weight:** 30 oz. (4" bbl.). **Length:** 9¼" overall (4" bbl.).
**Stocks:** Checkered Brazilian hardwood.
**Sights:** Serrated ramp front, square notch rear.
**Features:** Imported by Taurus International.
**Price:** Blue . . . . . . . . . . . . . . . . . . . . . . $229.00
**Price:** Stainless . . . . . . . . . . . . . . . . . . . . $282.00

## TAURUS MODEL 82 HEAVY BARREL REVOLVER
**Caliber:** 38 Spec., 6-shot.
**Barrel:** 3" or 4", heavy.
**Weight:** 34 oz. (4" bbl.). **Length:** 9¼" overall (4" bbl.).
**Stocks:** Checkered Brazilian hardwood.
**Sights:** Serrated ramp front, square notch rear.
**Features:** Imported by Taurus International.
**Price:** Blue . . . . . . . . . . . . . . . . . . . . . . $229.00
**Price:** Stainless . . . . . . . . . . . . . . . . . . . . $282.00

## TAURUS MODEL 85 REVOLVER
**Caliber:** 38 Spec., 5-shot.
**Barrel:** 2", 3".
**Weight:** 21 oz.
**Stocks:** Checkered Brazilian hardwood.
**Sights:** Ramp front, square notch rear.
**Features:** Blue, satin nickel finish or stainless steel. Introduced 1980. Imported by Taurus International.
**Price:** Blue, 2", 3" . . . . . . . . . . . . . . . . . . $251.00
**Price:** Stainless steel . . . . . . . . . . . . . . . . . $315.00

## TAURUS MODEL 83 REVOLVER
**Caliber:** 38 Spec., 6-shot.
**Barrel:** 4" only, heavy.
**Weight:** 34 oz.
**Stocks:** Oversize checkered Brazilian hardwood.
**Sights:** Ramp front, micro-click rear adjustable for windage and elevation.
**Features:** Blue or nickel finish. Introduced 1977. Imported by Taurus International.
**Price:** Blue . . . . . . . . . . . . . . . . . . . . . . $241.00
**Price:** Stainless . . . . . . . . . . . . . . . . . . . . $292.00

### Taurus Model 85CH Revolver
Same as the Model 85 except has 2" barrel only and concealed hammer. Smooth Brazilian hardwood stocks. Introduced 1991. Imported by Taurus International.
**Price:** Blue . . . . . . . . . . . . . . . . . . . . . . $251.00
**Price:** Stainless . . . . . . . . . . . . . . . . . . . . $315.00

Taurus Model 85CH

## TAURUS MODEL 86 REVOLVER

**Caliber:** 38 Spec., 6-shot.
**Barrel:** 6" only.
**Weight:** 34 oz. **Length:** 11¼" overall.
**Stocks:** Oversize target-type, checkered Brazilian hardwood.
**Sights:** Patridge front, micro-click rear adjustable for windage and elevation.
**Features:** Blue finish with non-reflective finish on barrel. Imported by Taurus International.
**Price:** . . . . . . . . . . . . . . . . . . . . . . . . . . . . . . . . . . . . . . **$326.00**

## TAURUS MODEL 94 REVOLVER

**Caliber:** 22 LR, 9-shot cylinder.
**Barrel:** 3", 4".
**Weight:** 25 oz.
**Stocks:** Checkered Brazilian hardwood.
**Sights:** Serrated ramp front, click-adjustable rear for windage and elevation.
**Features:** Floating firing pin, color case-hardened hammer and trigger. Introduced 1989. Imported by Taurus International.
**Price:** Blue . . . . . . . . . . . . . . . . . . . . . . . . . . . . **$264.00**
**Price:** Stainless . . . . . . . . . . . . . . . . . . . . . . . . **$314.00**

## TAURUS MODEL 96 REVOLVER

**Caliber:** 22 LR, 6-shot.
**Barrel:** 6".
**Weight:** 34 oz. **Length:** NA.
**Stocks:** Checkered Brazilian hardwood.
**Sights:** Patridge-type front, micrometer click rear adjustable for windage and elevation.
**Features:** Heavy solid barrel rib; target hammer; adjustable target trigger. Blue only. Imported by Taurus International.
**Price:** . . . . . . . . . . . . . . . . . . . . . . . . . . . . . . . . . . . . . . **$326.00**

## TAURUS MODEL 669 REVOLVER

**Caliber:** 357 Mag., 6-shot.
**Barrel:** 4", 6".
**Weight:** 37 oz., (4" bbl.).
**Stocks:** Checkered Brazilian hardwood.
**Sights:** Serrated ramp front, micro-click rear adjustable for windage and elevation.
**Features:** Wide target-type hammer, floating firing pin, full-length barrel shroud. Introduced 1988. Imported by Taurus International.
**Price:** Blue, 4", 6" . . . . . . . . . . . . . . . . . . . . . . **$301.00**
**Price:** Blue, 4", 6" compensated . . . . . . . . . . . . **$308.00**
**Price:** Stainless, 4", 6" . . . . . . . . . . . . . . . . . . **$379.00**
**Price:** Stainless, 4", 6" compensated . . . . . . . . . . **$386.00**

### Taurus Model 689 Revolver

Same as the Model 669 except has full-length ventilated barrel rib. Available in blue or stainless steel. Introduced 1990. From Taurus International.
**Price:** Blue, 4" or 6" . . . . . . . . . . . . . . . . . . . . **$313.00**
**Price:** Stainless, 4" or 6" . . . . . . . . . . . . . . . . . **$392.00**

## TAURUS MODEL 761 REVOLVER

**Caliber:** 32 H&R Magnum, 6-shot.
**Barrel:** 6", heavy, solid rib.
**Weight:** 34 oz.
**Stocks:** Checkered Brazilian hardwood.
**Sights:** Patridge-type front, micro-click rear adjustable for windage and elevation.
**Features:** Target hammer, adjustable target trigger. Blue only. Introduced 1991. Imported by Taurus International.
**Price:** . . . . . . . . . . . . . . . . . . . . . . . . . . . . . . . . . . . . . . **$326.00**

### Taurus Model 741 Revolver

Same as the Model 761 except with 3" or 4" heavy barrel only, serrated ramp front sight, micro click rear adjustable for windage and elevation. Introduced 1991. Imported by Taurus International.
**Price:** Blue, 3", 4" . . . . . . . . . . . . . . . . . . . . . . . **$254.00**
**Price:** Stainless, 3", 4" . . . . . . . . . . . . . . . . . . . **$342.00**

## TAURUS MODEL 941 REVOLVER

**Caliber:** 22 WMR, 8-shot.
**Barrel:** 3", 4".
**Weight:** 27.5 oz. (4" barrel). **Length:** NA.
**Stocks:** Checkered Brazilian hardwood.
**Sights:** Serrated ramp front, rear adjustable for windage and elevation.
**Features:** Solid rib heavy barrel with full-length ejector rod shroud. Blue or stainless steel. Introduced 1992. Imported by Taurus International.
**Price:** Blue . . . . . . . . . . . . . . . . . . . . . . . . . . . . **$290.00**
**Price:** Stainless . . . . . . . . . . . . . . . . . . . . . . . . **$346.00**

Taurus Model 86

## TAURUS MODEL 441/431 REVOLVERS

**Caliber:** 44 Special, 5-shot.
**Barrel:** 3", 4", 6".
**Weight:** 40.4 oz. (6" barrel). **Length:** NA.
**Stocks:** Checkered Brazilian hardwood.
**Sights:** Serrated ramp front, micrometer click rear adjustable for windage and elevation.
**Features:** Heavy barrel with solid rib and full-length ejector shroud. Introduced 1992. Imported by Taurus International.
**Price:** Blue, 3", 4", 6" . . . . . . . . . . . . . . . . . . . **$307.00**
**Price:** Stainless, 3", 4", 6" . . . . . . . . . . . . . . . . **$386.00**
**Price:** Model 431 (fixed sights), blue . . . . . . . . . . . **$281.00**
**Price:** Model 431 (fixed sights), stainless . . . . . . . . . . **$351.00**

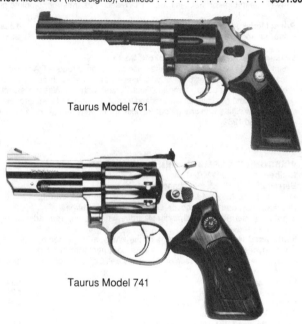

Taurus Model 761

Taurus Model 741

Consult our Directory pages for the location of firms mentioned.

Taurus Model 941

### THUNDER FIVE REVOLVER
**Caliber:** 45 Colt/410 shotshell, 2" and 3"; 5-shot cylinder.
**Barrel:** 2".
**Weight:** 48 oz. **Length:** 9" overall.
**Stocks:** Pachmayr checkered rubber.
**Sights:** Fixed.
**Features:** Double action with ambidextrous hammer-block safety; squared trigger guard; internal draw bar safety. Made of chrome moly steel, with matte blue finish. Announced 1991. From Tapco, Inc.
**Price:** ..................... **$379.00**

### WESSON FIREARMS MODEL 8 & MODEL 14
**Caliber:** 38 Special (Model 8-2); 357 (14-2), both 6-shot.
**Barrel:** 2½", 4", 6", 8"; interchangeable.
**Weight:** 30 oz. (2½"). **Length:** 9¼" overall (4" bbl.).
**Stocks:** Checkered, interchangeable.
**Sights:** ⅛" serrated front, fixed rear.
**Features:** Interchangeable barrels and grips; smooth, wide trigger; wide hammer spur with short double-action travel. Available in stainless or Brite blue. Contact Wesson Firearms for complete price list.
**Price:** Model 8-2, 2½", blue . . . . . . . . . . . **$267.00**
**Price:** As above except in stainless . . . . . . . **$311.00**
**Price:** Model 714-2 Pistol Pac, stainless . . . . **$522.00**

### Wesson Firearms Model 9-2, 15-2 & 32M Revolvers
Same as Models 8-2 and 14-2 except they have adjustable sight. Model 9-2 chambered for 38 Special, Model 15-2 for 357 Magnum. Model 32M is chambered for 32 H&R Mag. Same specs and prices as for 15-2 guns. Available in blue or stainless. Contact Wesson Firearms for complete price list.
**Price:** Model 9-2 or 15-2, 2½", blue . . . . . . . **$338.00**
**Price:** As above except in stainless . . . . . . . **$366.00**

### Wesson Firearms Model 15 Gold Series
Similar to the Model 15 except has smoother action to reduce DA pull to 8-10 lbs.; comes with either 6" or 8" vent heavy slotted barrel shroud with bright blue barrel. Shroud is stamped "Gold Series" with the Wesson signature engraved and gold filled. Hammer and trigger are polished bright; rosewood grips. New sights with orange dot Patridge front, white triangle on rear blade. Introduced 1989.
**Price:** 6" . . . . . . . . . . . . . . . . . . . . . **NA**
**Price:** 8" . . . . . . . . . . . . . . . . . . . . . **NA**

### WESSON FIREARMS MODEL 22 REVOLVER
**Caliber:** 22 LR, 22 WMR, 6-shot.
**Barrel:** 2½", 4", 6", 8"; interchangeable.
**Weight:** 36 oz. (2½"), 44 oz. (6"). **Length:** 9¼" overall (4" barrel).
**Stocks:** Checkered; undercover, service or over-size target.
**Sights:** ⅛" serrated, interchangeable front, white outline rear adjustable for windage and elevation.
**Features:** Built on the same frame as the Wesson 357; smooth, wide trigger with over-travel adjustment, wide spur hammer, with short double-action travel. Available in Brite blue or stainless steel. Contact Wesson Firearms for complete price list.
**Price:** 2½" bbl., blue . . . . . . . . . . . . . . **$349.00**
**Price:** As above, stainless . . . . . . . . . . . . **$391.00**
**Price:** With 4", vent. rib, blue . . . . . . . . . . **$357.00**
**Price:** As above, stainless . . . . . . . . . . . . **$399.00**
**Price:** Stainless Pistol Pac, 22 LR, blue . . . . . **$637.00**

Wesson Model 32M

### WESSON FIREARMS MODEL 41V, 44V, 45V REVOLVERS
**Caliber:** 41 Mag., 44 Mag., 45 Colt, 6-shot.
**Barrel:** 4", 6", 8", 10"; interchangeable.
**Weight:** 48 oz. (4"). **Length:** 12" overall (6" bbl.).
**Stocks:** Smooth.
**Sights:** ⅛" serrated front, white outline rear adjustable for windage and elevation.
**Features:** Available in blue or stainless steel. Smooth, wide trigger with adjustable over-travel; wide hammer spur. Available in Pistol Pac set also. Contact Wesson Firearms for complete price list.
**Price:** 41 Mag., 4", vent . . . . . . . . . . . . . **$433.55**
**Price:** As above except in stainless . . . . . . . **$508.30**
**Price:** 44 Mag., 4", blue . . . . . . . . . . . . . **$433.55**
**Price:** As above except in stainless . . . . . . . **$508.30**
**Price:** 45 Colt, 4", vent . . . . . . . . . . . . . . **$433.55**
**Price:** As above except in stainless . . . . . . . **$508.30**

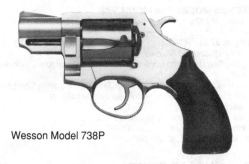

Wesson Model 738P

### WESSON FIREARMS MODEL 738P REVOLVER
**Caliber:** 38 Special +P, 5-shot.
**Barrel:** 2".
**Weight:** 24.6 oz. **Length:** 6.5" overall.
**Stocks:** Pauferro wood or rubber.
**Sights:** Blade front, fixed notch rear.
**Features:** Designed for +P ammunition. Stainless steel construction. Introduced 1992. Made in U.S. by Wesson Firearms Co., Inc.
**Price:** . . . . . . . . . . . . . . . . . . . . . . . **$270.00**

# HANDGUNS—SINGLE-ACTION REVOLVERS

Both classic six-shooters and modern adaptations for hunting and sport.

### AMERICAN ARMS REGULATOR SINGLE ACTIONS
**Caliber:** 357 Mag. 44-40, 45 Colt.
**Barrel:** 4¾", 5½", 7½".
**Weight:** 32 oz. (4¾" barrel) **Length:** 8⅛" overall (4¾" barrel).
**Stocks:** Smooth walnut.
**Sights:** Blade front, groove rear.
**Features:** Blued barrel and cylinder, brass trigger guard and backstrap. Introduced 1992. Imported from Italy by American Arms, Inc.
**Price:** Regulator, single cylinder . . . . . . . . . **$305.00**
**Price:** Regulator, dual cylinder (44-40/44 Spec. or 45 Colt/45 ACP) . **$349.00**

### American Arms Buckhorn Single Action
Similar to the Regulator single action except chambered for 44 Magnum. Available with 4¾", 6" or 7½" barrel. Overall length 11¾", weight is 44 oz. with 6" barrel. Introduced 1993. Imported from Italy by American Arms, Inc.
**Price:** . . . . . . . . . . . . . . . . . . . . . . . **$320.00**

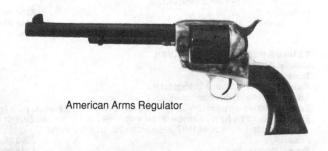

American Arms Regulator

**CAUTION:** PRICES CHANGE, CHECK AT GUNSHOP.

## CENTURY GUN DIST. MODEL 100 SINGLE ACTION
**Caliber:** 30-30, 375 Win., 444 Marlin, 45-70, 50-70.
**Barrel:** 6½" (standard), 8", 10", 12".
**Weight:** 6 lbs. (loaded). **Length:** 15" overall (8" bbl.).
**Stocks:** Smooth walnut.
**Sights:** Ramp front, Millett adjustable square notch rear.
**Features:** Highly polished high tensile strength manganese bronze frame, blue cylinder and barrel; coil spring trigger mechanism. Calibers other than 45-70 start at $1,500.00. Contact maker for full price information. Introduced 1975. Made in U.S. From Century Gun Dist., Inc.
**Price:** 6½" barrel, 45-70 . . . . . . . . . . . . . . . . . . . . . $1,250.00

Century Model 100

Cimarron Peacekeeper

## CIMARRON PEACEKEEPER REVOLVER
**Caliber:** 357 Mag., 44 WCF, 44 Spec., 45 Colt, 6-shot.
**Barrel:** 3½", 4¾", with ejector.
**Weight:** 38 oz. (3$E1/2" barrel). **Length:** NA.
**Stocks:** Hand-checkered walnut.
**Sights:** Blade front, notch rear.
**Features:** Thunderer grip; color case-hardened frame with balance blued, or nickel finish. Introduced 1993. Imported by Cimarron Arms.
**Price:** Color case-hardened . . . . . . . . . . . . . . . . . . . . . $459.00
**Price:** Nickeled . . . . . . . . . . . . . . . . . . . . . . . . . . . $559.00

## CIMARRON U.S. CAVALRY MODEL SINGLE ACTION
**Caliber:** 45 Colt.
**Barrel:** 7½".
**Weight:** 42 oz. **Length:** 13½" overall.
**Stocks:** Walnut.
**Sights:** Fixed.
**Features:** Has "A.P. Casey" markings; "U.S." plus patent dates on frame, serial number on backstrap, trigger guard, frame and cylinder, "APC" cartouche on left grip; color case-hardened frame and hammer, rest charcoal blue. Exact copy of the original. Imported by Cimarron Arms.
**Price:** . . . . . . . . . . . . . . . . . . . . . . . . . . . . . . . . $459.00

### Cimarron Artillery Model Single Action
Similar to the U.S. Cavalry model except has 5½" barrel, weighs 39 oz., and is 11½" overall. U.S. markings and cartouche, case-hardened frame and hammer; 45 Colt only.
**Price:** . . . . . . . . . . . . . . . . . . . . . . . . . . . . . . . . $459.00

> Consult our Directory pages for the location of firms mentioned.

## CIMARRON 1873 PEACEMAKER REPRO
**Caliber:** 22 LR, 22 WMR, 38 WCF, 357 Mag., 44 WCF, 44 Spec., 45 Colt.
**Barrel:** 4¾", 5½", 7½".
**Weight:** 39 oz. **Length:** 10" overall (4" barrel).
**Stocks:** Walnut.
**Sights:** Blade front, fixed or adjustable rear.
**Features:** Uses "old model" blackpowder frame with "Bullseye" ejector or New Model frame. Imported by Cimarron Arms.
**Price:** Peacemaker, 4¾" barrel . . . . . . . . . . . . . . . . . . $429.00
**Price:** Frontier Six Shooter, 5½" barrel . . . . . . . . . . . . . . $429.00
**Price:** Single Action Army, 7½" barrel . . . . . . . . . . . . . . . $429.00

Cimarron 1873 Peacemaker

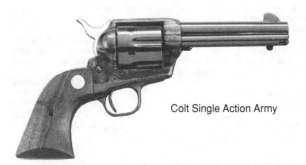

Colt Single Action Army

## COLT SINGLE ACTION ARMY REVOLVER
**Caliber:** 44-40, 45 Colt, 6-shot.
**Barrel:** 4¾", 5½", 7½".
**Weight:** 40 oz. (4¾" barrel). **Length:** 10¼" overall (4¾" barrel).
**Stocks:** American walnut.
**Sights:** Blade front, notch rear.
**Features:** Available in full nickel finish with nickel grip medallions, or Royal Blue with color case-hardened frame, gold grip medallions. Reintroduced 1992.
**Price:** . . . . . . . . . . . . . . . . . . . . . . . . . . . . . . . $1,273.95

## DAKOTA 1875 OUTLAW REVOLVER
**Caliber:** 357, 44-40, 45 Colt.
**Barrel:** 7½".
**Weight:** 46 oz. **Length:** 13½" overall.
**Stocks:** Smooth walnut.
**Sights:** Blade front, fixed groove rear.
**Features:** Authentic copy of 1875 Remington with firing pin in hammer; color case-hardened frame, blue cylinder, barrel, steel backstrap and brass trigger guard. Also available in nickel, factory engraved. Imported by E.M.F.
**Price:** All calibers . . . . . . . . . . . . . . . . . . . . . . . . . $465.00
**Price:** Nickel . . . . . . . . . . . . . . . . . . . . . . . . . . . . $550.00
**Price:** Engraved . . . . . . . . . . . . . . . . . . . . . . . . . . . $600.00
**Price:** Engraved Nickel . . . . . . . . . . . . . . . . . . . . . . . $710.00

### Dakota 1890 Police Revolver
Similar to the 1875 Outlaw except has 5½" barrel, weighs 40 oz., with 12½" overall length. Has lanyard ring in butt. No web under barrel. Calibers 357, 44-40, 45 Colt. Imported by E.M.F.
**Price:** All calibers . . . . . . . . . . . . . . . . . . . . . . . . . $470.00
**Price:** Nickel . . . . . . . . . . . . . . . . . . . . . . . . . . . . $560.00
**Price:** Engraved . . . . . . . . . . . . . . . . . . . . . . . . . . . $620.00
**Price:** Engraved nickel . . . . . . . . . . . . . . . . . . . . . . . $725.00

## E.A.A. BIG BORE BOUNTY HUNTER SA REVOLVERS
**Caliber:** 357 Mag., 41 Mag., 44-40, 44 Mag., 45 Colt, 6-shot.
**Barrel:** 4⅝", 5½", 7½".
**Weight:** 2.5 lbs. **Length:** 11" overall (5" barrel).
**Stocks:** Smooth walnut.
**Sights:** Blade front, grooved topstrap rear.
**Features:** Transfer bar safety; three position hammer; hammer forged barrel. Introduced 1992. Imported by European American Armory.
**Price:** Blue . . . . . . . . . . . . . . . . . . . . . . . . . . . . . . . . **$425.00**
**Price:** Color case-hardened frame . . . . . . . . . . . . . . . . . . **$440.00**
**Price:** Blue with gold-plated grip frame . . . . . . . . . . . . . . **$440.00**
**Price:** Chrome-plated . . . . . . . . . . . . . . . . . . . . . . . . . **$475.00**

E.A.A. Big Bore Bounty Hunter

## E.A.A. BOUNTY HUNTER REVOLVER
**Caliber:** 22 LR, 22 WMR, 6-shot cylinder.
**Barrel:** 4¾", 6", 9".
**Weight:** 32 oz. **Length:** 10" overall (4¾" barrel).
**Stocks:** European hardwood.
**Sights:** Blade front, rear adjustable for windage.
**Features:** Available in blue or blue/gold finish. Introduced 1991. From European American Armory Corp.
**Price:** 4¾", blue . . . . . . . . . . . . . . . . . . . . . . . . . . . . **$115.00**
**Price:** 4¾", blue, 22 LR/22 WMR combo . . . . . . . . . . . . **$135.00**
**Price:** 4¾", blue/gold, 22 LR/22 WMR combo . . . . . . . . . **$145.00**
**Price:** 6", blue, 22 LR/22 WMR combo . . . . . . . . . . . . . **$140.00**
**Price:** 6", blue/gold, 22 LR/22 WMR combo . . . . . . . . . . **$150.00**
**Price:** 9", blue, 22 LR/22 WMR combo . . . . . . . . . . . . . **$155.00**
**Price:** 9", blue/gold, 22 LR/22 WMR combo . . . . . . . . . . **$165.00**

E.A.A. Bounty Hunter

## FREEDOM ARMS PREMIER 454 CASULL
**Caliber:** 44 Mag., 45 Colt/45 ACP (optional cylinder), 454 Casull, 5-shot.
**Barrel:** 3", 4¾", 6", 7½", 10".
**Weight:** 50 oz. **Length:** 14" overall (7½" bbl.).
**Stocks:** Impregnated hardwood.
**Sights:** Blade front, notch or adjustable rear.
**Features:** All stainless steel construction; sliding bar safety system. Hunter Pak includes 7½" gun, sling and studs, aluminum carrying case with tool and cleaning kit. Lifetime warranty. Made in U.S.A.
**Price:** Field Grade (matte finish, Pachmayr grips), adjustable sights, 4¾", 6", 7½", 10" . . . . . . . . . . . . . . . . . . **$1,115.00**
**Price:** Field Grade, fixed sights, 4¾" only . . . . . . . . . . . **$1,035.00**
**Price:** Field Grade, 44 Rem. Mag., adjustable sights, all lengths **$1,115.00**
**Price:** Premier Grade (brush finish, impregnated hardwood grips) adjustable sights, 4¾", 6", 7½", 10" . . . . . . . . . . **$1,385.00**
**Price:** Premier Grade, fixed sights, 7½" only . . . . . . . . . **$1,298.00**
**Price:** Premier Grade, 44 Rem. Mag., adjustable sights, all lengths **$1,385.00**
**Price:** Premier Grade Hunter Pak, black micarta grips, no front sight base . . . . . . . . . . . . . . . . . . . . . . **$1,611.10**
**Price:** Premier Grade Hunter Pak, adjustable sight, black micarta grips . . . . . . . . . . . . . . . . . . . . . **$1,711.35**
**Price:** Field Grade Hunter Pak, Pachmayr grips, 2x Leupold scope, Leupold rings and base, no front sight base . . . . . . . . . . **$1,332.85**
**Price:** Field Grade Hunter Pak, Pachmayr grips, low-profile adjustable sight . . . . . . . . . . . . . . . . **$1,408.85**
**Price:** Fitted 45 ACP or 45 Colt cylinder, add . . . . . . . . . . **$213.00**

Freedom 454 Field Grade

## Freedom Arms Casull Model 353 Revolver
Similar to the Premier 454 Casull except chambered for 357 Magnum with 5-shot cylinder; 4¾", 6", 7½" or 9" barrel. Weighs 59 oz. with 7½" barrel. Standard model has adjustable sights, matte finish, Pachmayr grips, 7½" or 9" barrel; Silhouette has 9" barrel, Patridge front sight, Iron Sight Gun Works Silhouette adjustable rear, Pachmayr grips, trigger over-travel adjustment screw. All stainless steel. Introduced 1992.
**Price:** Field Grade . . . . . . . . . . . . . . . . . . . . . . . . . **$1,115.00**
**Price:** Premier Grade (brushed finish, impregnated hardwood grips, Premier Grade sights) . . . . . . . . . . . . . . . . . . . . . . . . **$1,385.00**
**Price:** Silhouette . . . . . . . . . . . . . . . . . . . . . . . . . . . **$1,213.80**

## Dakota New Model Single-Action Revolvers
Similar to the standard Dakota except has color case-hardened forged steel frame, black nickel backstrap and trigger guard. Calibers 357 Mag., 44-40, 45 Colt only.
**Price:** . . . . . . . . . . . . . . . . . . . . . . . . . . . . . . . . . . **$490.00**
**Price:** Nickel . . . . . . . . . . . . . . . . . . . . . . . . . . . . . . . **$636.00**

## DAKOTA HARTFORD SINGLE-ACTION REVOLVERS
**Caliber:** 22 LR, 357 Mag., 32-20, 38-40, 44-40, 44 Spec., 45 Colt.
**Barrel:** 4¾", 5½", 7½".
**Weight:** 45 oz. **Length:** 13" overall (7½" barrel).
**Stocks:** Smooth walnut.
**Sights:** Blade front, fixed rear.
**Features:** Identical to the origianl Colts with inspector cartouche on left grip, original patent dates and U.S. markings. All major parts serial numbered using original Colt-style lettering, numbering. Bullseye ejector head and color case-hardening on frame and hammer. Introduced 1990. From E.M.F.
**Price:** . . . . . . . . . . . . . . . . . . . . . . . . . . . . . . . . . . **$600.00**
**Price:** Cavalry or Artillery . . . . . . . . . . . . . . . . . . . . . . **$655.00**
**Price:** Nickel plated . . . . . . . . . . . . . . . . . . . . . . . . . . **$760.00**
**Price:** Cattlebrand engraved nickel . . . . . . . . . . . . . . . **$1,150.00**
**Price:** Scroll engraved . . . . . . . . . . . . . . . . . . . . . . . . **$840.00**
**Price:** Scroll engraved nickel . . . . . . . . . . . . . . . . . . . **$1,000.00**

Heritage Rough Rider

## HERITAGE ROUGH RIDER REVOLVER
**Caliber:** 22 LR, 22 LR/22 WMR combo, 6-shot.
**Barrel:** 3", 4¾", 6½", 9".
**Weight:** 31 to 38 oz. **Length:** NA
**Stocks:** Smooth walnut.
**Sights:** Blade front, fixed rear.
**Features:** Hammer block safety. High polish blue finish, gold-tone screws, polished hammer. Introduced 1993. Made in U.S. by Heritage Mfg., Inc.
**Price:** . . . . . . . . . . . . . . . . . . . . . . . . . . **$104.95 to $139.95**

**CAUTION:** PRICES CHANGE, CHECK AT GUNSHOP.

## MITCHELL SINGLE-ACTION ARMY REVOLVERS
**Caliber:** 357 Mag., 44 Mag., 45 ACP, 45 Colt, 6-shot.
**Barrel:** 4¾", 5½", 7½".
**Weight:** NA. **Length:** NA.
**Stocks:** One-piece walnut.
**Sights:** Serrated ramp front, fixed or adjustable rear.
**Features:** Color case-hardened frame, brass or steel backstrap/trigger guard; hammer-block safety. Bright nickel-plated model and dual cylinder models available. Contact importer for complete price list. Imported by Mitchell Arms, Inc.
**Price:** Cowboy, 4¾", Army 5½", Cavalry 7½", blue, 357,
45 Colt, 45 ACP . . . . . . . . . . . . . . . . . . . . . . . . **$399.00**
**Price:** As above, nickel . . . . . . . . . . . . . . . . . . . . **$439.00**
**Price:** 45 Colt/45 ACP dual cyl., blue . . . . . . . . . . . **$549.00**
**Price:** As above, nickel . . . . . . . . . . . . . . . . . . . . **$588.00**
**Price:** Bat Masterson model, 45 Colt, 4¾", nickel . . . . . . . **$439.00**

Mitchell Single Action

Navy Arms 1873

## NAVY ARMS 1873 SINGLE-ACTION REVOLVER
**Caliber:** 44-40, 45 Colt, 6-shot cylinder.
**Barrel:** 3", 4¾", 5½", 7½".
**Weight:** 36 oz. **Length:** 10¾" overall (5½" barrel).
**Stocks:** Smooth walnut.
**Sights:** Blade front, groove in topstrap rear.
**Features:** Blue with color case-hardened frame, or nickel. Introduced 1991. Imported by Navy Arms.
**Price:** Blue . . . . . . . . . . . . . . . . . . . . . . . . **$370.00**
**Price:** Nickel . . . . . . . . . . . . . . . . . . . . . . . **$435.00**
**Price:** 1873 U.S. Cavalry Model (7½", 45 Colt, arsenal markings) . . **$455.00**
**Price:** 1895 U.S. Artillery Model (as above, 5½" barrel) . . . . . . **$455.00**

## NORTH AMERICAN MINI-REVOLVERS
**Caliber:** 22 LR, 22 WMR, 5-shot.
**Barrel:** 1⅛", 1⅝".
**Weight:** 4 to 6.6 oz. **Length:** 3⅝" to 6⅛" overall.
**Stocks:** Laminated wood.
**Sights:** Blade front, notch fixed rear.
**Features:** All stainless steel construction. Polished satin and matte finish. Engraved models available. From North American Arms.
**Price:** 22 LR, 1⅛" bbl. . . . . . . . . . . . . . . . . . . . **$164.50**
**Price:** 22 LR, 1⅝" bbl. . . . . . . . . . . . . . . . . . . . **$164.50**
**Price:** 22 WMR, 1⅝" bbl. . . . . . . . . . . . . . . . . . . **$184.50**
**Price:** 22 WMR, 1⅛" or 1⅝" bbl. with extra 22 LR cylinder . . . . . **$219.50**

North American Mini

> Consult our Directory pages for the location of firms mentioned.

North American Mini-Master

## NORTH AMERICAN MINI-MASTER
**Caliber:** 22 LR, 22 WMR, 5-shot cylinder.
**Barrel:** 4".
**Weight:** 10.7 oz. **Length:** 7.75" overall.
**Stocks:** Checkered hard black rubber.
**Sights:** Blade front, white outline rear adjustable for elevation, or fixed.
**Features:** Heavy vent barrel; full-size grips. Non-fluted cylinder. Introduced 1989.
**Price:** Adjustable sight, 22 WMR or 22 LR . . . . . . . . . . . . **$267.50**
**Price:** As above with extra WMR/LR cylinder . . . . . . . . . . . **$302.50**
**Price:** Fixed sight, 22 WMR or 22 LR . . . . . . . . . . . . . . **$257.50**
**Price:** As above with extra WMR/LR cylinder . . . . . . . . . . . **$292.50**

### North American Black Widow Revolver
Similar to the Mini-Master except has 2" Heavy Vent barrel. Built on the 22 WMR frame. Non-fluted cylinder, black rubber grips. Available with either Millett Low Profile fixed sights or Millett sight adjustable for elevation only. Overall length 5⅞", weight 8.8 oz. From North American Arms.
**Price:** Adjustable sight, 22 LR or 22 WMR . . . . . . . . . . . . **$235.50**
**Price:** As above with extra WMR/LR cylinder . . . . . . . . . . . **$270.50**
**Price:** Fixed sight, 22 LR or 22 WMR . . . . . . . . . . . . . . **$225.50**
**Price:** As above with extra WMR/LR cylinder . . . . . . . . . . . **$260.50**

## PHELPS HERITAGE I, EAGLE I, GRIZZLY REVOLVERS
**Caliber:** 444 Marlin, 45-70, 50-70, 6-shot.
**Barrel:** 8", 12", 16" (45-70).
**Weight:** 5½ lbs. **Length:** 19½" overall (12" bbl.).
**Stocks:** Smooth walnut.
**Sights:** Ramp front, adjustable rear.
**Features:** Single action; polished blue finish; safety bar. From Phelps Mfg. Co.
**Price:** 8", 45-70 or 444 Marlin, about . . . . . . . . . **$1,085.00**
**Price:** 12", 45-70 or 444 Marlin, about . . . . . . . . . **$1,165.00**
**Price:** 8", 50-70, about . . . . . . . . . . . . . . . . **$1,550.00**

## RUGER BLACKHAWK REVOLVER
**Caliber:** 30 Carbine, 357 Mag./38 Spec., 41 Mag., 45 Colt, 6-shot.
**Barrel:** 4⅝" or 6½", either caliber; 7½" (30 Carbine, 45 Colt only).
**Weight:** 42 oz. (6½" bbl.). **Length:** 12¼" overall (6½" bbl.).
**Stocks:** American walnut.
**Sights:** ⅛" ramp front, micro-click rear adjustable for windage and elevation.
**Features:** Ruger interlock mechanism, independent firing pin, hardened chrome moly steel frame, music wire springs throughout.
**Price:** Blue, 30 Carbine (7½" bbl.), BN31 . . . . . . . . . . . . **$328.00**
**Price:** Blue, 357 Mag. (4⅝", 6½"), BN34, BN36 . . . . . . . . . **$328.00**
**Price:** Blue, 357/9mm Convertible (4⅝", 6½"), BN34X, BN36X . . . **$343.50**
**Price:** Blue, 41 Mag., 45 Colt (4⅝", 6½"), BN41, BN42, BN45 . . . **$328.00**
**Price:** Stainless, 357 Mag. (4⅝", 6½"), KBN34, KBN36 . . . . . . **$404.00**

Ruger Blackhawk

Ruger Bisley

Ruger New Super Bearcat

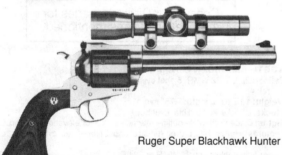

Ruger SSM Single-Six

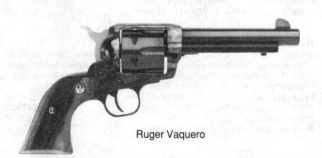

Ruger Super Blackhawk Hunter

Ruger Vaquero

### SPORTARMS MODEL HS21S SINGLE ACTION
**Caliber:** 22 LR or 22 LR/22 WMR combo, 6-shot.
**Barrel:** 5½".
**Weight:** 33.5 oz. **Length:** 11" overall.
**Stocks:** Smooth hardwood.
**Sights:** Blade front, rear drift adjustable for windage.
**Features:** Available in blue with imitation stag or wood stocks. Made in Germany by Herbert Schmidt; Imported by Sportarms of Florida.
**Price:** 22 LR, blue, "stag" grips, about . . . . . . . . . . . . . **$100.00**
**Price:** 22 LR/22 WMR combo, blue, wood stocks, about . . . . . . **$120.00**

### Ruger Bisley Single-Action Revolver
Similar to standard Blackhawk except the hammer is lower with a smoothly curved, deeply checkered wide spur. The trigger is strongly curved with a wide smooth surface. Longer grip frame has a hand-filling shape. Adjustable rear sight, ramp-style front. Has an unfluted cylinder and roll engraving, adjustable sights. Chambered for 357, 41, 44 Mags. and 45 Colt; 7½" barrel; overall length of 13". Introduced 1985.
**Price:** . . . . . . . . . . . . . . . . . . . . . . . . . . . . . . . . **$391.00**

### RUGER NEW SUPER BEARCAT SINGLE ACTION
**Caliber:** 22 LR/22 WMR, 6-shot.
**Barrel:** 4".
**Weight:** 23 oz. **Length:** 8⅞" overall.
**Stocks:** Smooth rosewood with Ruger medallion.
**Sights:** Blade front, fixed notch rear.
**Features:** Reintroduction of the Ruger Super Bearcat with slightly lengthened frame, Ruger patented transfer bar safety system. Comes with two cylinders. Available in blue or stainless steel. Introduced 1993. From Sturm, Ruger & Co.
**Price:** SBC4, blue . . . . . . . . . . . . . . . . . . . . . . . . . **$298.00**
**Price:** KSBC4, stainless . . . . . . . . . . . . . . . . . . . . . . **$325.00**

### RUGER SUPER SINGLE-SIX CONVERTIBLE
**Caliber:** 22 LR, 6-shot; 22 WMR in extra cylinder.
**Barrel:** 4⅝", 5½", 6½", or 9½" (6-groove).
**Weight:** 34½ oz. (6½" bbl.). **Length:** 11¹³⁄₁₆" overall (6½" bbl.).
**Stocks:** Smooth American walnut.
**Sights:** Improved Patridge front on ramp, fully adjustable rear protected by integral frame ribs.
**Features:** Ruger interlock mechanism, transfer bar ignition, gate-controlled loading, hardened chrome moly steel frame, wide trigger, music wire springs throughout, independent firing pin.
**Price:** 4⅝", 5½", 6½", 9½" barrel . . . . . . . . . . . . . . . . . **$281.00**
**Price:** 5½", 6½" bbl. only, stainless steel . . . . . . . . . . . . . **$354.00**

### Ruger SSM Single-Six Revolver
Similar to the Super Single-Six revolver except chambered for 32 H&R Magnum (also handles 32 S&W and 32 S&W Long). Weight is about 34 oz. with 6½" barrel. Barrel lengths: 4⅝", 5½", 6½", 9½". Introduced 1985.
**Price:** . . . . . . . . . . . . . . . . . . . . . . . . . . . . . . . . **$281.00**

### Ruger Bisley Small Frame Revolver
Similar to the Single-Six except frame is styled after the classic Bisley "flat-top." Most mechanical parts are unchanged. Hammer is lower and smoothly curved with a deeply checkered spur. Trigger is strongly curved with a wide smooth surface. Longer grip frame designed with a hand-filling shape, and the trigger guard is a large oval. Adjustable dovetail rear sight; front sight base accepts interchangeable square blades of various heights and styles. Has an unfluted cylinder and roll engraving. Weight about 41 oz. Chambered for 22 LR and 32 H&R Mag., 6½" barrel only. Introduced 1985.
**Price:** . . . . . . . . . . . . . . . . . . . . . . . . . . . . . . . . **$328.75**

### RUGER SUPER BLACKHAWK
**Caliber:** 44 Magnum, 6-shot. Also fires 44 Spec.
**Barrel:** 5½", 7½", 10½".
**Weight:** 48 oz. (7½" bbl.), 51 oz. (10½" bbl.). **Length:** 13⅜" overall (7½" bbl.).
**Stocks:** American walnut.
**Sights:** ⅛" ramp front, micro-click rear adjustable for windage and elevation.
**Features:** Ruger interlock mechanism, non-fluted cylinder, steel grip and cylinder frame, square back trigger guard, wide serrated trigger and wide spur hammer.
**Price:** Blue (S45N, S47N, S411N) . . . . . . . . . . . . . . . . . **$378.50**
**Price:** Stainless (KS45N, KS47N, KS411N) . . . . . . . . . . . . . **$413.75**
**Price:** Stainless KS47NH Hunter with scope rings, 7½" . . . . . . . **$479.50**

### RUGER VAQUERO SINGLE-ACTION REVOLVER
**Caliber:** 44-40, 44 Magnum, 45 Colt, 6-shot.
**Barrel:** 4⅝", 5½", 7½".
**Weight:** 41 oz. **Length:** 13⅜" overall (7½" barrel).
**Stocks:** Smooth rosewood with Ruger medallion.
**Sights:** Blade front, fixed notch rear.
**Features:** Uses Ruger's patented transfer bar safety system and loading gate interlock with classic styling. Blued model has color case-hardened finish on the frame, the rest polished and blued. Stainless model is polished. Introduced 1993. From Sturm, Ruger & Co.
**Price:** BNV44 (4⅝"), BNV445 (5½"), BNV45 (7½"), blue . . . . . **$394.00**
**Price:** KBNV44 (4⅝"), KBNV455 (5½"), KBNV45 (7½"), stainless . **$394.00**

## TEXAS LONGHORN ARMS GROVER'S IMPROVED NO. FIVE
**Caliber:** 44 Magnum, 6-shot.
**Barrel:** 5½".
**Weight:** 44 oz. **Length:** NA.
**Stocks:** Fancy AAA walnut.
**Sights:** Square blade front on ramp, fully adjustable rear.
**Features:** Music wire coil spring action with double locking bolt; polished blue finish. Handmade in limited 1,200-gun production. Grip contour, straps, over-sized base pin, lever latch and lockwork identical copies of Elmer Keith design. Lifetime warranty to original owner. Introduced 1988.
**Price:** . . . . . . . . . . . . . . . . . . . . . . . **$985.00**

Texas Longhorn Grover's No. Five

## TEXAS LONGHORN ARMS RIGHT-HAND SINGLE ACTION
**Caliber:** All centerfire pistol calibers.
**Barrel:** 4¾".
**Weight:** NA. **Length:** NA.
**Stocks:** One-piece fancy walnut, or any fancy AAA wood.
**Sights:** Blade front, grooved topstrap rear.
**Features:** Loading gate and ejector housing on left side of gun. Cylinder rotates to the left. All steel construction; color case-hardened frame; high polish blue; music wire coil springs. Lifetime guarantee to original owner. Introduced 1984. From Texas Longhorn Arms.
**Price:** South Texas Army Limited Edition—handmade, only 1,000 to be produced; "One of One Thousand" engraved on barrel . . . . . **$1,500.00**

### Texas Longhorn Arms Texas Border Special
Similar to the South Texas Army Limited Edition except has 3½" barrel, bird's-head style grip. Same special features. Introduced 1984.
**Price:** . . . . . . . . . . . . . . . . . . . . . . . **$1,500.00**

Texas Longhorn Border Special

### Texas Longhorn Arms Sesquicentennial Model Revolver
Similar to the South Texas Army Model except has ¾-coverage Nimschke-style engraving, antique golden nickel plate finish, one-piece elephant ivory grips. Comes with handmade solid walnut presentation case, factory letter to owner. Limited edition of 150 units. Introduced 1986.
**Price:** . . . . . . . . . . . . . . . . . . . . . . . **$2,500.00**

### Texas Longhorn Arms Cased Set
Set contains one each of the Texas Longhorn Right-Hand Single Actions, all in the same caliber, same serial numbers (100, 200, 300, 400, 500, 600, 700, 800, 900). Ten sets to be made (#1000 donated to NRA museum). Comes in hand-tooled leather case. All other specs same as Limited Edition guns. Introduced 1984.
**Price:** . . . . . . . . . . . . . . . . . . . . . . . **$5,750.00**
**Price:** With ¾-coverage "C-style" engraving . . . . . . . . . . . **$7,650.00**

## UBERTI 1873 CATTLEMAN SINGLE ACTIONS
**Caliber:** 38 Spec., 357 Mag., 44 Spec., 44-40, 45 Colt/45 ACP, 6-shot.
**Barrel:** 4¾", 5½", 7½"; 44-40, 45 Colt also with 3".
**Weight:** 38 oz. (5½" bbl.). **Length:** 10¾" overall (5½" bbl.).
**Stocks:** One-piece smooth walnut.
**Sights:** Blade front, groove rear; fully adjustable rear available.
**Features:** Steel or brass backstrap, trigger guard; color case-hardened frame, blued barrel, cylinder. Imported from Italy by Uberti USA.
**Price:** Steel backstrap, trigger guard, fixed sights . . . . . **$410.00**
**Price:** Brass backstrap, trigger guard, fixed sights . . . . . . . . . . **$365.00**

## UBERTI 1875 SA ARMY OUTLAW REVOLVER
**Caliber:** 357 Mag., 44-40, 45 Colt, 6-shot.
**Barrel:** 7½".
**Weight:** 44 oz. **Length:** 13¾" overall.
**Stocks:** Smooth walnut.
**Sights:** Blade front, notch rear.
**Features:** Replica of the 1875 Remington S.A. Army revolver. Brass trigger guard, color case-hardened frame, rest blued. Imported by Uberti USA.
**Price:** . . . . . . . . . . . . . . . . . . . . . . . **$405.00**
**Price:** 45 Colt/45 ACP convertible . . . . . . . . . . . . . . . . . **$450.00**

## UBERTI 1890 ARMY OUTLAW REVOLVER
**Caliber:** 357 Mag., 44-40, 45 Colt, 6-shot.
**Barrel:** 5½".
**Weight:** 37 oz. **Length:** 12½" overall.
**Stocks:** American walnut.
**Sights:** Blade front, groove rear.
**Features:** Replica of the 1890 Remington single action. Brass trigger guard, rest is blued. Imported by Uberti USA.
**Price:** . . . . . . . . . . . . . . . . . . . . . . . **$410.00**
**Price:** 45 Colt/45 ACP convertible . . . . . . . . . . . . . . . . . **$415.00**

### Texas Longhorn Arms West Texas Flat Top Target
Similar to the South Texas Army Limited Edition except choice of barrel length from 7½" through 15"; flat-top style frame; ⅛" contoured ramp front sight, old model steel micro-click rear adjustable for windage and elevation. Same special features. Introduced 1984.
**Price:** . . . . . . . . . . . . . . . . . . . . . . . **$1,500.00**

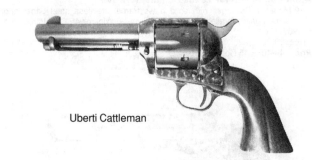

Uberti Cattleman

### Uberti 1873 Buckhorn Single Action
A slightly larger version of the Cattleman revolver. Available in 44 Magnum or 44 Magnum/44-40 convertible, otherwise has same specs.
**Price:** Steel backstrap, trigger guard, fixed sights . . . . . . . . . . **$410.00**
**Price:** Convertible (two cylinders) . . . . . . . . . . . . . . . . . **$460.00**

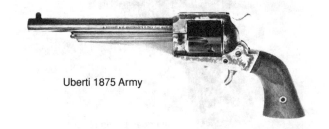

Uberti 1875 Army

Specially adapted single-shot and multi-barrel arms.

American Derringer Model 1

## AMERICAN DERRINGER MODEL 3
**Caliber:** 38 Special.
**Barrel:** 2.5".
**Weight:** 8.5 oz. **Length:** 4.9" overall.
**Stocks:** Rosewood.
**Sights:** Blade front.
**Features:** Made of stainless steel. Single shot with manual hammer block safety. Introduced 1985. From American Derringer Corp.
**Price:** . . . . . . . . . . . . . . . . . . . . . . . **$120.00**

## American Derringer Model 7 Ultra Lightweight
Similar to Model 1 except made of high strength aircraft aluminum. Weighs 7½ oz., 4.82" o.a.l., rosewood stocks. Available in 22 LR, 32 H&R Mag., 380 ACP, 38 Spec., 44 Spec. Introduced 1986.
**Price:** 22 LR . . . . . . . . . . . . . . . . . . . **$200.00**
**Price:** 38 Spec. . . . . . . . . . . . . . . . . . **$202.50**
**Price:** 380 ACP . . . . . . . . . . . . . . . . . **$199.95**
**Price:** 32 H&R Mag. . . . . . . . . . . . . . . **$202.50**
**Price:** 44 Spec. . . . . . . . . . . . . . . . . . **$500.00**

## American Derringer Texas Commemorative
A Model 1 Derringer with solid brass frame, stainless steel barrel and rosewood grips. Available in 38 Speical, 44-40 Win., or 45 Colt. Introduced 1987.
**Price:** 38 Spec. . . . . . . . . . . . . . . . . . **$215.00**
**Price:** 44-40 or 45 Colt . . . . . . . . . . . . **$320.00**

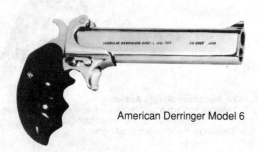

American Derringer Model 6

American Derringer Semmerling

## AMERICAN DERRINGER MODEL 1
**Caliber:** 22 LR, 22 WMR, 30 Luger, 30-30 Win., 32 ACP, 380 ACP, 38 Spec., 9mm Para., 357 Mag., 357 Maximum, 10mm, 40 S&W, 41 Mag., 38-40, 44-40 Win., 44 Spec., 44 Mag., 45 Colt, 45 ACP, 410-bore (2½").
**Barrel:** 3".
**Weight:** 15½ oz. (38 Spec.). **Length:** 4.82" overall.
**Stocks:** Rosewood, Zebra wood.
**Sights:** Blade front.
**Features:** Made of stainless steel with high-polish or satin finish. Two-shot capacity. Manual hammer block safety. Introduced 1980. Available in almost any pistol caliber. Contact the factory for complete list of available calibers and prices. From American Derringer Corp.
**Price:** 22 LR or WMR . . . . . . . . . . . . **$212.50 to $225.00**
**Price:** 38 Spec. . . . . . . . . . . . . . . . . . **$219.00**
**Price:** 357 Maximum . . . . . . . . . . . . . **$265.00**
**Price:** 357 Mag. . . . . . . . . . . . . . . . . . **$250.00**
**Price:** 9mm, 380, . . . . . . . . . . . . . . . . **$215.00**
**Price:** 10mm, 40 S&W . . . . . . . . . . . . **$250.00**
**Price:** 44 Spec., . . . . . . . . . . . . . . . . . **$320.00**
**Price:** 44-40 Win., 45 Colt, 45 Auto Rim . . **$320.00**
**Price:** 30-30, 41, 44 Mags., 45 Win. Mag. . **$375.00**
**Price:** 45-70, single shot . . . . . . . . . . . **$312.00**
**Price:** 45 Colt, 410, 2½" . . . . . . . . . . . **$320.00**
**Price:** 45 ACP, 10mm Auto . . . . . . . . . **$250.00**
**Price:** 125th Anniversary model (brass frame, stainless bbl., 44-40, 45 Colt, 38 Spec.) . . . . . . . . . . . . . . . . . . . **$320.00**
**Price:** Alaskan Survival model (45-70 upper, 410-45 Colt lower) . . . **$387.50**

## American Derringer Model 4
Similar to the Model 1 except has 4.1" barrel, overall length of 6", and weighs 16½ oz.; chambered for 3" 410-bore shotshells or 45 or 44 Magnum Colt. Can be had with 45-70 upper barrel and 3" 410-bore or 45 Colt bottom barrel. Made of stainless steel. Manual hammer block safety. Introduced 1985.
**Price:** 3" 410/45 Colt (either barrel) . . . . . . . . **$352.00**
**Price:** 3" 410/45 Colt or 45-70 (Alaskan Survival model) . . . . . . **$387.50**
**Price:** 44 Magnum with oversize grips . . . . . . . . **$422.00**

## American Derringer Model 6
Similar to the Model 1 except has 6" barrels chambered for 3" 410 shotshells or 45 Colt, rosewood stocks, 8.2" o.a.l. and weighs 21 oz. Shoots either round for each barrel. Manual hammer block safety. Introduced 1986.
**Price:** High polish or satin finish . . . . . . . . . . . . . . . . . **$387.50**
**Price:** Gray matte finish . . . . . . . . . . . . . . . . . . . . . . . **$362.50**

## American Derringer Model 10 Lightweight
Similar to the Model 1 except frame is of aluminum, giving weight of 10 oz. Available in 45 Colt or 45 ACP only. Matte gray finish. Introduced 1989.
**Price:** 45 Colt . . . . . . . . . . . . . . . . . . . . . . . . . . . . . **$320.00**
**Price:** 45 ACP . . . . . . . . . . . . . . . . . . . . . . . . . . . . . **$250.00**
**Price:** Model 11 (38 Spec., aluminum bbls., wgt. 11 oz.) . . . . . . . **$205.00**

## American Derringer Lady Derringer
Same as the Model 1 except has tuned action, is fitted with scrimshawed synthetic ivory grips; chambered for 32 H&R Mag. and 38 Spec.; 22 LR, 22 WMR, 380 ACP, 357 Mag., 9mm Para., 45 ACP, 45 Colt/410 shotshell available at extra cost. Deluxe Grade is highly polished; Deluxe Engraved is engraved in a pattern similar to that used on 1880s derringers. All come in a French fitted jewelry box. Introduced 1991.
**Price:** Deluxe Grade . . . . . . . . . . . . . . . . . . . . . . . . . **$235.00**
**Price:** Deluxe Engraved Grade . . . . . . . . . . . . . . . . . . . **$750.00**

## AMERICAN DERRINGER SEMMERLING LM-4
**Caliber:** 9mm Para., 7-shot magazine; 45 ACP, 5-shot magazine.
**Barrel:** 3.625".
**Weight:** 24 oz. **Length:** 5.2" overall.
**Stocks:** Checkered plastic on blued guns, rosewood on stainless guns.
**Sights:** Open, fixed.
**Features:** Manually-operated repeater. Height is 3.7", width is 1". Comes with manual, leather carrying case, spare stock screws, wrench. From American Derringer Corp.
**Price:** Blued . . . . . . . . . . . . . . . . . . . . . . . . . . . . . . **$1,750.00**
**Price:** Stainless steel . . . . . . . . . . . . . . . . . . . . . . . . . **$1,875.00**

**CAUTION:** PRICES CHANGE. CHECK AT GUNSHOP.

## AMERICAN DERRINGER DA 38 MODEL
**Caliber:** 9mm Para., 38 Spec., 357 Mag., 40 S&W.
**Barrel:** 3".
**Weight:** 14.5 oz. **Length:** 4.8" overall.
**Stocks:** Rosewood, walnut or other hardwoods.
**Sights:** Fixed.
**Features:** Double-action only; two-shots. Manual safety. Made of satin-finished stainless steel and aluminum. Introduced 1989. From American Derringer Corp.
**Price:** 38 Spec. . . . . . . . . . . . . . . . . . . . . . . $250.00
**Price:** 9mm Para. . . . . . . . . . . . . . . . . . . . . $275.00
**Price:** 357 Mag., 40 S&W . . . . . . . . . . . . . . $300.00

## ANSCHUTZ EXEMPLAR BOLT-ACTION PISTOL
**Caliber:** 22 LR, 5-shot; 22 Hornet, 5-shot.
**Barrel:** 10", 14".
**Weight:** 3½ lbs. **Length:** 17" overall.
**Stock:** European walnut with stippled grip and forend.
**Sights:** Hooded front on ramp, open notch rear adjustable for windage and elevation.
**Features:** Uses Match 64 action with left-hand bolt; Anschutz #5091 two-stage trigger set at 9.85 oz. Receiver grooved for scope mounting; open sights easily removed. Introduced 1987. Imported from Germany by Precision Sales International.
**Price:** 22 LR . . . . . . . . . . . . . . . . . . . . . . . $499.50
**Price:** 22 LR, left-hand . . . . . . . . . . . . . . . . $499.50
**Price:** 22 LR, 14" barrel . . . . . . . . . . . . . . . $522.00
**Price:** 22 Hornet (no sights, 10" bbl.) . . . . . . . $822.00

## DAVIS DERRINGERS
**Caliber:** 22 LR, 22 WMR, 25 ACP, 32 ACP.
**Barrel:** 2.4".
**Weight:** 9.5 oz. **Length:** 4" overall.
**Stocks:** Laminated wood.
**Sights:** Blade front, fixed notch rear.
**Features:** Choice of black Teflon or chrome finish; spur trigger. Introduced 1986. Made in U.S. by Davis Industries.
**Price:** . . . . . . . . . . . . . . . . . . . . . . . . . . . $64.90

Davis D-38

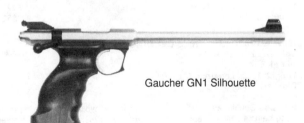

Gaucher GN1 Silhouette

## HIGH STANDARD DERRINGER
**Caliber:** 22 LR, 22 WMR, 2-shot.
**Barrel:** 3.5".
**Weight:** 11 oz. **Length:** 5.12" overall.
**Stocks:** Black composition.
**Sights:** Fixed.
**Features:** Double action, dual extraction. Hammer-block safety. Blue finish. Introduced 1990. Made in U.S. by American Derringer Corp.
**Price:** . . . . . . . . . . . . . . . . . . . . . . . . . . $169.50

## AMERICAN DERRINGER COP 357 DERRINGER
**Caliber:** 38 Spec. or 357 Mag., 4-shot.
**Barrel:** 3.14".
**Weight:** 16 oz. **Length:** 5.53" overall.
**Stocks:** Rosewood.
**Sights:** Fixed.
**Features:** Double-action only. Four shots. Made of stainless steel. Introduced 1990. Made in U.S. by American Derringer Corp.
**Price:** . . . . . . . . . . . . . . . . . . . . . . . . . . $375.00

## American Derringer Mini COP Derringer
Similar to the COP 357 except chambered for 22 WMR. Barrel length of 2.85", overall length of 4.95", weight is 16 oz. Double action with automatic hammer-block safety. Made of stainless steel. Grips of rosewood, walnut or other hardwoods. Introduced 1990. Made in U.S. by American Derringer Corp.
**Price:** . . . . . . . . . . . . . . . . . . . . . . . . . . $312.50

Anschutz Exemplar

## DAVIS D-38 DERRINGER
**Caliber:** 38 Special.
**Barrel:** 2.75".
**Weight:** 11.5 oz. **Length:** 4.65" overall.
**Stocks:** Textured black synthetic.
**Sights:** Blade front, fixed notch rear.
**Features:** Alloy frame, stee-lined barrels, steel breech block. Plunger-type safety with integral hammer block. Chrome or black Teflon finish. Introduced 1992. Made in U.S. by Davis Industries.
**Price:** . . . . . . . . . . . . . . . . . . . . . . . . . . $89.90

## FEATHER GUARDIAN ANGEL PISTOL
**Caliber:** 22 LR/22 WMR.
**Barrel:** 2".
**Weight:** 12 oz. **Length:** 5" overall.
**Stocks:** Black composition.
**Sights:** Fixed.
**Features:** Uses a pre-loaded two-shot drop-in "magazine." Stainless steel construction; matte finish. From Feather Industries. Introduced 1988.
**Price:** . . . . . . . . . . . . . . . . . . . . . . . . . . $119.95

## GAUCHER GN1 SILHOUETTE PISTOL
**Caliber:** 22 LR, single shot.
**Barrel:** 10".
**Weight:** 2.4 lbs. **Length:** 15.5" overall.
**Stock:** European hardwood.
**Sights:** Blade front, open adjustable rear.
**Features:** Bolt action, adjustable trigger. Introduced 1990. Imported from France by Mandall Shooting Supplies.
**Price:** About . . . . . . . . . . . . . . . . . . . . . . . $319.95
**Price:** Model GP Silhouette . . . . . . . . . . . . . $380.00

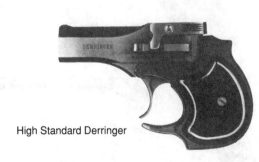

High Standard Derringer

**CAUTION:** PRICES CHANGE, CHECK AT GUNSHOP.

## HJS FRONTIER FOUR DERRINGER
**Caliber:** 22 LR.
**Barrel:** 2".
**Weight:** 5½ oz. **Length:** 3¹⁵⁄₁₆" overall.
**Stocks:** Black plastic.
**Sights:** None.
**Features:** Four barrels fire with rotating firing pin. Stainless steel construction. Introduced 1993. Made in U.S. by HJS Arms, Inc.
**Price:** . . . . . . . . . . . . . . . . . . . . . . . . . . . $160.00

## HJS LONE STAR DERRINGER
**Caliber:** 380 ACP, 38 S&W.
**Barrel:** 2".
**Weight:** 6 oz. **Length:** 3¹⁵⁄₁₆" overall.
**Stocks:** Black plastic.
**Sights:** Groove.
**Features:** Stainless steel Construction. Beryllium copper firing pin. Button-rifled barrel. Introduced 1993. Made in U.S. by HJS Arms, Inc.
**Price:** . . . . . . . . . . . . . . . . . . . . . . . . . . . $180.00

## ITHACA X-CALIBER SINGLE SHOT
**Caliber:** 22 LR, 44 Mag.
**Barrel:** 10", 15".
**Weight:** 3¼ lbs. **Length:** 15" overall (10" barrel).
**Stocks:** Goncalo Alves grip and forend on Model 20; American walnut on Model 30.
**Sights:** Blade on ramp front; Model 20 has adjustable, removable target-type rear. Drilled and tapped for scope mounting.
**Features:** Dual firing pin for RF/CF use. Polished blue finish.
**Price:** 22 LR, 10", 44 Mag., 10" or 15" . . . . . . . . $270.00
**Price:** 22 LR/44 Mag. combo, 10" and 15" . . . . . . . . . $365.00
**Price:** As above, both 10" barrels . . . . . . . . . $365.00

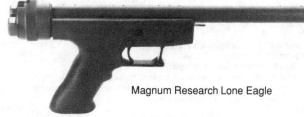

Magnum Research Lone Eagle

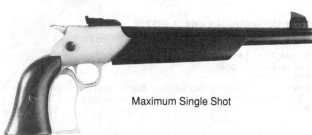

Maximum Single Shot

New Advantage Derringer

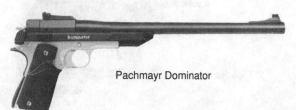

Pachmayr Dominator

HJS Frontier Four

## MANDALL/CABANAS PISTOL
**Caliber:** 177, pellet or round ball; single shot.
**Barrel:** 9".
**Weight:** 51 oz. **Length:** 19" overall.
**Stock:** Smooth wood with thumbrest.
**Sights:** Blade front on ramp, open adjustable rear.
**Features:** Fires round ball or pellets with 22 blank cartridge. Automatic safety; muzzlebrake. Imported from Mexico by Mandall Shooting Supplies.
**Price:** . . . . . . . . . . . . . . . . . . . . . . . . . . . $139.95

## MAGNUM RESEARCH LONE EAGLE SINGLE SHOT PISTOL
**Caliber:** 22 Hornet, 223, 22-250, 243, 7mm BR, 7mm-08, 30-30, 308, 30-06, 357 Max., 35 Rem., 358 Win., 44 Mag., 444 Marlin.
**Barrel:** 14", interchangable.
**Weight:** 4lbs., 3 oz. to 4 lbs., 7 oz. **Length:** 15" overall.
**Stocks:** Composition, with thumbrest.
**Sights:** None furnished; drilled and tapped for scope mounting and open sights. Open sights optional.
**Features:** Cannon-type rotating breech with spring-activated ejector. Ordnance steel with matte blue finish. Cross-bolt safety. External cocking lever on left side of gun. Introduced 1991. Available from Magnum Research, Inc.
**Price:** Complete pistol . . . . . . . . . . . . . . . . $344.00
**Price:** Barreled action only . . . . . . . . . . . . . . . . $254.00
**Price:** Scope base . . . . . . . . . . . . . . . . $14.00
**Price:** Adjustable open sights . . . . . . . . . . . . . . . . $35.00

## MAXIMUM SINGLE SHOT PISTOL
**Caliber:** 22 LR, 22 Hornet, 22 BR, 223 Rem., 22-250, 6mm BR, 6mm-223, 243, 250 Savage, 6.5mm-35, 7mm TCU, 7mm BR, 7mm-35, 7mm INT-R, 7mm-08, 7mm Rocket, 7mm Super Mag., 30 Herrett, 30 Carbine, 308 Win., 7.62 x 39, 32-20, 357 Mag., 357 Maximum, 358 Win., 44 Mag.
**Barrel:** 8¾", 10½", 14".
**Weight:** 61 oz. (10½" bbl.); 78 oz. (14" bbl.). **Length:** 15", 18½" overall (with 10½" and 14" bbl., respectively).
**Stocks:** Smooth walnut stocks and forend.
**Sights:** Ramp front, fully adjustable open rear.
**Features:** Falling block action; drilled and tapped for M.O.A. scope mounts; integral grip frame/receiver; adjustable trigger; Douglas barrel (interchangeable). Introduced 1983. Made in U.S. by M.O.A. Corp.
**Price:** Stainless receiver, blue barrel . . . . . . . . . . . . $622.00
**Price:** Stainless receiver, stainless barrel . . . . . . . . . . $677.00
**Price:** Extra blued barrel . . . . . . . . . . . . . . . . $164.00
**Price:** Extra stainless barrel . . . . . . . . . . . . . . . . $222.00
**Price:** Scope mount . . . . . . . . . . . . . . . . . . . . $52.00

## NEW ADVANTAGE ARMS DERRINGER
**Caliber:** 22 LR, 22 WMR, 4-shot.
**Barrel:** 2½".
**Weight:** 15 oz. **Length:** 4½" overall.
**Stocks:** Smooth walnut.
**Sights:** Fixed.
**Features:** Double-action mechanism, four barrels, revolving firing pin. Rebounding hammer. Blue or stainless. Reintroduced 1989. From New Advantage Arms Corp.
**Price:** 22 LR, 22 WMR, blue, about . . . . . . . . . . . . . . . . $199.00
**Price:** As above, stainless, about . . . . . . . . . . . . . . . . $229.00

## PACHMAYR DOMINATOR PISTOL
**Caliber:** 22 Hornet, 223, 7mm-06, 308, 35 Rem., 44 Mag., single shot.
**Barrel:** 10½" (44 Mag.), 14" all other calibers.
**Weight:** 4 lbs. (14" barrel). **Length:** 16" overall (14" barrel).
**Stocks:** Pachmayr Signature system.
**Sights:** Optional sights or drilled and tapped for scope mounting.
**Features:** Bolt-action pistol on 1911A1 frame. Comes as complete gun. Introduced 1988. From Pachmayr.
**Price:** Either barrel . . . . . . . . . . . . . . . . . . . . . . . $524.50

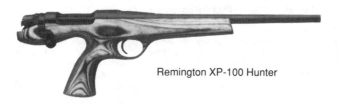

Remington XP-100 Hunter

Remington XP-100R KS

## RPM XL SINGLE SHOT PISTOL

**Caliber:** 22 LR, 22 WMR, 225 Win., 25 Rocket, 6.5 Rocket, 32 H&R Mag., 357 Max., 357 Mag., 30-30 Win., 30 Herrett, 357 Herrett, 41 Mag., 44 Mag., 454 Casull, 375 Win., 7mm UR, 7mm Merrill, 30 Merrill, 7mm Rocket, 270 Ren, 270 Rocket, 270 Max., 45-70.

**Barrel:** 8" slab, 10¾", 12", 14" bull; .450" wide rib, matted to prevent glare.

**Weight:** About 60 oz. **Length:** 12¼" overall (10¾" bbl.).

**Stocks:** Smooth Goncalo with thumb and heel rest.

**Sights:** Front .100" blade, Millett rear adjustable for windage and elevation. Hooded front with interchangeable post optional.

**Features:** Blue finish, hard chrome optional. Barrel is drilled and tapped for scope mounting. Cocking indicator visible from rear of gun. Has spring-loaded barrel lock, positive hammer block thumb safety. Trigger adjustable for weight of pull and over-travel. For complete price list contact RPM.

**Price:** Regular ¾" frame, right-hand action . . . . . . . . . . . . . . . **$807.50**
**Price:** As above, left-hand action . . . . . . . . . . . . . . . . . . . . . . **$832.50**
**Price:** Wide ⅞" frame, right-hand action . . . . . . . . . . . . . . . . . **$857.50**
**Price:** Extra barrel, 8", 10¾" . . . . . . . . . . . . . . . . . . . . . . . . . **$287.50**
**Price:** Extra barrel, 12", 14" . . . . . . . . . . . . . . . . . . . . . . . . . . **$357.50**

Texas Arms Defender

## TEXAS LONGHORN "THE JEZEBEL" PISTOL

**Caliber:** 22 Short, Long, Long Rifle, single shot.

**Barrel:** 6".

**Weight:** 15 oz. **Length:** 8" overall.

**Stocks:** One-piece fancy walnut grip (right- or left-hand), walnut forend.

**Sights:** Bead front, fixed rear.

**Features:** Handmade gun. Top-break action; all stainless steel; automatic hammer block safety; music wire coil springs. Barrel is half-round, half-octagon. Announced 1986. From Texas Longhorn Arms.

**Price:** About . . . . . . . . . . . . . . . . . . . . . . . . . . . . . . . . . . . **$250.00**

T/C Contender

## REMINGTON XP-100 HUNTER PISTOL

**Caliber:** 223 Rem., 7mm BR Rem., 7mm-08 Rem., 35 Rem., single shot.

**Barrel:** 14½".

**Weight:** 4½ lbs. **Length:** 21¼" overall.

**Stocks:** Laminated wood with contoured grip.

**Sights:** None furnished. Drilled and tapped for scope mounting.

**Features:** Mid-handle grip design with scalloped contours for right- or left-handed shooters; two-position safety. Matte blue finish. Introduced 1993.

**Price:** . . . . . . . . . . . . . . . . . . . . . . . . . . . . . . . . . . . . . . **$532.00**

## Remington XP-100 Custom HB Long Range Pistol

Similar to the XP-100 "Varmint Special" except chambered for 223 Rem., 22-250, 7mm-08 Rem., 35 Rem., 250 Savage, 6mm BR, 7mm BR, 308. Offered with standard 14½" barrel with adjustable rear leaf and front bead sights, or with heavy 15½" barrel without sights. Custom Shop 14½" barrel, Custom Shop English walnut stock in right- or left-hand configuration. Action tuned in Custom Shop. Weight is under 4½ lbs. (heavy barrel, 5½ lbs.). Introduced 1986.

**Price:** Right- or left-hand . . . . . . . . . . . . . . . . . . . . . . . . . **$945.00**

## Remington XP-100R KS Repeater Pistol

Similar to the Custom Long Range Pistol except chambered for 223 Rem., 22-250, 7mm-08 Rem., 250 Savage, 308, 350 Rem. Mag., and 35 Rem., and has a blind magazine holding 5 rounds (7mm-08 and 35), or 6 (223 Rem.). Comes with a rear-handle, synthetic stock of Du Pont Kevlar to eliminate the transfer bar between the forward trigger and rear trigger assembly. Fitted with front and rear sling swivel studs. Has standard-weight 14½" barrel with adjustable leaf rear sight, bead front. The receiver is drilled and tapped for scope mounts. Weight is about 4½ lbs. Introduced 1990. From Remington Custom Shop.

**Price:** . . . . . . . . . . . . . . . . . . . . . . . . . . . . . . . . . . . . . . **$840.00**

RPM XL Pistol

## TEXAS ARMS DEFENDER DERRINGER

**Caliber:** 9mm Para., 38 Spec., 357 Mag., 40 S&W, 44 Mag., 45 ACP, 45 Colt/410.

**Barrel:** 3", 3.5".

**Weight:** 21 oz. **Length:** 5" overall.

**Stocks:** Smooth wood.

**Sights:** Blade front, fixed rear.

**Features:** Interchangeable barrels; retracting firing pins; rebounding hammer; cross-bolt safety; removable trigger guard; automatic extractor. Matte finish stainless steel. Introduced 1993. Made in U.S. by Texas Arms.

**Price:** . . . . . . . . . . . . . . . . . . . . . . . . . . . . . . . . . . . . . . **$310.00**
**Price:** Extra barrel sets . . . . . . . . . . . . . . . . . . . . . . . . . . . . **$100.00**

## THOMPSON/CENTER CONTENDER

**Caliber:** 7mm TCU, 30-30 Win., 22 LR, 22 WMR, 22 Hornet, 223 Rem., 270 Ren, 7-30 Waters, 32-20 Win., 357 Mag., 357 Rem. Max., 44 Mag., 10mm Auto, 445 Super Mag., 45/410, single shot.

**Barrel:** 10", tapered octagon, bull barrel and vent. rib.

**Weight:** 43 oz. (10" bbl.). **Length:** 13¼" (10" bbl.).

**Stocks:** T/C "Competitor Grip." Right or left hand.

**Sights:** Under-cut blade ramp front, rear adjustable for windage and elevation.

**Features:** Break-open action with automatic safety. Single-action only. Interchangeable bbls., both caliber (rim & centerfire), and length. Drilled and tapped for scope. Engraved frame. See T/C catalog for exact barrel/caliber availability.

**Price:** Blued (rimfire cals.) . . . . . . . . . . . . . . . . . . . . . . . . . **$415.00**
**Price:** Blued (centerfire cals.) . . . . . . . . . . . . . . . . . . . . . . . . **$415.00**
**Price:** Extra bbls. (standard octagon) . . . . . . . . . . . . . . . . . . **$190.00**
**Price:** 45/410, internal choke bbl. . . . . . . . . . . . . . . . . . . . . . **$210.00**

T/C Stainless Super 14

**Thompson/Center Contender Hunter Package**
Package contains the Contender pistol in 223, 7-30 Waters, 30-30, 375 Win., 357 Rem. Maximum, 35 Rem., 44 Mag. or 45-70 with 12" or 14" barrel with T/C's Muzzle Tamer, a 2.5x Recoil Proof Long Eye Relief scope with lighted reticle, q.d. sling swivels with a nylon carrying sling. Comes with a suede leather case with foam padding and fleece lining. Introduced 1990. From Thompson/Center Arms.
Price: 12" barrel . . . . . . . . . . . . . . . . . . . . . . . . . . . **$695.00**
Price: 14" barrel . . . . . . . . . . . . . . . . . . . . . . . . . . . **$705.00**

**UBERTI ROLLING BLOCK TARGET PISTOL**
Caliber: 22 LR, 22 WMR, 22 Hornet, 357 Mag., single shot.
Barrel: 9⅞", half-round, half-octagon.
Weight: 44 oz. Length: 14" overall.
Stocks: Walnut grip and forend.
Sights: Blade front, fully adjustable rear.
Features: Replica of the 1871 rolling block target pistol. Brass trigger guard, color case-hardened frame, blue barrel. Imported by Uberti USA.
Price: . . . . . . . . . . . . . . . . . . . . . . . . . . . . . . . . **$380.00**

**ULTRA LIGHT ARMS MODEL 20 REB HUNTER'S PISTOL**
Caliber: 22-250 thru 308 Win. standard. Most silhouette calibers and others on request. 5-shot magazine.
Barrel: 14", Douglas No. 3.
Weight: 4 lbs.
Stock: Composite Kevlar, graphite reinforced. Du Pont Imron paint in green, brown, black and camo.
Sights: None furnished. Scope mount included.
Features: Timney adjustable trigger; two-position, three-function safety; benchrest quality action; matte or bright stock and metal finish; right- or left-hand action. Shipped in hard case. Introduced 1987. From Ultra Light Arms.
Price: . . . . . . . . . . . . . . . . . . . . . . . . . . . . . **$1,600.00**

**WICHITA MASTER PISTOL**
Caliber: 6mm BR, 7mm BR, 243, 7mm-08, 22-250, 308, 3 or 5-shot magazine.
Barrel: 13", 14.875".
Weight: 4.5 lbs. (13" barrel). Length: NA.
Stock: American walnut with oil finish; glass bedded.
Sights: Hooded post front, open adjustable rear.
Features: Comes with left-hand action with right-hand grip. round receiver and barrel. Wichita adjustable trigger. Introduced 1991. From Wichita Arms.
Price: . . . . . . . . . . . . . . . . . . . . . . . . . . . . . **$1,500.00**

**Thompson/Center Stainless Contender**
Same as the standard Contender except made of stainless steel with blued sights, black Rynite forend and ambidextrous finger-groove grip with a built-in rubber recoil cushion that has a sealed-in air pocket. Receiver has a different cougar etching. Available with 10" bull barrel in 22 LR, 22 LR Match, 22 Hornet, 223 Rem., 30-30 Win., 357 Mag., 44 Mag., 45 Colt/410. Introduced 1993.
Price: . . . . . . . . . . . . . . . . . . . . . . . . . . . . . . . **$445.00**
Price: 45 Colt/410 . . . . . . . . . . . . . . . . . . . . . . . . . **$465.00**

**Thompson/Center Stainless Super 14, Super 16 Contender**
Same as the standard Super 14 and Super 16 except they are made of stainless steel with blued sights. Both models have black Rynite forend and finger-groove, ambidextrous grip with a built-in rubber recoil cushion that has a sealed-in air pocket. Receiver has a different cougar etching. Available in 22 LR, 22 LR Match, 22 Hornet, 223 Rem., 30-30 Win., 35 Rem. (Super 14), 45-70 (Super 16 only), 45 Colt/410. Introduced 1993.
Price: 14" bull barrel . . . . . . . . . . . . . . . . . . . . . . . **$455.00**
Price: 16¼" bull barrel . . . . . . . . . . . . . . . . . . . . . . **$460.00**
Price: 45 Colt/410, 14" . . . . . . . . . . . . . . . . . . . . . . **$475.00**
Price: 45 Colt/410, 16" . . . . . . . . . . . . . . . . . . . . . . **$480.00**

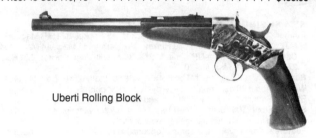

Uberti Rolling Block

Ultra Light Model 20

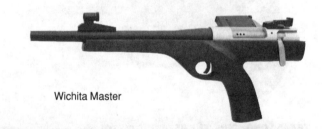

Wichita Master

# CENTERFIRE RIFLES—AUTOLOADERS

Includes models for hunting, adaptable to and suitable for certain competition.

Thompson M1

**Auto-Ordnance Thompson M1**
Similar to the Model 27 A-1 except is in the M-1 configuration with side cocking knob, horizontal forend, smooth unfinned barrel, sling swivels on butt and forend. Matte black finish. Introduced 1985.
Price: . . . . . . . . . . . . . . . . . . . . . . . . . . . . . . . **$712.50**

**AUTO-ORDNANCE 27 A-1 THOMPSON**
Caliber: 45 ACP, 30-shot magazine.
Barrel: 16".
Weight: 11½ lbs. Length: About 42" overall (Deluxe).
Stock: Walnut stock and vertical forend.
Sights: Blade front, open rear adjustable for windage.
Features: Recreation of Thompson Model 1927. Semi-auto only. Deluxe model has finned barrel, adjustable rear sight and compensator; Standard model has plain barrel and military sight. From Auto-Ordnance Corp.
Price: Deluxe . . . . . . . . . . . . . . . . . . . . . . . . . . . **$735.00**
Price: 1927A5 Pistol (M27A1 without stock; wgt. 7 lbs.) . . . . . . . **$704.00**
Price: 1927A1C Lightweight model . . . . . . . . . . . . . . . . . **$707.00**

## BARRETT LIGHT-FIFTY MODEL 82 A-1 AUTO
**Caliber:** 50 BMG, 10-shot detachable box magazine.
**Barrel:** 29".
**Weight:** 28.5 lbs. **Length:** 57" overall.
**Stock:** Composition with Sorbothane recoil pad.
**Sights:** Open, iron and 10x scope.
**Features:** Semi-automatic, recoil operated with recoiling barrel. Three-lug locking bolt; muzzlebrake. Self-leveling bipod. Fires same 50-cal. ammunition as the M2HB machinegun. Introduced 1985. From Barrett Firearms.
**Price:** From . . . . . . . . . . . . . . . . . . . . . . . . . . . . . . **$6,750.00**

> Consult our Directory pages for the location of firms mentioned.

Browning Mark II Safari

## BROWNING BAR MARK II SAFARI SEMI-AUTO RIFLE
**Caliber:** 243, 270, 30-06, 308.
**Barrel:** 22" round tapered.
**Weight:** 7⅜ lbs. **Length:** 43" overall.
**Stock:** French walnut p.g. stock and forend, hand checkered.
**Sights:** Gold bead on hooded ramp front, click adjustable rear, or no sights.
**Features:** Has new bolt release lever; removable trigger assembly with larger trigger guard; redesigned gas and buffer systems. Detachable 4-round box magazine. Scroll-engraved receiver is tapped for scope mounting. Mark II Safari introduced 1993. Imported from Belgium by Browning.
**Price:** Safari, with sights . . . . . . . . . . . . . . . . . . . **$664.95**
**Price:** Safari, no sights . . . . . . . . . . . . . . . . . . . . **$647.95**

## Browning BAR Mark II Safari Magnum Rifle
Same as the standard caliber model, except weighs 8⅜ lbs., 45" overall, 24" bbl., 3-round mag. Cals. 7mm Mag., 270 Wea. Mag., 300 Win. Mag., 338 Win. Mag. Introduced 1993.
**Price:** Safari, with sights . . . . . . . . . . . . . . . . . . . **$713.95**
**Price:** Safari, no sights . . . . . . . . . . . . . . . . . . . . **$697.95**

Calico Model M-951

## CALICO MODEL M-900 CARBINE
**Caliber:** 9mm Para., 50- or 100-shot magazine.
**Barrel:** 16.1".
**Weight:** 3.7 lbs. (empty). **Length:** 28½" overall (stock collapsed).
**Stock:** Sliding steel buttstock.
**Sights:** Post front adjustable for windage and elevation, fixed notch rear.
**Feature:** Helical feed 50- or 100-shot magazine. Ambidextrous safety, static cocking handle. Retarded blowback action. Glass-filled polymer grip. Introduced 1989. From Calico.
**Price:** . . . . . . . . . . . . . . . . . . . . . . . . . . . . . . . **$617.90**

## Calico Model M-951 Tactical Carbine
Similar to the M-900 Carbine except has an adjustable forward grip, long compensator, and 16.1" barrel. 9mm Para., 50- or 100-shot magazine. Introduced 1990. Made in U.S. by Calico.
**Price:** . . . . . . . . . . . . . . . . . . . . . . . . . . . . . . . **$661.90**
**Price:** M-951-S (as above except fixed buttstock) . . . . . . . . . . **$674.90**

Century FAL Sporter

## CENTURY INTERNATIONAL M-14 SEMI-AUTO RIFLE
**Caliber:** 308 Win., 20-shot magazine.
**Barrel:** 22".
**Weight:** 8.25 lbs. **Length:** 40.8" overall.
**Stock:** Walnut with rubber recoil pad.
**Sights:** Protected blade front, fully adjustable aperture rear.
**Features:** Gas-operated; forged receiver; Parkerized finish. Imported from China by Century International Arms.
**Price:** About . . . . . . . . . . . . . . . . . . . . . . . . . . . **$468.95**

## CENTURY INTERNATIONAL FAL SPORTER RIFLE
**Caliber:** 308 Win.
**Barrel:** 20.75".
**Weight:** 9 lbs., 13 oz. **Length:** 41.125" overall.
**Stock:** Bell & Carlson thumbhole sporter.
**Sights:** Protected post front, adjustable aperture rear.
**Features:** Matte blue finish; rubber butt pad. From Century International Arms.
**Price:** About . . . . . . . . . . . . . . . . . . . . . . . . . . . **$625.00**

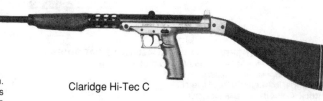

Claridge Hi-Tec C

## CLARIDGE HI-TEC C CARBINE
**Caliber:** 9mm Para., 18-shot magazine.
**Barrel:** 16.1".
**Weight:** 4 lbs., 9 oz. **Length:** 31.7" overall.
**Stock:** Walnut.
**Sights:** Adjustable post front in ring, open rear adjustable for windage.
**Features:** Aluminum or stainless frame. Telescoping bolt, floating firing pin. Safety locks the firing pin. Sight radius of 20.1". Accepts same magazines as Claridge Hi-Tec pistols. Can be equipped with scope or Aimpoint sight. Also available in 40 S&W and 45 ACP. Made in U.S. From Claridge Hi-Tec, Inc.
**Price:** . . . . . . . . . . . . . . . . . . . . . . . . . . . . . . . **$525.50**
**Price:** Model LEC-9 (as above with graphite composite stock) . . . **$579.00**
**Price:** Model ZLEC-9 (as above with laser sight) . . . . . . . . . **$898.50**

Colt Sporter Lightweight

## COLT SPORTER LIGHTWEIGHT RIFLE
**Caliber:** 9mm Para., 223 Rem., 7.62x39mm, 5-shot magazine.
**Barrel:** 16".
**Weight:** 6.7 lbs. (223); 7.1 lbs. (9mm Para.). **Length:** 34.5" overall extended.
**Stock:** Composition stock, grip, forend.
**Sights:** Post front, rear adjustable for windage and elevation.
**Features:** 5-round detachable box magazine, flash suppressor, sling swivels. Forward bolt assist included. Introduced 1991.
**Price:** . . . . . . . . . . . . . . . . . . . . . . . . . . . . . . $877.95
**Price:** 7.62x39mm . . . . . . . . . . . . . . . . . . . . . . . $859.95

Eagle Arms EA-15

## EAGLE ARMS EA-15 AUTO RIFLE
**Caliber:** 223 Rem., 30-shot magazine.
**Barrel:** 20".
**Weight:** About 7 lbs. **Length:** 39" overall.
**Stock:** Black composition; trapdoor-style buttstock.
**Sights:** Post front, fully adjustable rear.
**Features:** Upper and lower receivers have push-type pivot pin for easy takedown. Receivers hard coat anodized. E2-style forward assist mechanism. Integral raised M-16A2-type fence around magazine release button. Introduced 1989. Made in U.S. by Eagle Arms, Inc.
**Price:** . . . . . . . . . . . . . . . . . . . . . . . . . . . . . . $800.00

## Eagle Arms EA-15 Action Master Auto Rifle
Same as the EA-15 Standard Model except has a one-piece international-style upper receiver for scope mounting, no front sight; solid aluminum handguard tube; free-floating 20" Douglas Premium fluted barrel; muzzle compensator; NM trigger group and bolt carrier group. Weighs about 8 lbs., 5 oz. Introduced 1991. Made in U.S. by Eagle Arms, Inc.
**Price:** . . . . . . . . . . . . . . . . . . . . . . . . . . . . . . $1,075.00

## Eagle Arms EA-15 Golden Eagle Auto Rifle
Same as the EA-15 Standard Model except has E2-style National Match rear sight with ½-MOA adjustments, elevation-adjustable NM front sight with set screw; 20" Douglas Premium extra-heavy match barrel with 1:9" twist; NM trigger group and bolt carrier group. Weight about 12 lbs., 12 oz. Introduced 1991. Made in U.S. by Eagle Arms, Inc.
**Price:** . . . . . . . . . . . . . . . . . . . . . . . . . . . . . . $1,075.00

> Consult our Directory pages for the location of firms mentioned.

## Eagle Arms EA-15 E1, E2 Carbines
Same as the EA-15 Standard Model except has collapsible carbine-type buttstock, 16" heavy carbine barrel. Weighs about 5 lbs., 14 oz. (E1), 6 lbs., 2 oz. (E2). Introduced 1989. Made in U.S. by Eagle Arms, Inc.
**Price:** E1 Carbine . . . . . . . . . . . . . . . . . . . . . . . $845.00
**Price:** E2 Carbine (.73" dia. bbl., NM sights) . . . . . . . . . $895.00

## Eagle Arms EA-15 E2 H-BAR Auto Rifle
Same as the EA-15 Golden Eagle except has 20" standard heavy match barrel with 1:9" twist. Weighs about 8 lbs., 9 oz. Introduced 1989. Made in U.S. by Eagle Arms, Inc.
**Price:** . . . . . . . . . . . . . . . . . . . . . . . . . . . . . . $890.00
**Price:** With standard sights . . . . . . . . . . . . . . . . . . $895.00

Feather Model F9

## FEATHER AT-9 SEMI-AUTO CARBINE
**Caliber:** 9mm Para., 25-shot magazine.
**Barrel:** 17".
**Weight:** 5 lbs. **Length:** 35" overall (stock extended); 26½" (closed).
**Stock:** Telescoping wire, composition pistol grip.
**Sights:** Hooded post front, adjustable aperture rear.
**Features:** Semi-auto only. Matte black finish. From Feather Industries. Announced 1988.
**Price:** . . . . . . . . . . . . . . . . . . . . . . . . . . . . . . $499.95
**Price:** Model F9 (fixed stock) . . . . . . . . . . . . . . . . . $534.95

Federal XC900

## FEDERAL ENGINEERING XC900/XC450 AUTO CARBINES
**Caliber:** 9mm Para., 32-shot; 45 ACP, 16-shot magazine,
**Barrel:** 16.5" (with flash hider).
**Weight:** 8 lbs. **Length:** 34.5" overall.
**Stock:** Quick-detachable tube steel.
**Sights:** Hooded post front, Williams adjustable rear; sight bridge grooved for scope mounting.
**Features:** Quick takedown; all-steel Heli-arc welded construction; internal parts industrial hard chromed. Made in U.S. by Federal Engineering Corp.
**Price:** Includes receiver cap, sling, swivels . . . . . . . . . . . . $639.00

H&K SR9

## HECKLER & KOCH SR9 RIFLE
**Caliber:** 308 Win., 5-shot magazine.
**Barrel:** 19.7", bull.
**Weight:** 11 lbs. **Length:** 42.4" overall.
**Stock:** Kevlar reinforced fiberglass with thumbhole; wood grain finish.
**Sights:** Post front, aperture rear adjustable for windage and elevation.
**Features:** A redesigned version of the HK91 rifle. Comes standard with bull barrel with polygonal rifling. Uses HK clawlock scope mounts. Introduced 1990. Imported from Germany by Heckler & Koch, Inc.
**Price:** . . . . . . . . . . . . . . . . . . . . . . . . **$1,369.00**

## Heckler & Koch SR9(T) Target Rifle
Same as the SR9 rifle except has MSG90 adjustable buttstock, trigger group from the PSG1 Marksman's Rifle, and the PSG1 contoured pistol grip with palm shelf. Introduced 1992. Imported from Germany by Heckler & Koch, Inc.
**Price:** . . . . . . . . . . . . . . . . . . . . . . . . **$1,799.00**

## FEG SA-85M AUTOLOADING RIFLE
**Caliber:** 7.62x39, 6-shot magazine.
**Barrel:** 16.3".
**Weight:** 7 lbs., 10 oz. **Length:** 34.7" overall.
**Stock:** Hardwood handguard and thumbhole buttstock.
**Sights:** Cylindrical post front, tangent rear adjustable for windage and elevation.
**Features:** Matte finish. Chrome-lined barrel. Imported from Hungary by K.B.I., Inc.
**Price:** . . . . . . . . . . . . . . . . . . . . . **$499.00**

## IBUS M17S 223 BULLPUP RIFLE
**Caliber:** 223, 20-shot magazine.
**Barrel:** 22".
**Weight:** 8.8 lbs. **Length:** 31½" overall.
**Stock:** Zytel glass-filled nylon.
**Sights:** None furnished. Comes with scope mount for Weaver-type rings.
**Features:** Gas-operated, short-stroke piston system. Ambidextrous magazine release. Introduced 1993. Made in U.S. by Quality Parts Co.
**Price:** . . . . . . . . . . . . . . . . . . . . . **$975.00**

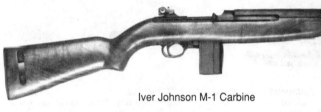

Iver Johnson M-1 Carbine

## IVER JOHNSON M-1 CARBINE
**Caliber:** 30 U.S. Carbine, or 9mm Para.
**Barrel:** 18" four-groove.
**Weight:** 6½ lbs. **Length:** 35½" overall.
**Stock:** Glossy-finished hardwood or walnut; or collapsible wire.
**Sights:** Click-adjustable peep rear.
**Features:** Gas-operated semi-auto carbine. 15-shot detachable magazine. Made in U.S.A.
**Price:** 30 cal., Parkerized finish, hardwood stock, metal handguard . **$349.95**
**Price:** 30 cal., Parkerized finish, walnut stock and handguard . . . . **$384.95**
**Price:** 9mm, hardwood stock, metal handguard . . . . . . . . . . . . **$365.00**
**Price:** 9mm, walnut stock and handguard . . . . . . . . . . . . . . . **$399.00**
**Price:** 30 cal., collapsible wire stock . . . . . . . . . . . . . . . . **$443.00**
**Price:** 9mm, collapsible wire stock . . . . . . . . . . . . . . . . **$448.95**

## Iver Johnson 50th Anniversary M-1 Carbine
Same as the standard Iver Johnson 30-caliber M-1 Carbine except has deluxe walnut stock with red, white and blue circular enameled American flag embedded in the stock, and gold-filled roll-engraving with the words "50th Anniversary 1941-1991" on the slide. Parkerized finish. Introduced 1991. From Iver Johnson Arms.
**Price:** . . . . . . . . . . . . . . . . . . . . . **$384.95**

## KIMEL AR9 SEMI-AUTOMATIC RIFLE
**Caliber:** 9mm Para., 20-shot magazine.
**Barrel:** 16¼".
**Weight:** 6.5 lbs. **Length:** 33" overall.
**Stock:** Folding buttstock, checkered plastic grip.
**Sights:** Adjustable post front in ring, fixed open rear.
**Features:** Fires from closed bolt; lever safety blocks trigger and sear; vented barrel shroud. Matte blue/black or nickel finish. Introduced 1991. Made in U.S. From Kimel Industries.
**Price:** Blue/black finish . . . . . . . . . . . . . . . . . . . . . **$369.00**

Kimel AR9

Marlin Model 9N

## MARLIN MODEL 9 CAMP CARBINE
**Caliber:** 9mm Para., 12-shot magazine.
**Barrel:** 16½", Micro-Groove® rifling.
**Weight:** 6¾ lbs. **Length:** 35½" overall.
**Stock:** Walnut-finished hardwood; rubber buttpad; Mar-Shield® finish; swivel studs.
**Sights:** Ramp front with orange post, cutaway Wide-Scan™ hood, adjustable open rear.
**Features:** Manual bolt hold-open; Garand-type safety, magazine safety; loaded chamber indicator; receiver drilled, tapped for scope mounting. Introduced 1985.
**Price:** . . . . . . . . . . . . . . . . . . . . . **$374.05**
**Price:** Model 9N (nickel-Teflon finish) . . . . . . . . . . . . . . . **$421.90**

## NORINCO MAK 90 SEMI-AUTO RIFLE
**Caliber:** 7.62x39, 5-shot magazine.
**Barrel:** 16.25".
**Weight:** 8 lbs., 3 oz. **Length:** 35.5" overall.
**Stock:** Walnut-finished thumbhole with recoil pad.
**Sights:** Adjustable post front, open adjustable rear.
**Features:** Chrome-lined barrel; forged receiver; black oxide finish. Comes with extra magazine, oil bottle, cleaning kit, sling. Imported from China by Century International Arms.
**Price:** About . . . . . . . . . . . . . . . . . . . . . **$312.00**

## Marlin Model 45 Carbine
Similar to the Model 9 except chambered for 45 ACP, 7-shot magazine. Introduced 1986.
**Price:** . . . . . . . . . . . . . . . . . . . . . **$374.05**

Olympic CAR-310

## QUALITY PARTS SHORTY E-2 CARBINE
**Caliber:** 223, 30-shot magazine.
**Barrel:** 16".
**Weight:** NA. **Length:** NA.
**Stock:** Telescoping buttstock.
**Sights:** Adjustable post front, adjustable aperture rear.
**Features:** Patterned after Colt M-16A2. Chrome-lined barrel with manganese phosphate finish. Has E-2 lower receiver with push-pin. From Quality Parts Co.
**Price:** . . . . . . . . . . . . . . . . . . . . . . . . . . . . . . . . **$850.00**
**Price:** E-2 Carbine Dissipator (M-16A2 handguard, E-2 sight, fixed or telescoping stock) . . . . . . . . . . . . . . . . . . . . . . . **$895.00**
**Price:** As above with A-1 sight, fixed or telescoping stock . . . . . . **$875.00**

## OLYMPIC ARMS CAR SERIES CARBINES
**Caliber:** 223, 20- or 30-shot; 9mm Para., 34-shot; 45 ACP, 16-shot; 10mm, 40 S&W, 41 A.E., 15-shot; 7.62x39mm, 5- or 30-shot.
**Barrel:** 16".
**Weight:** 7 lbs. **Length:** 34" overall (stock extended).
**Stock:** Telescoping butt.
**Sights:** Post front adjustable for elevation, rear adjustable for windage.
**Features:** Based on the AR-15 rifle. Has A2 Stowaway pistol grip and stock. Introduced 1982. Made in U.S. by Olympic Arms, Inc.
**Price:** CAR-15, 223 caliber . . . . . . . . . . . . . . . . . . . **$650.00**
**Price:** CAR-9, 9mm Para. . . . . . . . . . . . . . . . . . . . **$700.00**
**Price:** CAR-45, 45 ACP . . . . . . . . . . . . . . . . . . . . **$730.00**
**Price:** CAR-40, 40 S&W . . . . . . . . . . . . . . . . . . . . **$780.00**
**Price:** CAR-41, 41 A.E. . . . . . . . . . . . . . . . . . . . . **$780.00**
**Price:** CAR-310, 10mm . . . . . . . . . . . . . . . . . . . . **$850.00**
**Price:** 7.62x39mm . . . . . . . . . . . . . . . . . . . . **$700.00**

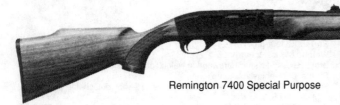

Remington 7400 Special Purpose

## Remington Model 7400 Special Purpose Auto Rifle
Similar to the standard Model 7400 except chambered only for 270 and 30-06, non-glare finish on the American walnut stock. All exposed metal has non-reflective matte black finish. Comes with quick-detachable sling swivels and camo-pattern Cordura carrying sling. Introduced 1993.
**Price:** . . . . . . . . . . . . . . . . . . . . . . . . . . . . . . . . **$503.00**

## REMINGTON MODEL 7400 AUTO RIFLE
**Caliber:** 243 Win., 270 Win., 280 Rem., 308 Win., 30-06, 35 Whelan, 4-shot magazine.
**Barrel:** 22" round tapered.
**Weight:** 7½ lbs. **Length:** 42" overall.
**Stock:** Walnut, deluxe cut checkered p.g. and forend. Satin or high-gloss finish.
**Sights:** Gold bead front sight on ramp; step rear sight with windage adjustable.
**Features:** Redesigned and improved version of the Model 742. Positive cross-bolt safety. Receiver tapped for scope mount. 4-shot clip mag. Introduced 1981.
**Price:** About . . . . . . . . . . . . . . . . . . . . . . . . . . **$503.00**
**Price:** Carbine (18½" bbl., 30-06 only) . . . . . . . . . . . . . . **$503.00**

Ruger Mini-14/5R

## Ruger Mini Thirty Rifle
Similar to the Mini-14 Ranch Rifle except modified to chamber the 7.62x39 Russian service round. Weight is about 7 lbs., 3 oz. Has 6-groove barrel with 1-10" twist, Ruger Integral Scope Mount bases and folding peep rear sight. Detachable 5-shot staggered box magazine. Blued finish. Introduced 1987.
**Price:** Blue . . . . . . . . . . . . . . . . . . . . . . . . . . . . **$530.00**
**Price:** Stainless . . . . . . . . . . . . . . . . . . . . . . . . . . **$580.00**

## RUGER MINI-14/5 AUTOLOADING RIFLE
**Caliber:** 223 Rem., 5-shot detachable box magazine.
**Barrel:** 18½". Rifling twist 1:7".
**Weight:** 6.4 lbs. **Length:** 37¼" overall.
**Stock:** American hardwood, steel reinforced.
**Sights:** Ramp front, fully adjustable rear.
**Features:** Fixed piston gas-operated, positive primary extraction. New buffer system, redesigned ejector system. Ruger S100RH scope rings included. 20-, 30-shot magazine available to police departments and government agencies only.
**Price:** Mini-14/5R, Ranch Rifle, blued, scope rings . . . . . . . . . **$530.00**
**Price:** K-Mini-14/5R, Ranch Rifle, stainless, scope rings . . . . . . **$580.00**
**Price:** Mini-14/5, blued, no scope rings . . . . . . . . . . . . . . **$491.50**
**Price:** K-Mini-14/5, stainless, no scope rings . . . . . . . . . . . . **$542.00**

Springfield M-1A

## SPRINGFIELD INC. M-1A RIFLE
**Caliber:** 7.62mm NATO (308), 5-, 10- or 20-shot box magazine.
**Barrel:** 25¹⁄₁₆" with flash suppressor, 22" without suppressor.
**Weight:** 8¾ lbs. **Length:** 44¼" overall.

**Stock:** American walnut with walnut colored heat-resistant fiberglass handguard. Matching walnut handguard available. Also available with fiberglass stock.
**Sights:** Military, square blade front, full click-adjustable aperture rear.
**Features:** Commercial equivalent of the U.S. M-14 service rifle with no provision for automatic firing. From Springfield Inc.
**Price:** Standard M-1A rifle, about . . . . . . . . . . . . . . . **$1,239.00**
**Price:** National Match about . . . . . . . . . . . . . . . . . . **$1,539.00**
**Price:** Super Match (heavy premium barrel) about . . . . . . . . . **$1,849.00**
**Price:** M1A-A1 Bush Rifle, walnut stock, about . . . . . . . . . . **$1,249.00**

**CAUTION:** PRICES CHANGE, CHECK AT GUNSHOP.

Stoner SR-25

### VOERE MODEL 2185 SEMI-AUTO RIFLE
**Caliber:** 7x64, 308, 30-06, 2-shot detachable magazine.
**Barrel:** 20".
**Weight:** 7¾ lbs. **Length:** 43½" overall.
**Stock:** European walnut with checkered grip and forend, ventilated rubber recoil pad. Oil finish.
**Sights:** Blade on ramp front, open adjustable rear. Receiver drilled and tapped for scope mounting.
**Features:** Gas-operated with three forward locking lugs; free-floating barrel; two-stage trigger; cocking indicator inside trigger guard. Imported from Austria by JagerSports, Ltd.
**Price:** About . . . . . . . . . . . . . . . . . . . . . . . **$1,950.00**
**Price:** With Mannlicher-style full stock, about . . . . . . . . . **$2,015.00**

### STONER SR-25 STANDARD RIFLE
**Caliber:** 7.62 NATO, 20-shot magazine, 5-shot optional.
**Barrel:** 20".
**Weight:** 8.8 lbs. **Length:** 40.75" overall.
**Stock:** Black synthetic AR-15A2 design, synthetic round forend.
**Sights:** Fixed AR-15-style front sight tower, rear is adjustable for windage and elevation.
**Features:** Merges designs of the AR-10 and AR-15 rifles. Upper and lower receivers made of lightweight aircraft aluminum alloy. Quick-detachable carrying handle/rear sight assembly. Introduced 1993. Made in U.S. by Knight's Mfg. Co.
**Price:** . . . . . . . . . . . . . . . . . . . . . . . . **$2,495.00**

### WILKINSON TERRY CARBINE
**Caliber:** 9mm Para., 31-shot magazine.
**Barrel:** 16³⁄₁₆".
**Weight:** 6 lbs., 3 oz. **Length:** 30" overall.
**Stock:** Maple stock and forend.
**Sights:** Protected post front, aperture rear.
**Features:** Semi-automatic blowback action fires from a closed breech. Bolt-type safety and magazine catch. Ejection port has automatic trap door. Receiver equipped with dovetail for scope mounting. Made in U.S. From Wilkinson Arms.
**Price:** . . . . . . . . . . . . . . . . . . . . . . . . . **$485.92**

# CENTERFIRE RIFLES—LEVER & SLIDE

Both classic arms and recent designs in American-style repeaters for sport and field shooting.

Browning Long Action BLR

### Browning Model 81 Long Action BLR
Similar to the standard Model 81 BLR except has long acton to accept 30-06, 270 and 7mm Rem. Mag. Barrel lengths are 22" for 30-06 and 270, 24" for 7mm Rem. Mag. Has six-lug rotary bolt; bolt and receiver are full-length fluted. Fold-down hammer at half-cock. Weight about 8½ lbs., overall length 42½" (22" barrel). Introduced 1991.
**Price:** . . . . . . . . . . . . . . . . . . . . . . . . . **$539.95**

### BROWNING MODEL 81 BLR LEVER-ACTION RIFLE
**Caliber:** 222, 223, 22-250, 243, 257 Roberts, 7mm-08, 308 Win. or 358 Win., 4-shot detachable magazine.
**Barrel:** 20" round tapered.
**Weight:** 6 lbs., 15 oz. **Length:** 39¾" overall.
**Stock:** Walnut. Checkered straight grip and forend, high-gloss finish.
**Sights:** Gold bead on hooded ramp front; low profile square notch adj. rear.
**Features:** Wide, grooved trigger; half-cock hammer safety; fold-down hammer. Receiver tapped for scope mount. Recoil pad installed. Imported from Japan by Browning.
**Price:** With sights . . . . . . . . . . . . . . . . . . . . **$509.95**

Browning 1886 Carbine

### CIMARRON 1860 HENRY REPLICA
**Caliber:** 44 WCF, 13-shot magazine.
**Barrel:** 24¼" (rifle), 22" (carbine).
**Weight:** 9½lbs. **Length:** 43" overall (rifle).
**Stock:** European walnut.
**Sights:** Bead front, open adjustable rear.
**Features:** Brass receiver amd buttplate. Uses original Henry loading system. Faithful to the original rifle. Introduced 1991. Imported by Cimarron Arms.
**Price:** . . . . . . . . . . . . . . . . . . . . . . . . . **$799.95**

### BROWNING MODEL 1886 LEVER-ACTION CARBINE
**Caliber:** 45-70, 8-shot magazine.
**Barrel:** 22".
**Weight:** 8 lbs., 3 oz. **Length:** 40.75" overall.
**Stock:** Satin-finished select walnut with metal crescent buttplate.
**Sights:** Blade front, open adjustable rear.
**Features:** Recreation of the original gun. Full-length magazine, classic-style forend with barrel band, saddle ring. Polished blue finish. Limited to 7000 guns. Introduced 1992. Imported from Japan by Browning.
**Price:** . . . . . . . . . . . . . . . . . . . . . . . . . **$749.95**

### Browning Model 1886 High Grade Carbine
Same as the standar Model 1886 Carbine except has high grade walnut with cut-checkered grip and forend and gloss finish. Receiver and lever are grayed steel. Receiver has scroll engraving and game scenes of mule deer and grizzly bear highlighted by a special gold plating and engraving process. Limited to 3000 guns. Introduced 1992.
**Price:** . . . . . . . . . . . . . . . . . . . . . . . . . **$1,175.00**

## CIMARRON 1866 WINCHESTER REPLICAS
**Caliber:** 22 LR, 22 WMR, 38 Spec., 44 WCF.
**Barrel:** 24¼" (rifle), 19" (carbine).
**Weight:** 9 lbs. **Length:** 43" overall (rifle).
**Stock:** European walnut.
**Sights:** Bead front, open adjustable rear.
**Features:** Solid brass receiver, buttplate, forend cap. Octagonal barrel. Faithful to the original Winchester '66 rifle. Introduced 1991. Imported by Cimarron Arms.
**Price:** Rifle . . . . . . . . . . . . . . . . . . . . . . . . . . **$689.95**
**Price:** Carbine . . . . . . . . . . . . . . . . . . . . . . . . . **$649.95**

## CIMARRON 1873 SHORT RIFLE
**Caliber:** 22 LR, 22 WMR, 357 Magnum, 44-40, 45 Colt.
**Barrel:** 20" tapered octagon.
**Weight:** 7.5 lbs. **Length:** 39" overall.
**Stock:** Walnut.
**Sights:** Bead front, adjustable semi-buckhorn rear.
**Features:** Has half "button" magazine. Original-type markings, including caliber, on barrel and elevator and "Kings" patent. From Cimarron Arms.
**Price:** . . . . . . . . . . . . . . . . . . . . . . . . . . . . **$799.95**

Cimarron 1873 30"

## CIMARRON 1873 30" EXPRESS RIFLE
**Caliber:** 22 LR, 22 WMR, 357 Mag., 38-40, 44-40, 45 Colt.
**Barrel:** 30", octagonal.
**Weight:** 8½ lbs. **Length:** 48" overall.
**Stock:** Walnut.
**Sights:** Blade front, semi-buckhorn ramp rear. Tang sight optional.
**Features:** Color case-hardened frame; choice of modern blue-black or charcoal blue for other parts. Barrel marked "Kings improvement." From Cimarron Arms.
**Price:** . . . . . . . . . . . . . . . . . . . . . . . . . . . . **$819.95**

## Cimarron 1873 Sporting Rifle
Similar to the 1873 Express except has 24" barrel with half-magazine.
**Price:** . . . . . . . . . . . . . . . . . . . . . . . . . . . . **$799.95**
**Price:** 1873 Saddle Ring Carbine, 19" barrel . . . . . . . . . . . . **$729.95**

Dixie 1873

## E.M.F. 1866 YELLOWBOY LEVER ACTIONS
**Caliber:** 38 Spec., 44-40.
**Barrel:** 19" (carbine), 24" (rifle).
**Weight:** 9 lbs. **Length:** 43" overall (rifle).
**Stock:** European walnut.
**Sights:** Bead front, open adjustable rear.
**Features:** Solid brass frame, blued barrel, lever, hammer, buttplate. Imported from Italy by E.M.F.
**Price:** Rifle . . . . . . . . . . . . . . . . . . . . . . . . . **$848.00**
**Price:** Carbine . . . . . . . . . . . . . . . . . . . . . . . . **$825.00**

## DIXIE ENGRAVED 1873 RIFLE
**Caliber:** 44-40, 11-shot magazine.
**Barrel:** 20", round.
**Weight:** 7¾ lbs. **Length:** 39" overall.
**Stock:** Walnut.
**Sights:** Blade front, adjustable rear.
**Features:** Engraved and case-hardened frame. Duplicate of Winchester 1873. Made in Italy. From Dixie Gun Works.
**Price:** . . . . . . . . . . . . . . . . . . . . . . . . . . . . **$995.00**
**Price:** Plain, blued carbine . . . . . . . . . . . . . . . . . **$895.00**

## E.M.F. MODEL 73 LEVER-ACTION RIFLE
**Caliber:** 357 Mag., 44-40, 45 Colt.
**Barrel:** 24".
**Weight:** 8 lbs. **Length:** 43¼" overall.
**Stock:** European walnut.
**Sights:** Bead front, rear adjustable for windage and elevation.
**Features:** Color case-hardened frame (blue on carbine). Imported by E.M.F.
**Price:** Rifle . . . . . . . . . . . . . . . . . . . . . . . . **$1,050.00**
**Price:** Carbine, 19" barrel . . . . . . . . . . . . . . . . . **$1,020.00**

## E.M.F. 1860 HENRY RIFLE
**Caliber:** 44-40 or 44 rimfire.
**Barrel:** 24.25".
**Weight:** About 9 lbs. **Length:** About 43.75" overall.
**Stock:** Oil-stained American walnut.
**Sights:** Blade front, rear adjustable for elevation.
**Features:** Reproduction of the original Henry rifle with brass frame and buttplate, rest blued. From E.M.F.
**Price:** Standard . . . . . . . . . . . . . . . . . . . . . . **$1,100.10**

Marlin Model 336CS

## MARLIN MODEL 336CS LEVER-ACTION CARBINE
**Caliber:** 30-30 or 35 Rem., 6-shot tubular magazine.
**Barrel:** 20" Micro-Groove®.
**Weight:** 7 lbs. **Length:** 38½" overall.
**Stock:** Select American black walnut, capped p.g. with white line spacers. Mar-Shield® finish; rubber buttpad; swivel studs.
**Sights:** Ramp front with Wide-Scan™ hood, semi-buckhorn folding rear adjustable for windage and elevation.
**Features:** Hammer-block safety. Receiver tapped for scope mount, offset hammer spur; top of receiver sand blasted to prevent glare.
**Price:** . . . . . . . . . . . . . . . . . . . . . . . . . . . . **$404.30**

## MARLIN MODEL 444SS LEVER-ACTION SPORTER
**Caliber:** 444 Marlin, 5-shot tubular magazine.
**Barrel:** 22" Micro-Groove®.
**Weight:** 7½ lbs. **Length:** 40½" overall.
**Stock:** American black walnut, capped p.g. with white line spacers, rubber rifle buttpad. Mar-Shield® finish; swivel studs.
**Sights:** Hooded ramp front, folding semi-buckhorn rear adjustable for windage and elevation.
**Features:** Hammer-block safety. Receiver tapped for scope mount; offset hammer spur.
**Price:** . . . . . . . . . . . . . . . . . . . . . . . . . . . . **$490.25**

## Marlin Model 30AS Lever-Action Carbine
Same as the Marlin 336CS except has walnut-finished hardwood p.g. stock, 30-30 only, 6-shot. Hammer-block safety. Adjustable rear sight, brass bead front.
**Price:** . . . . . . . . . . . . . . . . . . . . . . . . . . . . **$344.25**

Marlin Model 1894S

**Marlin Model 1894CS Carbine**
Similar to the standard Model 1894S except chambered for 38 Special/357 Magnum with full-length 9-shot magazine, 18½" barrel, hammer-block safety, brass bead front sight. Introduced 1983.
Price: . . . . . . . . . . . . . . . . . . . . . . . . . . . . . . . . . . $454.80

**MARLIN MODEL 1894S LEVER-ACTION CARBINE**
**Caliber:** 44 Special/44 Magnum, 10-shot tubular magazine.
**Barrel:** 20" Micro-Groove®.
**Weight:** 6 lbs. **Length:** 37½" overall.
**Stock:** American black walnut, straight grip and forend. Mar-Shield® finish. Rubber rifle buttpad; swivel studs.
**Sights:** Wide-Scan™ hooded ramp front, semi-buckhorn folding rear adjustable for windage and elevation.
**Features:** Hammer-block safety. Receiver tapped for scope mount, offset hammer spur, solid top receiver sand blasted to prevent glare.
Price: . . . . . . . . . . . . . . . . . . . . . . . . . . . $454.80

Marlin Model 1894CL

**Marlin Model 1894CL Classic**
Similar to the 1894CS except chambered for 218 Bee, 25-20 and 32-20 Win. Has 6-shot tubular magazine. 22" barrel with 6-groove rifling, brass bead front sight, adjustable semi-buckhorn folding rear. Hammer-block safety. Weighs 6¼ lbs., overall length of 38¾". Bee has rubber rifle butt pad, swivel studs. Introduced 1988.
Price: . . . . . . . . . . . . . . . . . . . . . . . . . . . . . . . . . . $488.00

**MARLIN MODEL 1895SS LEVER-ACTION RIFLE**
**Caliber:** 45-70, 4-shot tubular magazine.
**Barrel:** 22" round.
**Weight:** 7½ lbs. **Length:** 40½" overall.
**Stock:** American black walnut, full pistol grip. Mar-Shield® finish; rubber buttpad; q.d. swivel studs.
**Sights:** Bead front with Wide-Scan™ hood, semi-buckhorn folding rear adjustable for windage and elevation.
**Features:** Hammer-block safety. Solid receiver tapped for scope mounts or receiver sights; offset hammer spur.
Price: . . . . . . . . . . . . . . . . . . . . . . . . . . . $490.25

Mitchell 1858 Henry

**MITCHELL 1866 WINCHESTER REPLICA**
**Caliber:** 44-40, 13-shot.
**Barrel:** 24¼".
**Weight:** 9 lbs. **Length:** 43" overall.
**Stock:** European walnut.
**Sights:** Bead front, open adjustable rear.
**Features:** Solid brass receiver, buttplate, forend cap. Octagonal barrel. Faithful to the original Winchester '66 rifle. Introduced 1990. Imported by Mitchell Arms, Inc.
Price: . . . . . . . . . . . . . . . . . . . . . . . . . . . . . . . . . . $829.00

**MITCHELL 1858 HENRY REPLICA**
**Caliber:** 44-40, 13-shot magazine.
**Barrel:** 24¼".
**Weight:** 9.5 lbs. **Length:** 43" overall.
**Stock:** European walnut.
**Sights:** Bead front, open adjustable rear.
**Features:** Brass receiver and buttplate. Uses original Henry loading system. Faithful to the original rifle. Introduced 1990. Imported by Mitchell Arms, Inc.
Price: . . . . . . . . . . . . . . . . . . . . . . . . . . . $999.00

**MITCHELL 1873 WINCHESTER REPLICA**
**Caliber:** 45 Colt, 13-shot.
**Barrel:** 24¼".
**Weight:** 9.5 lbs. **Length:** 43" overall.
**Stock:** European walnut.
**Sights:** Bead front, open adjustable rear.
**Features:** Color case-hardened steel receiver. Faithful to the original Model 1873 rifle. Introduced 1990. Imported by Mitchell Arms, Inc.
Price: . . . . . . . . . . . . . . . . . . . . . . . . . . . $950.00

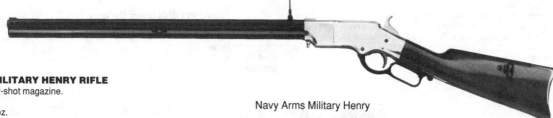

**NAVY ARMS MILITARY HENRY RIFLE**
**Caliber:** 44-40, 12-shot magazine.
**Barrel:** 24¼".
**Weight:** 9 lbs., 4 oz.
**Stock:** European walnut.
**Sights:** Blade front, adjustable ladder-type rear.
**Features:** Brass frame, buttplate, rest blued. Recreation of the model used by cavalry units in the Civil War. Has full-length magazine tube, sling swivels; no forend. Introduced 1991. Imported from Italy by Navy Arms.
Price: . . . . . . . . . . . . . . . . . . . . . . . . . . . . . . . . . . $875.00

Navy Arms Military Henry

**Navy Arms Iron Frame Henry**
Similar to the Military Henry Rifle except receiver is blued or color case-hardened steel. Introduced 1991. Imported by Navy Arms.
Price: . . . . . . . . . . . . . . . . . . . . . . . . . . . . . . . . . . $895.00

**Navy Arms Henry Trapper**
Similar to the Military Henry Rifle except has 16½" barrel, weighs 7½ lbs. Brass frame and buttplate, rest blued. Introduced 1991. Imported from Italy by Navy Arms.
Price: . . . . . . . . . . . . . . . . . . . . . . . . . . . $875.00

**Navy Arms Henry Carbine**
Similar to the Military Henry rifle except has 22" barrel, weighs 8 lbs., 12 oz., is 41" overall; no sling swivels. Caliber 44-40. Introduced 1992. Imported from Italy by Navy Arms.
Price: . . . . . . . . . . . . . . . . . . . . . . . . . . . $875.00

Consult our Directory pages for the location of firms mentioned.

Navy Arms 1873 Winchester-Style

## NAVY ARMS 1866 YELLOWBOY RIFLE
**Caliber:** 44-40, 12-shot magazine.
**Barrel:** 24", full octagon.
**Weight:** 8½ lbs. **Length:** 42½" overall.
**Stock:** European walnut.
**Sights:** Blade front, adjustable ladder-type rear.
**Features:** Brass frame, forend tip, buttplate, blued barrel, lever, hammer. Introduced 1991. Imported from Italy by Navy Arms.
**Price:** . . . . . . . . . . . . . . . . . . . . . . . . . $710.00
**Price:** Carbine, 19" barrel . . . . . . . . . . . . . . . . . . . $685.00

## Navy Arms 1873 Sporting Rifle
Similar to the 1873 Winchester-Style rifle except has checkered pistol grip stock, 30" octagonal barrel (24" available). Introduced 1992. Imported by Navy Arms.
**Price:** . . . . . . . . . . . . . . . . . . . . . . . . . $895.00

## NAVY ARMS 1873 WINCHESTER-STYLE RIFLE
**Caliber:** 44-40, 45 Colt, 12-shot magazine.
**Barrel:** 24".
**Weight:** 8¼ lbs. **Length:** 43" overall.
**Stock:** European walnut.
**Sights:** Blade front, buckhorn rear.
**Features:** Color case-hardened frame, rest blued. Full-octagon barrel. Introduced 1991. Imported by Navy Arms.
**Price:** . . . . . . . . . . . . . . . . . . . . . . . . . $840.00
**Price:** Carbine, 19" barrel . . . . . . . . . . . . . . . . . . . $815.00

Remington 7600 Special Purpose

## Remington Model 7600 Special Purpose Slide Action
Similar to the standard Model 7600 except chambered only for 270 and 30-06, non-glare finish on the American walnut stock. All exposed metal has non-reflective matte black finish. Comes with quick-detachable sling swivels and camo-pattern Cordura carrying sling. Introduced 1993.
**Price:** . . . . . . . . . . . . . . . . . . . . . . . . . $480.00

## REMINGTON 7600 SLIDE ACTION
**Caliber:** 243, 270, 280, 30-06, 308, 35 Whelen.
**Barrel:** 22" round tapered.
**Weight:** 7½ lbs. **Length:** 42" overall.
**Stock:** Cut-checkered walnut p.g. and forend, Monte Carlo with full cheekpiece. Satin or high-gloss finish.
**Sights:** Gold bead front sight on matted ramp, open step adjustable sporting rear.
**Feature:** Redesigned and improved version of the Model 760. Detachable 4-shot clip. Cross-bolt safety. Receiver tapped for scope mount. Also available in high grade versions. Introduced 1981.
**Price:** About . . . . . . . . . . . . . . . . . . . . . . . $480.00
**Price:** Carbine (18½" bbl., 30-06 only) . . . . . . . . . . . . . $480.00

Rossi SRC Carbine

## ROSSI M92 SRC SADDLE-RING CARBINE
**Caliber:** 38 Spec./357 Mag., 44 Spec./44-40, 44 Mag., 10-shot magazine.
**Barrel:** 20".
**Weight:** 5¾ lbs. **Length:** 37" overall.
**Stock:** Walnut.
**Sights:** Blade front, buckhorn rear.
**Features:** Recreation of the famous lever-action carbine. Handles 38 and 357 interchangeably. Has high-relief puma medallion inlaid in the receiver. Introduced 1978. Imported by Interarms.
**Price:** . . . . . . . . . . . . . . . . . . . . . . . . . $350.00
**Price:** 44 Spec./44 Mag. (Model 65) . . . . . . . . . . . . . . . $367.00

## Rossi M92 SRS Short Carbine
Similar to the standard M92 except has 16" barrel, overall length of 33", in 38/357 only. Puma medallion on side of receiver. Introduced 1986.
**Price:** . . . . . . . . . . . . . . . . . . . . . . . . . $350.00

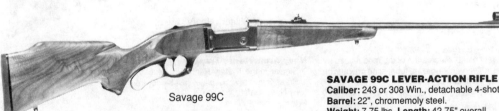

Savage 99C

## SAVAGE 99C LEVER-ACTION RIFLE
**Caliber:** 243 or 308 Win., detachable 4-shot magazine.
**Barrel:** 22", chromemoly steel.
**Weight:** 7.75 lbs. **Length:** 42.75" overall.
**Stock:** Walnut with checkered p.g. and forend, Monte Carlo comb.
**Sights:** Hooded ramp front, adjustable ramp rear sight. Tapped for scope mounts.
**Features:** Grooved trigger, top tang slide safety locks trigger and lever. Brown rubber buttpad, q.d. swivel studs, push-button magazine release.
**Price:** . . . . . . . . . . . . . . . . . . . . . . . . . $620.00

**CAUTION:** PRICES CHANGE, CHECK AT GUNSHOP.

## UBERTI HENRY RIFLE
**Caliber:** 44-40.
**Barrel:** 24¼", half-octagon.
**Weight:** 9.2 lbs. **Length:** 43¾" overall.
**Stock:** American walnut.
**Sights:** Blade front, rear adjustable for elevation.
**Features:** Frame, elevator, magazine follower, buttplate are brass, balance blue (also available in polished steel). Imported by Uberti USA.
**Price:** .............................................. $895.00
**Price:** Henry Carbine (22¼" bbl.) ............ $900.00
**Price:** Henry Trapper (16", 18" bbl.) ........ $900.00

## UBERTI 1873 SPORTING RIFLE
**Caliber:** 22 LR, 22 WMR, 38 Spec., 357 Mag., 44-40, 45 Colt.
**Barrel:** 24¼", 30", octagonal.
**Weight:** 8.1 lbs. **Length:** 43¼" overall.
**Stock:** Walnut.
**Sights:** Blade front adjustable for windage, open rear adjustable for elevation.

Winchester 94 Side Eject

## Winchester Model 94 Trapper Side Eject
Same as the Model 94 except has 16" barrel, 5-shot magazine in 30-30, 9-shot in 357 Magnum, 44 Magnum/44 Special, 45 Colt. Has stainless steel claw extractor, saddle ring, hammer spur extension, walnut wood.
**Price:** 30-30 ..................................... $335.00
**Price:** 357 Mag., 44 Mag./44 Spec., 45 Colt ........... $354.00

## WINCHESTER MODEL 94 BIG BORE SIDE EJECT
**Caliber:** 307 Win., 356 Win., 6-shot magazine.
**Barrel:** 20".
**Weight:** 7 lbs. **Length:** 38⅝" overall.
**Stock:** American walnut. Satin finish.
**Sights:** Hooded ramp front, semi-buckhorn rear adjustable for windage and elevation.
**Features:** All external metal parts have Winchester's deep blue finish. Rifling twist 1:12". Rubber recoil pad fitted to buttstock. Introduced 1983. From U.S. Repeating Arms Co.
**Price:** .............................................. $374.00

## UBERTI 1866 SPORTING RIFLE
**Caliber:** 22 LR, 22 WMR, 38 Spec., 44-40, 45 Colt.
**Barrel:** 24¼", octagonal.
**Weight:** 8.1 lbs. **Length:** 43¼" overall.
**Stock:** Walnut.
**Sights:** Blade front adjustable for windage, rear adjustable for elevation.
**Features:** Frame, buttplate, forend cap of polished brass, balance charcoal blued. Imported by Uberti USA.
**Price:** .............................................. $780.00
**Price:** Yellowboy Carbine (19" round bbl.) ............ $720.00

**Features:** Color case-hardened frame, blued barrel, hammer, lever, buttplate, brass elevator. Also available with pistol grip stock ($100.00 extra). Imported by Uberti USA.
**Price:** .............................................. $900.00
**Price:** 1873 Carbine (19" round bbl.) ........... $890.00

## WINCHESTER MODEL 94 SIDE EJECT LEVER-ACTION RIFLE
**Caliber:** 30-30, 7x30 Waters, 32 Win. Spec., 6-shot tubular magazine.
**Barrel:** 20".
**Weight:** 6½ lbs. **Length:** 37¾" overall.
**Stock:** Straight grip walnut stock and forend.
**Sights:** Hooded blade front, semi-buckhorn rear. Drilled and tapped for scope mount. Post front sight on Trapper model.
**Features:** Solid frame, forged steel receiver; side ejection; exposed rebounding hammer with automatic trigger-activated transfer bar. Introduced 1984.
**Price:** Checkered walnut ......................... $362.00
**Price:** No checkering, walnut .................... $335.00
**Price:** With WinTuff laminated hardwood stock, 30-30 only .... $335.00

## Winchester Model 94 Ranger Side Eject Lever-Action Rifle
Same as Model 94 Side Eject except has 5-shot magazine, American hardwood stock and forend, post front sight. Introduced 1985.
**Price:** .............................................. $296.00
**Price:** With 4x32 Bushnell scope, mounts ........... $348.00

Winchester 94 Wrangler

## Winchester Model 94 Wrangler Side Eject
Same as the Model 94 except has 16" barrel and large loop lever for large and/or gloved hands. Has 9-shot capacity (5-shot for 30-30), stainless steel claw extractor. Available in 30-30, 44 Magnum/44 Special. Reintroduced 1992.
**Price:** 30-30 ..................................... $354.00
**Price:** 44 Magnum/44 Special ..................... $374.00

# CENTERFIRE RIFLES—BOLT ACTION

Includes models for a wide variety of sporting and competitive purposes and uses.

Alpine Rifle

## ALPINE BOLT-ACTION RIFLE
**Caliber:** 22-250, 243 Win., 270, 30-06, 308, 7mm Rem. Mag., 8mm, 5-shot magazine (3 for magnum).
**Barrel:** 23" (std. cals.), 24" (mag.).
**Weight:** 7½ lbs.
**Stock:** European walnut. Full p.g. and Monte Carlo; checkered p.g. and forend; rubber recoil pad; white line spacers; sling swivels.
**Sights:** Ramp front, open rear adjustable for windage and elevation.
**Features:** Made by Firearms Co. Ltd. in England. Imported by Mandall Shooting Supplies.
**Price:** Custom Grade ............................. $395.00
**Price:** Supreme Grade ............................ $425.00

A-Square Hannibal

## A-SQUARE CAESAR BOLT-ACTION RIFLE

**Caliber:** 7mm Rem. Mag., 7mm STW, 30-06, 300 Win. Mag., 300 H&H, 300 Wea. Mag., 8mm Rem. Mag., 338 Win. Mag., 340 Wea. Mag., 338 A-Square, 9.3x62, 9.3x64, 375 Wea. Mag., 375 H&H, 375 JRS, 375 A-Square, 416 Hoffman, 416 Rem. Mag., 416 Taylor, 404 Jeffery, 425 Express, 458 Win. Mag., 458 Lott, 450 Ackley, 460 Short A-Square, 470 Capstick, 495 A-Square.
**Barrel:** 20" to 26" (no-cost customer option).
**Weight:** 8½ to 11 lbs.
**Stock:** Claro walnut with hand-rubbed oil finish; classic style with A-Square Coil-Chek® features for reduced recoil; flush detachable swivels. Customer choice of length of pull.
**Sights:** Choice of three-leaf express, forward or normal-mount scope, or combination (at extra cost).
**Features:** Matte non-reflective blue, double cross-bolts, steel and fiberglass reinforcement of wood from tang to forend tip; three-position positive safety; three-way adjustable trigger; expanded magazine capacity. Right- or left-hand. Introduced 1984. Made in U.S. by A-Square Co., Inc.
**Price:** Walnut stock . . . . . . . . . . . . . . . . . . . **$2,550.00**
**Price:** Synthetic stock . . . . . . . . . . . . . . . . . . . **$2,800.00**

## A-SQUARE HANNIBAL BOLT-ACTION RIFLE

**Caliber:** 7mm Rem. Mag., 7mm STW, 30-06, 300 Win. Mag., 300 H&H, 300 Wea. Mag., 8mm Rem. Mag., 338 Win. Mag., 340 Wea. Mag., 338 A-Square Mag., 9.3x62, 9.3x64, 375 H&H, 375 Wea. Mag., 375 JRS, 375 A-Square Mag., 378 Wea. Mag., 416 Taylor, 416 Rem. Mag., 416 Hoffman, 416 Rigby, 416 Wea. Mag., 404 Jeffery, 425 Express, 458 Win. Mag., 458 Lott, 450 Ackley, 460 Short A-Square Mag., 460 Wea. Mag., 470 Capstick, 495 A-Square Mag., 500 A-Square Mag.
**Barrel:** 20" to 26" (no-cost customer option).
**Weight:** 9 to 11¾ lbs.
**Stock:** Claro walnut with hand-rubbed oil finish; classic style with A-Square Coil-Chek® features for reduced recoil; flush detachable swivels. Customer choice of length of pull. Available with synthetic stock.
**Sights:** Choice of three-leaf express, forward or normal-mount scope, or combination (at extra cost).
**Features:** Matte non-reflective blue, double cross-bolts, steel and fiberglass reinforcement of wood from tang to forend tip; Mauser-style claw extractor; expanded magazine capacity; two-position safety; three-way target trigger. Right-hand only. Introduced 1983. Made in U.S. by A-Square Co., Inc.
**Price:** Walnut stock . . . . . . . . . . . . . . . . . . . **$2,495.00**
**Price:** Synthetic stock . . . . . . . . . . . . . . . . . . . **$2,645.00**

Anschutz 1700D Classic

## Anschutz 1700D Custom Rifles

Similar to the Classic models except have roll-over Monte Carlo cheekpiece, slim forend with Schnabel tip, Wundhammer palm swell on pistol grip, rosewood grip cap with white diamond insert. Skip-line checkering on grip and forend. Introduced 1988. Imported from Germany by PSI.
**Price:** . . . . . . . . . . . . . . . . . . . **$1,416.00**
**Price:** Meistergrade (select stock, gold engraved trigger guard) . . **$1,615.00**

## ANSCHUTZ 1700D CLASSIC RIFLES

**Caliber:** 22 Hornet, 5-shot clip; 222 Rem., 3-shot clip.
**Barrel:** 24", 13/16" dia. heavy.
**Weight:** 7¾ lbs. **Length:** 43" overall.
**Stock:** Select European walnut with checkered pistol grip and forend.
**Sights:** Hooded ramp front, folding leaf rear; drilled and tapped for scope mounting.
**Features:** Adjustable single stage trigger. Receiver drilled and tapped for scope mounting. Introduced 1988. Imported from Germany by Precision Sales International.
**Price:** . . . . . . . . . . . . . . . . . . . **$1,387.00**
**Price:** Meistergrade (select stock, gold engraved trigger guard) . . **$1,586.00**

Anschutz 1733D

## Anschutz 1733D Mannlicher Rifle

Similar to the 1700D Bavarian except chambered only for 22 Hornet and has Mannlicher stock. Uses improved Match 54 action with #5096 single-stage trigger with 2.6 lb. adjustable pull weight. Has 19.75" barrel, overall length of 39". Comes with sling swivels, Lyman folding rear sight and hooded ramp front, 4-shot magazine. Introduced 1993. Imported from Germany by Precision Sales International.
**Price:** . . . . . . . . . . . . . . . . . . . **$1,537.00**

## ANSCHUTZ 1700D BAVARIAN BOLT-ACTION RIFLE

**Caliber:** 22 Hornet, 222 Rem., detachable clip.
**Barrel:** 24".
**Weight:** 7¼ lbs. **Length:** 43" overall.
**Stock:** European walnut with Bavarian cheek rest. Checkered p.g. and forend.
**Sights:** Hooded ramp front, folding leaf rear.
**Features:** Uses the improved 1700 Match 54 action with adjustable trigger. Drilled and tapped for scope mounting. Introduced 1988. Imported from Germany by Precision Sales International.
**Price:** . . . . . . . . . . . . . . . . . . . **$1,416.00**
**Price:** Meistergrade (select stock, gold engraved trigger guard) . . **$1,615.00**

Beeman/HW 60J

## BARRETT MODEL 90 BOLT-ACTION RIFLE

**Caliber:** 50 BMG, 5-shot magazine.
**Barrel:** 29".
**Weight:** 22 lbs. **Length:** 45" overall.
**Stock:** Sorbothane recoil pad.
**Sights:** Scope optional.
**Features:** Bolt-action, bullpup design. Disassembles without tools; extendable bipod legs; match-grade barrel; high efficiency muzzlebrake. Introduced 1990. From Barrett Firearms Mfg., Inc.
**Price:** From . . . . . . . . . . . . . . . . . . . **$3,650.00**

## BEEMAN/HW 60J BOLT-ACTION RIFLE

**Caliber:** 222 Rem.
**Barrel:** 22.8".
**Weight:** 6.5 lbs. **Length:** 41.7" overall.
**Stock:** Walnut with cheekpiece; cut checkered p.g. and forend.
**Sights:** Hooded blade on ramp front, open rear.
**Features:** Polished blue finish; oil-finished wood. Imported from Germany by Beeman. Introduced 1988.
**Price:** . . . . . . . . . . . . . . . . . . . **$945.00**

**CAUTION:** PRICES CHANGE, CHECK AT GUNSHOP.

Blaser R84

## BRNO 537 SPORTER BOLT-ACTION RIFLE
**Caliber:** 243, 270, 30-06 (internal 5-shot magazine), 308 (detachable 5-shot magazine).
**Barrel:** 23.6".
**Weight:** 7 lbs., 9 oz. **Length:** 44.7" overall.
**Stock:** Checkered walnut or synthetic.
**Sights:** Hooded ramp front, adjustable folding leaf rear.
**Features:** Improved standard size Mauser-style action with non-rotating claw extractor; externally adjustable trigger, American-style safety; streamlined bolt shroud with cocking indicator. Introduced 1992. Imported from the Czech Republic by Action Arms Ltd.
**Price:** Walnut stock . . . . . . . . . . . . . . . . . . . . **$669.00**
**Price:** Synthetic stock . . . . . . . . . . . . . . . . . . . **$599.00**

## BLASER R84 BOLT-ACTION RIFLE
**Caliber:** Std. cals.—22-250, 243, 6mm Rem., 25-06, 270, 280, 30-06; magnum cals.—257 Wea., 264 Win. Mag., 7mm Rem. Mag., 300 Win. Mag., 300 Wea., 338 Win. Mag., 375 H&H.
**Barrel:** 23" (24" in magnum cals.).
**Weight:** 7-7¼ lbs. **Length:** Std. cals.—41" overall (23" barrel).
**Stock:** Two-piece Turkish walnut. Solid black buttpad.
**Sights:** None furnished. Comes with low-profile Blaser scope mountings.
**Features:** Interchangeable barrels (scope mountings on barrel), and magnum/standard caliber bolt assemblies. Left-hand models available in all calibers. Imported from Germany by Autumn Sales, Inc.
**Price:** Right-hand, standard or magnum calibers . . . . . . . . . **$2,300.00**
**Price:** Left-hand, standard or magnum calibers . . . . . . . . . . **$2,850.00**
**Price:** Interchangeable barrels, standard or magnum calibers . . . . **$600.00**

BRNO ZKB 527 Fox

## BRNO ZKB 527 FOX BOLT-ACTION RIFLE
**Caliber:** 22 Hornet, 222 Rem., 223 Rem., detachable 5-shot magazine.
**Barrel:** 23½".

**Weight:** 6 lbs., 1 oz. **Length:** 42½" overall.
**Stock:** European walnut, with Monte Carlo, or synthetic.
**Sights:** Hooded front, open adjustable rear.
**Features:** Improved mini-Mauser action with non-rotating claw extractor; grooved receiver. Imported from the Czech Republic by Action Arms Ltd.
**Price:** Walnut stock . . . . . . . . . . . . . . . . . . . . . **$655.00**
**Price:** Synthetic stock . . . . . . . . . . . . . . . . . . . . **$599.00**

BRNO ZKK 602

## BRNO ZKK 600, 601, 602 BOLT-ACTION RIFLES
**Caliber:** 7x57, 30-06, 270 (M600); 243, 308 (M601); 300 Win. Mag., 375 H&H, 458 Win. Mag. (M602), 5-shot magazine.
**Barrel:** 23½" (M600, 601); 25" (M602).

**Weight:** 7 lbs., 3 oz. to 9 lbs., 9 oz. **Length:** 43" overall (M601).
**Stock:** Classic-style checkered walnut.
**Sights:** Hooded ramp front, open folding leaf adjustable rear.
**Features:** Improved Mauser action with controlled feed, claw extractor; safety blocks triggers and locks bolt; sling swivels. Imported from the Czech Republic by Action Arms Ltd.
**Price:** Model 600, 601 . . . . . . . . . . . . . . . . . . . **$609.00**
**Price:** Model 602 . . . . . . . . . . . . . . . . . . . . . . **$835.00**

Browning A-Bolt Hunter

> Consult our Directory pages for the location of firms mentioned.

### Browning A-Bolt Stainless Stalker
Similar to the Hunter model A-Bolt except receiver is made of stainless steel; the rest of the exposed metal surfaces are finished with a durable matte silver-gray. Graphite-Fiberglass composite textured stock. No sights are furnished. Available in 270, 30-06, 7mm Rem. Mag., 375 H&H. Introduced 1987.
**Price:** . . . . . . . . . . . . . . . . . . . . . . . . . . . **$664.95**
**Price:** Composite Stalker (as above, checkered stock) . . . . . . **$524.95**
**Price:** Left-hand, no sights . . . . . . . . . . . . . . . . . . **$684.95**
**Price:** 375 H&H, with sights . . . . . . . . . . . . . . . . . **$764.95**
**Price:** 375 H&H, left-hand, with sights . . . . . . . . . . . . **$786.95**

## BROWNING A-BOLT RIFLE
**Caliber:** 25-06, 270, 30-06, 280, 7mm Rem. Mag., 300 Win. Mag., 338 Win. Mag., 375 H&H Mag.
**Barrel:** 22" medium sporter weight with recessed muzzle; 26" on mag. cals.
**Weight:** 6½ to 7½ lbs. **Length:** 44¾" overall (magnum and standard); 41¾" (short action).
**Stock:** Classic style American walnut; recoil pad standard on magnum calibers.
**Features:** Short-throw (60°) fluted bolt, three locking lugs, plunger-type ejector; adjustable trigger is grooved and gold-plated. Hinged floorplate, detachable box magazine (4 rounds std. cals., 3 for magnums). Slide tang safety. Medallion has glossy stock finish, rosewood grip and forend caps, high polish blue. Introduced 1985. Imported from Japan by Browning.
**Price:** Medallion, no sights . . . . . . . . . . . . . . . . . **$596.95**
**Price:** Hunter, no sights . . . . . . . . . . . . . . . . . . . **$509.95**
**Price:** Hunter, with sights . . . . . . . . . . . . . . . . . . **$574.95**
**Price:** Medallion, 375 H&H Mag., with sights . . . . . . . . . **$696.95**

### Browning A-Bolt Left Hand
Same as the Medallion model A-Bolt except has left-hand action and is available only in 270, 30-06, 7mm Rem. Mag., 375 H&H. Introduced 1987.
**Price:** . . . . . . . . . . . . . . . . . . . . . . . . . . . **$621.95**
**Price:** 375 H&H, with sights . . . . . . . . . . . . . . . . . **$721.95**

Browning Euro-Bolt

## Browning A-Bolt Short Action

Similar to the standard A-Bolt except has short action for 22 Hornet, 223, 22-250, 243, 257 Roberts, 7mm-08, 284 Win., 308 chamberings. Available in Hunter or Medallion grades. Weighs 6½ lbs. Other specs essentially the same. Introduced 1985.

Price: Medallion, no sights . . . . . . . . . . . . . . . . . . . **$596.95**
Price: Hunter, no sights . . . . . . . . . . . . . . . . . . . **$509.95**
Price: Hunter, with sights . . . . . . . . . . . . . . . . . . . **$574.95**
Price: Composite, no sights . . . . . . . . . . . . . . . . . . . **$524.95**

## Browning Euro-Bolt Rifle

Similar to the A-Bolt Hunter except has satin-finished walnut stock with Continental-style cheekpiece, palm-swell grip and schnabel forend, rounded bolt shroud and Mannlicher-style flattened bolt handle. Available in 30-06 and 270 with 22" barrel, 7mm Rem. Mag. with 26" barrel. Weighs about 6 lbs., 11 oz. Introduced 1993.

Price: . . . . . . . . . . . . . . . . . . . . . . . . . . . . . . . **$699.95**

## Browning A-Bolt Gold Medallion

Similar to the standard A-Bolt except has select walnut stock with brass spacers between rubber recoil pad and between the rosewood grip cap and forend tip; gold-filled barrel inscription; palm-swell pistol grip, Monte Carlo comb, 22 lpi checkering with double borders; engraved receiver flats. In 270, 30-06, 7mm Rem. Mag. only. Introduced 1988.

Price: . . . . . . . . . . . . . . . . . . . . . . . . . . . . . . . **$809.95**

Browning Micro Medallion

## Browning A-Bolt Micro Medallion

Similar to the standard A-Bolt except is a scaled-down version. Comes with 20" barrel, shortened length of pull (13⁵⁄₁₆"); three-shot magazine capacity; weighs 6 lbs., 1 oz. Available in 243, 308, 7mm-08, 257 Roberts, 223, 22-250. Introduced 1988.

Price: No sights . . . . . . . . . . . . . . . . . . . . . . . . . **$596.95**

Century Centuion 14

## CENTURY ENFIELD SPORTER #4

Caliber: 303 British, 10-shot magazine.
Barrel: 25.2".
Weight: 8 lbs., 5 oz. Length: 44.5" overall.
Stock: Beechwood with checkered p.g. and forend, Monte Carlo comb.
Sights: Blade front, adjustable aperture rear.
Features: Uses Lee-Enfield action; blue finish. Trigger pinned to receiver. Introduced 1987. From Century International Arms.
Price: About . . . . . . . . . . . . . . . . . . . . . . . . . . **$156.00**

## CENTURY CENTURION 14 SPORTER

Caliber: 7mm Rem. Mag., 300 Win. Mag., 5-shot magazine.
Barrel: 24".
Weight: NA. Length: 43.3" overall.
Stock: Walnut-finished European hardwood. Checkered p.g. and forend. Monte Carlo comb.
Sights: None furnished.
Features: Uses modified Pattern 14 Enfield action. Drilled and tapped; scope base mounted. Blue finish. From Century International Arms.
Price: About . . . . . . . . . . . . . . . . . . . . . . . . . . **$275.00**

Century Swedish #38

## CENTURY MAUSER 98 SPORTER

Caliber: 243, 270, 308, 30-06.
Barrel: 24".
Weight: NA. Length: 44" overall.
Stock: Black synthetic.
Sights: None furnished. Scope base installed.
Features: Mauser 98 action; bent bolt handle for scope use; low-swing safety; matte black finish; blind magazine. Introduced 1992. From Century International Arms.
Price: About . . . . . . . . . . . . . . . . . . . . . . . . . . **$288.00**

## DAKOTA 22 SPORTER BOLT-ACTION RIFLE

Caliber: 22 LR, 22 Hornet, 5-shot magazine.
Barrel: 22".
Weight: About 6.5 lbs. Length: NA.
Stock: Claro or English walnut in classic design; 13.5" length of pull. Choice of grade. Point panel hand checkering. Swivel studs. Black butt pad.
Sights: None furnished; comes with mount bases.
Features: Combines features of Winchester 52 and Dakota 76 rifles. Full-sized receiver; rear locking lugs and bolt machined from bar stock. Trigger and striker-blocking safety; adjustable trigger. Introduced 1992. From Dakota Arms, Inc.
Price: . . . . . . . . . . . . . . . . . . . . . . . . . . . . . **$1,500.00**

## CENTURY SWEDISH SPORTER #38

Caliber: 6.5x55 Swede, 5-shot magazine.
Barrel: 24".
Weight: NA. Length: 44.1" overall.
Stock: Walnut-finished European hardwood with checkered p.g. and forend; Monte Carlo comb.
Sights: Blade front, adjustable rear.
Features: Uses M38 Swedish Mauser action; comes with Holden Ironsighter see-through scope mount. Introduced 1987. From Century International Arms.
Price: About . . . . . . . . . . . . . . . . . . . . . . . . . . **$237.50**

## COOPER MODEL 38 CENTERFIRE SPORTER

Caliber: 17 CCM, 22 CCM, 3-shot magazine.
Barrel: 23¾" Shilen match.
Weight: 8 lbs. Length: 42½" overall.
Stock: Standard—AA Claro walnut with 22 lpi checkering, oil finish; Custom has AAA Claro or AA French walnut, beaded Monte Carlo cheekpiece.
Sights: None furnished.
Features: Action has three front locking lugs, 45-degree bolt rotation; fully adjustable single stage match trigger; swivel studs. Pachmayr butt pad. Introduced 1991. Made in U.S. by Cooper Arms.
Price: Standard . . . . . . . . . . . . . . . . . . . . . . **$1,095.00**
Price: Standard single shot . . . . . . . . . . . . . . . . **$995.00**
Price: Custom . . . . . . . . . . . . . . . . . . . . . . . **$1,295.00**

CAUTION: PRICES CHANGE, CHECK AT GUNSHOP.

Dakota 76 Classic

## DAKOTA 76 CLASSIC BOLT-ACTION RIFLE
**Caliber:** 257 Roberts, 270, 280, 30-06, 7mm Rem. Mag., 338 Win. Mag., 300 Win. Mag., 375 H&H, 458 Win. Mag.
**Barrel:** 23".
**Weight:** 7½ lbs. **Length:** NA.
**Stock:** Medium fancy grade walnut in classic style. Checkered p.g. and forend; solid buttpad.
**Sights:** None furnished; drilled and tapped for scope mounts.
**Features:** Has many features of the original Model 70 Winchester. One-piece rail trigger guard assembly; steel grip cap. Adjustable trigger. Many options available. Left-hand rifle available at same price. Introduced 1988. From Dakota Arms, Inc.
**Price:** . . . . . . . . . . . . . . . . . . . . . . . . . . . . . . . **$2,300.00**

### Dakota 76 Short Action Rifles
A scaled-down version of the standard Model 76. Standard chamberings are 22-250, 243, 6mm Rem., 250-3000, 7mm-08, 308, others on special order. Short Classic Grade has 21" barrel; Alpine Grade is lighter (6½ lbs.), has a blind magazine and slimmer stock. Introduced 1989.
**Price:** Short Classic . . . . . . . . . . . . . . . . . . . . . . $2,300.00

Dakota 76 Safari

## DAKOTA 76 SAFARI BOLT-ACTION RIFLE
**Caliber:** 338 Win. Mag., 300 Win. Mag., 375 H&H, 458 Win. Mag.
**Barrel:** 23".
**Weight:** 8½ lbs. **Length:** NA.
**Stock:** Fancy walnut with ebony forend tip; point-pattern with wraparound forend checkering.
**Sights:** Ramp front, standing leaf rear.
**Features:** Has many features of the original Model 70 Winchester. Barrel band front swivel, inletted rear. Cheekpiece with shadow line. Steel grip cap. Introduced 1988. From Dakota Arms, Inc.
**Price:** Wood stock . . . . . . . . . . . . . . . . . . . . . . **$3,000.00**

### Dakota 416 Rigby African
Similar to the 76 Safari except chambered for 404 Jeffery, 416 Rigby, 416 Dakota, 450 Dakota, 4-round magazine, select wood, two stock cross-bolts. Has 24" barrel, weight of 9-10 lbs. Ramp front sight, standing leaf rear. Introduced 1989.
**Price:** . . . . . . . . . . . . . . . . . . . . . . . . . . . . . . **$3,500.00**

E.A.A./Sabatti Rover

## E.A.A./SABATTI ROVER 870 BOLT-ACTION RIFLE
**Caliber:** 22-250, 243, 25-06, 270, 30-06, 308, 7mm Rem. Mag., 300 Win. Mag., 338 Win. Mag.
**Barrel:** 23".
**Weight:** 6.9 lbs. **Length:** 42.5" overall.
**Stock:** Walnut with straight comb, cut checkering on grip and forend.
**Sights:** Gold bead on ramp front, open adjustable rear.
**Features:** Blue finish. Positive safety locks trigger. Introduced 1986. Imported by European American Armory.
**Price:** . . . . . . . . . . . . . . . . . . . . . . . . . . . . . . **$550.00**

### AUGUSTE FRANCOTTE BOLT-ACTION RIFLES
**Caliber:** 243, 270, 7x64, 30-06, 308, 300 Win. Mag., 338, 7mm Rem. Mag., 375 H&H, 458 Win. Mag.; others on request.
**Barrel:** 23½" to 26½".
**Weight:** 8 to 10 lbs.
**Stock:** Fancy European walnut. To customer specs.
**Sights:** To customer specs.
**Features:** Basically a custom gun, Francotte offers many options. Imported from Belgium by Armes de Chasse.
**Price:** . . . . . . . . . . . . . . . . . $9,000.00 to $15,000.00

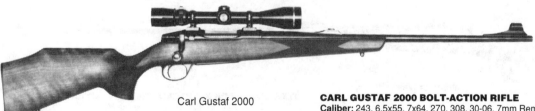

Carl Gustaf 2000

## CARL GUSTAF 2000 BOLT-ACTION RIFLE
**Caliber:** 243, 6.5x55, 7x64, 270, 308, 30-06, 7mm Rem. Mag., 300 Win. Mag., 9.3x62, 4-shot detachable magazine.
**Barrel:** 24".
**Weight:** 7.5 lbs. **Length:** 44 " overall.
**Stock:** Select European walnut with hand-rubbed oil finish; Monte Carlo cheekpiece; Wundhammar swell pistol grip; 18 l.p.i. checkering.
**Sights:** Optional. Drilled and tapped for scope mounting.
**Features:** Three-way adjustable single-stage, roller bearing trigger; three-position safety; triple front locking lugs; free-floating barrel; swivel studs. Comes with factory test target. Introduced 1991. Imported from Sweden by Precision Sales International.
**Price:** Without sights . . . . . . . . . . . . . . . . . . . . $1,875.00
**Price:** With sights . . . . . . . . . . . . . . . . . . . . . . . $1,985.00

Heym Express

**HEYM MAGNUM EXPRESS SERIES RIFLE**
**Caliber:** 338 Lapua Mag., 375 H&H, 378 Wea. Mag., 416 Rigby, 500 Nitro Express 3", 460 Wea. Mag., 500 A-Square, 450 Ackley, 600 N.E.
**Barrel:** 24".
**Weight:** About 9.9 lbs. **Length:** 45¼" overall.

**Stock:** Classic English design of AAA-grade European walnut with cheekpiece, solid rubber buttpad, steel grip cap.
**Sights:** Adjustable post front on ramp, three-leaf express rear.
**Features:** Modified magnum Mauser action, Timney single trigger; special hinged floorplate; barrel-mouted q.d. swivel, q.d. rear; vertical double recoil lug in rear of stock. Introduced 1989. Imported from Germany by JagerSport, Ltd.
**Price:** . . . . . . . . . . . . . . . . . . . . . . . . . . . . . . . . . **$6,500.00**
**Price:** For left-hand rifle, add . . . . . . . . . . . . . . . . . **$595.00**
**Price:** 600 Nitro Express . . . . . . . . . . . . . . . . . . . . **$11,350.00**

Howa Lightning

**HOWA LIGHTNING BOLT-ACTION RIFLE**
**Caliber:** 223, 22-250, 243, 270, 308, 30-06, 7mm Rem. Mag., 300 Win. Mag., 338 Win. Mag.
**Barrel:** 22", 24" magnum calibers.

**Weight:** 7½ lbs. **Length:** 42" overall (22" barrel).
**Stock:** Black Bell & Carlson Carbelite composite with Monte Carlo comb; checkered grip and forend.
**Sights:** None furnished. Drilled and tapped for scope mounting.
**Features:** Sliding thumb safety; hinged floorplate; polished blue/black finish. Introduced 1993. From Interarms.
**Price:** Standard calibers . . . . . . . . . . . . . . . . . . . . **$498.00**
**Price:** Magnum calibers . . . . . . . . . . . . . . . . . . . . . **$517.00**

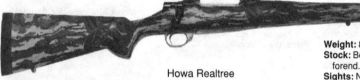

Howa Realtree

**HOWA REALTREE CAMO RIFLE**
**Caliber:** 270, 30-06, 5-shot magazine.
**Barrel:** 22".

**Weight:** 8 lbs. **Length:** 42¼" overall.
**Stock:** Bell & Carlson Carbelite composite. Straight comb; checkered grip and forend.
**Sights:** None furnished. Drilled and tapped for scope mouting.
**Features:** Completely covered with Realtree camo finish, except bolt. Sliding thumb safety, hinged floorplate; sling swivel studs, recoil pad. Introduced 1993. From Interarms.
**Price:** . . . . . . . . . . . . . . . . . . . . . . . . . . . . . . . . . **$620.00**

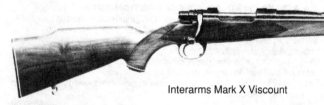

Interarms Mark X Viscount

**Interarms Mini-Mark X Rifle**
Scaled-down version of the Mark X Viscount. Uses miniature M98 Mauser-system action, chambered for 223 Rem. and 7.62x39; 20" barrel. Overall length of 39¾", weight 6.35 lbs. Drilled and tapped for scope mounting. Checkered hardwood stock. Adjustable trigger. Introduced 1987. Imported from Yugoslavia by Interarms.
**Price:** Either caliber . . . . . . . . . . . . . . . . . **$527.00**

**INTERARMS MARK X VISCOUNT BOLT-ACTION RIFLE**
**Caliber:** 22-250, 243, 25-06, 270, 7x57, 308, 30-06, 7mm Rem. Mag., 300 Win. Mag.
**Barrel:** 24".
**Weight:** 7 lbs. **Length:** 44" overall.
**Stock:** European hardwood with Monte Carlo comb, checkered grip and forend.
**Sights:** Blade on ramp front, open fully adjustable rear. Drilled and tapped for scope mounting.
**Features:** Polished blue finish. Uses Mauser system action with sliding thumb safety, hinged floorplate, adjustable trigger. Reintroduced 1987. Imported from Yugoslavia by Interarms.
**Price:** Standard calibers . . . . . . . . . . . . . . . . . . . . **$568.00**
**Price:** Magnum calibers . . . . . . . . . . . . . . . . . . . . . **$590.00**

Interarms Whitworth Express

**INTERARMS WHITWORTH EXPRESS RIFLE**
**Caliber:** 375 H&H, 458 Win. Mag.
**Barrel:** 24".
**Weight:** 7½-8 lbs. **Length:** 44".
**Stock:** Classic English Express rifle design of hand checkered, select European walnut.
**Sights:** Ramp front with removable hood, three-leaf open sight calibrated for 100, 200, 300 yards on ¼-rib.
**Features:** Solid rubber recoil pad, barrel-mounted sling swivel, adjustable trigger, hinged floorplate, solid steel recoil cross bolt. From Interarms.
**Price:** 375, 458, with express sights . . . . . . . . . . . . . . . . . **$870.00**

**INTERARMS MARK X WHITWORTH BOLT-ACTION RIFLE**
**Caliber:** 22-250, 243, 25-06, 270, 7x57, 308, 30-06, 7mm Rem. Mag., 300 Win. Mag., 5-shot magazine (3-shot for 300 Win. Mag.).
**Barrel:** 24".
**Weight:** 7 lbs. **Length:** 44" overall.
**Stock:** European walnut with checkered grip and forend, straight comb.
**Sights:** Hooded blade on ramp front, open fully adjustable rear.
**Features:** Uses Mauser system action with sliding thumb safety, hinged floorplate, adjustable trigger. Polished blue finish. Swivel studs. Imported from Yugoslavia by Interarms.
**Price:** Standard calibers . . . . . . . . . . . . . . . . . . . . **$700.00**
**Price:** Magnum calibers . . . . . . . . . . . . . . . . . . . . . **$722.00**

**CAUTION:** PRICES CHANGE, CHECK AT GUNSHOP.

Iver Johnson 5100A1

## KDF K15 AMERICAN BOLT-ACTION RIFLE
**Caliber:** 25-06, 257 Wea. Mag., 270, 270 Wea. Mag., 7mm Rem. Mag., 30-06, 300 Win. Mag., 300 Wea. Mag., 338 Win. Mag., 340 Wea. Mag., 375 H&H, 411 KDF Mag., 416 Rem. Mag., 458 Win. Mag.; 4-shot magazine for standard calibers, 3-shot for magnums.
**Barrel:** 22" standard, 24" optional.
**Weight:** About 8 lbs. **Length:** 44" overall (24" barrel).
**Stock:** Laminated standard; Kevlar composite or AAA walnut in classic, schnabel or thumbhole styles optional.
**Sights:** None furnished; optional. Drilled and tapped for scope mounting.
**Features:** Three-lug locking design with 60˚ bolt lift; ultra-fast lock time; fully adjustable trigger. Options available. Introduced 1991. Made in U.S. by KDF, Inc.
**Price:** Standard calibers . . . . . . . . . . . . . . . . . **$1,950.00**
**Price:** Magnum calibers . . . . . . . . . . . . . . . . . **$2,000.00**

## KRICO MODEL 700 BOLT-ACTION RIFLES
**Caliber:** 17 Rem., 222, 222 Rem. Mag., 223, 5.6x50 Mag., 243, 308, 5.6x57 RWS, 22-250, 6.5x55, 6.5x57, 7x57, 270, 7x64, 30-06, 9.3x62, 6.5x68, 7mm Rem. Mag., 300 Win. Mag., 8x68S, 7.5 Swiss, 9.3x64, 6x62 Freres.
**Barrel:** 23.6" (std. cals.); 25.5" (mag. cals.).
**Weight:** 7 lbs. **Length:** 43.3" overall (23.6" bbl.).
**Stock:** European walnut, Bavarian cheekpiece.

## IVER JOHNSON MODEL 5100A1 LONG-RANGE RIFLE
**Caliber:** 50 BMG.
**Barrel:** 29", fully fluted, free-floating.
**Weight:** 36 lbs. **Length:** 51.5" overall.
**Stocks:** Composition. Adjustable drop and comb.
**Sights:** None furnished. Optional Leupold Ultra M1 16x scope.
**Features:** Bolt-action long-range rifle. Adjustable trigger. Rifle breaks down for transport, storage. From Iver Johnson.
**Price:** . . . . . . . . . . . . . . . . . . . . . . . . . . **$5,000.00**

## KRICO MODEL 600 BOLT-ACTION RIFLE
**Caliber:** 222, 223, 22-250, 243, 308, 5.6x50 Mag., 4-shot magazine.
**Barrel:** 23.6".
**Weight:** 7.9 lbs. **Length:** 43.7" overall.
**Stock:** European walnut with Monte Carlo comb.
**Sights:** None furnished; drilled and tapped for scope mounting.
**Features:** Rubber recoil pad, sling swivels, checkered grip and forend. Polished blue finish. Imported from Germany by Mandall Shooting Supplies.
**Price:** . . . . . . . . . . . . . . . . . . . . . . . . . . **$1,295.00**

**Sights:** Blade on ramp front, open adjustable rear.
**Features:** Removable box magazine; sliding safety. Drilled and tapped for scope mounting. Imported from Germany by Mandall Shooting Supplies.
**Price:** Model 700 . . . . . . . . . . . . . . . . . . . . **$995.00**
**Price:** Model 700 Deluxe S . . . . . . . . . . . . . . **$1,495.00**
**Price:** Model 700 Deluxe . . . . . . . . . . . . . . . . **$1.025.00**
**Price:** Model 700 Stutzen (full stock) . . . . . . . . . **$1,295.00**

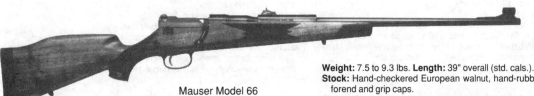

Mauser Model 66

## MAUSER MODEL 66 BOLT-ACTION RIFLE
**Caliber:** 243, 270, 308, 30-06, 5.6x57, 6.5x57, 7x64, 9.3x62, 7mm Rem. Mag., 300 Wea. Mag., 300 Win. Mag., 6.5x68, 8x68S, 9.3x64, 375 H&H, 458 Win. Mag. Three-shot magazine.
**Barrel:** 21" (Stutzen); 24" (standard cals.); 26" (magnum cals.).

**Weight:** 7.5 to 9.3 lbs. **Length:** 39" overall (std. cals.).
**Stock:** Hand-checkered European walnut, hand-rubbed oil finish. Rosewood forend and grip caps.
**Sights:** Blade front on ramp, open rear adjustable for windage and elevation.
**Features:** Telescopic short-stroke action; interchangeable, free-floated, medium-heavy barrels. Mini-claw extractor; adjustable single-stage trigger; internal magazine. Introduced 1989. Imported from Germany by Precision Imports, Inc.
**Price:** With Monte Carlo stock . . . . . . . . . . . . . **$1,783.00**
**Price:** Stutzen (full-length stock) . . . . . . . . . . . **$1,873.00**
**Price:** Safari model . . . . . . . . . . . . . . . . . . . **$2,079.00**

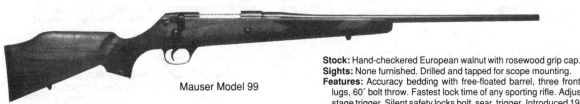

Mauser Model 99

## MAUSER MODEL 99 BOLT-ACTION RIFLE
**Caliber:** 243, 25-06, 270, 308, 30-06, 5.6x57, 6.5x57, 7x57, 7x64 (standard cals.); 7mm Rem. Mag., 257 Wea. Mag., 270 Wea. Mag., 300 Wea. Mag., 300 Win. Mag., 338 Win. Mag., 375 H&H, 8x68S, 9.3x64 (magnum cals.); removable 4-shot magazine (std. cals.), 3-shot (magnum cals.).
**Barrel:** 24" (std.), 26" (mag.).
**Weight:** About 8 lbs. **Length:** 44" overall (std. cals.).

**Stock:** Hand-checkered European walnut with rosewood grip cap.
**Sights:** None furnished. Drilled and tapped for scope mounting.
**Features:** Accuracy bedding with free-floated barrel, three front-locking bolt lugs, 60˚ bolt throw. Fastest lock time of any sporting rifle. Adjustable single-stage trigger. Silent safety locks bolt, sear, trigger. Introduced 1989. Imported from Germany by Precision Imports, Inc.
**Price:** Classic stock, oil finish, std. cals. . . . . . . . **$1,130.00**
**Price:** As above, magnum cals. . . . . . . . . . . . . . **$1,180.00**
**Price:** Classic stock, high luster finish, std. cals. . . . **$1,272.00**
**Price:** As above, magnum cals. . . . . . . . . . . . . . **$1,322.00**
**Price:** Monte Carlo stock, oil finish, std. cals. . . . . . **$1,130.00**
**Price:** As above, magnum cals. . . . . . . . . . . . . . **$1,180.00**
**Price:** Monte Carlo stock, high luster finish, std. cals. . . . . . . **$1,272.00**
**Price:** As above, magnum cals. . . . . . . . . . . . . . **$1,322.00**

## McMILLAN SIGNATURE CLASSIC SPORTER
**Caliber:** 22-250, 243, 6mm Rem., 7mm-08, 284, 308 (short action); 25-06, 270, 280 Rem., 30-06, 7mm Rem. Mag., 300 Win. Mag., 300 Wea. (long action); 338 Win. Mag., 340 Wea., 375 H&H (magnum action).
**Barrel:** 22", 24", 26".
**Weight:** 7 lbs. (short action).
**Stock:** McMillan fiberglass in green, beige, brown or black. Recoil pad and 1"

swivels installed. Length of pull up to 14¼".
**Sights:** None furnished. Comes with 1" rings and bases.
**Features:** Uses McMillan right- or left-hand action with matte black finish. Trigger pull set at 3 lbs. Four-round magazine for standard calibers; three for magnums. Aluminum floorplate. Fibergrain and wood stocks optional. Introduced 1987. From McMillan Gunworks, Inc.
**Price:** . . . . . . . . . . . . . . . . . . . . . . . . . . **$2,299.00**

McMillan Alaskan

## McMillan Signature Super Varminter

Similar to the Classic Sporter except has heavy contoured barrel, adjustable trigger, field bipod and special hand-bedded fiberglass stock (Fibergrain optional). Chambered for 223, 22-250, 220 Swift, 243, 6mm Rem., 25-06, 7mm-08 and 308. Comes with 1" rings and bases. Introduced 1989.
Price: . . . . . . . . . . . . . . . . . . . . . . . . . . . . . **$2,370.00**

## McMillan Signature Alaskan

Similar to the Classic Sporter except has match-grade barrel with single leaf rear sight, barrel band front, 1" detachable rings and mounts, steel floorplate, electroless nickel finish. Has wood Monte Carlo stock with cheekpiece, palm-swell grip, solid buttpad. Chambered for 270, 280 Rem., 30-06, 7mm Rem. Mag., 300 Win. Mag., 300 Wea., 358 Win., 340 Wea., 375 H&H. Introduced 1989.
Price: . . . . . . . . . . . . . . . . . . . . . . . . . . . . . **$3,225.00**

## McMillan Signature Titanium Mountain Rifle

Similar to the Classic Sporter except action made of titanium alloy, barrel of chromemoly steel. Stock is of graphite reinforced fiberglass. Weight is 5½ lbs. Chambered for 270, 280 Rem., 30-06, 7mm Rem. Mag., 300 Win. Mag. Fibergrain stock optional. Introduced 1989.
Price: . . . . . . . . . . . . . . . . . . . . . . . . . . . . . **$2,995.00**

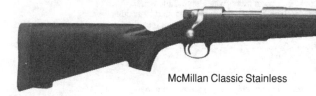

McMillan Classic Stainless

## McMILLAN TALON SAFARI RIFLE

**Caliber:** 300 Win. Mag., 300 Wea. Mag., 338 Win. Mag., 300 H&H, 340 Wea. Mag., 375 H&H, 404 Jeffery, 416 Rem. Mag., 458 Win. Mag. (Safari Magnum); 378 Wea. Mag., 416 Rigby, 416 Wea. Mag., 460 Wea. Mag. (Safari Super Magnum).
**Barrel:** 24".
**Weight:** About 9-10 lbs. **Length:** 43" overall.
**Stock:** McMillan fiberglass Safari.
**Sights:** Barrel band front ramp, multi-leaf express rear.
**Features:** Uses McMillan Safari action. Has q.d. 1" scope mounts, positive locking steel floorplate, barrel band sling swivel. Match-grade barrel. Matte black finish standard. Introduced 1989. From McMillan Gunworks, Inc.
**Price:** Talon Safari Magnum . . . . . . . . . . . . . . . . . **$3,570.00**
**Price:** Talon Safari Super Magnum . . . . . . . . . . . . . **$4,120.00**

## McMillan Classic Stainless Sporter

Similar to the Classic Sporter except barrel and action made of stainless steel. Same calibers, in addition to 416 Rem. Mag. Comes with fiberglass stock, right- or left-hand action in natural stainless, glass bead or black chrome sulfide finishes. Introduced 1990. From McMillan Gunworks, Inc.
Price: . . . . . . . . . . . . . . . . . . . . . . . . . . . . . **$2,450.00**

## McMILLAN TALON SPORTER RIFLE

**Caliber:** 25-06, 270, 280 Rem., 30-06 (Long Action); 7mm Rem. Mag., 300 Win. Mag., 300 Wea. Mag., 300 H&H, 338 Win. Mag., 340 Wea. Mag., 375 H&H, 416 Rem. Mag.
**Barrel:** 24" (standard).
**Weight:** About 7½ lbs. **Length:** NA.
**Stock:** Choice of walnut or McMillan fiberglass.
**Sights:** None furnished; comes with rings and bases. Open sights optional.
**Features:** Uses pre-'64 Model 70-type action with cone breech, controlled feed, claw extractor and three-position safety. Barrel and action are of stainless steel; chromemoly optional. Introduced 1991. From McMillan Gunworks, Inc.
**Price:** . . . . . . . . . . . . . . . . . . . . . . . . . . . . **$2,541.00**

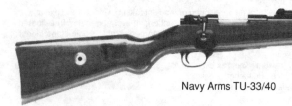

Navy Arms TU-33/40

## MIDLAND 1500S SURVIVOR RIFLE

**Caliber:** 308, 5-shot magazine.
**Barrel:** 22".
**Weight:** 7 lbs. **Length:** 43" overall.
**Stock:** Black composite with recoil pad, Monte Carlo cheekpiece.
**Sights:** Hooded ramp front, open rear adjustable for windage.
**Features:** Stainless steel barreled action with satin chromed bolt. Introduced 1993. Made by Gibbs Rifle Co., distributed by Navy Arms.
**Price:** . . . . . . . . . . . . . . . . . . . . . . . . . . . . **$450.00**
**Price:** Model 1500C clip model . . . . . . . . . . . . . . . . **$480.00**

## NAVY ARMS TU-33/40 CARBINE

**Caliber:** 7.62x39mm, 4-shot magazine.
**Barrel:** 20.75".
**Weight:** 9 lbs. **Length:** NA.
**Stock:** Hardwood.
**Sights:** Hooded barleycorn front, military V-notch adjustable rear.
**Features:** Miniature Mauser-style action. Comes with leather sling. Introduced 1992. Imported by Navy Arms.
**Price:** . . . . . . . . . . . . . . . . . . . . . . . . . . . . **NA**

Consult our Directory pages for the location of firms mentioned.

Parker-Hale 81 Classic

**Weight:** About 7¾ lbs. **Length:** 44½" overall.
**Stock:** European walnut in classic style with oil finish, hand-cut checkering; palm-swell pistol grip, rosewood grip cap.
**Sights:** Drilled and tapped for open sights and scope mounting. Scope bases included.
**Features:** Uses Mauser-style action; one-piece steel, Oberndorf-style trigger guard with hinged floorplate; rubber buttpad; quick-detachable sling swivels. Introduced 1984. Made by Gibbs Rifle Co., distributed by Navy Arms.
**Price:** . . . . . . . . . . . . . . . . . . . . . . . . . . . . **$900.00**

## PARKER-HALE MODEL 81 CLASSIC RIFLE

**Caliber:** 22-250, 243, 6mm Rem., 270, 6.5x55, 7x57, 7x64, 308, 30-06, 300 Win. Mag., 7mm Rem. Mag., 4-shot magazine.
**Barrel:** 24".

**CAUTION:** PRICES CHANGE, CHECK AT GUNSHOP.

### Parker-Hale Model 81 Classic African Rifle

Similar to the Model 81 Classic except chambered only for 375 H&H and 9.3x62. Has adjustable trigger, barrel band front swivel, African express rear sight, engraved receiver. Classic-style stock has a solid buttpad, checkered pistol grip and forend. Introduced 1986. Made by Gibbs Rifle Co., distributed by Navy Arms.

Price: . . . . . . . . . . . . . . . . . . . . . . . . . . . . **$1,050.00**

### Parker-Hale Model 1000 Rifle

Similar to the Model 81 Classic except has walnut Monte Carlo stock, 22" barrel (24" in 22-250), weighs 7.25 lbs. Not available in 300 Win. Mag. Introduced 1992. Made by Gibbs Rifle Co., distributed by Navy Arms.

Price: . . . . . . . . . . . . . . . . . . . . . . . . . . . . . **$495.00**
Price: Model 1000 Clip (detachable magazine) . . . . . . . . . . . **$535.00**

Parker-Hale 1100M

### Parker-Hale Model 1100 Lightweight Rifle

Similar to the Model 81 Classic except has slim barrel profile, hollow bolt handle, alloy trigger guard/floorplate. The Monte Carlo stock has a schnabel forend, hand-cut checkering, swivel studs, palm-swell pistol grip. Comes with hooded ramp front sight, open Williams rear adjustable for windage and elevation. Same calibers as Model 81. Overall length is 43", weight 6½ lbs., with 22" barrel. Introduced 1984. Made by Gibbs Rifle Co., distributed by Navy Arms.

Price: . . . . . . . . . . . . . . . . . . . . . . . . . . . . . **$510.00**

### PARKER-HALE MODEL 1100M AFRICAN MAGNUM

**Caliber:** 375 H&H, 458 Win. Mag.
**Barrel:** 24".
**Weight:** 9.5 lbs. **Length:** NA.
**Stock:** Checkered walnut with reinforcing lugs.
**Sights:** Hooded ramp front, shallow V open rear.
**Features:** Mauser-style 98 action with steel trigger guard, special lengthened steel magazine. Drilled and tapped for scope mounts. Made by Gibbs Rifle Co., distributed by Navy Arms.

Price: . . . . . . . . . . . . . . . . . . . . . . . . . . . . . **$930.00**

### PARKER-HALE MODEL 2100 MIDLAND RIFLE

**Caliber:** 22-250, 243, 6mm, 270, 6.5x55, 7x57, 7x64, 308, 30-06, 300 Win. Mag., 7mm Rem. Mag.
**Barrel:** 22".
**Weight:** About 7 lbs. **Length:** 43" overall.
**Stock:** European walnut, cut-checkered pistol grip and forend; sling swivels.
**Sights:** Hooded post front, flip-up open rear.
**Features:** Mauser-type action has twin front locking lugs, rear safety lug, and claw extractor; hinged floorplate; adjustable single-stage trigger; silent side safety. Introduced 1984. Made by Gibbs Rifle Co., distributed by Navy Arms.

Price: . . . . . . . . . . . . . . . . . . . . . . . . . . . . . **$390.00**
Price: Model 2600 (hardwood stock, no white spacers) . . . . . . **$375.00**

### PARKER-HALE MODEL 1200 SUPER RIFLE

**Caliber:** 22-250, 243, 6mm, 25-06, 270, 6.5x55, 7x57, 7x64, 308, 30-06, 8mm Mauser (standard action); 7mm Rem. Mag., 300 Win. Mag. (1200M Super Magnum).
**Barrel:** 24".
**Weight:** About 7½ lbs. **Length:** 44½" overall.
**Stock:** European walnut, rosewood grip and forend tips, hand-cut checkering; roll-over cheekpiece; palm-swell pistol grip; ventilated recoil pad; wraparound checkering.
**Sights:** Hooded post front, open rear.
**Features:** Uses Mauser-style action with claw extractor; gold-plated adjustable trigger; silent side safety locks trigger, sear and bolt; aluminum trigger guard. Introduced 1984. Made by Gibbs Rifle Co., distributed by Navy Arms.

Price: . . . . . . . . . . . . . . . . . . . . . . . . . . . . . **$595.00**

### Parker-Hale Midland Model 2700 Lightweight Rifle

Similar to the Model 2100 Midland except has tapered lightweight barrel, aluminum trigger guard, lightened stock. Receiver drilled and tapped for scope mounting. Weighs 6.5 lbs. Not available in 300 Win. Mag. Introduced 1992. Made by Gibbs Rifle Co., distributed by Navy Arms.

Price: . . . . . . . . . . . . . . . . . . . . . . . . . . . . . **$415.00**

### Parker-Hale Model 1200 Super Clip Rifle

Same as the Model 1200 Super except has a detachable steel box magazine and steel trigger guard. Introduced 1984. Made by Gibbs Rifle Co., distributed by Navy Arms.

. . . . . . . . . . . . . . . . . . . . . . . . . . . . . **$640.00**

Parker-Hale 1300C

### PARKER-HALE MODEL 1300C SCOUT RIFLE

**Caliber:** 243, 308, 10-shot magazine.
**Barrel:** 20".
**Weight:** 8.5 lbs. **Length:** 41" overall.
**Stock:** Checkered laminated birch.
**Sights:** None furnished. Drilled and tapped for scope mounting.
**Features:** Detachable magazine; muzzle brake; polished blue finish. Introduced 1992. Made by Gibbs Rifle Co., distributed by Navy Arms.

Price: . . . . . . . . . . . . . . . . . . . . . . . . . . . . . **$525.00**
Price: With fixed 5-shot magazine . . . . . . . . . . . . . . . . **$495.00**

### Parker-Hale Model 2800 Midland Rifle

Similar to the Model 2100 Midland except has Monte Carlo stock of laminated birch. Not available in 300 Win. Mag. Made by Gibbs Rifle Co., distributed by Navy Arms.

Price: . . . . . . . . . . . . . . . . . . . . . . . . . . . . . **$405.00**

Remington Model Seven

### REMINGTON MODEL SEVEN BOLT-ACTION RIFLE

**Caliber:** 17 Rem., 223 Rem. (5-shot); 243, 6mm Rem., 7mm-08, 6mm, 308 (4-shot).
**Barrel:** 18½".
**Weight:** 6¼ lbs. **Length:** 37½" overall.
**Stock:** Walnut, with modified schnabel forend. Cut checkering.
**Sights:** Ramp front, adjustable open rear.
**Features:** Short-action design; silent side safety; free-floated barrel except for single pressure point at forend tip. Introduced 1983.

Price: About . . . . . . . . . . . . . . . . . . . . . . . . . . **$524.00**
Price: 17 Rem., about . . . . . . . . . . . . . . . . . . . . . **$551.00**

### Remington Model Seven Youth Rifle

Similar to the Model Seven except has hardwood stock with 12³⁄₁₆" length of pull and chambered for 6mm Rem., 243, 7mm-08. Introduced 1993.

Price: About . . . . . . . . . . . . . . . . . . . . . . . . . . **$425.00**

Remington Model Seven MS

## Remington Model Seven Custom KS
Similar to the standard Model Seven except has custom finished stock of lightweight Kevlar aramid fiber and chambered for 223 Rem., 7mm-08, 308, 35 Rem. and 350 Rem. Mag. Barrel length is 20", weight 5¾ lbs. Comes with iron sights and is drilled and tapped for scope mounting. Special order through Remington Custom Shop. Introduced 1987.
**Price:** . . . . . . . . . . . . . . . . . . . . . . . . **$997.00**

## Remington Model Seven Custom MS Rifle
Similar to the Model Seven except has full-length Mannlicher-style stock of laminated wood with straight comb, solid black recoil pad, black steel forend tip, cut checkering, gloss finish. Barrel length 20", weight 6¾ lbs. Availabloe in 222 Rem., 223, 22-250, 243, 6mm Rem., 7mm-08 Rem., 308, 350 Rem. Mag. Calibers 250 Savage, 257 Roberts, 35 Rem. available on special order. Polished blue finish. Introduced 1993. From Remington Custom Shop.
**Price:** About . . . . . . . . . . . . . . . . . . . . **$1,001.00**

Remington 700 BDL

## Remington 700 BDL Bolt-Action Rifle
Same as the 700 ADL except chambered for 222, 223 (short action, 24" barrel), 22-250, 25-06, 6mm Rem. (short action, 22" barrel), 243, 270, 7mm-08, 280, 300 Savage, 30-06, 308; skip-line checkering; black forend tip and grip cap with white line spacers. Matted receiver top, quick-release floorplate. Hooded ramp front sight; q.d. swivels.
**Price:** About . . . . . . . . . . . . . . . . . . . . . **$524.00**
Also available in 17 Rem., 7mm Rem. Mag., 300 Win. Mag. (long action, 24" barrel), 338 Win. Mag., 35 Whelen (long action, 22" barrel). Overall length 44½", weight about 7½ lbs.
**Price:** About . . . . . . . . . . . . . . . . . . . . . **$551.00**
**Price:** Custom Grade, about . . . . . . . . . . . . . **$2,296.00**

## REMINGTON 700 ADL BOLT-ACTION RIFLE
**Caliber:** 243, 270, 308, 30-06 and 7mm Rem. Mag.
**Barrel:** 22" or 24" round tapered.
**Weight:** 7 lbs. **Length:** 41½" to 43½" overall.
**Stock:** Walnut. Satin-finished p.g. stock with fine-line cut checkering, Monte Carlo.
**Sights:** Gold bead ramp front; removable, step-adj. rear with windage screw.
**Features:** Side safety, receiver tapped for scope mounts.
**Price:** About . . . . . . . . . . . . . . . . . . . . . **$439.00**
**Price:** 7mm Rem. Mag., about . . . . . . . . . . . . **$465.00**
**Price:** Model 700 ADL/LS (laminated stock, 243, 270, 30-06 only) . . **$485.00**
**Price:** As above, 7mm Rem. Mag. . . . . . . . . . . **$512.00**

## Remington 700 BDL Varmint Special
Same as 700 BDL, except 24" heavy bbl., 43½" overall, weighs 9 lbs. Cals. 222, 223, 22-250, 243, 6mm Rem., 7mm-08 Rem. and 308. No sights.
**Price:** About . . . . . . . . . . . . . . . . . . . . . **$557.00**

Remington 700 BDL European

## Remington 700 BDL European Bolt-Action Rifle
Same as the 700 BDL except has oil-finished walnut stock and is chambered for 243, 270, 7mm-08, 280 Rem., 30-06 (22" barrel), 7mm Rem. Mag. (24" barrel). Introduced 1993.
**Price:** Standard calibers, about . . . . . . . . . . . **$524.00**
**Price:** 7mm Rem. Mag., about . . . . . . . . . . . . **$551.00**

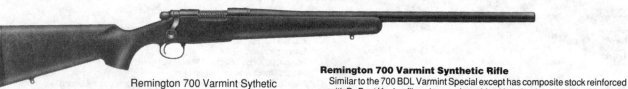

Remington 700 Varmint Sythetic

## Remington 700 BDL SS Rifle
Similar to the 700 Stainless Synthetic rifle except has hinged floorplate, 24" standard weight barrel in all calibers; magnum calibers have magnum-contour barrel. No sights supplied, but comes drilled and tapped. Has corrosion-resistant follower and fire control, stainless BDL-style barreled action with fine matte finish. Synthetic stock has straight comb and cheekpiece, textured finish, positive checkering, plated swivel studs. Short action calibers—223, 243, 6mm Rem., 7mm-08 Rem., 308; standard long action—25-06, 270, 280 Rem., 30-06; magnums—7mm Rem. Mag., 7mm Wea. Mag., 300 Win. Mag., 300 Wea. Mag., 338 Win. Mag. Weighs 6¾-7 lbs. Introduced 1993.
**Price:** Standard calibers, about . . . . . . . . . . . **$585.00**
**Price:** Magnum calibers, about . . . . . . . . . . . . **$612.00**

## Remington 700 MTRSS Rifle
Similar to the 700 BDL SS except stainless steel barreled action with 22" barrel; textured black synthetic stock profiled like the Mountain Rifle with positive checkering, straight comb and cheekpiece. Available in 25-06, 270, 280 Rem., 30-06. Weighs 6¾ lbs. Introduced 1993.
**Price:** . . . . . . . . . . . . . . . . . . . . . . . . . **$532.00**

## Remington 700 Varmint Synthetic Rifle
Similar to the 700 BDL Varmint Special except has composite stock reinforced with DuPont Kevlar, fiberglass and graphite. Has aluminum bedding block that runs the full length of the receiver. Free-floating barrel. Metal has black matte finish; stock has textured black and gray finish and swivel studs. Available in 220 Swift, 223, 22-250, 308. Introduced 1992.
**Price:** . . . . . . . . . . . . . . . . . . . . . . . . . **$632.00**

## Remington 700 Stainless Synthetic Rifle
Similar to the 700 BDL except has stainless barrel, bolt and receiver with synthetic stock profiled like the Mountain Rifle, with blind magazine, corrosion-resistant follower, black textured finish, checkered pistol grip and forend, swivel studs. Matte-finished metal. Introduced 1992.
**Price:** 25-06, 270, 280, 30-06 . . . . . . . . . . . . **$532.00**
**Price:** 7mm Wea. Mag., 7mm Rem. Mag., 300 Win. Mag., 338 Win. Mag. . . . . . . . . . . . . . . . . **$632.00**

## Remington 700 BDL Left Hand
Same as 700 BDL except mirror-image left-hand action, stock. Available in 22-250, 243, 308, 270, 30-06 only.
**Price:** About . . . . . . . . . . . . . . . . . . . . . **$548.00**
**Price:** 7mm Rem. Mag., 338 Win. Mag., about . . . . . . **$575.00**

**CAUTION:** PRICES CHANGE, CHECK AT GUNSHOP.

Remington 700 Camo Synthetic

## Remington 700 Safari

Similar to the 700 BDL except custom finished and tuned. In 8mm Rem. Mag., 375 H&H, 416 Rem. Mag. or 458 Win. Magnum calibers only with heavy barrel. Hand checkered, oil-finished stock in classic or Monte Carlo style with recoil pad installed. Delivery time is about 5 months.

**Price:** About . . . . . . . . . . . . . . . . . . . . . . . . . **$999.00**
**Price:** Classic stock, left-hand . . . . . . . . . . . . . **$1,063.00**
**Price:** Safari Custom KS (Kevlar stock), right-hand . . **$1,153.00**
**Price:** As above, left-hand . . . . . . . . . . . . . . . **$1,215.00**
**Price:** Custom KS wood-grained stock, right-hand . . . . **$1,265.00**
**Price:** As above, left-hand . . . . . . . . . . . . . . . **$1,327.00**

## Remington 700 Custom KS Mountain Rifle

Similar to the 700 "Mountain Rifle" except custom finished with Kevlar reinforced resin synthetic stock. Available in both left- and right-hand versions. Chambered for 270 Win., 280 Rem., 30-06, 7mm Rem. Mag., 300 Win. Mag., 300 Wea. Mag., 35 Whelen, 338 Win. Mag., 8mm Rem. Mag., 375 H&H, all with 24" barrel only. Weight is 6 lbs., 6 oz. Introduced 1986.

**Price:** Right-hand . . . . . . . . . . . . . . . . . . . . **$997.00**
**Price:** Left-hand . . . . . . . . . . . . . . . . . . . . . **$1,059.00**
**Price:** Stainless . . . . . . . . . . . . . . . . . . . . . **$1,137.00**
**Price:** With wood-grained Kevlar stock, right-hand . . . **$1,109.00**
**Price:** As above, left-hand . . . . . . . . . . . . . . . **$1,172.00**

## Remington 700 Camo Synthetic Rifle

Similar to the 700 BDL except has synthetic stock and the stock and metal (except bolt and sights) are fully camouflaged in Mossy Oak Bottomland camo. Comes with swivel studs, open adjustable sights. Available in 22-250, 243, 7mm-08, 270, 280, 30-06, 308, 7mm Rem. Mag., 300 Wea. Mag. Introduced 1992.

**Price:** Standard calibers . . . . . . . . . . . . . . . . **$568.00**
**Price:** Magnum calibers . . . . . . . . . . . . . . . . . **$595.00**

## Remington 700 Mountain Rifle

Similar to the 700 BDL except weighs 6¾ lbs., has a 22" tapered barrel. Redesigned pistol grip, straight comb, contoured cheekpiece, satin stock finish, fine checkering, hinged floorplate and magazine follower, two-position thumb safety. Chambered for 243, 257 Roberts, 270 Win., 7x57, 7mm-08, 25-06, 280 Rem., 30-06, 308, 4-shot magazine. Overall length is 42½". Introduced 1986.

**Price:** About . . . . . . . . . . . . . . . . . . . . . . . **$524.00**

## REMINGTON 700 CLASSIC RIFLE

**Caliber:** 222 Remington only, 5-shot magazine.
**Barrel:** 24".
**Weight:** About 7¾ lbs. **Length:** 44½" overall.
**Stock:** American walnut, 20 lpi checkering on p.g. and forend. Classic styling. Satin finish.
**Sights:** None furnished. Receiver drilled and tapped for scope mounting.
**Features:** A "classic" version of the M700 ADL with straight comb stock. Fitted with rubber recoil pad. Sling swivel studs installed. Hinged floorplate. Limited production in 1993 only.
**Price:** About . . . . . . . . . . . . . . . . . . . . . . . **$524.00**

Ruger M77 Express

## RUGER M77 MARK II MAGNUM RIFLE

**Caliber:** 375 H&H, 404 Jeffery, 4-shot magazine; 416 Rigby, 458 Win. Mag., 3-shot magazine.
**Barrel:** 26", with integral steel rib.
**Weight:** 9.25 lbs. (375, 404); 10.25 lbs. (416, 458). **Length:** 40.5" overall.
**Stock:** Circassian walnut with hand-cut checkering, swivel studs, steel grip cap, rubber butt pad.
**Sights:** Ramp front, three leaf express on serrated integral steel rib. Rib also serves as base for front scope ring.
**Features:** Uses an enlarged Mark II action with three-position safety, stainless bolt, steel trigger guard and hinged steel floorplate. Controlled feed. Introduced 1989.
**Price:** M77MKIIRSM . . . . . . . . . . . . . . . . . . . . **$1,550.00**

## RUGER M77 MARK II RIFLE

**Caliber:** 223, 243, 6mm Rem., 257 Roberts, 25-06, 6.5x55 Swedish, 270, 280 Rem., 308, 30-06, 7mm Rem. Mag., 300 Win. Mag., 338 Win. Mag., 4-shot magazine.
**Barrel:** 20", 22"; 24" (magnums).
**Weight:** About 7 lbs. **Length:** 39¾" overall.
**Stock:** Hand-checkered American walnut; swivel studs, rubber butt pad.
**Sights:** None furnished. Receiver has Ruger integral scope mount base, comes with Ruger 1" rings. Some models have iron sights.
**Features:** Short action with new trigger and three-position safety. New trigger guard with redesigned floorplate latch. Left-hand model available. Introduced 1989.
**Price:** M77MKIIR (no sights) . . . . . . . . . . . . . . . **$558.00**
**Price:** M77MKIIRS (open sights) . . . . . . . . . . . . . **$617.00**
**Price:** M77MKIILR (left-hand, 270, 30-06, 7mm Rem. Mag., 300 Win. Mag.) . . . . . . . . . . . . . . **$558.00**

Ruger M77RL

Ruger M77 All-Weather

## Ruger M77RL Ultra Light

Similar to the standard M77 except weighs only 6 lbs., chambered for 223, 243, 308, 270, 30-06, 257; barrel tapped for target scope blocks; has 20" Ultra Light barrel. Overall length 40". Ruger's steel 1" scope rings supplied. Introduced 1983.
**Price:** M77MKIIRL . . . . . . . . . . . . . . . . . . . . **$592.46**

## Ruger M77 Mark II All-Weather Stainless Rifle

Similar to the wood-stock M77 Mark II except all metal parts are of stainless steel, and has an injection-moulded, glass-fiber-reinforced Du Pont Zytel stock. Chambered for 223, 243, 270, 308, 30-06, 7mm Rem. Mag., 300 Win. Mag., 338 Win. Mag. Has the fixed-blade-type ejector, three-position safety, and new trigger guard with patented floorplate latch. Comes with integral Scope Base Receiver and 1" Ruger scope rings, built-in sling swivel loops. Introduced 1990.
**Price:** KM77MKIIRP . . . . . . . . . . . . . . . . . . . . **$558.00**

Ruger M77RSI International

## Ruger M77RSI International Carbine

Same as the standard Model 77 except has 18½" barrel, full-length Mannlicher-style stock, with steel forend cap, loop-type steel sling swivels. Integral-base receiver, open sights, Ruger 1" steel rings. Improved front sight. Available in 243, 270, 308, 30-06. Weighs 7 lbs. Length overall is 38⅜".
**Price:** M77MKIIRSI . . . . . . . . . . . . . . . . . . . . . . **$623.44**

## RUGER M77 MARK II EXPRESS RIFLE
**Caliber:** 270, 30-06, 7mm Rem. Mag., 300 Win. Mag., 4-shot magazine.
**Barrel:** 22", with integral steel rib; barrel-mounted front swivel stud.
**Weight:** 7.5 lbs. **Length:** 42.125" overall.
**Stock:** Hand-checkered medium quality walnut with steel grip cap, black rubber butt pad, swivel studs.
**Sights:** Ramp front, open rear adjustable for windage and elevation mounted on rib.
**Features:** Mark II action with three-position safety, stainless steel bolt, steel trigger guard, hinged steel floorplate. Introduced 1991.
**Price:** M77EXPMKII . . . . . . . . . . . . . . . . . . . . . **$1,550.00**

Ruger M77VT Target

## RUGER M77VT TARGET RIFLE
**Caliber:** 22 PPC, 22-250, 220 Swift, 223, 243, 6mm PPC, 25-06, 308.
**Barrel:** 26" heavy stainless steel with matte finish.

**Weight:** Approx. 9.25 lbs. **Length:** Approx. 44" overall.
**Stock:** Laminated American hardwood with flat forend, steel swivel studs; no checkering or grip cap.
**Sights:** Integral scope mount bases in receiver.
**Features:** Ruger diagonal bedding system. Ruger steel 1" scope rings supplied. Fully adjustable trigger. Steel floorplate and trigger guard. New version introduced 1992.
**Price:** KM77MKIIVT . . . . . . . . . . . . . . . . . . . . . . **$665.00**

Sako Hunter

## Sako Fiberclass Sporter
Similar to the Hunter except has a black fiberglass stock in the classic style, with wrinkle finish, rubber buttpad. Barrel length is 23", weight 7 lbs., 2 oz. Introduced 1985.
**Price:** 25-06, 270, 280 Rem., 30-06 . . . . . . . . . . **$1,310.00**
**Price:** 7mm Rem. Mag., 300 Win. Mag., 338 Win. Mag. . . . . . **$1,325.00**
**Price:** 375 H&H, 416 Rem. Mag. . . . . . . . . . . . . . . **$1,340.00**

## SAKO HUNTER RIFLE
**Caliber:** 17 Rem., 222, 223 (short action); 22-250, 243, 7mm-08, 308 (medium action); 25-06, 270, 30-06, 7mm Rem. Mag., 300 Win. Mag., 338 Win. Mag., 375 H&H Mag., 300 Wea. Mag., 416 Rem. Mag. (long action).
**Barrel:** 22" to 24" depending on caliber.
**Weight:** 5¾ lbs. (short); 6¼ lbs. (med.); 7¼ lbs. (long).
**Stock:** Hand-checkered European walnut.
**Sights:** None furnished.
**Features:** Adj. trigger, hinged floorplate. Imported from Finland by Stoeger.
**Price:** 17 Rem., 222, 223 . . . . . . . . . . . . . . . . . **$975.00**
**Price:** 22-250, 243, 308, 7mm-08 . . . . . . . . . . . . **$975.00**
**Price:** Long action cals. (except magnums) . . . . . . . . **$1,000.00**
**Price:** Magnum cals. . . . . . . . . . . . . . . . . . . . **$1,020.00**
**Price:** 375 H&H, 416 Rem. Mag., from . . . . . . . . . . **$1,035.00**
**Price:** 300 Wea. . . . . . . . . . . . . . . . . . . . . . **$1,035.00**

## Sako Safari Grade Bolt Action
Similar to the Hunter except available in long action, calibers 338 Win. Mag. or 375 H&H Mag. or 416 Rem. Mag. only. Stocked in French walnut, checkered 20 lpi, solid rubber buttpad; grip cap and forend tip; quarter-rib "express" rear sight, hooded ramp front. Front sling swivel band-mounted on barrel.
**Price:** . . . . . . . . . . . . . . . . . . . . . . . . . . . **$2,625.00**

## Sako Hunter Left-Hand Rifle
Same gun as the Sako Hunter except has left-hand action, stock with dull finish. Available in medium, long and magnum actions. Introduced 1987.
**Price:** Standard calibers, 22-250 to 7mm-08 . . . . . . . **$1,055.00**
**Price:** Magnum calibers . . . . . . . . . . . . . . . . . **$1,100.00**
**Price:** 375 H&H, 416 Rem. Mag. . . . . . . . . . . . . . **$1,115.00**
**Price:** Deluxe, standard calibers, 25-06, 30-06 . . . . . **$1,430.00**
**Price:** Deluxe, magnum calibers . . . . . . . . . . . . . **$1,445.00**
**Price:** Deluxe, 375 H&H, 416 Rem. Mag. . . . . . . . . . **$1,460.00**
**Price:** Long action, 25-06, 270, 280, 30-06 . . . . . . . **$1,085.00**

Sako Classic

## Sako Classic Bolt Action
Similar to the Hunter except has classic-style stock with straight comb. Has 21¾" barrel, weighs 6 lbs. Matte finish wood. Introduced 1993. Imported from Finland by Stoeger.
**Price:** 243 . . . . . . . . . . . . . . . . . . . . . . . . . **$975.00**
**Price:** 270, 30-06 . . . . . . . . . . . . . . . . . . . . . **$1,000.00**
**Price:** 7mm Rem. Mag. . . . . . . . . . . . . . . . . . . **$1,020.00**
**Price:** Left-hand, 270 . . . . . . . . . . . . . . . . . . . **$1,085.00**
**Price:** Left-hand, 7mm Rem. Mag. . . . . . . . . . . . . **$1,100.00**

## Sako Hunter LS Rifle
Same gun as the Sako Hunter except has laminated stock with dull finish. Chambered for same calibers. Also available in left-hand version. Introduced 1987.
**Price:** Medium action . . . . . . . . . . . . . . . . . . . **$1,190.00**
**Price:** Long action, from . . . . . . . . . . . . . . . . . **$1,155.00**
**Price:** Magnum cals., from . . . . . . . . . . . . . . . . **$1,175.00**
**Price:** 375 H&H, 416 Rem. Mag., from . . . . . . . . . . **$1,185.00**

## Sako Deluxe Lightweight
Same action as Hunter except has select wood, rosewood p.g. cap and forend tip. Fine checkering on top surfaces of integral dovetail bases, bolt sleeve, bolt handle root and bolt knob. Vent. recoil pad, skip-line checkering, mirror finish bluing.
**Price:** 17 Rem., 222, 223, 22-250, 243, 308, 7mm-08 . . . . . . **$1,325.00**
**Price:** 25-06, 270, 280 Rem., 30-06 . . . . . . . . . . . **$1,365.00**
**Price:** 7mm Rem. Mag., 300 Win. Mag., 338 Win. Mag. . . . . . **$1,380.00**
**Price:** 300 Wea., 375 H&H, 416 Rem. Mag. . . . . . . . . **$1,395.00**

Sako Mannlicher

## Sako Super Deluxe Sporter
Similar to Deluxe Hunter except has select European walnut with high-gloss finish and deep-cut oak leaf carving. Metal has super high polish, deep blue finish. Special order only.
**Price:** . . . . . . . . . . . . . . . . . . . . . **$2,790.00**

### Sako Mannlicher-Style Carbine
Same as the Hunter except has full "Mannlicher" style stock, 18½" barrel, weighs 7½ lbs., chambered for 243, 25-06, 270, 308 and 30-06, 7mm Rem. Mag., 300 Win. Mag., 338 Win. Mag., 375 H&H. Introduced 1977. From Stoeger.
**Price:** 243, 308 . . . . . . . . . . . . . . . . . . . **$1,130.00**
**Price:** 270, 30-06 . . . . . . . . . . . . . . . . . . **$1,165.00**
**Price:** 338 Win. Mag., 375 H&H . . . . . . . . . . **$1,180.00**
**Price:** 375 H&H . . . . . . . . . . . . . . . . . . . **$1,200.00**

Sako Heavy Barrel

### Sako Varmint Heavy Barrel
Same as std. Super Sporter except has beavertail forend; available in 17 Rem., 222, 223 (short action), 22 PPC, 6mm PPC (single shot), 22-250, 243, 308, 7mm-08 (medium action). Weight from 8¼ to 8½ lbs., 5-shot magazine capacity.
**Price:** 17 Rem., 222, 223 (short action) . . . . . . . . **$1,110.00**
**Price:** 22-250, 243, 308 (medium action) . . . . . . . **$1,110.00**
**Price:** 22 PPC, 6mm PPC (single shot) . . . . . . . . **$1,330.00**

Sako TRG-S

## SAKO TRG-S BOLT-ACTION RIFLE
**Caliber:** 243, 7mm-08, 270, 30-06, 7mm Rem. Mag., 300 Win. Mag., 338 Win. Mag., 375 H&H, 416 Rem. Mag., 5-shot magazine (4-shot for 375 H&H).
**Barrel:** 22", 24" (magnum calibers).

**Weight:** 7.75 lbs. **Length:** 45.5" overall.
**Stock:** Reinforced polyurethane with Monte Carlo comb.
**Sights:** None furnished.
**Features:** Resistance-free bolt with 60-degree lift. Recoil pad adjustable for length. Free-floating barrel, detachable magazine, fully adjustable trigger. Matte blue metal. Introduced 1993. Imported from Finland by Stoeger.
**Price:** 243, 7mm-08, 270, 30-06 . . . . . . . . . . **$730.00**
**Price:** Magnum calibers . . . . . . . . . . . . . . . **$765.00**

Sauer 90

## SAUER 90 BOLT-ACTION RIFLE
**Caliber:** 270, 25-06, 30-06, 7mm Rem. Mag., 300 Win. Mag., 300 Wea. Mag., 338 Win., 375 H&H, 458 Win. Mag., 4-shot magazine for standard calibers, 3-shot for magnums.
**Barrel:** 24" (standard calibers), 26" (magnum calibers).
**Weight:** 7.25 to 8 lbs. **Length:** 44" overall (24" barrel).

**Stock:** Monte Carlo style with sculptured cheekpiece, hand-checkered grip and forend, rosewood grip cap and forend tip. Lux is European walnut with oil finish, Supreme is American walnut with high-gloss lacquer finish.
**Sights:** None furnished; drilled and tapped for scope mount.
**Features:** Rear bolt cam activated locking lug action with 65° bolt lift, fully adjustable gold-plated trigger, chamber-loaded signal pin, cocking indicator, tang-mounted slide safety. Detachable box magazine. Introduced 1986. Imported from Germany by G.U., Inc.
**Price:** Lux or Supreme . . . . . . . . . . . . . . . **$1,495.00**
**Price:** With engraving LVL I . . . . . . . . . . . . . **$2,495.00**
**Price:** With engraving LVL II . . . . . . . . . . . . . **$3,095.00**
**Price:** With engraving LVL III . . . . . . . . . . . . **$3,395.00**
**Price:** With engraving LVL IV . . . . . . . . . . . . **$3,995.00**
**Price:** 458 Safari . . . . . . . . . . . . . . . . . . . **$1,995.00**

Savage 110G

### SAVAGE 110G BOLT-ACTION RIFLE
**Caliber:** 22-250, 223, 250 Savage, 25-06, 7mm-08, 270, 308, 30-06, 243, 5-shot; 7mm Rem. Mag., 300 Win. Mag., 338 Win. Mag., 4-shot.
**Barrel:** 22" round tapered, 24" for magnum.
**Weight:** 6¾ lbs. **Length:** 42⅜" (22" barrel).
**Stock:** Walnut-finished checkered hardwood with Monte Carlo; hard rubber buttplate.
**Sights:** Ramp front, step adjustable rear.
**Features:** Top tang safety, receiver tapped for scope mount. Full-floating barrel; adjustable trigger. Introduced 1989.
**Price:** . . . . . . . . . . . . . . . . . . . . . . . . **$340.00**
**Price:** Left-hand, 30-06, 270, 7mm Rem. Mag. only, M110GLNS . . **$400.00**
**Price:** Model 110GNS (no sights) . . . . . . . . . . . **$340.00**
**Price:** Model 110FNS (no sights, black composite stock) . . . . . **$370.00**
**Price:** Model 110GC (removable box magazine, 30-06, 270, 7mm Rem. Mag., 300 Win. Mag.) . . . . . . . . . . . . . . . . . . . . **$375.00**

Consult our Directory pages for the location of firms mentioned.

# CENTERFIRE RIFLES—BOLT ACTION

**Savage 110CY Youth/Ladies Rifle**
Similar to the Savage 110G except has walnut-finished hardwood stock with 12½" length of pull, and is chambered for 243 and 300 Savage. Comes with gun lock, ear plugs, sight-in target and shooting glasses. Introduced 1991.
Price: . . . . . . . . . . . . . . . . . . . . . . . . . . . . **$350.00**

**Savage 110GXP3 Bolt-Action Rifle**
Similar to the 110G except comes with 3-9x32 scope, rings and bases, Savage leather sling, swivels, gun lock, ear plugs, safety glasses and sight-in target. Available in 223, 22-250, 243, 270, 308, 30-06, 7mm Rem. Mag., 300 Win. Mag. Introduced 1991.
Price: . . . . . . . . . . . . . . . . . . . . . . . . . . . . **$397.00**

**Savage 110FXP3 Bolt-Action Rifle**
Same as the Savage 110F except has black composite stock and comes with a 3-9x32 scope, Kwik-Site rings and bases, Savage/Pathfinder leather sling, Uncle Mike's swivels, gun lock, ear plugs, shooting glasses and sight-in target. Chambered for 223, 22-250, 308, 243, 30-06, 270, 7mm Rem. Mag., 300 Win. Mag. Introduced 1991.
Price: . . . . . . . . . . . . . . . . . . . . . . . . . . . . **$390.00**

Savage 112FV

**Savage 114CU Classic Ultra Rifle**
Similar to the Savage 110G except comes with adjustable sights, a straight American walnut stock with high-gloss finish, cut checkering, grip cap and recoil pad. Removable box magazine hold five rounds (four for magnums). Chambered for 270, 30-06, 7mm Rem. Mag. and 300 Win. Mag. Introduced 1991.
Price: . . . . . . . . . . . . . . . . . . . . . . . . . . . . **$520.00**

Savage 112BV

**Savage Model 112FVS Varmint Rifle**
Similar to the Model 112 FV except is a single shot with rigid, solid-bottom receiver. Available in 223, 22-250 and 220 Swift. Introduced 1993.
Price: . . . . . . . . . . . . . . . . . . . . . . . . . . . . **$360.00**

Savage 116FSS

**Savage Model 116FSK Kodiak Rifle**
Similar to the Model 116FSS except has "Shock Suppressor" recoil reducer. Available only in 338 Win. Mag., 22" barrel. Introduced 1993.
Price: . . . . . . . . . . . . . . . . . . . . . . . . . . . . **$510.00**

Savage 110FP

**Savage 110WLE One of One Thousand Limited Edition Rifle**
Similar to the Savage 110G except is chambered for 7x57mm Mauser, 250-3000 Savage and 300 Savage, and comes with high-luster #2 fancy-grade American walnut stock with cut checkering, swivel studs, and recoil pad. Highly polished barrel; the bolt has a laser-etched Savage logo. Included are gun lock, ear plugs, sight-in target and shooting glasses. Introduced 1992.
Price: About . . . . . . . . . . . . . . . . . . . . . . . . **$475.00**

**Savage 110F Bolt-Action Rifle**
Similar to the Model 110G except has a black Du Pont Rynite® stock with black buttpad, swivel studs, removable open sights. Same calibers as the 110G except 250 Savage, 25-06, 7mm-08. Introduced 1988.
Price: Right-hand only . . . . . . . . . . . . . . . . . . **$360.00**

**Savage 110GV Varmint Rifle**
Similar to the Model 110G except has medium-weight varmint barrel, no sights, receiver drilled and tapped for scope mounting. Calibers 22-250, 223 only. Introduced 1989.
Price: . . . . . . . . . . . . . . . . . . . . . . . . . . . . **$400.00**

**Savage 112FV Varmint Rifle**
Similar to the Savage 110G except has 26" heavy barrel, chambered for 223 and 22-250, and comes with a DuPont Rynite stock. Drilled and tapped for scope mounts. Weight is 9 lbs. Included are gun lock, ear plugs, sight-in target and shooting glases. Reintroduced 1991.
Price: . . . . . . . . . . . . . . . . . . . . . . . . . . . . **$360.00**
Price: Model 112FVSS (as above except has stainless barrel, bolt handle, trigger guard, synthetic stock with positive checkering) . . . . . . **$460.00**

**Savage Model 112BV Heavy Barrel Varmint Rifle**
Same as the Model 112FV except has laminated wood stock with high comb, ambidextrous grip with palm swell. Available in 223, 22-250. Introduced 1993.
Price: . . . . . . . . . . . . . . . . . . . . . . . . . . . . **$460.00**

**Savage 116FSS Bolt-Action Rifle**
Similar to the Savage 110F except made of stainless steel. Has black DuPont Rynite stock. Drilled and tapped for scope mounts; no open sights supplied. In 223, 243, 30-06, 270, 7mm Rem. Mag., 300 Win. Mag., 338 Win. Mag.; 22" barrel for 30-06, 270; 24" for magnums. Introduced 1991.
Price: . . . . . . . . . . . . . . . . . . . . . . . . . . . . **$500.00**
Price: Model 116FCS (as above with removable box magazine; cals. 30-06, 270, 7mm Rem. Mag., 300 Win. Mag. only) . . . . . . . . . . **$510.00**

**SAVAGE 110FP POLICE RIFLE**
**Caliber:** 223, 308, 4-shot magazine.
**Barrel:** 24", heavy.
**Weight:** 9 lbs. **Length:** 45.5" overall.
**Stock:** Black Rynite composition.
**Sights:** None furnished. Receiver drilled and tapped for scope mounting.
**Features:** Matte finish on all metal parts. Double swivel studs on the forend for sling and/or bipod mount. Introduced 1990. From Savage Arms.
Price: . . . . . . . . . . . . . . . . . . . . . . . . . . . . **$400.00**

**CAUTION:** PRICES CHANGE, CHECK AT GUNSHOP.

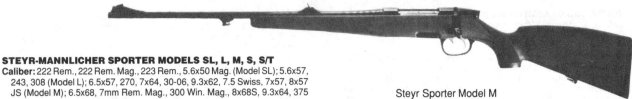

## STEYR-MANNLICHER SPORTER MODELS SL, L, M, S, S/T
**Caliber:** 222 Rem., 222 Rem. Mag., 223 Rem., 5.6x50 Mag. (Model SL); 5.6x57, 243, 308 (Model L); 6.5x57, 270, 7x64, 30-06, 9.3x62, 7.5 Swiss, 7x57, 8x57 JS (Model M); 6.5x68, 7mm Rem. Mag., 300 Win. Mag., 8x68S, 9.3x64, 375 H&H, 458 Win. Mag. (Model S).
**Barrel:** 20" (full-stock), 23.6" (half-stock), 26" (magnums).
**Weight:** 6.8 to 7.5 lbs. **Length:** 39" (full-stock), 43" (half-stock).
**Stock:** Hand-checkered European walnut. Full Mannlicher or standard half-stock with Monte Carlo comb and rubber recoil pad.
**Sights:** Ramp front, open adjustable rear.
**Features:** Choice of single- or double-set triggers. Detachable 5-shot rotary magazine. Drilled and tapped for scope mounting. Model M actions available in left-hand models; S (magnum) actions available in half-stock only. Imported by GSI, Inc.

Steyr Sporter Model M

| | |
|---|---|
| **Price:** Models SL, L, M, half-stock | **$2,023.00** |
| **Price:** As above, full-stock | **$2,179.00** |
| **Price:** Models SL, L Varmint, 26" heavy barrel | **$2,179.00** |
| **Price:** Model M left-hand, half-stock (270, 30-06, 7x64) | **$2,179.00** |
| **Price:** As above, full-stock (270, 7x57, 7x64, 30-06) | **$2,335.00** |
| **Price:** Model S Magnum | **$2,179.00** |
| **Price:** Model S/T, 26" heavy barrel (375 H&H, 9.3x64, 458 Win. Mag.) | **$2,335.00** |

Steyr Luxus

## Steyr-Mannlicher Model M Professional Rifle
Similar to the Sporter series except has black ABS Cycolac stock, Parkerized finish. Chambered for 6.5x57, 270, 7x64, 30-06, 9.3x62. Has 23.6" barrel, weighs 7.5 lbs. Imported by GSI, Inc.
**Price:** Without sights . . . . . . . . . . . . . . . . . . . . . . . . **$1,495.00**

## Steyr-Mannlicher Luxus Model L, M, S
Similar to the Sporter series except has single set trigger, detachable steel 3-shot, in-line magazine, rear tang slide safety. Calibers: 5.6x57, 243, 308 (Model L); 6.5x57, 270, 7x64, 30-06, 9.3x62, 7.5 Swiss (Model M); 6.5x68, 7mm Rem. Mag., 300 Win. Mag., 8x68S (Model S). S (magnum) calibers available in half-stock only. Imported by GSI, Inc.

| | |
|---|---|
| **Price:** Model L, M, half-stock | **$2,648.00** |
| **Price:** As above, full-stock | **$2,804.00** |
| **Price:** Model S (magnum) | **$2,804.00** |

Tikka Premium Grade

## Tikka Premium Grade Rifles
Similar to the standard grade Tikka except has stock with roll-over cheekpiece, select walnut, rosewood grip and forend caps. Hand-checkered grip and forend. Highly polished and blued barrel. Introduced 1990. Imported from Finland by Stoeger.
**Price:** Standard calibers . . . . . . . . . . . . . . . . . . . **$1,030.00**
**Price:** Magnum calibers . . . . . . . . . . . . . . . . . . . **$1,070.00**

## TIKKA BOLT-ACTION RIFLE
**Caliber:** 22-250, 223, 243, 270, 308, 30-06, 7mm Rem. Mag., 300 Win. Mag., 338 Win. Mag.
**Barrel:** 22½" (std. cals.), 24½" (magnum cals.).
**Weight:** 7⅛ lbs. **Length:** 43" overall (std. cals.).
**Stock:** European walnut with Monte Carlo comb, rubber buttpad, checkered grip and forend.
**Sights:** None furnished.
**Features:** Detachable four-shot magazine (standard calibers), three-shot in magnums. Receiver dovetailed for scope mounting. Introduced 1988. Imported from Finland by Stoeger Industries.
**Price:** Standard calibers . . . . . . . . . . . . . . . . . . . **$835.00**
**Price:** Magnum calibers . . . . . . . . . . . . . . . . . . . **$860.00**

## Tikka Varmint/Continental Rifle
Similar to the standard Tikka rifle except has heavy barrel, extra-wide forend. Chambered for 22-250, 223, 243, 308. Introduced 1991. Made in Finland by Sako. Imported by Stoeger.
**Price:** . . . . . . . . . . . . . . . . . . . . . . . . . . . . **$1,090.00**

## Tikka Whitetail/Battue Rifle
Similar to the standard Tikka rifle except has 20½" barrel with raised quarter-rib with wide V-shaped sight for rapid sighting. Chambered for 308, 270, 30-06, 7mm Rem. Mag., 300 Win. Mag., 338 Win. Mag. Made in Finland by Sako. Introduced 1991. Imported by Stoeger.
**Price:** 308, 270, 30-06 . . . . . . . . . . . . . . . . . . . **$860.00**
**Price:** 7mm Rem. Mag., 300 Win. Mag., 338 Win. Mag. . . . . . . . **$895.00**

Ultra Light Model 20

## Ultra Light Arms Model 28, Model 40 Rifles
Similar to the Model 20 except in 264, 7mm Rem. Mag., 300 Win. Mag., 338 Win. Mag. (Model 28), 300 Wea. Mag., 416 Rigby (Model 40). Both use 24" Douglas Premium No. 2 contour barrel. Weight 5½ lbs., 45" overall length. KDF or ULA recoil arrestor built in. Any custom feature available on any ULA product can be incorporated.
**Price:** Right-hand, Model 28 or 40 . . . . . . . . . . **$2,900.00**
**Price:** Left-hand, Model 28 or 40 . . . . . . . . . . **$3,000.00**

## ULTRA LIGHT ARMS MODEL 20 RIFLE
**Caliber:** 17 Rem., 22 Hornet, 222 Rem., 223 Rem. (Model 20S); 22-250, 6mm Rem., 243, 257 Roberts, 7x57, 7x57 Ackley, 7mm-08, 284 Win., 308 Savage. Improved and other calibers on request.
**Barrel:** 22" Douglas Premium No. 1 contour.
**Weight:** 4½ lbs. **Length:** 41½" overall.
**Stock:** Composite Kevlar, graphite reinforced. Du Pont imron paint colors—green, black, brown and camo options. Choice of length of pull.
**Sights:** None furnished. Scope mount included.
**Features:** Timney adjustable trigger; two-position three-function safety. Benchrest quality action. Matte or bright stock and metal finish. 3" magazine length. Shipped in a hard case. From Ultra Light Arms, Inc.
**Price:** Right-hand . . . . . . . . . . . . . . . . . . . **$2,400.00**
**Price:** Model 20 Left Hand (left-hand action and stock) . . . . . **$2,500.00**
**Price:** Model 24 (25-06, 270, 280 Rem., 30-06, 3⅜" magazine length) . . . . . . . . . . . . . . . . . . . **$2,500.00**
**Price:** Model 24 Left Hand (left-hand action and stock) . . . . . **$2,600.00**

## VOERE VEC 91 LIGHTNING BOLT-ACTION RIFLE

**Caliber:** 5.7x26mm UCC (223-cal.) caseless, 5-shot magazine.
**Barrel:** 20".
**Weight:** 6 lbs. **Length:** 39'Overall.
**Stock:** European walnut with cheekpiece, checkered grip and schnabel forend.
**Sights:** Blade on ramp front, open adjustable rear.
**Features:** Fires caseless ammunition via electric ignition; two batteries housed in the pistol grip last for about 5000 shot. Trigger is adjustable from 5 oz. to 7 lbs. Bolt action has twin forward locking lugs. Top tang safety. Drilled and tapped for scope mounting. Ammunition available from importer. Introduced 1991. Imported from Austria by JagerSport, Ltd.
**Price:** About . . . . . . . . . . . . . . . . . . . . . . . . . . . . . . **$2,730.00**

## Voere Model 2155, 2150 Bolt-Action Rifles

Similar to the Model 2165 except has conventional non-removable magazine, comes without sights (drilled and tapped); 22" barrel in standard calibers, 24" magnums. Imported from Austria by JagerSport, Ltd.
**Price:** Standard calibers—243, 270, 30-06, about . . . . . . . . . **$910.00**
**Price:** Magnum calibers—7mm Rem. Mag.,
300 Win. Mag. (M2155M), about . . . . . . . . . . . . . . **$975.00**
**Price:** Model 2150 (as above with sights, deluxe walnut stock with hand-rubbed finish, barrel-mounted swivel), standard calibers, about . **$1,685.00**
**Price:** Model 2150M, 7mm Rem. Mag., 300 Win. Mag., about . . **$1,755.00**

## VOERE MODEL 2165 BOLT-ACTION RIFLE

**Caliber:** 22-250, 243, 270, 7x57, 7x64, 308, 30-06 (standard), 7mm Rem. Mag., 300 Win. Mag., 9,3x64; 5-shot magazine for standard calibers, 3-shot for magnums.
**Barrel:** 22" (standard calibers), 24" (magnums).
**Weight:** 7-7½ lbs. **Length:** 44½" overall (22" barrel).
**Stock:** European walnut with Bavarian cheekpiece; schnabel forend tip; rosewood grip cap.
**Sights:** Ramp front, open adjustable rear.
**Features:** Built on Mauser 98-type action; tang safety; detachable box magazine. Comes with extra magazine. Imported from Austria by JagerSport, Ltd.
**Price:** Standard calibers, about . . . . . . . . . . . . . . . . . . **$1,425.00**
**Price:** Magnum calibers (Model 2165M), about . . . . . . . . . **$1,495.00**

> Consult our Directory pages for the location of firms mentioned.

Weatherby Mark V

## Weatherby Lazermark V Rifle

Same as standard Mark V except stock has extensive laser carving under cheekpiece on butt, p.g. and forend. Introduced 1981.
**Price:** 240, 257, 270, right-hand, 7mm, 300 Wea. Mag., right- or
left-hand, 24" . . . . . . . . . . . . . . . . . . . . . . . **$1,355.00**
**Price:** 240, 257, 270, 7mm Wea. Mag., 30-06, right-hand, 26" . . **$1,368.00**
**Price:** 300 Wea. Mag., right- or left-hand, 340 Wea. Mag., right-hand,
26" . . . . . . . . . . . . . . . . . . . . . . . . . . . . . **$1,403.00**
**Price:** 378 Wea. Mag., right-hand, 26" . . . . . . . . . . . . . . **$1,443.00**
**Price:** 416 Wea. Mag., right-hand, 26" . . . . . . . . . . . . . . **$1,489.00**
**Price:** 460 Wea. Mag., right-hand, 26" . . . . . . . . . . . . . . **$1,844.00**

## WEATHERBY MARK V DELUXE BOLT-ACTION RIFLE

**Caliber:** All Weatherby cals., plus 22-250, 270, 30-06, 7mm Rem. Mag., 375 H&H.
**Barrel:** 24" or 26" round tapered.
**Weight:** 6½-10½ lbs. **Length:** 43¼"-46½" overall.
**Stock:** Walnut, Monte Carlo with cheekpiece, high luster finish, checkered p.g. and forend, recoil pad.
**Sights:** Optional (extra).
**Features:** Cocking indicator, adjustable trigger, hinged floorplate, thumb safety, quick detachable sling swivels.
**Price:** 224 Wea. Mag., 22-250, 26" . . . . . . . . . . . . . . . **$1,196.00**
**Price:** 240, 257, 270, 7mm, 300 Wea. Mag., 30-06, right-hand, left-hand available, 24" . . . . . . . . . . . . . . . . . . . . . . **$1,225.00**
**Price:** 375 H&H, right-hand, 24" . . . . . . . . . . . . . . . . . **$1,377.00**
**Price:** 240, 257, 270, 7mm Wea. Mag., 30-06, right-hand, 26" . . . **$1,239.00**
**Price:** 300 Wea. Mag., left-hand available, 340 Wea. Mag., right-hand,
26" . . . . . . . . . . . . . . . . . . . . . . . . . . . . . **$1,270.00**
**Price:** 378 Wea. Mag., right-hand, 26" . . . . . . . . . . . . . . **$1,305.00**
**Price:** 416 Wea. Mag., right-hand, 26" . . . . . . . . . . . . . . **$1,346.00**

Weatherby Mark V Sporter

## Weatherby Mark V Crown Custom Rifles

Uses hand-honed, engraved Mark V barreled action with fully-checkered bolt knob, damascened bolt and follower. Floorplate is engraved "Weatherby Custom." Super fancy walnut stock with inlays and stock carving. Gold monogram with name or initials. Right-hand only. Available in 240, 257, 270, 7mm, 300 Wea. Mag. or 30-06. Introduced 1989.
**Price:** From . . . . . . . . . . . . . **$3,533.00** to **$4,933.00**
**Price:** For 340 Wea. Mag., add . . . . . . . . . . . . . . . **$20.00**

## Weatherby Weathermark Rifle

Similar to the Mark V rifle except has impregnated-color black composite stock with raised point checkering. Uses the Mark V action. Weighs 7.5 lbs. Right-hand only. Introduced 1992.
**Price:** 257, 270, 7mm, 300 Wea. Mag., 7mm Rem. Mag., 300 Win. Mag., 300
Win. Mag., right-hand, 24" . . . . . . . . . . . . . . . . **$599.00**
**Price:** 257, 270, 7mm Wea. Mag., right-hand, 26" . . . . . . . . . **$625.00**
**Price:** 375 H&H, right-hand, 24" . . . . . . . . . . . . . . . . . **$711.00**
**Price:** 270 Win., 30-06, right-hand, 22" . . . . . . . . . . . . . **$599.00**
**Price:** 300, 340 Wea. Mag., right-hand, 26" . . . . . . . . . . . **$625.00**

## Weatherby Mark V Sporter Rifle

Same as the Mark V Deluxe without the embellishments. Metal has low-luster blue, Stock is Claro walnut with high-gloss epoxy finish, Monte Carlo comb, recoil pad. Introduced 1993.
**Price:** 257 270, 7mm, 300 Wea. Mag., 7mm Rem. Mag., 300, 338 Win. Mag.,
right-hand, 24" . . . . . . . . . . . . . . . . . . . . . . **$732.00**
**Price:** 375 H&H, right-hand, 24" . . . . . . . . . . . . . . . . . **$833.00**
**Price:** 270 Win., 30-06, right-hand, 22" . . . . . . . . . . . . . **$732.00**
**Price:** 300, 340 Wea. Mag., right-hand, 26" . . . . . . . . . . . **$780.00**

## Weatherby Mark V Safari Grade Custom Rifles

Uses the Mark V barreled action. Stock is of European walnut with satin oil finish, rounded ebony tip and cap, black presentation recoil pad, no white spacers, and pattern #16 fine-line checkering. Matte finish bluing, floorplate is engraved "Weatherby Safari Grade"; 24" barrel. Standard rear stock swivel, barrel band front swivel. Has quarter-rib rear sight with a stationary leaf and one folding shallow V leaf. Front sight is a hooded ramp with brass bead. Right- or left-hand. Allow 8-10 months delivery. Introduced 1985.
**Price:** 300 W.M. . . . . . . . . . . . . . . . . . . . . . . . . . **$3,301.00**
**Price:** 340 W.M. . . . . . . . . . . . . . . . . . . . . . . . . . **$3,321.00**
**Price:** 378 W.M. . . . . . . . . . . . . . . . . . . . . . . . . . **$3,481.00**
**Price:** 416 W.M. . . . . . . . . . . . . . . . . . . . . . . . . . **$3,534.00**
**Price:** 460 W.M. . . . . . . . . . . . . . . . . . . . . . . . . . **$3,574.00**

**CAUTION:** PRICES CHANGE, CHECK AT GUNSHOP.

# CENTERFIRE RIFLES—BOLT ACTION

**Weatherby Weathermark Alaskan Rifle**
Same as the Weathermark except all metal plated with electroless nickel. Available in right-hand only. Introduced 1992.
Price: 257, 270, 7mm, 300 Wea. Mag., 7mm Rem. Mag., 300 Win. Mag., 338 Win. Mag.,right-hand, 24" . . . . . . . . . **$799.00**
Price: 257, 270, 7mm Wea. Mag., right-hand, 26" . . . . . . . . **$833.00**
Price: 375 H&H, right-hand, 24" . . . . . . . . . . . **$949.00**
Price: 270 Win., 30-06, right-hand, 22" . . . . . . . . . . **$799.00**
Price: 300, 340 Wea. Mag., right-hand, 26" . . . . . . . **$833.00**

**Weatherby Weatherguard Alaskan Rifle**
Same as the Vanguard Weatherguard except all metal finished with electroless nickel. Available in 223, 243, 7mm-08, 270 Win., 7mm Rem. Mag., 308, 30-06, right-hand only, 24" barrel. Introduced 1992.
Price: . . . . . . . . . . . . . . . . . . . **$699.00**

**Weatherby Classicmark No. 1 Rifle**
Similar to the Mark V except has straight comb stock of hand-selected American claro walnut with oil finish, 18 l.p.i. panel point checkering and a 1" Presentation recoil pad. All metal satin finished. Uses the Mark V action. Available in right- or left-hand versions. Introduced 1992.
Price: 240, 257, 270, 7mm, 300 Wea. Mag.,
7mm Rem. Mag., right-hand, 24" . . . . . . **$1,295.00**
Price: 375 H&H, right-hand, 26" . . . . . . . **$1,425.00**
Price: 240, 257, 270, 7mm Wea. Mag., right-hand, 26" . . . . **$1,310.00**
Price: 270 Win., 30-06, right-hand, 22" . . . . . . **$1,295.00**
Price: 300, 340 Wea. Mag., right-hand, 26" . . . . **$1,323.00**
Price: 378 Wea. Mag., right-hand, 26" . . . . **$1,356.00**
Price: 416 Wea. Mag., right-hand, 26" . . . . **$1,411.00**
Price: 460 Wea. Mag., right-hand, 26" . . . . **$1,573.00**

Weatherby Vanguard VGX

**Weatherby Vanguard Classic Rifle**
Similar to the Classicmark I except has rounded forend with black tip, black grip cap with walnut diamond inlay, 20 lpi checkering. Solid black recoil pad. Oil-finished stock. Available in 22-250, 243, 270, 7mm Rem. Mag., 30-06, 300 Win. Mag., 338 Win. Mag., 270 Wea. Mag., 300 Wea. Mag. Introduced 1989.
Price: . . . . . . . . . . . . . . . . . **$549.00**

**WEATHERBY VANGUARD VGX DELUXE RIFLE**
Caliber: 22-250, 243, 270, 270 Wea. Mag., 7mm Rem. Mag., 30-06, 300 Win. Mag., 300 Wea. Mag., 338 Win. Mag.; 5-shot magazine (3-shot for magnums).
Barrel: 24", No. 2 contour.
Weight: 7⅞-8½ lbs. Length: 44½" overall (22-250, 243 are 44").
Stock: Walnut with high luster finish; rosewood grip cap and forend tip.
Sights: Optional, available at extra cost.
Features: Fully adjustable trigger; side safety; rubber recoil pad. Introduced 1989. Imported from Japan by Weatherby.
Price: . . . . . . . . . . . . . . . . . **$699.00**

**Weatherby Vanguard Classic No. 1 Rifle**
Similar to the Vanguard VGX Deluxe except has a "classic" style stock without Monte Carlo comb, no forend tip. Has distinctive Weatherby grip cap. Satin finish on stock. Available in 223, 243, 270, 7mm-08, 7mm Rem. Mag., 30-06, 308; 24" barrel. Introduced 1989.
Price: . . . . . . . . . . . . . . . . . **$549.00**

**Weatherby Vanguard Weatherguard Rifle**
Has a forest green or black wrinkle-finished synthetic stock. All metal is matte blue. Has a 24" barrel, weighs 7½ lbs., measures 44½". In 223, 243, and 308; 40½" in 270, 7mm-08, 7mm Rem. Mag., 30-06. Accepts same scope mount bases as Mark V action. Introduced 1989.
Price: Right-hand only . . . . . . . . . . **$499.00**

Wichita Classic

**WICHITA VARMINT RIFLE**
Caliber: 222 Rem., 222 Rem. Mag., 223 Rem., 22 PPC, 6mm PPC, 22-250, 243, 6mm Rem., 308 Win.; other calibers on special order.
Barrel: 20⅛".
Weight: 9 lbs. Length: 40⅛" overall.
Stock: AAA Fancy American walnut. Hand-rubbed finish, hand checkered, 20 lpi pattern. Hand-inletted, glass bedded, steel grip cap. Pachmayr rubber recoil pad.
Sights: None. Drilled and tapped for scope mounts.
Features: Right- or left-hand Wichita action with three locking lugs. Available as a single shot or repeater with 3-shot magazine. Checkered bolt handle. Bolt is hand fitted, lapped and jeweled. Side thumb safety. Firing pin fall is 3⁄16". Non-glare blue finish. From Wichita Arms.
Price: Single shot . . . . . . . . . . **$2,250.00**

**WICHITA CLASSIC RIFLE**
Caliber: 17-222, 17-222 Mag., 222 Rem., 222 Rem. Mag., 223 Rem., 6x47; other calibers on special order.
Barrel: 21⅛".
Weight: 8 lbs. Length: 41" overall.
Stock: AAA Fancy American walnut. Hand-rubbed and checkered (20 lpi). Hand-inletted, glass bedded, steel grip cap. Pachmayr rubber recoil pad.
Sights: None. Drilled and tapped for scope mounting.
Features: Available as single shot or repeater. Octagonal barrel and Wichita action, right- or left-hand. Checkered bolt handle. Bolt is hand-fitted, lapped and jeweled. Adjustable trigger is set at 2 lbs. Side thumb safety. Firing pin fall is 3⁄16". Non-glare blue finish. From Wichita Arms.
Price: Single shot . . . . . . . . . . **$2,950.00**

Winchester Model 70 Sporter

**WINCHESTER MODEL 70 SPORTER**
Caliber: 22-250, 223, 243, 25-06, 270, 270 Wea., 30-06, 264 Win. Mag., 7mm Rem. Mag., 300 H&H, 300 Win. Mag., 300 Wea. Mag., 338 Win. Mag., 3-shot magazine.

Barrel: 24".
Weight: 7¾ lbs. Length: 44½" overall.
Stock: American walnut with Monte Carlo cheekpiece. Cut checkering and satin finish.
Sights: Optional hooded ramp front, adjustable folding leaf rear. Drilled and tapped for scope mounting.
Features: Three-position safety, stainless steel magazine follower; rubber buttpad; epoxy bedded receiver recoil lug. From U.S. Repeating Arms Co.
Price: With sights . . . . . . . . . . **$556.00**
Price: With bases and rings . . . . . . . . . . **$556.00**

**CAUTION:** PRICES CHANGE, CHECK AT GUNSHOP.

Winchester Model 70 Win Tuff

### Winchester Model 70 SM Sporter

Same as the Model 70 Sporter except has black composite, graphite-impregnated stock and matte-finished metal. Available in 223, 22-250, 243, 270, 308, 30-06, 7mm Rem. Mag., 300 Win. Mag., 338 Win. Mag., 375 H&H. Weighs about 7.8 lbs. Comes with scope bases and rings. Introduced 1992.
**Price:** . . . . . . . . . . . . . . . . . . . . . . . . . . . . . **$576.00**
**Price:** 375 H&H . . . . . . . . . . . . . . . . . . . . . . . . **$604.00**

### Winchester Model 70 Sporter WinTuff

Same as the Model 70 Sporter except has classic-style brown laminated stock with sculpted cheekpiece, diamond point checkering, sling swivel studs, and contoured rubber recoil pad. Available in 270, 30-06, 7mm Rem. Mag., 300 Win. Mag., 300 Wea. Mag., 338 Win Mag. Weighs about 7.8 lbs. Comes with scope bases and rings. Introduced 1992.
**Price:** . . . . . . . . . . . . . . . . . . . . . . . . . . . . . **$572.00**

Winchester Model 70 Stainless

### Winchester Model 70 Stainless Rifle

Same as the Model 70 Sporter except has stainless steel barrel and action with matte gray finish, black composite stock impregnated with fiberglass and graphite, contoured rubber recoil pad. Available in 270, 30-06, 7mm Rem. Mag., 300 Win. Mag., 338 Win. Mag. (24" barrel), 3- or 5-shot magazine. Weighs 6.75 lbs. Introduced 1992.
**Price:** . . . . . . . . . . . . . . . . . . . . . . . . . . . . . **$604.00**

Winchester Model 70 Heavy Varmint

### Winchester Model 70 Synthetic Heavy Varmint Rifle

Similar to the Model 70 Varmint except has fiberglass/graphite stock, 26" heavy stainless steel barrel, blued receiver. Weighs about 10¾ lbs. Available in 223, 22-250, 243, 308. Uses full-length Pillar Plus Accu Block bedding system. Introduced 1993.
**Price:** . . . . . . . . . . . . . . . . . . . . . . . . . . . . . **$700.00**

### Winchester Model 70 DBM Rifle

Same as the Model 70 Sporter except has detachable box magazine. Available in 223, 22-250, 243, 270, 308, 30-06, 7mm Rem. Mag., 300 Win. Mag. with 24" barrel. Introduced 1992.
**Price:** . . . . . . . . . . . . . . . . . . . . . . . . . . . . . **$598.00**

### Winchester Model 70 Varmint

Similar to the Model 70 Sporter except has heavy 26" barrel with counter-bored muzzle. Available in 22-250, 223, 243 and 308. Receiver bedded in sporter-style stock. Has rubber buttpad. Receiver drilled and tapped for scope mounting. Weight about 9 lbs., overall length 46". Introduced 1989.
**Price:** . . . . . . . . . . . . . . . . . . . . . . . . . . . . . **$580.00**

### Winchester Model 70 DBM-S Rifle

Same as the Model 70 DBM except has fiberglass/graphite composite stock. Available in 223, 22-250, 243, 270, 308, 30-06, 7mm Rem. Mag., 300 Win. Mag. Detachable box magazine, 24" barrel. Most calibers offered with choice of open sights or bases and rings. Introduced 1993.
**Price:** . . . . . . . . . . . . . . . . . . . . . . . . . . . . . **$618.00**

Winchester Model 70 Featherweight

### Winchester Model 70 Featherweight WinTuff

Same as the Model 70 Featherweight except has brown laminated stock. Available in 22-250, 223, 243, 270, 308, 30-06. Weighs 6.75-7 lbs. Comes with scope bases and rings. Introduced 1992.
**Price:** . . . . . . . . . . . . . . . . . . . . . . . . . . . . . **$572.00**

### Winchester Model 70 Featherweight

Available with standard action in 270 Win., 280 Rem., 30-06, 7mm Rem. Mag., 300 Win. Mag., short action in 22-250, 223, 243, 6.5x55, 7mm-08, 308; 22" tapered. Featherweight barrel; classic-style American walnut stock with Schnabel forend, wraparound checkering fashioned after early Model 70 custom rifle patterns. Red rubber buttpad, sling swivel studs. Weighs 6¾ lbs. (standard action), 6½ lbs. (short action). Introduced 1984.
**Price:** . . . . . . . . . . . . . . . . . . . . . . . . . . . . . **$562.00**

Winchester Model 70 Featherweight Classic

### Winchester Model 70 Featherweight Classic

Same as the Model 70 Featherweight except has claw controlled-round feeding system; action is bedded in a standard-grade walnut stock. Available in 270, 280 Rem., 30-06. Drilled and tapped for scope mounts; comes with rings and bases. Weighs 7.25 lbs. Introduced 1992.
**Price:** . . . . . . . . . . . . . . . . . . . . . . . . . . . . . **$749.00**

**CAUTION:** PRICES CHANGE, CHECK AT GUNSHOP.

# CENTERFIRE RIFLES—BOLT ACTION

**WINCHESTER MODEL 70 LIGHTWEIGHT RIFLE**
**Caliber:** 270, 280, 30-06 (standard action); 22-250, 223, 243, 308 (short action), both 5-shot magazine, except 6-shot in 223.
**Barrel:** 22".
**Weight:** 6¼ lbs. **Length:** 40½" overall (std.), 40" (short).
**Stock:** American walnut with satin finish, deep-cut checkering.
**Sights:** None furnished. Drilled and tapped for scope mounting.
**Features:** Three position safety; stainless steel magazine follower; hinged floorplate; sling swivel studs. Introduced 1984.
**Price:** Walnut . . . . . . . . . . . . . . . . . . . . . . . . . . . . . . . $485.00

**WINCHESTER MODEL 70 SUPER EXPRESS MAGNUM**
**Caliber:** 375 H&H Mag., 458 Win. Mag., 3-shot magazine.
**Barrel:** 24" (375), 22" (458).
**Weight:** 8½ lbs.
**Stock:** American walnut with Monte Carlo cheekpiece. Wraparound checkering and finish.
**Sights:** Hooded ramp front, open rear.
**Features:** Controlled round feeding. Two steel cross bolts in stock for added strength. Front sling swivel stud mounted on barrel. Contoured rubber buttpad. From U.S. Repeating Arms Co.
**Price:** . . . . . . . . . . . . . . . . . . . . . . . . . . . . . . . . . . . . $816.00

**Winchester Model 70 Custom Sporting Sharpshooter Rifle**
Similar to the Custom Sharpshooter except has McMillan sporter-style, gray-finished composite stock, stainless steel Schneider barrel with natural matte finish, blued receiver. Available in 270, (24"), 7mm STW and 300 Win. Mag. (26"). Comes with rings and bases. Introduced 1993.
**Price:** . . . . . . . . . . . . . . . . . . . . . . . . . . . . . . . $1,595.00

**Winchester Ranger Rifle**
Similar to Model 70 Lightweight except chambered only for 223, 243, 270, 30-06, with 22" barrel. American hardwood stock, no checkering, composition butt-plate. Metal has matte blue finish. Introduced 1985.
**Price:** . . . . . . . . . . . . . . . . . . . . . . . . . . . . . . . . $427.00
**Price:** Ranger Ladies/Youth, 243, 308 only, scaled-down stock . . . $443.00

**WINCHESTER MODEL 70 SUPER GRADE**
**Caliber:** 270, 30-06, 5-shot magazine; 7mm Rem. Mag., 300 Win. Mag., 338 Win. Mag., 3-shot magazine.
**Barrel:** 24".
**Weight:** About 7¾ lbs. **Length:** 44½" overall.
**Stock:** Walnut with straight comb, sculptured cheekpiece, wraparound cut checkering, tapered forend, solid rubber buttpad.
**Sights:** None furnished; comes with scope bases and rings.
**Features:** Controlled round feeding with stainless steel claw extractor, bolt guide rail, three-position safety; all steel bottom metal, hinged floorplate, stainless magazine follower. Introduced 1990. From U.S. Repeating Arms Co.
**Price:** . . . . . . . . . . . . . . . . . . . . . . . . . . . . . . . . $997.00

**WINCHESTER MODEL 70 CUSTOM SHARPSHOOTER**
**Caliber:** 223, 22-250, 308 Win., 300 Win. Mag.
**Barrel:** 24" (308), 26" (223, 22-250, 300 Win. Mag.).
**Weight:** 11 lbs. **Length:** 44.5" overall (24" barrel).
**Stock:** McMillan A-2 target style; glass bedded; recoil pad, swivel studs.
**Sights:** None furnished; comes with bases and rings.
**Features:** Hand-honed and fitted action, Schneider barrel. Matte blue finish. Introduced 1992. From U.S. Repeating Arms Co.
**Price:** . . . . . . . . . . . . . . . . . . . . . . . . . . . . . . . $1,650.00

# CENTERFIRE RIFLES—SINGLE SHOT

Classic and modern designs for sporting and competitive use.

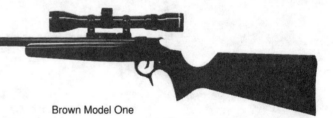

Brown Model One

**BROWN MODEL ONE SINGLE SHOT RIFLE**
**Caliber:** 22 LR, 357 Mag., 44 Mag., 7-30 Waters, 30-30 Win., 375 Win., 45-70; custom chamberings from 17 Rem. through 45-caliber available.
**Barrel:** 22" or custom, bull or tapered.
**Weight:** 6 lbs. **Length:** NA.
**Stock:** Smooth walnut; custom takedown design by Woodsmith. Palm swell for right- or left-hand; rubber butt pad.
**Sights:** Optional. Drilled and tapped for scope mounting.
**Features:** Rigid barrel/receiver; falling block action with short lock time, automatic case ejection; air-gauged barrels by Wilson and Douglas. Muzzle has 11-degree target crown. Matte black oxide finish standard, polished and electroless nickel optional. Introduced 1988. Made in U.S. by E.A. Brown Mfg.
**Price:** . . . . . . . . . . . . . . . . . . . . . . . . . . . . . . . . $750.00

**ARMSPORT 1866 SHARPS RIFLE, CARBINE**
**Caliber:** 45-70.
**Barrel:** 28", round or octagonal.
**Weight:** 8.10 lbs. **Length:** 46" overall.
**Stock:** Walnut.
**Sights:** Blade front, folding adjustable rear. Tang sight set optionally available.
**Features:** Replica of the 1866 Sharps. Color case-hardened frame, rest blued. Imported by Armsport.
**Price:** . . . . . . . . . . . . . . . . . . . . . . . . . . . . $860.00
**Price:** With octagonal barrel . . . . . . . . . . . . . . . . . $880.00
**Price:** Carbine, 22" round barrel . . . . . . . . . . . . . . . $830.00

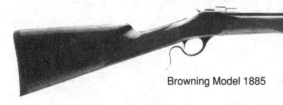

Browning Model 1885

**BROWNING MODEL 1885 SINGLE SHOT RIFLE**
**Caliber:** 223, 22-250, 30-06, 270, 7mm Rem. Mag., 45-70.
**Barrel:** 28".
**Weight:** About 8½ lbs. **Length:** 43½" overall.
**Stock:** Walnut with straight grip, schnabel forend.
**Sights:** None furnished; drilled and tapped for scope mounting.
**Features:** Replica of J.M. Browning's high-wall falling block rifle. Octagon barrel with recessed muzzle. Imported from Japan by Browning. Introduced 1985.
**Price:** . . . . . . . . . . . . . . . . . . . . . . . . . . . . . . . $809.95

**DAKOTA SINGLE SHOT RIFLE**
**Caliber:** Most rimmed and rimless commercial calibers.
**Barrel:** 23".
**Weight:** 6 lbs. **Length:** 39½" overall.
**Stock:** Medium fancy grade walnut in classic style. Checkered grip and forend.
**Sights:** None furnished. Drilled and tapped for scope mounting.

**Features:** Falling block action with under-lever. Top tang safety. Removable trigger plate for conversion to single set trigger. Introduced 1990. Made in U.S. by Dakota Arms.
**Price:** . . . . . . . . . . . . . . . . . . . . . . . . . . . . . $2,300.00
**Price:** Barreled action . . . . . . . . . . . . . . . . . . . . . $1,650.00
**Price:** Action only . . . . . . . . . . . . . . . . . . . . . . . $1,400.00

## DESERT INDUSTRIES G-90 SINGLE SHOT RIFLE
**Caliber:** 22-250, 220 Swift, 223, 6mm, 243, 25-06, 257 Roberts, 270 Win., 270 Wea. Mag., 280, 7x57, 7mm Rem. Mag., 30-06, 300 Win. Mag., 300 Wea. Mag., 338 Win. Mag., 375 H&H, 45-70, 458 Win. Mag.
**Barrel:** 20", 22", 24", 26"; light, medium, heavy.
**Weight:** About 7.5 lbs.

**Stock:** Walnut.
**Sights:** None furnished. Drilled and tapped for scope mounting.
**Features:** Cylindrical falling block action. All steel construction. Blue finish. Announced 1990. From Desert Industries, Inc.
**Price:** . . . . . . . . . . . . . . . . . . . . . . . . . . . . . . . . **$525.00**

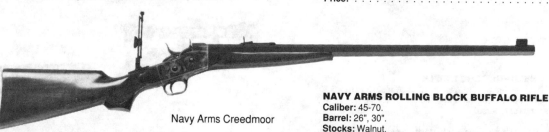

H&R Ultra Varmint

## HARRINGTON & RICHARDSON ULTRA VARMINT RIFLE
**Caliber:** 223, 22-250.
**Barrel:** 22", heavy.
**Weight:** About 7.5 lbs. **Length:** NA.
**Stock:** Hand-checkered curly maple with Monte Carlo comb.
**Sights:** None furnished. Drilled and tapped for scope mounting.
**Features:** Break-open action with side-lever release, positive ejection. Comes with scope mount. Blued receiver and barrel. Swivel studs. Introduced 1993. From H&R 1971, Inc.
**Price:** . . . . . . . . . . . . . . . . . . . . . . . . . . . . . . **$249.95**

Model 1885 High Wall

**Barrel:** 26" (30-40), 28" all others. Douglas Premium #3 tapered octagon.
**Weight:** NA. **Length:** NA.
**Stock:** Premium American black walnut.
**Sights:** Marble's standard ivory bead front, #66 long blade top rear with reversible notch and elevator.
**Features:** Recreation of early octagon top, thick-wall High Wall with Coil spring action. Tand drilled, tapped for High Wall tand sight. Receiver, lever, hammer and breechblock color case-hardened. Introduced 1991. Avaiable from Montana Armory, Inc.
**Price:** . . . . . . . . . . . . . . . . . . . . . . . . . . **$1,095.00**

## MODEL 1885 HIGH WALL RIFLE
**Caliber:** 30-40 Krag, 32-40, 38-55, 40-65 WCF, 45-70.

Navy Arms Creedmoor

## Navy Arms #2 Creedmoor Rifle
Similar to the Navy Arms Buffalo Rifle except has 30" tapered octagon barrel, checkered full-pistol grip stock, blade front sight, open adjustable rear sight and Creedmoor tang sight. Introduced 1991. Imported by Navy Arms.
**Price:** . . . . . . . . . . . . . . . . . . . . . . . . . . **$695.00**

## NAVY ARMS ROLLING BLOCK BUFFALO RIFLE
**Caliber:** 45-70.
**Barrel:** 26", 30".
**Stocks:** Walnut.
**Sights:** Blade front, adjustable rear.
**Features:** Reproduction of classic rolling block action. Available with full-octagon or half-octagon-half-round barrel. Color case-hardened action. From Navy Arms.
**Price:** . . . . . . . . . . . . . . . . . . . . . . . . . . **$510.00**

## Navy Arms Sharps Cavalry Carbine
Similar to the Sharps Plains Rifle except has 22" barrel, overall length of 39", and weighs 7¾ lbs. Has blade front sight, military ladder-style rear, barrel band on forend. Color case-hardened action, rest blued. Introduced 1991. Imported by Navy Arms.
**Price:** . . . . . . . . . . . . . . . . . . . . . . . . . . **$650.00**

## NAVY ARMS SHARPS PLAINS RIFLE
**Caliber:** 45-70.
**Barrel:** 28½".
**Weight:** 8 lbs., 10 oz. **Length:** 45¾" overall.
**Stock:** Checkered walnut butt and forend.
**Sights:** Blade front, open rear adjustable for windage.
**Features:** Color case-hardened action, rest blued. Introduced 1991. Imported by Navy Arms.
**Price:** . . . . . . . . . . . . . . . . . . . . . . . . . . **$715.00**

NEF Handi-Rifle

## NEW ENGLAND FIREARMS HANDI-RIFLE
**Caliber:** 22 Hornet, 22-250, 223, 243, 30-30, 270, 30-06, 45-70.
**Barrel:** 22".
**Weight:** 7 lbs.
**Stock:** Walnut-finished hardwood.
**Sights:** Ramp front, folding rear. Drilled and tapped for scope mount;22-250, 223, 243, 270, 30-06 have no open sights, come with scope mounts.
**Features:** Break-open action with side-lever release. The 243, 270 and 30-06 have recoil pad and Monte Carlo stock for shooting with scope. Swivel studs on all models. Blue finish. Introduced 1989. From New England Firearms.
**Price:** 22-250, 243, 270, 30-06 . . . . . . . . . . . . . . . . **$199.95**
**Price:** 22 Hornet, 223, 30-30, 45-70 . . . . . . . . . . . . . **$189.95**

**CAUTION:** PRICES CHANGE, CHECK AT GUNSHOP.

**Red Willow No. 5**

## RED WILLOW ARMORY BALLARD NO. 5 PACIFIC
**Caliber:** 32-40 Win., 38-55, 40-65 Win., 40-70 Ballard, 40-85 Ballard, 45-70; other calibers on special order.
**Barrel:** 30", tapered octagon.
**Weight:** 10-11.5 lbs. **Length:** NA.
**Stock:** Oil-finished American walnut with crescent butt, schnabel forend.
**Sights:** Blade front, buckhorn rear.
**Features:** Exact recreation of the Ballard No. 5 Pacific; double-set triggers; under-barrel wiping rod; drilled and tapped for tang sight; ring lever. Mid- and long range sights, fancy wood, single trigger optionally available. Made in U.S. Introduced 1992. From Red Willow Tool & Armory, Inc.
**Price:** Standard model . . . . . . . . . . . . . . . . . . . . . . . . . **$1,912.00**

## Red Willow Armory Ballard No. 8 Union Hill Rifle
Similar to the Ballard No. 5 Pacific except has 30" part round-part octagon barrel; weighs 10 lbs. Oil-finished checkered American walnut stock with cheek rest, pistol grip, nickeled off-hand-style buttplate. Swiss tube sight with bead front, drilled and tapped for tang sight. Exact recreation of the original, with double-set triggers. Options include mid- and long range tang sights, Lyman globe front, fancy wood, single trigger, buckhorn rear sight, customs. Made in U.S. Introduced 1992. From Red Willow Tool & Armory, Inc.
**Price:** Standard model . . . . . . . . . . . . . . . . . . . . . . . . . **$2,712.50**
**Price:** Deluxe model (has fancy wood and checkering, mid-range tang sight) . . . . . . . . . . . . . . . . . . . . . . . . . . . . . . . . **$3,212.50**

## REMINGTON-STYLE ROLLING BLOCK CARBINE
**Caliber:** 45-70.
**Barrel:** 30", octagonal.
**Weight:** 11¾ lbs. **Length:** 46½" overall.
**Stock:** Walnut.

## Red Willow Armory Ballard No. 1½ Hunting Rifle
Similar to the Ballard No. 5 Pacific except has 30" medium-heavy tapered round barrel, no wiping rod, weighs 9 lbs. Has S-type lever, single trigger. Same calibers as No. 5 Pacific. Options include mid- and long range tang sights, Swiss tube with bead of Lyman globe front, fancy wood, double-set triggers, custom rifles. Introduced 1992. From Red Willow Tool & Armory, Inc.
**Price:** Standard model . . . . . . . . . . . . . . . . . . . . . . . . . **$1,405.00**

## Red Willow Armory Ballard No. 4½ Target Rifle
Similar to the No. 5 Pacific except has single trigger, 30" part-round, part-octagon, medium-heavy barrel, full loop lever. Pistol grip stock has a checkered steel shotgun-style buttplate. Swiss bead front sight. Available in 32-40, 38-55, 40-63, 40-65, 40-85, 45-70. Introduced 1993. From Red Willow Tool & Armory, Inc.
**Price:** Standard model . . . . . . . . . . . . . . . . . . . . . . . . . **$2,437.50**
**Price:** Deluxe model (fancy wood, checkering, long range tang sight) . . . . . . . . . . . . . . . . . . . . . . . . . . . . . . . . . . **$2,968.75**

**Sights:** Blade front, adjustable rear.
**Features:** Color case-hardened receiver, brass trigger guard, buttplate and barrel band, blued barrel. Imported from Italy by E.M.F.
**Price:** . . . . . . . . . . . . . . . . . . . . . . . . . . . . . . . . . . . **$820.00**

**Ruger No. 1B**

## Ruger No. 1A Light Sporter
Similar to the No. 1B Standard Rifle except has lightweight 22" barrel, Alexander Henry-style forend, adjustable folding leaf rear sight on quarter-rib, dovetailed ramp front with gold bead. Calibers 243, 30-06, 270 and 7x57. Weight about 7¼ lbs.
**Price:** No. 1A . . . . . . . . . . . . . . . . . . . . . . . . . . . . . **$634.00**
**Price:** Barreled action . . . . . . . . . . . . . . . . . . . . . . . . **$429.50**

## Ruger No. 1H Tropical Rifle
Similar to the No. 1B Standard Rifle except has Alexander Henry forend, adjustable folding leaf rear sight on quarter-rib, ramp front with dovetail gold bead, 24" heavy barrel. Calibers 375 H&H, 404 Jeffery, 416 Rem. Mag. (weight about 8¼ lbs.), 416 Rigby, and 458 Win. Mag. (weight about 9 lbs.).
**Price:** No. 1H . . . . . . . . . . . . . . . . . . . . . . . . . . . . . **$634.00**
**Price:** Barreled action . . . . . . . . . . . . . . . . . . . . . . . . **$429.50**

## RUGER NO. 1B SINGLE SHOT
**Caliber:** 218 Bee, 22 Hornet, 220 Swift, 22-250, 223, 243, 6mm Rem., 25-06, 257 Roberts, 270, 280, 30-06, 7mm Rem. Mag., 300 Win. Mag., 338 Win. Mag., 270 Wea., 300 Wea.
**Barrel:** 26" round tapered with quarter-rib; with Ruger 1" rings.
**Weight:** 8 lbs. **Length:** 43⅜" overall.
**Stock:** Walnut, two-piece, checkered p.g. and semi-beavertail forend.
**Sights:** None, 1" scope rings supplied for integral mounts.
**Features:** Under-lever, hammerless falling block design has auto ejector, top tang safety.
**Price:** . . . . . . . . . . . . . . . . . . . . . . . . . . . . . . . . . . **$634.00**
**Price:** Barreled action . . . . . . . . . . . . . . . . . . . . . . . . **$429.50**

## Ruger No. 1S Medium Sporter
Similar to the No. 1B Standard Rifle except has Alexander Henry-style forend, adjustable folding leaf rear sight on quarter-rib, ramp front sight base and dovetail-type gold bead front sight. Calibers 218 Bee, 7mm Rem. Mag., 338 Win. Mag., 300 Win. Mag. with 26" barrel, 45-70 with 22" barrel. Weight about 7½ lbs. In 45-70.
**Price:** No. 1S . . . . . . . . . . . . . . . . . . . . . . . . . . . . . **$634.00**
**Price:** Barreled action . . . . . . . . . . . . . . . . . . . . . . . . **$429.50**

**Ruger No. 1 International**

## Ruger No. 1 RSI International
Similar to the No. 1B Standard Rifle except has lightweight 20" barrel, full-length Mannlicher-style forend with loop sling swivel, adjustable folding leaf rear sight on quarter-rib, ramp front with gold bead. Calibers 243, 30-06, 270 and 7x57. Weight is about 7¼ lbs.
**Price:** No. 1 RSI . . . . . . . . . . . . . . . . . . . . . . . . . . . . **$656.00**
**Price:** Barreled action . . . . . . . . . . . . . . . . . . . . . . . . **$429.50**

## Ruger No. 1V Special Varminter
Similar to the No. 1B Standard Rifle except has 24" heavy barrel. Semi-beavertail forend, barrel tapped for target scope block, with 1" Ruger scope rings. Calibers 22 PPC, 22-250, 220 Swift, 223, 6mm PPC, 25-06. Weight about 9 lbs.
**Price:** No. 1V . . . . . . . . . . . . . . . . . . . . . . . . . . . . . **$634.00**
**Price:** Barreled action . . . . . . . . . . . . . . . . . . . . . . . . **$429.50**

Consult our Directory pages for the location of firms mentioned.

C. Sharps 1875 Sporting

## C. SHARPS ARMS NEW MODEL 1874 OLD RELIABLE
**Caliber:** 40-50, 40-70, 40-90, 45-70, 45-90, 45-100, 45-110, 45-120, 50-70, 50-90, 50-140.
**Barrel:** 26", 28", 30" tapered octagon.
**Weight:** About 10 lbs. **Length:** NA.
**Stock:** American black walnut; shotgun butt with checkered steel buttplate; straight grip, heavy forend with schnabel tip.
**Sights:** Blade front, buckhorn rear. Drilled and tapped for tang sight.
**Features:** Recreation of the Model 1874 Old Reliable Sharps Sporting Rifle. Double set triggers. Reintroduced 1991. Made in U.S. by C. Sharps Arms. Available from Montana Armory, Inc.
**Price:** . . . . . . . . . . . . . . . . . . . . . . . . . . . . . . . . . . **$995.00**

## C. Sharps Arms 1875 Classic Sharps
Similar to the New Model 1875 Sporting Rifle except has 26", 28" or 30" full octagon barrel, crescent buttplate with toe plate, Hartford-style forend with cast German silver nose cap. Blade front sight, Rocky Mountain buckhorn rear. Weight is 10 lbs. Introduced 1987. From C. Sharps Arms Co. and Montana Armory, Inc.
**Price:** . . . . . . . . . . . . . . . . . . . . . . . . . . . . . **$1,075.00**

## C. SHARPS ARMS NEW MODEL 1875 RIFLE
**Caliber:** 22LR, 32-40 & 38-55 Ballard, 38-56 WCF, 40-65 WCF, 40-90 3¼", 40-90 2⅝", 40-70 2¹⁄₁₀", 40-70 2¼", 40-70 2½", 40-50 1¹¹⁄₁₆", 40-50 1⅞", 45-90, 45-70, 45-100, 45-110, 45-120. Also available on special order only in 50-70, 50-90, 50-140.
**Barrel:** 24", 26", 30" (standard); 32", 34" optional.
**Weight:** 8-12 lbs.
**Stocks:** Walnut, straight grip, shotgun butt with checkered steel buttplate.
**Sights:** Silver blade front, Rocky Mountain buckhorn rear.
**Features:** Recreation of the 1875 Sharps rifle. Production guns will have case colored receiver. Available in Custom Sporting and Target versions upon request. Announced 1986. From C. Sharps Arms Co. and Montana Armory, Inc.
**Price:** 1875 Carbine (24" tapered round bbl.) . . . . . . . . . . . **$725.00**
**Price:** 1875 Saddle Rifle (26" tapered oct. bbl.) . . . . . . . . . **$825.00**
**Price:** 1875 Sporting Rifle (30" tapered oct. bbl.) . . . . . . . . **$850.00**
**Price:** 1875 Business Rifle (28" tapered round bbl.) . . . . . . . **$775.00**

## C. Sharps Arms New Model 1875 Target & Long Range
Similar to the New Model 1875 except available in all listed calibers except 22 LR; 34" tapered octagon barrel; globe with post front sight, Long Range Vernier tang sight with windage adjustments. Pistol grip stock with cheek rest; checkered steel buttplate. Introduced 1991. From C. Sharps Arms Co. and Montana Armory, Inc.
**Price:** . . . . . . . . . . . . . . . . . . . . . . . . . . . . . **$1,165.00**

Shiloh Long Range Express

## Shiloh Sharps 1874 Montana Roughrider
Similar to the No. 1 Sporting Rifle except available with half-octagon or full-octagon barrel in 24", 26", 28", 30", 34" lengths; standard supreme or semi-fancy wood, shotgun, pistol grip or military-style butt. Weight about 8½ lbs. Calibers 30-40, 30-30, 40-50x1¹¹⁄₁₆" BN, 40-70x2¹⁄₁₀" BN, 45-70x2¹⁄₁₀" ST. Globe front and tang sight optional.
**Price:** Standard supreme . . . . . . . . . . . . . . . . . . . . . **$870.00**
**Price:** Semi-fancy . . . . . . . . . . . . . . . . . . . . . . . . **$950.00**

## Shiloh Sharps 1874 Military Carbine
Has 22" round barrel with blade front sight and full buckhorn ladder-type rear. Military-style buttstock with barrel band on military-style forend. Steel buttplate, saddle bar and ring. Standard supreme grade only. Weight is about 8½ lbs. Calibers 40-70 BN, 45-70, 50-70. Introduced 1989.
**Price:** . . . . . . . . . . . . . . . . . . . . . . . . . . . . . . . **$925.00**

## SHILOH SHARPS 1874 LONG RANGE EXPRESS
**Caliber:** 40-50 BN, 40-70 BN, 40-90 BN, 45-70 ST, 45-90 ST, 45-110 ST, 50-70 ST, 50-90 ST, 50-110 ST, 32-40, 38-55, 40-70 ST, 40-90 ST.
**Barrel:** 34" tapered octagon.
**Weight:** 10½ lbs. **Length:** 51" overall.
**Stock:** Oil-finished semi-fancy walnut with pistol grip, shotgun-style butt, traditional cheek rest and accent line. Schnabel forend.
**Sights:** Globe front, sporting tang rear.
**Features:** Recreation of the Model 1874 Sharps rifle. Double set triggers. Made in U.S. by Shiloh Rifle Mfg. Co.
**Price:** . . . . . . . . . . . . . . . . . . . . . . . . . . . . . . . **$995.00**
**Price:** Sporting Rifle No. 1 (similar to above except with 30" bbl., blade front, buckhorn rear sight) . . . . . . . . . . . . . . . . . **$970.00**
**Price:** Sporting Rifle No. 3 (similar to No. 1 except straight-grip stock, standard wood) . . . . . . . . . . . . . . . . . . . . . . . . **$870.00**
**Price:** 1874 Hartford model . . . . . . . . . . . . . . . . . . **$1,033.00**

## Shiloh Sharps 1874 Business Rifle
Similar to No. 3 Rifle except has 28" heavy round barrel, military-style buttstock and steel buttplate. Weight about 9½ lbs. Calibers 40-50 BN, 40-70 BN, 40-90 BN, 45-70 ST, 45-90 ST, 50-70 ST, 50-100 ST, 32-40, 38-55, 40-70 ST, 40-90 ST.
**Price:** . . . . . . . . . . . . . . . . . . . . . . . . . . . . . . . **$875.00**
**Price:** 1874 Carbine (similar to above except 24" round bbl., single trigger—double set avail.) . . . . . . . . . . . . . . . . . . . . . . . **$895.00**
**Price:** 1874 Saddle Rifle (similar to Carbine except has 26" octagon barrel, semi-fancy shotgun butt) . . . . . . . . . . . . . . . . . **$925.00**

Shiloh 1874 Military

## SHARPS 1874 OLD RELIABLE
**Caliber:** 45-70.
**Barrel:** 28", octagonal.
**Weight:** 9¼ lbs. **Length:** 46" overall.
**Stock:** Checkered walnut.
**Sights:** Blade front, adjustable rear.

## Shiloh Sharps 1874 Military Rifle
Has 30" round barrel. Iron block front sight and Lawrence-style rear ladder sight. Military butt, buttplate, patchbox assembly optional; three barrel bands; single trigger (double set available). Calibers 40-50x1¹¹⁄₁₆" BN, 40-70x2¹⁄₁₀" BN, 40-90 BN, 45-70x2¹⁄₁₀" ST, 50-70 ST.
**Price:** . . . . . . . . . . . . . . . . . . . . . . . . . . . . . . . **$995.00**

**Features:** Double set triggers on rifle. Color case-hardened receiver and buttplate, blued barrel. Imported from Italy by E.M.F.
**Price:** Rifle or carbine . . . . . . . . . . . . . . . . . . . . . . **$950.00**
**Price:** Military rifle, carbine . . . . . . . . . . . . . . . . . . . **$860.00**
**Price:** Sporting rifle . . . . . . . . . . . . . . . . . . . . . . . . **$860.00**

**CAUTION:** PRICES CHANGE, CHECK AT GUNSHOP.

Thompson/Center Stainless

### Thompson/Center Stainless Contender Carbine

Same as the blued Contender Carbine except made of stainless steel with blued sights. Available with walnut or Rynite stock and forend. Chambered for 22 LR, 22 Hornet, 223 Rem., 7-30 Waters, 30-30 Win., 410-bore. Youth model has walnut buttstock with 12" pull length. Introduced 1993.

**Price:** Walnut stock, forend . . . . . . . . . . . . . . . . . . . . . . $490.00
**Price:** Rynite stock, forend . . . . . . . . . . . . . . . . . . . . . $455.00
**Price:** Youth model . . . . . . . . . . . . . . . . . . . . . . . . . $455.00

### Thompson/Center Contender Carbine Survival System

Combines the Rynite-stocked Contender Carbine with two 16¼" barrels—one chambered for 223 Rem., the other for 45 Colt/410 bore. The frame/buttstock assembly store in the camouflage Cordura case, measuring 25½"x6¾". Introduced 1991.

**Price:** . . . . . . . . . . . . . . . . . . . . . . . . . . . . . . . . . $635.00

### THOMPSON/CENTER CONTENDER CARBINE

**Caliber:** 22 LR, 22 Hornet, 223 Rem., 7mm T.C.U., 7x30 Waters, 30-30 Win., 357 Rem. Maximum, 35 Rem., 44 Mag., 410, single shot.
**Barrel:** 21".
**Weight:** 5 lbs., 2 oz. **Length:** 35" overall.
**Stock:** Checkered American walnut with rubber buttpad. Also with Rynite stock and forend.
**Sights:** Blade front, open adjustable rear.
**Features:** Uses the T/C Contender action. Eleven interchangeable barrels available, all with sights, drilled and tapped for scope mounting. Introduced 1985. Offered as a complete Carbine only.
**Price:** Rifle calibers . . . . . . . . . . . . . . . . . . . . . . . . . $460.00
**Price:** Extra barrels, rifle calibers, each . . . . . . . . . . . . . $210.00
**Price:** 410 shotgun . . . . . . . . . . . . . . . . . . . . . . . . . $480.00
**Price:** Extra 410 barrel . . . . . . . . . . . . . . . . . . . . . . . $235.00
**Price:** Rynite stock, forend . . . . . . . . . . . . . . . . . . . . $425.00
**Price:** As above, 21" vent. rib smoothbore 410 bbl. . . . . . . . $450.00

### Thompson/Center Contender Carbine Youth Model

Same as the standard Contender Carbine except has 16¼" barrel, shorter buttstock with 12" length of pull. Comes with fully adjustable open sights. Overall length is 29", weight about 4 lbs., 9 oz. Available in 22 LR, 22 WMR, 223 Rem., 7x30 Waters, 30-30, 35 Rem., 44 Mag. Also available with 16¼", rifled vent. rib barrel chambered for 45/410.

**Price:** . . . . . . . . . . . . . . . . . . . . . . . . . . . . . . . . . $425.00
**Price:** With 45/410 barrel . . . . . . . . . . . . . . . . . . . . . . $455.00
**Price:** Extra barrels . . . . . . . . . . . . . . . . . . . . . . . . . $205.00
**Price:** Extra 45/410 barrel . . . . . . . . . . . . . . . . . . . . . $235.00
**Price:** Extra 45-70 barrel . . . . . . . . . . . . . . . . . . . . . . $210.00

Thompson/Center TCR '87

### UBERTI ROLLING BLOCK BABY CARBINE

**Caliber:** 22 LR, 22 WMR, 22 Hornet, 357 Mag., single shot.
**Barrel:** 22".
**Weight:** 4.8 lbs. **Length:** 35½" overall.
**Stock:** Walnut stock and forend.
**Sights:** Blade front, fully adjustable open rear.
**Features:** Resembles Remington New Model No. 4 carbine. Brass trigger guard and buttplate; color case-hardened frame, blued barrel. Imported by Uberti USA.
**Price:** . . . . . . . . . . . . . . . . . . . . . . . . . . . . . . . . . $460.00

### THOMPSON/CENTER TCR '87 SINGLE SHOT RIFLE

**Caliber:** 22 Hornet, 222 Rem., 223 Rem., 22-250, 243 Win., 270, 308, 7mm-08, 30-06, 32-40 Win., 12-ga. slug. Also 10-ga. and 12-ga. field barrels.
**Barrel:** 23" (standard), 25⅞" (heavy).
**Weight:** About 6¾ lbs. **Length:** 39½" overall.
**Stock:** American black walnut, checkered p.g. and forend.
**Sights:** None furnished.
**Features:** Break-open design with interchangeable barrels. Single-stage trigger. Cross-bolt safety. Introduced 1983. Made in U.S. by T/C. Available only through the T/C custom shop.
**Price:** With Medium Sporter barrel (223, 22-250, 7mm-08, 308, 32-40 Win.), about . . . . . . . . . . . . . . . . . . . . . . . . . $595.00
**Price:** With Light Sporter barrel (22 Hornet, 222, 223, 22-250, 243, 270, 7mm-08, 308, 30-06), about . . . . . . . . . . . . . . . . . . . . . $595.00
**Price:** 12-ga. slug barrel, about . . . . . . . . . . . . . . . . . . $275.00
**Price:** Extra Medium or Light Sporter barrel, about . . . . . . . . $250.00
**Price:** 10-, 12-ga. field barrels . . . . . . . . . . . . . . . . . . . $250.00

# DRILLINGS, COMBINATION GUNS, DOUBLE RIFLES

Designs for sporting and utility purposes worldwide.

Beretta 455EELL Express

### BERETTA EXPRESS SSO O/U DOUBLE RIFLES

**Caliber:** 375 H&H, 458 Win. Mag., 9.3x74R.
**Barrel:** 25.5".
**Weight:** 11 lbs.
**Stock:** European walnut with hand-checkered grip and forend.
**Sights:** Blade front on ramp, open V-notch rear.
**Features:** Sidelock action with color case-hardened receiver (gold inlays on SSO6 Gold). Ejectors, double triggers, recoil pad. Introduced 1990. Imported from Italy by Beretta U.S.A.
**Price:** SSO6 . . . . . . . . . . . . . . . . . . . . . . . . . . . . $21,600.00
**Price:** SSO6 Gold . . . . . . . . . . . . . . . . . . . . . . . . . $23,000.00

### BERETTA MODEL 455 SxS EXPRESS RIFLE

**Caliber:** 375 H&H, 458 Win. Mag., 470 NE, 500 NE 3", 416 Rigby.
**Barrel:** 23½" or 25½".
**Weight:** 11 lbs.
**Stock:** European walnut with hand-checkered grip and forend.
**Sights:** Blade front, folding leaf V-notch rear.
**Features:** Sidelock action with easily removable sideplates; color case-hardened finish (455), custom big game or floral motif engraving (455EELL). Double triggers, recoil pad. Introduced 1990. Imported from Italy by Beretta U.S.A.
**Price:** Model 455 . . . . . . . . . . . . . . . . . . . . . . . . . $36,000.00
**Price:** Model 455EELL . . . . . . . . . . . . . . . . . . . . . . $47,000.00

## CHAPUIS RGEXPRESS DOUBLE RIFLE
**Caliber:** 30-06, 7x65R, 8x57 JRS, 9.3x74R.
**Barrel:** 23.6".
**Weight:** 8-9 lbs. **Length:** NA.
**Stock:** Deluxe walnut with Monte Carlo comb, oil finish.
**Sights:** Bead on ramp front, adjustable express rear on quarter-rib.
**Features:** Boxlock action with long trigger guard, automatic ejectors, double hook Blitz system action with coil springs; coin metal finish; trap grip cap for extra front sight. Imported from France by Armes de Chasse.
**Price:** About . . . . . . . . . . . . . . . . . . . . . **$7,000.00 to $8,500.00**

## AUGUSTE FRANCOTTE BOXLOCK DOUBLE RIFLE
**Caliber:** 243, 270, 30-06, 7x64, 7x65R, 8x57JRS, 9.3x74R, 375 H&H, 470 N.E.; other calibers on request.
**Barrel:** 23.5" to 26".
**Weight:** NA. **Length:** NA.
**Stock:** Deluxe European walnut to customer specs; pistol grip or straight grip with Francotte cheekpiece; checkered butt; oil finish.
**Sights:** Bead front on long ramp, quarter-rib with fixed V rear.
**Features:** Side-by-side barrels; Anson & Deeley boxlock action with double triggers (front hinged), manual safety, floating firing pins and gas vent safety screws. Splinter or beavertail forend. English scroll engraving; coin finish or color case-hardening. Many options available. Imported from Belgium by Armes de Chasse.
**Price:** From about . . . . . . . . . . . . . . **$20,000.00 to $25,000.00**

## Heym Model 55FW O/U Combo Gun
Similar to Model 55B O/U rifle except chambered for 12-, 16-, or 20-ga. (2¾" or 3") over 7x65R, 308, 30-06, 8x57JRS, 8x75 RS, 9.3x74R, 375 H&H, 458 Win. Mag., 470 N.E. Has solid rib barrel. Available with interchangeable shotgun and rifle barrels.
**Price:** Model 55FW boxlock . . . . . . . . . . . . . . . **$3,900.00**
**Price:** Model 55BW (over/under rifle) . . . . . . . . . . . **$5,715.00**

## AUGUSTE FRANCOTTE SIDELOCK DOUBLE RIFLES
**Caliber:** 243, 7x64, 7x65R, 8x57JRS, 270, 30-06, 9.3x74R, 375 H&H, 470 N.E.; others on request.
**Barrel:** 23½" to 26".
**Weight:** 7.61 lbs. (medium calibers), 11.1 lbs. (mag. calibers).
**Stock:** Fancy European walnut; dimensions to customer specs. Straight or pistol grip style. Checkered butt, oil finish.
**Sights:** Bead on ramp front, leaf rear on quarter-rib; to customer specs.
**Features:** Custom made to customer's specs. Special extractor for rimless cartridges; back-action sidelocks; double trigger with hinged front trigger. Automatic or free safety. Wide range of options available. Imported from Belgium by Armes de Chasse.
**Price:** . . . . . . . . . . . . . . . . . . . . **$30,000.00 to $36,000**

## HEYM MODEL 55B O/U DOUBLE RIFLE
**Caliber:** 7x65R, 308, 30-06, 8x57JRS, 8x75 RS, 9.3x74R, 375 H&H, 458 Win. Mag., 470 N.E.
**Barrel:** 25".
**Weight:** About 8 lbs., depending upon caliber. **Length:** 42" overall.
**Stock:** Dark European walnut, hand-checkered p.g. and forend. Oil finish.
**Sights:** Silver bead ramp front, open V-type rear.
**Features:** Boxlock or full sidelock; Kersten double cross bolt, cocking indicators; hand-engraved hunting scenes. Options available include interchangeable barrels, Zeiss scopes in claw mounts, deluxe engravings and stock carving, etc. Imported from Germany by JagerSport, Ltd.
**Price:** Model 55B boxlock . . . . . . . . . . . . . . . . . **$10,800.00**

## HEYM MODEL 88B SIDE-BY-SIDE DOUBLE RIFLE
**Caliber:** 30-06, 8x57JRS, 9.3x74R, 375 H&H.
**Barrel:** 25".
**Weight:** 7½ lbs. (std. cals.), 8½ lbs. (mag.). **Length:** 42" overall.
**Stock:** Fancy French walnut, classic North American design.
**Sights:** Silver bead post on ramp front, fixed or three-leaf express rear.
**Features:** Action has complete coverage hunting scene engraving. Available as boxlock or with q.d. sidelocks. Imported from Germany by JagerSport, Ltd.
**Price:** Boxlock . . . . . . . . . . . . . . **$12,500.00 to $18,950.00**
**Price:** Sidelock, Model 88B-SS, from . . . . . . . . . . . . . . **$16,600.00**

Kodiak Mk. IV

## KODIAK MK. IV DOUBLE RIFLE
**Caliber:** 45-70.
**Barrel:** 24".
**Weight:** 10 lbs. **Length:** 42½" overall.
**Stock:** European walnut with semi-pistol grip.
**Sights:** Ramp front with bead, adjustable two-leaf rear.
**Features:** Exposed hammers, color case-hardened locks. Rubber recoil pad. Introduced 1988. Imported from Italy by Trail Guns Armory.
**Price:** About . . . . . . . . . . . . . . . . . . . **$1,895.00**

## KRIEGHOFF TECK O/U COMBINATION GUN
**Caliber/Gauge:** 12, 16, 20/22 Hornet, 222, 243, 270, 30-06, 308 and standard European calibers. O/U rifle also available in 458 Win. on special order.
**Barrel:** 25" on double rifle combo, 28" on O/U shotgun. Optional free-floating rifle barrel available.
**Weight:** 7-7½ lbs.
**Stock:** Hand-checkered European walnut with German-style grip and cheekpiece.
**Sights:** White bead front on shotgun, open or folding on rifle or combo.
**Features:** Boxlock action with non-selective single trigger or optional single/double trigger. Greener cross bolt. Ejectors standard on all but O/U rifle. Top tang safety. Light scroll engraving. Imported from Germany by Krieghoff International, Inc.
**Price:** From about . . . . . . . . . . . . . **$7,995.00 to $9,500.00**
**Price:** Ulm (full sidelock model), from about . . . . **$14,950.00 to 18,606.00**

## MERKEL OVER/UNDER COMBINATION GUNS
**Caliber/Gauge:** 12, 16, 20 (2¾" chamber) over 22 Hornet, 5.6x50R, 5.6x52R, 222 Rem., 243 Win., 6.5x55, 6.5x57R, 7x57R, 7x65R, 308 Win., 30-06, 8x57JRS, 9.3x74R, 375 H&H.
**Barrel:** 25.6".
**Weight:** About 7.6 lbs. **Length:** NA.
**Stock:** Oil-finished walnut; pistol grip, cheekpiece.
**Sights:** Bead front, fixed rear.

## KRIEGHOFF TRUMPF DRILLING
**Caliber/Gauge:** 12, 16, 20/22 Hornet, 222 Rem., 243, 270, 30-06, 308. Standard European calibers also available.
**Barrel:** 25". Shot barrels choked Imp. Mod. & Full. Optional free-floating rifle barrel available.
**Weight:** About 7½ lbs.
**Stock:** Hand-checkered European walnut with German-style grip and cheekpiece. Oil finish.
**Sights:** Bead front, automatic pop-up open rear.
**Features:** Boxlock action with double or optional single trigger, top tang shotgun safety. Fine, light scroll engraving. Imported from Germany by Krieghoff International, Inc.
**Price:** From about . . . . . . . . . . . . . . . . . . . **$8,875.00**
**Price:** Neptun (full sidelock drilling), from about . . . . . . . . **$19,750.00**

**Features:** Kersten double cross-bolt lock; scroll-engraved, color case-hardened receiver; Blitz action; double triggers. Imported from Germany by GSI.
**Price:** Model 210E . . . . . . . . . . . . . . . . . . . **$6,195.00**
**Price:** Model 211E (silver-grayed receivcer, fine hunting scene engraving) . . . . . . . . . . . . . . . . . . . **$7,895.00**
**Price:** Model 213E (sidelock action, English-style, large scroll Arabesque engraving) . . . . . . . . . . . . . . **$14,695.00**
**Price:** Model 313E (as above, medium-scroll engraving) . . . . . **$23,395.00**

## MERKEL DRILLINGS

**Caliber/Gauge:** 12, 20, 3" chambers, 16, 2¾" chambers; 22 Hornet, 5.6x50R Mag., 5.6x52R, 222 Rem., 243 Win., 6.5x55, 6.5x57R, 7x57R, 7x65R, 308, 30-06, 8x57JRS, 9.3x74R, 375 H&H.
**Barrel:** 25.6".
**Weight:** 7.9 to 8.4 lbs. depending upon caliber. **Length:** NA.
**Stock:** Oil-finished walnut with pistol grip; cheekpiece on 12-, 16-gauge.
**Sights:** Blade front, fixed rear.
**Features:** Double barrel locking lug with Greener cross-bolt; scroll-engraved, case-hardened receiver; automatic trigger safety; Blitz action; double triggers. Imported from Germany by GSI.
**Price:** Model 90 . . . . . . . . . . . . . . . . . . . . . **$6,895.00**
**Price:** Model 90S (as above except has selective sear safety) . . **$7,195.00**
**Price:** Model 90K (manually cocked rifle system) . . . . . . . . **$7,595.00**
**Price:** Model 95 (silver-grayed receiver with fine hunting scene
engraving) . . . . . . . . . . . . . . . . . . . . . . . . . **$7,895.00**
**Price:** Model 95S (selective sear safety) . . . . . . . . . . . . **$8,195.00**
**Price:** Model 95K (manually cocked rifle system) . . . . . . . . **$8,595.00**

## MERKEL OVER/UNDER DOUBLE RIFLES

**Caliber:** 22 Hornet, 5.6x50R Mag., 5.6x52R, 222 Rem., 243 Win., 6.5x55, 6.5x57R, 7x57R, 7x65R, 308, 30-06, 8x57JRS, 9.3x74R, 375 H&H.
**Barrel:** 25.6".
**Weight:** About 7.7 lbs, depending upon caliber. **Length:** NA.
**Stock:** Oil-finished walnut with pistol grip, cheekpiece.
**Sights:** Blade front, fixed rear.

Savage 24F-12T

## Savage 24F-12T Turkey Gun

Similar to Model 24F except has camouflage Rynite stock and Full, Imp. Cyl., Mod. choke tubes. Available only in 22 Hornet or 223 over 12-gauge with 3" chamber. Introduced 1989.
**Price:** . . . . . . . . . . . . . . . . . . . . . . . . . . . . . **$420.00**

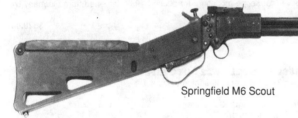

Springfield M6 Scout

## TIKKA MODEL 412S COMBINATION GUN

**Caliber/Gauge:** 12 over 222, 308.
**Barrel:** 24" (Imp. Mod.).
**Weight:** 7⅝ lbs.
**Stock:** American walnut, with recoil pad. Monte Carlo style. Standard measurements 14"x1⅜"x2"x2⅜".
**Sights:** Blade front, flip-up-type open rear.
**Features:** Barrel selector on trigger. Hand-checkered stock and forend. Barrels are screw-adjustable to change bullet point of impact. Barrels are interchangeable. Introduced 1980. Imported from Italy by Stoeger.
**Price:** . . . . . . . . . . . . . . . . . . . . . . . . . . . . . **$1,255.00**
**Price:** Extra barrels, from . . . . . . . . . . . . . . . . . . . **$720.00**

## TIKKA MODEL 412S DOUBLE RIFLE

**Caliber:** 9.3x74R.
**Barrel:** 24".
**Weight:** 8⅝ lbs.
**Stock:** American walnut with Monte Carlo style.
**Sights:** Ramp front, adjustable open rear.
**Features:** Barrel selector mounted in trigger. Cocking indicators in tang. Recoil pad. Valmet scope mounts available. Introduced 1980. Imported from Italy by Stoeger.
**Price:** With ejectors, 9.3x74R . . . . . . . . . . . . . . . . . **$1,470.00**

## MERKEL MODEL 160 SIDE-BY-SIDE DOUBLE RIFLE

**Caliber:** 22 Hornet, 5.6x50R Mag., 5.6x52R, 222 Rem., 243 Win., 6.5x55, 6.5x57R, 7x57R, 7x65R, 308, 30-06, 8x57JRS, 9.3x74R, 375 H&H.
**Barrel:** 25.6".
**Weight:** About 7.7 lbs, depending upon caliber. **Length:** NA.
**Stock:** Oil-finished walnut with pistol grip, cheekpiece.
**Sights:** Blade front on ramp, fixed rear.
**Features:** Sidelock action. Double barrel locking lug with Greener cross-bolt; fine engraved hunting scenes on sideplates; Holland & Holland ejectors; double triggers. Imported from Germany by GSI.
**Price:** . . . . . . . . . . . . . . . . . . . . . . . . . . . . . **$10,995.00**

**Features:** Kersten double cross-bolt lock; scroll-engraved, case-hardened receiver; Blitz action with double triggers. Imported from Germany by GSI.
**Price:** Model 220E . . . . . . . . . . . . . . . . . . . . . . **$10,795.00**
**Price:** Model 221 E (silver-grayed receiver finish, hunting scene
engraving) . . . . . . . . . . . . . . . . . . . . . . . . . **$12,295.00**
**Price:** Model 223E (sidelock action, English-style large-scroll Arabesque
engraving) . . . . . . . . . . . . . . . . . . . . . . . . . **$18,395.00**
**Price:** Model 323E (as above with medium-scroll engraving) . . **$27,595.00**

## SAVAGE 24F O/U COMBINATION GUN

**Caliber/Gauge:** 22 Hornet, 223, 30-30 over 12 (24F-12) or 22 LR, 22 Hornet, 223, 30-30 over 20-ga. (24F-20); 3" chambers.
**Action:** Takedown, low rebounding visible hammer. Single trigger, barrel selector spur on hammer.
**Barrel:** 24" separated barrels; 12-ga. has Full, Mod., Imp. Cyl. choke tubes, 20-ga. has fixed Mod. choke.
**Weight:** 7 lbs. **Length:** 40½" overall.
**Stock:** Black Rynite composition.
**Sights:** Ramp front, rear open adjustable for elevation. Grooved for tip-off scope mount.
**Features:** Removable butt cap for storage and accessories. Introduced 1989.
**Price:** 24F-12 . . . . . . . . . . . . . . . . . . . . . . . . . **$400.00**
**Price:** 24F-20 . . . . . . . . . . . . . . . . . . . . . . . . . **$400.00**

## SPRINGFIELD INC. M6 SCOUT RIFLE/SHOTGUN

**Caliber:** 22 LR or 22 Hornet over 410-bore.
**Barrel:** 18.25".
**Weight:** 4.5 lbs. **Length:** 32" overall.
**Stock:** Steel, folding, with storage for 15 22 LR, four 410 shells.
**Sights:** Blade front, military aperture for 22; V-notch for 410.
**Features:** All-metal construction. Designed for quick disassembly and minimum maintenance. Folds for compact storage. Introduced 1982; reintroduced 1991. Made in U.S. by Springfield Inc.
**Price:** 22 LR/410 . . . . . . . . . . . . . . . . . . . . . . . **$199.00**
**Price:** 22 Hornet/410 . . . . . . . . . . . . . . . . . . . . . **$219.00**

> Consult our Directory pages for
> the location of firms mentioned.

## A. ZOLI RIFLE-SHOTGUN O/U COMBO

**Caliber/Gauge:** 12-ga. over 222, 308 or 30-06.
**Barrel:** Combo—24"; shotgun—28" (Mod. & Full).
**Weight:** About 8 lbs. **Length:** 41" overall (24" bbl.).
**Stock:** European walnut.
**Sights:** Blade front, flip-up rear.
**Features:** Available with German claw scope mounts on rifle/shotgun barrels. Comes with set of 12/12 (Mod. & Full) barrels. Imported from Italy by Mandall Shooting Supplies.
**Price:** With two barrel sets . . . . . . . . . . . . . . . . . . **$1,695.00**
**Price:** As above with claw mounts, scope . . . . . . . . . . . . **$2,495.00**

Designs for hunting, utility and sporting purposes, including training for competition.

AMT Lightning Hunting II

## AMT LIGHTNING 25/22 RIFLE
**Caliber:** 22 LR, 30-shot magazine.
**Barrel:** 18", tapered.
**Weight:** 6 lbs. **Length:** 26½" (folded), 37" (open).
**Stock:** Folding stainless steel.
**Sights:** Ramp front, fixed rear.
**Features:** Made of stainless steel with matte finish. Receiver dovetailed for scope mounting. Extended magazine release. Adjustable rear sight optionally available. Youth stock available. Introduced 1984. From AMT.
**Price:** . . . . . . . . . . . . . . . . . . . . . . . . . . $295.99

## AMT MAGNUM HUNTER AUTO RIFLE
**Caliber:** 22 WMR, 10-shot rotary magazine.
**Barrel:** 22".
**Weight:** 6 lbs. **Length:** 40½" overall.
**Stock:** Black fiberglass-filled nylon; checkered grip and forend.

## AMT Lightning Small-Game Hunting Rifle II
Same as the Lightning 25/22 except has conventional stock of black fiberglass-filled nylon, checkered at the grip and forend, and fitted with Uncle Mike's swivel studs. Removable recoil pad provides storage for ammo, cleaning rod and survival knife. No sights—receiver grooved for scope mounting. Has a 22" full-floating target weight barrel, weighs 6¾ lbs., overall length of 40½", 10-shot rotary magazine. Introduced 1987; 22 WMR introduced 1992. From AMT.
**Price:** . . . . . . . . . . . . . . . . . . . . . . . . . . $299.99

**Sights:** None furnished; grooved for scope mounting.
**Features:** Stainless steel construction. Free-floating target-weight barrel. Removable recoil pad for storage of ammo, knife, etc. Introduced 1993. Made in U.S. by AMT.
**Price:** . . . . . . . . . . . . . . . . . . . . . . . . . . $449.99

Anschutz 525

## ANSCHUTZ 525 DELUXE AUTO
**Caliber:** 22 LR, 10-shot clip.
**Barrel:** 24".

**Weight:** 6½ lbs. **Length:** 43" overall.
**Stock:** European hardwood; checkered pistol grip, Monte Carlo comb, beavertail forend.
**Sights:** Hooded ramp front, folding leaf rear.
**Features:** Rotary safety, empty shell deflector, single stage trigger. Receiver grooved for scope mounting. Introduced 1982. Imported from Germany by PSI.
**Price:** . . . . . . . . . . . . . . . . . . . . . . . . . . $528.00

## ARMSCOR MODEL 1600 AUTO RIFLE
**Caliber:** 22 LR, 15-shot magazine.
**Barrel:** 19.5".
**Weight:** 6 lbs. **Length:** 38" overall.
**Stock:** Mahogany.
**Sights:** Post front, aperture rear.
**Features:** Resembles Colt AR-15. Matte black finish. Introduced 1987. Imported from the Philippines by Ruko Products.
**Price:** About . . . . . . . . . . . . . . . . . . . . . $189.00
**Price:** M1600R (as above except has retractable buttstock, ventilated forend), about . . . . . . . . . . . . . . . . . . . . $189.00

## ARMSCOR MODEL AK22 AUTO RIFLE
**Caliber:** 22 LR, 15- and 30-shot magazine.
**Barrel:** 18.5".
**Weight:** 7 lbs. **Length:** 36" overall.
**Stock:** Plain mahogany.
**Sights:** Post front, open rear adjustable for windage and elevation.
**Features:** Resembles the AK-47. Matte black finish. Introduced 1987. Imported from the Philippines by Ruko Products.
**Price:** About . . . . . . . . . . . . . . . . . . . . . $259.00
**Price:** With folding steel stock, about . . . . . . . . . . . . . . . . $289.00

Armscor Model 2000SC

## AUTO-ORDNANCE 1927A-3
**Caliber:** 22 LR, 10-, 30- or 50-shot magazine.
**Barrel:** 16", finned.
**Weight:** About 7 lbs.
**Stock:** Walnut stock and forend.
**Sights:** Blade front, open rear adjustable for windage and elevation.
**Features:** Recreation of the Thompson Model 1927, only in 22 Long Rifle. Alloy receiver, finned barrel.
**Price:** . . . . . . . . . . . . . . . . . . . . . . . . . . $487.50

## ARMSCOR MODEL 20P AUTO RIFLE
**Caliber:** 22 LR, 15-shot magazine.
**Barrel:** 21".
**Weight:** 6.5 lbs. **Length:** 39.75" overall.
**Stock:** Walnut-finished mahogany.
**Sights:** Hooded front, rear adjustable for elevation.
**Features:** Receiver grooved for scope mounting. Blued finish. Introduced 1990. Imported from the Philippines by Ruko Products.
**Price:** About . . . . . . . . . . . . . . . . . . . . . . $119.00
**Price:** With checkered stock . . . . . . . . . . . . . . . . $149.00
**Price:** Model 20C (carbine-style stock, steel barrel band, buttplate) . $139.00
**Price:** Model 2000SC (as above except has checkered stock, fully adjustable sight, rubber buttpad, forend tip), about . . . . . . . . . . . . NA
**Price:** Model 50S (similar to Model 20P except has ventilated barrel shroud, and 30-shot magazine) . . . . . . . . . . . . . . . . . . . . . . $199.00

**CAUTION:** PRICES CHANGE, CHECK AT GUNSHOP.

Browning Auto-22

## Browning Auto-22 Grade VI

Same as the Grade I Auto-22 except available with either grayed or blued receiver with extensive engraving with gold-plated animals: right side pictures a fox and squirrel in a woodland scene; left side shows a beagle chasing a rabbit. On top is a portrait of the beagle. Stock and forend are of high-grade walnut with a double-bordered cut checkering design. Introduced 1987.
**Price:** Grade VI, blue or gray receiver . . . . . . . . . . . . . . . **$708.95**

## CALICO MODEL M-100 CARBINE
**Caliber:** 22 LR, 100-shot magazine.
**Barrel:** 16".
**Weight:** 5.7 lbs. (loaded). **Length:** 35.8" overall (stock extended).
**Stock:** Folding steel.
**Sights:** Post front adjustable for elevation, notch rear adjustable for windage.
**Features:** Uses alloy frame and helical-feed magazine; ambidextrous safety; removable barrel assembly; pistol grip compartment; flash suppressor; bolt stop. Made in U.S. From Calico.
**Price:** . . . . . . . . . . . . . . . . . . . . . . . . . . . . . . . . . . **$346.90**

## E.A.A./SABATTI MODEL 1822 AUTO RIFLE
**Caliber:** 22 LR, 10-shot magazine.
**Barrel:** 18½" round tapered; bull barrel on Heavy and Thumbhole Heavy models.
**Weight:** 5¼ lbs. (Sporter). **Length:** 37" overall.
**Stock:** Stained hardwood; Thumbhole model has one-piece stock.
**Sights:** Bead front, folding leaf rear adjustable for elevation on Sporter model. Heavy and Thumbhole models only dovetailed for scope mount.
**Features:** Cross-bolt safety. Blue finish. Lifetime warranty. Introduced 1993. Imported from Italy by European American Armory.
**Price:** Sporter . . . . . . . . . . . . . . . . . . . . . . . . . . . . . **$199.95**
**Price:** Heavy . . . . . . . . . . . . . . . . . . . . . . . . . . . . . . **$224.95**
**Price:** Thumbhole Heavy . . . . . . . . . . . . . . . . . . . . . . . **$359.95**

Feather Model F2

## BROWNING AUTO-22 RIFLE
**Caliber:** 22 LR, 11-shot.
**Barrel:** 19¼".
**Weight:** 4¾ lbs. **Length:** 37" overall.
**Stock:** Checkered select walnut with p.g. and semi-beavertail forend.
**Sights:** Gold bead front, folding leaf rear.
**Features:** Engraved receiver with polished blue finish; cross-bolt safety; tubular magazine in buttstock; easy takedown for carrying or storage. Imported from Japan by Browning.
**Price:** Grade I . . . . . . . . . . . . . . . . . . . . . . . . . . . . . **$344.95**

Calico M-105

## Calico Model M-105 Sporter

Similar to the M-100 except has hand-rubbed wood buttstock and forend. Weight is 4¾ lbs. Introduced 1987.
**Price:** . . . . . . . . . . . . . . . . . . . . . . . . . . . . . . . . . . **$376.90**

## ERMA EM1 CARBINE
**Caliber:** 22 LR, 10-shot magazine.
**Barrel:** 18".
**Weight:** 5.6 lbs. **Length:** 35.5" overall.
**Stock:** Polished beech or oiled walnut.
**Sights:** Blade front, fully adjustable aperture rear.
**Features:** Blowback action. Receiver grooved for scope mounting. Imported from Germany by Mandall Shooting Supplies.
**Price:** . . . . . . . . . . . . . . . . . . . . . . . . . . . . . . . . . . **$499.95**

## FEATHER AT-22 SEMI-AUTO CARBINE
**Caliber:** 22 LR, 20-shot magazine.
**Barrel:** 17".
**Weight:** 3.25 lbs. **Length:** 35" overall (stock extended).
**Stock:** Telescoping wire; composition pistol grip.
**Sights:** Protected post front, adjustable aperture rear.
**Features:** Removable barrel. Length when folded is 26". Matte black finish. From Feather Industries. Introduced 1986.
**Price:** . . . . . . . . . . . . . . . . . . . . . . . . . . . . . . . . . . **$249.95**
**Price:** Model F2 (fixed stock) . . . . . . . . . . . . . . . . . . . **$279.95**

Federal XC222

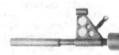

Consult our Directory pages for
the location of firms mentioned.

## FEDERAL ENGINEERING XC222 AUTO CARBINE
**Caliber:** 22 LR, 30-shot magazine.
**Barrel:** 16.5" (with flash hider).
**Weight:** 7.25 lbs. **Length:** 34.5" overall.
**Stock:** Quick-detachable tube steel.
**Sights:** Hooded post front, Williams adjustable rear; sight bridge grooved for scope mounting.
**Features:** Quick takedown; all-steel heli-arc welded construction; internal parts industrial hard chromed. Made in U.S. by Federal Engineering Corp.
**Price:** Includes receiver cap, sling, swivels . . . . . . . . . . . . **$459.00**

**CAUTION:** PRICES CHANGE, CHECK AT GUNSHOP.

Grendel R-31

## KRICO MODEL 260 AUTO RIFLE
**Caliber:** 22 LR, 5-shot magazine.
**Barrel:** 19.6".
**Weight:** 6.6 lbs. **Length:** 38.9" overall.
**Stock:** Beech.
**Sights:** Blade on ramp front, open adjustable rear.
**Features:** Receiver grooved for scope mounting. Sliding safety. Imported from Germany by Mandall Shooting Supplies.
**Price:** . . . . . . . . . . . . . . . . . . . . . . . . . . . . . . . . . . . $700.00

## GRENDEL R-31 AUTO CARBINE
**Caliber:** 22 WMR, 30-shot magazine.
**Barrel:** 16".
**Weight:** 4 lbs. **Length:** 23.5" overall (stock collapsed).
**Stock:** Telescoping tube, Zytel forend.
**Sights:** Post front adustable for windage and elevation, aperture rear.
**Features:** Blowback action with fluted chamber; ambidextrous safety. Steel receiver. Matte black finish. Muzzle brake. Scope mount optional. Introduced 1991. Made in U.S. by Grendel, Inc.
**Price:** . . . . . . . . . . . . . . . . . . . . . . . . . . . . . . . . . . . $385.00

> Consult our Directory pages for the location of firms mentioned.

Lakefield Arms Model 64B

## LAKEFIELD ARMS MODEL 64B AUTO RIFLE
**Caliber:** 22 LR, 10-shot magazine.
**Barrel:** 20".
**Weight:** 5½ lbs. **Length:** 40" overall.
**Stock:** Walnut-finished hardwood with Monte Carlo-type comb, checkered grip and forend.
**Sights:** Bead front, open adjustable rear. Receiver grooved for scope mounting.
**Features:** Thumb-operated rotating safety. Blue finish. Side ejection, bolt hold-open device. Introduced 1990. Made in Canada by Lakefield Arms Ltd.
**Price:** About . . . . . . . . . . . . . . . . . . . . . . . . . . . . . . . $132.95

Marlin Model 60SS

## Marlin Model 60SS Self-Loading Rifle
Same as the Model 60 except breech bolt, barrel and outer magazine tube are made of stainless steel; most other parts are either nickel-plated or coated to match the stainless finish. Monte Carlo stock is of black/gray Main birch laminate, and has nickel-plated swivel studs, rubber butt pad. Introduced 1993.
**Price:** . . . . . . . . . . . . . . . . . . . . . . . . . . . . . . . . . . . $221.95

## MARLIN MODEL 60 SELF-LOADING RIFLE
**Caliber:** 22 LR, 14-shot tubular magazine.
**Barrel:** 22" round tapered.
**Weight:** About 5½ lbs. **Length:** 40½" overall.
**Stock:** Walnut-finished Monte Carlo, full pistol grip; Mar-Shield® finish.
**Sights:** Ramp front, open adjustable rear.
**Features:** Matted receiver is grooved for scope mount. Manual bolt hold-open; automatic last-shot bolt hold-open.
**Price:** . . . . . . . . . . . . . . . . . . . . . . . . . . . . . . . . . . . $148.75

Marlin Model 70HC

## Marlin Model 990L Self-Loading Rifle
Similar to the Model 60 except has laminated hardwood stock with black rubber rifle butt pad and swivel studs, gold-plated steel trigger. Ramp front sight with brass bead and Wide-Scan hood, adjustable semi-buckhorn folding rear. Weighs 5.75 lbs. Introduced 1992. From Marlin.
**Price:** . . . . . . . . . . . . . . . . . . . . . . . . . . . . . . . . . . . $215.50

## MARLIN MODEL 70 HC AUTO
**Caliber:** 22 LR, 7- and 15-shot clip magazines.
**Barrel:** 18" (16-groove rifling).
**Weight:** 5 lbs. **Length:** 36¾" overall.
**Stock:** Walnut-finished hardwood with Monte Carlo, full p.g. Mar-Shield® finish.
**Sights:** Ramp front, adjustable open rear. Receiver grooved for scope mount.
**Features:** Receiver top has serrated, non-glare finish; cross-bolt safety; manual bolt hold-open.
**Price:** . . . . . . . . . . . . . . . . . . . . . . . . . . . . . . . . . . . $168.90

Marlin Model 70P Papoose

## Marlin Model 70P Papoose
Similar to the Model 70 HC except is a takedown model with easily removable barrel—no tools needed. Has 16¼" Micro-Groove® barrel, walnut-finished hardwood stock, ramp front, adjustable open rear sights, cross-bolt safety. Takedown feature allows removal of barrel without tools. Overall length is 35¼", weight is 3¼ lbs. Receiver grooved for scope mounting. Comes with zippered case. Introduced 1986.
**Price:** . . . . . . . . . . . . . . . . . . . . . . . . . . . . . . . . . . . $195.50

**CAUTION:** PRICES CHANGE, CHECK AT GUNSHOP.

Marlin Model 922

## MARLIN MODEL 922 MAGNUM SELF-LOADING RIFLE
**Caliber:** 22 WMR, 7-shot magazine.
**Barrel:** 20.5".

**Weight:** 6.5 lbs. **Length:** 39.75" overall.
**Stock:** American black walnut with Monte Carlo comb, swivel studs, rubber butt pad.
**Sights:** Ramp front with bead and removable Wide-Scan® hood, adjustable folding semi-buckhorn rear.
**Features:** Action based on the centerfire Model 9 Carbine. Receiver drilled and tapped for scope mounting. Automatic last-shot bolt holdopen; magazine safety. Introduced 1993.
**Price:** . . . . . . . . . . . . . . . . . . . . . . . . . . . . . **$362.95**

## MARLIN MODEL 995 SELF-LOADING RIFLE
**Caliber:** 22 LR, 7-shot clip magazine.
**Barrel:** 18" Micro-Groove®.
**Weight:** 5 lbs. **Length:** 36¾" overall.
**Stock:** American black walnut, Monte Carlo-style, with full pistol grip. Checkered p.g. and forend; white buttplate spacer; Mar-Shield® finish.

**Sights:** Ramp bead front with Wide-Scan™ hood; adjustable folding semi-buckhorn rear.
**Features:** Receiver grooved for scope mount; bolt hold-open device; cross-bolt safety. Introduced 1979.
**Price:** . . . . . . . . . . . . . . . . . . . . . . . . . . . . . **$198.80**

## MITCHELL GALIL/22 AUTO RIFLE
**Caliber:** 22 LR, 20-shot magazine; 22 WMR, 10-shot magazine.
**Barrel:** 18".
**Weight:** 6.5 lbs. **Length:** 36" overall.
**Stock:** European walnut grip and forend with metal folding stock.
**Sights:** Post front adjustable for elevation, rear adjustable for windage.
**Features:** Replica of the Israeli Galil rifle. Introduced 1987. Imported by Mitchell Arms, Inc.
**Price:** 22 LR, fixed or folding stock . . . . . . . . . . . . . . . . . . **$359.00**
**Price:** 22 WMR, fixed or folding stock . . . . . . . . . . . . . . . **$359.00**

## MITCHELL AK-22 SEMI-AUTO RIFLE
**Caliber:** 22 LR, 20-shot magazine; 22 WMR, 10-shot magazine.
**Barrel:** 18".
**Weight:** 6½ lbs. **Length:** 36" overall.
**Stock:** European walnut.
**Sights:** Post front, open adjustable rear.
**Features:** Replica of the AK-47 rifle. Wide magazine to maintain appearance. Imported from Italy by Mitchell Arms, Inc.
**Price:** 22 LR . . . . . . . . . . . . . . . . . . . . . . . . . . . . **$359.00**
**Price:** 22 WMR . . . . . . . . . . . . . . . . . . . . . . . . . . . **$359.00**

## MITCHELL PPS/50 RIFLE
**Caliber:** 22 LR, 20-shot magazine (50-shot drum optional).
**Barrel:** 16½".
**Weight:** 5½ lbs. **Length:** 33½" overall.
**Stock:** Walnut.
**Sights:** Blade front, adjustable rear.
**Features:** Full-length perforated barrel shroud. Matte finish. Introduced 1989. Imported by Mitchell Arms, Inc.
**Price:** With 20-shot "banana" magazine . . . . . . . . . . . . . . . **$359.00**
**Price:** With 50-shot drum magazine . . . . . . . . . . . . . . . . . **$459.00**

## MITCHELL MAS/22 AUTO RIFLE
**Caliber:** 22 LR, 20-shot magazine.
**Barrel:** 18".
**Weight:** 7½ lbs. **Length:** 28.5" overall.
**Stock:** Walnut butt, grip and forend.
**Sights:** Adjustable post front, flip-type aperture rear.
**Features:** Bullpup design resembles French armed forces rifle. Top cocking lever, flash hider. Introduced 1987. Imported by Mitchell Arms, Inc.
**Price:** 22 LR . . . . . . . . . . . . . . . . . . . . . . . . . . . . **$359.00**

Mitchell M-16A1/22

## Mitchell CAR-15/22 Semi-Auto Rifle
Similar to the M-16 A-1/22 rifle except has 16¾" barrel, telescoping butt, giving an overall length of 32" when collapsed. Adjustable post front sight, adjustable aperture rear. Scope mount available. Has 15-shot magazine. Replica of the CAR-15 rifle. Introduced 1990. Imported by Mitchell Arms, Inc.
**Price:** . . . . . . . . . . . . . . . . . . . . . . . . . . . . . **$359.00**

## MITCHELL M-16A-1/22 RIFLE
**Caliber:** 22 LR, 15-shot magazine.
**Barrel:** 20.5".
**Weight:** 7 lbs. **Length:** 38.5" overall.
**Stock:** Black composition.
**Sights:** Adjustable post front, adjustable aperture rear.
**Features:** Replica of the AR-15 rifle. Full width magazine. Comes with military-type sling. Introduced 1990. Imported by Mitchell Arms, Inc.
**Price:** 22 LR . . . . . . . . . . . . . . . . . . . . . . . . . . . . **$359.00**

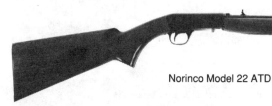

Norinco Model 22 ATD

## NORINCO MODEL 22 ATD RIFLE
**Caliber:** 22 LR, 11-shot magazine.
**Barrel:** 19.4".
**Weight:** 4.6 lbs. **Length:** 36.6" overall.
**Stock:** Checkered hardwood.
**Sights:** Blade front, open adjustable rear.
**Features:** Browning-design takedown action for storage, transport. Cross-bolt safety. Tube magazine loads through buttplate. Blue finish with engraved receiver. Introduced 1987. Imported from China by Interarms.
**Price:** . . . . . . . . . . . . . . . . . . . . . . . . . . . . . **$168.00**

**CAUTION:** PRICES CHANGE, CHECK AT GUNSHOP.

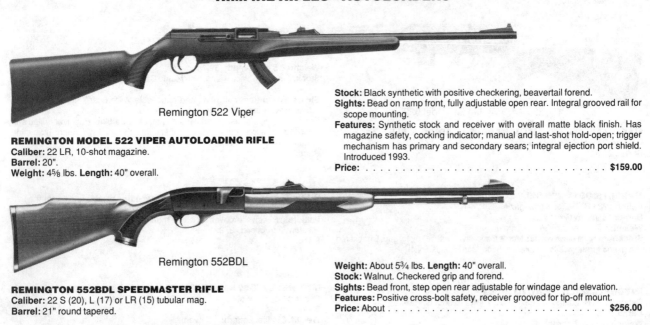

Remington 522 Viper

**REMINGTON MODEL 522 VIPER AUTOLOADING RIFLE**
**Caliber:** 22 LR, 10-shot magazine.
**Barrel:** 20".
**Weight:** 4⅝ lbs. **Length:** 40" overall.

**Stock:** Black synthetic with positive checkering, beavertail forend.
**Sights:** Bead on ramp front, fully adjustable open rear. Integral grooved rail for scope mounting.
**Features:** Synthetic stock and receiver with overall matte black finish. Has magazine safety, cocking indicator; manual and last-shot hold-open; trigger mechanism has primary and secondary sears; integral ejection port shield. Introduced 1993.
**Price:** . . . . . . . . . . . . . . . . . . . . . . . . . . . . . . . . . **$159.00**

Remington 552BDL

**REMINGTON 552BDL SPEEDMASTER RIFLE**
**Caliber:** 22 S (20), L (17) or LR (15) tubular mag.
**Barrel:** 21" round tapered.
**Weight:** About 5¾ lbs. **Length:** 40" overall.
**Stock:** Walnut. Checkered grip and forend.
**Sights:** Bead front, step open rear adjustable for windage and elevation.
**Features:** Positive cross-bolt safety, receiver grooved for tip-off mount.
**Price:** About . . . . . . . . . . . . . . . . . . . . . . . . . . . . . **$256.00**

Ruger K10/22RB

**Ruger 10/22 Deluxe Sporter**
Same as 10/22 Carbine except walnut stock with hand checkered p.g. and forend; straight buttplate, no barrel band, has sling swivels.
**Price:** Model 10/22 DSP . . . . . . . . . . . . . . . . . . . . . **$254.50**

**RUGER 10/22 AUTOLOADING CARBINE**
**Caliber:** 22 LR, 10-shot rotary magazine.
**Barrel:** 18½" round tapered.
**Weight:** 5 lbs. **Length:** 37¼" overall.
**Stock:** American hardwood with p.g. and bbl. band.
**Sights:** Brass bead front, folding leaf rear adjustable for elevation.
**Features:** Detachable rotary magazine fits flush into stock, cross-bolt safety, receiver tapped and grooved for scope blocks or tip-off mount. Scope base adaptor furnished with each rifle.
**Price:** Model 10/22 RB (blue) . . . . . . . . . . . . . . . . . **$201.50**
**Price:** Model K10/22RB (bright finish stainless barrel) . . . . . . . . **$236.00**

**SURVIVAL ARMS AR-7 EXPLORER RIFLE**
**Caliber:** 22 LR, 8-shot magazine.
**Barrel:** 16".
**Weight:** 2.5 lbs. **Length:** 34.5" overall; 16.5" stowed.
**Stock:** Moulded Cycolac; snap-on rubber butt cap.
**Sights:** Square blade front, aperture rear adjustable for elevation.
**Features:** Takedown design stores barrel and action in hollow stock. Light enough to float. Black, Silvertone or camouflage finish. Reintroduced 1992. From Survival Arms, Inc.
**Price:** Silver or camo . . . . . . . . . . . . . . . . . . . . . **$150.00**
**Price:** Sporter (black finish with telescoping stock, 25-shot magazine) **$200.00**
**Price:** Wildcat (black finish with wood stock) . . . . . . . . . . . . **$150.00**

**TEXAS REMINGTON REVOLVING CARBINE**
**Caliber:** 22 LR.
**Barrel:** 21".
**Weight:** 5¾ lbs. **Length:** 36" overall.
**Stock:** Smooth walnut.
**Sights:** Blade front, rear adjustable for windage and elevation.
**Features:** Brass frame, buttplate and trigger guard, blued cylinder and barrel. Introduced 1991. Imported from Italy by E.M.F.
**Price:** . . . . . . . . . . . . . . . . . . . . . . . . . . . . . . . . . **$420.00**

**VOERE MODEL 2115 AUTO RIFLE**
**Caliber:** 22 LR, 10-shot magazine.
**Barrel:** 18.1".
**Weight:** 5.75 lbs. **Length:** 37.7" overall.
**Stock:** Walnut-finished beechwood with cheekpiece; checkered pistol grip and forend.

**Sights:** Post front with hooded ramp, leaf rear.
**Features:** Clip-fed autoloader with single stage trigger, wing-type safety. Introduced 1984. Imported from Austria by JagerSport, Ltd.
**Price:** About . . . . . . . . . . . . . . . . . . . . . . . . . . . . . **$585.00**

# RIMFIRE RIFLES—LEVER & SLIDE ACTION

Classic and modern models for sport and utility, including training.

Browning BL-22

**BROWNING BL-22 LEVER-ACTION RIFLE**
**Caliber:** 22 S (22), L (17) or LR (15), tubular magazine.
**Barrel:** 20" round tapered.

**Weight:** 5 lbs. **Length:** 36¾" overall.
**Stock:** Walnut, two-piece straight grip Western style.
**Sights:** Bead post front, folding-leaf rear.
**Features:** Short throw lever, half-cock safety, receiver grooved for tip-off scope mounts. Imported from Japan by Browning.
**Price:** Grade I . . . . . . . . . . . . . . . . . . . . . . . . . . . **$301.50**
**Price:** Grade II (engraved receiver, checkered grip and forend) . . . **$343.50**

**CAUTION:** PRICES CHANGE, CHECK AT GUNSHOP.

Marlin 39TDS

## MARLIN 39TDS CARBINE

**Caliber:** 22 S (16), 22 L (12), 22 LR (11).
**Barrel:** 16½" Micro-Groove®.
**Weight:** 5¼ lbs. **Length:** 32⅝" overall.
**Stock:** American black walnut with straight grip; short forend with blued tip. Mar-Shield® finish.
**Sights:** Ramp front with Wide-Scan™ hood, adjustable semi-buckhorn folding rear.
**Features:** Takedown style, comes with carrying case. Hammer-block safety, rebounding hammer; blued metal, gold-plated steel trigger. Introduced 1988.
**Price:** With case . . . . . . . . . . . . . . . . . . . . . . . . . . . . . $418.85

## NORINCO EM-321 PUMP RIFLE

**Caliber:** 22 LR, 9-shot magazine.
**Barrel:** 19.5".
**Weight:** 6 lbs. **Length:** 37" overall.
**Stock:** Hardwood.
**Sights:** Blade front, open folding rear.
**Features:** Blue finish; grooved slide handle. Imported from China by China Sports, Inc.
**Price:** . . . . . . . . . . . . . . . . . . . . . . . . . . . . . . . . . . NA

Rossi Model 62 SAC

## Rossi Model 62 SAC Carbine

Same as standard model except 22 LR only, has 16¼" barrel. Magazine holds slightly fewer cartridges.
**Price:** Blue . . . . . . . . . . . . . . . . . . . . . . . . . . $227.00
**Price:** Nickel . . . . . . . . . . . . . . . . . . . . . . . . . $245.00

Winchester Model 9422

## Winchester Model 9422 Magnum Lever-Action Rifle

Same as the 9422 except chambered for 22 WMR cartridge, has 11-round mag. capacity.
**Price:** Walnut . . . . . . . . . . . . . . . . . . . . . . . . $393.00
**Price:** With WinCam green stock . . . . . . . . . . . . . . . . $393.00
**Price:** With WinTuff brown laminated stock . . . . . . . . . . . $393.00

## MARLIN MODEL 39AS GOLDEN LEVER-ACTION RIFLE

**Caliber:** 22 S (26), L (21), LR (19), tubular magazine.
**Barrel:** 24" Micro-Groove®.
**Weight:** 6½ lbs. **Length:** 40" overall.
**Stock:** American black walnut with white line spacers at p.g. cap and buttplate; Mar-Shield® finish. Swivel studs; rubber buttpad.
**Sights:** Bead ramp front with detachable Wide-Scan™ hood, folding rear semi-buckhorn adjustable for windage and elevation.
**Features:** Hammer-block safety; rebounding hammer. Takedown action, receiver tapped for scope mount (supplied), offset hammer spur; gold-plated steel trigger.
**Price:** . . . . . . . . . . . . . . . . . . . . . . . . . . . . . $405.45

## REMINGTON 572BDL FIELDMASTER PUMP RIFLE

**Caliber:** 22 S (20), L (17) or LR (14), tubular magazine.
**Barrel:** 21" round tapered.
**Weight:** 5½ lbs. **Length:** 42" overall.
**Stock:** Walnut with checkered p.g. and slide handle.
**Sights:** Blade ramp front; sliding ramp rear adjustable for windage and elevation.
**Features:** Cross-bolt safety; removing inner magazine tube converts rifle to single shot; receiver grooved for tip-off scope mount.
**Price:** About . . . . . . . . . . . . . . . . . . . . . . . . . . $269.00

## ROSSI MODEL 62 SA PUMP RIFLE

**Caliber:** 22 LR, 22 WMR.
**Barrel:** 23", round or octagonal.
**Weight:** 5¾ lbs. **Length:** 39¼" overall.
**Stock:** Walnut, straight grip, grooved forend.
**Sights:** Fixed front, adjustable rear.
**Features:** Capacity 20 Short, 16 Long or 14 Long Rifle. Quick takedown. Imported from Brazil by Interarms.
**Price:** Blue . . . . . . . . . . . . . . . . . . . . . . . . . . $227.00
**Price:** Nickel . . . . . . . . . . . . . . . . . . . . . . . . . $245.00
**Price:** Blue, with octagonal barrel . . . . . . . . . . . . . . . $253.00
**Price:** 22 WMR, as Model 59 . . . . . . . . . . . . . . . . . . $280.00

## WINCHESTER MODEL 9422 LEVER-ACTION RIFLE

**Caliber:** 22 S (21), L (17), LR (15), tubular magazine.
**Barrel:** 20½".
**Weight:** 6¼ lbs. **Length:** 37⅛" overall.
**Stock:** American walnut, two-piece, straight grip (no p.g.).
**Sights:** Hooded ramp front, adjustable semi-buckhorn rear.
**Features:** Side ejection, receiver grooved for scope mounting, takedown action. From U.S. Repeating Arms Co.
**Price:** Walnut . . . . . . . . . . . . . . . . . . . . . . . . $376.00
**Price:** With WinTuff laminated stock . . . . . . . . . . . . . . $376.00

# RIMFIRE RIFLES—BOLT ACTIONS & SINGLE SHOTS

Includes models for a variety of sports, utility and competitive shooting.

## ANSCHUTZ ACHIEVER BOLT-ACTION RIFLE

**Caliber:** 22 LR, single shot adaptor.
**Barrel:** 19½".
**Weight:** 5 lbs. **Length:** 35½" to 36⅔" overall.
**Stock:** Walnut-finished hardwood with adjustable buttplate, vented forend, stippled pistol grip. Length of pull adjustable from 11⅞" to 13".
**Sights:** Hooded front, open rear adjustable for windage and elevation.

**Features:** Uses Mark 2000-type action with adjustable two-stage trigger. Receiver grooved for scope mounting. Designed for training in junior rifle clubs and for starting young shooters. Introduced 1987. Imported from Germany by Precision Sales International.
**Price:** . . . . . . . . . . . . . . . . . . . . . . . . . . . . . $395.00
**Price:** Sight Set #1 . . . . . . . . . . . . . . . . . . . . . . . $67.00

Anschutz 1416D/1516D

### Anschutz 1418D/1518D Mannlicher Rifles
Similar to the 1416D/1516D rifles except has full-length Mannlicher-style stock, shorter 19¾" barrel. Weighs 5½ lbs. Stock has mahogany schnabel tip. Model 1418D chambered for 22 LR, 1518D for 22 WMR. Imported from Germany by Precision Sales International.
**Price: 1418D** . . . . . . . . . . . . . . . . . . . **$1,053.00**
**Price: 1518D** . . . . . . . . . . . . . . . . . . . **$1,073.00**

### ANSCHUTZ 1700D CLASSIC RIFLES
**Caliber:** 22 LR, 5-shot clip.
**Barrel:** 23½", ¹³⁄₁₆" dia. heavy.
**Weight:** 7¾ lbs. **Length:** 42½" overall.
**Stock:** Select European walnut with checkered pistol grip and forend.
**Sights:** Hooded ramp front, folding leaf rear; drilled and tapped for scope mounting.
**Features:** Adjustable single stage trigger. Receiver drilled and tapped for scope mounting. Introduced 1988. Imported from Germany by Precision Sales International.
**Price:** 22 LR . . . . . . . . . . . . . . . . . . . **$1,228.00**
**Price:** As above, Meistergrade (select walnut, gold engraved trigger guard), add . . . . . . . . . . . . . **$199.00**

### Anschutz 1700D Graphite Custom Rifle
Similar to the Model 1700D Custom except has McMillan graphite reinforced stock with roll-over cheekpiece. Has 22" barrel. No sights furnished, but drilled and tapped for scope mounting. Comes with embroidered sling, Michael's quick-detachable swivels. Introduced 1991.
**Price:** . . . . . . . . . . . . . . . . . . . . . **$1,183.00**

> Consult our Directory pages for the location of firms mentioned.

### ANSCHUTZ 1416D/1516D CLASSIC RIFLES
**Caliber:** 22 LR (1416D), 5-shot clip; 22 WMR (1516D), 4-shot clip.
**Barrel:** 22½".
**Weight:** 6 lbs. **Length:** 41" overall.
**Stock:** European walnut; Monte Carlo with cheekpiece, schnabel forend, checkered pistol grip and forend.
**Sights:** Hooded ramp front, folding leaf rear.
**Features:** Uses Model 1403 target rifle action. Adjustable single stage trigger. Receiver grooved for scope mounting. Imported from Germany by Precision Sales International.
**Price:** 1416D, 22 LR . . . . . . . . . . . . . **$690.00**
**Price:** 1516D, 22 WMR . . . . . . . . . . . . **$716.00**
**Price:** 1416D Classic left-hand . . . . . . . **$711.00**

### Anschutz 1700D Custom Rifles
Similar to the Classic models except have roll-over Monte Carlo cheekpiece, slim forend with schnabel tip, Wundhammer palm swell on pistol grip, rosewood grip cap with white diamond insert. Skip-line checkering on grip and forend. Introduced 1988. Imported from Germany by Precision Sales International.
**Price:** 22 LR . . . . . . . . . . . . . . . . . . **$1,258.00**
**Price:** Custom 1700 Meistergrade (select walnut, gold engraved trigger guard), add . . . . . . . . . . . **$199.00**

### Anschutz 1700 FWT Bolt-Action Rifle
Similar to the Anschutz Custom except has McMillan fiberglass stock with Monte Carlo, roll-over cheekpiece, Wundhammer swell, and checkering. Comes without sights but the receiver is drilled and tapped for scope mounting. Has 22" barrel, single stage #5095 trigger. Weighs 6.25 lbs. Introduced 1989.
**Price:** With fiberglass stock . . . . . . . . . **$1,118.00**
**Price:** As above, with Fibergrain stock . . . . **$1,327.00**

### ANSCHUTZ 1700D BAVARIAN BOLT-ACTION RIFLE
**Caliber:** 22 LR, 5-shot clip.
**Barrel:** 24".
**Weight:** 7¼ lbs. **Length:** 43" overall.
**Stock:** European walnut with Bavarian cheek rest. Checkered p.g. and forend.
**Sights:** Hooded ramp front, folding leaf rear.
**Features:** Uses the Improved 1700 Match 54 action with adjustable 5096 trigger. Drilled and tapped for scope mounting. Introduced in 1988. Imported from Germany by Precision Sales International.
**Price:** 22 LR . . . . . . . . . . . . . . . . . . **$1,258.00**
**Price:** Custom 1700D Meistergrade (select walnut, gold engraved trigger guard), add . . . . . . . . . . . **$199.00**

Armscor Model 14D

### Armscor Model 1500 Rifle
Similar to the Model 14P except chambered for 22 WMR. Has 21.5" barrel, double lug bolt, checkered stock, weighs 6.5 lbs. Introduced 1987.
**Price:** About . . . . . . . . . . . . . . . . . . **$189.00**

### ARMSCOR MODEL 14P BOLT-ACTION RIFLE
**Caliber:** 22 LR, 10-shot magazine.
**Barrel:** 23".
**Weight:** 7 lbs. **Length:** 41.5" overall.
**Stock:** Walnut-finished mahogany.
**Sights:** Bead front, rear adjustable for elevation.
**Features:** Receiver grooved for scope mounting. Blued finish. Introduced 1987. Imported from the Philippines by Ruko Products.
**Price:** About . . . . . . . . . . . . . . . . . . **$119.00**
**Price:** Model 14D Deluxe (checkered stock) . . . . . . . **$139.00**

BRNO ZKM 452 Deluxe

### BRNO ZKM 452 Deluxe
Same as the Standard except checked walnut stock with oil finish, sling swivels. Introduced 1992. Imported from the Czeck Republic by Action Arms, Ltd.
**Price:** . . . . . . . . . . . . . . . . . . . . . **$349.00**
**Price:** With synthetic stock . . . . . . . . . . **$305.00**

### BRNO ZKM-452 DELUXE BOLT-ACTION RIFLE
**Caliber:** 22 LR, detachable 5-shot magazine.
**Barrel:** 23.6".
**Weight:** 6.9 lbs. **Length:** 43.5" overall.
**Stock:** Checkered walnut.
**Sights:** Hooded bead front, open rear adjustable for windage and elevation.
**Features:** Dual claw extractors, safety locks firing pin. Blue finish; grooved receiver; oiled stock; sling swivels. Introduced 1992. Imported from the Czech Republic by Action Arms Ltd.
**Price:** . . . . . . . . . . . . . . . . . . . . . **$349.00**
**Price:** With synthetic stock . . . . . . . . . . **$305.00**

**CAUTION:** PRICES CHANGE, CHECK AT GUNSHOP.

## BEEMAN/HW 60J-ST BOLT-ACTION RIFLE
**Caliber:** 22 LR.
**Barrel:** 22.8".
**Weight:** 6.5 lbs. **Length:** 41.7" overall.
**Stock:** Walnut with cheekpiece, cut checkered p.g. and forend.

Browning A-Bolt 22

## Browning A-Bolt Gold Medallion
Similar to the standard A-Bolt except stock is of high-grade walnut with brass spacers between stock and rubber recoil pad and between the rosewood grip cap and forend. Medallion-style engraving covers the receiver flats, and the words "Gold Medallion" are engraved and gold filled on the right side of the barrel. High gloss stock finish. Introduced 1988.
**Price:** No sights . . . . . . . . . . . . . . . . . . . . . . . . . . . . **$496.95**

## CABANAS PHASER RIFLE
**Caliber:** 177.
**Barrel:** 19".
**Weight:** 6 lbs., 12 oz. **Length:** 42" overall.
**Stock:** Target-type thumbhole.
**Sights:** Blade front, open fully adjustable rear.
**Features:** Fires round ball or pellets with 22 blank cartridge. Imported from Mexico by Mandall Shooting Supplies.
**Price:** . . . . . . . . . . . . . . . . . . . . . . . . . . . . . . . . . **$159.95**

## Cabanas Espronceda IV Bolt-Action Rifle
Similar to the Leyre model except has full sporter stock, 18¾" barrel, 40" overall length, weighs 5½ lbs.
**Price:** . . . . . . . . . . . . . . . . . . . . . . . . . . . . . . . . . **$134.95**

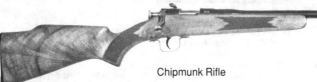

Chipmunk Rifle

## COOPER ARMS MODEL 36S SPORTER RIFLE
**Caliber:** 22 LR, 5-shot magazine.
**Barrel:** 23¾" Shilen match.
**Weight:** 8 lbs. **Length:** 42½" overall.
**Stock:** AA Claro walnut with 22 lpi checkering, oil finish; Custom has AAA Claro or AA French walnut.
**Sights:** None furnished.
**Features:** Action has three mid-bolt locking lugs, 45-degree bolt rotation; fully adjustable single stage match trigger; swivel studs. Pachmayr butt pad. Introduced 1991. Made in U.S. by Cooper Arms.
**Price:** Standard . . . . . . . . . . . . . . . . . . . . . . . . . . . **$995.00**
**Price:** Custom . . . . . . . . . . . . . . . . . . . . . . . . . . . . **$1,195.00**

Dakota 22 Sporter

## DAKOTA 22 SPORTER BOLT-ACTION RIFLE
**Caliber:** 22 LR, 22 Hornet, 5-shot magazine.
**Barrel:** 22".

**Sights:** Hooded blade on ramp front, open rear.
**Features:** Polished blue finish; oil-finished walnut. Imported from Germany by Beeman. Introduced 1988.
**Price:** . . . . . . . . . . . . . . . . . . . . . . . . . . . . . . . . . **$645.00**

## BROWNING A-BOLT 22 BOLT-ACTION RIFLE
**Caliber:** 22 LR, 22 WMR, 5-shot magazines standard.
**Barrel:** 22".
**Weight:** 5 lbs., 9 oz. **Length:** 40¼" overall.
**Stock:** Walnut with cut checkering, rosewood grip cap and forend tip.
**Sights:** Offered with or without open sights. Open sight model has ramp front and adjustable folding leaf rear.
**Features:** Short 60-degree bolt throw. Top tang safety. Grooved for 22 scope mount. Drilled and tapped for full-size scope mounts. Detachable magazines. Gold-colored trigger preset at about 4 lbs. Imported from Japan by Browning. Introduced 1986.
**Price:** A-Bolt 22, no sights . . . . . . . . . . . . . . . . . . **$374.95**
**Price:** A-Bolt 22, with open sights . . . . . . . . . . . . . . **$384.95**
**Price:** A-Bolt 22 WMR, no sights . . . . . . . . . . . . . . . **$429.95**
**Price:** As above, with sights . . . . . . . . . . . . . . . . . . **$439.95**

## CABANAS MASTER BOLT-ACTION RIFLE
**Caliber:** 177, round ball or pellet; single shot.
**Barrel:** 19½".
**Weight:** 8 lbs. **Length:** 45½" overall.
**Stocks:** Walnut target-type with Monte Carlo.
**Sights:** Blade front, fully adjustable rear.
**Features:** Fires round ball or pellet with 22-cal. blank cartridge. Bolt action. Imported from Mexico by Mandall Shooting Supplies. Introduced 1984.
**Price:** . . . . . . . . . . . . . . . . . . . . . . . . . . . . . . . . . **$159.95**
**Price:** Varmint model (has 21½" barrel, 4½ lbs., 41" o.a.l., varmint-type stock) . . . . . . . . . . . . . . . . . . . . . . . . . . . . . . **$119.95**

## Cabanas Leyre Bolt-Action Rifle
Similar to Master model except 44" overall, has sport/target stock.
**Price:** . . . . . . . . . . . . . . . . . . . . . . . . . . . . . . . . . **$149.95**
**Price:** Model R83 (17" barrel, hardwood stock, 40" o.a.l.) . . . . . . **$79.95**
**Price:** Mini 82 Youth (16½" barrel, 33" o.a.l., 3½ lbs.) . . . . . . . **$69.95**
**Price:** Pony Youth (16" barrel, 34" o.a.l., 3.2 lbs.) . . . . . . . . . . **$69.95**

## CHIPMUNK SINGLE SHOT RIFLE
**Caliber:** 22, S, L, LR, single shot.
**Barrel:** 16⅛".
**Weight:** About 2½ lbs. **Length:** 30" overall.
**Stocks:** American walnut, or camouflage.
**Sights:** Post on ramp front, peep rear adjustable for windage and elevation.
**Features:** Drilled and tapped for scope mounting using special Chipmunk base ($9.95). Made in U.S. Introduced 1982. From Oregon Arms.
**Price:** Standard . . . . . . . . . . . . . . . . . . . . . . . . . . . **$149.95**
**Price:** Deluxe (better wood, checkering) . . . . . . . . . . . . . **$199.95**

**Weight:** About 6.5 lbs. **Length:** NA.
**Stock:** Claro or English walnut in classic design; 13.6" length of pull. Choice of grade. Point panel hand checkering. Swivel studs. Black butt pad.
**Sights:** None furnished; comes with mount bases.
**Features:** Combines features of Winchester 52 and Dakota 76 rifles. Full-sized receiver; rear locking lug and bolt machined from bar stock. Trigger and striker-blocking safety; adjustable trigger. Introduced 1992. From Dakota Arms, Inc.
**Price:** . . . . . . . . . . . . . . . . . . . . . . . . . . . . . . . . . **$995.00**

## KRICO MODEL 300 BOLT-ACTION RIFLES

**Caliber:** 22 LR, 22 WMR, 22 Hornet.
**Barrel:** 19.6" (22 RF), 23.6" (Hornet).
**Weight:** 6.3 lbs. **Length:** 38.5" overall (22 RF).
**Stock:** Walnut-stained beech.
**Sights:** Blade on ramp front, open adjustable rear.

**Features:** Double triggers, sliding safety. Checkered grip and forend. Imported from Germany by Mandall Shooting Supplies.
**Price:** Model 300 Standard . . . . . . . . . . . . . . . . **$700.00**
**Price:** Model 300 Deluxe . . . . . . . . . . . . . . . . . . **$795.00**
**Price:** Model 300 Stutzen (walnut full-length stock) . . . . . . **$825.00**
**Price:** Model 300 SA (walnut Monte Carlo stock) . . . . . . . . **$750.00**

Lakefield Arms Mark II Left-Hand

## LAKEFIELD ARMS MARK II BOLT-ACTION RIFLE

**Caliber:** 22 LR, 10-shot magazine.
**Barrel:** 20½".
**Weight:** 5½ lbs. **Length:** 39½" overall.
**Stock:** Walnut-finished hardwood with Monte Carlo-type comb, checkered grip and forend.
**Sights:** Bead front, open adjustable rear. Receiver grooved for scope mounting.
**Features:** Thumb-operated rotating safety. Blue finish. Introduced 1990. Made in Canada by Lakefield Arms Ltd.
**Price:** About . . . . . . . . . . . . . . . . . . . . . . . . **$124.95**
**Price:** Mark II-Y (youth), 19" barrel, 37" overall, 5 lbs. . . . . . . . **$124.95**
**Price:** Mark II left-hand . . . . . . . . . . . . . . . . . . **$139.95**
**Price:** Mark II-Y (youth) left-hand . . . . . . . . . . . . . **$139.95**

## LAKEFIELD ARMS MARK I BOLT-ACTION RIFLE

**Caliber:** 22 LR, single shot.
**Barrel:** 20½".
**Weight:** 5½ lbs. **Length:** 39½" overall.
**Stock:** Walnut-finished hardwood with Monte Carlo-type comb, checkered grip and forend.
**Sights:** Bead front, open adjustable rear. Receiver grooved for scope mounting.
**Features:** Thumb-operated rotating safety. Blue finish. Rifled or smooth bore. Introduced 1990. Made in Canada by Lakefield Arms Ltd.
**Price:** About . . . . . . . . . . . . . . . . . . . . . . . . **$119.95**
**Price:** Mark I-Y (Youth), 19" barrel, 37" overall, 5 lbs. . . . . . . . **$119.95**

Magtech Model MT-22C

## MAGTECH MODEL MT-22C BOLT-ACTION RIFLE

**Caliber:** 22 S, L, LR, 6- and 10-shot magazines.
**Barrel:** 21" (six-groove).
**Weight:** 5¾ lbs. **Length:** 39" overall.
**Stock:** Brazilian hardwood.
**Sights:** Blade front, open rear adjustable for windage and elevation.
**Features:** Sliding wing-type safety; double extractors; red cocking indicator; receiver grooved for scope mount. Introduced 1991. Imported from Brazil by Magtech Recreational Products, Inc.
**Price:** About . . . . . . . . . . . . . . . . . . . . . . . . **$119.95**

Marlin Model 880

## MARLIN MODEL 880 BOLT-ACTION RIFLE

**Caliber:** 22 LR; 7-shot clip magazine.
**Barrel:** 22" Micro-Groove®.
**Weight:** 5½ lbs. **Length:** 41".
**Stock:** Monte Carlo American black walnut with checkered p.g. and forend. Rubber buttpad, swivel studs. Mar-Shield® finish.
**Sights:** Wide-Scan™ ramp front, folding semi-buckhorn rear adjustable for windage and elevation.
**Features:** Receiver grooved for scope mount. Introduced 1989.
**Price:** . . . . . . . . . . . . . . . . . . . . . . . . . . . . **$217.75**

### Marlin Model 881 Bolt-Action Rifle

Same as the Marlin 880 except tubular magazine, holds 17 Long Rifle, 19 Long, 25 Short cartridges. Weighs 6 lbs.
**Price:** . . . . . . . . . . . . . . . . . . . . . . . . . . . . **$226.85**

### Marlin Model 882 Bolt-Action Rifle

Same as the Marlin 880 except 22 WMR cal. only with 7-shot clip magazine; weight about 6 lbs. Comes with swivel studs.
**Price:** . . . . . . . . . . . . . . . . . . . . . . . . . . . . **$240.05**
**Price:** Model 882L (laminated hardwood stock) . . . . . . . . . **$254.55**

### Marlin Model 883 Bolt-Action Rifle

Same as Marlin 882 except tubular magazine holds 12 rounds of 22 WMR ammunition.
**Price:** . . . . . . . . . . . . . . . . . . . . . . . . . . . . **$248.90**
**Price:** Model 883N (nickel-Teflon finish) . . . . . . . . . . . . . **$274.70**

Marlin Model 883SS

### Marlin Model 883SS Bolt-Action Rifle

Same as the Model 883 except front breech bolt, striker knob, trigger stud, cartridge lifter stud and outer magazine tube are of stainless steel; other parts are nickel-plated. Has two-tone brown laminated Monte Carlo stock with swivel studs, rubber butt pad. Introduced 1993.
**Price:** . . . . . . . . . . . . . . . . . . . . . . . . . . . . **$263.70**

### Marlin Model 25MN Bolt-Action Rifle

Similar to the Model 25N except chambered for 22 WMR. Has 7-shot clip magazine, 22" Micro-Groove® barrel, walnut-finished hardwood stock. Introduced 1989.
**Price:** . . . . . . . . . . . . . . . . . . . . . . . . . . . . **$180.50**

### Marlin Model 25N Bolt-Action Repeater

Similar to Marlin 880, except walnut-finished p.g. stock, adjustable open rear sight, ramp front.
**Price:** . . . . . . . . . . . . . . . . . . . . . . . . . . . . **$158.00**

## MARLIN MODEL 15YN "LITTLE BUCKAROO"
**Caliber:** 22 S, L, LR, single shot.
**Barrel:** 16¼" Micro-Groove;rm.
**Weight:** 4¼ lbs. **Length:** 33¼" overall.
**Stock:** One-piece walnut-finished hardwood with Monte Carlo; Mar-Shield® finish.
**Sights:** Ramp front, adjustable open rear.
**Features:** Beginner's rifle with thumb safety, easy-load feed throat, red cocking indicator. Receiver grooved for scope mounting. Introduced 1989.
**Price:** . . . . . . . . . . . . . . . . . . . . . . . . . . . . . . . . . . . . **$152.15**

## MAUSER MOD
**Caliber:** 22 LR,
**Barrel:** 21".
**Weight:** About
**Stock:** Walnut-
ered grip and
**Sights:** Availa
**Features:** Ha
locking lug
trigger. Re

## Navy
Sim
Bas
Na
**Price**

## Na
ers
S
(
P

## MAUSER MODEL 107 BOLT-ACTION RIFLE
**Caliber:** 22 LR, 5-shot magazine.
**Barrel:** 21.6".
**Weight:** 5.1 lbs. **Length:** 40" overall.
**Stock:** Walnut-stained beechwood with Monte Carlo, checkered grip and forend; sling swivels.
**Sights:** Hooded blade front, adjustable open rear.
**Features:** Dual extractors, 60-degree bolt throw; steel trigger guard and floorplate. Grooved receiver for scope mounting. Satin blue finish. Introduced 1992. Imported from Germany by Precision Imports, Inc.
**Price:** . . . . . . . . . . . . . . . . . . . . . . . . . . . . . . . . . . . . **$330.00**

. . . ling. Introduced 1989. Imported from Germany by Precision Imports, Inc.
. 2 LR with sights . . . . . . . . . . . . . . . . . **$491.00**
As above, no sights . . . . . . . . . . . . . . . **$472.00**
22 WMR with sights . . . . . . . . . . . . . . . **$534.00**
As above, no sights . . . . . . . . . . . . . . . **$515.00**
Luxus, 22 LR with sights . . . . . . . . . . . . **$648.00**
As above, no sights . . . . . . . . . . . . . . . **$621.00**
Luxus, 22 WMR with sights . . . . . . . . . . **$698.00**

## AVY ARMS TU-KKW TRAINING RIFLE
**aliber:** 22 LR, 5-shot detachable magazine.
**arrel:** 26".
**eight:** 8 lbs. **Length:** 44" overall.
**Stock:** Walnut-stained hardwood.
**Sights:** Blade front, open rear adjustable for elevation; military style.
**Features:** Replica of the German WWII training rifle. Polished blue metal. Bayonet lug, cleaning rod, takedown disk in butt. Introduced 1991. Imported by Navy Arms.
**Price:** . . . . . . . . . . . . . . . . . . . . . . . . . . . . . . . . . . . . **$210.00**

Consult our Directory pages for
the location of firms mentioned.

## NORINCO JW-27 BOLT-ACTION RIFLE
**Caliber:** 22 LR, 5-shot magazine.
**Barrel:** 22.75".
**Weight:** 5 lbs., 14 oz. **Length:** 41.75" overall.
**Stock:** Walnut-finished hardwood with checkered grip and forend.
**Sights:** Dovetailed bead on blade front, fully adjustable rear.
**Features:** Receiver grooved for scope mounting. Blued finish. Introduced 1992. Imported from China by Century International Arms.
**Price:** About . . . . . . . . . . . . . . . . . . . . . . . . . . . . . . . . **$106.95**

. . . uced 1991.
. . . to $118.00

Remington 541-T

## REMINGTON 40-XR RIMFIRE CUSTOM SPORTER
**Caliber:** 22 LR.
**Barrel:** 24".
**Weight:** 10 lbs. **Length:** 42½" overall.
**Stock:** Full-sized walnut, checkered p.g. and forend.
**Sights:** None furnished; drilled and tapped for scope mounting.
**Features:** Custom Shop gun. Duplicates Model 700 centerfire rifle.
**Price:** Grade I . . . . . . . . . . . . . . . . . . . . . . . . . . . . . . **$2,186.00**

## REMINGTON 541-T
**Caliber:** 22 S, L, LR, 5-shot clip.
**Barrel:** 24".
**Weight:** 5⅞ lbs. **Length:** 42½" overall.
**Stock:** Walnut, cut-checkered p.g. and forend. Satin finish.
**Sights:** None. Drilled and tapped for scope mounts.
**Features:** Clip repeater. Thumb safety. Reintroduced 1986.
**Price:** About . . . . . . . . . . . . . . . . . . . . . . . . . . . . . . . . **$371.00**

Remington 541-T Heavy Barrel

## Remington 541-T HB Bolt-Action Rifle

Similar to the 541-T except has a heavy target-type barrel without sights. Receiver is drilled and tapped for scope mounting. American walnut stock with straight comb, satin finish, cut checkering, black checkered buttplate, black grip cap and forend tip. Weight is about 6½ lbs. Introduced 1993.

**Price:** . . . . . . . . . . . . . . . . . . . . . . . . . . . . . . **$397.00**

## REMINGTON 581-S SPORTSMAN RIFLE

**Caliber:** 22 S, L or LR, 5-shot clip magazine.
**Barrel:** 24" round.
**Weight:** 4¾ lbs. **Length:** 42⅜" overall.
**Stock:** Walnut-finished hardwood, Monte Carlo with p.g.
**Sights:** Bead post front, screw adjustable open rear.
**Features:** Sliding side safety, wide trigger, receiver grooved for tip-off scope mounts. Comes with single shot adaptor. Reintroduced 1986.
**Price:** About . . . . . . . . . . . . . . . . . . . . . . . . . . . . **$204.00**

Ruger K77/22RSP

## RUGER 77/22 RIMFIRE BOLT-ACTION RIFLE

**Caliber:** 22 LR, 10-shot rotary magazine; 22 WMR, 9-shot rotary magazine.
**Barrel:** 20".
**Weight:** About 5¾ lbs. **Length:** 39¾" overall.
**Stock:** Checkered American walnut or injection-moulded fiberglass-reinforced Du Pont Zytel with Xenoy inserts in forend and grip, stainless sling swivels.
**Sights:** Brass bead front, adjustable folding leaf rear or plain barrel with 1" Ruger rings.

**Features:** Mauser-type action uses Ruger's 10-shot rotary magazine. Three-position safety, simplified bolt stop, patented bolt locking system. Uses the dual screw barrel attachment system of the 10/22 rifle. Integral scope mounting system with 1" Ruger rings. Blued model introduced in 1983. Stainless steel model and blued model with the synthetic stock introduced in 1989.
**Price:** 77/22R (no sights, rings, walnut stock) . . . . . . . . . **$402.00**
**Price:** 77/22RS (open sights, rings, walnut stock) . . . . . . . . **$424.00**
**Price:** 77/22RSP (open sights, rings, synthetic stock) . . . . . . . **$353.00**
**Price:** K77/22RP (stainless, no sights, rings, synthetic stock) . . **$397.00**
**Price:** K77/22RSP (stainless, open sights, rings, synthetic stock) . . **$419.00**
**Price:** 77/22RM (22 WMR, blue, walnut stock) . . . . . . . . . **$402.00**
**Price:** K77/22RSMP (22 WMR, stainless, open sights, rings, synthetic stock) . . . . . . . . . . . . . . . . . . . . . . . . . . **$445.20**
**Price:** K77/22RMP (22 WMR, stainless, synthetic stock) . . . . . . **$419.00**
**Price:** 77/22RSM (22 WMR, blue, open sights, rings, walnut stock) . **$424.00**

Ruger K77/22 Varmint

## RUGER K77/22 VARMINT RIFLE

**Caliber:** 22 WMR, 9-shot detachable rotary magazine.
**Barrel:** 24", heavy.
**Weight:** 7.25 lbs. **Length:** 43.25" overall.
**Stock:** Laminated hardwood with rubber butt pad, quick-detachable swivel studs. No checkering or grip cap.
**Sights:** None furnished. Comes with Ruger 1" scope rings.
**Features:** Made of stainless steel with matte finish. Three-position safety, dual extractors. Stock has wide, flat forend. Introduced 1993.
**Price:** K77/22VBZ . . . . . . . . . . . . . . . . . . . . . . . . . . **$485.00**

Ultra Light Arms Model 20

## ULTRA LIGHT ARMS MODEL 20 RF BOLT-ACTION RIFLE

**Caliber:** 22 LR, single shot or 5-shot repeater.
**Barrel:** 22" Douglas Premium, #1 contour.
**Weight:** 5 lbs., 3 oz. **Length:** 41½" overall.
**Stock:** Composite Kevlar, graphite reinforced. Du Pont Imron paint; 13½" length of pull.
**Sights:** None furnished. Drilled and tapped for scope mounting.
**Features:** Available as either single shot or repeater with 5-shot removable magazine. Comes with scope mounts. Introduced 1993. Made in U.S. by Ultra Light Arms, Inc.
**Price:** . . . . . . . . . . . . . . . . . . . . . . . . . . . . . . . . **$800.00**

Winchester Model 52B

## WINCHESTER MODEL 52B SPORTING RIFLE

**Caliber:** 22 LR, 5-shot magazine.
**Barrel:** 24".
**Weight:** 7 lbs. **Length:** 42⅛" overall.
**Stock:** Walnut, with sculpted cheekpiece.
**Sights:** None furnished. Drilled and tapped for scope mounting.
**Features:** Uses the Model 52C mechanism with stock configuration of the Model 52B. Has Micro-Motion trigger system of the original. Production limited to 6000 rifles. Reintroduced 1993. From U.S. Repeating Arms Co.
**Price:** . . . . . . . . . . . . . . . . . . . . . . . . . . . . . . . . **$576.00**

Includes models for classic American and ISU target competition and other sporting and competitive shooting.

## ANSCHUTZ 64-MS, 64-MS LEFT SILHOUETTE
**Caliber:** 22 LR, single shot.
**Barrel:** 21½", medium heavy; ⅞" diameter.
**Weight:** 8 lbs. **Length:** 39½" overall.
**Stock:** Walnut-finished hardwood, silhouette-type.
**Sights:** None furnished. Receiver drilled and tapped for scope mounting.
**Features:** Uses Match 64 action. Designed for metallic silhouette competition. Stock has stippled checkering, contoured thumb groove with Wundhammer swell. Two-stage #5091 trigger. Slide safety locks sear and bolt. Introduced 1980. Imported from Germany by Precision Sales International.
**Price:** 64-MS . . . . . . . . . . . . . . . . . . . . . . . . . . . . **$912.00**
**Price:** 64-MS Left . . . . . . . . . . . . . . . . . . . . . . . . **$957.00**

## ANSCHUTZ 1827B BIATHLON RIFLE
**Caliber:** 22 LR, 5-shot magazine.
**Barrel:** 21½".
**Weight:** 8½ lbs. with sights. **Length:** 42½" overall.
**Stock:** Walnut-finished hardwood; cheekpiece, stippled pistol grip and forend.
**Sights:** Globe front specially designed for Biathlon shooting, micrometer rear with hinged snow cap.
**Features:** Uses Match 54 action and nine-way adjustable trigger; adjustable wooden buttplate, Biathlon butthook, adjustable hand-stop rail. **Special Order Only.** Introduced 1982. Imported from Germany by Precision Sales International.
**Price:** Right-hand . . . . . . . . . . . . . . . . . . . . . **$2,233.00**
**Price:** With Fortner straight-pull bolt . . . . . . . . . . . . . . . **$3,449.00**
**Price:** As above, left-hand . . . . . . . . . . . . . . . **$3,794.00**

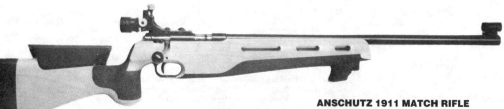

Anschutz 1803D

## Anschutz 1803D Intermediate Match
Similar to the Model 1903D except has blonde-finished European hardwood stock, buttplate and cheekpiece have fewer adjustments. Takes Anschutz #6825 sight set (optional). Weight is 9.5 lbs. Introduced 1991.
**Price:** . . . . . . . . . . . . . . . . . . . . . . . . . . . . **$1,012.00**
**Price:** #6825 sight set . . . . . . . . . . . . . . . . . . **$250.00**

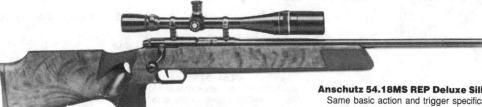

Anschutz 54.18MS REP

## Anschutz 1913 Super Match Rifle
Same as the Model 1911 except European walnut International-type stock with adjustable cheekpiece, adjustable aluminum hook buttplate, adjustable hand stop, weight 15½ lbs., 46" overall. Imported from Germany by Precision Sales International.
**Price:** Right-hand, no sights . . . . . . . . . . . . . . **$2,980.00**
**Price:** M1913 left-hand . . . . . . . . . . . . . . . . . . **$3,148.00**

## Anschutz 1907 Match Rifle
Same action as Model 1913 but with ⅞" diameter 26" barrel. Length is 44½" overall, weight 10 lbs. Blonde wood finish with vented forend. Designed for ISU requirements; suitable for NRA matches.
**Price:** Right-hand, no sights . . . . . . . . . . . . . . **$1,780.00**
**Price:** M1907-L (true left-hand action and stock) . . . . . . . . . **$1,888.00**

## ANSCHUTZ 1808D RT SUPER MATCH 54 TARGET
**Caliber:** 22 LR, single shot.
**Barrel:** 32½".
**Weight:** 9.4 lbs. **Length:** 50½" overall.
**Stock:** Walnut-finished European hardwood. Heavy beavertail forend; adjustable cheekpiece and buttplate. Stippled grip and forend.
**Sights:** None furnished. Grooved for scope mounting.
**Features:** Designed for Running Target competition. Nine-way adjustable single-stage trigger, slide safety. Introduced 1991. Imported from Germany by Precision Sales International.
**Price:** Right-hand . . . . . . . . . . . . . . . . . . . . . **$1,759.00**

## ANSCHUTZ 1903D MATCH RIFLE
**Caliber:** 22 LR, single shot.
**Barrel:** 25", ¾" diameter.
**Weight:** 8.6 lbs. **Length:** 43¾" overall.
**Stock:** Walnut-finished hardwood with adjustable cheekpiece; stippled grip and forend.
**Sights:** None furnished.
**Features:** Uses Anschutz Match 64 action and #5091 two-stage trigger. A medium weight rifle for intermediate and advanced Junior Match competition. Introduced 1987. Imported from Germany by Precision Sales International.
**Price:** Right-hand . . . . . . . . . . . . . . . . . . . . . **$1,070.00**
**Price:** Left-hand . . . . . . . . . . . . . . . . . . . . . . . **$1,143.00**
**Price:** #6823 sight set . . . . . . . . . . . . . . . . . . . **$270.00**

## ANSCHUTZ 1911 MATCH RIFLE
**Caliber:** 22 LR, single shot.
**Barrel:** 27¼" round (1" dia.).
**Weight:** 11 lbs. **Length:** 46" overall.
**Stock:** Walnut-finished European hardwood; American prone style with Monte Carlo, cast-off cheekpiece, checkered p.g., beavertail forend with swivel rail and adjustable swivel, adjustable rubber buttplate.
**Sights:** None. Receiver grooved for Anschutz sights (extra). Scope blocks.
**Features:** Two-stage #5018 trigger adjustable from 2.1 to 8.6 oz. Extremely fast lock time. Imported from Germany by Precision Sales International.
**Price:** Right-hand, no sights . . . . . . . . . . . . . . **$2,086.00**
**Price:** M1911-L (true left-hand action and stock) . . . . . . . . . **$2,209.00**

## Anschutz 54.18MS REP Deluxe Silhouette Rifle
Same basic action and trigger specifications as the Anschutz 1913 Super Match but with removable 5-shot clip magazine, 22" barrel extendable to 30" using optional extension and weight set. Receiver drilled and tapped for scope mounting. Silhouette stock with thumbhole grip is of fiberglass with walnut wood Fibergrain finish. Introduced 1990. Imported from Germany by Precision Sales International.
**Price:** 54.18MS REP Deluxe . . . . . . . . . . . . . . **$1,766.00**
**Price:** 54.18MS Standard with fiberglass stock . . . . . . . . . . . **$2,055.00**

## Anschutz 1910 Super Match II
Similar to the Super Match 1913 rifle except has a stock of European hardwood with tapered forend and deep receiver area. Hand and palm rests not included. Uses Match 54 action. Adjustable hook buttplate and cheekpiece. Sights not included. Introduced 1982. Imported from Germany by Precision Sales International.
**Price:** Right-hand . . . . . . . . . . . . . . . . . . . . . **$2,660.00**
**Price:** Left-hand . . . . . . . . . . . . . . . . . . . . . . . **$2,813.00**

### Anschutz 54.18MS Silhouette Rifle

Same basic features as Anschutz 1913 Super Match but with special metallic silhouette European hardwood stock and two-stage trigger. Has 22" barrel; receiver drilled and tapped.

Price: . . . . . . . . . . . . . . . . . . . . . . . . . . . **$1,488.00**
Price: 54.18MSL (true left-hand version of above) . . . . . . . . . **$1,594.00**

Consult our Directory pages for the location of firms mentioned.

Anschutz 2013

### Anschutz Super Match 54 Target Model 2007

Similar to the Model 2013 except has ISU Standard design European walnut stock. Sights optional. Introduced 1992. Imported from Germany by Precision Sales International.

Price: . . . . . . . . . . . . . . . . . . . . . . . . . . . **$2,650.00**
Price: M2007 left-hand . . . . . . . . . . . . . . . . . . . **$2,736.00**

### ANSCHUTZ SUPER MATCH 54 TARGET MODEL 2013

**Caliber:** 22 LR.
**Barrel:** 19.75" (26" with tube installed).
**Weight:** 15.5 lbs. **Length:** NA.
**Stock:** European walnut; target adjustable.
**Sights:** Optional. Uses #6820 sight set.
**Features:** Improved Super Match 54 action, #5018 trigger give fastest consistent lock time for a production target rifle. Barrel is micro-honed; trigger has nine points of adjustment, two stages. Slide safety. Comes with test target. Introduced 1992. Imported from Germany by Precision Sales International.
Price: . . . . . . . . . . . . . . . . . . . . . . . . . . . **$3,700.00**
Price: M2013 left-hand . . . . . . . . . . . . . . . . . . . **$3,905.00**

Beeman/FWB 2600

### BEEMAN/FEINWERKBAU 2600 TARGET RIFLE

**Caliber:** 22 LR, single shot.
**Barrel:** 26.3".
**Weight:** 10.6 lbs. **Length:** 43.7" overall.
**Stock:** Laminated hardwood and hard rubber.

**Sights:** Globe front with Interchangeable Inserts; micrometer match aperture rear.
**Features:** Identical smallbore companion to the Beeman/FWB 600 air rifle. Free floating barrel. Match trigger has fingertip weight adjustment dial. Introduced 1986. Imported from Germany by Beeman.
Price: Right-hand . . . . . . . . . . . . . . . . . . . **$1,695.00**
Price: Left-hand . . . . . . . . . . . . . . . . . . . **$1,855.00**
Price: Free rifle, right-hand . . . . . . . . . . . . **$2,498.00**
Price: Free rifle, left-hand . . . . . . . . . . . . . **$2,650.00**

Colt Sporter Competition HBAR

### Colt Sporter Competition HBAR Rifle

Similar to the Sporter Target except has flat-top receiver with integral Weaver-type base for scope mounting. Counter-bored muzzle, 1:9" rifling twist. Introduced 1991.
**Price:** Model R6700 . . . . . . . . . . . . . . . . . . . **$989.95**

### Colt Sporter Competition HBAR Range Selected Rifle

Same as the Sporter Competition HBAR #R6700 except is range selected for accuracy, and comes with 3-9x rubber armored scope, scope mount, carrying handle with iron sights, Cordura nylon carrying case. Introduced 1992.
**Price:** Model R6700CH . . . . . . . . . . . . . . . . . . . **$1,489.95**

### Colt Sporter Match HBAR Rifle

Similar to the Target Model except has heavy barrel, 800-meter rear sight adjustable for windage and elevation. Introduced 1991.
Price: . . . . . . . . . . . . . . . . . . . . . . . . . . . **$938.95**

### COLT SPORTER TARGET MODEL RIFLE

**Caliber:** 223 Rem., 5-shot magazine.
**Barrel:** 20".
**Weight:** 7.5 lbs. **Length:** 39" overall.
**Stock:** Composition stock, grip, forend.
**Sights:** Post front, aperture rear adjustable for windage and elevation.
**Features:** Five-round detachable box magazine, standard-weight barrel, flash suppressor, sling swivels. Has forward bolt assist. Military matte black finish. Model introduced 1991.
Price: . . . . . . . . . . . . . . . . . . . . . . . . . . . **$897.95**

### COOPER ARMS MODEL TRP-1 ISU STANDARD RIFLE

**Caliber:** 22 LR, single shot.
**Barrel:** 22".
**Weight:** 10 lbs. **Length:** 40.5" overall.
**Stock:** Walnut, competition style with adjustable cheekpiece and buttpad.
**Sights:** None furnished; accepts Anschutz sight packages.
**Features:** Action has three front locking lugs, 45-degree bolt rotation; fully adjustable single stage trigger; hand-lapped match grade Shilen stainless barrel. Introduced 1991. Made in U.S. by Cooper Arms.
Price: . . . . . . . . . . . . . . . . . . . . . . . . . . . **$1,095.00**
Price: BR-50 (benchrest-style stock) . . . . . . . . . . . **$995.00**
Price: MS-36 (oil-finished silhouette-style stock) . . . . . . . . **$995.00**

**CAUTION:** PRICES CHANGE, CHECK AT GUNSHOP.

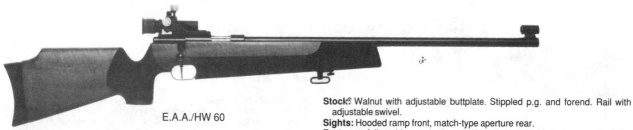

E.A.A./HW 60

**E.A.A./WEIHRAUCH HW 60 TARGET RIFLE**
**Caliber:** 22 LR, single shot.
**Barrel:** 26.8".
**Weight:** 10.8 lbs. **Length:** 45.7" overall.

**Stock:** Walnut with adjustable buttplate. Stippled p.g. and forend. Rail with adjustable swivel.
**Sights:** Hooded ramp front, match-type aperture rear.
**Features:** Adjustable match trigger with push-button safety. Left-hand version also available. Introduced 1981. Imported from Germany by European American Armory.
**Price:** Right-hand . . . . . . . . . . . . . . . . . . . . . . . . . . . **$798.00**
**Price:** Left-hand . . . . . . . . . . . . . . . . . . . . . . . . . . . . **$878.95**

E.A.A./HW 660

**E.A.A./HW 660 MATCH RIFLE**
**Caliber:** 22 LR.
**Barrel:** 26".

**Weight:** 10.7 lbs. **Length:** 45.3" overall.
**Stock:** Match-type walnut with adjustable cheekpiece and buttplate.
**Sights:** Globe front, match aperture rear.
**Features:** Adjustable match trigger; stippled p.g. and forend; forend accessory rail. Introduced 1988. Imported from Germany by European American Armory.
**Price:** About . . . . . . . . . . . . . . . . . . . . . . . . . . . . . . **$875.00**

**FINNISH LION STANDARD TARGET RIFLE**
**Caliber:** 22 LR, single shot.
**Barrel:** 27⅝".
**Weight:** 10½ lbs. **Length:** 44⁹⁄₁₆" overall.
**Stock:** French walnut, target style.
**Sights:** Globe front, International micrometer rear.
**Features:** Optional accessories: palm rest, hook buttplate, forend stop and swivel assembly, buttplate extension, five front sight aperture inserts, three rear sight apertures, Allen wrench. Adjustable trigger. Imported from Finland by Mandall Shooting Supplies.
**Price:** Without sights . . . . . . . . . . . . . . . . . . . . . . **$695.00**
**Price:** Sight set . . . . . . . . . . . . . . . . . . . . . . . . . . . **$195.00**

> Consult our Directory pages for the location of firms mentioned.

Heckler & Koch SR9 (TC)

**HECKLER & KOCH SR9 (TC) TARGET RIFLE**
**Caliber:** 308.
**Barrel:** 19.7" polygonal.
**Weight:** 10.9 lbs. **Length:** NA.
**Stock:** PSG1 adjustable buttstock.
**Sights:** Post front, aperture rear adjustable for windage and elevation.
**Features:** Target/competition version of the SR9 rifle. Has PSG1 butt, trigger group and contoured grip. Introduced 1993. Imported from Germany by Heckler & Koch, Inc.
**Price:** . . . . . . . . . . . . . . . . . . . . . . . . . . . . . . **$1,946.00**

**HECKLER & KOCH PSG-1 MARKSMAN RIFLE**
**Caliber:** 308, 5- and 20-shot magazines.
**Barrel:** 25.6", heavy.
**Weight:** 17.8 lbs. **Length:** 47.5" overall.
**Stock:** Matte black high impact plastic, adjustable for length, pivoting butt cap, vertically-adjustable cheekpiece; target-type pistol grip with adjustable palm shelf.
**Sights:** Hendsoldt 6x42 scope.
**Features:** Uses HK-91 action with low-noise bolt closing device; special forend with T-way rail for sling swivel or tripod. Gun comes in special foam-fitted metal transport case with tripod, two 20-shot and two 5-shot magazines, cleaning rod. Imported from Germany by Heckler & Koch, Inc. Introduced 1986.
**Price:** . . . . . . . . . . . . . . . . . . . . . . . . . . . . . . **$9,325.00**

**KRICO MODEL 360 S2 BIATHLON RIFLE**
**Caliber:** 22 LR, 5-shot magazine.
**Barrel:** 21.25".
**Weight:** 9 lbs., 15 oz. **Length:** 40.55" overall.
**Stock:** Biathlon design of black epoxy-finished walnut with pistol grip.
**Sights:** Globe front, fully adjustable Diana 82 match peep rear.
**Features:** Pistol-grip-activated action. Comes with five magazines (four stored in stock recess), muzzle/sight snow cap. Introduced 1991. Imported from Germany by Mandall Shooting Supplies.
**Price:** . . . . . . . . . . . . . . . . . . . . . . . . . . . . . . **$1,595.00**

**KRICO MODEL 400 MATCH RIFLE**
**Caliber:** 22 LR, 22 Hornet, 5-shot magazine.
**Barrel:** 23.2" (22 LR), 23.6" (22 Hornet).
**Weight:** 8.8 lbs. **Length:** 42.1" overall (22 RF).
**Stock:** European walnut, match type.
**Sights:** None furnished; receiver grooved for scope mounting.
**Features:** Heavy match barrel. Double-set or match trigger. Imported from Germany by Mandall Shooting Supplies.
**Price:** . . . . . . . . . . . . . . . . . . . . . . . . . . . . . . **$950.00**

Krico Model 360S Biathlon

**KRICO MODEL 500 KRICOTRONIC MATCH RIFLE**
**Caliber:** 22 LR, single shot.
**Barrel:** 23.6".
**Weight:** 9.4 lbs. **Length:** 42.1" overall.
**Stock:** European walnut, match type with adjustable butt.
**Sights:** Globe front, match micrometer aperture rear.
**Features:** Electronic ignition system for fastest possible lock time. Completely adjustable trigger. Barrel has tapered bore. Imported from Germany by Mandall Shooting Supplies.
**Price:** . . . . . . . . . . . . . . . . . . . . . . . . . . . . . . **$3,950.00**

**KRICO MODEL 360S BIATHLON RIFLE**
**Caliber:** 22 LR, 5-shot magazine.
**Barrel:** 21.25".
**Weight:** 9.26 lbs. **Length:** 40.55" overall.
**Stock:** Walnut with high comb, adjustable buttplate.
**Sights:** Globe front, fully adjustable Diana 82 match peep rear.
**Features:** Straight-pull action with 17.6-oz. match trigger. Comes with five magazines (four stored in stock recess), muzzle/sight snow cap. Introduced 1991. Imported from Germany by Mandall Shooting Supplies.
**Price:** . . . . . . . . . . . . . . . . . . . . . . . . . . . . **$1,695.00**

**KRICO MODEL 600 SNIPER RIFLE**
**Caliber:** 222, 223, 22-250, 243, 308, 4-shot magazine.
**Barrel:** 23.6".
**Weight:** 9.2 lbs. **Length:** 45.2" overall.
**Stock:** European walnut with adjustable rubber buttplate.
**Sights:** None supplied; drilled and tapped for scope mounting.
**Features:** Match barrel with flash hider; large bolt knob; wide trigger shoe. Parkerized finish. Imported from Germany by Mandall Shooting Supplies.
**Price:** . . . . . . . . . . . . . . . . . . . . . . . . . . . . **$2,645.00**

Krico Model 600 Match

Lakefield Model 92S

**KRICO MODEL 600 MATCH RIFLE**
**Caliber:** 222, 223, 22-250, 243, 308, 5.6x50 Mag., 4-shot magazine.
**Barrel:** 23.6".
**Weight:** 8.8 lbs. **Length:** 43.3" overall.
**Stock:** Match stock of European walnut with cheekpiece.
**Sights:** None furnished; drilled and tapped for scope mounting.
**Features:** Match stock with vents in forend for cooling, rubber recoil pad, sling swivels. Imported from Germany by Mandall Shooting Supplies.
**Price:** . . . . . . . . . . . . . . . . . . . . . . . . . . . . **$1,250.00**

**LAKEFIELD ARMS MODEL 90B TARGET RIFLE**
**Caliber:** 22 LR, 5-shot magazine.
**Barrel:** 21".
**Weight:** 8¼ lbs. **Length:** 39⅝" overall.
**Stock:** Natural finish hardwood with clip holder, carrying and shooting rails, butt hook, hand stop.
**Sights:** Target front with inserts, peep rear with ¼-minute click adjustments.
**Features:** Biathlon-style rifle with snow cap muzzle protector. Comes with five magazines. Introduced 1991. Made in Canada by Lakefield Arms.
**Price:** About . . . . . . . . . . . . . . . . . . . . . . . . **$534.95**
**Price:** left-hand, about . . . . . . . . . . . . . . . . . **$589.95**

**LAKEFIELD ARMS MODEL 91T TARGET RIFLE**
**Caliber:** 22 LR, single shot.
**Barrel:** 25".
**Weight:** 8 lbs. **Length:** 43⅝" overall.
**Stock:** Target-type, walnut-finished hardwood.
**Sights:** Target front with inserts, peep rear with ¼-minute click adjustments.
**Features:** Comes with shooting rail and hand stop. Also available as 5-shot repeater as Model 91-TR. Introduced 1991. Made in Canada by Lakefield Arms.
**Price:** Model 91T . . . . . . . . . . . . . . . . . . . . . . **$424.95**
**Price:** Model 91-TR (repeater) . . . . . . . . . . . . . **$454.95**
**Price:** Model 91-TR left-hand . . . . . . . . . . . . . . **$499.95**

**Lakefield Arms Model 92S Silhouette Rifle**
Similar to the Model 90B except has high-comb target-type stock of walnut-finished hardwood, one 5-shot magazine. Comes without sights, but receiver is drilled and tapped for scope base. Weight about 8 lbs. Introduced 1992. Made in Canada by Lakefield Arms.
**Price:** . . . . . . . . . . . . . . . . . . . . . . . . . . . . . **$364.95**
**Price:** left-hand . . . . . . . . . . . . . . . . . . . . . . . **$399.95**

Marlin Model 2000

**MARLIN MODEL 2000 TARGET RIFLE**
**Caliber:** 22 LR, single shot.
**Barrel:** 22" heavy, Micro-Groove® rifling, match chamber, recessed muzzle.
**Weight:** 8 lbs. **Length:** 41" overall.

**Stock:** High-comb fiberglass/Kevlar with stipple finish grip and forend.
**Sights:** Hooded front with seven aperture inserts, fully adjustable target rear peep.
**Features:** Stock finished with royal blue enamel. Buttplate adjustable for length of pull, height and angle. Aluminum forend rail with stop and quick-detachable swivel. Two-stage target trigger; red cocking indicator. Five-shot adaptor kit available. Introduced 1991. From Marlin.
**Price:** . . . . . . . . . . . . . . . . . . . . . . . . . . . . . **$559.50**

**CAUTION:** PRICES CHANGE, CHECK AT GUNSHOP.

### MAUSER MODEL 86-SR SPECIALTY RIFLE
**Caliber:** 308 Win., 9-shot detachable magazine.
**Barrel:** 25.6", fluted, 1:12 twist.
**Weight:** About 10.8 lbs. **Length:** 47.7" overall.
**Stock:** Laminated wood, fiberglass, or special match thumbhole wood. All have rail in forend and adjustable recoil pad.
**Sights:** None furnished. Competition metallic sights or scope mount optional.

**Features:** Match barrel with muzzlebrake. Action has two front bolt locking lugs. Action bedded in stock with free-floated barrel. Match trigger adjustable as single or two-stage; fully adjustable for weight, slack, and position. Silent safety locks bolt, firing pin. Introduced 1989. Imported from Germany by Precision Imports, Inc.
**Price:** With fiberglass stock . . . . . . . . . . . . . . . . . . . . **$3,921.00**
**Price:** With match thumbhole stock . . . . . . . . . . . . . . . **$4,145.00**

McMillan M-86

### McMILLAN COMBO M-87/M-88 50-CALIBER RIFLE
**Caliber:** 50 BMG, single shot.
**Barrel:** 29", with muzzlebrake.
**Weight:** About 21½ lbs. **Length:** 53" overall.
**Stock:** McMillan fiberglass.
**Sights:** None furnished.
**Features:** Right-handed McMillan stainless steel receiver, chromemoly barrel with 1:15 twist. Introduced 1987. From McMillan Gunworks, Inc.
**Price:** . . . . . . . . . . . . . . . . . . . . . . . . . . . . . . **$4,000.00**
**Price:** M-87R (5-shot repeater) "Combo" . . . . . . . . . . . . **$4,270.00**

### McMILLAN 300 PHOENIX LONG RANGE RIFLE
**Caliber:** 300 Phoenix.
**Barrel:** 28".
**Weight:** 12.5 lbs. **Length:** NA.
**Stock:** Fiberglass with adjustable cheekpiece, adjustable butt plate.
**Sights:** None furnished; comes with rings and bases.
**Features:** Matte black finish; textured stock. Introduced 1992. Made in U.S. by McMillan Gunworks, Inc.
**Price:** . . . . . . . . . . . . . . . . . . . . . . . . . . . . . . **$2,995.00**

### McMILLAN NATIONAL MATCH RIFLE
**Caliber:** 7mm-08, 308, 5-shot magazine.
**Barrel:** 24", stainless steel.
**Weight:** About 11 lbs. (std. bbl.). **Length:** 43" overall.
**Stock:** Modified ISU fiberglass with adjustable buttplate.
**Sights:** Barrel band and Tompkins front; no rear sight furnished.

### McMILLAN M-86 SNIPER RIFLE
**Caliber:** 308, 30-06, 4-shot magazine; 300 Win. Mag., 300 Phoenix, 3-shot magazine.
**Barrel:** 24", McMillan match-grade in heavy contour.
**Weight:** 11¼ lbs. (308), 11½ lbs. (30-06, 300). **Length:** 43½" overall.
**Stock:** Specially designed McHale fiberglass stock with textured grip and forend, recoil pad.
**Sights:** None furnished.
**Features:** Uses McMillan repeating action. Comes with bipod. Matte black finish. Sling swivels. Introduced 1989. From McMillan Gunworks, Inc.
**Price:** . . . . . . . . . . . . . . . . . . . . . . . . . . . . . . **$1,895.00**
**Price:** 300 Phoenix . . . . . . . . . . . . . . . . . . . . . . . . **$2,445.00**

### McMILLAN M-89 SNIPER RIFLE
**Caliber:** 308 Win., 5-shot magazine.
**Barrel:** 28" (with suppressor).
**Weight:** 15 lbs., 4 oz.
**Stock:** McMillan fiberglass; adjustable for length; recoil pad.
**Sights:** None furnished. Drilled and tapped for scope mounting.
**Features:** Uses McMillan repeating action. Comes with bipod. Introduced 1990. From McMillan Gunworks, Inc.
**Price:** Standard (non-suppressed) . . . . . . . . . . . . . . . **$2,200.00**

**Features:** McMillan repeating action with clip slot, Canjar trigger. Match-grade barrel. Available in right-hand only. Fibergrain stock, sight installation, special machining and triggers optional. Introduced 1989. From McMillan Gunworks, Inc.
**Price:** . . . . . . . . . . . . . . . . . . . . . . . . . . . . . . **$2,598.00**

McMillan Long Range

### McMILLAN LONG RANGE RIFLE
**Caliber:** 300 Win. Mag., 7mm Rem. Mag., 300 Phoenix, 338 Lapua, single shot.
**Barrel:** 26", stainless steel, match-grade.

**Weight:** 14 lbs. **Length:** 46½" overall.
**Stock:** Fiberglass with adjustable buttplate and cheekpiece. Adjustable for length of pull, drop, cant and cast-off.
**Sights:** Barrel band and Tompkins front; no rear sight furnished.
**Features:** Uses McMillan solid bottom single shot action and Canjar trigger. Barrel twist 1:12. Introduced 1989. From McMillan Gunworks, Inc.
**Price:** . . . . . . . . . . . . . . . . . . . . . . . . . . . . . . **$2,598.00**

Olymipc International

### OLYMPIC ARMS ULTRAMATCH/INTERNATIONAL MATCH RIFLES
**Caliber:** 223, 20- or 30-shot magazine.
**Barrel:** 20", 24", stainless steel.
**Weight:** 10 lbs., 3 oz. **Length:** 39½" overall (20" barrel).
**Stock:** A2 stowaway butt and grip.
**Sights:** Cut-off carrying handle with scope rail attached (Ultramatch); target peep on International Match.
**Features:** Based on the AR-15 rifle. Broach-cut, free-floating barrel with 1:10 or 1:8.5" twist; fluting optional. Introduced 1985. Made in U.S. by Olympic Arms, Inc.
**Price:** Ultramatch . . . . . . . . . . . . . . . . . . . . . . . . **$1,120.00**
**Price:** International Match . . . . . . . . . . . . . . . . . . . . **$1,200.00**

### Olympic Arms Intercontinental Match Rifle
Similar to the Ultramatch/International Match except 20" barrel only, has woodgrain thumbhole buttstock, magazine well floorplate, 5-shot magazine. Introduced 1992. Made in U.S. by Olympic Arms, Inc.
**Price:** . . . . . . . . . . . . . . . . . . . . . . . . . . . . . . **$1,330.00**

**CAUTION:** PRICES CHANGE, CHECK AT GUNSHOP.

Olympic Service Match

## OLYMPIC ARMS SERVICE MATCH RIFLE
**Caliber:** 223, 20- or 30-shot magazine.
**Barrel:** 20" stainless.
**Weight:** 8¾ lbs. **Length:** 39½" overall.
**Stock:** Black composition A2 standard stock.
**Sights:** Post front, fully adjustable aperture rear.
**Features:** Based on the AR-15 rifle. Conforms to all DCM standards. Barrel is broach-cut and free-floating with 1:10" or 1:8.5" twist; fluting optional. Introduced 1989. Made in U.S. by Olympic Arms, Inc.
**Price:** . . . . . . . . . . . . . . . . . . . . . . . . . . . . . **$875.00**

## OLYMPIC ARMS MULTIMATCH RIFLES
**Caliber:** 223, 20- or 30-shot magazine.
**Barrel:** 16" stainless steel.
**Weight:** 8 lbs., 2 oz. **Length:** 36" overall.
**Stock:** Telescoping or A2 stowaway butt and grip.
**Sights:** Post front, E2 rear (ML1); cut front, cut-off carrying handle with scope rail attached (ML2).
**Features:** Based on the AR-15 rifle. Barrel is broach-cut and free-floating with 1:10" or 1:8.5" twist. Introduced 1991. Made in U.S. by Olympic Arms, Inc.
**Price:** . . . . . . . . . . . . . . . . . . . . . . . . . . . . . **$890.00**

### Olympic Arms AR-15 Match Rifle
Similar to the Service Match except has cut-off carrying handle with scope rail attached, button-rifled 4140 ordnance steel or 416 stainless barrel with 1:9" twist standard, 1:7", 1:12", 1:14" twists optional. Weighs 8 lbs, 5 oz. Introduced 1993. Made in U.S. by Olympic Arms, Inc.
**Price:** . . . . . . . . . . . . . . . . . . . . . . . . . . . . . **$690.00**

Parker-Hale M-85

## PARKER-HALE M-87 TARGET RIFLE
**Caliber:** 308 Win., 243, 6.5x55, 308, 30-06, 300 Win. Mag. (other calibers on request), 5-shot detachable box magazine.
**Barrel:** 26" heavy.
**Weight:** About 10 lbs. **Length:** 45" overall.
**Stock:** Walnut target-style, adjustable for length of pull; solid buttpad; accessory rail with hand-stop. Deeply stippled grip and forend.
**Sights:** None furnished. Receiver dovetailed for Parker-Hale "Roll-Off" scope mounts.
**Features:** Mauser-style action with large bolt knob. Parkerized finish. Introduced 1987. Made by Gibbs Rifle Co., distributed by Navy Arms.
**Price:** . . . . . . . . . . . . . . . . . . . . . . . . **$1,500.00**

## PARKER-HALE M-85 SNIPER RIFLE
**Caliber:** 308 Win., 10-shot magazine.
**Barrel:** 24¼".
**Weight:** 12½ lbs (with scope). **Length:** 45" overall.
**Stock:** McMillan fiberglass (several color patterns available).
**Sights:** Post front adjustable for windage, fold-down rear adjustable for elevation.
**Features:** Comes with quick-detachable bipod, palm stop with rail; sling swivels; matte finish. Made by Gibbs Rifle Co., distributed by Navy Arms.
**Price:** Less scope . . . . . . . . . . . . . . . . . . . . . **$1,950.00**

## QUALITY PARTS V MATCH RIFLE
**Caliber:** 223, 30-shot magazine.
**Barrel:** 20", 24", 26"; 1:9" twist.
**Weight:** NA. **Length:** NA.
**Stock:** Composition.
**Sights:** None furnished; comes with scope mount base installed.
**Features:** Hand-built match gun. Barrel is .950" outside diameter with counterbored crown: integral flash suppressor; upper receiver has brass deflector; free-floating steel handguard accepts laser sight, flashlight, bipod; 5-lb. trigger pull. From Quality Parts Co.
**Price:** From . . . . . . . . . . . . . . . . . . . . . . . . . **$1,200.00**

## QUALITY PARTS XM-15-E2 TARGET MODEL RIFLE
**Caliber:** 223, 30-shot magazine.
**Barrel:** 20", 24", 26"; 1:7" or 1:9" twist; heavy.
**Weight:** NA. **Length:** NA.
**Stock:** Black composition.
**Sights:** Adjustable post front, adjustable aperture rear.
**Features:** Patterned after Colt M-16A2. Chrome-lined barrel with manganese phosphate exterior. Has E-2 lower receiver with push-pin. From Quality Parts Co.
**Price:** 20" match heavy barrel . . . . . . . . . . . . . . . . . **$895.00**
**Price:** 24" match heavy barrel . . . . . . . . . . . . . . . . . **$905.00**
**Price:** 26" match heavy barrel . . . . . . . . . . . . . . . . . **$915.00**

Remington 40-XB

## REMINGTON 40-XB RANGEMASTER TARGET CENTERFIRE
**Caliber:** 222 Rem., 222 Rem. Mag., 223, 220 Swift, 22-250, 6mm Rem., 243, 25-06, 7mm BR Rem., 7mm Rem. Mag., 30-338 (30-7mm Rem. Mag.), 300 Win. Mag., 7.62 NATO (308 Win.), 30-06, single shot.

**Barrel:** 27¼".
**Weight:** 11¼ lbs. **Length:** 47" overall.
**Stock:** American walnut or Kevlar with high comb and beavertail forend stop. Rubber non-slip buttplate.
**Sights:** None. Scope blocks installed.
**Features:** Adjustable trigger pull. Receiver drilled and tapped for sights.
**Price:** Standard s.s., stainless steel barrel, about . . . . . . . . . **$1,109.00**
**Price:** Left-hand . . . . . . . . . . . . . . . . . . . . . . . . **$1,171.00**
**Price:** Model 40-XB KS . . . . . . . . . . . . . . . . . . . . . **$1,265.00**
**Price:** Left-hand . . . . . . . . . . . . . . . . . . . . . . . . **$1,327.00**
**Price:** Extra for repeater model (KS) . . . . . . . . . . . . . . . **$92.00**
**Price:** Extra for 2-oz. trigger . . . . . . . . . . . . . . . . . . **$155.00**

**CAUTION:** PRICES CHANGE, CHECK AT GUNSHOP.

Remington 40-XR KS

## REMINGTON 40-XBBR KS
**Caliber:** 22 BR Rem., 222 Rem., 222 Rem. Mag., 223, 6mmx47, 6mm BR Rem., 7.62 NATO (308 Win.).
**Barrel:** 20" (light varmint class), 24" (heavy varmint class).
**Weight:** 7¼ lbs. (light varmint class); 12 lbs. (heavy varmint class).
**Length:** 38" (20" bbl.), 42" (24" bbl.).
**Stock:** Kevlar.
**Sights:** None. Supplied with scope blocks.
**Features:** Unblued stainless steel barrel, trigger adjustable from 1½ lbs. to 3½ lbs. Special 2-oz. trigger at extra cost. Scope and mounts extra.
**Price:** With Kevlar stock . . . . . . . . . . . . . . . . . . . . . . **$1,345.00**
**Price:** Extra for 2-oz. trigger, about . . . . . . . . . . . . . . . . . . . **$155.00**

## REMINGTON 40-XR KS RIMFIRE POSITION RIFLE
**Caliber:** 22 LR, single shot.
**Barrel:** 24", heavy target.
**Weight:** 10 lbs. **Length:** 43" overall.
**Stock:** Kevlar. Position-style with front swivel block on forend guide rail.
**Sights:** Drilled and tapped. Furnished with scope blocks.
**Features:** Meets all ISU specifications. Deep forend, buttplate vertically adjustable, wide adjustable trigger.
**Price:** About . . . . . . . . . . . . . . . . . . . . . . . . . . . . **$1,265.00**

## REMINGTON 40-XC KS NATIONAL MATCH COURSE RIFLE
**Caliber:** 7.62 NATO, 5-shot.
**Barrel:** 24", stainless steel.
**Weight:** 11 lbs. without sights. **Length:** 43½" overall.
**Stock:** Kevlar, position-style, with palm swell, handstop.
**Sights:** None furnished.
**Features:** Designed to meet the needs of competitive shooters firing the national match courses. Position-style stock, top loading clip slot magazine, anti-bind bolt and receiver, bright stainless steel barrel. Meets all ISU Army Rifle specifications. Adjustable buttplate, adjustable trigger.
**Price:** About . . . . . . . . . . . . . . . . . . . . . . . . . . . . **$1,345.00**

Sako TRG-21

## SAKO TRG-21 BOLT-ACTION RIFLE
**Caliber:** 308 Win., 10-shot magazine.
**Barrel:** 25.75".

**Weight:** 10.5 lbs. **Length:** 46.5" overall.
**Stock:** Reinforced polyurethane with full adjustable cheekpiece and buttplate.
**Sights:** None furnished. Optional quick-detachable, one-piece scope mount base, 1" or 30mm rings.
**Features:** Resistance-free bolt, free-floating heavy stainless barrel, 60-degree bolt lift. Two-stage trigger is adjustable for length, pull, horizontal or vertical pitch. Introduced 1993. Imported from Finland by Stoeger.
**Price:** . . . . . . . . . . . . . . . . . . . . . . . . . . . . . . . **$3,850.00**

Springfield M-1A Match

## STEYR-MANNLICHER MATCH SPG-UIT RIFLE
**Caliber:** 308 Win.
**Barrel:** 25.5".
**Weight:** 10 lbs. **Length:** 44" overall.
**Stock:** Laminated and ventilated. Special UIT Match design.
**Sights:** Steyr globe front, Steyr peep rear.
**Features:** Double-pull trigger adjustable for let-off point, slack, weight of first-stage pull, release force and length; buttplate adjustable for height and length. Meets UIT specifications. Introduced 1992. Imported from Austria by GSI, Inc.
**Price:** . . . . . . . . . . . . . . . . . . . . . . . . . . . . . . . **$3,995.00**

## SPRINGFIELD INC. M-1A SUPER MATCH
**Caliber:** 243, 7mm-08, 308 Win.
**Barrel:** 22", heavy Douglas Premium, or Hart stainless steel.
**Weight:** About 10 lbs. **Length:** 44.31" overall.
**Stock:** Heavy walnut competition stock with longer pistol grip, contoured area behind the rear sight, thicker butt and forend, glass bedded.
**Sights:** National Match front and rear.
**Features:** Has figure-eight-style operating rod guide. Introduced 1987. From Springfield Armory, Inc.
**Price:** About . . . . . . . . . . . . . . . . . . . . . . . . . . . . **$1,849.00**

Steyr-Mannlicher SSG P-I

## Steyr-Mannlicher SSG P-III Rifle
Similar to the SSG P-I except has 26" heavy barrel, diopter match sight bases. Available in 308 only. Has H-S Precision Pro-Series stock (black only). Introduced 1992. Imported from Austria by GSI, Inc.
**Price:** . . . . . . . . . . . . . . . . . . . . . . . . . . . . . . . **$3,162.00**

## STEYR-MANNLICHER SSG P-I RIFLE
**Caliber:** 243, 308 Win.
**Barrel:** 25.6".
**Weight:** 8.6 lbs. **Length:** 44.5" overall.
**Stock:** ABS Cycolac synthetic half-stock. Removable spacers in butt adjusts length of pull from 12¾" to 14".
**Sights:** Hooded blade front, folding leaf rear.
**Features:** Parkerized finish. Choice of interchangeable single- or double-set triggers. Detachable 5-shot rotary magazine (10-shot optional). Receiver grooved for Steyr and Bock Quick Detach mounts. Imported from Austria by GSI, Inc.
**Price:** Synthetic half-stock . . . . . . . . . . . . . . . . . . . . . **$2,043.00**
**Price:** SSG-PII (as above except has large bolt knob, heavy bbl., no sights, forend rail). . . . . . . . . . . . . . . . . . . . . . . . . . . **$2,229.00**

Steyr-Mannlicher SSG P-IV

**Steyr-Mannlicher SSG P-IV Rifle**
Similar to the SSG P-I except has 16.75" heavy barrel with flash hider. Available in 308 only. ABS Cycolac synthetic stock in green or black. Introduced 1992. Imported from Austria by GSI, Inc.
Price: .................................... **$2,603.00**

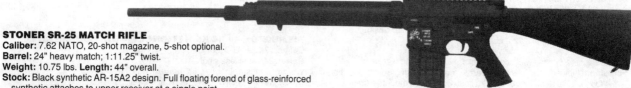

## STONER SR-25 MATCH RIFLE
**Caliber:** 7.62 NATO, 20-shot magazine, 5-shot optional.
**Barrel:** 24" heavy match; 1:11.25" twist.
**Weight:** 10.75 lbs. **Length:** 44" overall.
**Stock:** Black synthetic AR-15A2 design. Full floating forend of glass-reinforced synthetic attaches to upper receiver at a single point.
**Sights:** None furnished. Has integral Weaver-style rail.
**Features:** Modified AR-15 trigger is adjustable for over-travel and sear engagement; AR-15-style seven-lug rotating bolt. Gas block rail takes detachable front sight. Introduced 1993. Made in U.S. by Knight's Mfg. Co.
**Price:** ............... **$2,495.00**

Stoner SR-25 Match

## TANNER 50 METER FREE RIFLE
**Caliber:** 22 LR, single shot.
**Barrel:** 27.7".
**Weight:** 13.9 lbs. **Length:** 44.4" overall.
**Stock:** Seasoned walnut with palm rest, accessory rail, adjustable hook buttplate.
**Sights:** Globe front with interchangeable inserts, Tanner micrometer-diopter rear with adjustable aperture.
**Features:** Bolt action with externally adjustable set trigger. Supplied with 50-meter test target. Imported from Switzerland by Mandall Shooting Supplies. Introduced 1984.
**Price:** About ...................... **$4,000.00**

## TANNER STANDARD UIT RIFLE
**Caliber:** 308, 7.5mm Swiss, 10-shot.
**Barrel:** 25.9".
**Weight:** 10.5 lbs. **Length:** 40.6" overall.
**Stock:** Match style of seasoned nutwood with accessory rail; coarsely stippled pistol grip; high cheekpiece; vented forend.
**Sights:** Globe front with interchangeable inserts, Tanner micrometer-diopter rear with adjustable aperture.
**Features:** Two locking lug revolving bolt encloses case head. Trigger adjustable from ½ to 6½ lbs.; match trigger optional. Comes with 300-meter test target. Imported from Switzerland by Mandall Shooting Supplies. Introduced 1984.
**Price:** About ........................... **$4,700.00**

Tanner 300 Meter

## WICHITA SILHOUETTE RIFLE
**Caliber:** All standard calibers with maximum overall cartridge length of 2.800".
**Barrel:** 24" free-floated Matchgrade.
**Weight:** About 9 lbs.
**Stock:** Metallic gray fiberthane with ventilated rubber recoil pad.
**Sights:** None furnished. Drilled and tapped for scope mounts.
**Features:** Legal for all NRA competitions. Single shot action. Fluted bolt, 2-oz. Canjar trigger; glass-bedded stock. Introduced 1983. From Wichita Arms.
**Price:** ...................... **$2,250.00**
**Price:** Left-hand ............ **$2,400.00**

## TANNER 300 METER FREE RIFLE
**Caliber:** 308 Win., 7.5 Swiss, single shot.
**Barrel:** 27.58".
**Weight:** 15 lbs. **Length:** 45.3" overall.
**Stock:** Seasoned walnut, thumbhole style, with accessory rail, palm rest, adjustable hook butt.
**Sights:** Globe front with interchangeable inserts, Tanner-design micrometer-diopter rear with adjustable aperture.
**Features:** Three-lug revolving-lock bolt design; adjustable set trigger; short firing pin travel; supplied with 300-meter test target. Imported from Switzerland by Mandall Shooting Supplies. Introduced 1984.
**Price:** About ........................... **$4,900.00**

# SHOTGUNS—AUTOLOADERS

Includes a wide variety of sporting guns and guns suitable for various competitions.

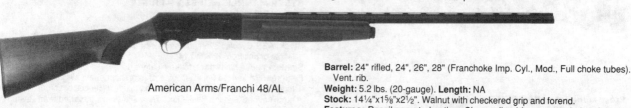

American Arms/Franchi 48/AL

**Barrel:** 24" rifled, 24", 26", 28" (Franchoke Imp. Cyl., Mod., Full choke tubes). Vent. rib.
**Weight:** 5.2 lbs. (20-gauge). **Length:** NA
**Stock:** 14¼"x1⅝"x2½". Walnut with checkered grip and forend.
**Features:** Recoil-operated action. Chrome-lined bore; cross-bolt safety. Imported from Italy by American Arms, Inc.

## AMERICAN ARMS/FRANCHI BLACK MAGIC 48/AL
**Gauge:** 12 or 20, 2¾" chamber.
**Price:** ................................. **$609.00**
**Price:** 12-ga., 24" rifled slug, open sights ............. **$640.00**

CAUTION: PRICES CHANGE, CHECK AT GUNSHOP.

Benelli Slug Gun

## Benelli Super Black Eagle Slug Gun
Similar to the Benelli Super Black Eagle except has 24" E.R. Shaw Custom rifled barrel with 3" chamber, and comes with scope mount base. Uses the Montefeltro inertia recoil bolt system. Matte-finish receiver. Weight is 7.5 lbs., overall length 45.5". Introduced 1992. Imported from Italy by Heckler & Koch, Inc.
**Price:** . . . . . . . . . . . . . . . . . . . . . . . . . . . **$1,079.00**

## BENELLI SUPER BLACK EAGLE SHOTGUN
**Gauge:** 12, 3½" chamber.
**Barrel:** 24", 26", 28" (Imp. Cyl., Mod., Imp. Mod., Full choke tubes).
**Weight:** 7 lbs., 5 oz. **Length:** 49⅝" overall (28" barrel).
**Stock:** European walnut with satin or gloss finish, or polumer. Adjustable for drop.
**Sights:** Bead front.
**Features:** Uses Montfeltro inertia recoil bolt system. Fires all 12-gauge shells from 2¾" to 3½" magnums. Introduced 1991. Imported from Italy by Heckler & Koch, Inc.
**Price:** . . . . . . . . . . . . . . . . . . . . . . . . . . . **$1,079.00**

Benelli M1 Super 90 Field

## Benelli Montefeltro Super 90 20-Gauge Shotgun
Similar to the 12-gauge Montefeltro Super 90 except chambered for 3" 20-gauge, 26" barrel (choke tubes), weighs 5 lbs., 12 oz. Has drop-adjustable walnut stock with gloss finish, blued receiver. Overall length 47.5". Introduced 1993. Imported from Italy by Heckler & Koch, Inc.
**Price:** . . . . . . . . . . . . . . . . . . . . . . . . . . . **$824.00**

## BENELLI M1 SUPER 90 FIELD AUTO SHOTGUN
**Gauge:** 12, 3" chamber.
**Barrel:** 21", 24", 26", 28" (choke tubes).
**Weight:** 7 lbs., 4 oz.
**Stock:** High impact polymer.
**Sights:** Metal bead front.
**Features:** Sporting version of the military & police gun. Uses the rotating Montefeltro bolt system. Ventilated rib; blue finish. Comes with set of five choke tubes. Imported from Italy by Heckler & Koch, Inc.
**Price:** . . . . . . . . . . . . . . . . . . . . . . . . . . . **$799.00**

Benelli Montefeltro Super 90

## BENELLI M1 SPORTING SPECIAL AUTO SHOTGUN
**Gauge:** 12, 3" chamber.
**Barrel:** 18.5" (Imp. Cyl. Mod., Full choke tubes).
**Weight:** 6 lbs., 8 oz. **Length:** 39.75" overall.
**Stock:** Sporting-style polymer with drop adjustment.
**Sights:** Ghost ring.
**Features:** Uses Montefeltro inertia recoil bolt system. Matte-finish receiver. Introduced 1993. Imported from Italy by Heckler & Koch, Inc.
**Price:** . . . . . . . . . . . . . . . . . . . . . . . . . . . **$829.00**

## Benelli Montefeltro Super 90 Shotgun
Similar to the M1 Super 90 except has checkered walnut stock with high-gloss finish. Uses the Montefeltro rotating bolt system with a simple inertia recoil design. Full, Imp. Mod., Mod., Imp. Cyl. choke tubes. Weight is 7-7½ lbs. Finish is matte black. Introduced 1987.
**Price:** 21", 24", 26", 28" . . . . . . . . . . . . . . . . **$824.00**
**Price:** Left-hand, 26", 28" . . . . . . . . . . . . . . . . **$844.00**
**Price:** 20-ga., Montefeltro Super 90, 26", 5¾ lbs. . . . . . . . . **$824.00**

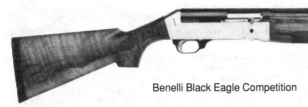

Benelli Black Eagle Competition

## BENELLI BLACK EAGLE COMPETITION AUTO SHOTGUN
**Gauge:** 12, 3" chamber.
**Barrel:** 26", 28" (Full, Mod., Imp. Cyl., Imp. Mod., Skeet choke tubes). Mid-bead sight.
**Weight:** 7.1 to 7.6 lbs. **Length:** 49⅝" overall (26" barrel).
**Stock:** European walnut with high-gloss finish. Special competition stock comes with drop adjustment kit.
**Features:** Uses the Montefeltro rotating bolt inertia recoil operating system with a two-piece steel/aluminum etched receiver (bright on lower, blue upper). Drop adjustment kit allows the stock to be custom fitted without modifying the stock. Black lower receiver finish, blued upper. Introduced 1989. Imported from Italy by Heckler & Koch, Inc.
**Price:** . . . . . . . . . . . . . . . . . . . . . . . . . . . **$1,099.00**

## BERETTA A-303 AUTO SHOTGUN
**Gauge:** 12, 20, 2¾" or 3" chamber.
**Barrel:** 26", 28", Mobilchoke choke tubes.
**Weight:** About 6½ lbs., 20-gauge; about 7½ lbs., 12-gauge.
**Stock:** American walnut; hand-checkered grip and forend.
**Features:** Gas-operated action, alloy receiver, magazine cut-off, push-button safety. Mobilchoke models come with three interchangeable flush-mounted screw-in choke tubes. Imported from Italy by Beretta U.S.A. Introduced 1983.
**Price:** Mobilchoke, 20-ga. . . . . . . . . . . . . . . . . **$755.00**
**Price:** 12-ga. trap with standard trap stock . . . . . . . . . **$735.00**
**Price:** 12- or 20-ga., Skeet . . . . . . . . . . . . . . . . **$735.00**
**Price:** A-303 Youth Gun, 20-ga., 2¾" or 3" chamber, 24" barrel . . . **$735.00**
**Price:** A-303 Sporting Clays with Mobilchoke, 12 or 20 . . . . . . . **$835.00**

### Beretta A-303 Upland Model
Similar to the field A-303 except 12- or 20-gauge, has 24" vent. rib barrel with Mobilchoke choke tubes, 2¾" chamber, straight English-style stock. Introduced 1989.
**Price:** . . . . . . . . . . . . . . . . . . . . . . . . . . . **$735.00**

Beretta A390 Super Trap

## Beretta 390 Super Trap, Super Skeet Shotguns

Similar to the 390 Field except have adjustable-comb stocks that allow height adjustments via interchangeable comb inserts. Rounded recoil pad system allows adjustments for length of pull. Wide ventilated rib with orange front sight. Factory ported barrels in 28" (fixed Skeet), 30", 32" (Mobilchoke tubes). Weight 7 lbs., 10 oz. In 12-gauge only, with 2¾" chamber. Introduced 1993. Imported from Italy by Beretta U.S.A.

**Price:** 390 Super Trap .............................. **$1,210.00**
**Price:** 390 Super Skeet .......................... **$1,160.00**

## BERETTA 390 FIELD AUTO SHOTGUN

**Gauge:** 12, 3" chamber.
**Barrel:** 24", 26", 28", 30", Mobilchoke choke tubes.
**Weight:** About 7 lbs.
**Stock:** Select walnut. Adjustable drop and cast.
**Features:** Gas-operated action with self-compensating valve allows shooting all loads without adjustment. Alloy receiver, reversible safety; chrome-plated bore; floating vent. rib. Matte-finish models for turkey/waterfowl and Deluxe with gold, engraving also available. Introduced 1992. Imported from Italy by Beretta U.S.A.
**Price:** .............................................. **$775.00**
**Price:** Model 390 Field (matte finish) ............... **$775.00**
**Price:** Deluxe model .............................. **$935.00**

Beretta Vittoria

## BERETTA MODEL 1201F AUTO SHOTGUN

**Gauge:** 12, 3" chamber.
**Barrel:** 24", 26", 28" vent. rib with Mobilchoke choke tubes.
**Weight:** 7 lbs., 4 oz.
**Stock:** Special strengthened technopolymer, matte black finish. Adjustable butt and recoil pad.
**Features:** Resists abrasion and adverse effects of water, salt and other damaging materials associated with tough field conditions. Imported from Italy by Beretta U.S.A. Introduced 1988.
**Price:** .............................................. **$625.00**

## BERETTA VITTORIA AUTO SHOTGUN

**Gauge:** 12, 3" chamber.
**Barrel:** 24" (Slug), 24", 26" (choke tubes).
**Weight:** 7 lbs.
**Stock:** Checkered walnut.
**Features:** Montefeltro-type short recoil action. Matte finish on wood and metal. Slug version has rifle sights and rifled choke tube. Comes with sling swivels. Introduced 1993. Imported from Italy by Beretta U.S.A.
**Price:** .............................................. **$700.00**

Browning BSA 10

## Browning BSA 10 Stalker Auto Shotgun

Same as the standard BSA 10 except has non-glare metal finish and black graphite-fiberglass composite stock with dull finish and checkering. Introduced 1993. Imported by Browning.
**Price:** .............................................. **$899.95**
**Price:** Extra barrel .............................. **$229.95**

## BROWNING BSA 10 AUTO SHOTGUN

**Gauge:** 10, 3½" chamber, 5-shot magazine.
**Barrel:** 26", 28", 30" (Imp. Cyl., Mod., Full standard Invector).
**Weight:** 10 lbs, 7 oz. (28" barrel).
**Stock:** 14⅜"x1½"x2⅜". Select walnut with gloss finish, cut checkering, recoil pad.
**Features:** Short-stroke, gas-operated action, cross-bolt safety. Forged steel receiver with polished blue finish. Introduced 1993. Imported by Browning.
**Price:** .............................................. **$899.95**
**Price:** Extra barrel .............................. **$229.95**

Browning A-500G

## BROWNING A-500G AUTO SHOTGUN

**Gauge:** 12, 3" chamber.
**Barrel:** 26", 28", 30", Invector choke tubes. Ventilated rib.
**Weight:** 7 lbs., 14 oz. (26" bbl.). **Length:** 47½" overall.
**Stock:** 14⅜"x1½"x2". Select walnut with gloss finish, rounded pistol grip. Recoil pad standard.
**Features:** Gas-operated action with four-lug rotary bolt, cross-bolt safety. Interchangeable barrels. High-polish blue finish with light engraving on receiver and "A-500G" in gold color. Patented gas metering system to handle all loads. Built-in buffering system to absorb recoil, reduce stress on internal parts. Introduced 1990. Imported by Browning.
**Price:** .............................................. **$652.95**
**Price:** Extra Invector barrels ..................... **$254.95**

## BROWNING A-500R AUTO SHOTGUN

**Gauge:** 12 only, 3" chamber.
**Barrel:** 24" Buck Special, 26", 28", 30" with Invector choke tubes.
**Weight:** 7 lbs., 7 oz. (30" bbl.). **Length:** 49½" overall (30" bbl.).
**Stock:** 14¼"x1½"x2½"; select walnut with gloss finish; checkered p.g. and forend; black vent., recoil pad.
**Sights:** Metal bead front.
**Features:** Uses a short-recoil action with four-lug rotary bolt and composite and coil spring buffering system. Shoots all loads without adjustment. Has a magazine cut-off, Invector chokes. Introduced 1987. Imported from Belgium by Browning.
**Price:** .............................................. **$559.95**
**Price:** A-500R Buck Special ....................... **$592.95**
**Price:** Extra Invector barrel ...................... **$199.95**
**Price:** 24" Buck Special barrel .................... **$232.95**

## Browning A-500G Sporting Clays

Same as the standard A-500G except has 28" or 30" Invector choke barrel, receiver has semi-gloss finish with "Sporting Clays" in gold lettering. Introduced 1992.
**Price:** .............................................. **$652.95**

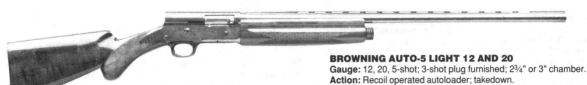

Browning Auto-5

## BROWNING AUTO-5 LIGHT 12 AND 20

**Gauge:** 12, 20, 5-shot; 3-shot plug furnished; 2¾" or 3" chamber.
**Action:** Recoil operated autoloader; takedown.
**Barrel:** 26", 28", 30" Invector (choke tube) barrel; also available with Light 20-ga. 28" (Mod.) or 26" (Imp. Cyl.) barrel.
**Weight:** 12-, 16-ga. 7¼ lbs.; 20-ga. 6⅜ lbs.
**Stock:** French walnut, hand checkered half-p.g. and forend. 14¼"x1⅝"x2½".
**Features:** Receiver hand engraved with scroll designs and border. Double extractors, extra bbls. Interchangeable without factory fitting; mag. cut-off; cross-bolt safety. All 12-gauge models except Buck Special and game guns have back-bored barrels with Invector Plus choke tubes. Imported from Japan by Browning.
**Price:** Light 12, 20, vent. rib., standard Invector . . . . . $719.95
**Price:** Extra Invector barrel . . . . . . . . . . . . . . . . . . . $249.95
**Price:** Light 12 Buck Special . . . . . . . . . . . . . . . . . . $724.95
**Price:** Extra fixed-choke barrel (Light 20 only) . . . . . . $194.95
**Price:** 12, 12 magnum, 20 Buck Special barrel . . . . . . $259.95
**Price:** Light 12, Hunting, Invector Plus . . . . . . . . . . . $734.95

Consult our Directory pages for the location of firms mentioned.

## Browning Auto-5 Stalker
Similar to the Auto-5 Light and Magnum models except has matte blue metal finish and black graphite-fiberglass stock and forend. Stock is scratch and impact resistant and has checkered panels. Light Stalker has 2¾" chamber, 26" or 28" vent. rib barrel with Invector choke tubes, weighs 8 lbs., 1 oz. (26"). Magnum Stalker has 3" chamber, 28" or 30" back-bored vent. rib barrel with Invector choke tubes, weighs 8 lbs., 11 oz. (28"). Introduced 1992.
**Price:** Light Stalker . . . . . . . . . . . . . . . . . . . . $734.95
**Price:** Magnum Stalker . . . . . . . . . . . . . . . . . . $756.95

## Browning Auto-5 Magnum 20
Same as Magnum 12 except 26" or 28" barrel with Invector choke tubes. With ventilated rib, 7½ lbs.
**Price:** Invector only . . . . . . . . . . . . . . . . . . . . . . $742.95
**Price:** Extra Invector barrel . . . . . . . . . . . . . . . . . $249.95

## CHURCHILL TURKEY AUTOMATIC SHOTGUN
**Gauge:** 12, 3" chamber, 5-shot magazine.
**Barrel:** 25" (Mod., Full, Extra Full choke tubes).
**Weight:** 7 lbs.. **Length:** NA.
**Stock:** Walnut with satin finish, hand checkering.
**Features:** Gas-operated action, magazine cut-off, non-glare metal finish. Gold-colored trigger. Introduced 1990. Imported by Ellett Bros.
**Price:** . . . . . . . . . . . . . . . . . . . . . . . . . . . . . . $569.95

## Browning Auto-5 Magnum 12
Same as standard Auto-5 except chambered for 3" magnum shells (also handles 2¾" magnum and 2¾" HV loads). 28" Mod., Full; 30" and 32" (Full) bbls. Back-bored barrel comes with Invector choke tubes. 14"x1⅝"x2½" stock. Recoil pad. Wgt. 8¾ lbs.
**Price:** With standard Invector choke tubes . . . . . . . . $742.95
**Price:** Extra standard Invector barrel . . . . . . . . . . . . $249.95
**Price:** With back-bored barrel, Invector Plus . . . . . . . $756.95
**Price:** Extra Invector Plus barrel . . . . . . . . . . . . . . . $269.95

## COSMI AUTOMATIC SHOTGUN
**Gauge:** 12 or 20, 2¾" or 3" chamber.
**Barrel:** 22" to 34". Choke (including choke tubes) and length to customer specs. Boehler steel.
**Weight:** About 6¼ lbs. (20-ga.).
**Stock:** Length and style to customer specs. Hand-checkered exhibition grade circassian walnut standard.
**Features:** Hand-made, essentially a custom gun. Recoil-operated auto with tip-up barrel. Made completely of stainless steel (lower receiver polished); magazine tube in buttstock holds 7 rounds. Double ejectors, double safety system. Comes with fitted leather case. Imported from Italy by Incor, Inc.
**Price:** From . . . . . . . . . . . . . . . . . . . . . . . . . . $7,400.00

Maverick Model 60

## MAVERICK MODEL 60 AUTO SHOTGUN
**Gauge:** 12, 2¾" or 3" chamber, 5-shot.
**Barrel:** 18½" (2¾" only, Cyl. bore), 24" (Full and Rifled choke tubes), 28" vent rib (Accu-Choke Mod. tube).

**Weight:** 7¼ lbs. **Length:** 48⅜" overall (28" barrel).
**Stock:** Black synthetic.
**Features:** Designated barrels for magnum and non-magnum loads. Blued receiver with action release button. Introduced 1993. Made in U.S. by Maverick Arms, Inc.
**Price:** 28" magnum or non-magnum . . . . . . . . . . . . . $279.00
**Price:** Combo with 18½" and 28" barrels . . . . . . . . . . $312.00
**Price:** Turkey/Deer, Ghost Ring sights, tube combo . . . . . . . . $324.00

Mossberg Model 9200

## MOSSBERG MODEL 9200 REGAL SEMI-AUTO SHOTGUN
**Gauge:** 12, 3" chamber.
**Barrel:** 24" (rifled bore), 28" (Accu-Choke tubes); vent. rib.
**Weight:** About 7.5 lbs. **Length:** 48" overall (28" bbl.).
**Stock:** Walnut with high-gloss finish.
**Features:** Shoots all 2¾" or 3" loads without adjustment. Alloy receiver, ambidextrous top safety. Introduced 1992.
**Price:** 28", vent rib . . . . . . . . . . . . . . . . . . . . . $374.00
**Price:** Turkey, 24" vent rib . . . . . . . . . . . . . . . . . $374.00
**Price:** Trophy, 24" with scope base, rifled bore, Dual-Comb stock . . $393.00
**Price:** 24", rifle sights, rifled bore . . . . . . . . . . . . . $374.00
**Price:** Combo 24" Trophy with scope base, rifled bore, Dual-Comb, and 28" vent rib with Accu-Choke tubes . . . . . . . . . . . . . $441.00
**Price:** Combo 24", rifle sights, rifled bore, and 28" vent rib, Accu-Choke tubes . . . . . . . . . . . . . . . . . . . $433.00

## Mossberg Model 9200 USST Auto Shotgun
Same as the Model 9200 Regal except has "United States Shooting Team" custom engraved receiver. Comes with 26" vent rib barrel with Accu-Choke tubes (including Skeet), walnut-finish stock and forend. Introduced 1993.
**Price:** . . . . . . . . . . . . . . . . . . . . . . . . . . . . . . $374.00

### Mossberg Model 9200 Camo Shotgun

Same as the Model 9200 Regal except completely covered with Mossy Oak Tree Stand or OFM camouflage finish. Available with 24" or 28" barrel with Accu-Choke tubes, or 24" rifled bore with rifle sights, and 28" vent rib with Accu-Choke tubes as Combo model. All have synthetic stock and forend. Introduced 1993.

Price: Turkey, 24" vent rib, Mossy Oak finish . . . . . . . . . . **$436.00**
Price: 28" vent rib, Accu-Chokes, OFM camo finish . . . . . . . **$393.00**
Price: Combo, 24", rifled bore, rifle sights, with 28" vent rib, Accu-Chokes, OFM camo finish . . . . . . . . . . . . . . . . . . . **$456.000**

### Mossberg Model 6000 Auto Shotgun

Similar to the Model 9200 Regal except comes only with 28" vent rib barrel—Magnum shoots 2¾" or 3" loads, Non-Magnum 2¾" only. Supplied with one Mod. Accu-Choke tube. Walnut-finish stock and forend. Introduced 1993.
Price: . . . . . . . . . . . . . . . . . . . . . . . . . . . . . . . . . **$321.00**

Remington 11-87 Sporting Clays

### REMINGTON 11-87 SPORTING CLAYS

Gauge: 12, 2¾" chamber.
Barrel: 26", 28", vent. rib, Rem Choke (Skeet, Imp. Cyl., Mod., Full); Light Contour barrel. Medium height rib.
Weight: 7.5 lbs. Length: 46.5" overall (26" barrel).
Stock: 14³⁄₁₆"x1½"x2¼". Walnut, with cut checkering; sporting clays butt pad.
Features: Top of receiver, barrel and rib have matte finish; shortened magazine tube and forend; lengthened forcing cone; ivory bead front sight; competition trigger. Special no-wrench choke tubes marked on the outside. Comes in two-barrel fitted hard case. Introduced 1992.
Price: . . . . . . . . . . . . . . . . . . . . . . . . . . . . . . . . . **$725.00**

### Remington 11-87 Premier Skeet

Similar to 11-87 Premier except Skeet dimension stock with cut checkering, satin finish, two-piece buttplate; 26" barrel with Skeet or Rem Chokes (Skeet, Imp. Skeet). Gas system set for 2¾" shells only. Introduced 1987.
Price: . . . . . . . . . . . . . . . . . . . . . . . . . . . . . . . . . **$669.00**
Price: Left-hand . . . . . . . . . . . . . . . . . . . . . . . . . . . **$735.00**

### REMINGTON 11-87 PREMIER SHOTGUN

Gauge: 12, 3" chamber.
Barrel: 26", 28", 30" Rem Choke tubes. Light Contour barrel.
Weight: About 8¼ lbs. Length: 46" overall (26" bbl.).
Stock: Walnut with satin or high-gloss finish; cut checkering; solid brown buttpad; no white spacers.
Sights: Bradley-type white-faced front, metal bead middle.
Features: Pressure compensating gas system allows shooting 2¾" or 3" loads interchangeably with no adjustments. Stainless magazine tube; redesigned feed latch, barrel support ring on operating bars; pinned forend. Introduced 1987.
Price: . . . . . . . . . . . . . . . . . . . . . . . . . . . . . . . . . **$637.00**
Price: Left-hand . . . . . . . . . . . . . . . . . . . . . . . . . . . **$699.00**
Price: Premier Cantilever Deer Barrel, scope rings, sling, swivels, Monte Carlo stock . . . . . . . . . . . . . . . . . . . . . . . . . . . **$679.00**

### Remington 11-87 Premier Trap

Similar to 11-87 Premier except trap dimension stock with straight or Monte Carlo combs; select walnut with satin finish and Tournament-grade cut checkering; 30" barrel with Rem Chokes (Trap Full, Trap Extra Full, Trap Super Full). Gas system set for 2¾" shells only. Introduced 1987.
Price: With straight stock, Rem Choke . . . . . . . . . . . . . . **$667.00**
Price: With Monte Carlo stock . . . . . . . . . . . . . . . . . . . **$692.00**
Price: Left-hand, straight stock . . . . . . . . . . . . . . . . . . **$745.00**
Price: Left-hand, Monte Carlo stock . . . . . . . . . . . . . . . **$761.00**

Remington 11-87 SPS-T Camo

### Remington 11-87 SPS-T Camo Auto Shotgun

Similar to the 11-87 Special Purpose Magnum except with synthetic stock, 21" vent rib barrel with Super-Full Turkey (.665" diameter with knurled extension) and Imp. Cyl. Rem Choke tubes. Completely covered with Mossy Oak Green Leaf camouflage. Bolt body, trigger guard and recoil pad are non-reflective black. Introduced 1993.
Price: . . . . . . . . . . . . . . . . . . . . . . . . . . . . . . . . . **$700.00**

### Remington 11-87 Special Purpose Magnum

Similar to the 11-87 Premier except has dull stock finish, Parkerized exposed metal surfaces. Bolt and carrier have dull blackened coloring. Comes with 26" or 28" barrel with Rem Chokes, padded Cordura nylon sling and q.d. swivels. Introduced 1987.
Price: . . . . . . . . . . . . . . . . . . . . . . . . . . . . . . . . . **$619.00**
Price: With synthetic stock and forend (SPS) . . . . . . . . . . **$619.00**
Price: Magnum-Turkey with synthetic stock (SPS-T) . . . . . . **$632.00**

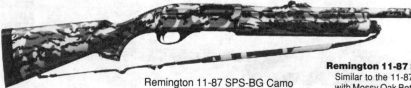

Remington 11-87 SPS-BG Camo

### Remington 11-87 Special Purpose Deer Gun

Similar to the 11-87 Special Purpose Magnum except has 21" barrel with rifle sights, rifled and Imp. Cyl. choke tubes. Gas system set to handle all 2¾" and 3" slug, buckshot, high velocity field and magnum loads. Not designed to function with light 2¾" field loads. Introduced 1987.
Price: . . . . . . . . . . . . . . . . . . . . . . . . . . . . . . . . . **$599.00**
Price: With cantilever scope mount, rings . . . . . . . . . . . . **$653.00**

### Remington 11-87 SPS-Deer Shotgun

Similar to the 11-87 Special Purpose Deer except has fully-rifled 21" barrel with rifle sights, black non-reflective, synthetic stock and forend, black carrying sling. Introduced 1993.
Price: . . . . . . . . . . . . . . . . . . . . . . . . . . . . . . . . . **$625.00**

### Remington 11-87 SPS-BG-Camo Deer/Turkey Shotgun

Similar to the 11-87 Special Purpose Deer Gun except completely covered with Mossy Oak Bottomland camouflage, comes with Super-Full Turkey Rem Choke tube of .665" diameter with knurled end-ring, Rifled choke tube insert, and an Imp. Cyl. tube. Synthetic stock and forend, quick-detachable swivels, camo Cordura carrying sling. Barrel is 21" with rifle sights, 3" chamber. Introduced 1993.
Price: . . . . . . . . . . . . . . . . . . . . . . . . . . . . . . . . . **$683.00**

### Remington 11-87 Special Purpose Synthetic Camo

Similar to the 11-87 Special Purpose Magnum except has synthetic stock and all metal (except bolt and trigger guard) surfaces covered with Mossy Oak Bottomland camo finish. In 12-gauge only, 26", 28" vent. rib, Rem Choke. Comes with camo sling, swivels. Introduced 1992.
Price: . . . . . . . . . . . . . . . . . . . . . . . . . . . . . . . . . **$687.00**

### Remington SP-10 Magnum Camo

**Remington SP-10 Magnum-Camo Auto Shotgun**
Similar to the SP-10 Magnum except buttstock, forend, receiver, barrel and magazine cap are covered with Mossy Oak Bottomland camo finish; bolt body and trigger guard have matte black finish. Comes with Extra-Full Turkey Rem Choke tube, 23" vent rib barrel with mid-rib bead and Bradley-style front sight, swivel studs and quick-detachable swivels, and a non-slip Cordura carrying sling in the same camo pattern. Introduced 1993.
**Price:** . . . . . . . . . . . . . . . . . . . . . . . . . . . . . . **$1,105.00**

**REMINGTON SP-10 MAGNUM AUTO SHOTGUN**
**Gauge:** 10, 3½" chamber, 3-shot magazine.
**Barrel:** 26", 30" (Full and Mod. Rem Chokes).
**Weight:** 11 to 11¼ lbs. **Length:** 47½" overall (26" barrel).
**Stock:** Walnut with satin finish. Checkered grip and forend.
**Sights:** Metal bead front.
**Features:** Stainless steel gas system with moving cylinder; ⅜" ventilated rib. Receiver and barrel have matte finish. Brown recoil pad. Comes with padded Cordura nylon sling. Introduced 1989.
**Price:** . . . . . . . . . . . . . . . . . . . . . . . . . . . . . . **$966.00**

**Remington SP-10 Magnum Turkey Combo**
Combines the SP 10 with 26" or 30" vent. rib barrel, plus extra 22" rifle-sighted barrel with Mod., Full, Extra-Full Turkey Rem Choke tubes. Comes with camo sling, swivels. Introduced 1991.
**Price:** . . . . . . . . . . . . . . . . . . . . . . . . . . . . . . **$1,104.00**

### Remington 1100 Special Field

**Remington 1100 Special Field**
Similar to standard Model 1100 except 12- and 20-ga. only, comes with 21" Rem Choke barrel. LT-20 version 6½ lbs.; has straight-grip stock, shorter forend, both with cut checkering. Comes with vent. rib only; matte finish receiver without engraving. Introduced 1983.
**Price:** 12- and 20-ga., 21" Rem Choke, about . . . . . . . . . **$589.00**

**Remington 1100 20-Gauge Deer Gun**
Same as 1100 except 20-ga. only, 21" barrel (Imp. Cyl.), rifle sights adjustable for windage and elevation; recoil pad with white spacer. Weight 7¼ lbs.
**Price:** About . . . . . . . . . . . . . . . . . . . . . . . . . . . . **$532.00**

**REMINGTON 1100 LT-20 AUTO**
**Gauge:** 20, 28, 410.
**Barrel:** 25" (Full, Mod.), 26", 28" with Rem Chokes.
**Weight:** 7½ lbs.
**Stock:** 14"x1½"x2½". American walnut, checkered p.g. and forend.
**Features:** Quickly interchangeable barrels. Matted receiver top with scroll work on both sides of receiver. Cross-bolt safety.
**Price:** With Rem Chokes, 20-ga. about . . . . . . . . . . . . **$589.00**
**Price:** 28 and 410 . . . . . . . . . . . . . . . . . . . . . . . . **$633.00**
**Price:** Youth Gun LT-20 (21" Rem Choke) . . . . . . . . . . . **$576.00**
**Price:** 20-ga., 3" magnum . . . . . . . . . . . . . . . . . . . . **$589.00**

**Remington 1100 LT-20 Tournament Skeet**
Same as the 1100 except 26" barrel, special Skeet boring, vent. rib, ivory bead front and metal bead middle sights. 14"x1½"x2½" stock. 20-, 28-gauge, 410-bore. Weight 7½ lbs., cut checkering, walnut, new receiver scroll.
**Price:** Tournament Skeet (28, 410), about . . . . . . . . . . . **$670.00**
**Price:** Tournament Skeet (20), about . . . . . . . . . . . . . . **$670.00**

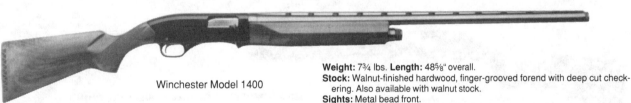

### Winchester Model 1400

**WINCHESTER MODEL 1400 SEMI-AUTO SHOTGUN**
**Gauge:** 12 and 20, 2¾" chamber.
**Barrel:** 22", 26", 28" vent. rib with Winchoke tubes (Imp. Cyl., Mod., Full).

**Weight:** 7¾ lbs. **Length:** 48⅝" overall.
**Stock:** Walnut-finished hardwood, finger-grooved forend with deep cut checkering. Also available with walnut stock.
**Sights:** Metal bead front.
**Features:** Cross-bolt safety, front-locking rotary bolt, black serrated buttplate, gas-operated action. From U.S. Repeating Arms Co., Inc.
**Price:** Ranger, vent. rib with Winchoke . . . . . . . . . . . . **$367.00**
**Price:** As above with walnut stock (1400 Walnut) . . . . . . . **$407.00**
**Price:** Ranger Deer barrel combo . . . . . . . . . . . . . . . . **$423.00**

# SHOTGUNS—SLIDE ACTIONS

Includes a wide variety of sporting guns and guns suitable for competitive shooting.

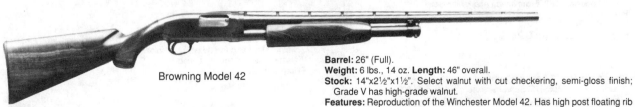

### Browning Model 42

**BROWNING MODEL 42 PUMP SHOTGUN**
**Gauge:** 410-bore, 3" chamber.

**Barrel:** 26" (Full).
**Weight:** 6 lbs., 14 oz. **Length:** 46" overall.
**Stock:** 14"x2½"x1½". Select walnut with cut checkering, semi-gloss finish; Grade V has high-grade walnut.
**Features:** Reproduction of the Winchester Model 42. Has high post floating rib with grooved sighting plane; cross-bolt safety in trigger guard; polished blue finish. Limited to 6000 Grade I and 6000 Grade V guns. Introduced 1991. Imported from Japan by Browning.
**Price:** Model 42, Grade I . . . . . . . . . . . . . . . . . . . . . **$799.95**
**Price:** Model 42, Grade V . . . . . . . . . . . . . . . . . . . . . **$1,360.00**

**CAUTION:** PRICES CHANGE, CHECK AT GUNSHOP.

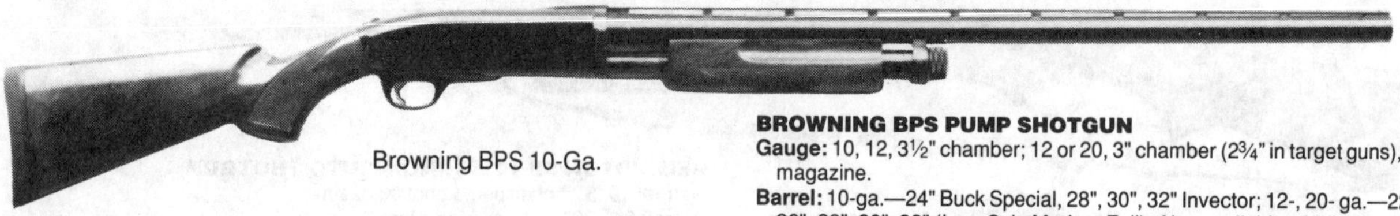

Browning BPS 10-Ga.

## Browning BPS Stalker Pump Shotgun
Same gun as the standard BPS except all exposed metal parts have a matte blued finish and the stock has a durable black finish with a black recoil pad. Available in 10-ga. (3½") and 12-ga. with 3" or 3½" chamber, 22", 28", 30" barrel with Invector choke system. Introduced 1987.
**Price:** 12-ga., 3" chamber, Invector Plus . . . . . . . . . . . . . . . **$462.95**
**Price:** 10-, 12-ga., 3½" chamber . . . . . . . . . . . . . . . . . . . . **$584.95**

## Browning BPS Pigeon Grade Pump shotgun
Same as the standard BPS except has select high grade walnut stock and forend, and gold-trimmed receiver. Available in 12-gauge only with 26" or 28" vent. rib barrels. Introduced 1992.
**Price:** . . . . . . . . . . . . . . . . . . . . . . . . . . . . . . . . . . . . . **$599.95**
**Price:** 10-gauge Waterfowl Model . . . . . . . . . . . . . . . . . . **$749.95**

## Browning BPS Pump Shotgun (Ladies and Youth Model)
Same as BPS Upland Special except 20-ga. only, 22" Invector barrel, stock has pistol grip with recoil pad. Length of pull is 13¼". Introduced 1986.
**Price:** . . . . . . . . . . . . . . . . . . . . . . . . . . . . . . . . . . . . . **$442.95**

## BROWNING BPS PUMP SHOTGUN
**Gauge:** 10, 12, 3½" chamber; 12 or 20, 3" chamber (2¾" in target guns), 5-shot magazine.
**Barrel:** 10-ga.—24" Buck Special, 28", 30", 32" Invector; 12-, 20- ga.—22", 24", 26", 28", 30", 32" (Imp. Cyl., Mod. or Full). Also available with Invector choke tubes, 12- or 20-ga.; Upland Special has 22" barrel with Invector tubes. BPS 3" and 3½" have back-bored barrel.
**Weight:** 7 lbs., 8 oz. (28" barrel). **Length:** 48¾" overall (28" barrel).
**Stock:** 14¼"x1½"x2½". Select walnut, semi-beavertail forend, full p.g. stock.
**Features:** All 12-gauge 3" guns except Buck Special and game guns have back-bored barrels with Invector Plus choke tubes. Bottom feeding and ejection, receiver top safety, high post vent. rib. Double action bars eliminate binding. Vent. rib barrels only. All 12- and 20-gauge guns with 3" chamber available with fully engraved receiver flats at no extra cost. Each gsuge has its own unique game scene. Introduced 1977. Imported from Japan by Browning.
**Price:** 10-ga., Hunting, Invector . . . . . . . . . . . . . . . . . . . . **$584.95**
**Price:** 12-ga., 3½" Mag., Hunting, Invector Plus . . . . . . . . . **$584.95**
**Price:** 12-ga., Hunting, Invector Plus . . . . . . . . . . . . . . . . . **$462.95**
**Price:** 12-, 20-ga., Upland Special, Invector . . . . . . . . . . . . **$442.95**
**Price:** 10-ga. and 3½" 12-ga. Mag., Buck Special . . . . . . . . **$589.95**
**Price:** 12-ga. Buck Special . . . . . . . . . . . . . . . . . . . . . . . . **$448.95**

## Browning BPS Game Gun Turkey Special
Similar to the standard BPS except has satin-finished walnut stock and dull-finished barrel and receiver. Receiver is drilled and tapped for scope mounting. Rifle-style stock dimensions and swivel studs. Has Extra-Full Turkey choke tube. Introduced 1992.
**Price:** . . . . . . . . . . . . . . . . . . . . . . . . . . . . . . . . . . . . . **$499.95**

Browning BPS Game Deer

## Browning BPS Game Gun Deer Special
Similar to the standard BPS except has newly designed receiver/magazine tube/barrel mounting system to eliminate play, heavy 20.5" barrel with rifle-type sights with adjustable rear, solid receiver scope mount, "rifle" stock dimensions for scope or open sights, sling swivel studs. Gloss-finish wood with checkering, polished blue metal. Introduced 1992.
**Price:** . . . . . . . . . . . . . . . . . . . . . . . . . . . . . . . . . . . . . **$527.95**

Ithaca Model 87 Supreme

## ITHACA MODEL 87 DEERSLAYER SHOTGUN
**Gauge:** 12, 20, 3" chamber.
**Barrel:** 20", 25" (Special Bore), or rifled bore.
**Weight:** 6 to 6¾ lbs.
**Stock:** 14"x1½"x2¼". American walnut. Checkered p.g. and slide handle.
**Sights:** Raybar blade front on ramp, rear adjustable for windage and elevation, and grooved for scope mounting.
**Features:** Bored for slug shooting. Bottom ejection, cross-bolt safety. Reintroduced 1988. From Ithaca Acquisition Corp.
**Price:** . . . . . . . . . . . . . . . . . . . . . . . . . . . . . . . . . . . . . **$391.00**
**Price:** Deluxe . . . . . . . . . . . . . . . . . . . . . . . . . . . . . . . . . **$430.00**
**Price:** Field Deerslayer, Basic . . . . . . . . . . . . . . . . . . . . . . **$363.00**

## Ithaca Model 87 Turkey Gun
Similar to the Model 87 Supreme except comes with 22" or 24" (fixed Full or Full choke tube) barrel, either Camoseal camouflage or matte blue finish, oiled wood, blued trigger.
**Price:** With fixed choke, blue . . . . . . . . . . . . . . . . . . . . . . **$380.00**
**Price:** With choke tube, blue . . . . . . . . . . . . . . . . . . . . . . . **$394.00**
**Price:** With fixed choke, Camoseal . . . . . . . . . . . . . . . . . . **$422.00**
**Price:** With choke tube, Camoseal . . . . . . . . . . . . . . . . . . . **$436.00**

## ITHACA MODEL 87 SUPREME PUMP SHOTGUN
**Gauge:** 12, 20, 3" chamber, 5-shot magazine.
**Barrel:** 26" (Imp. Cyl., Mod., Full tubes), 28" (Mod.), 30" (Full). Vent. rib.
**Weight:** 6¾ to 7 lbs.
**Stock:** 14"x1½"x2¼". Full fancy-grade walnut, checkered p.g. and slide handle.
**Sights:** Raybar front.
**Features:** Bottom ejection, cross-bolt safety. Polished and blued engraved receiver. Reintroduced 1988. From Ithaca Acquisition Corp.
**Price:** . . . . . . . . . . . . . . . . . . . . . . . . . . . . . . . . . . . . . **$668.00**
**Price:** M87 Camo Vent. (28", Mod. choke tube, camouflage finish) . **$457.00**
**Price:** M87 English (20-ga., 24", 26", choke tubes) . . . . . . . . . **$462.50**
**Price:** M87 Deluxe Vent, 12, 20, 26", 28", 30", choke tubes) . . . . . **$462.50**

## Ithaca Deerslayer II Rifled Shotgun
Similar to the Deerslayer except has rifled 25" barrel and checkered American walnut stock and forend with high-gloss finish and Monte Carlo comb. Solid frame construction. Introduced 1988.
**Price:** 12 or 20 . . . . . . . . . . . . . . . . . . . . . . . . . . . . . . . . **$525.00**

## Ithaca Model 87 Deluxe Pump Shotgun
Similar to the Model 87 Supreme Vent. Rib except comes with choke tubes in 25", 26", 28" (Mod.), 30" (Full). Standard-grade walnut.
**Price:** . . . . . . . . . . . . . . . . . . . . . . . . . . . . . . . . . . . . . **$463.00**

**CAUTION:** PRICES CHANGE, CHECK AT GUNSHOP.

Magtech Model 586-VR

**Weight:** 8.5 lbs. **Length:** 46.5" overall (26" barrel).
**Stock:** Brazilian hardwood.
**Features:** Double action slide bars. Ventilated rib with bead front sight. Polished blue finish. Introduced 1993. Imported from Brazil by Magtech Recreational Products.
**Price:** Model 586-VR, about . . . . . . . . . . . . . . . . . . . . **$255.00**
**Price:** Model 586 (as above, plain barrel), about . . . . . . . . **$225.00**
**Price:** Model 586-S (24" barrel, rifle sights), about . . . . . . . . **$235.00**

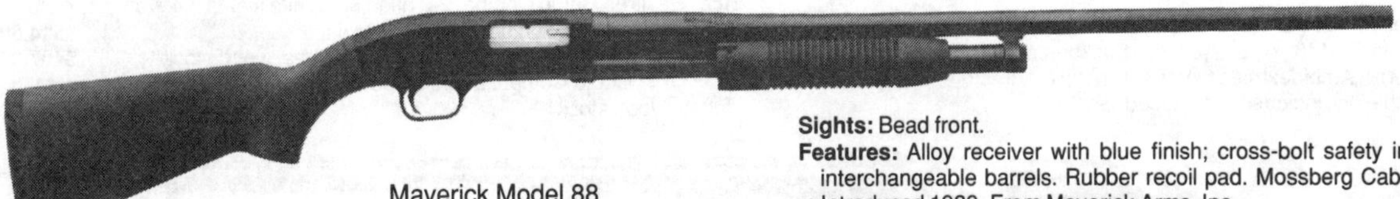

## MAGTECH MODEL 586-VR PUMP SHOTGUN
**Gauge:** 12, 3" chamber.
**Barrel:** 26", 28", choke tubes.

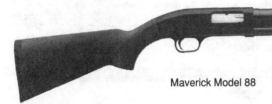

Maverick Model 88

**Sights:** Bead front.
**Features:** Alloy receiver with blue finish; cross-bolt safety in trigger guard; interchangeable barrels. Rubber recoil pad. Mossberg Cablelock included. Introduced 1989. From Maverick Arms, Inc.
**Price:** Model 88, synthetic stock, 28", 30" plain bbl. . . . . . . . **$205.00**
**Price:** Model 88, synthetic stock, 28", 30" vent. rib . . . . . . . . . **$212.00**
**Price:** Model 88, synthetic stock, 24" with rifle sights . . . . . . . . **$215.00**
**Price:** Model 88, synthetic stock, Combo 18½", 28" plain bbl. . . . . **$230.00**
**Price:** Model 88, synthetic stock, Combo 18½" (plain), 28" (vent. rib) **$238.00**
**Price:** Model 91, synthetic stock, 28" plain bbl. with one Full steel shot choke tube . . . . . . . . . . . . . . . . . . . . . . . . . . . **$226.00**
**Price:** As above, vent. rib bbl. . . . . . . . . . . . . . . . . . . . . **$234.00**

## MAVERICK MODELS 88, 91 PUMP SHOTGUNS
**Gauge:** 12, 3" chamber; 3½" chamber (Model 91).
**Barrel:** 18½" (Cyl.), 28" (Mod.), plain or vent. rib; 30" (Full), plain or vent. rib.
**Weight:** 7¼ lbs. **Length:** 48" overall with 28" bbl.
**Stock:** Black synthetic with ribbed synthetic forend.

Mossberg Model 500 Sporting

## Mossberg Model 500 Camo Pump
Same as the Model 500 Sporting Pump except 12-gauge only and entire gun is covered with special camouflage finish. Receiver drilled and tapped for scope mounting. Comes with q.d. swivel studs, swivels, camouflage sling, Mossberg Cablelock.
**Price:** From about . . . . . . . . . . . . . . . . . . . . . . . . . **$299.00**
**Price:** Camo Combo (as above with extra Slugster barrel), from about **$353.00**

## MOSSBERG MODEL 500 TROPHY SLUGSTER
**Gauge:** 12, 3" chamber.
**Barrel:** 24", rifled bore. Plain (no rib).
**Weight:** 7¼ lbs. **Length:** 44" overall.
**Stock:** 14" pull, 1⅜" drop at heel. Walnut; Dual Comb design for proper eye positioning with or without scoped barrels. Recoil pad and swivel studs.
**Features:** Ambidextrous thumb safety, twin extractors, dual slide bars. Comes with scope mount. Mossberg Cablelock included. Introduced 1988.
**Price:** Rifled bore, with scope mount . . . . . . . . . . . . . . . **$327.00**
**Price:** Rifled bore, rifle sights . . . . . . . . . . . . . . . . . . . **$300.00**
**Price:** Cyl. bore. rifle sights . . . . . . . . . . . . . . . . . . . . **$266.00**

## MOSSBERG MODEL 500 SPORTING PUMP
**Gauge:** 12, 20, 410, 3" chamber.
**Barrel:** 18½" to 28" with fixed or Accu-Choke, with Accu-II tubes or Accu-Steel tubes for steel shot, plain or vent. rib.
**Weight:** 6¼ lbs. (410), 7¼ lbs. (12). **Length:** 48" overall (28" barrel).
**Stock:** 14"x1½"x2½". Walnut-stained hardwood. Checkered grip and forend.
**Sights:** White bead front, brass mid-bead.
**Features:** Ambidextrous thumb safety, twin extractors, disconnecting safety, dual action bars. Mossberg Cablelock included. From Mossberg.
**Price:** From about . . . . . . . . . . . . . . . . . . . . . . . . . **$253.00**
**Price:** Sporting Combos (field barrel and Slugster barrel), from . . . **$281.00**

## Mossberg Model 500 Muzzleloader Combo
Same as the Model 500 Sporting Pump except comes with 28" vent. rib Accu-Choke barrel with Imp. Cyl., Mod. and Full choke tubes and 24" fully rifled 50-caliber muzzle-loading barrel and ramrod. Uses #209 standard primer. Introduced 1992.
**Price:** . . . . . . . . . . . . . . . . . . . . . . . . . . . . . . . **$399.00**

Mossberg Model 500 Bantam

## Mossberg Model 500 Bantam Pump
Same as the Model 500 Sporting Pump except 20-gauge only, 22" vent. rib Accu-Choke barrel with three choke tubes; has 1" shorter stock, reduced length from pistol grip to trigger, reduced forend reach. Introduced 1992.
**Price:** . . . . . . . . . . . . . . . . . . . . . . . . . . . . . . . **$253.00**
**Price:** Bantam Jake, Accu-Choke tubes, matte blue, Realtree camo on stock and forend . . . . . . . . . . . . . . . . . . . . . . . . . . **$318.00**

## Mossberg Turkey Model 500 Pump
Same as the Model 500 Sporting Pump except has overall OFM camo finish, Ghost-Ring sights, Accu-Choke barrel with Imp. Cyl., Mod., Full, Extra-Full lead shot choke tubes, 24" barrel, swivel studs, camo sling. Introduced 1992.
**Price:** . . . . . . . . . . . . . . . . . . . . . . . . . . . . . . . **$353.00**

## Mossberg Field Grade Model 835 Pump Shotgun
Same as the Model 835 Regal except has walnut-stained hardwood stock and comes only with Modified choke tube, 28" barrel. Introduced 1992.
**Price:** . . . . . . . . . . . . . . . . . . . . . . . . . . . . . . . **$284.00**
**Price:** Turkey, 24", Extra-Full choke tube . . . . . . . . . . . . . **$284.00**
**Price:** Combo, 24" Cyl. bore, rifle sights, and 28" vent rib with Mod. tube . . . . . . . . . . . . . . . . . . . . . . . . . . . **$321.00**

**CAUTION:** PRICES CHANGE, CHECK AT GUNSHOP.

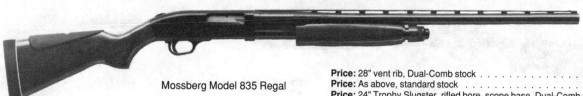

Mossberg Model 835 Regal

## MOSSBERG MODEL 835 REGAL ULTI-MAG PUMP
**Gauge:** 12, 3½" chamber.
**Barrel:** 24" rifled bore, 24", 28", Accu-Mag with four choke tubes for steel or lead shot.
**Weight:** 7¾ lbs. **Length:** 48½" overall.
**Stock:** 14"x1½"x2½". Dual Comb. Walnut or camo synthetic; both have recoil pad.
**Sights:** White bead front, brass mid-bead.
**Features:** Shoots 2¾", 3" or 3½" shells. Backbored barrel to reduce recoil, improve patterns. Ambidextrous thumb safety, twin extractors, dual slide bars. Mossberg Cablelock included. Introduced 1988.

**Price:** 28" vent rib, Dual-Comb stock . . . . . . . . . . . . . $381.00
**Price:** As above, standard stock . . . . . . . . . . . . . $374.00
**Price:** 24" Trophy Slugster, rifled bore, scope base, Dual-Comb stock $400.00
**Price:** Combo, 24" rifled bore, rifle sights, 28" vent rib, Accu-Mag choke tubes, Dual-Comb stock . . . . . . . . . . . . . $429.00
**Price:** Combo, 24" Trophy Slugster rifled bore, 28" vent rib, Accu-Mag choke tubes, Dual-Comb stock . . . . . . . . . . . . . $435.00
**Price:** Realtree Camo Turkey, 24" vent rib, Accu-Mag Extra-Full tube, synthetic stock . . . . . . . . . . . . . $436.00
**Price:** Realtree Camo, 28" vent rib, Accu-Mag tubes, synthetic stock $436.00
**Price:** Realtree Camo Combo, 24" rifled bore, rifle sights, 24" vent rib, Accu-Mag choke tubes, synthetic stock, hard case . . . . $514.00
**Price:** OFM Camo, 28" vent rib, Accu-Mag tubes, wood stock . . . . $407.00
**Price:** OFM Camo Combo, 24" rifled bore, rifle sights, 28" vent rib, Accu-Mag tubes, wood stock . . . . . . . . . . . . . $453.00

Remington 870 Wingmaster

### Remington 870 Special Purpose Deer Gun
Similar to the 870 Wingmaster except available with 20" barrel with rifled and Imp. Cyl. choke tubes; rifle sights or cantilever scope mount with rings. Metal has black, non-glare finish, satin finish on wood. Recoil pad, detachable sling of camo Cordura nylon. Introduced 1989.
**Price:** With rifle sights, Monte Carlo stock . . . . . . . . . . . . . $412.00
**Price:** With scope mount and rings, Monte Carlo stock . . . . . . $497.00

## REMINGTON 870 WINGMASTER
**Gauge:** 12, 3" chamber.
**Barrel:** 26", 28", 30" (Rem Chokes). Light Contour barrel.
**Weight:** 7¼ lbs. **Length:** 46½" overall (26" bbl.).
**Stock:** 14"x2½"x1". American walnut with satin or high-gloss finish, cut-checkered p.g. and forend. Rubber buttpad.
**Sights:** Ivory bead front, metal mid-bead.
**Features:** Double action bars; cross-bolt safety; blue finish. Available in right- or left-hand style. Introduced 1986.
**Price:** . . . . . . . . . . . . . $469.00
**Price:** Left-hand (28" only) . . . . . . . . . . . . . $529.00
**Price:** Deer Gun (rifle sights, 20" bbl.) . . . . . . . . . . . . . $439.00
**Price:** Deer Gun, left-hand, Monte Carlo stock . . . . . . . . . $495.00
**Price:** LW-20 20-ga., vent. rib, 26", 28" (Rem Choke) . . . . . . . $460.00

Remington 870 SPS-BG-Camo

### Remington 870 SPS-Deer Shotgun
Similar to the 870 Special Purpose Deer excet has fully-rifled 20" barrel with rifle sights, black non-reflective, synthetic stock and forend, black carrying sling. Introduced 1993.
**Price:** . . . . . . . . . . . . . $385.00

### Remington 870 Marine Magnum
Similar to the 870 Wingmaster except all metal is plated with electroless nickel and has black synthetic stock and forend. Has 18" plain barrel (Cyl.), bead front sight, 7-shot magazine. Introduced 1992.
**Price:** . . . . . . . . . . . . . $448.00

### Remington 870 SPS-BG-Camo Deer/Turkey Shotgun
Similar to the 870 Special Purpose Deer Gun except completely covered with Mossy Oak Bottomland camouflage, comes with Super-Full Turkey Rem Choke tube of .665" diameter with knurled end-ring, Rifled choke tube insert, and an Imp. Cyl. tube. Synthetic stock and forend, quick-detachable swivels, camo Cordura carrying sling. Barrel is 20" with rifle sights, 3" chamber. Introduced 1993.
**Price:** . . . . . . . . . . . . . $443.00

### Remington 870 TC Trap
Same as the Model 870 except 12-ga. only, 30" Rem Choke, vent. rib barrel, Ivory front and white metal middle beads. Special sear, hammer and trigger assembly. 14⅜"x1½"x1⅞" stock with recoil pad. Hand fitted action and parts. Weight 8 lbs.
**Price:** Model 870TC Trap, Rem Choke, about . . . . . . . . . . $613.00
**Price:** TC Trap with Monte Carlo stock, about . . . . . . . . . $628.00

Remington 870 SPS Camo

### Remington 870 Wingmaster Small Gauges
Same as the standard Model 870 Wingmaster except chambered for 20-ga. (2¾" and 3"), 28-ga., and 410-bore. The 20-ga. available with 26", 28" vent. rib barrel with Rem Choke tubes, high-gloss or satin wood finish; 28 and 410 available with 25" Full or Mod. fixed choke, satin finish only.
**Price:** 20-ga. . . . . . . . . . . . . . $460.00
**Price:** 20-ga. Deer Gun, rifle sights . . . . . . . . . . . . . $412.00
**Price:** 28 and 410 . . . . . . . . . . . . . $504.00

### Remington 870 Special Purpose Synthetic Camo
Similar to the 870 Special Purpose Magnum except has synthetic stock and all metal (except bolt and trigger guard) and stock covered with Mossy Oak Bottomland camo finish, In 12-gauge only, 26", 28" vent. rib, Rem Choke. Comes with camo sling, swivels. Introduced 1992.
**Price:** . . . . . . . . . . . . . $433.00

### Remington 870 Express Rifle-Sighted Deer Gun
Same as the Model 870 Express except comes with 20" barrel with fixed Imp. Cyl. choke, open iron sights, Monte Carlo stock. Introduced 1991.
**Price:** . . . . . . . . . . . . . $273.00
**Price:** With fully rifled barrel . . . . . . . . . . . . . $304.00

**CAUTION:** PRICES CHANGE, CHECK AT GUNSHOP.

## Remington 870 SPS Special Purpose Magnum

Similar to the Model 870 except chambered only for 12-ga., 3" shells, vent. rib. 26" or 28" Rem Choke barrel. All exposed metal surfaces are finished in dull, non-reflective black. Black synthetic stock and forend. Comes with padded Cordura 2" wide sling, quick-detachable swivels. Chrome-lined bores. Dark recoil pad. Introduced 1985.

**Price:** . . . . . . . . . . . . . . . . . . . **$367.00**
**Price:** Magnum-Turkey (synthetic stock, forend) SPS-T . . . . . . . **$393.00**

## Remington 870 SPS-T Camo Pump Shotgun

Similar to the 870 Special Purpose Magnum except with synthetic stock, 21" vent rib barrel with Super-Full Turkey (.665" diameter with knurled extension) and Imp. Cyl. Rem Choke tubes. Completely covered with Mossy Oak Green Leaf camouflage. Bolt body, trigger guard and recoil pad are non-reflective black. Introduced 1993.

**Price:** . . . . . . . . . . . . . . . . . . . **$447.00**

Remington 870 Special Field

## Remington 870 Special Field

Similar to the standard Model 870 except comes with 21" barrel only, 3" chamber, choked Imp. Cyl., Mod., Full and Rem Choke; 12-ga. weighs 6¾ lbs., LW-20 weighs 6 lbs.; has straight-grip stock, shorter forend, both with cut checkering. Vent. rib barrel only. Introduced 1984.

**Price:** 12- or 20-ga., Rem Choke, about . . . . . . . . . . . . . . **$460.00**

## Remington Model 870 Express Youth Gun

Same as the Model 870 Express except comes with 12½" length of pull, 21" barrel with Mod. Rem Choke tube. Hardwood stock with low-luster finish. Introduced 1991.

**Price:** . . . . . . . . . . . . . . . . . . . **$277.00**

## Remington 870 Express Turkey

Same as the Model 870 Express except comes with 3" chamber, 21" vent. rib turkey barrel and Extra-Full Rem Choke Turkey tube; 12-ga. only. Introduced 1991.

**Price:** . . . . . . . . . . . . . . . . . . . **$292.00**

## Remington 870 High Grades

Same as 870 except better walnut, hand checkering. Engraved receiver and barrel. Vent. rib. Stock dimensions to order.

**Price:** 870D, about . . . . . . . . . . . . . . **$2,509.00**
**Price:** 870F, about . . . . . . . . . . . . . . **$5,169.00**
**Price:** 870F with gold inlay, about . . . . . . . . . . . . . . . . **$7,752.00**

## Remington 870 Express

Similar to the 870 Wingmaster except has a walnut-toned hardwood stock with solid, black recoil pad and pressed checkering on grip and forend. Outside metal surfaces have a black oxide finish. Comes with 26" or 28" vent. rib barrel with a Mod. Rem Choke tube. Introduced 1987.

**Price:** 12 or 20 . . . . . . . . . . . . . . **$277.00**
**Price:** Express Combo (with extra 20" Deer barrel), 12 or 20 . . . . **$376.00**
**Price:** Express 20-ga., 28" with Mod. Rem Choke tubes . . . . . . **$277.00**
**Price:** 410-bore . . . . . . . . . . . . . . **$292.00**

Winchester Model 12

### WINCHESTER MODEL 12 PUMP SHOTGUN

**Gauge:** 20, 2¾" chamber, 5-shot magazine.
**Barrel:** 26" (Imp. Cyl.). Vent rib.

**Weight:** 7 lbs. **Length:** 45" overall.
**Stock:** 14"x2½"x1½". Select walnut with satin finish. Checkered grip and forend.
**Features:** Grade I has plain blued receiver; production limited to 4000 guns. Grade IV receiver has engraved game scenes and gold highlights identical to traditional Grade IV, and is limited to 1000 guns. Introduced 1993. From U.S. Repeating Arms Co.

**Price:** Grade I . . . . . . . . . . . . . . **$879.00**
**Price:** Grade IV . . . . . . . . . . . . . . **$1,431.00**

Winchester Model 42

### WINCHESTER MODEL 42 HIGH GRADE SHOTGUN

**Gauge:** 410, 2¾" chamber.
**Barrel:** 26" (Full).
**Weight:** 7 lbs. **Length:** 45" overall.
**Stock:** 14"x2½"x1½". High grade walnut with checkered grip and forend.
**Features:** Engraved receiver with gold inlays. Production of only 850 guns. Introduced 1993. From U.S. Repeating Arms Co.

**Price:** . . . . . . . . . . . . . . . . . . . **$1,617.00**

Winchester Model 1300 Walnut

### WINCHESTER MODEL 1300 WALNUT PUMP

**Gauge:** 12 and 20, 3" chamber, 5-shot capacity.
**Barrel:** 22", 26", 28", vent. rib, with Full, Mod., Imp. Cyl. Winchoke tubes.
**Weight:** 6⅜ lbs. **Length:** 42⅝" overall.
**Stock:** American walnut, with deep cut checkering on pistol grip, traditional ribbed forend; high luster finish.
**Sights:** Metal bead front.
**Features:** Twin action slide bars; front-locking rotary bolt; roll-engraved receiver; blued, highly polished metal; cross-bolt safety with red indicator. Introduced 1984. From U.S. Repeating Arms Co., Inc.

**Price:** . . . . . . . . . . . . . . . . . . . **$374.00**
**Price:** Model 1300 Ladies/Youth, 22" vent. rib . . . . . . . . . . . **$312.00**

Consult our Directory pages for the location of firms mentioned.

Winchester Model 1300 Slug Hunter Deer

## Winchester Model 1300 Slug Hunter Deer Gun
Same as the Model 1300 except has rifled 22" barrel, walnut stock, rifle-type sights. Introduced 1990.
**Price:** Walnut stock . . . . . . . . . . . . . . . . . . . . . . . . **$445.00**
**Price:** Whitetails Unlimited model . . . . . . . . . . . . . . . . . **$449.00**

## Winchester Model 1300 Ranger Pump Gun Combo & Deer Gun
Similar to the standard Ranger except comes with two barrels: 22" (Cyl.) deer barrel with rifle-type sights and an interchangeable 28" vent. rib Winchoke barrel with Full, Mod. and Imp. Cyl. choke tubes. Drilled and tapped; comes with rings and bases. Available in 12- and 20-gauge 3" only, with recoil pad. Introduced 1983.
**Price:** Deer Combo with two barrels . . . . . . . . . . . . . . **$368.00**
**Price:** 12- or 20-ga., 22" (Cyl.) . . . . . . . . . . . . . . . . . **$294.00**
**Price:** 12-ga., 22" rifled barrel . . . . . . . . . . . . . . . . . **$333.00**
**Price:** 12-ga., 22" (Imp. Cyl., rifled sabot tubes) . . . . . . . . **$345.00**
**Price:** Combo 12-ga. with 18" (Cyl.) and 28" (Mod. tube) . . . . . **$368.00**
**Price:** Rifled Deer Combo (22" rifled and 28" vent. rib barrels, 12 or 20-ga.) . . . . . . . . . . . . . . . . . . . . . . . . . **$390.00**

> Consult our Directory pages for the location of firms mentioned.

## Winchester Model 1300 Turkey Gun
Similar to the standard Model 1300 Walnut except 12-ga. only, 22" barrel with Mod., Full and Extra Full Winchoke tubes, matte finish wood and metal. Comes with recoil pad, Cordura sling and swivels.
**Price:** With WinCam green camo laminated stock, about . . . . . . **$435.00**
**Price:** National Wild Turkey Federation Series III and IV . . . . . . **$458.00**

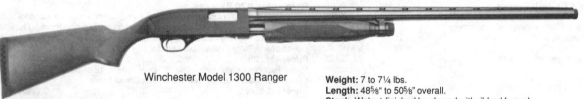

Winchester Model 1300 Ranger

## WINCHESTER MODEL 1300 RANGER PUMP GUN
**Gauge:** 12 or 20, 3" chamber, 5-shot magazine.
**Barrel:** 26", 28" vent. rib with Full, Mod., Imp. Cyl. Winchoke tubes.

**Weight:** 7 to 7¼ lbs.
**Length:** 48⅝" to 50⅝" overall.
**Stock:** Walnut-finished hardwood with ribbed forend.
**Sights:** Metal bead front.
**Features:** Cross-bolt safety, black rubber recoil pad, twin action slide bars, front-locking rotating bolt. From U.S. Repeating Arms Co., Inc.
**Price:** Vent. rib barrel, Winchoke . . . . . . . . . . . . . . . . **$294.00**

# SHOTGUNS—OVER/UNDERS

Includes a variety of game guns and guns for competitive shooting.

American Arms/Franchi Falconet

## AMERICAN ARMS/FRANCHI FALCONET 2000 O/U
**Gauge:** 12, 2¾" chambers.
**Barrel:** 26" (Imp. Cyl., Mod., Full Franchoke tubes).

**Weight:** 6 lbs.
**Stock:** Checkered walnut; 14¼" length of pull.
**Sights:** White flourescent bead front.
**Features:** Silvered boxlock action with gold-plated game scene; single selective trigger; automatic selective ejectors. Reintroduced 1992. Imported from Italy by American Arms, Inc.
**Price:** . . . . . . . . . . . . . . . . . . . . . . . . . . . . . **$1,419.00**

American Arms Silver I

## American Arms Silver II Shotgun
Similar to the Silver I except 26" barrel (Imp. Cyl., Mod., Full choke tubes, 12- and 20-ga.), 28" (Imp. Cyl., Mod., Full choke tubes, 12-ga. only), 26" (Imp. Cyl. & Mod. fixed chokes, 28 and 410), 26" two-barrel set (Imp. Cyl. & Mod. fixed, 28 and 410); automatic selective ejectors. Weight is about 6 lbs., 15 oz. (12-ga., 26").
**Price:** . . . . . . . . . . . . . . . . . . . . . . . . . . . . . . **$699.00**
**Price:** 28, 410 . . . . . . . . . . . . . . . . . . . . . . . . . . **$719.00**
**Price:** Two-barrel set (28, 410) . . . . . . . . . . . . . . . . . **$1,129.00**

## AMERICAN ARMS SILVER I O/U
**Gauge:** 12, 20, 28, 410, 3" chamber (28 has 2¾").
**Barrel:** 26" (Imp. Cyl. & Mod., all gauges), 28" (Mod. & Full, 12, 20).
**Weight:** About 6¾ lbs.
**Stock:** 14⅛"x1⅜"x2⅜". Checkered walnut.
**Sights:** Metal bead front.
**Features:** Boxlock action with scroll engraving, silver finish. Single selective trigger, extractors. Chrome-lined barrels. Manual safety. Rubber recoil pad. Introduced 1987. Imported from Italy and Spain by American Arms, Inc.
**Price:** 12- or 20-gauge . . . . . . . . . . . . . . . . . . . . . . **$549.00**
**Price:** 28 or 410 . . . . . . . . . . . . . . . . . . . . . . . . . **$609.00**

CAUTION: PRICES CHANGE, CHECK AT GUNSHOP.

# SHOTGUNS—OVER/UNDERS

## American Arms Silver Skeet O/U
Similar to the Silver II except has 28" ported barrels with elongated forcing cones, target-type vent. rib with two bead sights. Stock dimensions: 14⅜"x1⅜"x2⅜". Weighs 7 lbs., 6 oz. Comes with Skeet, Skeet, Imp. Cyl., Mod. choke tubes. Introduced 1992. Imported by American Arms, Inc.
**Price:** . . . . . . . . . . . . . . . . . . . . . . . . . . . . $899.00

American Arms Silver Sporting

## American Arms Silver Trap O/U
Similar to the Silver II except has 30" ported barrels with elongated forcing cones, target-type vent. rib with two sight beads. Stock dimensions: 14⅜"x1½"x1⅝". Weight is 7 lbs., 12 oz. Comes with Mod., Imp. Mod., Full, Full choke tubes. Introduced 1992. Imported by American Arms, Inc.
**Price:** . . . . . . . . . . . . . . . . . . . . . . . . . . . . $899.00

American Arms WS/OU 12

## American Arms WT/OU 10 Shotgun
Similar to the WS/OU 12 except chambered for 10-gauge 3½" shell, 26" (Full & Full, choke tubes) barrel. Single selective trigger, extractors. Non-reflective finish on wood and metal. Imported by American Arms, Inc.
**Price:** . . . . . . . . . . . . . . . . . . . . . . . . . . . . $945.00

## ARMSPORT 2700 O/U GOOSE GUN
**Gauge:** 10, 3½" chambers.
**Barrel:** 28" (Full & Imp. Mod.), 32" (Full & Full).
**Weight:** About 9.8 lbs.
**Stock:** European walnut.
**Features:** Boss-type action; double triggers; extractors. Introduced 1986. Imported from Italy by Armsport.
**Price:** Fixed chokes . . . . . . . . . . . . . . . . $1,190.00
**Price:** With choke tubes . . . . . . . . . . . . . $1,299.00

## ARMSPORT 2900 TRI-BARREL SHOTGUN
**Gauge:** 12, 3" chambers.
**Barrel:** 28" (Imp., Mod., Full).
**Weight:** 7¾ lbs.
**Stock:** European walnut.
**Features:** Has three barrels. Top-tang barrel selector; double triggers; silvered, engraved frame. Introduced 1986. Imported from Italy by Armsport.
**Price:** . . . . . . . . . . . . . . . . . . . . . . . . . $3,400.00

## AMERICAN ARMS/FRANCHI SPORTING 2000 O/U
**Gauge:** 12, 2¾" chambers.
**Barrel:** 28" (Skeet, Imp. Cyl., Mod., Full Franchoke tubes).
**Weight:** 7.75 lbs.
**Stock:** Checkered walnut.
**Sights:** White flourescent bead front.
**Features:** Blued boxlock action with single selective mechanical trigger, automatic selective ejectors; ported barrels. Introduced 1992. Imported from Italy by American Arms, Inc.
**Price:** . . . . . . . . . . . . . . . . . . . . . . . . . $1,619.00

## AMERICAN ARMS SILVER SPORTING O/U
**Gauge:** 12, 2¾" chambers.
**Barrel:** 28", 30" (Skeet, Imp. Cyl., Mod., Full choke tubes).
**Weight:** 7⅜ lbs. **Length:** 45½" overall.
**Stock:** 14⅜"x1½"x2⅜". Figured walnut, cut checkering; Sporting Clays quick-mount buttpad.
**Sights:** Target bead front.
**Features:** Boxlock action with single selective trigger, automatic selective ejectors; special broadway channeled rib; vented barrel rib; chrome bores. Chrome-nickel finish on frame, with engraving. Introduced 1990. Imported from Italy by American Arms, Inc.
**Price:** . . . . . . . . . . . . . . . . . . . . . . . . . . . $899.00

## AMERICAN ARMS WS/OU 12, TS/OU 12 SHOTGUNS
**Gauge:** 12, 3½" chambers.
**Barrel:** WS/OU—28" (Imp. Cyl., Mod., Full choke tubes); TS/OU—24" (Imp. Cyl., Mod., Full choke tubes).
**Weight:** 6 lbs., 15 oz. **Length:** 46" overall.
**Stock:** 14⅛"x1⅛"x2⅜". European walnut with cut checkering, black vented recoil pad, matte finish.
**Features:** Boxlock action with single selective trigger, automatic selective ejectors; chrome bores. Matte metal finish. Imported by American Arms, Inc.
**Price:** . . . . . . . . . . . . . . . . . . . . . . . . . . . $719.00

## ARMSPORT 2700 SERIES O/U
**Gauge:** 10, 12, 20, 28, 410.
**Barrel:** 26" (Imp. Cyl. & Mod.); 28" (Mod. & Full); vent. rib.
**Weight:** 8 lbs.
**Stock:** European walnut, hand-checkered p.g. and forend.
**Features:** Single selective trigger, automatic ejectors, engraved receiver. Imported by Armsport. Contact Armsport for complete list of models.
**Price:** M2733/2735 (Boss-type action, 12, 20, extractors) . . . . . $790.00
**Price:** M2741 (as above with ejectors) . . . . . . . . . . . . . $825.00
**Price:** M2730/2731 (as above with single trigger, screw-in chokes) . $975.00
**Price:** M2705 (410 bore, 26" Imp. & Mod., double triggers) . . . . . $785.00
**Price:** M2742 Sporting Clays (12-ga., 28", choke tubes) . . . . . . . $930.00
**Price:** M2744 Sporting Clays (20-ga., 26", choke tubes) . . . . . . . $930.00
**Price:** M2750 Sporting Clays (12-ga., 28", choke tubes, sideplates) $1050.00
**Price:** M2751 Sporting Clays (20-ga., 26", choke tubes, sideplates) $1050.00

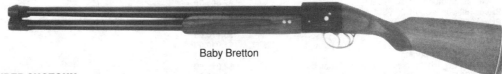
Baby Bretton

## BABY BRETTON OVER/UNDER SHOTGUN
**Gauge:** 12 or 20, 2¾" chambers.
**Barrel:** 27½" (Cyl., Imp. Cyl., Mod., Full choke tubes).
**Weight:** About 5 lbs.
**Stock:** Walnut, checkered pistol grip and forend, oil finish.
**Features:** Receiver slides open on two guide rods, is locked by a large thumb lever on the right side. Extractors only. Light alloy barrels. Imported from France by Mandall Shooting Supplies.
**Price:** . . . . . . . . . . . . . . . . . . . . . . . . . . . $895.00

Consult our Directory pages for the location of firms mentioned.

**CAUTION:** PRICES CHANGE, CHECK AT GUNSHOP.

26th EDITION, 1994  **213**

Beretta ASE 90 Trap

## BERETTA MODEL 686 ULTRALIGHT O/U
**Gauge:** 12, 2¾" chambers.
**Barrel:** 26", 28", Mobilchoke choke tubes.
**Weight:** About 5 lbs., 13 oz.
**Stock:** Select American walnut with checkered grip and forend.
**Features:** Low-profile aluminum alloy receiver with titanium breech face insert. Matte black receiver finish with gold P. Beretta signature inlay. Single selective trigger; automatic safety. Introduced 1992. Imported from Italy by Beretta U.S.A.
**Price:** . . . . . . . . . . . . . . . . . . . . . . . **$1,525.00**

## BERETTA ASE 90 COMPETITION O/U SHOTGUN
**Gauge:** 12, 2¾" chambers.
**Barrel:** 28" (Pigeon, Sporting Clays, Skeet), 30" (Sporting Clays, Trap), Mobilchoke choke tubes on Sporting Clays, Trap; fixed chokes on Trap, Skeet, Pigeon. Trap model also available as Top Combo (30", 32" barrels or 30", 34").
**Weight:** About 8 lbs., 6 oz.
**Stock:** High grade walnut.
**Features:** Has drop-out trigger assembly, wide ventilated top and side ribs, hard-chrome bores. Competition-style receiver with coin-silver finish, gold inlay Pietro Beretta initials. Comes with hard case. Introduced 1992. Imported from Italy by Beretta U.S.A.
**Price:** Pigeon, Trap, Skeet . . . . . . . . . . . . . **$8,070.00**
**Price:** Sporting Clays . . . . . . . . . . . . . . . **$8,140.00**

Beretta 686EL

## BERETTA ONYX HUNTER SPORT O/U SHOTGUN
**Gauge:** 12, 3" chambers.
**Barrel:** 28", 30" (Mobilchoke tubes).
**Weight:** 6 lbs., 13 oz.
**Stock:** Checkered American walnut.
**Features:** Intended for the beginning sporting clays shooter. Has wide, vented 12.5mm target rib, radiused recoil pad. Matte black finish on receiver and barrels. Introduced 1993. Imported from Italy by Beretta U.S.A.
**Price:** . . . . . . . . . . . . . . . . . . . . . . . **$1,385.00**
**Price:** 686 Hunter Sport (as above except coin silver receiver with scroll engraving; 12- or 20-ga.) . . . . . . . . . . **$1,425.00**

## BERETTA OVER/UNDER FIELD SHOTGUNS
**Gauge:** 12, 20, 28, and 410 bore, 2¾", 3" and 3½" chambers.
**Barrel:** 26" and 28" (Mobilchoke tubes).
**Stock:** Close-grained walnut.
**Features:** Highly-figured, American walnut stocks and forends, and a unique, weather-resistant finish on barrels. The 686 Onyx bears a gold P. Beretta signature on each side of the receiver. Imported from Italy by Beretta U.S.A.
**Price:** 686 Onyx . . . . . . . . . . . . . . . . . **$1,355.00**
**Price:** 686 two bbl. set . . . . . . . . . . . . . . **$2,085.00**
**Price:** 686 Field . . . . . . . . . . . . . . . . . **$1,355.00**
**Price:** 686L Silver (12, 20, polished silver receiver) . . **$1,385.00**
**Price:** 686EL (engraved sideplates, hard case) . . . **$2,200.00**
**Price:** 687L Field . . . . . . . . . . . . . . . . . **$1,870.00**
**Price:** 687 EL (gold inlays, sideplates) . . . . . . . **$3,180.00**
**Price:** 687 EELL (engraved sideplates) . . . . . **$4,625.00** to **$5,130.00**

Beretta Model SO6 EELL

## BERETTA SPORTING CLAYS SHOTGUNS
**Gauge:** 12 and 20, 2¾" chambers.
**Barrel:** 28", 30", Mobilchoke.
**Stock:** Close-grained walnut.
**Sights:** Luminous front sight and center bead.
**Features:** Equipped with Beretta Mobilchoke flush-mounted screw-in choke tube system. Models vary according to grade, from field-grade Beretta 686 Sporting with its floral engraving pattern, to competition-grade Beretta 682 Sporting with its brushed satin finish and adjustable length of pull to the 687 Sporting with intricately hand-engraved game scenes, fine line, deep-cut checkering. Imported from Italy by Beretta U.S.A.
**Price:** 682 Sporting, 30" (with case) . . . . . . . **$2,605.00**
**Price:** 682 Super Sport, 28", 30", tapered rib . . . **$2,715.00**
**Price:** 682 Sporting 20-gauge . . . . . . . . . . **$2,650.00**
**Price:** 682 Sporting Combo, 28" and 30" . . . . . **$3,470.00**
**Price:** 686 Sporting . . . . . . . . . . . . . . . **$1,940.00**
**Price:** 686 Onyx Sporting . . . . . . . . . . . . **$1,940.00**
**Price:** 686 English Course Sporting, 2¾" chambers, 28" . . . . **$2,015.00**
**Price:** 686 Sporting Combo, 28" and 30" . . . . . **$2,600.00**
**Price:** 687 Sporting . . . . . . . . . . . . . . . **$2,285.00**
**Price:** 687 Sporting (20-gauge) . . . . . . . . . **$2,285.00**
**Price:** 687 EELL Sporter (hand engraved sideplates, deluxe wood) **$4,705.00**
**Price:** 687 Sporting Combo, 28" and 30" . . . . . **$3,410.00**
**Price:** ASE 90 Sporting . . . . . . . . . . . . . **$8,140.00**

## BERETTA MODEL SO5, SO6, SO9 SHOTGUNS
**Gauge:** 12, 2¾" chambers.
**Barrel:** To customer specs.
**Stock:** To customer specs.
**Features:** SO5—Trap, Skeet and Sporting Clays models SO5 and SO5 EELL; SO6—SO6 and SO6 EELL are field models. SO6 has a case-hardened or silver receiver with contour hand engraving. SO6 EELL has hand-engraved receiver in a fine floral or "fine English" pattern or game scene, with bas-relief chisel work and gold inlays. SO6 and SO6 EELL are available with sidelocks removable by hand. Imported from Italy by Beretta U.S.A.
**Price:** SO5 Trap, Skeet, Sporting . . . . . . . . **$12,000.00**
**Price:** SO5 Combo, two-bbl. set . . . . . . . . . **$15,500.00**
**Price:** SO6 Trap, Skeet, Sporting . . . . . . . . . **$16,300.00**
**Price:** SO6 EELL Field, custom specs . . . . . . . **$26,000.00**
**Price:** SO9 (12, 20, 28, 410, 26", 28", 30", any choke) . . . **$28,500.00**

### Beretta 687EL Sporting O/U
Similar to the 687 Sporting except has sideplates with gold inlay game scene, vent side and top ribs, bright orange front sight. Stock and forend are of high grade walnut with fine-line checkering. Available in 12-gauge only with 28" or 30" barrels and Mobilchoke tubes. Weight is 6 lbs., 13 oz. Introduced 1993. Imported from Italy by Beretta U.A.S.
**Price:** . . . . . . . . . . . . . . . . . . . . . . . **$3,225.00**

### Beretta 682 Super Sporting O/U
Similar to the 682 Sporting except has stock with adjustable comb that allows height adjustments via interchangeable inserts. Accessory recoil pad system and adjustable trigger allow length of pull changes. Factory ported barrels, raised tapered top rib with mid-rib bead, bright orange front sight. Available in 12-gauge only, 2¾" chambers, 28" 30", Mobilchoke tubes. Introduced 1993. Imported from Italy by Beretta U.S.A.
**Price:** . . . . . . . . . . . . . . . . . . . . . . . **$2,925.00**

Beretta 682 Competition

## BERETTA SERIES 682 COMPETITION OVER/UNDERS
**Gauge:** 12, 2¾" chambers.
**Barrel:** Skeet—26" and 28"; trap—30" and 32", Imp. Mod. & Full and Mobil-choke; trap mono shotguns—32" and 34" Mobilchoke; trap top single guns—32" and 34" Full and Mobilchoke; trap combo sets—from 30" O/U, 32" unsingle to 32" O/U, 34" top single.
**Stock:** Close-grained walnut, hand checkered.
**Sights:** Luminous front sight and center bead.
**Features:** Trap Monte Carlo stock has deluxe trap recoil pad. Various grades available; contact Beretta U.S.A. for details. Imported from Italy by Beretta U.S.A.

| | |
|---|---|
| **Price:** 682 Skeet | $2,520.00 |
| **Price:** 682 Trap | $2,495.00 |
| **Price:** 682 Trap Mono shotguns | $3,400.00 |
| **Price:** 682 Trap Top Single shotguns | $2,650.00 |
| **Price:** 682 Trap Combo sets | $3,340.00 to $3,400.00 |
| **Price:** 682 Pigeon Silver | $2,760.00 |
| **Price:** 687 EELL Trap | $4,610.00 to $5,815.00 |
| **Price:** 687 EELL Skeet (4-bbl. set) | $8,040.00 |
| **Price:** 682 Super Skeet (adjustable comb and butt pads, bbl. porting) | $2,915.00 |
| **Price:** 682 Super Trap (adjustable comb and butt pad, bbl. porting) | $2,885.00 to $3,865.00 |

Browning Citori Gran Lightning

## Browning Superlight Citori Over/Under
Similar to the standard Citori except available in 12, 20 with 24", 26" or 28" Invector barrels, 28 or 410 with 26" barrels choked Imp. Cyl. & Mod. or 28" choked Mod. & Full. Has straight grip stock, schnabel forend tip. Superlight 12 weighs 6 lbs., 9 oz. (26" barrels); Superlight 20, 5 lbs., 12 oz. (26" barrels). Introduced 1982.

| | |
|---|---|
| **Price:** Grade I only, 28 or 410 | $1,220.00 |
| **Price:** Grade III, Invector, 12 or 20 | $1,750.00 |
| **Price:** Grade III, 28 or 410 | $1,920.00 |
| **Price:** Grade VI, Invector, 12 or 20 | $2,540.00 |
| **Price:** Grade VI, 28 or 410 | $2,700.00 |
| **Price:** Grade I Invector, 12 or 20 | $1,215.00 |
| **Price:** Grade I Invector, Upland Special (24" bbls.), 12 or 20 | $1,215.00 |

## Browning Lightning Sporting Clays
Similar to the Citori Lightning with rounded pistol grip and classic forend. Has high post tapered rib or lower hunting-style rib with 30" back-bored Invector Plus barrels, ported or non-ported, 3" chambers. Gloss stock finish, radiused recoil pad. Has "Lightning Sporting Clays Edition" engraved and gold filled on receiver. Introduced 1989.

| | |
|---|---|
| **Price:** Low-rib, ported | $1,300.00 |
| **Price:** High-rib, ported | $1,360.00 |
| **Price:** Pigeon Grade, low rib, ported | $1,550.00 |
| **Price:** Pigeon Grade, high rib, ported | $1,488.00 |

## Browning Citori Plus Trap Combo
Same as the Citori Plus Trap except comes with 34" single barrel with the 32" O/U model, or 32" or 34" single with the 30" O/U model. Introduced 1992.

| | |
|---|---|
| **Price:** With fitted luggage case | $3,300.00 |

## Browning Citori O/U Skeet Models
Similar to standard Citori except 26", 28", 12-gauge, Invector Plus, (Skeet & Skeet) only; stock dimensions of 14⅜"x1½"x2", fitted with Skeet-style recoil pad; conventional target rib and high post target rib.

| | |
|---|---|
| **Price:** Grade I Invector, 12-ga., Invector Plus (high post rib) | $1,380.00 |
| **Price:** Grade I, 20, 28 and 410 (high post rib) | $1,315.00 |
| **Price:** Grade III, 20, 28, 410 (high post rib) | $1,860.00 |
| **Price:** Grade VI, 20, 28, 410 (high post rib) | $2,650.00 |
| **Price:** Four barrel Skeet set—12, 20, 28, 410 barrels, with case, Grade I only | $4,250.00 |
| **Price:** Grade III, four-barrel set (high post rib) | $4,860.00 |
| **Price:** Grade VI, four-barrel set (high post rib) | $5,500.00 |
| **Price:** Grade I, three-barrel set | $2,960.00 |
| **Price:** Grade III, three-barrel set | $3,560.00 |
| **Price:** Grade VI, three-barrel set | $4,200.00 |
| **Price:** Grade III, 12-ga. Invector Plus | $1,896.00 |
| **Price:** Grade VI, 12-ga., Invector Plus | $2,690.00 |

## BROWNING CITORI O/U SHOTGUN
**Gauge:** 12, 20, 28 and 410.
**Barrel:** 26", 28" (Mod. & Full, Imp. Cyl. & Mod.), in 28 and 410. Also offered with Invector choke tubes. All 12-gauge models have back-bored barrels and Invector Plus choke system.
**Weight:** 6 lbs., 8 oz. (26" 410) to 7 lbs., 13 oz. (30" 12-ga.).
**Length:** 43" overall (26" bbl.).
**Stock:** Dense walnut, hand checkered, full p.g., beavertail forend. Field-type recoil pad on 12-ga. field guns and Skeet models.
**Sights:** Medium raised beads, German nickel silver.
**Features:** Barrel selector integral with safety, automatic ejectors, three-piece takedown. Imported from Japan by Browning. Contact Browning for complete list of models and prices.

| | |
|---|---|
| **Price:** Grade I, Hunting, Invector, 12 and 20 | $1,165.00 |
| **Price:** Grade III, Hunting, Invector, 12 and 20 | $1,715.00 |
| **Price:** Grade VI, Hunting, Invector, 12 and 20 | $2,485.00 |
| **Price:** Grade I, Hunting, 28 and 410, fixed chokes | $1,155.00 |
| **Price:** Grade III, Lightning, 28 and 410, fixed chokes | $1,900.00 |
| **Price:** Grade VI, 28 and 410 Lightning, fixed chokes | $2,695.00 |
| **Price:** Grade I, Lightning, Invector, 12, 20 | $1,198.00 |
| **Price:** Grade I, Hunting, 28", 30" only, 3½", Invector Plus | $1,240.00 |
| **Price:** Grade III, Lightning, Invector, 12, 20 | $1,745.00 |
| **Price:** Grade VI, Lightning, Invector, 12, 20 | $2,530.00 |
| **Price:** Gran Lightning, 26", 28", Invector | $1,630.00 |

## Browning Micro Citori Lightning
Similar to the standard Citori 20-ga. Lightning except scaled down for smaller shooter. Comes with 24" barrels with Invector choke system, 13¾" length of pull. Weighs about 6 lbs., 3 oz. Introduced 1991.

| | |
|---|---|
| **Price:** Grade I | $1,228.00 |
| **Price:** Grade III | $1,775.00 |
| **Price:** Grade VI | $2,515.00 |

## Browning Citori Plus Trap Gun
Similar to the Grade I Citori Trap except comes only with 30" barrels with .745" over-bore, Invector Plus choke system with Full, Imp. Mod. and Mod. choke tubes; high post, ventilated, tapered, target rib for adjustable impact from 3" to 12" above point of aim. Available with or without ported barrels. Select walnut stock has high-gloss finish, Monte Carlo comb, modified beavertail forend and is fully adjustable for length of pull, drop at comb and drop at Monte Carlo. Has Browning Recoil Reduction System. Introduced 1989.

| | |
|---|---|
| **Price:** Grade I, with ported barrel | $1,950.00 |
| **Price:** Grade I, non-ported barrel | $1,925.00 |
| **Price:** Pigeon Grade, ported barrels | $2,140.00 |

## Browning Citori O/U Trap Models
Similar to standard Citori except 12 gauge only; 30", 32" ported or non-ported (Full & Full, Imp. Mod. & Full, Mod. & Full) or Invector Plus, 34" single barrel in Combo Set (Full, Imp. Mod., Mod.), or Invector model; Monte Carlo cheek piece (14⅜"x1⅜"x1⅜"x2"); fitted with trap-style recoil pad; conventional target rib and high post target rib.

| | |
|---|---|
| **Price:** Grade I, Invector Plus, ported bbls. | $1,380.00 |
| **Price:** Grade VI, Invector, high post target rib | $2,520.00 |
| **Price:** Grade III, Invector Plus Ported | $1,896.00 |
| **Price:** Grade IV, Invector Plus Ported | $2,690.00 |

Browning Citori GTI

## Browning Special Sporting Clays
Similar to the GTI except has full pistol grip stock with palm swell, gloss finish, 28", 30" or 32" barrels with back-bored Invector Plus chokes (ported or non-ported); high post tapered rib. Also available as 28" and 30" two-barrel set. Introduced 1989.
**Price:** With ported barrels . . . . . . . . . . . . . . . . . . **$1,360.00**

## Browning Citori GTI Sporting Clays
Similar to the Citori Hunting except has semi-pistol grip with slightly grooved, semi-beavertail forend, satin-finish stock, radiused rubber buttpad. Has three interchangeable trigger shoes, trigger has three length of pull adjustments. Wide 13mm vent. rib, 28" or 30" barrels (ported or non-ported) with Invector Plus choke tubes. Ventilated side ribs. Introduced 1989.
**Price:** With ported barrels . . . . . . . . . . . . . . . . . . **$1,380.00**

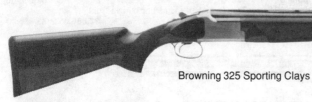

Browning 325 Sporting Clays

## BROWNING 325 SPORTING CLAYS
**Gauge:** 12, 20, 2¾" chambers.
**Barrel:** 12-ga.—28", 30", 32" (Invector Plus tubes), back-bored; 20-ga.—28", 30" (Imp. Mod. & Imp. Cyl.).
**Weight:** 7 lbs., 13 oz. (12-ga., 28").
**Stock:** 14¹³⁄₁₆" (+/-⅛")x1⁷⁄₁₆"x2³⁄₁₆" (12-ga.). Select walnut with gloss finish, cut checkering, schnabel forend.
**Features:** Grayed receiver with engraving, blued barrels. Barrels are ported on 12-gauge guns. Has 10mm wide vent rib. Comes with three interchangeable trigger shoes to adjust length of pull. Introduced in U.S. 1993. Imported by Browning.
**Price:** 12-ga. . . . . . . . . . . . . . . . . . . . . . . . . **$1,540.00**
**Price:** 20-ga. . . . . . . . . . . . . . . . . . . . . . . . . **$1,470.00**

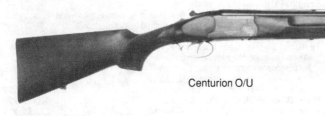

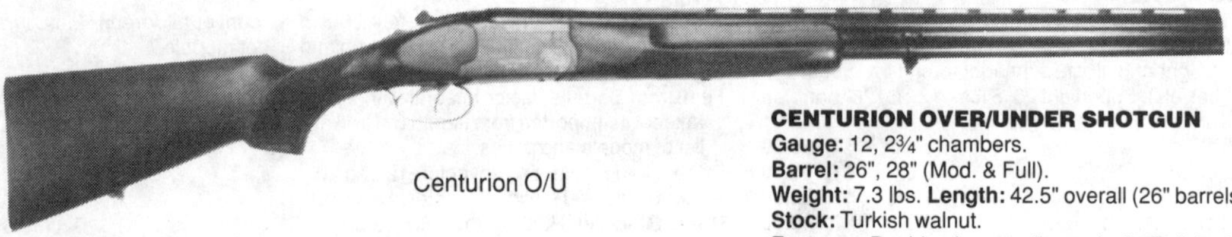

Centurion O/U

## CHAPUIS OVER/UNDER SHOTGUN
**Gauge:** 12, 16, 20.
**Barrel:** 22", 23.6", 26.8", 27.6", 31.5", chokes to customer specs.
**Weight:** 5 to 8 lbs. **Length:** NA.
**Stock:** French walnut, straight English or pistol grip.
**Features:** Double hook blitz system boxlock action with automatic ejectors or extractors. Long trigger guard (most models), choice of raised solid rib, vent. rib or ultra light rib. Imported from France by Armes de Chasse.
**Price:** About . . . . . . . . . . . . . . . . . . . . **$4,000.00** to **$5,000.00**

## CENTURION OVER/UNDER SHOTGUN
**Gauge:** 12, 2¾" chambers.
**Barrel:** 26", 28" (Mod. & Full).
**Weight:** 7.3 lbs. **Length:** 42.5" overall (26" barrels).
**Stock:** Turkish walnut.
**Features:** Double triggers; sling swivels. Polished blue finish. Introduced 1993. Imported by Century International Arms.
**Price:** About . . . . . . . . . . . . . . . . . . . . . . . . . **$350.00**

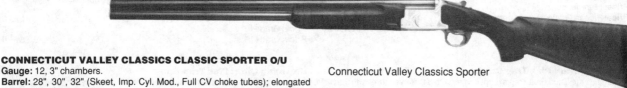

Connecticut Valley Classics Sporter

## CONNECTICUT VALLEY CLASSICS CLASSIC SPORTER O/U
**Gauge:** 12, 3" chambers.
**Barrel:** 28", 30", 32" (Skeet, Imp. Cyl. Mod., Full CV choke tubes); elongated forcing cones.
**Weight:** 7¾ lbs. **Length:** 44⅞" overall (28" barrels).
**Stock:** 14½"x1½"x2⅛". American black walnut with hand-checkered grip and forend.
**Features:** Receiver duplicates Classic Doubles M101 specifications. Nitrided grayed or stainless receiver with fine engraving. Chrome-lined bores and chambers suitable for steel shot. Optionally available are CV Plus (2⅜" tubes) or Competition (2¾" Briley) choke tubes. Introduced 1993. Made in U.S. by Connecticut Valley Classics.
**Price:** Classic Sporter . . . . . . . . . . . . . . . . . . **$2,195.00**
**Price:** Classic Sporter Stainless . . . . . . . . . . . . . **$2,395.00**

## Charles Daly Lux Over/Under
Similar to the Field Grade except available in 12, 20, 28, 410-bore, has automatic selective ejectors, antique silver finish on frame, and has choke tubes for Imp. Cyl., Mod. and Full. Introduced 1989.
**Price:** . . . . . . . . . . . . . . . . . . . . . . . . . . . . . **$699.00**

## Connecticut Valley Classics Classic Field Waterfowler
Similar to the Classic Sporter except with 30" barrel only, blued, non-reflective overall finish. Interchangeable CV choke tube system includes Skeet, Imp. Cyl., Mod. Full tubes. Introduced 1993. Made in U.S. by Connecticut Valley Classics.
**Price:** . . . . . . . . . . . . . . . . . . . . . . . . . . . . . **$1,895.00**

## CHARLES DALY FIELD GRADE O/U
**Gauge:** 12 or 20, 3" chambers.
**Barrel:** 12- and 20- ga.—26" (Imp. Cyl. & Mod.), 12-ga.—28" (Mod. & Full).
**Weight:** 6 lbs., 15 oz. (12-ga.); 6 lbs., 10 oz. (20-ga.). **Length:** 43½" overall (26" bbl.).
**Stock:** 14⅛"x1⅜"x2⅜". Walnut with cut-checkered grip and forend. Black, vent. rubber recoil pad. Semi-gloss finish.
**Features:** Boxlock action with manual safety; extractors; single selective trigger. Color case-hardened receiver with engraving. Introduced 1989. Imported from Europe by Outdoor Sports Headquarters.
**Price:** . . . . . . . . . . . . . . . . . . . . . . . . . . . . . **$475.00**

**CAUTION:** PRICES CHANGE, CHECK AT GUNSHOP.

## E.A.A./SABATTI SPORTING CLAYS PRO-GOLD O/U

**Gauge:** 12, 3" chambers.
**Barrel:** 28" or 30" with six choke tubes.
**Weight:** 7¼ lbs.
**Stock:** European walnut with gloss finish, checkered grip and forend. Special sporting clays recoil pad.
**Features:** Boxlock action with gold-plated single selective trigger, automatic ejectors. Engraved, blued receiver with gold inlays. Target-style flourescent bar front sight. Comes with lockable hard shell plastic case. Introduced 1993. Imported from Italy by European American Armory.
**Price:** . . . . . . . . . . . . . . . . . . . . . . . . . . . . . . . . . **$999.00**

E.A.A./Sabatti Sporting Clays

## E.A.A./SABATTI FALCON-MON OVER/UNDER

**Gauge:** 12, 20, 28, 410, 3" chambers.
**Barrel:** 26" or 28" (standard chokes).
**Weight:** 6.6 to 7.8 lbs.
**Stock:** Select walnut with cut checkering. Full pistol grip, beavertail forend. Gloss finish.
**Features:** Boxlock action with gold-plated single selective trigger, extractors; ventilated rib. Engraved, blued receiver. Lifetime warranty. Introduced 1993. Imported from Italy by European American Armory.
**Price:** 12 or 20 . . . . . . . . . . . . . . . . . . . . . . . . . **$599.00**
**Price:** 28 or 410 . . . . . . . . . . . . . . . . . . . . . . . . . **$675.00**

Kassnar Grade I

## KASSNAR GRADE I O/U SHOTGUN

**Gauge:** 12, 20, 28, 410, 3" chambers.
**Barrel:** 26" (Imp. Cyl. & Mod.), 28" (Mod. & Full), 28" (choke tubes).
**Weight:** 6.5 to 7.5 lbs.
**Stock:** European walnut with checkered grip and forend.
**Features:** Boxlock action with single selective trigger; blued and engraved receiver; vent. rib. Imported by K.B.I., Inc.
**Price:** . . . . . . . . . . . . . . . . . . . . . . . **$500.00 to $750.00**

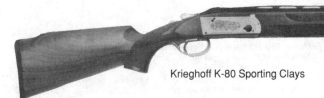

Krieghoff K-80 Sporting Clays

## KRIEGHOFF K-80 SKEET SHOTGUN

**Gauge:** 12, 2¾" chambers.
**Barrel:** 28" (Skeet & Skeet, optional Tula or choke tubes).
**Weight:** About 7¾ lbs.
**Stock:** American Skeet or straight Skeet stocks, with palm-swell grips. Walnut.
**Features:** Satin gray receiver finish. Selective mechanical trigger adjustable for position. Choice of ventilated 8mm parallel flat rib or ventilated 8-12mm tapered flat rib. Introduced 1980. Imported from Germany by Krieghoff International, Inc.
**Price:** Standard, Skeet chokes . . . . . . . . . . . . . . **$6,290.00**
**Price:** As above, Tula chokes . . . . . . . . . . . . . **$6,550.00**
**Price:** Lightweight model (weighs 7 lbs.), Standard . . . . . . . **$6,290.00**
**Price:** Two-Barrel Set (tube concept), 12-ga., Standard . . . . . **$10,935.00**
**Price:** Skeet Special (28", tapered flat rib, Skeet & Skeet choke tubes) . . . . . . . . . . . . . . . . . . . . . . . . . . . **$6,895.00**

## Krieghoff K-80 Four-Barrel Skeet Set

Similar to the Standard Skeet except comes with barrels for 12, 20, 28, 410. Comes with fitted aluminum case.
**Price:** Standard grade . . . . . . . . . . . . . . . . . . **$14,200.00**

## KRIEGHOFF K-80 SPORTING CLAYS O/U

**Gauge:** 12.
**Barrel:** 28" or 30" with choke tubes.
**Weight:** About 8 lbs.
**Stock:** #3 Sporting stock designed for gun-down shooting.
**Features:** Choice of standard or lightweight receiver with satin nickel finish and classic scroll engraving. Selective mechanical trigger adjustable for position. Choice of tapered flat or 8mm parallel flat barrel rib. Free-floating barrels. Aluminum case. Imported from Germany by Krieghoff International, Inc.
**Price:** Standard grade with five choke tubes . . . . . . . . . . . **$7,350.00**

## Krieghoff K-80 International Skeet

Similar to the Standard Skeet except has ½" ventilated Broadway-style rib, special Tula chokes with gas release holes at muzzle. International Skeet stock. Comes in fitted aluminum case.
**Price:** Standard grade . . . . . . . . . . . . . . . . . . **$6,995.00**

## Krieghoff K-80/RT Shotguns

Same as the standard K-80 shotguns except has a removable internally selective trigger mechanism. Can be considered an option on all K-80 guns of any configuration. Introduced 1990.
**Price:** RT (removable trigger) option on K-80 guns, add . . . . . . **$1,000.00**
**Price:** Extra pull trigger mechanisms . . . . . . . . . . . . . . **$1,275.00**

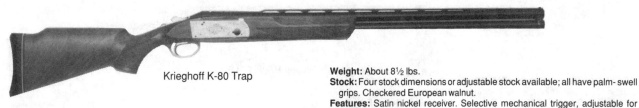

Krieghoff K-80 Trap

## KRIEGHOFF K-80 O/U TRAP SHOTGUN

**Gauge:** 12, 2¾" chambers.
**Barrel:** 30", 32" (Imp. Mod. & Full or choke tubes).

**Weight:** About 8½ lbs.
**Stock:** Four stock dimensions or adjustable stock available; all have palm-swell grips. Checkered European walnut.
**Features:** Satin nickel receiver. Selective mechanical trigger, adjustable for position. Ventilated step rib. Introduced 1980. Imported from Germany by Krieghoff International, Inc.
**Price:** K-80 O/U (30", 32", Imp. Mod. & Full), from . . . . . . **$6,695.00**
**Price:** K-80 Unsingle (32", 34", Full), Standard, from . . . . . . **$7,300.00**
**Price:** K-80 Combo (two-barrel set), Standard, from . . . . . . . **$9,380.00**

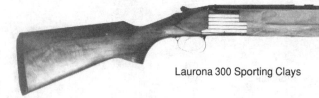

Laurona 300 Sporting Clays

## LAURONA SILHOUETTE 300 SPORTING CLAYS
**Gauge:** 12, 2¾" or 3" chambers.
**Barrel:** 28", 29" (Multichoke tubes, flush-type or knurled).
**Weight:** 7 lbs., 12 oz.
**Stock:** 14⅜"x1⅜"x2½". European walnut with full pistol grip, beavertail forend. Rubber buttpad.
**Features:** Selective single trigger, automatic selective ejectors. Introduced 1988. Imported from Spain by Galaxy Imports.
**Price:** . . . . . . . . . . . . . . . . . . . . . . . . . . . . . . $1,250.00
**Price:** Silhouette Ultra-Magnum, 3½" chambers . . . . . . . . . . $1,265.00

## LAURONA SILHOUETTE 300 TRAP
Same gun as the Silhouette 300 Sporting Clays except has 29" barrels, trap stock dimensions of 14⅜"x1⁷⁄₁₆"x1⅝", weighs 7 lbs., 15 oz. Available with flush or knurled Multichokes.
**Price:** . . . . . . . . . . . . . . . . . . . . . . $1,310.00

Laurona Super 85 MS Pigeon

## LAURONA SUPER MODEL OVER/UNDERS
**Gauge:** 12, 20, 2¾" or 3" chambers.
**Barrel:** 26", 28" (Multichoke), 29" (Multichokes and Full).
**Weight:** About 7 lbs.

**Stock:** European walnut. Dimensions vary according to model. Full pistol grip.
**Features:** Boxlock action, silvered with engraving. Automatic selective ejectors; choke tubes available on most models; single selective or twin single triggers; black chrome barrels. Has 5-year warranty, including metal finish. Imported from Spain by Galaxy Imports.
**Price:** Model 83 MG, 12- or 20-ga. . . . . . . . . . . . . . . . $1,215.00
**Price:** Model 84S Super Trap (fixed chokes) . . . . . . . . . . . $1,340.00
**Price:** Model 85 Super Game, 12- or 20-ga. . . . . . . . . . . . $1,215.00
**Price:** Model 85 MS Super Trap (Full/Multichoke) . . . . . . . . $1,390.00
**Price:** Model 85 MS Super Pigeon . . . . . . . . . . . . . . . . $1,370.00
**Price:** Model 85 S Super Skeet, 12-ga. . . . . . . . . . . . . . $1,300.00

Ljutic LM-6

## LJUTIC LM-6 DELUXE O/U SHOTGUN
**Gauge:** 12.
**Barrel:** 28" to 34", choked to customer specs for live birds, trap, International Trap.

**Weight:** To customer specs.
**Stock:** To customer specs. Oil finish, hand checkered.
**Features:** Custom-made gun. Hollow-milled rib, pull or release trigger, pushbutton opener in front of trigger guard. From Ljutic Industries.
**Price:** Super Deluxe LM-6 O/U . . . . . . . . . . . . . . . . . $14,995.00
**Price:** Over/under Combo (interchangeable single barrel, two trigger guards, one for single trigger, one for doubles) . . . . . . . . . . . $21,995.00
**Price:** Extra over/under barrel sets, 29"-32" . . . . . . . . . . $5,995.00

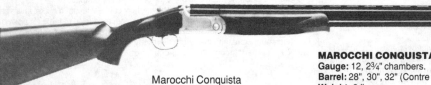

Marocchi Conquista

## MAROCCHI AVANZA O/U SHOTGUN
**Gauge:** 12 and 20, 3" chambers.
**Barrel:** 26" (Imp. Cyl. & Mod. or Imp. Cyl., Mod., Full Interchokes); 28" (Mod. & Full or Imp. Cyl. Mod., Full Interchokes).
**Weight:** 6 lbs., 6 oz. to 6 lbs., 13 oz.
**Stock:** 14"x2¼"x1½". Select walnut with cut checkering. Recoil pad.
**Features:** Single selective trigger, auto-mechanical barrel cycling, automatic selective ejectors, unbreakable firing pins. Ventilated top and middle ribs. Automatic safety. Introduced 1990. Imported from Italy by Precision Sales International.
**Price:** 12-ga., 26" or 28", fixed chokes . . . . . . . . . . . . . $769.00
**Price:** As above, with Interchokes . . . . . . . . . . . . . . . . $829.00

## MAROCCHI CONQUISTA OVER/UNDER SHOTGUN
**Gauge:** 12, 2¾" chambers.
**Barrel:** 28", 30", 32" (Contre choke tubes).
**Weight:** 8 lbs.
**Stock:** 14½"-14⅞"x2¼"x1½"; American walnut with checkered grip and forend; sporting clays butt pad.
**Sights:** 16mm luminescent front.
**Features:** Has lower monoblock and frame profile. Fast lock time. Ergonomically-shaped trigger is adjustable for pull length and weight. Automatic selective ejectors. Coin-finished receiver, blued barrels. Comes with five choke tubes, hard case, stock wrinch. Introduced 1993. Imported from Italy by Precision Sales International.
**Price:** Grade I . . . . . . . . . . . . . . . . . . . . . . . . . . $1,985.00
**Price:** Grade II . . . . . . . . . . . . . . . . . . . . . . . . . $2,450.00

Merkel Model 201E

## MERKEL MODEL 200E O/U SHOTGUN
**Gauge:** 12, 3" chambers, 16, 2¾" chambers, 20, 3" chambers.
**Barrel:** 12- , 16-ga.—28"; 20-ga.—26¾" (Imp. Cyl. & Mod., Mod. & Full). Solid rib.
**Weight:** About 7 lbs. (12-ga.).
**Stock:** Oil-finished walnut; straight English or pistol grip.
**Features:** Scroll engraved, color case-hardened receiver. Single selective or double triggers; ejectors. Imported from Germany by GSI.

**Price:** Model 200E . . . . . . . . . . . . . . . . . . . . . . . . $3,395.00
**Price:** Model 201E (as above except silver-grayed receiver with engraved hunting scenes) . . . . . . . . . . . . . . . . . . . . . . $4,195.00
**Price:** Model 202E (as above except has false sideplates, fine hunting scenes with Arabesque engraving) . . . . . . . . . . . . . . $7,995.00

### Merkel Model 200E Skeet, Trap Over/Unders

Similar to the Model 200E except in 12-gauge only with 2¾" chambers, tapered ventilated rib, competition stock with full pistol grip, half-coverage Arabesque engraving on silver-grayed receiver. Single selective trigger only. Model 200ES has 26¾" (Skeet & Skeet) barrels; Model 200ET has 30" (Full & Full) barrles. Imported from Germany by GSI.

**Price:** Model 200ES . . . . . . . . . . . . . . . . . . . . . . . **$4,995.00**
**Price:** Model 200ET . . . . . . . . . . . . . . . . . . . . . . . **$4,795.00**
**Price:** Model 201ES (full-coverage engraving) . . . . . . . . . **$5,595.00**
**Price:** Model 201ET (full-coverage engraving) . . . . . . . . . **$5,395.00**
**Price:** Model 203ES (sidelock action, Skeet) . . . . . . . . . . **$9,795.00**
**Price:** Model 203ET (sidelock action, Trap) . . . . . . . . . . **$9,795.00**

### Merkel Model 203E, 303E Over/Under Shotguns

Similar to the Model 200E except with Holland & Holland-style sidelocks, both quick-detachable: Model 203E with cranked screw, 303E with integral retracting hook. Model 203E has coil spring ejectors; 303E H&H ejectors. Both have silver-grayed receiver with English-style Arabesque engraving—large scrolls on 203E, medium on 303E. Imported from Germany by GSI.

**Price:** Model 203E . . . . . . . . . . . . . . . . . . . . . . . . **$9,695.00**
**Price:** Model 303E . . . . . . . . . . . . . . . . . . . . . . . . **$21,295.00**

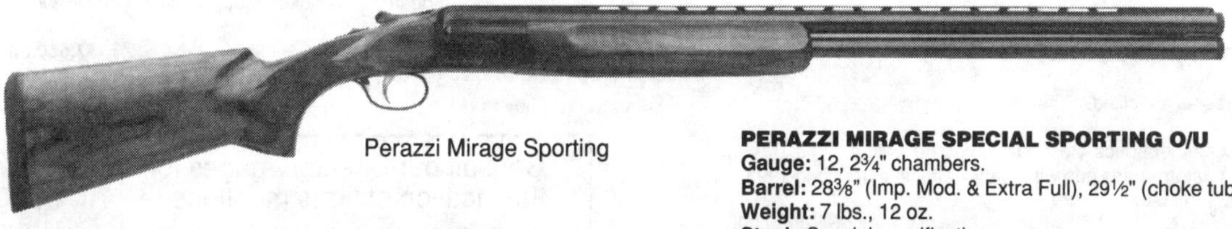

Perazzi Mirage Sporting

### Perazzi Mirage Special Four-Gauge Skeet

Similar to the Mirage Sporting model except has Skeet dimensions, interchangeable, adjustable four-position trigger assembly. Comes with four barrel sets in 12, 20, 28, 410, flat 5/16"x5/16" rib.
**Price:** From . . . . . . . . . . . . . . . . . . . . . . . . . . **$17,500.00**

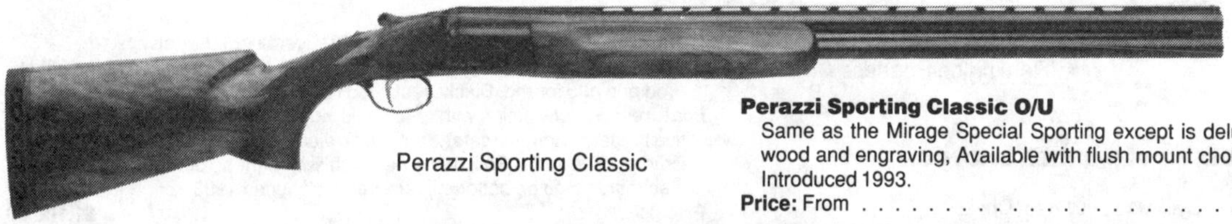

### PERAZZI MIRAGE SPECIAL SPORTING O/U

**Gauge:** 12, 2¾" chambers.
**Barrel:** 28⅜" (Imp. Mod. & Extra Full), 29½" (choke tubes).
**Weight:** 7 lbs., 12 oz.
**Stock:** Special specifications.
**Features:** Has single selective trigger; flat 7/16"x5/16" vent. rib. Many options available. Imported from Italy by Perazzi U.S.A., Inc.
**Price:** . . . . . . . . . . . . . . . . . . . . . . . . . . . . . **$8,100.00**

Perazzi Sporting Classic

### Perazzi Sporting Classic O/U

Same as the Mirage Special Sporting except is deluxe version with select wood and engraving, Available with flush mount choke tubes, 29.5" barrels. Introduced 1993.
**Price:** From . . . . . . . . . . . . . . . . . . . . . . . . . . **$9,150.00**

Perazzi MX7

### PERAZZI MX7 OVER/UNDER SHOTGUNS

**Gauge:** 12, 2¾" chambers.
**Barrel:** 29.5", 31.5", fixed or choke tubes.
**Weight:** NA.
**Stock:** To customer specifications.
**Features:** Has fixed coil spring trigger mechanism; selective firing order. Available in combo or over/under configurations. Introduced 1992. Imported from Italy by Perazzi U.S.A.
**Price:** From . . . . . . . . . . . . . . . . . . . . . . . **$6,100.00**

### Perazzi Mirage Special Skeet Over/Under

Similar to the MX8 Skeet except has adjustable four-position trigger, Skeet stock dimensions.
**Price:** From . . . . . . . . . . . . . . . . . . . . . . . . . . **$7,700.00**

### Perazzi MX8/20 Over/Under Shotgun

Similar to the MX8 except has smaller frame and has a removable trigger mechanism. Available in trap, Skeet, sporting or game models with fixed chokes or choke tubes. Stock is made to customer specifications. Introduced 1993.
**Price:** From . . . . . . . . . . . . . . . . . . . . . . . . . . **$7,300.00**

### PERAZZI MX8/MX8 SPECIAL TRAP, SKEET

**Gauge:** 12, 2¾" chambers.
**Barrel:** Trap—29½" (Imp. Mod. & Extra Full), 31½" (Full & Extra Full). Choke tubes optional. Skeet—27⅝" (Skeet & Skeet).
**Weight:** About 8½ lbs. (Trap); 7 lbs., 15 oz. (Skeet).
**Stock:** Interchangeable and custom made to customer specs.
**Features:** Has detachable and interchangeable trigger group with flat V springs. Flat 7/16" ventilated rib. Many options available. Imported from Italy by Perazzi U.S.A., Inc.
**Price:** From . . . . . . . . . . . . . . . . . . . . . . . **$7,300.00**
**Price:** MX8 Special (adj. four-position trigger), from . . . . . . . **$7,700.00**
**Price:** MX8 Special Single (32" or 34" single barrel, step rib), from **$7,300.00**
**Price:** MX8 Special Combo (o/u and single barrel sets), from . . . **$10,250.00**

> Consult our Directory pages for the location of firms mentioned.

### PERAZZI MX9 SINGLE, OVER/UNDER SHOTGUNS

**Gauge:** 12, 2¾" chambers.
**Barrel:** 29.5", 31.5" (choke tubes).
**Weight:** NA.
**Stock:** Walnut; cheekpiece adjustable for elevation and cast.
**Features:** Comes with six pattern adjustment rib inserts. Vent side rib. Externally selective trigger. Available in single barrel, combo, over/under trap, Skeet, pigeon and sporting models. Introduced 1993. Imported from Italy by Perazzi U.S.A.
**Price:** From . . . . . . . . . . . . . . . . . . . . . . . . . . **$9,200.00**
**Price:** MX10 (fixed chokes, different rib), from . . . . . . . . . . **$9,450.00**

### PERAZZI MX12 HUNTING OVER/UNDER

**Gauge:** 12, 2¾" chambers.
**Barrel:** 26", 27⅝", 28⅜", 29½" (Mod. & Full); choke tubes available in 27⅝", 29½" only (MX12C).
**Weight:** 7 lbs., 4 oz.
**Stock:** To customer specs; Interchangeable.
**Features:** Single selective trigger; coil springs used in action; schnabel forend tip. Imported from Italy by Perazzi U.S.A., Inc.
**Price:** From . . . . . . . . . . . . . . . . . . . . . . . . . . **$7,300.00**
**Price:** MX12C (with choke tubes), from . . . . . . . . . . . . . . **$7,700.00**

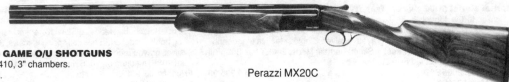

**PERAZZI MX28, MX410 GAME O/U SHOTGUNS**
**Gauge:** 28, 2¾" chambers, 410, 3" chambers.
**Barrel:** 26" (Imp. Cyl. & Full).
**Weight:** NA.
**Stock:** To customer specifications.
**Features:** Made on scaled-down frames proportioned to the gauge. Introduced 1993. Imported from Italy by Perazzi U.S.A.
**Price:** From . . . . . . . . . . . . . . . . . . . . . . . . . $14,600.00

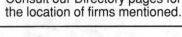

Perazzi MX20C

**PIOTTI BOSS OVER/UNDER SHOTGUN**
**Gauge:** 12, 20.
**Barrel:** 25" to 32", chokes as specified.
**Weight:** 6.5 to 8 lbs.
**Stock:** Dimensions to customer specs. Best quality figured walnut.
**Features:** Essentially a custom-made gun with many options. Introduced 1993. Imported from Italy by Wm. Larkin Moore.
**Price:** From . . . . . . . . . . . . . . . . . . . . . . . $34,0000.00

**Perazzi MX20 Hunting Over/Under**
Similar to the MX12 except 20-ga. frame size. Available in 20, 28, 410 with 2¾" or 3" chambers. 26" standard, and choked Mod. & Full. Weight is 6 lbs., 6 oz.
**Price:** From . . . . . . . . . . . . . . . . . . . . . . . $7,650.00
**Price:** MX20C (as above, 20-ga. only, choke tubes), from . . . . . $8,050.00

Consult our Directory pages for the location of firms mentioned.

Remington Peerless

**REMINGTON PEERLESS OVER/UNDER SHOTGUN**
**Gauge:** 12, 3" chambers.
**Barrel:** 26", 28", 30" (Imp. Cyl., Mod., Full Rem Chokes).

**Weight:** 7¼ lbs. (26" barrels). **Length:** 43" overall (26" barrels).
**Stock:** 14³/₁₆"x1½"x2¼". American walnut with Imron gloss finish, cut-checkered grip and forend. Black, ventilated recoil pad.
**Features:** Boxlock action with removable sideplates. Gold-plated, single selective trigger, automatic safety, automatic ejectors. Fast lock time. Mid-rib bead, Bradley-type front. Polished blue finish with light scrollwork on sideplates, Remington logo on bottom of receiver. Introduced 1993.
**Price:** . . . . . . . . . . . . . . . . . . . . . . . . . $1,105.00

Ruger English Field

**RUGER RED LABEL O/U SHOTGUN**
**Gauge:** 12 and 20, 3" chambers.
**Barrel:** 26", 28" (Skeet, Imp. Cyl., Full, Extra-Full, Mod. screw-in choke tubes). Proved for steel shot.
**Weight:** About 7 lbs. (20-ga.); 7½ lbs. (12-ga.). **Length:** 43" overall (26" barrels).
**Stock:** 14"x1½"x2½". Straight grain American walnut. Checkered pistol grip and forend, rubber butt pad.
**Features:** Choice of blue or stainless receiver. Single selective mechanical trigger, selective automatic ejectors; serrated free-floating vent. rib. Comes with two Skeet, one Imp. Cyl., one Mod., one Full choke tube and wrench; Extra-Full tube available at extra cost. Made in U.S. by Sturm, Ruger & Co.
**Price:** Red Label with pistol grip stock . . . . . . . . . . . . . . $1,157.50
**Price:** English Field with straight-grip stock . . . . . . . . . . . $1,157.50

**Ruger Sporting Clays O/U Shotgun**
Similar to the Red Label except 12-gauge only, 30" barrels back-bored to .744" diameter with stainless steel choke tubes. Weight is 7.75 lbs., overall length 47". Stock dimensions of 14⅛"x1½"x2½". Free-floating serrated vent. rib with brass front and mid-rib beads. No barrel side spacers. Comes with two Skeet, one Imp. Cyl., one Mod. choke tubes. Full and Extra-Full available at extra cost. Introduced 1992.
**Price:** . . . . . . . . . . . . . . . . . . . . . . . . . $1,285.00

San Marco 12-Gauge

**San Marco Field Special O/U Shotgun**
Similar to the 12-ga. Wildfowler except in 12-, 20- and 28-gauge with 3" chambers, 26" (Imp. Cyl. & Mod.) or 28" (Full & Mod.) barrels. Stock dimensions of 14¼"x1½"x1½". Weight of 5½ to 6 lbs. Engraved, silvered receiver, vented top and middle ribs, single trigger. Introduced 1990. Imported from Italy by Cape Outfitters.
**Price:** . . . . . . . . . . . . . . . . . . . . . . . . . $695.00

**SAN MARCO 10-GAUGE O/U SHOTGUN**
**Gauge:** 10, 3½" chambers.
**Barrel:** 28" (Mod. & Mod.), 32" (Mod. & Full). Chrome lined.
**Weight:** 9 to 9½ lbs.
**Stock:** 15"x1⅜"x2⅛". Walnut.

**SAN MARCO 12-GA. WILDFOWLER SHOTGUN**
**Gauge:** 12, 3½" chambers.
**Barrel:** 28" (Mod. & Mod., Full & Mod.), vented top and middle ribs.
**Weight:** 7 lbs., 12 oz.
**Stock:** 15"x1½"x2¼". Walnut, with checkered grip and forend.
**Features:** Chrome-lined bores with long forcing cones; single non-selective trigger; extractors on Standard, automatic ejectors on Deluxe; silvered, engraved action. Waterproof wood finish. Introduced 1990. Imported from Italy by Cape Outfitters.
**Price:** Standard . . . . . . . . . . . . . . . . . . . . . $595.00
**Price:** Deluxe . . . . . . . . . . . . . . . . . . . . . . $695.00

**Features:** Solid ⅜" barrel rib. Long forcing cones. Double triggers, extractors; Deluxe grade has automatic ejectors. Engraved receiver with game scenes, matte finish. Waterproof finish on wood. Introduced 1990. Imported from Italy by Cape Outfitters.
**Price:** Standard grade . . . . . . . . . . . . . . . . . . . . . $795.00
**Price:** Deluxe grade$895.00

SKB Model 685 Target

## SKB Model 685 Over/Under Shotgun

Similar to the Model 505 Deluxe except has gold-plated trigger, semi-fancy American walnut stock, jeweled barrel block and fine engraving in silvered receiver, top lever, and trigger guard. Gold inlay on receiver, better walnut, ventilated side ribs. All 12-gauge barrels are back-bored, have lengthened forcing cones and longer choke tube system.

**Price:** Field . . . . . . . . . . . . . . . . . . . . . . . . . . . . . . . . **$1,278.65**
**Price:** Two-barrel Field Set (12 & 20, 20 & 28 or 28 & 410) . . . . **$1,813.65**
**Price:** Trap, Skeet . . . . . . . . . . . . . . . . . . . . . . . . . . . . **$1,278.65**
**Price:** Two-barrel trap combo . . . . . . . . . . . . . . . . . . . . . **$1,706.65**
**Price:** Sporting Clays . . . . . . . . . . . . . . . . . . . . . . . . . . **$1,332.15**
**Price:** Sporting Clays two-barrel set . . . . . . . . . . . . . . . . . . . **NA**
**Price:** Skeet Set (20, 28, 410) . . . . . . . . . . . . . . . . . . . . . **$2,562.65**

## SKB Model 885 Over/Under Trap, Skeet, Sporting Clays

Similar to the Model 685 except has engraved sideplates, top lever and trigger guard, select American walnut stock. All 12-gauge barrels are back-bored, have lengthened forcing cones and longer choke tube system.

**Price:** Field, Skeet/Trap . . . . . . . . . . . . . . . . . . . . . . . . **$1,706.65**

## Stoeger/IGA ERA 2000 Over/Under Shotgun

Similar to the Condor I except available in 12-gauge only with 26" or 28" barrels, Full, Mod., and Imp. Cyl. choke tubes, single trigger. Introduced 1992. Imported from Brazil by Stoeger Industries.

**Price:** . . . . . . . . . . . . . . . . . . . . . . . . . . . . . . . . . . . . **$665.00**

Tikka Model 412S Field

## TECHNI-MEC MODEL 610 OVER/UNDER

**Gauge:** 10, 3½" chambers.
**Barrel:** 32" (Imp. Mod. & Full).
**Stocks:** Hand-checkered walnut.
**Features:** Single selective trigger; silvered engraved frame, blued barrels. Rubber recoil pad. Introduced 1991. Imported from Italy by Mandall Shooting Supplies.
**Price:** . . . . . . . . . . . . . . . . . . . . . . . . . . . . . . . . . . . **$1,200.00**

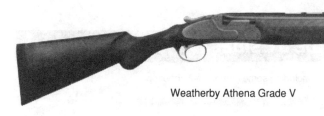

Weatherby Athena Grade V

## Weatherby Athena Grade V Classic Field O/U

Similar to the Athena Grade IV except has rounded pistol grip, slender forend, oil-finished Claro walnut stock with fine-line checkering, Old English recoil pad. Sideplate receiver has rose and scroll engraving. Available in 12-gauge, 26", 28", 30", 20-gauge, 26", 28", all with 3" chambers. Introduced 1993.
**Price:** . . . . . . . . . . . . . . . . . . . . . . . . . . . . . . . . . . . **$2,450.00**

## SKB MODEL 505 DELUXE OVER/UNDER SHOTGUN

**Gauge:** 12, or 3"; 20, 3"; 28, 2¾"; 410, 3".
**Barrel:** 12-ga.—26", 28", 30", 32", 34" (Inter-Choke tube); 20-ga.—26", 28" (Inter-Choke tube); 28—26", 28" (Inter-Choke tube); 410—26", 28" (Imp. Cyl. & Mod., Mod. & Full). Ventilated side ribs.
**Weight:** 6.6 to 8.5 lbs. **Length:** 43" to 51⅜" overall.
**Stock:** 14⅛"x1½"x2³⁄₁₆". Hand checkered walnut with high-gloss finish. Target stocks available in standard and Monte Carlo.
**Sights:** Metal bead front (field), target style on Skeet, trap, Sporting Clays.
**Features:** Boxlock action; silver nitride finish with Field or Target pattern engraving, gold inlay; manual safety, automatic ejectors, single selective trigger. All 12-gauge barrels are back-bored, have lengthened forcing cones and longer choke tube system. Introduced 1987. Imported from Japan by G.U., Inc.

**Price:** Field . . . . . . . . . . . . . . . . . . . . . . . . . . . . . . . **$1,064.65**
**Price:** Two-barrel Field Set (12 & 20, 20 & 28 or 28 & 410) . . . . **$1,599.65**
**Price:** Trap, Skeet . . . . . . . . . . . . . . . . . . . . . . . . . . . . **$1,064.65**
**Price:** Two-barrel trap combo . . . . . . . . . . . . . . . . . . . . . **$1,492.65**
**Price:** Sporting Clays model . . . . . . . . . . . . . . . . . . . . . . **$1,118.15**
**Price:** Skeet Set (20, 28, 410) . . . . . . . . . . . . . . . . . . . . . **$2,348.65**

**Price:** Skeet Set (20, 28, 410) . . . . . . . . . . . . . . . . . . . . . **$3,204.65**
**Price:** Trap Combo . . . . . . . . . . . . . . . . . . . . . . . . . . . . **$2,348.65**
**Price:** Field Set . . . . . . . . . . . . . . . . . . . . . . . . . . . . . . **$2,348.65**
**Price:** Sporting Clays . . . . . . . . . . . . . . . . . . . . . . . . . . **$1,760.15**

## STOEGER/IGA CONDOR I OVER/UNDER SHOTGUN

**Gauge:** 12, 20, 3" chambers.
**Barrel:** 26" (Full & Full, Imp. Cyl. & Mod.), 28" (Mod. & Full), or with choke tubes.
**Weight:** 6¾ to 7 lbs.
**Stock:** 14½"x1½"x2½". Oil-finished hardwood with checkered pistol grip and forend.
**Features:** Manual safety, single trigger, extractors only, ventilated top rib. Introduced 1983. Imported from Brazil by Stoeger Industries.
**Price:** . . . . . . . . . . . . . . . . . . . . . . . . . . . . . . . . . . . . **$540.00**
**Price:** With choke tubes . . . . . . . . . . . . . . . . . . . . . . . . . **$582.00**
**Price:** Condor II (sames as Condor I except has double triggers, moulded buttplate) . . . . . . . . . . . . . . . . . . . . . . . . . . . . **$432.00**

## TIKKA MODEL 412S FIELD GRADE OVER/UNDER

**Gauge:** 12, 20, 3" chambers.
**Barrel:** 24", 26", 28", 30" with stainless steel screw-in chokes (Imp. Cyl, Mod., Imp. Mod., Full); 20-ga., 28" only.
**Weight:** About 7¼ lbs.
**Stock:** American walnut. Standard dimensions—13⁹⁄₁₀"x1½"x2⅖". Checkered p.g. and forend.
**Features:** Free interchangeability of barrels, stocks and forends into double rifle model, combination gun, etc. Barrel selector in trigger; auto. top tang safety; barrel cocking indicators. Introduced 1980. Imported from Italy by Stoeger.
**Price:** Model 412S (ejectors) . . . . . . . . . . . . . . . . . . . . . **$1,155.00**
**Price:** Model 412S Sporting Clays, 12-ga., 28", choke tubes . . . . **$1,270.00**

## WEATHERBY ATHENA GRADE IV O/U SHOTGUNS

**Gauge:** 12, 20, 28, 410, 3" chambers; 2¾" on 28-ga. gun.
**Action:** Boxlock (simulated sidelock) top lever break-open. Selective auto ejectors, single selective trigger (selector inside trigger guard).
**Barrel:** 26", 28", 30", 12-ga.; 26", 28", 20-ga.; 26", 28-ga., IMC Multi-Choke tubes; 26" fixed Imp. Cyl. & Mod. on 410.
**Weight:** 12-ga., 7⅜ lbs.; 20-ga. 6⅞ lbs.
**Stock:** American walnut, checkered p.g. and forend (14¼"x1½"x2½").
**Features:** Mechanically operated trigger. Top tang safety, Greener cross bolt, fully engraved receiver, recoil pad installed. IMC models furnished with three interchangeable flush-fitting choke tubes. Imported from Japan by Weatherby. Introduced 1982.
**Price:** 12-ga., IMC, 26", 28", 30" . . . . . . . . . . . . . . . . . . . **$1,950.00**
**Price:** 20-ga., IMC, 26", 28" . . . . . . . . . . . . . . . . . . . . . . **$1,950.00**
**Price:** 28-ga., IMC, 26" . . . . . . . . . . . . . . . . . . . . . . . . . **$1,950.00**
**Price:** 410-bore, fixed Imp. Cyl & Mod., 26" . . . . . . . . . . . . . **$1,950.00**

Weatherby Orion II Classic Sporting

## Weatherby Orion II, III Classic Field O/Us
Similar to the Orion II, Orion III except with rounded pistol grip, slender forend, oil-finished Claro walnut stock with fine-line checkering, Old English recoil pad. Sideplate receiver has rose and scroll engraving. Available in 12-gauge, 26", 28", 30" (IMC tubes), 20-gauge, 26", 28" (IMC tubes), 28-gauge, 26" (IMC tubes), 3" chambers. Introduced 1993.
**Price:** Orion II Classic Field . . . . . . . . . . . . . . . . . . **$1,150.00**
**Price:** Orion III Classic Field (12 and 20 only) . . . . . . . . . **$1,350.00**

## Weatherby Orion II Classic Sporting Clays O/U
Similar to the Orion II Sporting Clays except has rounded pistol grip, slender forend, oil-finished wood. Silver-gray nitride receiver has scroll engraving with clay pigeon monogram in gold-plate overlay. Stepped Broadway-style competition vent rib, vent side rib. Available in 12-gauge, 28" with choke tubes. Introduced 1993.
**Price:** . . . . . . . . . . . . . . . . . . . . . . . . . . . . . . **$1,249.00**

## WEATHERBY ORION O/U SHOTGUNS
**Gauge:** 12, 20, 410, 3" chambers; 28, 2¾" chambers.
**Barrel:** Fixed choke, 12, 20, 28, 410—26", 28", 30" (Imp. Cyl. & Mod., Full & Mod., Skeet & Skeet); IMC Multi-Choke, 12, 20, Field models—26" (Imp. Cyl., Mod., Full, Skeet), 28" (Imp. Cyl., Mod., Full), 30" (Mod., Full); O/U Trap models—30", 32" (Imp. Mod., Mod., Full); Single bbl. Trap—32", 34" (Imp. Mod., Mod., Full).
**Weight:** 6½ to 9 lbs.
**Stock:** American walnut, checkered grip and forend. Rubber recoil pad. Dimensions for Field and Skeet models, 14¼"x1½"x2½".
**Features:** Selective automatic ejectors, single selective mechanical trigger. Top tang safety, Greener cross bolt. Orion I has plain blued receiver, no engraving; Orion II has engraved, blued receiver; Orion III has silver-gray receiver with engraving. Imported from Japan by Weatherby.
**Price:** Orion I, Field, 12, IMC, 26", 28", 30" . . . . . . . . . . . . **$1,050.00**
**Price:** Orion I, Field, 20, IMC, 26", 28" . . . . . . . . . . . . . . **$1,050.00**
**Price:** Orion II, Trap, 30", 32" . . . . . . . . . . . . . . . . . . **$1,207.00**
**Price:** Orion II, Single Barrel Trap, 32" . . . . . . . . . . . . . **$1,207.00**
**Price:** Orion II, Skeet, 12 or 20, fixed chokes, 26" . . . . . . . . **$1,193.00**
**Price:** Orion III, Field, 12, IMC, 26", 28", 30" . . . . . . . . . . . **$1,350.00**
**Price:** Orion III, Field, 20, IMC, 26", 28" . . . . . . . . . . . . . **$1,350.00**

Weatherby Orion II Sporting Clays

## Weatherby Orion II Sporting Clays O/U
Similar to the Orion II Field except in 12-gauge only with 2¾" chambers, 28", 30" barrels with Imp. Cyl., Mod., Full chokes. Stock dimensions are 14¼"x1½"x2¼"; weight 7.5 to 8 lbs. Matte finish, competition center vent. rib, mid-barrel and enlarged front beads. Rounded recoil pad. Receiver finished in silver nitride with acid-etched, gold-plate clay pigeon monogram. Barrels have lengthened forcing cones. Introduced 1992.
**Price:** . . . . . . . . . . . . . . . . . . . . . . . . . . . . . . **$1,249.00**

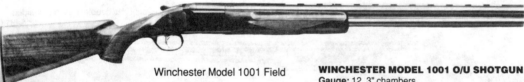

Winchester Model 1001 Field

## Winchester Model 1001 Sporting Clays O/U
Similar to the Model 1001 except has silver nitrate-finished receiver with special engraving incorporating a flying target, fuller pistol grip and radiused recoil pad. Ventilated rib is 10mm wide with mid-rib bead, white front bead. Available with 28" or 30" barrels with four WinPlus choke tubes. Stock dimensions are 14⅜"x1⅜"x2⅛"; weight 7¾ lbs. Introduced 1993.
**Price:** . . . . . . . . . . . . . . . . . . . . . . . . . . . . . . **$1,253.00**

## PIETRO ZANOLETTI MODEL 2000 FIELD O/U
**Gauge:** 12 only.
**Barrel:** 28" (Mod. & Full).
**Weight:** 7 lbs.
**Stock:** European walnut, checkered grip and forend.

## WINCHESTER MODEL 1001 O/U SHOTGUN
**Gauge:** 12, 3" chambers.
**Barrel:** 28" (Imp. Cyl., Mod., Imp. Mod., Skeet WinPlus choke tubes).
**Weight:** 7 lbs. **Length:** 45" overall.
**Stock:** 14¼"x1½"x2". Select walnut with checkered grip and forend.
**Features:** Single selective inertia trigger, automatic ejectors; wide vent rib; back-bored barrels; matte-finished receiver top; receiver is blued and has scroll engraving. Introduced 1993. From U.S. Repeating Arms Co.
**Price:** . . . . . . . . . . . . . . . . . . . . . . . . . . . . . . **$1,099.00**

**Sights:** Gold bead front.
**Features:** Boxlock action with auto ejectors, double triggers; engraved receiver. Imported from Italy by Mandall Shooting Supplies. Introduced 1984.
**Price:** . . . . . . . . . . . . . . . . . . . . . . . . . . . . . . **$895.00**

# SHOTGUNS—SIDE BY SIDES

Variety of models for utility and sporting use, including some competitive shooting.

American Arms Brittany

## AMERICAN ARMS BRITTANY SHOTGUN
**Gauge:** 12, 20, 3" chambers.
**Barrel:** 12-ga.—27"; 20-ga.—25" (Imp. Cyl., Mod., Full choke tubes).
**Weight:** 6 lbs., 7 oz. (20-ga.).
**Stock:** 14⅛"x1⅜"x2⅜". Hand-checkered walnut with oil finish, straight English-style with semi-beavertail forend.
**Features:** Boxlock action with case-color finish, engraving; single selective trigger, automatic selective ejectors; rubber recoil pad. Introduced 1989. Imported from Spain by American Arms, Inc.
**Price:** . . . . . . . . . . . . . . . . . . . . . . . . . . . . . . **$763.00**

**CAUTION:** PRICES CHANGE, CHECK AT GUNSHOP.

American Arms Gentry

## American Arms Derby Side-by-Side

Has sidelock action with English-style engraving on the sideplates. Straight-grip, hand-checkered walnut stock with splinter forend, hand-rubbed oil finish. Single non-selective trigger, automatic selective ejectors. Same chokes, rib, barrel lengths as the Gentry. Has 5-year warranty. From American Arms, Inc.
**Price:** 12- or 20-ga. . . . . . . . . . . . . . . . . . . . . . . . . . . . **$999.50**

American Arms Grulla

## AMERICAN ARMS WS/SS 10

**Gauge:** 10, 3½" chambers.
**Barrel:** 32" (Full & Full). Flat rib.
**Weight:** 10 lbs., 13 oz.
**Stock:** 14⁵⁄₁₆"x1³⁄₈"x2³⁄₈". Hand-checkered walnut with beavertail forend, full pistol grip, dull finish, rubber recoil pad.
**Features:** Boxlock action with double triggers and extractors. All metal has Parkerized finish. Comes with camouflaged sling, sling swivels, 5-year warranty. Introduced 1987. Imported from Spain by American Arms, Inc.
**Price:** . . . . . . . . . . . . . . . . . . . . . . . . . . . . . . . . . . **$639.00**

## American Arms TS/SS 12 Side-by-Side

Similar to the WS/SS 10 except in 12-ga. with 3½" chambers, 26" barrels with Imp. Cyl., Mod., Full choke tubes, single selective trigger, extractors. Comes with camouflage sling, swivels, 5-year warranty. From American Arms, Inc.
**Price:** . . . . . . . . . . . . . . . . . . . . . . . . . . . . . . . . . . **$639.00**

## ARMSPORT 1050 SERIES DOUBLE SHOTGUNS

**Gauge:** 12, 20, 410, 28, 3" chambers.
**Barrel:** 12-ga.—28" (Mod. & Full); 20-ga.—26" (Imp. & Mod.); 410—26" (Full & Full); 28-ga.—26" (Mod. & Full).
**Weight:** About 6¾ lbs.
**Stock:** European walnut.
**Features:** Chrome-lined barrels. Boxlock action with engraving. Imported from Italy by Armsport.
**Price:** 12, 20 . . . . . . . . . . . . . . . . . . . . . . . . . . . . . **$785.00**
**Price:** 28, 410 . . . . . . . . . . . . . . . . . . . . . . . . . . . . . **$860.00**

---

## AMERICAN ARMS GENTRY DOUBLE SHOTGUN

**Gauge:** 12, 20, 28, 410, 3" chambers except 16, 28, 2¾".
**Barrel:** 26" (Imp. Cyl. & Mod., all gauges), 28" (Mod., & Full, 12 and 20 gauges).
**Weight:** 6¼ to 6¾ lbs.
**Stock:** 14⅛"x1³⁄₈"x2³⁄₈". Hand-checkered walnut with semi-gloss finish.
**Sights:** Metal bead front.
**Features:** Boxlock action with English-style scroll engraving, color case-hardened finish. Double triggers, extractors. Independent floating firing pins. Manual safety. Five-year warranty. Introduced 1987. Imported from Spain by American Arms, Inc.
**Price:** 12 or 20 . . . . . . . . . . . . . . . . . . . . . . . . . . . . **$625.00**
**Price:** 28 or 410 . . . . . . . . . . . . . . . . . . . . . . . . . . . . **$655.00**

## AMERICAN ARMS GRULLA #2 DOUBLE SHOTGUN

**Gauge:** 12, 20, 28, 410.
**Barrel:** 12-ga.—28" (Mod. & Full); 26" (Imp. Cyl. & Mod.), all gauges.
**Weight:** 5 lbs., 13 oz. to 6 lbs., 4 oz.
**Stock:** Select walnut with straight English grip, splinter forend; hand-rubbed oil finish; checkered grip, forend, butt.
**Features:** True sidelock action with double triggers, detachable locks, automatic selective ejectors, cocking indicators, gas escape valves. Color case-hardened receiver with scroll engraving. English-style concave rib. Introduced 1989. Imported from Spain by American Arms, Inc.
**Price:** 12, 20, 28, 410 . . . . . . . . . . . . . . . . . . . . . . . **$2,943.00**
**Price:** Two-barrel sets . . . . . . . . . . . . . . . . . . . . . . . **$4,089.00**

## American Arms TS/SS 10 Double Shotgun

Similar to the WS/SS 10 except has 26" (Full & Full choke tubes) barrels, raised solid rib. Double triggers, extractors. All metal and wood has matte finish. Imported by American Arms, Inc.
**Price:** . . . . . . . . . . . . . . . . . . . . . . . . . . . . . . . . . . **$639.00**

## ARRIETA SIDELOCK DOUBLE SHOTGUNS

**Gauge:** 12, 16, 20, 28, 410.
**Barrel:** Length and chokes to customer specs.
**Weight:** To customer specs.
**Stock:** 14½"x1½"x2½" (standard dimensions), or to customer specs. Straight English with checkered butt (standard), or pistol grip. Select European walnut with oil finish.
**Features:** Essentially a custom gun with myriad options. Holland & Holland-pattern hand-detachable sidelocks, selective automatic ejectors, double triggers (hinged front) standard. Some have self-opening action. Finish and engraving to customer specs. Imported from Spain by Wingshooting Adventures.
**Price:** Model 557, auto ejectors, from . . . . . . . . . . . **$2,750.00**
**Price:** Model 570, auto ejectors, from . . . . . . . . . . . **$3,380.00**
**Price:** Model 578, auto ejectors, from . . . . . . . . . . . **$3,740.00**
**Price:** Model 600 Imperial, self-opening, from . . . . . . **$4,990.00**
**Price:** Model 601 Imperial Tiro, self-opening, from . . . **$5,750.00**
**Price:** Model 801, from . . . . . . . . . . . . . . . . . . . . . **$7,950.00**
**Price:** Model 802, from . . . . . . . . . . . . . . . . . . . . . **$7,950.00**
**Price:** Model 803, from . . . . . . . . . . . . . . . . . . . . . **$5,850.00**
**Price:** Model 871, auto ejectors, from . . . . . . . . . . . **$4,290.00**
**Price:** Model 872, self-opening, from . . . . . . . . . . . . **$9,790.00**
**Price:** Model 873, self-opening, from . . . . . . . . . . . . **$6,850.00**
**Price:** Model 874, self-opening, from . . . . . . . . . . . . **$7,950.00**
**Price:** Model 875, self-opening, from . . . . . . . . . . . **$13,950.00**

---

Consult our Directory pages for the location of firms mentioned.

---

Arizaga Model 31

## ARIZAGA MODEL 31 DOUBLE SHOTGUN

**Gauge:** 12, 16, 20, 28, 410.
**Barrel:** 26", 28" (standard chokes).
**Weight:** 6 lbs., 9 oz. **Length:** 45" overall.
**Stock:** Straight English style or pistol grip.
**Features:** Boxlock action with double triggers; blued, engraved receiver. Imported by Mandall Shooting Supplies.
**Price:** . . . . . . . . . . . . . . . . . . . . . . . . . . . . . . . . . . **$550.00**

**CAUTION:** PRICES CHANGE, CHECK AT GUNSHOP.

## AYA BOXLOCK SHOTGUNS

**Gauge:** 12, 16, 20, 28, 410.
**Barrel:** 26", 27", 28", depending upon gauge.
**Weight:** 5 to 7 lbs.
**Stock:** European walnut.
**Features:** Anson & Deeley system with double locking lugs; chopper lump barrels; bushed firing pins; automatic safety and ejectors; articulated front trigger. Imported by Armes de Chasse.
**Price:** Model XXV, 12 or 20 . . . . . . . . . . . . . . . . . . . **$3,300.00**
**Price:** Model 4 Deluxe, 12, 16, 20, 28, 410 . . . . . . . . . **$3,500.00**
**Price:** Model 4, 12, 16, 20, 28, 410 . . . . . . . . . . . . . **$2,000.00**

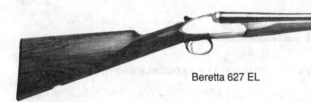

Beretta 627 EL

## BERETTA SIDE-BY-SIDE FIELD SHOTGUNS

**Gauge:** 12 and 20, 3" chambers.
**Barrel:** 26" and 28" (Mobilchoke tubes).
**Stock:** Close-grained American walnut.
**Features:** Front and center beads on a raised ventilated rib. Onyx has P. Beretta signature on each side of the receiver, while a gold gauge marking is inscribed atop the rib. Imported from Italy by Beretta U.S.A.
**Price:** 626 Onyx . . . . . . . . . . . . . . . . . . . . . . . . **$1,870.00**
**Price:** 627 EL (gold inlays, sideplates) . . . . . . . . . . . . **$3,270.00**
**Price:** 627 EELL (engraved sideplates, pistol grip or straight English stock) . . . . . . . . . . . . . . . . . . . . . . . . . . . **$5,405.00**

## CHAPUIS SIDE-BY-SIDE SHOTGUN

**Gauge:** 12, 16, 20.
**Barrel:** 22", 23.6", 26.8", 27.6", 31.5", chokes to customer specs.
**Weight:** 5 to 10 lbs. **Length:** NA.
**Stock:** French walnut, straight English or pistol grip.
**Features:** Double hook Blitz system center sidelock action with notched action zone, automatic ejectors or extractors. Long trigger guard (most models), choice of raised solid rib, vent. rib or ultra light rib. Imported from France by Armes de Chasse.
**Price:** About . . . . . . . . . . . . . . . . $4,000.00 to $5,000.00

## CHARLES DALY MODEL DSS DOUBLE

**Gauge:** 12, 20, 3" chambers.
**Barrel:** 26", choke tubes.
**Weight:** 6 lbs., 13 oz. (12-ga.). **Length:** 44.5" overall.
**Stock:** 14 1/8"x1 3/8"x2 3/8". Figured walnut; pistol grip; cut checkering; black rubber recoil pad; semi-beavertail forend.
**Features:** Boxlock action with automatic selective ejectors, automatic safety, gold single trigger. Engraved, silvered frame. Introduced 1990. Imported by Outdoor Sports Headquarters.
**Price:** . . . . . . . . . . . . . . . . . . . . . . . . . . . . . **$675.00**

## AYA SIDELOCK DOUBLE SHOTGUNS

**Gauge:** 12, 16, 20, 28, 410.
**Barrel:** 26", 27", 28", 29", depending upon gauge.
**Weight:** NA.
**Stock:** Figured European walnut; cut checkering; oil finish.
**Features:** Sidelock actions with double triggers (articulated front), automatic safety, automatic ejectors, cocking indicators, bushed firing pins, replaceable hinge pins, chopper lump barrels. Many options available. Imported by Armes de Chasse.
**Price:** Model 1, 12 or 20, exhibition-quality wood . . . . . . . . . **$7,000.00**
**Price:** Model 2, 12, 16, 20, 28, 410 . . . . . . . . . . . . . **$3,700.00**
**Price:** Model 53, 12, 16, 20 . . . . . . . . . . . . . . . . . **$5,300.00**
**Price:** Model 56, 12 only . . . . . . . . . . . . . . . . . . . **$8,200.00**
**Price:** Model XXV, 12 or 20, Churchill-type rib . . . . . . . . . **$4,300.00**
**Price:** Matador, 12 or 20, single selective trigger, pistol grip stock . **$2,000.00**

## BERETTA MODEL 452 SIDELOCK SHOTGUN

**Gauge:** 12, 2 3/4" or 3" chambers.
**Barrel:** 26", 28", 30", choked to customer specs.
**Weight:** 6 lbs., 13 oz.
**Stock:** Dimensions to customer specs. Highly figured walnut; Model 452 EELL has walnut briar.
**Features:** Full sidelock action with English-type double bolting; automatic selective ejectors, manual safety; double triggers, single or single non-selective trigger on request. Essentially custom made to specifications. Model 452 is coin finished without engraving; 452 EELL is fully engraved. Imported from Italy by Beretta U.S.A.
**Price:** 452 . . . . . . . . . . . . . . . . . . . . . . . . . . **$22,000.00**
**Price:** 452 EELL . . . . . . . . . . . . . . . . . . . . . . . **$30,500.00**

## CRUCELEGUI HERMANOS MODEL 150 DOUBLE

**Gauge:** 12, 16 or 20, 2 3/4" chambers.
**Action:** Greener triple cross bolt.
**Barrel:** 20", 26", 28", 30", 32" (Cyl. & Cyl., Full & Full, Mod. & Full, Mod. & Imp. Cyl., Imp. Cyl. & Full, Mod. & Mod.).
**Weight:** 5 to 7 1/4 lbs.
**Stock:** Hand-checkered walnut, beavertail forend.
**Features:** Double triggers; color case-hardened receiver; sling swivels; chrome-lined bores. Imported from Spain by Mandall Shooting Supplies.
**Price:** . . . . . . . . . . . . . . . . . . . . . . . . . . . . . **$450.00**

## E.A.A./SABATTI SABA-MON DOUBLE SHOTGUN

**Gauge:** 12, 20, 28, 410, 3" chambers.
**Barrel:** 26" or 28" (standard chokes).
**Weight:** NA.
**Stock:** European walnut, straight English or pistol grip.
**Features:** Anson & Deeley-type boxlock action, single selective trigger, automatic selective ejectors. Blue finish. Introduced 1993. Imported from Italy by European American Armory.
**Price:** . . . . . . . . . . . . . . . . . . . . . . . . . . . . **$1,095.00**

## FERLIB MODEL F VII DOUBLE SHOTGUN

**Gauge:** 12, 16, 20, 28, 410.
**Barrel:** 25" to 28".
**Weight:** 5 1/2 lbs. (20-ga.).
**Stock:** Oil-finished walnut, checkered straight grip and forend.
**Features:** Boxlock action with fine scroll engraving, silvered receiver. Double triggers standard. Introduced 1983. Imported from Italy by Wm. Larkin Moore.
**Price:** F.VII . . . . . . . . . . . . . . . . . . . . . . . . . . **$7,500.00**
**Price:** F.VII SC . . . . . . . . . . . . . . . . . . . . . . . . **$9,000.00**
**Price:** F.VII SP Sideplate with gold . . . . . . . . . . . . . . **$13,000.00**

Francotte Boxlock

## AUGUSTE FRANCOTTE BOXLOCK SHOTGUN

**Gauge:** 12, 16, 20, 28 and 410-bore, 2 3/4" or 3" chambers.
**Barrel:** 26" to 29", chokes to customer specs.
**Weight:** NA. **Length:** NA.
**Stock:** Deluxe European walnut to customer specs. Straight or pistol grip; checkered butt; oil finish; splinter or beavertail forend.
**Sights:** Bead front.
**Features:** Anson & Deeley boxlock action with double locks, double triggers (front hinged), manual or automatic safety, Holland & Holland ejectors. English scroll engraving, coin finish or color case-hardening. Many options available. Imported from Belgium by Armes de Chasse.
**Price:** From about . . . . . . . . . . . . . . . $16,000.00 to $20,000.00

## AUGUSTE FRANCOTTE SIDELOCK SHOTGUN
**Gauge:** 12, 16, 20, 28 and 410-bore, 2¾" or 3" chambers.
**Barrel:** 26" to 29", chokes to customer specs.
**Weight:** NA. **Length:** NA.
**Stock:** Deluxe European walnut to customer specs. Straight or pistol grip; checkered butt; oil finish; splinter or beavertail forend.

Garbi Model 100

## Garbi Model 101 Side-by-Side
Similar to the Garbi Model 100 except is hand engraved with scroll engraving, select walnut stock. Better overall quality than the Model 100. Imported from Spain by Wm. Larkin Moore.
**Price:** From . . . . . . . . . . . . . . . . . . . . . . . . . . . . . . **$5,750.00**

## Garbi Model 103A, B Side-by-Side
Similar to the Garbi Model 100 except has Purdey-type fine scroll and rosette engraving. Better overall quality than the Model 101. Model 103B has nickel-chrome steel barrels, H&H-type easy opening mechanism; other mechanical details remain the same. Imported from Spain by Wm. Larkin Moore.
**Price:** Model 103A, from . . . . . . . . . . . . . . . . . . . **$7,100.00**
**Price:** Model 103B, from . . . . . . . . . . . . . . . . . . . **$9,900.00**

## BILL HANUS BIRDGUN DOUBLES
**Gauge:** 16, 20, 28.
**Barrel:** 26" (Skeet & Skeet).
**Weight:** About 6¼ lbs. (16-ga.).
**Stock:** Hand-checkered walnut; straight grip, semi-beavertail forend.

## HATFIELD UPLANDER SHOTGUN
**Gauge:** 20, 3" chambers.
**Barrel:** 26" (Imp. Cyl. & Mod.).
**Weight:** 5¾ lbs.
**Stock:** Straight English style, special select XXX fancy maple. Hand-rubbed oil finish. Splinter forend.
**Features:** Double locking under-lug boxlock action; color case-hardened frame; single non-selective trigger. Grades differ in engraving, finish, gold work. Introduced 1988. From Hatfield.

Merkel Model 147E

| Consult our Directory pages for the location of firms mentioned. |
|---|

## MERKEL MODEL 47LSC SPORTING CLAYS DOUBLE
**Gauge:** 12, 3" chambers.
**Barrel:** 28" with Briley choke tubes.
**Weight:** 7.2 lbs.
**Stock:** Fancy figured walnut with pistol grip, recoil pad. Beavertail forend.
**Features:** Anson & Deeley boxlock action with single selective trigger adjsutable for length of pull; H&H-type ejectors; white front sight with mid-rib bead; manual safety; cocking indicators; lengthened forcing cones; color case-hardened receiver with Arabesque engraving. Comes with fitted leather luggage case. Introduced 1993. Imported from Germany by GSI.
**Price:** . . . . . . . . . . . . . . . . . . . . . . . . . . . . . . . **$2,995.00**

**Sights:** Bead front.
**Features:** True Holland & Holland sidelock action with double locks, double triggers (front hinged), manual or automatic safety, Holland & Holland ejectors. English scroll engraving, coin finish or color case-hardening. Many options available. Imported from Belgium by Armes de Chasse.
**Price:** From about . . . . . . . . . . . . . . **$20,000.00 to $25,000.00**

## GARBI MODEL 100 DOUBLE
**Gauge:** 12, 16, 20, 28.
**Barrel:** 26", 28", choked to customer specs.
**Weight:** 5½ to 7½ lbs.
**Stock:** 14½"x2¼"x1½". European walnut. Straight grip, checkered butt, classic forend.
**Features:** Sidelock action, automatic ejectors, double triggers standard. Color case-hardened action, coin finish optional. Single trigger; beavertail forend, etc. optional. Five other models are available. Imported from Spain by Wm. Larkin Moore.
**Price:** From . . . . . . . . . . . . . . . . . . . . . . . . . . . . **$4,500.00**

## Garbi Model 200 Side-by-Side
Similar to the Garbi Model 100 except has heavy-duty locks, magnum proofed. Very fine Continental-style floral and scroll engraving, well figured walnut stock. Other mechanical features remain the same. Imported from Spain by Wm. Larkin Moore.
**Price:** . . . . . . . . . . . . . . . . . . . . . . . . . . . . . . . **$9,400.00**

**Features:** Color case-hardened boxlock action; raised Churchill rib; single non-selective trigger; auto ejectors, auto safety. Introduced 1991. Imported by Precision Sports.
**Price:** 16-, 20-ga. . . . . . . . . . . . . . . . . . . . . . . . . . **$1,269.95**
**Price:** 28-ga. . . . . . . . . . . . . . . . . . . . . . . . . . . . . **$1,399.95**

Hatfield Uplander

**Price:** Grade I . . . . . . . . . . . . . . . . . . . . . . . . . . . **$1,995.00**
**Price:** Grade II . . . . . . . . . . . . . . . . . . . . . . . . . . . **$2,595.00**
**Price:** Grades III through VIII, from . . . . . . . . . . . . . . **$3,500.00**

## MERKEL MODEL 8, 47E SIDE-BY-SIDE SHOTGUNS
**Gauge:** 12, 3" chambers, 16, 2¾" chambers, 20, 3" chambers.
**Barrel:** 12-, 16-ga.—28"; 20-ga.—26¾" (Imp. Cyl. & Mod., Mod. & Full).
**Weight:** About 6¾ lbs. (12-ga.).
**Stock:** Oil-finished walnut; straight English or pistol grip.
**Features:** Anson & Deeley-type boxlock action with single selective or double triggers, automatic safety, cocking indicators. Color case-hardened receiver with standard Arabesque engraving. Imported from Germany by GSI.
**Price:** Model 8 (extractors only) . . . . . . . . . . . . . . . . **$1,295.00**
**Price:** Model 47E (H&H ejectors) . . . . . . . . . . . . . . . **$1,595.00**
**Price:** Model 147 (extractors, silver-grayed receiver with hunting scenes) . . . . . . . . . . . . . . . . . . . . . . . . . . . . **$1,795.00**
**Price:** Model 147E (as above with ejectors) . . . . . . . . . **$1,995.00**
**Price:** Model 122 (as above with false sideplates, fine engraving) . **$3,195.00**

## Merkel Model 47S, 147S Side-by-Sides
Similar to the Model 122 except with Holland & Holland-style sidelock action with cocking indicators, ejectors. Silver-grayed receiver and sideplates have Arabesque engraving, engraved border and screws (Model 47S), or fine hunting scene engraving (Model 147S). Imported from Germany by GSI.
**Price:** Model 47S . . . . . . . . . . . . . . . . . . . . . . . . . **$4,195.00**
**Price:** Model 147S . . . . . . . . . . . . . . . . . . . . . . . . . **$5,195.00**
**Price:** Model 247S (English-style engraving, large scrolls) . . . . **$6,895.00**
**Price:** Model 347S (English-style engraving, medium scrolls) . . . **$7,895.00**
**Price:** Model 447S (English-style engraving, small scrolls) . . . . **$8,995.00**

# SHOTGUNS—SIDE BY SIDES

**PARKER REPRODUCTIONS SIDE-BY-SIDE SHOTGUN**
**Gauge:** 12, 16/20 combo, 20, 28, 2¾" and 3" chambers.
**Barrel:** 26" (Skeet 1 & 2, Imp. Cyl. & Mod.), 28" (Mod. & Full, 2¾" and 3", 12, 20, 28; Skeet 1 & 2, Imp. Cyl. & Mod., Mod. & Full 16-ga. only).
**Weight:** 6¾ lbs. (12-ga.)
**Stock:** Checkered (26 lpi) AAA fancy California English or Claro walnut, skeleton steel and checkered butt. Straight or pistol grip, splinter or beavertail forend.
**Features:** Exact reproduction of the original Parker—parts interchange. Double or single selective trigger, selective ejectors, hard-chromed bores, designed

for steel shot. One, two or three (16-20, 20) barrel sets available. Hand-engraved snap caps included. Introduced 1984. Made by Winchester. Imported from Japan by Parker Division, Reagent Chemical.
**Price:** D Grade, one-barrel set . . . . . . . . . . $3,370.00
**Price:** Two-barrel set, same gauge . . . . . . . $4,200.00
**Price:** Two-barrel set, 16/20 . . . . . . . . . . . $4,870.00
**Price:** Three-barrel set, 16/20/20 . . . . . . . $5,630.00
**Price:** A-1 Special two-barrel set . . . . . . . $11,200.00
**Price:** A-1 Special three-barrel set . . . . . . $13,200.00

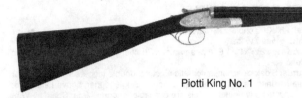

Piotti King No. 1

**PIOTTI KING NO. 1 SIDE-BY-SIDE**
**Gauge:** 12, 16, 20, 28, 410.
**Barrel:** 25" to 30" (12-ga.), 25" to 28" (16, 20, 28, 410). To customer specs. Chokes as specified.

**Piotti Lunik Side-by-Side**
Similar to the Piotti King No. 1 except better overall quality. Has Renaissance-style large scroll engraving in relief, gold crown in top lever, gold name and gold crest in forend. Best quality Holland & Holland-pattern sidelock ejector double with chopper lump (demi-bloc) barrels. Other mechanical specifications remain the same. Imported from Italy by Wm. Larkin Moore.
**Price:** From . . . . . . . . . . . . . . . . . . . . . $21,500.00

**Weight:** 6½ lbs. to 8 lbs. (12-ga. to customer specs.).
**Stock:** Dimensions to customer specs. Finely figured walnut; straight grip with checkered butt with classic splinter forend and hand-rubbed oil finish standard. Pistol grip, beavertail forend, satin luster finish optional.
**Features:** Holland & Holland pattern sidelock action, automatic ejectors. Double trigger with front trigger hinged standard; non-selective single trigger optional. Coin finish standard; color case-hardened optional. Top rib; level, file-cut standard; concave, ventilated optional. Very fine, full coverage scroll engraving with small floral bouquets, gold crown in top lever, name in gold, and gold crest in forend. Imported from Italy by Wm. Larkin Moore.
**Price:** From . . . . . . . . . . . . . . . . . . . . . $19,900.00

**Piotti King Extra Side-by-Side**
Similar to the Piotti King No. 1 except highest quality wood and metal work. Choice of either bulino game scene engraving or game scene engraving with gold inlays. Engraved and signed by a master engraver. Exhibition grade wood. Other mechanical specifications remain the same. Imported from Italy by Wm. Larkin Moore.
**Price:** From . . . . . . . . . . . . . . . . . . . . . $23,700.00

Piotti Piuma

**PIOTTI PIUMA SIDE-BY-SIDE**
**Gauge:** 12, 16, 20, 28, 410.
**Barrel:** 25" to 30" (12-ga.), 25" to 28" (16, 20, 28, 410).

**Weight:** 5½ to 6¼ lbs. (20-ga.).
**Stock:** Dimensions to customer specs. Straight grip stock with walnut checkered butt, classic splinter forend, hand-rubbed oil finish are standard; pistol grip, beavertail forend, satin luster finish optional.
**Features:** Anson & Deeley boxlock ejector double with chopper lump barrels. Level, file-cut rib, light scroll and rosette engraving, scalloped frame. Double triggers with hinged front standard, single non-selective optional. Coin finish standard, color case-hardened optional. Imported from Italy by Wm. Larkin Moore.
**Price:** From . . . . . . . . . . . . . . . . . . . . . $11,900.00

Precision Sports 640E

**PRECISION SPORTS MODEL 600 SERIES DOUBLES**
**Gauge:** 10, 3½" chambers; 12, 16, 20, 2¾" chambers; 28, 410, 3" chambers.
**Barrel:** 25", 26", 27", 28" (Imp. Cyl. & Mod., Mod. & Full).
**Weight:** 12-ga., 6¾-7 lbs.; 20-ga., 5¾-6 lbs.
**Stock:** 14½"x1½"x2½". Hand-checkered walnut with oil finish. "E" (English) models have straight grip, splinter forend, checkered butt. "A" (American) models have p.g. stock, beavertail forend, buttplate.
**Features:** Boxlock action; silvered, engraved action; automatic safety; ejectors or extractors. E-models have double triggers, concave rib (XXV models have Churchill-type rib); A-models have single, non-selective trigger, raised matte rib. Made in Spain by Ugartechea. Imported by Precision Sports. Introduced 1986.

**Price:** 640E (12, 16, 20; 26", 28"), extractors . . . . . . . . $849.95
**Price:** 640E (28, 410 only), extractors . . . . . . . . $939.95
**Price:** 640A (12, 16, 20; 26", 28"), extractors . . . . . . . . $964.95
**Price:** 640A (28, 410 only), ejectors . . . . . . . . $1,109.95
**Price:** 640M "Big Ten" (10-ga. 26", 30", 32", Full & Full) . . . . . . . . $999.95
**Price:** 640 Slug Gun (12, 25", Imp. Cyl. & Imp. Cyl.) . . . . . . . . $1,119.95
**Price:** 645E (12, 16, 20; 26", 28"), with ejectors . . . . . . . . $1,089.95
**Price:** 645E (28, 410), with ejectors . . . . . . . . $1,149.95
**Price:** 645A (12, 16, 20; 26", 28"), with ejectors . . . . . . . . $1,199.95
**Price:** 645A (28, 410), ejectors . . . . . . . . $1,309.95
**Price:** 645E-XXV (12, 16, 20; 25"), with ejectors . . . . . . . . $1,099.95
**Price:** 645E-XXV (28, 410), with ejectors . . . . . . . . $1,199.95
**Price:** 650E (12), extrators, choke tubes . . . . . . . . $919.95
**Price:** 650A (12), extractors, choke tubes . . . . . . . . $1,039.95
**Price:** 655E (12), ejectors, choke tubes . . . . . . . . $1,149.95
**Price:** 655A (12), ejectors, choke tubes . . . . . . . . $1,259.95

**RIZZINI BOXLOCK SIDE-BY-SIDE**
**Gauge:** 12, 16, 20, 28, 410.
**Barrel:** 25" to 30" (12-, 16-, 20-ga.), 25" to 28" (28, 410).
**Weight:** 5½ to 6¼ lbs. (20-ga.).
**Stock:** Dimensions to customer specs. Straight grip stock with checkered butt, classic splinter forend, hand-rubbed oil finish are standard; pistol grip, beavertail forend; satin luster finish optional.
**Features:** Anson & Deeley boxlock ejector double with chopper lump barrels. Level, file-cut rib, scalloped frame. Double triggers with hinged front optional, single non-selective standard. Coin finish standard. Imported from Italy by Wm. Larkin Moore.
**Price:** 12-, 20-ga., from . . . . . . . . . . . . . $23,000.00
**Price:** 28, 410 bore, from . . . . . . . . . . . . $25,500.00

**RIZZINI SIDELOCK SIDE-BY-SIDE**
**Gauge:** 12, 16, 20, 28, 410.
**Barrel:** 25" to 30" (12-, 16-, 20-ga.), 25" to 28" (28, 410). To customer specs. Chokes as specified.
**Weight:** 6½ lbs. to 8 lbs. (12-ga. to customer specs).
**Stock:** Dimensions to customer specs. Finely figured walnut; straight grip with checkered butt with classic splinter forend and hand-rubbed oil finish standard. Pistol grip, beavertail forend, satin luster finish optional.
**Features:** Holland & Holland pattern sidelock action, auto ejectors. Double triggers with front trigger hinged optional; non-selective single trigger standard. Coin finish standard. Top rib level, file cut standard; concave optional. Imported from Italy by Wm. Larkin Moore.
**Price:** 12-, 20-ga., from . . . . . . . . . . . . . $40,000.00
**Price:** 28, 410 bore, from . . . . . . . . . . . . $46,000.00

**CAUTION:** PRICES CHANGE, CHECK AT GUNSHOP.

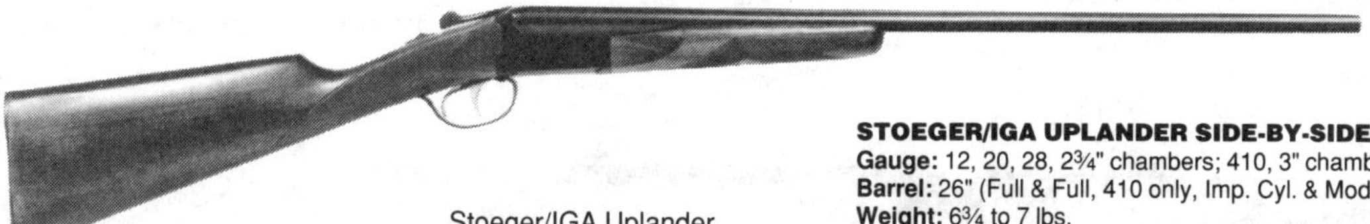

Stoeger/IGA Uplander

**STOEGER/IGA UPLANDER SIDE-BY-SIDE SHOTGUN**
**Gauge:** 12, 20, 28, $2\frac{3}{4}$" chambers; 410, 3" chambers.
**Barrel:** 26" (Full & Full, 410 only, Imp. Cyl. & Mod.), 28" (Mod. & Full).
**Weight:** $6\frac{3}{4}$ to 7 lbs.
**Stock:** $14\frac{1}{2}$"x$1\frac{1}{2}$"x$2\frac{1}{2}$". Oil-finished hardwood. Checkered pistol grip and forend.
**Features:** Automatic safety, extractors only, solid matted barrel rib. Double triggers only. Introduced 1983. Imported from Brazil by Stoeger Industries.
**Price:** . . . . . . . . . . **$383.00**
**Price:** With choke tubes . . . . . . . . . . **$425.00**
**Price:** Coach Gun, 12, 20, 410, 20" bbls. . . . . . . . . . **$367.00**

**UGARTECHEA 10-GAUGE MAGNUM SHOTGUN**
**Gauge:** 10, $3\frac{1}{2}$" chambers.
**Action:** Boxlock.
**Barrel:** 32" (Full).
**Weight:** 11 lbs.
**Stock:** $14\frac{1}{2}$"x$1\frac{1}{2}$"x$2\frac{5}{8}$". European walnut, checkered at pistol grip and forend.
**Features:** Double triggers; color case-hardened action, rest blued. Front and center metal beads on matted rib; ventilated rubber recoil pad. Forend release has positive Purdey-type mechanism. Imported from Spain by Mandall Shooting Supplies.
**Price:** . . . . . . . . . . **$699.50**

# SHOTGUNS—BOLT ACTIONS & SINGLE SHOTS

Variety of designs for utility and sporting purposes, as well as for competitive shooting.

**ARMSPORT SINGLE BARREL SHOTGUN**
**Gauge:** 20, 3" chamber.
**Barrel:** 26" (Mod.).
**Weight:** About $6\frac{1}{2}$ lbs.
**Stock:** Hardwood with oil finish.
**Features:** Chrome-lined barrel, manual safety, cocking indicator. Opening lever behind trigger guard. Imported by Armsport.
**Price:** . . . . . . . . . . **$100.00**

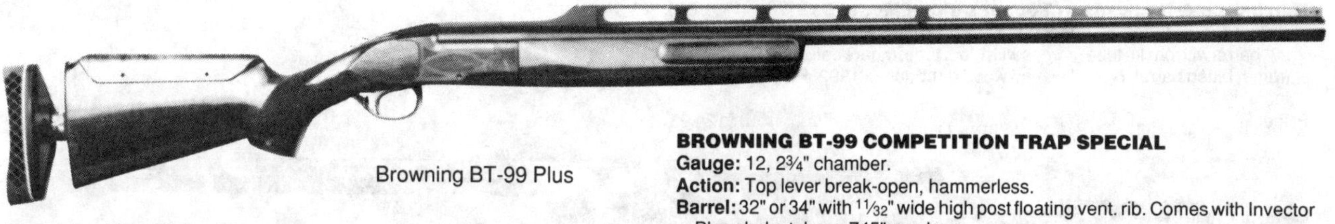

Browning BT-99 Plus

**Browning BT-99 Plus Trap Gun**
Similar to the Grade I BT-99 except comes with 32" or 34" barrel with .745" over bore, Invector Plus choke system with Full, Imp. Mod. and Mod. choke tubes; high post, ventilated, tapered, target rib adjustable from 3" to 12" above point of aim. Available with or without ported barrel. Select walnut stock has high-gloss finish, Monte Carlo comb, modified beavertail forend and is fully adjustable for length of pull, drop at comb and drop at Monte Carlo. Has Browning Recoil Reduction System. Introduced 1989.
**Price:** Grade I, with ported barrel . . . . . . . . . . **$1,780.00**
**Price:** Grade I, non-ported barrel . . . . . . . . . . **$1,765.00**
**Price:** Stainless, ported . . . . . . . . . . **$2,150.00**
**Price:** Pigeon Grade, ported . . . . . . . . . . **$1,985.00**
**Price:** Signature Painted, ported . . . . . . . . . . **$1,815.00**

**BROWNING BT-99 COMPETITION TRAP SPECIAL**
**Gauge:** 12, $2\frac{3}{4}$" chamber.
**Action:** Top lever break-open, hammerless.
**Barrel:** 32" or 34" with $\frac{11}{32}$" wide high post floating vent. rib. Comes with Invector Plus choke tubes; .745" overbore.
**Weight:** 8 lbs. (32" bbl.).
**Stock:** French walnut; hand-checkered, full pistol grip, full beavertail forend; recoil pad. Trap dimensions with M.C. $14\frac{3}{8}$"x$1\frac{3}{8}$"x$1\frac{3}{8}$"x2".
**Sights:** Ivory front and middle beads.
**Features:** Gold-plated trigger with $3\frac{1}{2}$-lb. pull, deluxe trap-style recoil pad, automatic ejector, no safety. Available with either Monte Carlo or standard stock. Imported from Japan by Browning.
**Price:** Grade I Invector, Plus Ported barrels . . . . . . . . . . **$1,225.00**
**Price:** Stainless, ported . . . . . . . . . . **$1,650.00**
**Price:** Pigeon Grade, ported . . . . . . . . . . **$1,430.00**
**Price:** Signature Painted . . . . . . . . . . **$1,260.00**

**Browning BT-99 Plus Micro**
Similar to the standard BT-99 Plus except scaled down for smaller shooters. Comes with 28", 30", 32" or 34" barrel with adjustable rib system and buttstock with adjustable length of pull range of $13\frac{1}{2}$" to 14". Also has Browning's recoil reducer system, ported barrels, Invector Plus choke system and back-bored barrel. Weight is about 8 lbs., 6 oz. Introduced 1991.
**Price:** With ported barrel . . . . . . . . . . **$1,780.00**
**Price:** With non-ported barrel . . . . . . . . . . **$1,765.00**
**Price:** Stainless, ported . . . . . . . . . . **$2,150.00**
**Price:** Pigeon Grade, ported . . . . . . . . . . **$1,985.00**
**Price:** Signature Painted**$1,815.00**

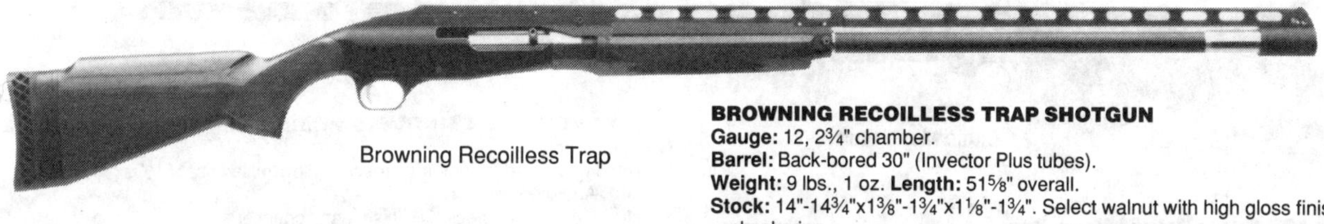

Browning Recoilless Trap

**BROWNING RECOILLESS TRAP SHOTGUN**
**Gauge:** 12, $2\frac{3}{4}$" chamber.
**Barrel:** Back-bored 30" (Invector Plus tubes).
**Weight:** 9 lbs., 1 oz. **Length:** $51\frac{5}{8}$" overall.
**Stock:** 14"-$14\frac{3}{4}$"x$1\frac{3}{8}$"-$1\frac{3}{4}$"x$1\frac{1}{8}$"-$1\frac{3}{4}$". Select walnut with high gloss finish, cut checkering.
**Features:** Eliminates up to 72 percent of recoil. Mass of the inner mechansim (barrel, receiver and inner bolt) is driven forward when trigger is pulled, cancelling most recoil. Forend is used to cock action when the action is forward. Ventilated rib adjusts to move point of impact; drop at comb and length of pull adjustable. Introduced 1993. Imported by Browning.
**Price:** . . . . . . . . . . **$1,670.00**

**Browning Micro Recoilless Trap Shotgun**
Same as the standard Recoilless Trap except has 27" barrel, weighs 8 lbs., 10 oz., and stock length of pull adjustable from 13" to $13\frac{3}{4}$", Overall length $47\frac{5}{8}$". Introduced 1993. Imported by Browning.
**Price:** . . . . . . . . . . **$1,670.00**

## DESERT INDUSTRIES BIG TWENTY SHOTGUN
**Gauge:** 20, 2¾" chamber.
**Barrel:** 19" (Cyl.).
**Weight:** 4¾ lbs. **Length:** 31¾" overall.
**Stock:** Fixed wire, with buttplate. Walnut forend and grip.

H&R Topper 098

## Harrington & Richardson Topper Classic Youth Shotgun
Similar to the Topper Junior 098 except available in 20-gauge (3", Mod.), 410-bore (Full) with 3" chamber; 28-gauge, 2¾" chamber (Mod.); all have 22" barrel. Stock is American black walnut with cut-checkered pistol grip and forend. Ventilated rubber recoil pad with white line spacers. Blued barrel, blued frame. Introduced 1992. From H&R 1871, Inc.
**Price:** . . . . . . . . . . . . . . . . . . . . . . . . . . . . **$139.95**

H&R N.W.T.F. Turkey

## Harrington & Richardson Topper Deluxe Model 098
Similar to the standard Topper 098 except 12-gauge only with 3½" chamber, 28" barrel with choke tube (comes with Mod. tube, others optional). Satin nickel frame, blued barrel, black-finished wood. Introduced 1992. From H&R 1871, Inc.
**Price:** . . . . . . . . . . . . . . . . . . . . . . . . . . . . **$124.95**

Krieghoff KS-5 Trap

## Krieghoff KS-5 Special
Same as the KS-5 except the barrel has a fully adjustable rib and adjustable stock. Rib allows shooter to adjust point of impact from 50%/50% to nearly 90%/10%. Introduced 1990.
**Price:** . . . . . . . . . . . . . . . . . . . . . . . . . . . . **$4,450.00**

## KRIEGHOFF K-80 SINGLE BARREL TRAP GUN
**Gauge:** 12, 2¾" chamber.
**Barrel:** 32" or 34" Unsingle; 34" Top Single. Fixed Full or choke tubes.
**Weight:** About 8¾ lbs.
**Stock:** Four stock dimensions or adjustable stock available. All hand-checkered European walnut.

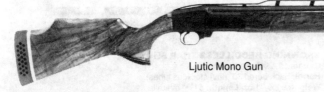

Ljutic Mono Gun

## Ljutic LTX Super Deluxe Mono Gun
Super Deluxe version of the standard Mono Gun with high quality wood, extra-fancy checkering pattern in 24 lpi, double recessed choking. Available in two weights: 8¼ lbs. or 8¾ lbs. Extra light 33" barrel; medium-height rib. Introduced 1984. From Ljutic Industries.
**Price:** . . . . . . . . . . . . . . . . . . . . . . . . . . . . **$5,595.00**
**Price:** With three screw-in choke tubes . . . . . . . . . . . . **$5,995.00**

---

**Stock:** Bead front.
**Features:** Single shot action of all steel construction. Blue finish. Announced 1990. From Desert Industries, Inc.
**Price:** . . . . . . . . . . . . . . . . . . . . . . . . . . . . **$189.95**

## HARRINGTON & RICHARDSON TOPPER MODEL 098
**Gauge:** 12, 20, 410, 3" chamber.
**Barrel:** 12 ga.—28" (Mod.); 20 ga.—26" (Mod.); 410 bore—26" (Full).
**Weight:** 5-6 lbs.
**Stock:** Black-finish hardwood with full pistol grip; semi-beavertail forend.
**Sights:** Gold bead front.
**Features:** Break-open action with side-lever release, automatic ejector. Satin nickel frame, blued barrel. Reintroduced 1992. From H&R 1871, Inc.
**Price:** . . . . . . . . . . . . . . . . . . . . . . . . . . . . **$109.95**
**Price:** Topper Junior 098 (as above except 22" barrel, 20-ga. (Mod.), 410-bore (Full), 12½" length of pull) . . . . . . . . . . . . . . **$114.95**

## Harrington & Richardson N.W.T.F Turkey Mag
Similar to the Topper 098 except covered with Mossy Oak camouflage. Chambered for 12-gauge 3½" chamber, 24" barrel (comes with Turkey Full choke tube, others available); weighs 6 lbs., overall length 40". Comes with Mossy Oak sling, swivels, studs. Introduced 1992. From H&R 1871, Inc.
**Price:** . . . . . . . . . . . . . . . . . . . . . . . . . . . . **$169.95**

## KRIEGHOFF KS-5 TRAP GUN
**Gauge:** 12, 2¾" chamber.
**Barrel:** 32", 34"; Full choke or choke tubes.
**Weight:** About 8½ lbs.
**Stock:** Choice of high Monte Carlo (1½"), low Monte Carlo (1⅜") or factory adjustable stock. European walnut.
**Features:** Ventilated tapered step rib. Adjustable trigger or optional release trigger. Satin gray electroless nickel receiver. Comes with fitted aluminum case. Introduced 1988. Imported from Germany by Krieghoff International, Inc.
**Price:** Fixed choke, cased . . . . . . . . . . . . . . . . . . . **$3,575.00**
**Price:** With choke tubes . . . . . . . . . . . . . . . . . . . **$3,975.00**

**Features:** Satin nickel finish with K-80 logo. Selective mechanical trigger adjustable for finger position. Tapered step vent. rib. Adjustable point of impact on Unsingle.
**Price:** Standard grade full Unsingle . . . . . . . . . . . . . . **$7,300.00**
**Price:** Standard grade full Top Single combo (special order), from **$9,380.00**
**Price:** RT (removable trigger) option, add . . . . . . . . . . . **$1,000.00**

## LJUTIC MONO GUN SINGLE BARREL
**Gauge:** 12 only.
**Barrel:** 34", choked to customer specs; hollow-milled rib, 35½" sight plane.
**Weight:** Approx. 9 lbs.
**Stock:** To customer specs. Oil finish, hand checkered.
**Features:** Totally custom made. Pull or release trigger; removable trigger guard contains trigger and hammer mechanism; Ljutic pushbutton opener on front of trigger guard. From Ljutic Industries.
**Price:** With standard, medium or Olympic rib, custom 32"-34" bbls. **$4,495.00**
**Price:** As above except with screw-in choke barrel . . . . . . . . **$4,695.00**

---

**CAUTION:** PRICES CHANGE, CHECK AT GUNSHOP.

# SHOTGUNS—BOLT ACTIONS & SINGLE SHOTS

## LJUTIC RECOILLESS SPACE GUN SHOTGUN
**Gauge:** 12 only, 2¾" chamber.
**Barrel:** 30" (Full). Screw-in or fixed-choke barrel.
**Weight:** 8½ lbs.
**Stock:** 14½" to 15" pull length; universal comb; medium or large p.g.

Marlin Model 55

## MARLIN MODEL 55 GOOSE GUN BOLT ACTION
**Gauge:** 12 only, 2¾" or 3" chamber.

**Sights:** Vent. rib.
**Features:** Pull trigger standard, release trigger available; anti-recoil mechanism. Revolutionary new design. Introduced 1981. From Ljutic Industries.
**Price:** From . . . . . . . . . . . . . . . . . . . . . . . . . . . **$5,995.00**

**Action:** Bolt action, thumb safety, detachable two-shot clip. Red cocking indicator.
**Barrel:** 36" (Full).
**Weight:** 8 lbs. **Length:** 56¾" overall.
**Stock:** Walnut-finished hardwood, p.g., ventilated recoil pad. Swivel studs, MarShield® finish.
**Features:** Brass bead front sight, U-groove rear sight.
**Price:** . . . . . . . . . . . . . . . . . . . . . . . . . . . . . . **$274.75**

## NEW ENGLAND FIREARMS TURKEY AND GOOSE GUN
**Gauge:** 10, 3½" chamber.
**Barrel:** 28" (Full).
**Weight:** 9.5 lbs. **Length:** 44" overall.
**Stock:** American hardwood with walnut, or matte camo finish; ventilated rubber recoil pad.
**Sights:** Bead front.
**Features:** Break-open action with side-lever release; ejector. Matte finish on metal. Introduced 1992. From New England Firearms.
**Price:** Walnut-finish wood . . . . . . . . . . . . . . . . . . . **$149.95**
**Price:** Camo finish, sling and swivels . . . . . . . . . . . . **$159.95**

New England Turkey

### New England Firearms N.W.T.F. Shotgun
Similar to the Turkey/Goose Gun except completely covered with Mossy Oak camouflage finish; 24" barrel with interchangeable choke tubes (comes with Turkey Full, others optional); comes with Mossy Oak sling. Drilled and tapped for long eye relief scope mount. Introduced 1992. From New England Firearms.
**Price:** . . . . . . . . . . . . . . . . . . . . . . . . . . . . . . **$199.95**
**Price:** 20-ga., 24" (Mod.), Mossy Oak camo . . . . . . . . . . . **$149.95**

New England Slug

## NEW ENGLAND FIREARMS TRACKER SLUG GUN
**Gauge:** 12, 20, 3" chamber.
**Barrel:** 24" (Cyl.).

**Weight:** 6 lbs. **Length:** 40" overall.
**Stock:** Walnut-finished hardwood with full pistol grip, recoil pad.
**Sights:** Blade front, fully adjustable rifle-type rear.
**Features:** Break-open action with side-lever release; blued barrel, color case-hardened frame. Introduced 1992. From New England Firearms.
**Price:** Tracker . . . . . . . . . . . . . . . . . . . . . . . . . . **$124.95**
**Price:** Tracker II (as above except fully rifled bore) . . . . . . . . **$129.95**

## NEW ENGLAND FIREARMS STANDARD PARDNER
**Gauge:** 12, 20, 410, 3" chamber; 16, 28, 2¾" chamber.
**Barrel:** 12-ga.—28" (Full, Mod.); 16-ga.—28" (Full); 20-ga.—26" (Full, Mod.); 28-ga.—26" (Mod.); 410-bore—26" (Full).
**Weight:** 5-6 lbs. **Length:** 43" overall (28" barrel).
**Stock:** Walnut-finished hardwood with full pistol grip.

**Sights:** Bead front.
**Features:** Transfer bar ignition; break-open action with side-lever release. Introduced 1987. From New England Firearms.
**Price:** . . . . . . . . . . . . . . . . . . . . . . . . . . . . . . **$99.95**
**Price:** Youth model (20-ga., 410, 22" barrel, recoil pad) . . . . . . **$104.95**

New England Survival

## NEW ENGLAND FIREARMS SURVIVAL GUN
**Gauge:** 12, 20, 3" chamber.
**Barrel:** 22" (Mod.).

**Weight:** 6 lbs. **Length:** 36" overall.
**Stock:** Black polymer with thumbhole/pistol grip, sling swivels.
**Sights:** Bead front.
**Features:** Buttplate swings open to expose storage for extra ammunition. Blue or nickel finish. Introduced 1993. From New England Firearms.
**Price:** Blue . . . . . . . . . . . . . . . . . . . . . . . . . . . . **$129.95**
**Price:** Nickel . . . . . . . . . . . . . . . . . . . . . . . . . . . **$149.95**

## PERAZZI TM1 SPECIAL SINGLE TRAP
**Gauge:** 12, 2¾" chambers.
**Barrel:** 32" or 34" (Extra Full).
**Weight:** 8 lbs., 6 oz.
**Stock:** To customer specs; interchangeable.
**Features:** Tapered and stepped high rib; adjustable four-position trigger. Also available with choke tubes. Imported from Italy by Perazzi U.S.A., Inc.

Perazzi TM1

**Price:** From . . . . . . . . . . . . . . . . . . . . . . . . . . . **$5,750.00**
**Price:** TMX Special Single (as above except special high rib), from **$5,950.00**

CAUTION: PRICES CHANGE, CHECK AT GUNSHOP.

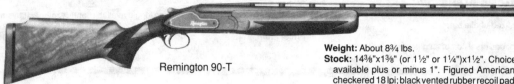

Remington 90-T

**Weight:** About 8¾ lbs.
**Stock:** 14⅜"x1⅜" (or 1½" or 1¼")x1½". Choice of drops at comb, pull length available plus or minus 1". Figured American walnut with low-luster finish, checkered 18 lpi; black vented rubber recoil pad. Cavity in forend and buttstock for added weight.
**Features:** Barrel is over-bored with elongated forcing cones. Removable sideplates can be ordered with engraving; drop-out trigger assembly. Metal has non-glare matte finish. Available with extra barrels in different lengths, chokes, extra trigger assemblies and sideplates, porting, stocks. Introduced 1990. From Remington.
**Price:** Depending on options . . . . . . . . . . . . . . . . . . . **$2,995.00**
**Price:** With high post adjustable rib and adjustable comb . . . . . . . . **NA**

## REMINGTON 90-T SUPER SINGLE SHOTGUN
**Gauge:** 12, 2¾" chamber.
**Barrel:** 30", 32", 34", fixed choke or Rem Choke tubes; ported or non-ported. Medium-high tapered, ventilated rib; white Bradley-type front bead, stainless center bead.

Snake Charmer II

## SNAKE CHARMER II SHOTGUN
**Gauge:** 410, 3" chamber.
**Barrel:** 18¼".
**Weight:** About 3½ lbs. **Length:** 28⅝" overall.
**Stock:** ABS grade impact resistant plastic.
**Features:** Thumbhole-type stock holds four extra rounds. Stainless steel barrel and frame. Reintroduced 1989. From Sporting Arms Mfg., Inc.
**Price:** . . . . . . . . . . . . . . . . . . . . . . . . . . . . . . . . **$139.00**
**Price:** New Generation Snake Charmer (as above except with black carbon steel bbl.) . . . . . . . . . . . . . . . . . . . . . . . . . . . **$129.00**

## STOEGER/IGA REUNA SINGLE BARREL SHOTGUN
**Gauge:** 12, 2¾" chamber; 20, 410, 3" chamber.
**Barrel:** 12-ga.—26" (Imp. Cyl.), 28" (Full); 20-ga.—26" (Full); 410 bore—26" (Full).
**Weight:** 5¼ lbs.
**Stock:** 14"x1½"x2½". Brazilian hardwood.

**Sights:** Metal bead front.
**Features:** Exposed hammer with half-cock safety; extractor; blue finish. Introduced 1987. Imported from Brazil by Stoeger Industries.
**Price:** . . . . . . . . . . . . . . . . . . . . . . . . . . . . . . . . **$115.00**
**Price:** 12-, 20-ga., Full choke tube . . . . . . . . . . . . . . . . . . **$132.00**
**Price:** Youth model (20-ga., 410, 22" Full) . . . . . . . . . . . . . **$127.00**

Thompson/Center Hunter

## THOMPSON/CENTER TCR '87 HUNTER SHOTGUN
**Gauge:** 10, 12, 3½".
**Barrel:** 25" (Full).
**Weight:** 8 lbs.
**Stock:** Uncheckered walnut.
**Sights:** Bead front.
**Features:** Uses same receiver as TCR '87 rifle models, and stock has extra ⁷⁄₁₆" drop at heel. Choke designed for steel shot. Available only through the T/C custom shop. Introduced 1989. From Thompson/Center.
**Price:** About . . . . . . . . . . . . . . . . . . . . . . . . . . . . . **$595.00**

# SHOTGUNS—MILITARY & POLICE

Designs for utility, suitable for and adaptable to competitions and other sporting purposes.

American Arms/Franchi SPAS-12

## AMERICAN ARMS/FRANCHI SPAS-12 SHOTGUN
**Gauge:** 12, 2¾" chamber.
**Barrel:** 21½" (Cyl.), with muzzle protector.
**Weight:** 8¾ lbs. **Length:** 41" overall.
**Stock:** Black nylon with full pistol grip.
**Sights:** Blade front, aperture rear.
**Features:** Gas-operated semi-auto converts instantly to pump action; cross-bolt safety and secondary tactical lever safety; 7-shot tubular magazine; matte phosphate finish. Choke tubes available as accessories. Imported from Italy by American Arms, Inc.
**Price:** . . . . . . . . . . . . . . . . . . . . . . . . . . . . . . . . **$713.00**
**Price:** LAW-12 (as above except gas-operated action only) . . . . . **$686.00**

Benelli M3 Super 90

## Benelli M1 Super 90
Similar to the M3 Super 90 except is semi-automatic only, has overall length of 41" and weighs 7 lbs. Introduced 1986.
**Price:** Slug Gun with standard stock . . . . . . . . . **$724.00**
**Price:** With pistol grip stock (Defense) . . . . . . . . **$764.00**
**Price:** With ghost ring sight system (standard stock) . . . . . . . **$764.00**
**Price:** With ghost ring sight system, pistol grip stock (Defense) . . . **$814.00**

## BENELLI M3 SUPER 90 PUMP/AUTO SHOTGUN
**Gauge:** 12, 3" chamber, 7-shot magazine.
**Barrel:** 19¾" (Cyl.).
**Weight:** 7 lbs., 8 oz. **Length:** 41" overall.
**Stock:** High-impact polymer with sling loop in side of butt; rubberized pistol grip on stock. Also folding stock model.
**Sights:** Post front, buckhorn rear adjustable for windage. Ghost ring system available.
**Features:** Combination pump/auto action. Alloy receiver with inertia recoil rotating locking lug bolt; matte finish; automatic shell release lever. Introduced 1989. Imported by Heckler & Koch, Inc.
**Price:** . . . . . . . . . . . . . . . . . . . . **$919.00**
**Price:** With Ghost Ring sight system . . . . . . . . **$949.00**
**Price:** With folding stock . . . . . . . . . . . . **$1,029.00**

Benelli M1 Super 90 Tactical

## Benelli M1 Super 90 Tactical Shotgun
Similar to the M1 Super 90 except has 18.5" barrel with Imp. Cyl., Mod., Full choke tubes, ghost ring sight system (tritium night sights optional), 7-shot magazine. In 12-gauge (3" chamber) only, matte-finish receiver. Overall length 39.75". Introduced 1993. Imported from Italy by Heckler & Koch, Inc.
**Price:** . . . . . . . . . . . . . . . . . . . . **$829.00**

Beretta Model 1201FP3

## ITHACA MODEL 87 M&P DSPS SHOTGUNS
**Gauge:** 12, 3" chamber, 5- or 8-shot magazine.
**Barrel:** 20" (Cyl.).
**Weight:** 7 lbs.
**Stock:** Walnut.
**Sights:** Bead front on 5-shot, rifle sights on 8-shot.
**Features:** Parkerized finish; bottom ejection; cross-bolt safety. Reintroduced 1988. From Ithaca Acquisition Corp.
**Price:** M&P, 5-shot . . . . . . . . . . . . . . **$322.00**
**Price:** DSPS, 8-shot . . . . . . . . . . . . . . **$322.00**
**Price:** DSPS, 5-shot, nickel . . . . . . . . . . . **$422.00**

## BERETTA MODEL 1201FP3 AUTO SHOTGUN
**Gauge:** 12, 3" chamber.
**Barrel:** 20" (Cyl.).
**Weight:** 7.3 lbs. **Length:** NA
**Stock:** Special strengthened technopolymer, matte black finish.
**Stock:** Fixed rifle type.
**Features:** Has 6-shot magazine. Introduced 1988. Imported from Italy by Beretta U.S.A.
**Price:** . . . . . . . . . . . . . . . . . . . . **$660.00**
**Price:** Pistol grip model . . . . . . . . . . . . . **$705.00**

## Ithaca Model 87 Hand Grip Shotgun
Similar to the Model 87 M&P except has black polymer pistol grip and slide handle. In 12- or 20-gauge, 18½" barrel (Cyl.), 5-shot magazine. Reintroduced 1988.
**Price:** . . . . . . . . . . . . . . . . . . . . **$323.00**

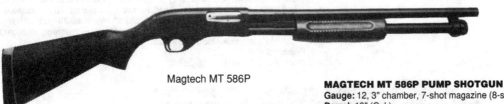

Magtech MT 586P

## MAVERICK MODEL 60 AUTO SHOTGUN
**Gauge:** 12, 2¾" chamber, 6-shot.
**Barrel:** 18½" (Cyl.).
**Weight:** 7 lbs. **Length:** 38⅜" overall.
**Stock:** Black synthetic.
**Sights:** Bead front.
**Features:** Shoots 2¾" loads only. Blue finish. Introduced 1993. From Maverick Arms, Inc.
**Price:** . . . . . . . . . . . . . . . . . . . . **$264.00**

## MAGTECH MT 586P PUMP SHOTGUN
**Gauge:** 12, 3" chamber, 7-shot magazine (8-shot with 2¾" shells).
**Barrel:** 19" (Cyl.).
**Weight:** 7.3 lbs. **Length:** 39.5" overall.
**Stock:** Brazilian hardwood.
**Sights:** Bead front.
**Features:** Dual action slide bars, cross-bolt safety. Blue finish. Introduced 1991. Imported from Brazil by Magtech Recreational Products.
**Price:** About . . . . . . . . . . . . . . . . . . **$219.00**

Maverick 88 Bullpup

### MAVERICK MODEL 88 PUMP SECURITY SHOTGUN
**Gauge:** 12, 3" chamber, 6-shot.
**Barrel:** 18½" (Cyl.).
**Weight:** 6 lbs. **Length:** 38⅜" overall.
**Stock:** Black synthetic. Regular butt or pistol grip only.
**Sights:** Bead front.
**Features:** Blue finish. Ribbed pump handle. Introduced 1993. From Maverick Arms, Inc.
**Price:** . . . . . . . . . . . . . . . . . . . . . . . . . . . . . . . . **$199.00**

### MAVERICK MODEL 88 BULLPUP SHOTGUN
**Gauge:** 12, 3" chamber; 6-shot magazine.
**Barrel:** 18½" (Cyl.).
**Weight:** 9½ lbs. **Length:** 26½" overall.
**Stock:** Bullpup design of high-impact plastics.
**Sights:** Fixed, mounted in carrying handle.
**Features:** Uses the Model 88 pump shotgun action. Cross-bolt and grip safeties. Mossberg Cablelock included. Introduced 1991. From Maverick Arms.
**Price:** . . . . . . . . . . . . . . . . . . . . . . . . . . . . . . . **$291.00**

### Maverick Model HS410 Shotgun
Similar to the Maverick Model 88 except chambered for 410, 3" shells; has pistol grip forend, thick recoil pad, muzzle brake and special spreader choke on the 18.5" barrel. Overall length is 37.5", weight is 6.25 lbs. Blue finish; synthetic field stock. Also available with integral Laser Sight forend. Cablelock included. Introduced 1993. From Maverick Arms, Inc.
**Price:** HS410 . . . . . . . . . . . . . . . . . . . . . . . . . . **$226.00**
**Price:** HS410 Laser . . . . . . . . . . . . . . . . . . . . . . **$366.00**

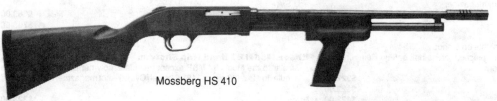

Mossberg 500 Security

### Mossberg Model 500, 590 Ghost-Ring Shotguns
Similar to the Model 500 Security except has adjustable blade front, adjustable Ghost-Ring rear sight with protective "ears." Model 500 has 18.5" (Cyl.) barrel, 6-shot capacity; Model 590 has 20" (Cyl.) barrel, 9-shot capacity. Both have synthetic field stock. Mossberg Cablelock included. Introduced 1990. From Mossberg.
**Price:** Model 500, blue . . . . . . . . . . . . . . . . . . . . **$300.00**
**Price:** As above, Parkerized . . . . . . . . . . . . . . . . . **$348.00**
**Price:** Model 590, blue . . . . . . . . . . . . . . . . . . . . **$359.00**
**Price:** As above, Parkerized . . . . . . . . . . . . . . . . . **$406.00**

### Mossberg Model 500, 590 Mariner Pump
Similar to the Model 500 or 590 Security except all metal parts finished with Marinecote, a Teflon and metal coating to resist rust and corrosion. Synthetic field stock; pistol grip kit included. Mossberg Cablelock included.
**Price:** 6-shot, 18½" barrel . . . . . . . . . . . . . . . . . . **$353.00**
**Price:** 9-shot, 20" barrel . . . . . . . . . . . . . . . . . . . **$353.00**

### MOSSBERG MODEL 500 PERSUADER/CRUISER SECURITY SHOTGUNS
**Gauge:** 12, 20, 410, 3" chamber.
**Barrel:** 18½", 20" (Cyl.).
**Weight:** 7 lbs.
**Stock:** Walnut-finished hardwood or synthetic field.
**Sights:** Metal bead front.
**Features:** Available in 6- or 8-shot models. Top-mounted safety, double action slide bars, swivel studs, rubber recoil pad. Blue, Parkerized, Marinecote finishes. Pistol grip kit and Mossberg Cablelock included. **Price list not complete—contact Mossberg for full list.**
**Price:** 12- or 20-ga., 18½", blue, wood or synthetic stock, 6-shot . . **$251.00**
**Price:** As above, Parkerized finish, synthetic stock, 6-shot . . . . . **$274.00**
**Price:** Cruiser, 12- or 20-ga., 18½", blue, pistol grip only . . . . . **$242.00**
**Price:** As above, 410-bore . . . . . . . . . . . . . . . . . . **$280.00**
**Price:** 12-ga., 8-shot, blue, wood or synthetic stock . . . . . . . . **$251.00**
**Price:** As above with rifle sights . . . . . . . . . . . . . . . **$272.00**

### Mossberg Model 500, 590 Intimidator Shotguns
Similar to the Model 500 or 590 Security with synthetic stock except has integral Laser Sight built into the forend. Mossberg Cablelock included. Introduced 1990.
**Price:** Model 500, blue, 6-shot . . . . . . . . . . . . . . . **$505.00**
**Price:** Model 500, Parkerized, 6-shot . . . . . . . . . . . . **$527.00**
**Price:** Model 590, blue, 9-shot . . . . . . . . . . . . . . . **$556.00**
**Price:** Model 590, Parkerized, 9-shot . . . . . . . . . . . . **$601.00**

Mossberg HS 410

### Mossberg Model HS410 Shotgun
Similar to the Model 500 Security pump except chambered for 410, 3" shells; has pistol grip forend, thick recoil pad, muzzle brake and has special spreader choke on the 18.5" barrel. Overall length is 37.5", weight is 6.25 lbs. Blue finish; synthetic field stock. Also available with integral Laser Sight forend. Mossberg Cablelock and video included. Introduced 1990.
**Price:** HS 410 . . . . . . . . . . . . . . . . . . . . . . . . . **$253.00**
**Price:** HS 410 Laser . . . . . . . . . . . . . . . . . . . . . . **$451.00**

Mossberg Model 590

### MOSSBERG MODEL 590 SHOTGUN
**Gauge:** 12, 3" chamber.
**Barrel:** 20" (Cyl.).
**Weight:** 7¼ lbs.
**Stock:** Synthetic field or Speedfeed.
**Sights:** Metal bead front.
**Features:** Top-mounted safety, double slide action bars. Comes with heat shield, bayonet lug, swivel studs, rubber recoil pad. Blue, Parkerized or Marinecote finish. Mossberg Cablelock included. From Mossberg.
**Price:** Blue, synthetic stock . . . . . . . . . . . . . . . . . **$305.00**
**Price:** Parkerized, synthetic stock . . . . . . . . . . . . . . **$351.00**
**Price:** Blue, Speedfeed stock . . . . . . . . . . . . . . . . . **$319.00**
**Price:** Parkerized, Speedfeed stock . . . . . . . . . . . . . . **$366.00**

Remington 870P

## REMINGTON 870P POLICE SHOTGUN
**Gauge:** 12, 3" chamber.
**Barrel:** 18", 20" (Police Cyl.), 20" (Imp. Cyl.).

**Weight:** About 7 lbs.
**Stock:** Lacquer-finished hardwood.
**Sights:** Metal bead front or rifle sights.
**Features:** Solid steel receiver, double action slide bars. Blued or Parkerized finish.
**Price:** 18" or 20", bead sight, about . . . . . . . . . . . . . . . . $356.00
**Price:** 20", rifle sights, about . . . . . . . . . . . . . . . . $383.00

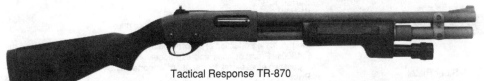

Tactical Response TR-870

## TACTICAL RESPONSE TR-870 SHOTGUN
**Gauge:** 12, 3" chamber, 7-shot magazine.
**Barrel:** 18" (Cyl.).
**Weight:** 9 lbs. **Length:** 38" overall.
**Stock:** Fiberglass-filled polypropolene with non-snag recoil absorbing butt pad. Nylon tactical forend houses flashlight.
**Sights:** Trak-Lock ghost ring sight system. Front sight has tritium insert.

**Features:** Highly modified Remington 870P with Parkerized finish. Comes with nylon three-way adjustable sling, high visibility non-binding follower, high performance magazine spring, Jumbo Head safety, and Side Saddle extended 6-shot shell carrier on left side of receiver. Introduced 1991. From Scattergun Technologies, Inc.
**Price:** Standard model . . . . . . . . . . . . . . . . . . . . $695.00
**Price:** FBI model, 5-shot . . . . . . . . . . . . . . . . . $665.00
**Price:** Patrol model, 5-shot, no Side Saddle . . . . . . . . . . . . $525.00
**Price:** Border Patrol model, 7-shot, standard forend . . . . . . $555.00
**Price:** Military model, 7-shot, bayonet lug . . . . . . . . . . $655.00
**Price:** K-9 model, 7-shot (Rem. 11-87 action) . . . . . . . . . $755.00
**Price:** Urban Sniper, 7-shot, rifled bbl., Burris Scout scope, Rem. 11-87 action . . . . . . . . . . . . . . . . . . . $1,095.00

Winchester Model 1300 Defender

## Winchester Model 1300 Stainless Marine Pump Gun
Same as the Defender except has bright chrome finish, stainless steel barrel, rifle-type sights only. Phosphate coated receiver for corrosion resistance.
**Price:** About . . . . . . . . . . . . . . . . . . . . . . $436.00

## Winchester 8-Shot Pistol Grip Pump Security Shotguns
Same as regular Defender Pump but with pistol grip and forend of high-impact resistant ABS plastic with non-glare black finish. Introduced 1984.
**Price:** Pistol Grip Defender, about . . . . . . . . . . . . . . . $270.00

## WINCHESTER MODEL 1300 DEFENDER PUMP GUN
**Gauge:** 12, 20, 3" chamber, 5- or 8-shot capacity.
**Barrel:** 18" (Cyl.).
**Weight:** 6¾ lbs. **Length:** 38⅝" overall.
**Stock:** Walnut-finished hardwood stock and ribbed forend, or synthetic; or pistol grip.
**Sights:** Metal bead front.
**Features:** Cross-bolt safety, front-locking rotary bolt, twin action slide bars. Black rubber buttpad. From U.S. Repeating Arms Co.
**Price:** 8-shot, wood or synthetic stock . . . . . . . . . . . . $270.00
**Price:** 5-shot, wood stock . . . . . . . . . . . . . . . . . $270.00

# BLACKPOWDER SINGLE SHOT PISTOLS—FLINT & PERCUSSION

Dixie Charleville

Consult our Directory pages for the location of firms mentioned.

## BLACK WATCH SCOTCH PISTOL
**Caliber:** 577 (.500" round ball).
**Barrel:** 7", smoothbore.
**Weight:** 1½ lbs. **Length:** 12" overall.
**Stock:** Brass.
**Sights:** None.
**Features:** Faithful reproduction of this military flintlock. From Dixie Gun Works, E.M.F.
**Price:** . . . . . . . . . . . . . . . . . . . . . . . $175.00 to $310.00

## CHARLEVILLE FLINTLOCK PISTOL
**Caliber:** 69 (.680" round ball).
**Barrel:** 7½".
**Weight:** 48 oz. **Length:** 13½" overall.
**Stock:** Walnut.
**Sights:** None.
**Features:** Brass frame, polished steel barrel, iron belt hook, brass buttcap and backstrap. Replica of original 1777 pistol. Imported by Dixie Gun Works, E.M.F.
**Price:** . . . . . . . . . . . . . . . . . . . . . . . $195.00 to $325.00

CVA Hawken

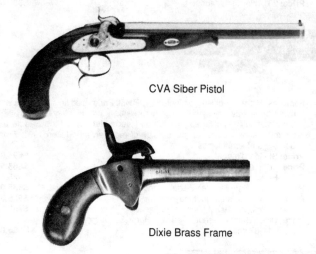

CVA Siber Pistol

Dixie Brass Frame

## DIXIE LINCOLN DERRINGER
**Caliber:** 41.
**Barrel:** 2", 8 lands, 8 grooves.
**Weight:** 7 oz. **Length:** 5½" overall.
**Stock:** Walnut finish, checkered.
**Sights:** Fixed.
**Features:** Authentic copy of the "Lincoln Derringer." Shoots .400" patched ball. German silver furniture includes trigger guard with pineapple finial, wedge plates, nose, wrist, side and teardrop inlays. All furniture, lockplate, hammer, and breech plug engraved. Imported from Italy by Dixie Gun Works.
**Price:** With wooden case . . . . . . . . . . . . . . . . . . . . . . . . . **$285.95**
**Price:** Kit (not engraved) . . . . . . . . . . . . . . . . . . . . . . . . **$89.95**

## FRENCH-STYLE DUELING PISTOL
**Caliber:** 44.
**Barrel:** 10".
**Weight:** 35 oz. **Length:** 15¾" overall.
**Stock:** Carved walnut.
**Sights:** Fixed.
**Features:** Comes with velvet-lined case and accessories. Imported by Mandall Shooting Supplies.
**Price:** . . . . . . . . . . . . . . . . . . . . . . . . . . . . . . . . . . **$295.00**

Dixie Tornado

## CVA HAWKEN PISTOL
**Caliber:** 50.
**Barrel:** 9¾"; ¹⁵⁄₁₆" flats.
**Weight:** 50 oz. **Length:** 16½" overall.
**Stock:** Select hardwood.
**Sights:** Beaded blade front, fully adjustable open rear.
**Features:** Color case-hardened lock, polished brass wedge plate, nose cap, ramrod thimbles, trigger guard, grip cap. Hooked breech. Imported by CVA.
**Price:** . . . . . . . . . . . . . . . . . . . . . . . . . . . . . . . . . . **$176.95**
**Price:** Kit . . . . . . . . . . . . . . . . . . . . . . . . . . . . . . . . . **$109.95**

## CVA SIBER PISTOL
**Caliber:** 45.
**Barrel:** 10½".
**Weight:** 34 oz. **Length:** 15½" overall.
**Stock:** High-grade French walnut, checkered grip.
**Sights:** Barleycorn front, micro-adjustable rear.
**Features:** Reproduction of pistol made by Swiss watchmaker Jean Siber in the 1800s. Precision lock and set-trigger give fast lock time. Has engraved, polished steel barrel, trigger guard. Imported by CVA.
**Price:** . . . . . . . . . . . . . . . . . . . . . . . . . . . . . . . . . . **$439.95**

## CVA VEST POCKET DERRINGER
**Caliber:** 44.
**Barrel:** 2½", brass.
**Weight:** 7 oz.
**Stock:** Two-piece walnut.
**Features:** All brass frame with brass ramrod. A muzzle-loading version of the Colt No. 3 derringer. Imported by CVA.
**Price:** Finished . . . . . . . . . . . . . . . . . . . . . . . . . . . . . . **$69.95**

## DIXIE BRASS FRAME DERRINGER
**Caliber:** 41.
**Barrel:** 2½".
**Weight:** 7 oz. **Length:** 5½" overall.
**Stock:** Walnut.
**Features:** Brass frame, color case-hardened hammer and trigger. Shoots .395" round ball. Engraved model available. From Dixie Gun Works.
**Price:** Plain model . . . . . . . . . . . . . . . . . . . . . . . . . . . . **$69.95**
**Price:** Engraved model . . . . . . . . . . . . . . . . . . . . . . . . . . **$95.50**

## DIXIE PENNSYLVANIA PISTOL
**Caliber:** 44 (.430" round ball).
**Barrel:** 10" (⅞" octagon).
**Weight:** 2½ lbs.
**Stock:** Walnut-stained hardwood.
**Sights:** Blade front, open rear drift-adjustable for windage; brass.
**Features:** Available in flint only. Brass trigger guard, thimbles, nosecap, wedgeplates; high-luster blue barrel. Imported from Italy by Dixie Gun Works.
**Price:** Finished . . . . . . . . . . . . . . . . . . . . . . . . . . . . . **$149.95**
**Price:** Kit . . . . . . . . . . . . . . . . . . . . . . . . . . . . . . . . . **$119.95**

## DIXIE SCREW BARREL PISTOL
**Caliber:** .445".
**Barrel:** 2½".
**Weight:** 8 oz. **Length:** 6½" overall.
**Stock:** Walnut.
**Features:** Trigger folds down when hammer is cocked. Close copy of the originals once made in Belgium. Uses No. 11 percussion caps. From Dixie Gun Works.
**Price:** . . . . . . . . . . . . . . . . . . . . . . . . . . . . . . . . . . **$89.00**
**Price:** Kit . . . . . . . . . . . . . . . . . . . . . . . . . . . . . . . . . **$74.95**

## DIXIE TORNADO TARGET PISTOL
**Caliber:** 44 (.430" round ball).
**Barrel:** 10", octagonal, 1:22 twist.
**Stocks:** Walnut, target-style. Left unfinished for custom fitting. Walnut forend.
**Sights:** Blade on ramp front, micro-type open rear adjustable for windage and elevation.
**Features:** Grip frame style of 1860 Colt revolver. Improved model of the Tingle and B.W. Southgate pistol. Trigger adjustable for pull. Frame, barrel, hammer and sights in the white, brass trigger guard. Comes with solid brass, walnut-handled cleaning rod with jag and nylon muzzle protector. Introduced 1983. From Dixie Gun Works.
**Price:** . . . . . . . . . . . . . . . . . . . . . . . . . . . . . . . . . . **$215.50**

**CAUTION:** PRICES CHANGE, CHECK AT GUNSHOP.

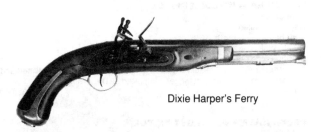

Dixie Harper's Ferry

## HAWKEN PERCUSSION PISTOL
**Caliber:** 54.
**Barrel:** 9", octagonal.
**Weight:** 40 oz. **Length:** 14" overall.
**Stock:** Checkered walnut.
**Sights:** Blade front, fixed notch rear.
**Features:** German silver trigger guard, blued barrel. Imported from Italy by E.M.F.
**Price:** . . . . . . . . . . . . . . . . . . . . . . . . . . . . $370.00

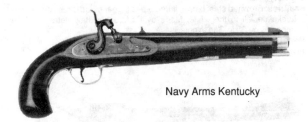

Navy Arms Kentucky

Lyman Plains Pistol

## CHARLES MOORE FLINTLOCK PISTOL
**Caliber:** 45.
**Barrel:** 10", octagonal.
**Weight:** 36 oz. **Length:** 15" overall.
**Stock:** Checkered hardwood.
**Sights:** Blade front, fixed notch rear.
**Features:** German silver trigger guard, rest blued. Imported from Italy by E.M.F.
**Price:** . . . . . . . . . . . . . . . . . . . . . . . . . . . . $400.00

## NAVY ARMS LE PAGE DUELING PISTOL
**Caliber:** 44.
**Barrel:** 9", octagon, rifled.
**Weight:** 34 oz. **Length:** 15" overall.
**Stock:** European walnut.
**Sights:** Adjustable rear.
**Features:** Single-set trigger. Polished metal finish. From Navy Arms.
**Price:** Percussion . . . . . . . . . . . . . . . . $475.00
**Price:** Single cased set, percussion . . . . . . . . $685.00
**Price:** Double cased set, percussion . . . . . . $1,290.00
**Price:** Flintlock, rifled . . . . . . . . . . . . . . $550.00
**Price:** Flintlock, smoothbore (45-cal.) . . . . . . . . $550.00
**Price:** Flintlock, single cased set . . . . . . . . . $760.00
**Price:** Flintlock, double cased set . . . . . . . $1,430.00

## HARPER'S FERRY 1806 PISTOL
**Caliber:** 58 (.570" round ball).
**Barrel:** 10".
**Weight:** 40 oz. **Length:** 16" overall.
**Stock:** Walnut.
**Sights:** Fixed.
**Features:** Case-hardened lock, brass-mounted browned barrel. Replica of the first U.S. Gov't.-made flintlock pistol. Imported by Navy Arms, Dixie Gun Works, E.M.F.
**Price:** . . . . . . . . . . . . . . . . . . $249.95 to $405.00
**Price:** Kit (Dixie) . . . . . . . . . . . . . . . . . . . $184.95

## KENTUCKY FLINTLOCK PISTOL
**Caliber:** 44, 45.
**Barrel:** 10⅛".
**Weight:** 32 oz. **Length:** 15½" overall.
**Stock:** Walnut.
**Sights:** Fixed.
**Features:** Specifications, including caliber, weight and length may vary with importer. Case-hardened lock, blued barrel; available also as brass barrel flint Model 1821. Imported by Navy Arms (44 only), The Armoury, E.M.F.
**Price:** . . . . . . . . . . . . . . . . . . $145.00 to $207.00
**Price:** Brass barrel (E.M.F.) . . . . . . . . . . . . . $265.00
**Price:** In kit form, from . . . . . . . . . . . $90.00 to $112.00
**Price:** Single cased set (Navy Arms) . . . . . . . . $300.00
**Price:** Double cased set (Navy Arms) . . . . . . . . $515.00

### Kentucky Percussion Pistol
Similar to flint version but percussion lock. Imported by The Armoury, E.M.F., Navy Arms, CVA (50-cal.).
**Price:** . . . . . . . . . . . . . . . . . . $141.95 to $250.00
**Price:** Brass barrel (E.M.F.) . . . . . . . . . . . . . $275.00
**Price:** Steel barrel (Armoury) . . . . . . . . . . . . $179.00
**Price:** Single cased set (Navy Arms) . . . . . . . . $300.00
**Price:** Double cased set (Navy Arms) . . . . . . . . $515.00

## LE PAGE PERCUSSION DUELING PISTOL
**Caliber:** 45.
**Barrel:** 10", rifled.
**Weight:** 40 oz. **Length:** 16" overall.
**Stock:** Walnut, fluted butt.
**Sights:** Blade front, notch rear.
**Features:** Double-set triggers. Blued barrel; trigger guard and buttcap are polished silver. Imported by Dixie Gun Works, E.M.F.
**Price:** . . . . . . . . . . . . . . . . . . $259.95 to $400.00

> Consult our Directory pages for the location of firms mentioned.

## LYMAN PLAINS PISTOL
**Caliber:** 50 or 54.
**Barrel:** 8", 1:30 twist, both calibers.
**Weight:** 50 oz. **Length:** 15" overall.
**Stock:** Walnut half-stock.
**Sights:** Blade front, square notch rear adjustable for windage.
**Features:** Polished brass trigger guard and ramrod tip, color case-hardened coil spring lock, spring-loaded trigger, stainless steel nipple, blackened iron furniture. Hooked patent breech, detachable belt hook. Introduced 1981. From Lyman Products.
**Price:** Finished . . . . . . . . . . . . . . . . . . . . $219.95
**Price:** Kit . . . . . . . . . . . . . . . . . . . . . . . . $179.95

## MOORE & PATRICK FLINT DUELING PISTOL
**Caliber:** 45.
**Barrel:** 10", rifled.
**Weight:** 32 oz. **Length:** 14½" overall.
**Stock:** European walnut, checkered.
**Sights:** Fixed.
**Features:** Engraved, silvered lockplate, blue barrel. German silver furniture. Imported from Italy by Dixie Gun Works.
**Price:** . . . . . . . . . . . . . . . . . . . . . . . . . $335.00

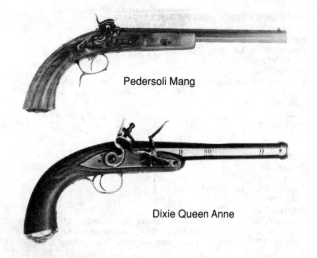

Pedersoli Mang

Dixie Queen Anne

## THOMPSON/CENTER SCOUT PISTOL
**Caliber:** 45, 50 and 54.
**Barrel:** 12", interchangeable.
**Weight:** 4 lbs., 6 oz. **Length:** NA.
**Stocks:** American black walnut stocks and forend.
**Sights:** Blade on ramp front, fully adjustable Patridge rear.
**Features:** Patented in-line ignition system with special vented breech plug. Patented trigger mechanism consists of only two moving parts. Interchangeable barrels. Wide grooved hammer. Brass trigger guard assembly. Introduced 1990. From Thompson/Center.
**Price:** 45-, 50- or 54-cal. . . . . . . . . . . . . . . . . . **$315.00**
**Price:** Extra barrel, 45-, 50- or 54-cal. . . . . . . . . . . . **$140.00**

## TRADITIONS BUCKSKINNER PISTOL
**Caliber:** 50.
**Barrel:** 10" octagonal, ¹⁵⁄₁₆" flats.
**Weight:** 40 oz. **Length:** 15" overall.
**Stocks:** Stained beech or laminated wood.
**Sights:** Blade front, rear adjustable for windage.
**Features:** Percussion ignition. Blackened furniture. Imported by Traditions, Inc.
**Price:** Beech stocks . . . . . . . . . . . . . . . . . . . . **$157.00**
**Price:** Laminated stocks . . . . . . . . . . . . . . . . . **$182.00**

Traditions Pioneer

## TRADITIONS TRAPPER PISTOL
**Caliber:** 50.
**Barrel:** 9¾", ⅞" flats.
**Weight:** 2¾ lbs. **Length:** 16" overall.
**Stock:** Beech.
**Sights:** Blade front, adjustable rear.
**Features:** Double-set triggers; brass buttcap, trigger guard, wedge plate, forend tip, thimble. From Traditions, Inc.
**Price:** . . . . . . . . . . . . . . . . . . . . . . . . . . . **$170.00**
**Price:** Kit . . . . . . . . . . . . . . . . . . . . . . . . . . **$130.00**

## TRADITIONS VEST POCKET DERRINGER
**Caliber:** 31.
**Barrel:** 2½", round.
**Weight:** 16 oz. **Length:** 5" overall.
**Stocks:** White composite.
**Sights:** Post front.
**Features:** Polished brass barrel and frame, blued trigger and screws. Imported by Traditions, Inc.
**Price:** . . . . . . . . . . . . . . . . . . . . . . . . . . . **$75.00**

## W. PARKER FLINTLOCK PISTOL
**Caliber:** 45.
**Barrel:** 11", rifled.
**Weight:** 40 oz. **Length:** 16½" overall.
**Stock:** Walnut.
**Sights:** Blade front, notch rear.
**Features:** Browned barrel, silver-plated trigger guard, finger rest, polished and engraved lock. Double-set triggers. Imported by Dixie Gun Works.
**Price:** . . . . . . . . . . . . . . . . . . . . . . . . . . . **$310.00**

## PEDERSOLI MANG TARGET PISTOL
**Caliber:** 38.
**Barrel:** 10.5", octagonal; 1:15" twist,
**Weight:** 2.5 lbs. **Length:** 17.25" overall.
**Stock:** Walnut with fluted grip.
**Sights:** Blade front, open rear adjustable for windage.
**Features:** Browned barrel, polished breech plug, rest color case-hardened. Imported from Italy by Dixie Gun Works.
**Price:** . . . . . . . . . . . . . . . . . . . . . . . . . . . **$595.00**

## QUEEN ANNE FLINTLOCK PISTOL
**Caliber:** 50 (.490" round ball).
**Barrel:** 7½", smoothbore.
**Stock:** Walnut.
**Sights:** None.
**Features:** Browned steel barrel, fluted brass trigger guard, brass mask on butt. Lockplate left in the white. Made by Pedersoli in Italy. Introduced 1983. Imported by Dixie Gun Works.
**Price:** . . . . . . . . . . . . . . . . . . . . . . . . . . . **$189.95**
**Price:** Kit . . . . . . . . . . . . . . . . . . . . . . . . . . **$138.50**

Thompson/Center Scout

## TRADITIONS PHILADELPHIA DERRINGER
**Caliber:** 45.
**Barrel:** 3¼" octagonal, ⅞" flats.
**Weight:** 16 oz. **Length:** 7⅛" overall.
**Stock:** Stained beech.
**Sights:** Blade front.
**Features:** Color case-hardened percussion lock has coil mainspring. Brass furniture, engraved wedge plate. Imported by Traditions, Inc.
**Price:** . . . . . . . . . . . . . . . . . . . . . . . . . . . **$109.00**
**Price:** Kit . . . . . . . . . . . . . . . . . . . . . . . . . . **$82.00**

## TRADITIONS PIONEER PISTOL
**Caliber:** 45.
**Barrel:** 9⅝", ¹³⁄₁₆" flats.
**Weight:** 36 oz. **Length:** 15" overall.
**Stock:** Beech.
**Sights:** Blade front, fixed rear.
**Features:** V-type mainspring; 1:18" twist. Single trigger. German silver furniture, blackened hardware. From Traditions, Inc.
**Price:** . . . . . . . . . . . . . . . . . . . . . . . . . . . **$169.00**
**Price:** Kit . . . . . . . . . . . . . . . . . . . . . . . . . . **$119.00**

## TRADITIONS WILLIAM PARKER PISTOL
**Caliber:** 45 and 50.
**Barrel:** 10⅜", ¹⁵⁄₁₆" flats; polished steel.
**Weight:** 40 oz. **Length:** 17½" overall.
**Stock:** Walnut with checkered grip.
**Sights:** Brass blade front, fixed rear.
**Features:** Replica dueling pistol with 1:18" twist, hooked breech. Brass wedge plate, trigger guard, cap guard; separate ramrod. Double-set triggers. Polished steel barrel, lock. Imported by Traditions, Inc.
**Price:** . . . . . . . . . . . . . . . . . . . . . . . . . . . **$265.00**

**CAUTION:** PRICES CHANGE, CHECK AT GUNSHOP.

Army 1851

## ARMY 1860 PERCUSSION REVOLVER

**Caliber:** 44, 6-shot.
**Barrel:** 8".
**Weight:** 40 oz. **Length:** 13⅝" overall.
**Stocks:** Walnut.
**Sights:** Fixed.
**Features:** Engraved Navy scene on cylinder; brass trigger guard; case-hardened frame, loading lever and hammer. Some importers supply pistol cut for detachable shoulder stock, have accessory stock available. Imported by American Arms, Cabela's, E.M.F., Navy Arms, The Armoury, Cimarron, Dixie Gun Works (half-fluted cylinder, not roll engraved), Euroarms of America (brass or steel model), Armsport, Mitchell, Traditions, Inc. (brass or steel), Uberti USA.
**Price:** About . . . . . . . . . . . . . . . . . . . . . . . . . . . **$92.95 to $300.00**
**Price:** Single cased set (Navy Arms) . . . . . . . . . . . . . . . **$265.00**
**Price:** Double cased set (Navy Arms) . . . . . . . . . . . . . . **$430.00**
**Price: 1861 Navy:** Same as Army except 36-cal., 7½" bbl., wgt. 41 oz., cut for shoulder stock; round cylinder (fluted avail.), from E.M.F., CVA (brass frame, 44-cal.), Cabela's, Mitchell . . . . . . . . . . **$99.95 to $249.00**
**Price:** Steel frame kit (E.M.F., Mitchell, Navy, Euroarms) **$125.00 to $187.00**
**Price:** Colt Army Police, fluted cyl., 5½", 36-cal. (Cabela's) . . . . . **$96.95**

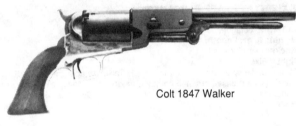

Colt 1847 Walker

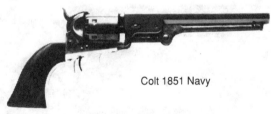

Colt 1851 Navy

Colt 1860 Army

## COLT 1860 ARMY PERCUSSION REVOLVER

**Caliber:** 44.
**Barrel:** 8", 7 groove, left-hand twist.
**Weight:** 42 oz.
**Stocks:** One-piece walnut.
**Sights:** German silver front sight, hammer notch rear.
**Features:** Steel backstrap cut for shoulder stock; brass trigger guard. Cylinder has Navy scene. Color case-hardened frame, hammer, loading lever. Reproduction of original gun with all original markings. From Colt Blackpowder Arms Co.
**Price:** . . . . . . . . . . . . . . . . . . . . . . . . . . . . . . . **$395.00**

## ARMY 1851 PERCUSSION REVOLVER

**Caliber:** 44, 6-shot.
**Barrel:** 7½".
**Weight:** 45 oz. **Length:** 13" overall.
**Stocks:** Walnut finish.
**Sights:** Fixed.
**Features:** 44-caliber version of the 1851 Navy. Imported by The Armoury, Armsport.
**Price:** . . . . . . . . . . . . . . . . . . . . . . . . . . . . . . . **$129.00**

American Arms 1860 Army

## BABY DRAGOON 1848, 1849 POCKET, WELLS FARGO

**Caliber:** 31.
**Barrel:** 3", 4", 5", 6"; seven-groove, RH twist.
**Weight:** About 21 oz.
**Stock:** Varnished walnut.
**Sights:** Brass pin front, hammer notch rear.
**Features:** No loading lever on Baby Dragoon or Wells Fargo models. Unfluted cylinder with stagecoach holdup scene; cupped cylinder pin; no grease grooves; one safety pin on cylinder and slot in hammer face; straight (flat) mainspring. From Armsport, Dixie Gun Works, Uberti USA, Cabela's.
**Price:** 6" barrel, with loading lever (Dixie Gun Works) . . . . . . . **$185.00**
**Price:** 4" (Uberti USA) . . . . . . . . . . . . . . . . . . . . . . **$295.00**

## CABELA'S PATERSON REVOLVER

**Caliber:** 36, 5-shot cylinder.
**Barrel:** 7½".
**Weight:** 24 oz. **Length:** 11½" overall.
**Stocks:** One-piece walnut.
**Sights:** Fixed.
**Features:** Recreation of the 1836 gun. Color case-hardened frame, steel backstrap; roll-engraved cylinder scene. Imported by Cabela's.
**Price:** . . . . . . . . . . . . . . . . . . . . . . . . . . . . . . . **$199.95**

## COLT 1847 WALKER PERCUSSION REVOLVER

**Caliber:** 44.
**Barrel:** 9", 7 groove, right-hand twist.
**Weight:** 73 oz.
**Stocks:** One-piece walnut.
**Sights:** German silver front sight, hammer notch rear.
**Features:** Made in U.S. Faithful reproduction of the original gun, including markings. Color case-hardened frame, hammer, loading lever and plunger. Blue steel backstrap, brass square-back trigger guard. Blue barrel, cylinder, trigger and wedge. From Colt Blackpowder Arms Co.
**Price:** . . . . . . . . . . . . . . . . . . . . . . . . . . . . . . . **$395.00**

## COLT 1849 POCKET DRAGOON REVOLVER

**Caliber:** 31.
**Barrel:** 4".
**Weight:** 24 oz. **Length:** 9½" overall.
**Stocks:** One-piece walnut.
**Sights:** Fixed. Brass pin front, hammer notch rear.
**Features:** Color case-hardened frame. No loading lever. Unfluted cylinder with engraved scene. Exact reproduction of original. From Colt Blackpowder Arms Co.
**Price:** . . . . . . . . . . . . . . . . . . . . . . . . . . . . . . . **$360.00**

## COLT 1851 NAVY PERCUSSION REVOLVER

**Caliber:** 36.
**Barrel:** 7½", octagonal, 7 groove left-hand twist.
**Weight:** 40½ oz.
**Stocks:** One-piece oiled American walnut.
**Sights:** Brass pin front, hammer notch rear.
**Features:** Faithful reproduction of the original gun. Color case-hardened frame, loading lever, plunger, hammer and latch. Blue cylinder, trigger, barrel, screws, wedge. Silver-plated brass backstrap and square-back trigger guard. From Colt Blackpowder Arms Co.
**Price:** . . . . . . . . . . . . . . . . . . . . . . . . . . . . . . . **$395.00**

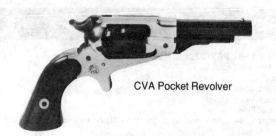

CVA Pocket Revolver

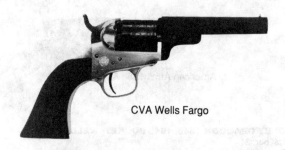

CVA Wells Fargo

Dixie Third Model Dragoon

## GRISWOLD & GUNNISON PERCUSSION REVOLVER
**Caliber:** 36 or 44, 6-shot.
**Barrel:** 7½".
**Weight:** 44 oz. (36-cal.). **Length:** 13" overall.
**Stocks:** Walnut.
**Sights:** Fixed.
**Features:** Replica of famous Confederate pistol. Brass frame, backstrap and trigger guard; case-hardened loading lever; rebated cylinder (44-cal. only). Rounded Dragoon-type barrel. Imported by Navy Arms (as Reb Model 1860), E.M.F.
**Price:** About . . . . . . . . . . . . . . . . . . . . . . . . . . **$229.00**
**Price:** Single cased set (Navy Arms) . . . . . . . . . . . **$205.00**
**Price:** Double cased set (Navy Arms) . . . . . . . . . . **$335.00**
**Price:** Reb 1860 (Navy Arms) . . . . . . . . . . . . . . **$110.00**
**Price:** As above, kit . . . . . . . . . . . . . . . . . . . . . **$90.00**

## LE MAT CAVALRY MODEL REVOLVER
**Caliber:** 44/65.
**Barrel:** 6¾" (revolver); 4⅞" (single shot).
**Weight:** 3 lbs., 7 oz.
**Stocks:** Hand-checkered walnut.
**Sights:** Post front, hammer notch rear.
**Features:** Exact reproduction with all-steel construction; 44-cal. 9-shot cylinder, 65-cal. single barrel; color case-hardened hammer with selector; spur trigger guard; ring at butt; lever-type barrel release. From Navy Arms.
**Price:** Cavalry model (lanyard ring, spur trigger guard) . . . . . . . **$595.00**
**Price:** Army model (round trigger guard, pin-type barrel release) . . **$595.00**
**Price:** Naval-style (thumb selector on hammer) . . . . . . . . . . **$595.00**

Uberti 1851 Squareback

## CVA POCKET REVOLVER
**Caliber:** 31.
**Barrel:** 4", octagonal.
**Weight:** 15½ oz. **Length:** 7½" overall.
**Stocks:** Two-piece walnut.
**Sights:** Post front, grooved topstrap rear.
**Features:** Spur trigger, brass frame with blued barrel and cylinder. Introduced 1984. Imported by CVA.
**Price:** Finished . . . . . . . . . . . . . . . . . . . . . . . . **$129.95**

## CVA WELLS FARGO MODEL
**Caliber:** 31.
**Barrel:** 4", octagonal.
**Weight:** 28 oz. (with extra cylinder). **Length:** 9" overall.
**Stocks:** Walnut.
**Sights:** Post front, hammer notch rear.
**Features:** Brass frame and backstrap; blue finish. Comes with extra cylinder. Imported by CVA.
**Price:** Brass frame, finished . . . . . . . . . . . . . . . . **$129.95**

## DIXIE THIRD MODEL DRAGOON
**Caliber:** 44 (.454" round ball).
**Barrel:** 7⅜".
**Weight:** 4 lbs., 2½ oz.
**Stocks:** One-piece walnut.
**Sights:** Brass pin front, hammer notch rear, or adjustable folding leaf rear.
**Features:** Cylinder engraved with Indian fight scene. This is the only Dragoon replica with folding leaf sight. Brass backstrap and trigger guard; color case-hardened steel frame, blue-black barrel. Imported by Dixie Gun Works.
**Price:** . . . . . . . . . . . . . . . . . . . . . . . . . . . . . **$149.95**

### CVA Third Model Dragoon
Similar to the Dixie Third Dragoon except has 7½" barrel, weighs 4 lbs., 6 oz., blade front sight. Overall length of 14". 44-caliber, 6-shot.
**Price:** . . . . . . . . . . . . . . . . . . . . . . . . . . . . . **$279.95**

## DIXIE WYATT EARP REVOLVER
**Caliber:** 44.
**Barrel:** 12" octagon.
**Weight:** 46 oz. **Length:** 18" overall.
**Stocks:** Two-piece walnut.
**Sights:** Fixed.
**Features:** Highly polished brass frame, backstrap and trigger guard; blued barrel and cylinder; case-hardened hammer, trigger and loading lever. Navy-size shoulder stock ($45) will fit with minor fitting. From Dixie Gun Works.
**Price:** . . . . . . . . . . . . . . . . . . . . . . . . . . . . . **$130.00**

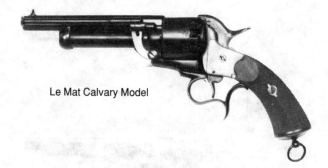

Le Mat Calvary Model

## NAVY MODEL 1851 PERCUSSION REVOLVER
**Caliber:** 36, 44, 6-shot.
**Barrel:** 7½".
**Weight:** 44 oz. **Length:** 13" overall.
**Stocks:** Walnut finish.
**Sights:** Post front, hammer notch rear.
**Features:** Brass backstrap and trigger guard; some have 1st Model squareback trigger guard, engraved cylinder with navy battle scene; case-hardened frame, hammer, loading lever. Imported by American Arms, The Armoury, Cabela's, Mitchell, Navy Arms, E.M.F., Dixie Gun Works, Euroarms of America, Armsport, CVA (36-cal. only), Traditions, Inc., Uberti USA.
**Price:** Brass frame . . . . . . . . . . . . . . **$125.00 to $280.00**
**Price:** Steel frame . . . . . . . . . . . . . . . **$130.00 to $285.00**
**Price:** Kit form . . . . . . . . . . . . . . . . . **$110.00 to $123.95**
**Price:** Engraved model (Dixie Gun Works) . . . . . . . . . **$139.95**
**Price:** Single cased set, steel frame (Navy Arms) . . . . . **$245.00**
**Price:** Double cased set, steel frame (Navy Arms) . . . . . **$405.00**
**Price:** Confederate Navy (Cabela's) . . . . . . . . . . . . . **$69.95**

CAUTION: PRICES CHANGE, CHECK AT GUNSHOP.

# BLACKPOWDER REVOLVERS

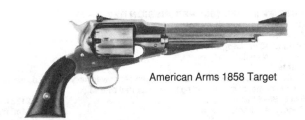

American Arms 1858 Target

### CVA 1858 Target Revolver
Similar to the New Model 1858 Army revolver except has ramp-mounted blade front sight on 8" barrel, adjustable rear sight, overall blue finish. Imported by CVA.
**Price:** . . . . . . . . . . . . . . . . . . . . **$239.95**

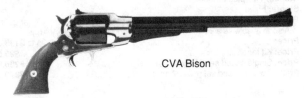

CVA Bison

### CVA Bison Revolver
Similar to the CVA 1858 Target except has 10¼" octagonal barrel, 44-caliber, brass frame.
**Price:** Finished . . . . . . . . . . . . . . **$247.95**
**Price:** From Armsport . . . . . . . . . . **$222.00**

### NAVY ARMS DELUXE 1858 REMINGTON-STYLE REVOLVER
**Caliber:** 44.
**Barrel:** 8".
**Weight:** 2 lbs., 13 oz.
**Stocks:** Smooth walnut.
**Sights:** Dovetailed blade front.
**Features:** First exact reproduction—correct in size and weight to the original, with progressive rifling; highly polished with blue finish, silver-plated trigger guard. From Navy Arms.
**Price:** Deluxe model . . . . . . . . . . . **$365.00**

> Consult our Directory pages for the location of firms mentioned.

### ROGERS & SPENCER PERCUSSION REVOLVER
**Caliber:** 44.
**Barrel:** 7½".
**Weight:** 47 oz. **Length:** 13¾" overall.
**Stocks:** Walnut.
**Sights:** Cone front, integral groove in frame for rear.
**Features:** Accurate reproduction of a Civil War design. Solid frame; extra large nipple cut-out on rear of cylinder; loading lever and cylinder easily removed for cleaning. From Euroarms of America (standard blue, engraved, burnished, target models), Navy Arms.
**Price:** . . . . . . . . . . . . **$160.00 to $240.00**
**Price:** Nickel-plated . . . . . . . . . . . **$215.00**
**Price:** Engraved (Euroarms) . . . . . . **$286.00**
**Price:** Kit version . . . . . . . . . . . . . **$95.00**
**Price:** Target version (Euroarms, Navy Arms) . **$260.00**
**Price:** Burnished London Gray (Euroarms, Navy Arms) . . . . . . **$260.00**

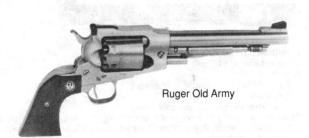

Ruger Old Army

### Uberti 1861 Navy Percussion Revolver
Similar to 1851 Navy except has round 7½" barrel, rounded trigger guard, German silver blade front sight, "creeping" loading lever. Available with fluted or round cylinder. Imported by Uberti USA.
**Price:** Steel backstrap, trigger guard, cut for stock . . . . . . . . . **$300.00**

### CVA Colt Sheriff's Model
Similar to the Uberti 1861 Navy except has 5½" barrel, brass or steel frame, semi-fluted cylinder. In 36-caliber only.
**Price:** Brass frame, finished . . . . . . . **$157.95**
**Price:** As above, brass frame, 44-cal. . . **$139.95**
**Price:** As above, kit . . . . . . . . . . . . **$129.95**
**Price:** Brass frame (Armsport) . . . . . . **$155.00**
**Price:** Steel frame (Armsport) . . . . . . **$193.00**

### NEW MODEL 1858 ARMY PERCUSSION REVOLVER
**Caliber:** 36 or 44, 6-shot.
**Barrel:** 6½" or 8".
**Weight:** 40 oz. **Length:** 13½" overall.
**Stocks:** Walnut.
**Sights:** Blade front, groove-in-frame rear.
**Features:** Replica of Remington Model 1858. Also available from some importers as Army Model Belt Revolver in 36-cal., a shortened and lightened version of the 44. Target Model (Uberti USA, Navy Arms) has fully adjustable target rear sight, target front, 36 or 44. Imported by American Arms, Cabela's, CVA (as 1858 Army), Dixie Gun Works, Navy Arms, The Armoury, E.M.F., Euroarms of America (engraved, stainless and plain), Armsport, Mitchell, Traditions, Inc., Uberti USA.
**Price:** Steel frame, about . . . . . **$99.95 to $280.00**
**Price:** Steel frame kit (Euroarms, Navy Arms) . . **$115.95 to $150.00**
**Price:** Single cased set (Navy Arms) . . . . . . **$255.00**
**Price:** Double cased set (Navy Arms) . . . . . . **$420.00**
**Price:** Stainless steel Model 1858 (American Arms, Euroarms, Uberti USA, Cabela's, Navy Arms, Armsport, Traditions) . . . . . **$169.95 to $380.00**
**Price:** Target Model, adjustable rear sight (Cabela's, Euroarms, Uberti USA, Navy Arms, E.M.F.) . . . . . **$95.95 to $399.00**
**Price:** Brass frame (CVA, Cabela's, Traditions, Navy Arms) **$79.95 to $212.95**
**Price:** As above, kit (CVA, Dixie Gun Works, Navy Arms) **$145.00 to $188.95**
**Price:** Remington "Texas" (Mitchell) . . . . . . **$199.00**
**Price:** Buffalo model, 44-cal. (Cabela's) . . . . . **$109.95**
**Price:** Lawman model, 44-cal. (Cabela's) . . . . . **$159.95**
**Price:** Police model, 36-cal. (Cabela's) . . . . . . **$99.95**
**Price:** Old Silver model, 44-cal. (Cabela's) . . . . **$199.95**

Euroarms Rogers & Spencer

### POCKET POLICE 1862 PERCUSSION REVOLVER
**Caliber:** 36, 5-shot.
**Barrel:** 4½", 5½", 6½", 7½".
**Weight:** 26 oz. **Length:** 12" overall (6½" bbl.).
**Stocks:** Walnut.
**Sights:** Fixed.
**Features:** Round tapered barrel; half-fluted and rebated cylinder; case-hardened frame, loading lever and hammer; silver or brass trigger guard and backstrap. Imported by CVA (7½" only), Navy Arms (5½" only), Uberti USA (5½", 6½" only).
**Price:** About . . . . . . . . **$143.95 to $310.00**
**Price:** Single cased set with accessories (Navy Arms) . . . . . . . . **$360.00**

### RUGER OLD ARMY PERCUSSION REVOLVER
**Caliber:** 45, 6-shot. Uses .457" dia. lead bullets.
**Barrel:** 7½" (6-groove, 16" twist).
**Weight:** 46 oz. **Length:** 13¾" overall.
**Stocks:** Smooth walnut.
**Sights:** Ramp front, rear adjustable for windage and elevation.
**Features:** Stainless steel; standard size nipples, chrome-moly steel cylinder and frame, same lockwork as in original Super Blackhawk. Also available in stainless steel. Made in USA. From Sturm, Ruger & Co.
**Price:** Stainless steel (Model KBP-7) . . . . . . **$428.00**
**Price:** Blued steel (Model BP-7) . . . . . . . . **$378.50**

# BLACKPOWDER REVOLVERS

Texas Paterson

## TEXAS PATERSON 1836 REVOLVER
**Caliber:** 36 (.376" round ball).
**Barrel:** 7½".
**Weight:** 42 oz.
**Stocks:** One-piece walnut.
**Sights:** Fixed.
**Features:** Copy of Sam Colt's first commercially-made revolving pistol. Has no loading lever but comes with loading tool. From Dixie Gun Works, Navy Arms, Uberti USA.
**Price:** About . . . . . . . . . . . . . . . . . . . $335.00 to $395.00
**Price:** With loading lever (Uberti USA) . . . . . . . . . . . . . . . $450.00
**Price:** Engraved (Navy Arms) . . . . . . . . . . . . . $465.00

## Uberti 2nd Model Dragoon Revolver
Similar to the 1st Model except distinguished by rectangular bolt cuts in the cylinder.
**Price:** . . . . . . . . . . . . . . . . . . . . . . $325.00

## Uberti 3rd Model Dragoon Revolver
Similar to the 2nd Model except for oval trigger guard, long trigger, modifications to the loading lever and latch. Imported by Uberti USA.
**Price:** Military model (frame cut for shoulder stock, steel backstrap) $330.00
**Price:** Civilian (brass backstrap, trigger guard) . . . . . . . . . $325.00

## UBERTI 1862 POCKET NAVY PERCUSSION REVOLVER
**Caliber:** 36, 5-shot.
**Barrel:** 5½", 6½", octagonal, 7-groove, LH twist.
**Weight:** 27 oz. (5½" barrel). **Length:** 10½" overall (5½" bbl.).
**Stocks:** One-piece varnished walnut.
**Sights:** Brass pin front, hammer notch rear.
**Features:** Rebated cylinder, hinged loading lever, brass or silver-plated backstrap and trigger guard, color-cased frame, hammer, loading lever, plunger and latch, rest blued. Has original-type markings. From Uberti USA.
**Price:** With brass backstrap, trigger guard . . . . . . . . . . . . . $310.00

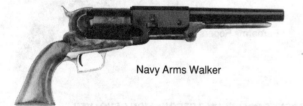

Navy Arms Walker

## SHERIFF MODEL 1851 PERCUSSION REVOLVER
**Caliber:** 36, 44, 6-shot.
**Barrel:** 5".
**Weight:** 40 oz. **Length:** 10½" overall.
**Stocks:** Walnut.
**Sights:** Fixed.
**Features:** Brass backstrap and trigger guard; engraved navy scene; case-hardened frame, hammer, loading lever. Imported by E.M.F.
**Price:** Steel frame . . . . . . . . . . . . . . . . . . . . . . . . . . $172.00
**Price:** Brass frame . . . . . . . . . . . . . . . . . . . . . . . . . . $140.00

## SPILLER & BURR REVOLVER
**Caliber:** 36 (.375" round ball).
**Barrel:** 7", octagon.
**Weight:** 2½ lbs. **Length:** 12½" overall.
**Stocks:** Two-piece walnut.
**Sights:** Fixed.
**Features:** Reproduction of the C.S.A. revolver. Brass frame and trigger guard. Also available as a kit. From Dixie Gun Works, Mitchell, Navy Arms.
**Price:** . . . . . . . . . . . . . . . . . . . . . . . $89.95 to $199.00
**Price:** Kit form . . . . . . . . . . . . . . . . . . . . . . . . . . . $95.00
**Price:** Single cased set (Navy Arms) . . . . . . . . . . . . . . . $230.00
**Price:** Double cased set (Navy Arms) . . . . . . . . . . . . . . $370.00

## UBERTI 1st MODEL DRAGOON
**Caliber:** 44.
**Barrel:** 7½", part round, part octagon.
**Weight:** 64 oz.
**Stocks:** One-piece walnut.
**Sights:** German silver blade front, hammer notch rear.
**Features:** First model has oval bolt cuts in cylinder, square-back flared trigger guard, V-type mainspring, short trigger. Ranger and Indian scene roll-engraved on cylinder. Color case-hardened frame, loading lever, plunger and hammer; blue barrel, cylinder, trigger and wedge. Available with old-time charcoal blue or standard blue-black finish. Polished brass backstrap and trigger guard. From Uberti USA.
**Price:** . . . . . . . . . . . . . . . . . . . . . . . . . . . $325.00

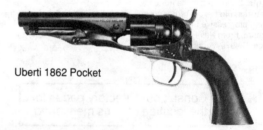

Uberti 1862 Pocket

## WALKER 1847 PERCUSSION REVOLVER
**Caliber:** 44, 6-shot.
**Barrel:** 9".
**Weight:** 84 oz. **Length:** 15½" overall.
**Stocks:** Walnut.
**Sights:** Fixed.
**Features:** Case-hardened frame, loading lever and hammer; iron backstrap; brass trigger guard; engraved cylinder. Imported by American Arms, Cabela's, CVA, Navy Arms, Dixie Gun Works, Uberti USA, E.M.F., Cimarron, Traditions, Inc.
**Price:** About . . . . . . . . . . . . . . . . . . . . . $225.00 to $360.00
**Price:** Single cased set (Navy Arms) . . . . . . . . . . . . . . . $385.00

# BLACKPOWDER MUSKETS & RIFLES

Armoury R140 Hawken

## ARMOURY R140 HAWKEN RIFLE
**Caliber:** 45, 50 or 54.
**Barrel:** 29".
**Weight:** 8¾ to 9 lbs. **Length:** 45¾" overall.
**Stock:** Walnut, with cheekpiece.
**Sights:** Dovetail front, fully adjustable rear.
**Features:** Octagon barrel, removable breech plug; double set triggers; blued barrel, brass stock fittings, color case-hardened percussion lock. From Armsport, The Armoury.
**Price:** . . . . . . . . . . . . . . . . . . . . . . . $225.00 to $245.00

**CAUTION:** PRICES CHANGE, CHECK AT GUNSHOP.

**ARMSPORT 1863 SHARPS RIFLE, CARBINE**
**Caliber:** 45, 54.
**Barrel:** 28", round.
**Weight:** 8.4 lbs. **Length:** 46" overall.
**Stock:** Walnut.
**Sights:** Blade front, folding adjustable rear. Tang sight set optionally available.
**Features:** Replica of the 1863 Sharps. Color case-hardened frame, rest blued. Imported by Armsport.
**Price:** . . . . . . . . . . . . . . . . . . . . . . . . . . . **$780.00**
**Price:** Carbine, 54 caliber, 22" barrel . . . . . . . . . . . . . . . **$755.00**

Cabela's Accura 9000

**CABELA'S ACCURA 9000 MUZZLELOADER**
**Caliber:** 50, 54.
**Barrel:** 27"; 1:54 twist.

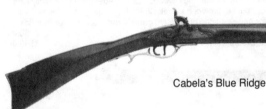

Cabela's Blue Ridge

**Cabela's Blue Ridge Carbine**
Similar to the Blue Ridge Rifle except has 28" barrel, weighs 6¼ lbs. Available in 50- or 54-caliber. From Cabela's.
**Price:** . . . . . . . . . . . . . . . . . . . . . . . . . . . **$259.95**

Cabela's Swivel-Barrel

**CABELA'S SWIVEL-BARREL RIFLE**
**Caliber:** 50, 54.
**Barrel:** 23.75".

**CABELA'S TAOS RIFLE**
**Caliber:** 45, 50.
**Barrel:** 28¼".
**Weight:** 6 lbs., 11 oz. **Length:** 43¼" overall.
**Stock:** Oil-finished walnut.
**Sights:** Blade front, rear adjustable for windage.
**Features:** Carbine version of the Pennsylvania rifle. Adjustable double-set triggers. Imported by Cabela's.
**Price:** Percussion . . . . . . . . . . . . . . . . . . . . . . . . **$229.95**
**Price:** Flintlock . . . . . . . . . . . . . . . . . . . . . . . . . . **$239.95**

> Consult our Directory pages for the location of firms mentioned.

**Cabela's Hawken's Hunter Rifle**
Similar to the Traditional Hawken's except has more modern stock style with rubber recoil pad, blued furniture, sling swivels. Percussion only, in 45-, 50-, 54- or 58-caliber.
**Price:** Right-hand . . . . . . . . . . . . . . . . . . . . . . . **$184.95**
**Price:** Left-hand . . . . . . . . . . . . . . . . . . . . . . . . **$189.95**

**BOSTONIAN PERCUSSION RIFLE**
**Caliber:** 45.
**Barrel:** 30", octagonal
**Weight:** 7¼ lbs. **Length:** 46" overall.
**Stock:** Walnut.
**Sights:** Blade front, fixed notch rear.
**Features:** Color case-hardened lock, brass trigger guard, buttplate, patchbox. Imported from Italy by E.M.F.
**Price:** . . . . . . . . . . . . . . . . . . . . . . . . . . . **$285.00**

**Weight:** About 7½ lbs. **Length:** 44" overall.
**Stock:** European walnut with Monte Carlo cheeckpiece, checkered grip and forend.
**Sights:** Hooded front with interchangeable blades, open rear adjustable for windage and elevation.
**Features:** In-line ignition system with removable breech plug. Automatic safety and half-cock. Quick detachable sling swivels, schnabel forend tip, recoil pad. From Cabela's.
**Price:** Right or left-hand . . . . . . . . . . . . . . . . . . **$399.95**

**CABELA'S BLUE RIDGE RIFLE**
**Caliber:** 32, 36, 45, 50, 54.
**Barrel:** 39", octagonal.
**Weight:** About 7¾ lbs. **Length:** 55" overall.
**Stock:** American black walnut.
**Sights:** Blade front, rear drift adjustable for windage.
**Features:** Color case-hardened lockplate and cock/hammer, brass trigger guard and buttplate, double set, double-phased triggers. From Cabela's.
**Price:** Percussion . . . . . . . . . . . . . . . . . . . . . . **$299.95**
**Price:** Flintlock . . . . . . . . . . . . . . . . . . . . . . . . **$319.95**
**Price:** Squirrel Rifle, 32-cal., percussion . . . . . . . . . **$299.95**
**Price:** As above, flintlock . . . . . . . . . . . . . . . . . . **$319.95**

**Weight:** 10 lbs. **Length:** 40" overall.
**Stock:** Checkered American walnut.
**Sights:** Blade front, open rear adjustable for windage and elevation; one set for each barrel.
**Features:** Barrel assembly rotates for second shot. Back action mechanism. Monte Carlo comb, rubber butt pad; checkered pistol grip and forend panels. Introduced 1992. From Cabela's.
**Price:** . . . . . . . . . . . . . . . . . . . . . . . . . . . **$379.95**

**CABELA'S TRADITIONAL HAWKEN'S**
**Caliber:** 45, 50, 54, 58.
**Barrel:** 29".
**Weight:** About 9 lbs.
**Stock:** Walnut.
**Sights:** Blade front, open adjustable rear.
**Features:** Flintlock or percussion. Adjustable double-set triggers. Polished brass furniture, color case-hardened lock. Imported by Cabela's.
**Price:** Percussion, right-hand . . . . . . . . . . . . . . . **$169.95**
**Price:** Percussion, right-hand, kit . . . . . . . . . . . . . **$139.95**
**Price:** Percussion, left-hand . . . . . . . . . . . . . . . . **$174.95**
**Price:** Flintlock, right-hand . . . . . . . . . . . . . . . . . **$189.95**
**Price:** Flintlock kit . . . . . . . . . . . . . . . . . . . . . . . **$164.95**

**Cabela's Synthetic Hawken's Hunter**
Similar to the Hawken's Hunter except has Bell & Carlson Carbelite black synthetic stock with rubber recoil pad. Available in percussion or flintlock, 50-, 54-, 58-caliber. From Cabela's.
**Price:** . . . . . . . . . . . . . . . . . . . . . . . . . . . **$179.95**

# BLACKPOWDER MUSKETS & RIFLES

**CABELA'S ROLLING BLOCK MUZZLELOADER**
**Caliber:** 50, 54.
**Barrel:** 26½" octagonal; 1:32" (50), 1:48" (54) twist.
**Weight:** About 9¼ lbs. **Length:** 43½" overall.
**Stock:** American walnut, rubber butt pad.
**Sights:** Blade front, adjustable buckhorn rear.
**Features:** Uses in-line ignition system, Brass trigger guard, color case-hardened hammer, block and buttplate; black-finished, engraved receiver; easily removable screw-in breech plug; black ramrod and thimble. From Cabela's.
**Price:** . . . . . . . . . . . . . . . . . . . . . . . . . . . . $269.95

**Cabela's Rolling Block Muzzleloader Carbine**
Similar to the rifle version except has 22¼" barrel, weighs 8¼ lbs. Has bead on ramp front sight, modern fully adjustable rear. From Cabela's.
**Price:** . . . . . . . . . . . . . . . . . . . . . . . . . . . . $249.95

Cook & Brother

**COOK & BROTHER CONFEDERATE CARBINE**
**Caliber:** 58.

CVA Apollo Carbelite

**CVA Apollo Shadow**
Similar to the Apollo Carbelite except has black textured epoxicoat hardwood stock. Rifle length only with 27" barrel, 50- or 54- caliber.
**Price:** . . . . . . . . . . . . . . . . . . . . . . . . . . . . $314.95

**CVA Apollo Sporter**
Similar to the Apollo Carbelite except has walnut-stained hardwood stock, composition buttplate. Available only in 50-caliber, 25" barrel.
**Price:** . . . . . . . . . . . . . . . . . . . . . . . . . . . . $269.95

CVA Express Rifle

**CVA FRONTIER CARBINE**
**Caliber:** 50.
**Barrel:** 24" octagon; ¹⁵⁄₁₆" flats.
**Weight:** 6½ lbs. **Length:** 40" overall.
**Stock:** Selected hardwood.
**Sights:** Brass blade front, fixed open rear.
**Features:** Color case-hardened lockplate, V-type mainspring. Early style brass trigger with tension spring. Brass buttplate, trigger guard, wedge plate, nose cap, thimble. From CVA.
**Price:** Percussion . . . . . . . . . . . . . . . . . . . . $189.95
**Price:** Flintlock rifle . . . . . . . . . . . . . . . . . . . $224.95
**Price:** Percussion Carbine kit . . . . . . . . . . . . . . $137.95

**CABELA'S SHARPS SPORTING RIFLE**
**Caliber:** 45, 54.
**Barrel:** 31", octagonal.
**Weight:** About 10 lbs. **Length:** 49" overall.
**Stock:** American walnut with checkered grip and forend.
**Sights:** Blade front, ladder-type adjustable rear.
**Features:** Color case-hardened lock and buttplate. Adjustable double set, double-phased triggers. From Cabela's.
**Price:** . . . . . . . . . . . . . . . . . . . . . . . . . . . . $595.00

**Barrel:** 24".
**Weight:** 7½ lbs. **Length:** 40½" overall.
**Stock:** Select walnut.
**Features:** Recreation of the 1861 New Orleans-made artillery carbine. Color case-hardened lock, browned barrel. Buttplate, trigger guard, barrel bands, sling swivels and nose cap of polished brass. From Euroarms of America.
**Price:** . . . . . . . . . . . . . . . . . . . . . . . . . . . . $366.00
**Price:** Cook & Brother rifle (33" barrel) . . . . . . . . . $550.00

**CVA APOLLO CARBELITE RIFLE**
**Caliber:** 50, 54.
**Barrel:** 25", blued, round; 1:32" rifling.
**Weight:** 7½ lbs. **Length:** 43" overall.
**Stock:** Black Carbelite composite with fluted Monte Carlo comb, cheekpiece, full pistol grip. Sling swivel studs.
**Sights:** Bead on ramp front, fully adjustable click rear. Drilled and tapped for scope mounting or peep sight.
**Features:** In-line percussion system with push-pull bolt block safety system. One-piece blued barrel/receiver. Has loading window and foul weather cover. Vented for gas escape. From CVA.
**Price:** . . . . . . . . . . . . . . . . . . . . . . . . . . . . $349.95

**CVA BUSHWACKER RIFLE**
**Caliber:** 50.
**Barrel:** 26", octagonal; ¹⁵⁄₁₆" flats; 1:48" twist.
**Weight:** 7.5 lbs. **Length:** 40" overall.
**Stock:** Walnut-stained hardwood.
**Sights:** Brass blade front, fixed semi-buckhorn open rear.
**Features:** Color case-hardened lockplate; single trigger with oversize blackened trigger guard; blued barrel, wedge plates. From CVA.
**Price:** Percussion only . . . . . . . . . . . . . . . . . $159.95

**CVA EXPRESS RIFLE**
**Caliber:** 50, 54.
**Barrel:** 28", round.
**Weight:** 9 lbs.
**Stock:** Walnut-stained hardwood.
**Sights:** Bead and post front, adjustable rear.
**Features:** Double rifle with twin percussion locks and triggers, adjustable barrels. Hooked breech. Introduced 1989. From CVA.
**Price:** Finished . . . . . . . . . . . . . . . . . . . . . . . $525.95

**CVA Frontier Hunter Carbine**
Similar to the CVA Frontier Carbine except has conventional-style black rubber butt pad, black chrome furniture. Barrel is drilled and tapped for scope mounting. Fully adjustable rear sight. Overall length 40", weight 7.5 lbs., 50-caliber only. From CVA.
**Price:** . . . . . . . . . . . . . . . . . . . . . . . . . . . . $209.95

**CAUTION:** PRICES CHANGE, CHECK AT GUNSHOP.

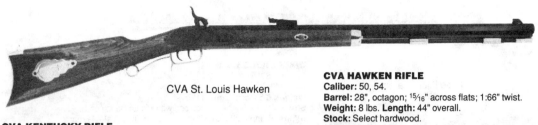

CVA St. Louis Hawken

## CVA KENTUCKY RIFLE
**Caliber:** 50.
**Barrel:** 33½", rifled, octagon; ⅞" flats.
**Weight:** 7½ lbs. **Length:** 48" overall.
**Stock:** Select hardwood.
**Sights:** Brass Kentucky blade-type front, fixed open rear.
**Features:** Available in percussion only. Stainless steel nipple included. From CVA.
**Price:** Percussion . . . . . . . . . . . . . . . . . . . . . . . **$262.95**
**Price:** Percussion kit . . . . . . . . . . . . . . . . . . . . . **$189.95**

## CVA STALKER RIFLE/CARBINE
**Caliber:** 50, 54.
**Barrel:** 24", 28"; octagonal; drilled and tapped for scope mounting; 1:32" twist.
**Weight:** 7.5 lbs. **Length:** 44" overall (rifle).
**Stock:** Walnut-stained hardwood with Monte Carlo comb, cheekpiece. Ventilated rubber recoil pad.
**Sights:** Beaded blade front, fully adjustable click rear.
**Features:** Color case-hardened lockplate; Hawken-style lock with bridle and fly, 45-degree offset hammer; single modern-style trigger. From CVA.
**Price:** 50, 54 rifle . . . . . . . . . . . . . . . . . . . . . . . **$217.95**
**Price:** 50, 54 carbine . . . . . . . . . . . . . . . . . . . . . **$217.95**
**Price:** Left-hand carbine . . . . . . . . . . . . . . . . . . . **$239.95**
**Price:** Sierra Stalker Rifle (28", not drilled, tapped, 50-cal. only) . . . **$189.95**

## CVA HAWKEN RIFLE
**Caliber:** 50, 54.
**Barrel:** 28", octagon; ¹⁵⁄₁₆" across flats; 1:66" twist.
**Weight:** 8 lbs. **Length:** 44" overall.
**Stock:** Select hardwood.
**Sights:** Beaded blade front, fully adjustable open rear.
**Features:** Fully adjustable double-set triggers; brass patch box, wedge plates, nosecap, thimbles, trigger guard and buttplate; blued barrel; color case-hardened, engraved lockplate. V-type mainspring. Percussion only. Hooked breech. Introduced 1981. From CVA.
**Price:** St. Louis Hawken, finished (50-, 54-cal.) . . . . . . . . . . **$214.95**
**Price:** As above, combo kit (50-, 54-cal. bbls.) . . . . . . . . . . . **$229.95**

## CVA TRACKER CARBINE
**Caliber:** 50.
**Barrel:** 21", half round, half octagon with ¹⁵⁄₁₆" flats; 1:32" twist.
**Weight:** 6.5 lbs. **Length:** 36" overall.
**Stock:** Matte finish walnut with straight grip; ventilated rubber recoil pad.
**Sights:** Beaded blade front, fully adjustable click rear.
**Features:** Color case-hardened lockplate, black-chromed furniture; drilled and tapped for scope mounting. From CVA.
**Price:** . . . . . . . . . . . . . . . . . . . . . . . . . . . . . . **$254.95**

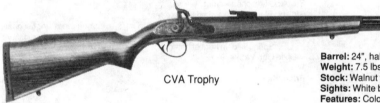

CVA Trophy

## CVA TROPHY CARBINE
**Caliber:** 50, 54.

## CVA VARMINT RIFLE
**Caliber:** 32.
**Barrel:** 24" octagonal; ⅞" flats; 1:48" rifling.
**Weight:** 6¾ lbs. **Length:** 40" overall.
**Stock:** Select hardwood.
**Sights:** Blade front, Patridge-style click adjustable rear.
**Features:** Brass trigger guard, nose cap, wedge plate, thinble and buttplate. Drilled and tapped for scope mounting. Color case-hardened lock. Single trigger. Imported by CVA.
**Price:** . . . . . . . . . . . . . . . . . . . . . . . . . . . . . . **$234.95**

**Barrel:** 24", half round, half octagon with ¹⁵⁄₁₆" flats; 1:32" twist.
**Weight:** 7.5 lbs. **Length:** 40" overall.
**Stock:** Walnut with Monte Carlo comb, cheekpiece.
**Sights:** White bead on blade front, fully adjustable click rear.
**Features:** Color case-hardened lockplate, blued barrel, thimble. Modern-style stock; modern rifle trigger with over-sized guard; drilled and tapped for scope mounting. From CVA.
**Price:** . . . . . . . . . . . . . . . . . . . . . . . . . . . . . . **$254.95**

## DIXIE DELUX CUB RIFLE
**Caliber:** 40.
**Barrel:** 28".
**Weight:** 6½ lbs.
**Stock:** Walnut.
**Sights:** Fixed.
**Features:** Short rifle for small game and beginning shooters. Brass patchbox and furniture. Flint or percussion. From Dixie Gun Works.
**Price:** Finished . . . . . . . . . . . . . . . . . . . . . . . . . **$335.00**
**Price:** Kit . . . . . . . . . . . . . . . . . . . . . . . . . . . . . **$205.00**

Dixie English Matchlock

## DIXIE ENGLISH MATCHLOCK MUSKET
**Caliber:** 72.
**Barrel:** 44".
**Weight:** 8 lbs. **Length:** 57.75" overall.
**Stock:** Walnut with satin oil finish.
**Sights:** Blade front, open rear adjustable for windage.
**Features:** Replica of circa 1600-1680 English matchlock. Getz barrel with 11" octagonal area at rear, rest is round with cannon-type muzzle. All steel finished in the white. Imported by Dixie Gun Works.
**Price:** . . . . . . . . . . . . . . . . . . . . . . . . . . . . . . **$825.00**

## DIXIE HAWKEN RIFLE
**Caliber:** 45, 50, 54.
**Barrel:** 30".
**Weight:** 8 lbs. **Length:** 46½" overall.
**Stock:** Walnut.
**Sights:** Blade front, adjustable rear.
**Features:** Blued barrel, double-set triggers, steel crescent buttplate. Imported by Dixie Gun Works.
**Price:** Finished . . . . . . . . . . . . . . . . . . . . . . . . . **$250.00**
**Price:** Kit . . . . . . . . . . . . . . . . . . . . . . . . . . . . . **$220.00**

Dixie Inline Carbine

## DIXIE TENNESSEE MOUNTAIN RIFLE

**Caliber:** 32 or 50.
**Barrel:** 41½", 6-groove rifling, brown finish. **Length:** 56" overall.
**Stock:** Walnut, oil finish; Kentucky-style.
**Sights:** Silver blade front, open buckhorn rear.
**Features:** Recreation of the original mountain rifles. Early Schultz lock, interchangeable flint or percussion with vent plug or drum and nipple. Tumbler has fly. Double-set triggers. All metal parts browned. From Dixie Gun Works.
**Price:** Flint or percussion, finished rifle, 50-cal. . . . . . . . . . . $495.00
**Price:** Kit, 50-cal. . . . . . . . . . . . . $395.00
**Price:** Left-hand model, flint or percussion . . . . . . . . . . $450.00
**Price:** Left-hand kit, flint or perc., 50-cal. . . . . . . . . . . $360.00
**Price:** Squirrel Rifle (as above except in 32-cal. with ¹³⁄₁₆" barrel flats), flint or percussion . . . . . . . . . . . . . . . . . . $495.00
**Price:** Kit, 32-cal., flint or percussion . . . . . . . . . . . . . . $395.00

## DIXIE INLINE CARBINE
**Caliber:** 50, 54.
**Barrel:** 24"; 1:32" twist.
**Weight:** 6.5 lbs. **Length:** 41" overall.
**Stock:** Walnut-finished hardwood with Monte Carlo comb.
**Sights:** Ramp front with red insert, open fully adjustable rear.
**Features:** Sliding "bolt" fully encloses cap and nipple. Fully adjustable trigger, automatic safety. Aluminum ramrod. Imported from Italy by Dixie Gun Works.
**Price:** . . . . . . . . . . . . . . . . . . . . . . . . . . . . . . $349.95

## DIXIE 1863 SPRINGFIELD MUSKET
**Caliber:** 58 (.570" patched ball or .575" Minie).
**Barrel:** 50", rifled.
**Stocks:** Walnut stained.
**Sights:** Blade front, adjustable ladder-type rear.
**Features:** Bright-finish lock, barrel, furniture. Reproduction of the last of the regulation muzzleloaders. Imported from Japan by Dixie Gun Works.
**Price:** Finished . . . . . . . . . . . . . . . . . . . . . . $475.00
**Price:** Kit . . . . . . . . . . . . . . . . . . . . . . . . . . $330.00

Dixie Model 1816

## DIXIE U.S. MODEL 1816 FLINTLOCK MUSKET
**Caliber:** 69.
**Barrel:** 42", smoothbore.
**Weight:** 9.75 lbs. **Length:** 56.5" overall.
**Stock:** Walnut with oil finish.
**Sights:** Blade front.
**Features:** All metal finished "National Armory Bright"; three barrel bands with springs; steel ramrod with buttom-shaped head. Imported by Dixie Gun Works.
**Price:** . . . . . . . . . . . . . . . . . . . . . . . . . . . . $725.00

## DIXIE U.S. MODEL 1861 SPRINGFIELD
**Caliber:** 58.
**Barrel:** 40".
**Weight:** About 8 lbs. **Length:** 55¹³⁄₁₆" overall.
**Stock:** Oil-finished walnut.
**Sights:** Blade front, step adjustable rear.
**Features:** Exact recreation of original rifle. Sling swivels attached to trigger guard bow and middle barrel band. Lockplate marked "1861" with eagle motif and "U.S. Springfield" in front of hammer; "U.S." stamped on top of buttplate. From Dixie Gun Works.
**Price:** . . . . . . . . . . . . . . . . . . . . . . . . . . . . $450.00
**Price:** Kit . . . . . . . . . . . . . . . . . . . . . . . . . . . $420.00

Euroarms Volunteer

## EUROARMS BUFFALO CARBINE
**Caliber:** 58.
**Barrel:** 26", round.
**Weight:** 7¾ lbs. **Length:** 42" overall.
**Stock:** Walnut.
**Sights:** Blade front, open adjustable rear.
**Features:** Shoots .575" round ball. Color case-hardened lock, blue hammer, barrel, trigger; brass furniture. Brass patchbox. Imported by Euroarms of America.
**Price:** . . . . . . . . . . . . . . . . . . . . . . . . . . . . $407.00

## EUROARMS VOLUNTEER TARGET RIFLE
**Caliber:** .451.
**Barrel:** 33" (two-band), 36" (three-band).
**Weight:** 11 lbs. (two-band). **Length:** 48.75" overall (two-band).
**Stock:** European walnut with checkered wrist and forend.
**Sights:** Hooded bead front, adjustable rear with interchangeable leaves.
**Features:** Alexander Henry-type rifling with 1:20" twist. Color case-hardened hammer and lockplate, brass trigger guard and nose cap, rest blued. Imported by Euroarms of America.
**Price:** Two-band . . . . . . . . . . . . . . . . . . . . . $670.00
**Price:** Three-band . . . . . . . . . . . . . . . . . . . . $700.00

Euroarms 1861

## EUROARMS 1861 SPRINGFIELD RIFLE
**Caliber:** 58.
**Barrel:** 40".
**Weight:** About 10 lbs. **Length:** 55.5" overall.
**Stock:** European walnut.
**Sights:** Blade front, three-leaf military rear.
**Features:** Reproduction of the original three-band rifle. Lockplate marked "1861" with eagle and "U.S. Springfield." Metal left in the white. Imported by Euroarms of America.
**Price:** . . . . . . . . . . . . . . . . . . . . . . . . . . . . $650.00

**CAUTION:** PRICES CHANGE, CHECK AT GUNSHOP.

Gonic GA-87

## GONIC GA-87 M/L RIFLE
**Caliber:** 30, 38, 44, 45, 50, 54, 20-ga.
**Barrel:** 26".
**Weight:** 6 to 6½ lbs. **Length:** 43" overall (Carbine).
**Stock:** American walnut with checkered grip and forend, or laminated stock.
**Sights:** Optional bead front, open or peep rear adjustable for windage and elevation; drilled and tapped for scope bases (included).
**Features:** Closed-breech action with straight-line ignition. Modern trigger mechanism with ambidextrous safety. Satin blue finish on metal, satin stock finish. Introduced 1989. From Gonic Arms, Inc.
**Price:** Standard rifle, no sights . . . . . . . . . . . . . . . . **$493.38**
**Price:** As above, with sights, from . . . . . . . . . . . . . . . **$535.95**
**Price:** Deluxe Rifle, no sights, from . . . . . . . . . . . . . . **$526.06**
**Price:** As above, with sights, from . . . . . . . . . . . . . . . **$568.64**
**Price:** Accessory 24" carbine barrel, from . . . . . . . . . . **$190.49**

## Gonic Model 93 Magnum M/L Rifle
Similar to the GA-87 except has open bolt mechanism, single safety, 22" barrel and comes only in 50-caliber with open sights. Stock is either black wrinkle-finish wood or gray laminate. Introduced 1993. From Gonic Arms, Inc.
**Price:** . . . . . . . . . . . . . . . . . . . . . . . . . . . . . . . **$310.00**

Hatfield Squirrel Rifle

## HATFIELD SQUIRREL RIFLE
**Caliber:** 36, 45, 50.
**Barrel:** 39½", octagon, 32" on half-stock.
**Weight:** 7½ lbs. (32-cal.).
**Stock:** American fancy maple.
**Sights:** Silver blade front, buckhorn rear.
**Features:** Recreation of the traditional squirrel rifle. Available in flint or percussion with brass trigger guard and buttplate. From Hatfield Rifle Works. Introduced 1983.
**Price:** Full stock, percussion, Grade II . . . . . . . . . . . **$650.00**
**Price:** As above, flintlock . . . . . . . . . . . . . . . . . . . **$650.00**
**Price:** As above, Grade III, flint or percussion . . . . . . . **$750.00**

## HARPER'S FERRY 1803 FLINTLOCK RIFLE
**Caliber:** 54 or 58.
**Barrel:** 35".
**Weight:** 9 lbs. **Length:** 59½" overall.
**Stock:** Walnut with cheekpiece.
**Sights:** Brass blade front, fixed steel rear.
**Features:** Brass trigger guard, sideplate, buttplate; steel patch box. Imported by Euroarms of America, Navy Arms (54-cal. only).
**Price:** . . . . . . . . . . . . . . . . . . . . . . . . . . . . . . . **$512.00**
**Price:** 54-cal. (Navy Arms) . . . . . . . . . . . . . . . . . . . **$555.00**

## HAWKEN RIFLE
**Caliber:** 45, 50, 54 or 58.
**Barrel:** 28", blued, 6-groove rifling.
**Weight:** 8¾ lbs. **Length:** 44" overall.
**Stock:** Walnut with cheekpiece.
**Sights:** Blade front, fully adjustable rear.
**Features:** Coil mainspring, double-set triggers, polished brass furniture. From Armsport, Ellett Bros., Navy Arms, E.M.F.
**Price:** . . . . . . . . . . . . . . . . . . . . . **$245.00 to $345.00**
**Price:** 50-, 54-cal., right-hand, percussion (Ellett Bros.) . . . . . . **$289.95**
**Price:** 50-, 54-cal., left-hand, percussion (Ellett Bros.) . . . . . . **$299.95**
**Price:** 50-cal., right-hand, flintlock (Ellett Bros.) . . . . . . . . . **$309.95**
**Price:** 50-cal., left-hand, flintlock (Ellett Bros.) . . . . . . . . . **$389.95**

## ITHACA-NAVY HAWKEN RIFLE
**Caliber:** 50.
**Barrel:** 32" octagonal, 1" dia.
**Weight:** About 9 lbs.
**Stocks:** Walnut.
**Sights:** Blade front, rear adjustable for windage.
**Features:** Hooked breech, 1⅞" throw percussion lock. Attached twin thimbles and under-rib. German silver barrel key inlays, Hawken-style toe and buttplates, lock bolt inlays, barrel wedges, entry thimble, trigger guard, ramrod and cleaning jag, nipple and nipple wrench. Introduced 1977. From Navy Arms.
**Price:** Complete, percussion . . . . . . . . . . . . . . . . . . **$400.00**
**Price:** Kit, percussion . . . . . . . . . . . . . . . . . . . . . . **$360.00**

Knight Mk-85 Hunter

## KENTUCKIAN RIFLE & CARBINE
**Caliber:** 44.
**Barrel:** 35" (Rifle), 27½" (Carbine).
**Weight:** 7 lbs. (Rifle), 5½ lbs. (Carbine). **Length:** 51" overall (Rifle), 43" (Carbine).
**Stock:** Walnut stain.
**Sights:** Brass blade front, steel V-ramp rear.
**Features:** Octagon barrel, case-hardened and engraved lockplates. Brass furniture. Imported by Dixie Gun Works.
**Price:** Rifle or carbine, flint, about . . . . . . . . . . . . . . **$259.95**
**Price:** As above, percussion, about . . . . . . . . . . . . . . **$249.95**

## Knight MK-85 Grand American Rifle
Similar to the MK-85 Hunter except comes with Shadow Black or Shadow Brown thumbhole stock. Hand-selected barrel and components. Comes with test target, hard gun case. Blue finish.
**Price:** . . . . . . . . . . . . . . . . . . . . . . . . . . . . . . . **$995.00**
**Price:** As above except in stainless steel . . . . . . . . . . **$1,095.00**

## KNIGHT MK-85 HUNTER RIFLE
**Caliber:** 50, 54.
**Barrel:** 24".
**Weight:** 7 lbs.
**Stock:** Classic walnut; recoil pad; swivel studs.
**Sights:** Hooded blade front on ramp, open adjustable rear.
**Features:** One-piece in-line bolt assembly with straight through in-line ignition system. Adjustable Featherweight trigger. Drilled and tapped for scope mounting. Made in U.S. From Modern Muzzle Loading, Inc.
**Price:** . . . . . . . . . . . . . . . . . . . . . . . . . . . . . . . **$529.95**
**Price:** Stalker (laminated, colored stock), 50 or 54 . . . . . **$579.95**
**Price:** Predator (stainless steel, composition stock), 50 or 54 . . . . **$649.95**
**Price:** Light Knight (20" barrel, walnut stock) . . . . . . . . . **$499.95**
**Price:** Light Knight (20" barrel, black composite stock) . . . . **$519.95**
**Price:** BK-92 Black Knight (blued, hardwood Monte Carlo stock) . . **$379.95**
**Price:** As above with black synthetic-coated stock . . . . . . **$349.95**
**Price:** As above with composite stock . . . . . . . . . . . . . **$399.95**
**Price:** LK-93 Knight Legend . . . . . . . . . . . . . . . . . . . **$289.95**

## KENTUCKY FLINTLOCK RIFLE
**Caliber:** 44, 45, or 50.
**Barrel:** 35".
**Weight:** 7 lbs. **Length:** 50" overall.
**Stock:** Walnut stained, brass fittings.
**Sights:** Fixed.
**Features:** Available in carbine model also, 28" bbl. Some variations in detail, finish. Kits also available from some importers. Imported by Navy Arms, The Armoury.
**Price:** About . . . . . . . . . . . . . . . . . **$217.95 to $345.00**
**Price:** Percussion, 45 or 50-cal. (Navy Arms) . . . . . . . . **$330.00**

## Kentucky Percussion Rifle
Similar to flintlock except percussion lock. Finish and features vary with importer. Imported by Navy Arms (45-cal.), The Armoury, CVA.
**Price:** About . . . . . . . . . . . . . . . . . . . . . . . . . **$259.95**
**Price:** 50-cal. (Navy Arms) . . . . . . . . . . . . . . . . . **$330.00**
**Price:** Kit, 50-cal. (CVA) . . . . . . . . . . . . . . . . . . **$189.95**

Navy Kodiak

## LONDON ARMORY 2-BAND ENFIELD 1858
**Caliber:** .577" Minie, .575" round ball.
**Barrel:** 33".
**Weight:** 10 lbs. **Length:** 49" overall.
**Stock:** Walnut.
**Sights:** Folding leaf rear adjustable for elevation.
**Features:** Blued barrel, color case-hardened lock and hammer, polished brass buttplate, trigger guard, nosecap. From Navy Arms, Euroarms of America, Dixie Gun Works.
**Price:** . . . . . . . . . . . . . . . . . . . **$385.00 to $450.00**
**Price:** Assembled kit (Euroarms of America) . . . . . . . . . . . **$364.00**

## LONDON ARMORY ENFIELD MUSKETOON
**Caliber:** 58, Minie ball.
**Barrel:** 24", round.
**Weight:** 7-7½ lbs. **Length:** 40½" overall.
**Stock:** Walnut, with sling swivels.
**Sights:** Blade front, graduated military-leaf rear.
**Features:** Brass trigger guard, nose cap, buttplate; blued barrel, bands, lockplate, swivels. Imported by Euroarms of America, Navy Arms.
**Price:** . . . . . . . . . . . . . . . . . . . **$300.00 to $370.00**
**Price:** Kit . . . . . . . . . . . . . . . . . . . . . . . . . **$345.00**

## KODIAK MK. III DOUBLE RIFLE
**Caliber:** 54x54, 58x58, 50x50.
**Barrel:** 28", 5-groove, 1:48 twist.
**Weight:** 9½ lbs. **Length:** 43¼" overall.
**Stock:** Czechoslovakian walnut, hand-checkered.
**Sights:** Adjustable bead front, adjustable open rear.
**Features:** Hooked breech allows interchangeability of barrels. Comes with sling, swivels, bullet mould and bullet starter. Engraved lockplates, top tang and trigger guard. Locks and top tang polished, rest browned. Introduced 1976. Imported from Italy by Trail Guns Armory, Inc., Navy Arms.
**Price:** 50-, 54-, 58-cal. SxS . . . . . . . . . . . . . . . . . **$650.00**
**Price:** Spare barrels, all calibers . . . . . . . . . . . . . . . **$395.50**
**Price:** Spare barrels, 12-ga.x12-ga. . . . . . . . . . . . . . . **$295.50**

## LONDON ARMORY 3-BAND 1853 ENFIELD
**Caliber:** 58 (.577" Minie, .575" round ball, .580" maxi ball).
**Barrel:** 39".
**Weight:** 9½ lbs. **Length:** 54" overall.
**Stock:** European walnut.
**Sights:** Inverted "V" front, traditional Enfield folding ladder rear.
**Features:** Recreation of the famed London Armory Company Pattern 1862 Enfield Musket. One-piece walnut stock, brass buttplate, trigger guard and nose cap. Lockplate marked "London Armoury Co." and with a British crown. Blued Baddeley barrel bands. From Dixie Gun Works, Euroarms of America, Navy Arms.
**Price:** About . . . . . . . . . . . . . . . . . **$350.00 to $485.00**
**Price:** Assembled kit (Dixie, Euroarms of America) . . . . . . . . . **$425.00**

Lyman Great Plains

> Consult our Directory pages for the location of firms mentioned.

## LYMAN GREAT PLAINS RIFLE
**Caliber:** 50- or 54-cal.
**Barrel:** 32", 1:66 twist.
**Weight:** 9 lbs.
**Stock:** Walnut.
**Sights:** Steel blade front, buckhorn rear adjustable for windage and elevation and fixed notch primitive sight included.
**Features:** Blued steel furniture. Stainless steel nipple. Coil spring lock, Hawken-style trigger guard and double-set triggers. Round thimbles recessed and sweated into rib. Steel wedge plates and toe plate. Introduced 1979. From Lyman.
**Price:** Percussion . . . . . . . . . . . . . . . . . . . . . **$409.95**
**Price:** Flintlock . . . . . . . . . . . . . . . . . . . . . . **$439.95**
**Price:** Percussion kit . . . . . . . . . . . . . . . . . . . . **$329.95**
**Price:** Flintlock kit . . . . . . . . . . . . . . . . . . . . . **$359.95**
**Price:** Left-hand percussion . . . . . . . . . . . . . . . . . **$409.95**
**Price:** Left-hand flintlock . . . . . . . . . . . . . . . . . . **$439.95**

## LYMAN DEERSTALKER RIFLE
**Caliber:** 50, 54.
**Barrel:** 24", octagonal; 1:48 rifling.
**Weight:** 7½ lbs.
**Stock:** Walnut with black rubber buttpad.
**Sights:** Lyman #37MA beaded front, fully adjustable fold-down Lyman #16A rear.
**Features:** Stock has less drop for quick sighting. All metal parts are blackened, with color case-hardened lock; single trigger. Comes with sling and swivels. Available in flint or percussion. Introduced 1990. From Lyman.
**Price:** 50- or 54-cal., percussion . . . . . . . . . . . . . . . **$339.95**
**Price:** 50- or 54-cal., flintlock . . . . . . . . . . . . . . . . **$359.95**
**Price:** 50- or 54-cal., percussion, left-hand . . . . . . . . . . . **$339.95**
**Price:** 50-cal., flintlock, left-hand . . . . . . . . . . . . . . . **$359.95**

## Lyman Deerstalker Custom Carbine
Similar to the Deerstalker rifle except in 50-caliber only with 21" stepped octagon barrel; 1:24 twist for optimum performance with conical projectiles. Comes with Lyman 37MA front sight, Lyman 16A folding rear. Weighs 6¾ lbs., measures 38½" overall. Percussion or flintlock. Comes with Delrin ramrod, modern sling and swivels. Introduced 1991.
**Price:** Percussion . . . . . . . . . . . . . . . . . . . . . **$349.95**
**Price:** Flintlock . . . . . . . . . . . . . . . . . . . . . . **$374.95**
**Price:** Percussion, left-hand . . . . . . . . . . . . . . . . . **$349.95**

**CAUTION:** PRICES CHANGE, CHECK AT GUNSHOP.

Lyman Trade Rifle

**LYMAN TRADE RIFLE**
**Caliber:** 50 or 54.
**Barrel:** 28" octagon, 1:48 twist.
**Weight:** 8¾ lbs. **Length:** 45" overall.

**Stock:** European walnut.
**Sights:** Blade front, open rear adjustable for windage or optional fixed sights.
**Features:** Fast twist rifling for conical bullets. Polished brass furniture with blue steel parts, stainless steel nipple. Hook breech, single trigger, coil spring percussion lock. Steel barrel rib and ramrod ferrules. Introduced 1980. From Lyman.
**Price:** Percussion . . . . . . . . . . . . . . . . . . . . . . . . . . . . . **$309.95**
**Price:** Kit, percussion . . . . . . . . . . . . . . . . . . . . . . . . . . **$249.95**
**Price:** Flintlock . . . . . . . . . . . . . . . . . . . . . . . . . . . . . . . **$339.95**
**Price:** Kit, flintlock . . . . . . . . . . . . . . . . . . . . . . . . . . . . **$284.95**

Mowrey Squirrel Rifle

**Mowrey Silhouette Rifle**
   Similar to the Squirrel Rifle except in 40-caliber with 32" barrel. Available in brass or steel frame.
**Price:** Brass frame . . . . . . . . . . . . . . . . . . . . . . . . . . **$350.00**
**Price:** Steel frame . . . . . . . . . . . . . . . . . . . . . . . . . . . **$350.00**
**Price:** Kit, brass or steel . . . . . . . . . . . . . . . . . . . . . . **$300.00**

**Mowrey 1 N 30 Conical Rifle**
   Similar to the Squirrel Rifle except in steel frame only, 45-, 50- or 54-caliber. Has special 1:24" twist barrel for conical- and sabot-style bullets. The 50- and 54-caliber barrels have 1" flats.
**Price:** . . . . . . . . . . . . . . . . . . . . . . . . . . . . . . . . . . . **$350.00**
**Price:** Kit . . . . . . . . . . . . . . . . . . . . . . . . . . . . . . . . . **$300.00**

**J.P. MURRAY 1862-1864 CAVALRY CARBINE**
**Caliber:** 58 (.577" Minie).
**Barrel:** 23".
**Weight:** 7 lbs., 9 oz. **Length:** 39" overall.
**Stock:** Walnut.

**MOWREY SQUIRREL RIFLE**
**Caliber:** 32, 36 or 45.
**Barrel:** 28"; 13/16" flats; 1:66" twist.
**Weight:** About 7.5 lbs. **Length:** 43" overall.
**Stock:** Curly maple; crescent buttplate.
**Sights:** German silver blade front, semi-buckhorn rear.
**Features:** Brass or steel boxlock action; cut-rifled barrel. Steel rifles have browned finish, brass have browned barrel. Adjustable sear and trigger pull. Made in U.S. by Mowrey Gun Works.
**Price:** Brass or steel . . . . . . . . . . . . . . . . . . . . . . . . . **$350.00**
**Price:** Kit . . . . . . . . . . . . . . . . . . . . . . . . . . . . . . . . . **$300.00**

**Mowrey Plains Rifle**
   Similar to the Squirrel Rifle except in 50- or 54-caliber with 32" barrel. Available in brass or steel frame.
**Price:** Brass frame . . . . . . . . . . . . . . . . . . . . . . . . . . **$350.00**
**Price:** Steel frame . . . . . . . . . . . . . . . . . . . . . . . . . . . **$350.00**
**Price:** Rocky Mountain Hunter (as above except 28" bbl.), brass . . . **$350.00**
**Price:** As above, steel frame . . . . . . . . . . . . . . . . . . . **$350.00**
**Price:** All above in kit form, ea. . . . . . . . . . . . . . . . . . **$300.00**

**Sights:** Blade front, rear drift adjustable for windage.
**Features:** Browned barrel, color case-hardened lock, blued swivel and band springs, polished brass buttplate, trigger guard, barrel bands. From Navy Arms, Euroarms of America.
**Price:** . . . . . . . . . . . . . . . . . . . . . . . . . . **$300.00 to $380.00**

Navy Arms Japanese Matchlock

**NAVY ARMS MORTIMER FLINTLOCK RIFLE**
**Caliber:** 54.
**Barrel:** 36".
**Weight:** 9 lbs. **Length:** 52¼" overall.
**Stock:** Checkered walnut.
**Sights:** Bead front, rear adjustable for windage.
**Features:** Waterproof pan, roller frizzen; sling swivels; browned barrel; external safety. Introduced 1991. Imported by Navy Arms.
**Price:** . . . . . . . . . . . . . . . . . . . . . . . . . . . . . . . . . . . **$690.00**

**NAVY ARMS JAPANESE MATCHLOCK RIFLE**
**Caliber:** 50.
**Barrel:** 41".
**Weight:** 8½ lbs. **Length:** 54¼" overall.
**Stock:** Stained hardwood.
**Sights:** Blade front, rear adjustable for windage.
**Features:** Replica of the matchlocks used by the Samurai. Brass lock, serpentine and trigger guard. Introduced 1991. Imported by Navy Arms.
**Price:** . . . . . . . . . . . . . . . . . . . . . . . . . . . . . . . . . . . **$495.00**

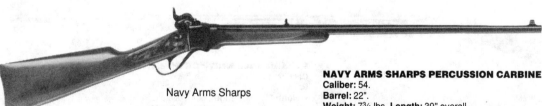

Navy Arms Sharps

**NAVY ARMS SHARPS PERCUSSION CARBINE**
**Caliber:** 54.
**Barrel:** 22".
**Weight:** 7¾ lbs. **Length:** 39" overall.
**Stock:** Walnut.
**Sights:** Blade front, military ladder-type rear.
**Features:** Color case-hardened action, blued barrel. Has saddle ring. Introduced 1991. Imported from Navy Arms.
**Price:** . . . . . . . . . . . . . . . . . . . . . . . . . . . . . . . . . . . **$715.00**
**Price:** Sharps Plains rifle (28.5" barrel) . . . . . . . . . . . . . **$715.00**

# BLACKPOWDER MUSKETS & RIFLES

## NAVY ARMS 1777 CHARLEVILLE MUSKET
**Caliber:** 69.
**Barrel:** 44⅝".
**Weight:** 10 lbs., 4 oz. **Length:** 59¾" overall.
**Stock:** Walnut.
**Sights:** Brass blade front.
**Features:** Exact copy of the musket used in the French Revolution. All steel is polished, in the white. Brass flashpan. Introduced 1991. Imported by Navy Arms.
**Price:** .................................................. $690.00
**Price:** 1763 Standard Charleville Musket, finished .......... $575.00
**Price:** As above, kit .......................................... $450.00
**Price:** 1816 M.T. Wickham Musket .......................... $690.00

## NAVY ARMS 1862 C.S. RICHMOND RIFLE
**Caliber:** 58.
**Barrel:** 40".
**Weight:** 10 lbs. **Length:** NA.
**Stock:** Walnut.
**Sights:** Blade front, adjustable rear.
**Features:** Copy of the three-band rifle musket made at Richmond Armory for the Confederacy. All steel polished bright. Imported by Navy Arms, Euroarms.
**Price:** .................................................. $550.00
**Price:** From Euroarms ....................................... $647.15

Navy Arms 1863

## NAVY ARMS 1863 SPRINGFIELD
**Caliber:** 58, uses .575" Minie.
**Barrel:** 40", rifled.
**Weight:** 9½ lbs. **Length:** 56" overall.
**Stock:** Walnut.
**Sights:** Open rear adjustable for elevation.
**Features:** Full-size three-band musket. Polished bright metal, including lock. From Navy Arms.
**Price:** Finished rifle ...................................... $550.00
**Price:** Kit ................................................... $450.00

## NAVY ARMS PENNSYLVANIA LONG RIFLE
**Caliber:** 32, 45.
**Barrel:** 40½".
**Weight:** 7½ lbs. **Length:** 56½" overall.
**Stock:** Walnut.
**Sights:** Blade front, fully adjustable rear.
**Features:** Browned barrel, brass furniture, polished lock with double-set triggers. Introduced 1991. Imported by Navy Arms.
**Price:** Percussion .......................................... $395.00
**Price:** Flintlock ............................................ $410.00

## NAVY ARMS SMITH CARBINE
**Caliber:** 50.
**Barrel:** 21½".
**Weight:** 7¾ lbs. **Length:** 39" overall.
**Stock:** American walnut.
**Sights:** Brass blade front, folding ladder-type rear.
**Features:** Replica of the breech-loading Civil War carbine. Color case-hardened receiver, rest blued. Cavalry model has saddle ring and bar, Artillery model has sling swivels. Introduced 1991. Imported by Navy Arms.
**Price:** Cavalry model ...................................... $600.00
**Price:** Artillery model ...................................... $600.00

Parker-Hale 1853

## PARKER-HALE ENFIELD 1853 MUSKET
**Caliber:** .577".
**Barrel:** 39", 3-groove cold-forged rifling.
**Weight:** About 9 lbs. **Length:** 55" overall.
**Stock:** Seasoned walnut.
**Sights:** Fixed front, rear step adjustable for elevation.
**Features:** Three-band musket made to original specs from original gauges. Solid brass stock furniture, color hardened lockplate, hammer; blued barrel, trigger. Made by Gibbs Rifle Co., distributed by Navy Arms.
**Price:** .................................................. $585.00

## PARKER-HALE ENFIELD PATTERN 1858 NAVAL RIFLE
**Caliber:** .577".
**Barrel:** 33".
**Weight:** 8½ lbs. **Length:** 48½" overall.
**Stock:** European walnut.
**Sights:** Blade front, step adjustable rear.
**Features:** Two-band Enfield percussion rifle with heavy barrel. Five-groove progressive depth rifling, solid brass furniture. All parts made exactly to original patterns. Made by Gibbs Rifle Co., distributed by Navy Arms.
**Price:** .................................................. $550.00

## PARKER-HALE ENFIELD 1861 MUSKETOON
**Caliber:** 58.
**Barrel:** 24".
**Weight:** 7 lbs. **Length:** 40½" overall.
**Stock:** Walnut.
**Sights:** Fixed front, adjustable rear.
**Features:** Percussion muzzleloader, made to original 1861 English patterns. Made by Gibbs Rifle Co., distributed by Navy Arms.
**Price:** .................................................. $450.00

Parker-Hale Whitworth

## Parker-Hale Limited Edition Whitworth Sniping Rifle
Same as the Parker-Hale Whitworth Military Target Rifle except has replica of the Model 1860 brass telescope sight in fully adjustable mount. Made by Gibbs Rifle Co., distributed by Navy Arms.
**Price:** .................................................. $995.00

## PARKER-HALE WHITWORTH MILITARY TARGET RIFLE
**Caliber:** 45.
**Barrel:** 36".
**Weight:** 9¼ lbs. **Length:** 52½" overall.
**Stock:** Walnut. Checkered at wrist and forend.
**Sights:** Hooded post front, open step-adjustable rear.
**Features:** Faithful reproduction of the Whitworth rifle, only bored for 45-cal. Trigger has a detented lock, capable of being adjusted very finely without risk of the sear nose catching on the half-cock bent and damaging both parts. Introduced 1978. Made by Gibbs Rifle Co., distributed by Navy Arms.
**Price:** .................................................. $815.00

# BLACKPOWDER MUSKETS & RIFLES

## PARKER-HALE VOLUNTEER RIFLE
**Caliber:** .451".
**Barrel:** 32".
**Weight:** 9½ lbs. **Length:** 49" overall.
**Stock:** Walnut, checkered wrist and forend.
**Sights:** Globe front, adjustable ladder-type rear.
**Features:** Recreation of the type of gun issued to volunteer regiments during the 1860s. Rigby-pattern rifling, patent breech, detented lock. Stock is glass bedded for accuracy. Made by Gibbs Rifle Co., distributed by Navy Arms.
**Price:** . . . . . . . . . . . . . . . . . . . . . . . **$750.00**
**Price:** Three-band Volunteer . . . . . . . . . . . . . . . . . . **$815.00**

## PENNSYLVANIA FULL-STOCK RIFLE
**Caliber:** 45 or 50.
**Barrel:** 32" rifled, ¹⁵⁄₁₆ dia.
**Weight:** 8½ lbs.
**Stock:** Walnut.
**Sights:** Fixed.
**Features:** Available in flint or percussion. Blued lock and barrel, brass furniture. Offered complete or in kit form. From The Armoury.
**Price:** Flint . . . . . . . . . . . . . . . . . . . . **$250.00**
**Price:** Percussion . . . . . . . . . . . . . . . . . **$225.00**

C.S. Richmond 1863

## C.S. RICHMOND 1863 MUSKET
**Caliber:** 58.
**Barrel:** 40".
**Weight:** 11 lbs. **Length:** 56¼" overall.
**Stock:** European walnut with oil finish.
**Sights:** Blade front, adjustable folding leaf rear.
**Features:** Reproduction of the three-band Civil War musket. Sling swivels attached to trigger guard and middle barrel band. Lock plate marked "1863" and "C.S. Richmond." All metal left in the white. Brass buttplate and forend cap. Imported by Euroarms of America.
**Price:** . . . . . . . . . . . . . . . . . . . . . . **$650.00**

## ROBERTS 98 MAUSER MUZZLE LOADER
**Caliber:** 45, 50, 54.
**Barrel:** 26".
**Weight:** 8 lbs. **Length:** 46" overall.
**Stock:** Walnut-finished hardwood.
**Sights:** None furnished; comes with Weaver-style one-piece scope mount.
**Features:** Uses 98 Mauser bolt action. Wilson #3 tapered barrel; Mark II low profile safety. Announced 1993. Made in U.S. Available from Sile Distributors.
**Price:** About . . . . . . . . . . . . . . . . . . . . **$336.00**

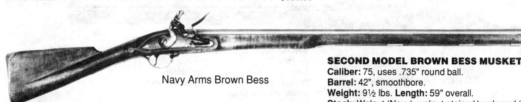

Navy Arms Brown Bess

## SECOND MODEL BROWN BESS MUSKET
**Caliber:** 75, uses .735" round ball.
**Barrel:** 42", smoothbore.
**Weight:** 9½ lbs. **Length:** 59" overall.
**Stock:** Walnut (Navy); walnut-stained hardwood (Dixie).
**Sights:** Fixed.
**Features:** Polished barrel and lock with brass trigger guard and buttplate. Bayonet and scabbard available. From Navy Arms, Dixie Gun Works.
**Price:** Finished . . . . . . . . . . . . **$475.00** to **$850.00**
**Price:** Kit (Dixie Gun Works, Navy Arms) . . . . . **$495.00** to **$510.00**
**Price:** Carbine (Navy Arms) . . . . . . . . . . . . . . **$635.00**

## SHARPS PERCUSSION RIFLES
**Caliber:** 54.
**Barrel:** 28".
**Weight:** 9 lbs. **Length:** 46" overall.
**Stock:** Checkered walnut.
**Sights:** Blade front, ladder-type adjustable rear.
**Features:** Blued barrel, color case-hardened receiver and buttplate. Imported from Italy by E.M.F.
**Price:** Rifle or carbine . . . . . . . . . . . . . . . **$860.00**

T/C Big Boar

## THOMPSON/CENTER BIG BOAR RIFLE
**Caliber:** 58.
**Barrel:** 26" octagon; 1:48 twist.
**Weight:** 7¾ lbs. **Length:** 42½" overall.
**Stock:** American black walnut; rubber buttpad; swivels.
**Sights:** Bead front, full adjustable open rear.
**Features:** Percussion lock; single trigger with wide bow trigger guard. Comes with soft leather sling. Introduced 1991. From Thompson/Center.
**Price:** . . . . . . . . . . . . . . . . . . . . . . . **$340.00**

T/C Grey Hawk

## THOMPSON/CENTER GREY HAWK PERCUSSION RIFLE
**Caliber:** 50.
**Barrel:** 24"; 1:48" twist.
**Weight:** 7 lbs. **Length:** 41" overall.
**Stock:** Black Rynite with rubber recoil pad.
**Sights:** Bead front, fully adjustable open hunting rear.
**Features:** Stainless steel barrel, lock, hammer, trigger guard, thimbles; blued sights. Percussion only. Introduced 1993. From Thompson/Center Arms.
**Price:** . . . . . . . . . . . . . . . . . . . . . . . **$275.00**

T/C Hawken

## THOMPSON/CENTER HAWKEN RIFLE
**Caliber:** 45, 50 or 54.
**Barrel:** 28" octagon, hooked breech.
**Stocks:** American walnut.
**Sights:** Blade front, rear adjustable for windage and elevation.
**Features:** Solid brass furniture, double-set triggers, button rifled barrel, coil-type mainspring. From Thompson/Center.
**Price:** Percussion model (45-, 50- or 54-cal.) . . . . . . . . . . . $375.00
**Price:** Flintlock model (50-cal.) . . . . . . . . . . . . . . . . $385.00
**Price:** Percussion kit . . . . . . . . . . . . . . . . . . . . . . $275.00
**Price:** Flintlock kit . . . . . . . . . . . . . . . . . . . . . . . $295.00

## THOMPSON/CENTER HIGH PLAINS SPORTER
**Caliber:** 50.
**Barrel:** 24".
**Weight:** 7 lbs. **Length:** 41" overall.
**Stock:** Black walnut with pistol grip, rubber recoil pad, sling swivel studs.
**Sights:** Blade front with open hunting-style rear, or T/C hunting-style tang peep sight.
**Features:** Percussion lock only. Single hunting-style trigger with wide bow trigger guard. Color case-hardened lock plate. Introduced 1992. From Thompson/Center.
**Price:** With open sights . . . . . . . . . . . . . . . . . . . $340.00
**Price:** With tang sight . . . . . . . . . . . . . . . . . . . . $345.00

## THOMPSON/CENTER NEW ENGLANDER RIFLE
**Caliber:** 50, 54.
**Barrel:** 28", round.
**Weight:** 7 lbs., 15 oz.
**Stock:** American walnut or Rynite.
**Sights:** Open, adjustable.
**Features:** Color case-hardened percussion lock with engraving, rest blued. Also accepts 12-ga. shotgun barrel. Introduced 1987. From Thompson/Center.
**Price:** Right-hand model . . . . . . . . . . . . . . . . . . $270.00
**Price:** As above, Rynite stock . . . . . . . . . . . . . . . $255.00
**Price:** Left-hand model . . . . . . . . . . . . . . . . . . . $290.00
**Price:** Accessory 12-ga. barrel, right-hand . . . . . . . . $130.00

T/C Pennsylvania Hunter

### Thompson/Center Pennsylvania Hunter Carbine
Similar to the Pennsylvania Hunter except has 21" barrel, weighs 6.5 lbs., and has an overall length of 38". Designed for shooting patched round balls. Available in percussion or flintlock styles. Introduced 1992. From Thompson/Center.
**Price:** Percussion . . . . . . . . . . . . . . . . . . . . . . $310.00
**Price:** Flintlock . . . . . . . . . . . . . . . . . . . . . . . $325.00
**Price:** Accessory barrels . . . . . . . . . . . . . . . . . . $155.00

### Thompson/Center Renegade Hunter
Similar to standard Renegade except has single trigger in a large-bow shotgun-style trigger guard, no brass trim. Available in 50- or 54-caliber. Color case-hardened lock, rest blued. Introduced 1987. From Thompson/Center.
**Price:** . . . . . . . . . . . . . . . . . . . . . . . . . . . . $310.00

## THOMPSON/CENTER SCOUT RIFLE
**Caliber:** 50 and 54.
**Barrel:** 21", interchangeable, 1:20 twist.
**Weight:** 7 lbs., 4 oz. **Length:** 38⅝" overall.
**Stocks:** American black walnut stock and forend.
**Sights:** Bead front, adjustable semi-buckhorn rear.
**Features:** Patented in-line ignition system with special vented breech plug. Patented trigger mechanism consists of only two moving parts. Interchange

## THOMPSON/CENTER PENNSYLVANIA HUNTER RIFLE
**Caliber:** 50.
**Barrel:** 31", half-octagon, half-round.
**Weight:** About 7½ lbs. **Length:** 48" overall.
**Stock:** Black walnut.
**Sights:** Open, adjustable.
**Features:** Rifled 1:66 for round ball shooting. Available in flintlock or percussion. From Thompson/Center.
**Price:** Percussion . . . . . . . . . . . . . . . . . . . . . . $320.00
**Price:** Flintlock . . . . . . . . . . . . . . . . . . . . . . . $335.00

## THOMPSON/CENTER RENEGADE RIFLE
**Caliber:** 50 and 54.
**Barrel:** 26", 1" across the flats.
**Weight:** 8 lbs.
**Stock:** American walnut.
**Sights:** Open hunting (Patridge) style, fully adjustable for windage and elevation.
**Features:** Coil spring lock, double-set triggers, blued steel trim. From Thompson/Center.
**Price:** Percussion model . . . . . . . . . . . . . . . . . . $335.00
**Price:** Flintlock model, 50-cal. only . . . . . . . . . . . . $345.00
**Price:** Percussion kit . . . . . . . . . . . . . . . . . . . . $245.00
**Price:** Flintlock kit . . . . . . . . . . . . . . . . . . . . . $260.00
**Price:** Left-hand percussion, 50- or 54-cal. . . . . . . . . $345.00

able barrels. Wide grooved hammer. Brass trigger guard assembly, brass barrel band and buttplate. Ramrod has blued hardware. Comes with q.d. swivels and suede leather carrying sling. Drilled and tapped for standard scope mounts. Introduced 1990. From Thompson/Center.
**Price:** 50- or 54-cal. . . . . . . . . . . . . . . . . . . . . . $395.00
**Price:** With black Rynite stock . . . . . . . . . . . . . . . $295.00
**Price:** Extra barrel, 50- or 54-cal. . . . . . . . . . . . . . $160.00

T/C Thunder Hawk

**Weight:** 6.75 lbs. **Length:** 38.75" overall.
**Stock:** American walnut with rubber recoil pad.
**Sights:** Bead on ramp front, adjustable leaf rear.
**Features:** Uses modern in-line ignition system, adjustable trigger. Knurled striker handle indicators for Safe and Fire. Black wood ramrod, Drilled and tapped for T/C scope mounts. Introduced 1993. From Thompson/Center Arms.
**Price:** . . . . . . . . . . . . . . . . . . . . . . . . . . . . $275.00

## THOMPSON/CENTER THUNDER HAWK RIFLE
**Caliber:** 50.
**Barrel:** 21"; 1:38" twist.

# BLACKPOWDER MUSKETS & RIFLES

T/C Tree Hawk

## THOMPSON/CENTER WHITE MOUNTAIN CARBINE
**Caliber:** 45, 50 and 54.
**Barrel:** 21", half-octagon, half-round.
**Weight:** 6½ lbs. **Length:** 38" overall.
**Stock:** American black walnut.
**Sights:** Open hunting (Patridge) style, fully adjustable rear.
**Features:** Percussion or flintlock. Single trigger, large trigger guard; rubber buttpad; rear q.d. swivel, front swivel mounted on thimble; comes with sling. Introduced 1989. From Thompson/Center.
**Price:** Percussion . . . . . . . . . . . . . . . . . . . . . . . . . **$335.00**
**Price:** Flintlock . . . . . . . . . . . . . . . . . . . . . . . . . . . **$355.00**

Traditions Buckskinner

## TRADITIONS DEERHUNTER RIFLE
**Caliber:** 50.
**Barrel:** 26", octagonal, ¹⁵/₁₆" flats; 1:48" or 1:66" twist.
**Weight:** 5 lbs., 14 oz. **Length:** 39¼" overall.
**Stock:** Stained beech with rubber buttpad, sling swivels.
**Sights:** Blade front, rear adjustable for windage.
**Features:** Flint or percussion with color case-hardened lock. Hooked breech, oversized trigger guard, blackened furniture, wood ramrod. Imported by Traditions, Inc.
**Price:** Percussion, 1:48" twist . . . . . . . . . . . . . . . **$165.00**
**Price:** Flintlock, 1:66" twist . . . . . . . . . . . . . . . . . **$182.00**
**Price:** Percussion kit . . . . . . . . . . . . . . . . . . . . . . **$149.00**

## Traditions Frontier Carbine
Similar to the Frontier Rifle except has 24" barrel, is 40½" overall, weighs 6½ lbs. Available in 50-caliber percussion only. From Traditions, Inc.
**Price:** . . . . . . . . . . . . . . . . . . . . . . . . . . . . . . . . **$254.00**

## THOMPSON/CENTER TREE HAWK CARBINE
**Caliber:** 50.
**Barrel:** 21".
**Weight:** 6.75 lbs. **Length:** 38" overall.
**Stock:** Rynite composition with choice of Realtree or Mossy Oak Bottomland camouflage.
**Sights:** Bead front, fully adjustable open hunting-style rear.
**Features:** All hardware (except sling swivels and barrel wedge) finished in camouflage, including the polymer-coated fiberglass ramrod. Single trigger, wide bow trigger guard, rubber recoil pad, camo sling. Introduced 1992. From Thompson/Center.
**Price:** 50-cal. percussion only . . . . . . . . . . . . . . . **$340.00**
**Price:** Accessory 12-gauge barrel . . . . . . . . . . . . . **$165.00**

## TRADITIONS BUCKSKINNER CARBINE
**Caliber:** 50.
**Barrel:** 21", ¹⁵/₁₆" flats, half octagon, half round.
**Weight:** 6 lbs. **Length:** 36¼" overall.
**Stock:** Beech or black laminated.
**Sights:** Beaded blade front, hunting-style open rear click adjustable for windage and elevation.
**Features:** Uses V-type mainspring, single trigger. Non-glare hardware. Comes with leather sling. From Traditions, Inc.
**Price:** Flintlock . . . . . . . . . . . . . . . . . . . . . . . . . . **$290.00**
**Price:** Flintlock, laminated stock . . . . . . . . . . . . . . **$337.00**
**Price:** Percussion . . . . . . . . . . . . . . . . . . . . . . . . . **$274.00**
**Price:** Percussion, laminated stock . . . . . . . . . . . . . **$320.00**
**Price:** Percussion, left-hand . . . . . . . . . . . . . . . . . . **$290.00**

## TRADITIONS FRONTIER SCOUT RIFLE
**Caliber:** 36, 45, 50.
**Barrel:** 24" (36-cal.), 26" (45, 50); ⅞" flats.
**Weight:** 6 lbs. **Length:** 39⅛" overall (24" barrel).
**Stock:** Beech.
**Sights:** Blade Front, primitive-style adjustable rear.
**Features:** Scaled-down version of the Frontier rifle for smaller shooters. Percussion only. Color case-hardened lock plate. From Traditions, Inc.
**Price:** . . . . . . . . . . . . . . . . . . . . . . . . . . . . . . . . **$232.00**

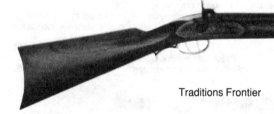

Traditions Frontier

## TRADITIONS HAWKEN RIFLE
**Caliber:** 50, 54.
**Barrel:** 32¼"; 1" flats.
**Weight:** 9 lbs. **Length:** 50" overall.
**Stock:** Walnut with cheekpiece.
**Sights:** Hunting style, click adjustable for windage and elevation.
**Features:** Fiberglass ramrod, double-set triggers, polished brass furniture. From Traditions, Inc.
**Price:** Percussion . . . . . . . . . . . . . . . . . . . . . . . . . **$412.00**

## TRADITIONS HAWKEN WOODSMAN RIFLE
**Caliber:** 50 and 54.
**Barrel:** 28"; ¹⁵/₁₆" flats.
**Weight:** 7 lbs. **Length:** 45.75" overall.
**Stock:** Walnut-stained hardwood.

## TRADITIONS FRONTIER RIFLE
**Caliber:** 45, 50.
**Barrel:** 28", ¹⁵/₁₆" flats.
**Weight:** 8 lbs. **Length:** 44¾" overall.
**Stock:** Beech.
**Sights:** Beaded blade front, hunting-style rear click adjustable for windage and elevation.
**Features:** Adjustable sear engagement with fly and bridle, V-type mainspring; double-set triggers. Brass furniture. From Traditions, Inc.
**Price:** Percussion . . . . . . . . . . . . . . . . . . . . . . . . . **$254.00**
**Price:** Flintlock . . . . . . . . . . . . . . . . . . . . . . . . . . . **$274.00**
**Price:** Kit, 50-caliber percussion . . . . . . . . . . . . . . . **$165.00**

**Sights:** Beaded blade front, hunting-style open rear adjustable for windage and elevation.
**Features:** Percussion only. Brass patchbox and furniture. Double triggers. From Traditions, Inc.
**Price:** 50 or 54 . . . . . . . . . . . . . . . . . . . . . . . . . . . **$292.00**
**Price:** 50-cal., left-hand . . . . . . . . . . . . . . . . . . . . . **$309.00**
**Price:** Kit . . . . . . . . . . . . . . . . . . . . . . . . . . . . . . . . **$210.00**

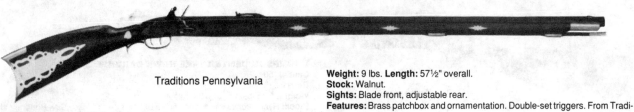

Traditions Pennsylvania

## TRADITIONS PENNSYLVANIA RIFLE
**Caliber:** 45, 50.
**Barrel:** 40¼", ⅞" flats.

## TRADITIONS PIONEER RIFLE/CARBINE
**Caliber:** 50, 54.
**Barrel:** 27¼"; ¹⁵⁄₁₆" flats.
**Weight:** 7 lbs. **Length:** 44" overall.
**Stock:** Beech with pistol grip, recoil pad.

## TRADITIONS WHITETAIL SERIES RIFLES
**Caliber:** 50, 54 (percussion only).
**Barrel:** 21", 26", ¹⁵⁄₁₆" flats.
**Weight:** 5 lbs., 14 oz. (rifle). **Length:** 39¼" overall (rifle).
**Stock:** Walnut-stained hardwood, rubber recoil pad; or synthetic.
**Sights:** Beaded blade front with flourescent dot, fully adjustable hunting-style rear.
**Features:** Flint or percussion. Color case-hardened, engraved lock with V-type mainspring, offset hammer. Barrel drilled and tapped for scope mounting (percussion only). Oversized trigger guard, sling swivels, blackened furniture, inletted wedge plates. Imported by Traditions, Inc.
**Price:** Flintlock, wood stock, rifle or carbine . . . . . . . . . . . $274.00
**Price:** Flintlock, synthetic stock, stainless barrel . . . . . . . . . . $337.00
**Price:** Percussion, wood stock, 50 or 54 . . . . . . . . . . . . . $257.00
**Price:** As above, synthetic stock . . . . . . . . . . . . . . . . $290.00
**Price:** Carbine, percussion, wood stock . . . . . . . . . . . . . $257.00
**Price:** As above, synthetic stock . . . . . . . . . . . . . . . . $290.00
**Price:** Carbine, percussion, synthetic stock, stainless barrel . . . . $320.00

Navy Arms Tryon

## Navy Arms Tryon Creedmoor Target Model
Similar to the standard Tryon rifle except 45-caliber only, 33" octagon barrel, globe front sight with inserts, fully adjustable match rear. Has double-set triggers, sling swivels. Imported by Navy Arms.
**Price:** . . . . . . . . . . . . . . . . . . . . . . . . . . . . $680.00

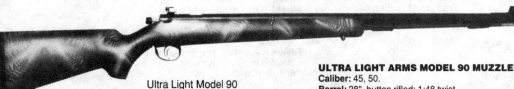

Ultra Light Model 90

## UBERTI SANTA FE HAWKEN RIFLE
**Caliber:** 50 or 54.
**Barrel:** 32", octagonal.
**Weight:** 9.8 lbs. **Length:** 50" overall.
**Stock:** Walnut, with beavertail cheekpiece.
**Sights:** German silver blade front, buckhorn rear.
**Features:** Browned finish, color case-hardened lock, double triggers, German silver ferrule, wedge plates. Imported by Uberti USA.
**Price:** . . . . . . . . . . . . . . . . . . . . . . . . . . . $495.00

**Weight:** 9 lbs. **Length:** 57½" overall.
**Stock:** Walnut.
**Sights:** Blade front, adjustable rear.
**Features:** Brass patchbox and ornamentation. Double-set triggers. From Traditions, Inc.
**Price:** Flintlock . . . . . . . . . . . . . . . . . . . . . . $495.00
**Price:** Percussion . . . . . . . . . . . . . . . . . . . . . . $467.00

**Sights:** German silver blade front, buckhorn rear with elevation ramp.
**Features:** V-type mainspring, adjustable single trigger; blackened furniture; color case-hardened lock; large trigger guard. From Traditions, Inc.
**Price:** Percussion only, rifle . . . . . . . . . . . . . . . . . $227.00
**Price:** Carbine. 24" barrel, 50-cal. only . . . . . . . . . . . . $227.00

## TRADITIONS T93 CUSTOM IN-LINE RIFLE, CARBINE
**Caliber:** 50.
**Barrel:** 21", 28", round.
**Weight:** 7 lbs., 14 oz. (rifle). **Length:** 44¼" overall (rifle).
**Stock:** Stained beech.
**Sights:** Beaded blade front, click adjustable rear.
**Features:** Closed breech in-line percussion action, ambidextrous and half-cock safety. Comes with blackened furniture, swivel studs, unbreakable ramrod, oversized trigger guard. Polished blue finish. From Traditions, Inc.
**Price:** Rifle or carbine . . . . . . . . . . . . . . . . . . . . $432.00

## TRYON RIFLE
**Caliber:** 50, 54.
**Barrel:** 34", octagon; 1:63 twist.
**Weight:** 9 lbs. **Length:** 49" overall.
**Stock:** European walnut with steel furniture.
**Sights:** Blade front, fixed rear.
**Features:** Reproduction of an American plains rifle with double-set triggers and back-action lock. Imported from Italy by Dixie Gun Works.
**Price:** . . . . . . . . . . . . . . . . . . . . . . . . . . . $595.00

## TRYON TRAILBLAZER RIFLE
**Caliber:** 50.
**Barrel:** 32", 1" flats.
**Weight:** 9 lbs. **Length:** 48" overall.
**Stock:** European walnut with cheekpiece.
**Sights:** Blade front, semi-buckhorn rear.
**Features:** Reproduction of a rifle made by George Tryon about 1820. Double-set triggers, back action lock, hooked breech with long tang. From Armsport, Navy Arms.
**Price:** About . . . . . . . . . . . . . . . . . . . . . . . . $455.00
**Price:** 50-, . . . ?8", 30" bbl. (Armsport) . . . . . . . . . . $825.00
**Price:** Del. . . . . . . . l with silver finish (Armsport) . . . . . . . . $895.00

## ULTRA LIGHT ARMS MODEL 90 MUZZLELOADER
**Caliber:** 45, 50.
**Barrel:** 28", button rifled; 1:48 twist.
**Weight:** 6 lbs.
**Stock:** Kevlar/graphite, colors optional.
**Sights:** Hooded blade front on ramp, Williams aperture rear adjustable for windage and elevation.
**Features:** In-line ignition system with top loading port. Timney trigger; integral side safety. Comes with recoil pad, sling swivels and hard case. Introduced 1990. Made in U.S. by Ultra Light Arms.
**Price:** . . . . . . . . . . . . . . . . . . . . . . . . . . . $950.00

# BLACKPOWDER MUSKETS & RIFLES

White Systems Super 91

## White Systems Original 68 Blackpowder Rifle
Similar to the Super 91 model except made of blued ordnance steel. Uses Insta-Fire Straight-Pull Hammer percussion ignition. Has 24" barrel, Posi-safe thumb safety, adjustable trigger. Fully adjustable hunting rear sight, black composite stock with recoil pad, swivel studs; Delron ramrod. Drilled and tapped for scope mounting. Weighs 7½ lbs. Available in 45-caliber (1:20" twist) or 50-caliber (1:24" twist). Reintroduced 1993. From White Systems, Inc.
**Price:** ............................................... **$599.00**

## WHITE SYSTEMS SUPER 91 BLACKPOWDER RIFLE
**Caliber:** 45 or 50.
**Barrel:** 26".
**Weight:** 7½ lbs. **Length:** 43.5" overall.
**Stock:** Black laminate or black composite; recoil pad, swivel studs.
**Sights:** Bead front on ramp, fully adjustable open rear.
**Features:** Insta-Fire straight-line ignition system; all stainless steel construction; side-swing safety; fully adjustable trigger; full barrel under-rib with two ramrod thimbles. Introduced 1991. Made in U.S. by White Systems, Inc.
**Price:** Laminated or composite stock ................. **$699.00**

## WHITE SYSTEMS WHITETAIL RIFLE
**Caliber:** 45 or 50.
**Barrel:** 22".
**Weight:** 6.5 lbs. **Length:** 39.5" overall.
**Stock:** Black composite; classic style; recoil pad, swivel studs.
**Sights:** Bead front on ramp, fully adjustable open rear.
**Features:** Insta-Fire straight-line ignition; action and trigger safeties; adjustable trigger; stainless steel. Introduced 1992. Made in U.S. by White Systems, Inc.
**Price:** Blue, composite stock ...................... **$499.00**
**Price:** Stainless, composite stock ................. **$549.00**

White Systems Whitetail

## White Systems Bison Blackpowder Rifle
Similar to the blued Whitetail model except in 50-caliber (1:24" twist) or 54-caliber (1:28" twist) with 22" ball barrel. Uses Insta-Fire in-line percussion system, double safety. Adjustable sight, walnut-finished hardwood stock, matte blue metal finish, Delron ramrod, swivel studs. Drilled and tapped for scope mounting. Weighs 7¼ lbs. Introduced 1993. From White Systems, Inc.
**Price:** ............................................. **$399.00**

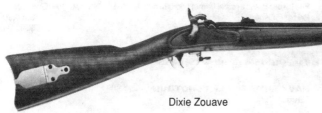

Dixie Zouave

## ZOUAVE PERCUSSION RIFLE
**Caliber:** 58, 59.
**Barrel:** 32½".
**Weight:** 9½ lbs. **Length:** 48½" overall.
**Stock:** Walnut finish, brass patchbox and buttplate.
**Sights:** Fixed front, rear adjustable for elevation.
**Features:** Color case-hardened lockplate, blued barrel. From Navy Arms, Dixie Gun Works, Euroarms of America (M1863), E.M.F.
**Price:** About ........................... **$325.00 to $540.00**
**Price:** Kit (Euroarms 58-cal. only) ................. **$263.00**

## Mississippi Model 1841 Percussion Rifle
Similar to Zouave rifle but patterned after U.S. Model 1841. Imported by Dixie Gun Works, Euroarms of America, Navy Arms.
**Price:** ................................. **$430.00 to $463.00**

# BLACKPOWDER SHOTGUNS

Cabela's 12-Gauge

## CVA TRAPPER PERCUSSION
**Gauge:** 12.
**Barrel:** 28". Choke tubes (Imp. Cyl., Mod., Full).
**Weight:** NA.
**Length:** 46" overall.
**Stock:** English-style straight grip of walnut-finished hardwood.
**Sights:** Brass bead front.
**Features:** Single blued barrel; color case-hardened lockplate and hammer; screw adjustable sear engagements, V-type mainspring; brass wedge plates; color case-hardened and engraved trigger guard and tang. From CVA.
**Price:** Finished ........................... **$339.95**

## CABELA'S BLACKPOWDER SHOTGUNS
**Gauge:** 10, 12, 20.
**Barrel:** 28½" (10-, 12-ga.), Imp. Cyl., Mod., Full choke tubes; 27½" (20-ga.), Imp. Cyl., Mod. choke tubes.
**Weight:** 6½ to 7 lbs. **Length:** 45" overall (28½" barrel).
**Stock:** American walnut with checkered grip; 12- and 20-gauge have straight stock, 10-gauge has pistol grip.
**Features:** Blued barrels, engraved, color case-hardened locks and hammers, brass ramrod tip. From Cabela's.
**Price:** 10-gauge ................................ **$379.95**
**Price:** 12-gauge ................................ **$359.95**
**Price:** 20-gauge ................................ **$329.95**

CAUTION: PRICES CHANGE, CHECK AT GUNSHOP.

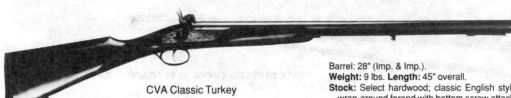

CVA Classic Turkey

**Barrel:** 28" (Imp. & Imp.).
**Weight:** 9 lbs. **Length:** 45" overall.
**Stock:** Select hardwood; classic English style with checkered straight grip, wrap-around forend with bottom screw attachment.
**Sights:** Bead front.
**Features:** Hinged double triggers; color case-hardened and engraved lock-plates, trigger guard and tang. Rubber recoil pad. Not suitable for steel shot. Introduced 1990. Imported by CVA.
**Price:** . . . . . . . . . . . . . . . . . . . . . . . . . . . . . . . . . . . . . $404.95

## CVA CLASSIC TURKEY DOUBLE SHOTGUN
**Gauge:** 12.

Dixie Magnum

**Barrel:** 30" (Imp. Cyl. & Mod.) in 10-ga.; 28" in 12-ga.
**Weight:** 6¼ lbs. **Length:** 45" overall.
**Stock:** Hand-checkered walnut, 14" pull.
**Features:** Double triggers, light hand engraving. Case-hardened locks in 12-ga.; polished steel in 10-ga. with sling swivels. From Dixie Gun Works.
**Price:** Upland . . . . . . . . . . . . . . . . . . . . . . . . . . . . . $399.00
**Price:** 12-ga. kit . . . . . . . . . . . . . . . . . . . . . . . . . . . $350.00
**Price:** 10-ga. . . . . . . . . . . . . . . . . . . . . . . . . . . . . . $495.00
**Price:** 10-ga. kit . . . . . . . . . . . . . . . . . . . . . . . . . . . $375.00

## DIXIE MAGNUM PERCUSSION SHOTGUN
**Gauge:** 10, 12.

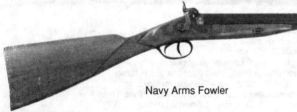

Mowrey Shotgun

**Barrel:** 28" (28-gauge, Cyl.); 32" (12-gauge, Cyl.); octagonal.
**Weight:** About 8 lbs. **Length:** 48" overall (32" barrel).
**Stock:** Curly maple.
**Sights:** Bead front.
**Features:** Brass or steel frame; shotgun butt. Made in U.S. by Mowrey Gun Works.
**Price:** Finished . . . . . . . . . . . . . . . . . . . . . . . . . . . . $350.00
**Price:** Kit . . . . . . . . . . . . . . . . . . . . . . . . . . . . . . . . $300.00

## MOWREY SHOTGUN
**Gauge:** 12, 28.

Navy Arms Fowler

## NAVY ARMS FOWLER SHOTGUN
**Gauge:** 12.
**Barrel:** 28".
**Weight:** 7 lbs., 12 oz. **Length:** 45" overall.
**Stock:** Walnut-stained hardwood.
**Features:** Color case-hardened lockplates and hammers; checkered stock. Imported by Navy Arms.
**Price:** Fowler model, 12-ga. only . . . . . . . . . . . . . . . . . . $325.00

## NAVY ARMS STEEL SHOT MAGNUM SHOTGUN
**Gauge:** 10.
**Barrel:** 28" (Cyl. & Cyl.).
**Weight:** 7 lbs., 9 oz. **Length:** 45½" overall.
**Stock:** Walnut, with cheekpiece.
**Features:** Designed specifically for steel shot. Engraved, polished locks; sling swivels; blued barrels. Introduced 1991. Imported by Navy Arms.
**Price:** . . . . . . . . . . . . . . . . . . . . . . . . . . . . . . . . . . $510.00

> Consult our Directory pages for the location of firms mentioned.

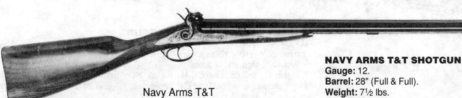

Navy Arms T&T

## NAVY ARMS T&T SHOTGUN
**Gauge:** 12.
**Barrel:** 28" (Full & Full).
**Weight:** 7½ lbs.
**Stock:** Walnut.
**Sights:** Bead front.
**Features:** Color case-hardened locks, double triggers, blued steel furniture. From Navy Arms.
**Price:** . . . . . . . . . . . . . . . . . . . . . . . . . . . . . . . . . . $480.00

## NAVY ARMS MORTIMER FLINTLOCK SHOTGUN
**Gauge:** 12.
**Barrel:** 36".
**Weight:** 7 lbs. **Length:** 53" overall.
**Stock:** Walnut, with cheekpiece.
**Features:** Waterproof pan, roller frizzen, external safety. Color case-hardened lock, rest blued. Introduced 1991. Imported by Navy Arms.
**Price:** . . . . . . . . . . . . . . . . . . . . . . . . . . . . . . . . . . $670.00

**CAUTION:** PRICES CHANGE, CHECK AT GUNSHOP.

T/C Tree Hawk

## THOMPSON/CENTER NEW ENGLANDER SHOTGUN
**Gauge:** 12.
**Barrel:** 28" (Imp. Cyl.), round.
**Weight:** 5 lbs., 2 oz.
**Stock:** Select American black walnut with straight grip.
**Features:** Percussion lock is color case-hardened, rest blued. Also accepts 26" round 50- and 54-cal. rifle barrel. Introduced 1986. From Thompson/Center.
**Price:** Right-hand . . . . . . . . . . . . . . . . . . . . . . . **$270.00**
**Price:** Right-hand, Rynite stock . . . . . . . . . . . . **$255.00**
**Price:** Left-hand . . . . . . . . . . . . . . . . . . . . . . . **$310.00**
**Price:** Accessory rifle barrel, right-hand, 50 or 54 . . . . . . . . **$130.00**
**Price:** As above, left-hand . . . . . . . . . . . . . . . **$140.00**

## THOMPSON/CENTER TREE HAWK SHOTGUN
**Gauge:** 12.
**Barrel:** 28" (Full choke tube).
**Weight:** 6.75 lbs. **Length:** 45" overall.
**Stock:** Rynite composition with choice of Realtree or Mossy Oak Bottomland camouflage.
**Sights:** Bead front.
**Features:** All hardware (except sling swivels and barrel wedge) finished in camouflage, including the polymer-coated fiberglass ramrod. Single trigger, wide bow trigger guard, rubber recoil pad, camo sling. Accessory Imp. Cyl. and Mod. choke tubes available. Introduced 1992. From Thompson/Center.
**Price:** 12-gauge, percussion only . . . . . . . . . . . . . . . **$345.00**
**Price:** Accessory 50-caliber barrel . . . . . . . . . . . . . . . **$160.00**

## TRAIL GUNS KODIAK 10-GAUGE DOUBLE
**Gauge:** 10.
**Barrel:** 20", 30¾" (Cyl. bore).
**Weight:** About 9 lbs. **Length:** 47⅛" overall.
**Stock:** Walnut, with cheek rest. Checkered wrist and forend.
**Features:** Chrome-plated bores; engraved lockplates, brass bead front and middle sights; sling swivels. Introduced 1980. Imported from Italy by Trail Guns Armory, Inc.
**Price:** . . . . . . . . . . . . . . . . . . . . . . . . . . . . **$425.00**

# AIRGUNS—HANDGUNS

## AIRROW MODEL 6A AIR PISTOL
**Caliber:** #2512 10.75" arrow.
**Barrel:** 10.75".
**Weight:** 1.75 lbs. **Length:** 16.5" overall.
**Power:** $CO_2$ or compressed air.
**Stocks:** Checkered composition.
**Sights:** Bead front, fully adjustable Williams rear.
**Features:** Velocity to 375 fps. Pneumatic air trigger. Floating barrel. All aircraft aluminum and stainless steel construction; Mil-spec materials and finishes. Announced 1993. From Swivel Machine Works, Inc.
**Price:** About . . . . . . . . . . . . . . . . . . . . . . . . **$499.00**

Airrow Model 6A

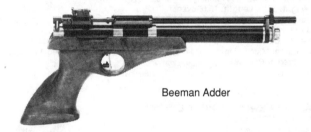

Beeman Adder

## BEEMAN P1 MAGNUM AIR PISTOL
**Caliber:** 177, 5mm, 22, single shot.
**Barrel:** 8.4".
**Weight:** 2.5 lbs. **Length:** 11" overall.
**Power:** Top lever cocking; spring piston.
**Stocks:** Checkered walnut.
**Sights:** Blade front, square notch rear with click micrometer adjustments for windage and elevation. Grooved for scope mounting.
**Features:** Dual power for 177 and 20-cal.: low setting gives 350-400 fps; high setting 500-600 fps. Rearward expanding mainspring simulates firearm recoil. All Colt 45 auto grips fit gun. Dry-firing feature for practice. Optional wooden shoulder stock. Introduced 1985. Imported by Beeman.
**Price:** 177, 5mm, 22-cal. . . . . . . . . . . . . . . . . **$384.50**
**Price:** 177, 5mm, stainless/blue finish . . . . . . . . . . . . . . . **$434.50**

## Beeman P2 Match Air Pistol
Similar to the Beeman P1 Magnum except shoots only 177 or 5mm pellets; completely recoilless single-stroke pnuematic action. Weighs 2.2 lbs. Choice of thumbrest match grips or standard style. Introduced 1990.
**Price:** 177, 5mm, standard grip . . . . . . . . . . . . . . . . **$425.00**
**Price:** 177, match grip . . . . . . . . . . . . . . . . . . . . . **$455.00**

## BEEMAN ADDER AIR PISTOL
**Caliber:** 20, 25, single shot.
**Barrel:** 10.5"; 12-groove rifling.
**Weight:** 3 lbs. **Length:** 16.5" overall.
**Power:** Pre-charged pneumatic, internal air chamber.
**Stocks:** Smooth, select hardwood.
**Sights:** Micrometer click adjustable. Built-in scope dovetail.
**Features:** Two-stage trigger. Steel body, highly polished, blued and accented with solid brass. Introduced 1992. Imported by Beeman.
**Price:** 20-, 25-cal. . . . . . . . . . . . . . . . . . . . . . . . . **$529.00**

Beeman P-1

## BEEMAN/FEINWERKBAU C5 CO₂ RAPID FIRE PISTOL

**Caliber:** 177.
**Barrel:** 7.25".
**Weight:** 2.42 lbs.
**Power:** NA.
**Stocks:** Anatomical match.
**Sights:** Match.
**Features:** Velocity 510 fps. Has special trigger shape with swivel action, longitudinal positioning. Introduced 1990. Imported by Beeman.
**Price:** Right-hand . . . . . . . . . . . . . . . . . . . . . . . **$1,485.00**
**Price:** Left-hand . . . . . . . . . . . . . . . . . . . . . . . . **$1,570.00**

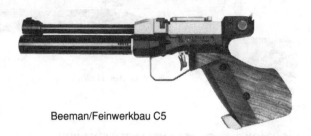

Beeman/Feinwerkbau C5

## BEEMAN/FEINWERKBAU C20 CO₂ PISTOL

**Caliber:** 177, single shot.
**Barrel:** 10.1", 12-groove rifling.
**Weight:** 2.5 lbs. **Length:** 16" overall.
**Power:** Special CO₂ cylinder.
**Stock:** Stippled walnut with adjustable palm shelf.
**Sights:** Blade front, open rear adjustable for windage and elevation. Notch size adjustable for width. Interchangeable front blades.
**Features:** Fully adjustable trigger; can be set for dry firing. Separate gas chamber for uniform power. Cylinders interchangeable even when full. Short-barrel model also available. Introduced 1988. Imported by Beeman.
**Price:** Right-hand, regular or Mini . . . . . . . . . . . . **$1,130.00**
**Price:** Left-hand . . . . . . . . . . . . . . . . . . . . . . . . **$1,195.00**

Beeman/Feinwerkbau 102

## BEEMAN/FEINWERKBAU C25 CO₂ PISTOL

**Caliber:** 177, single shot.
**Barrel:** 10.1"; 12-groove rifling.
**Weight:** 2.5 lbs. **Length:** 16.5" overall.
**Power:** Vertical, interchangeable CO₂ bottles.
**Stocks:** Stippled walnut with adjustable palm shelf.
**Sights:** Blade front, rear micrometer adjustable. Notch size adjustable for width; interchangeable front blades.
**Features:** Fully adjustable trigger; can be set for dry firing. Has special vertical CO₂ cylinder and weight rail for balance. Short-barrel model (C25 Mini) also available. Introduced 1992. Imported by Beeman.
**Price:** Right-hand . . . . . . . . . . . . . . . . . . . . . . **$1,295.00**
**Price:** Left-hand . . . . . . . . . . . . . . . . . . . . . . . . **$1,295.00**
**Price:** C25 Mini . . . . . . . . . . . . . . . . . . . . . . . . **$1,285.00**

## BEEMAN/FEINWERKBAU 102 PISTOL

**Caliber:** 177, single shot.
**Barrel:** 10.1", 12-groove rifling.
**Weight:** 2.5 lbs. **Length:** 16.5" overall.
**Power:** Single-stroke pneumatic, underlever cocking.
**Stocks:** Stippled walnut with adjustable palm shelf.
**Sights:** Blade front, open rear adjustable for windage and elevation. Notch size adjustable for width. Interchangeable front blades.
**Features:** Velocity 460 fps. Fully adjustable trigger. Cocking effort 12 lbs. Introduced 1988. Imported by Beeman.
**Price:** Right-hand . . . . . . . . . . . . . . . . . . . . . . **$1,325.00**
**Price:** Left-hand . . . . . . . . . . . . . . . . . . . . . . . . **$1,395.00**

## BEEMAN/FEINWERKBAU 65 MKII AIR PISTOL

**Caliber:** 177, single shot.
**Barrel:** 6.1" or 7.5", removable bbl. wgt. available.
**Weight:** 42 oz. **Length:** 13.3" or 14.1" overall.
**Power:** Spring, sidelever cocking.
**Stocks:** Walnut, stippled thumbrest; adjustable or fixed.
**Sights:** Front, interchangeable post element system, open rear, click adjustable for windage and elevation and for sighting notch width. Scope mount available.
**Features:** New shorter barrel for better balance and control. Cocking effort 9 lbs. Two-stage trigger, four adjustments. Quiet firing, 525 fps. Programs instantly for recoil or recoilless operation. Permanently lubricated. Steel piston ring. Special switch converts trigger from 17.6-oz. pull to 42-oz. let-off. Imported by Beeman.
**Price:** Right-hand . . . . . . . . . . . . . . . . . . . . . . **$1,065.00**
**Price:** Left-hand, 6.1" barrel . . . . . . . . . . . . . . . . **$1,149.00**
**Price:** Model 65 Mk. I (7.5" bbl.) . . . . . . . . . . . . . **$1,065.00**

## BEEMAN WOLVERINE PISTOL

**Caliber:** 177, 20, 25, single shot.
**Barrel:** 10.5"; 12-groove rifling.
**Weight:** 3 lbs. **Length:** 16.5" overall.
**Power:** Pre-charged pneumatic, internal air chamber.
**Stocks:** Stippled walnut.
**Sights:** Blade front, micrometer click adjustable rear. Built-in scope dovetail.
**Features:** Match trigger. Solid brass rear receiver cap. Introduced 1992. Imported by Beeman.
**Price:** 177, 20, 25 . . . . . . . . . . . . . . . . . . . . . . . **$698.00**

## BEEMAN HW70 AIR PISTOL

**Caliber:** 177, single shot.
**Barrel:** 6¼", rifled.
**Weight:** 38 oz. **Length:** 12¾" overall.
**Power:** Spring, barrel cocking.
**Stocks:** Plastic, with thumbrest.
**Sights:** Hooded post front, square notch rear adjustable for windage and elevation. HW70A has scope base.
**Features:** Adjustable trigger, 24-lb. cocking effort, 410 fps MV; automatic barrel safety. Imported by Beeman.
**Price:** HW70 (open sights) . . . . . . . . . . . . . . . . . **$189.98**
**Price:** HW70A (open sights, scope base) . . . . . . . . . . . **$194.50**

Beeman HW70

Benjamin Sheridan Pneumatic

## BENJAMIN SHERIDAN PNEUMATIC PELLET PISTOLS

**Caliber:** 177, 20, 22, single shot.
**Barrel:** 9⅜", rifled brass.
**Weight:** 38 oz. **Length:** 13⅛" overall.
**Power:** Under-lever pnuematic, hand pumped.
**Stocks:** Walnut stocks and pump handle.
**Sights:** High ramp front, fully adjustable notch rear.
**Features:** Velocity to 525 fps (variable). Bolt action with cross-bolt safety. Choice of black or nickel finish. Made in U.S. by Benjamin Sheridan Co.
**Price:** Black finish, HB17 (177), HB20 (20), HB22 (22) . . . . . . . . **$104.95**
**Price:** Nickel finish, H17 (177), H20 (20), H22 (22) . . . . . . . . . . **$111.50**

**CAUTION:** PRICES CHANGE, CHECK AT GUNSHOP.

Benjamin Sheridan CO₂

BRNO Aeron-Tau

## BSA SCORPION AIR PISTOL
**Caliber:** 177 or 22, single shot.
**Barrel:** 7¾".
**Weight:** 3½ lbs. **Length:** 15¾" overall.
**Power:** Spring piston, barrel cocking.
**Stocks:** Moulded synthetic with thumbrest.
**Sights:** Globe front, adjustable open rear.
**Features:** Velocity to 600 fps (177); 400 fps (22). Two-stage trigger. Barrel extension to ease cocking effort. Polished blue finish. Imported from England by Air Rifle Specialists.
**Price:** . . . . . . . . . . . . . . . . . . . . . . . . . . . $190.00

Crosman Auto Air II

Consult our Directory pages for the location of firms mentioned.

Crosman Model 1008

## BENJAMIN SHERIDAN CO₂ PELLET PISTOLS
**Caliber:** 177, 20, 22, single shot.
**Barrel:** 6⅜", rifled brass.
**Weight:** 29 oz. **Length:** 9.8" overall.
**Power:** 12-gram CO₂ cylinder.
**Stocks:** Walnut on nickeled model, checkered plastic on black guns.
**Sights:** High ramp front, fully adjustable notch rear.
**Features:** Velocity to 500 fps. Turn-bolt action with cross-bolt safety. Gives about 40 shots per CO₂ cylinder. Black or nickel finish. Made in U.S. by Benjamin Sheridan Co.
**Price:** Black finish, EB17 (177), EB20 (20), EB22 (22) . . . . . . . . $96.50
**Price:** Nickel finish, E17 (177), E20 (20), E22 (22) . . . . . . . . . $109.50

## BRNO AERON-TAU CO₂ PISTOL
**Caliber:** 177.
**Barrel:** 10".
**Weight:** 37 oz. **Length:** 12.5" overall.
**Power:** 12.5-gram CO₂ cartridges.
**Stocks:** Stippled hardwood with palm rest.
**Sights:** Blade front, open fully adjustable rear.
**Features:** Comes with extra seals and counterweight. Blue finish. Imported by Century International Arms.
**Price:** About . . . . . . . . . . . . . . . . . . . . . . . $299.00

BSA Scorpion

## CROSMAN AUTO AIR II PISTOL
**Caliber:** BB, 17-shot magazine, 177 pellet, single shot.
**Barrel:** 8⅝" steel, smoothbore.
**Weight:** 13 oz. **Length:** 10¾" overall.
**Power:** CO₂ Powerlet.
**Stocks:** Grooved plastic.
**Sights:** Blade front, adjustable rear; highlighted system.
**Features:** Velocity to 480 fps (BBs), 430 fps (pellets). Semi-automatic action with BBs, single shot with pellets. Silvered finish. Introduced 1991. From Crosman.
**Price:** About . . . . . . . . . . . . . . . . . . . . . . . . $28.00

## CROSMAN MODEL 357 AIR PISTOL
**Caliber:** 177, 6- and 10-shot pellet clips.
**Barrel:** 4" (Model 357-4), 6" (Model 357-6), rifled steel; 8" (Model 357-8), rifled brass.
**Weight:** 32 oz. (6"). **Length:** 11⅜" overall (357-6).
**Power:** CO₂ Powerlet.
**Stocks:** Checkered wood-grain plastic.
**Sights:** Ramp front, fully adjustable rear.
**Features:** Average 430 fps (Model 357-6). Break-open barrel for easy loading. Single or double action. Vent. rib barrel. Wide, smooth trigger. Two cylinders come with each gun. Model 357-8 has matte gray finish, black grips. From Crosman.
**Price:** 4" or 6", about . . . . . . . . . . . . . . . . . . $45.00
**Price:** 8", about . . . . . . . . . . . . . . . . . . . . . . $50.00
**Price:** Model 1357 (same gun as above, except shoots BBs, has 6-shot clip), about . . . . . . . . . . . . . . . . . . . . . . . . . . $45.00

## CROSMAN MODEL 1008 REPEAT AIR
**Caliber:** 177, 8-shot pellet clip
**Barrel:** 4.25", rifled steel.
**Weight:** 17 oz. **Length:** 8.625" overall.
**Power:** CO₂ Powerlet.
**Stocks:** Checkered plastic.
**Sights:** Post front, adjustable rear.
**Features:** Velocity about 430 fps. Break-open barrel for easy loading; single or double semi-automatic action; two 8-shot clips included. Optional carrying case available. Introduced 1992. From Crosman.
**Price:** About . . . . . . . . . . . . . . . . . . . . . . . . $43.00
**Price:** With case, about . . . . . . . . . . . . . . . . . . $50.00

Crosman 1322

Crosman SSP 250

CZ Model 3

## CROSMAN MODEL 1322, 1377 AIR PISTOLS
**Caliber:** 177 (M1377), 22 (M1322), single shot.
**Barrel:** 8", rifled steel.
**Weight:** 39 oz. **Length:** 13⅝".
**Power:** Hand pumped.
**Sights:** Blade front, rear adjustable for windage and elevation.
**Features:** Moulded plastic grip, hand size pump forearm. Cross-bolt safety. Model 1377 also shoots BBs. From Crosman.
**Price:** About . . . . . . . . . . . . . . . . . . . . . . . . . . . . . . . . . . $50.00

## CROSMAN MODEL SSP 250 PISTOL
**Caliber:** 177, 20, 22, single shot.
**Barrel:** 9⅞", rifled steel.
**Weight:** 3 lbs., 1 oz. **Length:** 14" overall.
**Power:** $CO_2$ Powerlet.
**Stocks:** Composition; black, with checkering.
**Sights:** Hooded front, fully adjustable rear.
**Features:** Velocity about 560 fps. Interchangeable accessory barrels. Two-stage trigger. High/low power settings. From Crosman.
**Price:** About . . . . . . . . . . . . . . . . . . . . . . . . . . . . . . . . . . $48.00

## CZ MODEL 3 AIR PISTOL
**Caliber:** 177, single shot.
**Barrel:** 7.25".
**Weight:** 44 oz. **Length:** 13.75" overall.
**Power:** Spring piston, barrel cocking.
**Stocks:** High-impact plastic; ambidextrous, with thumbrest.
**Sights:** Hooded front, fully adjustable rear.
**Features:** Velocity about 420 fps. Externally adjustable trigger; removable screwdriver threaded into receiver. Imported from the Czech Republic by Action Arms.
**Price:** . . . . . . . . . . . . . . . . . . . . . . . . . . . . . . . . . . . . . . $79.00

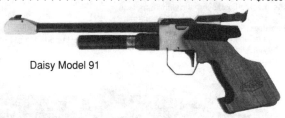

Daisy Model 91

## DAISY MODEL 91 MATCH PISTOL
**Caliber:** 177, single shot.
**Barrel:** 10.25", rifled steel.
**Weight:** 2.5 lbs. **Length:** 16.5" overall.
**Power:** $CO_2$, 12-gram cylinder.
**Stocks:** Stippled hardwood; anatomically shaped and adjustable.
**Sights:** Blade and ramp front, changeable-width rear notch with full micrometer adjustments.
**Features:** Velocity to 476 fps. Gives 55 shots per cylinder. Fully adjustable trigger. Introduced 1991. Imported by Daisy Mfg. Co.
**Price:** About . . . . . . . . . . . . . . . . . . . . . . . . . . . . . . $600.00

Daisy Model 288

## DAISY MODEL 188 BB PISTOL
**Caliber:** BB.
**Barrel:** 9.9", steel smoothbore.
**Weight:** 1.67 lbs. **Length:** 11.7" overall.
**Stocks:** Copolymer; checkered with thumbrest.
**Sights:** Blade and ramp front, open fixed rear.
**Features:** 24-shot repeater. Spring action with under-barrel cocking lever. Grip and receiver of Nylafil-copolymer material. Introduced 1979. From Daisy Mfg. Co.
**Price:** About . . . . . . . . . . . . . . . . . . . . . . . . . . . . . . . . . . $25.00

## DAISY MODEL 288 AIR PISTOL
**Caliber:** 177 pellets, 24-shot.
**Barrel:** Smoothbore steel.
**Weight:** .8 lb. **Length:** 12.1" overall.
**Power:** Single stroke spring air.
**Stocks:** Moulded resin with checkering and thumbrest.
**Sights:** Blade and ramp front, open fixed rear.
**Features:** Velocity to 215 fps. Cross-bolt trigger block safety. Black finish. Introduced 1993. From Daisy Mfg. Co.
**Price:** About . . . . . . . . . . . . . . . . . . . . . . . . . . . . . . . . . . $26.00

> Consult our Directory pages for the location of firms mentioned.

Daisy Model 500

## DAISY MODEL 500 RAVEN AIR PISTOL
**Caliber:** 177 pellets, single shot.
**Barrel:** Rifled steel.
**Weight:** 36 oz. **Length:** 8.5" overall.
**Power:** $CO_2$.
**Stocks:** Moulded plastic with checkering.
**Sights:** Blade front, fixed rear.
**Features:** Velocity up to 500 fps. Hammer-block safety. Resembles semi-auto centerfire pistol. Barrel tips up for loading. Introduced 1993. From Daisy Mfg. Co.
**Price:** About . . . . . . . . . . . . . . . . . . . . . . . . . . . . . . . . . . $65.00

**CAUTION:** PRICES CHANGE, CHECK AT GUNSHOP.

Daisy/Power Line 45

Daisy/Power Line 93

## DAISY/POWER LINE 717 PELLET PISTOL
**Caliber:** 177, single shot.
**Barrel:** 9.61".
**Weight:** 2.8 lbs. **Length:** 13½" overall.
**Stocks:** Moulded wood-grain plastic, with thumbrest.
**Sights:** Blade and ramp front, micro-adjustable notch rear.
**Features:** Single pump pneumatic pistol. Rifled steel barrel. Cross-bolt trigger
    block. Muzzle velocity 385 fps. From Daisy Mfg. Co. Introduced 1979.
**Price:** About . . . . . . . . . . . . . . . . . . . . . . . . . . . . . . . . . . . **$80.00**

### Daisy/Power Line 747 Pistol
    Similar to the 717 pistol except has a 12-groove rifled steel barrel by Lothar
Walther. Velocity of 360 fps. Manual cross-bolt safety.
**Price:** About . . . . . . . . . . . . . . . . . . . . . . . . . . . . . . . . . . **$160.00**

## DAISY/POWER LINE MATCH 777 PELLET PISTOL
**Caliber:** 177, single shot.
**Barrel:** 9.61" rifled steel by Lothar Walther.
**Weight:** 32 oz. **Length:** 13½" overall.
**Power:** Sidelever, single pump pneumatic.
**Stocks:** Smooth hardwood, fully contoured with palm and thumbrest.
**Sights:** Blade and ramp front, match-grade open rear with adjustable width
    notch, micro. click adjustments.
**Features:** Adjustable trigger; manual cross-bolt safety. MV of 385 fps. Comes
    with cleaning kit, adjustment tool and pellets. From Daisy Mfg. Co.
**Price:** About . . . . . . . . . . . . . . . . . . . . . . . . . . . . . . . . . . **$330.00**

Daisy/Power Line 1200

## DAISY/POWER LINE 44 REVOLVER
**Caliber:** 177 pellets, 6-shot.
**Barrel:** 6", rifled steel; interchangeable 4" and 8".
**Weight:** 2.7 lbs.
**Power:** $CO_2$.
**Stocks:** Moulded plastic with checkering.
**Sights:** Blade on ramp front, fully adjustable notch rear.
**Features:** Velocity up to 400 fps. Replica of 44 Magnum revolver. Has swingout
    cylinder and interchangeable barrels. Introduced 1987. From Daisy Mfg. Co.
**Price:** . . . . . . . . . . . . . . . . . . . . . . . . . . . . . . . . . . . . . . **$65.00**

## DAISY/POWER LINE 45 AIR PISTOL
**Caliber:** 177, 13-shot clip.
**Barrel:** 5", rifled steel.
**Weight:** 1.25 lbs. **Length:** 8.5" overall.
**Power:** $CO_2$.
**Stocks:** Checkered plastic.
**Sights:** Fixed.
**Features:** Velocity 400 fps. Semi-automatic repeater with double-action trigger.
    Manually operated lever-type trigger block safety; magazine safety. Intro-
    duced 1990. From Daisy Mfg. Co.
**Price:** About . . . . . . . . . . . . . . . . . . . . . . . . . . . . . . . . . . . **$75.00**
**Price:** Model 645 (nickel-chrome plated), about . . . . . . . . . . . **$83.00**

## DAISY/POWER LINE 93 PISTOL
**Caliber:** 177, BB, 15-shot clip.
**Barrel:** 5", steel.
**Weight:** 17 oz. **Length:** NA.
**Power:** $CO_2$.
**Stocks:** Checkered plastic.
**Sights:** Fixed.
**Features:** Velocity to 400 fps. Semi-automatic repeater. Manual lever-type
    trigger-block safety. Introduced 1991. From Daisy Mfg. Co.
**Price:** About . . . . . . . . . . . . . . . . . . . . . . . . . . . . . . . . . . . **$75.00**
**Price:** Model 693 (nickel-chrome plated), about . . . . . . . . . . . **$83.00**

Daisy/Power Line 717

Daisy/Power Line 777

## DAISY/POWER LINE CO₂ 1200 PISTOL
**Caliber:** BB, 177.
**Barrel:** 10½", smooth.
**Weight:** 1.6 lbs. **Length:** 11.1" overall.
**Power:** Daisy $CO_2$ cylinder.
**Stocks:** Contoured, checkered moulded wood-grain plastic.
**Sights:** Blade ramp front, fully adjustable square notch rear.
**Features:** 60-shot BB reservoir, gravity feed. Cross-bolt safety. Velocity of
    420-450 fps for more than 100 shots. From Daisy Mfg. Co.
**Price:** About . . . . . . . . . . . . . . . . . . . . . . . . . . . . . . . . . . . **$39.00**

## "GAT" AIR PISTOL
**Caliber:** 177, single shot.
**Barrel:** 7½" cocked, 9½" extended.
**Weight:** 22 oz.
**Power:** Spring piston.
**Stocks:** Cast checkered metal.
**Sights:** Fixed.
**Features:** Shoots pellets, corks or darts. Matte black finish. Imported from
    England by Stone Enterprises, Inc.
**Price:** . . . . . . . . . . . . . . . . . . . . . . . . . . . . . . . . . . . . . . **$21.95**

## MARKSMAN 1010 REPEATER PISTOL
**Caliber:** 177, 18-shot repeater.
**Barrel:** 2½", smoothbore.
**Weight:** 24 oz. **Length:** 8¼" overall.
**Power:** Spring.
**Features:** Velocity to 200 fps. Thumb safety. Black finish. Uses BBs, darts or pellets. Repeats with BBs only. From Marksman Products.
**Price:** Matte black finish . . . . . . . . . . . . . . . . . . . . . $24.95
**Price:** Model 1010X (as above except nickel-plated) . . . . . . . . $32.95

Marksman 1015

## MARKSMAN 1015 SPECIAL EDITION AIR PISTOL
**Caliber:** 177, 24-shot repeater.
**Barrel:** 3.8", rifled.
**Weight:** 22 oz. **Length:** 10.3" overall.
**Power:** Spring-air.
**Stocks:** Checkered brown composition.
**Sights:** Fixed.
**Features:** Velocity about 230 fps. Skeletonized trigger, extended barrel with "ported compensator." Shoots BBs, pellets, darts or bolts. From Marksman Products.
**Price:** . . . . . . . . . . . . . . . . . . . . . . . . . . . . . . $29.95

## RECORD JUMBO DELUXE AIR PISTOL
**Caliber:** 177, single shot.
**Barrel:** 6", rifled.
**Weight:** 1.9 lbs. **Length:** 7.25" overall.
**Power:** Spring-air, lateral cocking lever.
**Stocks:** Smooth walnut.
**Sights:** Blade front, fully adjustable open rear.
**Features:** Velocity to 322 fps. Thumb safety. Grip magazine compartment for extra pellet storage. Introduced 1983. Imported from Germany by Great Lakes Airguns.
**Price:** . . . . . . . . . . . . . . . . . . . . . . . . . . . . . . $107.50

Record Jumbo

## RWS/DIANA MODEL 5G AIR PISTOL
**Caliber:** 177, single shot.
**Barrel:** 7".
**Weight:** 2¾ lbs. **Length:** 16" overall.
**Power:** Spring-air, barrel cocking.
**Stocks:** Plastic, thumbrest design.
**Sights:** Tunnel front, micro-click open rear.
**Features:** Velocity of 410 fps. Two-stage trigger with automatic safety. Imported from Germany by Dynamit Nobel-RWS, Inc.
**Price:** . . . . . . . . . . . . . . . . . . . . . . . . . . . . . . $200.00

RWS/Diana Model 5G

## RWS/DIANA MODEL 6M MATCH AIR PISTOL
**Caliber:** 177, single shot.
**Barrel:** 7".
**Weight:** 3 lbs. **Length:** 16" overall.
**Power:** Spring-air, barrel cocking.
**Stocks:** Walnut-finished hardwood with thumbrest.
**Sights:** Adjustable front, micro. click open rear.
**Features:** Velocity of 410 fps. Recoilless double piston system, movable barrel shroud to protect from sight during cocking. Imported from Germany by Dynamit Nobel-RWS, Inc.
**Price:** Right-hand . . . . . . . . . . . . . . . . . . . . . . . . $475.00
**Price:** Left-hand . . . . . . . . . . . . . . . . . . . . . . . . . $530.00

### RWS/Diana Model 6G Air Pistols
Similar to the Model 6M except does not have the movable barrel shroud. Has click micrometer rear sight, two-stage adjustable trigger, interchangeable tunnel front sight. Available in right- or left-hand models.
**Price:** Right-hand . . . . . . . . . . . . . . . . . . . . . . . . $350.00
**Price:** Left-hand . . . . . . . . . . . . . . . . . . . . . . . . . $390.00

## RWS GAMO PR-45 AIR PISTOL
**Caliber:** 177, single shot.
**Barrel:** 8.3".
**Weight:** 25 oz. **Length:** 11" overall.
**Power:** Pre-compressed air.
**Stocks:** Composition.
**Sights:** Blade front, adjustable rear.
**Features:** Velocity to 430 fps. Recoilless and vibration free. Manual safety. Imported from Spain by Dynamit Nobel-RWS, Inc.
**Price:** . . . . . . . . . . . . . . . . . . . . . . . . . . . . . . $130.00
**Price:** Compact model (adjustable walnut grips, adjustable trigger, swiveling trigger shoe) . . . . . . . . . . . . . . . . . . . . . . . . . $200.00

## SHARP MODEL U-FP CO₂ PISTOL
**Caliber:** 177, single shot.
**Barrel:** 8", rifled steel.
**Weight:** 2.4 lbs. **Length:** 11.6" overall.
**Power:** 12-gram $CO_2$ cylinder.
**Stocks:** Smooth hardwood. Walnut target stocks available.
**Sights:** Post front, fully adjustable target rear.
**Features:** Variable power adjustment up to 545 fps. Adjustable trigger. Also available with adjustable field sight. Imported from Japan by Great Lakes Airguns.
**Price:** . . . . . . . . . . . . . . . . . . . . . . . . . . . . . . $228.50
**Price:** With walnut target grips . . . . . . . . . . . . . . . . . . $257.00

Sharp Model U-FP

## STEYR CO₂ MATCH 91 PISTOL
**Caliber:** 177, single shot.
**Barrel:** 9".
**Weight:** 38.7 oz. **Length:** 15.3" overall.
**Power:** Pre-compressed $CO_2$ cylinders.
**Stocks:** Fully adjustable Morini match with palm shelf; stippled walnut.
**Sights:** Interchangeable blade in 4mm, 4.5mm or 5mm widths, fully adjustable open rear with interchangeable 3.5mm or 4mm leaves.
**Features:** Velocity about 500 fps. Adjustable trigger, adjustable sight radius from 12.4" to 13.2". Imported from Austria by Nygord Precision Products.
**Price:** About . . . . . . . . . . . . . . . . . . . . . . . . . . . $1,050.00

**CAUTION:** PRICES CHANGE, CHECK AT GUNSHOP.

### STEYR LP5 MATCH PISTOL
**Caliber:** 177, 5-shot magazine.
**Barrel:** NA.
**Weight:** 40.2 oz. **Length:** 13.39" overall.
**Power:** Pre-compressed $CO_2$ cylinders.
**Stocks:** Adjustable Morini match with palm shelf; stippled walnut.
**Sights:** Movable 2.5mm blade front; 2-3mm interchangeable in .2mm increments; fully adjustable open match rear.
**Features:** Velocity about 500 fps. Fully adjustable trigger; has dry-fire feature. Barrel and grip weights available. Introduced 1993. Imported from Austria by Nygord Precision Products.
**Price:** About . . . . . . . . . . . . . . . . . . . . . . . . . . . . . . . . . . . **$1,250.00**

### WALTHER CP 3 AIR PISTOL
**Caliber:** 177, single shot.
**Barrel:** 9".
**Weight:** 40 oz. **Length:** 14¾" overall.
**Power:** $CO_2$.
**Stocks:** Full target-type stippled wood with adjustable hand shelf.
**Sights:** Target post front, fully adjustable target rear.
**Features:** Velocity of 520 fps, $CO_2$ powered; target-quality trigger; comes with adaptor for charging with standard $CO_2$ air tanks, case, and accessories. Introduced 1983. Imported from Germany by Interarms.
**Price:** . . . . . . . . . . . . . . . . . . . . . . . . . . . . . . . . . . . . . . . **$1,360.00**
**Price:** Model LPM-1 Match . . . . . . . . . . . . . . . . . . . . . . . . **$1,667.00**
**Price:** Model CPM-1 . . . . . . . . . . . . . . . . . . . . . . . . . . . . . . **$1,405.00**

## AIRGUNS—LONG GUNS

### AIR ARMS SM 100 AIR RIFLE
**Caliber:** 177, 22, single shot.
**Barrel:** 22", 12-groove Lothar Walther.
**Weight:** 8½ lbs. **Length:** 39½" overall.
**Power:** Pre-charged compressed air from diving tank.
**Stock:** Walnut-finished beech.
**Sights:** None furnished.
**Features:** Velocity to 1000 fps (177), 800 fps (22). PFTE-coated lightweight striker for consistent shots. Blued barrel and air chamber. Imported from England by Air Rifle Specialists.
**Price:** . . . . . . . . . . . . . . . . . . . . . . . . . . . . . . . . . . . . . . . . . **$750.00**
**Price:** For left-hand stock add . . . . . . . . . . . . . . . . . . . . . . . . **$60.00**
**Price:** Model XM 100 (same as SM100 except walnut stock) . . . . **$940.00**
**Price:** For left-hand stock add . . . . . . . . . . . . . . . . . . . . . . . . **$60.00**

### Air Arms TM 100 Air Rifle
Similar to the SM 100 except is target model with hand-picked barrel for best accuracy. Target-type walnut stock with adjustable cheekpiece and adjustable buttplate. Stippled grip and forend. Available in 177 or 22 (special order), right- or left-hand models. Variable power settings. Two-stage adjustable trigger; 22" barrel. Imported from England by Air Rifle Specialists.
**Price:** . . . . . . . . . . . . . . . . . . . . . . . . . . . . . . . . . . . . . . . **$1,170.00**
**Price:** Left-hand . . . . . . . . . . . . . . . . . . . . . . . . . . . . . . . . . **$1,230.00**

### Air Arms NJR 100 Air Rifle
Similar to the SM 100 except designed for Field Target competition. Hand-picked Walther barrel for best accuracy. Walnut Field Target thumbhole stock has adjustable forend, cheekpiece and buttpad. Has lever-type bolt, straight blade trigger. Imported from England by Air Rifle Specialists, Beeman.
**Price:** . . . . . . . . . . . . . . . . . . . . . . . . . . . . . . . . . . . . . . . **$1,670.00**
**Price:** Left-hand . . . . . . . . . . . . . . . . . . . . . . . . . . . . . . . . . **$1,730.00**
**Price:** Right-hand (Beeman) . . . . . . . . . . . . . . . . . . . . . . . . **$1,795.00**
**Price:** Left-hand (Beeman) . . . . . . . . . . . . . . . . . . . . . . . . . **$1,895.00**

Airrow Model 8S1P

### AIRROW MODEL 8S1P STEALTH AIR GUN
**Caliber:** #2512 16" arrow.
**Barrel:** 16".
**Weight:** 4.4 lbs. **Length:** 30.1" overall.
**Power:** $CO_2$ or compressed air; variable power.
**Stock:** Telescoping CAR-15-type.
**Sights:** 1.5-5x variable power scope.
**Features:** Velocity to 650 fps with 260-grain arrow. Pneumatic air trigger. All aircraft aluminum and stainless steel construction. Mil-spec materials and finishes. Waterproof case. Introduced 1991. From Swivel Machine Works, Inc.
**Price:** About . . . . . . . . . . . . . . . . . . . . . . . . . . . . . . . . . . **$1,699.00**

### ARS AR6 REPEATING AIR RIFLE
**Caliber:** 22, 6-shot repeater.
**Barrel:** 23¼".
**Weight:** 6¾ lbs. **Length:** 38¼" overall.
**Power:** Pre-compressed air from diving tank or $CO_2$.
**Stock:** Walnut with checkered grip; rubber buttpad.
**Sights:** Blade front, adjustable peep rear.
**Features:** Velocity to 1100 fps with 25-grain pellet. Receiver grooved for scope mounting. Imported from Korea by Air Rifle Specialists.
**Price:** . . . . . . . . . . . . . . . . . . . . . . . . . . . . . . . . . . . . . . . . . **$550.00**

### AIRROW MODEL 8SRB STEALTH AIR GUN
**Caliber:** 177, 22, 25, 38.
**Barrel:** 19.7".
**Weight:** 6 lbs. **Length:** 34" overall.
**Power:** $CO_2$ or compressed air; variable power.
**Stock:** Telescoping CAR-15-type.
**Sights:** 3.5-10x A.O. variable power scope.
**Features:** Velocity 1100 fps in all calibers. Pneumatic air trigger. All aircraft aluminum and stainless steel construction. Mil-spec materials and finishes. Introduced 1992. From Swivel Machine Works, Inc.
**Price:** About . . . . . . . . . . . . . . . . . . . . . . . . . . . . . . . . . . **$2,599.00**

ARS/Farco Shotgun

### ARS/FARCO $CO_2$ AIR SHOTGUN
**Caliber:** 51 (28-gauge).
**Barrel:** 30".
**Weight:** 7 lbs. **Length:** 48½" overall.
**Power:** 10-oz. refillable $CO_2$ tank.
**Stock:** Hardwood.
**Sights:** Bead front, fixed dovetail rear.
**Features:** Gives over 100 ft. lbs. energy for taking small game. Imported from Korea by Air Rifle Specialists.
**Price:** . . . . . . . . . . . . . . . . . . . . . . . . . . . . . . . . . . . . . . . . . **$395.00**

Anschutz 2002

## ANSCHUTZ 2002 MATCH AIR RIFLE
**Caliber:** 177, single shot.
**Barrel:** 26".
**Weight:** 10½ lbs. **Length:** 44½" overall.

**Stock:** European walnut; stippled grip and forend.
**Sights:** Globe front, #6824 Micro Peep rear.
**Features:** Balance, weight match the 1907 ISU smallbore rifle. Uses #5019 match trigger. Recoil and vibration free. Fully adjustable cheekpiece and buttplate. Introduced 1988. Imported from Germany by Precision Sales International.
**Price:** Right-hand . . . . . . . . . . . . . . . . . . . . . . . . . . $1,999.00
**Price:** Left-hand, hardwood stock . . . . . . . . . . . . . $2,039.00
**Price:** Model 2002D RT (Running Target) . . . . . . . . $2,094.00

## BEEMAN AIR WOLF AIR RIFLE
**Caliber:** 177, 20, 22, 25, single shot.
**Barrel:** 21"; 12-groove rifling.
**Weight:** 5.7 lbs. **Length:** 37" overall.
**Power:** Pre-charged pneumatic, internal air chamber.
**Stock:** Select walnut, adult-scaled stock; hand checkered.
**Sights:** None furnished; grooved for scope mounting
**Features:** Up to 150 shots per air charge. Imported by Beeman.
**Price:** . . . . . . . . . . . . . . . . . . . . . . . . . . . . . . . . $659.98
**Price:** Wolf Pup (15.5" bbl., 5 lbs.) . . . . . . . . . . . . $659.98
**Price:** Wolf Pup Deluxe (thumbhole stock) . . . . . . . $859.98
**Price:** For 20-cal., add . . . . . . . . . . . . . . . . . . . . . $20.00

Beeman Wolf Pup Deluxe

Beeman Classic

## BEEMAN CLASSIC MAGNUM AIR RIFLE
**Caliber:** 20, 25, single shot.
**Barrel:** 15"; 12-groove rifling.
**Weight:** 8.6 lbs. **Length:** 44.5" overall.
**Power:** Gas-spring; barrel cocking action. Adjustable power.
**Stock:** Walnut.
**Sights:** None furnished. Built-in base and 1" rings included.
**Features:** Two-stage adjustable trigger. Automatic safety. Also available in 22-caliber on special order. Imported by Beeman.
**Price:** Special order only . . . . . . . . . . . . . . . . . . . . $965.00

## BEEMAN CARBINE MODEL C1
**Caliber:** 177 or 22, single shot.
**Barrel:** 14", 12-groove rifling.
**Weight:** 6¼ lbs. **Length:** 38" overall.
**Power:** Spring-piston, barrel cocking.
**Stock:** Walnut-stained beechwood with rubber buttpad.
**Sights:** Blade front, rear click-adjustable for windage and elevation.
**Features:** Velocity 830 fps. Adjustable trigger. Receiver grooved for scope mounting. Imported by Beeman.
**Price:** . . . . . . . . . . . . . . . . . . . . . . . . . . . . . . . . $289.98

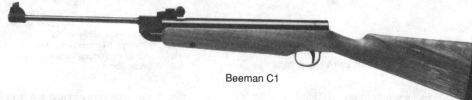

Beeman C1

Beeman Crow Magnum

## BEEMAN CROW MAGNUM AIR RIFLE
**Caliber:** 20, 25, single shot.
**Barrel:** 16"; 10-groove rifling.
**Weight:** 8.5 lbs. **Length:** 46" overall.
**Power:** Gas-spring; adjustable power to 32 foot pounds muzzle energy. Barrel-cocking.
**Stock:** Classic-style walnut; hand checkered.
**Sights:** For scope use only; built-in base and 1" rings included.
**Features:** Adjustable two-stage trigger. Automatic safety. Also available in 22-caliber on special order. Introduced 1992. Imported by Beeman.
**Price:** . . . . . . . . . . . . . . . . . . . . . . . . . . . . . . . $1,195.00

## BEEMAN FX-1 AIR RIFLE
**Caliber:** 177, single shot.
**Barrel:** 18", rifled.
**Weight:** 6.6 lbs. **Length:** 43" overall.
**Power:** Spring-piston, barrel cocking.
**Stock:** Walnut-stained hardwood.
**Sights:** Tunnel front with interchangeable inserts; rear with rotating disc to give four sighting notches.
**Features:** Velocity 680 fps. Match-type adjustable trigger. Receiver grooved for scope mounting. Imported by Beeman.
**Price:** . . . . . . . . . . . . . . . . . . . . . . . . . . . . . . . . $189.95

**CAUTION:** PRICES CHANGE, CHECK AT GUNSHOP.

Beeman Kodiak

## BEEMAN KODIAK AIR RIFLE
**Caliber:** 25, single shot.
**Barrel:** 17.6".
**Weight:** 9 lbs. **Length:** 45.6" overall.
**Power:** Barrel cocking.
**Stock:** Stained hardwood.
**Sights:** Blade front, open fully adjustable rear.
**Features:** Velocity to 820 fps. Up to 30 foot pounds muzzle energy. Introduced 1993. Imported by Beeman.
**Price:** . . . . . . . . . . . . . . . . . . . . . . . . . . . . . . . . . . **$549.95**

## BEEMAN R1 AIR RIFLE
**Caliber:** 177, 20 or 22, single shot.
**Barrel:** 19.6", 12-groove rifling.
**Weight:** 8.5 lbs. **Length:** 45.2" overall.
**Power:** Spring-piston, barrel cocking.
**Stock:** Walnut-stained beech; cut-checkered pistol grip; Monte Carlo comb and cheekpiece; rubber buttpad.
**Sights:** Tunnel front with interchangeable inserts, open rear click-adjustable for windage and elevation. Grooved for scope mounting.
**Features:** Velocity of 940-1050 fps (177), 860 fps (20), 800 fps (22). Non-drying nylon piston and breech seals. Adjustable metal trigger. Milled steel safety. Right- or left-hand stock. Available with adjustable cheekpiece and buttplate at extra cost. Custom and Super Laser versions available. Imported by Beeman.
**Price:** Right-hand, 177, 20, 22 . . . . . . . . . . . . . . . . **$489.95**
**Price:** Left-hand, 177, 20, 22 . . . . . . . . . . . . . . . . . **$549.95**
**Price:** Field Target, right-hand, 177, 20 . . . . . . . . . **$669.95**
**Price:** 177, 20, with Tyrolean walnut stock . . . . . . . . **$649.95**

## BEEMAN R1 LASER AIR RIFLE
**Caliber:** 177, 20, 22, 25, single shot.
**Barrel:** 16.1" or 19.6".
**Weight:** 8.4 lbs. **Length:** 41.7" overall (16.1" barrel).
**Power:** Spring-piston, barrel cocking.
**Stock:** Laminated wood with Monte Carlo comb and cheekpiece; checkered p.g. and forend; rubber buttpad.
**Sights:** Tunnel front with interchangeable inserts, open adjustable rear.
**Features:** Velocity up to 1150 fps (177). Special powerplant components. Built from the Beeman R1 rifle by Beeman.
**Price:** 177, 20, 22, 25 . . . . . . . . . . . . . . . . . . . . . . **$979.50**

## Beeman R7 Air Rifle
Similar to the R8 model except has lighter ambidextrous stock, match-grade trigger block; velocity of 680-700 fps; barrel length 17"; weight 5.8 lbs. Milled steel safety. Imported by Beeman.
**Price:** 177, 20 . . . . . . . . . . . . . . . . . . . . . . . . . . . . **$299.98**

## BEEMAN RX-1 GAS-SPRING MAGNUM AIR RIFLE
**Caliber:** 177, 20, 22, 25, single shot.
**Barrel:** 19.6"; 12-groove rifling.
**Weight:** 8.8 lbs.
**Power:** Gas-spring piston air; single stroke barrel cocking.
**Stock:** Walnut-finished hardwood, hand checkered, with cheekpiece. Adjustable cheekpiece and buttplate.
**Sights:** Tunnel front, click-adjustable rear.
**Features:** Velocity adjustable to about 1200 fps. Uses special sealed chamber of air as a mainspring. Gas-spring cannot take a set. Introduced 1990. Imported by Beeman.
**Price:** 177 or 22, regular, right-hand . . . . . . . . . . . **$539.95**
**Price:** 20 or 25, regular, right hand . . . . . . . . . . . . . **$539.95**

## BEEMAN SUPER 7 AIR RIFLE
**Caliber:** 22, 7-shot repeater.
**Barrel:** 19"; 12-groove rifling.
**Weight:** 7.2 lbs. **Length:** 41" overall.
**Power:** Pre-charged pneumatic, external air reservoir.
**Stock:** Walnut; high cheekpiece; rubber buttpad.
**Sights:** None furnished; drilled and tapped; 1" ring scope mounts included.
**Features:** Two-stage adjustable trigger; 7-shot rotary magazine. Receiver of anodized aircraft aluminum. All working parts either hardened or stainless steel. Imported by Beeman.
**Price:** . . . . . . . . . . . . . . . . . . . . . . . . . . . . . . . . . **$1,560.00**

## BEEMAN R1 CARBINE
**Caliber:** 177, 20, 22, 25, single shot.
**Barrel:** 16.1".
**Weight:** 8.6 lbs. **Length:** 41.7" overall.
**Power:** Spring-piston, barrel cocking.
**Stock:** Stained beech; Monte Carlo comb and checkpiece; cut checkered p.g.; rubber buttpad.
**Sights:** Tunnel front with interchangeable inserts, open adjustable rear; receiver grooved for scope mounting.
**Features:** Velocity up to 1050 fps (177). Non-drying nylon piston and breech seals. Adjustable metal trigger. Machined steel receiver end cap and safety. Right- or left-hand stock. Imported by Beeman.
**Price:** 177, 20, 22, 25, right-hand . . . . . . . . . . . . . . **$489.95**
**Price:** As above, left-hand . . . . . . . . . . . . . . . . . . . . **$549.95**

Beeman R1 Laser

## BEEMAN R8 AIR RIFLE
**Caliber:** 177, single shot.
**Barrel:** 18.3".
**Weight:** 7.2 lbs. **Length:** 43.1" overall.
**Power:** Barrel cocking, spring-piston.
**Stock:** Walnut with Monte Carlo cheekpiece; checkered pistol grip.
**Sights:** Globe front, fully adjustable rear; interchangeable inserts.
**Features:** Velocity of 735 fps. Similar to the R1. Nylon piston and breech seals. Adjustable match-grade, two-stage, grooved metal trigger. Milled steel safety. Rubber buttpad. Imported by Beeman.
**Price:** . . . . . . . . . . . . . . . . . . . . . . . . . . . . . . . . . . **$379.98**

---

Consult our Directory pages for the location of firms mentioned.

---

## BEEMAN R10 AIR RIFLES
**Caliber:** 177, 20, 22, single shot.
**Barrel:** 16.1"; 12-groove rifling.
**Weight:** 7.9 lbs. **Length:** 46" overall.
**Power:** Spring-piston, barrel cocking.
**Stock:** Standard—walnut-finished hardwood with Monte Carlo comb, rubber buttplate; Deluxe has white spacers at grip cap, buttplate, checkered grip, cheekpiece, rubber buttplate.
**Sights:** Tunnel front with interchangeable inserts, open rear click adjustable for windage and elevation. Receiver grooved for scope mounting.
**Features:** Over 1000 fps in 177-cal. only; 26-lb. cocking effort; milled steel safety and body tube. Right- and left-hand models. Similar in appearance to the Beeman R8. Introduced 1986. Imported by Beeman.
**Price:** 177, 20 or 22 Standard . . . . . . . . . . . . . . . . **$389.98**
**Price:** 20, Standard . . . . . . . . . . . . . . . . . . . . . . . . **$389.98**
**Price:** 177, 20, 22, Deluxe, right-hand . . . . . . . . . . . **$439.88**
**Price:** 177, 20, 22, Deluxe, left-hand . . . . . . . . . . . . **$498.50**

---

**CAUTION:** PRICES CHANGE, CHECK AT GUNSHOP.

Beeman/Feinwerkbau C60

**BEEMAN/FEINWERKBAU C60 CO₂ RIFLE**
**Caliber:** 177.
**Barrel:** 16.9". With barrel sleeve, 25.4".
**Weight:** 10 lbs. **Length:** 42.6" overall.

**Stock:** Laminated hardwood and hard rubber.
**Sights:** Tunnel front with interchangeable inserts, quick release micro. click match aperture rear.
**Features:** Similar features, performance as Beeman/FWB 601. Virtually no cocking effort. Right- or left-hand. Running target version available. Introduced 1987. Imported from Germany by Beeman.
**Price:** Right-hand . . . . . . . . . . . . . . . . . . . . . . . . . . . . . . . $1,495.00
**Price:** Left-hand . . . . . . . . . . . . . . . . . . . . . . . . . . . . . . . . $1,655.00
**Price:** Running Target, right-hand . . . . . . . . . . . . . . . . . . $1,475.00
**Price:** Running Target, left-hand . . . . . . . . . . . . . . . . . . . $1,599.00
**Price:** Mini C60, right-hand . . . . . . . . . . . . . . . . . . . . . . . $1,495.00

Beeman/Feinwekrbau 300-S

**BEEMAN/FEINWERKBAU 300-S MINI-MATCH**
**Caliber:** 177, single shot.
**Barrel:** 17⅛".
**Weight:** 8.8 lbs. **Length:** 40" overall.
**Power:** Spring piston, single stroke sidelever cocking.
**Stock:** Walnut. Stippled grip, adjustable buttplate. Scaled-down for youthful or slightly built shooters.
**Sights:** Globe front with interchangeable inserts, micro. adjustable rear. Front and rear sights move as a single unit.
**Features:** Recoilless, vibration free. Grooved for scope mounts. Steel piston ring. Cocking effort about 9½ lbs. Barrel sleeve optional. Left-hand model available. Introduced 1978. Imported by Beeman.
**Price:** Right-hand . . . . . . . . . . . . . . . . . . . . . . . . . . . . . . $1,195.00
**Price:** Left-hand . . . . . . . . . . . . . . . . . . . . . . . . . . . . . . . $1,298.00

**BEEMAN/HW30 AIR RIFLE**
**Caliber:** 177, 22, single shot.
**Barrel:** 17" (177), 16.9" (20); 12-groove rifling.
**Weight:** 5.5 lbs.
**Power:** Spring piston; single-stroke barrel cocking.
**Stock:** Walnut-finished hardwood.
**Sights:** Blade front, adjustable rear.
**Features:** Velocity about 660 fps (177). Double-jointed cocking lever. Cast trigger guard. Synthetic non-drying breech and piston seals. Introduced 1990. Imported by Beeman.
**Price:** 177 . . . . . . . . . . . . . . . . . . . . . . . . . . . . . . . . . . . . . $196.50
**Price:** 20 . . . . . . . . . . . . . . . . . . . . . . . . . . . . . . . . . . . . . . $209.95

**BEEMAN/FEINWERKBAU 300-S SERIES MATCH RIFLE**
**Caliber:** 177, single shot.
**Barrel:** 19.9", fixed solid with receiver.
**Weight:** Approx. 10 lbs. with optional bbl. sleeve. **Length:** 42.8" overall.
**Power:** Single stroke sidelever, spring piston.
**Stock:** Match model—walnut, deep forend, adjustable buttplate.
**Sights:** Globe front with interchangeable inserts. Click micro. adjustable match aperture rear. Front and rear sights move as a single unit.
**Features:** Recoilless, vibration free. Five-way adjustable match trigger. Grooved for scope mounts. Permanent lubrication, steel piston ring. Cocking effort 9 lbs. Optional 10-oz. barrel sleeve. Available from Beeman.
**Price:** Right-hand . . . . . . . . . . . . . . . . . . . . . . . . . . . . . . $1,195.00
**Price:** Left-hand . . . . . . . . . . . . . . . . . . . . . . . . . . . . . . . $1,298.00

**BEEMAN/FEINWERKBAU MODEL 601 AIR RIFLE**
**Caliber:** 177, single shot.
**Barrel:** 16.6".
**Weight:** 10.8 lbs. **Length:** 43" overall.
**Power:** Single stroke pneumatic.
**Stock:** Special laminated hardwoods and hard rubber for stability.
**Sights:** Tunnel front with interchangeable inserts, click micrometer match apperture rear.
**Features:** Recoilless action; double supported barrel; special, short rifled area frees pellet from barrel faster so shooter's motion has minimum effect on accuracy. Fully adjustable match trigger. Trigger and sights blocked when loading latch is open. Imported by Beeman. Introduced 1984.
**Price:** Right-hand . . . . . . . . . . . . . . . . . . . . . . . . . . . . . . $1,598.00
**Price:** Left-hand . . . . . . . . . . . . . . . . . . . . . . . . . . . . . . . $1,765.00
**Price:** Right-hand, walnut stock . . . . . . . . . . . . . . . . . . . $1,598.00

**Beeman/Feinwerkbau 601 Running Target**
Similar to the standard Model 601. Has 16.9" barrel (33.7" with barrel sleeve); special match trigger, short loading gate which allows scope mounting. No sights—built for scope use only. Introduced 1987.
**Price:** Right-hand . . . . . . . . . . . . . . . . . . . . . . . . . . . . . . $1,595.00
**Price:** Left-hand . . . . . . . . . . . . . . . . . . . . . . . . . . . . . . . $1,725.00
**Price:** Running target scope mounts . . . . . . . . . . . . . . . . $159.95

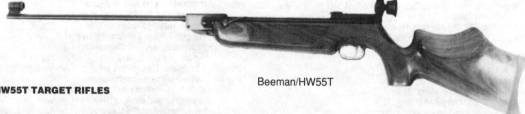

Beeman/HW55T

**BEEMAN/HW55MM, HW55T TARGET RIFLES**
**Caliber:** 177, single shot.
**Barrel:** 18½".
**Weight:** 7.8 lbs. **Length:** 43½" overall.
**Power:** Spring piston, barrel cocking.
**Stock:** Walnut. Pistol grip, high comb, beavertail forend on 55MM; 55T has Tyrolean style.
**Sights:** Globe front with four interchangeable inserts, fully adjustable match aperture rear.

**Features:** Trigger fully adjustable and removable. Nylon piston seals. Imported by Beeman.
**Price:** HW55MM . . . . . . . . . . . . . . . . . . . . . . . . . . . . . . . $609.95
**Price:** HW55T . . . . . . . . . . . . . . . . . . . . . . . . . . . . . . . . . $679.95

# AIRGUNS—LONG GUNS

Beeman/HW77

## BEEMAN/HW77 DELUXE AIR RIFLE & CARBINE
**Caliber:** 177, 20 or 22, single shot.
**Barrel:** 14.5" or 18.5", 12-groove rifling.
**Weight:** 8.9 lbs. **Length:** 39.7" or 43.7" overall.
**Power:** Spring-piston; under-lever cocking.
**Stocks:** Walnut-stained beech; rubber buttplate, cut checkering on grip; cheek-piece.
**Sights:** Blade front, open adjustable rear.
**Features:** Velocity 830 fps. Fixed-barrel with fully opening, direct loading breech. Extended under-lever gives good cocking leverage. Adjustable trigger. Grooved for scope mounting. Carbine has 14.5" barrel, weighs 8.7 lbs., and is 39.7" overall. Imported by Beeman.
**Price:** Right-hand, 177, 20, 22 . . . . . . . . . . . . . . . . . $529.00
**Price:** Left-hand, 177, 20, 22 . . . . . . . . . . . . . . . . . $579.00
**Price:** With Tyrolean walnut stock, right-hand . . . . . . . . . $645.00

## BEEMAN/HW50 LIGHT/SPORTER TARGET RIFLE
**Caliber:** 177, single shot.
**Barrel:** 18.4"; 12-groove rifling.
**Weight:** 6.9 lbs. **Length:** 43.1" overall.
**Power:** Spring piston; single-stroke barrel cocking.
**Stock:** Walnut-finished hardwood.
**Sights:** Blade front, adjustable rear.
**Features:** Velocity about 705 fps. Synthetic non-drying breech and piston seals. Double-jointed cocking lever. Introduced 1990. Imported by Beeman.
**Price:** . . . . . . . . . . . . . . . . . . . . . . . . . . . . . $214.98

Benjamin Sheridan CO₂

## BENJAMIN SHERIDAN PNEUMATIC (PUMP-UP) AIR RIFLES
**Caliber:** 177 or 22, single shot.
**Barrel:** 19⅜", rifled brass.
**Weight:** 5½ lbs. **Length:** 36¼" overall.
**Power:** Under-lever pneumatic, hand pumped.
**Stock:** American walnut stock and forend.
**Sights:** High ramp front, fully adjustable notch rear.
**Features:** Variable velocity to 800 fps. Bolt action with ambidextrous push-pull safety. Black or nickel finish. Introduced 1991. Made in the U.S. by Benjamin Sheridan Co.
**Price:** Black finish, Model 397 (177), Model 392 (22) . . . . $125.50
**Price:** Nickel finish, Model S397 (177), Model S392 (22) . . . $134.00

## BENJAMIN SHERIDAN CO₂ AIR RIFLES
**Caliber:** 177, 20 or 22, single shot.
**Barrel:** 19⅜", rifled brass.
**Weight:** 5 lbs. **Length:** 36½" overall.
**Power:** 12-gram CO₂ cylinder.
**Stock:** American walnut with buttplate.
**Sights:** High ramp front, fully adjustable notch rear.
**Features:** Velocity to 680 fps (177). Bolt action with ambidextrous push-pull safety. Gives about 40 shots per cylinder. Black or nickel finish. Introduced 1991. Made in the U.S. by Benjamin Sheridan Co.
**Price:** Black finish, Model G397 (177), Model G392 (22) . . . . . $114.50
**Price:** Nickel finish, Model GS397 (177), Model GS392 (22) . . . . $122.00
**Price:** Black finish, Model FB9 (20) . . . . . . . . . . . . . $124.00
**Price:** Nickel finish, Model F9 (20) . . . . . . . . . . . . . $131.95

BRNO Aeron-Tau

## BRNO AERON-TAU-2000 AIR RIFLE
**Caliber:** 177, single shot
**Barrel:** 23".
**Weight:** 6 lbs., 8 oz. **Length:** 40" overall.
**Power:** 12.5-gram CO₂ cartridges.
**Stock:** Synthetic match style with adjustable comb and buttplate.
**Sights:** Globe front with interchangeable inserts, fully adjustable open rear.
**Features:** Adjustable trigger. Rear sight converts to aperture on receiver. Comes with sling, extra seals, CO₂ cartridges, large CO₂ bottle, counterweight. Introduced 1993. Imported by Century International Arms.
**Price:** About . . . . . . . . . . . . . . . . . . . . . . . . . $312.00

BRNO Model 631

## BRNO 630 SERIES AIR RIFLES
**Caliber:** 177 single shot.
**Barrel:** 20.75".
**Weight:** 6 lbs., 15 oz. **Length:** 45.75" overall.
**Power:** Spring piston, barrel cocking.
**Stock:** Beechwood (Model 630); checkered, walnut stained (Model 631).
**Sights:** Hooded front, fully adjustable rear; grooved for scope mount.
**Features:** Velocity about 600 fps. Automatic safety; externally adjustable trigger; sling swivels. Imported from the Czech Republic by Action Arms, Ltd.
**Price:** Model 630 (Standard) . . . . . . . . . . . . . . . . . $95.00
**Price:** Model 631 (Deluxe) . . . . . . . . . . . . . . . . . $119.00

## BSA SUPERSTAR AIR RIFLE
**Caliber:** 177 or 22, single shot.
**Barrel:** 18½".
**Weight:** 7¾ lbs. **Length:** 42½" overall.
**Power:** Under-lever cocking spring piston or optional sealed gas Ram.
**Stock:** Walnut-stained European beech; checkered grip, rubber buttpad.
**Sights:** Globe front, open adjustable rear.
**Features:** Velocity up to 1000 fps (177); 800 fps (22). Adjustable two-stage trigger. Polished blue finish. Introduced 1991. Imported from England by Air Rifle Specialists.
**Price:** Spring piston model . . . . . . . . . . . . . . . . . $385.00
**Price:** With sealed gas Ram . . . . . . . . . . . . . . . . . $510.00

**CAUTION:** PRICES CHANGE, CHECK AT GUNSHOP.

**BSA Supersport**

## BSA SUPERSPORT AIR RIFLE
**Caliber:** 177, 22 or 25, single shot.
**Barrel:** 18½".
**Weight:** 7 lbs. **Length:** 41¾" overall.
**Power:** Spring piston or optional sealed gas Ram.
**Stock:** Walnut-stained European beech.
**Sights:** Globe front, adjustable open rear.
**Features:** Velocity up to 1010 fps (177); 830 fps (22); 700 fps (25). Adjustable two-stage trigger. Polished blue finish. Checkered pistol grip, rubber buttpad.

Introduced 1991. Imported from England by Air Rifle Specialists.
**Price:** Spring piston model . . . . . . . . . . . . . . . . . . . . **$250.00**
**Price:** With sealed gas Ram . . . . . . . . . . . . . . . . . . . **$375.00**

Crosman Model 664X

## CROSMAN MODEL 66 POWERMASTER
**Caliber:** 177 (single shot pellet) or BB, 200-shot reservoir.
**Barrel:** 20", rifled steel.

**Weight:** 3 lbs. **Length:** 38½" overall.
**Power:** Pneumatic; hand pumped.
**Stock:** Wood-grained ABS plastic; checkered p.g. and forend.
**Sights:** Ramp front, fully adjustable open rear.
**Features:** Velocity about 645 fps. Bolt action, cross-bolt safety. Introduced 1983. From Crosman.
**Price:** About . . . . . . . . . . . . . . . . . . . . . . . . . . . . **$42.00**
**Price:** Model 66RT (as above with Realtree camo finish), about . . . . **$50.00**
**Price:** Model 664X (as above, with 4x scope) . . . . . . . . . . . . **$50.00**

Crosman Model 262

## CROSMAN MODEL 262 SPORTER AIR RIFLE
**Caliber:** 177 pellet, single shot.
**Barrel:** 21.75", rifled steel.

**Weight:** 4 lbs. 14 oz.
**Power:** $CO_2$ Powerlet.
**Stock:** Hardwood.
**Sights:** Fixed front, adjustable rear.
**Features:** Easy-loading pellet port, two-stage trigger. Also available as Youth model with overall length of 33.75". Introduced 1990. From Crosman.
**Price:** About . . . . . . . . . . . . . . . . . . . . . . . . . . . . **$80.00**

Crosman Model 760

## CROSMAN MODEL 760 PUMPMASTER
**Caliber:** 177 pellets (single shot) or BB (200-shot reservoir).
**Barrel:** 19½", rifled steel.
**Weight:** 2 lbs., 12 oz. **Length:** 33.5" overall.
**Power:** Pneumatic, hand pumped.
**Stock:** Walnut-finished ABS plastic stock and forend
**Features:** Velocity to 590 fps (BBs, 10 pumps). Short stroke, power determined by number of strokes. Post front sight and adjustable rear sight. Cross-bolt safety. Introduced 1966. From Crosman.
**Price:** About . . . . . . . . . . . . . . . . . . . . . . . . . . . . **$32.00**

## CROSMAN MODEL 781 SINGLE PUMP
**Caliber:** 177 pellets (5-shot pellet clip) or BB (195-shot BB reservoir).
**Barrel:** 19½"; steel.
**Weight:** 2 lbs., 14 oz. **Length:** 35.8" overall.
**Power:** Pneumatic, single pump.
**Stock:** Wood-grained ABS plastic; checkered pistol grip and forend.
**Sights:** Blade front, open adjustable rear.
**Features:** Velocity of 405 fps (pellets). Uses only one pump. Hidden BB reservoir holds 195 shots; pellets loaded via 5-shot clip. Introduced 1984. From Crosman.
**Price:** About . . . . . . . . . . . . . . . . . . . . . . . . . . . . **$35.00**

## CROSMAN MODEL 782 BLACK DIAMOND AIR RIFLE
**Caliber:** 177 pellets (5-shot clip) or BB (195-shot reservoir).
**Barrel:** 18", rifled steel.
**Weight:** 3 lbs.
**Power:** $CO_2$ Powerlet.
**Stock:** Wood-grained ABS plastic; checkered grip and forend.
**Sights:** Blade front, open adjustable rear.
**Features:** Velocity up to 595 fps (pellets), 650 fps (BB). Black finish with white diamonds. Introduced 1990. From Crosman.
**Price:** About . . . . . . . . . . . . . . . . . . . . . . . . . . . . **$40.00**

## CROSMAN MODEL 788 BB SCOUT RIFLE
**Caliber:** BB only, 20-shot magazine.
**Barrel:** 14", steel.
**Weight:** 2 lbs. 7 oz. **Length:** 31½" overall.
**Power:** Pneumatic; hand pumped.
**Stock:** Wood-grained ABS plastic, checkered p.g. and forend.
**Sights:** Blade front, open adjustable rear.
**Features:** Variable pump power—three pumps give MV of 330 fps, six pumps 437 fps, 10 pumps 465 fps (BBs, average). Steel barrel, cross-bolt safety. Introduced 1978. From Crosman.
**Price:** About . . . . . . . . . . . . . . . . . . . . . . . . . . . . **$25.00**

## CROSMAN MODEL 1077 REPEATAIR RIFLE
**Caliber:** 177 pellets, 12-shot clip
**Barrel:** 20.3", rifled steel.
**Weight:** 3 lbs., 11 oz. **Length:** 38.8" overall.
**Power:** $CO_2$ Powerlet.
**Stock:** Textured synthetic.
**Sights:** Blade front, fully adjustable rear.
**Features:** Velocity 590 fps. Removable 12-shot clip. True semi-automatic action. Introduced 1993. From Crosman.
**Price:** About . . . . . . . . . . . . . . . . . . . . . . . . . . . . **$60.00**

Crosman Backpacker

## CROSMAN MODEL 2100 CLASSIC AIR RIFLE
**Caliber:** 177 pellets (single shot), or BB (200-shot BB reservoir).
**Barrel:** 21", rifled.
**Weight:** 4 lbs., 13 oz. **Length:** 39¾" overall.
**Power:** Pump-up, pneumatic.
**Stock:** Wood-grained checkered ABS plastic.
**Features:** Three pumps give about 450 fps, 10 pumps about 755 fps (BBs). Cross-bolt safety; concealed reservoir holds over 200 BBs. From Crosman.
**Price:** About . . . . . . . . . . . . . . . . . . . . . . . . . . . . $55.00

Crosman Model 2200

## CROSMAN MODEL 2200 MAGNUM AIR RIFLE
**Caliber:** 22, single shot.
**Barrel:** 19", rifled steel.

## DAISY/POWER LINE 130 AIR RIFLE
**Caliber:** 177, single shot.
**Barrel:** 18", rifled steel.
**Weight:** 5.9 lbs. **Length:** 41" overall.
**Power:** Spring-air, barrel cocking.
**Stock:** European-style hardwood.
**Sights:** Hooded front with blade on ramp, micrometer adjustable open rear.
**Features:** Velocity up to 800 fps. Introduced 1990. Imported from Spain by Daisy Mfg. Co.
**Price:** About . . . . . . . . . . . . . . . . . . . . . . . . . . . $175.00

Daisy Model 840

## DAISY MODEL 840
**Caliber:** 177 pellet single shot; or BB 350-shot.
**Barrel:** 19", smoothbore, steel.

Daisy/Power Line 856

## DAISY/POWER LINE 880 PUMP-UP AIRGUN
**Caliber:** 177 pellets, BB.
**Barrel:** Rifled steel with shroud.
**Weight:** 4.5 lbs. **Length:** 37¾" overall.
**Power:** Pneumatic pump-up.
**Stock:** Wood-grain moulded plastic with Monte Carlo cheekpiece.
**Sights:** Ramp front, open rear adjustable for elevation.
**Features:** Crafted by Daisy. Variable power (velocity and range) increase with pump strokes. 10 strokes for maximum power. 100-shot BB magazine. Cross-bolt trigger safety. Positive cocking valve. From Daisy Mfg. Co.
**Price:** About . . . . . . . . . . . . . . . . . . . . . . . . . . . $60.00

## CROSMAN MODEL 1389 BACKPACKER RIFLE
**Caliber:** 177, single shot.
**Barrel:** 14", rifled steel.
**Weight:** 3 lbs. 3 oz. **Length:** 31" overall.
**Power:** Hand pumped, pneumatic.
**Stock:** Composition, skeletal type.
**Sights:** Blade front, rear adjustable for windage and elevation.
**Features:** Velocity to 560 fps. Detachable stock. Receiver grooved for scope mounting. Metal parts blued. From Crosman.
**Price:** About . . . . . . . . . . . . . . . . . . . . . . . . . . . $54.00

**Weight:** 4 lbs., 12 oz. **Length:** 39" overall.
**Stock:** Full-size, wood-grained ABS plastic with checkered grip and forend.
**Sights:** Ramp front, open step-adjustable rear.
**Features:** Variable pump power—three pumps give 395 fps, six pumps 530 fps, 10 pumps 595 fps (average). Full-size adult air rifle. Has white line spacers at pistol grip and buttplate. Introduced 1978. From Crosman.
**Price:** About . . . . . . . . . . . . . . . . . . . . . . . . . . . $55.00

## DAISY/POWER LINE 753 TARGET RIFLE
**Caliber:** 177, single shot.
**Barrel:** 20.9", Lothar Walther.
**Weight:** 6.4 lbs. **Length:** 39.75" overall.
**Power:** Recoilless pneumatic, single pump.
**Stock:** Walnut with adjustable cheekpiece and buttplate.
**Sights:** Globe front with interchangeable inserts, diopter rear with micro. click adjustments.
**Features:** Includes front sight reticle assortment, web shooting sling. From Daisy Mfg. Co.
**Price:** About . . . . . . . . . . . . . . . . . . . . . . . . . . . $350.00

**Weight:** 2.7 lbs. **Length:** 36.8" overall.
**Stock:** Moulded wood-grain stock and forend.
**Sights:** Ramp front, open, adjustable rear.
**Features:** Single pump pneumatic rifle. Muzzle velocity 335 fps (BB), 300 fps (pellet). Steel buttplate; straight pull bolt action; cross-bolt safety. Forend forms pump lever. Introduced 1978. From Daisy Mfg. Co.
**Price:** About . . . . . . . . . . . . . . . . . . . . . . . . . . . $40.00

## DAISY/POWER LINE 856 PUMP-UP AIRGUN
**Caliber:** 177 pellets (single shot) or BB (100-shot reservoir).
**Barrel:** Rifled steel with shroud.
**Weight:** 2.7 lbs. **Length:** 37.4" overall.
**Power:** Pneumatic pump-up.
**Stock:** Moulded wood-grain with Monte Carlo cheekpiece.
**Sights:** Ramp and blade front, open rear adjustable for elevation.
**Features:** Velocity from 315 fps (two pumps) to 650 fps (10 pumps). Shoots BBs or pellets. Heavy die-cast metal receiver. Cross-bolt trigger-block safety. Introduced 1984. From Daisy Mfg. Co.
**Price:** About . . . . . . . . . . . . . . . . . . . . . . . . . . . $45.00

## DAISY MODEL 990 DUAL-POWER AIR RIFLE
**Caliber:** 177 pellets (single shot) or BB (100-shot magazine).
**Barrel:** Rifled steel.
**Weight:** 4.1 lbs. **Length:** 37.4" overall.
**Power:** Pneumatic pump-up and 12-gram $CO_2$.
**Stock:** Moulded woodgrain.
**Sights:** Ramp and blade front, adjustable open rear.
**Features:** Velocity to 650 fps (BB), 630 fps (pellet). Choice of pump or $CO_2$ power. Shoots BBs or pellets. Heavy die-cast receiver dovetailed for scope mount. Cross-bolt trigger block safety. Introduced 1993. From Daisy Mfg. Co.
**Price:** About . . . . . . . . . . . . . . . . . . . . . . . . . . . $65.00

Daisy Model 1894

**DAISY MODEL 1894**
**Caliber:** BB, 40-shot magazine.
**Barrel:** 17.5".

**Weight:** 2.2 lbs. **Length:** 39.5" overall.
**Power:** Spring air.
**Stock:** Moulded woodgrain plastic.
**Sights:** Blade on ramp front, adjustable open rear.
**Features:** Velocity 300 fps. Side loading port; slide safety; die-cast receiver. Made in U.S. From Daisy Mfg. Co.
**Price:** . . . . . . . . . . . . . . . . . . . . . . . . . . . $50.00

Daisy Red Ryder

**DAISY 1938 RED RYDER CLASSIC**
**Caliber:** BB, 650-shot repeating action.
**Barrel:** Smoothbore steel with shroud.

**Weight:** 2.2 lbs. **Length:** 35.4" overall.
**Stock:** Walnut stock burned with Red Ryder lariat signature.
**Sights:** Post front, adjustable V-slot rear.
**Features:** Walnut forend. Saddle ring with leather thong. Lever cocking. Gravity feed. Controlled velocity. One of Daisy's most popular guns. From Daisy Mfg. Co.
**Price:** About . . . . . . . . . . . . . . . . . . . . . . . $44.00

**DAISY/POWER LINE 853**
**Caliber:** 177 pellets.
**Barrel:** 20.9"; 12-groove rifling, high-grade solid steel by Lothar Walther™, precision crowned; bore size for precision match pellets.
**Weight:** 5.08 lbs. **Length:** 38.9" overall.
**Power:** Single-pump pneumatic.
**Stock:** Full-length, select American hardwood, stained and finished; black buttplate with white spacers.
**Sights:** Globe front with four aperture inserts; precision micrometer adjustable rear peep sight mounted on a standard ⅜" dovetail receiver mount.
**Features:** Single shot. From Daisy Mfg. Co.
**Price:** About . . . . . . . . . . . . . . . . . . . . $200.00

**DAISY/POWER LINE 922**
**Caliber:** 22, 5-shot clip.
**Barrel:** Rifled steel with shroud.
**Weight:** 4.5 lbs. **Length:** 37¾" overall.
**Stock:** Moulded wood-grained plastic with checkered p.g. and forend, Monte Carlo cheekpiece.
**Sights:** Ramp front, fully adjustable open rear.
**Features:** Muzzle velocity from 270 fps (two pumps) to 530 fps (10 pumps). Straight-pull bolt action. Separate buttplate and grip cap with white spacers. Introduced 1978. From Daisy Mfg. Co.
**Price:** About . . . . . . . . . . . . . . . . . . . . . $75.00
**Price:** Models 970/920 (same as Model 922 except with hardwood stock and forend), about . . . . . . . . . . . . . . . $120.00

**DAISY/POWER LINE EAGLE 7856 PUMP-UP AIRGUN**
**Caliber:** 177 (pellets), BB, 100-shot BB magazine.
**Barrel:** Rifled steel with shroud.
**Weight:** 2¾ lbs. **Length:** 37.4" overall.
**Power:** Pneumatic pump-up.
**Stock:** Moulded wood-grain plastic.
**Sights:** Ramp and blade front, open rear adjustable for elevation.
**Features:** Velocity from 315 fps (two pumps) to 650 fps (10 pumps). Finger grooved forend. Cross-bolt trigger-block safety. Introduced 1985. From Daisy Mfg. Co.
**Price:** With 4x scope, about . . . . . . . . . . . . . . $60.00

> Consult our Directory pages for the location of firms mentioned.

Daisy Model 95

**DAISY/YOUTH LINE RIFLES**

| Model: | 95 | 111 | 105 |
|---|---|---|---|
| Caliber: | BB | BB | BB |
| Barrel: | 18" | 18" | 13½" |
| Length: | 35.2" | 34.3" | 29.8" |
| Power: | Spring | Spring | Spring |
| Capacity: | 700 | 650 | 400 |
| Price: About | $40.00 | $35.00 | $30.00 |

**Features:** Model 95 stock and forend are wood; 105 and 111 have plastic stocks. From Daisy Mfg. Co.

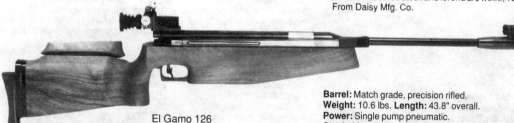

El Gamo 126

**EL GAMO 126 SUPER MATCH TARGET RIFLE**
**Caliber:** 177, single shot.

**Barrel:** Match grade, precision rifled.
**Weight:** 10.6 lbs. **Length:** 43.8" overall.
**Power:** Single pump pneumatic.
**Stock:** Match-style, hardwood, with stippled grip and forend.
**Sights:** Hooded front with interchangeable elements, fully adjustable match rear.
**Features:** Velocity of 590 fps. Adjustable trigger; easy loading pellet port; adjustable buttpad. Introduced 1984. Imported from Spain by Daisy Mfg. Co.
**Price:** About . . . . . . . . . . . . . . . . . . . . . $750.00

**CAUTION:** PRICES CHANGE, CHECK AT GUNSHOP.

## FAMAS SEMI-AUTO AIR RIFLE

**Caliber:** 177, 10-shot magazine.
**Barrel:** 19.2".
**Weight:** About 8 lbs. **Length:** 29.8" overall.
**Power:** 12 gram $CO_2$.
**Stock:** Synthetic bullpup design.
**Sights:** Adjustable front, aperture rear.
**Features:** Velocity of 425 fps. Duplicates size, weight and feel of the centerfire MAS French military rifle in caliber 223. Introduced 1988. Imported from France by Century International Arms.
**Price:** About . . . . . . . . . . . . . . . . . . . . . . . . **$275.00**

## "GAT" AIR RIFLE

**Caliber:** 177, single shot.
**Barrel:** 17¼" cocked, 23¼" extended.
**Weight:** 3 lbs.
**Power:** Spring piston.
**Stock:** Composition.
**Sights:** Fixed.
**Features:** Velocity about 450 fps. Shoots pellets, darts, corks. Imported from England by Stone Enterprises, Inc.
**Price:** . . . . . . . . . . . . . . . . . . . . . . . . . . . . **$34.95**

Marksman/Anschutz 380

## MARKSMAN 28 INTERNATIONAL AIR RIFLE

**Caliber:** 177, single shot.
**Barrel:** 17".
**Weight:** 5¾ lbs.
**Power:** Spring-air, barrel cocking.
**Stock:** Hardwood.
**Sights:** Hooded front, adjustable rear.
**Features:** Velocity of 580-620 fps. Introduced 1989. Imported from Germany by Marksman Products.
**Price:** . . . . . . . . . . . . . . . . . . . . . . . . . . . **$199.00**

## MARKSMAN 40 INTERNATIONAL AIR RIFLE

**Caliber:** 177, single shot.
**Barrel:** 18⅜".
**Weight:** 7⅓ lbs.
**Power:** Spring-air, barrel cocking.
**Stock:** Hardwood.
**Sights:** Hooded front, adjustable rear.
**Features:** Velocity of 700-720 fps. Introduced 1989. Imported from Germany by Marksman Products.
**Price:** . . . . . . . . . . . . . . . . . . . . . . . . . . . **$225.00**

## MARKSMAN/ANSCHUTZ MODEL 380 MATCH AIR RIFLE

**Caliber:** 177, single shot.
**Barrel:** 20.75".
**Weight:** 10.75 lbs.
**Power:** Spring piston, sidelever cocking.
**Stock:** Match-style, walnut, with adjustable cheekpiece, adjustable buttplate.
**Sights:** Tunnel front with interchangeable inserts, match diopter rear.
**Features:** Velocity of 600-640 fps. Fully adjustable trigger. Recoilless and vibration free. Introduced 1990. Imported from Germany by Marksman Products.
**Price:** Right-hand only . . . . . . . . . . . . . . . . . **$1,250.00**

## MARKSMAN MODEL 45 AIR RIFLE

**Caliber:** 177, single shot.
**Barrel:** 19.1".
**Weight:** 7.3 lbs. **Length:** 46.75" overall.
**Power:** Spring-air, barrel cocking.
**Stock:** Stained hardwood with Monte Carlo cheekpiece, butt pad.
**Sights:** Hooded front, fully adjustable micrometer rear.
**Features:** Velocity 900-930 fps. Adjustable trigger; automatic safety. Introduced 1993. Imported from Spain by Marksman Products.
**Price:** . . . . . . . . . . . . . . . . . . . . . . . . . . . **$189.00**

## MARKSMAN 58-S SILHOUETTE RIFLE

**Caliber:** 177, single shot.
**Barrel:** 16".
**Weight:** 8.5 lbs.
**Power:** Spring-air, barrel cocking.
**Stock:** Hardwood with stippled grip; ambidextrous.
**Sights:** None furnished.
**Features:** Velocity 910-940 fps. Adjustable Rekord trigger. Removable full-length barrel sleeve. Introduced 1989. Imported from Germany by Marksman Products.
**Price:** . . . . . . . . . . . . . . . . . . . . . . . . . . . **$390.00**

Marksman 58-S

> Consult our Directory pages for
> the location of firms mentioned.

## MARKSMAN 56-FTS FIELD TARGET RIFLE

**Caliber:** 177, single shot.
**Barrel:** 19⅝".
**Weight:** 8.8 lbs.
**Power:** Spring-air, barrel cocking.
**Stock:** Hardwood with stippled grip; ambidextrous, with adjustable cheekpiece, adjustable buttplate.
**Sights:** None furnished.
**Features:** Velocity 910-940 fps. Introduced 1989. Imported from Germany by Marksman Products.
**Price:** . . . . . . . . . . . . . . . . . . . . . . . . . . . **$450.00**

## MARKSMAN MODEL 60 AIR RIFLE

**Caliber:** 177, single shot.
**Barrel:** 18.5", rifled.
**Weight:** 8.9 lbs. **Length:** 44.75" overall.
**Power:** Spring piston, under-lever cocking.
**Stock:** Walnut-stained beech with Monte Carlo comb, hand-checkered pistol grip, rubber butt pad.
**Sights:** Blade front, open, micro. adjustable rear.
**Features:** Velocity of 810-840 fps. Automatic button safety on rear of receiver. Receiver grooved for scope mounting. Fully adjustable Rekord trigger. Introduced 1990. Imported from Germany by Marksman Products.
**Price:** . . . . . . . . . . . . . . . . . . . . . . . . . . . **$439.00**
**Price:** Model 61 Carbine (14.5" barrel) . . . . . . . . . . . . . . **$439.00**

Marksman Model 60

# AIRGUNS—LONG GUNS

## MARKSMAN 70 AIR RIFLE
**Caliber:** 177, 20 or 22, single shot.
**Barrel:** 19.75".
**Weight:** 8 lbs. **Length:** 45.5" overall.
**Power:** Spring air, barrel cocking.
**Stock:** Stained hardwood with Monte Carlo cheekpiece, rubber buttpad, cut checkered p.g.
**Sights:** Hooded front, open fully adjustable rear.
**Features:** Velocity of 910-940 fps (177), 810-840 fps (20), 740-780 fps (22); adjustable Rekord trigger. Introduced 1988. Imported from Germany by Marksman Products.
**Price:** 177 (Model 70T) . . . . . . . . . . . . . . . . . . . . $329.00
**Price:** 20 (Model 72) . . . . . . . . . . . . . . . . . . . . . $345.00
**Price:** (Model 71) . . . . . . . . . . . . . . . . . . . . . . . $329.00

### Marksman 55 Air Rifle
Similar to the Model 70T except has uncheckered hardwood stock, no cheekpiece, plastic buttplate. Adjustable Rekord trigger. Overall length is 45.25", weight is 7½ lbs. Available in 177-caliber only.
**Price:** . . . . . . . . . . . . . . . . . . . . . . . . . . . . . . $279.00
**Price:** Model 59T (as above, carbine) . . . . . . . . . . $279.00

## MARKSMAN 1740 AIR RIFLE
**Caliber:** 177 or 18-shot BB repeater.
**Barrel:** 15½", smoothbore.
**Weight:** 5 lbs., 1 oz. **Length:** 36½" overall.
**Power:** Spring, barrel cocking.
**Stock:** Moulded high-impact ABS plastic.
**Sights:** Ramp front, open rear adjustable for elevation.
**Features:** Velocity about 450 fps. Automatic safety; fixed front, adjustable rear sight; positive feed BB magazine; shoots 177-cal. BBs, pellets and darts. From Marksman Products.
**Price:** . . . . . . . . . . . . . . . . . . . . . . . . . . . . . . $47.95
**Price:** Model 1780 (deluxe sights, rifled barrel, shoots only pellets) . . $62.95

Marksman 1750 BB

## MARKSMAN 1790 BIATHLON TRAINER
**Caliber:** 177, single shot.
**Barrel:** 15", rifled.
**Weight:** 4.7 lbs.
**Power:** Spring-air, barrel cocking.
**Stock:** Synthetic.
**Sights:** Hooded front, match-style diopter rear.
**Features:** Velocity of 450 fps. Endorsed by the U.S. Shooting Team. Introduced 1989. From Marksman Products.
**Price:** . . . . . . . . . . . . . . . . . . . . . . . . . . . . . . $66.95

## MARKSMAN 1750 BB BIATHLON REPEATER RIFLE
**Caliber:** BB, 18-shot magazine.
**Barrel:** 15", smoothbore.
**Weight:** 4.7 lbs.
**Power:** Spring piston, barrel cocking.
**Stock:** Moulded composition.
**Sights:** Tunnel front, open adjustable rear.
**Features:** Velocity of 450 fps. Automatic safety. Positive Feed System loads a BB each time gun is cocked. Introduced 1990. From Marksman Products.
**Price:** . . . . . . . . . . . . . . . . . . . . . . . . . . . . . . $54.95

## RWS/DIANA MODEL 24 AIR RIFLE
**Caliber:** 177, 22, single shot.
**Barrel:** 17", rifled.
**Weight:** 6 lbs. **Length:** 42" overall.
**Power:** Spring air, barrel cocking.
**Stock:** Beech.
**Sights:** Hooded front, adjustable rear.
**Features:** Velocity of 700 fps (177). Easy cocking effort; blue finish. Imported from Germany by Dynamit Nobel-RWS, Inc.
**Price:** . . . . . . . . . . . . . . . . . . . . . . . . . . . . . . $185.00
**Price:** Model 24C . . . . . . . . . . . . . . . . . . . . . . . $185.00

### RWS/Diana Model 34 Air Rifle
Similar to the Model 24 except has 19" barrel, weighs 7.5 lbs. Gives velocity of 1000 fps (177), 800 fps (22). Adjustable trigger, synthetic seals. Comes with scope rail.
**Price:** 177 or 22 . . . . . . . . . . . . . . . . . . . . . . . . $245.00

### RWS/Diana Model 26 Air Rifle
Similar to the Model 24 except weighs 6.25 lbs., gives velocity of 750 fps (177), 500 fps (22). Automatic safety, scope rail, synthetic seals.
**Price:** 177 or 22 . . . . . . . . . . . . . . . . . . . . . . . . $195.00

### RWS/Diana Model 28 Air Rifle
Similar to the Model 26 except has Monte Carlo stock with cheekpiece, rubber recoil pad and two-stage trigger. Velocity of 750 fps (177), 500 fps (22).
**Price:** 177 or 22 . . . . . . . . . . . . . . . . . . . . . . . . $205.00

## RWS/DIANA MODEL 36 AIR RIFLE
**Caliber:** 177, 22, single shot.
**Barrel:** 19", rifled.
**Weight:** 8 lbs. **Length:** 45" overall.
**Power:** Spring air, barrel cocking.
**Stock:** Beech.
**Sights:** Hooded front (interchangeable inserts avail.), adjustable rear.
**Features:** Velocity of 1000 fps (177-cal.). Comes with scope mount; two-stage adjustable trigger. Imported from Germnay by Dynamit Nobel-RWS, Inc.
**Price:** . . . . . . . . . . . . . . . . . . . . . . . . . . . . . . $345.00
**Price:** Model 36 Carbine (same as Model 36 except has 15" barrel) $345.00

## RWS/DIANA MODEL 45 AIR RIFLE
**Caliber:** 177, single shot.
**Weight:** 7¾ lbs. **Length:** 46" overall.
**Power:** Spring air, barrel cocking.
**Stock:** Walnut-finished hardwood with rubber recoil pad.
**Sights:** Globe front with interchangeable inserts, micro. click open rear with four-way blade.
**Features:** Velocity of 820 fps. Dovetail base for either micrometer peep sight or scope mounting. Automatic safety. Imported from Germany by Dynamit Nobel-RWS, Inc.
**Price:** . . . . . . . . . . . . . . . . . . . . . . . . . . . . . . $280.00

RWS/Diana 52

## RWS/DIANA MODEL 52 AIR RIFLE
**Caliber:** 177, 22, single shot.
**Barrel:** 17", rifled.
**Weight:** 8½ lbs. **Length:** 43" overall.

**Power:** Spring air, sidelever cocking.
**Stock:** Beech, with Monte Carlo, cheekpiece, checkered grip and forend.
**Sights:** Ramp front, adjustable rear.
**Features:** Velocity of 1100 fps (177). Blue finish. Solid rubber buttpad. Imported from Germany by Dynamit Nobel-RWS, Inc.
**Price:** . . . . . . . . . . . . . . . . . . . . . . . . . . . . . . $450.00
**Price:** Model 48 (same as Model 52 except no Monte Carlo, cheekpiece or checkering) . . . . . . . . . . . . . . . . . . . . . . . $400.00
**Price:** Model 54, recoilless action . . . . . . . . . . . . . $635.00

CAUTION: PRICES CHANGE, CHECK AT GUNSHOP.

## RWS/DIANA MODEL 70 MATCH AIR RIFLE
**Caliber:** 177, single shot.
**Barrel:** 13.5".
**Weight:** 4.5 lbs. **Length:** 33 overall.
**Power:** Spring air, barrel cocking.
**Stock:** Beech, match-type.
**Sights:** Tunnel front with interchangeable inserts, fully adjustable peep rear.
**Features:** Velocity of 450 fps. Adjustable trigger. Designed and scaled for junior shooters. Introduced 1990. Imported from Germany by Dynamit Nobel-RWS, Inc.
**Price:** . . . . . . . . . . . . . . . . . . . . . . **$190.00**

### RWS/Diana Model 72 Air Rifle
Similar to the Model 70 except has recoilless action. Introduced 1990.
**Price:** . . . . . . . . . . . . . . . . . . . . . . **$340.00**

RWS/Diana 75 T01

## RWS/DIANA MODEL 75 T01 MATCH AIR RIFLE
**Caliber:** 177, single shot.
**Barrel:** 19".
**Weight:** 11 lbs. **Length:** 43.7" overall.
**Power:** Spring air, sidelever cocking.
**Stock:** Oil-finished beech with stippled grip, adjustable buttplate, accessory rail. Conforms to ISU rules.
**Sights:** Globe front with five inserts, fully adjustable match peep rear.
**Features:** Velocity of 574 fps. Fully adjustable trigger. Model 75 HV has stippled forend, adjustable cheekpiece. Uses double opposing piston system for recoilless operation. Imported from Germany by Dynamit Nobel-RWS, Inc.
**Price:** Model 75 T01 . . . . . . . . . . . . . . . . . . . . . . **$950.00**

### RWS/Diana Model 75S T01 Air Rifle
Similar to the Model 75 T01 except has beech stock specially shaped for standing and three-position shooting. Buttplate is vertically adjustable with curved and straight spacers for individual fit, adjustable cheekpiece. Introduced 1990.
**Price:** Right-hand . . . . . . . . . . . . . . . . . . **$1,150.00**
**Price:** Left-hand . . . . . . . . . . . . . . . . . . . **$1,245.00**

RWS/Diana 100

**Power:** Spring air, sidelever cocking.
**Stock:** Walnut.
**Sights:** Tunnel front, fully adjustable match rear.
**Features:** Velocity of 580 fps. Single-stroke cocking; cheekpiece adjustable for height and length; recoilless operation. Cocking lever secured against rebound. Introduced 1990. Imported from Germany by Dynamit Nobel-RWS, Inc.
**Price:** Right-hand only . . . . . . . . . . . . . . . . . . . . **$1,400.00**

## RWS/DIANA MODEL 100 MATCH AIR RIFLE
**Caliber:** 177, single shot.
**Barrel:** 19".
**Weight:** 11 lbs. **Length:** 43" overall.

## RWS GAMO CF-20 AIR RIFLE
**Caliber:** 177, single shot.
**Barrel:** 17.7".
**Weight:** 6.6 lbs. **Length:** 43.3" overall.
**Power:** Barrel cocking, spring piston.
**Stock:** Hardwood.
**Sights:** Blade on ramp front, fully adjustable open rear.
**Features:** Velocity to 800 fps. Cocking effort of 33 lbs. Grooved receiver, synthetic seals, dual safeties; sdjustable two-stage trigger. Imported from Spain by Dynamit Nobel-RWS, Inc.
**Price:** . . . . . . . . . . . . . . . . . . . . . . **$190.00**

## RWS GAMO EXPOMATIC 2000 AIR RIFLE
**Caliber:** 177, 25-shot magazine.
**Barrel:** 17.7".
**Weight:** 5.5 lbs. **Length:** 40.9" overall.
**Power:** Barrel cocking, spring piston.
**Stock:** Hardwood.
**Sights:** Blade front, fully adjustable open rear.
**Features:** Velocity to 600 fps. Cocking effort of 20 lbs. Dual safeties, grooved receiver, synthetic seals. Magazine tube holds 25 pellets, loads automatically. Imported from Spain by Dynamit Nobel-RWS, Inc.
**Price:** . . . . . . . . . . . . . . . . . . . . . . **$150.00**

RWS Gamo Delta

## RWS GAMO DELTA AIR RIFLE
**Caliber:** 177.
**Barrel:** 15.73".
**Weight:** 5.3 lbs. **Length:** 37" overall.
**Power:** Barrel cocking, spring piston.
**Stock:** Carbon fiber.
**Sights:** Blade front, fully adjustable open rear.
**Features:** Velocity to 565 fps. Has 20-lb. cocking effort. Synthetic seal; dual safeties; grooved for scope mounting. Imported from Spain by Dynamit Nobel-RWS, Inc.
**Price:** . . . . . . . . . . . . . . . . . . . . . . **$105.00**

## RWA GAMO HUNTER 440 AIR RIFLE
**Caliber:** 177, single shot.
**Barrel:** 18".
**Weight:** 6.75 lbs. **Length:** 43" overall.
**Power:** Spring piston, barrel cocking.
**Stock:** Hardwood.
**Sights:** Hooded blade on ramp front, fully adjustable rear.
**Features:** Velocity 1000 fps. Monte Carlo stock with cheekpiece; scope rail; dual safeties. Imported from Spain by Dynamit Nobel-RWS.
**Price:** . . . . . . . . . . . . . . . . . . . . . . **$205.00**

## SHERIDAN PNEUMATIC (PUMP-UP) AIR RIFLES

**Caliber:** 20 (5mm), single shot.
**Barrel:** 19⅜", rifled brass.
**Weight:** 6 lbs. **Length:** 36½" overall.
**Power:** Under-lever pneumatic, hand pumped.
**Stock:** Walnut with buttplate and sculpted forend.

**Sights:** High ramp front, fully adjustable notch rear.
**Features:** Variable velocity to 675 fps. Bolt action with ambidextrous push-pull safety. Blue finish (Blue Streak) or nickel finish (Silver Streak). Introduced 1991. Made in the U.S. by Benjamin Sheridan Co.
**Price:** Blue Streak, Model CB9 . . . . . . . . . . . . . . . . . **$139.95**
**Price:** Silver streak, Model C9 . . . . . . . . . . . . . . . . . **$148.50**

Sterling HR81

## STERLING SPRING PISTON AIR RIFLES

**Caliber:** 177, 20, 22, single shot.
**Barrel:** 18½", Lothar Walther, steel.
**Weight:** 9 lbs. **Length:** 42" overall.
**Power:** Spring piston with under-barrel lever.

**Stock:** American walnut (HR81); HR83 has walnut with checkpiece and hand-checkered grip. Rubber buttpad.
**Sights:** Standard—tunnel-type front, fully adjustable open rear; Deluxe has tunnel-type front, Williams fully adjustable peep rear with ¼-minute click-stop knobs.
**Features:** Velocity to 740 fps (177). Spring-loaded bolt action with adjustable single stage match trigger. Introduced 1983. Made in the U.S. by Benjamin Sheridan Co.
**Price:** Standard models, HR81-17 (177), HR81-20 (20), HR81-22 (22) **$341.95**
**Price:** Deluxe models, HR83-17W (177), HR83-20W (20), HR83-22W (22) . . . . . . . . . . . . . . . . . . . . . . . . **$481.95**

Steyr $CO_2$ Match

## STEYR $CO_2$ MATCH AIR RIFLE MODEL 91

**Caliber:** 177, single shot.
**Barrel:** 23.75", (13.75" rifled).
**Weight:** 10.5 lbs. **Length:** 51.7" overall.
**Power:** $CO_2$.

**Stock:** Match. Laminated wood. Adjustable buttplate and cheekpiece.
**Sights:** None furnished; comes with scope mount.
**Features:** Velocity 577 fps. $CO_2$ cylinders are refillable; about 320 shots per cylinder. Designed for 10-meter shooting. Introduced 1990. Imported from Austria by Nygord Precision Products.
**Price:** About . . . . . . . . . . . . . . . . . . . . . . . . . . **$1,300.00**
**Price:** Left-hand, about . . . . . . . . . . . . . . . . . . . . **$1,400.00**
**Price:** Running Target Rifle, right-hand, about . . . . . . . . **$1,325.00**
**Price:** As above, left-hand, about . . . . . . . . . . . . . . . **$1,425.00**

## THEOBEN CLASSIC AIR RIFLE

**Caliber:** 177 or 22, single shot.
**Barrel:** 19½".
**Weight:** 7¾ lbs. **Length:** 44" overall.
**Power:** Gas ram piston. Variable power.
**Stock:** Walnut with checkered grip and forend.
**Sights:** None furnished. Comes with scope mount.
**Features:** Velocity to 1100 fps (177) and 900 fps (22). Barrel-cocking action. Polished blue finish on metal, oil-finished stock. Adjustable trigger. Imported from England by Air Rifle Specialists.
**Price:** . . . . . . . . . . . . . . . . . . . . . . . . . . . . . **$830.00**
**Price:** For left-hand stock add . . . . . . . . . . . . . . . . . **$60.00**
**Price:** Grand Prix model (same as Classic except has thumbhole stock with adjustable buttplate) . . . . . . . . . . . . . . **$940.00**
**Price:** For left-hand stock add . . . . . . . . . . . . . . . . . **$60.00**

### Theoben Eliminator Air Rifle

Similar to the Theoben Classic except has a longer, more sturdily built action with longer piston stroke for more power. Has walnut thumbhole stock with adjustable buttplate and comes with sling. Imported from England by Air Rifle Specialists.
**Price:** . . . . . . . . . . . . . . . . . . . . . . . . . . . . **$1,500.00**
**Price:** Left-hand stock, add . . . . . . . . . . . . . . . . . . **$60.00**

### Theoben Imperator SLR 88 Air Rifle

Sporter version of the Theoben Imperator FT in 22-caliber only. Has conventional sporter stock of oil-finished walnut with checkered grip and forend. Has 7-shot clip. Velocity up to 725 fps. Imported from England by Air Rifle Specialists.
**Price:** . . . . . . . . . . . . . . . . . . . . . . . . . . . . **$1,680.00**

## THEOBEN IMPERATOR FT AIR RIFLE

**Caliber:** 177, single shot.
**Barrel:** 16".
**Weight:** 8½ lbs. **Length:** 42" overall.
**Power:** Under-lever cocking gas Ram piston. Variable power.
**Stock:** Hand-checkered European walnut, thumbhole design with adjustable forend block, roll-over cheekpiece, adjustable rubber buttpad.
**Sights:** None furnished. Comes with scope mount.
**Features:** Velocity up to 900 fps. Stippled grip and forend panels. Adjustable match-grade trigger. Imported from England by Air Rifle Specialists.
**Price:** . . . . . . . . . . . . . . . . . . . . . . . . . . . . **$1,500.00**

| Consult our Directory pages for the location of firms mentioned. |
| :---: |

## WALTHER CG90 AIR RIFLE

**Caliber:** 177, single shot.
**Barrel:** 18.9".
**Weight:** 10.2 lbs. **Length:** 44" overall.
**Power:** $CO_2$ cartridge.
**Stock:** Match type of European walnut; stippled grip.
**Sights:** Globe front, fully adjustable match rear.
**Features:** Uses tilting-block action. Introduced 1989. Imported from Germany by Interarms.
**Price:** . . . . . . . . . . . . . . . . . . . . . . . . . . . . **$1,748.00**

## WALTHER LG-90 MATCH AIR RIFLE

**Caliber:** 177, single shot.
**Barrel:** 25.5".
**Weight:** 13 lbs. **Length:** 44¾" overall.
**Power:** Spring air, barrel cocking.
**Stock:** Walnut match design with stippled grip and forend, adjustable cheekpiece, rubber buttpad.
**Features:** Has the same weight and contours as the Walther U.I.T. rimfire target rifle. Comes complete with sights, accessories and muzzle weight. Imported from Germany by Interarms.
**Price:** . . . . . . . . . . . . . . . . . . . . . . . . . . . . **$1,317.00**

**CAUTION:** PRICES CHANGE, CHECK AT GUNSHOP.

# METALLIC SIGHTS

## Sporting Leaf and Open Sights

**BURRIS SPORTING REAR SIGHT** Made of spring steel, supplied with multi-step elevator for coarse adjustments and notch plate with lock screw for finer adjustments.
Price: . . . . . . . . . . . . . . . . . . . . . . . . . . . **$15.95**

**LYMAN No. 16** Middle sight for barrel dovetail slot mounting. Folds flat when scope or peep sight is used. Sight notch plate adjustable for elevation. White triangle for quick aiming. 3 heights: A—.400" to .500", B—.345" to .445", C—.500" to .600".
Price: . . . . . . . . . . . . . . . . . . . . . . . . . . . **$13.50**

**MARBLE FALSE BASE #72, #73, #74** New screw-on base for most rifles replaces factory base. ⅜" dovetail slot permits installation of any folding rear sight. Can be had in sweat-on models also.
Price: . . . . . . . . . . . . . . . . . . . . . . . . . . . **$7.25**

**MARBLE CONTOUR RAMP #14R** For late model Rem. 725, 740, 760, 742 rear sight mounting. ⁹⁄₁₆" between mounting screws. Accepts all sporting rear sights.
Price: . . . . . . . . . . . . . . . . . . . . . . . . . . . **$14.40**

**MARBLE FOLDING LEAF** Flat-top or semi-buckhorn style. Folds down when scope or peep sights are used. Reversible plate gives choice of "U" or "V" notch. Adjustable for elevation.
Price: . . . . . . . . . . . . . . . . . . . . . . . . . . . **$13.35**
Price: Also available with both windage and elevation adjustment . . . **$15.30**

**MARBLE SPORTING REAR** With white enamel diamond, gives choice of two "U" and two "V" notches or different sizes. Adjustment in height by means of double step elevator and sliding notch piece. For all rifles; screw or dovetail installation.
Price: . . . . . . . . . . . . . . . . . . . . . . . **$13.35-$15.20**

**MARBLE #20 UNIVERSAL** New screw or sweat-on base. Both have .100" elevation adjustment. In five base sizes. Three styles of U-notch, square notch, peep. Adjustable for windage and elevation.
Price: Screw-on . . . . . . . . . . . . . . . . . . . . . . **$20.55**
Price: Sweat-on . . . . . . . . . . . . . . . . . . . . . . **$18.90**

**MILLETT RIFLE SIGHT** Open, fully adjustable rear sight fits standard ⅜" dovetail cut in barrel. Choice of white outline or target rear blades, .360". Front with white or orange bar, .343", .400", .430", .460", .500", .540".
Price: Rear sight . . . . . . . . . . . . . . . . . . . . . . **$52.95**
Price: Front sight . . . . . . . . . . . . . . . . . . . . . . **$11.75**

**MILLETT SCOPE-SITE** Open, adjustable or fixed rear sights dovetail into a base integral with the top scope-mounting ring. Blaze orange front ramp sight is integral with the front ring half. Rear sights have white outline aperture. Provides fast, short-radius, Patridge-type open sights on the top of the scope. Can be used with all Millett rings, Weaver-style bases, Ruger 77 (also fits Redhawk), Ruger Ranch Rifle, No. 1, No. 3, Rem. 870, 1100; Burris, Leupold and Redfield bases.
Price: Scope-Site top only, windage only . . . . . . . . . **$29.65**
Price: As above, fully adjustable . . . . . . . . . . . . . . **$62.95**
Price: Scope-Site Hi-Turret, fully adjustable, low, medium, high . . . . **$62.95**

**WICHITA MULTI RANGE SIGHT SYSTEM** Designed for silhouette shooting. System allows you to adjust the rear sight to four repeatable range settings, once it is pre-set. Sight clicks to any of the settings by turning a serrated wheel. Front sight is adjustable for weather and light conditions with one adjustment. Specify gun when ordering.
Price: Rear sight . . . . . . . . . . . . . . . . . . . . . . **$93.50**
Price: Front sight . . . . . . . . . . . . . . . . . . . . . . **$69.95**

**WILLIAMS DOVETAIL OPEN SIGHT (WDOS)** Open rear sight with windage and elevation adjustment. Furnished with "U" notch or choice of blades. Slips into dovetail and locks with gib lock. Heights from .281" to .531".
Price: With blade . . . . . . . . . . . . . . . . . . . . . . **$14.95**
Price: Less Blade . . . . . . . . . . . . . . . . . . . . . . **$9.35**

**WILLIAMS GUIDE OPEN SIGHT (WGOS)** Open rear sight with windage and elevation adjustment. Bases to fit most military and commercial barrels. Choice of square "U" or "V" notch blade, ³⁄₁₆", ¼", ⁵⁄₁₆", or ⅜" high.
Price: With blade . . . . . . . . . . . . . . . . . . . . . . **$19.95**
Price: Extra blades, each . . . . . . . . . . . . . . . . . . **$5.60**
Price: Less blade . . . . . . . . . . . . . . . . . . . . . . **$14.35**

**WILLIAMS WGOS OCTAGON** Open rear sight for 1" octagon barrels. Installs with two 6-48 screws and uses same hole spacing as most T/C muzzleloading rifles. Four heights, choice of square, U, V, B blade.
Price: . . . . . . . . . . . . . . . . . . . . . . . . . . . **$19.95**

## Micrometer Receiver Sights

**BEEMAN/WEIHRAUCH MATCH APERTURE SIGHT** Micrometer ¼-minute click adjustment knobs with settings indicated on scales.
Price: . . . . . . . . . . . . . . . . . . . . . . . . . . . **$119.95**

**BEEMAN/FEINWERKBAU MATCH APERTURE SIGHTS** Locks into one of four eye-relief positions. Micrometer ¼-minute click adjustments; may be set to zero at any range. Extra windage scale visible beside eyeshade. Primarily for use at 5 to 20 meters.
Price: . . . . . . . . . . . . . . . . . . . . . . . . . . . **$199.98**

**BEEMAN SPORT APERTURE SIGHT** Positive click micrometer adjustments. Standard units with flush surface screwdriver adjustments. Deluxe version has target knobs. For air rifles with grooved receivers.
Price: Standard . . . . . . . . . . . . . . . . . . . . . . **$34.98**
Price: Deluxe . . . . . . . . . . . . . . . . . . . . . . . **$44.98**

**LYMAN No. 57** ¼-minute clicks. Stayset knobs. Quick release slide, adjustable zero scales. Made for almost all modern rifles.
Price: . . . . . . . . . . . . . . . . . . . . . . . . . . . **$65.00**

**LYMAN No. 66** Fits close to the rear of flat-sided receivers, furnished with Stayset knobs. Quick release slide, ¼-min. adjustments. For most lever or slide action or flat-sided automatic rifles.
Price: . . . . . . . . . . . . . . . . . . . . . . . . . . . **$65.00**

**LYMAN No. 66U** Light weight, designed for most modern shotguns with a flat-sided, round-top receiver. ¼-minute clicks. Requires drilling, tapping. Not for Browning A-5, Rem. M11.
Price: . . . . . . . . . . . . . . . . . . . . . . . . . . . **$65.00**

**LYMAN 90MJT RECEIVER SIGHT** Mounts on standard Lyman and Williams FP bases. Has ¼-minute audible micrometer click adjustments, target knobs with direction indicators. Adjustable zero scales, quick release slide. Large ⅞" diameter aperture disk.
Price: . . . . . . . . . . . . . . . . . . . . . . . . . . . **$79.95**

**MILLETT ASSAULT RIFLE SIGHTS** Fully adjustable, heat-treated nickel steel peep aperture receiver sight for Mini-14. Has fine windage and elevation adjustments; replaces original.
Price: Rear sight . . . . . . . . . . . . . . . . . . . . . . **$51.45**
Price: Front sight . . . . . . . . . . . . . . . . . . . . . . **$17.85**

**WILLIAMS FP** Internal click adjustments. Positive locks. For virtually all rifles, T/C Contender, Heckler & Koch HK-91, Ruger Mini-14, plus Win., Rem. and Ithaca shotguns.
Price: From . . . . . . . . . . . . . . . . . . . . . . . . . **$53.25**
Price: With Target Knobs . . . . . . . . . . . . . . . . . . **$63.25**
Price: With Square Notched Blade . . . . . . . . . . . . . **$56.00**
Price: With Target Knobs & Square Notched Blade . . . . . **$66.15**
Price: FP-GR (for dovetail-grooved receivers, 22s and air guns) . . . **$53.25**

**WILLIAMS TARGET FP** Similar to the FP series but developed for most bolt-action rimfire rifles. Target FP High adjustable from 1.250" to 1.750" above centerline of bore; Target FP Low adjustable from .750" to 1.250". Attaching bases for Rem. 540X, 541-S, 580, 581, 582 (#540); Rem. 510, 511, 512, 513-T, 521-T (#510); Win. 75 (#75); Savage/Anschutz 64 and Mark 12 (#64). Some rifles require drilling, tapping.
Price: High or Low, with Base . . . . . . . . . . . . . . . . **$84.10**
Price: As above, less Base . . . . . . . . . . . . . . . . . **$72.00**
Price: Base only . . . . . . . . . . . . . . . . . . . . . . **$12.10**
Price: FP-T/C Scout rifle, from . . . . . . . . . . . . . . . **$53.25**

**WILLIAMS 5-D SIGHT** Low cost sight for shotguns, 22s and the more popular big game rifles. Adjustment for windage and elevation. Fits most guns without drilling or tapping. Also for British SMLE, Winchester M94 Side Eject.
Price: From . . . . . . . . . . . . . . . . . . . . . . . . . **$29.95**
Price: With Shotgun Aperture . . . . . . . . . . . . . . . . **$29.95**

**WILLIAMS GUIDE (WGRS)** Receiver sight for 30 M1 Carbine, M1903A3 Springfield, Savage 24s, Savage-Anschutz rifles and Weatherby XXII. Utilizes military dovetail; no drilling. Double-dovetail windage adjustment, sliding dovetail adjustment for elevation.
Price: . . . . . . . . . . . . . . . . . . . . . . . . . . . **$29.95**

## Front Sights

**LYMAN HUNTING SIGHTS** Made with gold or white beads ¹⁄₁₆" to ³⁄₃₂" wide and in varying heights for most military and commercial rifles. Dovetail bases.
Price: . . . . . . . . . . . . . . . . . . . . . . . . . . . **$9.80**

**MARBLE STANDARD** Ivory, red, or gold bead. For all American-made rifles, ¹⁄₁₆" wide bead with semi-flat face which does not reflect light. Specify type of rifle when ordering.
Price: . . . . . . . . . . . . . . . . . . . . . . . . . . . **$8.00**

**MARBLE-SHEARD "GOLD"** Shows up well even in darkest timber. Shows same color on different colored objects; sturdily built. Medium bead. Various models for different makes of rifles so specify type of rifle when ordering.
Price: . . . . . . . . . . . . . . . . . . . . . . . . . . . **$10.18**

**MARBLE CONTOURED** Same contour and shape as Marble-Sheard but uses standard ¹⁄₁₆" or ³⁄₃₂" bead, ivory, red or gold. Specify rifle type.
Price: . . . . . . . . . . . . . . . . . . . . . . . . . . . **$9.25**

**MARBLE PATRIDGE** Gold-faced Patridge front sight is available in .250" or .34" widths and heights from .260" to .538".
Price: . . . . . . . . . . . . . . . . . . . . . . . . . . . **$10.18**

**POLY-CHOKE** Rifle front sights available in six heights and two widths. Model A designed to be inserted into the barrel dovetail; Model B is for use with standard .350" ramp; both have standard ⅜" dovetails. Gold or ivory color ¹⁄₁₆" bead. From Marble Arms.
Price: . . . . . . . . . . . . . . . . . . . . . . . . . . . . . . . . . . . . . . . . . **$6.45**

**WILLIAMS RISER BLOCKS** For adding .250" height to front sights when using a receiver sight. Two widths available: .250" for Williams Streamlined Ramp or .340" on all standard ramps having this base width. Uses standard ⅜" dovetail.
Price: . . . . . . . . . . . . . . . . . . . . . . . . . . . . . . . . . . . . . . . . . **$4.95**

## Globe Target Front Sights

**LYMAN 20 MJT TARGET FRONT** Has ⅞" diameter, one-piece steel globe with ⅜" dovetail base. Height is .700" from bottom of dovetail to center of aperture; height on 20 LJT is .750". Comes with seven Anschutz-size steel inserts—two posts and five apertures .126" through .177".
Price: 20 MJT or 20 LJT . . . . . . . . . . . . . . . . . . . . . . . . . **$36.00**

**LYMAN No. 17A TARGET** Includes seven interchangeable inserts: four apertures, one transparent amber and two posts .50" and .100" in width.
Price: . . . . . . . . . . . . . . . . . . . . . . . . . . . . . . . . . . . . . . . . . **$28.00**
Price: Insert set . . . . . . . . . . . . . . . . . . . . . . . . . . . . . . . . . **$9.95**

**LYMAN NO. 93 MATCH** Has ⅞" diameter, fits any rifle with a standard dovetail mounting block. Comes with seven target inserts and accepts most Anschutz accessories. Hooked locking bolt and nut allows quick removal, installation. Base available in .860" (European) and .562" (American) hole spacing.
Price: . . . . . . . . . . . . . . . . . . . . . . . . . . . . . . . . . . . . . . . . . **$45.00**

## Ramp Sights

**LYMAN SCREW-ON RAMP** Used with 8-40 screws but may also be brazed on. Heights from .10" to .350". Ramp without sight.
Price: . . . . . . . . . . . . . . . . . . . . . . . . . . . . . . . . . . . . . . . . **$15.95**

**MARBLE FRONT RAMPS** Available in either screw-on or sweat-on style, five heights: ³⁄₁₆", ⁵⁄₁₆", ⅜", ⁷⁄₁₆", ⁹⁄₁₆". Standard ⅜" dovetail slot.
Price: . . . . . . . . . . . . . . . . . . . . . . . . . . . . . . . . . . . . . . . . **$15.40**
Price: Hoods for above ramps . . . . . . . . . . . . . . . . . . . . . . **$3.35**

**WILLIAMS SHORTY RAMP** Companion to "Streamlined" ramp, about ½" shorter. Screw-on or sweat-on. It is furnished in ⅛", ³⁄₁₆", ⁹⁄₃₂", and ⅜" heights without hood only.
Price: . . . . . . . . . . . . . . . . . . . . . . . . . . . . . . . . . . . . . . . . **$12.50**
Price: With dovetail lock . . . . . . . . . . . . . . . . . . . . . . . . . . **$14.85**

**WILLIAMS STREAMLINED RAMP** Available in screw-on or sweat-on models. Furnished in ⁹⁄₁₆", ⁷⁄₁₆", ⅜", ⁵⁄₁₆", ³⁄₁₆" heights.
Price: . . . . . . . . . . . . . . . . . . . . . . . . . . . . . . . . . . . . . . . . **$14.95**
Price: Sight hood . . . . . . . . . . . . . . . . . . . . . . . . . . . . . . . . **$3.50**

**WILLIAMS STREAMLINED FRONT SIGHTS** Narrow (.250" width) for Williams Streamlined ramps and others with ¼" top width; medium (.340" width) for all standard factory ramps. Available with white, gold or flourescent beads, ¹⁄₁₆" or ³⁄₃₂".
Price: . . . . . . . . . . . . . . . . . . . . . . . . . . . **$7.90 to $8.20**

## Handgun Sights

**BO-MAR DELUXE BMCS** Gives ⅜" windage and elevation adjustment at 50 yards on Colt Gov't 45; sight radius under 7". For GM and Commander models only. Uses existing dovetail slot. Has shield-type rear blade.
Price: . . . . . . . . . . . . . . . . . . . . . . . . . . . . . . . . . . . . . . . . **$65.95**

**BO-MAR LOW PROFILE RIB & ACCURACY TUNER** Streamlined rib with front and rear sights; 7⅛" sight radius. Brings sight line closer to the bore than standard or extended sight and ramp. Weight 5 oz. Made for Colt Gov't 45, Super 38, and Gold Cup 45 and 38.
Price: . . . . . . . . . . . . . . . . . . . . . . . . . . . . . . . . . . . . . . . **$123.00**

**BO-MAR COMBAT RIB** For S&W Model 19 revolver with 4" barrel. Sight radius 5¾", weight 5½ oz.
Price: . . . . . . . . . . . . . . . . . . . . . . . . . . . . . . . . . . . . . . . **$110.00**

**BO-MAR FAST DRAW RIB** Streamlined full-length rib with integral Bo-Mar micrometer sight and serrated fast draw sight. For Browning 9mm, S&W 39, Colt Commander 45, Super Auto and 9mm.
Price: . . . . . . . . . . . . . . . . . . . . . . . . . . . . . . . . . . . . . . . **$110.00**

**BO-MAR HUNTER REAR SIGHT** Replacement rear sight in two models— S&W K and L frames use 2¾" Bo-Mar base with ⁷⁄₁₆" overhang, has two screw holes; S&W N frame has 3" base, three screw holes. A .200" taller front blade is required.
Price: . . . . . . . . . . . . . . . . . . . . . . . . . . . . . . . . . . . . . . . **$86.00**

**BO-MAR WINGED RIB** For S&W 4" and 6" length barrels—K-38, M10, HB 14 and 19. Weight for the 6" model is about 7¼ oz.
Price: . . . . . . . . . . . . . . . . . . . . . . . . . . . . . . . . . . . . . . . **$123.00**

**BO-MAR COVER-UP RIB** Adjustable rear sight, winged front guards. Fits right over revolver's original front sight. For S&W 4" M-10HB, M-13, M-58, M-64 & 65, Ruger 4" models SDA-34, SDA-84, SS-34, SS-84, GF-34, GF-84.
Price: . . . . . . . . . . . . . . . . . . . . . . . . . . . . . . . . . . . . . . . **$117.00**

**C-MORE SIGHTS** Replacement front sight blades offered in two types and five styles. Made of Du Pont Acetal, they come in a set of five high-contrast

colors: blue, green, pink, red and yellow. Easy to install. Patridge style for Colt Python (all barrels), Ruger Super Blackhawk (7½"), Ruger Blackhawk (4⅝"); ramp style for Python (all barrels), Blackhawk (4⅝"), Super Blackhawk (7½" and 10½"). From Mag-na-port Int'l.
Price: Per set . . . . . . . . . . . . . . . . . . . . . . . . . . . . . . . . . . **$19.95**

**MMC COMBAT FIXED REAR SIGHT (Colt 1911-Type Pistols)** This veteran MMC sight is well known to those who prefer a true combat sight for "carry" guns. Steel construction for long service. Choose from a wide variety of front sights.
Price: Combat Fixed Rear, plain . . . . . . . . . . . . . . . . . . . **$18.45**
Price: As above, white outline . . . . . . . . . . . . . . . . . . . . . **$23.65**
Price: Combat Front Sight for above, six styles, from . . . . . . . . **$5.15**

**MMC M/85 ADJUSTABLE REAR SIGHT** Designed to be compatible with the Ruger P-85 front sight. Fully adjustable for windage and elevation.
Price: M/85 Adjustable Rear Sight, plain . . . . . . . . . . . . . **$52.45**
Price: As above, white outline . . . . . . . . . . . . . . . . . . . . . **$57.70**

**MMC STANDARD ADJUSTABLE REAR SIGHT** Available for Colt 1911 type, Ruger Standard Auto, and now for S&W 469, and 659 pistols. No front sight change is necessary, as this sight will work with the original factory front sight.
Price: Standard Adjustable Rear Sight, plain leaf . . . . . . . **$46.05**
Price: Standard Adjustable Rear Sight, white outline . . . . . **$51.15**

**MMC MINI-SIGHT** Miniature size for carrying, fully adjustable, for maximum accuracy with your pocket auto. MMC's Mini-Sight will work with the factory front sight. No machining is necessary; easy installation. Available for Walther PP, PPK, and PPK/S pistols. Will also fit fixed sight Browning Hi-Power (P-35).
Price: Mini-Sight, plain . . . . . . . . . . . . . . . . . . . . . . . . . . **$58.45**
Price: Mini-Sight, white bar . . . . . . . . . . . . . . . . . . . . . . . **$63.45**

**MEPROLIGHT SIGHTS** Replacement tritium open sights for popular handguns and AR-15/M-16 rifles. Both front and rear sights have tritium inserts for illumination in low-light conditions. Inserts give constant non-glare green light for 5 years, even in cold weather. For most popular auto pistols, revolvers, some rifles and shotguns. Contact Hesco, Inc. for complete details.
Price: Shotgun bead front sight . . . . . . . . . . . . . . . . . . . . **$22.95**
Price: M-16 front sight only . . . . . . . . . . . . . . . . . . . . . . . **$32.95**
Price: H&K SR9, MP5 front sight only . . . . . . . . . . . . . . . . **$49.95**
Price: Colt Python, King Cobra, Ruger GP-100 adj. sights . . . . **$124.95**
Price: Most other front and rear sights . . . . . . . . . . . . . . . **$89.95**
Price: Adj. sights for Beretta, Browning, Colt Gov't., Glock, Ruger P-Series, SIG, Taurus PT-92 . . . . . . . . . . . . . . . . . . . . . . . . . . . . . . **$139.95**

**MILLETT BAR-DOT-BAR TRITIUM SIGHTS** Combo set uses the Series 100 fully adjustable sight system with horizontal tritium inserts on the rear, a single insert on the front. Available for: Ruger P-85, SIG Sauer P220, P225/226, Browning Hi-Power, Colt GM, CZ/TZ, TA-90, Glock 17, 19, 20, 21, 22, 23, S&W (2nd, 3rd generations), Beretta 84, 85, 92SB, Taurus PT-92.
Price: . . . . . . . . . . . . . . . . . . . . . . . . . . . . . . . . . . . . . . . **$135.00**
Price: Beretta, Taurus . . . . . . . . . . . . . . . . . . . . . . . . . . . **$143.50**

**MILLETT 3-DOT SYSTEM SIGHTS** The 3-Dot System sights use a single white dot on the front blade and two dots flanking the rear notch. Fronts available in Dual-Crimp and Wide Stake-On styles, as well as special applications. Adjustable rear sight available for most popular auto pistols and revolvers.
Price: Front, from . . . . . . . . . . . . . . . . . . . . . . . . . . . . . . . **$15.25**
Price: Adjustable rear, from . . . . . . . . . . . . . **$46.96 to $52.95**

**MILLETT REVOLVER FRONT SIGHTS** All-steel replacement front sights with either white or orange bar. Easy to install. For Ruger GP-100, Redhawk, Security-Six, Police-Six, Speed-Six, Colt Trooper, Diamondback, King Cobra, Peacemaker, Python, Dan Wesson 22 and 15-2.
Price: . . . . . . . . . . . . . . . . . . . . . . . . . . . . **$12.95 to $15.25**

**MILLETT DUAL-CRIMP FRONT SIGHT** Replacement front sight for automatic pistols. Dual-Crimp uses an all-steel two-point hollow rivet system. Available in eight heights and four styles. Has a skirted base that covers the front sight pad. Easily installed with the Millett Installation Tool Set. Available in Blaze Orange Bar, White Bar, Serrated Ramp, Plain Post.
Price: . . . . . . . . . . . . . . . . . . . . . . . . . . . . . . . . . . . . . . . **$15.25**

**MILLETT STAKE-ON FRONT SIGHT** Replacement front sight for automatic pistols. Stake-On sights have skirted base that covers the front sight pad. Easily installed with the Millet Installation Tool Set. Available in seven heights and four styles—Blaze Orange Bar, White Bar, Serrated Ramp, Plain Post.
Price: . . . . . . . . . . . . . . . . . . . . . . . . . . . . . . . . . . . . . . . **$15.25**

**OMEGA OUTLINE SIGHT BLADES** Replacement rear sight blades for Colt and Ruger single action guns and the Interarms Virginian Dragoon. Standard Outline available in gold or white notch outline on blue metal. From Omega Sales, Inc.
Price: . . . . . . . . . . . . . . . . . . . . . . . . . . . . . . . . . . . . . . . . **$8.95**

**OMEGA MAVERICK SIGHT BLADES** Replacement "peep-sight" blades for Colt, Ruger SAs, Virginian Dragoon. Three models available—No. 1, Plain; No. 2, Single Bar; No. 3, Double Bar Rangefinder. From Omega Sales, Inc.
Price: Each . . . . . . . . . . . . . . . . . . . . . . . . . . . . . . . . . . . . **$6.95**

**TRIJICON NIGHT SIGHTS** Three-dot night sight system uses tritium inserts in the front and rear sights. Tritium "lamps" are mounted in silicone rubber inside a metal cylinder. A polished crystal sapphire provides protection and clarity. Inlaid white outlines provide 3-dot aiming in daylight also. Available for most popular handguns with fixed or adjustable sights. From Trijicon, Inc.
Price: . . . . . . . . . . . . . . . . . . . . . . . . . . **$19.95 to $175.00**

**THOMPSON/CENTER SILHOUETTE SIGHTS** Replacement front and rear sights for the T/C Contender. Front sight has three interchangeable blades. Rear sight has three notch widths. Rear sight can be used with existing soldered front sights.
Price: Front sight . . . . . . . . . . . . . . . . . . . . . . . **$30.40**
Price: Rear sight . . . . . . . . . . . . . . . . . . . . . . . **$77.25**
**WICHITA SERIES 70/80 SIGHT** Provides click windage and elevation adjustments with precise repeatability of settings. Sight blade is grooved and angled back at the top to reduce glare. Available in Low Mount Combat or Low Mount Target styles for Colt 45s and their copies, S&W 645, Hi-Power, CZ 75 and others.
Price: Rear sight, target or combat . . . . . . . . . . . . **$66.75**
Price: Front sight, Patridge or ramp . . . . . . . . . . . **$10.45**
**WICHITA GRAND MASTER DELUXE RIBS** Ventilated rib has wings machined into it for better sight acquisition. Made of stainless steel, sights blued. Uses Wichita Multi-Range rear sight, adjustable front sight. Made for revolvers with 6" barrel.
Price: Model 301 (adj. sight K-frames with custom bbl. of 1.000"-1.032" dia., L- and N-frames with 1.062"-1.100" bbl.) . . . . . . . . . . . . . . **$160.00**
Price: Model 302 (fixed sight K-frames; M10, 65, 13 with 1.000" bbl., N-frame with 1.062" bbl.) . . . . . . . . . . . . . . . . . . . **$160.00**
Price: Model 303 (Model 29, 629 with factory bbl., adj. sight K-, L-, N-frames) . . . . . . . . . . . . . . . . . . . . . **$160.00**
**WICHITA DOUBLE MASTER RIB** Ventilated rib has wings machined on either side of fixed front post sight for better acquisition and is relieved for Mag-na-ports. Milled to accept Weaver See-Thru-style rings. Made of blued steel. Has Wichita Multi-Range rear sight system. Made for Model 29/629 with factory barrel, and all adjustable-sight K-, L- and N-frames.
Price: Model 403 . . . . . . . . . . . . . . . . . . . . . . . **$140.00**

## Shotgun Sights

**ACCURA-SITE** For shooting shotgun slugs. Three models to fit most shotguns—"A" for vent. rib barrels, "B" for solid ribs, "C" for plain barrels. Rear sight has windage and elevation provisions. Easily removed and replaced. Includes front and rear sights. From All's, The Jim Tembeils Co.
Price: . . . . . . . . . . . . . . . . . . . . . **$27.95 to $34.95**
**FIRE FLY EM-109 SL SHOTGUN SIGHT** Made of aircraft-grade aluminum, this ¼-oz. "channel" sight has a thick, sturdy hollowed post between the side rails to give a Patridge sight picture. All shooting is done with both eyes open, allowing the shooter to concentrate on the target, not the sights. The hole in the sight post gives reduced-light shooting capability and allows for fast, precise aiming. For sport or combat shooting. Model EM-109 fits all vent. rib and double barrel shotguns and muzzleloaders with octagon barrel. Model MOC-110 fits all plain barrel shotguns without screw-in chokes. From JAS, Inc. Add $3 postage.
Price: . . . . . . . . . . . . . . . . . . . . . . . . . . . . **$29.95**
**LYMAN** Three sights of over-sized ivory beads. No. 10 Front (press fit) for double barrel or ribbed single barrel guns...**$5.00**; No. 10D Front (screw fit) for non-ribbed single barrel guns (comes with wrench)...**$6.50**; No. 11 Middle (press fit) for double and ribbed single barrel guns...**$5.00**.
**MMC M&P COMBAT SHOTGUN SIGHT SET** A durable, protected ghost ring aperture, combat sight made of steel. Fully adjustable for windage and elevation.
Price: M&P Sight Set (front and rear) . . . . . . . . . . . **$73.45**
Price: As above, installed . . . . . . . . . . . . . . . . . . **$83.95**
**MARBLE SHOTGUN BEAD SIGHTS** No. 214—Ivory front bead, 11/64", tapered shank...**$3.70**; No. 223—Ivory rear bead, .080", tapered shank...**$3.75**; No. 217—Ivory front bead, 11/64", threaded shank...**$4.00**; No.

223-T—Ivory rear bead, .080", threaded shank...**$5.30**. Reamers, taps and wrenches available from Marble Arms.
**MILLETT SHURSHOT SHOTGUN SIGHT** A sight system for shotguns with ventilated rib. Rear sight attaches to the rib, front sight replaces the front bead. Front has an orange face, rear has two orange bars. For 870, 1100 or other models.
Price: Front and rear . . . . . . . . . . . . . . . . . . . . **$20.95**
Price: Adjustable front and rear . . . . . . . . . . . . . . **$27.40**
**POLY-CHOKE** Replacement front shotgun sights in four styles—Xpert, Poly Bead, Xpert Mid Rib sights, and Bev-L-Block. Xpert Front available in 3x56, 6x48 thread, 3/32" or 5/32" shank length, gold, ivory...**$4.55**; or Sun Spot orange bead...**$4.85**; Poly Bead is standard replacement 1/8" bead, 6x48...**$2.75**; Xpert Mid Rib in tapered carrier (ivory only) **$4.00**, or 3x56 threaded shank (gold only)...**$2.75**; Hi and Lo Blok sights with 6x48 thread, gold or ivory...**$4.55** or Sun Spot Orange...**$4.85**. From Marble Arms.
**SLUG SIGHTS** Made of non-marring black nylon, front and rear sights stretch over and lock onto the barrel. Sights are low profile with blaze orange front blade. Adjustable for windage and elevation. For plain-barrel (non-ribbed) guns in 12-, 16- and 20-gauge, and for shotguns with 5/16" and 3/8" ventilated ribs. From Innovision Ent.
Price: . . . . . . . . . . . . . . . . . . . . . . . . . . . . **$11.95**
**WILLIAMS GUIDE BEAD SIGHT** Fits all shotguns, 1/8" ivory, red or gold bead. Screws into existing sight hole. Various thread sizes and shank lengths.
Price: . . . . . . . . . . . . . . . . . . . . . . . . . . . . **$4.50**
**WILLIAMS SLUGGER SIGHTS** Removable aluminum sights attach to the shotgun rib. High profile front, fully adjustable rear. Fits ¼", 5/16" or 3/8" (special) ribs.
Price: . . . . . . . . . . . . . . . . . . . . . . . . . . . . **$34.95**

## Sight Attachments

**MERIT IRIS SHUTTER DISC** Eleven clicks give 12 different apertures. No. 3 Disc and Master, primarily target types, 0.22" to .125"; No. 4, ½" dia. hunting type, .025" to .155". Available for all popular sights. The Master Deluxe, with flexible rubber light shield, is particularly adapted to extension, scope height, and tang sights. All Merit Deluxe models have internal click springs; are hand fitted to minimum tolerance.
Price: Master Deluxe . . . . . . . . . . . . . . . . . . . . **$63.00**
Price: No. 3 Disc . . . . . . . . . . . . . . . . . . . . . . **$52.00**
Price: No. 4 Hunting Disc . . . . . . . . . . . . . . . . . **$45.00**
**MERIT LENS DISC** Similar to Merit Iris Shutter (Model 3 or Master) but incorporates provision for mounting prescription lens integrally. Lens may be obtained locally from your optician. Sight disc is 7/16" wide (Model 3), or ¾" wide (Master). Model 3 Target.
Price: . . . . . . . . . . . . . . . . . . . . . . . . . . . . **$65.00**
Price: Master Deluxe . . . . . . . . . . . . . . . . . . . . **$75.00**
**MERIT OPTICAL ATTACHMENT** For revolver and pistol shooters, instantly attached by rubber suction cup to regular or shooting glasses. Any aperture .020" to .156".
Price: Deluxe (swings aside) . . . . . . . . . . . . . . . . **$63.00**
**WILLIAMS APERTURES** Standard thread, fits most sights. Regular series 3/8" to ½" O.D., .050" to .125" hole. "Twilight" series has white reflector ring. .093" to .125" inner hole.
Price: Regular series . . . . . . . . . . . . . . . . . . . . **$4.50**
Price: Twilight series . . . . . . . . . . . . . . . . . . . . **$6.15**
Price: Wide open 5/16" aperture for shotguns fits 5-D or Foolproof sights (specify model) . . . . . . . . . . . . . . **$7.95**

| Maker and Model | Magn. | Field at 100 Yds. (feet) | Relative Bright- ness | Eye Relief (in.) | Length (in.) | Tube Dia. (in.) | W&E Adjust- ments | Weight (ozs.) | Price | Other Data |
|---|---|---|---|---|---|---|---|---|---|---|
| **ACTION ARMS** | | | | | | | | | | [1]56mm objective. Variable intensity LED red aiming dot. Average battery life 20 to 4500 hours. Waterproof, nitrogen-filled aluminum tube. Fits most standard 1" rings. Both Ultra Dot models avail. in black and satin chrome. Imported by Action Arms Ltd. |
| **Micro-Dot** | | | | | | | | | | |
| 1.5-4.5x LER Pistol | 1.5-4.5 | 80-26 | — | 12-24 | 8.8 | 1 | Int. | 9.5 | $255.00 | |
| 1.5-4.5x Rifle | 1.5-4.5 | 80-26 | — | 3 | 9.8 | 1 | Int. | 10.5 | 259.00 | |
| 2-7x32 | 2-7 | 54-18 | — | 3 | 11 | 1 | Int. | 12.1 | 275.00 | |
| 3-9x40 | 3-9 | 40-14 | — | 3 | 12.2 | 1 | Int. | 13.3 | 289.00 | |
| 4x-12x[1] | 4-12 | — | — | 3 | 14.3 | 1 | Int. | 18.3 | 395.00 | |
| Ultra-Dot 25 1x | — | — | — | — | 5.1 | 1 | Int. | 4.0 | 139.00 | |
| Ultra-Dot 30 1x | — | — | — | — | 5.1 | 30mm | Int. | 3.9 | 179.00 | |
| **ADCO** | | | | | | | | | | [1]Multi-Color Dot system changes from red to green. [2]For airguns, paintball, rimfires. Uses common lithium wafer battery. All come with extension tube for mounting. Black or matte nickel finish. Optional 2x booster available. Five year warranty. From ADCO Sales. |
| MiRAGE Ranger 1" | 0 | — | — | — | 5.2 | 1 | Int. | 4.5 | 139.00 | |
| MiRAGE Ranger 30mm | 0 | — | — | — | 5.5 | 30mm | Int. | 5.5 | 165.00 | |
| MiRAGE Sportsman[1] | 0 | — | — | — | 5.2 | 1 | Int. | 4.5 | 219.00 | |
| MiRAGE Competitor[1] | 0 | — | — | — | 5.5 | 30mm | Int. | 5.5 | 249.00 | |
| IMP Sight[2] | 0 | — | — | — | 4.5 | — | Int. | 2 | 35.00 | |
| **AIMPOINT** | | | | | | | | | | Illuminates red dot in field of view. Noparallax (dot does not need to be centered). Unlimited field of view and eye relief. On/off, adj. intensity. Dot covers 3" @ 100 yds. Mounts avail. for all sights and scopes. [1]Comes with 30mm rings, battery, lens cloth. [2]Requires 1" rings. Black or stainless finish. 3x scope attachment for rifles only), **$129.95**. [3]Projects red dot of visible laser light onto target. Black finish (LSR-2B) or stainless (LSR-2S); or comes with rings and accessories. Optional toggle switch, **$34.95**. Lithium battery life up to 15 hours. [4]Black finish (AP 5000-B) or stainless (AP 5000-S); avail. with regular 3-min. or 10-min. Mag Dot as B2 or S2. [5]Black finish; 2x magnification scope with floating dot. [6]For Beretta, Browning, Colt Gov't., Desert Eagle, Glock, Ruger, SIG-Sauer, S&W. [7]For Colt, S&W. From Aimpoint. |
| Series 3000 Short[2] | 0 | — | — | — | 5.5 | 1 | Int. | 5.5 | 269.00 | |
| Series 3000 Long[2] | 0 | — | — | — | 6⅞ | 1 | Int. | 5.8 | 269.95 | |
| Laserdot[3] | — | — | — | — | 3.5 | 1 | Int. | 4.0 | 319.95 | |
| Series 5000[4] | 0 | — | — | — | 5.75 | 30mm | Int. | 5.8 | 319.95 | |
| Series 5000/2x[1] | 2 | — | — | — | 7 | 30mm | Int. | 9 | 399.95 | |
| AP 2P[5] | 2 | — | — | — | 8.5 | 1 | Int. | 8.3 | 324.95 | |
| Autolaser[6] | — | — | — | — | 3.75 | 1 | Int. | 4.3 | 351.00 | |
| Revolver Laser[7] | — | — | — | — | 3.5 | 1 | Int. | 3.6 | 339.00 | |
| **APPLIED LASER SYSTEMS** | | | | | | | | | | Visible laser diode with 100,000 hour life. Class IIIa; deep red color; 80% of beam image in 1" square at 50ft.; 100-yd. effective range; all metal construction; over 2½-hour battery life at continuous duty. From Applied Laser Systems. |
| T2 | — | — | — | — | 2.8 | — | Int. | 2.2 | 210.00 | |
| AR15 | — | — | — | — | 2 | — | Int. | 3 | 315.00 | |
| Colt 1911 | — | — | — | — | 2 | — | Int. | 4 | 315.00 | |
| Beretta 92F | — | — | — | — | 2 | — | Int. | 4 | 315.00 | |
| RM 870 | — | — | — | — | 3 | — | Int. | 3 | 315.00 | |
| Glock | — | — | — | — | .75 | — | Int. | .8 | 385.00 | |
| Mini Aimer | — | — | — | — | 1.5 | — | Int. | .8 | 370.00 | |
| **ARMSON O.E.G.** | | | | | | | | | | Shows red dot aiming point. No batteries needed. Standard model fits 1" ring mounts (not incl.). Other models available for many popular shotguns, para-military rifles and carbines. [1]Daylight Only Sight with ⅜" dovetail mount for 22s. Does not contain tritium. From Trijicon, Inc. |
| Standard | 0 | — | — | — | 5⅛ | 1 | Int. | 4.3 | 211.00 | |
| 22 DOS[1] | 0 | — | — | — | 3¾ | — | Int. | 3.0 | 121.00 | |
| 22 Day/Night | 0 | — | — | — | 3¾ | — | Int. | 3.0 | 167.00 | |
| M16/AR-15 | 0 | — | — | — | 5⅛ | — | Int. | 5.5 | 250.00 | |
| Colt Pistol | 0 | — | — | — | 3¾ | — | Int. | 3.0 | 250.00 | |
| **BAUSCH & LOMB** | | | | | | | | | | [1]Adj. objective, sunshade. [2]Also in matte finish, **$533.95**. [3]Also in matte finish, **$499.95**. [4]Also in matte finish, **$319.95**; silver finish, **$319.95**. [5]Also in matte finish, **$297.95**. [6]50mm objective; matte finish **$369.95**. **Contact Bushnell for details.** |
| **Elite 4000** | | | | | | | | | | |
| 40-6244A[1] | 6-24 | 18-4.5 | — | 3 | 16.9 | 1 | Int. | 20.2 | 587.95 | |
| 40-2104G[2] | 2.5-10 | 41.5-10.8 | — | 3 | 13.5 | 1 | Int. | 16 | 513.95 | |
| 40-1636G[3] | 1.5-6 | 61.8-16.1 | — | 3 | 12.8 | 1 | Int. | 15.4 | 479.95 | |
| 40-1040 | 10 | 10.5 | — | 3.6 | 13.8 | 1 | Int. | 22.1 | 1,389.95 | |
| **Elite 3000** | | | | | | | | | | |
| 30-4124A | 4-12 | 26.9-9 | — | 3 | 13.2 | 1 | Int. | 15.2 | 349.95 | |
| 30-3940G[4] | 3-9 | 33.8-11.5 | — | 3 | 12.6 | 1 | Int. | 13.1 | 301.95 | |
| 30-2732G[5] | 2-7 | 44.6-12.7 | — | 3 | 11.6 | 1 | Int. | 11.7 | 281.95 | |
| 30-3950G[6] | 3-9 | 31.5-10.5 | — | 3 | 15.7 | 1 | Int. | 19 | 359.95 | |
| **BEEMAN** | | | | | | | | | | All scopes have 5-pt. reticle, all glass, fully coated lenses. [1]Pistol scope; cast mounts included. [2]Pistol scope; silhouette knobs. [3]Rubber armor coating; built-in double adj. mount, parallax-free setting. [4]Objective focus; built-in double-adj. mount; matte finish. [5]Objective focus. [6]Also available with color reticle. [7]Includes cast mounts. [8]Objective focus; silhouette knobs; matte finish. [9]Also in "L" models with reticle lighted by ambient light or tiny add-on illuminator. Lighted models slightly higher priced. Imported by Beeman. |
| Blue Ring 20[1] | 1.5 | 14 | 150 | 11-16 | 8.3 | ¾ | Int. | 3.6 | 59.95 | |
| Blue Ribbon 25[2] | 2 | 19 | 150 | 10-24 | 9¹⁄₁₆ | 1 | Int. | 7.4 | 154.95 | |
| SS-1[3,7] | 2.5 | 30 | 61 | 3.25 | 5½ | 1 | Int. | 7 | 198.50 | |
| SS-2[4,6,7,8,9] | 3 | 34.5 | 74 | 3.5 | 6.8 | 1.38 | Int. | 13.6 | 285.95 | |
| Blue Ribbon 50R[5] | 2.5 | 33 | 245 | 3.5 | 12 | 1 | Int. | 11.8 | 198.95 | |
| Blue Ring 10 | 4 | 27 | 69 | 3.0 | 10.6 | 1 | Int. | 9.5 | 109.95 | |
| Blue Ribbon 66R[6,8,9] | 2-7 | 62-16 | 384-31 | 3 | 11.4 | 1 | Int. | 14.9 | 298.50 | |
| Blue Ring 12 | 3-9 | 39-13 | 172-20 | 3.0 | 12.8 | 1 | Int. | 12.7 | 129.95 | |
| SS-3[3,4] | 1.5-4 | 44.6-24.6 | 172-24 | 3 | 5.75 | ⅞ | Int. | 8.5 | 299.95 | |
| Blue Ribbon 68R | 4-12 | 30.5-11 | 150-13.5 | 3 | 14.4 | 1 | Int. | 15.2 | 429.95 | |
| Blue Ribbon 54R[5] | 4 | 29 | 96 | 3.5 | 12 | 1 | Int. | 12.3 | 229.95 | |
| SS-2[4,6,8] | 4 | 24.6 | 41 | 5 | 7 | 1.38 | Int. | 13.7 | 299.95 | |
| **B-SQUARE** | | | | | | | | | | |
| BSL-1 | — | — | — | — | 2.75 | .75 | Int. | 2.25 | 259.95 | Blue or stainless finish. From B-Square. |

**CAUTION:** PRICES CHANGE, CHECK AT GUNSHOP.

| Maker and Model | Magn. | Field at 100 Yds. (feet) | Relative Bright-ness | Eye Relief (in.) | Length (in.) | Tube Dia. (in.) | W&E Adjust-ments | Weight (ozs.) | Price | Other Data |
|---|---|---|---|---|---|---|---|---|---|---|
| **BURRIS** | | | | | | | | | | All scopes avail. in Plex reticle. Steel-on-steel click adjustments. [1]Dot reticle $13 extra. [2]Post crosshair reticle $13 extra. [3]Matte satin finish $20 extra. [4]Available with parallax adjustment $28 extra (standard on 10x, 12x, 4-12x, 6-12x, 6-18x, 6x HBR and 3-12x Signature). [5]Silver Safari finish $30 extra. [6]Target knobs $20 extra, standard on silhouette models, LER and XER with P.A., 6x HBR. [7]Sunshade avail. [8]Avail. with Fine Plex reticle. [9]Available with Heavy Plex reticle. [10]Available with Posi-Lock. [11]Available with Peep Plex reticle. |
| **Fullfield** | | | | | | | | | | |
| 1½x[9] | 1.6 | 62 | — | 3¼ | 10¼ | 1 | Int. | 9.0 | 229.95 | |
| 2½x[9] | 2.5 | 55 | — | 3¼ | 10¼ | 1 | Int. | 9.0 | 237.95 | |
| 4x[1,2,3] | 3.75 | 36 | — | 3¼ | 11¼ | 1 | Int. | 11.5 | 255.95 | |
| 6x[1,3] | 5.8 | 23 | — | 3¼ | 13 | 1 | Int. | 12.0 | 274.95 | |
| 12x[1,4,6,7,8] | 11.8 | 10.5 | — | 3¼ | 15 | 1 | Int. | 15 | 346.95 | |
| 1¾-5x[1,2,9] | 1.7-4.6 | 66-25 | — | 3¼ | 10⅞ | 1 | Int. | 13 | 295.95 | |
| 2-7x[1,2,3] | 2.5-6.8 | 47-18 | — | 3¼ | 12 | 1 | Int. | 14 | 322.95 | |
| 3-9x[1,2,3] | 3.3-8.7 | 38-15 | — | 3¼ | 12⅝ | 1 | Int. | 15 | 331.95 | |
| 3.7-10x50mm[3,5] | 3.7-9.7 | 29.5-11 | — | 3-3.25 | 14 | 1 | Int. | 19 | 408.95 | |
| 4-12x[1,4,8,11] | 4.4-11.8 | 27-10 | — | 3¼ | 15 | 1 | Int. | 18 | 406.95 | |
| 6-18x[1,3,4,6,7,8] | 6.5-17.6 | 16-7 | — | 3¼ | 15.8 | 1 | Int. | 18.5 | 422.95 | |
| **Mini Scopes** | | | | | | | | | | |
| 4x[4,5] | 3.6 | 24 | — | 3¾-5 | 8¼ | 1 | Int. | 7.8 | 205.95 | |
| 6x[1,4] | 5.5 | 17 | — | 3¾-5 | 9 | 1 | Int. | 8.2 | 219.95 | |
| 6x HBR P.A.[1,5,8] | 6.0 | 13 | — | 4.5 | 11¼ | 1 | Int. | 13.0 | 283.95 | |
| 2-7x | 2.5-6.9 | 32-14 | — | 3¾-5 | 12 | 1 | Int. | 10.5 | 281.95 | |
| 3-9x[5] | 3.6-8.8 | 25-11 | — | 3¾-5 | 12⅝ | 1 | Int. | 11.5 | 289.95 | |
| 4-12x[1,4,6] | 4.5-11.6 | 19-8 | — | 3¾-4 | 15 | 1 | Int. | 15 | 383.95 | |
| **Signature Series** | | | | | | | | | | LER=Long Eye Relief; IER=Intermediate Eye Relief; XER=Extra Eye Relief. From Burris. |
| 1.5-6x[2,3,5,9,10] | 1.7-5.8 | 70-20 | — | 3½-4 | 10.8 | 1 | Int. | 13.0 | 381.95 | |
| 4x[3] | 4.0 | 30 | — | 3 | 12⅛ | 1 | Int. | 14 | 325.95 | |
| 6x[3] | 6.0 | 20 | — | 3 | 12⅛ | 1 | Int. | 14 | 353.95 | |
| 2-8x[3,5,11] | 2.1-7.7 | 53-17 | — | 3-3.25 | 11.75 | 1 | Int. | 14 | 443.95 | |
| 3-9x[3,5,10] | 3.3-8.8 | 36-14 | — | 3 | 12⅞ | 1 | Int. | 15.5 | 455.95 | |
| 2½-10x[3,5,10] | 2.7-9.5 | 37-10.5 | — | 3-3¾ | 14 | 1 | Int. | 19.0 | 511.95 | |
| 3-12x[3,10] | 3.3-11.7 | 34-9 | — | 3 | 14¼ | 1 | Int. | 21 | 369.95 | |
| 6-24x[1,3,5,6,8,10] | 6.6-23.8 | 17-6 | — | 3-2½ | 16.0 | 1 | Int. | 22.7 | 600.95 | |
| **Handgun** | | | | | | | | | | |
| 1½-4x LER[1,5] | 1.6-3. | 16-11 | — | 11-25 | 10¼ | 1 | Int. | 11 | 315.95 | |
| 2½-7x LER[3,4,5] | 2-6.5 | 21-7 | — | 7-27 | 9.5 | 1 | Int. | 12.6 | 308.95 | |
| 3-9x LER[4,5] | 3.4-8.4 | 12-5 | — | 22-14 | 11 | 1 | Int. | 14 | 347.95 | |
| 1x LER[1] | 1.1 | 27 | — | 10-24 | 8¾ | 1 | Int. | 6.8 | 194.95 | |
| 2x LER[4,5,6] | 1.7 | 21 | — | 10-24 | 8¾ | 1 | Int. | 6.8 | 201.95 | |
| 3x LER[4,6] | 2.7 | 17 | — | 10-20 | 8⅞ | 1 | Int. | 6.8 | 217.95 | |
| 4x LER[1,4,5,6] | 3.7 | 11 | — | 10-22 | 9⅝ | 1 | Int. | 9.0 | 224.95 | |
| 7x IER[1,4,5,6] | 6.5 | 6.5 | — | 10-16 | 11¼ | 1 | Int. | 10 | 248.95 | |
| 10x IER[1,4,6] | 9.5 | 4 | — | 8-12 | 13½ | 1 | Int. | 14 | 308.95 | |
| **Scout Scope** | | | | | | | | | | |
| 1½x XER[3,9] | 1.5 | 22 | — | 7-18 | 9 | 1 | Int. | 7.3 | 199.95 | |
| 2¾x XER[3,9] | 2.7 | 15 | — | 7-14 | 9⅜ | 1 | Int. | 7.5 | 205.95 | |
| **BUSHNELL** | | | | | | | | | | [1]45mm objective. [2]Wide angle. [3]Also silver finish, **$175.95**. [4]Also silver finish, **$209.95**. [5]56mm objective. [6]Selective red L.E.D. dot for low light hunting. **Only selected models shown. Contact Bushnell for details.** |
| **Trophy** | | | | | | | | | | |
| 73-2545[1] | 2.5-10 | 39-10 | — | 3 | 13.75 | 1 | Int. | 14 | 259.95 | |
| 73-1500[2] | 1.75-5 | 68-23 | — | 3.5 | 10.8 | 1 | Int. | 12.3 | 209.95 | |
| 73-2733[2] | 2-7 | 63-18 | — | 3 | 10 | 1 | Int. | 11.3 | 177.95 | |
| 73-4124[2] | 4-12 | 32-11 | — | 3 | 12.5 | 1 | Int. | 16.1 | 245.95 | |
| 73-3940[2] | 3-9 | 42-14 | — | 3 | 11.7 | 1 | Int. | 13.2 | 169.95 | |
| 73-6184 | 6-18 | 17.3-6 | — | 3 | 14.8 | 1 | Int. | 17.9 | 277.95 | |
| **Trophy Handgun** | | | | | | | | | | |
| 73-0232[3] | 2 | 20 | — | 9-26 | 8.7 | 1 | Int. | 7.7 | 163.95 | |
| 73-2632[4] | 2-6 | 21-7 | — | 9-26 | 9.1 | 1 | Int. | 9.6 | 199.95 | |
| **Banner Armor-Sight** | | | | | | | | | | |
| 65-3940 | 3-9 | 39-13 | — | 3 | 12 | 1 | Int. | 12.5 | 349.95 | |
| **Banner Standard** | | | | | | | | | | |
| 71-2520 | 2.5 | 44 | — | 3.6 | 10 | 1 | Int. | 7.5 | 78.95 | |
| 71-3956[5] | 3-9 | 37-12 | — | 3.5 | 13.7 | 1 | Int. | 17.3 | 241.95 | |
| 71-1040 | 10 | 12 | — | 3 | 14.7 | 1 | Int. | 14.3 | 197.95 | |
| **Lite-Site** | | | | | | | | | | |
| 71-3940[6] | 3-9 | 36-13 | — | 3.1 | 12.8 | 1 | Int. | 15.5 | 289.95 | |
| **Sportview** | | | | | | | | | | |
| 74-1545 | 1.5-4.5 | 69-24 | — | 3 | 10.7 | 1 | Int. | 8.6 | 78.95 | |
| 74-2532 | 2.5 | 44 | — | 3.5 | 10.75 | 1 | Int. | 9 | 78.95 | |
| 74-3145 | 3.5-10 | 36-13 | — | 3 | 12.75 | 1 | Int. | 13.9 | 125.90 | |
| 74-1403 | 4 | 29 | — | 4 | 11.75 | 1 | Int. | 9.2 | 47.95 | |
| 74-3938 | 3-9 | 42-14 | — | 3 | 12.7 | 1 | Int. | 12.5 | 98.95 | |
| 74-3720 | 3-7 | 23-11 | — | 2.6 | 11.3 | .75 | Int. | 5.7 | 37.95 | |
| **CHARLES DALY** | | | | | | | | | | [1]Pistol scope. [2]Adj. obj. From Outdoor Sports Headquarters. |
| 4x32 | 4 | 28 | — | 3.25 | 11.75 | 1 | Int. | 9.5 | 70.00 | |
| 4x32[2] | 4 | 28 | — | 3 | 9 | 1 | Int. | 8.5 | 129.00 | |
| 4x40 WA | 4 | 36 | — | 3.25 | 13 | 1 | Int. | 11.5 | 98.00 | |
| 2.5x20[1] | 2.5 | 17 | — | 3 | 7.3 | 1 | Int. | 7.25 | 80.00 | |
| 2.5x32 | 2.5 | 47 | — | 3 | 12.25 | 1 | Int. | 10 | 80.00 | |
| 2-7x32 WA | 2-7 | 56-17 | — | 3 | 11.5 | 1 | Int. | 12 | 125.00 | |
| 3-9x40 | 3-9 | 35-14 | — | 3 | 12.5 | 1 | Int. | 11.25 | 77.00 | |
| 3-9x40 WA | 3-9 | 36-13 | — | 3 | 12.75 | 1 | Int. | 12.5 | 125.00 | |
| 4-12x40 WA | 4-12 | 30-11 | — | 3 | 13.75 | 1 | Int. | 14.5 | 133.00 | |
| 2x20[1] | 2 | 16 | — | 16-25 | 8.75 | 1 | Int. | 6.5 | 107.00 | |

| Maker and Model | Magn. | Field at 100 Yds. (feet) | Relative Brightness | Eye Relief (in.) | Length (in.) | Tube Dia. (in.) | W&E Adjustments | Weight (ozs.) | Price | Other Data |
|---|---|---|---|---|---|---|---|---|---|---|
| **FROM JENA** | | | | | | | | | | |
| 4x36 | 4 | 39 | — | 3.5 | 11.6 | 26mm | Int. | 14 | 695.00 | [1]Military scope with adjustable parallax. Fixed powers have 26mm tubes, variables have 30mm tubes. Some models avail. with steel tubes. All lenses multi-coated. Dust and water tight |
| 6x36 | 6 | 21 | — | 3.5 | 12 | 26mm | Int. | 14 | 795.00 | |
| 6x42 | 6 | 21 | — | 3.5 | 13 | 26mm | Int. | 15 | 860.00 | |
| 8x56 | 8 | 18 | — | 3.5 | 14.4 | 26mm | Int. | 20 | 890.00 | |
| 1.5-6x42 | 1.5-6 | 61.7-23 | — | 3.5 | 12.6 | 30mm | Int. | 17 | 975.00 | |
| 2-8x42 | 2-8 | 52-17 | — | 3.5 | 13.3 | 30mm | Int. | 17 | 1,050.00 | |
| 2.5-10x56 | 2.5-10 | 40-13.6 | — | 3.5 | 15 | 30mm | Int. | 21 | 1,195.00 | |
| 3-12x56 | 3-12 | NA | — | NA | NA | 30mm | Int. | NA | 1,195.00 | |
| 4-16x56 | 4-16 | NA | — | NA | NA | 30mm | Int. | NA | 1,225.00 | |
| 3-9x40 | 3-9 | NA | — | NA | NA | 1 | Int. | NA | 1,120.00 | |
| 2.5-10x46 | 2.5-10 | NA | — | NA | NA | 30mm | Int. | NA | 1,150.00 | |
| 4-16x56[1] | 4-16 | NA | — | NA | NA | 30mm | Int. | NA | 1,490.00 | |
| **GLOBAL INDUSTRIES** | | | | | | | | | | |
| **30mm Superb Series WA** | | | | | | | | | | [1]With adj. obj.; [2]Also 4x40, 4x40 with adj. obj.; [3]Also with adj. obj.; [4]Also 2-7x40, 2-7x40 with adj. obj.; [5]Also 3-9x40, 3-9x40 with adj. obj.; [6]Also 4x30, 4x40; [7]Also 10x40. |
| 1.5x20 | 1.5 | 78.73 | 69.64 | 3.9 | 9.4 | 1.18 | Int. | 12.3 | 318.56 | |
| 4x42 | 4 | 31.16 | 43.40 | 4.5 | 12.2 | 1.18 | Int. | 14.6 | 392.27 | |
| 6x42 | 6 | 19 | 19.29 | 3.7 | 12.2 | 1.18 | Int. | 14.6 | 408.51 | |
| 8x56 | 8 | 13.12 | 19.29 | 3.7 | 13.5 | 1.18 | Int. | 19.0 | 449.74 | |
| 15x56[1] | 15 | 8.5 | 5.38 | 3.3 | 15.9 | 1.18 | Int. | 25.7 | 673.13 | |
| **30mm Variables** | | | | | | | | | | **30mm Superb Series:** All models can be ordered with target or external knobs, magnifying reticle (European style), objective adjustment (O.A.), and choice of six reticles. Variables—IPC, extra-heavy construction of 6061 T-6 alloy. Fogproof, recoil-proof coated optics. **American Series:** Special reticles (12), target knobs, BDC objective lens adjustment feature can be added to any scope at extra cost. Sunshades also avail. 12x thru 24x can be made on special order. German-type speed focus avail. as option on all American Series scopes. Waterproof, fogproof, recoil-proof, fully coated. **European 1":** All wide angle with choice of 12 reticless, obj. adj. avail. on some models. BDC and target knobs avail. on all as options. Sunshades, locking lens covers, speed focus also optional. **Partial listing of models shown.** Contact Global Industries for full details. |
| 1-4x20 | 1-4 | 101-30.1 | 157-9.8 | 4.3-3.3 | 9.4 | 1.18 | Int. | 11.1 | 460.98 | |
| 2-8x42 | 2-8 | 46.9-16 | 173-11 | 4.5-3.5 | 13.3 | 1.18 | Int. | 17.4 | 522.82 | |
| 2.5-10 | 2.5-10 | 42.6-13 | 111.1-69 | 4.3-3.3 | 13.3 | 1.18 | Int. | 17.4 | 541.56 | |
| 3-12x56 | 3-12 | 37.7-10.8 | 137-16 | 3.9-3.3 | 14.3 | 1.18 | Int. | 25.7 | 673.13 | |
| 4-20x42 | 4-20 | 26-6 | 40-4 | 3.3-3.0 | 17.7 | 1.18 | Int. | 23.8 | 704.50 | |
| **American 1" Series WA** | | | | | | | | | | |
| Adirondack 1x20 | 1 | — | — | — | — | 1 | Int | — | 168.65 | |
| Raton 2.5x32 | 2.5 | 33.0 | 161 | 3.5 | 11.7 | 1 | Int. | 9.2 | 169.60 | |
| Las Vegas 4x32[2] | 4 | 29.0 | 64 | 3.3 | 11.7 | 1 | Int. | 9.2 | 172.40 | |
| Kalispell 6x40[3] | 6 | 18.5 | 45 | 3.2 | 13.0 | 1 | Int. | 10.2 | 198.29 | |
| Pecos 8x40 O.A. | 8 | 13.5 | 25 | 3.0 | 13.0 | 1 | Int. | 10.2 | 253.83 | |
| San Antonio 10x40 O.A. | 10 | 12.5 | 16 | 3.0 | 13.0 | 1 | Int. | 10.4 | 257.23 | |
| **Variables** | | | | | | | | | | |
| Abeline 1-3x20 | 1-3 | — | — | — | — | 1 | Int. | — | 237.98 | |
| Shiloh 1.5-4.5x20 | 1.5-4.5 | — | — | — | — | 1 | Int. | — | 241.73 | |
| Denver 2-7x32[4] | 2-7 | — | — | — | — | 1 | Int. | — | 226.24 | |
| Santa Fe 3-9x32[5] | 3-9 | 43.5-15 | 114-13 | 3.3-3.0 | 12.2 | 1 | Int. | 12.0 | 221.91 | |
| Sutter's Creek 4-12x40 O.A. | 4-12 | 30.5-11 | 100-12.3 | 3.0 | 15.8 | 1 | Int. | 15.0 | 301.71 | |
| **European 1" Series** | | | | | | | | | | |
| Jutland 4x20[6] | 4 | 33 | 25 | 3.2 | 11.0 | 1 | Int. | 10.5 | 208.82 | |
| Grenoble 6x40 | 6 | 26 | 43.56 | 3 | 13.2 | 1 | Int. | 13.7 | 244.29 | |
| Rhineland 8x56 | 8 | 20 | 49 | 3.2 | 13.5 | 1 | Int. | 17.2 | 310.05 | |
| Hamburg 10x56 O.A.[7] | 10 | — | — | 3.2 | 13.5 | 1 | Int. | 17.2 | 375.46 | |
| Brunswick 15x56 O.A. | 15 | — | — | 3.1 | 13.5 | 1 | Int. | 17.6 | 414.30 | |
| **INTERAIMS** | | | | | | | | | | Intended for handguns. Comes with rings. Dot size less than 1½" @ 100 yds. Waterproof. Battery life 50-10,000 hours. Black or nickel finish Imported by Stoeger. |
| One V | 0 | — | — | 4.5 | 1 | Int. | 4 | 139.95 | | |
| One V | 0 | — | — | 4.5 | 1 | Int. | 4 | 139.95 | | |
| **KAHLES** | | | | | | | | | | [1]Steel tube. [2]Ballistic cam system with military rangefinder. Waterproof, fogproof, nitrogen filled. Choice of reticles. Imported from Austria by Kahles USA. |
| K4x32-L | 4 | 33 | — | — | 11.3 | 1 | Int. | 11.2 | 555.00 | |
| K6x42-L | 6 | 23 | — | — | 12.5 | 1 | Int. | 13 | 615.00 | |
| K7x56-L | 7 | 19.7 | — | — | 14.4 | 26mm | Int. | 16.1 | 695.00 | |
| K8x56-L | 8 | 17.1 | — | — | 14.4 | 1 | Int. | 16.1 | 715.00 | |
| K1.1-4.5x20-L | 1.1-4.5 | 78.7-30 | — | — | 10.5 | 30mm | Int. | 12.6 | 685.00 | |
| K1.5-6x42-L | 1.5-6 | 61-21 | — | — | 12.5 | 30mm | Int. | 15.8 | 785.00 | |
| K2.2-9x42-L | 2.2-9 | 39.5-15 | — | — | 13.3 | 30mm | Int. | 15.5 | 945.00 | |
| K3-12x56-L | 3-12 | 30-11 | — | — | 15.2 | 30mm | Int. | 18 | 1,045.00 | |
| K2.5x20-S[1] | 2.5 | 54 | — | — | 9.6 | 1 | Int. | 12.6 | 525.00 | |
| KZF84-6[1,2] | 6 | 23 | — | — | 12.5 | 1 | Int. | 17.6 | 995.00 | |
| KZF84-10[1,2] | 10 | 13 | — | — | 13.25 | 1 | Int. | 18 | 1,045.00 | |
| **KASSNAR VISTASCOPES** | | | | | | | | | | Waterproof, fogproof, shockproof. Four-post reticle. From K.B.I. |
| HI0405 | 4 | 26 | — | 4 | 12 | 1 | Int. | 9.1 | NA | |
| HI0413 | 3-9 | 28-12 | — | 3.4-2.9 | 12 | 1 | Int. | 9.8 | NA | |
| HI0480 Compact | 4 | 21 | — | 4.1 | 9.9 | 1 | Int. | 9.1 | NA | |
| HI0499 Pistol | 4 | 9 | — | 14.5 | 9.5 | 1 | Int. | 9.5 | NA | |
| HI0502 Pistol | 2.5 | 12.6 | — | 13 | 8.9 | 1 | Int. | 9.1 | NA | |
| **KILHAM** | | | | | | | | | | Unlimited eye relief; internal click adjustments; crosshair reticle. Fits Thompson/Center rail mounts, for S&W K, N, Ruger Blackhawk, Super, Super Single-Six, Contender. |
| Hutson Handgunner II | 1.7 | 8 | — | 5½ | 7/8 | Int. | 5.1 | 119.95 | | |
| Hutson Handgunner | 3 | 8 | — | 10-12 | 6 | 7/8 | Int. | 5.3 | 119.95 | |
| **LASER AIM** | | | | | | | | | | [1]Laser sight. Battery life 45 min. Dot size 2" @ 300 ft. [2]Dot size 1" @ 300 ft. [3]Red dot sight. Dot size 3" @ 300 ft. (LA99), 6" (LA9750), 10" (LA9750-10). From Emerging Technologies, Inc. |
| LA5[1] | — | — | — | — | 2 | .75 | Int. | 1.2 | 239.00 | |
| LA5 Magnum[1,2] | — | — | — | — | 2.75 | .75 | Int. | 1.3 | 265.00 | |
| LA7[1] | — | — | — | — | 1.5 | 1.5 | Int. | 1.7 | 265.00 | |
| LA99[3] | — | — | — | — | 5.25 | 1 | Int. | NA | 135.00 | |
| LA9750[3] | — | — | — | — | 5.25 | 50mm | Int. | NA | 230.00 | |
| LA-9750-10[3] | — | — | — | — | 5.25 | 50mm | Int. | NA | 230.00 | |
| **LASER DEVICES** | | | | | | | | | | Projects high intensity beam of laser light onto target as an aiming point. Adj. for w. & e. [1]Diode laser system. From Laser Devices, Inc. |
| He Ne FA-6 | — | — | — | — | 6.2 | — | Int. | 11 | 229.50 | |
| He Ne FA-9 | — | — | — | — | 12 | — | Int. | 16 | 299.00 | |
| He Ne FA-9P | — | — | — | — | 9 | — | Int. | 14 | 299.00 | |

**CAUTION:** PRICES CHANGE, CHECK AT GUNSHOP.

| Maker and Model | Magn. | Field at 100 Yds. (feet) | Relative Brightness | Eye Relief (in.) | Length (in.) | Tube Dia. (in.) | W&E Adjustments | Weight (ozs.) | Price | Other Data |
|---|---|---|---|---|---|---|---|---|---|---|
| **Laser Devices** (cont.) | | | | | | | | | | |
| FA-4[1] | — | — | — | — | 4.5 | — | Int. | 3.5 | 299.00 | |
| **LASERSIGHT** | | | | | | | | | | Projects a highly visible beam of concentrated laser light onto the target. Adjustable for w. & e. Visible up to 500 yds. at night. For handguns, rifles, shotguns. Uses two standard 9V batteries. From Imatronic Lasersight. |
| LS45 | 0 | — | — | — | 7.5 | — | Int. | 8.5 | 245.00 | |
| LS25 | 0 | — | — | — | 6 | ¾ | Int. | 3.5 | 270.00 | |
| LS55 | 0 | — | — | — | 7 | 1 | Int. | 7 | 299.00 | |
| **LEATHERWOOD** | | | | | | | | | | Compensates for bullet drop via external circular cam. Matte gray finish. Designed specifically for the M1A/M-14 rifle. Quick Detachable model for rifles with Weaver-type bases. From North American Specialties. |
| ART II | 3.0-8.8 | 31-12 | — | 3.5 | 13.9 | 1 | Int. | 42 | 750.00 | |
| **LEATHERWOOD-MEOPTA, INC.** | | | | | | | | | | ART CZ-4 and CZ-6 have range-finding reticles with hold-over marks, multi-coated optics. Black or gray finish. From Leatherwood-Meopta, Inc. |
| ART II | 3.0-8.8 | 31-12 | — | 3.5 | 13.9 | 1 | Int. | 42 | 750.00 | |
| ART CZ-4 | 4 | 32 | — | — | 11 | 1 | Int. | 13.4 | 257.90 | |
| ART CZ-6 | 6 | 21 | — | — | 13.7 | 1 | Int. | 18.3 | 287.90 | |
| **LEUPOLD** | | | | | | | | | | Constantly centered reticles, choice of Duplex, tapered CPC, Leupold Dot, Crosshair and Dot. CPC and Dot reticles extra. [1]2x and 4x scopes have from 12"-24" of eye relief and are suitable for handguns, top ejection arms and muzzleloaders. [2]3x9 Compact, 6x Compact, 12x, 3x9, 3.5x10 and 6.5x20 come with adjustable objective. [3]Target scopes have 1-min. divisions with ¼-min. clicks, and adjustable objectives. 50-ft. Focus Adaptor available for indoor target ranges, **$51.80**. Sunshade available for all adjustable objective scopes, **$19.60-37.50**. [4]Also available in matte finish for about **$22.00** extra. [5]Silver finish about **$22.00** extra. [6]Matte finish. Partial listing shown. **Contact Leupold for complete details.** |
| Vari-X III 3.5x10 STD Police | 3.5-10 | 29.5-10.7 | — | 3.6-4.6 | 12.5 | 1 | Int. | 13.5 | 610.70 | |
| M8-2X EER[1] | 1.7 | 21.2 | — | 12-24 | 7.9 | 1 | Int. | 6.0 | 246.40 | |
| M8-2X EER Silver[1] | 1.7 | 21.2 | — | 12-24 | 7.9 | 1 | Int. | 6.0 | 267.90 | |
| M8-4X EER[1] | 3.7 | 9 | — | 12-24 | 8.4 | 1 | Int. | 7.0 | 333.90 | |
| M8-4X EER Silver[1] | 3.7 | 9 | — | 12-24 | 8.4 | 1 | Int. | 7.0 | 333.90 | |
| Vari-X 2.5-8 EER | 2.5-8.0 | 13-4.3 | — | 11.7-12 | 9.7 | 1 | Int. | 10.9 | 501.10 | |
| M8-2.5X Compact | 2.3 | 39.5 | — | 4.9 | 8.0 | 1 | Int. | 6.5 | 273.20 | |
| M8-4X Compact | 3.6 | 25.5 | — | 4.5 | 9.2 | 1 | Int. | 7.5 | 292.90 | |
| 2-7x Compact | 2.5-6.6 | 41.7-16.5 | — | 5-3.7 | 9.9 | 1 | Int. | 8.5 | 373.20 | |
| 3-9x Compact | 3.2-8.6 | 34-13.5 | — | 4.0-3.0 | 11-11.3 | 1 | Int. | 11.0 | 387.50 | |
| M8-4X[4] | 4.0 | 24 | — | 4.0 | 10.7 | 1 | Int. | 9.3 | 292.90 | |
| M8-6X[6] | 5.9 | 17.7 | — | 4.3 | 11.4 | 1 | Int. | 10.0 | 310.90 | |
| M8-6x 42mm | 6.0 | 17 | — | 4.5 | 12 | 1 | Int. | 11.3 | 408.90 | |
| M8-12x A.O. Varmint | 11.6 | 9.1 | — | 4.2 | 13.0 | 1 | Int. | 13.5 | 508.90 | |
| BR-24X[3] | 24.0 | 4.7 | — | 3.2 | 13.8 | 1 | Int. | 15.3 | 803.60 | |
| BR-36X[3] | 36.0 | 3.2 | — | 3.4 | 14.1 | 1 | Int. | 15.6 | 841.10 | |
| Vari-X 3-9x Compact EFR A.O. | 3.8-8.6 | 34.0-13.5 | — | 4.0-3.0 | 11.0 | 1 | Int. | 11 | 442.90 | |
| Vari-X-II 1x4 | 1.6-4.2 | 70.5-28.5 | — | 4.3-3.8 | 9.2 | 1 | Int. | 9.0 | 330.40 | |
| Vari-X-II 2x7[4] | 2.5-6.6 | 42.5-17.8 | — | 4.9-3.8 | 11.0 | 1 | Int. | 10.5 | 373.20 | |
| Vari-X-II 3x9[1,4,5] | 3.3-8.6 | 32.3-14.0 | — | 4.1-3.7 | 12.3 | 1 | Int. | 13.5 | 376.80 | |
| Vari-X-II 3-9x50mm[4] | 3.3-8.6 | 32.3-14 | — | 4.7-3.7 | 12 | 1 | Int. | 13.6 | 437.50 | |
| Vari-X-II 4-12 A.O. Matte | 4.4-11.6 | 22.8-11.0 | — | 5.0-3.3 | 12.3 | 1 | Int. | 13.5 | 489.30 | |
| Vari-X-III 1.5x5 | 1.5-4.5 | 66.0-23.0 | — | 5.3-3.7 | 9.4 | 1 | Int. | 9.5 | 487.50 | |
| Vari-X-III 1.75-6x 32 | 1.9-5.6 | 47-18 | — | 4.8-3.7 | 9.8 | 1 | Int. | 11 | 507.10 | |
| Vari-X-III 2.5x8[4] | 2.6-7.8 | 37.0-13.5 | — | 4.7-3.7 | 11.3 | 1 | Int. | 11.5 | 525.00 | |
| Vari-X-III 3.5-10x50 A.O. | 3.3-9.7 | 29.5-10.7 | — | 4.6-3.6 | 12.4 | 1 | Int. | 13.0 | 696.40 | |
| Vari-X-III 3.5-10x50[2,4] | 3.3-9.7 | 29.5-10.7 | — | 4.6-3.6 | 12.4 | 1 | Int. | 14.4 | 641.10 | |
| Vari-X-III 4.5-14 | 4.7-13.7 | 20.8-7.4 | — | 5.0-3.7 | 12.4 | 1 | Int. | 14.5 | 632.10 | |
| Vari-X-III 6.5-20 A.O. Varmint | 6.5-19.2 | 14.2-5.5 | — | 5.3-3.6 | 14.2 | 1 | Int. | 17.5 | 717.90 | |
| Vari-X-III 6.5-20x Target EFR A.O. | 6.5-19.2 | — | — | 5.3-3.6 | 14.2 | 1 | Int. | 16.5 | 708.90 | |
| Mark 4 M3-6x | 6 | 17.7 | — | 4.5 | 13.1 | 30mm | Int. | 21 | 1,419.60 | |
| Mark 4 M1-10x[6] | 10 | 11.1 | — | 3.6 | 13⅛ | 1 | Int. | 21 | 1,419.60 | |
| Mark 4 M1-16x[6] | 16 | 6.6 | — | 4.1 | 12⅞ | 1 | Int. | 22 | 1,419.60 | |
| Mark 4 M3-10x[6] | 10 | 11.1 | — | 3.6 | 13⅛ | 1 | Int. | 21 | 1,419.60 | |
| Vari-X-III 6.5x20[2] | 6.5-19.2 | 14.2-5.5 | — | 5.3-3.6 | 14.2 | 1 | Int. | 16.0 | 637.50 | |
| **Rimfire** | | | | | | | | | | |
| Vari-X-II 2-7x RF Special | 3.6 | 25.5 | — | 4.5 | 9.2 | 1 | Int. | 7.5 | 373.20 | |
| **Shotgun** | | | | | | | | | | |
| M8 2x EER | 1.7 | 21.2 | — | 12-24 | 7.9 | 1 | Int. | 6.0 | 269.60 | |
| M8 4x | 3.7 | 9.0 | — | 12-24 | 8.4 | 1 | Int. | 6.0 | 314.30 | |
| Vari-X-II 1x4 | 1.6-4.2 | 70.5-28.5 | — | 4.3-3.8 | 9.2 | 1 | Int. | 9.0 | 353.60 | |
| Vari-X-II 2x7 | 2.5-6.6 | 42.5-17.8 | — | 4.9-3.8 | 11.0 | 1 | Int. | 9.0 | 398.20 | |
| **McMILLAN** | | | | | | | | | | 42mm obj. lens; ¼-MOA clicks; nitrogen filled, fogproof, waterproof; etched duplex-type reticle. [1]Tactical Scope with external adj. knobs, military reticle; 60+ min. adj. |
| Vision Master 2.5-10x | 2.5-10 | 14.2-4.4 | — | 4.3-3.3 | 13.3 | 30mm | Int. | 17.0 | $1,500 | |
| Vision Master Model I[1] | 2.5-10 | 14.2-4.4 | — | 4.3-3.3 | 13.3 | 30mm | Int. | 17.0 | $1,200 | |
| **MIRADOR** | | | | | | | | | | [1]Wide Angle scope. Multi-coated objective lens. Nitrogen filled; waterproof; shockproof. From Mirador Optical Corp. |
| RXW 4x40[1] | 4 | 37 | — | 3.8 | 12.4 | 1 | Int. | 12 | 179.95 | |
| RXW 1.5-5x20[1] | 1.5-5 | 46-17.4 | — | 4.3 | 11.1 | 1 | Int. | 10 | 188.95 | |
| RXW 3-9x40 | 3-9 | 43-14.5 | — | 3.1 | 12.9 | 1 | Int. | 13.4 | 251.95 | |
| **NICHOLS** | | | | | | | | | | [1]Matte finish; also avail. with high gloss. [2]Adj. obj. [3]Stainless; also 3-9x40, blue, **$144.00**. [4]50-yd. parallax, with 22 rings; also with adj. obj., **$130.00**. [5]Also in stainless. [6]50-yd. parallax, **$90.00**. [7]Also 3-9x40, **$124.00**. Imported by G.U., Inc. |
| **"Light" Series** | | | | | | | | | | |
| 1.5-5x20 WA | 1.5-5 | 80.8-24.2 | — | 3.2-4.5 | 9.5 | 1 | Int. | 10.1 | 264.00 | |
| 2-7x32 WA | 2-7 | 60.4-17.5 | — | 3.3-4.2 | 10.0 | 1 | Int. | 11.3 | 280.00 | |
| 3-9x40 WA | 3-9 | 40.2-13.3 | — | 3.2-3.9 | 11.7 | 1 | Int. | 12.9 | 290.00 | |
| 3-10x40 WA | 3-10 | 40.2-12.1 | — | 3.1-4.0 | 11.9 | 1 | Int. | 14.1 | 310.00 | |
| 4-12x44 WA A.O. | 4-12 | 30.1-10 | — | 3.1-3.6 | 12.3 | 1 | Int. | 16.7 | 320.00 | |
| **"Magnum Target"** | | | | | | | | | | |
| 12x44[2] | 12 | 8.7 | — | 3.1 | 14.3 | 1 | Int. | 19.1 | 525.00 | |
| 24x44[2] | 24 | 4.3 | — | 2.9 | 14.3 | 1 | Int. | 18.4 | 525.00 | |
| 6-20x44[2] | 6-20 | 17.4-5.4 | — | 3.1-3.0 | 14.4 | 1 | Int. | 19.8 | 577.00 | |
| **"Classic"** | | | | | | | | | | |
| 4x40 WA | 4 | 37.0 | — | 3.8 | 13.0 | 1 | Int. | 11.6 | 140.00 | |

| Maker and Model | Magn. | Field at 100 Yds. (feet) | Relative Brightness | Eye Relief (in.) | Length (in.) | Tube Dia. (in.) | W&E Adjustments | Weight (ozs.) | Price | Other Data |
|---|---|---|---|---|---|---|---|---|---|---|
| **Nichols (cont.)** | | | | | | | | | | |
| 6x40 WA | 6 | 24.5 | — | 3.3 | 13.0 | 1 | Int. | 11.6 | 142.00 | |
| 1.5-4.5x WA | 1.5-4.5 | 54.0-22.0 | — | 3.4-3.3 | 11.5 | 1 | Int. | 10.9 | 163.00 | |
| 2-7x32 WA | 2-7 | 36.7-15.8 | — | 2.8-2.6 | 11.7 | 1 | Int. | 10.9 | 163.00 | |
| 3-9x32 WA[3] | 3-9 | 39.3-13.1 | — | 3.4-2.9 | 11.4 | 1 | Int. | 10.5 | 163.00 | |
| 4-12x40 | 4-12 | 30.0-11.0 | — | 3.9-3.2 | 12.3 | 1 | Int. | 12.3 | 170.00 | |
| **"Air Gun/Rimfire"** | | | | | | | | | | |
| 4x32[4] | 4 | 28.5 | — | 3.1 | 12.2 | 1 | Int. | 10.7 | 105.00 | |
| 2-7x32 WA A.O. | 2-7 | 36.7-15.7 | — | 2.8-2.6 | 11.8 | 1 | Int. | 10.5 | 187.00 | |
| **"Classic Handgun"** | | | | | | | | | | |
| 2x20[5] | 2 | 17.0 | — | 8.6-19.5 | 7.4 | 1 | Int. | 7.5 | 135.00 | |
| 2-7x28[5] | 2-7 | 40.0-9.7 | — | 8.9-19.5 | 9.0 | 1 | Int. | 9.0 | 260.00 | |
| **"Bullet"** | | | | | | | | | | |
| 4x32[6] | 4 | 28.5 | — | 3.1 | 12.2 | 1 | Int. | 10.7 | 82.00 | |
| 3-9x32[7] | 3-9 | 34.5-23.6 | — | 3.1-3.0 | 12.6 | 1 | Int. | 11.2 | 118.00 | |
| **NIKON** | | | | | | | | | | |
| 4x40 | 4 | 26.7 | — | 3.5 | 11.7 | 1 | Int. | 11.7 | 295.00 | Super multi-coated lenses and blackening of all internal metal parts for maximum light gathering capability; positive 1/4-MOA; fogproof; waterproof; shockproof; luster and matte finish. [1]Also available in matte silver finish, $448.00. From Nikon, Inc. |
| 1.5-4.5x20 | 1.5-4.5 | 67.8-22.5 | — | 3.7-3.2 | 10.1 | 1 | Int. | 9.5 | 387.00 | |
| 1.5-4.5x24 EER | 1.5-4.4 | 13.7-5.8 | — | 24-18 | 8.9 | 1 | Int. | 9.3 | 387.00 | |
| 2-7x32 | 2-7 | 46.7-13.7 | — | 3.9-3.3 | 11.3 | 1 | Int. | 11.3 | 426.00 | |
| 3-9x40[1] | 3-9 | 33.8-11.3 | — | 3.6-3.2 | 12.5 | 1 | Int. | 12.5 | 433.00 | |
| 3.5-10x50 | 3.5-10 | 25.5-8.9 | — | 3.9-3.8 | 13.7 | 1 | Int. | 15.5 | 653.00 | |
| 4-12x40 A.O. | 4-12 | 25.7-8.6 | — | 3.6-3.2 | 14 | 1 | Int. | 16.6 | 563.00 | |
| 4-12x50 A.O. | 4-12 | 25.4-8.5 | — | 3.6-3.5 | 14.0 | 1 | Int. | 18.3 | 712.00 | |
| 6.5-20x44 | 6.5-19.4 | 16.2-5.4 | — | 3.5-3.1 | 14.8 | 1 | Int. | 19.6 | 653.00 | |
| 2x20 EER | 2 | 22 | — | 26.4 | 8.1 | 1 | Int. | 6.3 | 234.00 | |
| **OAKSHORE ELECTRONICS** | | | | | | | | | | |
| UltraDOT | 0 | — | — | — | 5 | 1 | Int. | 3.9 | 139.00 | [1]Also 30mm tube, $199. [2]Variable intensity red dot appears in center of the duplex crosshair. Waterproof; nitrogen filled; coated lenses; 1/2-MOA dot at 100 yds. From Oakshore Electronic Sights, Inc. |
| MicroDOT 1.5-4.5x LER[2] | 1.5-4.5 | 14.9-6.9 | — | 12-24 | 9 | 1 | Int. | 10 | 259.00 | |
| MicroDOT 1.5-4.5x[2] | 1.5-4.5 | 73.8-24.6 | — | 3 | 9.8 | 1 | Int. | 10.5 | 259.00 | |
| MicroDOT 2-7x[2] | 2-7 | 48.2-13.8 | — | 3 | 11 | 1 | Int. | 12 | 279.00 | |
| MicroDOT 3-9x[2] | 3-9 | 37-12.5 | — | 3 | 12.3 | 1 | Int. | 13.4 | 299.00 | |
| MicroDOT 4-12x[2] | 1.5-4.5 | 28.1-9.2 | — | 3 | 14.4 | 1 | Int. | 21 | 399.00 | |
| **PENTAX** | | | | | | | | | | |
| 1.5-5x | 1.5-5 | 66-25 | — | 3-3 1/4 | 11 | 1 | Int. | 13 | 310.00 | Multi-coated lenses, fogproof, waterproof, nitrogen-filled. Penta-Plex reticle. Click 1/3-1/2-MOA adjustments. Matte finish $20.00 extra. [1]Also in matte chrome $260.00. [2]Also in matte chrome $390.00. [3]ProFinish (matte) $500. [4]ProFinish (matte) $530.00; satin chrome $550.00. [5]Chrome-Matte finish $400.00. [6]ProFinish (matte) $460.00; satin chrome $480.00. [7]Gloss finish; matte, $290.00. [8]Gloss finish; mattte $560.00. Imported by Pentax Corp. |
| 4x | 4 | 35 | — | 3 1/4 | 11.6 | 1 | Int. | 12.2 | 280.00 | |
| 6x | 6 | 20 | — | 3 1/4 | 13.4 | 1 | Int. | 13.5 | 310.00 | |
| 2-7x | 2-7 | 42.5-17 | — | 3-3 1/4 | 12 | 1 | Int. | 14 | 360.00 | |
| 3-9x | 3-9 | 33-13.5 | — | 3-3 1/4 | 13 | 1 | Int. | 15 | 380.00 | |
| 2.5x Lightseeker[7] | 2.5 | 55 | — | 3-3.5 | 10 | 1 | Int. | 9 | 280.00 | |
| 2-8x Lightseeker[6] | 2-8 | 53-17 | — | 3.5 | 11 7/8 | 1 | Int. | 14 | 450.00 | |
| 3-9x Lightseeker[4] | 3-9 | 36-14 | — | 3 | 12.7 | 1 | Int. | 15 | 540.00 | |
| 3-10x Lightseeker[8] | 3.5-10 | 29.5-11 | — | 3-3.25 | 14 | 1 | Int. | 19.5 | 540.00 | |
| 3-9x Mini | 3-9 | 26.5-10.5 | — | 3 3/4 | 10.4 | 1 | Int. | 13 | 320.00 | |
| 4-12x Mini[3] | 4-12 | 19-8 | — | 3.75-4 | 11.3 | 1 | Int. | 11.3 | 410.00 | |
| 6-18x[3] | 6-18 | 16-7 | — | 3-3.25 | 15.8 | 1 | Int. | 15.8 | 460.00 | |
| **Pistol** | | | | | | | | | | |
| 2x LER[1] | 2 | 21 | — | 10-24 | 8 3/4 | 1 | Int. | 6.8 | 240.00 | |
| 1.5-4x LER[2] | 1.5-4 | 16-11 | — | 11-25 | 10 | 1 | Int. | 11 | 360.00 | |
| 2 1/2-7x[5] | 2.5-7 | 12.0-7.5 | — | 11-28 | 12 | 1 | Int. | 12.5 | 400.00 | |
| **RWS** | | | | | | | | | | |
| 300 | 4 | — | — | 8 | 12 3/4 | 1 | Int. | 11 | 160.00 | Air gun scopes. All have Dyna-Plex reticle. Model 800 is for air pistols. Imported from Japan by Dynamit Nobel-RWS. |
| 350 | 4 | — | — | 8 | 10 | 1 | Int. | 10 | 125.00 | |
| 400 | 2-7 | — | — | 8 | 12 3/4 | 1 | Int. | 12 | 170.00 | |
| CS-10 | 2.5 | — | — | 8 | 5 3/4 | 1 | Int. | 7 | 125.00 | |
| **REDFIELD** | | | | | | | | | | |
| Ultimate Illuminator 3-9x | 3.4-9.1 | 27-9 | — | 3-3.5 | 15.1 | 30mm | Int. | 20.5 | 652.95 | *Accutrac feature avail. on these scopes at extra cost. Traditionals have round lenses. 4-Plex reticle is standard. [1]"Magnum Proof." Specially designed for magnum and auto pistols. Uses "Double Dovetail" mounts. Also in nickel-plated finish, 2 1/2x, $204.95, 4x, $253.95. [2]With matte finish $545.95. [3]Also available with matte finish at extra cost. [4]All Golden Five Star scopes come with Butler Creek flip-up lens covers. [5]Black anodized finish, also in nickel finish, $303.95. [6]56mm adj. objective; European #4 or 4-Plex reticle; comes with 30mm steel rings with Rotary Dovetail System. 1/4-min. click adj. Also in matte finish $754.95. [7]Also available nickel-plated $342.95. [8]Also with RealTree camo finish $581.95. [9]With RealTree camo finish $426.95. [10]Also available with RealTree camo finish $196.95. [11]With RealTree camo finish $264.95. [12]Also with RealTree camo finish $412.95; with matte finish $403.95. [13]With RealTree camo finish $314.95. Selected models shown. **Contact Redfield for full data.** |
| Ultimate Illuminator 3-12x[6] | 2.9-11.7 | 27-10.5 | — | 3-3 1/2 | 15.4 | 30mm | Int. | 23 | 745.95 | |
| Illuminator Trad. 3-9x | 2.9-8.7 | 33-11 | — | 3 1/2 | 12 3/4 | 1 | Int. | 17 | 505.95 | |
| Illuminator Widefield 4x | 4.2 | 28 | — | 3-3.5 | 11.7 | 1 | Int. | 13.5 | 376.95 | |
| Illuminator Widefield 2-7x | 2.0-6.8 | 56-17 | — | 3-3.5 | 11.7 | 1 | Int. | 13.5 | 498.95 | |
| Illuminator Widefield 3-9x[2,8] | 2.9-8.7 | 38-13 | — | 3 1/2 | 12 3/4 | 1 | Int. | 17 | 560.95 | |
| Tracker 4x[3,10] | 3.9 | 28.9 | — | 3 1/2 | 11.02 | 1 | Int. | 9.8 | 169.95 | |
| Tracker 6x[3] | 6.2 | 18 | — | 3.5 | 12.4 | 1 | Int. | 11.1 | 190.95 | |
| Tracker 2-7x[3] | 2.3-6.9 | 36.6-12.2 | — | 3 1/2 | 12.20 | 1 | Int. | 11.6 | 216.95 | |
| Tracker 3-9x[3,11] | 3.0-9.0 | 34.4-11.3 | — | 3 1/2 | 14.96 | 1 | Int. | 13.4 | 244.95 | |
| Traditional 4x 3/4" | 4 | 24 1/2 | 27 | 3 1/2 | 9 3/8 | 3/4 | Int. | — | 161.95 | |
| Traditional 2 1/2x | 2 1/2 | 43 | 64 | 3 1/2 | 10 1/4 | 1 | Int. | 8 1/2 | 161.95 | |
| Golden Five Star 4x[4] | 4 | 28.5 | 58 | 3.75 | 11.3 | 1 | Int. | 9.75 | 236.95 | |
| Golden Five Star 6x[4] | 6 | 18 | 40 | 3.75 | 12.2 | 1 | Int. | 11.5 | 254.95 | |
| Golden Five Star 2-7x[4] | 2.4-7.4 | 42-14 | 207-23 | 3-3.75 | 11.25 | 1 | Int. | 12 | 303.95 | |
| Golden Five Star 3-9x[4,7] | 3.0-9.1 | 34-11 | 163-18 | 3-3.75 | 12.50 | 1 | Int. | 13 | 372.95 | |
| Golden Five Star 3-9x 50mm[4,12] | 3.0-9.1 | 36.0-11.5 | — | 3-3.5 | 12.8 | 1 | Int. | 16 | 359.95 | |
| Golden Five Star 4-12x A.O.*[4] | 3.9-11.4 | 27-9 | 112-14 | 3-3.75 | 13.8 | 1 | Int. | 16 | 416.95 | |
| Golden Five Star 6-18x A.O.*[4] | 6.1-18.1 | 18.6 | 50-6 | 3-3.75 | 14.3 | 1 | Int. | 18 | 439.95 | |

| Maker and Model | Magn. | Field at 100 Yds. (feet) | Relative Bright-ness | Eye Relief (in.) | Length (in.) | Tube Dia. (in.) | W&E Adjust-ments | Weight (ozs.) | Price | Other Data |
|---|---|---|---|---|---|---|---|---|---|---|
| **Redfield (cont.)** | | | | | | | | | | |
| I.E.R. 1-4x Shotgun[13] | 1.3-3.8 | 48-16 | — | 6 | 10.2 | 1 | Int. | 12 | **297.95** | |
| **Compact Scopes** | | | | | | | | | | |
| Golden Five Star Compact 4x | 3.8 | 28 | — | 3.5 | 9.75 | 1 | Int. | 8.8 | **225.95** | |
| Golden Five Star Compact 6x | 6.3 | 17.6 | — | 3.5 | 10.70 | 1 | Int. | 9.5 | **252.95** | |
| Golden Five Star Compact 2-7x | 2.4-7.1 | 40-16 | — | 3-3.5 | 9.75 | 1 | Int. | 9.8 | **300.95** | |
| Golden Five Star Compact 3-9x | 3.3-9.1 | 32-11.25 | — | 3-3.5 | 10.7 | 1 | Int. | 10.5 | **317.95** | |
| Golden Five Star Compact 4-12x | 4.1-12.4 | 22.4-8.3 | — | 3-3.5 | 12 | 1 | Int. | 13 | **402.95** | |
| **Pistol Scopes** | | | | | | | | | | |
| 2½xMP[1] | 2.5 | 9 | 64 | 14-19 | 9.8 | 1 | Int. | 10.5 | **224.95** | |
| 4xMP[1] | 3.6 | 9 | — | 12-22 | 9¹¹⁄₁₆ | 1 | Int. | 11.1 | **239.95** | |
| 2-6x[5] | 2-5.5 | 25-7 | — | 10-18 | 10.4 | 1 | Int. | 11 | **283.95** | |
| **Widefield Low Profile Compact** | | | | | | | | | | |
| Widefield 4xLP Compact | 3.7 | 33 | — | 3.5 | 9.35 | 1 | Int. | 10 | **279.95** | |
| Widefield 3-9x LP Compact | 3.3-9 | 37.0-13.7 | — | 3-3.5 | 10.20 | 1 | Int. | 13 | **355.95** | |
| **Low Profile Scopes** | | | | | | | | | | |
| Widefield 2¾xLP | 2¾ | 55½ | 69 | 3½ | 10½ | 1 | Int. | 8 | **260.95** | |
| Widefield 4xLP | 3.6 | 37½ | 84 | 3½ | 11½ | 1 | Int. | 10 | **290.95** | |
| Widefield 6xLP | 5.5 | 23 | — | 3½ | 12¾ | 1 | Int. | 11 | **315.95** | |
| Widefield 1¾x-5xLP | 1¾-5 | 70-27 | 136-21 | 3½ | 10¾ | 1 | Int. | 11½ | **357.95** | |
| Widefield 2x-7xLP* | 2-7 | 49-19 | 144-21 | 3½ | 11¾ | 1 | Int. | 13 | **366.95** | |
| Widefield 3x-9xLP*[9] | 3-9 | 39-15 | 112-18 | 3½ | 12½ | 1 | Int. | 14 | **407.95** | |
| **SCHMIDT & BENDER** | | | | | | | | | | |
| Vari-M 1¼-4x20[1] | 1¼-4 | 96-16 | — | 3¼ | 10.4 | 30mm | Int. | 12.3 | **619.99** | [1]All steel. 30-year warranty. All have ⅓-min. click adjustment, centered reticles, nitrogen filling. Most models avail. in aluminum with mounting rail. Available from Paul Jaeger, Inc./Dunn's. |
| Vari-M 1½-6x42 | 1½-6 | 60-19.5 | — | 3¼ | 12.2 | 30mm | Int. | 17.5 | **684.99** | |
| Vari-M 2½-10x56 | 2½-10 | 37.5-12 | — | 3¼ | 14.6 | 30mm | Int. | 21.9 | **804.99** | |
| All Steel 4-12x42 | 4-12 | 34.7-12 | — | 3¼ | 13.25 | 30mm | Int. | 23 | **736.99** | |
| **SHEPHERD** | | | | | | | | | | |
| 3940-E | 3-9 | 43.5-15 | 178-20 | 3.3 | 13 | 1 | Int. | 17 | **597.00** | [1]Also avail. as 310-1, 310-E, **$453.28**. [2]Also avail. as 310-P1, 310-P2, 310-P3, 310-Pla, 310-PE1, 310-P22, 310-P22 Mag., 310-PE, **453.28** [3]27-4 has 9" stadia circles, traj. for 22 rifles. [4]Click adj. for shotgun, carbine, blackpowder. All have patented Dual Reticle system with rangefinder bullet drop compensation; multi-coated lenses, waterprooof, shockproof, nitrogen filled, matte finish. From Shepherd Scope, Ltd. |
| 310-21[1,2] | 3-10 | 35.3-11.6 | 178-16 | 3-3.75 | 12.8 | 1 | Int. | 21 | **453.28** | |
| 27-4[3] | 2.5-7.5 | 42-14 | 164-18 | 2.5-3 | 11.6 | 1 | Int. | 16.3 | **389.00** | |
| CBS[4] | 1.5-5 | 82.5-27.5 | 45.5-40.9 | 2.5-3.25 | 11 | 1 | Int. | 14.9 | **500.00** | |
| **SIMMONS** | | | | | | | | | | |
| **44 Mag** | | | | | | | | | | |
| M-1043 | 2-7 | 56-16 | — | 3.3 | 11.8 | 1 | Int. | 13 | **256.95** | [1]Matte; also polished finish. [2]Silver; also black matte or polished. [3]Black polish finish. [4]Granite finish; black polish **$216.95**; silver $218.95; also with 50mm obj., black granite **$336.95**. [5]Camouflage. [6]Black polish. [7]With ring mounts. **Only selected models shown. Contact Simmons Outdoor Corp. for complete details.** |
| M-1044 | 3-10 | 36.2-10.5 | — | 3.4-3.3 | 13.1 | 1 | Int. | 16.3 | **268.95** | |
| M-1045 | 4-12 | 27-9 | — | 3 | 12.6 | 1 | Int. | 19.5 | **280.95** | |
| **Prohunter** | | | | | | | | | | |
| 7700[1] | 2-7 | 58-17 | — | 3.25 | 11.6 | 1 | Int. | 12.4 | **159.95** | |
| 7710[2] | 3-9 | 40-15 | — | 3 | 12.6 | 1 | Int. | 13.4 | **169.95** | |
| 7715[3] | 4-12 | — | — | — | — | 1 | Int. | — | **179.95** | |
| 7720 | 6-18 | 38-13 | — | 2.5 | 12.5 | 1 | Int. | 13.5 | **209.95** | |
| 7725 | 4.5 | 26 | — | 3 | 9.9 | 1 | Int. | 9.9 | **109.95** | |
| **Whitetail Classic** | | | | | | | | | | |
| WTC10[4] | 4 | 36.8 | — | 4 | 12.3 | 1 | Int. | 9.8 | **139.95** | |
| WTC11[4] | 1.5-5 | 80-23.5 | — | 3.4-3.2 | 12.6 | 1 | Int. | 11.8 | **174.95** | |
| WTC12[4] | 2.5-8 | 46.5-14.5 | — | 3.2-3 | 12.6 | 1 | Int. | 12.8 | **189.95** | |
| WTC13[4] | 3.5-10 | 35-12 | — | 3.2-3 | 12.4 | 1 | Int. | 12.8 | **209.95** | |
| WTC14[4] | 2-10 | 50-11 | — | 3 | 12.8 | 1 | Int. | 16.9 | **256.95** | |
| **Deerfield** | | | | | | | | | | |
| 21006 | 4 | 28 | — | 4 | 12.0 | 1 | Int. | 9.1 | **74.95** | |
| 21010 | 3-9 | 38-12 | — | 3.4 | 12.6 | 1 | Int. | 12.3 | **91.95** | |
| 21029 | 3-9 | 32-11 | — | 3.4 | 12.6 | 1 | Int. | 12.3 | **104.95** | |
| 21031 | 4-12 | 28-11 | — | 3-2.8 | 13.9 | 1 | Int. | 14.6 | **139.95** | |
| **Gold Medal Silhouette** | | | | | | | | | | |
| 23000 | 12 | 8.7 | — | 3.1-3 | 14.5 | 1 | Int. | 18.3 | **449.95** | |
| 23001 | 24 | 4.3 | — | 3 | 14.5 | 1 | Int. | 18.3 | **455.95** | |
| 23002 | 6-20 | 17.4-5.4 | — | 3 | 14.5 | 1 | Int. | 18.3 | **499.95** | |
| **Gold Medal Handgun** | | | | | | | | | | |
| 22002[6] | 2.5-7 | 9.7-4.0 | — | 8.9-19.4 | 9.25 | 1 | Int. | 9.0 | **319.95** | |
| 22004[6] | 2 | 3.9 | — | 8.6-19.5 | 7.3 | 1 | Int. | 7.4 | **219.95** | |
| 22006[6] | 4 | 8.9 | — | 9.8-18.7 | 9 | 1 | Int. | 8.8 | **249.95** | |
| **Shotgun** | | | | | | | | | | |
| 21005 | 2.5 | 29 | — | 4.6 | 7.1 | 1 | Int. | 7.2 | **85.95** | |
| 7790 | 4 | 16 | — | 5.5 | 8.8 | 1 | Int. | 9.2 | **139.95** | |
| **Rimfire** | | | | | | | | | | |
| 1022[7] | 4 | 36 | — | 3.5 | 11.5 | ¾ | Int. | 10 | **74.95** | |
| 21007[7] | 4 | 29 | — | 3.5 | 12.0 | ¾ | Int. | 11.5 | **108.95** | |
| **STEINER** | | | | | | | | | | |
| **Penetrator** | | | | | | | | | | |
| 6x42 | 6 | 20.4 | — | 3.1 | 14.8 | 26mm | Int. | 14 | **889.00** | Waterproof, fogproof, nitrogen filled, accordion-type eye cup. From Pioneer Marketing & Research, Inc. |
| 1.5x6x42 | 1.5-6 | 64-21 | — | 3.1 | 12.8 | 30mm | Int. | 17 | **1,099.00** | |

| Maker and Model | Magn. | Field at 100 Yds. (feet) | Relative Brightness | Eye Relief (in.) | Length (in.) | Tube Dia. (in.) | W&E Adjustments | Weight (ozs.) | Price | Other Data |
|---|---|---|---|---|---|---|---|---|---|---|
| **Steiner** (cont.) | | | | | | | | | | |
| 3-12x56 | 3-12 | 29-10 | — | 3.1 | 14.8 | 30mm | Int. | 21 | 1,299.00 | |
| **SWAROVSKI HABICHT** | | | | | | | | | | |
| 4x32 | 4 | 33 | — | 3¼ | 11.3 | 1 | Int. | 15 | 625.00 | All models offered in either steel or lightweight alloy tubes. Weights shown are for lightweight versions. Choice of nine constantly centered reticles. Eyepiece recoil mechanism and rubber ring shield to protect face. American-style plex reticle available in 2.2-9x42 and 3-12x56 traditional European scopes. Imported by Swarovski Optik North America Ltd. |
| 6x42 | 6 | 23 | — | 3¼ | 12.6 | 1 | Int. | 17.9 | 690.00 | |
| 8x56 | 8 | 17 | — | 3¼ | 14.4 | 1 | Int. | 23 | 819.00 | |
| 1.5-6x42 | 1.5-6 | 61-21 | — | 3¼ | 12.6 | 30mm | Int. | 16 | 900.00 | |
| 2.2-9x42 | 2.2-9 | 39.5-15 | — | 3¼ | 13.3 | 30mm | Int. | 15.5 | 1,050.00 | |
| 3-12x56 | 3-12 | 30-11 | — | 3¼ | 15.25 | 1 | Int. | 18 | 1,165.00 | |
| **AL Scopes** | | | | | | | | | | |
| 4x32A | 4 | 30 | — | 3.2 | 11.5 | 1 | Int. | 10.8 | 495.00 | |
| 6x36A | 6 | 21 | — | 3.2 | 11.9 | 1 | Int. | 11.5 | 530.00 | |
| 1.5-4.5x20A | 1.5-4.5 | 75-25.8 | — | 3.5 | 9.53 | 1 | Int. | 10.6 | 595.00 | |
| 3-9x36 | 3-9 | 39-13.5 | — | 3.3 | 11.9 | 1 | Int. | 13 | 640.00 | |
| **SWIFT** | | | | | | | | | | |
| 600 4x15 | 4 | 16.2 | — | 2.4 | 11 | ¾ | Int. | 4.7 | 22.00 | All Swift scopes, with the exception of the 4x15, have Quadraplex reticles and are fogproof and waterproof. The 4x15 has crosshair reticle and is non-waterproof. [1]Available in black or silver finish—same price. From Swift Instruments. |
| 601 3-7x20 | 3-7 | 25-12 | — | 3-2.9 | 11 | 1 | Int. | 5.6 | 52.00 | |
| 650 4x32 | 4 | 29 | — | 3.5 | 12 | 1 | Int. | 9 | 78.00 | |
| 653 4x40WA[1] | 4 | 35.5 | — | 3.75 | 12.25 | 1 | Int. | 12 | 95.00 | |
| 654 3-9x32 | 3-9 | 35.75-12.75 | — | 3 | 12.75 | 1 | Int. | 13.75 | 94.00 | |
| 656 3-9x40WA[1] | 3-9 | 42.5-13.5 | — | 2.75 | 12.75 | 1 | Int. | 14 | 102.00 | |
| 657 6x40 | 6 | 18 | — | 3.75 | 13 | 1 | Int. | 10 | 99.50 | |
| 660 4x20 | 4 | 25 | — | 4 | 11.8 | 1 | Int. | 9 | 79.00 | |
| 664 4-12x40[1] | 4-12 | 27-9 | — | 3-2.8 | 13.3 | 1 | Int. | 14.8 | 142.00 | |
| 665 1.5-4.5x21 | 1.5-4.5 | 69-24.5 | — | 3.5-3 | 10.9 | 1 | Int. | 9.6 | 97.50 | |
| 666 Shotgun 1x20 | 1 | 113 | — | 3.2 | 7.5 | 1 | Int. | 9.6 | 99.50 | |
| **Pistol Scopes** | | | | | | | | | | |
| 661 4x32 | 4 | 90 | — | 10-22 | 9.2 | 1 | Int. | 9.5 | 110.50 | |
| 662 2.5x32 | 2.5 | 14.3 | — | 9-22 | 8.9 | 1 | Int. | 9.3 | 99.95 | |
| 663 2x20[1] | 2 | 18.3 | — | 9-21 | 7.2 | 1 | Int. | 8.4 | 105.00 | |
| **TASCO** | | | | | | | | | | |
| **World Class** | | | | | | | | | | |
| WA4x40 | 4 | 36 | 100.0 | 3 | 13 | 1 | Int. | 11.5 | 160.00 | [1]Water, fog & shockproof; fully coated optics; ¼-min. click stops; haze filter caps; lifetime warranty. [2]30/30 range finding reticle. [3]World Class Wide Angle; Supercon multi-coated optics; Opti-Centered® 30/30 range finding reticle; lifetime warranty. [4]⅓ greater zoom range. [5]Trajectory compensating scopes, Opti-Centered® stadia reticle. [6]Anodized finish. [7]True one-power scope. [8]Coated optics; crosshair reticle; ring mounts included to fit most 22, 10mm receivers. [9]Fits Remington 870, 1100, 11-87. [10]Electronic dot reticle with rheostat; coated optics; adj. for windage and elevation; waterproof, shockproof, fogproof; Lithium battery; 3x power booster avail.; matte black or matte aluminum finish; dot or T-3 reticle. [11]TV view. [12]Also matte aluminum finish. [13]Also with crosshair reticle. [14]Also 30/30 reticle. [15]Dot size 1.5" at 100 yds.; waterproof. [16]Stainless finish. [17]Black matte or stainless finish. **Contact Tasco for details on complete line.** |
| WA4x32ST[16] | 4 | 34 | — | 3 | — | 1 | Int. | 10.5 | 160.00 | |
| WA13.5x20[1,3,10] | 1-3.5 | 115-31 | 400.0-32.4 | 3.5 | 9.75 | 1 | Int. | 10.2 | 229.00 | |
| WA1.75-5x20[1,3] | 1.75-5 | 72-24 | 129.9-16.0 | 3 | 10⅝ | 1 | Int. | 9.8 | 257.00 | |
| WA2.5x40 | 2.5-8 | 44-14 | — | 3 | — | 1 | Int. | 14.25 | 199.00 | |
| WA27x32[1,3,9] | 2-7 | 56-17 | 256.0-20.2 | 3.25 | 11.5 | 1 | Int. | 12 | 191.00 | |
| WA39x40[1,3,6,11] | 3-9 | 43.5-15 | 176.8-19.3 | 3⅛ | 12.75 | 1 | Int. | 12.5 | 199.00 | |
| **World Class Compact** | | | | | | | | | | |
| CW4x32LE | 4 | 25 | 64 | 5 | 10.0 | 1 | Int. | 9.5 | 183.00 | |
| CW28x32 | 2-8 | 55-16 | — | 3 | 10.5 | 1 | Int. | 11.5 | 214.00 | |
| **World Class Airgun** | | | | | | | | | | |
| AG4x40A | 4 | 36 | — | 3 | 13 | 1 | Int. | 14 | 267.00 | |
| AG39x50WA | 3-9 | 41-14 | — | 3 | 15 | 1 | Int. | 17.5 | 428.00 | |
| **World Class Electronic** | | | | | | | | | | |
| ER39x40WA | 3-9 | 41-14 | 176.8-19.3 | 3 | 12.75 | 1 | Int. | 16 | 458.00 | |
| **World Class Mag IV-44** | | | | | | | | | | |
| WC2510x44[6] | 2.5-10 | 41-11 | — | 3.5 | 12.5 | 1 | Int. | 14.4 | 272.00 | |
| **World Class TS** | | | | | | | | | | |
| TS24x44 | 24 | 4.5 | — | 3 | 14 | 1 | Int. | 17.9 | 430.00 | |
| TS624x44 | 6-24 | 15-4.5 | — | 3 | 14 | 1 | Int. | 18.5 | 510.00 | |
| **World Class TR** | | | | | | | | | | |
| TR39x40WA | 3-9 | 41-14 | — | 3 | 12.75 | 1 | Int. | 12.5 | 275.00 | |
| **World Class Pistol** | | | | | | | | | | |
| PWC2x22[12] | 2 | 25 | — | 11-20 | 8.75 | 1 | Int. | 7.3 | 206.00 | |
| PWC4x28[12] | 4 | 8 | — | 12-19 | 9.45 | 1 | Int. | 7.9 | 252.00 | |
| **Mag IV** | | | | | | | | | | |
| W312x40[1,2,4] | 3-12 | 33-11 | 176.8-10.8 | 3 | 12⅛ | 1 | Int. | 12 | 183.00 | |
| W416x40[1,2,4] | 4-16 | 25.5-7 | 100.0-6.2 | 3 | 14.25 | 1 | Int. | 16.75 | 229.00 | |
| W624x40 | 6-24 | 17-4 | — | 3 | 15.25 | 1 | Int. | 16.8 | 290.00 | |
| **Titan** | | | | | | | | | | |
| TT1.56x42 | 1.5-6 | 59-20 | 748-49 | 3.5-4 | 12 | 30mm | Int. | 16.4 | 612.00 | |
| TT39x42 | 3-9 | 37-13 | 196-22 | 3.5-4 | 12.5 | 30mm | Int. | 16.8 | 733.00 | |
| **Golden Antler** | | | | | | | | | | |
| GA4x32TV | 4 | 32 | — | 3 | 13 | 1 | Int. | 12.7 | 79.00 | |
| GA2.510x44TV | 2.5-10 | 35-9 | — | 3.5 | 12.5 | 1 | Int. | 14.4 | 214.00 | |
| GA39x32TV[11] | 3-9 | 39-13 | — | 3 | — | 1 | Int. | 12.2 | 102.00 | |
| **Silver Antler** | | | | | | | | | | |
| SA2.5x32 | 2.5 | 42 | — | 3¼ | 11 | 1 | Int. | 10 | 86.00 | |
| SA4x40 | 4 | 32 | — | 3 | 12 | 1 | Int. | 12.5 | 99.00 | |
| SA39x40 | 3-9 | 39-13 | — | 3 | 12.5 | 1 | Int. | 13 | 135.00 | |
| SA2.150x44 | 2.5-10 | 35-9 | — | 3.5 | — | 1 | Int. | 14.4 | 214.00 | |
| **Rubber Armored** | | | | | | | | | | |
| RC39x40A | 3-9 | 35-12 | — | 3.25 | 12.5 | 1 | Int. | 14.3 | 206.00 | |
| **TR Scopes** | | | | | | | | | | |
| TR39x40WA | 3-9 | 41-14 | — | 3 | 13 | 1 | Int. | 12.5 | 275.00 | |
| TR416x40 | 4-16 | 26-7 | — | 3 | 14.25 | 1 | Int. | 16.8 | 298.00 | |
| TR624x40 | 6-24 | 17-4 | — | 3 | 15.5 | 1 | Int. | 17.5 | 336.00 | |
| **Shotgun Scopes** | | | | | | | | | | |
| WA1.75-5x20[9] | 1.75-5 | 74-24 | — | 3 | 10.5 | 1 | Int. | 10 | 257.00 | |

**CAUTION:** PRICES CHANGE, CHECK AT GUNSHOP.

| Maker and Model | Magn. | Field at 100 Yds. (feet) | Relative Brightness | Eye Relief (in.) | Length (in.) | Tube Dia. (in.) | W&E Adjustments | Weight (ozs.) | Price | Other Data |
|---|---|---|---|---|---|---|---|---|---|---|
| **Tasco** (cont.) | | | | | | | | | | |
| WA13.5x20[9] | 1-3.5 | 103-31 | — | 3 | 9 | 1 | Int. | 12 | 229.00 | |
| **Airgun** | | | | | | | | | | |
| AG4x20 | 4 | 20 | — | 2.5 | 10.75 | .75 | Int. | 5 | 48.00 | |
| AG4x32 | 4 | 28 | — | 3 | 12 | 1 | Int. | 13 | 220.00 | |
| AG4x32N | 4 | 30 | — | 3 | — | 1 | Int. | 13.5 | 128.00 | |
| AG39x50WA | 3-9 | 27-9 | — | 3 | 15 | 1 | Int. | 17.5 | 428.00 | |
| **Rimfire** | | | | | | | | | | |
| RF4x15[6] | 4 | 22.5 | 13.6 | 2.5 | 11 | .75 | Int. | 4 | 17.00 | |
| RF4x32 | 4 | 31 | — | 3 | 12.5 | 1 | Int. | 12.6 | 91.00 | |
| RF37x20 | 3-7 | 24-11 | — | 2.5 | 11.5 | .75 | Int. | 5.7 | 49.00 | |
| P1.5x15 | 1.5 | 22.5 | — | 9.5-20.75 | 8.75 | .75 | Int. | 3.25 | 37.00 | |
| **Propoint** | | | | | | | | | | |
| PDP2[10,12] | 1 | 25-12 | — | — | 5 | 30mm | Int. | 5.5 | 267.00 | |
| PDP3[10,12] | 1 | 40 | — | — | 5 | 30mm | Int. | 5.5 | 367.00 | |
| PDP4[17] | 1 | 82 | — | — | — | 45mm | Int. | 6.14 | 458.00 | |
| PB1[13] | 3 | 35 | — | 3 | 5.5 | 30mm | Int. | 6.3 | 183.00 | |
| PB3 | 2 | 30 | — | — | 1.25 | 30mm | Int. | 2.6 | 214.00 | |
| **Proclass** | | | | | | | | | | |
| P2x22S[14] | 2 | 23-18 | — | 10-24 | 6.5 | 30mm | Int. | 7.7 | 291.00 | |
| P3x22[14,17] | 3 | 13-6 | — | 12-24 | 8.25 | 30mm | Int. | 8.5 | 283.00 | |
| **World Class Plus** | | | | | | | | | | |
| WCP4x44 | 4 | 32 | — | 3¼ | 12.75 | 1 | Int. | 13.5 | 310.00 | |
| WCP3.510x50 | 3.5-10 | 30-10.5 | — | 3¾ | 13 | 1 | Int. | 17.1 | 489.00 | |
| WCP6x44 | 6 | 21 | — | 3.25 | 12.75 | 1 | Int. | 13.6 | 310.00 | |
| WCP39x44 | 3-9 | 39-14 | — | 3.5 | 12.75 | 1 | Int. | 15.8 | 370.00 | |
| **LaserPoint[15]** | — | — | — | — | 2 | ⅝ | Int. | .75 | 458.00 | |
| **THOMPSON/CENTER RECOIL PROOF PISTOL SCOPES** | | | | | | | | | | [1]Also silver finish, **$265.00** (#8316); with rail mount, black, **$257.00** (#8317); with lighted reticle, black, **$295.00** (#8326); with rail, lighted reticle, black, **$300.00** (#8327). [2]With lighted reticle, **$225.00** (#8322); silver, **$235.00** (#8323); with lighted reticle, rail mount, black, **$235.00** (#8320). [3]With lighted reticle, **$295.00** (#8626). [4]With rail mount, lighted reticle, **$170** (#8640). From Thompson/Center. |
| 8312 Compact Rail[2] | 2.5 | 15 | 64 | 9-21 | 7.25 | 1 | Int. | 6.6 | 160.00 | |
| 8315 Compact[1] | 2.5-7 | 15-5 | 125-16 | 8-21 | 9.25 | 1 | Int. | 9.2 | 250.00 | |
| **Rifle Scopes** | | | | | | | | | | |
| 8621 Compact | 1.5-5 | 61-20 | 177-16 | 3 | 10 | 1 | Int. | 8.5 | 220.00 | |
| 8623 Compact WA[3] | 3-9 | 33-11 | 113-13 | 3 | 10.75 | 1 | Int. | 9.9 | 241.00 | |
| 8624 Compact[4] | 4 | 26 | 64 | 3 | 10 | 1 | Int. | 8.2 | 183.00 | |
| **TRIJICON SPECTRUM** | | | | | | | | | | [1]Self-luminous low-light reticle glows in poor light; allows choice of red, amber or green via a selector ring on objective end. [2]Advanced Combat Optical Gunsight for AR-15, M-16, with integral mount. [3]Reticle glows red in low light. From Trijicon, Inc. |
| 6x56[1] | 6 | 24 | — | 3.0 | 14.1 | 1 | Int. | 20.3 | 579.00 | |
| 1-3x20[1] | 1-3 | 94-33 | — | 3.7-4.9 | 9.6 | 1 | Int. | 13.2 | 594.00 | |
| 3-9x40[1] | 3-9 | 35-14 | — | 3.3-3.0 | 13.1 | 1 | Int. | 16.0 | 569.00 | |
| 3-9x56[1] | 3-9 | 35-14 | — | 3.3-3.0 | 14.2 | 1 | Int. | 21.5 | 649.00 | |
| ACOG 3.5x35 | 3.5 | 29 | — | 2.4 | 8.0 | — | Int. | 14.0 | 995.00 | |
| ACOG 4x32[2] | 4 | 37 | — | 1.5 | 5.8 | — | Int. | 9.7 | 695.00 | |
| 4x32 Red[3] | 4 | 29 | — | 3.3 | 11.6 | 1 | Int. | 10.2 | 298.00 | |
| **UNERTL** | | | | | | | | | | [1]Dural ¼-MOA click mounts. Hard coated lenses. Non-rotating objective lens focusing. [2]¼-MOA click mounts. [3]With target mounts. [4]With calibrated head. [5]Same as 1" Target but without objective lens focusing. [6]Price with ¼-MOA click mounts. [7]With new Posa mounts. [8]Range focus unit near rear of tube. Price is with Posa or standard mounts. Magnum clamp. From Unertl. |
| 1" Target | 6,8,10 | 16-10 | 17.6-6.25 | 2 | 21½ | ¾ | Ext. | 21 | 233.00 | |
| 1¼" Target[1] | 8,10,12,14 | 12-16 | 15.2-5 | 2 | 25 | ¾ | Ext. | 21 | 302.00 | |
| 1½" Target | 8,10,12,14, 16,18,20 | 11.5-3.2 | — | 2¼ | 25½ | ¾ | Ext. | 31 | 326.00 | |
| 2" Target[2] | 8,10,12,14, 16,18,24, 30,36 | 8 | 22.6-2.5 | 2¼ | 26¼ | 1 | Ext. | 44 | 431.00 | |
| Varmint, 1¼"[3] | 6,8,10,12 | 1-7 | 28-7.1 | 2½ | 19½ | ⅞ | Ext. | 26 | 296.00 | |
| Ultra Varmint, 2"[4] | 8,10,12,15 | 12.6-7 | 39.7-11 | 2½ | 24 | 1 | Ext. | 34 | 420.00 | |
| Small Game[5] | 4,6 | 25-17 | 19.4-8.4 | 2¼ | 18 | ¾ | Ext. | 16 | 175.00 | |
| Vulture[6] | 8 | 11.2 | 29 | 3-4 | 15⅝ | 1 | Ext. | 15½ | 333.00 | |
| | 10 | 10.9 | 18½ | — | 16⅛ | 1 | | | | |
| Programmer 200[7] | 8,10,12,14, 16,18,20, 24,30,36 | 11.3-4 | 39-1.9 | — | 26½ | 1 | Ext. | 45 | 532.00 | |
| BV-20[8] | 20 | 8 | 4.4 | 4.4 | 17⅞ | 1 | Ext. | 21¼ | 390.00 | |
| **U.S. OPTICS** | | | | | | | | | | Extra-heavy thickness tubes; extra-long turrets; recoil shoulder on turret; individual adj. w&e rebound spring; up to 300 m.o.a. elevation travel; ranging reticles; front or rear focal plane reticle location; up to 40mm dia. tube; up to 77mm obj. lens; multi-coated lenses. Made in U.S. by United States Optical Technologies, Inc. |
| **SN/TR-1 System** | | | | | | | | | | |
| 10x | 10 | 11.3 | — | 3.8 | 14.5 | 30mm | Int. | 24 | 695.00 | |
| 15x | 15 | 8.6 | — | 4.3 | 16.5 | 30mm | Int. | 27 | 749.00 | |
| 20x | 20 | 5.8 | — | 3.8 | 18.0 | 30mm | Int. | 29 | 795.00 | |
| 24x | 24 | 5.0 | — | 3.4 | 18.0 | 30mm | Int. | 31 | 849.00 | |
| 30x | 30 | 4.6 | — | 3.5 | 18.0 | 30mm | Int. | 32 | 895.00 | |
| 36x | 36 | 4.0 | — | 3.6 | 18.0 | 30mm | Int. | 32 | 949.00 | |
| 40x | 40 | 3.6 | — | 3.7 | 18.0 | 30mm | Int. | 32 | 1,020.00 | |
| 50x | 50 | 3.0 | — | 3.8 | 18.0 | 30mm | Int. | 32 | 1,099.00 | |
| **Variables** | | | | | | | | | | |
| 4-20x | 4-20 | 26.8-5.8 | — | 5.4-3.8 | 18.0 | 30mm | Int. | 24 | 884.71 | |
| 12-48x | 12-48 | — | — | 4.4-4.8 | 18.4 | 30mm | Int. | 36 | 1,250.00 | |
| 8-36x | 8-36 | — | — | 4.6-4.9 | 18.0 | 30mm | Int. | 35 | 1,105.00 | |
| **Tactical Format** | | | | | | | | | | |
| 2.5-10x | 2.5-10 | — | — | 43-11 | 12.8 | 30mm | Int. | 18 | 924.48 | |
| 1-4x | 1-4 | 118-25 | — | 4.8-4.4 | 9.4 | 30mm | Int. | 18 | 535.00 | |
| SN-6 | 6,8,10 | — | — | 4.2-4.8 | 9.2 | 30mm | Int. | 18 | 748.00 | |
| SN-7 | 4 | 27.5 | — | 5.2 | 7 | 30mm | Int. | 18 | 426.00 | |
| SN-8 | 4 | 28.8 | — | 5.2 | 7 | 30mm | Int. | 18 | 642.00 | |
| **WEATHERBY** | | | | | | | | | | Lumiplex reticle in all models. Blue-black, nonglare finish. From Weatherby. |
| Supreme 1¾-5x20 | 1.7-5 | 66.6-21.4 | — | 3.4 | 10.7 | 1 | Int. | 11 | 254.00 | |

| Maker and Model | Magn. | Field at 100 Yds. (feet) | Relative Brightness | Eye Relief (in.) | Length (in.) | Tube Dia. (in.) | W&E Adjustments | Weight (ozs.) | Price | Other Data |
|---|---|---|---|---|---|---|---|---|---|---|
| **Weatherby (cont.)** | | | | | | | | | | |
| Supreme 2-7x34 | 2.1-6.8 | 59-16 | — | 3.4 | 11¼ | 1 | Int. | 10.4 | 263.00 | |
| Supreme 4x44 | 3.9 | 32 | — | 3 | 12½ | 1 | Int. | 11.6 | 263.00 | |
| Supreme 3-9x44 | 3.1-8.9 | 36-13 | — | 3.5 | 12.7 | 1 | Int. | 11.6 | 310.00 | |
| **WEAVER** | | | | | | | | | | Micro-Trac adjustment system with ¼-minute clicks on all models. All have Dual-X reticle. One-piece aluminum tube, satin finish, nitrogen filled, multi-coated lenses, waterproof. ¹Also avilable in matte finish: K4, **$133.95**; V9, **$174.41**; V10, **$185.57**. From Weaver. |
| K2.5 | 2.5 | 35 | — | 3.7 | 9.5 | 1 | Int. | 7.3 | 117.61 | |
| K4¹ | 3.7 | 26.5 | — | 3.3 | 11.3 | 1 | Int. | 10 | 127.52 | |
| K6 | 5.7 | 18.5 | — | 3.3 | 11.4 | 1 | Int. | 10 | 138.95 | |
| V3 | 1.1-2.8 | 88-32 | — | 3.9-3.7 | 9.2 | 1 | Int. | 8.5 | 154.13 | |
| V9¹ | 2.8-8.7 | 33-11 | — | 3.5-3.4 | 12.1 | 1 | Int. | 11.1 | 166.10 | |
| V10¹ | 2.2-9.6 | 38.5-9.5 | — | 3.4-3.3 | 12.2 | 1 | Int. | 11.2 | 176.64 | |
| KT15 | 14.6 | 7.5 | — | 3.2 | 12.9 | 1 | Int. | 14.7 | 276.84 | |
| **WILLIAMS** | | | | | | | | | | ¹Matte or glossy black finish. TNT models. From Williams Gunsight Co. |
| Twilight Crosshair TNT | 1½-5 | 57¾-21 | 177-16 | 3½ | 10¾ | 1 | Int. | 10 | 206.65 | |
| Twilight Crosshair TNT | 2½ | 32 | 64 | 3¾ | 11¼ | 1 | Int. | 8½ | 146.25 | |
| Twilight Crosshair TNT | 4 | 29 | 64 | 3½ | 11¾ | 1 | Int. | 9½ | 152.90 | |
| Twilight Crosshair TNT | 2-6 | 45-17 | 256-28 | 3 | 11½ | 1 | Int. | 11½ | 206.65 | |
| Twilight Crosshair TNT | 3-9 | 36-13 | 161-18 | 3 | 12¾ | 1 | Int. | 13½ | 217.15 | |
| **Guideline II** | | | | | | | | | | |
| 4x¹ | 4 | 29 | 64 | 3.6 | 11¾ | 1 | Int. | 9½ | 222.00 | |
| 1.5-5x¹ | 1.5-5 | 57¾-21 | 177-16 | 3.5 | 10¾ | 1 | Int. | 10 | 267.00 | |
| 2-6x¹ | 2-6 | 45½-10¾ | 256-28 | 3 | 11½ | 1 | Int. | 11½ | 267.00 | |
| 3-9x¹ | 3-9 | 36½-12¾ | 161.2-17.6 | 3.1-2.9 | 12¾ | 1 | Int. | 13½ | 296.00 | |
| **Pistol Scopes** | | | | | | | | | | |
| Twilight 1.5x TNT | 1.5 | 19 | 177 | 18-25 | 8.2 | 1 | Int. | 6.4 | 151.25 | |
| Twilight 2x TNT | 2 | 17.5 | 100 | 18-25 | 8.5 | 1 | Int. | 6.4 | 153.50 | |
| **ZEISS** | | | | | | | | | | All scopes have ¼-minute click-stop adjustments. Choice of Z-Plex or fine crosshair reticles. Rubber armored objective bell, rubber eyepiece ring. Lenses have T-Star coating for highest light transmission. Z-Series scopes offered in non-rail tubes with duplex reticles only; 1" and 30mm. Imported from Germany by Carl Zeiss Optical, Inc. |
| Diatal C 4x32 | 4 | 30 | — | 3.5 | 10.6 | 1 | Int. | 11.3 | 680.00 | |
| Diatal C 6x32 | 6 | 20 | — | 3.5 | 10.6 | 1 | Int. | 11.3 | 715.00 | |
| Diatal C 10x36 | 10 | 12 | — | 3.5 | 12.7 | 1 | Int. | 14.1 | 835.00 | |
| Diatal Z 6x42 | 6 | 22.9 | — | 3.5 | 12.7 | 1.02 (26mm) | Int. | 13.4 | 910.00 | |
| Diatal Z 8x56 | 8 | 18 | — | 3.5 | 13.8 | 1.02 (26mm) | Int. | 17.6 | 1,015.00 | |
| Diavari C 1.5-4.5 | 1.5-4.5 | 72-27 | — | 3.5 | 11.8 | 1 | Int. | 13.4 | 930.00 | |
| Divari Z 2.5x10x48 | 2.5-10 | 33-11.7 | — | 3.2 | 14.5 | 30mm | Int. | 24 | 1,405.00 | |
| Diavari C 3-9x36 | 3-9 | 36-13 | — | 3.5 | 11.2 | 1 | Int. | 15.2 | 975.00 | |
| Diavari ZA 1.5-6x42 | 1.5-6 | 65.5-22.9 | — | 3.5 | 12.4 | 1.18 (30mm) | Int. | 18.5 | 1,230.00 | |
| Diavari Z 3-12x56 | 3-12 | 27.6-9.9 | — | 3.2 | 15.3 | 1.18 (30mm) | Int. | 25.8 | 1,405.00 | |

Hunting scopes in general are furnished with a choice of reticle—crosshairs, post with crosshairs, tapered or blunt post, or dot crosshairs, etc. The great majority of target and varmint scopes have medium or fine crosshairs but post or dot reticles may be ordered. W—Windage E—Elevation MOA—Minute of angle or 1" (approx.) at 100 yards, etc.

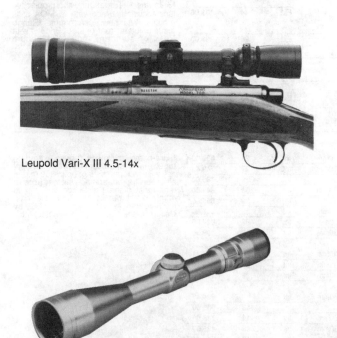

Leupold Vari-X III 4.5-14x

Nikon 3-9x40 Silver Matte

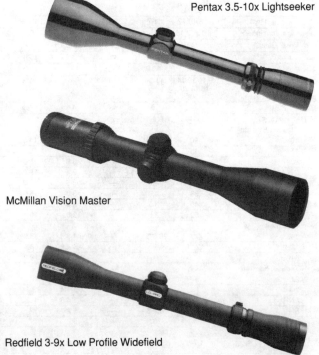

Pentax 3.5-10x Lightseeker

McMillan Vision Master

Redfield 3-9x Low Profile Widefield

**CAUTION:** PRICES CHANGE, CHECK AT GUNSHOP.

# SCOPE·MOUNTS

| Maker, Model, Type | Adjust. | Scopes | Price |
|---|---|---|---|
| **ACTION ARMS** | No | 1" split rings | From $12.00 |

For UZI, Galil, Ruger Mk. II, Mini-14, Win. 94, AR-15, Rem. 870, Ithaca 37, and many other popular rifles, handguns. Accept Weaver rings. All allow use of iron sights; some include rings; many in satin stainless finish. **Partial list shown. From Action Arms.**

| Maker, Model, Type | Adjust. | Scopes | Price |
|---|---|---|---|
| **AIMPOINT** | No | 1" | 49.95-89.95 |
| Laser Mounts[1] | No | 1", 30mm | 51.95 |

Mounts/rings for all Aimpoint sights and 1" scopes. For many popular revolvers, auto pistols, shotguns, military-style rifles/carbines, sporting rifles. Most require no gunsmithing. [1]Mounts Aimpoint Laser-dot below barrel; many popular handguns, military-style rifles. Contact Aimpoint.

| Maker, Model, Type | Adjust. | Scopes | Price |
|---|---|---|---|
| **AIMTECH** | | | |
| **Handguns** | | | |
| AMT Auto Mag II, III | No | 1" | 56.99-64.95 |
| Auto Mag IV | No | 1" | 64.95 |
| Astra revolvers | No | 1" | 63.25 |
| Beretta/Taurus auto | No | 1" | 63.25 |
| Browning Buck Mark/Challenger II | No | 1" | 56.99 |
| Browning Hi-Power | No | 1" | 63.25 |
| Glock 17, 17L, 19, 22, 23 | No | 1" | 63.25 |
| Govt. 45 Auto | No | 1" | 63.25 |
| Rossi revolvers | No | 1" | 63.25 |
| Ruger Blackhawk/Super | No | 1" | 63.25 |
| Ruger Mk I, Mk II | No | 1" | 49.95 |
| S&W K,L,N frame | No | 1" | 63.25 |
| S&W Model 41 Target | No | 1" | 63.25 |
| S&W Model 52 Target | No | 1" | 63.25 |
| S&W 45, 9mm autos | No | 1" | 56.99 |
| S&W 422/622/2206 | No | 1" | 56.99 |
| Taurus revolvers | No | 1" | 63.25 |
| TZ/CZ/P9 9mm | No | 1" | 63.25 |
| **Rifles** | | | |
| AR-15 | No | 1" | 21.95 |
| Browning A-Bolt | No | 1" | 19.95 |
| Knight MK85 | No | 1" | 21.95 |
| Remington 700 | No | 1" | 19.95 |
| Ruger 10/22 | No | 1" | 19.95 |
| Savage 110G | No | 1" | 19.95 |
| Winchester 70 | No | 1" | 19.95 |
| Winchester 94 | No | 1" | 19.95 |
| **Shotguns** | | | |
| Benelli Super 90 | No | 1" | 37.95 |
| Ithaca 37 | No | 1" | 37.95 |
| Mossberg 500 | No | 1" | 37.95 |
| Mossberg 835 Ultimag | No | 1" | 37.95 |
| Mossberg 5500 | No | 1" | 37.95 |
| Remington 870/1100 | No | 1" | 37.95 |
| Winchester 1300/1400 | No | 1" | 37.95 |

Mount scopes, lasers, electronic sights using Weaver-style base. All mounts allow use of iron sights; no gunsmithing. Available in satin black or satin stainless finish. **Partial listing shown.** Contact maker for full details. From L&S Technologies, Inc.

| Maker, Model, Type | Adjust. | Scopes | Price |
|---|---|---|---|
| **A.R.M.S.** | | | |
| FN FAL LAR | No | Weaver-type rail | 98.00 |
| FN FAL LAR Para. | No | — | 120.00 |
| M21/14 | No | — | 135.00 |
| M16A1/A2/AR-15 | No | Weaver-type rail | 59.95 |
| Multibase Weaver Rail[1] | No | — | 59.95 |
| Ring Inserts | No | 30mm to 1" | 29.00 |
| STANAG Rings | No | 30mm | 65.00 |
| Throw Lever Weaver Rings | No | 1" | 78.75 |
| #19 Weaver/STANAG Throw Lever Rail | No | — | 140.00 |

[1]For rifles with detachable carry handle, other Weaver rails. From A.R.M.S., Inc.

| Maker, Model, Type | Adjust. | Scopes | Price |
|---|---|---|---|
| **ARMSON** | | | |
| AR-15[1] | No | 1" | 39.00 |
| Mini-14[2] | No | 1" | 56.00 |
| H&K[3] | No | 1" | 74.00 |
| UZI[4] | No | 1" | 74.00 |

[1]Fastens with one nut. [2]Models 181, 182, 183, 184, etc. [3]Claw mount. [4]Claw mount, bolt cover still easily removable. From Trijicon, Inc.

| Maker, Model, Type | Adjust. | Scopes | Price |
|---|---|---|---|
| **ARMSPORT** | | | |
| 100 Series[1] | No | 1" rings. Low, med., high | 10.75 |
| 104 22-cal. | No | 1" | 10.75 |
| 201 See-Thru | No | 1" | 13.00 |
| 1-Piece Base[2] | No | — | 5.50 |
| 2-Piece Base[2] | No | — | 2.75 |

[1]Weaver-type rings. [2]Weaver-type base; most popular rifles. Made in U.S. From Armsport.

| Maker, Model, Type | Adjust. | Scopes | Price |
|---|---|---|---|
| **B-SQUARE** | | | |
| **Pistols** | | | |
| Beretta/Taurus 92/99[6] | — | 1" | 69.95 |
| Browning Buck Mark[6] | No | 1" | 49.95 |
| Colt 45 Auto | E only | 1" | 69.95 |
| Colt Python/MkIV, 4",6",8"[1,6] | E | 1" | 59.95 |
| Dan Wesson Clamp-On[2,6] | E | 1" | 59.95 |
| Ruger 22 Auto Mono-Mount[3] | No | 1" | 49.95 |
| Ruger Single-Six[4] | No | 1" | 49.95 |
| Ruger Blackhawk, Super B'hwk[8] | W&E | 1" | 59.95 |
| Ruger GP-100[9] | No | 1" | 59.95 |
| Ruger Redhawk[8] | W&E | 1" | 59.95 |
| S&W 422/2206[9] | No | 1" | 59.95 |
| Taurus 66[9] | No | 1" | 59.95 |
| S&W K, L, N frame[2,6] | No | 1" | 59.95 |
| T/C Contender (Dovetail Base) | W&E | 1" | 49.95 |
| **Rifles** | | | |
| Charter AR-7 | No | 1" | 49.95 |
| Mini-14 (dovetail/NATO Stanag)[5,6] | W&E | 1" | 59.95 |
| M-94 Side Mount | W&E | 1" | 49.95 |
| RWS, Beeman/FWB Air Rifles | E only | — | 69.95 |
| SMLE Side Mount with rings | W&E | 1" | 69.95 |
| Rem. Model Seven, 600, 660, etc.[6] | No | 1" One-piece base | 9.95 |
| **Military** | | | |
| AK-47/AKM/AKS/SKS-56[10] | No | 1" | 59.95 |
| AK-47, SKS-56[11] | No | 1" | 69.95 |
| M1-A[7] | W&E | 1" | 99.50 |
| AR-15/16[7] | W&E | 1" | 59.95 |
| FN-LAR/FAL[6,7] | E only | 1" | 149.50 |
| HK-91/93/94[6,7] | E only | 1" | 99.50 |
| **Shotguns**[6] | | | |
| Ithaca 37[6] | No | 1" | 49.95 |
| Mossberg 500, 712, 5500[6] | No | 1" | 49.95 |
| Rem. 870/1100 (12 & 20 ga.)[6] | No | 1" | 49.95 |
| Rem. 870, 1100 (and L.H.)[6] | No | 1" | 49.95 |
| **BSL Laser Mounts** | | | |
| Scope Tube Clamp[12,13,16] | No | — | 39.95 |
| 45 Auto[12,13,16] | No | — | 69.95 |
| SIG P226[12,13,16] | No | — | 69.95 |
| Beretta 92F/Taurus PT99[12,13,16] | No | — | 69.95 |
| Colt King Cobra, Python, MkV[12,13,16] | No | — | 39.95 |
| S&W L Frame[13,16] | No | — | 39.95 |
| Taurus 66/69[12,14,16] | No | — | 69.95 |
| S&W K,L,N Frames[12,14,16] | No | — | 69.95 |
| Beretta 92F/Taurus PT99[12,15,16] | No | — | 79.95 |
| Ruger P85[12,15,16] | No | — | 79.95 |

[1]Clamp-on, blue finish; stainless finish **$59.95.** [2]Blue finish; stainless finish **$59.95.** [3]Clamp-on, blue; stainless finish **$59.95.** [4]Dovetail; stainless finish **$59.95.** [5]No gunsmithing, no sight removal; blue; stainless finish **$79.95.** [6]Weaver-style rings. Rings not included with Weaver-type bases; stainless finish add $10. [7]NATO Stanag dovetail model, **$99.50.** [8]Blue; stainless **$69.95.** [9]Blue; stainless **$69.95.** [10]Handguard mounts. [11]Receiver mounts. [12]Stainless finish add $10. [13]Under-barrel mount, no gunsmithing. [14]Ejector rod mount. [15]Guide rod mount. [16]Used with B-Square BSL-1 Laser Sight only. Mounts for many shotguns, airguns, military and law enforcement guns also available. **Partial listing of mounts shown here. Contact B-Square for more data.**
B-Square makes mounts for the following military rifles: AK47/AKS, Egyptian Hakim, French MAS 1936, M91 Argentine Mauser, Model 98 Brazilian and German Mausers, Model 93, Spanish Mauser (long and short), Model 1916 Mauser, Model 38 and 96 Swedish Mausers, Model 91 Russian (round and octagon receivers), Chinese SKS 56, SMLE No. 1, Mk. III, 1903 Springfield, U.S. 30-cal. Carbine, and others. Those following replace gun's rear sight: AK47/AKS, P14/1917 Enfield, FN49, M1 Garand, M1-A/M14 (no sight removal), SMLE No. 1, Mk III/No. 4 & 5, Mk. 1, 1903/1903-A3 Springfield, Beretta AR 70 (no sight removal).

| Maker, Model, Type | Adjust. | Scopes | Price |
|---|---|---|---|
| **BEEMAN** | | | |
| Double Adjustable | W&E | 1" | 29.98 |
| Deluxe Ring Mounts | No | 1" | 29.98 |
| Professional Mounts | W&E | 1" | 149.95 |
| Dampamount | No | 1" | 89.95 |

All grooved receivers and scope bases on all known air rifles and 22-cal. rimfire rifles (1/2" to 5/8"—6mm to 15mm).

| Maker, Model, Type | Adjust. | Scopes | Price |
|---|---|---|---|
| **BOCK** | | | |
| Swing ALK[1] | W&E | 1", 26mm, 30mm | 224.00 |
| Safari KEMEL[2] | W&E | 1", 26mm, 30mm | 149.00 |
| Claw KEMKA[3] | W&E | 1", 26mm, 30mm | 224.00 |
| ProHunter Fixed[4] | No | 1", 26mm, 30mm | 95.00 |

| Maker, Model, Type | Adjust. | Scopes | Price |
|---|---|---|---|
| **BOCK** (cont.) | | | |
| Dovetail 22[5] | No | 1", 26mm | 59.00 |

[1]Q.D.; pivots right for removal. For Steyr-Mannlicher, Win. 70, Rem. 700, Mauser 98, Dakota, Sako, Sauer 80, 90. Magnum has extra-wide rings, same price. [2]Heavy-duty claw-type; reversible for front or rear removal. For Steyr-Mannlicher rifles. [3]True claw mount for bolt-action rifles. Also in extended model. For Steyr-Mannlicher, Win. 70, Rem. 700. Also avail. as Gunsmith Bases—bases not drilled or contoured—same price. [4]Extra-wide rings. [5]Fit most 22 rimfires with dovetail receivers. Imported from Germany by GSI, Inc.

| Maker, Model, Type | Adjust. | Scopes | Price |
|---|---|---|---|
| **BUEHLER** | | | |
| One Piece (T)[1] | W only | 1" split rings, 3 heights | Complete—89.50 |
| | | 1" split rings, engraved | Rings only—140.00 |
| | | 26mm split rings, 2 heights | Rings only—59.00 |
| | | 30mm split rings, 1 height | Rings only—77.00 |
| One Piece Micro Dial (T)[1] | W&E | 1" split rings | Complete—115.50 |
| Two Piece (T)[1] | W only | 1" split rings | Complete—89.50 |
| Two Piece Dovetail (T)[2] | W only | 1" split rings | Complete—110.50 |
| One Piece Pistol (T)[3] | W only | 1" split rings | Complete—$89.50 |
| One Piece Pistol Stainless (T)[1] | W only | 1" stainless rings | Complete—115.50 |
| One Piece Ruger Mini-14 (T)[4] | W only | 1" split rings | Complete—110.50 |
| One Piece Pistol M83 Blue[4,5] | W only | 1" split rings | Complete—102.50 |
| One Piece Pistol M83 Silver[4,5] | W only | 1" stainless rings | Complete—118.50 |

[1]Most popular models. [2]Sako dovetail receivers. [3]15 models. [4]No drilling & tapping. [5]Aircraft alloy, dyed blue or to match stainless; for Colt Diamondback, Python, Trooper, Ruger Blackhawk, Single-Six, Security-Six, S&W K-frame, Dan Wesson.

| Maker, Model, Type | Adjust. | Scopes | Price |
|---|---|---|---|
| **BURRIS** | | | |
| Supreme One Piece (T)[1] | W only | 1" split rings, 3 heights | 1 piece base—25.95 |
| Trumount Two Piece (T) | W only | 1" split rings, 3 heights | 2 piece base—23.95 |
| Trumount Two Piece Ext. | W only | 1" split rings | 29.95 |
| Browning Auto Mount[2] | No | 1" split rings | 19.95 |
| Rings Mounts[3] | No | 1" split rings | 1" rings—20.95 |
| L.E.R. Mount Bases[4] | W only | 1" split rings | 23.95 |
| L.E.R. No Drill-No Tap Bases[4,7,8] | W only | 1" split rings | 37.95-48.95 |
| Extension Rings[5] | No | 1" scopes | 41.95-48.95 |
| Ruger Ring Mount[6] | W only | 1" split rings | 36.95-41.95 |
| Std. 1" Rings | — | Low, medium, high heights | 33.95-41.95 |
| Zee Rings | — | Fit Weaver bases; medium and high heights | 27.95-35.95 |

[1]Most popular rifles. Universal rings, mounts fit Burris, Universal, Redfield, Leupold and Browning bases. Comparable prices. [2]Browning Standard 22 Auto rifle. [3]Grooved receivers. [4]Universal dovetail; accept Burris, Universal, Redfield, Leupold rings. For Dan Wesson, S&W, Virginian, Ruger Blackhawk, Win. 94. [5]Medium standard front, extension rear, per pair. Low standard front, extension rear, per pair. [6]Mini scopes, scopes with 2" bell, for M77R. [7]Selected rings and bases available with matte Safari or silver finish. [8]For S&W K,L,N frames, Colt Python, Dan Wesson with 6" or longer barrels.

| Maker, Model, Type | Adjust. | Scopes | Price |
|---|---|---|---|
| **BUSHNELL** | | | |
| Detachable (T) mounts only[1] | W only | 1" split rings, uses Weaver base | Rings—15.95 |
| 22 mount | No | 1" only | Rings—6.95 |

[1]Most popular rifles. Includes windage adjustment.

| Maker, Model, Type | Adjust. | Scopes | Price |
|---|---|---|---|
| **CAPE OUTFITTERS** | | | |
| Quick Detachable | No | 1" split rings, lever quick detachable | 99.95 |

Double rifles; Rem. 700-721, Colt Sauer, Sauer 200, Kimber, Win. 61-63-07-100-70, Browning High Power, 22, BLR, BAR, BBR, A-Bolt; Wea. Mark V, Vanguard; Modern Muzzle Loading, Knight, Thompson/Center, CVA rifles, Dixie rifles. All steel; returns to zero. From Cape Outfitters.

| Maker, Model, Type | Adjust. | Scopes | Price |
|---|---|---|---|
| **CLEAR VIEW** | | | |
| Universal Rings, Mod. 101[1] | No | 1" split rings | 21.95 |
| Standard Model[2] | No | 1" split rings | 21.95 |
| Broad View[3] | No | 1" | 21.95 |
| 22 Model[4] | No | 3/4", 7/8", 1" | 13.95 |
| SM-94 Winchester[5] | No | 1" split rings | 23.95 |
| 94 EJ[6] | No | 1" split rings | 21.95 |

[1]Most rifles by using Weaver-type base; allows use of iron sights. [2]Most popular rifles; allows use of iron sights. [3]Most popular rifles; low profile, wide field of view. [4]22 rifles with grooved receiver. [5]Side mount. [6]For Winchester Angle Eject. From Clear View Mfg.

| Maker, Model, Type | Adjust. | Scopes | Price |
|---|---|---|---|
| **CONETROL** | | | |
| Huntur[1] | W only | 1", 26mm, 26.5mm solid or split rings, 3 heights | 59.91 |
| Gunnur[2] | W only | 1", 26mm, 26.5mm solid or split rings, 3 heights | 74.91 |
| Custum[3] | W only | 1", 26mm, 26.5mm solid or split rings, 3 heights | 89.91 |
| One Piece Side Mount Base[4] | W only | 1", 26mm, 26.5mm solid or split rings, 3 heights | — |
| DapTar Bases[5] | W only | 1", 26mm, 26.5mm solid or split rings, 3 heights | — |
| Pistol Bases, 2 or 3-ring[6] | W only | 1" scopes | — |
| Fluted Bases[7] | W only | Standard Conetrol rings | 99.99 |
| 30mm Rings[8] | W only | 30mm | 49.98-69.96 |

[1]All popular rifles, including metric-drilled foreign guns. Price shown for base, two rings. Matte finish. [2]Gunnur grade has mirror-finished rings, satin-finish base. Price shown for base, two rings. [3]Custum grade has mirror-finished rings and mirror-finished, streamlined base. Price shown for base, two rings. [4]Win. 94, Krag, older split-bridge Mannlicher-Schoenauer, Mini-14, etc. Prices same as above. [5]For all popular guns with integral mounting provision, including Sako, BSA, Ithacagun, Ruger, Tikka, H&K, BRNO—$29.97-$44.97—and many others. Also for grooved-receiver rimfires and air rifles. Prices same as above. [6]For XP-100, T/C Contender, Colt SAA, Ruger Blackhawk, S&W. [7]Sculptured two-piece bases as found on fine custom rifles. Price shown is for base alone. Also available unfinished—$74.91, or finished but unblued—$87.95. [8]30mm rings made in projectionless style, medium height only. Three-ring mount available for T/C Contender and other pistols in Conetrol's three grades.

| Maker, Model, Type | Adjust. | Scopes | Price |
|---|---|---|---|
| **EAW** | | | |
| Quick Detachable Top Mount | W&E | 1", 26mm | 259.99 |
| | W&E | 1"/26mm with front extension ring | 259.99 |
| | W&E | 30mm | 279.99 |
| | W&E | 30mm with front extension ring. | 279.99 |

Also 30mm rings to fit Burris, Redfield or Leupold-type bases, low and high, **$112.00**; 1" or 26mm rings only, **$95.00** Most popular rifles. Elevation adjusted with variable-height sub-bases for rear ring. Imported by Paul Jaeger, Inc.

| Maker, Model, Type | Adjust. | Scopes | Price |
|---|---|---|---|
| **GENTRY** | | | |
| Feather-Light Rings | No | 1", 30mm | 75.00 |

| Maker, Model, Type | Adjust. | Scopes | Price |
|---|---|---|---|
| **GRACE** | | | |
| Swan G-3 | No | Weaver-type | 259.95 |

For HK G-3 guns. All-steel; provides iron sight see-through. From Grace Tool, Inc.

| Maker, Model, Type | Adjust. | Scopes | Price |
|---|---|---|---|
| **GRIFFIN & HOWE** | | | |
| Standard Double Lever (S) | No | 1" or 26mm split rings. | 305.00 |

All popular models (Garand $215). All rings $75. Top ejection rings available. Price installed for side mount.

| Maker, Model, Type | Adjust. | Scopes | Price |
|---|---|---|---|
| **HOLDEN** | | | |
| Wide Ironsighter™ | No | 1" split rings | 27.95 |
| Ironsighter Center Fire[1] | No | 1" split rings | 27.95 |
| Ironsighter S-94 | No | 1" split rings | 32.95 |
| **Ironsighter 22-Cal. Rimfire** | | | |
| Model #500[2] | No | 1" split rings | 19.95 |
| Model #600[3] | No | 7/8" split rings also fits 3/4" | 15.95 |
| Series #700[5] | No | 1" split rings | 27.95 |
| Model 732, 777[6] | No | 1" split rings | 56.95 |
| Ironsighter Handguns[4] | No | 1" split rings | 32.95-56.95 |
| Blackpowder Mount[7] | No | 1" | 27.95-56.95 |

[1]Most popular rifles, including Ruger Mini-14, H&R M700, and muzzleloaders. Rings have oval holes to permit use of iron sights. [2]For 1" dia. scopes. [3]For 3/4" or 7/8" dia. scopes. [4]For 1" dia. extended eye relief scopes. [5]702—Browning A-Bolt; 709—Marlin 39A. [6]732—Ruger 77/22 R&RS, No. 1, Ranch Rifle; 777 fits Ruger 77R, RS. Both 732, 777 fit Ruger integral bases. [7]Fits most popular blackpowder rifles; one model for Holden Ironsighter mounts, one for Weaver rings. Adj. rear sight is integral. Some models in stainless finish. From J.B. Holden Co.

| Maker, Model, Type | Adjust. | Scopes | Price |
|---|---|---|---|
| **KENPATABLE MOUNT** | | | |
| Shotgun Mount | No | 1", laser or red dot device | 49.95 |

Wrap-around design; no gunsmithing required. Models for Browning BPS, A-5 12-ga., Sweet 16, 20, Rem. 870/1100 (LTW and L.H.), S&W 916, Mossberg 500, Ithaca 37 & 51 12-ga., S&W 1000/3000, Win. 1400. From KenPatable Ent.

| Maker, Model, Type | Adjust. | Scopes | Price |
|---|---|---|---|
| **KRIS MOUNTS** | | | |
| Side-Saddle[1] | No | 1", 26mm split rings | 12.98 |
| Two Piece (T)[2] | No | 1", 26mm split rings | 8.98 |

**CAUTION:** PRICES CHANGE, CHECK AT GUNSHOP.

| Maker, Model, Type | Adjust. | Scopes | Price |
|---|---|---|---|
| **Kris** (cont.) | | | |
| One Piece (T)[3] | No | 1", 26mm split rings | 12.98 |

[1]One-piece mount for Win. 94. [2]Most popular rifles and Ruger. [3]Blackhawk revolver. Mounts have oval hole to permit use of iron sights.

| Maker, Model, Type | Adjust. | Scopes | Price |
|---|---|---|---|
| **KWIK-SITE** | | | |
| KS-See-Thru[1] | No | 1" | 25.95 |
| KS-22 See-Thru[2] | No | 1" | 22.95 |
| KS-W94[3] | No | 1" | 30.95 |
| Imperial Bench Rest | No | 1" | 30.95 |
| KS-WEV | No | 1" | 21.95 |
| KS-WEV-HIGH | No | 1" | 21.95 |
| KS-T22 1"[4] | No | 1" | 22.95 |
| KS-FL Flashlite[5] | No | Mini or C cell flashlight | 49.95 |
| KS-T88[6] | No | 1" | 10.95 |
| KS-T89 | No | 30mm | 14.95 |
| KSN 22 See-Thru | No | 1", 7⁄8" | 19.95 |
| KSN-T22 | No | 1", 7⁄8" | 19.95 |
| KSN-M16 See-Thru | No | 1" | 99.95 |
| KSB Base Set | — | — | 5.65 |
| Combo Bases & Rings | No | 1" | 26.75 |

[1]Most rifles. Allows use of iron sights. [2]22-cal. rifles with grooved receivers. Allows use of iron sights. [3]Model 94, 94 Big Bore. No drilling or tapping. Also in adjustable model **$49.95.** [4]Non-see-through model for grooved receivers. [5]Allows Mag Lite or C or D, Mini Mag Lites to be mounted atop See-Thru mounts. [6]Fits any Redfield, Tasco, Weaver or universal-style Kwik-Site dovetail base. Bright blue, black matte or satin finish. Standard, high heights.

| Maker, Model, Type | Adjust. | Scopes | Price |
|---|---|---|---|
| **LASER AIM** | No | Laser Aim | 29.00-69.00 |

Mounts Laser Aim above or below barrel. Avail. for most popular handguns, rifles, shotguns, including militaries. From Emerging Technologies, Inc.

| Maker, Model, Type | Adjust. | Scopes | Price |
|---|---|---|---|
| **LASERSIGHT** | No | LS45 only | 29.95-149.00 |

For the LS45 Lasersight. Allows LS45 to be mounted alongside any 1" scope. Universal adapter attaches to any full-length Weaver-type base. For most popular military-type rifles, Mossberg, Rem. shotguns, Python, Desert Eagle, S&W N frame, Colt 45ACP. From Imatronic Lasersight.

| Maker, Model, Type | Adjust. | Scopes | Price |
|---|---|---|---|
| **LEUPOLD** | | | |
| STD Bases[1] | W only | One- or two-piece bases | 22.90 |
| STD Rings[2] | — | 1" super low, low, medium, high | 32.00 |
| STD Handgun mounts[3] | No | — | 57.90 |
| Dual Dovetail Bases[1,4] | No | — | 22.90 |
| Dual Dovetail Rings[10] | — | 1", super low, low | 32.00 |
| Ring Mounts[5,6,7] | No | 7⁄8", 1" | 81.10 |
| 22 Rimfire[10] | No | 7⁄8", 1" | 60.00 |
| Gunmaker Base[8] | W only | 1" | 16.00 |
| Gunmaker Ring Blanks[9] | — | 1" | 22.00 |
| Quick Release Rings | — | 1", low, med., high | 32.00 |
| Quick Release Bases[11] | No | 1", one- or two-piece | 66.00 |
| Airgun Ringmount[12] | No | 1" | 92.00 |

[1]Rev. front and rear combinations; matte finish **$22.90.** [2]Avail. polished, matte or silver (low, med. only) finish. [3]Base and two rings; Casull, Ruger, S&W, T/C; add $5.00 for silver finish. [4]Rem. 700, Win. 70-type actions. [5]For Ruger No. 1, 77, 77/22; interchangeable with Ruger units. [6]For dovetailed rimfire rifles. [7]Sako; high, medium, low. [8]Must be drilled, tapped for each action. [9]Unfinished bottom, top completed; sold singly. [10]Most dovetail-receiver 22s. [11]BSA Monarch, Rem. 40X, 700, 721, 725, Ruger M77, S&W 1500, Weatherby Mark V, Vanguard, Win M70. [12]Receiver grooves 9.5mm to 11.0mm; matte finish.

| Maker, Model, Type | Adjust. | Scopes | Price |
|---|---|---|---|
| **LEATHERWOOD** | | | |
| Bridge Bases[1] | No | ART II or all dovetail rings | 15.00 |
| M1A/M-14 Q.D. | No | ART II or all dovetail rings | 105.00 |
| AR-15/M-16 Base | No | ART II or all dovetail rings | 25.00 |
| FN-FAL Base | No | ART II or all dovetail rings | 100.00 |
| FN Para. Base | No | ART II or all dovetail rings | 110.00 |
| Steyr SSG Base | No | ART II or all dovetail rings | 55.00 |

[1]Many popular bolt actions. Mounts accept Weaver or dovetail-type rings. From North American Specialties.

| Maker, Model, Type | Adjust. | Scopes | Price |
|---|---|---|---|
| **MARLIN** | | | |
| One Piece QD (T) | No | 1" split rings | 14.95 |

Most Marlin lever actions.

| Maker, Model, Type | Adjust. | Scopes | Price |
|---|---|---|---|
| **MILLETT** | | | |
| Black Onyx Smooth | — | 1", low, medium, high | 29.65 |
| Chaparral Engraved | — | 1", high engraved | 43.95 |
| One-Piece Bases[6] | Yes | 1" | 23.95 |
| **Universal Two-Piece Bases** | | | |
| 700 Series | W only | Two-piece bases | 23.95 |

| Maker, Model, Type | Adjust. | Scopes | Price |
|---|---|---|---|
| **Millett** (cont.) | | | |
| FN Series | W only | Two-piece bases | 23.95 |
| 70 Series[1] | W only | 1", two-piece bases | 23.95 |
| Angle-Loc Rings[2] | W only | 1", low, medium, high | 30.65-44.95 |
| Ruger 77 Rings[3] | — | 1" | 44.95 |
| Shotgun Rings[4] | — | 1" | 26.95 |
| Handgun Bases, Rings[5] | — | 1" | 32.95-61.35 |
| 30mm Rings[7] | — | 30mm | 35.95 |
| Extension Rings[8] | — | 1" | 33.95 |

Rem. 40X, 700, 722, 725, Ruger 77 (round top), Weatherby, FN Mauser, FN Brownings, Colt 57, Interarms Mark X, Parker-Hale, Sako (round receiver), many others. [1]Fits Win. M70, 70XTR, 670, Browning BBR, BAR, BLR, A-Bolt, Rem. 7400/7600, Four, Six, Marlin 336, Win. 94 A.E., Sav. 110. [2]To fit Weaver-type bases. [3]Engraved. Smooth $30.65. [4]For Rem. 870, 1100; smooth. [5]Two and three-ring sets for Colt Python, Trooper, Diamondback, Peacekeeper, Dan Wesson, Ruger Redhawk, Super Redhawk, XP-100 pistols. [6]Both Weaver and turn-in styles; three heights. [7]Med. or high; ext. front—std. rear, ext. rear—std. front, ext. front—ext. rear; **$38.95** for double extension. Some models available in nickel at extra cost. From Millett Sights.

| Maker, Model, Type | Adjust. | Scopes | Price |
|---|---|---|---|
| **OAKSHORE** | | | |
| **Handguns** | | | |
| Browning Buck Mark | No | 1" | 29.00 |
| Colt Cobra, Diamondback, Python, 1911 | No | 1" | 38.00-52.00 |
| Ruger 22 Auto, GP100 | No | 1" | 33.00-49.00 |
| S&W N Frame | No | 1" | 45.00-60.00 |
| S&W 422 | No | 1" | 35.00-38.00 |
| **Rifles** | | | |
| Colt AR-15 | No | 1" | 26.00-34.00 |
| H&K 91, 93, 94, MP-5, G-3 | No | 1" | 56.00 |
| Galil | No | 1" | 75.00 |
| Marlin 336 & 1800 Series | No | 1" | 21.00 |
| Win. 94 | No | 1" | 39.00 |
| **Shotguns** | | | |
| Mossberg 500 | No | 1" | 40.00 |
| Rem. 870, 1100 | No | 1" | 33.00-52.00 |
| Rings | — | 1", med., high | 5.20-9.80 |

See Through offered in some models. Black or silver finish; 1" rings also avail. for 3⁄8" grooved receivers (See Through). From Oakshore Electronic Sights, Inc.

| Maker, Model, Type | Adjust. | Scopes | Price |
|---|---|---|---|
| **PEM'S** | | | |
| 22T Mount[1] | No | 1" | 17.95 |
| The Mount[2] | Yes | 1" | 27.50 |

[1]Fit all 3⁄8" dovetail on rimfire rifles. [2]Base and ring set; for over 100 popular rifles; low, medium rings. From Pem's.

| Maker, Model, Type | Adjust. | Scopes | Price |
|---|---|---|---|
| **RAM-LINE** | | | |
| Mini-14 Mount | Yes | 1" | 24.97 |

No drilling or tapping. Use std. dovetail rings. Has built-in shell deflector. Made of solid black polymer. From Ram-Line, Inc.

| Maker, Model, Type | Adjust. | Scopes | Price |
|---|---|---|---|
| **REDFIELD** | | | |
| American Rings[8] | No | 1", low, med., high | 16.95 |
| American Bases[8] | No | — | 2.65-5.09 |
| American Widefield See-Thru[9] | No | 1" | 16.95 |
| JR-SR (T)[1] | W only | 3⁄4", 1", 26mm, 30mm | JR—20.95-52.95 SR—20.95-39.95 |
| Ring (T)[2] | No | 3⁄4" and 1" | 27.95 |
| Three-Ring Pistol System SMP[3] | No | 1" split rings (three) | 56.95-62.95 |
| Widefield See-Thru Mounts | No | 1" | 16.95 |
| Ruger Rings[4] | No | 1", med., high | 35.95 |
| Ruger 30mm[5] | No | 1" | 46.95 |
| Midline Ext. Rings | No | 1" | 20.95 |
| Steel "WS" Rings[6] | W | 1", 30mm | 26.95-39.95 |
| Steel 22 Ring Mount, Base[7] | No | 3⁄4", 1" | 13.95-29.95 |

[1]Low, med. & high; split rings. Reversible extension front rings for 1". 2-piece bases for Sako. Colt Sauer bases $39.95. Med. Top Access JR rings nickel-plated, $29.95. SR two-piece ABN mount nickel-plated, **$22.95**; RealTree Camo rings, med., high **$31.95**; RealTree Camo JR bases **$25.95**; RealTree Camo rings **$25.95**. [2]Split rings for grooved 22s. See-Thru mounts **$16.95.** [3]Used with MP scopes for: S&W K, L or N frame, XP-100, T/C Contender, Ruger receivers. [4]For Ruger Model 77 rifles, medium and high; medium only for M77/22. [5]For Model 77. Also in matte finish, **$44.95.** [6]Nickel-plated, **$37.95**. [7]For 22 rifles with grooved receivers. Fits all radius dovetails. [8]Aluminum 22 groove mount **$14.95**; base and medium rings **$17.95.** [9]Fits American or Weaver-style base.

| Maker, Model, Type | Adjust. | Scopes | Price |
|---|---|---|---|
| **S&K** | | | |
| Insta-Mount (T) bases and rings[1] | W only | Use S&K rings only | 25.00-99.00 |
| Conventional rings and bases[2] | W only | 1" split rings | From 50.00 |
| Sculptured Bases, Rings[2] | W only | 1", 26mm, 30mm | From 50.00 |

[1]1903, A3, M1 Carbine, Lee Enfield #1, Mk. III, #4, #5, M1917, M98 Mauser, FN Auto, AR-15, AR-180, M-14, M-1, Ger. K-43, Mini-14, M1-A, Krag, AKM, AK-47, Win. 94, SKS Type 56, Daewoo, H&K. [2]Most popular rifles already drilled and tapped. Horizontally and vertically split rings, matte or high gloss.

| Maker, Model, Type | Adjust. | Scopes | Price |
|---|---|---|---|
| **SSK INDUSTRIES** | | | |
| T'SOB | No | 1" | 65.00-145.00 |
| Quick Detachable | No | 1" | From 160.00 |

Custom installation using from two to four rings (included). For T/C Contender, most 22 auto pistols, Ruger and other S.A. revolvers, Ruger, Dan Wesson, S&W, Colt DA revolvers. Black or white finish. Uses Kimber rings in two- or three-ring sets. In blue or SSK Khrome. For T/C Contender or most popular revolvers. Standard, non-detachable model also available, from $65.00.

| Maker, Model, Type | Adjust. | Scopes | Price |
|---|---|---|---|
| **SAKO** | | | |
| QD Dovetail | W only | 1" only | 67.00-140.00 |

Sako, or any rifle using Sako action, 3 heights available. Stoeger, importer.

| Maker, Model, Type | Adjust. | Scopes | Price |
|---|---|---|---|
| **TASCO** | | | |
| **World Class** | | | |
| Universal "W" Ringmount[1] | No | 1", 30mm | 27.00-59.00 |
| Ruger[2] | No | 1", 30mm | 35.00-59.00 |
| 22, Air Rifle[3] | No | 1", 30mm | 28.00-66.00 |
| Center-Fire Ringmount[4] | No | 1", 26mm, 30mm | 46.00-66.00 |
| Desert Eagle Ringmount[5] | No | 1", 30mm | 51.00-72.00 |
| Ringsets[6] | No | 1", 26mm, 30mm | 26.00-56.00 |
| Bases[7] | Yes | — | 26.00-46.00 |
| Pro-Mount Handgun Base[8] | No | — | 9.00-37.00 |

[1]Steel; low, high only; also high-profile see-through; fit Tasco, Weaver, other universal bases; black gloss or satin chrome. [2]Low, high only; for Redhawk and Super, No.1, Mini-14 & Thirty, 77, 77/22; blue or stainless. [3]Low, med., high; 3/8" grooved receivers; black or satin chrome. [4]Low, med., high; for Tasco W.C. bases, some dovetail; black gloss only. [5]For Desert Eagle pistols, 22s, air rifles with deep dovetails. [6]Low, med., high; black gloss, matte satin chrome; also Traditional Ringsets $31.00 (1"), $42.00 (26mm), $53.00 (30mm). [7]For popular rifles and shotguns; one-piece, two-piece, Q.D., long and short action, extension. Handgun bases have w&e adj. [8]For many popular handguns, blue or stainless. From Tasco.

| Maker, Model, Type | Adjust. | Scopes | Price |
|---|---|---|---|
| **THOMPSON/CENTER** | | | |
| Contender 9741[1] | No | 2½, 4 RP | 17.00 |
| S&W 9747[2] | No | Lobo or RP | 17.00 |
| Ruger 9748[3] | No | Lobo or RP | 17.00 |
| Hawken 9749[4] | No | Lobo or RP | 17.00 |
| Hawken/Renegade 9754[5] | No | Lobo or RP | 17.00 |
| New Englander 9757 | No | Lobo or RP | 17.00 |
| Quick Release System[6] | No | 1" | Rings 48.00 Base 24.50 |

[1]T/C rail mount scopes; all Contenders except vent. rib. [2]All S&W K and Combat Masterpiece, Hi-Way Patrolman, Outdoorsman, 22 Jet, 45 Target 1955. Requires drilling, tapping. [3]Blackhawk, Super Blackhawk, Super Single-Six. Requires drilling, tapping. [4]45 or 50 cal.; replaces rear sight. [5]Rail mount scopes; 54-cal. Hawken, 50, 54, 56-cal. Renegade. Replaces rear sight. [6]For Contender pistol, Carbine, Scout, all M/L long guns. From Thompson/Center.

| Maker, Model, Type | Adjust. | Scopes | Price |
|---|---|---|---|
| **UNERTL** | | | |
| ¼ Click[1] | Yes | ¾", 1" target scopes | Per set 115.00 |

[1]Unertl target or varmint scopes. Posa or standard mounts, less bases. From Unertl

| Maker, Model, Type | Adjust. | Scopes | Price |
|---|---|---|---|
| **WARNE** | | | |
| Quick Detachable Thumb Knob | No | 1", 3 heights | 67.80 |
| | | 26mm 2 heights | 82.80 |
| | | 30mm 2 heights | 82.80 |
| Traditional Double Lever | No | 1", 3 heights | 89.50 |
| | | 26mm 2 heights | 103.00 |
| | | 30mm 2 heights | 103.00 |
| Adjustable Double Lever | No | 1", 3 heights | 99.50 |
| | | 26mm 2 heights | 111.50 |
| | | 30mm 2 heights | 111.50 |
| Grooved Receiver[1] | No | 1", 3 heights | 67.80-99.50 |
| Machine Screw[2] | — | | 67.80-99.50 |
| BRNO[3] | No | ZKK[4] 1", 3 heights | 99.50 |
| | | ZKK[4] 30mm 2 heights | 111.50 |
| | | MDL 1[5] 1" 2 heights | 99.50 |
| | | MDL 1[5] 30mm 2 heights | 111.50 |
| | | MDL 2 | 67.80-99.50 |
| Ruger[3,6] | No | M77 1", 2 heights | 99.50 |
| | | M77 30mm, 2 heights | 111.50 |
| | | Other 1", 4 heights | 99.50 |
| | | Other 30mm, 3 heights | 111.50 |
| Sako[3,6,7] | No | 1", 4 heights | 99.50 |
| | | 30mm, 3 heights | 111.50 |

| Maker, Model, Type | Adjust. | Scopes | Price |
|---|---|---|---|
| **Warne (cont.)** | | | |
| Steyr[3,6] | No | SSG 1", 2 heights | 99.50 |
| | | SSG 30mm, 2 heights | 111.50 |
| Two-Piece Bases (pr.) | — | — | 25.00 |
| One-Piece Base | — | — | 32.00 |
| Ruger Pistol Kit[8,9] | — | — | 47.00 |

Vertically split rings with dovetail clamp, precise repeat to zero. Fit most popular rifles, handguns. Regular blue, matte blue, silver finish. [1]In 3 styles for 22-cal. 3/8" dovetailed receivers. [2]Non q.d. [3]Adjustable double lever only. [4]19mm dovetail. [5]16mm dovetail. [6]Use standard rings if bases required. [7]For dovetail receiver. [8]For Bull barrel only. [9]Not including rings. From Warne Mfg. Co.

| Maker, Model, Type | Adjust. | Scopes | Price |
|---|---|---|---|
| **WEAVER** | | | |
| **Detachable Mounts** | | | |
| Top Mount[1] | No | ⅞", 1" | 25.49-26.51 |
| Side Mount[2] | No | 1", 1" Long | 31.18-36.87 |
| Pivot Mount[3] | No | 1" | 39.96 |
| Tip-Off Mount[4] | No | ⅞", 1" | 22.69-28.93 |
| **See-Thru Mount** | | | |
| Traditional[6] | No | 1" | 26.51 |
| Symmetrical[6] | No | 1" | 17.61-21.44 |
| Detachable[5] | No | 1" | 26.51 |
| Tip-Off[4] | No | 1", ⅞" | 17.67-21.51 |
| Pro View[6] | No | 1" | 17.67-18.44 |
| **Mount Base System[7]** | | | |
| Blue Finish | No | 1" | 76.71 |
| Stainless Finish | No | 1" | 107.31 |
| Shotgun Converta-Mount System[8] | No | 1" | 76.71 |
| Rifle Mount System[9] | No | 1" | 34.02 |
| **Paramount Mount Systems[10]** | | | |
| Bases, pair | Yes | 1" | 26.36 |
| Rings, pair | No | 1" | 34.22 |

[1]Nearly all modern rifles. Low, med., high. 1" extension $30.96. 1" low, med., high stainless steel $40.53. [2]Nearly all modern rifles, shotguns. [3]Most modern big bore rifles; std., high. [4]22s with 3/8" grooved receivers. [5]Nearly all modern rifles. 1" See-Thru extension $30.96. [6]Most modern big bore rifles. Some in stainless finish, $20.22-21.44. [7]No drilling, tapping. For Colt Python, Trooper, 357, Officer's Model, Ruger Blackhawk & Super, Mini-14, Security-Six, 22 auto pistols, Single-Six 22, Redhawk, Blackhawk SRM 357, S&W current K, L with adj. sights. [8]For Rem. 870, 1100, 11-87, Browning A-5, BPS, Ithaca 37, 87, Beretta A303, Beretta A-390, Winchester 1200-1500, Mossberg 500. [9]For some popular sporting rifles. [10]Dovetail design mount for Rem. 700, Win. 70, FN Mauser, low, med., high rings; std., extension bases. From Weaver.

| Maker, Model, Type | Adjust. | Scopes | Price |
|---|---|---|---|
| **WIDEVIEW** | | | |
| Premium 94 Angle Eject | No | 1" | 24.00 |
| Premium See-Thru | No | 1" | 22.00 |
| 22 Premium See-Thru | No | ¾", 1" | 16.00 |
| Universal Ring Angle Cut | No | 1" | 24.00 |
| Universal Ring Straight Cut | No | 1" | 22.00 |
| **Solid Mounts** | | | |
| Lo Ring Solid[1] | No | 1" | 16.00 |
| Hi Ring Solid[1] | No | 1" | 16.00 |
| SR Rings | — | 1", 30mm | 16.00 |
| 22 Grooved Receiver | No | 1" | 16.00 |
| 94 Side Mount | No | 1" | 26.00 |
| Blackpowder Mounts[2] | No | 1" | 30.00 |

[1]For Weaver-type bases. Models for many popular rifles. Low ring, high ring and grooved receiver types. [2]No drilling, tapping; for T/C Renegade, Hawken, CVA guns; for guns drilled and tapped, $16.00. From Wideview Scope Mount Corp.

| Maker, Model, Type | Adjust. | Scopes | Price |
|---|---|---|---|
| **WILLIAMS** | | | |
| Sidemount with HCO Rings[1] | No | 1", split or extension rings | 69.25 |
| Sidemount, offset rings[2] | No | Same | 57.00 |
| Sight-Thru Mounts[3] | No | 1", ⅞" sleeves | 23.95 |
| Streamline Mounts | No | 1" (bases form rings). | 23.95 |
| Guideline Handgun[4] | No | 1" split rings. | 79.95 |

[1]Most rifles, Br. S.M.L.E. (round rec.) $13.45 extra. [2]Most rifles including Win. 94 Big Bore. [3]Many modern rifles, including CVA Apollo, others with 1" octagon barrels. [4]No drilling, tapping required; heat treated alloy. For Ruger Blackhawk, Super Blackhawk, Redhawk; S&W N frame, M29 with 10⅝" barrel ($79.95); S&W K, L frames; Colt Python, King Cobra; Ruger MkII Bull Barrel; Streamline Top Mount for T/C Contender, Scout Rifle, CVA Apollo ($39.95), High Top Mount with sub-base ($49.95). From Williams Gunsight Co.

| Maker, Model, Type | Adjust. | Scopes | Price |
|---|---|---|---|
| **YORK** | | | |
| M-1 Garand | Yes | 1" | 39.95 |

Centers scope over the action. No drilling, tapping or gunsmithing. Uses standard dovetail rings. From York M-1 Conversions.

**NOTES**

(S)—Side Mount (T)—Top Mount; 22mm=.866"; 25.4mm=1.024"; 26.5mm=1.045"; 30mm=1.81"

**CAUTION:** PRICES CHANGE, CHECK AT GUNSHOP.

# DIRECTORY OF THE ARMS TRADE

The **Product Directory** contains a total of 53 product categories. This year we have changed Guns, Foreign to **Guns, Foreign— Manufacturers** and have added a new category **Guns, Foreign—Importers**. The two are cross-referenced to aid you in finding the U.S. importers of any foreign-manufactured firearm.

The **Manufacturer's Directory** lists the manufacturers alphabetically, their addresses, phone numbers and FAX numbers.

# PRODUCT DIRECTORY

## AMMUNITION, COMMERCIAL

Action Arms Ltd.
ACTIV Industries, Inc.
A-Square Co., Inc.
Black Hills Ammunition
Blammo Ammo
Blount, Inc. Sporting Equipment
  Division
Bottom Line Shooting Supplies
Buck Stix
Buck-X, Inc
The BulletMakers Workshop
California Magnum
CBC
Century International Arms, Inc.
ChinaSports, Inc.
Cor-Bon Bullet & Ammo Co.
Daisy Mfg. Co.
Diana
Denver Bullets, Inc.
Dynamit Nobel-RWS, Inc.
Eley Ltd.
Elite Ammunition
Enguix Import-Export
Estate Cartridge, Inc.
Federal Cartridge Co.
Fiocchi of America, Inc.
FN Herstal
Gamo
Garrett Cartridges, Inc.
GDL Enterprises
Glaser Safety Slug, Inc.
"Gramps"Antique Cartridges
Hansen Cartridge Co.
Hirtenberger Aktiengesellschaft
Hornady Mfg. Co.
ICI-America
IMI
Jones, J.D.
Kent Cartridge Mfg. Co. Ltd.
Lapua Ltd.

Lethal Force Institute
M&D Munitions Ltd.
Maionchi-L.M.I.
MAGTECH Recreational
  Products, Inc.
Markell, Inc.
Master Class Bullets
Men—Metallwerk
  Elisenhuette, GmbH
Midway Arms, Inc.
New England Ammunition Co.
Neutralizer Police Munitions
Old Western Scrounger, Inc.
Omark Industries
Paragon Sales & Services, Inc.
PMC/Eldorado Cartridge Corp.
Police Bookshelf
Pony Express Reloaders
Precision Delta Corp.
Precision Prods. of Wash., Inc.
Pro Load Ammunition, Inc.
Ravell Ltd.
Remington Arms Co., Inc.
Rocky Fork Enterprises
Royal Arm International Products
Rucker Ammunition Co.
RWS
Safari Gun Co.
Sherwood Intl. Export Corp.
SOS Products Co.
Speer Products
Star Reloading Co., Inc.
3-D Ammunition & Bullets
3-Ten Corp.
USAC
Valor Corp.
Weatherby, Inc.
Winchester Div., Olin Corp.
Wosenitz VHP, Inc.
Zero Ammunition Co., Inc.

## AMMUNITION, CUSTOM

AFSCO Ammunition
All American Bullets
Ballistica Maximus North
Ballistica Maximus South
Beeman Precision Airguns, Inc.
Bertram Bullet Co.
Bottom Line Shooting Supplies
Brynin, Milton
Buck Stix
The BulletMakers Workshop
Cartridges Unlimited
Country Armourer, The
Cubic Shot Shell Co., Inc.
Custom Hunting Ammo & Arms
Custom Tackle & Ammo
Dakota Arms
Deadeye Sport Center
DKT, Inc.
E.A.A. Corp.
Eagle Flight Bullet Co.
Elite Ammunition
Elko Arms, L. Kortz
Ellis Sport Shop, E.W.
Epps "Orillia" Ltd., Ellwood
Estate Cartridge, Inc.
Fitz Pistol Grip Co.
Freedom Arms, Inc.
Gammog, Gregory B. Gally
GDL Enterprises
"Gramps" Antique Cartridges
Granite Custom Bullets
Hardin Specialty Dist.
Heidenstrom Bullets
Hindman, Ace
Hirtenberger Aktiengesellschaft
Horizons Unlimited
Jensen's Custom Ammunition

Jensen's Firearm Academy
Jett & Co., Inc.
Kaswer Custom, Inc.
Keeler, R.H.
Kent Cartridge Mfg. Co. Ltd.
KJM Brass Group
Lindsley Arms Cartridge Co.
Lomont Precision Bullets, Kent
MagSafe Ammo Co.
Marple & Associates, Dick
McMurdo, Lynn
M&D Munitions Ltd.
Monte Kristo Pistol Grip Co.
Mountain South
Newman Gunshop
Old Western Scrounger, Inc.
Personal Protection Systems Ltd.
Precision Delta Corp.
Precision Munitions, Inc.
Sanders Custom Gun Service
Sandia Die & Cartridge Co.
SOS Products Co.
Specialty Gunsmithing
Spence, George W.
SSK International
Star Custom Bullets
State Arms Gun Co.
Stewart's Gunsmithing
3-D Ammunition & Bullets
Three-Ten Corp.
Vitt/Boos
Weaver Arms Corp.
Westley Richards & Co.
Worthy Products, Inc.
Wosenitz VHP, Inc.
Wyoming Armory, Inc.

## AMMUNITION, FOREIGN

Action Arms Ltd.
AFSCO Ammunition
Bertram Bullet Co.
Bottom Line Shooting Supplies

Brenneke KG, Wilhelm
The BulletMakers Workshop
Cartridges Unlimited
CBC

Champion's Choice, Inc.
Cubic Shot Shell Co., Inc.
Diana
Dynamit Nobel-RWS, Inc.
Enguix Import-Export
Estate Cartridge, Inc.
Fiocchi of America, Inc.
FN Herstal
Gamo
"Gramps" Antique Cartridges
Hansen Cartridge Co.
Hirtenberger Aktiengesellschaft
IMI
K.B.I., Inc.
Lapua Ltd.
Maionchi-L.M.I.

MAGTECH Recreational
  Products, Inc.
Merkuria Ltd.
New England Arms Co.
Old Western Scrounger, Inc.
Paragon Sales & Services, Inc.
PMC/Eldorado Cartridge Corp.
Precision Delta Corp.
R.E.T. Enterprises
Rocky Fork Enterprises
RWS
Safari Gun Co.
Sako, Ltd.
Samco Global Arms, Inc.
T.F.C. S.p.A.

## AMMUNITION COMPONENTS—BULLETS, POWDER, PRIMERS

Acadian Ballistic Specialties
Accuracy Unlimited (Glendale, AZ)
Accurate Arms Co., Inc.
ACTIV Industries, Inc.
Alaska Bullet Works
Allred Bullet Co.
Alpha LaFranck
American Bullets
A-Square Co., Inc.
American Products Co.
Armfield Custom Bullets
Ballard Built Custom Bullets
Ballistic Products, Inc.
Banaczkowski Bullets
Barnes Bullets, Inc.
Bell Reloading, Inc.
Berger Bullets, Ltd.
Berry's Bullets
Bertram Bullet Co.
Bitterroot Bullet Co.
Black Hills Shooters Supply
Black Mountain Bullets
Blount, Inc. Sporting Equipment
  Division
Blue Mountain Bullets
Brenneke KG, Wilhelm
Brown Co., E. Arthur
Brownells, Inc.
BRP, Inc.
Bruno Shooters Supply
Buckeye Custom Bullets
Buck Stix
Buffalo Bullet Co., Inc.
Buffalo Rock Shooters Supply
Bullet, Inc.
Bull-X, Inc.
Bullseye Bullets
Burling Bullets
Buzztail Brass
Calhoon Varmint Bullets, James
Canadian Custom Bullets
Carnahan Bullets
Cartridge Co., C.W.
Cartridges Unlimited
Canyon Cartridge Corp.
CFVentures
Champion's Choice, Inc.
Cheddite France S.A.
CheVron Bullets
Circle M Custom Bullets
Classic Brass
Competitor Corp., Inc.
Cook Bullets
Cook Engineering Service
Cor-Bon Bullet & Ammo Co.
Crawford Co., Inc., R.M.
Creative Cartridge Co.
Cummings Bullets
Custom Bullets by Hoffman
Cutsinger Benchrest Bullets
D&J Bullet Co. & Custom
  Gun Shop, Inc.
Denver Bullets, Inc.
DKT, Inc.
Dohring Bullets
DuPont
E.A.A. Corp.
Ed's Custom Bullets
Eichelberger Bullets, Wm.
Eiland Custom Bullets
Enguix Import-Export

Eureka Bullets
Federal Cartridge Co.
Finch Custom Bullets
Fiocchi of America, Inc.
Fitz Pistol Grip Co.
Fowler Bullets
Foy Custom Bullets
Freedom Arms, Inc.
Fusilier Bullets
G&C Bullet Co., Inc.
Gise Bullets
GOEX, Inc.
Gotz Bullets
Grand Falls Bullets
Granite Custom Bullets
Green Bay Bullets
Greenwalt Rifles
Grizzly Bullets
Group Tight Bullets
Gun City
Hammets VLD Bullets
Hansen Cartridge Co.
Harris Enterprises
Harrison Bullet Works
Hawk Co.
Hawk Laboratories, Inc.
Heidenstrom Bullets
Hercules, Inc.
Higgs Bullets
High Country Custom Bullets
Hirtenberger Aktiengesellschaft
Hobson Precision
  Manufacturing Co.
Hodgdon Powder Co., Inc.
Hornady Mfg. Co.
HT Bullets
Idaho Bullets
Imperical Magnum Corp.
IMR Powder Co.
IMI
J-4, Inc.
Jensen Bullets
Jensen's Custom Ammunition
Jensen's Firearms Acadamy
Jester Bullets
JLK Bullets
Ka Pu Kapili
Kasmarsnik Bullets
Kaswer Custom, Inc.
Keith's Bullets
Ken's Kustom Kartridge
Kent Cartridge Mfg. Co. Ltd.
Keystone Bullets
KJM Brass Group
Kodiak Custom Bullets
Kustom Kast Bullets
Lachaussee, S.A.
Lage Uniwad, Inc.
Lane Bullets
Lapua Ltd.
Lathrop's, Inc.
Lindsley Arms Cartridge Co.
Lomont Precision Bullets, Kent
Magnus Bullets
Maine Custom Bullets
Maionchi-L.M.I.
Marchmon Bullets
Master Class Bullets
McKenzie Bullet Co.
McMurdo, Lynn
M&D Munitions Ltd.

MEC
Merkuria Ltd.
Michael's Antiques
Miller Enterprises, Inc.
Mitchell Bullets, R.F.
MoLoc Bullets
Montana Precision Swaging
Mulhern, Rick
Mullins Ammo
Murmur Corp.
Mushroom Express Bullet Co.
Nagel's Bullets
NAK Custom Bullets
National Bullet Co.
Naval Ordanance Works
Necromancer Industries, Inc.
Newman Gunshop
Norma
Northern Precision Custom
   Swaged Bullets
Nosler, Inc.
O'Connor Rifle Products Co., Ltd.
Old Wagon Bullets
Old Western Scrounger, Inc.
Omark Industries
Ordnance Works, The
Pace Marketing, Inc.
Page Custom Bullets
Patchbox & Museum of
   the Great Divide, The
Patrick Bullets
Patriot Manufacturing
Pattern Control
Phillippi Custom Bullets, Justin
Polywad, Inc.
Pomeroy, Robert
Pony Express Reloaders
Precision Components & Guns
Precision Delta Corp.
Precision Munitions, Inc.
Precision Reloading, Inc.
Prescott Projectile Co.
Price Bullets, Patrick W.
Rainier Ballistic Corp.
Ranch Products
Ravell Ltd.
Red Willow Tool & Armory, Inc.
Redwood Bullet Works
Reloading Specialties
Remington Arms Co., Inc.
Rencher Bullets
Renner Co., R.J./Radical Concepts
R.I.S. Co., Inc.
Rolston, Jr., Fred
Rossi, Amadeo

Rubright Bullets
Rucker Ammunition Co.
Sako, Ltd.
Scharch Mfg., Inc.
Scot Powder Co. of Ohio, Inc.
Schmidtman Custom Ammunition
Schneider Bullets
Shappy Bullets
Sheidan USA, Inc., Austin
Sioux Bullets
Small Group Bullets
SOS Products Co.
Southern Ammunition Co., Inc.
Specialty Gunsmithing
Stanley Bullets
Star Custom Bullets
Stark's Bullets Manufacturing
Stevi Machine, Inc.
Stewart's Gunsmithing
Swift Bullet Co.
Taracorp Industries
TCCI
T.F.C. S.p.A.
3-D Ammunition & Bullets
Thompson Precision
TMI Products
Tooley, David
Trico Plastics
Trophy Bonded Bullets, Inc.
True Flight Bullet Co.
USAC
Vann Custom Bullets
Vihtavuori Oy
Vincent's Shop
Vitt/Boos
Warren Muzzleloading Co., Inc.
Watson Trophy Match Bullets
Weisner Bullets
Whitestone Lumber Corp.
White Systems, Inc.
Widener's Reloading &
   Shooting Supply
Williams Bullet Co., J.R.
Winchester Div., Olin Corp.
Windjammer Tournament
   Wads, Inc.
Winkle Bullets
Woodland Bullets
Worthy Products, Inc.
Wosenitz VHP, Inc.
Wyant Bullets
Wyoming Casting Co.
Wyoming Custom Bullets
Zero Ammunition Co., Inc.

## ANTIQUE ARMS DEALERS

Ad Hominem
Ammunition Consulting
   Services, Inc.
Antique American Firearms
Antique Arms Co.
Aplan Antiques & Art, James O.
Arms, Jackson
Beeman Precision Airguns, Inc.
Boggs, Wm.
British Arms Co. Ltd.
Buckskin Machine Works
Cape Outfitters
Carlson, Douglas R.
Chadick's Ltd.
Champlin Firearms, Inc.
Classic Guns, Inc.
Colonial Repair
Condon, Inc., David
Corry, John
Cullity Restoration, Daniel
D&D Gunsmiths, Ltd.
Dilliott Gunsmithing, Inc.
Dyson & Son Ltd., Peter
Ed's Gun House
Epps "Orillia" Ltd., Ellwood
Fagan & Co., William
Fish, Marshall F.
Flayderman & Co., N.
Flintlock Muzzle Loading
   Gun Shop, The
Frielich Police Equipment
Fulmer's Antique Firearms, Chet
Glass, Herb
Goergen Gun Shop, Inc.
Golden Age Arms Co.
Gun Works, The

Hallowell & Co.
Hansen & Co.
Hunkeler, A.
Jackson Arms
Kelley's
Ledbetter Airguns, Riley
LeFever Arms Co., Inc.
Lever Arms Service Ltd.
Lock's Philadelphia Gun Exchange
Log Cabin Sport Shop
Martin's Gun Shop
Mendez, John A.
Montana Outfitters
Museum of Historical Arms, Inc.
Muzzleloaders Etcetera, Inc.
New England Arms Co.
New Orleans Arms Co.
Paragon Sales & Services, Inc.
Patchbox & Museum
   of the Great Divide, The
Pioneer Guns
Pony Express Sport Shop, Inc.
P.S.M.G. Gun Co.
Ravell Ltd.
Retting, Inc., Martin B.
Rutgers Book Center
Semmer, Charles
Sherwood Intl. Export Corp.
S&S Firearms
Steves House of Guns
Stott's Creek Armory, Inc.
Ward & Van Valkenburg
Wiest, M.C.
Wood, Frank S.
Yearout, Lewis E.

## APPRAISERS—GUNS, ETC.

Ahlman Guns
Ammunition Consulting
   Services, Inc.
Amodei, Jim
Antique Arms Co.
Aplan Antiques & Art, James O.
Beeman Precision Airguns, Inc.
Blue Book Publications, Inc.
Bustani Appraisers, Leo
Butterfield & Butterfield
Camilli, Lou
Cannon's Guns
Chadick's Ltd.
Christie's East
Christopher Firearms Co., Inc., E.
Clark Firearms Engraving
Classic Guns, Inc.
Clements' Custom
   Leathercraft, Chas
Condon, Inc., David
Cullity Restoration, Daniel
Custom Tackle & Ammo
D&D Gunsmiths, Ltd.
Dixon Muzzleloading Shop, Inc.
D.O.C. Specialists, Inc.
Ed's Gun House
Ellis Sport Shop, E.W.
Epps "Orillia" Ltd., Ellwood
Eversull Co., Inc., K.
Fagan & Co., William
Fish, Marshall F.-Mfg. Gunsmith
Flayderman & Co., Inc., N.
Forgett, Valmore J., Jr.
Fredrick Gun Shop
Frontier Arms Co., Inc.
Goergen's Gun Shop, Inc.
Golden Age Arms Co.
Gonzalez Guns, Ramon B.
Goodwin, Fred
Greenwald, Leon E. "Bud"
Griffin & Howe, Inc.
Guns
Hallowell & Co.
Hansen & Co.
Holster Shop, The
Hughes, Steven Dodd
Irwin, Campbell H.
Jaeger, Inc., Paul/Dunn's
Jonas Appraisals & Taxidermy, Jack

Kelley's
Ledbetter Airguns, Riley
LeFever Arms Co., Inc.
Lock's Philadelphia Gun Exchange
Mack's Sport Shop
Mac's .45 Shop
Marple & Associates, Dick
Martin's Gun Shop
McGowan Rifle Barrels
Montana Outfitters
Museum of Historical Arms, Inc.
Muzzleloaders Etcetera, Inc.
Navy Arms Co.
Novak's .45 Shop, Wayne
Orvis Co., The
Parke-Bernet
Parker-Hale
Pentheny de Pentheny
Perazzi U.S.A., Inc.
Pettinger Books, Gerald
Pony Express Sport Shop, Inc.
Precision Arms International, Inc.
P.S.M.G. Gun Co.
R.E.T. Enterprises
Richards, John
Safari Outfitters Ltd.
Shell Shack
Shooting Gallery, The
Silver Ridge Gun Shop
S.K. Guns, Inc.
Sotheby's
S&S Firearms
Stott's Creek Armory, Inc.
Stratco, Inc.
Strawbridge, Victor W.
Thurston Sports, Inc.
Tillinghast, James C.
Ulrich, Doc & Bud
Unick's Gunsmithing
Vic's Gun Refinishing
Vintage Industries, Inc.
Wayne Firearms for Collectors and
   Investors, James
Whildin & Sons Ltd., E.H.
Whitestone Lumber Corp.
Wiest, M.C.
Wood, Frank S.
Yearout, Lewis E.

## AUCTIONEERS—GUNS, ETC.

Ammunition Consulting
   Services, Inc.
Bourne Co., Inc., Richard A.
Butterfield & Butterfield
Christie's East
Fagan & Co., William
Goodwin, Fred

Kelley's
"Little John's" Antique Arms
Parke-Bernet
Silver Ridge Gun Shop
Sotheby's
Tillinghast, James C.

## BOOKS (Publishers and Dealers)

ADC, Inc.
American Handgunner Magazine
Aplan Antiques & Art, James O.
Armory Publications
Arms & Armour Press, Ltd.
Beeman Precision Airguns, Inc.
Blacksmith Corp.
Blacktail Mountain Books
Blue Book Publications, Inc.
Brownell's, Inc.
Calibre Press, Inc.
Colorado Sutlers Arsenal
Corbin, Inc.
DBI Books, Inc.
Executive Protection Institute
Flores Publications, Inc., J.
Fortress Publications, Inc.
Golden Age Arms Co.
"Gramps" Antique Cartridges
Gun City
Guncraft Sports, Inc.
Gun Hunter Books
Gun Room Press, The
GUNS Magazine
Gunnerman Books
Handgun Press
H&P Publishing
Hodgdon Powder Co., Inc.
Hungry Horse Books
Ironside International
   Publishers, Inc.
Jackson Arms
King & Co.

Krause Publications
Lane Publishing
LBT
Madis, David
Magma Engineering Co.
Martin, J.
McKee Publications
Mountain South
NECO
New Win Publishing, Inc.
NgraveR Co., The
North American Pine
   Training Center
Old Western Scrounger, Inc.
Outdoorsman's Bookstore, The
Paladin Press
Pease Accuracy, Bob
Pejsa Ballistics
Petersen Publishing Co.
Pettinger Books, Gerald
PFRB Co.
Pranger, Ed G.
Quack Decoy Corp.
Ravell Ltd.
R.G.-G., Inc.
Riling Arms Books Co., Ray
Rutgers Book Center
Rutgers Gun & Boat Center
Safari Press, Inc.
S.A.F.E.
Shootin' Accessories, Ltd.
Stackpole Books
Stoeger Publishing Co.

Survival Books/The Larder
Thomas, Charles C.
Threat Management Institute
Trafalgar Square
Trotman, Ken
Vintage Industries, Inc.

VSP Publishers
Wahl Corp., Paul
Weisz Antique Gun Parts
Wilderness Sound Productions Ltd.
Wolfe Publishing Co.

## BULLET AND CASE LUBRICANTS

Armite Laboratories
Blackhawk East
Blackhawk Mountain
Blackhawk West
Blount, Inc. Sporting Equipment
  Division
Bullet Swaging Supply, Inc.
Camp-Cap Products
CFVentures
Cooper-Woodward
Corbin, Inc.
Dillon Precision Prods., Inc.
Fitz Pistol Grip Co.
GAR
Gozon Corp.
Guardsman Products
Hollywood Engineering
Hornady Mfg. Co.
Huntington Die Specialties
INTEC International, Inc.
Javelina Products
Lane Bullets, Inc.
LBT

Lee Precision, Inc.
Lighthouse Mfg. Co., Inc.
Lithi Bee Bullet Lube
Magma Engineering Co.
Micro-Lube
Monte Kristo Pistol Grip Co.
M&N Bullet Lube
Ox-Yoke Originals, Inc.
Ravell Ltd.
RCBS
Reardon Products
SAECO
Shay's Gunsmithing
Shooters Accessory Supply
Slipshot MTS Group
Small Custom Mould & Bullet Co.
Tamarack Products, Inc.
Thompson Bullet Lube Co.
Thompson/Center Arms
Watson Trophy Match Bullets
White Systems, Inc.
Young Country Arms

## BULLET SWAGE DIES AND TOOLS

Advance Car Mover Co.
Blount, Inc. Sporting Equipment
  Division
Bruno Shooters Supply
Brynin, Milton
Bullet Swaging Supply, Inc.
C-H Tool & Die Corp./4-D Custom
  Die Co.
Corbin, Inc.
Fitz Pistol Grip Co.

Hollywood Engineering
Lachaussee, S.A.
MoLoc Bullets
Monte Kristo Pistol Grip Co.
NECO
Necromancer Industries, Inc.
Rorschach Precision Products
Speer Products
Sport Flite Manufacturing Co.

## CARTRIDGES FOR COLLECTORS

Ad Hominem
Ammunition Consulting
  Services, Inc.
Baekgaard Ltd.
Cameron's
Campbell, Dick
Duffy, Chas. E.
Ed's Gun House
Eichelberger Bullets, Wm.
Epps "Orillia" Ltd., Ellwood
First Distributors, Inc., Jack
Forty Five Ranch Enterprises
Gun City
"Gramps" Antique Cartridges
Hansen & Co.

Idaho Ammunition Service
Kelley's
Lock's Philadelphia Gun Exchange
Montana Outfitters
Mountain Bear Rifle Works, Inc.
Muzzleloaders Etcetera, Inc.
Old Western Scrounger, Inc.
Paragon Sales & Services, Inc.
Ranch Products
Ravell Ltd.
San Francisco Gun Exchange
Tillinghast, James C.
Ward & Van Valkenburg
Yearout, Lewis E.

## CASES, CABINETS, RACKS AND SAFES—GUN

A&B Industries, Inc.
Abel Safe & File, Inc.
Airmold, W.R. Grace & Co.-Conn.
Alco Carrying Cases
Allen Co., Bob
Allen Co., Inc.
Allen Sportswear, Bob
American Display Co.
American Security Products Co.
Americase
Ansen Enterprises
Arizona Custom Case
Arkfeld Mfg. & Dist. Co., Inc.
Art Jewel Enterprises Ltd.
Ashby Turkey Calls
Bandera Gun Locker
Barramundi Corp.
Bill's Custom Cases
Big Sky Racks, Inc.
Big Spring Enterprises "Bore Stores"
Black Sheep Brand
Boyt
Brauer Bros. Mfg. Co.
Browning Arms Co.
Brunsport, Inc.
Bucheimer, J.M.
Bushmaster Hunting & Fishing
Cannon Safe, Inc.
Cascade Fabrication
Chipmunk
CoBalt Mfg., Inc.

Crane & Crane Ltd.
Dara-Nes, Inc.
Dee Zee Alumna Sports
Doskocil Mfg. Co., Inc.
DTM International, Inc.
Elk River, Inc.
EMF Co., Inc.
English Inc., A.G.
Enhanced Presentations, Inc.
Epps "Orillia" Ltd., Ellwood
Eversull Co., Inc., K.
Fort Knox Security Products
Frontier Safe Co.
Galati Internationl
GAR
Granite Custom Bullets
Gun-Ho Sports Cases
Gun Vault, Inc.
Gusdorf Corp.
Hafner Creation, Inc.
Hall Plastics, Inc., John
Harrison-Hurtz Enterprises, Inc.
Homak Mfg. Co., Inc.
Huey Gun Cases, Marvin
Hugger Hooks Co.
Hunter Co., Inc.
Hunting Classics Ltd.
Impact Case Co.
Johnson Gunsmithing, Inc., Neal G.
Johnston Bros.
Jumbo Sports Products

Kalispel Case Line
Kane Products, Inc.
KK Air International
Knock on Wood Antiques
Kodiak Safe
Kolpin Mfg., Inc.
Lakewood Products, Inc.
Liberty Safe
Maloni, Russ
Marsh, Mike
Maximum Security Corp.
McGuire, Bill
McWelco Products
Morton Booth Co.
Mountain States Engraving
M/S Deepeeka Exports Pvt. Ltd.
National Security Safe Co., Inc.
Nesci Enterprises, Inc.
Nielsen Custom Cases
Oregon Arms, Inc.
Otto, Tim
Outa-Site Gun Carriers
Outdoor Connection, Inc., The
Palmer Metal Products
Penguin Industries, Inc.
Perazzi U.S.A., Inc.
Pflumm Gun Mfg. Co.
PistolPAL Products

Protecto Plastics
Prototech Industries, Inc.
Quality Arms, Inc.
Red Head, Inc.
Russwood Custom Pistol Grips
San Angelo Sports Products, Inc.
Savana Sports, Inc.
Schulz Industries
Sonderman, Robert B.
Sportsman's Communicators
Sun Welding Safe Co.
Sweet Home, Inc.
Tinks & Ben Lee Hunting Products
Tread Corp.
Unick's Gunsmithing
Verdemont Fieldsports
Waller & Son, Inc., W.
WAMCO, Inc.
Warren, Kenneth W.
Weatherby, Inc.
Weather Shield Sports
  Equipment, Inc.
Wellington Outdoors
Wilson Case, Inc.
Woodstream
Zanotti Armor
Ziegel Engineering

## CHOKE DEVICES, RECOIL ABSORBERS AND RECOIL PADS

Action Products, Inc.
Answer Products Co.
Arms Ingenuity Co.
Baker, Stan
B-Square Co.
Briley Mfg., Inc.
Butler Creek Corp.
C&H Research
Cape Outfitters
Cation
Cellini, Inc., Vito Francesca
Clinton River Gun Serv., Inc.
Colonial Arms, Inc.
Danuser Machine Co.
Delta Vectors, Inc.
E.A.A. Corp.
Fabian Bros. Sporting Goods, Inc.
FAPA Corp.
Franchi S.p.A., Luigi
Frontier Arms Co., Inc.
Gentry Custom Gunmaker, David
Great 870 Co., The
Griggs Products
Harper, William E.
Hastings Barrels
Intermountain Arms
Jaeger, Inc., Paul/Dunn's

Jenkins Recoil Pads, Inc.
KDF, Inc.
Kick Eez
LaRocca Gun Works, Inc.
London Guns Ltd.
Mag-Na-Port Int'l, Inc.
Marble Arms Corp.
McGowen Rifle Barrels
MCRW Associates
Moneymaker Guncraft Corp.
Morrow, Bud
Nelson/Weather-rite
Nu-Line Guns, Inc.
Oakland Custom Arms, Inc.
One Of A Kind
Pachmayr Ltd.
Palsa Outdoor Products
Pro-Port Ltd.
Protektor Model Co.
Ravell Ltd.
Royal Arm International Products
Shotguns Unlimited
S.K. Guns, Inc.
Thompson/Center Arms
Trulock Tool
Upper Missouri Trading Co.

## CHRONOGRAPHS AND PRESSURE TOOLS

Canons Delcour
Chronotech
Competition Electronics, Inc.
Custom Chronograph, Inc.
D&H Precision Tooling
Dedicated Systems

Lachaussee, S.A.
Oehler Research, Inc.
P.A.C.T., Inc.
Shooting Chrony, Inc.
Stratco, Inc.
Tepeco

## CLEANING AND REFINISHING SUPPLIES

Acculube II, Inc.
Accupro Gun Care
Accuracy Products, S.A.
ADCO International
American Gas & Chemical Co., Ltd.
Armoloy Co. of Ft. Worth
Belltown, Ltd.
Beretta, Dr. Franco
Big 45 Frontier Gun Shop
Bill's Gun Repair
Birchwood Laboratories, Inc.
Blount, Inc. Sporting Equipment
  Division
Break-Free
Bridgers Best
Brobst, Jim
Browning Arms Co.
Bruno Shooters Supply
Chopie Mfg., Inc.
Clenzoil Corp.
Corbin, Inc.
Crane & Crane Ltd.
Creedmoor Sports, Inc.
Crouse's Country Cover
Custom Products
Decker Shooting Products
M/S Deepeeka Exports Pvt. Ltd.

Dewey Mfg. Co., Inc., J.
Dri-Slide, Inc.
Du-Lite Corp.
Dutchman's Firearms, Inc., The
Dykstra, Doug
Eezox, Inc.
Faith Associates, Inc.
Flitz International Ltd.
Flouramics, Inc.
Forster Products
Forty-Five Ranch
Frontier Products Co.
G96 Products Co., Inc.
Golden Age Arms Co.
Gozon Corp.
Graves Co.
Guardsman Products
Gun Works, The
Half Moon Rifle Shop
Heatbath Corp.
Hoppe's Div.
INTEC International, Inc.
Iosso Marine Products
Jantz Supply
J-B Bore Cleaner
Johnson Gunsmithing, Inc., Neal G.
Johnston Bros.

Jonad Corp.
Kleen-Bore, Inc.
Kopp, Terry K.
Lee Supplies, Mark
LEM Gun Specialties, Inc.
LPS Laboratories, Inc.
LT Industries, Inc.
Marble Arms Corp.
Micro Sight Co.
Mountain View Sports, Inc.
Munger, Robert D.
Muscle Products Corp./Firepower
  Lubricants
Nesci Enterprises, Inc.
Northern Precision Custom
  Swaged Bullets
Old World Oil Products
Omark Industries
Outers Laboratories, Div. of Blount
Ox-Yoke Originals, Inc.
Parker Gun Finishes
Pendleton Royal
Pflumm Gun Mfg. Co.
P&M Sales and Service
Precision Sports
Prolix®
Pro-Shot Products, Inc.
Radiator Specialty Co.
Ravell Ltd.
R&S Industries Corp.
Rice, Keith

Richards Classic Oil Finish, John
Rickard, Inc., Pete
RIG Products Co.
Robar Co.'s, Inc., The
Rusteprufe Laboratories
Rusty Duck Premium Gun Care
  Products
San Angelo Sports Products, Inc.
Scott, Inc., Tyler
Shooter's Choice
Shootin' Accessories, Ltd.
Slipshot MTS Group
Speer Products
Sports Support Systems, Inc.
Stoney Point Products, Inc.
Svon Corp.
TDP Industries, Inc.
TETRA Gun Lubricants
Texas Platers Supply Co.
T.F.C. S.p.A.
Treso, Inc.
United States Products Co.
Valor Corp.
Van Gorden & Son, Inc., C.S.
Verdemont Fieldsports
Watson Trophy Match Bullets
WD-40 Co.
White Rock Tool & Die
Williams Shootin' Iron Service
Young Country Arms
Z-Coat Industrial Coatings, Inc.

## COMPUTER SOFTWARE—BALLISTICS

ADC, Inc.
AmBr Software Group Ltd.
Arms, Peripheral Data Systems
Ballistic Program Co., Inc., The
Best Load
Blount, Inc. Sporting Equipment
  Division
Canons Delcour
Corbin Applied Technology
Corbin, Inc.
Country Armourer, The
Data Tech Software Systems
Destination North Software
Exe, Inc.

Ford, Jack
J.I.T. Ltd.
Lachaussee, S.A.
Lee Precision, Inc.
Load From A Disk
Magma Engineering Co.
Maionchi-L.M.I.
Oehler Research, Inc.
P.A.C.T., Inc.
Pejsa Ballistics
Ravell Ltd.
Regional Associates
Sierra Bullets
Vancini, Carl A./Bestload

## CUSTOM GUNSMITHS

Accuracy Gun Shop
Accuracy Unlimited (Glendale, AZ)
Accurate Plating & Weaponry, Inc.
Ackley Rifle Barrels, P.O.
Adair Custom Shop, Bill
Ahlman Guns
Ahrends, Kim
Aldis Gunsmithing & Shooting
  Supply
Alpine's Precision Gunsmithing &
  Indoor Shooting Range
American Custom Gunmakers Guild
Amrine's Gun Shop
Answer Products Co.
Apel, Dietrich
Armament Gunsmithing Co., Inc.
Arms Craft Gunsmithing
Arms Ingenuity Co.
Armscorp. USA, Inc.
Armurier Hiptmayer
Arrieta, S.L.
Art's Gun & Sport Shop, Inc.
A&W Repair
AWC Systems Technology
B&C
Bain & Davis, Inc.
Baity's Custom Gunworks
Barnes Bullets, Inc.
Barton Technology
Barta's Gunsmithing
Baumannize, Inc.
Beaver Lodge
Beeman Precision Airguns, Inc.
Behlert Precision
Beitzinger, George
Belding's Custom Gun Shop
Bell & Carlson, Inc.
Bellm Contenders
Benchmark Guns
Bengtson Arms Co., L.
Biesen, Al
Biesen, Roger
Billeb, Stephen L.
Billings Gunsmiths, Inc.
Bolden's
Boltin, John M.

Borovnik KG, Ludwig
Bowerly, Kent
Brace, Larry D.
Brgoch, Frank
Briganti & Co., A.
Briley Mfg., Inc.
Broken Gun Ranch
Brown Precision, Inc.
Bruno Shooters Supply
Buck Stix
Buckhorn Gun Works
Buckskin Machine Works
Budin, Dave
Burgess and Son Gunsmiths, R.W.
Burkhart Gunsmithing, Don
Burres, Jack
Bustani Appraisers, Leo
Cache La Poudre Rifleworks
CAM Enterprises
Camilli, Lou
Campbell, Dick
Cannon's Guns
Carter's Gun Shop
Caywood, Shane J.
Chicasaw Gun Works
Christopher Firearms Co., Inc., E.
Chuck's Gun Shop
Clark Custom Guns, Inc.
Clark Firearms Engraving
Classic Arms Corp.
Classic Guns, Inc.
Clinton River Gun Service, Inc.
Cloward's Gun Shop
Cochran, Oliver
Colonial Repair
Competitive Pistol Shop, The
Conrad, C.A.
Cook, John
Corkys Gun Clinic
Costa, David
Cox, C. Ed
Creekside Gun Shop, Inc.
Cumberland Knife & Gun Works
Curtis Custom Shop
Custom Barrel Electropolishing
Custom Checkering Service

Custom Firearms
Custom Gun Products
Custom Gunsmiths
Custom Gun Stocks
Custom Shop, The
Dangler, Homer L.
Darlington Gun Works, Inc.
Davis Service Center, Bill
D.D. Custom Rifles
D&D Gunsmiths, Ltd.
Dever Co., Jack
Devereaux, R.H. "Dick"
DGS, Inc.
Dilliott Gunsmithing, Inc.
Donnelly, C.P.
Dowtin Gunworks
Duffy, Charles E.
Duncan's Gun Works, Inc.
Dyson & Son Ltd., Peter
E.A.A. Corp.
Eagle Flight Bullet Co.
Echols & Co., D'Arcy
Eckelman Gunsmithing
Echols & Co., D'Arcy
Eggleston, Jere D.
EMF Co., Inc.
Emmons, Bob
Erhardt, Dennis
Eversull Co., Inc., K.
Eyster Heritage Gunsmiths, Inc.,
  Ken
Fanzoj GmbH
Farmer-Dressell, Sharon
Fautheree, Andy
Fellowes, Ted
Ferris Firearms
First Distributors, Inc., Jack
Fish, Marshall F.-Mfg. Gunsmith
Fisher, Jerry A.
Flaig's
Fleming Firearms
Flynn's Custom Guns
Fogle, James W.
Forster, Kathy
Forster, Larry L.
Forthofer's Gunsmithing &
  Knifemaking
Forty-Niner Trading Co.
Francesca Stabilizer's, Inc.
Francotte & Cie S.A., Auguste
Frank Custom Gun Service, Ron
Fredrick Gun Shop
Frontier Arms Co., Inc.
Furr Arms
Gander Mountain, Inc.
Garrett Accur-Lt. D.F.S. Co.
Gator Guns & Repair
Genecco Gun Works, K.
Gentry Custom Gunmaker, David
Gillmann, Edwin
Gilman-Mayfield, Inc.
Giron, Robert E.
Goens, Dale W.
Goodling's Gunsmithing
Goodwin, Fred
Gordie's Gun Shop
Grace, Charles E.
Graybill's Gun Shop
Green, Roger M.
Greenwalt Rifles
Greg Gunsmithing Repair
Griffin & Howe, Inc.
Gun Shop, The
Guns
Gunsite Gunsmithy
Gunsmithing Ltd.
Gun Works, The
Gutridge, Inc.
Hagn Rifles & Actions, Martin
Hallberg Gunsmith, Fritz
Hammans, Charles E.
Hammond Custom Guns Ltd., Guy
Hank's Gun Shop
Hanson's Gun Center, Dick
Hardison, Charles
Hart & Son, Inc., Robert W.
Hecht, Hubert J.
Heilmann, Stephen
Heinie Specialty Products
Hensler, Jerry
Hensley, Darwin
Heppler, Keith
Heppler's Machining
High Bridge Arms, Inc.
Hill, Loring F.
Hiptmayer, Klaus
H&L Gun Works

Hoag, James W.
Hobaugh, Wm.
Hobbie Gunsmithing, Duane A.
Hodgson, Richard
Hoehn's Shooting Supply
Hoenig & Rodman
Hofer Jagdwaffen, P.
Holland, Dick
Hollis Gun Shop
Horst, Alan K.
Huebner, Corey O.
Hughes, Steven Dodd
Hunkeler, Al
Huntington Die Specialties
Hyper-Single, Inc.
Intermountain Arms
Irwin, Campbell H.
Ivanoff, Thomas G.
Jackalope Gun Shop
Jaeger, Inc., Paul/Dunn's
Jarrett Rifles, Inc.
Jet Comp Systems
Jim's Gun Shop
Johnson Gunsmithing, Inc., Neal G.
Johnston, James
Jones, J.D.
Juenke, Vern
Jurras, L.E.
K-D, Inc.
KDF, Inc.
Kehr, Roger
Keith's Custom Gunstocks
Ken's Gun Specialties
King's Gun Works
Klein Custom Guns, Don
Kleinendorst, K.W.
Kneiper Custom Rifles, Jim
Knippel, Richard
Kopp, Terry K.
Korzinek Riflesmith, J.
LaFrance Specialties
Lair, Sam
Lampert, Ron
LaRocca Gun Works, Inc.
Lawson Co., Harry
Lee's Red Ramps
LeFever Arms Co., Inc.
Liberty Antique Gunworks
Lilja Precision Rifle Barrels
Lind Custom Guns, Al
Linebaugh Custom Sixguns
  & Rifle Works
Lock's Philadelphia Gun Exchange
Long, George F.
Mac's .45 Shop
Mag-Na-Port Int'l, Inc.
Mahoney, Philip Bruce
Mahony, Philip Bruce
Makinson, Nicholas
Mandarino, Monte
Manley Shooting Supplies, Lowell
Marent, Rudolf
Martin's Gun Shop
Masker, Seely
Mathews & Son, Inc., Geo. E.
Mazur Restoration, Pete
McCament, Jay
McGowen Rifle Barrels
McGuire, Bill
McMillan Gunworks, Inc.
MCS, Inc.
Mercer Custom Stocks, R.M.
Mid-America Recreation, Inc.
Miller Arms, Inc.
Miller Co., David
Miller Custom
Miller, Tom
Mills Jr., Hugh B.
Moeller, Steve
Monell Custom Guns
Moneymaker Guncraft Corp.
Moreton/Fordyce Enterprises
Morrison Custom Rifles, J.W.
Morrow, Bud
Mountain Bear Rifle Works, Inc.
Mowreys Guns & Gunsmithing
Mullis Guncraft
Mustra's Custom Guns, Inc., Carl
Nastoff's 45 Shop Inc., Steve
Nelson, Stephen E.
Nettestad Gun Works
New England Custom Gun Service
Newman Gunshop
Nickels, Paul R.
Nicklas, Ted
Nolan, Dave
Norman Custom Gunstocks, Jim

North American Shooting Systems
North Fork Custom Gunsmithing
Novak's .45 Shop, Wayne
Nowlin Custom Barrels Mfg.
Nu-Line Guns, Inc.
Oakland Custom Arms, Inc.
Old World Gunsmithing
Olson, Vic
Orvis Co., The
Ottmar, Maurice
Pace Marketing, Inc.
Pachmayr Ltd.
Pagel Gun Works, Inc.
Pasadena Gun Center
Paterson Gunsmithing
Pell, John T.
PEM's Mfg. Co.
Pence Precision Barrels
Penrod Precision
Pentheny de Pentheny
Peterson Gun Shop, Inc., A.W.
Powell & Son (Gunmakers) Ltd., William
Power Custom, Inc.
Practical Tools, Inc.
Precision Arms International, Inc.
Professional Gunsmiths of America
Pro-Port Ltd.
P&S Gun Service
Quality Firearms of Idaho, Inc.
Rice, Keith
Ridgetop Sporting Goods
Ries, Chuck
Rifle Shop, The
Rigby & Co., John
Rizzini Battista
RMS Custom Gunsmithing
Robar Co.'s, Inc., The
Roberts Jr., Wm. A.
Robinson, Don
Rocky Mountain Rifle Works Ltd.
Rogers Gunsmithing, Bob
Royal Arm International Products
Rupert's Gun Shop
Russell's Rifle Shop
Ryan, Chad L.
Sanders Custom Gun Service
Sandy's Custom Gunshop
Schaefer, Roy V.
Schiffman, Curt
Schiffman, Mike
Schiffman, Norman
Schumakers Gun Shop, William
Schwartz Custom Guns, Wayne E.
Scott Fine Guns, Inc., Thad
Scott/McDougall Custom Gunsmiths
Shane's Gunsmithing
Shaw, Inc., E.R.
Shaw's Finest in Guns
Shay's Gunsmithing
Shell Shack
Shockley, Harold H.
Shootin' Shack, Inc.
Shooting Gallery, The
Shooting Specialties
Shotgun Shop, The
Shotguns Unlimited
Silver Ridge Gun Shop
Sipes Gun Shop
Siskiyou Gun Works
S.K. Guns, Inc.
Sklany, Steve
Skeoch, Brian R.
Slezak, Jerome F.

Small Arms Mfg. Co.
Smith, Art
Snapp's Gunshop
SOS Products Co.
Spender Reblue Service
Sportsmen's Exchange & Western Gun Traders, Inc.
Spradlin's
Springfield, Inc.
SSK Industries
Starnes, Ken
Steelman's Gun Shop
Steffens, Ron
Storey, Dale A.
Stott's Creek Armory, Inc.
Strawbridge, Victor W.
Stroup, Earl R.
Swann, D.J.
Swenson's 45 Shop, A.D.
S.W.I.F.T.
Swift River Gunworks, Inc.
Szweda, Robert
300 Gunsmith Service, Inc.
Talmage, William G.
Tank's Rifle Shop
Taylor & Robbins
Tennessee Valley Mfg.
Ten-Ring Precision, Inc.
Tertin, James A.
Texas Platers Supply
Thurston Sports, Inc.
Titus, Daniel
Tom's Gun Repair
Tom's Gunshop
Tooley, David
Trevallion Gunstocks
T.S.W. Conversion, Inc.
Unick's Gunsmithing
Upper Missouri Trading Co.
Van Epps, Milton
Van Horn, Gil
Vest, John
Vic's Gun Refinishing
Vintage Arms, Inc.
Volquartsen Custom Ltd.
Waffen-Weber Custom Gunsmithing
Walker Arms Co., Inc.
Wallace's
Wardell Precision Handguns Ltd.
Weaver Arms Corp.
Weaver's Gun Shop
Weems, Cecil
Wells Custom Gunsmith, R.A.
Wells Sport Store
Werth, T.W.
Wessinger Custom Guns & Engraving
West, Robert G.
Westchester Carbide
Western Ordnance Int'l Corp.
Westley Richards & Co.
White Owl Enterprises
White Rock Tool & Die
White Systems, Inc.
Wichita Arms, Inc.
Wiebe, Duane
Williams Gun Sight Co.
Williamson Precision Gunsmithing
Wilson's Gun Shop
Winter, Robert M.
Wisner's Gun Shop, Inc.
Wood, Frank S.
Yankee Gunsmith
Zeeryp, Russ

## CUSTOM METALSMITHS

Ackley Rifle Barrels, P.O.
Ahlman Guns
Aldis Gunsmithing & Shooting Supply
Apel, Dietrich
Armurier Hiptmayer
Baron Technology, Inc.
Barta's Gunsmithing
Beitzinger, George
Bellm Contenders
Benchmark Guns
Biesen, Al
Billingsley & Brownell
Brace, Larry D.
Briganti & Co., A.
Brown Precision, Inc.
Bustani Appraisers, Leo
Campbell, Dick
Carter's Gun Shop
Checkmate Refinishing

Chuck's Gun Shop
Classic Guns, Inc.
Clinton River Gun Serv., Inc.
Colonial Repair
Condor Mfg. Co.
Costa, David
Craftguard
Crandall Tool & Machine Co.
Cullity Restoration, Daniel
Custom Gun Products
Custom Gunsmiths
D&D Gunsmiths, Ltd.
D&H Precision Tooling
Duncan's Gunworks, Inc.
Dyson & Son Ltd., Peter
Eyster Heritage Gunsmiths, Inc., Ken
First Distributors, Inc., Jack
Flaig's
Fisher, Jerry A.

Francesca Stabilizer's, Inc.
Fullmer, Geo. M.
Gentry Custom Gunmaker, David
Goodwin, Fred
Gordie's Gun Shop
Graybill's Gun Shop
Green, Roger M.
Greenwalt Rifles
Griffin & Howe, Inc.
Guns
Gunsmithing Ltd.
Gutridge, Inc.
Hagn Rifles & Actions, Martin
Hecht, Hubert J.
Heilmann, Stephen
Heppler's Machining
Hiptmayer, Klaus
Hoag, James W.
Highline Machine Co.
Hobaugh, Wm. H.
Hyper-Single, Inc.
Intermountain Arms
Ivanoff, Thomas G.
Jaeger, Inc., Paul/Dunn's
Jamison's Forge Works
Jeffredo Gunsight
Johnson Gunsmithing, Inc., Neal G.
Johnston, James
Jones, Neil
K-D, Inc.
Kilham & Co.
Klein Custom Guns, Don
Kleinendorst, K.W.
Kopp, Terry K.
Lampert, Ron
Lawson Co., Harry
Lock's Philadelphia Gun Exchange
Mac's .45 Shop
Mains Enterprises, Inc.
McCament, Jay
McCormick's Custom Gun Bluing
McFarland, Stan
Mid-America Recreation, Inc.
Morrison Custom Rifles, J.W.
Morrow, Bud
Mullis Guncraft
Nettestad Gun Works
New England Custom Gun Service
Noreen, Peter H.
North Fork Custom Gunsmithing
Pace Marketing, Inc.

Pagel Gun Works, Inc.
Parker Gun Finishes
Pasadena Gun Center
Penrod Precision
Pentheny de Pentheny
Precise Metal Finishing
Precise Metalsmithing Enterprises
Precision Metal Finishing, John Westrom
Precision Specialties
P&S Gun Service
Rice, Keith
Rifle Shop, The
Robar Co.'s, Inc., The
Royal Arm International Products
Shell Shack
Shirley Co. Gun & Riflemakers Ltd., J.A.
Shockley, Harold H.
Silver Ridge Gun Shop
S.K. Guns, Inc.
Skeoch, Brian R.
Smith, Art
Snapp's Gunshop
Sportsmatch Ltd.
Strawbridge, Victor W.
Steffens, Ron
Talley, Dave
Ten-Ring Precision, Inc.
Tom's Gun Repair
Thompson, Randall
T.S.W. Conversions, Inc.
Unick's Gunsmithing
Van Horn, Gil
Van Patten, J.W.
Vic's Gun Refinishing
Waffen-Weber Custom Gunsmithing
Waldron, Herman
Wallace's
Westchester Carbide
Wells Sport Store
Werth, T.W.
Wessinger Custom Guns & Engraving
Western Design
White Owl Enterprises
White Rock Tool & Die
Wiebe, Duane
Wisner's Gun Shop, Inc.
Westrom, John
Wood, Frank S.

## DECOYS

A&M Waterfowl, Inc.
Ammunition Consulting Services, Inc.
Baekgaard Ltd.
Belding's Custom Gun Shop
Burnham Bros.
Carry-Lite, Inc.
Deer Me Products Co.
Fair Game International
Farm Form, Inc.
Feather Flex Decoys
Flambeau Products Corp.
G&H Decoys, Inc.
Herter's Manufacturing, Inc.

Hiti-Schuch, Atelier Wilma
Iron Mountain Knife Co.
Klingler Woodcarving
Molin Industries, Tru-Nord Division
North Wind Decoys Co.
Penn's Woods Products, Inc.
Quack Decoy Corp.
Ravell Ltd.
Robinson Firearms Mfg. Ltd.
Royal Arms
Sports Innovations, Inc.
Tanglefree Industries
Waterfield Sports, Inc.
Woods Wise Products

## ENGRAVERS, ENGRAVING TOOLS

Adair Custom Shop, Bill
Adams, John J.
Ahlman Guns
Alfano, Sam
Allard, Gary
Altamont Co.
Anthony and George Ltd.
Artistic Engraving
Baron Technology, Inc.
Bates Engraving, Billy
Bell Originals, Sid
Bledsoe, Weldon
Bleile, C. Roger
Boessler, Erich
Bone Engraving, Ralph
Bratcher, Dan
Brgoch, Frank
Brooker, Dennis
Brownell Checkering Tools, W.E.
Burgess, Byron
CAM Enterprises
Christopher Firearms Co., Inc., E.
Churchill, Winston
Clark Firearms Engraving
Clark, Frank
Creek Side Metal & Woodcrafters

Davidson, Jere
Delorge, Ed
Dolbare, Elizabeth
Drain, Mark
Dubber, Michael W.
Dyson & Son Ltd., Peter
Engraving Artistry
Evans Engraving, Robert
Eversull Co., Inc., K.
Eyster Heritage Gunsmiths, Inc., Ken
Fanzoj GesmbH
Firearms Engraver's Guild of America
Flannery Engraving Co., Jeff W.
Floatstone Mfg. Co.
Fogle, James W.
Fountain Products
Francolini, Leonard
Frank Knives
French, J.R.
Gene's Custom Guns
George, Tim and Christy
Glimm, Jerome C.
Golden Age Arms Co.
Gournet, Geoffroy

Grant, Howard V.
Griffin & Howe, Inc.
GRS Corp.
Gun Room, The
Guns
Gurney, F.R.
Gwinnell, Bryson J.
Hale, Peter
Hand Engravers Supply Co.
Hands, Barry Lee
Harris Hand Engraving, Paul A.
Harwood, Jack O.
Hendricks, Frank E.
Hiptmayer, Heidemarie
Horst, Alan K.
Ingle, Ralph W.
Jaeger, Inc., Paul/Dunn's
Johns, Bill
Kamyk Engraving Co., Steve
Kehr, Roger
Kelly, Lance
Klingler Woodcarving
Koevenig's Engraving Service
Kudlas, John M.
Leibowitz, Leonard
Letschnig, Franz
Lindsay, Steve
Lutz Engraving, Ron
Mains Enterprises, Inc.
Maki School of Engraving, Robert E.
Marek, George
Master Engravers, Inc.
McDonald, Dennis
McKenzie, Lynton
Mele, Frank
Mid-America Recreation, Inc.
Mittermeier, Inc., Frank
Moschetti, Mitchell R.
Mountain States Engraving
Nelson, Gary K.
New Orleans Arms Co.
New Orleans Jewelers Supply Co.
NgraveR Co., The
Oker's Engraving
Old Dominion Engravers
Pachmayr Ltd.
Palmgren Steel Products

Pedersen & Son, C.R.
Pilgrim Pewter, Inc.
Pilkington, Scott
Piquette, Paul R.
Potts, Wayne E.
Pranger, Ed G.
P&S Gun Service
Rabeno, Martin
Ravell Ltd.
Reed, Dave
Reno, Wayne & Karen
Riggs, Jim
Roberts, J.J.
Rohner, Hans and John
Rosser, Bob
Rundell's Gun Shop
Runge, Robert P.
Sampson, Roger
Schiffman, Mike
Shaw's Finest in Guns
Sherwood, George
Sinclair, W.P.
Singletary, Kent
Skaggs, R.E.
Smith, Mark A.
Smith, Ron
Theis, Terry
Thiewes, George W.
Thirion Hand Engraving, Denise
Tuscano, Tony
Valade, Robert B.
Vest, John
Viramontez, Ray
Vohres, David
Waffen-Weber Custom Gunsmithing
Wagoner, Vernon G.
Wallace's
Wallace, Terry
Warenski, Julie
Warren, Kenneth W.
Welch, Sam
Wells, Rachel
Wessinger Custom Guns & Engraving
Willig Custom Engraving, Claus
Wood, Mel

## GAME CALLS

Adventure Game Calls
Arkansas Mallard Duck Calls
Ashby Turkey Calls
Baekgaard Ltd.
Blakemore Game Calls, Jim
Bostick Wildlife Calls, Inc.
Buck Stix
Burnham Bros.
Carter's Wildlife Calls, Inc., Garth
Cedar Hill Game Call Co.
Crawford Co., Inc., R.M.
D-Boone Ent., Inc.
Dr. O's Products Ltd.
Duck Call Specialists
Faulk's Game Call Co., Inc.
Flow-Rite of Tennessee, Inc.
Green Head Game Call Co.
Hally Caller
Haydel's Game Calls, Inc.
Hunter's Specialties, Inc.
Keowee Game Calls
Kingyon, Paul L.
Knight & Hale Game Calls
Lohman Mfg. Co., Inc.
Mallardtone Game Calls
Marsh, Johnny
Moss Double Tone, Inc.
Mountain Hollow Game Calls

M/S Deepeeka Exports Pvt. Ltd.
Oakman Turkey Calls
Olt Co., Philip S.
Penn's Woods Products, Inc.
Primos Wild Game Calls, Inc.
Quaker Boy, Inc.
Rickard, Inc., Pete
Robbins Scent, Inc.
Safari Gun Co.
Salter Calls, Inc., Eddie
San Angelo Sports Products, Inc.
Savana Sports, Inc.
Sceery Co., E.J.
Scobey Duck & Goose Calls, Glynn
Scotch Hunting Products Co., Inc.
Scruggs' Game Calls, Stanley
Simmons Outdoor Corp.
SOS Products Co.
Sports Innovations, Inc.
Stewart Game Calls, Inc., Johnny
Sure-Shot Game Calls, Inc.
Tanglefree Industries
Tink's & Ben Lee Hunting Products
Tink's Safariland Hunting Corp.
Wellington Outdoors
Wilderness Sound Productions Ltd.
Wittasek, Dipl.-Ing. Norbert
Woods Wise Products
Wyant's Outdoor Products, Inc.

## GUN PARTS, U.S. AND FOREIGN

Ad Hominem
Amherst Arms
Armscorp. USA, Inc.
Aztec International Ltd.
Badger Shooters Supply, Inc.
Baumannize, Inc.
Behlert Precision
Bob's Gun Shop
Bustani Appraisers, Leo
Can Am Enterprises
Caspian Arms
Century International Arms, Inc.
Clark Custom Guns, Inc.
Colonial Repair
Condor Mfg. Co.

Defense Moulding Enterprises
Delta Arms Ltd.
Dibble, Derek A.
Dressel Jr., Paul G.
Duffy, Charles E.
Eagle International, Inc.
Ed's Gun House
EMF Co., Inc.
Fabian Bros. Sporting Goods, Inc.
FAPA Corp.
Farmer-Dressel, Sharon
Federal Ordnance, Inc.
First Distributors, Inc., Jack
Fleming Firearms
Forrest, Inc., Tom

Frazier Brothers Enterprises
Gentry Custom Gunmaker, David
Global Industries
Greider Precision
Gun Parts Corp., The
Guns
Gun Shop, The
Hallberg Gunsmith, Fritz
Hastings Barrels
Hoehn's Shooting Supply
Irwin, Campbell H.
Jaeger, Inc., Paul/Dunn's
J.O. Arms & Ammunition Co.
GJohnson Gunsmithing, Inc., Neal G.
K&T Co.
Keng's Firearms Specialty, Inc.
Kimber, Inc.
Kopp, Terry K.
Krico/Kriegeskorte GmbH, A.
Lock's Philadelphia Gun Exchange
Lodewick, Walter H.
London Guns Ltd.
Mac's .45 Shop
Mag-Pack Corp.
Markell, Inc.
McCormick Corp., Chip
McKee Publications
MEC-GAR S.R.L.
Merkuria Ltd.
Morrow, Bud
Nu-Line Guns, Inc.
Old Western Scrounger, Inc.
Olympic Arms, Inc.
Pace Marketing, Inc.
Parts & Surplus
Perazzi U.S.A., Inc.
Pre-Winchester 92-90-62 Parts Co.
Quality Firearms of Idaho, Inc.

Quality Parts Co.
Ram-Line, Inc.
Ranch Products
Randco UK
Ravell Ltd.
Retting, Inc., Martin B.
Rizzini Battista
Ruvel & Co., Inc.
Safari Arms, Inc./SGW
Sarco, Inc.
Shell Shack
Scherer
Sheridan USA, Inc., Austin
Sherwood Intl. Export Corp.
Smires, Clifford L.
Southern Ammunition Co., Inc.
Southern Armory, The
Springfield, Inc.
Springfield Sporters, Inc.
S&S Firearms
Starnes, Ken
Su-Press-On, Inc.
Tank's Rifle Shop
Taurus, S.A., Forjas
Tradewinds, Inc.
Triple-K Mfg. Co., Inc.
T.S.W. Conversions, Inc.
Twin Pine Armory
Vintage Industries, Inc.
Walker Arms Co., Inc.
Wardell Precision Handguns Ltd.
Weaver's Gun Shop
Weisz Antique Gun Parts
Westfield Engineering
Wisner's Gun Shop, Inc.
Wolff Co., W.C.
Zoli USA, Inc., Antonio

## GUNS, AIR

Action Arms Ltd.
Airgun Repair Centre
Air Rifle Specialists
Air Venture
Beeman Precision Airguns, Inc.
Benjamin/Sheridan Co.
Brass Eagle, Inc.
BSA Guns Ltd.
Champion's Choice, Inc.
Component Concepts, Inc.
Crawford Co., Inc., R.M.
Creedmoor Sports, Inc.
Crosman Corp.
Crosman Products of Canada Ltd.
Daisy Mfg. Co.
Diana
Dynamit Nobel-RWS, Inc.
FWB
Gamo
GFR Corp.
Great Lakes Airguns
GZ Paintball Sports Products
Hartmann & Weiss GMBH
Hebard Guns, Gil
Hy-Score Arms Co. Ltd.
Interarms
I.S.S.

•Mac-1 Distributors
•Marksman Products
Merkuria Ltd.
National Survival Game, Inc.
Nationwide Airgun Repairs
•Old Western Scrounger, Inc.
•Pardini Armi Commerciale Srl
Penguin Industries, Inc.
•PSI, Inc.
Ravell Ltd.
•RWS
Savana Sports, Inc.
S.G.S. Sporting Guns Srl
Sheridan USA, Inc., Austin
Specialized Weapons, Inc.
Sportsmatch Ltd.
•Steyr-Mannlicher
Stone Enterprises Ltd.
•Swivel Machine Works, Inc.
Tapco, Inc.
•Taurus, S.A., Forjas
Tippman Pneumatics, Inc.
Valor Corp.
•Walther GmbH, Carl
Webley and Scott Ltd.
•Weihrauch KG, Hermann

## GUNS, FOREIGN—IMPORTERS (Manufacturers)

Action Arms Ltd. (BRNO; CZ)
Air Rifle Specialists (Air Arms; BSA Guns Ltd.; Theoben Engineering)
Air Venture (airguns)
American Arms, Inc. (Fausti & Figlie s.n.c., Stefano; Franchi S.p.A., Luigi; Grulla Armes; Hermanos S.A., Zabala; INDESAL; Norica, Avnda Otaloa; blackpowder arms)
Armes de Chasse (AYA; Chapuis Armes; Francotte & Cie S.A., Auguste)
Armoury, Inc., The (blackpowder)
Armscorp USA, Inc.
Armsport, Inc. (Armsport, Inc.; blackpowder arms)
Autumn Sales, Inc. (Blaser Jagdwaffen GmbH)
Beauchamp & Son, Inc. (Pedersoli Davide & C.)
Beeman Precision Airguns, Inc. (Air Arms; Beeman Precision Airguns, Inc.; FWB; Weihrauch KG, Hermann)
Bell's Legendary Country Wear

(Miroku, B.C./Daly, Charles; Powell & Son, Ltd., William)
Beretta U.S.A. Corp. (Beretta Firearms, Pietro)
Bohemia Arms Co. (BRNO)
British Arms Co. Ltd.
British Sporting Arms (Miroku, B.C./Daly, Charles)
Browning Arms Co. (Browning Arms Co.)
B-West Imports, Inc.
Cabela's (Pedersoli Davide & C.; blackpowder arms)
California Armory, Inc.
Cape Outfitters (San Marco; blackpowder arms)
Century International Arms, Inc. (BRNO; Famas; FEG; Norinco)
ChinaSports, Inc. (Norinco)
Cimarron Arms (Uberti, Aldo; blackpowder arms)
CVA (blackpowder arms)
Daisy Mfg. Co. (Daisy Mfg. Co.; Gamo)
Dixie Gun Works (Pedersoli Davide & C.; blackpowder arms)

Dynamit Nobel-RWS, Inc. (Diana, Gamo, RWS)
E.A.A. Corp. (Astra-Unceta Y Cia, S.A.; Benelli Armi S.p.A.; Fabrica D'Armi Sabatti S.R.L.; Tanfoglio S.r.l., Fratelli/Witness; Weihrauch KG, Hermann)
Eagle Imports, Inc. (Bersa S.A.)
Ellett Bros. (Churchill)
EMF Co., Inc. (Dakota, Pedersoli Davide & C.; blackpowder arms)
Euroarms of America, Inc. (blackpowder arms)
Firstshot, Inc. (Daewoo Precision Industries Ltd.)
Glock, Inc. (Glock GmbH)
Griffin & Howe, Inc. (Rigby & Co., John)
Great Lakes Airguns (Sharp airguns)
GSI, Inc. (Merkel Freres, Steyr-Daimler-Puch, Steyr-Mannlicher AG)
G.U., Inc. (Sauer, SKB Arms Co.)
Hammerli USA (Hammerli Ltd.)
Hanus Birdguns, Bill (Grulla Armes; Merkel Freres; SKB Arms Co.; Ugartechea S.A., Ignacio; Weatherby, Inc.)
Heckler & Koch, Inc. (Benelli Armi S.p.A.; Heckler & Koch, GmbH)
Interarms (Helwan; Howa Machinery Ltd.; Interarms; Norinco; Rossi, Amadeo; Star Bonifacio Echeverria S.A.; Walther GmbH, Carl; Zastava Arms)
JägerSport, Ltd. (Heym GmbH & Co., Friedrich Wilh.; Voere-KGH m.b.H.)
J.O. Arms & Ammunition Co. (J.O. Arms & Ammunition Co.)
K.B.I., Inc. (FEG; Kassnar; K.B.I., Inc.; Norica, Avnda Otaola)
Keng's Firearms Specialty, Inc. (Poly Technologies, Inc.)
Krieghoff International, Inc. (Krieghoff Gun Co., H.)
K-Sports Imports, Inc.
London Guns Ltd.
Magnum Research, Inc. (Bernardelli Vincenzo S.p.A.; IMI/Desert Eagle)
MAGTECH Recreational Products, Inc. (CBC)
Mandall Shooting Supplies, Inc. (Ariziga; Bretton; Cabanas; Crucelegoi, Hermanos; Erma Werke GmbH; Firearms Co. Ltd./Alpine; Gaucher Armes S.A.; Korth; Krico/Kriegeskorte GmbH, A.; SIG; Tanner; Ugartechea S.A., Ignacio; Zanoletti, Pietro; Zoli, Antonio; blackpowder arms)
Marent, Rudolf (Hammerli Ltd.)
Marksman Products (Marksman Products)
McMillan Gunworks, Inc. (Peters Stahl GmbH)
MCS, Inc. (Pardini Armi Commerciale Srl)
MEC-Gar U.S.A., Inc. (MEC-Gar s.r.l.)

Midwest Sport Distributors (Norinco)
Mitchell Arms, Inc. (Mitchell Arms, Inc.; blackpowder arms)
Moore & Co., Wm. Larkin (Bertuzzi; Garbi, Armas Urki; Perugini-Visini & Co. s.r.l.; Piotti; Rizzini, F.LLI)
Navy Arms Co. (Navy Arms Co; Pedersoli Davide & C.; Uberti, Aldo; blackpowder arms)
New England Arms Co. (Cosmi Americo & Figlio s.n.c.; FERLIB; premium high-grade shotguns)
Nygord Precision Products (FAS, Morini; Steyr airguns, Unique/M.A.P.F.; Vostok)
Outdoor Sports Headquarters, Inc. (Miroku, B.C./Daly, Charles)
Para-Ordnance Mfg., Inc. (Para-Ordnance Mfg., Inc.)
Parker Div. Reagent Chemicals (Parker Reproductions)
Perazzi U.S.A., Inc. (Perazzi m.a.p. S.p.A)
Pragotrade (BRNO, CZ)
Precision Imports, Inc. (Mauser-Werke)
PSI, Inc. (Anschutz GmbH; Erma Werke GmbH; Gustaf, Carl; Marocchi F.lli S.p.A.)
Precision Sports (Ugartechea S.A., Ignacio)
Quality Arms, Inc. (Arrieta, S.L.; FERLIB)
Ruko Products (Armscor)
Safari Arms/SGW (Peters Stahl GmbH)
SGS Importers International, Inc. (Llama Gabilondo Y Cia)
Sigarms, Inc. (SIG-Sauer)
Sile Distributors (Benelli Armi S.p.A.; Marocchi F.lli S.p.A.; Solothurn)
Simmons Enterprises, Ernie (Sauer, SKB Arms Co.)
Specialty Shooters Supply, Inc. (JSL Ltd.)
Sportarms of Florida (Norinco; Schmidt, Herbert; Tokarav)
St. Lawrence Sales, Inc. (Fabarm S.p.A.)
Springfield, Inc. (Springfield, Inc.)
Stoeger Industries (IGA, Sako Ltd., Tikka)
Stone Enterprises Ltd. (air guns)
Swarovski Optik North America Ltd. (Heym GmbH & Co., Friedrich Wilh.; Voere-KGH m.b.H.)
Taurus Firearms, Inc. (Taurus International Firearms)
Tradewinds, Inc. (blackpowder arms)
Trail Guns Armory, Inc. (Pedersoli Davide & C.; blackpowder arms)
Uberti USA, Inc. (Uberti, Aldo; blackpowder arms)
Vintage Arms, Inc.
Weatherby, Inc. (Howa Machinery Ltd.; Weatherby, Inc.)
Wingshooting Adventures (Arrieta, S.L.)
Zoli U.S.A., Inc., Antonio (Zoli, Antonio)

## GUNS, FOREIGN—MANUFACTURERS (Importers)

Air Arms (Air Rifle Specialists; Beeman Precision Airguns, Inc.)
Anschutz GmbH (PSI, Inc.)
Ariziga (Mandall Shooting Supplies, Inc.)
Armscor (Ruko Products)
Armsport, Inc. (Armsport, Inc.)
Arrieta, S.L. (Quality Arms, Inc.; Wingshooting Adventures)
Astra-Unceta Y Cia, S.A. (E.A.A. Corp.)
ATIS Armi S.A.S.
AYA (Armes de Chasse)
Beeman Precision Airguns, Inc. (Beeman Precision Airguns, Inc.)
Benelli Armi S.p.A. (E.A.A. Corp.; Heckler & Koch, Inc.; Sile Distributors)
Beretta Firearms, Pietro (Beretta U.S.A. Corp.)
Beretta, Dr. Franco
•Bernardelli Vincenzo S.p.A. (Magnum Research, Inc.)
•Bersa S.A. (Eagle Imports, Inc.)
•Bertuzzi (Moore & Co., Wm. Larkin)
•Blaser Jagdwaffen GmbH (Autumn Sales, Inc.)
Bondini Paolo (blackpowder arms)
•Bretton (Mandall Shooting Supplies, Inc.)
•BRNO (Action Arms Ltd.; Bohemia Arms Co.; Century International Arms, Inc.)
•Browning Arms Co. (Browning Arms Co.)
•BSA Guns Ltd. (Air Rifle Specialists)
•Cabanas (Mandall Shooting Supplies, Inc.)
•CBC (MAGTECH Recreational Products, Inc.)
•Chapuis Armes (Armes de Chasse)
•Churchill (Ellett Bros.)

Cosmi Americo & Figlio s.n.c. (New England Arms Co.)
Crucelegui Hermanos (Mandall Shooting Supplies, Inc.)
CVA (blackpowder arms)
CZ (Action Arms Ltd.)
Daewoo Precision Industries Ltd. (Firstshot, Inc.)
Dakota (EMF Co., Inc.)
Daisy Mfg. Co. (Daisy Mfg. Co.)
Diana (Dynamit Nobel-RWS, Inc.)
Dumoulin, Ernest
Elko Arms, L. Kortz
Erma Werke GmbH (Mandall Shooting Supplies, Inc.; PSI, Inc.)
Fabarm S.p.A. (St. Lawrence Sales, Inc.)
Fabrica D'Armi Sabatti S.R.L. (E.A.A. Corp.)
Famas (Century International Arms, Inc.)
FAS (Nygord Precision Products)
Fausti & Figlie s.n.c., Stefano (American Arms, Inc.)
FEG (Century International Arms, Inc.; K.B.I., Inc.)
FERLIB (New England Arms Co.; Quality Arms, Inc.)
Firearms Co. Ltd./Alpine (Mandall Shooting Supplies, Inc.)
FN Herstal
Frankonia Jagd
Franchi S.p.A., Luigi (American Arms, Inc.)
Francotte & Cie S.A., Auguste (Armes de Chasse)
FWB (Beeman Precision Airguns, Inc.)
Gamba S.p.A., Renato
Gamo (Daisy Mfg. Co.; Dynamit Nobel-RWS, Inc.)
Garbi, Armas Urki (Moore & Co., Wm. Larkin)
Gaucher Armes S.A. (Mandall Shooting Supplies, Inc.)
Glock GmbH (Glock, Inc.)
Grulla Armes (American Arms, Inc.; Hanus Birdguns, Bill)
Gustaf, Carl (PSI, Inc.)
Hammerli Ltd. (Hammerli USA; Marent, Rudolph)
Hartmann & Weiss GmbH
Heckler & Koch, GmbH (Heckler & Koch, Inc.)
Helwan (Interarms)
Heym GmbH & Co., Friedrich Wilh. (JägerSport, Ltd.; Swarovski Optik North America Ltd.)
Howa Machinery Ltd. (Interarms; Weatherby, Inc.)
IGA (Stoeger Industries)
IMI/Desert Eagle (Magnum Research, Inc.)
INDESAL (American Arms, Inc.)
Interarms (Interarms)
J.O. Arms & Ammunition Co. (J.O. Arms & Ammunition Co.)
JSL Ltd. (Specialty Shooters Supply, Inc.)
Kassnar (K.B.I., Inc.)
K.B.I., Inc. (K.B.I., Inc.)
Korth (Mandall Shooting Supplies, Inc.)
Krico/Kriegeskorte GmbH, A. (Mandall Shooting Supplies, Inc.)
Krieghoff Gun Co., H. (Krieghoff International, Inc.)
Lakefield Arms Ltd.
Lanber Armes S.A.
Laurona Armes S.A.
Lebeau-Courally
Llama Gabilondo Y Cia (SGS Importers International, Inc.)
Marksman Products (Marksman Products)
Marocchi F.lli S.p.A. (PSI, Inc.; Sile Distributors)
Mauser-Werke (Precision Imports, Inc.)
MEC-Gar s.r.l. (MEC-Gar U.S.A., Inc.)
Merkel Freres (GSI, Inc.; Hanus Birdguns, Bill)
Miroku, B.C./Daly, Charles (Bell's Legendary Country Wear; British Sporting Arms; Outdoor Sports Headquarters)

Mitchell Arms, Inc. (Mitchell Arms, Inc.)
Morini (Nygord Precision Products)
Navy Arms Co. (Navy Arms Co.)
Norica, Avnda Otaola (American Arms, Inc.; K.B.I., Inc.)
Norinco (Century International Arms, Inc.; ChinaSports, Inc.; Interarms; Midwest Sport Distributors; Sportarms of Florida)
Para-Ordnance Mfg., Inc. (Para-Ordnance Mfg., Inc.)
Pardini Armi Commerciale Srl (MCS, Inc.)
Parker Reproductions (Parker Div. Reagent Chemical)
Pedersoli Davide & C. (Beauchamp & Son, Inc.; Cabela's; Dixie Gun Works; EMF Co., Inc.; Navy Arms Co.; Trail Guns Armory, Inc.)
Perazzi m.a.p. S.p.A. (Perazzi U.S.A., Inc.)
Perugini-Visini & Co. s.r.l. (Moore & Co., Wm. Larkin)
Peters Stahl GmbH (McMillan Gunworks, Inc.; Safari Arms/SGW)
Piotti (Moore & Co., Wm. Larkin)
Poly Technologies, Inc. (Keng's Firearms Specialty, Inc.)
Powell & Son (Gunmakers) Ltd., William (Bell's Legendary Country Wear)
Rigby & Co., John (Griffin & Howe, Inc.)
Rizzini, F.LLI (Moore & Co., Wm. Larkin)
Rossi, Amadeo (Interarms)
RWS (Dynamit Nobel-RWS, Inc.)
Sako Ltd. (Stoeger Industries)
San Marco (Cape Outfitters)
Sardius Industries Ltd.
Sauer (G.U., Inc.; Simmons Enterprises, Ernie)
Schmidt, Herbert (Sportarms of Florida)
SIG (Mandall Shooting Supplies, Inc.)
SIG-Sauer (Sigarms, Inc.)
SKB Arms Co. (G.U., Inc.; Hanus Birdguns, Bill; Simmons Enterprises, Ernie)
Solothurn (Sile Distributors)
Springfield, Inc. (Springfield, Inc.)
Star Bonifacio Echeverria S.A. (Interarms)
Steyr airguns (Nygord Precision Products)
Steyr-Daimler-Puch (GSI, Inc.)
Steyr-Mannlicher AG (GSI, Inc.)
Tanfoglio S.r.l., Fratelli/Witness (E.A.A. Corp.)
Tanner (Mandall Shooting Supplies, Inc.)
Taurus International Firearms (Taurus Firearms, Inc.)
Techni-Mec
T.F.C. S.p.A.
Theoben Engineering (Air Rifle Specialists)
Tikka (Stoeger Industries)
Tokarav (Sportarms of Florida)
Uberti, Aldo (Cimarron Arms; Navy Arms Co.; Uberti USA, Inc.)
Ugartechea S.A., Ignacio (Hanus Birdguns, Bill; Mandall Shooting Supplies, Inc.; Precision Sports)
Unique/M.A.P.F. (Nygord Precision Products)
Verney-Carron
Voere-KGH m.b.H. (JägerSport, Ltd.; Swarovski Optik North America Ltd.)
Vostok (Nygord Precision Products)
Walther GmbH, Carl (Interarms)
Weatherby, Inc. (Hanus Birdguns, Bill; Weatherby, Inc.)
Weihrauch KG, Hermann (Beeman Precision Airguns, Inc.; E.A.A. Corp.)
Westley Richards & Co.
Zanoletti, Pietro (Mandall Shooting Supplies, Inc.)
Zabala Hermanos S.A. (American Arms, Inc.)
Zastava Arms (Interarms)
Zoli, Antonio (Mandall Shooting Supplies, Inc.; Zoli USA, Inc., Antonio)

## GUNS, U.S.-MADE

Accu-Tek
AMAC
American Arms, Inc.
American Derringer Corp.
AMT
Armscorp USA, Inc.
A-Square Co., Inc.
Auto-Ordnance Corp.
Barrett Firearms Mfg., Inc.
Beretta U.S.A. Corp.
Brown Co., E. Arthur
Browning Arms Co. (Parts & Service)
Bryco Arms
Calico Light Weapon Systems
California Armory, Inc.
Century Gun Dist., Inc.
Century International Arms, Inc.
Charter Arms
Claridge Hi-Tec, Inc.
Clifton Arms
Colt Blackpower Arms Co.
Colt's Mfg. Co., Inc.
Competitor Corp., Inc.
Connecticut Valley Classics
Coonan Arms, Inc.
Cooper Arms
CVA
Dakota Arms, Inc.
Davis Industries
Desert Industries, Inc.
Eagle Arms, Inc.
EMF Co., Inc.
Falcon Industries, Inc.
Feather Industries, Inc.
Federal Engineering Corp.
Freedom Arms, Inc.
Gentry Custom Gunmaker, David
Gibbs Rifle Co., Inc.
Gilbert Equipment Co., Inc.
Gonic Arms, Inc.
Grendel, Inc.
H&R 1871, Inc.
Hatfield Gun Co., Inc.
Hawken Shop, The
HJS Arms, Inc.
H-S Precision, Inc.
IAI
Intratec
Ithaca Aquisition Corp./Ithaca Gun Co.
Jennings Firearms Inc.
J.O. Arms & Ammunition Co.
Johnson, Iver
Jones, J.D.
KDF, Inc.
Kimber, Inc.
Kimel Industries
Knight's Mfg. Co.
L.A.R. Manufacturing, Inc.

Laseraim Arms
Ljutic Industries, Inc.
Lorcin Engineering Co., Inc.
Magnum Research, Inc.
Marlin Firearms Co.
Maverick Arms, Inc.
McMillan Gunworks, Inc.
Mitchell Arms, Inc.
MK Arms, Inc.
M.O.A. Corp.
Montana Armory, Inc.
Mossberg & Sons, Inc., O.F.
Mowrey Gun Works
Navy Arms Co.
New Advantage Arms Corp.
New England Firearms
North American Arms
Olympic Arms, Inc.
Oregon Arms, Inc.
Parker-Hale
Phelps Mfg. Co.
Phoenix Arms
Precision Arms International, Inc.
Quality Parts Co.
Ram-Line, Inc.
Ravell Ltd.
Red Willow Tool & Armory, Inc.
Remington Arms Co., Inc.
Rocky Mountain Arms, Inc.
RPM
Safari Arms/SGW
Savage Arms, Inc.
Scattergun Technologies, Inc.
Seecamp Co., Inc., L.W.
Sharps Arms Co., Inc., C.
Shilen Rifles, Inc.
Shiloh Rifle Mfg.
Smith & Wesson
Sporting Arms Mfg., Inc.
Springfield, Inc.
SSK Industries
Sturm, Ruger & Co., Inc.
Sundance Industries, Inc.
Survival Arms, Inc.
Taurus Firearms, Inc.
Texas Arms
Texas Longhorn Arms, Inc.
Thompson/Center Arms
Ultra Light Arms, Inc.
U.S. Arms Corp.
U.S. Repeating Arms Co.
Valor Corp.
Wesson Firearms Co., Inc.
White Systems, Inc.
Wichita Arms, Inc.
Wildey, Inc.
Wilkinson Arms
Wyoming Armory, Inc.

## GUNS AND GUN PARTS, REPLICA AND ANTIQUE

Antique Arms Co.
Armi San Paolo
Armsport, Inc.
Beauchamp & Son, Inc.
Bondini Paolo
Bill's Gun Repair
Billings Gunsmiths, Inc.
Buckskin Machine Works
Burgess & Son Gunsmiths, R.W.
Cache La Poudre Rifleworks
Champlin, R. MacDonald
Century International Arms, Inc.
Colonial Repair
Day & Sons, Inc., Leonard
Delhi Gun House
Delta Arms Ltd.
Dilliott Gunsmithing, Inc.
Dixie Gun Works
Dixon Muzzleloading Shop, Inc.
Dyson & Son Ltd., Peter
EMF Co., Inc.
Federal Ordnance, Inc.
First Distributors, Inc., Jack
Flintlocks, Inc.
Forster Products
Franchi S.p.A., Luigi
Furr Arms
Getz Barrel Co.
Global Industries
Golden Age Arms Co.
Goodwin, Fred
Gun Parts Corp., The
Guns

Gun Works, The
Hallberg Gunsmith, Fritz
House of Muskets, Inc., The
Hunkeler, A.
Ken's Gun Specialties
Kopp, Terry K.
Liberty Antique Gunworks
Lock's Philadelphia Gun Exchange
Lodewick, Walter H.
Log Cabin Sport Shop
Lucas, Edw. E.
Mowrey Gun Works
Munsch Gunsmithing, Tommy
Muzzleloaders Etcetera, Inc.
Navy Arms Co.
OMR Feinmechanik, Jagd-und Sportwaffen, GmbH
Parker-Hale
PEM's Mfg. Co.
Pony Express Sport Shop, Inc.
Precise Metalsmithing Enterprises
Pre-Winchester Parts Co.
Quality Firearms of Idaho, Inc.
Ram-Line, Inc.
Randco UK
Ravell Ltd.
Sarco, Inc.
Shiloh Rifle Mfg.
Silver Ridge Gun Shop
Sklany, Steve
S&S Firearms
Stott's Creek Armory, Inc.
Taylor's & Co., Inc.

Track of the Wolf, Inc.
Unick's Gunsmithing
Upper Missouri Trading Co.
Vintage Industries, Inc.

Wayne Firearms for Collectors & Investors, James
Wescombe
Winchester Sutler, Inc., The

## GUNS, SURPLUS—PARTS AND AMMUNITION

Ammunition Consulting Services, Inc.
Armscorp. USA, Inc.
Aztec International Ltd.
Ballistica Maximus North
Ballistica Maximus South
Bondini Paolo
Braun, M.
British Arms Co. Ltd.
Century International Arms, Inc.
ChinaSports, Inc.
Delta Arms Ltd.
Ed's Gun House
Federal Ordnance, Inc.
First Distributors, Inc., Jack
Fleming Firearms
Forrest, Inc., Tom
Garcia National Gun Traders, Inc.
Gibbs Rifle Co., Inc.
Gun Parts Corp., The
Hallberg Gunsmith, Fritz
Interarms
Lever Arms Service Ltd.

Lock's Philadelphia Gun Exchange
Moreton/Fordyce Enterprises
Navy Arms Co.
Oil Rod and Gun Shop
Old Western Scrounger, Inc.
Paragon Sales & Services, Inc.
Parker-Hale
Parts & Surplus
Pre-Winchester Parts Co.
Quality Firearms of Idaho, Inc.
Randall Firearms Research
Ravell Ltd.
Sarco, Inc.
Shell Shack
Sherwood Intl. Export Corp.
Southern Ammunition Co., Inc.
Springfield Sporters, Inc.
T.F.C. S.p.A.
Thurston Sports, Inc.
U.S. Arms Corp.
Westfield Engineering
Whitestone Lumber Corp.

## GUNSMITHS, CUSTOM (see Custom Gunsmiths)

## GUNSMITHS, HANDGUN (see Pistolsmiths)

## GUNSMITH SCHOOLS

Brooker, Dennis
Colorado School of Trades
Cylinder & Slide, Inc.
Lassen Community College, Gunsmithing Dept.
Modern Gun Repair School
Montgomery Community College
Murray State College
North American Correspondence Schools
Nowlin Custom Barrels Mfg.

Pennsylvania Gunsmith School
Piedmont Community College
Pine Technical College
Professional Gunsmiths of America, Inc.
Ravell Ltd.
Southeastern Community College
Trinidad State Junior College Gunsmithing Dept.
Yavapai College

## GUNSMITH SUPPLIES, TOOLS, SERVICES

Ackley Rifle Barrels
Aldis Gunsmithing & Shooting Supply
Alley Supply Co.
American Pistolsmiths Guild
Atlantic Mills, Inc.
Bald Eagle Precision Machine Co.
Bellm Contenders
Bengtson Arms Co., L.
Biesen, Al
Biesen, Roger
Blue Ridge Machinery & Tools, Inc.
Brownell's, Inc.
Brown Products, Inc., Ed
B-Square Co.
Buckhorn Gun Works
Buehler Scope Mounts
Can Am Enterprises
C-H Tool & Die Corp./4-D Custom Die
Chapman Manufacturing Co., The
Choate Machine & Tool Co., Inc.
Clymer Manufacturing Co., Inc.
Colonial Arms, Inc.
Conetrol Scope Mounts
Crouse's Country Cover
Cumberland Arms
Custom Checkering Service
Custom Gun Products
D&D Gunsmiths, Ltd.
Dan's Whetstone Co., Inc.
Davidson Products, Inc.
Dayton Traister
Decker Shooting Products
Dem-Bart Hand Checkering Tools, Inc.
de Treville & Co., Stan
Dremel Mfg. Co.
Duffy, Charles E.
Du-Lite Corp.
The Dutchman's Firearms, Inc.
E.A.A. Corp.
Echols & Co., D'Arcy
Edmund Scientific Co.
Ed's Gun House

Eilan S.A.L.
Faith Associates, Inc.
FERLIB di Ferraglio Libero & Co.
First Distributors, Inc., Jack
Fisher, Jerry A.
Flashette Co.
Flitz International Ltd.
Forgreens Tool Mfg., Inc.
Forster, Kathy
Forster Products
Frazier Brothers Enterprises
Garrett Accur-Lt. D.F.S. Co.
Global Industries
Grace Metal Products, Inc.
Graybill's Gun Shop
Greenwalt Rifles
GRS Corp.
Gunline Tools
Guns
Gun-Tec
Gutridge, Inc.
Half Moon Rifle Shop
Henriksen Tool Co., Inc.
Huey Gun Cases, Marvin
Iosso Marine Products
Ivanoff, Thomas G.
Jantz Supply
JGS Precision Tool Mfg.
K-D, Inc.
Kasenit Co., Inc.
Kleinendorst, K.W.
Kopp, Terry K.
Korzinek Riflesmith, J.
LaRocca Gun Works, Inc.
Lea Mfg. Co.
Lee Supplies, Mark
Lortone, Inc.
Marsh, Mike
MCRW Associates
MCS, Inc.
MDS, Inc.
Menck, Thomas W.
Metalife Industries
Millett Sights
Milliron Custom Mittermeier, Inc.

MMC
Morrow, Bud
Newman Gunshop
NGraveR Co., The
Nitex, Inc.
N&J Sales
Nowlin Custom Barrels Mfg.
Ole Frontier Gunsmith Shop
Pace Marketing, Inc.
Palmgren Steel Products
PanaVise Products, Inc.
Pease Accuracy, Bob
PEM's Mfg. Co.
Power Custom, Inc.
Precise Metal Finishing
Precision Arms International, Inc.
Precision Specialties
Prolix®
Ravell Ltd.
Reardon Products
Robar Co.'s, Inc., The
Roto/Carve
Russell Knives, Inc., A.G.
Scott/McDougall Custom Gunsmiths
Shaw's Finest in Guns
Sheridan USA, Inc., Austin

Shirley Co. Gun & Riflemakers Ltd.
S.K. Guns, Inc.
Smith Whetstone Co., Inc.
Spyderco, Inc.
Starrett Co., L.S.
Stoney Point Products, Inc.
Stuart Products, Inc.
Sure Shot of LA, Inc.
TDP Industries, Inc.
Texas Platers Supply
Tom's Gun Repair
Trulock Tool
Turnbull Restoration, Doug
Unick's Gunsmithing
Walker Arms Co., Inc.
Washita Mountain Whetstone Co.
Weaver's Gun Shop
Wessinger Custom Guns &
 Engraving
Westfield Engineering
Westrom, John
Wilcox All-Pro Tools & Supply
Will-Burt Co.
Williams Gun Sight Co.
Williams Shootin' Iron Service
Yavapai College

## HANDGUN ACCESSORIES

Action Arms Ltd.
ADCO International
Adventurer's Outpost
Ajax Custom Grips, Inc.
American Bullets
American Pistolsmiths Guild
Ansen Enterprises
Auto-Ordnance Corp.
Bar-Sto Precision Machine
Baumannize, Inc.
Behlert Precision
Bob's Tactical Indoor Shooting
 Range & Gun Shop
Boonie Packer Products
Brauer Bros. Mfg. Co.
Brownells, Inc.
Brown Products, Inc., Ed
B-Square Co.
Bucheimer, J.M.
Centaur Systems, Inc.
Central Specialties Ltd.
Champion's Choice, Inc.
Clark Custom Guns, Inc.
Clymer Manufacturing Co., Inc.
Cobra Gunskin
C3 Systems
Dade Screw Machine Products
Doskocil Mfg. Co., Inc
E.A.A. Corp.
Eagle Imports, Inc.
Eagle International, Inc.
E&L Mfg., Inc.
EMF Co., Inc.
Faith Associates, Inc.
Feminine Protection, Inc.
Ferris Firearms
Fleming Firearms
Frielich Police Equipment
Glock, Inc.
Greider Precision
Gremmel Enterprises
Gun-Alert/Master Products, Inc.
Guncraft Sports, Inc.
Gunfitters, The
Gun-Ho Sports Cases
Hebard Guns, Gil
Heinie Specialty Products
Hill Speed Leather, Ernie
H.K.S. Products
Holster Shop, The
Jeffredo Gunsight
Jet Comp Systems
Jett & Co., Inc.
J.O. Arms & Ammunition Co.
Johnson Gunsmithing, Inc., Neal G.
Jones, J.D.
Jumbo Sports Products
Keller Co., The
King's Gun Works
K&K Ammo Wrist Band
KLP, Inc.
Kopp, Terry K.
Lakewood Products, Inc.
La Prade

LaRocca Gun Works, Inc.
Laseraim
Lee's Red Ramps
Lighthouse Mfg. Co., Inc.
Loch Leven Industries
Lohman Mfg. Co., Inc.
Mac's .45 Shop
Mag-Na-Port Int'l, Inc.
Magnolia Sports, Inc.
Magnum Research, Inc.
Mag-Pack Corp.
Maloni, Russ
Markell Inc.
Masen Co., John
Master Products, Inc.
McCormick Corp., Chip
MEC-Gar S.R.L.
Menck, Thomas W.
Merit Corp.
Merkuria Ltd.
Michaels of Oregon Co.
MTM Molded Products Co., Inc.
Mustra's Custom Guns, Inc., Carl
N.C. Ordnance Co.
Nielsen Custom Cases
No-Sho Mfg. Co.
Novak's .45 Shop, Wayne
Owen, Harry
Pace Marketing, Inc.
Pachmayr Ltd.
Pardini Armi Commerciale Srl
Peregrine Industries, Inc.
PistolPAL Products
Power Custom, Inc.
Practical Tools, Inc.
Precision Arms International, Inc.
Ranch Products
Ravell Ltd.
Royal Arm International Products
Russwood Custom Pistol Grips
Sheridan USA, Inc., Austin
Sile Distributors
Sling 'N Things, Inc.
Sonderman, Robert
Southwind Sanctions
Specialized Weapons, Inc.
Sport Specialties
SSK Industries
TacTell, Inc.
Tapco, Inc.
Taurus, S.A., Forjas
T.F.C. S.p.A.
Thompson/Center Arms
Triple-K Mfg. Co.
Tyler Mfg.-Dist., Melvin
Valor Corp.
Volquartsen Custom Ltd.
Wessinger Custom Guns &
 Engraving
Western Design
Whitestone Lumber Corp.
Wilson's Gun Shop
Wichita Arms, Inc.

## HANDGUN GRIPS

African Import Co.
Ahrends, Kim
Ajax Custom Grips, Inc.
Altamont Co.
American Gripcraft
Art Jewel Enterprises Ltd.
Barami Corp.
Bear Hug Grips, Inc.
Bell Originals, Inc., Sid
Bob's Gun Shop
Boone's Custom Ivory Grips, Inc.
CAM Enterprises
Champion's Choice, Inc.
Cobra Gunskin
Cole-Grip
Colonial Repair
Custom Firearms
Desert Industries, Inc.
E.A.A. Corp.
Eagle Imports, Inc.
EMF Co., Inc.
Eyears
Fitz Pistol Grip Co.
Forrest, Inc., Tom
Greene, M.L.
Guns
Harrison-Hurtz Enterprises, Inc.
Herrett's Stocks, Inc.
Hogue Grips
Holster Shop, The
Johnson Gunsmithing, Inc., Neal G.
Linebaugh Custom Sixguns & Rifle
 Works
Logan Security Products Co.

Mac's .45 Shop
Maloni, Russ
Masen Co., John
Monte Kristo Pistol Grip Co.
N.C. Ordnance Co.
Newell, Robert H.
Old Western Scrounger, Inc.
Pace Marketing, Inc.
Pachmayr Ltd.
Pardini Armi Commerciale Srl
Pilgrim Pewter, Inc.
Ravell Ltd.
Renner Co., R.J./Radical Concepts
Rosenberg & Sons, Jack A.
Royal Arm International Products
Royal Arms
Roy's Custom Grips
Russwood Custom Pistol Grips
Safari Gun Co.
Safariland Ltd., Inc.
Savana Sports, Inc.
Sheridan USA, Inc., Austin
Sile Distributors
Sonderman, Robert B.
Spegel, Craig
Taurus, S.A., Forjas
Taurus Firearms, Inc.
Tyler Mfg.-Dist., Melvin
Valor Corp.
Vintage Industries, Inc.
Volquartsen Custom Ltd.
Wallace's
Wayland Precision Wood Products

## HEARING PROTECTORS

Bausch & Lomb, Inc.
Bilsom Intl., Inc.
Blount, Inc. Sporting Equipment
 Division
Champion's Choice, Inc.
Clark Co., Inc., David
Cobra Gunskin
E-A-R, Inc.
Fitz Pistol Grip Co.
Flents Products Co., Inc.
Johnson Gunsmithing, Inc., Neal G.
MCRW Associates

North Specialty Products
Paterson Gunsmithing
Peltor, Inc.
R.E.T. Enterprises
Rockwood Corp., Speedwell Div.
Safari Gun Co.
Safariland Ltd., Inc.
Safety Direct
Smith & Wesson
Valor Corp.
Willson Safety Prods. Div.

## HOLSTERS AND LEATHER GOODS

A&B Industries, Inc.
Action Products, Inc.
Aker Leather Products
Alessi Holsters, Inc.
American Sales & Mfg. Co.
Arratoonian, Andy
Artistry in Leather
Baker's Leather Goods, Roy
Bandcor Industries
Barami Corp.
Beeman Precision Airguns, Inc.
Bianchi International, Inc.
Blocker's Custom Holsters, Ted
Bob's Tactical Indoor Shooting
 Range & Gun Shop
Brauer Bros. Mfg. Co.
Brown, H.R.
Brownells, Inc.
Browning Arms Co.
Bucheimer, J.M.
Carvajal Belts & Holsters
Cathey Enterprises, Inc.
Chace Leather Products
Clements' Custom Leathercraft,
 Chas
Cobra Gunskin
Cobra Line SRL
Cobra Sport
Colonial Repair
Crawford Co., Inc., R.M.
Creedmoor Sports, Inc.
Dakota Corp.
Davis Leather Co., G. Wm.
Delhi Gun House
DeSantis Holster & Leather Goods
Easy Pull/Outlaw Products
Ekol Leather Care
El Paso Saddlery Co.
EMF Co., Inc.
Epps "Orillia" Ltd., Ellwood
Eutaw Co., Inc., The
Faust, Inc., T.G.
Fobus International Ltd.

Fury Cutlery
Galati International
GALCO International Ltd.
Glock, Inc.
GML Products, Inc.
Gould & Goodrich
Gunfitters, The
Gun Leather Limited
Gusty Winds Corp.
Gun Works, The
Hafner Creations, Inc.
Hebard Guns, Gil
Henigson & Associates, Steve
High North Products, Inc.
Hill Speed Leather, Ernie
Holster Outpost
Holster Shop, The
Horseshoe Leather Products
Hoyt Holster Co., Inc.
Hume, Don
Hunter Co., Inc.
J.O. Arms & Ammunition Co.
John's Custom Leather
Jumbo Sports Products
Kane Products, Inc.
Kirkpatrick Leather Co.
KLP, Inc.
Kolpin Mfg., Inc.
L.A.R. Manufacturing, Inc.
Law Concealment Systems, Inc.
Lawrence Leather Co.
Leather Arsenal
Lethal Force Institute
Lone Star Gunleather
Magnolia Sports, Inc.
Markell, Inc.
MCRW Associates
Michaels of Oregon Co.
Mixson Leathercraft, Inc.
Nelson Combat Leather, Bruce
Nielsen Custom Cases
Noble Co., Jim
No-Sho Mfg. Co.

Null Holsters Ltd., K.L.
October Country
Ojala Holsters, Arvo
Oklahoma Leather Products, Inc.
Old West Reproductions, Inc.
Pace Marketing, Inc.
Pathfinder Sports Leather
Police Bookshelf
Proline Handgun Leather
PW Gunleather
Red Head, Inc.
Red River Frontier Outfitters
Renegade
Ringler Custom Leather Co.
Rybka Custom Leather Equipment, Thad
Safari Gun Co.
Safariland Ltd., Inc.
Safety Speed Holster, Inc.
Savana Sports, Inc.
Schulz Industries
Shadow Concealment Systems
Sheridan USA, Inc., Austin
Shoemaker & Sons, Inc., Tex

Shurkatch Corp.
Sile Distributors
Silhouette Leathers
Smith Saddlery, Jesse W.
Southwind Sanctions
Sparks, Milt
Stalker, Inc.
Strong Holster Co.
Stuart, V. Pat
Tabler Marketing
Texas Longhorn Arms, Inc.
Torel, Inc.
Triple-K Mfg. Co., Inc.
Tyler Mfg.-Dist., Melvin
Uberti USA, Inc.
Valor Corp.
Venus Industries
Viking Leathercraft, Inc.
Walt's Custom Leather
Whinnery, Walt
Wild Bill's Originals
Whitestone Lumber Corp.
Winchester Sutler, Inc., The

## HUNTING AND CAMP GEAR, CLOTHING, ETC.

Ace Sportswear, Inc.
Action Products, Inc.
Adventure 16, Inc.
All Weather Outerwear
Allen Co., Bob
Allen Sportswear, Bob
American Import Co., The
Armor
Atsko/Sno-Seal, Inc.
Bagmaster Mfg. Inc.
Barbour, Inc.
Barteaux Machetes, Inc.
Bauer, Eddie
Bausch & Lomb, Inc.
Bean, L.L.
Bear Archery
Beaver Park Products, Inc
Better Concepts Co.
Bilsom Intl., Inc.
Boss Manufacturing Co.
Brell Mar Products
Browning Arms Co.
Brown Manufacturing
Brunton U.S.A.
Buck Stop Lure Co., Inc.
Cabela's
Camofare Co.
Camp-Cap Products
Carhartt, Inc.
Catoctin Cutlery
Chameleon Camouflage Systems
Coulston Int. Corp.
Chimere, Inc.
Chippewa Shoe Co.
Churchill Glove Co., James
Clarkfield Enterprises, Inc.
Cobra Gunskin
Coghlan's Ltd.
Crawford Co., Inc., R.M.
Creedmoor Sports, Inc.
Coleman Co., Inc.
Counter Assault
Dakota Corp.
Danner Shoe Mfg. Co.
DeckSlider of Florida
Deer Me Products
Dr. O's Products Ltd.
Dunham Co.
Duofold, Inc.
Duxbak, Inc.
Dynalite Products, Inc.
E-A-R, Inc.
Erickson's Mfg., Inc., C.W.
Finerty, Raymond F.
Fish-N-Hunt, Inc.
Forrest Tool Co.
Fox River Mills, Inc.
Frankonia Jagd
Fury Cutlery
Game Winner, Inc.
Gander Mountain, Inc.
G&H Decoys, Inc.
Gerber Legendary Blades
Glacier Glove
Gozon Corp.
Hawken Shop, The
Herrett's Stocks, Inc.
Hinman Outfitters, Bob
Hodgman, Inc.
Houtz & Barwick

Hunter's Specialties, Inc.
Hunting Classics Ltd.
Innovision Enterprises
Johanssons Vapentillbehor, Bert
Just Brass, Inc.
Kamik Outdoor Footwear
K&M Industries, Inc.
Keowee Game Calls
LaCrosse Footwear, Inc.
Langenberg Hat Co.
Mack's Sport Shop
MAG Instrument, Inc.
Marathon Rubber Prods. Co., Inc.
Melton Shirt Co., Inc.
Millenium Safety Products
Molin Industries
Nelson/Weather-Rite
Noble Co., Jim
Northlake Boot Co.
Original Mink Oil, Inc.
Orvis Co., The
Palsa Outdoor Products
Partridge Sales Ltd., John
PAST Sporting Goods, Inc
Pendleton Woolen Mills
Porta Blind, Inc.
Primos Wild Game Calls, Inc.
Pro-Mark
Pyromid, Inc.
Randolph Engineering, Inc.
Ranger Footwear
Ranger Mfg. Co., Inc.
Rattlers Brand
Red Ball
Red Head, Inc.
Red River Frontier Outfitters
Refrigiwear, Inc.
Re-Heater, Inc.
Remington Footwear Co.
Rocky
Safari Gun Co.
Safesport Manufacturing Co.
Safety Direct
San Angelo Sports Products, Inc.
Savana Sports, Inc.
Scansport, Inc.
Scotch Hunting Products Co., Inc.
Servus Footwear Co.
Slings 'N Things, Inc.
Smith Whetstone Co., Inc.
Streamlight, Inc.
Survival Books/The Larder
Swanndri New Zealand
Torel, Inc.
Trail Timer Co.
Teledyne Co.
10-X Products Group
Thompson, Norm
Tink's Safariland Hunting Corp.
Torel, Inc.
Venus Industries
Wakina by Pic
Walker Shoe Co.
Walls Industries
Willson Safety Prods. Div.
Wolverine Boots & Shoes Div.
Woolrich Woolen Mills
Wyoming Knife Corp.
Yellowstone Wilderness Supply

## KNIVES AND KNIFEMAKER'S SUPPLIES FACTORY AND MAIL ORDER

Adventure 16, Inc.
African Import Co.
Aitor-Cuchilleria Del Norte, S.A.
American Target Knives
Aristocrat Knives
Art Jewel Enterprises Ltd.
Atlanta Cutlery Corp.
B&D Trading Co., Inc.
Barteaux Machetes, Inc.
Bean, L.L.
Benchmark Knives
Beretta U.S.A. Corp.
Blackjack Knives
Blue Ridge Knives
Blue Ridge Machinery & Tools, Inc.
Boker USA, Inc.
Bowen Knife Co.
Browning Arms Co.
Brunton U.S.A.
Buck Knives, Inc.
Buster's Custom Knives
CAM Enterprises
Camillus Cutlery Co.
Campbell, Dick
Case & Sons Cutlery Co., W.R.
Catoctin Cutlery
Chicago Cutlery Co.
Christopher Firearms Co., Inc., E.
Clements' Custom Leathercraft, Chas
Coast Cutlery Co.
Cold Steel, Inc.
Coleman Co., Inc.
Collins Brothers Div.
Colonial Knife Co.
Compass Industries, Inc.
Crawford Co., Inc., R.M.
Creative Craftsman, Inc., The
Crosman Blades
Cutco Cutlery
Cutlery Shoppe
Damascus-U.S.A.
Dan's Whetstone Co., Inc.
Degen Knives
Delhi Gun House
Diamontd Machining Technology, Inc.
EdgeCraft Corp.
EK Knife Co.
Empire Cutlery Corp.
Eze-Lap Diamond Prods.
Fitz Pistol Grip Co.
Forrest Tool Co.
Forthofer's Gunsmithing & Knifemaking
Fortune Products, Inc.
Frank Knives
Frost Cutlery Co.
Fury Cutlery
Gerber Legendary Blades
Golden Age Arms Co.
Gutmann Cutlery Co., Inc.
Hawken Shop, The
H&B Forge Co.
Harrington Cutlery, Inc., Russell
Henckels Zwillingswerk, Inc., J.A.

Hubertus Schneidwarenfabrik
Hunting Classics Ltd.
Hy-Score Arms Co. Ltd.
Ibberson (Sheffield) Ltd., George
Iron Mountain Knife Co.
J.A. Blades, Inc.
Jantz Supply
Jenco Sales, Inc.
KA-BAR Knives
Kasenit Co., Inc.
Kellogg's Professional Products
Ken's Finn Knives
Kershaw Knives
Knife Importers, Inc.
Koval Knives, Inc.
Lamson & Goodnow Mfg. Co.
Lansky Sharpeners & Crock Stick
Leatherman Tool Group, Inc.
Linder Solingen Knives
Mar Knives, Inc., Al
Matthews Cutlery
Molin Industries
Monte Kristo Pistol Grip Co.
Murphy Co., Inc., R.
Normark Corp.
North American Specialties
Outdoor Edge Cutlery Corp.
Plaza Cutlery, Inc.
Precise International
Queen Cutlery Co.
Randall-Made Knives
R&C Knives & Such
Ravell Ltd.
Reno, Wayne and Karen
Russell Knives, Inc., A.G.
Safesport Manufacturing Co.
Scansport, Inc.
Schiffman, Mike
Schrade Cutlery Corp.
Schrimsher's Custom Knifemaker's Supply, Bob
Sheffield Knifemakers Supply
Sheridan USA, Inc., Austin
Smith & Wesson
Smith Saddlery, Jesse W.
Smith Whetstone Co., Inc.
Soque River Knives
Spyderco, Inc.
Survival Books/The Larder
Swiss Army Knives, Inc.
T.F.C. S.p.A.
Track of the Wolf, Inc.
Tru-Balance Knife Co.
United Cutlery Corp.
Utica Cutlery Co.
Valor Corp.
Venus Industries
Walt's Custom Leather
Washita Mountain Whetstone Co.
Weber Jr., Rudolf
Wenoka/Seastyle
Western Cutlery Co.
Whinnery, Walt
White Owl Enterprises
Wostenholm
Wyoming Knife Corp.

## LABELS, BOXES, CARTRIDGE HOLDERS

Accuracy Products, S.A.
Anderson Manufacturing Co., Inc.
Arkfeld Mfg. & Dist. Co., Inc.
Cabinet Mtn. Outfitter
Del Rey Products
Fitz Pistol Grip Co.
Flambeau Products Corp.
Huey Gun Cases, Marvin
J&J Products Co.

KLP, Inc.
Kolpin Mfg., Inc.
Lakewood Products, Inc.
Monte Kristo Pistol Grip Co.
Peterson Instant Targets Co.
Ravell Ltd.
Scharch Mfg., Inc.
Stalwart Corp.

## LOAD TESTING AND PRODUCT TESTING, (Chronographing, Ballistic Studies)

ADC, Inc.
Ballistic Research
Bustani Appraisers, Leo
Clerke Co., J.A.
Corbin Applied Technology
D&H Precision Tooling
Farr Studio, Inc.
Jensen Bullets
Jones, J.D.
Jurras, L.E.
Lachaussee, S.A.
Lomont Precision Bullets

Maionchi-L.M.I.
McMurdo, Lynn
Neutralizer Police Munitions
Pejsa Ballistics
Rupert's Gun Shop
Russell's Rifle Shop
Schumakers Gun Shop, William
SSK Industries
Star Custom Bullets
White Laboratory, Inc., H.P.
Wildcatters, The

## MISCELLANEOUS

*Actions, Rifle*
  Hall Manufacturing
*Accurizing, Rifle*
  Stoney Baroque Shooters Supply
*Adapters, Cartridge*
  Alex, Inc.
  Owen, Harry
*Adapters, Shotshell*
  PC Co. (Plummer 410 conversion)
*Airgun Accessories*
  Beeman Precision Airguns, Inc.
    (Beeman Pell Seat, Pell Size)
  BSA Guns Ltd.
*Assault Rifle Accessories*
  Feather Industries, Inc.
  Ram-Line, Inc.
*Body Armor*
  A&B Industries, Inc.
  Faust, Inc., T.G.
  Second Chance Body Armor
*Bore Collimator*
  Alley Supply Co. (Sweany
    Site-A-Line)
*Bore Illuminator*
  Flashette Co. (gun cleaning aid)
*Bore Lights*
  MDS, Inc.
*Brass Catcher*
  M.A.M. Products, Inc. (free
    standing for all auto pistols
    and/or semi-auto rifles)
*Bullets, Rubber*
  CIDCO
*Calendar, Gun Show*
  Stott's Creek Armory, Inc.
*Cannons, Miniature Replicas*
  Furr Arms
  R.G.-G., Inc.
*Convert-A-Pell*
  Jett & Co., Inc.
*Dehumidifiers*
  Buenger Enterprises
  Hydrosorbent Products
*Deer Drag*
  D&H Prods. Co., Inc.
*Dryers*
  Buenger Enterprises
    (thermo-electric)
  Peet Shoe Dryer, Inc. (electric
    boot, shoe, hip, chest wader)
*E-Z Loader*
  Del Rey Products (for 22-cal.
    rifles)
*Firearm Historian*
  Kennerknecht, Rick "KK"
*Firearm Restoration*
  Adair Custom Shop, Bill
  Border Guns & Leather
  Johns, Bill
  Liberty Antique Gunworks
  Mazur Restoration, Pete
  Moeller, Steve
*FFL Record Keeping*
  Basics Information Systems, Inc.
  R.E.T. Enterprises
*Flares*
  Aztec International Ltd.
*Gatling Guns*
  Furr Arms
*Hunting Trips*
  J/B Adventures & Safaris, Inc.
  Professional Hunter Specialties
    (African safaris)
  Mongaso Wild Life Safaris
*Hypodermic Rifles/Pistols*
  Multipropulseurs
*Insert Barrels*
  Owen, Harry/Sport Specialties
*IR Detection Systems*
  GTS Enterprises, Inc.
*Locks, Gun*
  Brown Manufacturing
  Master Lock Co.
*Military Equipment/Accessories*
  Alpha 1 Drop Zone
*Monte Carlo Pad*
  Hoppe's Div.
*Photographers, Gun*
  Bilal, Mustafa
  Hanusin, John
  Macbean, Stan
  Payne Photography, Robert
  Semmer, Charles
  Smith, Michael
  Weyer International

*Power Tools, Rotary Flexible Shaft*
  Foredom Electric Co.
*Racks, Gun and Bow*
  All Rite Products, Inc.
*Saddle Rings, Studs*
  Silver Ridge Gun Shop
*Safety Devices*
  Gun-Alert/Master Products, Inc.
    (gun safety cover)
  P&M Sales and Service
*Safeties*
  Harper, William E./The Great 870
    Co. (for Rem. 870P)
  Taylor & Robbins (sidelever f. rifle)
*Scents and Lures*
  Buck Stop Lure Co., Inc.
  Cabinet Mtn. Outfitter
  Dr. O's Products Ltd.
  Mountain Hollow Game Calls
  Rickard, Inc., Pete
  Robbins Scent, Inc.
  Tink's Safariland Hunting Corp.
  Wildlife Research Center, Inc.
*Scoring Plug*
  RIG Products
*Scrimshaw*
  Boone's Custom Ivory Grips, Inc.
  Dolbare, Elizabeth
  Gun Room, The
  Marek, George
  Reno, Wayne and Karen
  Sherwood, George
*Self-Defense Sprays*
  Counter Assault
*Shell Catcher*
  Condor Mfg. Co.
*Shell Dispenser*
  Loadmaster
*Shooting Range Equipment*
  Caswell International Corp.
*Silencers*
  AWC Systems Technology
  Ciener, Jonathan Arthur
  Developmental Concepts
  DLO Mfg.
  Fleming Firearms
  Norrell Arms, John
  Precision Arms International, Inc.
  S&H Arms Mfg. Co.
  S.C.R.C.
  Sound Technology
  Ward Machine
*Slings and Swivels*
  Boonie Packer Products
  Butler Creek Corp.
  DTM International, Inc.
  Leather Arsenal
  Michaels of Oregon Co.
  Outdoor Connection, Inc., The
  Palsa Outoor Products
  Pathfinder Sports Leather
  Schulz Industries
  Sile Distributors
  Torel, Inc.
*Speedloader, Shotgun*
  Armstec, Inc.
*Treestands and Steps*
  A&J Products
  Amacker International, Inc.
  Apache Products, Inc.
  Dr. O's Products Ltd.
  Silent Hunter
  Summit Specialties, Inc.
  Trax America, Inc.
  Treemaster
  Warren & Sweat Mfg. Co.
*Trophies*
  Blackinton & Co., Inc., V.H.
*Ventilation*
  ScanCo Environmental Systems
    (indoor range filtration)
*Video Tapes*
  Calibre Press, Inc. (police survival)
  Dangler, Homer L. (Kentucky
    rifles)
  Eastman Products, R.T. (outdoor
    adventure)
  Foothills Video Productions, Inc.
  MagSafe Ammo Co.
  New Historians Productions, The
    (muzzle-loading)
  Trail Visions (woodcock hunting)
  Wilderness Sound Productions
*Xythos-Miniature Revolver*
  Andres & Dworsky

## MUZZLE-LOADING GUNS, BARRELS AND EQUIPMENT

Accuracy Unlimited (Littleton, CO)
Adkins, Luther
All American Bullets
Anderson Manufacturing Co., Inc.
Armi San Paolo
Armoury, Inc., The
Armsport, Inc.
Barton, Michael D.
Beauchamp & Son, Inc.
Beaver Lodge
Bentley, John
Blackhawk East
Blackhawk Mountain
Blackhawk West
Blount, Inc. Sporting Equipment
  Division
Bridgers Best
Buckskin Machine Works
Buffalo Bullet Co., Inc.
Burgess and Son Gunsmiths, R.W.
Butler Creek Corp.
Cache La Poudre Rifleworks
Camas Hot Springs Mfg.
Chopie Mfg., Inc.
CONKKO
Cousin Bob's Mountain Products
Cumberland Arms
Cumberland Knife & Gun Works
CVA
Dangler, Homer L.
Dan's Whetstone Co., Inc.
Day & Sons, Inc., Leonard
Dayton Traister
deHaas Barrels
Denver Arms, Ltd.
DGS, Inc.
Dixon Muzzleloading Shop, Inc.
Ed's Gun House
EMF Co., Inc.
Euroarms of America, Inc.
Eutaw Co., Inc., The
Fautheree, Andy
Fellowes, Ted
Fish, Marshall F.-Mfg. Gunsmith
Flintlock Muzzle Loading Gun
  Shop, The
Flintlocks, Etc.
Forster Products
Frontier
Getz Barrel Co.
Gibbs Rifle Co., Inc.
Golden Age Arms Co.
Gonic Arms, Inc.
Green Bay Bullets
Gun Works, The
Hatfield Gun Co., Inc.
Hawken Shop, The
Hege Jagd-u. Sporthandels, GmbH
Hodgdon Powder Co., Inc.
Hornady Mfg. Co.
House of Muskets, Inc., The
Hunkeler, A.
Jamison's Forge Works
K&M Industries, Inc.
Kolpin Mfg., Inc.

Kwik-Site Co.
Lite Tek International
Log Cabin Sport Shop
Lyman Products Corp.
McCann's Muzzle-Gun Works
Mitchell Arms, Inc.
Modern MuzzleLoading, Inc.
Montana Armory, Inc.
Mossberg & Sons, Inc., O.F.
Mountain State Muzzleloading
  Supplies
Mowrey Gun Works
MMP
Mt. Alto Outdoor Products
Mushroom Express Bullet Co.
Muzzleloaders Etcetera, Inc.
Neumann GmbH
Newman Gunshop
October Country
Oklahoma Leather Products, Inc.
Olde Pennsylvania
Ox-Yoke Originals, Inc.
Parker Gun Finishes
Patchbox & Museum of the Great
  Divide, The
Pedersoli Davide & C.
Peterson Gun Shop, Inc., A.W.
Peterson Instant Targets, Inc.
Phyl-Mac
Robinson Firearms Mfg. Ltd.
R.V.I.
Scott, Inc., Tyler
Selsi Co., Inc.
Safari Gun Co.
S&B Industries
Sharps Arms Co., Inc., C.
Shooter's Choice
Sile Distributors
Siler Locks
Single Shot, Inc.
Slings 'N Things, Inc.
South Bend Replicas, Inc.
Southern Bloomer Mfg. Co.
SPG Bullet Lubricant
Storey, Dale A.
Sturm, Ruger & Co., Inc.
Taylor's & Co., Inc.
TDP Industries, Inc.
Tennessee Valley Mfg.
TETRA Gun Lubricants
Thompson/Center Arms
Thunder Mountain Arms
Tiger-Hunt
Track of the Wolf, Inc.
Traditions, Inc.
Trail Guns Armory, Inc.
Uberti USA, Inc.
Ultra Light Arms, Inc.
Upper Missouri Trading Co.
Warren Muzzleloading Co., Inc.
Wescombe
White Systems, Inc.
Winchester Sutler, Inc., The
Young Country Arms
Ziegel Engineering

## PISTOLSMITHS

Accuracy Gun Shop
Accuracy Unlimited (Glendale, AZ)
Accurate Plating & Weaponry, Inc.
Ahlman Guns
Aldis Gunsmithing & Shooting
  Supply
Alpha Precision, Inc.
American Pistolsmiths Guild
Amodei, Jim
Armament Gunsmithing Co., Inc.
Bain & Davis, Inc.
Baity's Custom Gunworks
Banks, Ed
Bar-Sto Precision Machine
Barta's Gunsmithing
Bengtson Arms Co., L.
Border Guns & Leather
Bowen Classic Arms Corp.
Brian, C.T.
Briley Mfg., Inc.
Broken Gun Ranch
Brown Products, Inc., Ed
Campbell, Dick
Cannon's Guns
Caraville Manufacturing
Carter's Gun Shop

Cellini, Inc., Vito Francesca
Chesire & Perez Dist.
Chuck's Gun Shop
Clark Custom Guns, Inc.
Colonial Repair
Corkys Gun Clinic
Curtis Custom Shop
Custom Gunsmiths
Cylinder & Slide, Inc.
Davis Service Center, Bill
D&D Gunsmiths, Ltd.
D&L Sports
D.O.C. Specialists, Inc.
Duncan's Gunworks, Inc.
E.A.A. Corp.
EMF Co., Inc.
Ferris Firearms
First Distributors, Inc., Jack
Fisher Custom Firearms
Francesca Stabilizer's, Inc.
Frielich Police Equipment
Frontier Arms Co., Inc.
Garthwaite, Jim
Greider Precision
Guncraft Sports, Inc.
Gunsite Gunsmithy

Gunsmithing Ltd.
Gutridge, Inc.
Hamilton, Keith
Hank's Gun Shop
Hanson's Gun Center, Dick
Hardison, Charles
Hebard Guns, Gil
Heinie Specialty Products
High Bridge Arms, Inc.
Highline Machine Co.
Hindman, Ace
Hoag, James W.
Irwin, Campbell H.
Ivanoff, Thomas G.
Ken's Gun Specialties
Jarvis Gunsmithing, Inc.
Johnston, James
Jones, J.D.
Jungkind, Reeves C.
Kilham & Co.
Kimball, Gary
Kopec Enterprises, John
Kopp, Terry K.
La Clinique du .45
LaFrance Specialties
LaRocca Gun Works, Inc.
Laughridge, William R.
Lawson, John G.
Lee's Red Ramps
Linebaugh Custom Sixguns & Rifle
  Works
Lock's Philadelphia Gun Exchange
Long, George F.
Mac's .45 Shop
Mahony, Philip Bruce
Martz, John V.
Marvel, Alan
McMillan Gunworks, Inc.
MCS, Inc.
Mid-America Recreation, Inc.
Miller Custom
Mitchell's Accuracy Shop
MJK Gunsmithing, Inc.
Moran, Jerry
Mountain Bear Rifle Works, Inc.
Mullis Guncraft
Mustra's Custom Guns, Inc., Carl
Nastoff's 45 Shop Inc., Stev
North Fork Custom Gunsmithing
Novak's .45 Shop, Wayne
Nowlin Custom Barrels Mfg.
Nu-Line Guns, Inc.
Nygord Precision Products
Oglesby & Oglesby
  Gunmakers, Inc.

Old West Reproductions
Pace Marketing, Inc.
Pachmayr Ltd.
Pardini Armi Commerciale Srl
Paris, Frank J.
Peacemaker Specialists
PEM's Mfg. Co.
Performance Specialists
Phillips & Bailey, Inc.
Pierce Pistols
Plaxco, J. Michael
Practical Tools, Inc.
Precision Arms International, Inc.
Precision Specialties
Randco UK
Ravell Ltd.
Ries, Chuck
Riggs, Jim
Robar Co.'s, Inc., The
Rogers Gunsmithing, Bob
Scott/McDougall Custom Gunsmiths
Seecamp Co., Inc., L.W.
Shell Shack
Shooter Shop, The
Singletary, Kent
Sipes Gun Shop
Sight Shop, The
S.K. Guns, Inc.
Slings & Arrows
Spokhandguns, Inc.
Springfield, Inc.
SSK Industries
Starnes, Ken
Steger, James R.
Strawbridge, Victor W.
Stroup, Earl R.
Swenson's 45 Shop, A.D.
300 Gunsmith Service, Inc.
Ten-Ring Precision, Inc.
Thompson, Randall
Thurston Sports, Inc.
Tom's Gun Repair
T.S.W. Conversions, Inc.
Ulrich, Doc & Bud
Unick's Gunsmithing
Vic's Gun Refinishing
Volquartsen Custom Ltd.
Wallace's
Walters Industries
Wardell Precision Handguns Ltd.
Wessinger Custom Guns &
  Engraving
Williamson Precision Gunsmithing
Woods Pistolsmithing
Yavapai College

G&C Bullet Co., Inc.
"Gramps" Antique Cartridges
Graphics Direct
Green, Arthur S.
Hanned Line, The
HEBB Resources
Heidenstrom Bullets
Hensley & Gibbs
Hindman, Ace
Hoehn's Shooting Supply
Hollywood Engineering
Hondo Industries
Hornady Mfg. Co.
Huntington Die Specialties
INTEC International, Inc.
Iosso Marine Products
JGS Precision Tool Mfg.
Jones, Neil
KAPRO MFG. Co., Inc.
King & Co.
K&M Services
Lachaussee, S.A.
LeClear Industries
Lee Precision, Inc.
Liberty Metals
Lighthouse Mfg. Co., Inc.
Lortone, Inc.
Loweth Firearms, Richard
Lyman Products Corp.
Magma Engineering Co.
McKillen & Heyer, Inc.
MCRW Associates
MCS, Inc.
MEC
Midway Arms, Inc.
MMP
Monte Kristo Pistol Grip Co.
Mountain South
MTM Molded Products Co., Inc.
Multi-Scale Charge Ltd.
NECO
Necromancer Industries, Inc.
Newman Gunshop
Niemi Enterprises, W.B.
Old West Bullet Moulds
Old Western Scrounger, Inc.
Omark Industries
Pattern Control
Pend Oreille Sport Shop
Peterson Instant Targets, Inc.
Plum City Ballistic Range
Ponsness/Warren
Precision Castings & Equipment,
  Inc.
Precision Reloading, Inc.

Quinetics Corp.
Rapine Bullet Mould Mfg. Co.
Ravell Ltd.
Raytech
•RCBS
•R.D.P. Tool Co., Inc.
•Redding Reloading, Inc.
Riebe Co., W.J.
Roberts Products
Rochester Lead Works, Inc.
Rooster Laboratories
Rorschach Precision Products
Rucker Ammunition Co.
SAECO
Safari Gun Co.
Sandia Die & Cartridge Co.
S.C.A.P. Industries
•Scharch Mfg., Inc.
Scot Powder Co. of Ohio, Inc.
Shooters Accessory Supply
Sierra Bullets
Sierra Specialty Prod. Co.
Silver Eagle Machining
Simmons, Jerry
Sinclair International, Inc.
Skip's Machine
Slipshot MTS Group
Small Custom Mould & Bullet Co.
SOS Products Co.
Speer Products
Sportsman Supply Co.
•Stalwart Corp.
•Star Machine Works
Stoney Point Products, Inc.
Taracorp Industries
TETRA Gun Lubricants
Thompson Bullet Lube Co.
Timber Heirloom Products
Trammco, Inc.
Tru-Square Metal Products
T&S Industries, Inc.
Varner's Service
Vega Tool Co.
VibraShine, Inc.
Vibra-Tek Co.
Webster Scale Mfg. Co.
Welsh, Bud
Westfield Engineering
Whitestone Lumber Corp.
Whitetail Design & Engineering Ltd.
Widener's Reloading & Shooting
  Supply
•William's Gun Shop, Ben
Wilson, Co, L.E.
Young Country Arms

## REBORING AND RERIFLING

Ackley Rifle Barrels, P.O.
Bellm Contenders
Chuck's Gun Shop
DKT, Inc.
H&S Liner Service
Ivanoff, Thomas G.
Jackalope Gun Shop
Jaeger, Inc., Paul/Dunn's
K-D, Inc.
Kopp, Terry K.
LaBounty Precision Reboring
Matco, Inc.
Mid-America Recreation, Inc.

Morrow, Bud
Ozark Gun Works
Pac-Nor Barreling
Pence Precision Barrels
Redman's Rifling & Reboring
Ridgetop Sporting Goods
Sharon Rifle Barrel Co.
Shaw, Inc., E.R.
Swift River Gunworks, Inc.
300 Gunsmith Service, Inc.
Tom's Gun Repair
Van Patten, J.W.
West, Robert G.

## RELOADING TOOLS AND ACCESSORIES

Accuracy Components Co.
Advance Car Mover Co., Inc.
Ammo Load, Inc.
AMT
Andela Tool & Machinery, Inc.
ASI
Ballisti-Cast, Inc.
Ballistic Products, Inc.
Barlett, J.
Ben's Machines
Blount, Inc. Sporting Equipment
  Division
Brown Co., E. Arthur
Brynin, Milton
Buck Stix
C&D Special Products
Camdex, Inc.
Carbide Die & Mfg. Co., Inc.
C-H Tool & Die Corp./4-D Custom
  Die Co.
CheVron Case Master
Claybuster
Coats, Mrs. Lester

Colorado Shooter's Supply
Competitor Corp., Inc.
Conetrol Scope Mounts
CONKKO
•Corbin, Inc.
Custom Products
•Dakota Arms
D.C.C. Enterprises
•Denver Instrument Co.
•Destination North Software
Dever Co., Jack
Dewey Mfg. Co., Inc., J.
•Dillon Precision Prods., Inc.
Eagan, Donald V.
Efemes Enterprises
Engineered Accessories
Enguix Import-Export
Fisher Enterprises
Fitz Pistol Grip Co.
Flambeau Products Corp.
Forgreens Tool Mfg., Inc.
•Forster Products
•Fremont Tool Works

## RESTS—BENCH, PORTABLE—AND ACCESSORIES

Adventure 16, Inc.
Armor Metal Products
Bald Eagle Precision Machine Co.
Blount, Inc. Sporting Equipment
  Division
B-Square Co.
Champion's Choice, Inc.
Clift Mfg., L.R.
Clifton Arms, Inc.
Cravener's Gun Shop
Davidson Products, Inc.
Desert Mountain Mfg.
Forster Products
Greenwalt Rifles
Harris Engineering, Inc.
Hart & Son, Inc., Robert W.
Hidalgo, Tony

Holden Co., J.B.
Hoppe's Div.
Johnson Gunsmithing, Inc., Neal G.
MCRW Associates
Millett Sights
Newman Gunshop
Protektor Model Co.
Ransom International Corp
Sinclair International, Inc.
Sportsman Supply Co.
Sports Support Systems, Inc.
Sure Shot of LA, Inc.
Thompson Target Technology
Ultra Light Arms, Inc.
Verdemont Fieldsports
World of Targets

## RIFLE BARREL MAKERS (See also Muzzle-Loading Guns, Barrels and Equipment)

Ackley Rifle Barrels, P.O.
American Bullets
Bellm Contenders
Borovnik KG, Ludwig
Bullberry Barrel Works, Ltd.
Bustani Appraisers, Leo
Carter's Gun Shop
Camas Hot Springs Mfg.
Cincinnati Swaging
Clark Custom Guns, Inc.
Clerke Co., J.A.
Competition Limited
DKT, Inc.
Donnelly, C.P.
Douglas Barrels, Inc.
Federal Ordnance, Inc.
Frank Custom Gun Service, Ron
Getz Barrel Co.

Graybill's Gun Shop
Green Mountain Rifle Barrel Co.,
  Inc.
H-S Precision, Inc.
Half Moon Rifle Shop
Hart Rifle Barrels, Inc.
Hastings Barrels
K-D, Inc.
KOGOT
Kopp, Terry K.
Krieger Barrels, Inc.
LaBounty Precision Reboring
Lilja Precision Rifle Barrels
Lock's Philadelphia Gun Exchange
Marquart Precision Co., Inc.
Matco, Inc.
McGowen Rifle Barrels
McMillan Rifle Barrels

Mid-America Recreation, Inc.
Oakland Custom Arms, Inc.
Obermeyer Rifled Barrels
Olympic Arms, Inc.
Pell, John T.
Pence Precision Barrels
Ravell Ltd.
Robar Co.'s, Inc., The
Rocky Mountain Rifle Works Ltd.
Safari Arms, Inc./SGW
Schneider Rifle Barrels, Inc., Gary
Sharon Rifle Barrel Co.

Shaw, Inc., E.R.
Shilen Rifles, Inc.
Small Arms Mfg. Co.
Siskiyou Gun Works
Societa Armi Bresciane Srl
Springfield, Inc.
Strutz Rifle Barrels, Inc., W.C.
Unique/M.A.P.F.
Verney-Carron
White Systems, Inc.
Wilson Arms Co., The

## SCOPES, MOUNTS, ACCESSORIES, OPTICAL EQUIPMENT

Ackley Rifle Barrels
Action Arms Ltd.
ADCO International
Adventurer's Outpost
Aimpoint, Inc.
Aimtech Mount Systems
Air Venture
Ajax Custom Grips, Inc.
Alley Supply Co.
Anderson Manufacturing Co., Inc.
Apel GmbH, Ernst
Applied Laser Systems, Inc.
A.R.M.S., Inc.
Armscorp. USA, Inc.
Armurier Hiptmayer
Baumannize, Inc.
Bausch & Lomb, Inc.
Beaver Park Products, Inc.
Beeman Precision Airguns, Inc.
Bellm Contenders
Blount, Inc. Sporting Equipment
  Division
B.M.F. Activator, Inc.
Brownells, Inc.
Brunton U.S.A.
B-Square Co.
Buehler Scope Mounts
Burris Co., Inc.
Bushnell
Butler Creek Corp.
California Armory, Inc.
California Grip
Camp-Cap Products
Cape Outfitters
Celestron International
Clark Custom Guns, Inc.
Clearview Mfg. Co., Inc.
Combat Military Ordnance Ltd.
Compass Industries, Inc.
Conetrol Scope Mounts
Creedmoor Sports, Inc.
Del-Sports, Inc.
D&H Prods. Co., Inc.
E.A.A. Corp.
E&L Mfg., Inc.
Ednar, Inc.
Eggleston, Jere D.
Europtik Ltd.
Farr Studio, Inc.
Flaig's
Forster Products
Fujinon, Inc.
Galati International
Global Industries
Grace Tool, Inc.
Greenwalt Rifles
Griffin & Howe, Inc.
GSI, Inc.
G.U., Inc.
Hakko Co. Ltd.
Hermann Leather Co., H.J.
Hertel & Reuss
Hiptmayer, Klaus
Holden Co., J.B.
Imatronic, Inc.
Jaeger, Inc., Paul/Dunn's
Jason Empire, Inc.
Jeffredo Gunsight
Johnson Gunsmithing, Inc., Neal G.
Kahles USA
K-D, Inc.
Keng's Firearms Specialty, Inc.
KenPatable Ent., Inc.
Kesselring Gun Shop
Kilham & Co.
Kimber, Inc.
Kmount
Kowa Optimed, Inc.
Kris Mounts
KVH Industries, Inc.
Kwik Mount Corp.
Kwik-Site Co.

L&S Technologies, Inc.
Laseraim
Laser Devices, Inc.
Leatherwood-Meopta, Inc.
Lectro Science, Inc.
Lee Supplies, Mark
Lee Co., T.K.
Leica USA, Inc.
Leupold
Lite Tek International
Lohman Mfg. Co., Inc.
London Guns Ltd.
Mac-1 Distributors
Mac's .45 Shop
McKee, Arthur
McMillan Optical Gunsight Co.
Meier Works
Midway Arms, Inc.
Military Armament Corp.
Millett Sights
Mirador Optical Corp.
Muzzle-Nuzzle Co.
New Democracy, Inc.
Newman Gunshop
Nichols Sports Optics
Night Vision Equipment Co., Inc.
Nikon, Inc.
North American Specialties
Nygord Precision Products
Oakshore Electronic Sights, Inc.
Old Western Scrounger, Inc.
Olympic Optical Co.
OMR Feinmechanik, Jagd-und
  Sportwaffen, GmbH
Optolyth-USA, Inc.
Orchard Park Enterprise
Outdoor Connection, Inc., The
Pace Marketing, Inc.
Pachmayr Ltd.
PECAR Herbert Schwarz, GmbH
PEM's Mfg. Co.
Pentax Corp.
Pilkington Gun Co.
Precise Metalsmithing Enterprises
Precision Sport Optics
Premier Reticles
Ram-Line, Inc.
Ranch Products
Randolph Engineering, Inc.
Ranging, Inc.
Ravell Ltd.
Redfield, Inc.
Robar Co.'s, Inc., The
Rocky Mountain High Sports
  Glasses
Royal Arm International Products
Sanders Custom Gun Service
Schmidt & Bender
Seattle Binocular & Scope Repair
  Co.
Selsi Co,, Inc.
Shepherd Scope Ltd.
Sheridan USA, Inc., Austin
Shooters Supply
Simmons Enterprises, Ernie
Simmons Outdoor Corp.
S&K Mfg. Co.
Societa Armi Bresciane Srl.
Specialized Weapons, Inc.
Speer Products
Sportsmatch Ltd.
Springfield, Inc.
Sure Shot of LA, Inc.
Swift Instruments, Inc.
Tapco, Inc.
Tasco Sales, Inc.
Tele-Optics
Tele-Optics, Inc.
Thompson/Center Arms
Trijicon, Inc.
Unertl Optical Co., Inc., John
United Binocular Co.

United States Optics Technologies,
  Inc.
Valor Corp.
Warne Manufacturing Co.
WASP Shooting Systems
Weatherby, Inc.
Weaver Products
Weaver Scope Repair Service

Wells Custom Gunsmith, R.A.
Western Design
Westfield Engineering
•White Systems, Inc.
Wideview Scope Mount Corp.
•Williams Gun Sight Co.
York M-1 Conversions
•Zeiss Optical, Inc., Carl

## SHOOTING/TRAINING SCHOOLS

Alpine Precision Gunsmithing &
  Indoor Shooting Range
American Pistol Institute
American Small Arms Academy
Auto Arms
Bob's Tactical Indoor Shooting
  Range & Gun Shop
Chapman Academy of Practical
  Shooting
Chelsea Gun Club of New York
  City, Inc.
CQB Training
Daisy Mfg. Co.
Defense Training International, Inc.
Dowtin Gunworks
Executive Protection Institute
Firearm Training Center, The
Firearms Academy of Seattle
Francesca Stabilizer's, Inc.
G.H. Enterprises Ltd.
Guardian Group International
Guncraft Sports, Inc.
Gunfitters, The
InSights Training Center, Inc.
International Shootists, Inc.
Jensen's Firearms Acadamy
Lethal Force Institute

McMurdo, Lynn
Mendez, John A.
North American Shooting Systems
Northeast Training Institute, Inc.
North Mountain Pine Training
  Center
Pacific Pistolcraft
Police Bookshelf
Quack Decoy Corp.
Quigley's Personal Protection
  Strategies, Paxton
River Road Sporting Clays
Robar Co.'s, Inc., The
Rossi S.A. Metalurgica E
  Municoes, Amadeo
S.A.F.E.
Shooter's World
Shotgun Shop, The
Sipes Gun Shop
Slings & Arrows
Specialty Gunsmithing
Starlight Training Center, Inc.
S.W.I.F.T.
Tactical Training Center
Threat Management Institute
Western Missouri Shooters Alliance
Yavapai Firearms Academy Ltd.

## SIGHTS, METALLIC

Alley Supply Co.
All's, The Jim J. Tembelis Co., Inc.
Alpec Team, Inc.
Andela Tool & Machine, Inc.
Armurier Hiptmayer
Bo-Mar Tool & Mfg. Co.
Bradley Gunsight Co.
Burris Co., Inc.
Cape Outfitters
Carter's Gun Shop
Champion's Choice, Inc.
Colonial Repair
E.A.A. Corp.
Engineered Accessories
Fausti & Figlie s.n.c., Stefano
Fautheree, Andy
Francesca Stabilizer's, Inc.
Guardian Group International
Gun Doctor, The
Heinie Specialty Products
Hesco-Meprolight
Hiptmayer, Klaus
Imatronic, Inc.
Innovision Enterprises
Jaeger, Inc., Paul/Dunn's
J.O. Arms & Ammunition Co.
Johnson Gunsmithing, Inc., Neal G.
Kopp, Terry K.
Lofland, James W.
London Guns Ltd.

L.P.A. Snc
Lyman Products Corp.
Marble Arms Corp.
McKee, Arthur
MCS, Inc.
Meier Works
Meprolight
Merit Corp.
Mid-America Recreation, Inc.
Millett Sights
MMC
Newman Gunshop
Novak's .45 Shop, Wayne
OMR Feinmechanik, Jagd-und
  Sportwaffen, GmbH
Pachmayr Ltd.
PEM's Mfg. Co.
Peterson Instant Targets, Inc.
Ravell Ltd.
Robar Co.'s, Inc., The
RPM
Sheridan USA, Inc., Austin
Slug Site Co.
Tanfoglio S.r.l., Fratelli
T.F.C. S.p.A.
Trijicon, Inc.
Vintage Arms, Inc.
WASP Shooting Systems
Wichita Arms, Inc.
Williams Gun Sight Co.

## STOCKS (Commercial and Custom)

Angelo & Little Custom Gun Stock
  Blanks
Apel, Dietrich
Arms Ingenuity Co.
Armurier Hiptmayer
Balickie, Joe
Barta's Gunsmithing
Bartlett, Don
Barton, Michael D.
Beeman Precision Airguns, Inc.
Belding's Custom Gun Shop
Benchmark Guns
Biesen, Al
Biesen, Roger
Billeb, Stephen L.
Bishop, E.C.
B.M.F. Activator, Inc.
Bob's Gun Shop
Boltin, John M.
Borovnik KG, Ludwig
Bowerly, Kent
Boyds' Gunstock Industries, Inc.
Brace, Larry D.

Brgoch, Frank
Brown Precision, Inc.
Buckhorn Gun Works
Bullberry Barrel Works, Ltd.
Burkhart Gunsmithing, Don
Burres, Jack
Butler Creek Corp.
Cali'co Hardwoods, Inc.
Camilli, Lou
Campbell, Dick
Cape Outfitters
Caywood, Shane J.
Chicasaw Gun Works
Churchill, Winston
Clifton Arms, Inc.
Clinton River Gun Serv., Inc.
Cloward's Gun Shop
Cochran, Oliver
Coffin, Charles H.
Coffin, Jim
Conrad, C.A.
Costa, David
Crane Sales Co., George S.

Creedmoor Sports, Inc.
Custom Checkering Service
Custom Gun Products
Custom Gun Stocks
Dahl's Custom Stocks
Dangler, Homer L.
D&D Custom Rifles
D&D Gunsmiths, Ltd.
Desert Industries, Inc.
Dever Co., Jack
Devereaux, R.H. "Dick"
Dillon, Ed
Dowtin Gunworks
Dressel Jr., Paul G.
Duane Custom Stocks, Randy
Dutchman's Firearms, Inc., The
Duncan's Gunworks, Inc.
E.A.A. Corp.
Echols & Co., D'Arcy
Eggleston, Jere D.
Emmons, Bob
Erhardt, Dennis
Eversull Co., Inc., K.
Fajen, Inc., Reinhart
Farmer-Dressel, Sharon
Fiberpro Rifle Stocks
Fibron Products
Fisher, Jerry A.
Flaig's
Folks, Donald E.
Forster, Kathy
Forster, Larry L.
Frank Custom Gun Service, Ron
Game Haven Gunstocks
Garrett Accur-Lt. D.F.S. Co.
Gene's Custom Guns
Gentry Custom Gunmaker, David
Glaser Safety Slug, Inc.
Goens, Dale W.
Golden Age Arms Co.
Gordie's Gun Shop
Goudy Classic Stocks, Gary
Grace, Charles E.
Green, Roger M.
Greene, M.L.
Greenwalt Rifles
Griffin & Howe, Inc.
Gun Shop, The
Gunsmithing Ltd.
Halstead, Rick
Hank's Gun Shop
Hanson's Gun Center, Dick
Harper's Custom Stocks
Hecht, Hubert J.
Heilmann, Stephen
Hensley, Darwin
Heppler, Keith M.
Heydenberk, Warren R.
Hillmer Custom Gunstocks, Paul D.
Hiptmayer, Klaus
Hoenig & Rodman
H-S Precision, Inc.
Huebner, Corey O.
Hughes, Steven Dodd
Intermountain Arms
Ivanoff, Thomas G.
Jackalope Gun Shop
Jaeger, Inc., Paul/Dunn's
Jamison's Forge Works
Jarrett Rifles, Inc.
Johnson Gunsmithing, Inc., Neal G.
Johnson Wood Products
Keith's Custom Gunstocks
Ken's Rifle Blanks
Klein Custom Guns, Don
Klingler Woodcarving
Knippel, Richard
Kopp, Terry K.
Lawson Co., Harry
Lind Custom Guns, Al
Lynn's Custom Gunstocks
Makinson, Nicholas
Mandarino, Monte
Masen Co., John
McCullough, Ken
McCament, Jay

McDonald, Dennis
McFarland, Stan
McGuire, Bill
McMillan Fiberglass Stocks, Inc.
McMillan Rifle Barrels
Mercer Custom Stocks, R.M.
Mid-America Recreation, Inc.
Miller Gun Woods
Monell Custom Guns
Morrison Custom Rifles, J.W.
Morrow, Bud
MPI Stocks
Muzzelite Corp.
Nettestad Gun Works
New England Custom Gun Service
Newman Gunshop
Nickels, Paul R.
Nicklas, Ted
Norman Custom Gunstocks, Jim
Oakland Custom Arms, Inc.
Old World Gunsmithing
One Of A Kind
Or-Ün
Orvis Co., The
Ottmar, Maurice
Pachmayr Ltd.
Pasadena Gun Center
Paulsen Gunstocks
PEM's Mfg. Co.
Pentheny de Pentheny
Perazzi U.S.A., Inc.
P&S Gun Service
Reiswig, Wallace E.
Richards Micro-Fit Stocks
R&J Gun Shop
RMS Custom Gunsmithing
Robar Co.'s, Inc., The
Robinson, Don
Robinson Firearms Mfg. Ltd.
Roto Carve
Royal Arm International Products
Royal Arms
Ryan, Chad L.
Schaefer, Roy V.
Schiffman, Curt
Schiffman, Mike
Schwartz Custom Guns, David W.
Shaw's Finest in Guns
Sherk, Dan A.
Shooting Gallery, The
Sile Distributors
Six Enterprises
Skeoch, Brian R.
Snider Stocks, Walter S.
Speedfeed, Inc.
Speiser, Fred D.
Strawbridge, Victor W.
Swan, D.J.
Szweda, Robert
Talmage, William G.
Tecnolegno S.p.A.
T.F.C. S.p.A.
Tiger-Hunt
Tirelli
Tom's Gun Repair
Tom's Gun Shop
Trevallion Gunstocks
Tucker, James C.
Vest, John
Vic's Gun Refinishing
Vintage Industries, Inc.
Waffen-Weber Custom Gunsmithing
Wallace's
Weatherby, Inc.
Weems, Cecil
Wenig Custom Gunstocks, Inc.
Werth, T.W.
West, Robert G.
Western Gunstock Mfg. Co.
Westminster Arms Ltd.
Windish, Jim
Winter, Robert M.
Wright's Hardwood Sawmill
Yee, Mike
York M-1 Conversions
Zeeryp, Russ

## TARGETS, BULLET AND CLAYBIRD TRAPS

Abbott Industries
Action Target, Inc.
Aldis Gunsmithing & Shooting Supply
American Whitetail Target Systems
Applied Laser Systems
Armor Metal Products
Aztec International Ltd.
Barsotti, Bruce
Birchwood Laboratories, Inc.
Blount, Inc. Sporting Equipment Division
Caswell International Corp.
Champion's Choice, Inc.
Champion Target Co.
Clay Target Enterprises
Cunningham Co., Eaton
Dapkus Co., J.G.
Datumtech Corp.
Detroit-Armor Corp.
Diamond Mfg. Co.
Dutchman's Firearms, Inc., The
Epps "Orillia" Ltd., Ellwood
Federal Champion Target Co.
Freeman Animal Targets
G.H. Enterprises Ltd.
Hiti-Schuch, Atelier Wilma
Hunterjohn
Innovision Enterprises
Johnson Gunsmithing, Inc., Neal G.

Kennebec Journal
Kleen-Bore, Inc.
Littler Sales Co.
Maki Industries
MTM Molded Products Co., Inc.
National Target Co.
North American Shooting Systems
Nu-Teck
Outers Laboratories
Ox-Yoke Originals, Inc.
Primos Wild Game Calls, Inc.
Quack Decoy Corp.
Red Star Target Co.
Remington Arms Co., Inc.
Richards, John
River Road Sporting Clays
Rockwood Corp., Speedwell Div.
Rocky Mountain Target Co.
R-Tech Corp.
Schaefer Shooting Sports
Seligman Shooting Products
Shooting Arts Ltd
Shotgun Shop, The
Stoney Baroque Shooters Supply
Thompson Target Technology
Verdemont Fieldsports
White Flyer
White Flyer Targets
World of Targets

## TAXIDERMY

Jonas Appraisals & Taxidermy, Jack
Kulis Freeze Dry Taxidermy
Shell Shack

Parker, Mark D.
Piedmont Community College
World Trek, Inc.

## TRAP AND SKEET SHOOTER'S EQUIPMENT

Allen Sportswear, Bob
Baker, Stan
Blount, Inc. Sporting Equipment Division
C&H Research
Clymer Manufacturing Co., Inc.
D&H Prods. Co., Inc.
Danuser Machine Co.
F.A.I.R. Tecni-Mec SNC di Isidoro Rizzini
Ganton Manufacturing Ltd.
G.H. Enterprises Ltd.
Great 870 Co., The
Griggs Products
Hafner Creations, Inc.
Hall Plastics, Inc., John
Harper, William E.
Hoppe's Div.
Jenkins Recoil Pads, Inc.
K&T Co.
Loadmaster
Lynn's Custom Gunstocks
Magnum Research, Inc.
Maionchi-L.M.I.

Meadow Industries
Moneymaker Guncraft Corp.
MTM Molded Products Co., Inc.
Noble Co., Jim
Outers Laboratories
PAST Sporting Goods, Inc.
Perazzi U.S.A., Inc.
Pro-Port Ltd.
Protektor Model Co.
Quack Decoy Corp.
Ravell Ltd.
Remington Arms Co., Inc.
Rhodeside, Inc.
Shootin' Accessories, Ltd.
Shooting Specialties
Shotgun Shop, The
Speer Products
10-X Products Group
Titus, Daniel
Trius Traps
Universal Clay Pigeon Traps
Winchester Div., Olin Corp.
Ziegel Engineering

## TRIGGERS, RELATED EQUIPMENT

Boyds' Gunstock Industries, Inc.
Canjar Co., M.H.
Central Specialties Ltd.
Clark Custom Guns, Inc.
Custom Products
Cycle Dynamics, Inc.
Dayton Traister
E.A.A. Corp.
Electronic Trigger Systems, Inc.
Flaig's
Forster Products
Gentry Custom Gunmaker, David
Greenwalt Rifles
Hart & Son, Inc., Robert W.
Johnson Gunsmithing, Inc., Neal G.
Jones, Neil
Krieger Barrels, Inc.
Lee's Red Ramps

London Guns, Ltd.
Mac's .45 Shop
Mahony, Philip Bruce
Mid-America Recreation, Inc.
Miller Single Trigger Mfg. Co.
Newman Gunshop
Pace Marketing, Inc.
Pachmayr Ltd.
Pease Accuracy, Bob
PEM's Mfg. Co.
Penrod Precision
Perazzi U.S.A., Inc.
Royal Arms
S&B Industries
Shilen Rifles, Inc.
Taurus, S.A., Forjas
Timney Mfg., Inc.
Tyler Mfg.-Dist., Melvin

## A

A&B Industries, Inc., 7920-28 Hamilton Ave., Cincinnati, OH 45231/513-522-2992, 800-346-6699/FAX: 513-522-0916
A&J Products, Inc., 5791 Hall Rd., Muskegon, MI 49442-1964
A&M Waterfowl, Inc., 301 Burke Dr., Ripley, TN 38063/901-635-4003; FAX: 901-635-2320
A&W Repair, 2930 Schneider Dr., Arnold, MO 63010/314-287-3725
Abbott Industries, 3368 Miller St., Philadelphia, PA 19134/215-426-3435; FAX: 215-426-1718
Abel Safe & File, Inc., 124 West Locust St., Fairbury, IL 61739/815-692-2131; FAX: 815-692-3350
A.B.S. III, 9238 St. Morritz Dr., Fern Creek, KY 40291
Acadian Ballistic Specialties, Rt. 1, Box 1-D, Galliano, LA 70354
Accu-Tek, 4525 Carter Ct., Chino, CA 91710/714-627-2404; FAX: 714-627-7817
Acculube II, Inc., 22261 68th Ave. S., Kent, WA 98032-1914/206-395-7171
Accupro Gun Care, 15512-109 Ave., Surrey, BC U3R 7E8, CANADA/604-583-7807
Accuracy Components Co., P.O. Box 60034, Renton, WA 98058/206-255-4577
Accuracy Den, The, 25 Bitterbrush Rd., Reno, NV 89523/702-345-0225
Accuracy Gun Shop, 3651 University Ave., San Diego, CA 92104/619-282-8500
Accuracy Products, S.A., 14 rue de Lawsanne, Brussels, 1060 BELGIUM/32-2-539-34-42; FAX: 32-2-539-39-60
Accuracy Unlimited, 7479 S. DePew St., Littleton, CO 80123
Accuracy Unlimited, 16036 N. 49 Ave., Glendale, AZ 85306/602-978-9089
Accura-Site (See All's, The Jim Tembellis Co., Inc.)
Accurate Arms Co., Inc., Rt. 1, Box 167, McEwen, TN 37101/615-729-4207; FAX 615-729-4217
Accurate Plating & Weaponry, Inc., 1937 Calumet St., Clearwater, FL 34625/813-449-9112
Ace Sportswear, Inc., 700 Quality Rd., Fayetteville, NC 28306/919-323-1223
Ackley Rifle Barrels, P.O. (See Bellm Contenders)
Action Ammo Ltd. (See Action Arms Ltd.)
Action Arms Ltd., P.O. Box 9573, Philadelphia, PA 19124/215-744-0100; FAX: 215-533-2188
Action Products, Inc., 22 N. Mulberry St., Hagerstown, MD 21740/301-797-1414
Action Target, P.O. Box 636, Provo, UT 84603/801-377-8033; FAX: 801-377-8096
Actions by "T", Teddy Jacobson, 16315 Redwood Forest Ct., Sugarland, TX 77478/713-277-4008
ACTIV Industries, Inc., 1000 Zigor Rd., P.O. Box 339, Kearneysville, WV 25430/304-725-0451; FAX: 304-725-2080
Ad Hominem, RR 3, Orillia, Ont. L3V 6H3, CANADA/705-689-5303
Adair Custom Shop, Bill,, 2886 Westridge, Carrollton, TX 75006
Adams, John J., P.O. Box 467, Corinth, VT 05039/802-439-5904
ADC, Inc., 32654 Coal Creek Rd., Scappoose, OR 97056-2601/503-543-5088
ADCO International, 1 Wyman St., Woburn, MA 01801-2341/617-935-1799; FAX: 617-932-4807
Adkins, Luther, 1292 E. McKay Rd., Shelbyville, IN 46176-9353/317-392-3795
Advance Car Mover Co., Rowell Div., P.O. Box 1, 240 N. Depot St., Juneau, WI 53039/414-386-4464
Adventure 16, Inc., 4620 Alvarado Canyon Rd., San Diego, CA 92120/619-283-6314
Adventure Game Calls, R.D. 1, Leonard Rd., Spencer, NY 14883/607-589-4611
Adventurer's Outpost, P.O. Box 70, Cottonwood, AZ 86326/800-762-7471; FAX: 602-634-8781
African Import Co., 20 Braunecker Rd., Plymouth, MA 02360/508-746-8552
AFSCO Ammunition, 731 W. Third St., P.O. Box L, Owen, WI 54460/715-229-2516
Ahlman Guns, Rt. 1, Box 20, Morristown, MN 55052/507-685-4243; FAX: 507-685-4247
Ahrends, Kim, Custom Firearms, Box 203, Clarion, IA 50525/515-532-3449
Aimpoint, Inc., 580 Herndon Parkway, Suite 500, Herndon, VA 22070/703-471-6828; FAX: 703-689-0575
Aimtech Mount Systems, 101 Inwood Acres, Thomasville, GA 31792/912-226-4313; FAX: 912-227-0222
Air Arms (See U.S. importers—Air Rifle Specialists; Beeman Precision Airguns, Inc.)
Air Rifle Specialists, 311 East Water St., Elmira, NY 14901/607-734-7340; FAX: 607-733-3261
Air Venture, 9752 E. Flower St., Bellflower, CA 90706/213-867-6344
Airgun Repair Centre, 3227 Garden Meadows, Lawrenceburg, IN 47025/812-637-1463
Airmold, W.R. Grace & Co.-Conn., Becker Farms Ind. Park, P.O. Box 610, Roanoke Rapids, NC 27870/919-536-2171; FAX: 919-536-2201
Airrow (See Swivel Machine Works, Inc.)
Aitor-Cuchilleria Del Norte, S.A., Izelaieta, 17, 48260 Ermua (Vizcaya), SPAIN/43-17-08-50; FAX: 43-17-00-01
Ajax Custom Grips, Inc., Div. of A. Jack Rosenberg & Sons, 9130 Viscount Row, Dallas, TX 75247/214-630-8893
Aker Leather Products, 2248 Main St., Suite 6, Chula Vista, CA 91911/619-423-5182
Alaska Bullet Works, P.O. Box 54, Douglas, AK 99824/907-789-3834
Alcas Cutlery Corp. (See Cutco Cutlery)
Alco Carrying Cases, 601 W. 26th St., New York, NY 10001/212-675-5820
Aldis Gunsmithing & Shooting Supply, 502 S. Montezuma St., Prescott, AZ 86303/602-445-6723; FAX: 602-445-6763
Alessi Holsters, Inc., 2465 Niagara Falls Blvd., Amherst, NY 14228-3527/716-691-5615
Alex, Inc., Box 3034, Bozeman, MT 59772/406-282-7396; FAX: 406-282-7396
Alfano, Sam, 36180 Henry Gaines Rd., Pearl River, LA 70452/504-863-3364; FAX: 504-863-7715
All American Bullets, 889 Beatty St., Medford, OR 97501/503-770-5649
All American Lead Shot Corp., P.O. Box 224566, Dallas, TX 75062
All Rite Products, Inc., 5752 N. Silver Stone Circle, Mountain Green, UT 84040/801-586-7100
All Weather Outerwear, 1270 Broadway, Rm 1005, New York, NY 10001/212-244-2690
All's, The Jim J. Tembelis Co., Inc., 280 E. Fernau Ave., Oshkosh, WI 54901/414-426-1080; FAX: 414-426-1080
Allard, Gary, Creek Side Metal & Woodcrafters, Fishers Hill, VA 22626/703-465-3903
Allen Co., Bob, 214 SW Jackson, Des Moines, IA 50315/515-283-2191; 800-685-7020
Allen Sportswear, Bob, P.O. Box 477, Des Moines, IA 50302
Allen Co., Inc., 525 Burbank St., Broomfield, CO 80020/303-469-1857
Alley Supply Co., P.O. Box 848, Gardnerville, NV 89410/702-782-3800
Allred Bullet Co., 932 Evergreen Drive, Logan, UT 84321/801-752-6983
American Display Co., 55 Cromwell St., Providence, RI 02907/401-331-2464; FAX: 401-421-1264
Alpec Team, Inc., 55 Oak Ct., Danville, CA 94526/510-820-1763; FAX: 510-820-8738
Alpha LaFranck Enterprises, P.O. Box 81072, Lincoln, NE 68501/402-466-3193
Alpha 1 Drop Zone, 2121 N. Tyler, Wichita, KS 67212/316-729-0800

Alpha Precision, Inc., 2765-B Preston Rd. NE, Good Hope, GA 30641/404-267-6163
Alpine's Precision Gunsmithing & Indoor Shooting Range, 2401 Government Way, Coeur d'Alene, ID 83814/208-765-3559
Altamont Co., 901 N. Church St., P.O. Box 309, Thomasboro, IL 61878/217-643-3125; FAX: 217-643-7973
AMAC, Iver Johnson, 2202 Redmond Rd., Jacksonville, AR 72076/501-982-1633; FAX: 501-982-8075
Amacker International, Inc., 1212 Main St., Amacker Park, Delhi, LA 71232/318-878-9061; FAX: 318-878-5532
AmBr Software Group Ltd., The, 2205 Maryland Ave., Baltimore, MD 21218/301-243-7717; FAX: 301-366-8742
American Arms, Inc., 715 E. Armour Rd., N. Kansas City, MO 64116/816-474-3161; FAX: 816-474-1225
American Bullets, 2190 C. Coffee Rd., Lithonia, GA 30058/404-482-4253
American Custom Gunmakers Guild, P.O. Box 812, Burlington, IA 52601/319-752-6114
American Derringer Corp., P.O. Box 8983, Waco, TX 76714/800-642-7817, 817-799-9111; FAX: 817-799-7935
American Gas & Chemical Co., Ltd., 220 Pegasus Ave., Northvale, NJ 07647/201-767-7300
American Gripcraft, 3230 S. Dodge 2, Tucson, AZ 85713/602-790-1222
American Handgunner Magazine, 591 Camino de la Reina, Suite 200, San Diego, CA 92108/619-297-5350; FAX: 619-297-5353
American Import Co., The, 1453 Mission St., San Francisco, CA 94103/415-863-1506
American Military Arms Corp. (See AMAC)
American Pistol Institute, P.O. Box 401, Paulden, AZ 86334/602-636-4565; FAX: 602-636-1236
American Pistolsmiths Guild, P.O. Box 67, Louisville, TN 37777/615-984-3583
American Products Co., 14729 Spring Valley Road, Morrison, IL 61270/815-772-3336; FAX: 815-772-7921
American Sales & Mfg. Co., P.O. Box 677, Laredo, TX 78042/210-723-6893; FAX: 210-725-0672
American Security Products Co., 11925 Pacific Ave., Fontana, CA 92335/714-685-9680, 800-421-6142
American Small Arms Academy, P.O. Box 12111, Prescott, AZ 86304/602-778-5623
American Target Knives, 1030 Brownwood NW, Grand Rapids, MI 49504/616-453-1998
American Whitetail Target Systems, P.O. Box 41, 106 S. Church St., Tennyson, IN 47637/812-567-4527
Americase, P.O. Box 271, Waxahachie, TX 75165/800-972-2737
Amherst Arms, P.O. Box 1457, Englewood, FL 34295/813-475-2020
Ammo Load, Inc., 1560 East Edinger, Suite G., Santa Ana, CA 92705/714-558-8858; FAX: 714-569-0319
Amm-O-Mart, Ltd., P.O. Box 125, Hawkesbury, Ont., K6A 2R8 CANADA/613-632-9300
Ammunition Consulting Services, Inc., P.O. Box 1303, St. Charles, IL 60174/708-377-4625; FAX: 708-377-4680
Amodei, Jim (See D.O.C. Specialists, Inc.)
Amrine's Gun Shop, 937 La Luna, Ojai, CA 93023/805-646-2376
AMT, 6226 Santos Diaz St., Irwindale, CA 91702/818-334-6629; FAX: 818-969-5247
Analog Devices, Box 9106, Norwood, MA 02062
Andela Tool & Machine, Inc., RD3, Box 246, Richfield Springs, NY 13439
Anderson Manufacturing Co., Inc., P.O. Box 2640, 2741 N. Crosby Rd., Oak Harbor, WA 98277/206-675-7300; FAX: 206-675-3939
Andres & Dworsky, Bergstrasse 18, A-3822 Karlstein, Thaya, Austria, EUROPE, 0 28 44-285
Angelo & Little Custom Gun Stock Blanks, Chaffin Creek Rd., Darby, MT 59829/406-821-4530
Anschutz GmbH, Postfach 1128, D-7900 Ulm, Donau, GERMANY (U.S. importer—PSI, Inc.)
Ansen Enterprises, Inc., 1506 W. 228th St., Torrance, CA 90501-5105/213-534-1837
Answer Products Co., 1519 Westbury Drive, Davison, MI 48423/313-653-2911
Anthony and George Ltd., Rt. 1, P.O. Box 45, Evington, VA 24550/804-821-8117
Antique American Firearms (See Carlson, Douglas R.)
Antique Arms Co., 1110 Cleveland Ave., Monett, MO 65708/417-235-6501
AO Safety Products, Div. of American Optical Corp. (See E-A-R, Inc.)
Apache Products, Inc., 2208 Mallory Place, Monroe, LA 71201/318-325-1761; FAX: 318-325-4873
Apel GmbH, Ernst, Am Kirschberg 3, D-8708 Gerbrunn, GERMANY/0(9 31)-70 71 91; FAX: 0(9 31)70 71 92
Apel, Dietrich, New England Custom Gun Service, RR 2, Box 122W, Brook Rd., W. Lebanon, NH 03784/603-469-3565; FAX: 603-469-3471
Aplan Antiques & Art, James O., HC 80, Box 793-25, Piedmont, SD 57769/605-347-5016
Applied Case Systems, Inc., 2160 NW Vine St., Bldg. A, Grants Pass, OR 97526/503-479-0484; FAX: 503-476-5105
Applied Laser Systems, 2160 NW Vine St., Grants Pass, OR 97526/503-479-0484; FAX: 503-476-5105
Arcadia Machine & Tool, Inc. (See AMT)
Aristocrat Knives, 9608 Van Nuys Blvd.,104, Panorama City, CA 91402/818-892-6534; FAX: 818-830-7333
Arizaga (See U.S. importer—Mandall Shooting Supplies, Inc.)
Arizona Ammo & Arms, 2611 Sierra Lane, Kingman, AZ 86401
Arizona Custom Case, 1015 S. 23rd St., Phoenix, AZ 85034/602-273-0220
Arkansas Mallard Duck Calls, Rt. Box 182, England, AR 72046/501-842-3597
Arkfeld Mfg. & Dist. Co., Inc., P.O. Box 54, Norfolk, NE 68702-0054/402-371-9430; 800-533-0076
Armament Gunsmithing Co., Inc., 525 Rt. 22, Hillside, NJ 07205/908-686-0960
Armes de Chasse, P.O. Box 827, Chadds Ford, PA 19317/215-388-1146; FAX: 215-388-1147
Armfield Custom Bullets, 4775 Caroline Drive, San Diego, CA 92115/619-582-7188
Armi San Paolo, via Europa 172-A, I-25060 Concesio, (BS) ITALY/030-2751725
Armite Laboratories, 1845 Randolph St., Los Angeles, CA 90001/213-587-7768; FAX: 213-587-5075
Armoloy Co. of Ft. Worth, 204 E. Daggett St., Fort Worth, TX 76104/817-332-5604; FAX: 817-335-6517
Armor (See Buck Stop Lure Co., Inc.)
Armor Metal Products, P.O. Box 4609, Helena, MT 59604/406-442-5560
Armory Publications, P.O. Box 4206, Oceanside, CA 92052-4206/619-757-3930; FAX: 619-722-4108
Armoury, Inc., The, Rt. 202, Box 2340, New Preston, CT 06777/203-868-0001
A.R.M.S., Inc., 375 West St., West Bridgewater, MA 02379/508-584-7816; FAX: 508-588-8045
Arms, Peripheral Data Systems, 15110 SW Boones Ferry Rd., Suite 225, Lake Oswego, OR 97035/800-366-5559, 503-697-0533; FAX: 503-697-3337
Arms & Armour Press, Ltd., Villiers House, 41-47 Strand, London WC2N 5JE/ENGLAND
Arms Corp. of the Phillipines, 550E Delos Santos Ave., Cubau, Quezon City, PHILLIPINES

Arms Craft Gunsmithing, 1106 Linda Dr., Arroyo Grande, CA 93420/805-481-2830
Arms Ingenuity Co., P.O. Box 1, 51 Canal St., Weatogue, CT 06089/203-658-5624
Armscor (See U.S. importer—Ruko Products)
Armscor Precision, 225 Lindbergh St., San Mateo, CA 94401/415-347-9556; FAX: 415-347-7634
Armscorp USA, Inc., 4424 John Ave., Baltimore, MD 21227/301-247-6200
Armsport, Inc., 3950 NW 49th St., Miami, FL 33142/305-635-7850; FAX: 305-633-2877
Armstec, Inc., 339 East Ave., Rochester, NY 14604/800-262-2832
Armurier Hiptmayer, RR 112 750, P.O. Box 136, Eastman, Quebec JOE 1P0 CANADA/514-297-2492
Arratoonian, Andy (See Horseshoe Leather Products)
Arrieta, S.L., Morkaiko, 5, Elgoibar, E-20870, SPAIN/(43) 74 31 50; FAX: (43) 74 31 54 (U.S. importers—Quality Arms, Inc.; Wingshooting Adventures)
Artistry in Leather (See Stuart, V. Pat)
Art Jewel Enterprises Ltd., Eagle Business Ctr., 460 Randy Rd., Carol Stream, IL 60188/708-260-0400
Art's Gun & Sport Shop, Inc., 6008 Hwy. Y, Hillsboro, MO 63050
ASI, 6226 Santos Dias St., Irwindale, CA 91706/818-334-6629
A-Square Co., Inc., RR2, Box 357D, Bedford, KY 40006-9667/502-255-7456; FAX: 502-255-7657
Ashby Turkey Calls, HCR 5, Box 345, Houston, MO 65483/417-967-3787
Astra-Unceta Y Cia, S.A., Apartado 3, 48300 Guernica, Espagne, SPAIN (U.S. importer—E.A.A. Corp.)
ATIS Armi S.A.S., via Gussalli 24, Zona Industriale-Loc. Fornaci, 25020, Brescia, ITALY
Atlanta Cutlery Corp., 2143 Gees Mill Rd., Box 839XE, Conyers, GA 30207/800-241-3595
Atlanta Discount Ammo (See Bottom Line Shooting Supplies)
Atlantic Mills, Inc., 1325 Washington Ave., Asbury Park, NJ 07712/201-774-4882
Atlantic Research Marketing Systems (See A.R.M.S., Inc.)
Atsko/Sno-Seal, Inc., 2530 Russell SE, Orangeburg, SC 29115/803-531-1820; FAX: 803-531-2139
Audette, Creighton, 19 Highland Circle, Springfield, VT 05156/802-885-2331
Auto Arms, 738 Clearview, San Antonio, TX 78228/512-434-5450
Automatic Equipment Sales, 627 E. Railroad Ave., Salesburg, MD 21801
Auto-Ordnance Corp., Williams Lane, West Hurley, NY 12491/914-679-7225; FAX: 914-679-2698
Automatic Weaponry (See Scattergun Technologies, Inc.)
Autumn Sales, Inc. (Blaser), 1320 Lake St., Fort Worth, TX 76102/817-335-1634; FAX: 817-338-0119
AWC Systems Technology, P.O. Box 41938, Phoenix, AZ 85080-1938/602-780-1050
AYA (See U.S. importer—Armes de Chasse)
Aztec International Ltd., P.O. Box 1384, Clarkesville, GA 30523/404-754-8282

# B

B&C (See Bell & Carlson, Inc.)
B&D Trading Co., Inc., 3935 Fair Hill Rd., Fair Oaks, CA 95628/916-967-9366
Badger Shooters Supply, Inc., 202 N. Harding, Owen, WI 54460/715-229-2101; FAX: 715-229-2332
Baer Custom, Inc., Les, 3737 14th Ave., Rock Island, IL 61201/309-794-1166; FAX: 309-794-9882
Baekgaard Ltd., 1855 Janke Dr., Northbrook, IL 60062/708-498-3040; FAX: 708-493-3106
Bagmaster Mfg., Inc., 2731 Sutton Ave., St. Louis, MO 63143/314-781-8002
Bain & Davis, Inc., 307 E. Valley Blvd., San Gabriel, CA 91776-3522/818-573-4241, 213-283-7449
Baity's Custom Gunworks, 414 2nd St., N. Wilkesboro, NC 28659/919-667-8785
Baker's Leather Goods, Roy, P.O. Box 893, Magnolia, AR 71753/501-234-0344
Baker, Stan, 10,000 Lake City Way, Seattle, WA 98125/206-522-4575
Balaance Co., 340-39 Ave. S.E. Box 505, Calgary, AB, T2G 1X6 CANADA
Bald Eagle Precision Machine Co., 101 Allison St., Lock Haven, PA 17745/717-748-6772; FAX: 717-748-4443
Balickie, Joe, 408 Trelawney Lane, Apex, NC 27502/919-362-5185
Ballard Built, P.O. Box 1443, Kingsville, TX 78364/512-592-0853
Ballisti-Cast, Inc., Box 383, Parshall, ND 58770/701-862-3324
Ballistic Products, Inc., 20015 75th Ave. North, Corcoran, MN 55340/612-494-9237; FAX: 612-494-9236
Ballistic Program Co., Inc., The, 2417 N. Patterson St., Thomasville, GA 31792/912-228-5739, 800-368-0835
Ballistic Research, 1108 W. May Ave., McHenry, IL 60050/815-385-0037
Ballistica Maximus North, 107 College Park Plaza, Johnstown, PA 15904/814-266-8380
Ballistica Maximus South, 3242 Mary St., Suite S-318, Miami, FL 33133/305-446-5549
Banaczkowski Bullets, 56 Victoria Dr., Mount Barker, S.A. 5251 AUSTRALIA
Bandcor Industries, Div. of Man-Sew Corp., 6108 Sherwin Dr., Port Richey, FL 34668/813-848-0432
Bandera Gun Locker, 2146 NE 4th St., Bend, OR 97701/800-441-6773
Bang-Bang Boutique (See Holster Shop, The)
Banks, Ed, 2762 Hwy. 41 N., Ft. Valley, GA 31030/912-987-4665
Barnes Bullets, Inc., P.O. Box 215, American Fork, UT 84003/801-756-4222
Bar-Sto Precision Machine, 73377 Sullivan Rd., P.O. Box 1838, Twentynine Palms, CA 92277/619-367-2747; FAX: 619-367-2407
Barami Corp., 6250 E. 7 Mile Rd., Detroit, MI 48234/313-891-2536
Barbour, Inc., 55 Meadowbrook Dr., Milford, NH 03055/603-673-1313; FAX: 603-673-6510
Barlett, J., 6641 Kaiser Ave., Fontana, CA 92336-3265
Barnett International, P.O. Box 934, 1967 Gunn Highway, Odessa, FL 33556/813-920-2241
Baron Technology, 62 Spring Hill Rd., Trumbull, CT 06611/203-452-0515; FAX: 203-452-0663
Barramundi Corp., P.O. Drawer 4259, Homosassa Springs, FL 32687/904-628-0200
Barrett Firearms Mfg., Inc., P.O. Box 1077, Murfreesboro, TN 37133/615-896-2938; FAX: 615-896-7313
Barsotti, Bruce (See River Road Sporting Clays)
Barta's Gunsmithing, 10231 US Hwy. 10, Cato, WI 54206/414-732-4472
Barteaux Machete, 1916 SE 50th Ave., Portland, OR 97215-3238/503-233-5880
Bartlett, Don, 3704 E. Pine Needle Ave., Colbert, WA 99005/509-467-5009
Barton, Michael D. (See Tiger-Hunt)
Basics Information Systems, Inc., 1141 Georgia Ave., Suite 515, Wheaton, MD 20902/301-949-1070
Bates Engraving, Billy, 2302 Winthrop Dr., Decatur, AL 35603/205-355-3690
Bauer, Eddie, 15010 NE 36th St., Redmond, WA 98052
Baumannize Custom, 4784 Sunrise Hwy., Bohemia, NY 11716/800-472-4387; FAX: 516-567-0001
Baumgartner Bullets, 3011 S. Alane St., W. Valley City, UT 84120
Bausch & Lomb Sports Optics Div. (See Bushnell)
Bausch & Lomb, Inc., 42 East Ave., Rochester, NY 14603/800-828-5423
Bean, L.L., 386 Main St., Freeport, ME 04032/207-865-3111
Bear Archery, RR 4, 4600 Southwest 41st Blvd., Gainesville, FL 32601/904-376-2327
Bear Hug Grips, Inc., 17230 County Rd. 338, Buena Vista, CO 81211/800-232-7710
Bear Machine Co., 1108 Society Building, 159 S. Main, Akron, OH 44308/216-376-3747
Beauchamp & Son, Inc., 160 Rossiter Rd., Richmond, MA 01254
Beaver Lodge (See Fellowes, Ted)
Beaver Park Products, Inc., 840 J St., Penrose, CO 81240/719-372-6744
Beeman Precision Airguns, Inc., 3440 Airway Dr., Santa Rosa, CA 95403/707-578-7900; FAX: 707-578-4751
Behlert Precision, P.O. Box 288, 7067 Easton Rd., Pipersville, PA 18947/215-766-8681; FAX: 215-766-8681
Beitzinger, George, 116-20 Atlantic Ave., Richmond Hill, NY 11419/718-847-7661
Belding's Custom Gun Shop, 10691 Sayers Rd., Munith, MI 49259/517-596-2388
Bell & Carlson, Inc., 509 N. 5th St., Atwood, KS 67730/913-626-3204; FAX: 913-626-9602
Bell Originals, Inc., Sid, 7776 Sharkham Rd., Tully, NY 13159-9333/607-842-6431
Bell Reloading, Inc., 1725 Harlin Lane Rd., Villa Rica, GA 30180
Bell's Legendary Country Wear, 22 Circle Dr., Bellmore, NY 11710/516-679-1158
Bell's Gun & Sport Shop, 3309-19 Mannheim Rd, Franklin Park, IL 60131
Bellm Contenders, P.O. Ackley Rifle Barrels, P.O. Box 459, Cleveland, UT 84518/801-653-2530
Belltown, Ltd., 11 Camps Rd., Kent, CT 06757/203-354-5750
Ben's Machines, 1151 S. Cedar Ridge, Duncanville, TX 75137/214-780-1807
Benchmark Guns, 12593 S. Ave. 5 East, Yuma, AZ 85365
Benchmark Knives (See Gerber Legendary Blades)
Benchrest & Bucks, 6601 Kirby Drive 527, Houston, TX 77005/713-669-0925
Benelli Armi, S.p.A., Via della Stazione, 61029 Urbino, ITALY (U.S. importers—E.A.A. Corp.; Heckler & Koch, Inc.; Sile Distributors)
Bengtson Arms Co., L., 6345-B E. Akron St., Mesa, AZ 85205/602-981-6375
Benjamin Air Rifle Co. (See Benjamin/Sheridan Co.)
Benjamin/Sheridan Co., 2600 Chicory Rd., Racine, WI 53403/414-554-7900
Bentley, John, 128-D Watson Dr., Turtle Creek, PA 15145
Beretta Firearms, Pietro, 25063 Gardone V.T., ITALY (U.S. importer—Beretta U.S.A. Corp.)
Beretta U.S.A. Corp., 17601 Beretta Drive, Accokeek, MD 20607/301-283-2191
Beretta, Dr. Franco, via Rossa, 4, Concesio (BC), Italy I-25062/030-2751955; FAX: 030-218-0414
Berger Bullets, Ltd., 4234 N. 63rd Ave., Phoenix, AZ 85033/602-846-5791; FAX: 602-848-0780
Bergman & Williams, 2450 Losee Rd., Suite F, Las Vegas, NV 89030/702-642-1901
Bernardelli Vincenzo S.p.A., Via Matteotti 125, Gardone V.T., ITALY I-25063/30-8912851-2-3 (U.S. importer—Magnum Research, Inc.)
Berry's Bullets, Div. of Berry's Mfg., Inc., Box 100, Bloomington, CA 92316/714-823-5222; FAX: 714-823-4715
Bersa S.A., Gonzales Castillo 312, 1704 Ramos Mejia, ARGENTINA (U.S. importer—Eagle Imports, Inc.)
Bertram Bullet Co., P.O. Box 313, Seymour, Victoria 3660, AUSTRALIA/61-57-922912; FAX: 61-47-991650
Best Load, P.O. Box 4354, Stamford, CT 06907
Better Concepts Co., 663 New Castle Rd., Butler, PA 16001/412-285-9000
Bertuzzi (See U.S. importer—Moore & Co., Wm. Larkin)
Bianchi International, Inc., 100 Calle Cortez, Temecula, CA 92590/714-676-5621
Biesen, Al, 5021 Rosewood, Spokane, WA 99208/509-328-9340
Biesen, Roger, 5021 W. Rosewood, Spokane, WA 99208/509-328-9340
Big 45 Frontier Gun Shop, 515 Cliff Ave., Valley Springs, SD 57068/605-757-6248; FAX: 605-757-6248
Big Sky Racks, Inc., P.O. Box 729, Bozeman, MT 59771-0729/406-586-9393
Big Spring Enterprises "Bore Stores", P.O. Box 1115, Big Spring Rd., Yellville, AR 72687/501-449-5297; FAX: 501-449-4446
Bilal, Mustafa, 5429 Russell Ave. NW, Suite 202, Seattle, WA 98107/206-782-4164
Bill's Custom Cases, P.O. Box 2, Dunsmuir, CA 96025/916-235-0177
Bill's Gun Repair, 1007 Burlington St., Mendota, IL 61342/815-539-5786
Billeb, Stephen L., 1100 N. 7th St., Burlington, IA 52601/319-753-2110
Billings Gunsmiths, Inc., 1940 Grand Ave., Billings, MT 59102/406-652-3104
Billingsley & Brownell, P.O. Box 25, Dayton, WY 82836/307-655-9344
Bilsom Intl., Inc., 109 Carpenter Dr., Sterling, VA 20164/703-834-1070
Birchwood Laboratories, Inc., 7900 Fuller Rd., Eden Prairie, MN 55344/612-937-7933; FAX: 612-937-7979
Bishop, E.C., P.O. Box 7, Warsaw, MO 65355/816-438-5121; FAX: 816-4387-2201
Bismuth Cartridge Co., 3500 Maple Ave., Suite 1650, Dallas, TX 75129/800-759-3333; 214-521-5882
Bitterroot Bullet Co., Box 412, Lewiston, ID 83501-0412/208-743-5635
Black Hills Ammunition, P.O. Box 3090, Rapid City, SD 57709/605-348-5150; FAX: 605-348-9827
Black Hills Shooters Supply, P.O. Box 4220, Rapid City, SD 57709/605-348-4477; FAX: 605-348-5037
Black Sheep Brand, 3220 W. Gentry Parkway, Tyler, TX 75702/214-592-3853
Blackhawk East, P.O. Box 2274, Loves Park, IL 61131
Blackhawk Mountain, P.O. Box 210, Conifer, CO 80433
Blackhawk West, P.O. Box 285, Hiawatha, KS 66434
Blackinton & Co., Inc., V.H., 221 John L. Dietsch, Attleboro Falls, MA 02763-3000/508-699-4436; FAX: 508-695-5349
Blackjack Knives, 1307 W. Wabash, Effingham, IL 62401/217-347-7700; FAX: 217-347-7737
Blacksmith Corp., 830 N. Road 1 E.,Box 1752, Chino Valley, AZ 86323/602-636-4456; FAX: 602-636-4457
Blacktail Mountain Books, 42 First Ave. West, Kalispell, MT 59901/406-257-5573
Blakemore Game Calls, Jim, Rt. 2, Box 544, Cape Girardeau, MO 63701
Blammo Ammo, P.O. Box 1677, Seneca, SC 29679/803-882-1768
Blaser Jagdwaffen GmbH, D-7972 Isny Im Allgau, GERMANY (U.S. importer—Autumn Sales, Inc.)
Bledsoe, Weldon, 6812 Park Place Dr., Fort Worth, TX 76118/817-589-1704
Bleile, C. Roger, 5040 Ralph Ave., Cincinnati, OH 45238/513-251-0249
Blocker's Holsters, Inc., Ted, 5360 NE 112, Portland, OR 97220/503-254-9950
Blount, Inc., Sporting Equipment Div., 2299 Snake River Ave., P.O. Box 856, Lewiston, ID 83501/800-627-3640, 208-746-2351
Blue and Gray Products, Inc. (See Ox-Yoke Originals, Inc.)
Blue Book Publications, Inc., One Appletree Square, Minneapolis, MN 55425/800-877-4867; FAX: 612-853-1486
Blue Mountain Bullets, HCR 77, P.O. Box 231, John Day, OR 97845/503-820-4594
Blue Point Mfg., Co., P.O. Box 722, Massena, NY 13662
Blue Ridge Knives, Rt. 6, Box 185, Marion, VA 24354/703-783-6143; FAX: 703-783-9298
Blue Ridge Machinery & Tools, Inc., P.O. Box 536-GD, Hurricane, WV 25526/304-562-3538; FAX: 304-562-5311
Bluebonnet Specialty, P.O. Box 737, Palestine, TX 75802/214-723-2075
BMC Supply, Inc., 26051-179th Ave. S.E., Kent, WA 98042
B.M.F. Activator, Inc., 803 Mill Creek Run, Plantersville, TX 77363/409-894-2005, 800-527-2881
Bo-Mar Tool & Mfg. Co., Rt. 12, Box 405, Longview, TX 75605/903-759-4784; FAX: 903-759-9141
Bob's Gun Shop, P.O. Box 200, Royal, AR 71968/501-767-1970
Bob's Tactical Indoor Shooting Range & Gun Shop, 122 Lafayette Rd., Salisbury, MA 01952/508-465-5561
Boessler, Erich, Am Vogeltal 3, 8732 Munnerstadt, GERMANY/9733-9443
Boggs, Wm., 1816 Riverside Dr. C, Columbus, OH 43212/614-486-6965
Bohemia Arms Co., 17101 Los Modelos, Fountain Valley, CA 92708/714-963-0809; FAX: 714-963-0809
Boker USA, Inc., 14818 West 6th Ave., Suite 10A, Golden, CO 80401-5045/303-279-5997; FAX: 303-279-5919
Bolden's, 1295 Lassen Dr., Hanford, CA 93230/209-582-6937
Boltin, John M., P.O. Box 644, Estill, SC 29918/803-625-2185
Bondini Paolo, Via Sorrento, 345, San Carlo di Cesena, ITALY I-47020/0547 663 240; FAX: 0547 663 780
Bone Engraving, Ralph, 718 N. Atlanta, Owasso, OK 74055/918-272-9745
Boone's Custom Ivory Grips, Inc., 562 Coyote Rd., Brinnon, WA 98320/206-796-4330

Boonie Packer Products, P.O. Box 12204, Salem, OR 97309/800-477-3244; FAX: 503-581-3191
Border Guns & Leather, P.O. Box 1423, 110 E. Spruce St., Deming, NM 88031
Borovnik KG, Ludwig, 9170 Ferlach, Bahnhofstrasse 7, AUSTRIA
Boss Manufacturing Co., 221 W. First St., Kewanee, IL 61443/309-852-2131
Bostick Wildlife Calls, Inc., P.O. Box 728, Estill, SC 29918/803-625-2210, 803-625-4512
Bottom Line Shooting Supplies, P.O. Box 258, Clarkesville, GA 30523/706-754-9000; FAX: 706-754-7263
Bourne Co., Inc., Richard A., P.O. Box 141, Hyannis Port, MA 02647/508-775-0797
Bowen Classic Arms Corp., P.O. Box 67, Louisville, TN 37777/615-984-3583
Bowen Knife Co., P.O. Box 590, Blackshear, GA 31516/912-449-4794
Bowerly, Kent, HCR Box 1903, Camp Sherman, OR 97730/503-595-6028
Bowlin, Gene, Rt. 1, Box 890, Snyder, TX 79549
Boyds' Gunstock Industries, Inc., 3rd & Main, Box 305, Geddes, SD 57342/605-337-2123; FAX: 605-337-3363
Boyt, 509 Hamilton, Iowa Falls, IA 50126/515-648-4626
Brace, Larry D., 771 Blackfoot Ave., Eugene, OR 97404/503-688-1278
Bradley Gunsight Co., P.O. Box 140, Plymouth, VT 05056/203-589-0531; FAX: 203-582-6294
Brass Eagle, Inc., 7050A Bramalea Rd., Unit 19, Mississauga, Ont. L4Z 1C7, CANADA/416-848-4844
Bratcher, Dan, 311 Belle Air Pl., Carthage, MO 64836/417-358-1518
Brauer Bros. Mfg. Co., 2020 Delmar Blvd., St. Louis, MO 63103/314-231-2864; FAX: 314-249-4952
Braun, M., 32, rue Notre-Dame, 2440 LUXEMBURG
Break-Free, P.O. Box 25020, Santa Ana, CA 92799/714-953-1900
Brell Mar Products, Inc., 5701 Hwy. 80 West, Jackson, MS 39209
Brenneke KG, Wilhelm, Ilmenauweg 2, P.O. Box 16 46, D-3012 Langenhagen, GERMANY/1-772288
Bretton, 19 rue Victor Grignard, Z.I. Montreynaud, 42-St. Et., FRANCE (U.S. importer—Mandall Shooting Supplies, Inc.)
Brgoch, Frank, 1580 S. 1500 East, Bountiful, UT 84010/801-295-1885
Brian, C.T., 1101 Indiana Ct., Decatur, IL 62521/217-429-2290
Bricker Bullets, Box 509M RD3, Manheim, PA 17545/717-665-4332
Bridgers Best, P.O. Box 1410, Berthoud, CO 80513
Briganti & Co., A., 475 Rt. 32, Highland Mills, NY 10930/914-928-9573
Briley Mfg., Inc., 1230 Lumpkin, Houston, TX 77043/B713-932-6995; FAX: 713-932-1043
British Arms Co. Ltd., P.O. Box 7, Latham, NY 12110/518-783-0773
British Sporting Arms, RR1, Box 130, Millbrook, NY 12545/914-677-8303
BRNO (See U.S. importers—Action Arms Ltd.; Bohemia Arms Co.; Century International Arms, Inc.)
Brobst, Jim, 299 Poplar St., Hamburg, PA 19526/215-562-2103
Broken Gun Ranch, RR2, Box 92, Spearville, KS 67876/316-385-2587
Brooker, Dennis, Rt. 1, Box 12A, Derby, IA 50068/515-533-2103
Brown Manufacturing, P.O. Box 9219, Akron, OH 44305/800-837-GUNS
Brown Co., E. Arthur, 3404 Pawnee Dr., Alexandria, MN 56308/612-762-8847
Brown Precision, Inc., 7786 Molinos Ave., Los Molinos, CA 96055/916-384-2506; FAX: 916-384-1638
Brown Products, Ed, Inc., Rt. 2, Box 2922, Perry, MO 63462/314-565-3261; FAX: 565-2791
Brown, H.R. (See Silhouette Leathers)
Brownell Checkering Tools, W.E., 9390 Twin Moutain Circle, San Diego, CA 92126/619-695-2479; FAX: 619-695-2479
Brownells, Inc., 200 S. Front St., Montezuma, IA 50171/515-623-5401; FAX: 515-623-3896
Browning Arms Co. (Gen. Offices), 1 Browning Place, Morgan, UT 84050/801-876-2711; FAX: 801-876-3331
Browning Arms Co. (Parts & Service), 3005 Arnold Tenbrook Rd., Arnold, MO 63010-9406/314-287-6800; FAX: 314-287-9751
BRP, Inc. High Performance Cast Bullets, 1210 Alexander Rd., Colorado Springs, CO 80909/719-633-0658
Bruno Shooters Supply, 106 N. Wyoming St., Hazleton, PA 18201/717-455-2211; FAX: 717-455-2211
Brunsport, Inc., 1131 Bayview Dr., Quincy, IL 62301/217-223-8844
Brunton U.S.A., 620 E. Monroe Ave., Riverton, WY 82501/307-856-6559; FAX: 307-856-1840
Bryco Arms (See U.S. distributor—Jennings Firearms, Inc.)
Bryant, A.V., 72 Whiting Road, E. Hartford, CT 06118
Brynin, Milton, P.O. Box 383, Yonkers, NY 10710/914-779-4333
BSA Guns Ltd., Armoury Rd. Small Heath, Birmingham, ENGLAND B11 2PX/(011)21 772 8543; FAX: (011)21 773-0845 (U.S. importer—Air Rifle Specialists)
B-Square Co., P.O. Box 11281, 2708 St. Louis Ave., Ft. Worth, TX 76110/817-923-0964, 800-433-2909; FAX: 817-926-7012
Bucheimer, J.M., Jumbo Sports Products, 721 N. 20th St., St. Louis, MO 63103/314-241-1020
Buck Knives, Inc., 1900 Weld Blvd., El Cajon, CA 92020/619-449-1100; FAX: 619-562-5774
Buck Stix—SOS Products Co., Box 3, Neenah, WI 54956
Buck Stop Lure Co., Inc., 3600 Grow Rd. NW, P.O. Box 636, Stanton, MI 48888/517-762-5091; FAX: 517-762-5124
Buckeye Custom Bullets, 6490 Stewart Rd., Elida, OH 45807/419-641-4463
Buckhorn Gun Works, Rt. 6, Box 2230, Rapid City, SD 57702/605-787-6289
Buckskin Machine Works, A. Hunkeler, 3235 S. 358th St., Auburn, WA 98001/206-927-5412
Budin, Dave, Main St., Margaretville, NY 12455/914-568-4103; FAX: 914-586-4105
Buehler Scope Mounts, 17 Orinda Way, Orinda, CA 94563/510-254-3201; FAX: 510-254-9720
Buenger Enterprises, Box 5286, Oxnard, CA 93031/805-985-0541
Buffalo Bullet Co., Inc., 12637 Los Nietos Rd. Unit A, Santa Fe Springs, CA 90670/310-944-0322; FAX: 310-944-5054
Buffalo Rock Shooters Supply, R.R. 1, Ottawa, IL 61350/815-433-2471
Bullberry Barrel Works, Ltd., 2430 W. Bullberry Ln. 67-5, Hurricane, UT 84737/801-635-9866
Bull-X, Inc., 520 N. Main St., Farmer City, IL 61842/309-928-2574, 800-248-3845 orders only
Bullet, Inc., 3745 Hiram Alworth Rd., Dallas, GA 30132
Bullet Swaging Supply, Inc., P.O. Box 1056, 303 McMillan Rd, West Monroe, LA 71291/318-387-7257; FAX: 318-387-7779
The BulletMakers Workshop, RFD 1 Box 1755, Brooks, ME 04921
Bullseye Bullets, 1610 State Road 60, Suite 12, Valrico, FL 33594/813-654-6563
Burgess, Byron, 1816 Gathe Dr., San Luis Obispo, CA 93405/805-543-7274
Burgess & Son Gunsmiths, R.W., P.O. Box 3364, Warner Robins, GA 31099/912-328-7487
Burkhart Gunsmithing, Don, P.O. Box 852, Rawlins, WY 82301/307-324-6007
Burling Bullets, 306 Range St., Elizabethton, TN 37643/615-542-8162
Burnham Bros., P.O. Box 669, 912 Hi-way 1431 West, Marble Falls, TX 78654/512-693-3112
Burres, Jack, 10333 San Fernando Rd., Pacoima, CA 91331/818-899-8000
Burris Co., Inc., P.O. Box 1747, Greeley, CO 80631/303-356-1670; FAX: 303-356-8702
Bushmann Hunters/Safaris, P.O. Box 110639, Aurora, CO 80011
Bushmaster Hunting & Fishing, 451 Alliance Ave., Toronto, Ont. M6N 2J1 CANADA/416-763-4040; FAX: 416-763-0623
Bushnell, Bausch & Lomb Sports Optics Div., 9200 Cody, Overland Park, KS 66214/913-888-0220
Bushwacker Backpack & Supply Co. (See Counter Assault)
Bustani Appraisers, Leo, P.O. Box 8125, W. Palm Beach, FL 33407/305-622-2710
Buster's Custom Knives, P.O. Box 214, Richfield, UT 84701/801-896-5319
Butler Creek Corp., 290 Arden Dr., Belgrade, MT 59714/406-388-1356; FAX: 406-388-7204
Butterfield & Butterfield, 220 San Bruno Ave., San Francisco, CA 94103/415-861-7500
Buzztail Brass, 5306 Bryant Ave., Klamath Falls, OR 97603/503-884-1072
B-West Imports, Inc., 5132 E. Pima St., Tucson, AZ 85712/602-881-3525; FAX: 602-322-5704

## C

C3 Systems, 678 Killingly St., Johnston, RI 02919
C&D Special Products (Claybuster), 309 Sequoya Dr., Hopkinsville, KY 42240/800-922-6287, 800-284-1746
C&H Research, 115 Sunnyside Dr., Box 351, Lewis, KS 67552/316-324-5445
Cabanas (See U.S. importer—Mandall Shooting Supplies, Inc.)
Cabela's, 812-13th Ave., Sidney, NE 69160/308-254-5505; FAX: 308-254-7809
Cabinet Mtn. Outfitter, P.O. Box 766, Plains, MT 59859/406-826-3970
Cache La Poudre Rifleworks, 140 N. College, Ft. Collins, CO 80524/303-482-6913
Cadre Supply (See Parts & Surplus)
Calhoon Varmint Bullets, James, 6035 Penworth Rd., S.E., Calgary, Alberta, T2A 4E9 CANADA/403-235-2959
Calibre Press, Inc., 666 Dundee Rd., Suite 1607, Northbrook, IL 60062-2760/800-323-0037; FAX: 708-498-6869
Cali'co Hardwoods, Inc., 1648 Airport Blvd., Windsor, CA 95492/707-546-4045; FAX: 707-546-4027
Calico Light Weapon Systems, 405 E. 19th St., Bakersfield, CA 93305/805-323-1327; FAX: 805-323-7844
California Armory, Inc., 881 W. San Bruno Ave., San Bruno, CA 94066/415-871-4886; FAX: 415-871-0713
California Grip, 1323 Miami Ave., Clovis, CA 93612/209-299-1316
California Magnum, 20746 Dearborn St., Chatsworth, CA 91313/818-341-7302; FAX: 818-341-7304
California Sight, P.O. Box 4607, Pagosa Springs, CO 81157/303-731-5003
CAM Enterprises, 5090 Iron Springs Rd., Box 2, Prescott, AZ 86301/602-776-9640
Camas Hot Springs Mfg., P.O. Box 639, Hot Springs, MT 59845/406-741-3756
Camdex, Inc., 2330 Alger, Troy, MI 48083/313-528-2300
Cameron's, 16690 W. 11th Ave., Golden, CO 80401/303-279-7365; FAX: 303-628-5413
Camilli, Lou, 4700 Oahu Dr. NE, Albuquerque, NM 87111/505-293-5259
Camillus Cutlery Co./Western Cutlery Co., 54 Main St., Camillus, NY 13031/315-672-8111; FAX: 315-672-8832
Camofare Co., 712 Main St. 2800, Houston, TX 77002/713-229-9253
Camp-Cap Products, P.O. Box 173, Chesterfield, MO 63006/314-532-4340
Campbell, Dick, 20,000 Silver Ranch Rd., Conifer, CO 80433/303-697-0150
Canadian Custom Bullets, Box 52, Anola Man. R0E 0A0 CANADA
Can Am Enterprises, Box 27, Fruitland, Ont. LOR ILO, CANADA/416-643-4357
Canjar Co., M.H., 500 E. 45th Ave., Denver, CO 80216/303-295-2638
Cannon Safe, Inc., 9358 Stephens St., Pico Rivera, CA 90660/213-692-0636, 800-242-1055, 800-222-1055 (CA)
Cannon's Guns, Box 1036, Polson, MT 59860/406-883-3583
Canons Delcour, Rue J.B. Cools, B-4040 Herstal, BELGIUM/32.(0)41.40.13.40; FAX: 32(0)412.40.22.88
Canyon Cartridge Corp., P.O. Box 152, Albertson, NY 11507/FAX: 516-294-8946
Cape Outfitters, Rt. 2, Box 437C, Cape Girardeau, MO 63701/314-335-4103; FAX: 314-335-1555
Caraville Manufacturing, P.O. Box 4545, Thousand Oaks, CA 91359/805-499-1234
Carbide Die & Mfg. Co., Inc., 15615 E. Arrow Hwy., Irwindale, CA 91706/818-337-2518
Carhartt, Inc., P.O. Box 600, Dearborn, MI 48121/800-358-3825; FAX: 313-271-3455
Carlson, Douglas R., Antique American Firearms, P.O. Box 71035, Dept. GD, DesMoines, IA 50325/515-224-6552
Carnahan Bullets, 17645 110th Ave. SE, Renton, WA 98055
Carry-Lite, Inc., 5203 W. Clinton Ave., Milwaukee, WI 53223/414-355-3520
Carter's Gun Shop, 225 G St., Penrose, CO 81240/719-372-6240
Carter's Wildlife Calls, Inc., Garth, P.O. Box 821, Cedar City, UT 84720/801-586-7639
Cartridges Unlimited, 190 Bull's Bridge Rd., South Kent, CT 06785/203-927-3053
Carvajal Belts & Holsters, 422 Chestnut, San Antonio, TX 78202/210-222-1634
Cascade Bullet Co., Inc., 413 Main St., Klamath Falls, OR 97601/503-884-9316
Cascade Fabrication, 1090 Bailey Hill Rd. Unit A, Eugene, OR 97402/503-485-3433; FAX: 503-485-3543
Cascade Shooters, 2155 N.W. 12th St., Redwood, OR 97756
Case & Sons Cutlery Co., W.R., Owens Way, Bradford, PA 16701/814-368-4123; FAX: 814-362-4877
Caspian Arms, 14 North Main St., Hardwick, VT 05843/802-472-6454
Cast Bullet Assoc., Inc., The, 4103 Foxcraft Dr., Traverse City, MI 49684
Caswell International Corp., 1221 Marshall St. NE, Minneapolis, MN 55413/612-379-2000
Catco-Ambush, Inc., P.O.Box 300, Corte Madera, CA 94926
Cathey Enterprises, Inc., P.O. Box 2202, Brownwood, TX 76804/915-643-2553; FAX: 915-643-3653
Cation, 32360 Edward, Madison Heights, MI 48071/313-588-0160
Catoctin Cutlery, P.O. Box 188, Smithsburg, MD 21783/301-824-7416; FAX: 301-824-6138
Caywood, Shane J., P.O. Box 321, Minocqua, WI 54548
CBC, Avenida Industrial, 3330, Santo Andre-SP-BRAZIL 09080/11-449-5600 (U.S. importer—MAGTECH Recreational Products, Inc.)
CCI, Div. of Blount, Inc., 2299 Snake River Ave., P.O. Box 856, Lewiston, ID 83501/800-627-3640, 208-746-2351
Cedar Hill Game Call Co., Rt. 2, Box 236, Downsville, LA 71234/318-982-5632
Celestron International, P.O. Box 3578, Torrance, CA 90503
Centaur Systems, Inc., 1602 Foothill Rd., Kalispell, MT 59901/406-755-8609; FAX: 406-755-8609
Central Specialties Ltd., 1122 Silver Lake Road, Cary, IL 60013/708-537-3300; FAX: 708-537-3615
Century Gun Dist., Inc., 1467 Jason Rd., Greenfield, IN 46140/317-462-4524
Century International Arms, Inc., 48 Lower Newton St., St. Albans, VT 05478/802-527-1252; FAX: 802-527-0470
CF Ventures, 509 Harvey Dr., Bloomington, IN 47403-1715
C-H Tool & Die Corp. (See 4-D Custom Die Co.)
Chace Leather Products, 507 Alden St., Fall River, MA 02722/508-678-7556; FAX: 508-675-9666
Chadick's Ltd., P.O. Box 100, Terrell, TX 75160/214-563-7577
Chameleon Camouflage Systems, 15199 S. Maplelane Rd., Oregon City, OR 97045/503-657-2266
Champion Target Co., 232 Industrial Parkway, Richmond, IN 47374/800-441-4971
Champion's Choice, Inc., 223 Space Park South, Nashville, TN 37211/615-834-6666; FAX: 615-831-2753
Champlin Firearms, Inc., P.O. Box 3191, Woodring Airport, Enid, OK 73701/405-237-7388; FAX: 405-242-6922
Champlin, R. MacDonald, P.O. Box 132, Candia, NH 03034
Chapman Academy of Practical Shooting, 4350 Academy Rd., Hallsville, MO 65255/314-696-5544; FAX: 314-696-2266
Chapman Manufacturing Co., The, 471 New Haven Rd., P.O. Box 250, Durham, CT 06422/203-349-9228; FAX: 203-349-0084
Chapuis Armes, 21 La Gravoux, BP15, 42380 St. Bonnet-le-Chateau, FRANCE/(33)77.50.06.96 (U.S. importer—Armes de Chasse)
CHARCO, 26 Beaver St., Ansonia, CT 06401/203-377-8080

Charter Arms (See CHARCO)
Checkmate Refinishing, 8232 Shaw Rd., Brooksville, FL 34602/904-799-5774
Cheddite France, S.A., 99 Route de Lyon, F-26500 Bourg Les Valence, FRANCE/75 56 45 45; FAX: 75 56 98 89
Chelsea Gun Club of New York City, Inc., 237 Ovington Ave., Apt. D53, Brooklyn, NY 11209/718-836-9422, 718-833-2704
Chem-Pak, Inc., 11 Oates Ave., P.O. Box 1685, Winchester, VA 22601/800-336-9828; FAX: 703-722-3993
Cherokee Gun Accessories (See Glaser Safety Slug, Inc.)
Chesapeake Importing & Distributing Co. (See CIDCO)
Chesire & Perez Dist., 425 W. Allen Ave., San Dimas, CA 91773-1485
CheVron Bullets, RR1, Ottawa, IL 61350/815-433-2471
CheVron Case Master (See CheVron Bullets)
Chicago Cutlery Co., 1536 Beech St., Terre Haute, IN 47804/800-457-2665
Chicasaw Gun Works (See Cochran, Oliver)
Chimere, Inc., 4406 Exchange Ave., Naples, FL 33942/813-643-4222
ChinaSports, Inc., 2010 S. Lynx Place, Ontario, CA 91761/714-923-1411; FAX: 714-923-0775
Chipmunk (See Oregon Arms, Inc.)
Chippewa Shoe Co., P.O. Box 2521, Ft. Worth, TX 76113/817-332-4385
Choate Machine & Tool Co., Inc., P.O. Box 218, Bald Knob, AR 72010/501-724-6193, 800-972-6390; FAX: 501-724-5873
Chopie Mfg., Inc., 700 Copeland Ave., LaCrosse, WI 54603/608-784-0926
Christie's East, 219 E. 67th St., New York, NY 10021/212-606-0400
Christopher Firearms Co., Inc., E., Route 128 & Ferry St., Miamitown, OH 45041/513-353-1321
Chronotech, 1655 Siamet Rd. Unit 6, Mississauga, Ont. L4W 1Z4 CANADA/416-625-5200; FAX: 416-625-5190
Chuck's Gun Shop, P.O. Box 597, Waldo, FL 32694/904-468-2264
Churchill (See U.S. importer—Ellett Bros.)
Churchill Glove Co., James, P.O. Box 298, Centralia, WA 98531
Churchill, Winston, Twenty Mile Stream Rd., RFD P.O. Box 29B, Proctorsville, VT 05153/802-226-7772
Chu Tani Ind., Inc., Box 3782, Chula Vista, CA 92011
CIDCO, 21480 Pacific Blvd., Sterling, VA 22170/703-444-5353
Ciener, Inc., Jonathan Arthur, 8700 Commerce St., Cape Canaveral, FL 32920/407-868-2200; FAX: 407-868-2201
Cimarron Arms, 1106 Wisterwood G, Houston, TX 77043/713-468-2007; FAX: 713-461-8320
Cincinnati Swaging, 2605 Marlington Ave., Cincinnati, OH 45208
Circle M Custom Bullets, 2718 Button Willow Parkway, Abilene, TX 97606/915-698-3106
Claridge Hi-Tec, Inc., 19350 Business Center Dr., Northridge, CA 91324/818-700-9093; FAX: 818-700-0026
Clark Co., Inc., David, P.O. Box 15054, Worcester, MA 01615-0054/508-756-6216; FAX: 508-753-5827
Clark Custom Guns, Inc., P.O. Box 530, 11462 Keatchie Rd., Keithville, LA 71047/318-925-0836; FAX: 318-925-9425
Clark Firearms Engraving, P.O. Box 80746, San Marino, CA 91118/818-287-1652
Clark, Frank, 3714-27th St., Lubbock, TX 79410/806-799-1187
Clarkfield Enterprises, Inc., 1032 10th Ave., Clarkfield, MN 56223/612-669-7140
Classic Arms Corp., P.O. Box 106, Dunsmuir, CA 96025-0106/916-235-2000
Classic Brass, 14 Grove St., Plympton, MA 02367/FAX: 617-585-5673
Classic Guns, Inc., Frank S. Wood, 3230 Medlock Bridge Rd., Suite 110, Norcross, GA 30092/404-242-7944
Clay Target Enterprises, 300 Railway Ave., Campbell, CA 95008/408-379-4829
Clearview Mfg. Co., Inc., 413 S. Oakley St., Fordyce, AR 71742/501-352-8557; FAX: 501-352-8557
Clements' Custom Leathercraft, Chas, 1741 Dallas St., Aurora, CO 80010-2018/303-364-0403
Clenzoil Corp., P.O. Box 80226, Canton, OH 44708/216-833-9758
Clerke Co., J.A., P.O. Box 627, Pearblossom, CA 93553-0627/805-945-0713
Clift Welding Supply & Cases, 1332-A Colusa Hwy., Yuba City, CA 95993/916-755-3390; FAX: 916-755-3393
Clifton Arms, Inc., P.O. Box 1471, Medina, TX 78055/210-589-2666; FAX: 210-589-2661
Clinton River Gun Serv., Inc., 30016 S. River Rd., Mt. Clemens, MI 48045/313-468-1090
Cloward's Gun Shop, 4023 Aurora Ave. N, Seattle, WA 98103/206-632-2072
Clymer Manufacturing Co., Inc., 1645 W. Hamlin Rd., Rochester Hills, MI 48309/313-853-5555; FAX: 313-853-1530
Coast Cutlery Co., 609 SE Ankeny, Portland, OR 97214/503-234-4545
Coats, Mrs. Lester, 300 Luman Rd., Space 125, Phoenix, OR 97535/503-535-1611
CoBalt Mfg., Inc., 15121 35 W., Unit 106-07, Denton, TX 76205/817-382-8986
Cobra Gunskin, 133-30 32nd Ave., Flushing, NY 11354/718-762-8181; FAX: 718-762-0890
Cobra Sport s.r.l., Via Caduti Nei Lager No. 1, 56020 San Romano, Montopoli v/Arno (Pi), ITALY/0039-571-450490; FAX: 0039-571-450492
Cochran, Oliver, Box 868, Shady Spring, WV 25918
Coffin, Charles H., 3719 Scarlet Ave.,Odessa, TX 79762/915-366-4729
Coffin, Jim, 250 Country Club Lane, Albany, OR 97321/503-928-4391
Coghlan's Ltd., 121 Irene St., Winnipeg, Man., CANADA R3T 4C7/204-284-9550
Cold Steel, Inc., 2128 Knoll Dr., Unit D, Ventura, CA 93003/800-255-4716, 800-624-2363
Cole-Grip, 16135 Cohasset St., Van Nuys, CA 91406/818-782-4424
Coleman Co., Inc., 250 N. St. Francis, Wichita, KS 67201
Collins Brothers Div. (See Bowen Knife Co.)
Colonial Arms, Inc., P.O. Box 636, Selma, AL 36702-0636/205-872-9455; FAX: 205-872-9540
Colonial Knife Co., P.O. Box 3327, Providence, RI 02909/401-421-1600; FAX: 401-421-2047
Colonial Repair, P.O. Box 372, Hyde Park, MA 02136-9998/617-469-4951
Colorado School of Trades, 1575 Hoyt St., Lakewood, CO 80215/800-234-4594; FAX: 303-233-4723
Colorado Shooter's Supply, 138 S. Plum, P.O. Box 132, Fruita, CO 81521/303-858-9191
Colorado Sutlers Arsenal, Box 991, Granby, CO 80446/303-887-3813
Colt Blackpowder Arms Co., 5 Centre Market Place, New York, NY 10013/212-925-4881; FAX: 212-966-4986
Colt's Mfg. Co., Inc., P.O. Box 1868, Hartford, CT 06144-1868/203-236-6311; FAX: 203-244-1449
Combat Military Ordnance Ltd., 3900 Hopkins St., Savannah, GA 31405/912-238-1900; FAX: 912-236-7570
Combat Shop, The (See Jet Comp Systems)
Companhia Brasileira de Cartuchos (See CBC)
Compass Industries, Inc., 104 East 25th St., New York, NY 10010/212-473-2614
Competition Electronics, Inc., 3469 Precision Dr., Rockford, IL 61109/815-874-8001; FAX: 815-874-8181
Competition Limited, 1664 S. Research Loop Rd., Tucson, AZ 85710/602-722-6455
Competitive Pistol Shop, The, 5233 Palmer Dr., Ft. Worth, TX 76117-2433/817-834-8479
Competitor Corp., Inc., P.O. Box 244, 293 Townsend Rd., West Groton, MA 01472/508-448-3521; FAX: 603-673-4540
Component Concepts, Inc., 10240 SW Nimbus Ave., Suite L-8, Portland, OR 97223/503-684-9262; FAX: 503-620-4285
Condon, Inc., David, P.O. Box 312, 14502-G Lee Rd., Chatilly, VA 22021/703-631-7748 or 109 E. Washington St., Middleburg, VA 22117/703-687-5642
Condor Mfg. Co., 418 W. Magnolia Ave., Glendale, CA 91204/818-240-3173
Conetrol Scope Mounts, 10225 Hwy. 123 S., Seguin, TX 78155/210-379-3030, 800-CONETROL
CONKKO, P.O. Box 40, Broomall, PA 19008/215-356-0711
Connecticut Valley Arms Co. (See CVA)
Connecticut Valley Classics, P.O. Box 2068, 12 Taylor Lane, Westport, CT 06880/203-435-4600
Conrad, C.A., 3964 Ebert St., Winston-Salem, NC 27127/919-788-5469
Continental Kite & Key (See CONKKO)
Cook Bullets, 1846 Rosemeade Parkway 188, Carrollton, TX 75007/214-394-8725
Cook Engineering Service, 891 Highbury Rd., Vermont VICT 3133 AUSTRALIA
Coonan Arms, Inc., 830 Hampden Ave., St. Paul, MN 55114/612-646-0902; FAX: 612-646-0902
Cooper Arms, P.O. Box 114, Stevensville, MT 59870/406-777-5534
Cooper-Woodward, P.O. Box 1788, East Helena, MT 59635/406-475-3321
Cor-Bon, Inc., 4828 Michigan Ave.,P.O. Box 10126, Detroit, MI 48210/313-894-2373
Corbin Applied Technology, P.O. Box 2171, White City, OR 97503/503-826-5211
Corbin, Inc., 600 Industrial Circle, P.O. Box 2659, White City, OR 97503/503-826-5211; FAX: 503-826-8669
Corkys Gun Clinic, 111 North 11th Ave., Greeley, CO 80631/303-330-0516
Corry, John, 861 Princeton Ct., Neshanic Station, NJ 08853/308-369-8019
Cosmi Americo & Figlio s.n.c., Via Flaminia 307, Ancona, ITALY I-60020/071-888208; FAX: 071-887008 (U.S. importer—New England Arms Co.)
Costa, David, P.O. Box 428, Island Pond, VT 05846
Coulston Products, Inc., P.O. Box 30, Easton, PA 18044-0030/215-253-0167; FAX: 215-252-1511
Counter Assault, Box 4721, Missoula, MT 59806/406-728-6241; FAX: 406-728-8800
Country Armourer, The, P.O. Box 308, Ashby, MA 01431/508-386-7789
Cousin Bob's Mountain Products, 7119 Ohio River Blvd., Ben Avon, PA 15202/412-766-5114; FAX: 412-766-5114
Cox, C. Ed, RD 2, Box 192, Prosperity, PA 15329/412-228-4984
CP Specialties, 1814 Mearns Rd., Warminster, PA 18974
CQB Training, P.O. Box 1739, Manchester, MO 63011
Craftguard, 3624 Logan Ave., Waterloo, IA 50703/319-232-2959
Crandall Tool & Machine Co., 1545 N. Mitchell St., P.O. Box 569, Cadillac, MI 49601/616-775-5562
Crane & Crane Ltd., 105 N. Edison Way 6, Reno, NV 89502-2355/702-856-1516; FAX: 702-856-1616
Crane Sales Co., George S., P.O. Box 385, Van Nuys, CA 91409/818-505-8337
Cravener's Gun Shop, 1627-5th Ave., Ford City, PA 16226/412-763-8312
Crawford Co., Inc., R.M., P.O. Box 277, Everett, PA 15537/814-652-6536; FAX: 814-652-9526
Creative Cartridge Co., 56 Morgan Rd., Canton, CT 06019/203-693-2529
Creative Craftsman, Inc., The, 95 Highway 29 North, P.O. Box 331, Lawrenceville, GA 30246/404-963-2112
Creedmoor Sports, Inc., P.O. Box 1040, Oceanside, CA 92051/619-757-5529
Creek Side Metal & Woodcrafters (See Allard, Gary)
Creekside Gun Shop, Inc., Main St., Holcomb, NY 14469/716-657-6338; FAX: 716-657-7900
Crosman Blades (See Coleman Co., Inc.)
Crosman Corp., Rt. 5 and 20, E. Bloomfield, NY 14443/716-657-6161; FAX: 716-657-5405
Crosman Products of Canada Ltd., 1173 N. Service Rd. West, Oakville, Ontario, LCM 2V9 CANADA/416-827-1822
Crouse's Country Cover, P.O. Box 160, Storrs, CT 06268/203-423-0702
Crucelegui Hermanos (See U.S. importer—Mandall Shooting Supplies, Inc.)
CRW Products, Inc., Box 2123, Des Moines, IA 50310
Cubic Shot Shell Co., Inc., 98 Fatima Dr., Campbell, OH 44405/216-755-0349; FAX: 216-755-0349
Cullity Restoration, Daniel, 209 Old County Rd., East Sandwich, MA 02537/508-888-1147
Cumberland Arms, Rt. I, Box 1150 Shafer Rd., Blantons Chapel, Manchester, TN 37355
Cumberland Knife & Gun Works, 5661 Bragg Blvd., Fayetteville, NC 28303/919-867-0009
Cummings Bullets, 1417 Esperanza Way, Escondido, CA 92027
Cummingham Co., Eaton, Admiral Blvd. at Oak, Kansas City, MO 64106/816-842-2600
Curtis Custom Shop, RR1, Box 193A, Wallingford, KY 41093/703-659-4265
Custom Barrel Electropolishing, 11609 Galayda St., Houston, TX 77086/713-448-5300; FAX: 713-448-7298
Custom Bullets by Hoffman, 2604 Peconic Ave., Seaford, NY 11783
Custom Checkering Service, Kathy Forster, 2124 SE Yamhill St., Portland, OR 97214/503-236-5874
Custom Chronograph, Inc., 5305 Reese Hill Rd., Sumas, WA 98295/206-988-7801
Custom Firearms (See Ahrends, Kim)
Custom Gun Products, 5021 W. Rosewood, Spokane, WA 99208/509-328-9340
Custom Gun Stocks, Rt. 6, P.O. Box 177, McMinnville, TN 37110/615-668-3912
Custom Gunsmiths, 4303 Friar Lane, Colorado Springs, CO 80907/719-599-3366
Custom Hunting Ammo & Arms, 2900 Fisk Rd., Howell, MI 48843/517-546-9498
Custom Shop, The, 890 Cochrane Crescent, Peterborough, Ont. K9H 5N3 CANADA/705-742-6693
Custom Tackle and Ammo, P.O. Box 1886, Farmington, NM 87499/505-632-3539
Cutco Cutlery, P.O. Box 810, Olean, NY 14760/716-372-3111
Cutlery Shoppe, 5461 Kendall St., Boise, ID 83706-1248/800-231-1272
Cutsinger Bench Rest Bullets, RR 8, Box 161-A, Shelbyville, IN 46176/317-729-5360
CVA, 5988 Peachtree Corners East, Norcross, GA 30071/404-449-4687; FAX: 404-242-8546
C.W. Cartridge Co., 242 Highland Ave., Kearney, NJ 07032/201-998-1030 or 71 Hackensack St., Wood-Ridge, NJ 07075
Cycle Dynamics, Inc., 74 Garden St., Feeding Hills, MA 01030/413-786-0141
Cylinder & Slide, Inc., William R. Laughridge, 245 E. 4th St., Fremont, NE 68025/402-721-4277; FAX: 402-721-0263
CZ (See U.S. importer—Action Arms Ltd.)

## D

D&D Gunsmiths, Ltd., 363 E. Elmwood, Troy, MI 48083/313-583-1512
D&H Precision Tooling, 7522 Barnard Mill Rd., Ringwood, IL 60072/815-653-4011
D&H Prods. Co., Inc., 465 Denny Rd., Valencia, PA 16059/412-898-2840
D&J Bullet Co. & Custom Gun Shop, Inc., Rt. 1, Box 223 A-1, Flatwoods, KY 41139/606-836-2663; FAX: 606-836-2663
D&L Sports, P.O. Box 651, Gillette, WY 82717/307-686-4008
D&R Distributing, 308 S.E. Valley St., Myrtle Creek, OR 97457/503-863-6850
Dade Screw Machine Products, 2319 NW 7th Ave., Miami, FL 33127/305-573-5050
Daewoo Precision Industries Ltd., 34-3 Yeoeuido-Dong, Yeongdeungeo-GU, 15th Fl., Seoul, KOREA (U.S. importer—Firstshot, Inc.)
Dahl's Custom Stocks, Rt. 4, P.O. Box 558, Lake Geneva, WI 53147/414-248-2464
Daisy Mfg. Co., P.O. Box 220, Rogers, AR 72756
Dakota (See U.S. importer—EMF Co., Inc.)
Dakota Arms, HC55, Box 326, Sturgis, SD 57785/605-347-4686; FAX: 605-347-4459
Dakota Corp., P.O. Box 543, Rutland, VT 05702/800-451-4167; FAX: 802-773-3919
Daly, Charles (See Miroku, B.C./Daly, Charles)
Damascus-U.S.A., RR 3, Box 39-A, Edenton, NC 27932/919-482-4992; FAX: 919-482-4723
Dan's Whetstone Co., Inc., 109 Remington Terrace, Hot Springs, AR 71913/501-767-1616; FAX: 501-767-9598
Dangler, Homer L., Box 254, Addison, MI 49220/517-547-6745
Danner Shoe Mfg. Co., 12722 NE Airport Way, Portland, OR 97230/503-251-1100; FAX: 503-251-1119
Danuser Machine Co., 550 E. Third St., P.O. Box 368, Fulton, MO 65251/314-642-2246; FAX: 314-642-2240
Dapkus Co., J.G., P.O. Box 293, Durham, CT 06422

Dara-Nes, Inc. (See Nesci Enterprises, Inc.)
Darlington Gun Works, Inc., P.O. Box 698, 516 S. 52 Bypass, Darlington, SC 29532/803-393-3931
Data Tech Software Systems, 19312 East Eldorado Drive, Aurora, CO 80013
Datumtech Corp., 2275 Wehrle Dr., Buffalo, NY 14221
Davidson Products, 2020 Huntington Dr., Las Cruces, NM 88801/505-522-5612
Davidson's, 2703 High Point Rd., Greensboro, NC 27403/800-367-4867, 919-292-5161; FAX: 919-252-2552
Davidson, Jere, Rt. 1, Box 132, Rustburg, VA 24588/804-821-3637
Davis Industries, 11186 Venture Dr., Mira Loma, CA 91752/909-360-5598
Davis Leather Co., G. Wm., 3990 Valley Blvd., Unit D, Walnut, CA 91789/714-598-5620
Davis Products, Mike, 643 Loop Dr., Moses Lake, WA 98837/509-765-6178, 800-765-6178 orders only
Davis Service Center, Bill, 10173 Croydon Way 9, Sacramento, CA 95827/916-369-6789
Day & Sons, Inc., Leonard, P.O. Box 122, Flagg Hill Rd., Heath, MA 01346/413-337-8369
Dayton Traister, P.O. Box 593, Oak Harbor, WA 98277
DBASE Consultants (See Peripheral Data Systems)
DBI Books, Inc., 4092 Commercial Ave., Northbrook, IL 60062/708-272-6310; FAX: 708-272-2051
D-Boone Ent., Inc., 5900 Colwyn Dr., Harrisburg, PA 17109
D.C.C. Enterprises, 259 Wynburn Ave., Athens, GA 30601
D.D. Custom Rifles, R.H. "Dick" Devereaux, 5240 Mule Deer Dr., Colorado Springs, CO 80919/719-548-8468
Dead Eyes Sport Center, RD 1, Box 147B, Shickshin, PA 18655/717-256-7432
de Treville & Co., Stan, 4129 Normal St., San Diego, CA 92103/619-298-3393
Decker Shooting Products, 1729 Laguna Ave., Schofield, WI 54476/715-359-5873
DeckSlider of Florida, 27641-2 Reahard Ct., Bonita Springs, FL 33923/800-782-1474
Dedicated Systems, 105-B Cochrane Circle, Morgan Hill, CA 95037/408-779-2808; FAX: 408-779-2673
Deepeeka Exports Pvt. Ltd., D-78, Saket, Meerut-250-006, INDIA/0121-74483; FAX: 0121-74483
Deer Me Products Co., Box 34, 1208 Park St., Anoka, MN 55303/612-421-8971; FAX: 612-422-0536
Dee Zee Alumna Sports, 1572 NE 58th Ave., P.O. Box 3090, Des Moines, IA 50316/515-265-7331
Defense Moulding Enterprises, 16781 Daisey Ave., Fountain Valley, CA 92708/714-842-5062
Defense Training International, Inc., 749 S. Lemay, Ste. A3-337, Ft. Collins, CO 80524/303-482-2520
Degen Knives, 9608 Van Nuys Blvd., 104, Panorama City, CA 91402/818-892-6534; FAX: 818-830-7333
deHaas Barrels, RR 3, Box 77, Ridgeway, MO 64481/816-872-6308
Del Rey Products, P.O. Box 91561, Los Angeles, CA 90009/213-823-0494
Del-Sports, Inc., Box 685, Main St., Margaretville, NY 12455/914-586-4103; FAX: 914-586-4105
Delhi Gun House, 1374 Kashmere Gate, Delhi, INDIA 110 006/(011)237375 239116; FAX: 91-11-2917344
Delorge, Ed, 2231 Hwy. 308, Thibodaux, LA 70301/504-447-1633
Delta Co. Ammo Bunker, 1209 16th Place, Yuma, AZ 85364/602-783-4563
Delta Arms Ltd., P.O. Box 68, Sellers, SC 29592-0068/803-752-7426, 800-677-0641; 800-274-1611
Delta Enterprises, 284 Hagemann Drive, Livermore, CA 94550
Delta Vectors, Inc., 7119 W. 79th St., Overland Park, KS 66204/913-642-0307
Dem-Bart Checkering Tools, Inc., 6807 Hwy. 2, Bickford Ave., Snohomish, WA 98290/206-568-7356; FAX: 206-568-3134
Denver Arms, Ltd., P.O. Box 4640, Pagosa Springs, CO 81157/303-731-2295
Denver Bullets, Inc., 1811 W. 13th Ave., Denver, CO 80204/303-893-3146
Denver Instrument Co., 6542 Fig St., Arvada, CO 80004/800-321-1135, 303-431-7255
DeSantis Holster & Leather Goods, P.O. Box 2039, New Hyde Park, NY 11040-0701/516-354-8000; FAX: 516-354-7501
Desert Industries, Inc., 3245 E. Patrick Ln., Suite H, Las Vegas, NV 89120/702-597-1066; FAX: 702-434-9495
Desert Mountain Mfg., P.O. Box 184, Coram, MT 59913/406-387-5381
Destination North Software, 804 Surry Road, Wenatchee, WA 98801/509-662-6602
Detroit-Armor Corp., 720 Industrial Dr. 112, Cary, IL 60013/708-639-7666
Developmental Concepts, Rt. 4, New Henderson Rd., Clinton, TN 37716/615-945-1428
Dever Co., Jack, 8590 NW 90, Oklahoma City, OK 73132/405-721-6393
Devereaux, R.H. "Dick" (See D.D. Custom Rifles)
Dewey Mfg. Co., Inc., J., P.O. Box 2014, Southbury, CT 06488/203-598-7912; FAX: 203-598-3119
DGS, Inc., Dale A. Storey, 1117 E. 12th, Casper, WY 82601/307-237-2414
Diamond Machining Technology, Inc., 85 Hayes Memorial Dr., Marlborough, MA 01752/508-481-5944; FAX: 508-485-3924
Diamond Mfg. Co., P.O. Box 174, Wyoming, PA 18644/800-233-9601
Diana (See U.S. importer—Dynamit Nobel-RWS, Inc.)
Dibble, Derek A., 555 John Downey Dr., New Britain, CT 06051/203-224-2630
Dilliott Gunsmithing, Inc., 657 Scarlett Rd., Dandridge, TN 37725/615-397-9204
Dillon Precision Products, Inc., 7442 E. Butherus Dr., Scottsdale, AZ 85260/602-948-8009
Dillon, Ed, 1035 War Eagle Dr. N., Colorado Springs, CO 80919/719-598-4929; FAX: 719-598-4929
Division Lead Co., 7742 W. 61st Pl., Summit, IL 60502
Dixie Gun Works, Hwy. 51 South, Union City, TN 38261/901-885-0700, order 800-238-6785; FAX: 901-885-0440
Dixon Muzzleloading Shop, Inc., RD 1, Box 175, Kempton, PA 19529/215-756-6271
DKT, Inc., 14623 Vera Drive, Union, MI 49130-9744/616-641-7120; FAX: 616-641-2015
DLO Mfg., 415 Howe Ave., Shelton, CT 06484/203-924-2952
Dohring Bullets, 100 W. 8 Mile Rd., Ferndale, MI 48220
Dolbare, Elizabeth, 39 Dahlia, Casper, WY 82604/307-266-5924
Donnelly, C.P., 405 Kubli Rd., Grants Pass, OR 97527/503-846-6604
Doskocil Mfg. Co., Inc., P.O. Box 1246, Arlington, TX 76004/817-467-5116
Douglas Barrels, Inc., 5504 Big Tyler Rd., Charleston, WV 25313-1398/304-776-1341; FAX: 304-776-8560
Dowtin Gunworks, Rt. 4, Box 930A, Flagstaff, AZ 86001/602-779-1898
Dr. O's Products Ltd., P.O. Box 111, Niverville, NY 12130/518-784-3333; FAX: 518-784-2800
Drain, Mark, SE 3211 Kamilche Point Rd., Shelton, WA 98584/206-426-5452
Dremel Mfg. Co., 4915-21st St., Racine, WI 53406
Dressel Jr., Paul G., 209 N. 92nd Ave., Yakima, WA 98908/509-966-9233
Dri-Slide, Inc., 411 N. Darling, Fremont, MI 49412/616-924-3950
DTM International, Inc., 40 Joslyn Rd., P.O. Box 5, Lake Orion, MI 48035/313-693-6670
D.O.C. Specialists, Inc., Doc & Bud Ulrich, Jim Amodei, 2209 S. Central Ave., Cicero, IL 60650/708-652-3606; FAX: 708-652-2516
Du-Lite Corp., 171 River Rd., Middletown, CT 06457/203-347-2505
Duane Custom Stocks, Randy, 110 W. North Ave., Winchester, VA 22601/703-667-9461; FAX: 703-722-3993
Dubber, Michael W., P.O. Box 312, Evansville, IN 47702/812-424-9000; FAX: 812-424-6551
Duck Call Specialists, P.O. Box 124, Jerseyville, IL 62052/618-498-4692
Duffy, Charles E., Williams Lane, West Hurley, NY 12491/914-679-2997
Dumoulin, Ernest, Rue Florent Boclinville 8-10, 13-4041 Votten, BELGIUM/41 27 78 92
Duncan's Gun Works, Inc., 1619 Grand Ave., San Marcos, CA 92069/619-727-0515
Dunham Co., P.O. Box 813, Brattleboro, VT 05301/802-254-2316
Duofold, Inc., 120 W. 45th St., 15th Floor, New York, NY 10036
DuPont (See IMR Powder Co.)

Durward, John, 448 Belgreen Way, Waterloo, Ontario N2L 5X5 CANADA
Dutchman's Firearms, Inc., The, 4143 Taylor Blvd., Louisville, KY 40215/502-366-0555
Duxbak, Inc., 903 Woods Rd., Cambridge, MD 21613/301-228-2990, 800-334-1845
Dybala Gun Shop, P.O. Box 1024, FM 3156, Bay City, TX 77414/409-245-0866
Dykstra, Doug, 411 N. Darling, Fremont, MI 49412/616-924-3950
Dynalite Products, Inc., 215 S. Washington St., Greenfield, OH 45123/513-981-2124
Dynamit Nobel-RWS, Inc., 81 Ruckman Rd., Closter, NJ 07624/201-767-1995; FAX: 201-767-1589
Dyson & Son Ltd., Peter, 29-31 Church St., Honley, Huddersfield, W. Yorkshire HD7 2AH, ENGLAND/0484-661062; FAX: 0484 663709

# E

E&L Mfg., Inc., 39042 N. School House Rd., Cave Creek, AZ 85331/602-488-2598; FAX: 602-488-0813
E.A.A. Corp., 4480 E. 11th Ave., Hialeah, FL 33013/305-688-4442; FAX: 305-688-5656
Eagan, Donald V., P.O. Box 196, Benton, PA 17814/717-925-6134
Eagle Arms, Inc., 131 E. 22nd Ave., P.O. Box 457, Coal Valley, IL 61240/309-799-5619; FAX: 309-799-5150
Eagle Flight Bullet Co., 925 Lakeville St., Suite 123, Petaluma, CA 94954/707-762-6955
Eagle Imports, Inc., 1907 Highway 35, Ocean, NJ 07712/908-531-8375; FAX: 908-531-1520
Eagle International, Inc., 5195 W. 58th Ave., Suite 300, Arvada, CO 80002/303-426-8100
Eagle Products Co., 1520 Adelia Ave., S. El Monte, CA 91733
E-A-R, Inc., Div. of Cabot Safety Corp., 5457 W. 79th St., Indianapolis, IN 46268/800-327-3431; FAX: 800-488-8007
Eastman Products, R.T., P.O. Box 1531, Jackson, WY 83001
Easy Pull Outlaw Products, 316 1st St. East, Polson, MT 59860/406-883-6822
Echols & Co., D'Arcy, 164 W. 580 S., Providence, UT 84332/801-753-2367
Eckelman Gunsmithing, 3125 133rd St. SW, Fort Ripley, MN 56449/218-829-3176
Edenpine, Inc. c/o Six Enterprises, Inc., 320 D Turtle Creek Ct., San Jose, CA 95125/408-999-0201; FAX: 408-999-0216
Ed's Gun House, Rt. 1, Box 62, Minnesota City, MN 55959/507-689-2925
EdgeCraft Corp., P.O. Box 3000, Avondale, PA 19311/215-268-0500, 800-342-3255; FAX: 215-268-3545
Edmisten Co., P.O. Box 1293, Boone, NC 28607
Edmund Scientific Co., 101 E. Gloucester Pike, Barrington, NJ 08033/609-543-6250
Ednar, Inc., 2-4-8 Kayabacho, Nihonbashi, Chuo-ku, Tokyo, JAPAN/81(Japan)-3-3667-1651
Eds Custom Bullets, 431 North 75 East, North Salt Lake, UT 84054/801-295-3960
Eezox, Inc., P.O. Box 772, Waterford, CT 06385-0772/203-447-8282; FAX: 203-447-3484
Efemes Enterprises, P.O. Box 691, Colchester, VT 05446
Eggleston, Jere D., 400 Saluda Ave., Columbia, SC 29205/803-799-3402
Eichelberger Bullets, Wm., 158 Crossfield Rd., King of Prussia, PA 19406
Eilan S.A.L., Paseo San Andres N8, Eibar, SPAIN 20600/(34)43118916; FAX: (34)43 114038
Eiland Custom Bullets, P.O. Box 688, Buena Vista, CO 81211/303-429-8850
EK Knife Co., 601 N. Lombardy St., Richmond, VA 23220/804-257-7272
Ekol Leather Care, P.O. Box 2652, West Lafayette, IN 47906/317-463-2250; FAX: 317-463-7004
El Paso Saddlery Co., P.O. Box 27194, El Paso, TX 79926/915-544-2233; FAX: 915-544-2535
Eldorado Cartridge Corp. (See PMC/Eldorado Cartridge Corp.)
Electronic Trigger Systems, Inc., 4124 Thrushwood Lane, Minnetonka, MN 55345/612-935-7829
Electro Prismatic Collimators, Inc., 1441 Manatt St., Lincoln, NE 68521
Eley Ltd., P.O. Box 705, Witton, Birmingham, B6 7UT, ENGLAND/21-356-8899; FAX: 21-331-4173
Elite Ammunition, P.O. Box 3251, Oakbrook, IL 60522/708-366-9006
Elk River, Inc., 1225 Paonia St., Colorado Springs, CO 80915/719-574-4407
Elko Arms, Dr. L. Kortz, 28 rue Ecole Moderne, B-7060 Soignies, BELGIUM/(32)67-33-29-34
Ellett Bros., P.O. Box 128, Columbia, SC 29036/803-345-1820; FAX: 803-345-1820
Ellis Sport Shop, E.W., RD 1, Route 9N, P.O. Box 315, Corinth, NY 12822/518-654-6444
EMF Co., Inc., 1900 E. Warner Ave. Suite 1-D, Santa Ana, CA 92705/714-261-6611; FAX: 714-956-0133
Empire Cutlery Corp., 12 Kruger Ct., Clifton, NJ 07013/201-472-5155; FAX: 201-779-0759
Engineered Accessories, 1307 W. Wabash Ave., Effingham, IL 62401/217-347-7700; FAX: 217-347-7737
English, Inc., A.G., 708 S. 12th St., Broken Arrow, OK 74012/918-251-3399
Englishtown Sporting Goods Co., Inc., David J. Maxham, 38 Main St., Englishtown, NJ 07726/201-446-7717
Engraving Artistry, 36 Alto Rd., RFD 2, Burlington, CT 06013/203-673-6837
Enguix Import-Export, Alpujarras 58, Alzira, Valencia, SPAIN 46600/(96) 241 43 95; FAX: (96) 241 43 95
Enhanced Presentations, Inc., 5929 Market St., Wilmington, NC 28405/919-799-1622; FAX: 919-799-5004
The Ensign-Bickford Co., 660 Hopmeadow St., Simsbury, CT 06070
Epps "Orillia" Ltd., Ellwood, RR 3, Hwy. 11 North, Orillia, Ont. L3V 6H3, CANADA/705-689-5333
Erhardt, Dennis, 3280 Green Meadow Dr., Helena, MT 59601/406-442-4533
Erickson's Mfg., Inc., C.W., 530 Garrison Ave. N.E., Buffalo, MN 55313/612-682-3665; FAX: 612-682-4328
Erma Werke GmbH, Johan Ziegler St., 13/15/FeldiglSt., D-8060 Dachau, GERMANY (U.S. importers—Mandall Shooting Supplies, Inc.; PSI, Inc.)
Essex Arms, P.O. Box 345, Island Pond, VT 05846/802-723-4313
Estate Cartridge, Inc., 2778 FM 830, Willis, TX 77378/409-856-7277; FAX: 409-856-5486
Eureka Bullets, Hill House, Taylors Arm, NSW 2447 AUSTRALIA
Euroarms of America, Inc., 208 E. Piccadilly St., Winchester, VA 22601/703-662-1863; FAX: 703-662-4464
European American Armory Corp. (See E.A.A. Corp.)
Europtik Ltd., P.O. Box 319, Dunmore, PA 18512/717-347-6049, 800-873-5362; FAX: 717-969-4330
Eutaw Co., Inc., The, P.O. Box 608, U.S. Hwy. 176 West, Holly Hill, SC 29059/803-496-3341
Evans Engraving, Robert, 332 Vine St., Oregon City, OR 97045/503-656-5693
Eversull Co., Inc., K., 1 Tracemont, Boyce, LA 71409/318-793-8728; FAX: 318-793-5483
Exe, Inc., 18830 Partridge Circle, Eden Prairie, MN 55346/612-944-7662
Executive Protection Institute, Rt. 2, Box 3645, Berryville, VA 22611/703-955-1128
Eyears Insurance, 4926 Annhurst Rd., Columbus, OH 43228-1341
Eyster Heritage Gunsmiths, Inc., Ken, 6441 Bishop Rd., Centerburg, OH 43011/614-625-6131
Eze-Lap Diamond Prods., P.O. Box 2229, 15164 Weststate St., Westminster, CA 92683//714-847-1555

# F

4-D Custom Die Co., 711 N. Sandusky St., P.O. Box 889, Mt. Vernon, OH 43050-0889/614-397-7214; FAX: 614-397-6600
Fabarm S.p.A., Via G. Zola N.33, Brescia, ITALY 25136/(030)2004805; FAX: (030)2004816 (U.S. importer—St. Lawrence Sales, Inc.)
Fabian Bros. Sporting Goods, Inc., 1510 Morena Blvd., Suite G, San Diego, CA 92110/619-275-0816; FAX: 619-276-8733

Fabrica D'Armi Sabatti S.R.L., via Dante 179, 25068 Sarezzo, Brescia, ITALY (U.S. importer—E.A.A. Corp.)
Fagan & Co., William, 22952 15 Mile Rd., Mt. Clemens, MI 48043/313-465-4637; FAX: 313-792-6996
Fair Game International, P.O. Box 77234-34053, Houston, TX 77234/713-941-6269
F.A.I.R. Techni-Mec s.n.c. Di Isidoro Rizzini & C., Via Gitti 41, 25060 Marcheno (BS), ITALY
Faith Associates, Inc., 1139 S. Greenville Hwy., Hendersonville, NC 28792/704-692-1916; FAX: 704-697-6827
Fajen, Inc., Reinhart, 1000 Red Bud Dr., P.O. Box 338, Warsaw, MO 65355/816-438-5111; FAX: 816-438-5175
Falcon Industries, Inc., P.O. Box 1310, Huntington Beach, CA 92647-1310/714-847-4700; 714-847-4141
Famas (See U.S. importer—Century International Arms, Inc.)
Fanzoj GmbH, Griesgasse 1, 9170 Ferlach, AUSTRIA 9170/(43) 04227-2283; FAX: (43) 04227-2867
FAPA Corp., P.O. Box 1439, New London, NH 03257/603-735-5652; FAX: 603-735-5154
Farm Form Decoys, Inc., 1602 Biovu, Galveston, TX 77551/409-744-0762, 409-765-6361; FAX: 409-765-8513
Farmer-Dressel, Sharon, 209 N. 92nd Ave., Yakima, WA 98908/509-966-9233
Far North Outfitters, Box 1252, Bethel, AK 99559
Farr Studio, Inc., 1231 Robinhood Rd., Greeneville, TN 37743/615-638-8825
FAS, Via E. Fermi, 8, 20019 Settimo Milanese, Milano, ITALY (U.S. importer—Nygord Precision Products)
Faulk's Game Call Co., Inc., 616 18th St., Lake Charles, LA 70601/318-436-9726
Faust, Inc., T.G., 544 Minor St., Reading, PA 19602/215-375-8549; FAX: 215-375-4488
Fausti & Figlie s.n.c., Stefano, Via Martini Zudipeudente, 70, Marcheno, 25060 ITALY (U.S. importer—American Arms, Inc.)
Fautheree, Andy, P.O. Box 4607, Pagosa Springs, CO 81157/303-731-5003
Feather Flex Decoys, 1655 Swan Lake Rd., Bossier City, LA 71111/318-746-8596; FAX: 318-742-4815
Feather Industries, Inc., 2300 Central Ave. K, Boulder, CO 80301/303-442-7021; FAX: 303-447-0944
Federal Cartridge Co., 900 Ehlen Dr., Anoka, MN 55303/612-422-2840
Federal Champion Target Co., 232 Industrial Parkway, Richmond, IN 47374/800-441-4971; FAX: 317-966-7747
Federal Engineering Corp., 1090 Bryn Mawr, Bensenville, IL 60106/708-860-1938
Federal Ordnance, Inc., 1443 Potrero Ave., S. El Monte, CA 91733/818-350-4161; FAX: 818-444-3875
FEG, Budapest, Soroksariut 158, H-1095 HUNGARY (U.S. importers—Century International Arms, Inc; K.B.I., Inc.)
Feinwerkbau Westinger & Altenburger GmbH & Co. KG (See FWB)
Fellowes, Ted, Beaver Lodge, 9245 16th Ave. SW, Seattle, WA 98106/206-763-1698
Feminine Protection, Inc., 10514 Shady Trail, Dallas, TX 75220/214-351-4500
Ferdinand, Inc., P.O. Box 5, 201 Main St., Harrison, ID 83833/208-689-3012; FAX: 208-689-3142
Ferguson, Bill, P.O. Box 1238, Sierra Vista, AZ 85636/602-452-0533; FAX: 602-458-9125
FERLIB di Ferraglio Libero & C., Via Costa 46, 25063 Gardone V.T. (Brescia), ITALY/30 89 12 586; FAX: 30 89 12 586 (U.S. importers—New England Arms Co., Quality Arms, Inc.)
Ferris Firearms, 1827 W. Hildebrand, San Antonio, TX 78201/210-734-0304
Fiberpro Rifle Stocks, Div. of Fibers West, 10977 San Diego Mission Rd., San Diego, CA 92108/619-282-4211; FAX: 619-282-0598
Fibron Products, Inc., 170 Florida St., Buffalo, NY 14208/716-886-2378; FAX: 716-886-2394
Finch Custom Bullets, 40204 La Rochelle, Prairieville, LA 70769
Finerty, Raymond F., 803 N. Downing St., P.O. Box 914, Piqua, OH 45356/800-543-8952
Fiocchi of America, Inc., Rt. 2, P.O. Box 90-8, Ozark, MO 65721/417-725-4118; FAX: 417-725-1039
Firearm Training Center, The, 9555 Blandville Rd., West Paducah, KY 42086/502-554-5886
Firearms Academy of Seattle, P.O. Box 6691, Lynnwood, WA 98036/206-827-0533
Firearms Co. Ltd./Alpine (See U.S. importer—Mandall Shooting Supplies, Inc.)
Firearms Engraver's Guild of America, 332 Vine St., Oregon City, OR 97045/503-656-5693
Firearms Safety Products, Inc. (See FSPI)
First Distributors, Jack, Inc., 44633 Sierra Hwy., Lancaster, CA 93534/805-945-6981; FAX: 805-942-0844
Firstshot, Inc., 4101 Far Green Rd., Harrisburg, PA 17110/717-238-2575
Fish, Marshall F., Rt. 22 N., P.O. Box 2439, Westport, NY 12993/518-962-4897
Fish-N-Hunt, Inc., 5651 Beechnut St., Houston, TX 77096/713-777-3285; FAX: 713-777-9884
Fisher Custom Firearms, 2199 S. Kittredge Way, Aurora, CO 80013/303-755-3710
Fisher Enterprises, 655 Main St. 305, Edmonds, WA 98020/206-776-4365
Fisher, Jerry A., 535 Crane Mt. Rd., Big Fork, MT 59911/406-837-1024
Fitz Pistol Grip Co., P.O. Box 610, Douglas City, CA 96024/916-623-4019
Flaig's, 2200 Evergreen Rd., Millvale, PA 15209/412-821-1717
Flambeau Products Corp., P.O. Box 97, Middlefield, OH 44062/216-632-1631; FAX: 216-632-1581
Flannery Engraving Co., Jeff W., 11034 Riddles Run Rd., Union, KY 41091/606-384-3127
Flashette Co., 4725 S. Kolin Ave., Chicago, IL 60632/312-927-1302
Flayderman & Co., Inc., N., P.O. Box 2446, Ft. Lauderdale, FL 33303/305-761-8855
Fleming Firearms, 7720 E. 126 St. N., Collinsville, OK 74021/918-665-3624
Flents Products Co., Inc., P.O. Box 2109, Norwalk, CT 06852/203-866-2581; FAX: 203-854-9322
Flintlock Muzzle Loading Gun Shop, The, 1238 "G" S. Beach Blvd., Anaheim, CA 92804/714-821-6655
Flintlocks, Etc. (See Beauchamp & Son, Inc.)
Flitz International Ltd., 821 Mohr Ave., Waterford, WI 53185/414-534-5898; FAX: 414-534-2991
Floatstone Mfg. Co., 106 Powder Mill Rd., P.O. Box 765, Canton, CT 06019/203-693-1977
Flores Publications, J., P.O. Box 830131, Miami, FL 33283/305-559-4652
Flouramics, Inc., 103 Pleasant Ave., Upper Saddle River, NJ 07458/201-825-8110
Flow-Rite of Tennessee, Inc., 107 Allen St., Bruceton, TN 38317/901-586-2271; FAX: 901-586-2300
Flynn's Custom Guns, P.O. Box 7461, Alexandria, LA 71306/318-455-7130
FN Herstal, Voie de Liege 33, Herstal 4040, BELGIUM/(32)41.40.82.83; FAX: (32)40.86.79
Fobus International Ltd., Kfar Hess, ISRAEL 40692/FAX: 972-52-911716
Fogle, James W., RR 2, P.O. Box 258, Herrin, IL 62948/618-988-1795
Folks, Donald E., 205 W. Lincoln St., Pontiac, IL 61764/815-844-7901
Foothills Video Productions, Inc., P.O. Box 651, Spartanburg, SC 29304/803-573-7023, 800-782-5358
Ford, Jack, 1430 Elkwood, Missouri City, TX 77489/713-499-9984
Foredom Electric Co., Rt. 6, 16 Stony Hill Rd., Bethel, CT 06801/203-792-8622
Forgett Jr., Valmore J., 689 Bergen Blvd., Ridgefield, NJ 07657/201-945-2500
Forgreens Tool Mfg., Inc., P.O. Box 990, Robert Lee, TX 76945/915-453-2800
Forrest Tool Co., P.O. Box 768, 44380 Gordon Lane, Mendocino, CA 95460/707-937-2141; FAX: 717-937-1817
Forrest, Inc., Tom, P.O. Box 326, Lakeside, CA 92040/619-561-5800; FAX: 619-561-0227
Forster, Kathy (See Custom Checkering Service)
Forster Products, 82 E. Lanark Ave., Lanark, IL 61046/815-493-6360; FAX: 815-493-2371
Forster, Larry L., P.O. Box 212, 220 First St. NE, Gwinner, ND 58040-0212/701-678-2475
Fort Knox Security Products, 1051 N. Industrial Park Rd., Orem, UT 84057/801-224-7233
Forthofer's Gunsmithing & Knifemaking, 711 Spokane Ave., Whitefish, MT 59937/406-862-2674
Fortress Publications, Inc., P.O. Box 9241, Stoney Creek, Ont. L8G 3X9, CANADA/416-662-3505
Fortune Products, Inc., Box 1308, Friendswood, TX 77546/713-996-0729; FAX: 713-996-1034
Forty Five Ranch Enterprises, Box 1080, Miami, OK 74355-1080/918-542-5875
Forty-Niner Trading Co., P.O. Box 792, Manteca, CA 95336/209-823-7263
Fouling Shot, The, 6465 Parfet St., Arvada, CO 80004
Fountain Products, 492 Prospect Ave., West Springfield, MA 01089/413-781-4651; FAX: 413-733-8217
Fowler Bullets, 4003 Linwood Rd., Gastonia, NC 28052/704-867-3259
Fox River Mills, Inc., P.O. Box 298, 227 Poplar St., Osage, IA 50461/515-732-3798; FAX: 515-732-5128
Foy Custom Bullets, 104 Wells Ave., Daleville, AL 36322
Francesca, Inc., 3115 Old Ranch Rd., San Antonio, TX 78217/512-826-2584; FAX: 512-826-8211
Francesca Stabilizer's, Inc., 3115 Old Ranch Rd., San Antonio, TX 78217/512-826-2584
Franchi S.p.A., Luigi, Via del Serpente, 12, 25020 Fornaci, ITALY (U.S. importer—American Arms, Inc.)
Francolini, Leonard, 106 Powder Mill Rd., P.O. Box 765, Canton, CT 06019/203-693-1977
Francotte & Cie S.A., Auguste, rue du Trois Juin 109, 4400 Herstal-Liege, BELGIUM/41-48.13.18 (U.S. importer—Armes de Chasse)
Frank Custom Gun Service, Ron, 7131 Richland Rd., Ft. Worth, TX 76118/817-284-4426
Frank Knives, Box 984, Whitefish, MT 59937/406-862-2681; FAX: 406-862-2681
Frankonia Jagd, Hofmann & Co., P.O. Box 6780, D-8700 Wurzburg 1, GERMANY/09302-200; FAX: 09302-20200
Frazier Brothers Enterprises, 1118 N. Main St., Franklin, IN 46131/317-736-4000; FAX: 317-736-4000
Fredrick Gun Shop, 10 Elson Dr., Riverside, RI 02915/401-433-2805
Freedom Arms, Inc., P.O. Box 1776, Freedom, WY 83120/307-883-2468; FAX: 307-883-2005
Freeman Animal Targets, 2559 W. Morris St., Plainsfield, IN 46168/317-271-5314; FAX: 317-271-9106
Fremont Tool Works, 1214 Prairie, Ford, KS 67842/316-369-2338
French, J.R., 1712 Creek Ridge Ct., Irving, TX 75060/214-254-2654
Frielich Police Equipment, 211 East 21st St., New York, NY 10010/212-254-3045
Frontier, 2910 San Bernardo, Laredo, TX 78040/512-723-5409
Frontier Arms Co., Inc., 401 W. Rio Santa Cruz, Green Valley, AZ 85614-3932
Frontier Products Co., 164 E. Longview Ave., Columbus, OH 43202/614-262-9357
Frontier Safe Co., Envirotemp Corp., 1317 Chute St., Fort Wayne, IN 46803/219-422-4801
Frost Cutlery Co., P.O. Box 21353, Chattanooga, TN 37421/615-894-6079; FAX: 615-894-9576
FSPI, 5885 Glenridge Dr. Suite 220A, Atlanta, GA 30328/404-843-2881; FAX: 404-843-0271
Fujinon, Inc., 10 High Point Dr., Wayne, NJ 07470/201-633-5600
Fullmer, Geo M., 2499 Mavis St., Oakland, CA 94601/510-533-4193
Fulmer's Antique Firearms, Chet, P.O. Box 792, Rt. 2 Buffalo Lake, Detroit Lakes, MN 56501/218-847-7712
Furr Arms, 91 N. 970 W., Orem, UT 84057/801-226-3877; FAX: 801-226-0085
Fury Cutlery, 801 Broad Ave., Ridgefield, NJ 07657/201-943-5920; FAX: 201-943-1579
Fusilier Bullets, 10010 N. 6000 W., Highland, UT 84003/801-756-6813
FWB, Neckarstrasse 43, 7238 Oberndorf a. N., GERMANY/07423-814-0; FAX: 07423-814-89 (U.S. importer—Beeman Precision Airguns, Inc.)

## G

G96 Products Co., Inc., 237 River St., Paterson, NJ 07524/201-684-4050; FAX: 201-684-3848
G&C Bullet Co., Inc., 8835 Thornton Rd., Stockton, CA 95209
G&H Decoys, Inc., P.O. Box 1208, Hwy. 75 North, Henryetta, OK 74437/918-652-3314
Galati International, P.O. Box 326, Catawissa, MO 63015/314-257-4837; FAX: 314-257-2268
Galaxy Imports Ltd., Inc., P.O. Box 3361, Victoria, TX 77903/512-573-4867; FAX: 512-576-9622
GALCO International Ltd., 2019 W. Quail Ave., Phoenix, AZ 85027/602-258-8295; FAX: 602-582-6854
Gamba S.p.A., Renato, Via Artigiani, 93, 25063 Gardone V.T. (Brescia), ITALY
Game Haven Gunstocks, 13750 Shire Rd., Wolverine, MI 49799/616-525-8257
Game Winner, Inc., 2625 Cumberland Parkway, Suite 220, Atlanta, GA 30339/404-434-9210; FAX: 404-434-9215
Gammog, Gregory B. Gally, 16009 Kenny Rd., Laurel, MD 20707/301-725-3838
Gamo (See U.S. importers—Daisy Mfg. Co.; Dynamit Nobel-RWS, Inc.)
Gander Mountain, Inc., P.O. Box 128, Hwy."W,", Wilmot, WI 53192/414-862-2331,Ext. 6425
Ganton Manufacturing Ltd., Depot Lane, Seamer Rd., Scarborough, North Yorkshire, Y012 4EB ENGLAND/0723-371910; FAX: 0723-501671
GAR, 139 Park Lane, Wayne, NJ 07470/201-256-7641
Garbi, Armas Urki, 12-14, 20.600 Eibar (Guipuzcoa) SPAIN/43-11 38 73 (U.S. importer—Moore & Co. Wm. Larkin)
Garcia National Gun Traders, Inc., 225 SW 22nd Ave., Miami, FL 33135/305-642-2355
Garrett Accur-Lt. D.F.S. Co., P.O. Box 8675, 1413B East Olive Ct., Ft. Collins, CO 80524/303-224-3067
Garrett Cartridges, Inc., P.O. Box 178, Chehalis, WA 98532/206-736-0702
Garthwaite, Jim, Rt. 2, Box 310, Watsontown, PA 17777/717-538-1566
Gator Guns & Repair, 6255 Spur Hwy., Kenai, AK 99611/907-283-7947
Gaucher Armes, S.A., 46, rue Desjoyaux, 42000 Saint-Etienne, FRANCE/77 33 38 92 (U.S. importer—Mandall Shooting Supplies, Inc.)
GDL Enterprises, 409 Le Gardeur, Slidell, LA 70460/504-649-0693
Genco, P.O. Box 5704, Asheville, NC 28803
Gene's Custom Guns, P.O. Box 10534, White Bear Lake, MN 55110/612-429-5105
Gene's Gun Shop, Rt. 1 Box 890, Snyder, TX 79549/915-573-2323
Genecco Gun Works, K., 10512 Lower Sacramento Rd., Stockton, CA 95210/209-951-0706
General Lead, Inc., 1022 Grand Ave., Phoenix, AZ 85007
Gentry Custom Gunmaker, David, 314 N. Hoffman, Belgrade, MT 59714/406-388-4867
George & Ray's Primer Sealant, 2950 NW 29th, Portland, OR 97210/800-553-3022
George, Tim, Rt. 1, P.O. Box 45, Evington, VA 24550/804-821-8117
Gerber Legendary Blades, 14200 SW 72nd Ave., Portland, OR 97223/503-639-6161; FAX: 503-684-7008
Getz Barrel Co., P.O. Box 88, Beavertown, PA 17813/717-658-7263
GFR Corp., P.O. Box 430, Andover, NH 03216/603-735-5300
G.H. Enterprises Ltd., Bag 10, Okotoks, Alberta T0L 1T0 CANADA/403-938-6070
Gibbs Rifle Co., Inc., Cannon Hill Industrial Park, Rt. 2, Box 214 Hoffman Rd., Martinsburg, WV 25401/304-274-0458; FAX: 304-274-0078
Gilbert Equipment Co., Inc., 960 Downtowner Rd., Mobile, AL 36609/205-344-3322
Gillmann, Edwin, 33 Valley View Dr., Hanover, PA 17331/717-632-1662
Gilman-Mayfield, Inc., 3279 E. Shields, Fresno, CA 93703/209-237-2500
Giron, Robert E., 1328 Pocono St., Pittsburgh, PA 15218/412-731-6041
Gise Bullets, P.O. Box 772, Santa Clara, CA 95052
Glacier Glove, 4890 Aircenter Circle 206, Reno, NV 89502/702-825-8225; FAX: 702-825-6544
Glaser Safety Slug, Inc., P.O. Box 8223, Foster City, CA 94404/415-345-7677; FAX: 415-345-8217
Glass, Herb, P.O. Box 25, Bullville, NY 10915/914-361-3021

Glimm, Jerome C., 19 S. Maryland, Conrad, MT 59425/406-278-3574
Global Industries, 1501 E. Chapman Ave., 306, Fullerton, CA 92631/714-879-8922
Glock GmbH, P.O. Box 50, A-2232 Deutsch Wagram, AUSTRIA (U.S. importer—Glock, Inc.)
Glock, Inc., 6000 Highlands Parkway, Smyrna, GA 30082/404-432-1202
GML Products, Inc., 394 Laredo Dr., Birmingham, AL 35226/205-979-4867
Goens, Dale W., P.O. Box 224, Cedar Crest, NM 87008/505-281-5419
Goergen's Gun Shop, Inc., Rt. 2, Box 182BB, Austin, MN 55912/507-433-9280
GOEX, Inc., 1002 Springbrook Ave., Moosic, PA 18507/717-457-6724; FAX: 717-457-1130
Golden Age Arms Co., 115 E. High St., Ashley, OH 43003/614-747-2488
Gonic Arms, Inc., 134 Flagg Rd., Gonic, NH 03839/603-332-8456, 603-332-8457
Gonzalez Guns, Ramon B., P.O. Box 370, Monticello, NY 12701/914-794-4515
Goodling's Gunsmithing, R.D. 1, Box 1097, Spring Grove, PA 17362/717-225-3350
Goodwin, Fred, Silver Ridge Gun Shop, Sherman Mills, ME 04776/207-365-4451
Gordie's Gun Shop, 1401 Fulton St., Streator, IL 61364/815-672-7202
Gotz Bullets, 7313 Rogers St., Rockford, IL 61111
Goudy Classic Stocks, Gary, 263 Hedge Rd., Menlo Park, CA 94025-1711/415-322-1338
Gould & Goodrich, P.O. Box 1479, Lillington, NC 27546/919-893-2071; FAX: 919-893-4742
Gozon Corp., P.O. Box 6278, Fulsom, CA 95763/916-983-1807; FAX: 916-983-9500
Gournet, Geoffroy, 820 Paxinosa Ave., Easton, PA 18042/215-559-0710
Gozon Corp., P.O. Box 6278, Folsom, CA 95630/FAX: 916-983-9500
Grace & Co.-Conn., W.R. (See Airmold, W.R. Grace & Co.-Conn.)
Grace, Charles E., 10144 Elk Lake Rd., Williamsburg, MI 49690/616-264-9483
Grace Metal Products, Inc., P.O. Box 67, Elk Rapids, MI 49629/616-264-8133
Grace Tool, Inc., 3661 E. 44th St., Tucson, AZ 85713/602-747-0213
"Gramps" Antique Cartridges, Box 341, Washago, Ont. L0K 2B0 CANADA/705-689-5348
Grand Falls Bullets, Inc., 1120 Forest Dr., Blue Springs, MO 64015/816-229-0112
Granger, Georges, 66 cours Fauriel, 42100 Saint Etienne, FRANCE/(77)25 14 73
Granite Custom Bullets, Box 190, Philipsburg, MT 59858/406-859-3245
Grant, Howard V., Hiawatha 15, Woodruff, WI 54568/715-356-7146
Graphics Direct, 18336 Gault St., Reseda, CA 91335/818-344-9002
Graves Co., 1800 Andrews Av., Pompano Beach, FL 33069/800-327-9103; FAX: 305-960-0301
Graybill's Gun Shop, 1035 Ironville Pike, Columbia, PA 17512/717-684-6220
The Great 870 Co., P.O. Box 6309, El Monte, CA 91734
Great Lakes Airguns, 6175 S. Park Ave., Hamburg, NY 14075/716-648-6666; FAX: 716-648-0393
Green, Arthur S., 485 S. Rovertson Blvd., Beverly Hills, CA 90211/310-274-1283
Green Bay Bullets, 1860 Burns Ave., Green Bay, WI 54313/414-494-5166
Green Genie, Box 114, Cusseta, GA 31805
Green Head Game Call Co., RR 1, Box 33, Lacon, IL 61540/309-246-2155
Green Mountain Rifle Barrel Co., Inc., RFD 2, Box 8 Center, Conway, NH 03813/603-356-2047; FAX: 603-356-2048
Green, Roger M., P.O. Box 984, 435 E. Birch, Glenrock, WY 82637/307-436-9804
Greene, M.L., 17200 W. 57th Ave., Golden, CO 80403/303-279-2383
Greenwald, Leon E. "Bud", 2553 S. Quitman St., Denver, CO 80219/303-935-3850
Greg Gunsmithing Repair, 3732 26th Ave. North, Robbinsdale, MN 55422/612-529-8103
Greg's Superior Products, P.O. Box 46219, Seattle, WA 98146
Greider Precision, 431 Santa Marina Ct., Escondido, CA 92029/619-480-8892
Gremmel Enterprises, 271 Sterling Dr., Eugene, OR 97404/503-688-3319
Grendel, Inc., P.O. Box 560909, Rockledge, FL 32953/800-274-7427, 407-636-1211; FAX: 407-633-6710
Griffin & Howe, Inc., 33 Claremont Rd., Bernardsville, NJ 07924/908-766-2287; FAX: 908-766-1068
Griffin & Howe, Inc., 36 W. 44th St., Suite 1011, New York, NY 10036/212-921-0980
Grifon, Inc., 58 Guinam St., Waltham, MS 02154
Griggs Products, P.O. Box 789, 270 S. Main St., Suite 103, Bountiful, UT 84010/801-295-9696
Grip-Master, P.O. Box 32, Westbury, NY 11490/800-752-0164; FAX: 516-997-5142
Grizzly Bullets, 2137 Hwy. 200, Trout Creek, MT 59874/406-847-2627
Group Tight Bullets, 482 Comerwood Court, San Francisco, CA 94080/415-583-1550
GRS Corp., Glendo, P.O. Box 1153, 900 Overlander St., Emporia, KS 66801/316-343-1084
Grulla Armes, Apartado 453, Avda Otaloa, 12, Eiber, SPAIN (U.S. importers—American Arms, Inc.; Hanus Birdguns, Bill)
GSI, Inc., 108 Morrow Ave., P.O. Box 129, Trussville, AL 35173/205-655-8299; FAX: 205-655-7078
GTS Enterprises, Inc., Dynaray Marketing Div., 50 W. Hillcrest Dr., Suite 215, Thousand Oaks, CA 91360/805-373-0921
G.U., Inc., 4325 S. 120th St., Omaha, NE 68137/402-330-4492
Guardian Group International, 21 Warren St., Suite 3E, New York, NY 10007/212-619-3838
Guardsman Products, 411 N. Darling, Fremont, MI 49412/616-924-3950
Gun City, 212 W. Main Ave., Bismarck, ND 58501/701-223-2304
Gun Doctor, The, 435 East Maple, Roselle, IL 60172/708-894-0668
Gun Doctor, The, P.O. Box 39242, Downey, CA 90242
Gun Hunter Books, Div. of Gun Hunter Trading Co., 5075 Heisig St., Beaumont, TX 77705/409-835-3006
Gun Leather Limited, 116 Lipscomb, Ft. Worth, TX 76104/817-334-0225; 800-247-0609
Gun List (See Krause Publications)
Gun Parts Corp., The, Williams Lane, West Hurley, NY 12491/914-679-2417; FAX: 914-679-5849
Gun Room, The, 1121 Burlington, Muncie, IN 47302/317-282-9073; FAX: 317-282-9073
Gun Room Press, The, 127 Raritan Ave., Highland Park, NJ 08904/908-545-4344; FAX: 908-545-6686
Gun Shop, The, 5550 S. 900 East, Salt Lake City, UT 84117/801-263-3633
Gun Shop, The, 62778 Spring Creek Rd., Montrose, CO 81401
Gun Shop, The, Shop 31 320 West St., Durban 4001 SOUTH AFRICA
Gun South, Inc. (See GSI, Inc.)
Gun Vault, Inc., 200 Larkin Dr., Unit E, Wheeling, IL 60090/708-215-6606; FAX: 708-215-7550
Gun Works, The, 236 Main St., Springfield, OR 97477/503-741-4118
Gun-Alert/Master Products, Inc., 1010 N. Maclay Ave., San Fernando, CA 91340/818-365-0864; FAX: 818-365-1308
Gun-Ho Sports Cases, 110 E. 10th St., St. Paul, MN 55101/612-224-9491
Gun-Tec, P.O. Box 8125, W. Palm Beach, FL 33407
Guncraft Books (See Guncraft Sports, Inc.)
Guncraft Sports, Inc., 10737 Dutchtown Rd., Knoxville, TN 37932/615-966-4545
Gunfitters, The, P.O. 426, Cambridge, WI 53523-0426/608-764-8128
Gunline Tools, P.O. Box 478, Placentia, CA 92670/714-528-5252; FAX: 714-572-4128
Gunnerman Books, P.O. Box 214292, Auburn Hills, MI 48321/313-879-2779
Guns, 81 E. Streetsboro St., Hudson, OH 44236/216-650-4563
GUNS Magazine, 591 Camino de la Reina, Suite 200, San Diego, CA 92108/619-297-5350; FAX: 619-297-5353
Guns Unlimited, Inc. (See G.U., Inc.)
Gunsight, The, 1712 North Placentia Ave., Fullerton, CA 92631
Gunsite Gunsmithy, P.O. Box 451, Paulden, AZ 86334/602-636-4565; FAX: 602-636-1236
The Gunsmith in Elk River, 14021 Victoria Lane, Elk River, MN 55330/612-441-7761
Gunsmithing Ltd., 57 Unquowa Rd., Fairfield, CT 06430/203-254-0436
Gurney, F.R., Box 13, Sooke, BC V0S 1N0 CANADA/604-642-5282
Gusdorf Corp., 11440 Lackland Rd., St. Louis, MO 63146/314-567-5249
Gustaf, Carl (See U.S. importer—PSI, Inc.)
Gusty Winds Corp., 2950 Bear St., Suite 120, Costa Mesa, CA 92626/714-536-3587
Gutmann Cutlery Co., Inc., 120 S. Columbus Ave., Mt. Vernon, NY 10553/914-699-4044
Gutridge, Inc., 2143 Gettler St., Dyer, IN 46311/219-865-8617
Gwinnell, Bryson J., P.O. Box 248C, Maple Hill Rd., Rochester, VT 05767/802-767-3664
GZ Paintball Sports Products, P.O. Box 430, Andover, NH 03216/603-735-5300; FAX: 603-735-5154

## H

H&B Forge Co., Rt. 2 Geisinger Rd., Shiloh, OH 44878/419-895-1856
H&H Engineering, Box 642, Narberty, PA 19072
H&L Gun Works, 817 N. Highway 90 1109, Sierra Vista, AZ 85635/602-452-0702
H&P Publishing, 7174 Hoffman Rd., San Angelo, TX 76905/915-655-5953
H&R 1871, Inc., 60 Industrial Rowe, Gardner, MA 01440/508-632-9393; FAX: 508-632-2300
H&S Liner Service, 515 E. 8th, Odessa, TX 79761/915-332-1021
Hafner Creations, Inc., Rt. 1, P.O. Box 248A, Lake City, FL 32055/904-755-6481
Hagn Rifles & Actions, Martin, P.O. Box 444, Cranbrook, B.C. VIC 4H9, CANADA/604-489-4861
Hakko Co. Ltd., 5F Daini-Tsunemi Bldg., 1-13-12, Narimasu, Itabashiku Tokyo 175, JAPAN/(03)5997-7870-2
Hale, Peter, 800 E. Canyon Rd., Spanish Fork, UT 84660/801-798-8215
Half Moon Rifle Shop, 490 Halfmoon Rd., Columbia Falls, MT 59912/406-892-4409
Hall Manufacturing, 1801 Yellow Leaf Rd., Clanton, AL 35045/205-755-4094
Hall Plastics, Inc., John, P.O. Box 1526, Alvin, TX 77512/713-489-9709
Hallberg Gunsmith, Fritz, 33 S. Main, Payette, ID 83661
Hallowell & Co., 340 W. Putnam Ave., Greenwich, CT 06830/203-869-2190; FAX: 203-869-0692
Hally Caller, 443 Wells Rd., Doylestown, PA 18901/215-345-6354
Halstead, Rick, P.O. Box 63, Grinnell, IA 50112/515-236-5904
Hamilton, Keith, P.O. Box 871, Gridley, CA 95948/916-846-2316
Hammans, Charles E., P.O. Box 788, 2022 McCracken, Stuttgart, AR 72106/501-673-1388
Hammerli USA, 19296 Oak Grove Circle, Groveland, CA 95321/209-962-5311; FAX: 209-962-5931
Hämmerli Ltd., Seonerstrasse 37, CH-5600 Lenzburg, SWITZERLAND/064-50 11 44; FAX: 064-51 38 27 (U.S. importer—Hammerli USA; Marent, Rudolph)
Hammets VLD Bullets, P.O. Box 479, Rayville, LA 71269/318-728-2019
Hammond Custom Guns Ltd., Guy, 619 S. Pandora, Gilbert, AZ 85234/602-892-3437
Hand Engravers Supply Co., 601 Springfield Dr., Albany, GA 31707/912-432-9683
Handgun Press, P.O. Box 406, Glenview, IL 60025/708-657-6500
HandiCrafts Unltd. (See Clements' Custom Leathercraft, Chas)
Handloader's Journal, 60 Cottage St. 11, Hughesville, PA 17737
Hands, Barry Lee, 26184 E. Shore Route, Bigfork, MT 59911/406-837-0035
Hank's Gun Shop, Box 370, 50 West 100 South, Monroe, UT 84754/801-527-4456
Hanned Line, The, P.O. Box 161565, Cupertino, CA 95016-1565/916-324-9089
Hanned Precision (See Hanned Line, The)
Hansen & Co. (See Hansen Cartridge Co.)
Hansen Cartridge Co., 244 Old Post Rd., Southport, CT 06490/203-789-7337
Hanson's Gun Center, Dick, 233 Everett Dr., Colorado Springs, CO 80911
Hanus Birdguns, Bill, P.O. Box 533, Newport, OR 97365
Hanusin, John, 3306 Commercial, Northbrook, IL 60062/708-564-2706
Hardin Specialty Dist., P.O. Box 338, Radcliff, KY 40159-0338/502-351-6649
Hardison, Charles, P.O. Box 356, 200 W. Baseline Rd., Lafayette, CO 80026 0356/303-666-5171
Harper, William E. (See Great 870 Co., The)
Harper's Custom Stocks, 928 Lombrano St., San Antonio, TX 78207/512-732-5780
Harrington & Richardson (See H&R 1871, Inc.)
Harrington Cutlery, Inc., Russell, Subs. of Hyde Mfg. Co., 44 River St., Southbridge, MA 01550/617-765-0201
Harris Engineering, Inc., Rt. 1, Barlow, KY 42024/502-334-3633; FAX: 502-334-3000
Harris Enterprises, P.O. Box 105, Bly, OR 97622/503-353-2625
Harris Hand Engraving, Paul A., 10630 Janet Lee, San Antonio, TX 78230/512-391-5121
Harrison Bullet Works, 6437 E. Hobart Street, Mesa, AZ 85205/602-985-7844
Harrison-Hurtz Enterprises, Inc., P.O. Box 268, Wymore, NE 68466/402-645-3378; FAX: 402-645-3606
Hart & Son, Inc., Robert W., 401 Montgomery St., Nescopeck, PA 18635/717-752-3655; FAX: 717-752-1088
Hart Rifle Barrels, Inc., RD 2, Apulia Rd., P.O. Box 182, Lafayette, NY 13084/315-677-9841
Hartmann & Weiss GmbH, Rahlstedter Bahnhofstr. 47, 2000 Hamburg 73, GERMANY/(40) 677 55 85; FAX: (40) 677 55 92
Harwood, Jack O., 1191 S. Pendlebury Lane, Blackfoot, ID 83221/208-785-5368
Haselbauer Products, Jerry, P.O. Box 27629, Tucson, AZ 85726/602-883-3391
Hastings Barrels, 320 Court St., Clay Center, KS 67432/913-632-3169; FAX: 913-632-6554
Hatfield Gun Co., Inc., 224 N. 4th St., St. Joseph, MO 64501/816-279-8688; FAX: 816-279-2716
Hawk Co., P.O. Box 1843, Glenrock, WY 82637/307-436-5561
Hawk Laboratories, Inc., P.O. Box 1843, Glenrock, WY 82637/307-436-5561
Hawken Shop, The (See Dayton Traister)
Haydel's Game Calls, Inc., 5018 Hazel Jones Rd., Bossier City, LA 71111/318-746-3586; FAX: 318-746-3711
Heatbath Corp., P.O. Box 2978, Springfield, MA 01101/413-543-3381
Hebard Guns, Gil, 125-129 Public Square, Knoxville, IL 61448
HEBB Resources, P.O. Box 999, Mead, WA 99021-09996/509-466-1292
Hecht, Hubert J., Waffen-Hecht, P.O. Box 2635, Fair Oaks, CA 95628/916-966-1020
Heckler & Koch GmbH, Postfach 1329, D-7238 Oberndorf, Neckar, GERMANY (U.S. importer—Heckler & Koch, Inc.)
Heckler & Koch, Inc., 21480 Pacific Blvd., Sterling, VA 20166/703-450-1900; FAX: 703-450-8160
Hege Jagd-u. Sporthandels, GmbH, P.O. Box 101461, W-7770 Ueberlingen a.Bodensee, GERMANY
Heidenstrom Bullets, Urds GT 1 Heroya, 3900 Porsgrunn, NORWAY
Heilmann, Stephen, P.O. Box 657, Grass Valley, CA 95945/916-272-8758
Heinie Specialty Products, 323 W. Franklin St., Havana, IL 62644/309-543-4535; FAX: 309-543-2521
Helwan (See U.S. importer—Interarms)
Henckels Zwillingswerk, Inc., J.A., 9 Skyline Dr., Hawthorne, NY 10532/914-592-7370
Hendricks, Frank E., Master Engravers, Inc., HC03, Box 434, Dripping Springs, TX 78620/512-858-7828
Henigson & Associates, Steve, 2049 Kerwood Ave., Los Angeles, CA 90025/213-305-8288
Henriksen Tool Co., Inc., 8515 Wagner Creek Rd., Talent, OR 97540/503-535-2309
Henry Customs, J., P.O. Box 3281, Texas City, TX 77592
Hensler, Jerry, 6614 Country Field, San Antonio, TX 78240
Hensley & Gibbs, Box 10, Murphy, OR 97533/503-862-2341
Hensley, Darwin, P.O. Box 179, Brightwood, OR 97011/503-622-5411
Heppler, Keith's Custom Gunstocks, Keith M., 540 Banyan Circle, Walnut Creek, CA 94598/510-934-3509
Heppler's Machining, 2240 Calle Del Mundo, Santa Clara, CA 95054/408-748-9166; FAX: 408-988-7711
Hercules, Inc., Hercules Plaza, 1313 N Market St., Wilmington, DE 19894/302-594-5000
Heritage Firearms, 4600 NW 135th St., Opa Locka, FL 33054/305-687-6721
Hermann Leather Co., H.J., Rt. 1, P.O. Box 525, Skiatook, OK 74070/918-396-1226
Herrett's Stocks, Inc., P.O. Box 741, Twin Falls, ID 83303/208-733-1498
Hertel & Reuss, Werk für Optik und Feinmechanik GmbH, Quellhofstrabe 67, 3500 Kassel, GERMANY/0561-83006; FAX: 0561-893308

Herter's Manufacturing, Inc., 111 E. Burnett St., P.O. Box 518, Beaver Dam, WI 53916/414-887-1765; FAX: 414-887-8444
Hesco-Meprolight, 2821 Greenville Rd., LaGrange, GA 30240/706-884-7967; FAX: 706-882-4683
Heydenberk, Warren R., 1059 W. Sawmill Rd., Quakertown, PA 18951/215-538-2682
Heym GmbH & Co., Friedrich Wilh, Coburger Str.8, D-8732 Munnerstadt, GERMANY (U.S. importers—JägerSport, Ltd.; Swarovski Optik North America Ltd.)
Hickman, Jaclyn, Box 1900, Glenrock, WY 82637
Hidalgo, Tony, 12701 SW 9th Pl., Davie, FL 33325/305-476-7645
Higgs Bullets, 403 E. Broadway, Denver City, TX 79323/806-592-8794
High Bridge Arms, Inc., 3185 Mission St., San Francisco, CA 94110/415-282-8358
High Country Custom Bullet, 19822 NW Sauvie Island Rd., Portland, OR 97231/503-621-3721
High North Products, Inc., P.O. Box 2, Antigo, WI 54409
Highline Machine Co., 654 Lela Place, Grand Junction, CO 81504/303-434-4971
Hill, Loring F., 304 Cedar Rd., Elkins Park, PA 19117
Hill Speed Leather, Ernie, 4507 N. 195th Ave., Litchfield Park, AZ 85340/602-853-9222; FAX: 602-853-9235
Hillmer Custom Gunstocks, Paul D., 7251 Hudson Heights, Hudson, IA 50643/319-988-3941
Hindman, Ace, 1880 1/2 Upper Turtle Creek Rd., Kerrville, TX 78028/512-257-4290
Hinman Outfitters, Bob, 1217 W. Glen, Peoria, IL 61614/309-691-8132
Hiptmayer, Heidemarie, RR 112 750, P.O. Box 136, Eastman, Quebec J0E 1PO, CANADA/514-297-2492
Hiptmayer, Klaus, RR 112 750, P.O. Box 136, Eastman, Quebec J0E 1P0, CANADA/514-297-2492
Hirtenberger Aktiengesellschaft, Leobersdorferstrasse 31, A-2552 Hirtenberg, AUSTRIA
HiTek International, 490 El Camino Real, Redwood City, CA 94063/800-54-NIGHT; FAX: 415-363-1408
Hiti-Schuch, Atelier Wilma, A-8863 Predlitz, Pirming Y1 AUSTRIA/0353418278
HJS Arms, Inc., P.O. Box 3711, Brownsville, TX 78523-3711/800-453-2767, 210-542-2767
H.K.S. Products, 7841 Founion Dr., Florence, KY 41042/606-342-7841
Hoag, James W., 8523 Canoga Ave., Suite C, Canoga Park, CA 91304/818-998-1510
Hobaugh, Wm. H. (See Rifle Shop, The)
Hobbie Gunsmithing, Duane A., 2412 Pattie Ave., Wichita, KS 67216/316-264-8266
Hobson Precision Mfg. Co., Rt. 1, Box 220-C, Brent, AL 35034/205-926-4662
Hodgdon Powder Co., Inc., P.O. Box 2932, Shawnee Mission, KS 66201/913-362-9455; FAX: 913-362-1307
Hodgman, Inc., 1750 Orchard Rd., Montgomery, IL 60538/708-897-7555; FAX: 708-897-7558
Hodgson, Richard, 9081 Tahoe Lane, Boulder, CO 80301
Hoehn's Shooting Supply, 75 Greensburg Ct., St. Charles, MO 63304/314-441-4231
Hoenig & Rodman, 6521 Morton Dr., Boise, ID 83704/208-375-1116
Hofer Jagdwaffen, Buchsenmachermeister,P., F.-Lange Strasse 13, A-9170, Ferlach, AUSTRIA/04227-3683
Hoffman New Ideas, 821 Northmoor Rd., Lake Forest, IL 60045/312-234-4075
Hogue Grips, P.O. Box 2038, Atascadero, CA 93423/FAX: 805-466-7329
Holden Co., J.B., P.O. Box 700320, 975 Arthur, Plymouth, MI 48170/313-455-4850; FAX: 313-455-4212
Holland, Dick, 422 NE 6th St., Newport, OR 97365/503-265-7556
Hollis Gun Shop, 917 Rex St., Carlsbad, NM 88220/505-835-3782
Hollywood Engineering, 10642 Arminta St., Sun Valley, CA 91352/818-842-8376
Holster Outpost, 950 Harry St., El Cajon, CA 92020/619-588-1222
Holster Shop, The, 720 N. Flagler Dr., Ft. Lauderdale, FL 33304/305-463-7910; FAX: 305-761-1483
Homak Mfg. Co., Inc., 3800 W. 45th, Chicago, IL 60632/312-523-3100
Hondo Ind., 510 S. 52nd St.,I04, Tempe, AZ 85281
Hoppe's Div., Penguin Industries, Inc., Airport Industrial Mall, Coatesville, PA 19320/251-384-6000
Horizons Unlimited, 8351 Roswell Rd., Suite 168, Atlanta, GA 30350/404-683-1269; FAX: 404-993-9770
Hornady Mfg. Co., P.O. Box 1848, Grand Island, NE 68801/800-338-3220, 308-382-1390
Horseshoe Leather Products, Andy Arratoonian, The Cottage Sharow, Ripon HG4 5BP ENGLAND/0765-605858
Horst, Alan K., 3221 2nd Ave. N., Great Falls, MT 59401/406-454-1831
Horton Dist. Co., Inc., Lew, 15 Walkup Dr., Westboro, MA 01581/508-366-7400
House of Muskets, Inc., The, P.O. Box 4640, Pagosa Springs, CO 81157/303-731-2295
Houtz & Barwick, P.O. Box 435, W. Church St., Elizabeth City, NC 27909/800-775-0337, 919-335-4191; FAX: 919-335-1152
Howa Machinery, Ltd., Sukaguchi, Shinkawa-cho, Nishikasugai-gun, Aichi 452, JAPAN (U.S. importers—Interarms; Weatherby, Inc.)
Howell Machine, 815 1/2 D St., Lewiston, ID 83501/208-743-7418
Hoyt Holster Co., Inc., P.O. Box 69, Coupeville, WA 98239-0069/206-678-6640; FAX: 206-678-6549
H-S Precision, Inc., 1301 Turbine Dr., Rapid City, SD 57701/605-341-3006; FAX: 605-342-8964
HT Bullets, 244 Belleville Rd., New Bedford, MA 02745/508-999-3338
Hubertus Schneidwarenfabrik, P.O. Box 180 106, Solingen, D-W-5650 GERMANY/01149-212-59-19-94; FAX: 01149-212-59-19-92
Huebner, Corey O., P.O. Box 2074, Missoula, MT 59804/406-721-9647
Huey Gun Cases, Marvin, P.O. Box 22456, Kansas City, MO 64113/816-444-1637
Hugger Hooks Co., 3900 Easley Way, Golden, CO 80403/303-279-0600
Hughes, Steven Dodd, P.O. Box 11455, Eugene, OR 97440/503-485-8869
Hume, Don, P.O. Box 351, Miami, OK 74355/918-542-6604
Hungry Horse Books, 4605 Hwy. 93 South, Whitefish, MT 59937/406-862-7997
Hunkeler, A. (See Buckskin Machine Works)
Hunter Co., Inc., 3300 W. 71st Ave., Westminster, CO 80030/303-427-4626
Hunter's Specialties, Inc., 6000 Huntington Ct. NE, Cedar Rapids, IA 52402-1268/319-395-0321
Hunterjohn, P.O. Box 477, St. Louis, MO 63166/314-531-7250
Hunting Classics Ltd., P.O. Box 2089, Gastonia, NC 28053/704-867-1307; FAX: 704-867-0491
Huntington Die Specialties, 601 Oro Dam Blvd., Oroville, CA 95965/916-534-1210; FAX: 916-534-1212
Hy-Score Arms Co. Ltd., 40 Stonar Industrial Estate, Sandwich, Kent CT13 9LN, ENGLAND/0304-61.12.21
Hydrosorbent Products, P.O. Box 437, Ashley Falls, MA 01222/413-229-2967; FAX: 413-229-8743
Hyper-Single, Inc., 520 E. Beaver, Jenks, OK 74037/918-299-2391

## I

IAI, 6226 Santos Diaz St., Irwindale, CA 91702/818-334-1200
Ibberson (Sheffield) Ltd., George, 25-31 Allen St., Sheffield, S3 7AW ENGLAND/0742-766123; FAX: 0742-738465
ICI-America, P.O. Box 751, Wilmington, DE 19897/302-575-3000
Idaho Ammunition Service, 2816 Mayfair Dr., Lewiston, ID 83501/208-743-0270
Idaho Bullets, Box 2532, Orofino, ID 83544/208-476-5046
IGA (See U.S. importer—Stoeger Industries)
Illinois Lead Shop, 7742 W. 61st Place, Summit, IL 60501
Imatronic, Inc., 1275 Paramount Pkwy., P.O. Box 520, Batavia, IL 60510/708-406-1920; FAX: 708-879-6749
IMI, P.O. Box 1044, Ramat Hasharon 47100, ISRAEL/972-3-5485222 (U.S. importer—Magnum Research, Inc.)
Impact Case Co., P.O. Box 9912, Spokane, WA 99209-0912/509-467-3303; FAX: 509-326-5436
Imperial Magnum Corp., 1417 Main St., Oroville, WA 98844/604-495-3131; FAX: 604-495-2816
IMR Powder Co., Box 247E, Xplo Complex, RTS, Plattsburgh, NY 12901/518-561-9530; FAX: 518-563-0044
I.N.C., Inc. (See Kick Eez)
Incor, Inc., P.O. Box 132, Addison, TX 75001/214-931-3500; FAX: 214-458-1626
Independent Machine & Gun Shop, 1416 N. Hayes, Pocatello, ID 83201
INDESAL, P.O. Box 233, Eibar, SPAIN 20600/43-751800; FAX: 43-751962 (U.S. importer—American Arms, Inc.)
Industria de la Escopeta S.A.L. (See INDESAL)
Info-Arm, P.O. Box 1262, Champlain, NY 12919
Ingle, Ralph W., 4 Missing Link, Rossville, GA 30741/404-866-5589
Innovision Enterprises, 728 Skinner Dr., Kalamazoo, MI 49001/616-382-1681; FAX: 616-382-1830
InSights Training Center, Inc., 240 NW Gilman Blvd., Issaquah, WA 98027/206-391-4834
INTEC International, Inc., P.O. Box 5828, Sparks, NV 89432-5828
Interarms, 10 Prince St., Alexandria, VA 22314/703-548-1400
Intermountain Arms & Tackle, Inc., 105 E. Idaho St., Meridian, ID 83642/208-888-4911; FAX: 208-888-4381
International Shooters Service (See I.S.S.)
International Shootists, Inc., P.O. Box 5354, Mission Hills, CA 91345/818-891-1723
Intratec, 12405 SW 130th St., Miami, FL 33186/305-232-1821; FAX: 305-253-7207
Iosso Products, 1485 Lively Blvd., Elk Grove Village, IL 60007/708-437-8400
Iron Mountain Knife Co., P.O. Box 2146, Sparks, NV 89432-2146/800-22-KNIFE, 702-356-3632
Ironside International Publishers, Inc., P.O. Box 55, 800 Slaters Lane, Alexandria, VA 22313/703-684-6111; FAX: 703-683-5486
Irwin, Campbell H., 140 Hartland Blvd., East Hartland, CT 06027/203-653-3901
Irwindale Arms, Inc. (See IAI)
Israel Military Industries Ltd. (See IMI)
I.S.S., P.O. Box 185234, Ft. Worth, TX 76181/817-595-2090
I.S.W., 106 E. Cairo Dr., Tempe, AZ 85282
Ithaca Aquisition Corp., Ithaca Gun Co., 891 Route 34B, King Ferry, NY 13081/315-364-7171; FAX: 315-364-5134
Ivanoff, Thomas G. (See Tom's Gun Repair)

## J

J-4, Inc., 1700 Via Burton, Anaheim, CA 92806
J&J Products Co., 9240 Whitmore, El Monte, CA 91731/818-571-5228; FAX: 818-571-8704
J&R Enterprises, 4550 Scotts Valley Rd., Lakeport, CA 95453
J.A. Blades, Inc. (See Christopher Firearms Co., Inc., E.)
Jackalope Gun Shop, 1048 S. 5th St., Douglas, WY 82633/307-358-3441
Jackson Arms, 6209 Hillcrest Ave., Dallas, TX 75205
JACO Precision Co., 11803 Indian Head Dr., Austin, TX 78753/512-836-4418
Jaeger, Inc., Paul/Dunn's, P.O. Box 449, 1 Madison Ave., Grand Junction, TN 38039/800-223-8667; FAX: 901-764-6503
JägerSport, Ltd., One Wholesale Way, Cranston, RI 02920/401-944-9682; FAX: 401-946-2587
Jamison's Forge Works, 4527 Rd. 6.5 NE, Moses Lake, WA 98837/509-762-2659
Jantz Supply, P.O. Box 584-GD, Davis, OK 73030/405-369-2316; FAX: 405-369-3082
Jarrett Rifles, Inc., 383 Brown Rd., Jackson, SC 29831/803-471-3616
Jarvis Gunsmithing, Inc., 1123 Cherry Orchard Lane, Hamilton, MT 59840/406-961-4392
JAS, Inc., P.O. Box 0, Rosemount, MN 55068/612-890-7631
Jason Empire, Inc., 9200 Cody, Overland Park, KS 66214-3259/913-888-0220; FAX: 913-888-0222
Javelina Products, P.O. Box 337, San Bernardino, CA 92402/714-882-5847; FAX: 714-434-6937
J/B Adventures & Safaris, Inc., P.O. Box 3397, Englewood, CO 80155/303-771-0977
J-B Bore Cleaner, 299 Poplar St., Hamburg, PA 19526/215-562-2103
Jeffredo Gunsight, P.O. Box 669, San Marcos, CA 92079/619-728-2695
Jenco Sales, Inc., P.O. Box 1000, Manchaca, TX 78652/512-282-2800; FAX: 512-282-7504
Jenkins Recoil Pads, Inc., RR 2, P.O. Box 471, Olney, IL 62450/618-395-3416
Jennings Firearms, Inc., 17692 Cowan, Irvine, CA 92714/714-252-7621; FAX: 714-252-7626
Jensen Bullets, 86 North, 400 West, Blackfoot, ID 83221/208-785-5590
Jensen's Custom Ammunition, 5146 E. Pima, Tucson, AZ 85712/602-325-3346; FAX: 602-322-5704
Jensen's Firearms Academy, 1280 W. Prince, Tucson, AZ 85705/602-293-8516
Jerry's Sport Center, P.O. Box 121 Main St., Forest City, PA 18421
Jester Bullets, Rt. 1 Box 27, Orienta, OK 73737
Jet Comp Systems, Rt. 1, Box 112-C, Surry, VA 23883/804-357-0881
Jett & Co., Inc., RR 3, Box 167-B, Litchfield, IL 62056/217-324-3779
JGS Precision Tool Mfg., 1141 S. Summer Rd., Coos Bay, OR 97420/503-267-4331; FAX:503-267-5996
Jim's Gun Shop (See Spradlin's)
Jim's Precision, Jim Ketchum, 1725 Moclips Dr., Petaluma, CA 94952/707-762-3014
J.I.T., Ltd., P.O. Box 749, Glenview, IL 60025/708-998-0937
JLK Bullets, RR1, Box 310C, Dover, AR 72837/501-331-4194
J.O. Arms & Ammunition Co., 5709 Hartsdale, Houston, TX 77036/713-789-0745; FAX: 713-789-7513
Johanssons Vapentillbehor, Bert, S-430 20 Veddige, SWEDEN
John's Custom Leather, 523 S. Liberty St., Blairsville, PA 15717/412-459-6802
Johns, Bill, 1412 Lisa Rae, Round Rock, TX 78664/512-255-8246
Johnson Gunsmithing, Inc., Neal G., 111 Marvin Dr., Hampton, VA 23666/804-838-8091; FAX: 804-838-8157
Johnson Wood Products, RR 1, Strawberry Point, IA 52076/319-933-4930
Johnson, Iver (See AMAC)
Johnston Bros., 1889 Rt. 9, Unit 22, Toms River, NJ 08755/800-257-2595; FAX: 800-257-2534
Johnston, James (See North Fork Custom Gunsmithing)
Jonad Corp., 2091 Lakeland Ave., Lakewood, OH 44107/216-226-3161
Jonas Appraisals & Taxidermy, Jack, 10050 E. Harvard Ave. B711, Denver, CO 80231/303-368-1939
Jones Custom Products, Neil, RD 1, Box 483A, Saegertown, PA 16443/814-763-2769; FAX: 814-763-4228
J.D. Jones, 721 Woodvue Lane, Wintersville, OH 43952/614-264-0176
Joy Enterprises (See Fury Cutlery)
J.P. Enterprises, Inc., P.O. Box 26324, Shoreview, MN 55126
JP Sales, Box 307, Anderson, TX 77830
JRW, 2425 Taffy Ct., Nampa, ID 83687
JSL Ltd., 35 Church St., Hereford HR1 2LR ENGLAND/0432-355416; FAX: 0432-355242 (U.S. importer—Specialty Shooters Supply, Inc.)
Juenke, Vern, 25 Bitterbush Rd., Reno, NV 89523/702-345-0225
Jumbo Sports Products (See Bucheimer, J.M.)

Jungkind, Reeves C., 5001 Buckskin Pass, Austin, TX 78745/512-442-1094
Jurras, L.E., P.O. Box 680, Washington, IN 47501/812-254-7698
Just Brass, Inc., 121 Henry St., P.O. Box 112, Freeport, NY 11520/516-378-8588
J.V.B., Inc., 109 6th St. NE, Little Falls, MN 56345/612-632-5120

# K

K&K Ammo Wrist Band, R.D. 1, P.O. Box 448-CA18, Lewistown, PA 17044/717-242-2329
K&M Industries, Inc., Box 66, 510 S. Main, Troy, ID 83871/208-835-2281; FAX: 208-835-5211
K&M Services, P.O. Box 363, 2525 Primrose Lane, York, PA 17404/717-764-1461
K&T Co., Div. of T&S Industries, Inc., 1027 Skyview Dr., W. Carrollton, OH 45449/513-859-8414
KA-BAR Knives, 31100 Solon Rd., Solon, OH 44139/216-248-7000; 800-321-9336; FAX: 216-248-8651
Kahles USA, P.O. Box 81071, Warwick, RI 02888/800-752-4537: FAX: 717-540-8567
Kalispel Case Line, P.O. Box 267, Cusick, WA 99119/509-445-1121
Kamik Outdoor Footwear, 554 Montee de Liesse, Montreal, Quebec, H4T 1P1 CANADA/514-341-3950
Kamyk Engraving Co., Steve, 9 Grandview Dr., Westfield, MA 01085/413-568-0457
Kane Products, Inc., 5572 Brecksville Rd., Cleveland, OH 44131/216-524-9962
Ka Pu Kapili, P.O. Box 745, Honokaa, HI 96727/808-776-1644; FAX: 808-776-1731
Kapro Mfg. Co., Inc., P.O. Box 88, Tallevast, FL 34270/813-755-0085
Kasenit Co., Inc., 13 Park Ave., Highland Mills, NY 10930/914-928-9595; FAX: 914-928-7292
Kasmarsik Bullets, 152 Crstler Rd., Chehalis, WA 98532
Kassnar (See U.S. importer—K.B.I., Inc.)
Kaswer Custom, Inc., 13 Surrey Drive, Brookfield, CT 06804/203-775-0564; FAX: 203-775-6872
K.B.I., Inc., P.O. Box 6346, Harrisburg, PA 17112/717-540-8518; FAX: 717-540-8567
K-D, Inc., 665 W. 300 South, Price, UT 84501/801-653-2530
KDF, Inc., 2485 Hwy. 46 N., Seguin, TX 78155/512-379-8141; FAX: 512-379-5420
Keeler, R.H., 817 "N" St., Port Angeles, WA 98362/206-457-4702
Kehr, Roger, 2131 Agate Ct. SE, Lacy, WA 98503/206-456-0831
Keith's Bullets, 942 Twisted Oak, Algonquin, IL 60102/708-658-3520
Keith's Custom Gunstocks (See Heppler, Keith M.)
Keller Co., The, 4215 McEwen Rd., Dallas, TX 75244/214-788-4254
Kelley's, P.O. Box 125, Woburn, MA 01801/617-935-3389
Kellogg's Professional Products, 325 Pearl St., Sandusky, OH 44870/419-625-6551; FAX: 419-625-6167
Kelly, Lance, 1723 Willow Oak Dr., Edgewater, FL 32132/904-423-4933
Ken's Kustom Kartridges, 331 Jacobs Rd., Hubbard, OH 44425/216-534-4595
Ken's Finn Knives, Rt. 1, Box 338, Republic, MI 49879/906-376-2132
Ken's Gun Specialties, Rt. 1, Box 147, Lakeview, AR 72642/501-431-5606
Ken's Rifle Blanks, Ken McCullough, Rt. 2, P.O. Box 85B, Weston, OR 97886/503-566-3879
Keng's Firearms Specialty, Inc., 875 Wharton Dr. SW, Atlanta, GA 30336/404-691-7611; FAX: 404-505-8445
Kennebec Journal, 274 Western Ave., Augusta, ME 04330/207-622-6288
Kennerknecht, Rick, "KK", Randall Firearms Historian, P.O. Box 1586, Lomita, CA 90717/5586/310-781-9199; FAX: 310-781-9266
KenPatable Ent., Inc., P.O. Box 19422, Louisville, KY 40219/502-239-5447
Kent Cartridge Mfg. Co. Ltd., Unit 16, Branbridges Industrial Estate, East Peckham, Tonbridge, Kent, TN12 5HF ENGLAND/622-872255; FAX: 622-873645
Keowee Game Calls, 608 Hwy. 25 North, Travelers Rest, SC 29690/803-834-7204
Kershaw Knives, 25300 SW Parkway Ave., Wilsonville, OR 97070/503-682-1966; FAX: 503-682-7168
Kesselring Gun Shop, 400 Hwy. 99 North, Burlington, WA 98233/206-724-3113; FAX: 206-724-7003
Keystone Bullets, RD 1, Box 312, New Bloomfield, PA 17068/717-582-8347
Kick Eez, P.O. Box 12767, Wichita, KS 67277/316-721-9570; FAX: 316-721-5260
Kilham & Co., Main St., P.O. Box 37, Lyme, NH 03768/603-795-4112
Kimball, Gary, 1526 N. Circle Dr., Colorado Springs, CO 80909/719-634-1274
Kimber, Inc., 16709 NE Union Rd., Ridgefield, WA 98642/206-573-4783
Kimel Industries, 3800 Old Monroe Rd., P.O. Box 335, Matthews, NC 28105/800-438-9288
King & Co., P.O. Box 1242, Bloomington, IL 61701/309-473-3964
King's Gun Works, 1837 W. Glenoaks Blvd., Glendale, CA 91201/818-956-6010
Kingyon, Paul L., 607 N. 5th St., Burlington, IA 52601/319-752-4465
Kirkpatrick Leather Co., 1910 San Bernardo, Laredo, TX 78040/512-723-6631; FAX: 512-725-0672
KJM Brass Group, P.O. Box 162, Marietta, GA 30061
KK Air International (See Impact Case Co.)
K.K. Arms Co., Star Route Box 671, Kerrville, TX 78028/512-257-4718
Kleen-Bore, Inc., 20 Ladd Ave., Northampton, MA 01060/413-586-7240; FAX: 413-586-0236
Klein Custom Guns, Don, 433 Murray Park Dr., Ripon, WI 54971/414-748-2931
Kleinendorst, K.W., RR 1, Box 1500, Hop Bottom, PA 18824/717-289-4687; FAX: 717-289-4687
Klingler Woodcarving, P.O. Box 141, Thistle Hill, Cabot, VT 05647/802-426-3811
KLP, Inc., 215 Charles Dr., Holland, MI 49424/616-396-2575; FAX: 616-396-1287
Kmount, P.O. Box 19422, Louisville, KY 40259/502-239-5447
Kneiper Custom Gums, Jim, 334 Summit Vista, Carbondale, CO 81623/303-963-9880
Knife Importers, Inc., P.O. Box 1000, Manchaca, TX 78652/512-282-6860
Knight & Hale Game Calls, Box 468 Industrial Park, Cadiz, KY 42211/502-522-3651; FAX: 502-522-0211
Knight's Mfg. Co., 7750 9th St. SW, Vero Beach, FL 32968/407-562-5697; FAX: 407-569-2955
Knippel, Richard, 5924 Carnwood, Riverbank, CA 95367/209-869-1469
Knock on Wood Antiques, 355 Post Rd., Darien, CT 06820/203-655-9031
Kodiak Custom Bullets, 8261 Henry Circle, Anchorage, AK 99507/907-349-2282
Kodiak Safe, 468 N. 1200 W., Lindon, UT 84042/801-785-9113
Koevenig's Engraving Service, Box 55 Rabbit Gulch, Hill City, SD 57745/605-574-2239
KOGOT, 410 College, Trinidad, CO 81082/719-846-9406
Kolbe Precision, Riccarton Farm, Newcastleton SCOTLAND U.K.
Kolpin Mfg., Inc., P.O. Box 107, 205 Depot St., Fox Lake, WI 53933/414-928-3118; FAX: 414-928-3687
Kopec Enterprises, John (See Peacemaker Specialists)
Kopp Publishing Co., Div. of Koppco Industries, 1301 Franklin, Lexington, MO 64067/816-259-2636
Kopp, Terry, 1301 Franklin, Lexington, MO 64067/816-259-2636
Korth, Robert-Bosch-Str. 4, P.O. Box 1320, 2418 Ratzeburg, GERMANY/0451-4991497; FAX: 0451-4993230 (U.S. importer—Mandall Shooting Supplies, Inc.)
Korzinek Riflesmith, J., RD 2, Box 73, Canton, PA 17724/717-673-8512
Koval Knives, 460 D Schrock Rd., Columbus, OH 43229/614-888-6486; FAX: 614-888-8218
Kowa Optimed, Inc., 20001 S. Vermont Ave., Torrance, CA 90502/310-327-1913; FAX: 310-327-4177
Krause Publications, 700 E. State St., Iola, WI 54990/715-445-2214; FAX: 715-445-4087
Krico/Kriegeskorte GmbH, A., Kronacherstr. 63, 85 W. Fürth-Stadeln, D-8510 GERMANY/0911-796092; FAX: 0911-796074 (U.S. importer—Mandall Shooting Supplies, Inc.)
Krieger Barrels, Inc., N114 W18697 Clinton Dr., Germantown, WI 53022/414-255-9593; FAX: 414-255-9586

Kriegeskorte GmbH., A. (See Krico/Kriegeskorte GmbH., A.)
H. Krieghoff Gun Co., Bosch Str. 22, 7900 Ulm, GERMANY (U.S. importer—Krieghoff International, Inc.)
Krieghoff International, Inc., 7528 Easton Rd., Ottsville, PA 18942/215-847-5173; FAX: 215-847-8691
Kris Mounts, 108 Lehigh St., Johnstown, PA 15905
K-Sports Imports, Inc., 290 Pioneer Place, Pomona, CA 91768/909-468-5871; FAX: 909-468-5870
Kudlas, John M., 622 14th St. SE, Rochester, MN 55904/507-288-5579
Kulis Freeze Dry Taxidermy, 725 Broadway Ave., Bedford, OH 44146/216-232-8352; FAX: 216-232-7305
Kustom Kast Bullets, 18533 Roscoe Blvd. S. 137, Northridge, CA 91324
KVH Industries, Inc., 110 Enterprise Center, Middletown, RI 02840/401-847-3327; FAX: 401-849-0045
Kwik Mount Corp., P.O. Box 19422, Louisville, KY 40259/502-239-5447
Kwik-Site Co., 5555 Treadwell, Wayne, MI 48184/313-326-1500; FAX: 313-326-4120

# L

L&S Technologies, Inc. (See Aimtech Mount Systems)
La Clinique du .45, 1432 Rougemont, Chambly, Quebec, J3L 2L8 CANADA/514-658-1144
La Prade, Rt. 5, P.O. Box 240AD, Tazewell, TN 37879
LaBounty Precision Reboring, P.O. Box 186, 7968 Silver Lk. Rd., Maple Falls, WA 98266/206-599-2047
Lachaussee, S.A., 29 Rue Kerstenne, Ans, B-4430 BELGIUM/041-63 88 77
LaCrosse Footwear, Inc., P.O. Box 1328, La Crosse, WI 54602/608-782-3020
LaFrance Specialties, P.O. Box 178211, San Diego, CA 92117/619-293-3373
Lage Uniwad, Inc., P.O. Box 446, Victor, IA 52327/319-647-3232
Lair, Sam, 520 E. Beaver, Jenks, OK 74037/918-299-2391
Lake Center, P.O. Box 38, St. Charles, MO 63302/314-946-7500
Lakefield Arms Ltd., 248 Water St., Lakefield, Ont. K0L 2H0, CANADA/705-652-6735, 705-652-8000; FAX: 705-652-8431
Lakewood Products, Inc., P.O. Box 1527, 1445 Eagle St., Rhinelander, WI 54501/715-369-3445
Ron Lampert, Rt. 1, Box 177, Guthrie, MN 56461/218-854-7345
Lamson & Goodnow Mfg. Co., 45 Conway St., Shelburne Falls, MA 03170/413-625-6331
Lanber Armes S.A., Calle Zubiaurre 5, Zaldibar, SPAIN/34-4-6827702; FAX: 34-4-6827999
Lane Bullets, Inc., 1011 S. 10th St., Kansas City, KS 66105/913-621-6113, 800-444-7468
Lane Publishing, P.O. Box 759, Hot Springs, AR 71902/501-623-4951; FAX: 501-623-9832
Langenberg Hat Co., P.O. Box 1860, Washington, MO 63090/800-428-1860; FAX: 314-239-3151
Lan Orchards, 3601 10th St. SE, Ewenatchee, WA 98801
Lansky Sharpeners & Crock Stick, P.O. Box 800, Buffalo, NY 14231/716-877-7511; FAX: 716-877-6955
Lapua Ltd., P.O. Box 5, Lapua, FINLAND SF-62101/64-310111
L.A.R. Manufacturing, Inc., 4133 W. Farm Rd., West Jordan, UT 84088/801-255-7106; FAX: 801-569-1972
LaRocca Gun Works, Inc., 51 Union Place, Worcester, MA 01608/508-754-2887; FAX: 508-754-2887
Laseraim (Emerging Technologies, Inc.), P.O. Box 3548, Little Rock, AR 72203/501-375-2227; FAX: 501-372-1445
Laseraim Arms, Sub. of Emerging Technologies, Inc., P.O. Box 3548, Little Rock, AR 72203/501-375-2227; FAX: 501-372-1445
Laser Devices, Inc., 2 Harris Ct. A-4, Monterey, CA 93940/408-373-0701; FAX: 408-373-0903
Lassen Community College, Gunsmithing Dept., P.O. Box 3000, Hwy. 139, Susanville, CA 96130/916-257-6181 ext. 109; FAX: 916-257-8964
Lathrop's, Inc., 5146 E. Pima, Tucson, AZ 85712/602-881-0226, 800-875-4867
Laughridge, William R. (See Cylinder & Slide, Inc.)
Laurona Armas S.A., Apartado 260, Avda Otaloa 25, Eibar, SPAIN/34-43-700600; FAX: 34-43-700616
Law Concealment Systems, Inc., P.O. Box 3952, Wilmington, NC 28406/919-791-6656, 800-373-0116 orders
Lawrence Leather Co., P.O. Box 1479, Lillington, NC 27546/919-893-2071; FAX: 919-893-4742
Lawson Co., Harry, 3328 N. Richey Blvd., Tucson, AZ 85716/602-326-1117
Lawson, John G. (See Sight Shop, The)
LBT, HCR 62, Box 145, Moyie Springs, ID 83845/208-267-3588
Lea Mfg. Co., 237 E. Aurora St., Waterbury, CT 06720/203-753-5116
Lead Bullets Technology (See LBT)
Leather Arsenal, 27549 Middleton Rd., Middleton, ID 83644/208-585-6212
Leatherman Tool Group, Inc., P.O. Box 20595, Portland, OR 97220/503-253-7826; FAX: 503-253-7830
Leatherwood-Meopta, Inc., 719 Ryan Plaza, Suite 103, Arlington, TX 76011/817-965-3253
Lebeau-Courally, Rue St. Gilles, 386, 4000 Liege, BELGIUM/041 52 48 43; FAX: 041 52 20 08
LeClear Industries, 1126 Donald Ave., P.O. Box 484, Royal Oak, MI 48068/313-588-1025
Lectro Science, Inc., 6410 W. Ridge Rd., Erie, PA 16506/814-833-6487; FAX: 814-833-0447
Ledbetter Airguns, Riley, 1804 E. Sprague St., Winston Salem, NC 27107-3521/919-784-0676
Leding Loader, RR 1, Box 645, Ozark, AR 72949
Lee Precision, Inc., 4275 Hwy. U, Hartford, WI 53027/414-673-3075
Lee Supplies, Mark, 9901 France Ct., Lakeville, MN 55044/612-461-2114
Lee's Red Ramps, Box 291240, Phelan, CA 92329-1240/619-868-5731
Lee Co., T.K., One Independence Plaza, Suite 520, Birmingham, AL 35209
LeFever Arms Co., Inc., RD 2, Box 31, Lee Center, NY 13363/315-337-6722; FAX: 315-337-1543
Leibowitz, Leonard, 1205 Murrayhill Ave., Pittsburgh, PA 15217/412-361-5455
Leica USA, Inc., 156 Ludlow Ave., Northvale, NJ 07647/201-767-7500; FAX: 201-767-8666
LEM Gun Specialties, P.O. Box 87031, College Park, GA 30337
Lenahan Family Enterprise, P.O. Box 46, Manitou Springs, CO 80829
Lethal Force Institute (See Police Bookshelf)
Letschnig, Franz, RR 1, Martintown, Ont. K0C 1S0, CANADA/613-528-4843
Leupold, P.O. Box 688, Beaverton, OR 97075/503-526-1491
Lever Arms Service Ltd., 2131 Burrard St., Vancouver, B.C. V6J 3H7 CANADA/604-736-0004; FAX: 604-738-3503
Liberty Antique Gunworks, 19 Key St., P.O. Box 183, Eastport, ME 04631/207-853-4116
Liberty Metal, 2233 East 16th St., Los Angeles, CA 90021/213-581-9171
Liberty Safe, 316 W. 700 S., Provo, UT 84601/801-373-0727
Lighthouse Mfg. Co., Inc., 443 Ashwood Place, Boca Raton, FL 33431/407-394-6011
Lilja Precision Rifle Barrels, P.O. Box 372, Plains, MT 59859/406-826-3084; FAX: 406-826-3083
Lincoln, Dean, Box 1886, Farmington, NM 87401
Lind Custom Guns, Al, 7821 76th Ave. SW, Tacoma, WA 98498/206-584-6361
Linder Solingen Knives, 4401 Sentry Dr., Tucker, GA 30084/404-939-6915
Lindner Custom Bullets, 325 Bennetts Pond La., Mattituck, NY 11952
Lindsay, Steve, RR 2 Cedar Hills, Kearney, NE 68847/308-236-7885
Lindsley Arms Ctg. Co., P.O. Box 757, 20 College Hill Rd., Henniker, NH 03242/603-428-3127
Linebaugh Custom Sixguns & Rifle Works, P.O. Box 1263, Cody, WY 82414/307-587-8010
Lite Tek International, 133-30 32nd Ave., Flushing, NY 11354/718-463-0650; FAX: 718-762-0890
Lithi Bee Bullet Lube, 2161 Henry St., Muskegon, MI 49441/616-755-4707
"Little John's" Antique Arms, 1740 W. Laveta, Orange, CA 92668

Littler Sales Co., 20815 W. Chicago, Detroit, MI 48228/313-273-6888; FAX: 313-273-1099
Ljutic Industries, Inc., 732 N. 16th Ave., Yakima, WA 98902/509-248-0476; FAX: 509-457-5141
Llama Gabilondo Y Cia, Apartado 290, E-01080, Victoria, SPAIN (U.S. importer—SGS Importers International, Inc.)
Load From A Disk, 9826 Sagedale, Houston, TX 77089/713-484-0935
Loadmaster, P.O. Box 1209, Warminster, Wilts. BA12 9XJ ENGLAND/(0985)218544; FAX: (0985)214111
Loch Leven Industries, P.O. Box 2751, Santa Rosa, CA 95405/707-573-8735
Lock's Philadelphia Gun Exchange, 6700 Rowland Ave., Philadelphia, PA 19149/215-332-6225; FAX: 215-332-4800
Lodewick, Walter H., 2816 NE Halsey St., Portland, OR 97232/503-284-2554
Lofland, James W., 2275 Larkin Rd., Boothwyn, PA 19061/215-485-0391
Log Cabin Sport Shop, 8010 Lafayette Rd., Lodi, OH 44254/216-948-1082
Logan, Harry M., Box 745, Honokaa, HI 96727/808-776-1644
Logan Security Products Co., 4926 Annhurst Rd., Columbus, OH 43228-1341
Lohman Mfg. Co., Inc., 4500 Doniphan Dr., P.O. Box 220, Neosho, MO 64850/417-451-4438; FAX: 417-451-2576
Lomont Precision Bullets, 4236 W. 700 South, Poneto, IN 46781/219-694-6792; FAX: 219-694-6797
London Guns Ltd., Box 3750, Santa Barbara, CA 93130/805-683-4141; FAX: 805-683-1712
Lone Star Gunleather, 1301 Brushy Bend Dr., Round Rock, TX 78681/512-255-1805
Long, George F., 1500 Rogue River Hwy., Ste. F, Grants Pass, OR 97527/503-476-7552
Lorcin Engineering Co., Inc., 10427 San Sevaine Way, Ste. A, Mira Loma, CA 91752/714-360-1406; FAX: 714-360-0623
Lortone, Inc., 2856 NW Market St., Seattle, WA 98107/206-789-3100
Loweth, Richard, 29 Hedgegrow Lane, Kirby Muxloe, Leics. LE9 9BN ENGLAND
L.P.A. Snc, Via V. Alfieri 26, Gardone V.T. BS, ITALY 25063/(30)8911481; FAX: (30)8910951
LPS Laboratories, Inc., 4647 Hugh Howell Rd., P.O. Box 3050, Tucker, GA 30084/404-934-7800
LT Industries, Inc., 20504 Hillgrove Ave., Maple Heights, OH 44137/216-587-5005
Lucas, Edward E., 32 Garfield Ave., East Brunswick, NJ 08816/201-251-5526
Lutz Engraving, Ron, E. 1998 Smokey Valley Rd., Scandinavia, WI 54977/715-467-2674
Lyman Products Corp., Rt. 147 West St., Middlefield, CT 06455
Lynn's Custom Gunstocks, RR 1, Brandon, IA 52210/319-474-2453

# M

M&D Munitions Ltd., 127 Verdi St., Farmingdale, NY 11735/516-752-1038; FAX: 516-752-1905
M&M Engineering (See Hollywood Engineering)
M&N Bullet Lube, P.O. Box 495, 151 NE Jefferson St., Madras, OR 97741/503-255-3750
MA Systems, P.O. Box 489, Chouteau, OK 74337/918-479-6378
Mac-1 Distributors, 13972 Van Ness Ave., Gardena, CA 90249/310-327-3582
Mac's .45 Shop, P.O. Box 2028, Seal Beach, CA 90740/310-438-5046
Macbean, Stan, 754 North 1200 West, Orem, UT 84057/801-224-6446
Macks Sport Shop, P.O. Box 1155, Kodiak, AK 99615/907-486-4276
Madis, David, 2453 West Five Mile Pkwy., Dallas, TX 75233/214-330-7169
MAG Instrument, Inc., 1635 S. Sacramento Ave., Ontario, CA 91761/714-947-1006; FAX: 714-947-3116
Mag-Na-Port International, Inc., 41302 Executive Dr., Harrison Twp., MI 48045-3448/313-469-6727; FAX: 313-469-0723
Mag-Pack Corp., P.O. Box 846, Chesterland, OH 44026
Magma Engineering Co., P.O. Box 161, Queen Creek, AZ 85242/602-987-9008; FAX: 602-987-0148
Magnolia Sports, Inc., 211 W. Main, Magnolia, AR 71753/800-530-7816; FAX: 501-234-8117
Magnum Power Products, Inc., P.O. Box 17768, Fountain Hills, AZ 85268
Magnum Research, Inc., 7110 University Ave., Minneapolis, MN 55432/612-574-1868; FAX: 612-574-0109
Magnus Bullets, P.O.Box 239, Toney, AL 35773/205-828-5089
MagSafe Ammo Co., Box 5692, 2725 Friendly Grove Rd NE, Olympia, WA 98506/206-357-6383
MAGTECH Recreational Products, Inc., 5030 Paradise Rd., Suite C211, Las Vegas, NV 89119/702-795-7191, 800-460-7191; FAX: 702-795-2769
Mahony, Philip Bruce, 67 White Hollow Rd., Lime Rock, CT 06039-2418/203-435-9341
Maine Custom Bullets, RFD 1, Box 1755, Brooks, ME 04921
Mains Enterprises, Inc., 3111 S. Valley View Blvd., Suite B120, Las Vegas, NV 89102-7790/702-876-6278; FAX: 702-876-1269
Maionchi-L.M.I., Via Di Coselli-Zona Industriale Di Guamo, Lucca, ITALY 55060/011 39-583 94291
Maki Industries, 26-10th St. SE, Medicine Hat, AB T1A 1P7 CANADA/403-526-7997
Maki School of Engraving, Robert E., P.O. Box 947, Northbrook, IL 60065/708-724-8238
Makinson, Nichola, RR 3, Komoka, Ont. N0L 1R0 CANADA/519-471-5462
Malcolm Enterprises, 1023 E. Prien Lake Rd., Lake Charles, LA 70601
Mallardtone Game Calls, 2901 16th St., Moline, IL 61265/309-762-8089
M.A.M. Products, Inc., 153 B Cross Slope Court, Englishtown, NJ 07726/908-536-3604
Mandall Shooting Supplies, Inc., 3616 N. Scottsdale Rd., Scottsdale, AZ 85252/602-945-2553; FAX: 602-949-0734
Maxi-Mount, 2405 Somrack Dr., Willoughby Hills, OH 44094/216-946-3105
Mandarino, Monte, 205 Fifth Ave. East, Kalispell, MT 59901/406-257-6208
Manley Shooting Supplies, Lowell, 3684 Pine St., Deckerville, MI 48427/313-376-3665
Manufacture D'Armes Des Pyrenees Francaises (See Unique/M.A.P.F.)
Mar Knives, Inc., Al, 5755 SW Jean Rd., Suite 101, Lake Oswego, OR 97035/503-635-9229
Marathon Rubber Prods. Co., Inc., 510 Sherman St., Wausau, WI 54401/715-845-6255
Marble Arms Corp., 420 Industrial Park, P.O. Box 111, Gladstone, MI 49837/906-428-3710; FAX: 906-428-3711
Marchmon Bullets, 8191 Woodland Shore Dr., Brighton, MI 48116
Marek, George, 55 Arnold St., Westfield, MA 01085/413-562-5673
Marent, Rudolf, 9711 Tiltree St., Houston, TX 77075/713-946-7028
Markell, Inc., 422 Larkfield Center 235, Santa Rosa, CA 95403/707-573-0792; FAX: 707-573-9867
Marksman Products, 5482 Argosy Dr., Huntington Beach, CA 92649/714-898-7535, 800-822-8005; FAX: 714-891-0782
Marlin Firearms Co., 100 Kenna Dr., New Haven, CT 06473/203-239-5621; FAX: 203-234-7991
Marocchi F.lli S.p.A., Via Galileo Galilei, I-25068 Zanano di Sarezzo, ITALY (U.S. importers—PSI, Inc.; Sile Distributors)
Marple & Associates, Dick, 21 Dartmouth St., Hooksett, NH 03106/603-627-1837; FAX: 603-641-4837
Marquart Precision Co., Inc., Rear 136 Grove Ave., Box 1740, Prescott, AZ 86302/602-445-5646
Marsh, Johnny, 1007 Drummond Dr., Nashville, TN 37211/615-833-3259
Marsh, Mike, Croft Cottage, Main St., Elton, Derbyshire DE4 2BY, ENGLAND/0629 650 669
Marshall Enterprises, 792 Canyon Rd., Redwood City, CA 94062
Martin Bookseller, J., P.O. Drawer AP, Beckley, WV 25802/304-255-4073; FAX: 304-255-4077
Martin's Gun Shop, 937 S. Sheridan Blvd., Lakewood, CO 80226/303-922-2184
Martz, John V., 8060 Lakeview Lane, Lincoln, CA 95648/916-645-2250
Marvel, Alan, 3922 Madonna Rd., Jarretsville, MD 21084/301-557-6545
Masen Co., John, P.O. Box 5050, Suite 165, Lewisville, TX 75057/817-430-8732
Masker, Seely, 54 Woodshire S., Getzville, NY 14068/716-689-8894
Master Class Bullets, 4110 Alder St., Eugene, OR 97405/503-687-1263
Master Engravers, Inc. (See Hendricks, Frank E.)
Master Lock Co., 2600 N. 32nd St., Milwaukee, WI 53245/414-444-2800
Master Products, Inc. (See Gun-Alert/Master Products, Inc.)
Matco, Inc., 1003-2nd St., N. Manchester, IN 46962/219-982-8282
Mathews & Son, Inc., George E., 10224 S. Paramount Blvd., Downey, CA 90241/310-862-6719
Matthews Cutlery, 4401 Sentry Dr., Tucker, GA 30084
Mauser-Werke Oberndorf, P.O. Box 1349, 7238 Oberndorf, Neckar, GERMANY (U.S. importer—Precision Imports, Inc.)
Maverick Arms, Inc., 7 Grasso Ave., P.O. Box 497, North Haven, CT 06473/203-288-6491; FAX: 203-288-2404
Maximum Security Corp., 32841 Calle Perfecto, San Juan Capistrano, CA 92675/714-493-3684; FAX: 714-496-7733
Mayville Engineering Co. (See MEC)
Mazur Restoration, Pete, 13083 Drummer Way, Grass Valley, CA 95949/916-268-2412
MCA Sports, P.O. Box 8868, Palm Springs, CA 92263/619-770-2005
McCament, Jay, 1730-134th St. Ct. S., Tacoma, WA 98444/206-531-8832
McCann's Muzzle-Gun Works, 14 Walton Dr., New Hope, PA 18938/215-862-9180
McCormick Corp., Chip, 1825 Fortview Rd., Ste. 115, Austin, TX 78704/512-462-0004; FAX: 512-462-0009
McCormick's Custom Gun Bluing, 609 NE 104th Ave., Vancouver, WA 98664/206-896-4232
McCullough, Ken (See Ken's Rifle Blanks)
McDonald, Dennis, 8359 Brady St., Peosta, IA 52068/319-556-7940
McFarland, Stan, 2221 Idella Ct., Grand Junction, CO 81505/303-243-4704
McGowen Rifle Barrels, 5961 Spruce Lane, St. Anne, IL 60964/815-937-9816; FAX: 815-937-4024
McGuire, Bill, 1600 N. Eastmont Ave., East Wenatchee, WA 98802/509-884-6021
McKee Publications, 121 Eatons Neck Rd., Northport, NY 11768/516-575-8850
McKee, Arthur, 121 Eatons Neck Rd., Northport, NY 11768/516-757-8850
McKenzie, Lynton, 6940 N. Alvernon Way, Tucson, AZ 85718/602-299-5090
McKillen & Heyer, Inc., 35535 Euclid Ave. Suite 11, Willoughby, OH 44094/216-942-2044
McMillan Fiberglass Stocks, Inc., 21421 N. 14th Ave., Phoenix, AZ 85027/602-582-9635; FAX: 602-581-3825
McMillan Gunworks, Inc., 302 W. Melinda Lane, Phoenix, AZ 85027/602-582-9627; FAX: 602-582-5178
McMillan Optical Gunsight Co., 28638 N. 42nd St., Cave Creek, AZ 85331/602-585-7868; FAX: 602-585-7872
McMillan Rifle Barrels, Bill Wiseman & Co., Inc., P.O. Box 3427, Bryan, TX 77805/409-690-3456; FAX: 409-690-0156
McMurdo, Lynn (See Specialty Gunsmithing)
MCRW Associates, R.R. 1 Box 1425, Sweet Valley, PA 18656
MCS, Inc., 34 Delmar Dr., Brookfield, CT 06804/203-775-1013; FAX: 203-775-9462
McWelco Products, 6730 Santa Fe Ave., Hesperia, CA 92345/619-244-8876; FAX: 619-244-9398
MDS, Inc., 1640 Central Ave., St. Petersburg, FL 33712/813-894-3512
Meadow Industries, P.O. Box 754, Locust Grove, VA 22508/703-972-2175
Measurement Group, Inc., Box 27777, Raleigh, NC 27611
MEC, Inc., 715 South St., Mayville, WI 53050/414-387-4500
MEC-Gar S.R.L., Via Madonnina 64, Gardone V.T. (BS), ITALY 25063/39-30-8911719; FAX: 39-30-8910065 (U.S. importer—MEC-Gar U.S.A., Inc.)
MEC-Gar U.S.A., Inc., Box 112, 500B Monroe Turnpike, Monroe, CT 06468/203-635-8662; FAX: 203-635-8662
Meier Works, P.O. Box 423, Tijeras, NM 87059/505-281-3783
Mele, Frank, Rt. 1 P.O. Box 349, Springfork Rd., Granville, TN 38564/615-653-4414
Melton Shirt Co., Inc., 56 Harvester Ave., Batavia, NY 14020/716-343-8750
Men-Metallwerk Elisenhuette, GmbH, P.O. Box 1263, W-5408 Nassau, GERMANY/2604-7819
Menck, Thomas W., 5703 S. 77th St., Ralston, NE 68127-4201
Mendez, John A., P.O. Box 1534, Radio City Station, New York, NY 10019/212-315-2580
Meprolight (See Hesco-Meprolight)
Mercer Custom Stocks, R.M., 216 S. Whitewater Ave., Jefferson, WI 53549/414-674-3839
Merit Corp., Box 9044, Schenectady, NY 12309/518-346-1420
Merkel Freres, Strasse 7 October, 10, Suhl, GERMANY (U.S. importers—GSI, Inc.; Hanus Birdguns, Bill)
Merkuria Ltd., Argentinska 38, 17005 Praha 7, CZECH REPUBLIC/422-875117; FAX: 422-809152
Metalife Industries, Box 53 Mong Ave., Reno, PA 16343/814-436-7747; FAX: 814-676-5662
Michael's Antiques, Box 591, Waldoboro, ME 04572
Michaels of Oregon Co., P.O. Box 13010, Portland, OR 97213/503-255-6890; FAX: 503-255-0746
Micro Sight Co., 242 Harbor Blvd., Belmont, CA 94002/415-591-0769; FAX: 415-591-7531
Micro-Lube, Rt. 2, P.O. Box 201, Deming, NM 88030/505-546-9116
Mid-America Recreation, Inc., 1328 5th Ave., Moline, IA 52807/309-764-5089; FAX: 309-764-2722
Midway Arms, Inc., P.O. Box 1483, Columbia, MO 65205/314-445-6363; FAX: 314-446-1018
Midwest Gun Sport, 1108 Herbert Dr., Zebulon, NC 27597/919-269-5570
Midwest Sport Distributors, Box 129, Fayette, MO 65248
Military Armament Corp., P.O. Box 120, Mt. Zion Rd., Lingleville, TX 76461/817-965-3253
Millenium Safety Products, P.O. Box 9802-916, Austin, TX 78766/512-346-3876
Miller Arms, Inc., P.O. Box 260 Purl St., St. Onge, SD 57779/605-642-5160
Miller Custom, 210 E. Julia, Clinton, IL 61727/217-935-9362
Miller Co., David, 3131 E. Greenlee Rd., Tucson, AZ 85716/602-326-3117
Miller Engineering, R&D Engineering & Manufacturing, P.O. Box 6342, Virginia Beach, VA 23456/804-468-1402
Miller Enterprises, Inc., 1557 E. Main St., Brownsburg, IN 46112/317-852-8187
Miller Gun Woods, 1440 Peltier Dr., Point Roberts, WA 98281/206-945-7014
Miller Single Trigger Mfg. Co., R.D.1, P.O. Box 99, Millersburg, PA 17061/717-692-3704
Miller, Tom (See Huntington Die Specialties)
Millett Sights, 16131 Gothard St., Huntington Beach, CA 92647/714-842-5575, 714-847-5245; FAX: 714-843-5707
Milliron Custom Machine Carving, Earl, 1249 NE 166th Ave., Portland, OR 97230/503-252-3725
Mills Jr., Hugh B., 3615 Canterbury Rd., New Bern, NC 28560/919-637-4631
Miniature Machine Co. (See MMC)
Mirador Optical Corp., 4501 Glencoe Ave., Marina Del Rey, CA 90292/310-821-5587; FAX: 310-305-0386
Miroku, B.C./Daly, Charles (See U.S. importers—Bell's Legendary Country Wear; British Sporting Arms; Outdoor Sports Headquarters)
Mitchell Arms, Inc., 3400 W. MacArthur Blvd., Ste. 1, Santa Ana, CA 92704/714-957-5711; FAX: 714-957-5732
Mitchell Bullets, R.F., 430 Walnut St., Westernport, MD 21562
Mitchell's Accuracy Shop, 68 Greenridge Dr., Stafford, VA 22554/703-659-0165
Mittermeier, Inc., Frank, P.O. Box 2G, 3577 E. Tremont Ave., Bronx, NY 10465/718-828-3843
Mixson Leathercraft, Inc., 7435 W. 19th Ct., Hialeah, FL 33014/305-821-5190; FAX: 305-558-9318
MJK Gunsmithing, Inc., 417 N. Huber Ct., E. Wenatchee, WA 98802/509-884-7683
MK Arms, Inc., 9112 Hyde Park Dr., Huntington Beach, CA 92646-2327/714-261-2767

MKS Supply, Inc., 1015 Springmill Rd., Mansfield, OH 44906/419-747-1088
MMC, 606 Grace Ave., Ft. Worth, TX 76111/817-831-0837
MMP, Rt. 6, Box 384, Harrison, AR 72601/501-741-5019; FAX: 501-741-3104
M.O.A. Corp., 2451 Old Camden Pike, Eaton, OH 45320/513-456-3669
M.O.A. Maximum, P.O. Box 185, Dayton, OH 45404/513-456-3669
Modern Gun Repair School, 2538 N. 8th St., P.O. Box 5338, Dept. GJY94, Phoenix, AZ 85010/602-990-8346
Modern MuzzleLoading, Inc., 234 Airport Rd., P.O. Box 130, Centerville, IA 52544/515-856-2626; FAX: 515-856-2628
Moeller, Steve, 1213 4th St., Fulton, IL 61252/815-589-2300
Molin Industries, Tru-Nord Division, P.O. Box 365, 204 North 9th St., Brainerd, MN 56401/218-829-2870
MoLoc Bullets, P.O. Box 2810, Turlock, CA 95381/209-632-1644
Monell Custom Guns, Red Mill Road, Pine Bush, NY 12566/914-744-3021
Moneymaker Guncraft Corp., 1420 Military Ave., Omaha, NE 68131/402-556-0226
Mongaso Wild Life Safaris, P.O. Box 67641 Station O, Vancouver B.C., V5W 3V1 CANADA
Montana Armory, Inc., 100 Centennial Dr., Big Timber, MT 59011/406-932-4353
Montana Outfitters, Lewis E. Yearout, 308 Riverview Dr. E., Great Falls, MT 59404/406-761-0859
Montana Precision Swaging, P.O. Box 4746, Butte, MT 59702/406-782-7502
Monte Kristo Pistol Grip Co., P.O. Box 85, Whiskeytown, CA 96095/916-623-4019
Montgomery Community College, P.O. Box 787, Troy, NC 27371/919-572-3691
Moore & Co., Wm. Larkin, 31360 Via Colinas, Suite 109, Westlake Village, CA 91361/818-889-4160; FAX: 818-889-1986
Moran, Jerry, P.O. Box 357, Mt. Morris, MI 45458-0357
Moreton/Fordyce Enterprises, P.O. Box 940, Saylorsburg, PA 18353/717-992-5742
Morini (See U.S. importer—Nygord Precision Products)
Morrison Custom Rifles, J.W., 4015 W. Sharon, Phoenix, AZ 85029/602-978-3754
Morrow, Bud, 11 Hillside Lane, Sheridan, WY 82801-9729/307-674-8360
Morton Booth Co., P.O. Box 123, Joplin, MO 64802/417-673-1962
Mo's Competitor Supplies (See MCS, Inc.)
MPC, 188 Freeport Rd., Butler, PA 16001/800-227-7049, 412-283-0567; FAX: 412-283-8310
Moschetti, Mitchell R. , P.O. Box 27065, Denver, CO 80227/303-733-9593
Moss Double Tone, Inc., P.O. Box 1112, 2101 S. Kentucky, Sedalia, MO 65301/816-827-0827
Mossberg & Sons, Inc., O.F, 7 Grasso Ave., North Haven, CT 06473/203-288-6491; FAX: 203-288-2404
Mountain Bear Rifle Works, Inc., 100 B Ruritan Rd., Sterling, VA 20164/703-430-0420
Mountain Hollow Game Calls, Box 121, Cascade, MD 21719/301-241-3282
Mountain South, P.O. Box 381, Barnwell, SC 29812/FAX: 803-259-3227
Mountain State Muzzleloading Supplies, Box 154-1, Rt. 2, Williamstown, WV 26187/304-375-7842; FAX: 304-375-3737
Mountain States Engraving, Kenneth W. Warren, P.O. Box 2842, Wenatchee, WA 98802/509-663-6123
Mountain View Sports, Inc., Box 188, Troy, NH 03465/603-357-9690; FAX: 603-357-9691
Mowreys Guns and Gunsmithing, P.O. Box 246, Waldron, IN 46182/317-525-6181; FAX: 317-525-6181
Mowreys Guns & Supplies, RD 1, Box 82, Canajoharie, NY 13317/518-673-3483
MPI Stocks, P.O. Box 83266, Portland, OR 97283-0266/503-226-1215
Mt. Alto Outdoor Products, Rt. 735, Howardsville, VA 24562
MTM Molded Products Co., Inc., 3370 Obco Ct., Dayton, OH 45414/513-890-7461; FAX: 513-890-1747
Mulhern, Rick, Rt. 5, Box 152, Rayville, LA 71269/318-728-2688
Mullins Ammo, Rt. 2, Box 304K, Clintwood, VA 24228/703-926-6772
Mullis Guncraft, 3523 Lawyers Road E., Monroe, NC 28110/704-283-6683
Multipax, 8086 S. Yale, Suite 286, Tulsa, OK 74136/918-496-1999; FAX: 918-492-7465
Multiplex International, 26 S. Main St., Concord, NH 03301/FAX: 603-796-2223
Multipropulseurs, La Bertrandiere, 42580 L'Etrat, FRANCE/77 74 01 30; FAX: 77 93 19 34
Multi-Scale Charge Ltd., P.O. Box 101 LP, Niagara Falls, NY14303/416-566-1255; FAX: 416-276-6295
Mundy, Thomas A., 69 Robbins Road, Somerville, NJ 08876/201-722-2199
Munger, Robert D. (See Rusteprufe Laboratories)
Munsch Gunsmithing, Tommy, Rt. 2, P.O. Box 248, Little Falls, MN 56345/612-632-6695
Murmur Corp., 2823 N. Westmoreland Ave., Dallas, TX 75222/214-630-5400
Murphy Co., Inc., R., 13 Groton-Harvard Rd., P.O. Box 376, Ayer, MA 01432/617-772-3481
Murray State College, 100 Faculty Dr., Tishomingo, OK 73460/405-371-2371
Muscle Products Corp. (See MPC)
Museum of Historical Arms, Inc., 1038 Alton Rd., Miami Beach, FL 33139/305-672-7480
Mushroom Express Bullet Co., 601 W. 6th St., Greenfield, IN 46140/317-462-6332
Mustra's Custom Guns, Inc., Carl, 1002 Pennsylvania Ave., Palm Harbor, FL 34683/813-785-1403
Muzzle-Nuzzle Co., 609 N. Virginia Ave., Roswell, NM 88201/505-624-1260
Muzzlelite Corp., P.O. Box 987, DeLeon Springs, FL 32130
Muzzleload Magnum Products (See MMP)
Muzzleloaders Etcetera, Inc., 9901 Lyndale Ave. S., Bloomington, MN 55420/612-884-1161

## N

N&J Sales, Lime Kiln Rd., Northford, CT 06472/203-484-0247
Nagel's Bullets, 9 Wilburn, Baytown, TX 77520
Nastoff's 45 Shop, Inc., Steve, 12288 Mahoning Ave., P.O. Box 446, North Jackson, OH 44451
National Bullet Co., 1585 E. 361 St., Eastlake, OH 44095/216-951-1854; FAX: 216-951-7761
National Security Safe Co., Inc., P.O. Box 39, 620 S. 380 E., American Fork, UT 84003/801-756-7706
National Survival Game, Inc., P.O. Box 1439, New London, NH 03257/603-735-6165; FAX: 603-735-5154
National Target Co., 4690 Wyaconda Rd., Rockville, MD 20852/800-827-7060, 301-770-7060; FAX: 301-770-7892
Nationwide Airgun Repairs (See Airgun Repair Centre)
Naval Ordnance Works, Rt. 2, Box 919, Sheperdstown, WV 25443/304-876-0998
Navy Arms Co., 689 Bergen Blvd., Ridgefield, NJ 07657/201-945-2500; FAX: 201-945-6859
N.C. Ordnance Co., P.O. Box 3254, Wilson, NC 27895/919-237-2440
Necessary Concepts, Inc., P.O. Box 571, Deer Park, NY 11729/516-321-8509
NECO, 1316-67th St., Emeryville, CA 94608/510-450-0420
Necromancer Industries, Inc., 14 Communications Way, West Newton, PA 15089/412-872-8722
Nelson Combat Leather, Bruce, P.O. Box 8691 CRB, Tucson, AZ 85738/602-825-9047
Nelson, Gary K., 975 Terrace Dr., Oakdale, CA 95361/209-847-4590
Nelson, Stephen, 7365 NW Spring Creek Dr., Corvallis, OR 97330/503-745-5232
Nelson/Weather-Rite, 14760 Santa Fe Trail Dr., Lenexa, KS 66215/913-492-3200
Nesci Enterprises, Inc., P.O. Box 119, Summit St., East Hampton, CT 06424/203-267-2588
Nettestad Gun Works, RR 1, Box 160, Pelican Rapids, MN 56572/218-863-4301
Neumann GmbH, Untere Ringstr. 17, 8506 Langenzenn, GERMANY/09101-8258
Neutralizer Police Munitions, 5029 Middle Rd., Horseheads, NY 14845-9568/607-739-8362; FAX: 607-594-3900
New Advantage Arms Corp., 2843 N. Alvernon Way, Tucson, AZ 85712/602-881-7444; FAX: 602-323-0949
New Democracy, Inc., 719 Ryan Plaza, Suite 103, Arlington, TX 76011
New England Ammunition Co., 1771 Post Rd. East, Suite 223, Westport, CT 06880/203-254-8048
New England Arms Co., Box 278, Lawrence Lane, Kittery Point, ME 03905/207-439-0593; FAX: 207-439-6726
New England Custom Gun Service (See Apel, Dietrich)
New England Firearms, 60 Industrial Rowe, Gardner, MA 01440/508-632-9393; FAX: 508-632-2300
New Historians Productions, The, 131 Oak St., Royal Oak, MI 48067/313-544-7544
New Orleans Arms Co., 5001 Treasure St., New Orleans, LA 70186/504-944-3371
New Orleans Jewelers Supply Co., 206 Charters St., New Orleans, LA 70130/504-523-3839
New Win Publishing, Inc., Box 5159, Clinton, NJ 08809/201-735-9701; FAX: 201-735-9703
Newark Electronics, 4801 N. Ravenswood Ave., Chicago, IL 60640
Newell, Robert H., 55 Coyote, Los Alamos, NM 87544/505-662-7135
Newman Gunshop, Rt. 1, Box 90F, Agency, IA 52530/515-937-5775
NgraveR Co., The, 67 Wawecus Hill Rd., Bozrah, CT 06334/203-823-1533
Nichols Sports Optics, P.O. Box 37669, Omaha, NE 68137/402-339-3530; FAX: 402-330-8029
Nickels, Paul R., 4789 Summerhill Rd., Las Vegas, NV 89121/702-435-5318
Nicklas, Ted, 5504 Hegel Rd., Goodrich, MI 48438/313-797-4493
Nielsen Custom Cases, P.O. Box 26297, Las Vegas, NV 89126/800-377-1341, 702-878-5611; FAX: 702-877-4433
Niemi Engineering, W.B., Box 126 Center Road, Greensboro, VT 05841/802-533-7180 days, 802-533-7141 evenings
Night Vision Equipment Co., Inc., P.O. Box 266, Emmaus, PA 18049/215-391-9101
Nikon, Inc., 1300 Walt Whitman Rd., Melville, NY 11747/516-547-4200
Nitex, Inc., P.O. Box 1706, Uvalde, TX 78801/512-278-8843
No-Sho Mfg. Co., 10727 Glenfield Ct., Houston, TX 77096/713-723-5332
Noble Co., Jim, 1305 Columbia St., Vancouver, WA 98660/206-695-1309
Nolan, Dave, Fox Valley Range, P.O. Box 155, Dundee, IL 60118/708-426-5921
Noreen, Peter H., 5075 Buena Vista Dr., Belgrade, MT 59714/406-586-7383
Norica, Avnda Otaola, 16, Apartado 68, 20600 Eibar, SPAIN (U.S. importers—American Arms, Inc.; K.B.I., Inc.)
Norinco, 7A, Yun Tan N Beijing, CHINA (U.S. importers—Century International Arms, Inc.; ChinaSports, Inc.; Interarms; Midwest Sport Distributors; Sportarms of Florida)
Norma (See U.S. importer—Paul Co., The)
Norman Custom Gunstocks, Jim, 14281 Cane Rd., Valley Center, CA 92082/619-749-6252
Normark Corp., 1710 E. 78th St., Minneapolis, MN 55423/612-869-3291
Normington Co., Box 6, Rathdrum, ID 83858
Norrell Arms, John, 2608 Grist Mill Rd., Little Rock, AR 72207/501-225-7864
North American Arms, 1800 North 300 West, Spanish Fork, UT 84660/800-821-5783, 801-897-7401; FAX: 801-798-9418
North American Correspondence Schools, The Gun Pro School, Oak & Pawney St., Scranton, PA 18515/717-342-7701
North American Shooting Systems, P.O. Box 306, Osoyoos, B.C. V0H 1V0 CANADA
North American Specialties, 25442 Trabuco Rd., 105-328, El Torro, CA 92630/714-979-4867; FAX: 714-979-1520
North Fork Custom Gunsmithing, James Johnston, 428 Del Rio Rd., Roseburg, OR 97470/503-673-4467
North Mountain Pine Training Center (See Executive Protection Institute)
North Specialty Products, 2664-B Saturn St., Brea, CA 92621/714-524-1665
North Wind Decoys Co., 1005 N. Tower Rd., Fergus Falls, MN 56537/218-736-4378; FAX: 218-736-4378
Northeast Training Institute, Inc., 1142 Rockland St., Suite 380, Reading, PA 19604/215-373-1940
Northern Precision Custom Swaged Bullets, 337 S. James St., Carthage, NY 13619/315-493-3456
Northlake Boot Co., 1810 Columbia Ave., Franklin, TN 37064/615-794-1556
Nosler, Inc., P.O. Box 671, Bend, OR 97709/800-285-3701, 503-382-3921; FAX: 503-388-4667
Novak's .45 Shop, Wayne, 1206 1/2 30th St., P.O. Box 4045, Parkersburg, WV 25101/304-485-9295
Nowlin Custom Barrels Mfg., Rt. 1, Box 308, Claremore, OK 74017/918-342-0689; FAX: 918-342-0624
Nu-Line Guns, Inc., 1053 Caulks Hill Rd., Harvester, MO 63303/314-441-4500; FAX: 314-447-5018
Null Holsters Ltd., K.L., Hill City Station, Resaca, GA 30735/404-625-5643; FAX: 404-625-9392
Numrich Arms Corp., 203 Broadway, W. Hurley, NY 12491
Nu-Teck, 30 Industrial Park Rd., Box 37, Centerbrook, CT 06409/203-767-3573; FAX: 203-767-9137
NW Sinker and Tackle, P.O. Box 1931, Myrtle Creek, OR 97457
Nygord Precision Products, P.O. Box 8394, La Crescenta, CA 91224/818-352-3027; FAX: 818-352-3027

## O

Oakland Custom Arms, Inc., 4690 W. Walton Blvd., Waterford, MI 48329/313-674-8261
Oakman Turkey Calls, RD 1, Box 825, Harrisonville, PA 17228/717-485-4620
Oakshore Electronic Sights, Inc., P.O. Box 4470, Ocala, FL 32678-4470/904-629-7112; FAX: 904-629-1433
Obermeyer Rifled Barrels, 23122 60th St., Bristol, WI 53104/414-843-3537; FAX: 414-843-2129
O'Connor Rifle Products Co., Ltd., 2008 Maybank Hwy., Charleston, SC 29412/803-795-8590
October Country, P.O. Box 969, Dept. GD, Hayden Lake, ID 83835/208-772-2068
Oehler Research, Inc., P.O. Box 9135, Austin, TX 78766/512-327-6900
Oglesby & Oglesby Gunmakers, Inc., RR 5, Springfield, IL 62707/217-487-7100
Oil Rod and Gun Shop, 69 Oak St., East Douglas, MA 01516/508-865-2005
Ojala Holsters, Arvo, P.O. Box 98, N. Hollywood, CA 91603/503-669-1404
Oker's Engraving, 365 Bell Rd., P.O. Box 126, Shawnee, CO 80475/303-838-6042
Oklahoma Leather Products, Inc., 500 26th NW, Miami, OK 74354/918-542-6651
Old Dominion Engravers, 100 Progress Drive, Lynchburg, VA 24502/804-237-4450
Old Wagon Bullets, 32 Old Wagon Rd., Wilton, CT 06897
Old West Bullet Moulds, P.O. Box 519, Flora Vista, NM 87415
Old West Reproductions, Inc., 446 Florence S. Loop, Florence, MT 59833/406-273-2615
Old Western Scrounger, Inc., 12924 Hwy. A-12, Montague, CA 96064/916-459-5445
Old World Gunsmithing, 2901 SE 122nd St., Portland, OR 97236/503-760-7681
Old World Oil Products, 3827 Queen Ave. N., Minneapolis, MN 55412/612-522-5037
Olde Pennsylvania, P.O. Box 912, New Kensington, PA 15068/412-337-1552
Ole Frontier Gunsmith Shop, 2617 Hwy. 29 S., Cantonment, FL 32533/904-477-8074
Olsen Development Lab, 111 Lakeview Ave., Blackwood, NJ 08012
Olson, Vic, 5002 Countryside Dr., Imperial, MO 63052/314-296-8086
Olt Co., Philip S., P.O. Box 550, Pekin, IL 61554/309-348-3633; FAX: 309-348-3300
Olympic Arms, Inc., 624 Old Pacific Hwy. SE, Olympia, WA 98503/206-456-3471; FAX: 206-491-3447
Olympic Optical Co., P.O. Box 752377, Memphis, TN 38175-2377/901-794-3890
Omark, Div. of Blount, Inc., 2299 Snake River Ave., P.O. Box 856, Lewiston, ID 83501/800-627-3640, 208-746-2351
Omnishock, 2219 Verde Oak Drive, Hollywood, CA 90068
OMR Feinmechanik, Jagd-und Sportwaffen, GmbH, Postfach 1231, Schutzenstr. 20, D-5400 Koblenz, GERMANY/0261-31865-15351
One Of A Kind, 15610 Purple Sage, San Antonio, TX 78255/512-695-3364

Optolyth-USA, Inc., 18805 Melvista Lane, Hillsboro, OR 97123/503-628-0246; FAX: 503-628-0797
Orchard Park Enterprise, P.O. Box 563, Orchard Park, NY 14227/616-656-0356
Ordnance Works, The, 2969 Pidgeon Point Road, Eureka, CA 95501/707-443-3252
Oregon Arms, Inc., 114 E. Jackson, P.O. Box 1104, Medford, OR 97501/503-560-4040
Original Mink Oil, Inc., P.O. Box 20191, 11021 NE Beach St., Portland, OR 97220/503-255-2814
Or-Ün, Tahtakale Menekse Han 18, Istanbul, TURKEY 34460/901-522-5912; FAX: 901-522-7973
Orvis Co., The, Rt. 7, Manchester, VT 05254/802-362-3622 ext. 283; FAX: 802-362-3525
Ottmar, Maurice, Box 657, 113 E. Fir, Coulee City, WA 99115/509-632-5717
Otto, Tim, 320 Fairhaven Rd., Alameda, CA 94501-5963
Outa-Site Gun Carriers, 219 Market, Laredo, TX 78040/210-722-4678; FAX: 210-726-4858
Outdoor Connection, Inc., The, 201 Douglas, P.O. Box 7751, Waco, TX 76712/800-533-6076; 817-772-5575; FAX: 817-776-6076
Outdoor Edge Cutlery Corp., 2888 Bluff St., Suite 130, Boulder, CO 80301/303-530-3855; FAX: 303-530-3855
Outdoor Sports Headquarters, Inc., 967 Watertower Lane, Dayton, OH 45449/513-865-5855; FAX: 513-865-5962
Outdoorsman's Bookstore, The, Llangorse, Brecon, County Powys LD3 7UE, U.K./44-87484-660; FAX: 44-87484-650
Outers Laboratories, Div. of Blount, Inc., Route 2, Onalaska, WI 54650/608-781-5800
Owen, Harry, Sport Specialties, 100 N. Citrus Ave. 412, W. Covina, CA 91791-1614/818-968-5806
Ox-Yoke Originals, Inc., 34 Main St., Milo, ME 04463/800-231-8313; FAX: 207-943-2416
Ozark Gun Works, 335 Cemetary Rd., Rogers, AR 72756/FAX: 501-631-6944

# P

P&M Sales and Service, 5724 Gainsborough Pl., Oak Forest, IL 60452/708-687-7149
P&P Tool Co., 125 W. Market St., Morrison, IL 61270/815-772-7618
P&S Gun Service, 2138 Old Shepardsville Rd., Louisville, KY 40218/502-456-9346
Pac-Nor Barreling, 99299 Overlook Rd., P.O. Box 6188, Brookings, OR 97415/503-469-7330; FAX: 503-469-7331
Pace Marketing, Inc., 9474 NW 48th St., Sunrise, FL 33351-5137/305-741-4361; FAX: 305-741-2901
Pachmayr Ltd., 1875 S. Mountain Ave., Monrovia, CA 91016/818-357-7771, 800-423-9704; FAX: 818-358-7251
Pacific Pistolcraft, 1810 E. Columbia Ave., Tacoma, WA 98404/206-474-5465
Pacific Tool Co., P.O. Box 2048, Ordnance Plant Rd., Grand Island, NE 68801
Paco's (See Small Custom Mould & Bullet Co.)
P.A.C.T., Inc., P.O. Box 531525, Grand Prairie, TX 75053/214-641-0049
Page Custom Bullets, P.O. Box 25, Port Moresby Papua, NEW GUINEA
Pagel Gun Works, Inc., 1407 4th St. NW, Grand Rapids, MN 55744/218-326-3003
Palmer Manufacturing Co., C., Inc., P.O. Box 220, West Newton, PA 15089/412-872-8200; FAX: 412-872-8302
Palmer Metal Products, 2930 N. Campbell Ave., Chicago, IL 60618/800-788-7725; FAX: 312-267-8080
Palmgren Steel Products, 8383 S. Chicago Ave., Chicago, IL 60617/312-721-9675; FAX: 312-721-9739
Palsa Outdoor Products, P.O. Box 81336, Lincoln, NE 68501/402-456-9281, 800-456-9281; FAX: 402-488-2321
PanaVise Products, Inc., 1485 Southern Way, Sparks, NV 89431/702-353-2900; FAX: 702-353-2929
Para-Ordnance Mfg., Inc., 3411 McNicoll Ave., Unit 14, Scarborough, Ont. M1V 2V6, CANADA/416-297-7855; FAX: 416-297-1289
Paragon Sales & Services, Inc., P.O. Box 2022, Joliet, IL 60434/815-725-9212; FAX: 815-725-8974
Pardini Armi Commerciale Srl, Via Italica 154, 55043 Lido Di Camaiore Lu, ITALY/584-90121; FAX: 584-90122 (U.S. importer—MCS, Inc.)
Paris, Frank J., 13945 Minock Dr., Redford, MI 48239/313-255-0888
Parke-Bernet (See Sotheby's)
Parker Div. Reageant Chemical (See Parker Reproductions)
Parker Gun Finishes, 9337 Smokey Row Rd., Strawberry Plains, TN 37871/615-933-3286
Parker Reproductions, 124 River Rd., Middlesex, NJ 08846/908-469-0100; FAX: 908-469-9692
Parker, Mark D., 1240 Florida Ave. 7, Longmont, CO 80501/303-772-0214
Parker-Hale (See U.S. distributor-Navy Arms Co.)
Parts & Surplus, P.O. Box 22074, Memphis, TN 38122/901-683-4007
Partridge Sales Ltd., John, Trent Meadows, Rugeley, Staffordshire, WS15 2HS ENGLAND/0889-584438
Pasadena Gun Center, 206 E. Shaw, Pasadena, TX 77506/713-472-0417; FAX: 713-472-1322
PAST Sporting Goods, Inc., P.O. Box 1035, Columbia, MO 65205/314-445-9200
Patchbox & Museum of the Great Divide, The, 600 Farm Rd., Kalispell, MT 59901/406-756-8851
Paterson Gunsmithing, 438 Main St., Paterson, NJ 07502/201-345-4100
Pathfinder Sports Leather, 2920 E. Chambers St., Phoenix, AZ 85040/602-276-0016
Patrick Bullets, P.O. Box 172, Warwick QSLD 4370 AUSTRALIA
Patriot Manufacturing, P.O. Box 50065, Lighthouse Point, FL 33074/305-783-4849
Pattern Control, 114 N. Third St., Garland, TX 75040/214-494-3551
Paul Co., The, Rt. 1, Box 177A, Wellsville, KS 66092/913-883-4444
Paulsen Gunstocks, Rt. 71, Box 11, Chinook, MT 59523/406-357-3403
Payne Photography, Robert, P.O. Box 141471, Austin, TX 78714/512-272-4554; FAX: 512-929-0714
PC Co., 5942 Secor Rd., Toledo, OH 43623/419-472-6222
Peacemaker Specialists, John Kopec Enterprises, P.O. Box 157, Whitmore, CA 96096/916-472-3438
Pease Accuracy, Bob, P.O. Box 310787, New Braunfels, TX 78131/210-625-1342
Peasley, David, P.O. Box 604, 2067 S. Hiway 17, Alamosa, CO 81101
PECAR Herbert Schwarz, GmbH, Kreuzbergstrasse 6, Berlin 61, 1000 GERMANY/004930-785-7383; FAX: 004930-785-1934
Pedersen & Son, C.R., 2717 S. Pere Marquette Hwy., Ludington, MI 49431/616-843-2061
Pedersoli Davide & C., Via Artigiani 53, Gardone V.T. (BS) ITALY 25063/030-8912402; FAX: 030-8911019 (U.S. importers—Beauchamp & Son, Inc.; Cabela's; Dixie Gun Works, EMF Co., Inc.; Navy Arms Co.; Trail Guns Armory, Inc.)
Peet Shoe Dryer, Inc., 130 S. 5th St., St. Maries, ID 83861/800-222-PEET; FAX: 208-245-5441
Pejsa Ballistics, 2120 Kenwood Pkwy., Minneapolis, MN 55405/612-374-3337; FAX: 612-374-3337
Pell, John T., 410 College, Trinidad, CO 81082/719-846-9406
Peltor, Inc., 63 Commercial Way, E. Providence, RI 02914/401-438-4800; FAX: 800-EAR-FAX1
PEM's Mfg. Co., 5063 Waterloo Rd., Atwater, OH 44201/216-947-3721
Pence Precision Barrels, 7567 E. 900 S., S. Whitley, IN 46787/219-839-4745
Pend Oreille Sport Shop, 3100 Hwy. 200 East, Sandpoint, ID 83864/208-263-2412
Pendleton Royal, 4/7 Highgate St., Birmingham, ENGLAND B12 0X5/44 21 440 3060; FAX: 44 21 446 4165
Pendleton Woolen Mills, P.O. Box 3030, 220 N.W. Broadway, Portland, OR 97208/503-226-4801
Penguin Industries, Inc., Airport Industrial Mall, Coatesville, PA 19320/215-384-6000
Penn's Woods Products, Inc., 19 W. Pittsburgh St., Delmont, PA 15626/412-468-8311
Pennsylvania Gunsmith School, 812 Ohio River Blvd., Avalon, Pittsburgh, PA 15202/412-766-1812
Penrod Precision, 312 College Ave., P.O. Box 307, N. Manchester, IN 46962/219-982-8385
Pentax Corp., 35 Inverness Dr. E., Englewood, CO 80112/303-799-8000
Pentheny de Pentheny, 2352 Baggett Ct., Santa Rosa, CA 95401/707-573-1390
Pepperbox Gun Shop, P.O. Box 922, E. Moline, IL 61244
Perazzi m.a.p. S.P.A., Via Fontanelle 1/3, 1-25080 Botticino Mattina, ITALY (U.S. importer—Perazzi USA, Inc.)
Perazzi USA, Inc., 1207 S. Shamrock Ave., Monrovia, CA 91016/818-303-0068
Peregrine Industries (See Falcon Industries, Inc.)
Performance Specialists, 308 Eanes School Rd., Austin, TX 78746/512-327-0119
Peripheral Data Systems (See Arms)
Personal Protection Systems, RD 5, Box 5027-A, Moscow, PA 18444/717-842-1766
Perugini Visini & Co. s.r.l., Via Camprelle, 126, 25080 Nuvolera (Bs.), ITALY (U.S. importer—Moore & Co., Wm. Larkin)
Peters Stahl GmbH, Stettiner Str. 42, D-4790 Paderborn, GERMANY/05251-750025-27; FAX: 05251-75611 (U.S. importers—McMillan Gunworks, Inc.; Safari Arms/SGW)
Petersen Publishing Co., 6420 Wilshire Blvd., Los Angeles, CA 90048
Peterson Gun Shop, Inc., A.W., 4255 W. Old U.S. 441, Mt. Dora, FL 32757-3299/904-383-4258
Peterson Instant Targets, Inc. (See Lyman Products Corp.)
Pettinger Books, Gerald, Rt. 2, Box 125, Russell, IA 50238/515-535-2239
Pflumm Gun Mfg. Co., 6139 Melrose Ln., Shawnee, KS 66203/800-888-4867
PFRB Co., P.O. Box 1242, Bloomington, IL 61701/309-473-3964
Phelps Mfg. Co., Box 2266, Evansville, IN 47714/812-476-8791
Phillippi Custom Bullets, Justin, P.O. Box 773, Ligonier, PA 15658/412-238-9671
Phillips & Bailey, Inc., 815A Yorkshire St., Houston, TX 77022/713-699-4288
Phoenix Arms Co. Ltd. (See Hy-Score Arms Co. Ltd.)
Phoenix Arms, 1420 S. Archibald Ave., Ontario, CA 91761/714-947-4843
Phyl-Mac, 609 NE 104th Ave., Vancouver, WA 98664/206-256-0579
Piedmont Community College, P.O. Box 1197, Roxboro, NC 27573/919-599-1181
Pierce Pistols, 2326 E. Hwy. 34, Newnan, GA 30263/404-253-8192
Pilgrim Pewter, Inc. (See Bell Originals, Sid)
Pilkington Gun Co., P.O. Box 1296, Muskogee, OK 74402/918-683-9418
Pilkington, Scott, Little Trees Ramble, P.O. Box 97, Monteagle, TN 37356/615-924-3475; FAX: 615-924-3442
Pine Technical College, 1100 4th St., Pine City, MN 55063/800-521-7463; FAX: 612-629-6766
Pioneer Guns, 5228 Montgomery Rd., Norwood, OH 45212/513-631-4871
Piotti (See U.S. importer—Moore & Co., Wm. Larkin)
Piquette, Paul R., 80 Bradford Dr., Feeding Hills, MA 01030/413-781-8300, Ext. 682
PistolPAL Products, 2930 N. Campbell Ave., Chicago, IL 60618/800-788-7725; FAX: 312-267-8080
Plaxco, J. Michael, Rt. 1, P.O. Box 203, Roland, AR 72135/501-868-9787
Plaza Cutlery, Inc., 3333 Bristol, 161, South Coast Plaza, Costa Mesa, CA 92626/714-549-3932
Plum City Ballistic Range, N2162 80th St., Plum City, WI 54761-8622/715-647-2539
PMC/Eldorado Cartridge Corp., P.O. Box 62508, 12801 U.S. Hwy. 95 S., Boulder City, NV 89006-2508/702-294-0025; FAX: 702-294-0121
Police Bookshelf, P.O. Box 122, Concord, NH 03301/603-224-6814; FAX: 603-226-3554
Poly Technologies, Inc. (See U.S. importer—Keng's Firearms Specialty, Inc.)
Polywad, Inc., P.O. Box 7916, Macon, GA 31209/912-477-0669
Pomeroy, Robert, RR1, Box 50, E. Corinth, ME 04427/207-285-7721
Ponsness/Warren, P.O. Box 8, Rathdrum, ID 83858/208-687-2231; FAX: 208-687-2233
Pony Express Reloaders, 608 E. Co. Rd. D, Suite 3, St. Paul, MN 55117/612-483-9406
Pony Express Sport Shop, Inc., 16606 Schoenborn St., North Hills, CA 91343/818-895-1231
Porta Blind, Inc., 2700 Speedway, Wichita Falls, TX 76308/800-842-5545
Potts, Wayne E., 912 Poplar St., Denver, CO 80220/303-355-5462
Powder Horn, Inc., The, P.O. Box 114 Patty Drive, Cusseta, GA 31805/404-989-3257
Powell & Son (Gunmakers) Ltd., William, 35-37 Carrs Lane, Birmingham B4 7SX ENGLAND/21-643-0689; FAX: 21-631-3504 (U.S. importer—Bell's Legendary Country Wear)
Power Custom, Inc., RR 2, P.O. Box 756AB, Gravois Mills, MO 65037/314-372-5684
Power Plus Enterprises, P.O. Box 6070, Columbus, GA 31907-0058/404-561-1717
PPC Corp., 627 E. 24th St., Paterson, NJ 07514/201-278-5428
Practical Tools, Inc., Austin Behlerts, P.O. Box 133, Pipersville, PA 18947/215-766-7301
Pragotrade, 307 Humberline Dr., Rexdale, Ontario, CANADA M9W 5V1/416-675-1322
Pranger, Ed G., 1414 7th St., Anacortes, WA 98221/206-293-3488
Pre-Winchester 92-90-62 Parts Co., P.O. Box 8125, W. Palm Beach, FL 33407
Precise International, 15 Corporate Dr., Orangeburg, NY 10962/914-365-3500
Precise Metalsmithing Enterprises, 146 Curtis Hill Rd., Chehalis, WA 98532/206-748-3743; FAX: 206-748-8102
Precision Airgun Sales, Inc., 5139 Center Rd., Maple Hts., OH 44137-1906
Precision Arms International, Inc., Rt. 17, Box 456, Bldg. 810, Saluda, VA 23149/804-758-5233; FAX: 804-758-2690
Precision Cartridge, 176 Eastside Rd., Deer Lodge, MT 59722/800-397-3901, 406-846-3900
Precision Cast Bullets, 101 Mud Creek Lane, Ronan, MT 59864/406-676-5135
Precision Castings & Equipment, Inc., P.O. Box 326, Jasper, IN 47547-0135/812-634-9167
Precision Components and Guns, Rt. 55, P.O. Box 337, Pawling, NY 12564/914-855-3040
Precision Delta Corp., P.O. Box 128, Ruleville, MS 38771/601-756-2810; FAX: 601-756-2590
Precision Imports, Inc., 5040 Space Center Dr., San Antonio, TX 78218/512-666-3033; FAX: 512-666-2723
Precision Metal Finishing, John Westrom, P.O. Box 3186, Des Moines, IA 50316/515-288-8680; FAX: 515-288-8680
Precision Munitions, Inc., P.O. Box 326, Jasper, IN 47547
Precision Ordnance, 1316 E. North St., Jackson, MI 49202
Precision Reloading, Inc., P.O. Box 122, Stafford Springs, CT 06076/203-684-7979; FAX: 203-684-6788
Precision Sales International, Inc. (See PSI, Inc.)
Precision Shooting, 102 Brandon Rd., Yonkers, NY 10704/914-776-1581
Precision Shooting, Inc., 5735 Sherwood Forest Dr., Akron, OH 44319
Precision Small Parts, Inc., 155 Carlton Rd., Charlottesville, VA 22902/804-293-6124
Precision Specialties, 131 Hendom Dr., Feeding Hills, MA 01030/413-786-3365; FAX: 413-786-3365
Precision Sport Optics, 15571 Producer Lane, Unit G, Huntington Beach, CA 92649/714-891-1309; FAX: 714-892-6920
Precision Sports, 3736 Kellogg Rd., P.O. Box 5588, Cortland, NY 13045-5588/607-756-2851, 800-847-6787; FAX: 607-753-8835
Premier Reticles, 920 Breckenridge Lane, Winchester, VA 22601-6707
Prescott Projectile Co., 1808 Meadowbrook Road, Prescott, AZ 86303
Price Bullets, Patrick W., 16520 Worthley Drive, San Lorenzo, CA 94580/415-278-1547
Primos Wild Game Calls, Inc., P.O. Box 12785, Jackson, MS 39236-2785/601-366-1288; FAX: 601-362-3274
Pro Load Ammunition, Inc., 5180 E. Seltice Way, Post Falls, ID 83854/208-773-9444; FAX: 208-773-9441
Pro-Mark, Div. of Wells Lamont, 6640 W. Touhy, Chicago, IL 60648/312-647-8200
Pro-Port Ltd., 41302 Executive Dr., Harrison Twp., MI 48045-3448/313-469-7323; FAX: 313-469-0425
Pro-Shot Products, Inc., P.O. Box 763, Taylorville, IL 62568/217-824-9133; FAX: 217-824-8861
Professional Firearms Record Book Co. (See PFRB Co.)

Professional Gunsmiths of America, Inc., 1301 Franklin, P.O. Box 224E, Lexington, MO 64067/816-259-2636
Professional Hunter Supplies (See Star Custom Bullets)
Proline Handgun Leather, P.O. Box 112154, Tacoma, WA 98411/206-564-6652
Prolix®, 15578 Mojave Dr. Unit D, Victorville, CA 92392/800-248-LUBE, 619-243-3129; FAX: 619-241-0148
Protecto Plastics, Div. of Penguin Ind., Airport Industrial Mall, Coatesville, PA 19320/215-384-6000
Protektor Model Co., 7 Ash St., Galeton, PA 16922/814-435-2442
Prototech Industries, Inc., Rt. 1, Box 81, Delia, KS 66418/913-771-3571
ProWare,Inc., 15847 NE Hancock St., Portland, OR 97230/503-239-0159
PSI, Inc., P.O. Box 1776, Westfield, MA 01086/413-562-5055; FAX: 413-562-5056
P.S.M.G. Gun Co., 10 Park Ave., Arlington, MA 02174/617-646-8845; FAX: 617-646-2133
PW Gunleather, P.O. Box 450432, Atlanta, GA 30345/404-822-1640; FAX: 404-822-1704
Pyromid, Inc., 3292 S. Highway 97, Redmond, OR 97786

## Q

Quack Decoy Corp., 4 Mill St., Cumberland, RI 02864/401-723-8202
Quaker Boy, Inc., 5455 Webster Rd., Orchard Parks, NY 14127/716-662-3979
Qualigraphics, Inc., 25 Ruta Ct., P.O. Box 2306, S. Hackensack, NJ 07606/201-440-9200
Quality Arms, Inc., Box 19477, Dept. GD, Houston, TX 77224/713-870-8377; FAX: 713-870-8524
Quality Firearms of Idaho, Inc., 114 13th Ave. S., Nampa, ID 83651/208-466-1631
Quality Parts Co., 999 Roosevelt Trail, Bldg. 3, Windham, ME 04062/800-556-7928, 207-892-2005; FAX: 207-892-8068
Quartz-Lok, 13137 N. 21st Lane, Phoenix, AZ 85029
Queen Cutlery Co., 507 Chestnut St., Titusville, PA 16354/800-222-5233
Quigley's Personal Protection Strategies, Paxton, 9903 Santa Monica Blvd., 300 Beverly Hills, CA 90212/310-281-1762
Quinetics Corp., P.O. Box 13237, San Antonio, TX 78213/512-684-8561; FAX: 512-684-2912

## R

R&C Knives & Such, P.O. Box 1047, Manteca, CA 95336/209-239-3722
R&J Gun Shop, 133 W. Main St., John Day, OR 97845/503-575-2130
R&S Industries Corp., 8255 Brentwood Industrial Dr., St. Louis, MO 63144/314-781-5400
Rabeno, Martin, 92 Spook Hole Rd., Ellenville, NY 12428/914-647-4567
Radiator Specialty Co., 1900 Wilkinson Blvd., P.O. Box 34689, Charlotte, NC 28234/800-438-6947; FAX: 800-421-9525
Radical Concepts, 19205 Parthenia St., Suite D, Northridge, CA 91324
Radix Research & Mktg., Box 247, Woodland Park, CO 80863
Rainier Ballists Corp., 4500 15th St. East, Tacoma, WA 98424/800-638-8722; FAX: 206-922-7854
Ram-Line, Inc., 10601 W. 48th Ave., Wheat Ridge, CO 80033/303-467-0300; FAX: 303-467-9833
Ranch Products, P.O. Box 145, Malinta, OH 43535/313-277-3118; FAX: 313-565-8536
Randall Firearms Research, P.O. Box 1586, Lomita, CA 90717-5586/310-325-0102; FAX: 310-325-0298
Randall-Made Knives, P.O. Box 1988, Orlando, FL 32802/407-855-8075
Randco UK, 286 Gipsy Rd., Welling, Kent DA16 1JJ, ENGLAND/44 81 303 4118
Randolph Engineering, Inc., 275 Centre St., Unit 17, Holbrook MA 02343/617-961-6070, 800-541-1405; FAX: 617-767-5239
Ranger Footwear, 1100 E. Main St., Endicott, NY 13760/800-688-6148
Ranger Mfg. Co., Inc., 1536 Crescent Dr., Augusta, GA 30919/404-738-3469
Ranger Shooting Glasses, 275 Centre St., Unit 17, Holbrook, MA 02343/800-541-1405, 617-961-6070; FAX: 617-767-5239
Ranging, Inc., Routes 5 & 20, East Bloomfield, NY 14443/716-657-6161
Ransom International Corp., P.O. Box 3845, 1040-A Sandretto Dr., Prescott, AZ 86302/602-778-7899; FAX: 602-778-7993
Rapine Bullet Mould Mfg. Co., P.O. Box 1119, East Greenville, PA 18041/215-679-5413
Rattlers Brand, P.O. Box 311, Thomaston, GA 30286/800-652-1341; FAX: 404-647-2742
Ravell Ltd., 289 Diputacion St., 08009, Barcelona SPAIN
Raytech, Div. of Lyman Products Corp., Rt. 32 Stafford Ind. Park, Box 6, Stafford Springs, CT 06076/203-684-4273; FAX: 203-684-7938
RCBS, Div. of Blount, Inc., 605 Oro Dam Blvd., Oroville, CA 95965/800-533-5000, 916-533-5191
R.D.P. Tool Co., Inc., 49162 McCoy Ave., East Liverpool, OH 43920/216-385-5129
Reagent Chemical & Research, Inc. (See Calico Hardwoods, Inc.)
Reardon Products, P.O. Box 126, Morrison, IL 61270/815-772-3155
Rebec's Reloading, P.O. Box 30550, Santa Barbara, CA 93130
Re-Heater, Inc., 15828 S. Broadway, C, Gardena, CA 90248
Red Ball, 100 Factory St., Nashua, NH 03060/603-881-4420
Red Diamond Dist. Co., 1304 Snowdon Dr., Knoxville, TN 37912
Red Head, Inc., P.O. Box 7100, Springfield, MO 65801/417-864-5430
Red River Frontier Outfitters, P.O. Box 241, Dept. GD, Tujunga, CA 91043/818-821-3167
Red Star Target Co., 4519 Brisebois Dr. NW, Calgary AB T2L 2G3 CANADA/403-289-7939; FAX: 403-289-3275
Red Willow Tool & Armory, Inc., 4004 Hwy. 93 North, Stevensville, MT 59870/406-777-5401; FAX: 406-777-5402
Redding Reloading, Inc., 1089 Starr Rd., Cortland, NY 13045/607-753-3331; FAX: 607-756-8445
Redfield, Inc., 5800 E. Jewell Ave., Denver, CO 80224/303-757-6411; FAX: 303-756-2338
Redman's Rifling & Reboring, Rt. 3, Box 330A, Omak, WA 98841/509-826-5512
Redwood Bullet Works, 3559 Bay Rd., Redwood City, CA 94063/415-367-6741
Reed, Dave, Rt. 1, Box 374, Minnesota City, MN 55959/507-689-2944
Refrigiwear, Inc., 71 Inip Dr., Inwood, Long Island, NY 11696
Regional Associates, P.O. Box 9849, Alexandria, VA 22304/703-780-6189
Reiswig, Wallace E., Claro Walnut Gunstock Co., 1235 Stanley Ave., Chico, CA 95928/916-342-5188
Reloaders Equipment Co., 4680 High St., Ecorse, MI 48229
Reloading Specialties, Inc., 209 S.W. 2nd Ave. Box 1130, Pine Island, MN 55963/507-356-8500
Remington Arms Co., Inc., 1007 Market St., Wilmington, DE 19898/302-773-5291
Remington Footwear Co., 1810 Columbia Ave., Franklin, TN 37604/800-332-2688
Rencher Bullets, 5161 NE 5th St., Redmond, OR 97756
Renegade, P.O. Box 31546, Phoenix, AZ 85046/602-482-6777
Renner Co./Radical Concepts, R.J., P.O. Box 10731, Canoga Park, CA 91309/818-700-8131
Reno, Wayne, 2808 Stagestop Rd., Jefferson, CO 80456/719-836-3452
R.E.T. Enterprises, 2608 S. Chestnut, Broken Arrow, OK 74012/918-251-GUNS; FAX: 918-251-0587
Retting, Inc., Martin B., 11029 Washington, Culver City, CA 90232/213-837-2412
R.G.-G., Inc., P.O. Box 1261, Conifer, CO 80433-1261
Rhodeside, Inc., 1704 Commerce Dr., Piqua, OH 45356/513-773-5781
Rice, Keith (See White Rock Tool & Die)
Richards Classic Oil Finish, John, Rt. 2, Box 325, Bedford, KY 40006/502-255-7222
Richards Micro-Fit Stocks, 8331 N. San Fernando Rd., P.O. Box 1066, Sun Valley, CA 91352/818-767-6097
Rickard, Inc., Pete, RD 1, Box 292, Cobleskill, NY 12043/800-282-5663; FAX: 518-234-2454
Ridgetop Sporting Goods, P.O. Box 306, 42907 Hilligoss Ln. East, Eatonville, WA 98328/206-832-6422
Riebe Co., W.J., 3434 Tucker Rd., Boise, ID 83703
Ries, Chuck, 415 Ridgecrest Dr., Grants Pass, OR 97527/503-476-5623
Rifle Shop, The, Wm. H. Hobaugh, P.O. Box M, Philipsburg, MT 59858/406-859-3515
RIG Products, 87 Coney Island Dr., Sparks, NV 89431-1990/702-331-5666; FAX: 702-331-5669
Rigby & Co., John, 66 Great Suffolk St., London SE1 OBU, ENGLAND (U.S. importer—Griffin & Howe, Inc.)
Riggs, Jim, 206 Azalea, Boerne, TX 78006/210-249-8567
Riling Arms Books Co., Ray, 6844 Gorsten St., P.O. Box 18925, Philadelphia, PA 19119/215-438-2456
Ringler Custom Leather Co., P.O. Box 206, Cody, WY 82414/307-645-3255
R.I.S. Co., Inc., 718 Timberlake Circle, Richardson, TX 75080/214-235-0933
River Road Sporting Clays, Bruce Barsotti, P.O. Box 3016, Gonzales, CA 93926/408-675-2473
Rizzini Battista, Via 2 Giugno 7/7Bis-25060 Marcheno (Brescia), ITALY
Rizzini, F.LLI (See U.S. importer—Moore & Co. Wm. Larkin)
RLCM Enterprises, 110 Hill Crest Drive, Burleson, TX 76028
RMS Custom Gunsmithing, 4120 N. Bitterwell, Prescott Valley, AZ 86314/602-772-7626
Robar Co.'s, Inc., The, 21438 N. 7th Ave., Suite B, Phoenix, AZ 85027/602-581-2648; FAX: 602-582-0059
Robbins Scent, Inc., P.O. Box 779, Connellsville, PA 15425/412-628-2529; FAX: 412-628-9598
Roberts Jr., William A., Rt. 14, P.O. Box 75, Athens, AL 35611/205-232-7027
Roberts Products, 25238 SE 32nd, Issaquah, WA 98027/206-392-8172
Roberts, J.J., 7808 Lake Dr., Manassas, VA 22111/703-330-0448
Robinson Firearms Mfg. Ltd., RR2, Suite 51, Comp. 24, Winfield, B.C. CANADA V0H 2C0/604-766-5353
Robinson, Don, Pennsylvania Hse., 36 Fairfax Crescent, Southowram, Halifax, W. Yorkshire HX3 9SQ, ENGLAND/0422-364458
Rochester Lead Works, 76 Anderson Ave., Rochester, NY 14607/716-442-8500
Rockwood Corp., Speedwell Division, 136 Lincoln Blvd., Middlesex, NJ 08846/908-560-7171
Rocky Fork Enterprises, P.O. Box 427, 878 Battle Rd., Nolensville, TN 37135/615-941-1307
Rocky Mountain Arms, Inc., 600 S. Sunset, Unit C, Longmont, CO 80501/303-768-8522; FAX: 303-678-8766
Rocky Mountain High Sports Glasses, 8121 N. Central Park Ave., Skokie, IL 60076/708-679-1012; FAX: 708-679-0184
Rocky Mountain Rifle Works Ltd., 1707 14th St., Boulder, CO 80302/303-443-9189
Rocky Mountain Target Co., 3 Aloe Way, Leesburg, FL 34788/904-365-9598
Rocky, Div. of Wm. Brooks Shoe Co., 294 Harper St., Nelsonville, OH 45764/614-753-1951; FAX: 614-753-4042
Rogers Gunsmithing, Bob, P.O. Box 305, 344 S. Walnut St., Franklin Grove, IL 61031/815-456-2685; FAX: 815-288-7142
Rohner, Hans and John, 710 Sunshine Canyon, Boulder, CO 80302/303-444-3841
Rolston Jr., Fred, 210 E. Cummins, Tecumseh, MI 49286/517-423-6002
Rooster Laboratories, P.O. Box 412514, Kansas City, MO 64141/816-474-1622; FAX: 816-474-1307
Rorschach Precision Products, P.O. Box 151613, Irving, TX 75015/214-790-3487
Rosenberg & Sons, Jack A., 12229 Cox Lane, Dallas, TX 75234/214-241-6302
Rosser, Bob, 142 Ramsey Dr., Albertville, AL 35950/205-878-5388
Rossi S.A. Metalurgica E Municoes, Amadeo, Rua Amadeo Rossi, 143, Sao Leopoldo, RS, BRAZIL 93 030/0512-92-5566 (U.S. importer—Interarms)
Roto Carve, 2754 Garden Ave., Janesville, IA 50647
Royal Arms, 5126 3rd Ave. N., Great Falls, MT 59401/406-453-1149
Royal Labs, Ltd., P.O. Box 2043, 710 Elm St., Truth or Consequences, NM 87901
Roy's Custom Grips, Rt. 3, Box 174-E, Lynchburg, VA 24504/804-385-6667
RPM, 15481 N. Twin Lakes Dr., Tucson, AZ 85737/602-825-1233; FAX: 602-825-3333
RSR Corp., 1111 West Mocking Bird Lane, Dallas, TX 75247
R-Tech Corp., P.O. Box 1281, Cottage Grove, OR 97424/503-942-5126; FAX: 503-942-8624
Rubright Bullets, 1008 S. Quince Rd., Walnutport, PA 18088/215-767-1339
Rucker Ammunition Co., P.O. Box 479, Terrell, TX 75160
Ruger (See Sturm, Ruger & Co.)
Ruko Products, Inc., 2245 Kenmore Ave., Suite 102, Buffalo, NY 14207/716-874-2707; FAX: 416-826-1353
Rundell's Gun Shop, 6198 Frances Rd., Clio, MI 48420/313-687-0559
Robert P. Runge, 94 Grove St., Ilion, NY 13357/315-894-3036
Rupert's Gun Shop, 2202 Dick Rd., Suite B, Fenwick, MI 48834/517-248-3252
Russell Knives, Inc., A.G., 1705 Hwy. 71 North, Springdale, AR 72764/501-751-7341
Russell's Rifle Shop, Rt. 5, P.O. Box 92, Georgetown, TX 78626/512-778-5338
Rusteprufe Laboratories, Robert D. Munger, 1319 Jefferson Ave., Sparta, WI 54656/608-269-4144
Rusty Duck Premium Gun Care Products, 7785 Founion Dr., Florence, KY 41042/606-342-5553
Rutgers Book Center, 127 Raritan Ave., Highland Park, NJ 08904/908-545-4344; FAX: 908-545-6686
Rutgers Gun & Boat Center, 127 Raritan Ave., Highland Park, NJ 08904/908-545-4344; FAX: 908-545-6686
Ruvel & Co., Inc., 4128-30 W. Belmont Ave., Chicago, IL 60641/312-286-9494
R.V.I., P.O. Box Q-1, 300 Boblett St., Blaine, WA 98230/206-595-2933
RWS (See U.S. importer—Dynamit Nobel-RWS, Inc.)
Ryan, Chad L., RR 3, Box 72, Cresco, IA 52136/319-547-4384
Rybka Custom Leather Equipment, Thad, 32 Havilah Hill, Odenville, AL 35120

## S

S&B Industries, 11238 McKinley Rd., Montrose, MI 48457/313-639-5491
S&H Arms Mfg. Co., Rt. 3, Box 689, Berryville, AR 72616/501-545-3511
S&K Mfg. Co., P.O. Box 247, Pittsfield, PA 16340/814-563-7808; FAX: 814-563-7808
S&S Firearms, 74-11 Myrtle Ave., Glendale, NY 11385/718-497-1100
SAECO (See Redding Reloading, Inc.)
Safari Arms/SGW (See Olympic Arms, Inc.)
Safari Gun Co., 6410 Brandon Ave., Springfield, VA 22150/703-569-1097
Safari Outfitters Ltd., 71 Ethan Allan Hwy., Ridgefield, CT 06877/203-544-9505
Safari Press, Inc., 15621 Chemical Lane B, Huntington Beach, CA 92649/714-894-9080; FAX: 714-894-4949
Safariland Ltd., Inc., 3120 E. Mission Blvd., P.O. Box 51478, Ontario, CA 91761/714-923-7300; FAX: 714-923-7400
S.A.F.E., P.O. Box 864, Post Falls, ID 83854/208-773-3624
Safesport Manufacturing Co., 1100 W. 45th Ave., Denver, CO 80211/303-433-6506; FAX: 303-433-4112
Safety Direct, 56 Coney Island Dr., Sparks, NV 89431/702-354-4451
Safety Speed Holster, Inc., 910 S. Vail Ave., Montebello, CA 90640/213-723-4140; FAX: 213-726-6973
Sako Ltd., P.O. Box 149, SF-11101, Riihimaki, FINLAND (U.S. importer—Stoeger Industries)
Salter Calls, Inc., Eddie, Hwy. 31 South-Brewton Industrial Park, Brewton, AL 36426/205-867-2584; FAX: 206-867-9005

Samco Global Arms, Inc., 6995 NW 43rd St., Miami, FL 33166/305-593-9782
Sampson, Roger, 430 N. Grove, Mora, MN 55051/612-679-4868
San Angelo Sports Products, Inc., 909 W. 14th St., San Angelo, TX 76903/915-655-7126; FAX: 915-653-6720
San Francisco Gun Exchange, 124 Second St., San Francisco, CA 94105/415-982-6097
San Marco (See U.S. importer—Cape Outfitters)
Sanders Custom Gun Service, 2358 Tyler Ln., Louisville, KY 40205/502-454-3338
Sanders Gun and Machine Shop, 145 Delhi Road, Manchester, IA 52057
Sandia Die & Ctg. Co., 37 Atancacio Rd. NE, Albuquerque, NM 87123/505-298-5729
Sandy's Custom Gunshop, Rt. 1, P.O. Box 4, Rockport, IL 62370/217-437-4241
Sarco, Inc., 323 Union St., Stirling, NJ 07980/908-647-3800
Sardius Industries Ltd., 72 Rokach St., Ramat Gan, ISRAEL 52542/972-3-7521353
Sauer (See U.S. importers—G.U., Inc.; Simmons Enterprises, Ernie)
Sauer Sporting Rifles, P.O. Box 37669, Omaha, NE 68137
Saunders Gun & Machine Shop, R.R. 2, Delhi Road, Manchester, IA 52057
Savage Arms, Inc., Springdale Rd., Westfield, MA 01085/413-568-7001; FAX: 413-562-7764
Savana Sports, Inc., 5763 Ferrier St., Montreal, Quebec, CANADA/514-739-1753; FAX: 514-739-1755
Scanco Environmental Systems, 5000 Highlands Parkway, Suite 180, Atlanta, GA 30082/404-431-0025; FAX: 404-431-0028
Scansport, Inc., P.O. Box 700, Enfield, NH 03748/603-632-7654
Scattergun Technologies, Inc., 518 3rd Ave. S., Nashville, TN 37210/615-254-1441
Sceery Co., E.J., 2308 Cedros Circle, Sante Fe, NM 87505/505-983-2125
Schaefer Shooting Sports, 2280 Grand Ave., Baldwin, NY 11510/516-379-4900; FAX: 516-379-6701
Schaefer, Roy V., 101 Irving Rd., Eugene, OR 97404/503-688-4333
Scharch Mfg., Inc., 10325 Co. Rd. 120, Unit C, Salida, CO 81201/719-539-7242
Scherer, Box 250, Ewing, VA 24248/615-733-2615; FAX: 615-733-2073
Schiffman, Curt, 3017 Kevin Cr., Idaho Falls, ID 83402/208-524-4684
Schiffman, Mike, 8233 S. Crystal Springs, McCammon, ID 83250/208-254-9114
Schiffman, Norman, 3017 Kevin Cr., Idaho Falls, ID 83402/208-524-4684
Schmidpke, Karl, P.O. Box 51692, New Berlin, WI 53151
Schmidt & Bender (See Jaeger, Inc., Paul/Dunn's)
Schmidt, Herbert (See U.S. importer—Sportarms of Florida)
Schmidtman Custom Ammunition, 6 Gilbert Court, Cotati, CA 94931
Schneider Bullets, 3655 West 214th St., Fairview Park, OH 44126
Schneider Rifle Barrels, Inc., Gary, 12202 N. 62nd Pl., Scottsdale, AZ 85254/602-948-2525
Schrade Cutlery Corp., Rt. 209 North, Ellenville, NY 12428/914-647-7600
Schrimsher's Custom Knifemaker's Supply, Bob, P.O. Box 308, Emory, TX 75440/903-473-3330; FAX: 903-473-2235
Schulz Industries, 16247 Minnesota Ave., Paramount, CA 90723/213-439-5903
Schumakers Gun Shop, William, 512 Prouty Corner Lp. A, Colville, WA 99114/509-684-4848
Schwartz Custom Guns, David W., 2505 Waller St., Eau Claire, WI 54703/715-832-1735
Schwartz Custom Guns, Wayne E., 970 E. Britton Rd., Morrice, MI 48857/517-625-4079
Scobey Duck & Goose Calls, Glynn, Rt. 3, Box 37, Newbern, TN 38059/901-643-6241
Scot Powder Co., 1200 Talley Road, Wilmington, DE 19809/302-764-9779
Scot Powder Co of Ohio, Inc., 430 Powder Plant Rd., McArthur, OH 45651/614-596-2706; FAX: 614-596-4050
Scotch Hunting Products Co., Inc., 6619 Oak Orchard Rd., Elba, NY 14058/716-757-9958; FAX: 716-757-9066
Scott Fine Guns, Inc., Thad, P.O. Box 412, Indianola, MS 38751/601-887-5929
Scott, Inc., Tyler, 313 Rugby Ave., Terrace Park, OH 45174/513-831-7603
Scott/McDougall Custom Gunsmiths, 880 Piner Rd., Suite 50, Santa Rosa, CA 95403/707-546-2264
S.C.R.C., P.O. Box 660, Kary, TX 77492-0660/713-492-6332; FAX: 713-578-3134
Scruggs' Game Calls, Stanley, Rt. 1, Hwy. 661, Cullen, VA 23934/804-542-4241, 800-323-4828
Seattle Binocular & Scope Repair Co., P.O. Box 46094, Seattle, WA 98146/206-932-3733
Second Chance Body Armor, P.O. Box 578, Central Lake, MI 49622/616-544-5721; FAX: 616-544-9824
Security Awareness & Firearms Education (See S.A.F.E.)
Seebeck Assoc., R.E., P.O. Box 59752, Dallas, TX 75229
Seecamp Co., Inc., L.W., P.O. Box 255, New Haven, CT 06502/203-877-3429
Seligman Shooting Products, Box 133, Seligman, AZ 86337/602-422-3607
Selsi Co., Inc., 40 Veterans Blvd., Carlstadt, NJ 07072-0497/201-935-5851
Semmer, Charles, 7885 Cyd Dr., Denver, CO 80221/303-429-6947
Service Armament, 689 Bergen Blvd., Ridgefield, NJ 07657
Servus Footwear Co., 1136 2nd St., Rock Island, IL 61204-3610/309-786-7741; FAX: 309-786-9808
SGS Importers International, Inc., 1907 Hwy. 35, Ocean, NJ 07712/908-531-9424; FAX: 908-531-1520
S.G.S. Sporting Guns Srl., F1 Milanofiori, Assago, 20090 ITALY/2-8241144-5; FAX: 2-8254644
Shane's Gunsmithing, P.O. Box 321, Hwy. 51 S., Minocqua, WI 54548/715-356-5414
Shappy Bullets, 76 Milldale Ave., Plantsville, CT 06479/203-621-3704
Sharon Rifle Barrel Co., 14396 D. Tuolumne Rd., Sonora, CA 95370/209-532-4139
Sharps Arms Co., Inc., C. (See Montana Armory, Inc.)
Shaw's Finest in Guns, 1255 N. Broadway 351, Escondido, CA 92026-2858
Shaw, Inc., E.R. (See Small Arms Mfg. Co.)
Shay's Gunsmithing, 931 Marvin Ave., Lebanon, PA 17042
Sheffield Knifemakers Supply, P.O. Box 141, Deland, FL 32721/904-775-6453; FAX: 904-774-5754
Shell Shack, 113 E. Main, Laurel, MT 59044/406-628-8986
Shepherd Scope Ltd., Box 189, Waterloo, NE 68069/402-779-2424; FAX: 402-779-4010
Sheridan Products, Inc. (See Benjamin/Sheridan Co.)
Sheridan USA, Inc., Austin, P.O. Box 577, Durham, CT 06422
Sherk, Dan A., 1311-105 Ave., Dawson Creek, B.C. V1G 2L9, CANADA/604-782-3720
Sherwood Intl. Export Corp., 18714 Parthenia St., Northridge, CA 91324/818-349-7600
Sherwood, George, 46 N. River Dr., Roseburg, OR 97470/503-672-3159
Shilen Rifles, Inc., P.O. Box 1300, 205 Metro Park Blvd., Ennis, TX 75119/214-875-5318; FAX: 214-875-1442
Shiloh Rifle Mfg., 201 Centennial Dr., Big Timber, MT 59011/406-932-4454; FAX: 406-932-5627
Shirley Co. Gun & Riflemakers Ltd., J.A., P.O. Box 368, High Wycombe, Bucks. HP13 6YN, ENGLAND/0494-446883; FAX: 0494-463685
Shockley, Harold H., 204 E. Farmington Rd., Hanna City, IL 61536/309-565-4524
Shoemaker & Sons, Inc., Tex, 714 W. Cienega Ave., San Dimas, CA 91750/714-592-2071; FAX: 714-592-2378
Shooter Shop, The, 221 N. Main, Butte, MT 59701/406-723-3842
Shooter's Choice, 16770 Hilltop Park Place, Chagrin Falls, OH 44022/216-543-8808; FAX: 216-543-8811
Shooter's Edge, Inc., P.O.Box 769, Trinidad, CO 81082
Shooter's World, 3828 N. 28th Ave., Phoenix, AZ 85017/602-266-0170
Shooters Accessory Supply (See Corbin, Inc.)
Shooters Supply, 1120 Tieton Dr., Yakima, WA 98902/509-452-1181
Shootin Accessories, Ltd., P.O. Box 6810, Auburn, CA 95604/916-889-2220
Shootin' Shack, Inc., 1065 Silver Beach Rd., Riviera Beach, FL 33403/407-842-0990
Shooting Arts Ltd., Box 621399, Littleton, CO 80162/303-933-2539
Shooting Chrony, Inc., P.O. Box 101 LP, Niagara Falls, NY 14304/416-276-6292; FAX: 416-276-6295
Shooting Gallery, The, 8070 Southern Blvd., Boardman, OH 44512/216-726-7788

Shooting Specialties (See Titus, Daniel)
Shotgun Shop, The, 14145 Proctor Ave., Suite 3, Industry, CA 91746/818-855-2737; FAX: 818-855-2735
Shotguns Unlimited, 2307 Fon Du Lac Rd., Richmond, VA 23229/804-752-7115
Shurkatch Corp., P.O. Box 850, Richfield Springs, NY 13439/315-858-1470; FAX: 315-858-2969
Siegrist Gun Shop, 8754 Turtle Road, Whittemore, MI 48770
Sierra Bullets, 1400 W. Henry St., Sedalia, MO 65301/816-827-6300; FAX: 816-827-4999
Sierra Specialty Prod. Co., 1344 Oakhurst Ave., Los Altos, CA 94024
SIG, CH-8212 Neuhausen, SWITZERLAND (U.S. importer—Mandall Shooting Supplies, Inc.)
SIG-Sauer (See U.S. importer—Sigarms, Inc.)
Sigarms, Inc., Industrial Drive, Exeter, NH 03833/603-772-2302; FAX: 603-772-9082
Sight Shop, The, John G. Lawson, 1802 E. Columbia Ave., Tacoma, WA 98404/206-474-5465
Sile Distributors, Inc., 7 Centre Market Pl., New York, NY 10013/212-925-4389; FAX: 212-925-3149
Silencio (See Safety Direct)
Silent Hunter, 1100 Newton Ave., W. Collingswood, NJ 08107/609-854-3276
Siler Locks, 7 Acton Woods Rd., Candler, NC 28715/704-667-9991
Silhouette Leathers, P.O. Box 1161, Gunnison, CO 81230/303-641-6639
Silver Eagle Machining, 18007 N. 69th Ave., Glendale, AZ 85308
Silver Ridge Gun Shop (See Goodwin, Fred)
Silver-Tip Corp., Rt. 1, Box 211-C, Liberty, MS 39645/601-384-5830
Simmons Enterprises, Ernie, 709 East Elizabethtown Rd., Manheim, PA 17545/717-664-4040
Simmons, Jerry, 715 Middlebury St., Goshen, IN 46526/219-533-8546
Simmons Outdoor Corp., 2571 Executive Ctr. Circle E, Tallahassee, FL 32301/904-878-5100; FAX: 904-878-0300
Sinclair, Fred, 2330 Wayne Haven St., Fort Wayne, IN 46803/219-493-1858
Sinclair International, Inc., 2330 Wayne Haven St., Fort Wayne, IN 46803/219-493-1858; FAX: 219-493-2530
Sinclair, W.P., Box 1209, Warminster, Wiltshire BA12 9XJ, ENGLAND/01044-985-218544; FAX: 01044-985-214111
Single Shot, Inc. (See Montana Armory, Inc.)
Singletary, Kent, 7516 W. Sells, Phoenix, AZ 85033/602-789-6004
Sioux Bullets, P.O. Box 3696, Midland, TX 79702
Sipes Gun Shop, 7415 Asher Ave., Little Rock, AR 72204/501-565-8480
Siskiyou Gun Works (See Donnelly, C.P.)
Six Enterprises, 320-D Turtle Creek Ct., San Jose, CA 95125/408-999-0201; FAX: 408-999-0216
Skaggs, R.E., P.O. Box 34, 1217 S. Church, Princeton, IL 61356/815-875-8207
SKB Arms Co., C.P.O. Box 1401, Tokyo, JAPAN (U.S. importers—G.U., Inc.; Hanus Birdguns, Bill; Simmons Enterprises, Ernie)
S.K. Guns, Inc., 3041A Main Ave., Fargo, ND 58103/701-293-4867; FAX: 701-232-0001
Skeoch, Brian R., P.O. Box 279, Glenrock, WY 82637/307-436-9804
Skip's Machine, 364 29 Road, Grand Junction, CO 81501/303-245-5417
Sklany, Steve, 566 Birch Grove Dr., Kalispell, MT 59901/406-755-4257
SKR Industries, POB 1382, San Angelo, TX 76902/915-658-3133
S.L.A.P. Industries, P.O. Box 1121, Parklands 2121, SOUTH AFRICA
Slezak, Jerome F., 1290 Marlowe, Lakewood (Cleveland), OH 44107/216-221-1668
Slings & Arrows, RD 1, Box 91A, Barnet, VT 05821/802-633-3314; FAX: 802-684-1108
Slings 'N Things, Inc., 8909 Bedford Circle, Suite 11, Omaha, NE 68134/402-571-6954; FAX: 402-571-7082
Slipshot MTS Group, P.O. Box 5, Postal Station D, Etobicoke, Ont., CANADA M9A 4X1/FAX: 416-762-0962
Slug Site Co., Ozark Wilds, Rt. 2, Box 158, Versailles, MO 65084/314-378-6430
Small Arms Mfg. Co., 611 Thoms Run Rd., Bridgeville, PA 15017/412-221-4343; FAX: 412-221-8443
Small Custom Mould & Bullet Co., Box 17211, Tucson, AZ 85731
Small Group Bullets, P.O. Box 20, Mertzon, TX 76941/915-835-4751
Smires, Clifford L., 28269 Old Schoolhouse Rd., Columbus, NJ 08022/609-298-3158
Smith & Wesson, 2100 Roosevelt Ave., Springfield, MA 01102/413-781-8300
Smith Saddlery, Jesse W., N. 1325 Division, Spokane, WA 99202/509-325-0622
Smith Whetstone Co., Inc., 1700 Sleepy Valley Rd., P.O. Box 5095, Hot Springs, AR 71902-5095/501-321-2244; FAX: 501-321-9232
Smith, Art, 4124 Thrushwood Lane, Minnetonka, MN 55345/612-935-7829
Smith, Mark A., 200 N. 9th, Sinclair, WY 82334/307-324-7929
Smith, Michael, 620 Nye Circle, Chattanooga, TN 37405/615-267-8341
Smith, Ron, 5869 Straley, Ft. Worth, TX 76114/817-732-6768
Smokey Valley Rifles (See Lutz Engraving, Ron)
Snapp's Gunshop, 6911 E. Washington Rd., Clare, MI 48617/517-386-9226
Snider Stocks, Walter S., Rt. 2 P.O. Box 147, Denton, NC 27239
Sno-Seal (See Atsko, Sno-Seal)
Societa Armi Bresciane Srl., Via Artigiani 93, Gardone Val Trompia, ITALY 25063/30-8911640, 30-8911648
Solothurn (See U.S. importer—Sile Distributors)
Sonderman, Robert, 735 Kenton Dr., Charleston, IL 61920/217-345-5429
Soque River Knives, P.O. Box 880, Clarkesville, GA 30523/706-754-8500
SOS Products Co. (See Buck Stix—SOS Products Co.)
Sotheby's, 1334 York Ave. at 72nd St., New York, NY 10021
Sound Technology, P.O. Box 1132, Kodiak, AK 99615/907-486-8448
South Bend Replicas, Inc., 61650 Oak Rd., South Bend, IN 46614/219-289-4500
South Central Research Corp. (See S.C.R.C.)
Southeastern Community College, 1015 S. Gear Ave., West Burlington, IA 52655/319-752-2731
Southern Ammunition Co., Inc., Rt. 1, Box 6B, Latta, SC 29565/803-752-7751; FAX: 803-752-2022
Southern Armory, The, Rt. 2, Box 134, Woodlawn, VA 24381/703-236-7835; FAX: 703-236-3714
Southern Bloomer Mfg. Co., P.O. Box 1621, Bristol, TN 37620/615-878-6660
Southwest Institute of Firearms Training (See S.W.I.F.T.)
Southwind Sanctions, P.O. Box 445, Aledo, TX 76008/817-441-8917
Sparks, Milt, 605 E. 44th St. No. 2, Boise, ID 83714-4800
Specialized Weapons, Inc. (See Tapco, Inc.)
Specialty Gunsmithing, Lynn McMurdo, P.O. Box 404, Afton, WY 83110/307-886-5535
Specialty Shooters Supply, Inc., 3325 Griffin Rd., Suite 9mm, Fort Lauderdale, FL 33317
Speedfeed, Inc., P.O. Box 258, Lafayette, CA 94549/510-284-2929; FAX: 510-284-2879
Speer Products, Div. of Blount, Inc., P.O. Box 856, Lewiston, ID 83501/208-746-2351
Spegel, Craig, P.O. Box 108, Bay City, OR 97107/503-377-2697
Speiser, Fred D., 2229 Dearborn, Missoula, MT 59801/406-549-8133
Spence, George W., 115 Locust St., Steele, MO 63877/314-695-4916
Spencer Reblue Service, 1820 Tupelo Trail, Holt, MI 48842/517-694-7474
SPG Lubricants, Box 761-H, Livingston, MT 59047
Sphinx Engineering SA, Ch. des Grandes-Vies 2, CH-2900 Porrentruy, SWITZERLAND/41 66 66 73 81; FAX: 41 66 66 30 90
SPI, 215 Poppleton St., Birmingham, MI 48009-5725
Spokhandguns, Inc., 1206 Fig St., Benton City, WA 99320/509-588-5255
Sport Flite Manufacturing Co., P.O. Box 1082, Bloomfield Hills, MI 48303/313-647-3747
Sport Specialties (See Owen, Harry)
Sportarms of Florida, 5555 NW 36 Ave., Miami, FL 33142/305-635-2411; FAX: 305-634-4536
Sporting Arms Mfg., Inc., 801 Hall Ave., Littlefield, TX 79339/806-385-5665; FAX: 806-385-3394

Sports Innovations, Inc., P.O. Box 5181, 8505 Jacksboro Hwy., Wichita Falls, TX 76307/817-723-6015
Sports Support Systems, Inc., 28416 Pacheco, Mission Viejo, CA 92692/714-367-0343
Sportsman Supply Co., 714 East Eastwood, P.O. Box 650, Marshall, MO 65340/816-886-9393
Sportsman's Communicators, 588 Radcliffe Ave., Pacific Palisades, CA 90272/800-538-3752
Sportsmatch Ltd., 16 Summer St., Leighton Buzzard, Bedfordshire, LU7 8HT ENGLAND/0525-381638; FAX: 0525-851236
Sportsmen's Exchange & Western Gun Traders, Inc., 560 S. "C" St., Oxnard, CA 93030/805-483-1917
Spradlin's, 113 Arthur St., Pueblo, CO 81004/719-543-9462
Springfield, Inc., 25144 Ridge Rd., Colona, IL 61241/309-441-6002; FAX: 309-441-6003
Springfield Sporters, Inc., RD 1, Penn Run, PA 15765/412-254-2626; FAX: 412-254-9173
Spyderco, Inc., P.O. Box 800, Golden, CO 80402/800-525-7770
SSK Co., 220 N. Belvidere Ave., York, PA 17404/717-854-2897
SSK Industries, 721 Woodvue Lane, Wintersville, OH 43952/614-264-0176; FAX: 614-264-2257
St. Lawrence Sales, Inc., 12 W. Fint St., Lake Orion, MI 48035/313-693-7760; 313-693-7718
Stackpole Books, P.O. Box 1831, Harrisburg, PA 17105/717-234-5041; FAX: 717-234-1359
Stafford Bullets, 1920 Tustin Ave., Philadelphia, PA 19152
Stalker, Inc., P.O. Box 21, Fishermans Wharf Rd., Malakoff, TX 75148/903-489-1010
Stalwart Corp., P.O. Box 357, Pocatello, ID 83204/208-232-7899
Stanley Bullets, 2085 Heatheridge Ln., Reno, NV 89509
Star Bonifacio Echeverria S.A., Torrekva 3, Eibar, SPAIN 20600/43-117340; FAX: 43-111524 (U.S. importer—Interarms)
Star Custom Bullets, P.O. Box 608, 468 Main St., Ferndale, CA 95536/707-786-4040; FAX: 707-786-9117
Star Machine Works, 418 10th Ave., San Diego, CA 92101/619-232-3216
Star Reloading Co., Inc., 5520 Rock Hampton Ct., Indianapolis, IN 46268/317-872-5840
Stark's Bullet Mfg., 2580 Monroe St., Eugene, OR 97405
Starlight Training Center, Inc., Rt. 1, P.O. Box 88, Bronaugh, MO 64728/417-843-3555
Starnes, Ken, 32900 SW Laurelview Rd., Hillsboro, OR 97123/503-628-0705
Starrett Co., L.S., 121 Crescent St., Athol, MA 01331/617-249-3551
Starshot Holduxa, Bolognise 125, Miraflores, Lima PERU
State Arms Gun Co., 815 S. Division St., Waunakee, WI 53597/608-849-5800
Steel Reloading Components Inc., P.O. Box 812, Washington, IN 47501/812-254-3775; FAX: 812-254-7269
Steelman's Gun Shop, 10465 Beers Rd., Swartz Creek, MI 48473/313-735-4884
Steffens, Ron, 18396 Mariposa Creek Rd., Willits, CA 95490/707-485-0873
Stegall, James B., 26 Forest Rd., Wallkill, NY 12589
Steger, James R., 1131 Dorsey Pl., Plainfield, NJ 07062
Steves House of Guns, Rt. 1, Minnesota City, MN 55959/507-689-2573
Stevi Machine, Inc., 4004 Hwy. 93 North, Stevensville, MT 59870/406-777-5401
Stewart Game Calls, Inc., Johnny, P.O. Box 7954, 5100 Fort Ave., Waco, TX 76714/817-772-3261
Stewart's Gunsmithing, P.O. Box 5854, Pietersburg North 0750, Transvaal, SOUTH AFRICA/01521-89401
Steyr Mannlicher AG, Mannlicherstrasse 1, P.O.B. 1000, A-4400 Steyr, AUSTRIA/0043-7252-67331; FAX: 0043-7252-68621 (U.S. importer—GSI, Inc.)
Steyr-Daimler-Puch, Schonauerstrasse 5, A-4400 Steyr AUSTRIA (U.S. importer—GSI, Inc.)
Stoeger Industries, 55 Ruta Ct., S. Hackensack, NJ 07606/201-440-2700, 800-631-0722; FAX: 201-440-2707
Stoeger Publishing Co. (See Stoeger Industries)
Stone Enterprises Ltd., Rt. 609, P.O. Box 335, Wicomico Church, VA 22579/804-580-5114; FAX: 804-580-8421
Stoney Baroque Shooters Supply, John Richards, Rt. 2, Box 325, Bedford, KY 40006/502-255-7222
Stoney Point Products, Inc., 124 Stoney Point Rd., Courtland, MN 56021/507-354-3360; FAX: 507-354-7236
Storey, Dale A. (See DGS, Inc.)
Stott's Creek Armory, Inc., RR1, Box 70, Morgantown, IN 46160/317-878-5489
Stratco, Inc., 200 E. Center St., Kalispell, MT 59901/406-755-4034; FAX: 406-257-4753
Strawbridge, Victor W., 6 Pineview Dr., Dover, NH 03820/603-742-0013
Streamlight, Inc., 1030 W. Germantown Pike, Norristown, PA 19403/215-631-0600
Strong Holster Co., 105 Maplewood Ave., Gloucester, MA 01930/508-281-3300; FAX: 508-281-6321
Stroup, Earl R., 30506 Flossmoor Way, Hayward, CA 94544/415-471-1549
Strutz Rifle Barrels, Inc., W.C., P.O. Box 611, Eagle River, WI 54521/715-479-4766
Stuart Products, Inc., P.O. Box 1587, Easley, SC 29641/803-859-9360
Stuart, V. Pat, Rt. 1, Box 242-B, P.O. Box 232, Weyers Cave, VA 24486/703-234-0816
Sturm, Ruger & Co., Inc., Lacey Place, Southport, CT 06490/203-259-7843
Su-Press-On, Inc., P.O. Box 09161, Detroit, MI 48209/313-842-4222 7:30-11p.m. Mon-Thurs.
Summit Specialties, Inc., P.O. Box 786, Decatur, AL 35602/205-353-0634
Sundance Industries, Inc., 25163 W. Avenue Stanford, Valencia, CA 91355/805-257-4807
Sun Jammer Products, Inc., 9600 N. IH-35, Austin, TX 78753/512-837-8696
Sun Welding Safe Co., 290 Easy St. No.3, Simi Valley, CA 93065/805-584-6678
Super Vel, Hamilton Rd., Rt. 2, P.O. Box 1398, Fond du Lac, WI 54935
Sure Shot of LA, Inc., 103 Coachman Dr., Houma, LA 70360/504-876-6709
Sure-Shot Game Calls, Inc., P.O. Box 816, 6835 Capitol, Groves, TX 77619/409-962-1636; FAX: 409-962-5465
Survival Arms, Inc., 4500 Pine Cone Place, Cocoa, FL 32922/407-633-4880; FAX: 407-633-4975
Survival Books, The Larder, 11106 Magnolia Blvd., North Hollywood, CA 91601/818-763-0804
Svon Corp., 280 Eliot St., Ashland, MA 01721/508-881-8852
Swampfire Shop, The (See Peterson Gun Shop, Inc., A.W.)
Swann, D.J., 5 Orsova Close, Eltham North, Vic. 3095, AUSTRALIA/03-431-0323
Swanndri New Zealand, 152 Elm Ave., Burlingame, CA 94010/415-347-6158
SwaroSports, Inc. (See JägerSports, Ltd.)
Swarovski Optik North America Ltd., One Wholesale Way, Cranston, RI 02920/401-946-2220; FAX: 800-426-3089
Sweet Home, Inc., P.O. Box 900, Orrville, OH 44667-0900
Swenson's 45 Shop, A.D., P.O. Box 606, Fallbrook, CA 92028
S.W.I.F.T., 4610 Blue Diamond Rd., Las Vegas, NV 89118/702-897-1100
Swift Bullet Co., P.O. Box 27, 201 Main St., Quinter, KS 67752/913-754-3959; FAX: 913-754-2359
Swift Instruments, Inc., 952 Dorchester Ave., Boston, MA 02125/617-436-2960; FAX: 617-436-3232
Swift River Gunworks, Inc., 450 State St., Belchertown, MA 01007/413-323-4052
Swiss Army Knives, Inc., 151 Long Hill Crossroads, 37 Canal St., Shelton, CT 06484/800-243-4032
Swivel Machine Works, Inc., 167 Cherry St., Suite 286, Milford, CT 06460/203-926-1840; FAX: 203-726-9431
Szweda, Robert (See RMS Custom Gunsmithing)

## T

3-D Ammunition & Bullets, 112 W. Plum St., P.O. Box J, Doniphan, NE 68832/402-845-2285; FAX: 402-845-6546
3-Ten Corp., P.O. Box 269, Feeding Hills, MA 01030/413-789-2086
10-X Products Group, 2915 Lyndon B. Johnson Freeway, Suite 133, Dallas, TX 75234/214-243-4016
300 Gunsmith Service, Inc., 6850 S. Yosemite Ct., Englewood, CO 80112/303-773-0300
Tabler Marketing, 2554 Lincoln Blvd. 555, Marina Del Rey, CA 90291-5082/818-366-7485; FAX: 818-831-3441
TacTell, Inc., P.O. Box 5654, Maryville, TN 37802/615-982-7855
Tactical Training Center, 574 Miami Bluff Ct., Loveland, OH 45140/513-677-8229
Talley, Dave, P.O. Box 821, Glenrock, WY 82637/307-436-8724
Talmage, William G., RR16, Box 102A, Brazil, IN 47834/812-442-0804
Tamarack Prods.,Inc., P.O. Box 625, Wauconda, IL 60084/708-526-9333
Tanfoglio S.r.l., Fratelli, via Valtrompia 39, 41, 25068 Gardone V.T., Brescia, ITALY/30-8910361; FAX: 30-8910183 (U.S. importer—E.A.A. Corp.)
Tanglefree Industries, 16102 Duggans Rd., Grass Valley, CA 95949
Tank's Rifle Shop, 1324 Ohio St., P.O. Box 474, Fremont, NE 68025/402-727-1317
Tanner (See U.S. importer—Mandall Shooting Supplies, Inc.)
Tapco, Inc., P.O. Box 546, Smyrna, GA 30081/404-435-9782, 800-359-6195; FAX: 404-333-9798
Taracorp Industries, Inc., 16th & Cleveland Blvd., Granite City, IL 62040/618-451-4400
Targot Man, Inc., 49 Gerald Dr., Manchester, CT 06040/203-646-8335; FAX: 203-646-8335
Tasco Sales, Inc., 7600 NW 84th Ave., Miami, FL 33122/305-591-3670; FAX: 305-592-5895
Taurus Firearms, Inc., 16175 NW 49th Ave., Miami, FL 33014/305-624-1115; FAX: 305-623-7506
Taurus International Firearms (See U.S. importer—Taurus Firearms, Inc.)
Taurus, S.A., Forjas, Avenida Do Forte 511, Porto Alegre, BRAZIL 91360/55 512-40 22 44
Taylor & Robbins, P.O. Box 164, Rixford, PA 16745/814-966-3233
Taylor's & Co., Inc., 299 Broad Ave., Winchester, VA 22602/703-722-2017; FAX: 703-722-2018
TCCI. P.O. Box 302, Phoenix, AZ 85001/602-237-3823; FAX: 602-237-3858
TDP Industries, Inc., 603 Airport Blvd., Doylestown, PA 18901/215-345-8687
Techni-Mec, Via Gitti s.n., 25060 Marcheno, ITALY
Tecnolegno S.p.A., Via A. Locatelli, 6, 10, 24019 Zogno, ITALY/0345-91114; FAX: 0345-93254
Tele-Optics, 5514 W. Lawrence Ave., Chicago, IL 60630/312-283-7757
Tele-Optics, Inc., P.O. Box 176, 219 E. Higgins Rd., Gilberts, IL 60136/708-426-7444
Teledyne Co., 290 E. Prairie St., Crystal Lake, IL 60014
Ten-Ring Precision, Inc., 1449 Blue Crest Lane, San Antonio, TX 78232/512-494-3063; FAX: 512-494-3066
Tennessee Valley Mfg., P.O. Box 1175, Corinth, MS 38834/601-286-5014
Tepeco, P.O. Box 342, Friendswood, TX 77546/713-482-2702
Testing Systems, Inc., 220 Pegasus Ave., Northvale, NJ 07647
TETRA Gun Lubricants, 1812 Margaret Ave., Annapolis, MD 21401/410-268-6451; FAX: 410-268-8377
Texas Arms, P.O. Box 154906, Waco, TX 76715/817-776-5294
Texas Longhorn Arms, Inc., 5959 W. Loop South, Suite 424, Bellaire, TX 77401/713-660-6323; FAX: 713-660-0493
Texas Platers Supply, 2453 W. Five Mile Parkway, Dallas, TX 75233/214-330-7168
T.F.C. S.p.A., Via G. Marconi 118, B, Villa Carcina, Brescia 25069, ITALY/030-881271; FAX: 030-881826
Theis, Terry, P.O. Box 535, Fredericksburg, TX 78624/512-997-6778
Theoben Engineering (See U.S. importer—Air Rifle Specialists)
Thiewes, George W., 1846 Allen Lane, St. Charles, IL 60174/708-584-1383
Things Unlimited, 235 N. Kimbau, Casper, WY 82601/307-234-5277
Thirion Hand Engraving, Denise, P.O. Box 408, Graton, CA 95444/707-829-1876
Thomas, Charles C., 2600 S. First St., Springfield, IL 62794/217-789-8980; FAX: 217-789-9130
Thompson Bullet Lube Co., P.O. Box 472343, Garland, TX 75047/214-271-8063; FAX: 214-840-6743
Thompson Precision, 110 Mary St., P.O. Box 251, Warren, IL 61087/815-745-3625
Thompson Target Technology, 618 Roslyn Ave., SW, Canton, OH 44710/216-453-7707; FAX: 216-478-4723
Thompson, Norm, 18905 NW Thurman St., Portland, OR 97209
Thompson, Randall (See Highline Machine Co.)
Thompson/Center Arms, Farmington Rd., P.O. Box 5002, Rochester, NH 03867/603-332-2394
Threat Management Institute, 1 St. Francis Place 2801, San Francisco, CA 94107/415-777-0303
Thunder Mountain Arms, P.O. Box 593, Oak Harbor, WA 98277/206-679-4657; FAX: 206-675-1114
Thunderbird Cartridge Co., Inc., (See TCCI)
Thurston Sports, Inc., RD 3 Donovan Rd., Auburn, NY 13021/315-253-0966
Tiger-Hunt, Michael D. Barton, Box 379, Beaverdale, PA 15921/814-472-5161
Tikka (See U.S. importer—Stoeger Industries)
Tillinghast, James C., P.O. Box 405DG, Hancock, NH 03449/603-525-4049
Timber Heirloom Products, 618 Roslyn Ave. SW, Canton, OH 44710/216-453-7707; FAX: 216-478-4723
Timney Mfg., Inc., 3065 W. Fairmont Ave., Phoenix, AZ 85017/602-274-2999; FAX: 602-241-0361
Tink's Safariland Hunting Corp., P.O. Box 244, Madison, GA 30650/404-342-4915
Tinks & Ben Lee Hunting Products (See Wellington Outdoors)
Tioga Engineering Co., Inc., P.O. Box 913, 13 Cone St., Wellsboro, PA 16901/717-662-2730
Tippman Pneumatics, Inc., 3518 Adams Center Rd., Fort Wayne, IN 46806/219-749-6022; FAX: 219-749-6619
Tirelli, Snc Di Tirelli Primo E.C., Via Matteotti No. 359, Gardone V.T., Brescia, ITALY 25063/030-8912819; FAX: 030-832240
Titus, Daniel, Shooting Specialties, 872 Penn St., Bryn Mawr, PA 19010/215-525-8829
TMI Products, 930 S. Plumer Ave., Tucson, AZ 85719/602-792-1075; FAX: 602-792-0093
Tokarav (See U.S. importer—Sportarms of Florida)
Tom's Gun Repair, Thomas G. Ivanoff, 76-6 Rt. Southfork Rd., Cody, WY 82414/307-587-6949
Tom's Gunshop, 3601 Central Ave., Hot Springs, AR 71913/501-624-3856
Tomboy, Inc., P.O. Box 846, Dallas, OR 97338/503-623-8405
Tooley, David, 516 Creek Meadow Dr., Gastonia, NC 28054
Torel, Inc., 1053 N. South St., P.O. Box 592, Yoakum, TX 77995/512-293-2341; FAX: 512-293-3413
Totally Dependable Products (See TDP Industries, Inc.)
Track of the Wolf, Inc., P.O. Box 6, Osseo, MN 55369-0006/612-424-2500; FAX: 612-424-9860
Tradewinds, Inc., P.O. Box 1191, 2339-41 Tacoma Ave. S., Tacoma, WA 98401/206-272-4887
Traditions, P.O. Box 235, Deep River, CT 06417/203-526-9555; FAX: 203-526-4564
Trafalgar Square, P.O. Box 257, N. Pomfret, VT 05053/802-457-1911
Traft Gunshop, P.O. Box 1078, Buena Vista, CO 81211
Trail Guns Armory, Inc., 1422 E. Main St., League City, TX 77573/713-332-5833; FAX: 713-332-5833
Trail Timer Co., 1992-A Suburban Ave., P.O. Box 19722, St. Paul, MN 55119/612-738-0925

Trail Visions, 5800 N. Ames Terrace, Glendale, WI 53209/414-228-1328
Trammco, 839 Gold Run Rd., Boulder, CO 80302
Trappers Trading, P.O. Box 26946, Austin, TX 78755/800-788-9334
Trax America, Inc., P.O. Box 898, 1150 Eldridge, Forrest City, AR 72335/800-232-2327
Tread Corp., 1764 Granby St. NE, Roanoke, VA 24012/703-982-6881
Treemaster, P.O. Box 247, Guntersville, AL 35976/205-878-3597
Treso, Inc., P.O. Box 4640, Pagosa Springs, CO 81157/303-731-2295
Trevallion Gunstocks, 9 Old Mountain Rd., Cape Neddick, ME 03902/207-361-1130
Trico Plastics, 590 S. Vincent Ave., Azusa, CA 91702
Trijicon, Inc., P.O. Box 2130, Farmington Hills, MI 48333/313-553-4960; FAX: 313-553-6129
Trinidad State Junior College, Gunsmithing Dept., 600 Prospect St., Trinidad, CO 81082/719-846-5631; FAX: 719-846-5667
Triple-K Mfg. Co., Inc., 2222 Commercial St., San Diego, CA 92113/619-232-2066; FAX: 619-232-7675
Trius Traps, P.O. Box 25, 221 S. Miami Ave., Cleves, OH 45002/513-941-5682; FAX: 513-941-7970
Trophy Bonded Bullets, Inc., 900 S. Loop W., Suite 190, Houston, TX 77054/713-645-4499; FAX: 713-741-6393
Trotman, Ken, 135 Ditton Walk, Unit 11, Cambridge CB5 8QD, ENGLAND/0223-211030; FAX: 0223-212317
Tru-Balance Knife Co., 2155 Tremont Blvd. NW, Grand Rapids, MI 49504/616-453-3679
Tru-Square Metal Prods., Inc., 640 First St. SW, P.O. Box 585, Auburn, WA 98001/206-833-2310
True Flight Bullet Co., 5581 Roosevelt St., Whitehall, PA 18052/800-875-3625; FAX: 215-262-7806
Trulock Tool, Broad St., Whigham, GA 31797/912-762-4678
T.S.W. Conversions, Inc., E. 115 Crain Rd., Paramus, NJ 07650-4017/201-265-1618
Tucker, James C., P.O. Box 38790, Sacramento, CA 95838/916-923-0571
Turnbull Restoration, Doug, 6426 County Rd. 30, Holcomb, NY 14469/716-657-6338
Tuscano, Tony, P.O. Box 461, Wickliffe, OH 44092/216-943-1175
Twin Pine Armory, P.O. Box 58, Hwy. 6, Adna, WA 98522/206-748-4590; FAX: 205-748-7011
Tyler Mfg.-Dist., Melvin, 1326 W. Britton Rd., Oklahoma City, OK 73114/405-842-8044

## U

Uberti USA, Inc., 362 Limerock Rd., P.O. Box 469, Lakeville, CT 06039/203-435-8068; FAX: 203-435-8146
Uberti, Aldo, Casella Postale 43, I-25063 Gardone V.T., ITALY (U.S. importers—Cimarron Arms; Navy Arms Co; Uberti USA, Inc.)
Ugartechea S.A., Ignacio, Chonta 26, Eibar, SPAIN 20600/43-121257; FAX: 43-121669 (U.S. importers—Hanus Birdguns, Bill; Mandall Shooting Supplies, Inc.; Precision Sports)
Ulrich, Doc & Bud (See D.O.C. Specialists, Inc.)
Ultra Light Arms, Inc., P.O. Box 1270, 214 Price St., Granville, WV 26534/304-599-5687
Uncle Mike's (See Michaels of Oregon Co.)
Unertl Optical Co., Inc., John, 308 Clay Ave., P.O. Box 818, Mars, PA 16046-0818/412-625-3810
Unick's Gunsmithing, 5005 Center Rd., Lowellville, OH 44436/216-536-8015
Unique/M.A.P.F., 10, Les Allees, 64700 Hendaye, FRANCE 64700/33-59 20 71 93 (U.S. importer—Nygord Precision Products)
United Binocular Co., 9043 S. Western Ave., Chicago, IL 60620
United Cutlery Corp., 1425 United Blvd., Sevierville, TN 37862/615-428-2532
United States Ammunition Co. (See USAC)
United States Products Co., 518 Melwood Ave., Pittsburgh, PA 15213/412-621-2130
Universal Clay Pigeon Traps, Unit 5, Dalacre Industrial Estate, Wilbarston,ENGLAND LE16 8QL/011-44536771625; FAX: 011-44536771625
Upper Missouri Trading Co., 304 Harold St., Crofton, NE 68730/402-388-4844
USAC, 4500-15th St. East, Tacoma, WA 98424/206-922-7589
U.S. Arms Corp., 444 Brickell Ave., Suite P-26, Miami, FL 33131/305-371-7211
U.S. Optics Technologies, Inc., Div. of Zeitz Optics, U.S.A., 1501 E. Chapman Ave., Suite 306, Fullerton, CA 92631/714-879-8922; FAX: 714-449-0941
U.S. Repeating Arms Co., Inc., 275 Winchester Ave., New Haven, CT 06511/203-789-5000; FAX: 203-789-5071
Utica Cutlery Co., 820 Noyes St., Utica, NY 13503/315-733-4663
Uvalde Machine & Tool, P.O. Box 1604, Uvalde, TX 78802

## V

Valade, Robert B., 931 3rd Ave., Seaside, OR 97138/503-738-7672
Valmet (See Tikka/U.S. importer—Stoeger Industries)
Valor Corp., 5555 NW 36th Ave., Miami, FL 33142/305-633-0127
Van Epps, Milton, Rt. 69-A, Parish, NY 13131/315-625-7251
Van Gorden & Son, Inc., C.S., 1815 Main St., Bloomer, WI 54724/715-568-2612
Van Horn, Gil, P.O. Box 207, Llano, CA 93544
Van Patten, J.W., P.O. Box 145, Foster Hill, Milford, PA 18337/717-296-7069
Vancini/Bestload, Carl A., P.O. Box 4354, Stamford, CT 06907/FAX: 203-978-0796
Vann Custom Bullets, 330 Grandview Ave., Novato, CA 94947
Varner's Service, 102 Shaffer Rd., Antwerp, OH 45813/419-258-8631
Vega Tool Co., 1840 Commerce St. Unit H, Boulder, CO 80301/303-443-4750
Venco Industries, Inc. (See Shooter's Choice)
Venus Industries, P.O. Box 246, Sialkot-1, PAKISTAN/FAX: 92 432 85579
Verdemont Fieldsports, P.O. Box 9337, San Bernardino, CA 92427/714-880-8255; FAX: 714-880-8255
Verney-Carron, B.P. 72, 54 Boulevard Thiers, 42002 St. Etienne Cedex 1, FRANCE/33-77791500; FAX: 33-77790702
Vest, John, P.O. Box 1552, Susanville, CA 96130/916-257-7228
VibraShine, Inc., Rt. 1, P.O. Box 64, Mt. Olive, MS 39119/601-733-5614; FAX: 601-733-2226
Vibra-Tek Co., 1844 Arroya Rd., Colorado Springs, CO 80906/719-634-8611; FAX: 719-634-6886
Vic's Gun Refinishing, 6 Pineview Dr., Dover, NH 03820/603-742-0013
Vihtavuori Oy, SF-41330 Vihtavouri, FINLAND/358-41-779-211; FAX: 358-41-771643
Vihtavuori Oy/Kaltron-Pettibone, 1241 Ellis St., Bensenville, IL 60106/708-350-1116; FAX: 708-350-1606
Viking Leathercraft, Inc., 1579A Jayken Way, Chula Vista, CA 91911/800-262-6666; FAX: 619-429-8268
Viking Video Productions, P.O. Box 251, Roseburg, OR 97470
Vincent's Shop, 210 Antoinette, Fairbanks, AK 99701
Vintage Arms, Inc., 6003 Saddle Horse, Fairfax, VA 22030/703-968-0779
Vintage Industries, Inc., P.O. Box 872, Casselberry, FL 32718-0872/FAX: 407-699-4919; FAX: 407-699-8419
Viramontez, Ray, 601 Springfield Dr., Albany, GA 31707/912-432-9683
Vitt/Boos, 2178 Nichols Ave., Stratford, CT 06497/203-375-6859
Voere-KGH m.b.H., P.O. Box 416, A-6333 Kufstein, Tirol, AUSTRIA/05372-62547; FAX: 5372-65752 (U.S. importers—JagerSport, Ltd.; Swarovski Optik North America Ltd.)
Volquartsen Custom Ltd., RR 1, Box 33A, P.O. Box 271, Carroll, IA 51401/712-792-4238; FAX: 712-792-2542
Vorhes, David, 3042 Beecham St., Napa, CA 94558/707-226-9116
Vostok (See U.S. importer—Nygord Precision Products)
VSP Publishers, P.O. Box 887, McCall, ID 83638/208-634-4104

## W

Waffen-Frankonia (See Frankonia Jagd)
Waffen-Weber Custom Gunsmithing, 4-1691 Powick Rd., Kelowna, B.C. CANADA V1X 4L1/604-762-7575; FAX: 604-861-3655
Wagoner, Vernon G., 2325 E. Encanto, Mesa, AZ 85213/602-835-1307
Wahl Corp., Paul, P.O. Box 6, Bogota, NJ 07603-0006/201-342-9245; FAX: 201-487-9329
Wakina by Pic, 24813 Alderbrook Dr., Santa Clarita, CA 91321/805-295-8194
Waldron, Herman, Box 475, 80 N. 17th St., Pomeroy, WA 99347/509-843-1404
Walker Arms Co., Inc., 499 County Rd. 820, Selma, AL 36701/205-872-6231
Walker Mfg., Inc., 8296 S. Channel, Harsen's Island, MI 48028
Walker Shoe Co., P.O. Box 1167, Asheboro, NC 27203-1167/919-625-1380
Wallace's, Star Rt.1, Box 76, Grandin, MO 63943/314-593-4773
Wallace, Terry, 385 San Marino, Vallejo, CA 94589/707-642-7041
Waller & Son, Inc., W., 142 New Canaan Ave., Norwalk, CT 06850/203-838-4083
Walls Industries, P.O. Box 98, Cleburne, TX 76031/817-645-4366
Walt's Custom Leather, Walt Whinnery, 1947 Meadow Creek Dr., Louisville, KY 40218/502-458-4361
Walters Industries, 6226 Park Lane, Dallas, TX 75225/214-691-6973
Walther GmbH, Carl, B.P. 4325, D-89033 Ulm, GERMANY (U.S. importer—Interarms)
WAMCO, Inc., Mingo Loop, P.O. Box 337, Oquossoc, ME 04964-0337/207-864-3344
Ward & Van Valkenburg, 114 32nd Ave. N., Fargo, ND 58102/701-232-2351
Ward Machine, 5620 Lexington Rd., Corpus Christi, TX 78412/512-992-1221
Wardell Precision Handguns Ltd., 48851 N. Fig Springs Rd., New River, AZ 85027/602-465-7995
Warenski, Julie, 590 E. 500 N., Richfield, UT 84701/801-896-5319; FAX: 801-896-5319
Warne Manufacturing Co., 9039 SE Jannsen Rd., Clackamas, OR 97015/503-657-5590; FAX: 503-657-5695
Warren & Sweat Mfg. Co., P.O. Box 350440, Grand Island, FL 32735/904-669-3166; FAX: 904-669-7272
Warren Muzzleloading Co., Inc., Hwy. 21 North, Ozone, AR 72854/501-292-3268
Warren, Kenneth W. (See Mountain States Engraving)
Washita Mountain Whetstone Co., P.O. Box 378, Lake Hamilton, AR 71951/501-525-3914
WASP Shooting Systems, Rt. 1, Box 147, Lakeview, AR 72642/501-431-5606
Waterfield Sports, Inc., 13611 Country Lane, Burnsville, MN 55337/612-435-8339
Watson Trophy Match Bullets, 2404 Wade Hampton Blvd., Greenville, SC 29615/803-244-7948
Wayland Precision Wood Products, P.O. Box 1142, Mill Valley, CA 94942/415-381-3543
Wayne Firearms for Collectors and Investors, James, 2608 N. Laurent, Victoria, TX 77901/512-578-1258; FAX: 512-578-3559
Wayne Specialty Services, 260 Waterford Drive, Florissant, MO 63033/413-831-7083
WD-40 Co., P.O. Box 80607, San Diego, CA 92138/619-275-1400; FAX: 619-275-5823
Weather Shield Sports Equipment, Inc., Rt. 3, Petoskey Rd., Charlevoix, MI 49720
Weatherby, Inc., 2781 Firestone Blvd., South Gate, CA 90280/213-569-7186, 800-227-2023; FAX: 213-569-5025
Weaver Arms Corp., P.O. Box 8, Dexter, MO 63841/314-568-3101
Weaver Products, Div. of Blount, Inc., P.O. Box 39, Onalaska, WI 54650/800-635-7656; FAX: 608-781-0368
Weaver Scope Repair Service, 1121 Larry Mahan Dr., Suite B, El Paso, TX 79925/915-593-1005
Weaver's Gun Shop, P.O. Box 8, Dexter, MO 63841/314-568-3101
Weber Jr., Rudolf, P.O. Box 160106, D-5650 Solingen, GERMANY/0212-592136
Webley and Scott Ltd., Frankley Industrial Park, Tay Rd., Rubery Rednal, Birmingham B45 OPA, U.K./021-453-1864; FAX: 021-457-7846
Webster Scale Mfg. Co., P.O. Box 188, Sebring, FL 33870/813-385-6362
Weems, Cecil, P.O. Box 657, Mineral Wells, TX 76067/817-325-1462
Weihrauch KG, Hermann, Industriestrasse 11, 8744 Mellrichstadt, GERMANY/09776-497-498 (U.S. importers—Beeman Precision Airguns, Inc.; E.A.A. Corp.)
Weisz Antique Gun Parts, P.O. Box 311, Arlington, VA 22210/703-243-9161
Welch, Sam, CVSR 2110, Moab, UT 84532/801-259-8131
Wellington Outdoors, P.O. Box 244, Madison, GA 30650/404-342-4915; FAX: 404-342-4656
Wells Sport Store, 110 N. Summit St., Prescott, AZ 86301/602-445-3655
Wells Custom Gunsmith, R.A., 3452 1st Ave., Racine, WI 53402/414-639-5223
Wells, Rachel, 110 N. Summit St., Prescott, AZ 86301/602-445-3655
Wells Creek Knife & Gun Works, 32956 State Hwy. 38, Scottsburg, OR 97473/503-587-4202
Welsh, Bud, 80 New Road, E. Amherst, NY 14051/716-688-6344
Wenig Custom Gunstocks, Inc., 103 N. Market St., Lincoln, MO 65338/816-547-3334; FAX: 816-547-2881
Wenoka/Seastyle, P.O. Box 10969, Riviera Beach, FL 33419/407-845-6155; FAX: 407-842-4247
Werth, T.W., 1203 Woodlawn Rd., Lincoln, IL 62656/217-732-1300
Wescombe, P.O. Box 488, Glencoe, CA 95232/209-293-7010
Wessinger Custom Guns & Engraving, 268 Limestone Rd., Chapin, SC 29036/803-345-5677
Wesson Firearms Co., Inc., Maple Tree Industrial Center, Rt. 20, Wilbraham Rd., Palmer, MA 01069/413-267-4081; FAX: 413-267-3601
West, Robert G., 3973 Pam St., Eugene, OR 97402/503-344-3700
Westchester Carbide, 148 Wheeler Ave., Pleasantville, NY 10570/914-769-1445
Western Design, 1629 Via Monserate, Fallbrook, CA 92028/619-723-9279
Western Gunstock Mfg. Co., 550 Valencia School Rd., Aptos, CA 95003/408-688-5884
Western Missouri Shooters Alliance, P.O. Box 11144, Kansas City, MO 64119/816-597-3950; FAX: 816-229-7350
Western Ordnance Int'l Corp., 325 S. Westwood St. 1, Mesa, AZ 85210/602-964-1799
Westfield Engineering, 6823 Watcher St., Commerce, CA 90040/FAX: 213-928-8270
Westley Richards & Co., 40 Grange Rd., Birmingham, ENGLAND B29 6AR/010-214722953
Westminster Arms Ltd., 9375 Freemont Way, Reno, NV 89506/916-827-2179
Westrom, John (See Precise Metal Finishing)
Weyer International, 2740 Nebraska Ave., Toledo, OH 43607/419-534-2020; FAX: 419-534-2697
Whildin & Sons Ltd., E.H., 76 Autumn Dr., Tolland, CT 06084/203-870-8713
Whinnery, Walt (See Walt's Custom Leather)
White Flyer Targets, 124 River Rd., Middlesex, NJ 08846/908-469-0100; FAX: 908-469-9692
White Flyer, Div. of Reagent Chemical & Research, Inc., 9139 W. Redfield Rd., Peoria, AZ 85381/800-647-2898
White Laboratory, Inc., H.P., 3114 Scarboro Rd., Street, MD 21154/410-838-6550; FAX: 410-838-2802
White Owl Enterprises, Rt. 4, Box 266 GD, Abilene, KS 67410/913-263-2613, 2616; FAX: 913-263-1426
White Rock Tool & Die, 6400 N. Brighton Ave., Kansas City, MO 64119/816-454-0478
White Systems, Inc., P.O. Box 190, Roosevelt, UT 84066/801-722-3085; FAX: 801-722-3085
Whitehead, James D., 204 Cappucino Way, Sacramento, CA 95838
Whitestone Lumber Corp., 148-02 14th Ave., Whitestone, NY 11357/718-746-4400; FAX: 718-767-1748
Whitetail Design & Engineering Ltd., 9421 E. Mannsiding Rd., Clare, MI 48617/517-386-3932

Whits Shooting Stuff, Box 1340, Cody, WY 82414
Wichita Arms, Inc., 923 E. Gilbert, P.O. Box 11371, Wichita, KS 67211/316-265-0661; FAX: 316-265-0760
Widener's Reloading & Shooting Supply, Inc., P.O. Box 3009 CRS, Johnson City, TN 37602/615-282-6786; FAX: 615-282-6651
Wideview Scope Mount Corp., 26110 Michigan Ave., Inkster, MI 48141/313-274-1238; FAX: 313-274-2814
Wiebe, Duane, Casper Mt. Rt., Box 40, Casper, WY 82601/307-237-0615; FAX: 307-266-4143
Wiest, M.C., 10737 Dutchtown Rd., Knoxville, TN 37932/615-966-4545
Wilcox All-Pro Tools & Supply, RR 1, Montezuma, IA 50171/515-623-3138
Wild Bill's Originals, P.O. Box 13037, Burton, WA 98013/206-463-5738
Wildcatters, The, P.O. Box 170, Greenville, WI 54942
Wilderness Sound Products Ltd., 4015 Main St. A, Springfield, OR 97478/503-741-0263; FAX: 503-741-7648
Wildey, Inc., P.O. Box 475, Brookfield, CT 06804/203-355-9000; FAX: 203-354-7759
Wildlife Research Center, Inc., 4345 157th Ave. NW, Anoka, MN 55304/612-427-3350
Wilkinson Arms, 26884 Pearl Rd., Parma, ID 83660/208-722-6771
Will-Burt Co., 169 S. Main, Orrville, OH 44667
William's Gun Shop, Ben, 1151 S. Cedar Ridge, Duncanville, TX 75137/214-780-1807
Williams Bullet Co., J.R., 2008 Tucker Rd., Perry, GA 31069/912-987-0274
Williams Gun Sight Co., 7389 Lapeer Rd., Box 329, Davison, MI 48423/313-653-2131, 800-530-9028; FAX: 313-658-2140
Williams Shootin' Iron Service, The Lynx-Line, 8857 Bennett Hill Rd., Central Lake, MI 49622/616-544-6615
Williamson Precision Gunsmithing, 117 W. Pipeline, Hurst, TX 76053/817-285-0064
Willig Custom Engraving, Claus, D-97422 Schweinfurt, Siedlerweg 17, GERMANY/01149-9721-41446
Willson Safety Prods. Div., P.O. Box 622, Reading, PA 19603
Wilson Arms Co., The, 63 Leetes Island Rd., Branford, CT 06405/203-488-7297; FAX: 203-488-0135
Wilson Case, Inc., P.O. Box 1106, Hastings, NE 68902-1106/800-322-5493; FAX: 402-463-5276
Wilson, Inc., L.E., Box 324, 404 Pioneer Ave., Cashmere, WA 98815/509-782-1328
Wilson's Gun Shop, Box 578, Rt. 3, Berryville, AR 72616/501-545-3635; FAX: 501-545-3310
Winchester (See U.S. Repeating Arms Co., Inc.)
Winchester Div., Olin Corp., 427 N. Shamrock, E. Alton, IL 62024/618-258-3566; FAX: 618-258-3180
Winchester Press (See New Win Publishing, Inc.)
Winchester Sutler, Inc., The, 270 Shadow Brook Lane, Winchester, VA 22603/703-888-3595
Windish, Jim, 2510 Dawn Dr., Alexandria, VA 22306/703-765-1994
Windjammer Tournament Wads, Inc., 750 W. Hampden Ave. Suite 170, Englewood, CO 80110/303-781-6329
Wingshooting Adventures, 4320 Kalamazoo Ave. SE, Grand Rapids, MI 49508/616-455-7810; FAX: 616-455-5212
Winkle Bullets, R.R. 1 Box 316, Heyworth, IL 61745
Winter & Associates (See Olde Pennsylvania)
Winter, Robert M., RR 2, P.O. Box 484, Menno, SD 57045/605-387-5322
Wisner's Gun Shop, Inc., 287 NW Chehalis Ave., Chehalis, WA 98532/206-748-8942; FAX: 206-748-7011
Wittasek, Dipl.-Ing. Norbert, Seilergasse 2, Wien, 1010 AUSTRIA/0222-513-7001
Wolfe Publishing Co., 6471 Airpark Dr., Prescott, AZ 86301/602-445-7810, 800-899-7810; FAX: 602-778-5124
W.C. Wolff Co., P.O. Box I, Newtown Square, PA 19073/215-359-9600
Wolverine Boots & Shoes Div., Wolverine World Wide, 9341 Courtland Dr., Rockford, MI 49351/616-866-1561
Wood, Frank (See Classic Guns)
Wood, Mel, P.O. Box 1255, Sierra Vista, AZ 85636/602-455-5541

Woodland Bullets, 638 Woodland Dr., Manheim, PA 17545/717-665-4332
Woods Pistolsmithing, 3840 Dahlgren Ct., Ellicott City, MD 21042/410-465-7979
Woods Wise Products, P.O. Box 681552, 2200 Bowman Rd., Franklin, TN 37068/800-735-8182; FAX: 615-790-3581
Woodstream, P.O. Box 327, Lititz, PA 17543/717-626-2125; FAX: 717-626-1912
Woolrich Woolen Mills, Mill St., Woolrich, PA 17779/717-769-6464
World of Targets, Div. of Steidle Corp., 9200 Floral Ave., Cincinnati, OH 45242/513-791-0917; FAX: 513-792-0004
World of Targets (See Birchwood Laboratories, Inc.)
World Trek, Inc., 2648 McCormick Ave., Pueblo, CO 81001/719-546-2121; FAX: 719-543-6886
Worthy Products, Inc., RR 1, P.O. Box 213, Martville, NY 13111/315-324-5298
Wosenitz VHP, Inc., Box 741, Dania, FL 33004/305-923-3748; FAX: 305-925-2217
Wostenholm (See Ibberson [Sheffield] Ltd., George)
Wright's Hardwood Sawmill, 8540 SE Kane Rd., Gresham, OR 97080/503-666-1705
Wyant Bullets, Gen. Del., Swan Lake, MT 59911
Wyant's Outdoor Products, Inc., P.O. Box 1325, Harrisonburg, VA 22801-1325/FAX: 702-833-4021
Wyoming Armory, Inc., Box 28, Farson, WY 82932/307-273-5556
Wyoming Casting Co., 305 Commerce Dr. 10D, P.O. Box 1492, Gillette, WY 82717/307-687-7779, 800-821-2167
Wyoming Custom Bullets, 1626 21st St., Cody, WY 82414
Wyoming Knife Corp., 101 Commerce Dr., Ft. Collins, CO 80524/303-224-3454

## Y

Yankee Gunsmith, 2901 Deer Flat Dr., Copperas Cove, TX 76522/817-547-8433
Yavapai College, 1100 E. Sheldon St., Prescott, AZ 86301/602-776-2359; FAX: 602-776-2193
Yavapai Firearms Academy Ltd., P.O. Box 27290, Prescott Valley, AZ 86312/602-772-8262
Yearout, Lewis E. (See Montana Outfitters)
Yee, Mike, 29927 56 Pl. S., Auburn, WA 98001/206-839-3991
Yellowstone Wilderness Supply, P.O. Box 129, W. Yellowstone, MT 59758/406-646-7613
York M-1 Conversions, 803 Mill Creek Run, Plantersville, TX 77363/800-527-2881, 713-477-8442
Young Country Arms, P.O. Box 3615, Simi Valley, CA 93093

## Z

Zabala Hermanos S.A., P.O. Box 97, Eibar, SPAIN 20600 (U.S. importer—American Arms, Inc.)
Zanoletti, Pietro, Via Monte Gugielpo, 4, I-25063 Gardone V.T., ITALY (U.S. importer—Mandall Shooting Supplies, Inc.)
Zanotti Armor, 123 W. Lone Tree Rd., Cedar Falls, IA 50613/319-232-9650
Zastava Arms (See U.S. importer—Interarms)
Z-Coat Industrial Coatings, Inc., 3375 U.S. Hwy. 98 S. No. A, Lakeland, FL 33803-8365/813-665-1734
Zeeryp, Russ, 1601 Foard Dr., Lynn Ross Manor, Morristown, TN 37814/615-586-2357
Zeiss Optical, Inc., Carl, 1015 Commerce St., Petersburg, VA 23803/804-861-0033; FAX: 804-862-3734
Zero Ammunition Co., Inc., 1601 22nd St. SE, P.O. Box 1188, Cullman, AL 35055-1188/800-545-9376; FAX: 205-739-4683
Ziegel Engineering, 2108 Lomina Ave., Long Beach, CA 90815/310-596-9481; FAX: 310-598-4734
Zim's Inc., 4370 S. 3rd West, Salt Lake City, UT 84107
Zoli USA, Inc., Antonio, P.O. Box 6190, Fort Wayne, IN 46896/219-447-4603
Zoli, Antonio, Via Zanardelli 39, Casier Postal 21, 23, I-25063 Gardone V.T., ITALY (U.S. importers—Mandall Shooting Supplies, Inc.; Zoli USA, Inc., Antonio)